The SAGE
Handbook *of*
Leadership

The SAGE
Handbook *of*
Leadership

Edited by
Alan Bryman, David Collinson, Keith Grint, Brad Jackson and Mary Uhl-Bien

Los Angeles | London | New Delhi
Singapore | Washington DC

SAGE Publications Ltd
1 Oliver's Yard
55 City Road
London EC1Y 1SP

SAGE Publications Inc.
2455 Teller Road
Thousand Oaks, California 91320

SAGE Publications India Pvt Ltd
B 1/I 1 Mohan Cooperative Industrial Area
Mathura Road
New Delhi 110 044

SAGE Publications Asia-Pacific Pte Ltd
33 Pekin Street #02-01
Far East Square
Singapore 048763

Library of Congress Control Number: 2010931598

British Library Cataloguing in Publication data

A catalogue record for this book is available from the British Library

ISBN 978-1-84860-146-8

Typeset by Glyph International
Printed by MPG Books Group, Bodmin, Cornwall
Printed on paper from sustainable resources

FSC

SA-COC-1565
© 1996 Forest Stewardship Council A.C.
'The Global Benchmark for
Responsible Forest Management'

Contents

Preface

It is an exciting and challenging time to be researching and studying leadership. In recent years there has been a significant expansion of theoretical, empirical, and policy-centred contributions to leadership studies. Invariably one of the most extensively researched topics in management, business and organization studies, recent interest in leadership has also emerged from across the social sciences. Leadership perspectives and research increasingly draw on a broad range of disciplines, including (social) psychology, sociology, history, political science, anthropology, cultural studies, philosophy, education, military studies, health and social welfare and religious studies. As an intellectual discipline, an area of research and indeed as a practical activity, leadership is increasingly recognized as a critical factor in all forms of organization: formal and informal, business and public, civilian and military, historical and contemporary, the arts as well as the sciences, and 'for profit', 'not for profit' and voluntary. Equally, recent financial crises and numerous high-profile scandals in Western societies have raised fundamental questions about the nature and integrity of contemporary business and political leadership practices.

The study of leadership has certainly come a long way since Thomas Carlyle wrote about heroes and hero worship in 1841. Leadership research is now a fertile field that is increasingly seen as an important and highly relevant area of inter-disciplinary contemporary scholarship. Studies of leadership continue to grow apace to the degree that current research can sustain a journal that has grown from four to six issues in the space of a decade (*The Leadership Quarterly*) and two new journals (*Leadership* and *Journal of Leadership Studies*) are now well established. Leadership also continues to figure prominently in journals in areas like organizational behaviour and organizational psychology. Precisely because it is such a productive field, it is difficult for even specialist scholars to keep up with its breadth and it is even more difficult for new scholars to break into it.

Informed by these new, more diverse theoretical frameworks, empirical findings and research methodologies, recent contributions have produced innovative ways of thinking about longstanding leadership issues and dilemmas. Increasingly, they have sought to develop international, cross-cultural perspectives and multi-disciplinary approaches to leadership. Alongside the predominant traditional approaches to leadership studies, that tend to draw mainly on functionalism, positivism and quantitative methodologies, more interpretive, discursive and phenomenological perspectives are increasingly influential. Emphasizing the socially constructed and relational nature of leadership, many of these approaches depart from the traditional association of leadership with designated hierarchical position to explore coordination through informal leaders. Such dynamics may emerge in particular within dispersed and distributed leadership forms where group-based processes and self-organizing systems are encouraged. These alternative perspectives have established a much richer, more diverse and increasingly pluralistic field of theoretically-informed research on which leadership studies is now being established.

Indeed there is far more optimism about leadership studies nowadays than in the 1970s and early 1980s when dismissive accounts often persisted. At the same time, new topics and approaches are continually being developed. The time would therefore seem ripe for a book which provides a state-of-the-art overview of the field and which shares in and reflects this optimism. The *SAGE Handbook of Leadership* has been compiled precisely for this reason, to provide an up-to-date overview of contemporary leadership studies in its many rich and diverse forms. This volume comprises a compilation of current theory and research on a broad range of important leadership topics and themes. At the same time as intending to cover the extant field, the Handbook is also designed to stretch its domain by including chapters on areas and topics that are beginning to surface and which are attracting more and more attention.

Initially, Kiren Shoman from Sage contacted David and Keith, as co-editors of the Sage journal *Leadership*, asking them to consider the possibility of producing a *Handbook of Leadership* as part of the Sage series of this name. David and Keith in turn talked with Brad, Mary and Alan and the project was soon up and running. We five editors discussed at great length the key themes that needed to be included in the Handbook. Originally, we identified many more potential chapters, authors and sections. After extensive debates across continents and time zones, and the implementation of a complicated voting system (installed by Brad), we were able to narrow the volume down to five main sections and approximately 40 chapters. Early on it was agreed that several excellent handbooks and encyclopaedias had previously been published which to some extent precluded the need to spend too much time covering old ground (e.g. Antonakis et al., 2004; Bass & Bass, 2008; Billsberry, 2009; English 2005; Goethals et al., 2004; Hooper, 2006; Storey, 2004; Wren et al., 2004). A primary concern was, therefore, to integrate an understanding of past research, with a more detailed analysis of contemporary theory and practices on current leadership issues.

Hence, in advance of contacting potential authors, the co-editors identified each of the five sections and individual chapters that needed to be addressed and covered. Once the structure of the Handbook had been agreed, we then discussed who should be invited to author individual chapters. Invitations to write chapters were sent to leadership researchers in different parts of the world based on their expertise in particular areas and the significant impact they had already made on the leadership field. We were delighted that very few invitations to be part of this project were declined and we are very grateful to all the authors for their major contributions to this collection. Each of the five editors was assigned primary responsibility for liaising with a number of specified authors and handling the editorial process. We asked chapter authors to explore the key issues addressed by leadership writers in the area covered by their chapter: the main theories, research findings, controversies and chief protagonists, as well as current hot issues and future possible directions. Once draft chapters were produced, they were reviewed by two of the five editors and in most cases extensive feedback was provided. This editorial division of labour and subsequent feedback processes proved to be extremely productive, facilitating stimulating dialogue and illuminating interactions for all involved.

The Handbook includes 38 contributions from 64 authors covering a vast array of key contemporary leadership issues. It is divided into five primary sections. Each of these parts represents a distinctive dimension on leadership deriving primarily from its disciplinary focus. Part I presents a number of overview chapters that explore general themes such as history, research methods, the elusive quest for a general theory, and leadership development. Part II addresses an area somewhat under-explored in traditional leadership studies: namely, the macro view. Drawing predominantly on economics and sociology, this section examines key issues such as the relationship of leadership to organization theory, strategy, charisma, gender, trust, networks and culture. Part III examines political and philosophical perspectives, looking particularly at more critical approaches that examine the power dynamics of leadership, as well as those drawn from ethics, philosophy and politics, aesthetics and the analysis of leadership and cults.

In Part IV, we present contributions from the discipline that has so far contributed most to the study of leadership, namely psychology. This section examines personality-based approaches, contingency theories, transformational leadership, leader–member exchange, leadership within teams, authentic leadership, the relationship between leadership and creativity and innovation, the role of emotions and the 'shadow side' of leadership and psychoanalytic approaches. The final section of the Handbook, Part V, examines some of the more promising emerging issues within the leadership field, recognizing that all avenues of leadership research continue to be in an emergent and evolving state. This section examines emergent concerns such as followership and follower-centred approaches, hybridity, relational approaches, complexity leadership, spirituality, discursive perspectives, social identity and virtual leadership.

To guide the reader, the main arguments contained within each of the 38 chapters that comprise this volume are briefly outlined in the chapter summaries section below.

In conclusion, we believe that, together, the chapters that comprise this Handbook provide a powerful statement about the rich, diverse and creative state of contemporary leadership research. Accordingly, we hope that this volume can reinforce the process of broadening out and stretching the theoretical and empirical agenda of leadership studies, exploring important leadership issues in ways that not only reflect but also generate new lines of enquiry and theorizing. We recognize that the issues raised here are by no means exhaustive of what is or needs to be researched in terms of leadership in all its diverse manifestations and different contexts. However, we believe that the contents of this volume illustrate and embody the kinds of innovative work that can shed new light on leadership issues in theory, research, development and practice. We also hope that the Handbook provides a key point of reference for researchers, postgraduate students, and practitioners for many years to come. As we outlined at the beginning of this Preface, leadership is a field that is changing rapidly as new perspectives and methodological styles proliferate. It is difficult not to be struck by the difference between the field's current diversity and its relative homogeneity in the period between the 1950s and the early 1990s. At a time of such heterogeneity, the need for a book such as this, which assesses the state of the field, is all the more necessary.

Finally, we would like to close by thanking Kiren Shoman and Alan Maloney from Sage Publications, Shruti Vasishta from Glyph International, all of the contributors to this volume and our respective spouses and families for their support during the co-editing of this Handbook.

Alan Bryman
David Collinson
Keith Grint
Brad Jackson
Mary Uhl-Bien

REFERENCES

Antonakis, J., Cianciolo, A.T. and Sternberg, R.J. (eds), (2004). *The Nature of Leadership*, Thousand Oaks, CA, Sage.

Bass, B.M. & Bass, R. (2008) *The Bass handbook of leadership: theory, research & managerial applications.* New York: Free Press.

Billsberry, J. (ed.) (2009) *Discovering leadership.* Basingstoke: Palgrave Macmillan/Open University.

English, F. W. (ed.) (2005) *The Sage handbook of educational leadership: advances in theory, research, and practice.* Thousand Oaks, CA: Sage.

Goethals, G., Sorenson, G. and Burns, J.M., (eds.) 2004. *The Encyclopedia of Leadership.* Thousand Oaks, CA: SAGE.

Hooper, A. (ed.) (2006) *Leadership perspectives.* Aldershot: Ashgate.

Storey, J. (ed.) (2004) *Leadership in organizations.* London: Routledge.

Wren, J.T., Hicks, D.A., & Price, T.L. (eds) (2004) *The international library of leadership.* Cheltenham: Edward Elgar.

Chapter Summaries

PART I   OVERVIEW PERSPECTIVES

1 A History of Leadership
Keith Grint

While situations are always changing, there are perennial issues in leadership and our historical knowledge of these can play a role in preventing the repetition of mistakes, even if we cannot guarantee success. Moreover, what we think leadership is, is necessarily related to the cultural mores that prevail at the time. An awareness of how often in the past leadership has failed or appeared terminally flawed does not necessarily mean that we should abandon the task of generating leadership for the public good; it just means that we need to be more alert to what is likely to happen unless we actively prevent it.

2 Research Methods in the Study of Leadership
Alan Bryman

There is considerable diversity in methodological approach within the field of leadership and that diversity is increasingly driven, in part, by the greater acceptance of qualitative methods. The appreciation of qualitative and other under-used methods has stimulated leadership researchers to think about leadership in new ways and suggested new research questions. Leadership researchers have been engaged for some time in a collective *mea culpa* about the dominance and limitations of the questionnaire in their field. Now is the time to do something.

3 The Enduring and Elusive Quest for a General Theory of Leadership: Initial Efforts and New Horizons
Georgia Sorenson, George Goethals and Paige Haber

The search for a General Theory of Leadership is one that has bedevilled leadership research for many years. Whether or not a general theory is ever found and whether or not a general theory is an intended goal, continued work on the synthesis and integration of leadership studies opens the conversation to interdisciplinary examination of leadership in a clear and needed way. However, leadership studies must continue to be challenged to move beyond the leader–follower–shared goal conversation. The discussion of power needs to be expanded; more attention needs to be given to the purpose of the leadership process and room must be made for more organic, systemic, and integrative ideas and approaches.

4 Leadership Development
David V. Day

While leadership development is a big business, the sheer number of research-related publications on leader and leadership development is still relatively small. Over the past decade there has been increasing attention paid to theorizing about the leadership development process, especially in terms of moving beyond any single, bounded theoretical approach to conceptualizing leadership. Research designs that incorporate multiple measurement perspectives, mixed methods, as well as a longitudinal component are more likely to yield scientific insight into the leadership development process. Efforts must also be devoted to translating ideas into action and science into sound practice.

PART II MACRO AND SOCIOLOGICAL PERSPECTIVES

5 Leadership and Organization Theory
Ken W. Parry

Organization theory and organizational behaviour are the chief areas within which leadership theory and research have developed. However, these fields are more uncoupled than they perhaps should be. A number of conceptual similarities exist between organization theory and leadership studies, but more paradoxes emerge than there are inherent similarities to be identified. A paradox within these parallel studies is that organizational power is usually generated within a structure, whereas leadership power is often generated from relations and processes that go on between people. Organization theory is more usually studied as a formal creation, while leadership increasingly is studied as the result of relationships between people and social processes at play in organizations.

6 Perspectives on Strategic Leadership
Jean-Louis Denis, Veronika Kisfalvi, Ann Langley and Linda Rouleau

Leadership is frequently seen as occupying an especially crucial role in relation to strategic management. The study of strategic leadership involves not only understanding the relationships between leaders and followers but also how strategic leaders go about orchestrating the decisions and activities that will orient the future of the organization. Four different perspectives on strategic leadership have developed in the literature: the first two perspectives place the greatest emphasis on the characteristics of leaders (who they are); the other two perspectives focus more on what strategic leaders do and how they do it. These four perspectives are applied to an illustrative case study of a Canadian grocery firm.

7 Charismatic Leadership
Jay A. Conger

Charismatic leadership is a rich and complex pheneomenon. Our understanding of the topic has advanced significantly since Max Weber proposed the formal theory of charismatic leadership. While political scientists and sociologists grappled with some of the more critical questions of why certain leaders are seen as charismatic, it was the field of organizational behaviour that advanced the theory and research to the greatest degree. However, important areas of the topic remain only partially understood. Significantly more research and theory building are required, especially to deepen our understanding of the interaction effects between context and charismatic leadership, institutionalization and succession dynamics, and the liabilities of this important form of leadership.

8 Gender and Leadership
Linda L. Carli and Alice H. Eagly

There is little evidence that the gender gap in leadership can be explained by inherent differences between men and women in abilities, traits or styles. Women's advancement remains obstructed to some extent by competing responsibilities and by gender stereotypes and discrimination as well as the inimicable structure and culture of many organizations. Although serious obstacles remain, there are signs that leadership opportunities will continue to expand for women. Women's personalities have become more assertive, dominant, and masculine, and their preference for careers that provide authority has increased and is now comparable to men. As women have changed, so too have ideas about leadership. These changes should facilitate women's advancement in leadership in the future.

9 A Network Approach to Leader Cognition and Effectiveness
Martin Kilduff and Prasad Balkundi

Leadership research from a network perspective provides a new understanding of the interplay between the psychology of individuals and the complexity of the networks through which actors exchange information, affect, and other resources. It also enables a renewed understanding of how patterns of informal leadership complement or detract from the work of formally appointed leaders and recognizes the role of actors within the network who may or may not be connected with the leader, but whose actions can affect leader outcomes by changing the structures within which the leader operates. Given its emphasis upon social relations, embeddedness, social capital, and social structure, the network perspective points to new directions for leadership research.

10 Trust and Distrust in the Leadership Process: A Review and Assessment of Theory and Evidence
Roderick M. Kramer

Although trust is generally seen to be a critical component of any effective leadership relationship, the fields of leadership and trust have largely developed in parallel. Research crossing these two fields provides scientific support for the central importance that trust plays in effective leadership processes. Considerable progress has been made with respect to clarifying the nature of this relationship, its benefits, as well as some of the difficulties that attend it; and identifying the cognitive, social and behavioural antecedents or underpinnings of trust in this process. Future research should focus on identifying the structural underpinnings of trust in leader–constituent relations; the gender effects of the leader and/or constituent; and cross-cultural differences in the trust–leadership process.

11 Leadership and Organizational Culture
Mats Alvesson

A cultural understanding of leadership calls for appreciating local shared meanings associated with the context of leadership relations and acts. Leadership can be defined as about influencing the construction of reality – the ideas, beliefs and interpretations of what and how things can and should be done in light of what the world looks like. A cultural view on leadership balances academic a priori definitions of leadership with openness to the meanings of the people being studied. In most cases leadership is better understood as taking place within and as an outcome of the cultural context. Only under extraordinary circumstances can leaders transcend parts of existing cultural patterns or contribute to the creation or radical change of organizational culture.

12 Cross-Cultural Leadership Revisited
Eric Guthey and Brad Jackson

Most cross-cultural leadership research has been dedicated to describing similarities and difference between societal cultures with a view towards helping leaders adapt to different and increasingly diverse cultural contexts within a globalized business arena. More recent humanities-based research has pushed the discussion of the relationship between leadership and culture in new and productive directions, away from deterministic generalizations about national culture and its influence towards a recognition of the very significant ways in which leadership and followership shape and influence cultures – and contribute significantly to the shaping of local, national and global cultural identities – rather than the other way around.

PART III POLITICAL AND PHILOSOPHICAL PERSPECTIVES

13 Critical Leadership Studies
David Collinson

Focusing particularly on the situated power relations between leaders, managers and followers, critical leadership studies suggest that constructivist and dialectical perspectives can facilitate new ways of thinking about the complex, shifting dynamics of leadership. More critical approaches recognize that leaders exercise considerable control and their power can have contradictory and ambiguous outcomes which leaders either do not always understand or of which they are unaware. Critical perspectives view control and resistance as mutually reinforcing and potentially contradictory processes. Questioning the prevailing view that leader-led relations are inherently consensual, they also highlight the importance of differences and inequalities like gender, race and class for understanding leadership dialectics.

14 Leadership and Power
Raymond Gordon

When viewed through a power lens, mainstream approaches to leadership can be challenged because they neglect to consider how historically constituted power relations unobtrusively shape behaviour in organizations. They also neglect the manner in which power is embedded in an organization's antecedents and meaning systems; how power is embedded in the sociocultural norms and discourses that organizational members reflect upon to make sense of their work relations and settings. Leadership researchers need to adopt a comprehensive approach to power. If they do not, leadership studies will continue to miss the contextual complexities associated with the shift in power relations currently occurring within organizations and broader social systems across the globe.

15 Political Leadership
Jean Hartley and John Benington

Research on political leadership is disparate, under-theorized and under-researched. Leadership scholars have largely ignored the complex world of political leadership, favouring managerial leadership. Studying political leadership emphasizes the fact that while initial formal legitimacy may be conferred by election or appointment, the variety of voices and the existence of opposing views means that authorization to lead has to be continually rewon. Neo-institutional theory is perhaps the most widely used framework for understanding political leadership, because it brings together in one conceptual framework the influence of structural conditions with informal practices and assumptions, while allowing for agency and change. Understanding political leadership is critical to the functioning of a democratic society. It has much to teach in relation to leadership studies and practice more generally.

16 Leadership and Cults
Dennis Tourish

Leadership scholars have largely ignored the cultic phenomenon, despite the fact that power relations are manifest within it in a more pristine form than most other organizational contexts. Cult leaders exercise their influence by manipulating well-known techniques of influence, persuasion and the exercise of charismatic authority, albeit to an extreme extent. It is useful to view cults as a continuum rather than in dichotomous categories. A greater awareness of these dynamics would both insulate people more fully from cultic influence, and alert organizations and their leaders to potentially dysfunctional aspects of their own practice that, ultimately, are likely to have socially harmful consequences.

17 Leadership Ethics
Joanne B. Ciulla and Donelson R. Forsyth

Ethical assumptions, expectations, and implications lie deeply embedded in every facet of the concept of leadership: from the way that leaders behave, to their relationships with followers, to the results of their initiatives. Leadership ethics is an applied field that examines the distinctive set of ethical challenges and problems related to the role of a leader. It draws upon the philosophic literature on ethics as well as psychology in order to develop an empirically-based overarching theory as to how a leader will act with regards to the moral order. A successful leader is someone who not only does the right thing but also does so in the right way and for the right reasons.

18 Philosophy of Leadership
Peter Case, Robert French and Peter Simpson

It is vital to engage in the task of *doing* philosophy of leadership. Four strategies of enquiry for doing leadership are suggested: (1) to consider the explicit and implicit philosophies informing contemporary leadership studies; (2) to examine the semantics and meaning-in-use of the terms 'lead', 'leader', 'leadership' and their putative relationship to 'philosophy'; (3) to consider the explicit and implicit philosophies of leadership that may be discovered through an examination of the history of ideas pertaining to 'leadership'; and (4) to suggest ways in which 'leadership philosophy', in contrast to 'philosophy of leadership', might be developed. There may be no philosophy of leadership but this in no way discounts or detracts from the challenge of establishing such a philosophy or philosophies.

19 Aesthetics and Leadership
Hans Hansen and Ralph Bathurst

An aesthetic approach to leadership entails an exploration of sensory experience and sensemaking, and the felt meanings that are both produced by and guided by our interactions and decisions. We act on, and 'go by' these tacit aesthetic meanings just as often as we are guided by ethical and instrumental understandings. The agenda underpinning critical studies is to understand power relationships and encourage emancipation from dominant or constraining power structures and worldviews. To this end, contemporary organizational aesthetics has introduced an alternative perspective to leadership studies involving the non-rational, felt meanings that pervade everyday organizational life and which form the basis of emancipatory efforts.

PART IV PSYCHOLOGICAL PERSPECTIVES

20 Predictors of Leadership: The Usual Suspects and the Suspect Traits
John Antonakis

In this chapter, the literature on traits (i.e. individual differences) and their links to leader outcomes are reviewed. An integrated model entitled 'the ascription-actuality trait theory of leadership' is presented in order to explain two routes to leader outcomes that stem from traits: the route that objectively matters and the route that appears to matter but objectively does not. Drawing on criteria to judge the validity of trait models, traits that really matter to effective leadership (e.g. ability and personality) are distinguished from those that do not seem to matter that much (e.g. emotional intelligence, MBTI) and those that do not matter at all (i.e. HBDI, DISC and NLP).

21 Contingency Theories of Effective Leadership
Gary Yukl

Contingency theories generated extensive research for two decades, but were eventually eclipsed by leadership theories that emphasized leader influence on emotions as well as cognitions, and influence by single and multiple leaders. One major reason for the declining popularity of the early contingency theories is the lack of strong empirical support for them. The lack of strong, consistent results in the research does not justify the conclusion that situational variables are irrelevant for understanding effective leadership. In an increasingly turbulent world, the idea that leaders must adapt their behavior to changing conditions seems even more relevant today than it was decades ago when the theories were first proposed.

22 Transformational Leadership
Hector R. Diaz-Saenz

Transformational leadership is the process whereby a leader fosters group or organizational performance beyond expectation by virtue of the strong emotional attachment with his or her followers, combined with the collective commitment to a higher moral cause. For the past 30 years transformational leadership has been the single most studied and debated idea within the field of leadership studies. Transformational leadership studies have also been conducted in the widest range of empirical contexts. However, efforts to progress the theory to its next level of development are hampered by an overreliance on quantitative data, most especially survey-generated data, as well as fragmentation and limited cross-fertilization between scholars who choose to rely on one particular survey instrument.

23 Leader–Member Exchange: Recent Findings and Prospects for the Future
Smriti Anand, Jia Hu, Robert C. Liden and Prajya R. Vidyarthi

In the past decade interest in studying leader–member exchange (LMX) has not diminished. Indeed many encouraging developments have taken place, most importantly: (1) increased attention to the context surrounding LMX relationship (e.g. work group dynamics); (2) many investigations are now exploring LMX from a multi-level perspective; and (3) there has been an increment in the number of studies conducted with non-US samples, especially those conducted in Asia, with a concurring focus on cultural variables that impinge on LMX relationships. Despite the progress, several concerns remain. Most notably, there continues to be a need for research that enhances our understanding of (1) LMX development and change/maintenance over time and (2) the way in which the constellation of social network relationships influence specific LMX dyads.

24 Leadership and Attachment Theory: Understanding Interpersonal Dynamics in Leader–Follower Relations
Annilee M. Game

There is growing interest in the relational dynamics of leadership and there is increased recognition that attachment theory, which previously has had limited influence of the field, may have a significant role in this connection. Attachment theory examines the ways in which people's reflections on and feelings about relationships are significantly affected by reflections on and feelings about their experiences of relationships with other important figures in their lives – both past and present. The limited theory and research that explores possible links between attachment theory and leadership have tended to be leader-centric, for example, examining attachment styles and leadership emergence or potential. However, this chapter also examines follower attachment styles and their significance for leadership relationships. The application of attachment theory does not generate a new theory of leadership. Instead, it enables established ideas and findings about leadership to be viewed differently and for leader-follower relational dynamics to be illuminated.

25 Team Leadership: A Review and Look Ahead
C. Shawn Burke, Deborah DiazGranados and Eduardo Salas

Conceptual and empirical work on team leadership has exploded within the last 10 years, paralleling the dramatic increase in the use of teams in organizations. Team leadership can be defined as the enactment of the affective, cognitive, and behavioural processes needed to facilitate performance management (i.e., adaptive, coordinated, integrated action) and team development. Team leadership is a complex, multilevel, and cyclical process that takes many forms. Four primary leadership foci are highlighted and illustrated with reference to empirical findings: leadership of co-located teams, virtual teams, networked teams (i.e. multi-team systems), and shared leadership. A critical analysis is presented of the research methodologies used both within the specific foci as well as across the broader team leadership domain.

26 Authentic Leadership
Arran Caza and Brad Jackson

Rooted in the positive psychology movement, authentic leadership builds on transformational leadership by bringing to the fore the central importance for leadership effectiveness of transparency, moral and ethical behaviour, openness and self-awareness. While relatively nascent, authentic leadership has attracted considerable theoretical attention and continues to figure prominently in practitioners' discussions of leadership. Its validity and efficacy as well as its purpose have also become the focus for considerable debate among leadership psychologists and critical leadership scholars.

27 A Multi-Level View of Leadership and Emotions: Leading with Emotional Labor
Neal M. Ashkanasy and Ronald H. Humphrey

Emotions and leadership are intimately bound concepts. Understanding leadership, therefore, requires an understanding of the role emotion plays at all levels of organizational functioning. This is addressed in three parts. In Part 1, leadership and emotion are linked at five levels of organizational analysis, going from affective events and within-person emotional fluctuations, to individual differences and emotion communication in interpersonal relationships, and then to consideration of emotion in groups and the organization as a whole. Part 2 deals in detail with three topics that arose from Part 1: leaders as managers of members' mood states, emotional intelligence, and the emotional underpinnings of charismatic and transformational leadership. Part 3 takes this line a step further, arguing that good leadership necessarily incorporates emotional labor.

28 The Shadow Side of Leadership
Manfred Kets De Vries and Katharina Balazs

Most leadership research endeavors to depict the leader as a paragon of virtue and speaks in glowing terms of the attributes that constitute leadership. The aim of this chapter is to counterbalance this preoccupation by providing insights into the darker, shadow side of leadership. The clinical paradigm which draws upon concepts such as transference and narcissism offers compelling explanations for leadership derailment, the contributions that psychological pressures play in promoting dysfunctional behavioral patterns and defensive reactions that leaders tend to fall prey to. Unconscious dynamics have a significant impact on life in organizations. Organizational leaders are, therefore, urged to recognize and plan for these dynamics.

29 Psychoanalytic Approaches to Leadership
Yiannis Gabriel

The distinguishing feature of psychoanalytic approaches is the assumption of an unconscious dimension to social and individual life. In line with Freud, leadership involves a powerful relation between leaders and followers; one based on the identification of followers with the leaders and his/her idealization. The leadership romance, the powerful bond that links leaders and their followers, which in so many ways is akin to being in love, frequently goes awry with leaders lapsing into dysfunctional modes such as narcissism and authoritarianism. From a psychoanalytic perspective, leading is defined as 'imagining, willing, inspiring and driving'. Psychoanalytic approaches acknowledge the relational aspect of leadership, but in the last resort insist on the asymmetrical relation between leaders and followers.

30 Creativity, Innovation and Leadership: Models and Findings
Michael D. Mumford, Isaac C. Robledo and Kimberly S. Hester

The impact of innovation on organizational performance has resulted in a new concern with the leadership of creative, innovative, efforts. Seven major theoretical models have been proposed to account for leader performance in innovative work: (1) cognition, (2) control, (3) climate, (4) motivation, (5) interactions, (6) teams, and (7) systems exchange. All of these theories have evidenced some validity as models of what leaders must do to ensure creativity and innovation. Research suggests that three unique aspects of leadership take on special significance when one examines innovation: first, in leading creative work, leader cognition becomes especially important; secondly, the leader's ability to define a climate that will support innovation becomes of great concern; and thirdly, how leaders go about integrating creative work with other ongoing organizational activities appears uniquely important.

PART V   EMERGING PERSPECTIVES

31 Followership and Follower-Centred Approaches
Michelle C. Bligh

The role of followers in determining leadership behaviour and effectiveness has been widely acknowledged for several decades. Yet only recently have a critical mass of scholars placed followers' perceptions, expectations and behaviours at the forefront of their concerns. Research into followers typically falls into three broad categories: (1) follower attributes relevant to the leadership process, including follower perceptions, affect, identity, motivation, and values; (2) leader–follower relations, such as the active role followers play in dynamic leadership processes; and (3) follower outcomes of leadership behaviors such as performance, creativity, or other dependent variables and unspecified effects that leaders have on followers. In light of this research, organizations should consider adopting policies and practices that encourage proactive followership.

32 Hybrid Configurations of Leadership
Peter Gronn

Configuration should be considered as the new unit of leadership analysis in order to try to transcend the individual–distributed divide that currently characterizes leadership research. While evidence from existing studies points towards leadership hybridity, its patternings are unclear: these might indicate that hybrid mixtures narrow around a small handful of gestalts or that they diverge in unpredictable ways. Future research should seek to understand the contribution particular ways of configuring leadership make to the overall performance effectiveness of organizations. Efforts should also be made to track leadership hybridity over time to ascertain broad developmental trajectories. Finally, increased recognition may have to be accorded to the peculiar factors which constrain and enable the work of different categories of leaders.

33 Moving Relationality: Meditations on a Relational Approach to Leadership
Dian Marie Hosking

Interest in relational approaches to leadership is blossoming. The term 'relational' is given many different meanings in the context of very different social science perspectives. It is important that such differences be recognized and respected rather than glossed or subjected to a universalizing 'better/worse' critique. It is hoped that there will be continuing exploration of *eco*-logical constructions and relational processes as they make and re-make self–other and relations. This must give more space to the body, to feelings and the senses, to what some would call wisdom, and to ways of opening up to otherness. Increasingly, world leaders, managers and consultants are (re)connecting 'sacred' and secular. It is possible that 'relationally engaged leadership' can provide the difference that really makes a difference.

34 Complexity Leadership Theory
Mary Uhl-Bien and Russ Marion

Complexity leadership draws from physical science principles of complexity theory to consider how we can view leadership as being dynamic, processual, contextual and multi-level (fractal). As with biology and physics, where complexity radically transformed views regarding orderliness of the universe, complexity is helping leadership scholars overcome the limits of bureaucratic logics in thinking about the dynamics of order in organizational life. Complexity provides a new lexicon for leadership research and practice – one that considers leadership as occurring in both formal *and* informal processes, and as emerging in and interacting with complex interactive dynamics. Complexity leadership theory brings to the fore the learning, creative, and adaptive capacity of complex adaptive systems (CAS) within a context of knowledge-producing organizations.

35 Spirituality and Leadership
Mario Fernando

Over the past decade, the relationship between spirituality and leadership has become a major preoccupation for a small but growing group of leadership researchers who draw on religious, non-denominational and secular perspectives. Interest has been fuelled by the spate of well-publicised irresponsible business practices linked to the global financial crisis and corporate collapses. In order for the field of spiritual leadership studies to fulfil its goal of promoting spiritually-enlightened responsible leadership, its researchers should begin to actively incorporate more concepts and constructs from other fields that are linked to spirituality; they should pursue more qualitative research and conduct research in empirical contexts beyond North America and Europe.

36 Discursive Approaches to Leadership
Gail T. Fairhurst

Scholars who study organizational discourse within a broadly social constructionist framework have rethought the concept of leadership with a social and cultural lens. A social and cultural lens emphasizes leadership discourse, communication, and relational stances. Not all social constructionists are interpretive, critical, and/or poststructuralists in orientation, but discursive leadership scholars typically are. Discursive leadership research focuses on localized problems, issues, or tensions in which there is meaning (negotiation) work and coordinated action of some kind. In a very visceral sense discursive approaches to leadership and leadership psychology undertake different kinds of research. However, there is the possibility for complementarity to exist between these two kinds of research, even if there are currently few exemplary of studies of this nature to draw upon.

37 Being Leaders: Identities and Identity Work in Leadership
Amanda Sinclair

A central concern of social theorizing for several decades, identity has only recently become a preoccupation within leadership studies. Two broad and very different sets of understandings and prescriptions have emerged from this work. On the one hand are more critical accounts of the production of leadership identities. This research examines the political and discursive processes by which manager and leader identities are manufactured, controlled and occasionally resisted. On the other hand is a substantial and growing popular literature which offers advice on how leaders can be more effective by adapting, presenting and projecting an authentic leadership persona. Leadership scholars should strive to explore the construction of leadership identities in a critical and more mindful way and become more explicit about their own identity work.

38 The Virtual Leader
David M. Boje, Alison Pullen, Carl Rhodes and Grace Ann Rosile

A virtual leader is a leader who is not actually an embodied person even though still performing leadership functions for the leader's organization. With virtualization, leadership can be enhanced and empowered such that it is no longer about the actions of persons, but rather is performed for and on the organization by the cultural 'imaginary' of what leadership signifies. This 'hyper-real' leadership is a potent fantasy of leadership, where leadership is disembodied in practice yet accelerated in effectivity. The virtual leader can enhance the capacity for transformational leadership in organizations, and for organizational transformation. Virtual leadership also has the capacity to transcend the persistent gender dualisms prevalent in leadership research, even though this potential is largely waiting to be realized.

List of Contributors

Mats Alvesson is Professor of Business Administration at the University of Lund, Sweden and at the University of Queensland Business School, Australia. He is Honorary Professor at the University of St Andrews and Visiting Professor at Exeter University. Research interests include critical theory, gender, power, management of professional service (knowledge-intensive) organizations, leadership, identity, organizational image, organizational culture and symbolism, qualitative methods and philosophy of science. Recent books include *Metaphors we lead by* (Routledge, 2010, edited with Andre Spicer), *Oxford Handbook of Critical Management Studies* (Oxford University Press, edited with Todd Bridgman and Hugh Willmott). *Understanding gender and organizations* (Sage, 2009, 2nd edn with Yvonne Billing), *Reflexive methodology* (Sage, 2009, 2nd edn, with Kaj Skoldberg), *Changing organizational culture* (Routledge, 2008, with Stefan Sveningsson), *Knowledge work and knowledge-intensive firms* (Oxford University Press, 2004), *Postmodernism and social research* (Open University Press, 2002), and *Understanding organizational culture* (Sage, 2002).

Smriti Anand is a doctoral candidate in organizational behavior/human resource management at the University of Illinois at Chicago. Her research interests include leadership, diversity, and non-traditional work arrangements with particular focus on multi-level and cross-cultural frameworks. Smriti has presented her research at several meetings of the Academy of Management and the Southern Management Association. Her research has also been published in the *Academy of Management Journal* and the *Journal of Applied Psychology.*

John Antonakis is Professor of Organizational Behaviour in the Faculty of Business and Economics of the University of Lausanne, Switzerland. He received his PhD from Walden University in Applied Management and Decision Sciences and was a postdoctoral fellow in the Department of Psychology at Yale University. He has published in world-class international journals such as *Science, The Leadership Quarterly, Journal of Operations Management, Personality and Individual Differences, Journal of the American Society for Information Science and Technology,* and *Human Relations,* among others. He has also published two books (*The Nature of Leadership* and *Being there even when you are not: Leading through strategy, structures, and systems*). He is Associate Editor of *The Leadership Quarterly,* and is on the editorial boards of *Academy of Management Review, Human Relations, Journal of Management Studies, Leadership, Organizational Psychology Review,* and *Organizational Research Methods.* Professor Antonakis' expertise is on predictors and outcomes of leadership, psychometrics, and social cognition. He frequently consults for government and private organizations on leadership and human resources issues. His research is quoted regularly in the media, both in Switzerland and internationally.

Neal M. Ashkanasy is Professor of Management in the UQ Business School at the University of Queensland. His PhD is in Social and Organizational Psychology, also from the University of Queensland. He is a Fellow of the Association for Psychological Science, the Society for Industrial and Organizational Psychology, and the Australia and New Zealand Academy of Management. His research focuses on the role of emotion in organizational life, as well as leadership, culture, and ethics. He has published over 100 articles, including in leading peer-reviewed journals such as the *Academy of Management Journal*, the *Academy of Management Review*, and the *Journal of Management*. Professor Ashkanasy is Editor-in-Chief of the *Journal of Organizational Behavior*, Associate Editor for *Emotion Review*, and series editor for *Research on Emotion in Organizations*. He administers two ListServs (Orgcult – The Organizational Culture Caucus; and Emonet – Emotions in Organizations) with a combined subscription of over 1500.

Katharina Balazs is Associate Professor of Leadership and Organizational Behavior at ESCP Europe (The European School of Management), Paris, France. She holds a PhD in Business Administration from HEC, Jouy en Josas and an MBA and MSc from INSEAD, Fontainebleau. She is author and co-author of several books and articles on outstanding leadership, organizational transformation, change, entrepreneurship and excellence (e.g., 'Some Like it *Haute:* Leadership Lessons from France's Great Chefs'). She has worked as a strategic management consultant in Scandinavia, France, Austria, Germany and Hungary, specializing on cross-cultural management issues in international mergers and acquisitions. Among her current organizational interests are leadership development, executive coaching, entrepreneurship, cross-cultural management, innovation and organizational excellence. She also does executive development and coaching work in international companies on leadership and cross-cultural management in different countries.

Prasad Balkundi is an Assistant Professor of Management in the State University of New York at Buffalo. He received his PhD in business administration from Pennsylvania State University. His research interests include social networks and leadership in teams and his work has appeared in the *Academy of Management Journal, Academy of Management Review* and *The Leadership Quarterly*.

Ralph Bathurst is a musician turned organizational theorist. His PhD is in Management from Victoria University of Wellington and his primary research interests focus on how artistic engagement assists management practice and organizational revitalization.

John Benington is Emeritus Professor at Warwick University, where for over 20 years he led Warwick Business School's research, development and teaching work in the fields of public policy and management. He has 20 years prior experience as a public manager, is a non-executive member of the Board of the UK's National School of Government, and is a member of their Sunningdale Institute. He is National Chair of the UK Local Authorities and Research Councils Initiative, and is on the editorial boards of two journals. His research and publications are on community and economic development, networked governance, public value and public leadership.

Michelle C. Bligh is an Associate Professor in the School of Behavioral and Organizational Sciences at Claremont Graduate University. Her research interests include charismatic leadership, interpersonal trust, and political leadership. Her work has been published in *Journal of Applied Psychology, Leadership, Employee Relations, The Leadership Quarterly, Applied*

Psychology: An International Review, Group and Organization Management, Journal of Managerial Psychology, and the *Journal of Business Ethics.* She was awarded the *2007 Sage Best Paper Award* in *Group and Organization Management* and the *2003 Sage Outstanding Paper Award for Research Methods.* She also serves on the editorial review board of *the Leadership Quarterly* and *Leadership,* and co-edited a recent book titled *Follower-Centered Perspectives on Leadership: A Tribute to the Memory of James R. Meindl.* Dr Bligh has also helped a variety of public and private sector organizations to assess and improve their effectiveness in the areas of leadership development, organizational culture, and change management.

David M. Boje is currently Bill Daniels Ethics Fellow, former Bank of America Endowed Professorship of Management (awarded September 2006–2010), and past Arthur Owens Professorship in Business Administration (June 2003–June 2006) in the Management Department at New Mexico State University. His focus is on study of ethics, critical theory ethics, feminism, and power of language, discourse, and storytelling and antinarratives in organizations (see Calling All Storytellers). As of 2010 he is co-chair of the steering committee of NMSU American Association of University Professors. His reputation in corporate social responsibility ethics in academia and industry is widely known and respected in the United States and internationally. Professor Boje is described by his peers as an international scholar in the areas of narrative, storytelling, postmodern theory and critical storytelling ethics. He has published 17 books and 123 articles in journals, including the top-tier journals such as *Management Science, Administrative Science Quarterly, Academy of Management Journal, Academy of Management Review, The Leadership Quarterly,* and the international *Journal of Organization Studies.*

Alan Bryman is Professor of Organizational and Social Research, School of Management, University of Leicester, UK. He is author/co-author of numerous articles and books, including *The Disneyization of Society* (Sage, 2004), *Social Research Methods* (3rd edition, Oxford University Press, 2008) and *Business Research Methods* (with Emma Bell, revised edition, Oxford University Press, 2007). He is co-editor of *The SAGE Encyclopedia of Social Science Research Methods* (Sage, 2004), *Handbook of Data Analysis* (Sage, 2004), and *SAGE Handbook of Organizational Research Methods* (Sage, 2009). Research interests include research methodology, leadership, and organizational analysis. His current research interests include mixed methods research and leadership in higher education.

C. Shawn Burke is a research scientist at the Institute for Simulation and Training of the University of Central Florida. Her expertise includes teams and their leadership, team adaptability, team training, measurement, evaluation, and team effectiveness. Dr Burke has published over 60 articles and book chapters related to the above topics and has had work accepted at over 100 peer-reviewed conferences. She is currently investigating team adaptability, issues related to multi-cultural team performance, and multiteam systems. All of the above work is conducted with an interest in team leadership and the training of teams operating in complex environments. Dr Burke earned her doctorate in Industrial/Organizational Psychology from George Mason University. Dr Burke serves as an ad-hoc reviewer for *Human Factors, Leadership Quarterly, Journal of Applied Psychology*, and *Human Resource Management.* She has co-edited a book on adaptability and one on advances in team effectiveness research.

Linda L. Carli holds a PhD in social psychology from the University of Massachusetts at Amherst. She was a faculty member at the College of the Holy Cross and Mount Holyoke College before joining Wellesley College, where she teaches courses in organizational, social and applied psychology. Dr Carli, a social psychologist, has been a faculty member at Wellesley College since 1991. An authority on gender discrimination and the challenges faced by professional women, she is the author (with Alice Eagly) of *Through the Labyrinth: The Truth About How Women Become Leaders* (Harvard Business School Press, 2007). Dr Carli's research is on the effects of gender on women's leadership, group interaction, communication, influence, and reactions to adversity. She has developed and conducted diversity training workshops and negotiation and conflict resolution workshops for women leaders and has lectured widely on gender and diversity for business, academic, and other organizations.

Peter Case is Professor of Organization Studies, Bristol Business School, University of the West of England and Director of the Bristol Centre for Leadership and Organizational Ethics. He is general co-editor of *Culture & Organization* and a member of the editorial boards of *Leadership, Leadership & Organizational Development Journal* and the *Journal of Management, Spirituality and Religion*. His research interests encompass the ethics of leadership, organization theory and technologically-mediated organization. Recent publications include *The Speed of Organization* (with S. Lilley and T. Owens, 2006: CBS & Liber) and *John Adair: the Fundamentals of Leadership* (with J. Gosling and M. Witzel, 2007: Palgrave).

Arran Caza is an Assistant Professor of Business Administration in the Wake Forest University Schools of Business. He earned his PhD at the University of Michigan and is a research affiliate of the New Zealand Leadership Institute. Arran's research focuses on leaders and followers in organizations, with a particular emphasis on how leaders' discretionary behaviors influence follower outcomes.

Joanne B. Ciulla is Professor and Coston Family Chair in Leadership and Ethics at the Jepson School of Leadership Studies, University of Richmond, where she is one of the founding faculty. She is also a Visiting Professor at Nyenrode Business Universiteit in the Netherlands and Fort Hare University in South Africa. Professor Ciulla has held the UNESCO Chair in Leadership Studies at the United Nations International Leadership Academy in Jordan, and had academic appointments at Harvard Business School and The Wharton School. She has a BA, MA, and PhD in philosophy, and teaches, writes, and consults on leadership ethics, business ethics, and the philosophy of work. Professor Ciulla has published extensively: recently, she edited a three-volume set called *Leadership at the Crossroads*. She sits on the editorial boards of *The Business Ethics Quarterly*, and *Leadership,* and is an Associate Editor of *The Leadership Quarterly*. Professor Ciulla is the president of The Society for Business.

David Collinson is Professor of Leadership & Organization at Lancaster University Management School. Previously at the universities of Warwick, Manchester, St Andrews and South Florida, David is the founding co-editor of the journal *Leadership* and the founding co-organizer of the International Conference on Studying Leadership. He has published eight books, including *Managing the Shopfloor* (1992) and *Managing to Discriminate* (1990) and over 100 journal articles, chapters and reports that contribute to critical perspectives on leadership, management and organization, exploring in particular issues of power, gender, resistance and identity. David's current research focuses on the development of critical approaches to leadership. Recent publications include: 'Dialectics of Leadership', 'Re-thinking Followership', 'Questions of Leadership Distance', 'Identities and Insecurities', 'Leadership, Humour and Satire' and 'Conformist, Resistant and Disguised Selves'.

Jay A. Conger is the Henry Kravis Research Professor of Leadership Studies at Claremont McKenna College. He is also Senior Research Scientist at the Center for Effective Organizations at the University of Southern California in Los Angeles and visiting Professor of Organizational Behavior at the London Business School. He has authored or co-authored 12 books including *Boardroom Realities, The Practice of Leadership, Shared Leadership, Spirit at Work,* and *Charismatic Leadership.* Jay is also a former Associate Editor of *Leadership Quarterly.*

Jean-Louis Denis, PhD is Full Professor at the École Nationale d'Administration Publique (ÉNAP) member at the Institute of Research in Public Health at Université de Montréal. He is visiting professor EuroMed Management in Marseille. He pursues research on governance and processes of change in health care organizations and systems. His current research looks at the implementation of healthcare networks, the development of primary care and the role of scientific evidence in the adoption and implementation of clinical and managerial innovations. He is a member of the Royal Society of Canada, fellow of the Canadian Academy of Health Sciences and chair of the advisory board of CIHR's Institute of Health Services and Policy Research.

David V. Day is the Woodside Professor of Leadership and Management at the University of Western Australia Business School. Professor Day has published more than 75 journal articles, books, and book chapters, many pertaining to his primary research interests in leadership and leadership development. He is the lead author on the recently published book titled, *An Integrative Approach to Leader Development: Connecting Adult Development, Identity and Expertise* (Routledge, 2009) and is presently editing *The Oxford Handbook of Leadership and Organizations.* Professor Day serves as an Associate Editor of the *Journal of Applied Psychology* and *Leadership Quarterly,* and is on the editorial boards of *Human Performance, Organizational Behavior and Human Decision Processes,* and *Journal of Management.* He is a Fellow of the American Psychological Association and the Society for Industrial and Organizational Psychology.

Deborah DiazGranados is a doctoral candidate in the Industrial/Organizational Psychology program at the University of Central Florida and is a graduate research associate at the Institute for Simulation and Training. Ms DiazGranados received her BS degrees in Psychology and Management from the University of Houston, and her MS in Industrial/Organizational Psychology from the University of Central Florida. Her research interests include team processes and effectiveness, training, motivation, leadership, and the multicultural issues that surround these topics. Ms. DiazGranados is currently investigating leadership and the issues related to multicultural team processes and performance.

Héctor R. Díaz-Sáenz is Professor at EGADE Business School, Monterrey, Mexico. He received his PhD in Organizational Communication from the University of Texas at Austin. He is leading a research group studying leadership and organizational behavior. He has a special interest in studying behaviors pertaining to transformational leaders, their communication interactions, and the applicability of this leadership focus on organizations of emerging economies. He is also involved in communication research initiatives that include diverse topics such as the sense of community in organizations, the impact of psychological contracts in labor relations, and the impact of leadership communication on creating a sense of community in organizations. In addition, he is involved in research projects that explore the sense of community as a social organizational context which fosters knowledge sharing and innovation. He participates in training programs focusing on the development of leadership, communication and teamwork skills, applying the experiential learning method. He was Director of Executive Programs of EGADE and performs assessments to help organizations to improve organizational communication, leadership, and culture.

Alice H. Eagly is Professor of Psychology, James Padilla Chair of Arts and Sciences, Professor of Management & Organizations, and Faculty Fellow in the Institute for Policy Research, all at Northwestern University. She received her PhD from the University of Michigan and has held faculty positions at Michigan State University, University of Massachusetts in Amherst, and Purdue University. Her research interests include the study of leadership, gender, attitudes, prejudice, and stereotyping. She is the author of several books and numerous journal articles and chapters in edited books. Her most recent book is *Through the Labyrinth: The Truth About How Women Become Leaders*, co-authored with Linda Carli. She has won several awards, most recently the 2008 Gold Medal for Life Achievement in the Science of Psychology from the American Psychological Foundation and the 2009 Distinguished Scientific Contribution Award from the American Psychological Association.

Gail T. Fairhurst is a Professor of Communication at the University of Cincinnati, USA. Her research interests are in organizational communication, specifically in language and discourse-based approaches to the study of leadership. She has published over 60 articles in communication and management journals as well as book chapters. She is the author of three books, including *Discursive Leadership: in Conversation with Leadership Psychology* (Sage, 2007) and *The Power of Framing: Creating the Language of Leadership* (Jossey-Bass, 2010). Her work has been the recipient of numerous awards. She is also a Fellow of the International Communication Association, a Fulbright Scholar, and an Associate Editor for *Human Relations*.

Mario Fernando is a Senior Lecturer at the School of Management and Marketing, University of Wollongong, Australia. His research explores spiritual well-being and ethical ideologies of senior managers, the virtuousness of corporate social responsibility and spiritual leadership. He has published his work in academic journals including the *Journal of Business Ethics, Technovation, International Journal of Project Management, Leadership and Organization Development Journal* and the *European Management Journal*. Mario has published a book titled *Spiritual Leadership in the Entrepreneurial Business: a Multifaith Study* (2007, Edward Elgar) and serves on the Editorial Review Board of the *Leadership and Organization Development Journal*.

Donelson R. Forsyth holds the Colonel Leo K. and Gaylee Thorsness Endowed Chair in Ethical Leadership in the Jepson School of Leadership Studies at the University of Richmond. A social psychologist, his research focuses on leadership, group processes, and the interpersonal foundations of morality, environmentalism, and social cognition, published in such journals as *Journal of Personality and Social Psychology* and the *American Psychologist*. His books include *Our Social World* (1998) and *Group Dynamics* (5th edn, 2010), and he was the founding editor of the journal *Group Dynamics: Theory, Research, and Practice*. He is a fellow of the American Psychological Association and the Society of Experimental Social Psychologists.

Robert French is Reader in Organization Studies at Bristol Business School, UWE, and also works as an independent organizational consultant. He has a particular interest in issues of teaching and learning, in leadership and in the application of psychoanalysis in group and organizational contexts. He has written widely in these areas and recently edited the papers of David Armstrong (*Organization in the Mind*, Karnac, 2005), and has co-edited two earlier books, *Rethinking Management Education* (Sage, 1996, with Chris Grey), and *Group Relations, Management, and Organization* (Oxford University Press, 1999, with Russ Vince).

Yiannis Gabriel is Professor of Organizational Theory and Deputy Dean of the School of Management at Bath University. Yiannis is known for his work into organizational storytelling and narratives, leadership, management learning, psychoanalytic studies of work, and the culture and politics of contemporary consumption. He has used stories as a way of studying numerous social and organizational phenomena, including leader–follower relations, group dynamics and fantasies, nostalgia, insults, and apologies. More recently, Yiannis has carried out research on leadership and patient care in the hospital sector and on the experiences of sacked leaders and senior professionals. He is the author of 10 books and has been editor of *Management Learning* and associate editor of *Human Relations*. His enduring fascination as a researcher lies in what he describes as the unmanageable qualities of life in and out of organizations.

Annilee M. Game is a Lecturer in Organisational Behaviour and Business Ethics in Norwich Business School at the University of East Anglia, UK. She obtained her PhD in 2003 from Aston Business School, UK. Her current research interests focus on leader–follower relations, the application of attachment theory to organisational life, and emotions at work.

George R. Goethals holds the E. Claiborne Robins Distinguished Professorship in Leadership Studies at the University of Richmond. Previously he taught at Williams College, where he was Chair of the Department of Psychology, founding Chair of the Program in Leadership Studies, Acting Dean of the Faculty, and Provost. A social psychologist by training, Goethals explores leadership from psychological and historical perspectives. With Georgia Sorenson and James MacGregor Burns he edited the *Encyclopedia of Leadership* (Sage, 2004), and with Sorenson, *The Quest for a General Theory of Leadership* (Elgar, 2006). His recent research focuses on presidential debates, the presidency of Ulysses S. Grant, and the role of biography in shaping our understanding of leadership. With Scott Allison, he is author of *Heroes, What They Do & Why We Need Them*, to be published in October 2010 by Oxford University Press.

Ray Gordon is a Professor of Organisation Behaviour and the current Dean of the Faculty of Business, Technology and Sustainable Business at Bond University, Queensland, Australia. His research interests include power in organizations, leadership and ethics, behavioural control systems, ethnography and discourse methods. He has published extensively in academic journals such as the *Leadership Quarterly, Organization Studies,* the *Journal of Public Administration* and the *Organization Management Journal*. He authored a book entitled *Power, Knowledge and Domination*, which was published in 2007 by Libre: Copenhagen Business School Press as part of its Advances in Organizations Studies series. His paper entitled *Ethics, Discourse and Power: An Empirical Analysis into Ethics in Practice* was nominated by the Social Issues in Management division for the All Academy Newman Award for excellence at the 2005 Academy of Management Conference, and in 2006 his paper entitled *Power, Authority and Legitimacy* won the best paper award for the Critical Management Studies stream and received an All Academy Highly Commended Paper Award at the Australia and New Zealand Academy of Management Conference.

Keith Grint is Professor of Public Leadership at Warwick University Business School. Previously he has held chairs at Cranfield University and Lancaster University. Before that he was Director of Research at the Saïd Business School, Oxford University. Keith spent 10 years in industry before switching to an academic career. He is a founding co-editor of the journal *Leadership* published by Sage and founding co-organizer of the International Conference in Leadership Research. He is an Academician of the Academy of Social Science, a Visiting

Research Professor at Lancaster, an Associate Fellow of the Saïd Business School and Green Templeton College, Oxford, a Fellow of the Sunningdale Institute, a research arm of the UK's National School of Government, a Fellow of the Windsor Leadership Trust, and a Fellow of the Leadership Trust. His books include *Leadership* (ed.) (1997); *Fuzzy Management* (1997); *The Machine at Work: Technology, Work and Society* (with Steve Woolgar) (1997); *The Arts of Leadership* (2000); *Organizational Leadership* (with John Bratton and Debra Nelson); *Leadership: Limits and Possibilities* (2005), *Leadership, Management and Command: Rethinking D-Day* (2008), and *Leadership: A Very Short Introduction* (2010).

Peter Gronn is a professor in the Faculty of Education, University of Cambridge, where he is also a Fellow of Hughes Hall. Previously he held professorial appointments at the University of Glasgow (2007–2008) and Monash University, where he was appointed to a personal chair (2003–2007). His research interests encompass a number of aspects of general leadership and management; educational policy, leadership and management; organization processes and behaviour; and educational history and biography. He is an editorial board member of a number of journals, including *Leadership, Leadership Quarterly, Leadership and Organization Development Journal, Leadership and Policy in Schools* and *Educational Administration Quarterly*. Recently he was part of a 21-country OECD study 'Improving School Leadership', and he has co-authored two research reports into leadership recruitment and retention, and leadership coaching for the Scottish Government. Currently, he is completing a biography of an Australian educational leader and public figure of influence.

Eric Guthey is an Associate Professor in the Department of Intercultural Communication and Management at the Copenhagen Business School in Denmark. His research explores how leadership concepts and practices interact with the social, institutional and commercial dynamics of their own production, distribution and consumption. He most recently published *Demystifying Business Celebrities* (together with Timothy Clark and Brad Jackson), and he is the author of numerous articles that develop interdisciplinary perspectives on the social and cultural dynamics of leadership and management.

Paige Haber is an instructor for the Department of Leadership Studies at the University of San Diego and for the Department of Organizational Leadership at Chapman University. Paige is also a doctoral candidate in the Leadership Studies Program at the University of San Diego. Her professional work is in the area of college student leadership development, the development of formal leadership programs, women's leadership, and emotional intelligence. Paige is the author of chapters in the *Handbook for Student Leadership Programs, Peer Education Sourcebook, Leadership in Nonprofit Organizations*, and *The Emotionally Intelligent Leadership Facilitator's Guide*.

Hans Hansen, PhD, Management, Rawls College of Business, Texas Tech University.

Jean Hartley is Professor of Organizational Analysis at Warwick Business School, University of Warwick. Her research is on public leadership (political, managerial/professional and social movement leadership), and on innovation, improvement and organizational change in public service organizations. Research with both national and local politicians has led to a number of publications on political leadership and the creation of leadership development tools for politicians. Research on managerial leadership has included a major research project on leadership with political awareness for managers as they lead across diverse and sometimes competing interests with multiple organizations and stakeholders. Jean has published six books, the two most recent being *Leadership for Healthcare* (2010) with John Benington and as co-author of *Managing to Improve Public Services* (2008). She has published a wide range of articles and reports on leadership, innovation and improvement, and organizational and cultural change and improvement in public services.

Kimberly S. Hester is a doctoral student in the Industrial and Organizational Psychology Program at the University of Oklahoma. Her research interests include leadership, affect, creativity, and innovation.

Dian Marie Hosking is Professor in Relational Processes at Utrecht University School of Governance, The Netherlands. Her books include *A Social Psychology of Organizing* (with Ian Morley), *Management and Organisation: Relational Alternatives to Individualism* (edited with Peter Dachler and Ken Gergen), *The Social Construction of Organisation* (with Sheila McNamee) and, most recently, *Transforming Inquiry* (also with Sheila McNamee). Her work embraces a continuing interest in possible alternatives to hard self/other differentiation. This is reflected in explorations of ongoing processes (rather than static entities), in ongoing development and transformation (rather than change), in distributed leadership, networking and self-organizing (rather than hierarchy, structures and control), and in constructions of the sacred. She is currently involved in a number of projects that further extend her explorations of possible connections between relational constructionism, Tibetan Buddhism, the warrior tradition of Shambhala and leadership. In recognition of her work on leadership, Turku School of Economics awarded her the degree of DSc (Econ) honoris causa.

Jia (Jasmine) Hu is a doctoral candidate in organizational behavior and human resource management at the University of Illinois at Chicago. Her research interests focus on leadership within work teams, especially the role of leader–member exchange and servant leadership in team motivation processes and team effectiveness. Jasmine has presented several papers in national meetings of the Academy of Management and Society for Industrial and Organizational Psychology. Her work has appeared in the *Journal of Vocational Behavior*.

Ronald H. Humphrey is a Professor of Management at Virginia Commonwealth University. Much of his research is on leadership and emotions. He recently edited (2008) *Affect and Emotion: New Directions in Management Theory and Research*. He is busy writing a forthcoming book (2011), *Modern Leadership,* to be published by Sage. Dr Humphrey has published in a wide range of journals, including the *Academy of Management Review, Research in Organizational Behavior, Leadership Quarterly, American Sociological Review, Social Psychology Quarterly, Human Relations, Organization Science*, and *Journal of Organizational Behavior.*

Brad Jackson is the Fletcher Building Education Trust Chair in Leadership at the University of Auckland Business School. His research explores the role of communication in the social construction of leadership, most especially visual communication; the relationship between leadership and governance processes; and the application of geographic perspectives to leadership research and teaching. Jackson has published five books – *Management Gurus and Management Fashions, The Hero Manager, Organisational Behaviour in New Zealand, A Very Short, Fairly Interesting and Reasonably Cheap Book About Studying Leadership* and *Demystifying Business Celebrity*. He serves on the board of the International Leadership Association, is a Fellow of the Leadership Trust and a Research Fellow of the Australian and New Zealand Academy of Management.

Manfred F. R. Kets de Vries holds the Raoul de Vitry d'Avaucourt Chair of Leadership Development at INSEAD. He is the Director of INSEAD's Global Leadership Centre. In addition, he is the Distinguished Professor of Leadership Development Research at the European Institute of Management and Technology in Berlin. He is the author of more than 30 books and 300 articles. His books and articles have been translated into 27 languages. Kets de Vries is a consultant on organizational change to leading European, US, Canadian, Australian, African, and Asian companies. He is a member of 17 editorial boards. He is a Fellow of the Academy of Management. In addition, he is a founding member of the International Society for the Psychoanalytic Study of Organizations and in 2009 he became a Lifetime Distinguished Member of ISPSO. Kets de Vries is also the recipient of the International Leadership Association Lifetime Achievement Award for his contributions to leadership research and development. He is listed as one of the world's leading thinkers on management.

Martin Kilduff (PhD, Cornell) is Diageo Professor of Management Studies at Judge Business School, Cambridge University, and former editor of *AMR*. Previously he served on the faculties of University of Texas at Austin, Penn State, and Insead. His work focuses on social networks and includes the co-authored books *Social Networks and Organizations* (Sage: 2003) and *Interpersonal networks in organizations: Cognition, personality, dynamics and culture* (Cambridge University Press: 2008). Current research relates personality to network structure (e.g., *Journal of Applied Psychology*, 2008) and perceived networks to actual networks (e.g., *Organizational Behavior and Human Decision Processes*, 2008). He has co-authored a review of social network research forthcoming in *Academy of Management Annals*.

Veronika Kisfalvi (PhD, McGill University) is an Associate Professor at HEC Montréal where she has been teaching courses on leadership, management skills and decision making since 1986. Her research focuses on the relationships between personality, emotions and strategic decision-making in top management teams. She has given executive seminars in Switzerland, Holland, Tunisia, West Africa, Bulgaria, Trinidad, Romania and the USA. Professor Kisfalvi currently holds the position of Director of the Graduate Diploma Program at HEC.

Roderick M. Kramer is the William R. Kimball Professor of Organizational Behavior at the Stanford University Graduate School of Business. He is the author or co-author of more than 100 scholarly articles. His work has appeared in leading academic journals as well as popular journals, such as the *Harvard Business Review*. He is also the author or co-author of a number of books, including *Negotiation in Social Contexts, Psychology of the Social Self, Trust in Organizations, Power and Influence in Organizations, Psychology of Leadership, Trust and Distrust within Organizations, Trust and Distrust,* and *Social Decision Making*. He also teaches at Harvard's Kennedy School of Government and has been a visiting scholar at Oxford, London Business School, Harvard Business School, Kellogg Graduate School of Management, the Bellagio Center, and Hoover Institution. Professor Kramer has consulted with a variety of organizations on issues of trust, leadership, power, group decision making, and creativity.

Ann Langley is Professor of Management at HEC Montréal and Canada Research Chair in Strategic Management in Pluralistic Settings. Her research focuses on strategic change, leadership, innovation and the use of management tools in complex organizations with an emphasis on processual research approaches. She has published over 50 articles and two books, most recently *Strategy as Practice: Research Directions and Resources* with Gerry Johnson, Leif Melin and Richard Whittington (Cambridge University Press, 2007).

Robert C. Liden is Professor of Management at the University of Illinois at Chicago where he is also Coordinator of the OB/HR Doctoral program and Director of Doctoral Programs for the College of Business Administration. He earned his PhD at the University of Cincinnati. His research focuses on interpersonal processes within the context of such topics as leadership, groups, and career progression. He won awards with coauthors for the best articles published in the *Academy of Management Journal* and *Human Resource Management* during 2001, and for the best organizational behavior article published in any journal during 2005, awarded by the Organizational Behavior Division of the Academy of Management. In 2000–01 he was Chair of the Academy of Management's Organizational Behavior Division.

Russ Marion is a Professor of Educational Leadership at Clemson University. His research explores complexity and educational leadership. He is author of numerous articles on leadership, including one that was honored in 2001 as best paper of the year by *The Leadership Quarterly* and the Center for Creative Leadership. He has authored two books, *The Edge of Organization* (1999) and *Leadership in Education* (2001), and co-edited the book *Complexity Leadership*. He serves on the editorial board of *The Leadership Quarterly,* and edited a special issue of that journal on leadership and complexity. Dr Marion has presented on complexity leadership at the India Institute of Technology, the Institute for Management Development in Switzerland, in workshops on destructing complex movements at the US Department of Defense, and in a number of conference venues.

Michael D. Mumford is the George Lynn Cross Distinguished Research Professor of Psychology at the University of Oklahoma, where he directs the Center for Applied Social Research. He received his doctoral degree from the University of Georgia in 1983 in the fields of industrial and organizational psychology and psychometrics. Dr Mumford is a fellow of the American Psychological Association (Divisions 3, 5, 14), the Society for Industrial and Organizational Psychology, and the American Psychological Society. He has written more than 250 articles on creativity, innovation, planning, leadership, and ethics. He serves as senior editor of the *The Leadership Quarterly* and is on the editorial boards of the *Creativity Research Journal*, the *Journal of Creative Behavior, IEEE Transactions on Engineering Management,* and the *Journal of Business Ethics*. Dr. Mumford has served as principal investigator on grants totaling more than 30 million from the National Science Foundation, the National Institutes of Health, the Department of Defense, the Department of Labor, and the Department of State. He is a recipient of the Society for Industrial and Organizational Psychology's M. Scott Myers Award for Applied Research in the Workplace.

Ken Parry is Professor of Leadership and Director of the Centre for Leadership Studies at Bond University, on Australia's Gold Coast. He is author or editor of several books, most recently *A Short, Interesting and Reasonably Cheap Book about Studying Leadership* (with Brad Jackson, 2010). He was founding editor of the *Journal of Management & Organization*, the journal of the Australian and New Zealand Academy of Management. Ken is former founding director of the Centre for the Study of Leadership in New Zealand. His current research interests involve corporate governance and leadership, critical realist approaches to grounded theory, autoethnography and the aesthetics of leadership and management.

Alison Pullen publishes widely around the broad areas of identity, gender, and organizations. Some of her current writing projects include critical appraisals of feminism in organization, gendered ethical and political behaviour in organizations, and feminist methodologies. Alison works at Swansea University, Wales teaching gender and organizations to undergraduate and postgraduate students – most have aspirations to be 'leaders' and some try to acknowledge that leadership is gendered. Alison is author of *Managing Identity* (Palgrave) and co-editor of *Identity and Organization* (Routledge), *Bits of Organization* (Liber), *Thinking Organization* (Routledge) and *Exploring Identity* (Palgrave). Alison appreciates the fragility of leadership when she is with her infant son, Elliot.

Carl Rhodes is Professor of Organization Studies at Swansea University, UK. His current research focuses on critically interrogating the narration and representation of organizational experience in practice and popular culture, with a particular concern with the possibilities for organizational ethics and responsibility. Carl's most recent books are *Bits of Organization* (Liber, 2009, co-edited with Alison Pullen) and *Critical Representations of Work and Organization in Popular Culture* (Routledge, 2008, co-authored with Robert Westwood).

Isaac C. Robledo is a doctoral student in the Industrial and Organizational Psychology Program at the University of Oklahoma. His research interests include creativity, innovation, and leadership.

Linda Rouleau is Professor of Management at HEC Montreal. She teaches strategic management and organization theory. She obtained her Ph.D. at HEC Montreal. Her research focuses on micro-strategy and strategizing and on the transformation of control and identity of middle managers in a context of restructuring. Recently, she has published her work in journals such as *Journal of Management Studies, Human Relations, Journal of Management Inquiry, Strategic Organization* and *Organization Science*. She is co-director of the Strategy as Practice Study Group at HEC Montreal, and a member of the CRIMT (Canadian Research Centre on Globalization and Work).

Grace Ann Rosile is Associate Professor of Management at New Mexico State University. Her primary interest is narrative approaches to organizational studies, including organizational storytelling, theatrics, pedagogy, ethics, and academic integrity. She received the Champion of Integrity award in 2005 from Duke University's Center for Academic Integrity. Her work has been published in the *Journal of Applied Behavioral Science, Management Communication Quarterly, Organization Studies, Ephemera, Journal of Management Inquiry, Journal of Management Education, Journal of Organizational Change Management*, and *Communication Research*, in addition to a book and several book chapters. She likes to teach embodied leadership by having people work with horses. Her website is Horse Sense At Work, at www.horsesenseatwork.com

Eduardo Salas is University Trustee Chair and Pegasus Professor of Psychology at the University of Central Florida where he also holds an appointment as Program Director for the Human Systems Integration Research Department at the Institute for Simulation and Training. Dr Salas has co-authored over 350 journal articles and chapters and has co-edited 20 books. His expertise includes teamwork, team training strategies, training effectiveness, decision making under stress, simulation-based training, patient safety, and performance measurement tools. Dr Salas is a Fellow of the American Psychological Association, the Human Factors and Ergonomics Society, the Association for Psychological Science, and is currently President of the Society for Industrial and Organizational Psychology.

Peter Simpson is Reader in Organization Studies at Bristol Business School, University of the West of England. He is Director of MBA and Executive Education and Deputy Director of the Bristol Centre for Leadership and Organizational Ethics. His current areas of interest are spirituality, psychodynamics and complexity applied to issues of organizational leadership and strategic change. He has published on these themes in a range of journals, including *Human Relations, Management Learning, Leadership*, and the *Journal of Organizational Change Management*. He serves on the Editorial Review Board for the *Leadership and Organization Development Journal*.

Amanda Sinclair is Foundation Professor of Management (Diversity and Change), Melbourne Business School, at the University of Melbourne, Australia. Her research and teaching is in leadership, gender and diversity, organizational culture, change and ethics. She is the author of several books, including *Doing Leadership Differently* (1998, 2005), *New Faces of Leadership* (2002) and *Leadership for the Disillusioned* (2007), which argues for leadership that frees both followers and leaders. Amanda also coaches individuals and teams and, with colleagues, has developed new approaches to teaching and researching leadership, incorporating insights from meditative traditions, mindfulness research and her practice as a yoga and meditation teacher. Her particular interests are in the less-inspected corners of leadership territory, such as indigenous leadership and the tactile place of bodies and physicality. In drawing insights from outside leadership studies, she is keen to explore how leadership might be understood, embodied and written differently.

Georgia Sorenson PhD is Visiting Research Professor in Leadership Studies at the University of Maryland School of Law and was the founder and Distinguished Leadership Scholar at the James MacGregor Burns Academy of Leadership. Sorenson served as the Inaugural Chair and Professor of Transformation of the US Army in 2005–2006. From 2002–2004, she served as the Visiting Senior Scholar at the Jepson School of Leadership Studies, University of Richmond. She is also co-founder (with Larraine Matusak and James MacGregor Burns) of the International Leadership Association. An architect of the leadership studies field, Sorenson is co-editor (with George Goethals and James MacGregor Burns) of the four-volume award-winning *Encyclopedia of Leadership*, published by Sage Books (2004). Her most recent theoretical work (with Goethals) is *The Quest for a General Theory of Leadership* (Elgar, 2006). Sorenson serves on the editorial board of numerous refereed journals, including *Leadership* (US Editor), *Leadership Quarterly* (Associate Editor) and *Leadership Review*. Her most recent book, *Strategic Leadership, A General's Art* (with Mark Grandstaff) on military leadership, came out in early 2009. Before joining academia, Sorenson was a Senior Policy Analyst in the White House and served on the President's Productivity Council.

Dennis Tourish is Professor of Leadership at the University of Kent. His research explores the dynamics of leadership development, the dysfunctional sides of leadership, and organizational communication. He has published seven books, and is presently working on a new book entitled *Leadership: A Voyage Around the Dark Side*. He is a Visiting Professor at the University of Ulster and Robert Gordon University, and is a Fellow of the Leadership Trust Foundation. He is also an Associate Editor of the journals *Management Communication Quarterly* and *Leadership*.

Mary Uhl-Bien is Howard Hawks Chair in Business Ethics and Leadership and Co-Director of the Institute for Innovative Leadership at the University of Nebraska. Her research interests are complexity leadership, relational leadership, and followership. Dr. Uhl-Bien has received best paper awards for her work on complexity leadership (*The Leadership Quarterly*, 2001) and implicit followership theories (Southern Management Association, 2009). She is senior editor of the Leadership Horizons series for Information Age Publishers and is on the editorial boards of *Academy of Management Journal, Academy of Management Review, The Leadership Quarterly, Leadership,* and *International Journal of Complexity in Leadership and Management.* She is a founding member of the Network of Leadership Scholars in the Academy of Management, and has been a Visiting Professor at Lund University in Sweden, Catolica/Nova in Lisbon, Portugal, and Pablo de Olavide University in Seville, Spain.

Prajya R. Vidyarthi is Assistant Professor of Management at the Indiana University Kokomo. He earned his PhD from the University of Illinois at Chicago. His primary research interests include leadership, social exchange, employment relationship, and culture, especially in the international context. Prajya is an active researcher, as evidenced by his publications in the *Academy of Management Journal* and the *Journal of Applied Psychology.*

Gary Yukl received a PhD in Industrial-Organizational Psychology from the University of California at Berkeley. He is currently a Professor of Management at University of Albany, and his research interests include leadership, power and influence, and management development. He has published many articles in professional journals and has received several awards for his research. Dr Yukl is also the author or co-author of several books, including *Leadership in Organizations,* 7th edition (Prentice-Hall, 2010) and *Flexible Leadership* (Jossey-Bass, 2004). He is a fellow of the American Psychological Association, the American Psychological Society, the Society for Industrial-Organizational Psychology, and the Academy of Management. His leadership development programmes have been used in many organizations.

PART I

Overview Perspectives

A History of Leadership

Keith Grint

INTRODUCTION

Why bother with the beginning? Is history, as Henry Ford said, 'just one damned thing after another'? Well it might be, though note that Ford proceeded to build his own museum of the Ford Motor Company – to make sure his version of one damned thing after another was the accepted version. It might also be worth considering whether history provides us with examples of failed and successful leadership that we might learn from; as, George Santayana (1954) suggested, 'Those who do not learn from history are condemned to repeat it.' But does history repeat itself? Marx certainly thought there was something in this with the opening line of his work on the *18th Brumaire of Louis Napoleon*; for 'Hegel remarks somewhere that all great world-historic facts and personages appear, so to speak, twice. He forgot to add the first time as tragedy, the second time as farce.' Yet if history did repeat itself we should be able to predict events rather better than we currently do. We should, for example, have seen the current economic problems coming if we were historians of the interwar period. Yet even though events are not identical and are thus not repeated, are there patterns that might give us clues as to what might and might not happen? Indeed, does not almost every academic journal article start with a potted history of some sorts to explain why the author has decided to focus on whatever follows?

Perhaps, but, what counts as the beginning anyway? Well we can start by agreeing that 'the beginning' for leadership scholars is the beginning of recorded history, not the beginning of *Homo sapiens*. As far as it is possible to tell, all organizations and societies of any significant size and longevity have had some form of leadership, often, but not always, embodied in one person, usually – but not always – a man. This does not necessarily mean that leadership has always been, and will always be, critical or essential but it does imply that we have always had leaders. How, then, can we establish whether leadership *is* crucial or whether the forms and styles of leadership have changed across space and time? We have an inordinate amount of information on 'management', as constituted in the last 200 years, and we have an increasing pool of knowledge about contemporary leadership, but what do we know about leadership in classical times?

To a very large extent our knowledge of leadership in ancient times is crucially dependent upon the existence of written texts, and here lies the first lesson of leadership: history is written, generally speaking, by the winners. This goes for both successful military leaders and for successful political groups. In the former category we might consider how we know so much about Alexander the Great's or Julius Caesar's victories, so little about Spartacus, and almost nothing about the hundreds of other slave revolts that regularly shook slave societies throughout antiquity (Grint, 2005; Wiedemann, 1995). The answer, of course, is that Alexander and Julius Caesar either wrote their own histories or had them professionally written on their behest, while Spartacus left no written accounts and very few other slave leaders even get a mention in the accounts of their slave owners. Thus, a preliminary warning in reading any account of classical leadership – and indeed any account of contemporary leadership – is to be wary of the sources. Accounts are not neutral carriers of factual information; rather, they are partial accounts intended to achieve a particular purpose. Horatio Nelson, for example, was known to have written his own account of the various battles he engaged in, and then have his subordinate officers attach their names to the account and send them off to the newspapers and the British Admiralty as if they were written by these subordinates (Grint, 2000: p. 247). If you want to increase your chances of appearing a good leader in the media, write the story yourself.

Whether that story ever gets written in the first place depends, to some extent, on whether the narrative contains something regarded as significant: that is to say, we tend to record only those events that are unusual or extraordinary to some degree. As a consequence we do not have vast tracts on how to run a small farm in China 2,000 years ago nor on leadership in an era of peace amongst the Celtic tribes of Gaul at the same time. But we do have records of the Celtic wars against the Romans at the time and we do have some accounts of Chinese warlords in the same period. However, the texts relating to the wars between the Gauls and the Romans are Roman texts: first, because the Celts were largely a non-literate society where oral cultures prevailed and second, because, by and large, the Romans were victorious. Again, what tend to survive over long periods of time are material texts and artefacts rather than oral narratives, so our understanding of the leadership of non-literate societies is often reconstructed from the often pejorative accounts of others. From what we know of preliterate ancient civilizations from the archaeological records, any periods of peaceful coexistence with neighbouring tribes led by humanitarian leaders are few and far between: as Keeley (1996, p. 174) suggests, 'Peaceful pre-state societies were very rare; warfare between them was very frequent, and most adult men in such groups saw combat repeatedly in a lifetime.'

It should already be clear that war is a critical component in the early developments in the practice of leadership. From Sargon of Akkad (*c.* 2334–2279 BC) in what is now the Middle East, to Ramesses II (Ramesses the Great) of Egypt and from the early Cretan civilizations from around 3000 BC to the Harappan civilization in the Indus valley at the same time, and across to the Huang Ho walled settlements in China, we know that military leadership played a crucial role in the quest for survival and domination. Again, this is not to insist that leadership has its origins in war or that military leadership is the most important element in classical leadership – we simply do not know enough about these times to confirm or deny this. But it remains the case that some of the most important classical writings on leadership pertain either to the conduct of war or the conduct of politics: what Clausewitz referred to as 'the continuation of war by other means.' This is particularly so for the Classical and Renaissance periods

that we shall consider first, before turning to the more modern literature.

CLASSICAL LEADERSHIP STUDIES

Outside Europe, Kautilya's *The Arthrasastra*, written around 321 BC for the Mauryan dynasty in what is now India, provided an array of practical tips for leaders to consider. But probably the first prescriptive text that achieved significant success in both its own time and space – ancient China – and *continues* to beguile business executives to this day is Sun Tzu's (400–320 BC) *The Art of War*. This became mandatory reading for the military leaders not just of China but of Japan under the Taiho Code of 701 (Farris, 1999, pp. 52–53), where, as in many non-Western societies, war in general and military leadership in particular became tightly incorporated into the state's governance systems. In contrast, Western approaches tended to maintain a markedly higher degree of decentralization and independence from the central authorities (Hanson and Strauss, 1999, pp. 446–448).

In fact, it is not clear who the author of the aphorisms that comprise *The Art of War* really is, and it may be that many were written by Sun Tzu's disciples and students; indeed, the text reproduces this assumption is its conversational format with several characters participating in the discussion under 'Master Sun's' facilitation. Nevertheless, the central message about leadership – though obscure in parts – is clear: 'The responsibility for a martial host of a million men lies in one man. He is the trigger of its spirit' (*Manoeuvre* 20). Once this is established, *The Art of War* sets out to provide conversational sketches of the most crucial elements of strategy and tactics for military leaders.

Ironically, to Western minds, but appropriately for the minimalist essence of its Taoist origins, one of the most important lessons in *The Art of War* is that fighting is the last thing military leaders should engage in, for: 'those who win every battle are not really skilful – those who render others' armies helpless without fighting are the best of all' ('Planning A Siege'). Sun Tzu then insists that strategy is critical to success, for the art of war is the art of avoiding *unnecessary* conflict.

'The Golden Bridge' is a natural consequence of this philosophy: if you must fight then avoid head-on conflicts if at all possible, since these are both expensive in resources and casualties and are far riskier than simply attacking the enemy's plans or supply lines. And if you must attack the enemy head on – but you cannot be confident about a complete rout – then you should leave a 'golden bridge', an escape route for your enemy to retreat across, otherwise your enemy will be forced to fight to the finish, and again the consequences could be problematic. For those involved in leading negotiations, this is clearly an important piece of advice: if you cannot allow your opponent to leave the negotiating table with something they value, you will find it hard to lead them to a deal.

A second and paradoxical piece of advice is to burn your own bridges: in other words, commit yourself or suffer the penalty. 'When a leader establishes a goal with the troops', suggests Sun Tzu, 'he is like one who climbs to a high place and then tosses away the ladder'. This is an inversion of the golden bridge rule, but that is for your enemies not your allies and followers, for if your colleagues feel threatened but see an easy escape route they may well take it. If, however, there is no escape – what Sun Tzu refers to as 'Dead Ground' – then they will have to commit themselves to the fight for survival, and it is this commitment by followers to their leader that again reflects the Taoist roots of Sun Tzu's work. As he puts it, in 'Nine Grounds': 'Put them in a spot where they have no place to go and they will die before fleeing.' This might be a useful phrase for all leaders – if their own survival or fortunes are tied into the organizations they lead, they might find it much harder to fail and walk away with a golden parachute.

Sun Tzu is also adamant that military matters should be left to the military specialist and not to their political controllers: 'To say that a general must await commands of the sovereign in such circumstances is like informing a superior that you wish to put out a fire' ('Offensive Strategy'). Or as is suggested in 'The Nine Variables', 'There are occasions when the commands of the sovereign need not be obeyed.... When you see the correct course act; do not wait for orders.' Now there's a radical thought – not waiting for permission for something that obviously needs doing!

At roughly the same time that Sun Tzu was teaching military leadership in China, Plato (?429–347 BC) was warning the Greeks that the rise of political leadership rooted in democracy did not represent the flowering of Greek culture so much as a direct threat to Greek civilization. The electoral system for selecting leaders generated a circus rather than a forum for serious consideration, as far as Plato was concerned, for it encouraged potential leaders to pander to the basest instincts of the mob – 'the large and dangerous animal' – that pervades much of his writing in this sphere. The mob, suggests Plato, in his *Republic,* would be willing to risk their society (represented as a ship) by electing whichever person promised them most. Thus, rather than sailing under the person who was best qualified to be the ship's captain (one of Plato's Philosopher Kings), democracy ensures that the popular demagogue prevails – and, of necessity, leads the ship straight onto the rocks of catastrophe. This, of course, legitimizes the leadership form used in business, where democracy is absent; though financial leadership by people best qualified to lead us (financial experts) seems to have steered us straight onto, rather than away from, the rocks of catastrophe, and only the elected political leaders seem to have saved us.

But how is the best person to lead recognized? For Plato it is self-evident that we recognize the skills of people by considering their expertise: we would not ask a gardener to build us a boat any more than we would ask a farmer to run the economy. But, to Plato's intense frustration, where 'moral' knowledge is concerned, the mob assumes that everyone is an expert and therefore no-one is. The result is that the mob assumes they can recognize good political leadership when they see and hear it and are keen to put themselves forward for office, even though they would not dream of building a ship unless they were a shipbuilder. It was for precisely this reason that Plato was so firmly opposed to the Sophists and Isocrates who taught the skills of rhetoric, or public speaking, because this would simply encourage the domination of form over content. Above all, Plato feared that even those who intended to lead in a moral way for the benefit of the community would be corrupted by the system and, since leaders were vital to the health of the community, a corrupted leader would inevitably destroy 'his' own community.

Aristotle (384–322 BC), one of Plato's students, agreed that Athens was indeed under attack from corrupt leaders but differed in his response to the problem. His book *Rhetorica* was written in part as an exposé of 'the tricks of public speaking', which Aristotle believed were already corrupting Athenian public life. In its earliest form 'rhetoric', from the Greek ρήτωρ (*rh• tōr*) (speaker in the assembly), was the art of using speech to persuade. It is not coincidental that the art of rhetoric and the rule of democracy evolved simultaneously. As Lawson-Tancred (1991, p. 3) suggests, when political rule is through naked force, or inherited tradition, there is little need to *persuade* the people of one's right to rule, though in fact Ancient Greek society held oratorical skills almost as high as military prowess. The origins of rhetorical skill appear to lie in Syracuse, a Greek colonial city, and the skill moved rapidly throughout Greek society where the political and the legal system depended upon rhetorical skill. By the time of the Peloponnesian War (431–404 BC), professional teachers of rhetoric and speech writers (*logographoi*) had appeared, and training in rhetoric became commonplace, especially for potential leaders.

Classical theoreticians (Georgias, Plato, Aristotle and Cicero) were very divided in their debates about the nature of rhetoric, in particular whether it was an essential part of life and leadership or a sleight of hand (Wardy, 1996). Georgias had originally argued that rhetoric, the art of persuasion in which emotion and power were influential features, was an inevitable element of all human life. For Plato, the use of rhetoric – as an act of manipulative persuasion – was both inferior to, and subversive of, philosophy, in particular the dialectical questioning method used by Socrates to establish truth through reason and rational debate. Plato was vehemently opposed to democracy and regarded the teaching of rhetoric as a dangerous malpractice: it was the mischievous tool of the demagogue – it enslaved the masses and it pleased rather than benefited the mob, for it provided even the worst political leaders with the technical skill to manipulate the masses in whatever direction they chose (Grint, 1997a; Wardy, 1996, p. 81). For Plato, the direction was crucial and rhetorical skill should always be subordinated to the direction, and not vice versa. But for Georgias, the Athenian right to free speech and the rule of democracy (for male citizens at least) made rhetoric a principle skill for all to master; however, it was a skill that could be used for good or evil as it did not embody any values in and of itself. Of course, heroic deeds were also important, but without their recording in rhetoric they were soon lost to history. Furthermore, Plato's representation of Socrates suggests that the teacher of philosophical dialectic did not pretend to know – as he suggests rhetoricians did – the answers, but merely taught the techniques for understanding, to attain knowledge for its own sake, and increase one's own knowledge in the dialectical process with the student (Wardy, 1996, pp. 54–70.) Whatever the results of the battle in any theoretical sense, in the hands of Aristotle, the construction of rules for rhetoric became formalized, and these rules changed little between Cicero and the late eighteenth, early nineteenth, centuries when the formal teaching of rhetoric as a university subject generally fell from favour.

Aristotle had four explanations for this apparent betrayal of his teacher: First, he still maintained that since truth and justice were stronger than lies and injustice, then 'false' rhetoric would not be able to overturn the former. Truth and justice, then, had a 'natural advantage' (Wardy, 1996, p. 110). Secondly, his arch opponent and intellectual competitor, Isocrates, had developed a very successful school based on the study of rhetoric – which shaded Aristotle's school with its pulling power – and, with the decline of Athenian democracy, the utility of persuasion took on a different meaning. For Aristotle, the reality that rhetoric was *already* being taught meant that he now had a duty to educate people about the tricks that rhetoricians would use to persuade them of falsehoods. Thirdly, Aristotle argued that rhetoric could be studied, but only in the context of its philosophical foundations and formations. Rhetoric, at the hands of Aristotle, was to become not the pragmatic bag of tricks he associated with its Isocratic version, but with the scientific roots of knowledge that Aristotle inherited from Plato and Socrates. Fourthly, although Plato was adamant that rhetoric persuaded through emotion not reason – and hence his dislike of it— Aristotle suggested that one could appeal to the listeners' emotions – if, but only if, the intent and effect was to enable them to see the rationality of the argument.

Unfortunately for Aristotle, his efforts had a limited effect in their time, not through any lack of skill on his part but because within five years of his death the great Athenian experiment in democracy had been plunged into darkness with the rise of the tyrant Demetrius (an ex-pupil of Aristotle), and with the subsequent restructuring of the legal system the requirements for rhetorical skill were marginal at best. Yet, the last 100 years have demonstrated without parallel that the ability to persuade people through rhetoric has altered the world beyond our wildest dreams or nightmares: would Hitler or Churchill or Obama have made such an impact without this ancient skill?

RENAISSANCE LEADERSHIP STUDIES

One thousand and eight hundred years after Aristotle there emerged from that same area of the Mediterranean a book that came to dominate prescriptive writing on leadership, not just in its own time but in our time too. Not that Machiavelli's *The Prince* was popular: on the contrary, it was the most *unpopular* prescriptive text of the sixteenth century. No doubt Machiavelli would have found this doubly ironic: first, because *The Prince* was written to regain some political credibility and popularity with his former employers; secondly, because Machiavelli wrote it as descriptive, rather than a prescriptive, work. In other words, Machiavelli insisted that he wrote about the world of politics as it was, not as it should be in some mystical and unachievable utopia. It was the political realism that infused *The Prince* that led to its instant condemnation by the religious and political leaders of the day but which also explains its popularity today (see, for example, Ledeen, 1999; McAlpine, 1997). It was, according to Machiavelli, rooted not in theory but in historical fact, yet it was prohibited by the Catholic Church under its Index of Books. It was nothing but 'A handbook for gangsters' according to Bertrand Russell, though Napoleon was rather more positive, suggesting it was 'The only book worth reading.'

The Prince was written in 1513–1514, probably after Machiavelli started writing his *Discourses on Livy*, though the latter was not published until 1531, while the former was published the following year. As his homeland fell apart under civil war and foreign invasion, Machiavelli sought to write a guidebook for all political leaders but, in particular, for the Medicis, his patrons and erstwhile leaders of Florence. *The Prince*, then, was not simply a book to ingratiate the favour of the Medicis, but a call to arms to defend Florence and – through Florentine domination – Italy, from the 'Barbarians', by whom he meant the Spanish and French invaders.

Machiavelli had lived through the golden age of Florence, but also through some of the excesses, invoked by critics like the Dominican preacher Girolamo Savonarola who encouraged the Florentines to burn their worldly goods – their books, pictures and jewels – in a 'pyre of vanities.' Eventually, Savonarola was himself burned at the stake, but it taught Machiavelli a lesson about the vulnerability of the 'unarmed prophet'. In 1498, Machiavelli was appointed to a senior position within the Florentine civil service as Secretary to the Ten, the committee concerned with foreign and military policy. However, his attempt to organize the recovery of Pisa using mercenary troops failed miserably and his antagonism to them – and desire to displace them with a citizens' army – played a significant part in regaining Pisa in 1509, and cemented his views in *The Prince*.

Also important was his next mission, to fend off Cesare Borgia, the illegitimate son of Cardinal Rodrigo Borgia, who had become Pope Alexander VI in 1492. Cesare Borgia led the papal armies and threatened Florentine independence, but Machiavelli soon recognized a different category of leader in Cesare: for here was a man who murdered his own lieutenant (Remirro Orco), when he appeared to be unnecessarily cruel in his control over the Romagna. As Machiavelli recalled, '... one morning Remirro's body was found cut in two pieces on the piazza at Cesena, with a block of wood and a bloody knife besides it. The brutality of this spectacle kept the people of the Romagna at once appeased and stupified.' (VII). Cesare subsequently invited those conspiring against him to dinner, only to have them all slaughtered as they ate. Machiavelli, then, used Cesare as a good example of the *real politik* of life; for he believed Cesare had restored peace through the selective use of violence. The alternative, as professed in public by most leaders at the time, was to act nobly and morally, but for Machiavelli the consequence of acting morally in an immoral world was simply to allow the most immoral to dominate. 'The fact is,' he suggests in *The Prince*, 'that a man who wants to act virtuously in every way necessarily comes to grief among so many who are not virtuous. Therefore, if a prince wants to maintain his rule he must learn how not to be virtuous, and to make use of this or not according to need.' (XV)

> Cesare Borgia was accounted cruel; nevertheless, this cruelty of his reformed the Romagna, brought it unity and restored order and obedience. On reflection, it will be seen that there was more compassion in Cesare than in the Florentine people who, to escape being called cruel, allowed Pistoia to be devastated...(XVII)

In effect, Machiavelli – and Machiavellians – are not necessarily suggesting that leaders should act immorally, but that to protect the interests of a community a prince has to do whatever is necessary – for the greater good. Thus, the act should be contextualized and not analysed against some mythical moral world. The problem, of course, is defining 'the greater good' and that problem continues to plague us.

And, in answer to his rhetorical question 'Whether it is better to be loved or feared, or the reverse', Machiavelli unequivocally sides with the fear factor.

> The answer is that one would like to be the one and the other; but because it is difficult to combine them, it is far better to be feared than loved if you cannot be both. One can make this generalization about men; they are ungrateful, fickle, liars and deceivers... when you are in danger they turn against you. Any prince who has come to depend entirely on promises and has taken no other precautions ensures his own ruin.... The bond of love is one which men... break when it is to their advantage to do so; but fear is strengthened by a dread of punishment which is always effective. The prince must nonetheless make himself feared in such a way that, if he is not loved, at least he escapes being hated. (XVII)

Mrs Thatcher might well have taken Machiavelli's advice here, for although she never did court popularity in the sense of wanting to be liked (often regarded as a fatal flaw in some accounts of leadership), she did generate so many political enemies within her own political party that eventually she ran out of allies and had no more punishments to hand out.

As far as Machiavelli was concerned, his ideas amounted to no more than disclosing what was already happening rather than advocating something radically new. However, he has usually been interpreted – and certainly was at the time – as suggesting that leaders should always act immorally and subordinate the means to the end, since this would generate an advantage over others. But he actually insists, more clearly in *The Discourses* than in *The Prince*, that this can only be legitimated by reference to the greater good of the community, and not to the benefit of the individual. Of course, how this greater good is defined is a moot question, but in *The Discourses* Machiavelli sets himself firmly on the side of the republic and the populace (though he was not a democrat) and against princes and those who led for their own self-interest (especially the 'idle' aristocracy). But he also suggests that there are times when the ruthlessness of a prince is necessary to restore a society back to health, something which republics find difficult to do. Thus, in the long term (and for Machiavelli the long term could only exist within an expansionist state), a republic is preferable, but an occasional prince may be a necessary evil. We might extend this idea to suggest that sometimes (in a crisis) leaders need to be ruthless commanders, but other times (facing a Wicked Problem) they need to exhibit the more collaborative style conducive to engaging disparate interests (Grint, 2005). Machiavelli drew many of his examples of leadership from the classical period of Rome and Ancient Greece and suggested that historical patterns and lessons of the kind we began with were clear for all to see. In the next section I consider modern leadership studies, not in any detail (that is well covered in other chapters of this book), but sufficiently to establish whether such historical leadership patterns can be discerned at all.

MODERN LEADERSHIP STUDIES

Ironically, Thomas Carlyle – for many the first 'modern' writer on leadership – had spoken warmly at his inaugural address as Rector of Edinburgh University in 1866 of both Machiavelli and Oliver Cromwell. The latter Carlyle likened to a Machiavellian prince who was absolutely necessary at the time of the English Civil War. The irony lies in both Cromwell's refusal to take the crown after the execution of Charles I and in Cromwell's delivery of the only period in English history when England was a republic. In fact we can trace the rise of leadership studies to the modern era – that is the rise of industrial societies – to then. In the beginning was perhaps not God, but rather the god-like creatures that peppered the 1840 lectures of Thomas Carlyle, whose fascination

with the 'Great Men' of history effectively reduced the role of mere mortals to 'extras'. Despite Carlyle's dislike of the early industrial entrepreneurs of Britain – the 'millocracy' as he called them – the model of individual heroism that he constructed personified a popular assumption about leadership in Victorian times: it was irredeemably masculine, heroic, individualist and normative in orientation and nature.

That model seems to have prevailed throughout the latter half of the nineteenth century and was not really challenged until the first professional managerial group began displacing the original – and 'heroic' – owner-managers towards the end of the nineteenth century. Then, the argument runs, the context – and thus the requirement – for leadership shifted from heroic individuals to rational systems and processes, as the scale of industry and the level of backward integration began generating huge industries (especially in the United States) that needed significant numbers of administrators to retain organizational coherence. Many of the models for such organizational leadership were derived from the army, civil service, post office and railroads and most constituted leadership as administrative positions within formal hierarchies. In turn, as the productive growth unleashed by these giants began to encourage significant market competition and eat into profit margins, attention quickly turned to cost-reduction strategies and to Scientific Management. F.W. Taylor concentrated on the control of knowledge by management at the expense of the workforce and the deskilling of jobs in line with the expansion of the division of labour. In this case, leadership was configured as knowledge leadership, with the leaders as repositories of knowledge of production that generated power over production – in contrast to the control over production, formerly wielded by craft workers.

The economic depression of the 1920s coincided with the next major shift in leadership models and, for our purposes, it was a major shift back to the role of normative power and away from the rationality of scientific systems and processes that had dominated for the previous two decades. This 'return' to a previous normative model was derived initially from the Hawthorne experiments in the 1920s and 1930s at the General Electric (GE) plant near Chicago. There, Taylorist scientific experiments in the development of the optimum environmental working conditions had allegedly generated first perplexity and then a realization that work could not be measured objectively because the very act of measurement altered the experience and thus the behaviour of those being measured. This 'Hawthorne Effect', as it was called then, spawned a whole series of related experiments that eventually persuaded first

GE and then whole swathes of American management that workers were normatively not rationally motivated and group- not individually-oriented in culture.

Arguably, these alternating or dualist models of leadership – first the 'normative' model of Carlyle of the second half of the nineteenth century, followed by the 'rational' model of Taylor and Ford in the first two decades of the twentieth century, in turn superseded by a return to the 'normative' model of the Hawthorn experiments that solidified into the Human Relations approach of the 1930s and 1940s – reflect two broader phenomena: first, the economic cycles of the period; and, second, the political models of the period. The economic cycles formed the basis of Kondratiev's controversial theory of Long Economic Waves or Cycles; the political cycles are less controversial and more intriguing, for it seems unlikely that industry could have isolated itself from the global rise of the mass movements of communism and fascism in the late 1920s and 1930s and more likely that the leadership models embodied in these were refracted in industry through a Zeitgeist that made sense at the time. In other words, in an era when mass political movements driven by normative adherence to the collective will – but manifest in cult-like loyalty to the party leader – were so prominent, it seemed perfectly natural to assume that the best way to lead an industrial organization was to mirror this assumption: work should be normatively rather than rationally organized – by groups led by leaders who prototypically embody the same apparent desires as those held by the mass.

By the time the Second World War was over, and the economic boom returned, the model that began to dominate in the West shifted once again from the normative cult of mass and heroes – that had reflected the power of communism and fascism – to one dominated by rational analysis of the situation – a scientific approach more conducive to the war-fighting capabilities of the pre-eminent victor, the United States, and one located within its individualist culture. Thus we see the rise of the American self-actualization movement, manifest particularly in Maslow's (1954) 'Hierarchy of Needs' and in McGregor's (1960) displacement of Theory X with Theory Y.

The movement away from norms and back towards the rational understanding of contexts followed the critiques of traits by Jenkins (1947) and Stogdill (1948, 1974), as well as the work of the University of Michigan and the Ohio State studies. These provided the framework for a radical development: contingency theory. Under the general umbrella provided by Fred Fieldler's (1964) contingency theory, and Robert Blake and Jane Mouton's (1964) Managerial Grid, the theoretical fragility of relying upon a potentially endless list of traits and superhuman charismatics was, ostensibly, dealt a crippling blow. From then on what really mattered was not having the most charismatic leader, leading the most adoring mass of followers, but having a rational understanding of the situation and responding appropriately. These leadership theories that eschewed the dominant and proactive role of the individual leader in favour of more social or structural accounts tended to assume that the context or situation should determine how leaders respond; thus, in terms of the early contingency theories, situation X requires leadership X to ensure an appropriate – and thus rational – response. More recent developments in contingency theory, for all their more sophisticated accumulation of significant and independent variables, still reproduce this assumption that the 'correct' response is determined by the correct analysis of the situation.

Since the early days of this contingency approach, we have 'progressed' by returning to the importance of leaders working with the (normative) 'strong cultures' beloved of Peters and Waterman (1982), then on to the (rational) pedagogy of the Reengineering revolution of the 1990s, and finally on to the contemporary development of transformational and inspirational leadership theories silhouetted by the rise of terrorism, global warming and political and religious fundamentalism. Such transformations also invoke the New Public Management, since the 1980s, under which the public sector was ostensibly transformed from a lethargic and bureaucratic leviathan to an agile service deliverer through the encroachment of the market and the discipline of targets and performance management systems.

Coupled with concerns about the importance of emotional intelligence, identity leadership, and the development of inspiring visions and missions, this seems to have ensured the return of the original normative trait approaches: we seem to have gone forward to the past. Thus, we were recently (back) in thrall to inspirational individuals, endowed with what list of essential competencies the contemporary leaders happen to have that are adjudged to be responsible for the results. That the competencies are decontextualized, ahistorical and, at best, only correlated with, rather than determinants of, success, seems to be irrelevant. Indeed, we appear to have an amazing capacity to attribute organizational success to individual competence on the basis of virtually no evidence at all. Many political commentators describe the global political situation in similar terms – dominated by the role of individual politicians. Others simply report that politicians are the world's least trusted people, again implying that it is the individual leader that matters not the situation. Yet there is considerable support for the

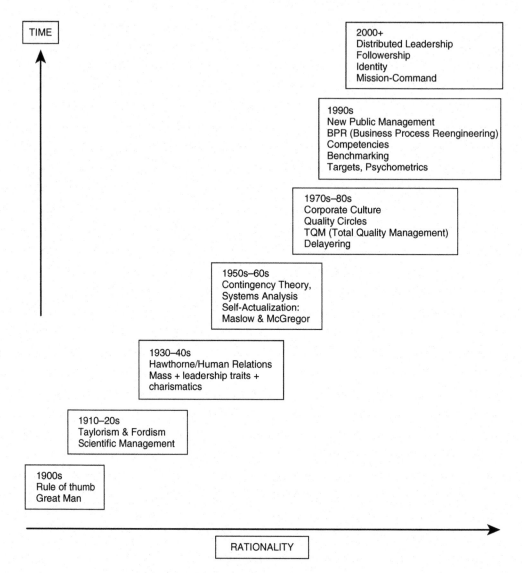

Figure 1.1 Increasingly rational leadership over time.

latter approach, within which even if individual leaders do make a difference, that difference is only marginal in comparison to the influence of more structural features like the economy or religion or political party or social class or gender or any other of the myriad variables on offer.

The current leadership fashion also manifests itself in some form of distributed leadership: we now need a collective approach to decision-making to counter the romance of (individual) leadership and to better cope with an increasingly complex world. Much of this work actually relates to specific contexts – either education, where professionalism is high, or the military, whose Mission-Command doctrine of highly decentralized operational leadership, combined with centralized strategic leadership, is designed to cope with the shift from conventional war-fighting to asymmetric conflict and peace keeping where decentralized decision-making is a prerequisite of success. Yet Mission-Command has been practised by the German army since the nineteenth century. It may be, then, that assumptions about the necessity of rigid command and control systems under all (military) circumstances have always been as dubious as assumptions that suggest the opposite.

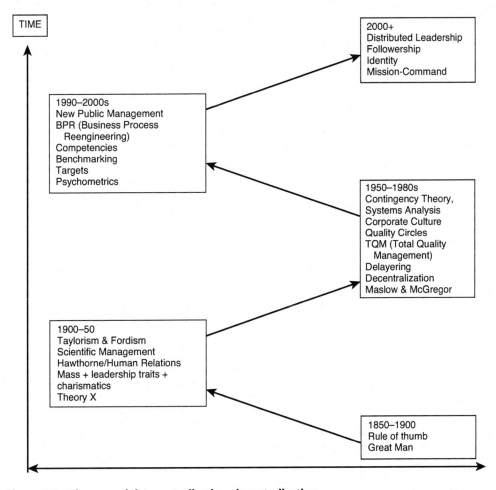

Figure 1.2 Binary model A: centralization–decentralization.

We might, therefore, be in as much danger of pursuing the romance of collaborative leadership (Leonard, 2007) as we previously were of pursuing the romance of individual leadership.

PATTERNS OF LEADERSHIP

The argument for these dualist shifts between forms of leadership is not universally accepted. Indeed, there are many ways to understand this pattern – if indeed there is a pattern. First, what we have is simply an increasingly sophisticated and rational approach to leadership across time represented by the incremental enhancements manifest in Figure 1.1. Students of history will recognize this as a Whig variant on progress across time. Of course there will be setbacks and

hiccups along the way, but the future is eternally rosy and will be preferable to the past.

Alternatively, there are two binary models that suggest a rather different explanation for change. Figure 1.2 suggests that the pattern is represented by a pendulum swinging between centralized and decentralized models of leadership – usually premised on assumptions about organizational learning and game playing so that what was once efficient becomes inefficient as institutional sclerosis sets in. Figure 1.3, on the other hand, retains the binary model but the causal mechanism relates to the structural binaries that constitute language: night/day, black/white, dead/alive and so forth. Here it is the relationship between science and culture as the binary pairing of linguistic opposites which provides the natural barriers to change and once the efficiencies of one leadership style are expended the pendulum swings in the opposite

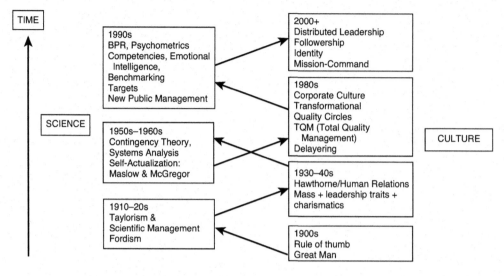

Figure 1.3   Binary model B: science vs culture.

linguistic direction until that mode is also exhausted.

Fourthly, a political model situates the changes not against the binary limits of language but rather the political machinations of the wider context, in which what seems 'normal' only appears so when framed by the political ideologies of the day. This approach, represented in Figure 1.4, is effectively locked into, and explained by, the Zeitgeist of the day: 'the spirit of the times'. Thus, Taylorism emerged as the norm, not because it was scientific and therefore rational, but because in an era where scientific breakthroughs were changing the world of work and where the eugenics movements started to dominate American culture, it seemed natural to assume that there was one best way to allocate, control and lead labour, and that allocation should be based on 'natural' differences that should be exploited for the benefit of all. In effect, as Taylor argued, if you could design jobs requiring virtually no intelligent action on the part of the worker, and where no communal interest prevailed, then you could minimize the cost of labour, the rate of error, and the possibilities of trade unionism.

Similarly, when communism and fascism began to ensnare European politics, it probably seemed inevitable that the best way to lead was not through scientific management of the individual but through the manipulation of the emotional mass by the charismatic leader.

Once the Second World War was over, the dominant power – the United States – reproduced its own scientific and individualist approach as the default leadership model and only when the threat from Japan (re)emerged in the 1980s was there a

significant shift towards a more cultural approach to leadership. Once again, when these ran out of steam in the 1990s, the move was back towards the scientific end of the spectrum, as New Public Management and target measurement took over to be toppled only now as the spread of moral panics about global warming, terrorism, swine flu, the credit crunch and so on shift the debate back towards the cultural school.

Finally, of course, it might well be that there is no pattern at all in the data itself as an object fact, but rather the patterns are more likely to be the consequence of the prior assumptions and cultures of the analyst. In effect, the more scientifically inclined amongst us might be inclined to see greater rationality in leadership styles across time; the more liberal amongst us might see the spread of collaborative styles as proof positive of their deeply held antipathy to individual leadership manifest in heroic men; the more cynical amongst us might perceive none of these patterns but just an accumulation of historical detritus strewn around by academics and consultants hoping, at most, to make sense of a senseless shape or, at least, to make a living from constructing patterns to sell. Now there's a thought....

CONCLUSIONS

Attempting to cover 3,000 years of history in less than 8,000 words or so inevitably requires a significant degree of omission, but what might the critical points of this review be?

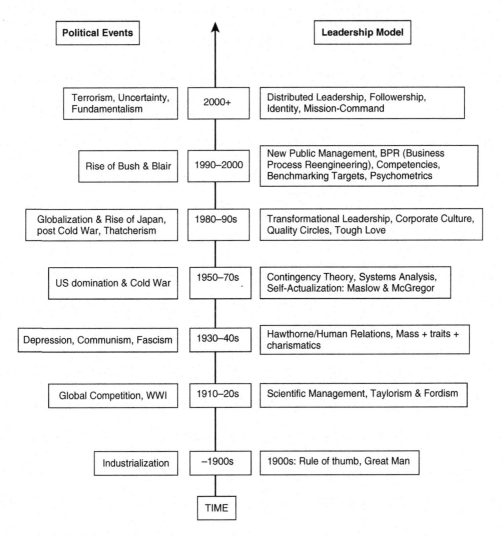

Figure 1.4   Political Zeitgeist.

First, that while situations are always changing, there are perennial issues in leadership and our historical knowledge of these can play a role in preventing the repetition of mistakes, even if we cannot guarantee success. So perhaps one of the reasons history does not repeat itself precisely is because we have some capacity to learn from our mistakes and stop it repeating itself.

Secondly, what we think leadership is, is necessarily related to the cultural mores that prevail at the time. Thus, what appears 'normal' at the time – for example, using targets to ensure compliance with the requirement of political leaders – can often appear extraordinarily naive when considered retrospectively. The problem, of course, is that we cannot step outside our own

milieu to reflect upon ourselves as disembodied and disinterested scholars. This, surely, is where the study of history comes into its own: not in analysing ourselves against an objective system of measurements, but in recognizing that we have been heading somewhere similar before – and if we do not take certain kinds of action we might end up in a very similar place.

Thirdly, that an awareness of how often in the past leadership has failed or appeared terminally flawed does not necessarily mean that we should abandon the task of generating leadership for the public good; it just means that we need to be more alert to what is likely to happen unless we actively prevent it. That includes recognizing that flawed leadership is part of the human condition, that there are no perfect leaders or perfect leadership systems out there to be imitated and, to quote an old Hopi Indian saying, 'We are the ones we have been waiting for.'

REFERENCES

Blake, R.R. and Mouton, J.S. (1964) *The Managerial Grid* (Houston: Gulf).

Farris, W.W. (1999) 'Japan to 1300'. In K. Raaflaub and N. Rosenstein (eds), *War and Society in the Ancient and Medieval Worlds* (London: Harvard University Press).

Fieldler, F.E. (1964) *A Theory of Leader Effectiveness* (New York: McGraw-Hill).

Grint, K. (1997a) *Fuzzy Management* (Oxford: Oxford University Press).

Grint, K. (2000) *The Arts of Leadership* (Oxford: Oxford University Press).

Grint, K. (2005) 'Problems, Problems, Problems: The Social Construction of Leadership', *Human Relations*, 58(11); 1467–1494.

Hanson, V.D. and Strauss, B.S. (1999) 'Epilogue'. In K. Raaflaub, and N. Rosenstein (eds), *War and Society in the Ancient and Medieval Worlds* (London: Harvard University Press).

Jenkins, W.O. (1947) `A review of leadership studies with particular reference to military problems', *Psychological Bulletin*, 44: 54–79.

Keeley, L.H. (1996) *War Before Civilization* (Oxford: Oxford University Press).

Lawson-Tancred-H. (1991) 'Introduction'. In Aristotle's *The Art of Rhetoric* (Harmondsworth: Penguin).

Ledeen, M.A. (1999) *Machiavelli on Modern Leadership* (New York: Truman Talley Books).

Leonard, P. (2007) 'The Romance of Collaborative Leadership'. Paper given at the British Academy of Management Conference (Warwick University).

McAlpine, A. (1997) *The New Machiavelli* (London: Aurum).

McGregor, D. (1960) *The Human Side of Enterprise* (New York: McGraw-Hill).

Maslow, A. (1954) *Motivation and Personality* (New York: Harper).

Peters, T. and Waterman, R.H. (1982) *In Search of Excellence* (London: Harper & Row).

Santayana, G. (1954) *The Life of Reason or The Phases of Human Progress* (New York: Charles Scribner's Sons).

Stogdill, R.M. (1948) 'Personal Factors Associated with Leadership: A Survey of the Literature', *Journal of Psychology*, 25, 35–71.

Stogdill, R.M. (1974) *Handbook of Leadership: A Survey of Theory and Research* (New York: Free Press).

Wardy, R. (1996) The Birth of Rhetoric: Georgias, Plato and Their Successors (London: Routledge).

Wiedemann, T.E.J. (1995) *Emperors and Gladiators* (London: Routledge).

2

Research Methods in the Study of Leadership

Alan Bryman

INTRODUCTION

In this chapter, I intend to review and comment upon the range of research methods that are employed by leadership researchers. This will require a consideration of broader issues such as epistemology that abut and relate to discussions of research methodology. I am by no means the first writer to review the methods employed by leadership researchers and, early on in this article, other reviews will be examined.

Leadership researchers employ a wide range of research methods, although the diversity of those methods is of relatively recent origin since the field has largely been dominated by a single method of data collection – the self-completion/self-administered questionnaire. As Avolio et al. have observed: 'The quantitative strategies for studying leadership have dominated the literature over the past 100 years' (2009a; p. 442). The self-administered questionnaire has been one of the most commonly employed tools among the quantitative strategies to which Avolio et al. refer and has been the instrument employed in traditions that have defined the field of leadership research over the years; for example, the Ohio State tradition. When Lowe and Gardner (2000) reviewed the research methods employed in articles during the first 10 years of the life of *The Leadership Quarterly*, they found that 64% employed a questionnaire-based approach. Thus, the leadership field is significantly reliant upon a single research method for its findings. It is not surprising, therefore, that Hunter et al. (2007) and Friedrich et al. (2009) refer to the questionnaire-based approach as the 'typical leadership study'.

The dominance of this tool and other quantitative instruments reflects the wider epistemological orientation of many leadership researchers in that it exemplifies the commitment to a natural science model of the research process and to positivism in particular. This predilection is also significant for its consequences, because it has implications for the evaluation of research, especially research employing qualitative methods. It has also meant that the field of leadership research is a relatively late adopter of such methods (Bryman, 2004), although it is probably not significantly later in this regard than the other areas of organization studies and organizational behaviour.

However, it could be argued that the account of the typical leadership study provided in the previous paragraph represents a North American view of the methodological state of the field. Thus, when David Collinson and Keith Grint, both co-editors of this volume, started the Europe-based journal *Leadership*, they outlined in their opening editorial that among their aims was that of increasing the field's methodological diversity. They wrote:

> In our view the understanding of leadership is best enhanced by the encouragement of a diversity of theoretical positions *and research methods* and the exploration of a great variety of research contexts and settings. Our vision is inclusive, not exclusive; one of radical heterogeneity, not simply a different form of homogeneity. (Collinson and Grint, 2005, p. 7, emphasis added)

Thus, their mission for the new journal was not the eradication of the typical leadership article, but instilling greater diversity of methodological approach in the field. An analysis of all empirical articles published in *Leadership* in its first five years of publication revealed that it had a different methodological profile from *The Leadership Quarterly*, as gleaned from Lowe and Gardner's (2000) article (Bryman, 2011). Whereas Lowe and Gardner found 64% of articles to contain data derived from questionnaires, only 22% of articles in *Leadership* included data from this same method. By contrast, 51% of the articles in *Leadership* contained data derived from semi-structured interviewing. Lowe and Gardner did not have a special category for this method, but they do report that 20% of all articles included interview data. This latter figure is likely to include data from other kinds of interview (e.g. structured interview). Thus, there is a considerable difference between articles published in *The Leadership Quarterly* during its first decade and articles in *Leadership* in terms of the methods of data collection used. However, the data for *The Leadership Quarterly* relate to the period up to 1999. An analysis by Gardner et al. (Unpublished work) of articles published in *The Leadership Quarterly* in its second decade does not allow a comparison with the proportion of articles based on questionnaire data, although the authors do note that the typical empirical article is based on a single method – the survey. Further, the analysis revealed that quantitative research intensified its hold in the second decade when compared to the first decade's articles.

PREVIOUS OVERVIEWS OF LEADERSHIP RESEARCH METHODS

There have been a small number of overviews of the research methods employed in leadership research. Because there are different ways of classifying research approaches, these reviews have employed different categorizations. For example, Antonakis et al. (2004) began their review by distinguishing between quantitative and qualitative research methods for studying leadership but then note: 'Because the vast majority of research that is conducted in the leadership domain is quantitative in nature and because theory can be tested appropriately only with quantitative methods…' they focus upon the latter (Antonakis et al., 2004, p. 55). Within the category of quantitative research methods they distinguish the following: laboratory experiments; field experiments; field studies; and survey research. Essentially, this classification operates at the level of research design rather than research method – for example, the questionnaire

can be (and indeed has been) used in connection with all four of these designs.

Kroeck et al. (2004) also use the quantitative/qualitative distinction as a starting point but have more to say about the nature of qualitative research and its underlying research methods. They distinguish between qualitative research based on ethnography, content analysis and observation. Under the umbrella of quantitative methods, they distinguish between paper-and-pencil questionnaire, computer-based questionnaire and simulation/assessment centre. In contrast to Antonakis et al., these distinctions emphasize methods of data collection rather than research design but are not without problems. First, content analysis is regarded by many writers as a quantitative rather than a qualitative method when it is implemented in the traditional fashion. More will be said about this issue below. Secondly, a similar point may be made about the category of 'observation'. Kroeck et al. associate observation with the qualitative research technique of participant observation, but there are also structured forms of observation, such as that used by Luthans and Lockwood (1984), which are typically viewed as associated with quantitative research (Bryman & Bell, 2007).

A more recent contribution by Mumford et al. (2009) provides what is probably the most detailed overview by distinguishing between the following methods: survey studies of leader behaviour; attribute studies; experimental studies; qualitative studies; and historiometric studies. It is not obvious where observational studies of leadership would fit into this scheme and it could be argued that it is a classification based on two different things – leadership foci (e.g. behaviour and attributes) and diverse research designs and methods. However, it is a comprehensive approach and provides a reasonably balanced account of qualitative research.

It is striking that these classifications often work with a distinction – either explicitly or implicitly – between quantitative and qualitative research. The quantitative/qualitative distinction is also implicit in the reviews of qualitative leadership research by some writers (e.g. Bryman, 2004; Klenke, 2008). Qualitative research methods tend to be grouped together and juxtaposed against several quantitative research methods. This is not unreasonable given the heavy reliance on the latter in leadership research, but a difficulty with the category 'qualitative research' in the leadership field (as well as elsewhere) is that it is very broad and as such does not fully take account of the fact that it relates to quite widely differing studies (Bryman, 2004). Examples of qualitative study might include: cross-sectional designs using qualitative interviews which can look very much like survey studies but without the numbers; single or multiple case studies using participant observation; single or multiple case studies using qualitative interviews; and single or multiple case studies using documents. Thus, the category 'qualitative research' obscures considerable variety in approach and its growing use in and contribution to the leadership field may require a rethink concerning such issues as the evaluation of studies prior to publication.

The classification of research methods in the leadership field presented in this chapter are summarized in Table 2.1. The listing is not exhaustive and it is doubtful whether any classification could be. Further, while the approaches are largely to do with research methods for the collection and/or analysis of data, experiments are strictly speaking a research *design* (Bryman and Bell, 2007). However, they are worth identifying separately for reasons that will hopefully become apparent during the discussion. It is also worth pointing out that single and multiple case studies will be discussed *en passant* as they are often linked to particular research methods. Thus, ethnographies are almost always single or multiple case studies; also, semi-structured interview studies may be conducted either within a cross-sectional or a case study design. Some of these distinctions will be brought out in the discussion below.

QUESTIONNAIRE STUDIES

As previously noted, the use of the self-administered or self-completion questionnaire in leadership research is pervasive. Questionnaire instruments like the Leader Behavior Description Questionnaire (LBDQ) used by the Ohio State leadership researchers, the Least-Preferred Co-worker (LPC) used to measure leadership orientations within Fiedler's Contingency Model, and the Multifactor Leadership Questionnaire (MLQ) used to measure transactional and transformational leadership are among the most intensively used and well-known scales in the field of organizational behaviour. Such instruments more or less define the field of leadership research. They have been widely used because their known psychometric qualities (their reliability and validity) have meant that researchers have been able to use them with an awareness of the advantages and limitations of doing so. The research streams associated with these questionnaires are covered in this volume in Chapters 17 and 22 by Diaz-Saenz and Yukl, respectively. Questionnaire instruments like the LBDQ and MLQ are employed to provide measures of leader behaviour. Typically, subordinates/followers complete questionnaires for each leader in a sample and the questionnaire scores are aggregated for each leader to give him or her an overall profile in terms of the leader behaviour dimensions.

Questionnaire data are subject to some well-known limitations, some of which are outlined in the remainder of this paragraph. Response rates to questionnaires can be low, especially when administered by mail. Data from scales used in questionnaires can be affected by response sets, like acquiescence effects (e.g. a tendency either to agree or disagree with Likert-type inventories). One particular kind of effect that is well attested in leadership research is the role of implicit leadership theories, whereby it has been shown that when answering batches of questions about a

Table 2.1 Methodological approaches to leadership discussed in the chapter

Methodological approach	Example(s) discussed in this chapter
Questionnaire	Greene (1975)
Experiment	Barling et al. (1996); Howell and Frost (1989); Lowin and Craig (1968); Rush et al. (1977)
Observation – structured observation	Luthans and Lockwood (1984)
Observation – observation in qualitative studies	Maitlis and Lawrence (2007); Roberts and Bradley (1988)
Interview – structured interview	Mizrahi and Rosenthal (2001)
Interview – qualitative interview	Maitlis and Lawrence (2007); Roberts and Bradley (1988); Treviño et al. (2003)
Content analysis – traditional content analysis	Bligh et al. (2004); Meindl et al. (1985)
Content analysis – historiometric studies	Mumford (2006)
Content analysis – qualitative/textual content analysis	Boje et al. (this volume – Chapter 38); Jackson and Guthey (2007); Mumford and Van Doorn (2001)
Discourse analysis	Alvesson and Sveningsson (2003)
Meta-analysis/systematic review	Avolio et al. (2009b); DeGroot et al. (2001); Lord et al. (1986)
Mixed methods research	Berson and Avolio (2004); Holmberg et al. (2008); Rowland and Parry (2009)

leader's style, questionnaire respondents reply in terms of known characteristics of that leader. Thus, if a leader is believed to be ineffective, their answers with respect to that leader will be affected by this knowledge, regardless of the leader's actual behaviour. The problem of common method (or same-source) variance/bias is also recognized in questionnaire surveys. This problem arises when respondents supply data relating to both the leadership variables (e.g. leader behaviour) and the outcome measures (e.g. organizational commitment or effectiveness of the leader) in a study. There is some disagreement over how problematic common method bias is (Spector and Brannick, 2009) but, to the extent that it is regarded as a problem, possible remedies have been proposed (Podsakoff et al., 2003). Because of beliefs in some quarters that in common method studies of leadership the relationships between leadership variables and outcomes tend to be inflated, research that uses measures of outcome that are not based on the same method and source are more robust.

One difficulty with the process of aggregation of followers' scores for each leader is the suggestion that it ignores crucial differences between subordinates in their relationships with the leader, an insight that played a significant role in the development of the leader–member exchange (LMX) model discussed by Smriti Anand and colleagues in Chapter 23. Further, with questionnaire research based on a cross-sectional design, a recurring problem is the question of causality. It has been shown that the so-called outcomes of leadership variables that have been identified in much cross-sectional survey research may actually be independent variables, because leaders are likely to change their behaviour as a result of the performance of their followers. It is precisely for this reason that some methodologists deny that it is ever possible to establish causality in organizational behaviour studies through non-experimental studies (e.g. Stone-Romero, 2009).

Questionnaires offer several advantages to the researcher and this endears them to many leadership researchers in spite of their limitations. They are invariably relatively cheap and quick to administer. A questionnaire is also a very flexible instrument that can be used to collect data on both leadership and various other variables which might be outcomes of leader behaviour or moderators of the leadership–outcome relationship. Respondents tend to be familiar with the instrument, so they do not require familiarization to use it. It can be administered to quite large samples at relatively little additional cost and because it rarely takes long to complete, a questionnaire is usually acceptable to organizations whose senior managers might otherwise worry about implications of

completing questionnaires for getting work done. Questionnaires usually contain large numbers of closed questions, so coding is unlikely to be time-consuming and the risks associated with coding inconsistencies are reduced. Also, questionnaires have proved flexible in terms of the context of completion – they can be completed in a variety of locations and with different media (e.g. pens, computer, online). The absence of an interviewer removes the risk of interviewer effects arising from interviewers' characteristics and the demand effects arising from the presence of an interviewer. These advantages must be regarded as sufficiently compelling to leadership researchers for them to be used so extensively, given the limitations of this instrument outlined above.

Questionnaires can be administered within the context of a longitudinal design as well as a cross-sectional design. Indeed, some of the problems with inferring causality from cross-sectional surveys have come to light as a result of the use of a longitudinal design. An early example of the use of this design is that of Greene (1975), who administered the LBDQ and measures of job satisfaction and subordinate performance (rated by peers) on three occasions with one month between each wave of data collection to two of the subordinates of each of 103 first-line managers in three firms. The findings confirmed the causal inference that consideration influences the job satisfaction of subordinates, but also that subordinate performance has an impact on both consideration and initiating structure. Such findings point to the internal validity problems of cross-sectional survey design studies based on questionnaires. However, the longitudinal design does not get over the causality problem according to writers who valorize the experimental approach. As Stone-Romero (2009, p. 312) suggests, the issue of temporal precedence is not addressed by a longitudinal design because the apparent causal connection between an earlier measure (e.g. performance) and a later one (e.g. consideration) is a sequence that is part of an ongoing series of interconnections that includes prior and subsequent variables that have not been observed.

EXPERIMENTAL RESEARCH

Experimental studies would seem to provide the obvious solution to the causality problem identified in the previous section in relation to questionnaire research. In an experiment, the researcher manipulates the putative independent variable and observes its effects. The issue of temporal precedence and the problem that there could be rival explanations of the causal relationship are eliminated provided that there is equivalence in the experimental manipulations and random assignment to experimental and control groups. Indeed, one of the early studies to draw attention to the possibility that leadership researchers using cross-sectional designs were incorrectly inferring causality was based on experimental research. Lowin and Craig (1968) manipulated levels of 'subordinate' performance in a laboratory experiment. They found that when confronted with a poor performance level, 'leaders' exhibited higher levels of initiating structure and closer supervision and lower levels of consideration. Such a finding casts doubt on the notion that studies showing that leader behaviour and performance are related imply that leadership is necessarily the independent variable. Since then, experimental studies have been employed to show how large an impact different types of leader behaviour have on a variety of dependent variables. The experimental manipulation can be achieved in different ways, such as by using actors to deliver different styles of behaviour or by using different written scenarios that are presented to experimental participants. As an example of the former, Howell and Frost (1989) used actors to simulate charismatic leadership, consideration, and initiating structure and observed the relative impacts of these three styles on task performance among students carrying out a business task.

Rush et al. (1977) provide an example of the use of a scenario within the context of an experiment. Undergraduate students at a US university were given a brief description of a person in a supervisory role. No indication was given of the nature of the individual's behaviour *qua* leader. Students were randomly assigned to one of the three conditions: high, average or low departmental performance. The student participants were then asked to describe the leader in terms of the Ohio State LBDQ. Rush et al. found that the performance cue affected the ratings of the leader: for example, with the high departmental performance scenario, participants were more likely to describe the leader as high in terms of both consideration and initiating structure. Since one of the fairly consistent findings of the Ohio researchers was that leaders high in terms of consideration and initiating structure were most effective, a finding like this implies that when people answer questions about their leaders using an instrument like the LBDQ, they are at the very least partly affected by their prior knowledge of the leader's performance or that of his/her section. In other words, when such questionnaires are being completed, followers are only partly answering questions in terms of the actual behaviour of the leaders concerned.

Field experiments are also found in the leadership field. One of the main difficulties for a field experiment, as compared to a laboratory one, is that the experimenter usually enjoys less control over experimental arrangements, which can have adverse implications for the internal validity of the study. Most notably, it can be difficult to ensure that participants are randomly assigned to the different treatment conditions, so that frequently such studies are better referred to as quasi-experiments (Stone-Romero, 2009). An example of a field experiment that did entail random assignment can be found in a study of the impact on managers in Canadian bank branches of training in transformational leadership (Barling et al., 1996). Managers were randomly assigned to a control group and to an experimental group that received training in transformational leadership. Managers trained in transformational leadership were found to be more likely than those not trained to be perceived as transformational and to have followers who were committed to the organization. There was also evidence that the financial performance of their branches was superior.

As noted above, experiments are often rooted within a quantitative research paradigm because the researcher is more likely to be able to impute causality by eliminating rival explanations of an apparent causal relationship than with a cross-sectional design. However, this advantage is frequently viewed as at a cost – a low level of mundane realism, particularly when the experiment is a laboratory one. Further, it is likely that only a limited range of leadership issues are likely to be amenable to experimental manipulation, whereas the use of questionnaires within a cross-sectional design is open to a wide range of research questions. In addition, the frequent use of students as experimental participants in laboratory studies has often been taken to place limits on the external validity of the study.

OBSERVATION

Given that much of the study of leadership is actually about the behaviour of leaders, it is perhaps surprising that observation is rarely used. Instead, researchers typically use questionnaires to tap leaders' behaviour. Lowe and Gardner (2000) found in their review of a decade of articles in *The Leadership Quarterly* that in only 8% of articles was observation used for the collection of data. It is worth drawing a distinction between structured observation, which is invariably conducted within a quantitative research approach, and participant observation, which is a qualitative research method.

Structured observation

Luthans and Lockwood (1984) devised the Leader Observation System (LOS). This instrument was developed following extensive informal observation of managers. Following this phase, leaders' behaviour was grouped into 12 categories (e.g. planning/coordinating, staffing, exchanging routine information). Each of these is broken down into components ('behavioural descriptors') that allow observers to code the presence or absence of each form of behaviour within a 10-minute time slot. Each manager was observed for a 10-minute period every hour for two weeks. The authors were then able to relate managers' behaviour to their performance. It was found that leaders who gave greater emphasis to conflict management, socializing/politicking, interacting with outsiders and decision-making, but who were less concerned with staffing, motivating/reinforcing and monitoring, were more likely to be successful (Luthans et al., 1985). Such findings are highly redolent of those engendered by questionnaire researchers, but are based on actual behaviour. There are likely to be advantages to using a research method that emphasizes what leaders do rather than what they or others say they do, but it tends to be difficult to code behaviour in a reliable manner. It is also far more time-consuming than data collection through questionnaires and this has almost certainly played a significant part in the lack of take-up of structured observation. On the other hand, it gets around some of the problems that have been identified thus far concerning cross-sectional design studies using questionnaires, such as common method bias and contamination through implicit leadership theories, though it does not get around the problem of causal direction.

Observation in qualitative studies

Observation in the course of qualitative case studies is sometimes employed by qualitative researchers, but it is rarely the sole or even the main method of data collection in such studies (Bryman, 2004). Maitlis and Lawrence (2007) conducted multiple case study research on three British symphony orchestras. The researchers were interested in the circumstances that prompt leaders and others to engage in organizational sensegiving and the circumstances that are favourable to sensegiving. In addition to semi-structured interviewing and examination of documents, the researchers engaged in 'observation of meetings, rehearsals, and orchestra tours' (Maitlis and Lawrence, 2007, p. 60). The authors go on to write:

The first author observed 107 meetings, including meetings of various groups within each organization (e.g., the executive team, the board) and meetings between orchestra leaders and external stakeholders (e.g., funders, collaborating organizations).... The meeting observation provided many rich opportunities to witness leaders and stakeholders engaging in sensegiving on a range of topics and to observe conditions associated with these instances of sensegiving. (Maitlis and Lawrence, 2007, p. 60)

As with this study, it is unusual for observation to be the primary method. A rare example of a leadership study in which observation figures sufficiently strongly for it to be considered an ethnography is Roberts and Bradley's (1988) case study of someone who was a superintendent of a suburban school district in the USA and who later became a commissioner at state level. The research was conducted over several years and at state level, Roberts was a participant observer in a task force and the commissioner was also observed 'making presentations to teachers and superintendents on both formal and informal occasions' and 'as she conducted meetings with her cabinet and staff and during legislative hearings, press conferences, and informal interactions with members of the Department of Education' (Roberts and Bradley, 1988, p. 259). In addition, numerous interviews were conducted over the years with the focal leader as well as with others. The research was able to show how, in her earlier role, she had been a highly charismatic leader who inspired others but, in her later role, she lost a good deal of her lustre. The authors were therefore able to examine the conditions that inhibited the transfer of charisma to her new role.

There are several reasons for the lack of use of observation in qualitative studies (Bryman, 2004), but a key reason is that (possibly), it is not always clear what is to be observed. It is one thing to observe leaders; it is quite another thing to observe leader*ship*. How is the observer to know when leadership is being exercised or exhibited? In some instances, it may be obvious, but in others it may not be clear whether what is being witnessed is leadership. If the view is taken that everything a leader does is suffused with symbolism, it could be argued that every act is a potential act of leadership, but that too causes possible difficulties for the researcher because it is then difficult to know what *not* to observe. Such considerations, along with the time-consuming nature of intensive observation, have almost certainly limited the use of the method, even since calls for its greater use (Conger, 1998). However, participant observation offers great potential to leadership researchers because it could be especially helpful in gaining an appreciation of contextual factors and how these interact with the tasks of leadership. Further, it is especially likely to be able to offer insights into informal leadership, an area that has been neglected by the tendency for questionnaire researchers to concentrate their attention on formally designated leaders.

INTERVIEW STUDIES

In a similar way to observation, interviews can be categorized as either structured interviews, which are employed mainly within a quantitative research approach, or various kinds of qualitative interview (e.g. the semi-structured or unstructured interview). The structured interview is not a prominent technique in leadership research, in spite of the dominance of the quantitative research approach. Lowe and Gardner (2000) calculated that 20% of *The Leadership Quarterly* articles were based on interviews, but this figure almost certainly included the small number of articles based on qualitative interviewing that had appeared in the journal during the period in question.

Structured interviewing

Mizrahi and Rosenthal (2001) employed a structured interview in their study of social change coalitions in the New York/New Jersey area. The researchers interviewed leaders about their leadership strategies in seeking to develop successful coalitions and how they themselves defined success. The researchers were interested in how leaders overcame the obstacles to the formation of coalitions. An interview schedule of over 600 items (most of which were closed questions) was used to interview 41 coalition leaders. Through the interviews, Mizrahi and Rosenthal were able to establish that persistence and vision play a crucial role in successful coalition formation.

The relative lack of use of structured interviewing in leadership research is possibly surprising in view of the popularity of the method in some social sciences such as sociology. It may be that this reflects the way in which psychology has played a particularly prominent role in the field and the relative lack of use of the method among psychologists.

Qualitative interviewing

Among qualitative studies of leadership, the situation could hardly be more different. Of the 66 articles based on qualitative research on leadership uncovered by Bryman (2004), 56 derived at least in part from qualitative interviewing. The reason for its popularity among qualitative leadership researchers is similar to the reasons for the popularity of questionnaires among quantitative researchers: it is a flexible research instrument that can be applied to a diversity of topics. It can also be applied to different research design contexts. Thus, it can be employed in the context of a single case study (e.g. Roberts and Bradley, 1988) or a multiple case study (e.g. Maitlis and Lawrence, 2007) or it can be employed within the context of either a cross-sectional or longitudinal design, though the latter is very rare.

A good example of the use of qualitative interviewing in the context of a cross-sectional design is the study by Treviño et al. (2003) of 20 corporate ethics/compliance officers and 20 senior executives. The goal of the study was to uncover what is meant by ethical leadership. The researchers used a semi-structured interview administered to question their 40 informants. Three-quarters of the interviews were conducted by telephone and the rest in person. The interviews suggest that an ethical leadership orientation is revealed in a focus on people, role modelling of ethical behaviour, having integrity, creating and institutionalizing values and using rewards and punishments to influence ethical behaviour. Also, the qualitative interview yields data that can be applied to a number of different analytic strategies, such as qualitative thematic textual analysis, traditional quantitative content analysis, discourse analysis and narrative analysis. As such, it is capable of generating data that are amenable to different kinds of analytic approach. This feature contributes to its popularity among leadership researchers inclined towards a qualitative research approach.

CONTENT ANALYSIS

The term 'content analysis' often refers to a range of different techniques. According to one of the earliest texts on the subject, traditional content analysis is a 'research technique for the objective, systematic and quantitative description of the manifest content of communication' (Berelson, 1952, p. 18). Given this definition, it is puzzling that it is referred to as a *qualitative* method by several writers (e.g. Insch et al., 1997; Lowe and Gardner, 2000). Content analysts may work on unstructured, qualitative material, but the approach to analysis is emphatically quantitative, as Berelson's classic definition demonstrates. Indeed, there is a sense in which content analysis exemplifies quantitative research, with its emphasis on quantification and the reliability and validity of measurement. Further, the application of techniques like structural equation modelling and log-linear analysis to the quantitative data (Insch et al., 1997) is far more redolent of quantitative than qualitative research.

Traditional content analysis

Content analysis can be, and indeed has been, applied to a diversity of raw materials in the leadership field. Newspaper and magazine articles, speeches, mission statements, and letters have provided some of the more common types of media to which content analysis has been applied in the leadership field. For example, Meindl et al. (1985) content analysed newspaper articles and dissertations to examine the degree to which a focus on leadership fluctuated in terms of how well the economy or particular firms or industries were faring. This analysis provided the foundation for the influential notion of the romance of leadership. Bligh et al. (2004) used computerized content analysis to examine how far the rhetoric and speeches of President George W. Bush changed after 9/11. The researchers were able to show that Bush displayed more charismatic imagery after the crisis and indeed that he was portrayed in the media in more charismatic terms than previously.

Content analysis offers many advantages to the researcher, one of the most significant of which is that when applied to materials like speeches or media articles, unlike the research methods discussed thus far, it is a non-reactive measure (Bryman and Bell, 2007). It also lends itself, where the data are available, to studies of changes in communication and other kinds of content. Its chief limitation is essentially that it is difficult to determine the meaning of the findings. This can be discerned in the following passage in which Bligh et al. grapple with the meaning of their findings on Bush's charismatic imagery:

> But what does this shift in rhetoric imply about his charismatic stature? Did the President's underlying personality actually become more charismatic since the early days of his administration, finally blossoming during the days and weeks following the crisis?.... It may be that the President had the 'right stuff' all along, with the crisis of 9/11 finally revealing a side of his (charismatic) personality not previously exposed to the American public. (Bligh et al., 2004, p. 227)

However, if content analysts are cautious not to overinterpret their findings, content analysis offers considerable potential to the leadership researcher. There is always a risk that the content analyst is tempted to draw more inferences about the results than are warranted. It is for this reason that Berelson's definition emphasizes the *manifest* content of the material being examined. The search for latent content carries the risk of drawing unsustainable inferences, as well as creating potential coding problems.

Historiometric research

Historiometric studies have gained in popularity in recent years and are in many ways a form of content analysis. According to Mumford et al. (2009, p.120): 'Historiometric studies represent an attempt to quantify historic observations on historic data bearing on leadership behavior and performance'. Mumford (2006) reports the results of such an examination. He analysed the biographies of 120 outstanding leaders, which allowed him to categorize the leaders into one of three types (charismatic, ideological and pragmatic). The behaviour and accomplishments of the leaders were examined, as well as some of the defining features of their earlier years. Leaders' biographies were coded in terms of a host of different dimensions. For example, the quality of leader–follower relations was coded in terms of whether the leader kept in contact with close followers after leaving power and whether the leader remained close to followers after leaving power (Mumford, 2006, p. 93). Prologue or epilogue chapters were scrutinized for this information and then coded. Socialized leaders were more likely than personalized leaders to maintain relationships (and were also found to perform better more generally – see Howell [1988] on the personalized/socialized distinction).

One issue with an analysis such as this is whether a single biography of a leader can ever be a sufficient proxy for the individual's life as a leader. To take as an example one of the leaders in Mumford's sample of 120 in which the present author has a long-standing interest – Walt Disney (Bryman, 1995) – the biography used (Mosley, 1985) was very controversial at the time it was published and the Disney family were reportedly distressed about it, though an even less flattering biography was still to come (Eliot, 1993). Relatedly, Mumford et al. (2009) point out that historiometric studies tend to be leader-centric in that they will focus on what the leader said and did but will relatively rarely provide the perspective of the follower. Therefore, historiometric studies will typically not provide significant insights into followers' reactions to leaders. On the other hand, such studies do provide an understanding of very creative leaders to whom access is normally difficult or impossible. Further, they allow us to study leadership over time, in that they give us access to such topics as formative influences and changes in leadership orientation over the individual's life course.

Qualitative/textual content analysis of texts

Qualitative/textual content analysis is not a distinct method like traditional content analysis. It comes in several guises, but the various approaches exhibit the common feature of the researcher extracting themes from the data. It can be discerned in Jackson and Guthey's (2007) analysis of visual images to explore what they call the 'celebrity CEO backlash', the process by which CEOs who would at one time have been shown in photographs as powerful superstars are increasingly being depicted in unflattering ways. Mumford and Van Doorn (2001) analysed various primary sources to examine 10 cases of exceptional leadership exhibited by Benjamin Franklin. Through this exercise, the researchers were able to explore Franklin's credentials as a pragmatic leader. As Mumford and Van Doorn point out, this is a significant issue because of a tendency to associate outstanding leadership with charismatic or transformational leaders. Mumford's (2006) previously mentioned historiometric study also makes this point. A further example of qualitative/textual content analysis can be discerned in Chapter 38, in which David Boje and his co-authors use a variety of sources, such as periodical articles, television and newspaper articles, and web sources, to develop the notion of virtual leadership.

Such studies can be very fertile in terms of generating new concepts or areas of enquiry (e.g. CEO celebrity backlash or virtual leadership) and in developing notions like pragmatic leadership. As such, they can be a source of theoretical creativity. The close relationship between the sources and the conceptualization provides a strong sense of the face validity of the concepts. It is sometimes suggested that the work lacks robustness: what, for example, might provide counter-examples or material that might shed doubt on the findings that are developed?

DISCOURSE ANALYSIS

Discourse analysis is a family of techniques used to examine the part played by language in human affairs. There is no one version of discourse analysis (Alvesson and Kärreman, 2000) but all the approaches share a predilection for analyses of language in use. 'Language' here may involve natural language in the course of conversations, the linguistic framing of answers to interview questions, rhetorical devices used in speeches, or the ways in which issues are framed in documents. Crucial to discourse analysis is the notion that discourse is not 'just' a neutral medium of communication. Instead, discourse analysts view social reality as socially constructed and propose that discourse plays a central role in the constitution of the social world. As such, the orientation of discourse analysis is somewhat different from that of many other qualitative methods. Instead of treating the social world as given, practitioners emphasize how everyday notions and objects are constituted through discourse.

In Chapter 36 of this volume, Gail Fairhurst makes a distinction between Big D and Little D discourse. Studies working within the latter (*dis*course) approach tend to emphasize fairly fine-grained analyses of language in the context of interaction within organizations. By contrast, *D*iscourse studies derive from a Foucauldian tradition that focuses on 'historical constellations of talk patterns, ideas, logics, and assumptions that constitute objects and subjects in particular ways'. Such studies, while attending to the detail of language, tend to be somewhat more broad brush in orientation.

An interesting example of a discourse analytic study is Alvesson and Sveningsson's (2003) research on the language of leadership and management. This article begins with a Big D issue – the way in which in the 1980s and early 1990s the popular literature on leadership developed a Discourse of leadership that distinguished it from management and in the process positioned leadership as essentially effective leadership. Alvesson and Sveningsson report a discourse analysis of qualitative interview transcripts of the accounts by managers of the nature of their leadership. They note that managers, when describing their leadership, were inconsistent in their accounts. For example, managers often repeated and claimed adherence to the Discourse of the day that positioned leadership (as distinct from management) as vision, but, when given the opportunity to elaborate on what that entails and how it is done, they turned to an emphasis on administrative and operational issues. It would seem that the managers were attracted to the Discourse of the day which positioned them as strategic masters but that when discussing their own leadership in some detail, the emphasis on vision gave way to the very immediate organizational demands and constraints they faced. In this study then, the authors undertook a *d*iscourse study of the *D*iscourse of leadership.

One of the chief arguments often levelled at discourse analysis generally is that its focus tends to occlude the operation of wider structures and the use of power (e.g. Reed, 2000). This orientation does not sit well with leadership theorists and organizational researchers more generally of a critical persuasion. However, as can be seen in the Alvesson and Sveningsson (2003) study, discourse analysis can be deployed in such a way that it can interrogate and illuminate larger-scale issues and concerns such as the capacity of wider Discourses to influence and, in this case, confuse the discourses of managers. Also, writers whose research is influenced by critical discourse analysis tend to be less implicated in this accusation (Phillips and Di Domenico, 2009).

META-ANALYSIS

Reviews of leadership literature have long played a significant role in leadership research. For example, the negative reviews by Stogdill (1948) and Mann (1959) of extant trait research on leadership have often been held responsible for sounding its death knell and for ushering in the emphasis on leadership style (e.g. Bryman, 1986). However, by pooling the findings from groups of studies investigating a topic, meta-analyses can often provide a better overview. Thus, as John Antonakis points out in Chapter 20, when Lord et al. (1986) conducted a meta-analysis of the same studies as those reviewed by Mann (1959), intelligence was found *contra* Mann to be related to leadership emergence.

Leadership is a field that lends itself quite well to meta-analysis because researchers are interested in impacts of leadership variables on various outcomes. Meta-analysis can also add to understanding because its capacity to pool a large number of studies can mean that moderating factors (e.g. research method used or situational factors) that are not revealed through individual studies can be examined. An example of a meta-analysis in the field of leadership is the review of published studies of the organizational outcomes related to charismatic leadership (DeGroot et al. 2000). Most of the measures of charismatic leadership were based on the Multifactor Leadership Questionnaire (MLQ), referred to by Jay Conger in this volume in Chapter 7. The meta-analysis was able to confirm that charismatic leadership is related to: leader effectiveness; subordinate effectiveness; subordinate satisfaction; and subordinate commitment. The authors were able to identify

that common method bias had some impact on the findings, with evidence of the relationship between charismatic leadership and job satisfaction being especially affected.

Meta-analysis suffers from certain difficulties, most notably the 'file drawer' problem, which refers to the fact that not all research gets into the public domain and that it is likely that research studies showing weak or no impacts may be particularly affected. DeGroot et al. did try to find unpublished research but were unsuccessful. However, they did adjust their data for the possible effects of this problem. The file drawer problem would have been a particular difficulty for Avolio et al. (2009b) who conducted a meta-analysis of experimental and quasi-experimental studies of the impact of leadership interventions. In addition to searching databases, Avolio et al. wrote emails to 670 people who worked in leadership and related areas, asking them to review for inclusiveness a list of leadership impact studies. The authors found 200 studies that met their criteria and, of these, 16% were unpublished, suggesting that at least in part the researchers had been able to address the file drawer problem. Interestingly, one of the main findings of this review was that while leadership interventions do have demonstrable impacts, those impacts tended to be stronger when the research was underpinned by a leadership theory that emphasized behavioural change rather than when the theory emphasized emotional or cognitive change.

MIXED METHODS RESEARCH

Mixed methods research has increasingly come to refer to research that combines quantitative and qualitative research. Methods can be and often are mixed within these two research strategies but with the arrival of a mixed methods industry in the form of a journal, handbook, a regular conference, and several books, it tends to denote a mixture of quantitative and qualitative approaches (Bryman, 2009). Mixed methods research is also being advocated by leadership researchers (e.g. Hunt and Conger, 1999), and others see it as likely to be an increasingly important approach. Avolio et al. (2009a, pp. 441–2), for example, write: 'We expect to see a greater use of mixed-methods designs in future research…. [I]ncreasing attention is being paid to cases and qualitative research that should now be integrated with quantitative approaches'.

When Bryman (2004) reviewed qualitative research on leadership, he uncovered 12 articles that used a mixed methods approach. It is striking that nine of these articles were published during the brief period 2000–03. This evidence of growing popularity reflects a growing openness among leadership researchers to both the use and the publication of qualitative research and an increased awareness among researchers generally in the potential of mixed methods research (Bryman, 2009). There are a number of ways of combining quantitative and qualitative research. In his review, Bryman (2004) used the scheme for classifying mixed methods research developed by Greene et al. (1989) and found that three approaches were particularly prominent: triangulation (using quantitative and qualitative research to cross-validate findings); expansion and complementarity (one set of data is used to expand on or complement the other set); and different issues (using quantitative and qualitative research to examine different aspects of the research topic). The last of these approaches was not a feature of the Greene et al. scheme (Bryman, 2009).

Mixed methods studies typically involve a cross-sectional survey design that combines either a structured interview or more usually a self-administered questionnaire for the quantitative data with semi-structured interviews for the qualitative data (Bryman, 2006), and the leadership field seems to fit with this tendency (Bryman, 2004). For example, in a study that was published in 2004, and which was therefore outside the date range of the review, Berson and Avolio (2004) report the results of a study of transformational leadership and the dissemination of organizational goals in a large Israeli telecommunications company. This investigation entailed a self-administered questionnaire completed by managers and others to collect data on managers' leadership styles (using the MLQ) and communication style. In addition, semi-structured interviews were carried out with managers and their direct reports. They write: 'By using both quantitative and qualitative methods, we were able to depict specific relationships, and then to provide a deeper examination of those relationships' (Berson and Avolio, 2004, p. 642), which is indicative of using one data set to expand on and complement the other. This article was highlighted as one of a number that could be used as a template for exploring the levels of analysis issue that has preoccupied many leadership researchers in recent years, but not always in a technically appropriate manner (Yammarino et al., 2005). Rowland and Parry (2009) included observation of team meetings, semi-structured interviews and questionnaires in their grounded theory-based study of organizational design and leadership in teams in Australian higher education, as did Holmberg et al. (2008) in their investigation of the role of leadership in the implementation of evidence-based treatment practices for drug abuse and criminal behaviour in Sweden.

A rather striking mixed methods approach can be discerned in Goodall's (2009) study of the leadership of top universities and business schools. Against a background in which it is sometimes argued that universities would be better led by non-academics, Goodall shows that better universities and business schools tend to be led by top scholars. The study combines quantitative and qualitative data. The former are derived from a secondary analysis of biographical information on leaders gleaned from publications like *Who's Who* and from the examination of citations, an approach usually referred to as bibliometrics. The qualitative data derived from interviews with 26 top leaders of universities in the UK and USA (vice-chancellors/principals/presidents) or deans of business schools. She also conducted 12 interviews in connection with a case study of the hiring of a UK vice-chancellor. The quantitative bibliometric data provided the confirmation of the relationship between the excellence in scholarship and university performance, while the qualitative data allowed some of the factors lying behind this relationship to surface.

While there has undoubtedly been a noticeable increase in mixed methods research to examine leadership, it is also the case that in much of it, the qualitative research component occupies a handmaiden role (Bryman, 2007), largely being used to illustrate or add to or support the quantitative findings rather than for what it can offer in its own right. Rowland and Parry's (2009) study represents an exception in adopting a clear constructionist orientation. The tendency for qualitative research to assume a somewhat subsidiary role in many studies probably reflects the training and general orientation of many leadership researchers and the perceived expectations of journals.

CONCLUSIONS

Although it is possible, and almost certainly valid, to write about a typical leadership study (Friedrich et al., 2009), it is clear that this is considerable diversity in methodological approach within the field and one gets a sense that that diversity is increasing. In part, the growing diversity reflects a greater acceptance of qualitative methods. It is likely that the growing awareness of research methods which have been neglected by leadership researchers, like qualitative ones, will also suggest new ways of thinking about leadership. When qualitative research methods have been used in leadership research, it has often been in a way that is either subsidiary to the quantitative component in mixed methods research or mimics some of the features of quantitative research so that it looks like quantitative research but without numbers (Bryman, 2004). However, an investigation like that of Alvesson and Sveningsson (2003), which was discussed above, treats leadership as a social construction and, as such, is more in tune with the ethos of qualitative research. Thus, as the appreciation of qualitative research grows and intensifies, it is feasible that the growing awareness of the potential of qualitative and other underused methods will stimulate leadership researchers to think about leadership in new ways and suggest new research questions.

However, it is important not to characterize the field's growing diversity as purely methodologically driven. As the leadership field becomes more theoretically diverse, writers are likely to feel impelled to explore more methods and to be innovative. For example, seeking to apply complexity theory to leadership led Dooley and Lichtenstein (2008) to develop methods to observe in real time events and interaction that take place in very, very brief time slots. By studying numerous time slots and the bits of interaction that take place within them, the researchers expect to be able to examine how far particular leadership patterns are influenced by context or are constant. As we have seen, observation is not uncommon in leadership research (and indeed was behind Bales and Slater's [1955] classic study of leadership emergence), but the microscopic approach taken by Dooley and Lichtenstein in their working through of some of the implications of complexity theory points to considerable experimentation. Similarly, towards the end of their chapter (Chapter 34) on complexity theory in the present volume, Uhl-Bien and Marion note that the working through of the implications of this perspective is likely to be more reliant on 'more qualitative and agent-based modeling approaches' than on the traditional questionnaire approach. They suggest that this is likely to be so because the ontology of the notion of complexity does not lend itself to the positivism with which the questionnaire approach is associated. Their suggestion that the complexity theory approach is likely to be more reliant on a process than a variance theory stance (Langley, 2009) further points to a greater reliance on qualitative research. In this way, the emergence of a new theoretical stance is acting as a spur to methodological innovation.

To take another example, heavily influenced by process philosophy, Wood and Ladkin (2008) developed the idea of the 'leaderful moment', a slice of time in which leadership emerges and comes into being. Such a view departs significantly, as in Dooley and Lichtenstein, from the more common view of leadership as part of an ongoing set of relationships that are founded on influence. To gain some leverage on the notion of the leaderful moment, the authors asked managers to 'photograph things, people or moments they perceived as inextricably linked with the experience of leadership, but which might usually go unnoticed' (Wood and Ladkin, 2008, p. 18). The managers were later interviewed about their photographs, a method often called 'photo-elicitation'. Thus, the development of new theoretical approaches frequently prompts researchers to develop new ways of collecting data about their object of interest, especially when, as with these two research areas, more conventional ways of collecting data do not look promising.

Leadership researchers have long been aware that the field is probably over-reliant on questionnaire studies. Nowadays, that awareness is being accompanied by a preparedness to explore new or different ways of getting to grips with the complex and elusive phenomenon of leadership. At the same time, little has changed since Conger's (1998) call for greater use of participant observation in the study of leadership. As noted above, ethnographic studies have considerable potential in the field in helping us to appreciate how leadership takes place, the 'leaderful moments' that undoubtedly occur in organizations, how context and leadership are intertwined, and the fact that leadership may occur anywhere and be exhibited by anyone – not just where leadership researchers assume it will take place. Leadership researchers have been engaged for some time in a collective *mea culpa* about the dominance and limitations of the questionnaire in their field. Now it is time to do something about it, particularly at a juncture at which new theoretical approaches and influences appear to be influencing the field more and more.

REFERENCES

Alvesson, M. and Kärreman, D. (2000) 'Varieties of discourse: on the study of organization through discourse analysis', *Human Relations*, 53(9), 1125–49.

Alvesson, M. and Sveningsson, S. (2003) 'Good visions, bad micro-management and ugly ambiguity, contradictions of (non-)leadership in a knowledge-intensive organization', *Organization Studies*, 24(6), 961–88.

Antonakis, J., Schriesheim, C.A., Donovan, J.A., et al. (2004) 'Methods for studying leadership'. In J. Antonakis, A.T. Cianciolo and R.J. Sternberg (eds), *The Nature of Leadership*. Thousand Oaks, CA: Sage, pp. 48–70.

Avolio, B.J., Walumbwa, F.O. and Weber, T.J. (2009a) 'Leadership: current theories, research, and future directions', *Annual Review of Psychology*, 60, 421–49.

Avolio, B.J., Reichard, R.J., Hannah, S.T., Walumbwa, F.O. and Chan, A. (2009b) 'A meta-analytic review of leadership impact research: experimental and quasi-experimental studies', *The Leadership Quarterly*, 20, 764–84.

Bales, R.F. and Slater, P.E. (1955) 'Role differentiation in small decision-making groups'. In T. Parsons and R.F. Bales (eds), *Family, Socialization and Interaction Process*. New York: Free Press.

Barling, J., Weber, T. and Kelloway, E.K. (1996) 'Effects of transformational leadership training on attitudinal and financial outcomes: a field experiment', *Journal of Applied Psychology*, 81(6), 827–32.

Berelson, B. (1952) *Content Analysis in Communication Research*. New York: Free Press.

Berson, Y. and Avolio, B.J. (2004) 'Transformational leadership and the dissemination of organizational goals: a case study of a telecommunications firm', *The Leadership Quarterly*, 15(5), 625–46.

Bligh, M.C., Kohles, J.C. and Meindl, J.R. (2004) 'Charisma under crisis: presidential leadership, rhetoric, and media responses before and after the September 11th terrorist attacks', *The Leadership Quarterly*, 15(2), 211–39.

Bryman, A. (1986) *Leadership and Organizations*. London: Routledge.

Bryman, A. (1995) *Disney and His Worlds*. London: Routledge.

Bryman, A. (2004) 'Qualitative research on leadership: a critical but appreciative review', *The Leadership Quarterly*, 15(6), 729–69.

Bryman, A. (2006) 'Integrating quantitative and qualitative research: How is it done?', *Qualitative Research*, 6(1), 97–113.

Bryman, A. (2007) 'Barriers to integrating quantitative and qualitative research', *Journal of Mixed Methods Research*, 1(1), 8–22.

Bryman, A. (2009) 'Mixed methods in organizational research'. In D.A. Buchanan and A. Bryman (eds), *Handbook of Organizational Research Methods*. London: Sage, pp. 516–31.

Bryman, A. (2011) 'Mission accomplished? Research methods in the first five years of *Leadership*', *Leadership*, 7(1).

Bryman, A. and Bell, E. (2007) *Business Research Methods*, revised ed. Oxford: Oxford University Press.

Collinson, D. and Grint, K. (2005) 'Editorial: the leadership agenda', *Leadership*, 1(1), 5–9.

Conger, J.A. (1998) 'Qualitative research as a cornerstone methodology for understanding leadership', *The Leadership Quarterly*, 9(1), 107–21.

DeGroot, T., Kiker, D.S. and Cross, T.C. (2000) 'A meta-analysis to review organizational outcomes related to charismatic leadership', *Canadian Review of Administrative Sciences*, 17(4), 356–71.

Dooley, K.J. and Lichtenstein, B. (2008) 'Research methods for studying the dynamics of leadership'. In M. Uhl-Bien and R. Marion (eds), *Complexity Leadership. Part 1: Conceptual Foundations*. Charlotte, NC: Information Age, pp. 269–90.

Eliot, M. (1993) *Walt Disney: Hollywood's Dark Prince*. New York: Birch Lane.

Friedrich, T.L., Byrne, C.L. and Mumford, M.D. (2009) 'Methodological and theoretical considerations in survey research', *The Leadership Quarterly*, 20(2), 57–60.

Gardner, W.L., Lowe, K.B., Moss, T.W., Mahoney, K.T. and Cogliser, C.C. (Unpublished work) 'Scholarly leadership of the study of leadership: a review of *The Leadership Quarterly*'s second decade, 2000–2009', unpublished MS.

Goodall, A.H. (2009) *Socrates in the Boardroom: Why Research Universities Should be Led by Top Scholars*. Princeton: Princeton University Press.

Greene, C.N. (1975) 'The reciprocal nature of influence between leader and subordinate', *Journal of Applied Psychology*, 60(2), 187–93.

Greene, J.C., Caracelli, V.J. and Graham, W. F. (1989) 'Toward a conceptual framework for mixed-method evaluation designs', *Educational Evaluation and Policy Analysis*, 11(3), 255–74.

Holmberg, R., Fridell, M., Arnesson, P. and Bäckvall, M. (2008) 'Leadership and implementation of evidence-based practices', *Leadership in Health Services*, 21(3), 168–84.

Howell, J. M. (1988) 'Two faces of charisma: Socialized and personalized leadership in organizations,' in J. Conger & R. Kanungo (eds.), *Charismatic leadership: The elusive factor in organizational effectiveness* (pp. 213–236). San Francisco: Jossey-Bass.

Howell, J.M. and Frost, P.J. (1989), 'A laboratory study of charismatic leadership', *Organizational Behavior and Human Decision Processes*, 43(2), 243–69.

Hunt, J.G. and Conger, J.A. (1999) 'From where we sit: an assessment of charismatic and transformational leadership research', *The Leadership Quarterly*, 10(3), 335–43.

Hunter, S.T., Bedell-Avers, K. and Mumford, M.D. (2007) 'The typical leadership study: assumptions, implications, and potential remedies', *The Leadership Quarterly*, 18(5), 436–46.

Insch, G.S., Moore, J.E. and Murphy, L.D. (1997) 'Content analysis in leadership research: example, procedures, and suggestions for further use', *The Leadership Quarterly*, 8(1), 1–25.

Jackson, B. and Guthey, E. (2007) 'Putting the visual into the social construction of leadership'. In B. Shamir, R. Pillai, M.C. Bligh and M. Uhl-Bien (eds), *Follower-Centered Perspectives on Leadership: a Tribute to the Memory of James R. Meindl*. Greenwich, CN: Information Age, pp. 167–86.

Klenke, K. (2008) *Qualitative Research in the Study of Leadership*. Bingley: Emerald.

Kroeck, K.G. Lowe, K.B. and Brown, K.W. (2004), 'The assessment of leadership'. In J. Antonakis, A.T. Cianciolo and R.J. Sternberg (eds), *The Nature of Leadership*. Thousand Oaks, CA: Sage, pp. 71–97.

Langley, A. (2009) 'Studying processes in and around organizations'. In D.A. Buchanan and A. Bryman (eds), *Handbook of Organizational Research Methods*. London: Sage, pp. 409–29.

Lord, R.G. De Vader, C.L. and Alliger, G.M. (1986) 'A meta-analysis of the relation between personality traits and leadership perceptions: an application of validity generalization procedures', *Journal of Applied Psychology*, 71(3), 402–10.

Lowe, K.B. and Gardner, W. L. (2000) 'Ten years of *The Leadership Quarterly*: contributions and challenges for the future', *The Leadership Quarterly*, 11(4), 459–514.

Lowin, A. and Craig, C.R. (1968) 'The influence of performance on managerial style: an experimental object lesson in the ambiguity of correlational data', *Organizational Behavior and Human Performance*, 3, 440–58.

Luthans, F. and Lockwood, D.L. (1984) 'Toward an observation system for measuring leader behavior'. In J.G. Hunt, D-M. Hosking, C.A. Schriesheim and R. Stewart (eds), *Leaders and Managers: International Perspectives on Managerial Behavior and Leadership*. New York: Pergamon.

Luthans, F., Rosenkrantz, S.A. and Hennessey, H.W. (1985) 'What do successful managers really do? An observation study of managerial activities', *Journal of Applied Behavioral Science*, 21: 255–70.

Maitlis, S. and Lawrence, T.B. (2007) 'Triggers and enablers of sensegiving in organizations', *Academy of Management Journal*, 50(1), 57–84.

Mann, R.D. (1959) 'A review of the relationship between personality and performance in small groups', *Psychological Bulletin*, 56(4), 241–70.

Meindl, J.R., Ehrlich, S.B. and Dukerich, J.M. (1985) 'The romance of leadership', *Administrative Science Quarterly*, 30, 78–102.

Mizrahi, T. and Rosenthal, B.B. (2001) 'Complexities of coalition building: leaders' successes, strategies, struggles, and solutions', *Social Work*, 46(1), 63–78.

Mosley, L. (1985) *Disney's World*. Briarcliff Manor, NY: Stein and Day.

Mumford, M.D. (2006) *Pathways to Outstanding Leadership: A Comparative Analysis of Charismatic, Ideological and Pragmatic Leaders*. Mahwah, NJ: Erlbaum.

Mumford, M.D. and Van Doorn, J.R. (2001) 'The leadership of pragmatism: reconsidering Franklin in the age of charisma', *The Leadership Quarterly*, 12(3), 279–309.

Mumford, M.D., Friedrich, T.L., Caughron, J.J. and Antes, A.L. (2009) 'Leadership research: traditions, developments, and current directions'. In D.A. Buchanan and A. Bryman (eds), *Handbook of Organizational Research Methods*. London: Sage, pp. 111–27.

Phillips, N. and Di Domenico, M.L. (2009) 'Discourse analysis in organizational research: methods and debates'. In D.A. Buchanan and A. Bryman (eds), *Handbook of Organizational Research Methods*. London: Sage, pp. 549–65.

Podsakoff, P.M., MacKenzie, S.B., Lee, J.Y. and Podsakoff, N.P. (2003) 'Common method biases in behavioral research: a critical review of the literature and recommended remedies', *Journal of Applied Psychology*, 88(5), 879–903.

Reed, M. (2000) 'The limits of discourse analysis in organizational analysis', *Organization*, 7(3): 524–30.

Roberts, N.C. and Bradley, R.T. (1988) 'The limits of charisma'. In J.A. Conger and R.N. Kanungo (eds), *Charismatic Leadership: The Elusive Factor in Organizational Effectiveness*. San Francisco: Jossey-Bass, pp. 253–75.

Rowland, P. and Parry, K. (2009) 'Consensual commitment: a grounded theory of the meso- level influence of organizational design on leadership and decision-making', *The Leadership Quarterly*, 20(4), 535–53.

Rush, M.D., Thomas, J.C. and Lord, R.G. (1977) 'Implicit leadership theory: a potential threat to the internal validity of leader behavior questionnaires', *Organizational Behavior and Human Performance*, 20(1), 93–110.

Spector, P.E. and Brannick, M.T. (2009) 'Common method variance or measurement bias? The problem and possible solutions'. In D.A. Buchanan and A. Bryman (eds), *Handbook of Organizational Research Methods*. London: Sage, pp. 346–62.

Stogdill, R.M. (1948) 'Personal factors associated with leadership: a survey of the literature', *Journal of Psychology*, 25, pp. 35–71.

Stone-Romero, E.F. (2009) 'Implications of research design options for the validity of inferences derived from organizational research'. In D.A. Buchanan and A. Bryman (eds), *Handbook of Organizational Research Methods*. London: Sage, pp. 302–27.

Treviño, L.K., Brown, M. and Pincus Hartman, L. (2003) 'A qualitative investigation of perceived executive ethical leadership: perceptions from inside and outside the executive suite', *Human Relations*, 56(1), 5–37.

Wood, M. and Ladkin, D. (2008) 'The event's the thing: brief encounters with the leaderful moment'. In K.T. Jones and J. Collins (eds), *Leadership Perspectives: Knowledge into Action*. Houndmills: Palgrave-Macmillan, pp. 15–28.

Yammarino, F.J., Dionne, S.D., Chun, J.U. and Danserau, F. (2005) 'Leadership and levels of analysis: a state-of-the-science review', *The Leadership Quarterly*, 16(6), 879–919.

3

The Enduring and Elusive Quest for a General Theory of Leadership: Initial Efforts and New Horizons

Georgia Sorenson, George R. Goethals and Paige Haber

This is my quest, to follow that star, no matter how hopeless, no matter how far... 'The Impossible Dream' from Man of La Mancha (Darion, 2008)

THE QUEST

When the idea of convening a group of scholars to formulate a general theory of leadership was first proposed, one of those who eventually became a key member remarked that the idea of such a project was 'quixotic.' Professor Joanne Ciulla used the term exactly as it is defined – as the *American Heritage Dictionary* (2009) has it, 'idealistic or romantic without regard to practicality.' What a charming, silly idea. And in the end, the quest and idealism endures but the goal of a general theory remains elusive. However, as Ciulla herself documents, we went far, and learned a great deal along the way.

The Quest for a General Theory of Leadership (GTOL) involves a story about process, and another about product. The story begins with James MacGregor Burns. Burns is a restless scholar who began thinking more generally about the phenomenon of leadership after his Pulitzer Prize and National Book Award-winning classic

Roosevelt: The Soldier of Freedom was published in 1970. He believed that he would need to expand beyond his familiar disciplines of political science and history in order to fully comprehend the subject. Accordingly, he immersed himself in the fields of philosophy and psychology and in 1978, at age 60, published one of his most influential works, *Leadership*. Burns then became increasingly interested in fostering the study of leadership. He laid the groundwork for the Program in Leadership Studies at Williams College, his *alma mater*, and, in the early 1990s, became closely involved with shaping and establishing the Jepson School of Leadership Studies at the University of Richmond and the Center for Political Leadership and Participation at the University of Maryland. In 1997 the center's name was changed to The James MacGregor Burns Academy of Leadership to honor his lasting contribution to the field.

Writing about leadership and promoting its study was not enough for Burns. He perceived a need for greater intellectual coherence in an extremely wide-ranging field of study and practice. In an interview with Sorenson and Goethals on July 5, 2009, Professor Burns stated that studying leadership in the early years was liberating and took him beyond a focus on biography and politics. He added that the study of leadership demanded intellectual creativity and reach. After publishing books on Bill Clinton and 'the three Roosevelts' in 1999 and 2001, with Georgia Sorenson and Susan Dunn, respectively, he directly took on the need for theoretical integration in leadership studies. He first approached Sorenson at the Burns Academy and then Al Goethals at Williams College about launching a project to formulate a general theory of leadership. Whatever doubts Sorenson and Goethals may have had about the enterprise were put aside. Both were energized at the prospect of working on another ambitious project with Burns.

The three scholars had learned of each others' work in leadership through the Kellogg Leadership Studies Project (KLSP), a four-year initiative funded by the W.K. Kellogg Foundation from 1994 to 1998 at the Burns Academy, that for the first time created a community of scholars in the field of leadership studies. In many ways, this research and community of scholars was the seed that made the work on the General Theory possible. What made it necessary was another mutual work by Goethals, Sorenson and Burns, Sage's four-volume 2 million-word *Encyclopedia of Leadership*, which we were just finishing up around the time of the Quest (Goethals and Sorenson, 2004). The encyclopedia had 'morsalized' (to use Burns' term) leadership – there was now a responsibility to pull it back together.

For these and other reasons, Burns, Sorenson and Goethals were all well-acquainted with the faculty at the Jepson School and decided immediately to test the waters of those professors' interest in the endeavor. The Jepson response was characteristic of the whole project. In November 2001, the entire Jepson faculty (then Professors Ciulla, Richard Cuoto, Elizabeth Faier, Gill Hickman, Douglas Hicks, Frederic Jablin, Terry Price and Thomas Wren) met with Burns, Goethals, and Sorenson in Richmond to decide whether it made sense to proceed. Many, if not most, of the Jepson faculty were skeptical, but they all engaged. Ciulla remarked that she had no inclination to work on such an enterprise, but she was curious about why some of her colleagues did. Price was initially extremely dubious about the whole idea, but he wanted to be involved in the discussions, so he joined the party.

During the November meeting a range of difficult questions was discussed in response to Burns' challenge to come up with a general theory, to be used by people studying or practicing leadership, that would provide 'a general guide or orientation – a set of principles that are universal which can then be adapted to different situations.' Keep in mind that this group of scholars was from a wide range of disciplines and perspectives: it included political scientists, anthropologists, historians, philosophers, and psychologists and scholars from professional schools of education and public administration. At the outset, discussions focused on the nature of theory, on what made a good theory, and whether a theory similar to those in the natural sciences, economics, or other social sciences might serve as a useful model. Many felt that leadership was too multifaceted to be captured in a single theory. Some expressed worry that anything that was generated would exclude something else. Others felt that the multidisciplinary nature of leadership studies and everyone's varying implicit assumptions about human beings, social relations, organizations, and societies doomed the enterprise. But some consensus emerged. The group agreed that a systems approach, incorporating post-Newtonian ideas of causality, was probably more apt to succeed than any linear model. However, many of the most vexing issues were simply set aside. For example, the group talked about the need to clarify whether the theory should be descriptive or prescriptive. The group felt that determining this would be important, but ultimately proceeded without really grappling with that central question.

Strangely perhaps, given that so many reservations and cautions were expressed, the group cheerfully pledged itself to push forward. No one abandoned the project. Rather, the group made specific commitments as to next steps. There would be another meeting at Jepson the following March, of 2002 (which was covered by reporter Katherine Mangan of the *Chronicle of Higher Education*) and then a three-day 'no kidding around' working session at Williams College's estate at Mount Hope Farm over the 2002 summer solstice in Williamstown, Massachusetts. Between the initial November meeting and the subsequent March meeting, each member of the working group wrote a short paper outlining principles or phenomena that she or he believed were essential to incorporate, in one way or another, into a general theory. In the March meeting the group continued their discussion of the difficult overarching questions, with no resolution, but also identified the issues they would discuss at Mount Hope. They decided that they must clarify the role of values, leader–follower relations, and power and context, including culture, in the general theory. These, in effect, were seen as the building blocks of an integrated theory.

It is important to note the leader–follower dynamics that carried the group through the first two meetings. Burns was the clear leader, though he insisted on not taking part in the various group discussions but rather joined the group for meals and general conversation. The Mount Hope gathering was managed by Sorenson and Goethals, but what held the group together was Burns' vision.

That vision was that a general theory was attainable, and that this was the group that could formulate it. Even if the goal was unreachable, the effort itself would produce useful results. The group members had enough respect and admiration for all that Burns had achieved that they put their doubts aside and worked as hard as they could to accomplish the mission. Without the group's willingness to follow its leader, despite misgivings, the project would have been abandoned in its very early stages.

So we beat on.... When the group members convened at Mount Hope in June, they were joined by another leadership scholar, Michael Harvey of Washington College in Maryland. Also, Gary Yukl from SUNY Albany was invited to join in some of the discussions. Before the work began, the group completely revised its agenda. Rather than discuss power, values, leader–follower relations, and context, as planned in March, and confirmed in correspondence between the March and June meetings, they decided that they had to address more fundamental questions first: What makes leadership necessary? What makes leadership possible? and What processes characterize the emergence, maintenance, and transformation of leadership?

Addressing these questions took the group back to a theme that was touched on occasionally in earlier meetings, but never fully grappled with. That is: What about the human condition defines the nature of leadership? At first, this question seemed both too basic and too difficult, so the group simply sidestepped it, without explicitly agreeing to do so. But as they thought harder about the overall goal, they knew they must consider the human condition in its most general sense, followed by the question: What about the human condition makes leadership both necessary and possible?

The group worked at Mount Hope for all or parts of five days. At his suggestion, the group worked independently of Burns, who joined them for meals. The group self-organized into three teams and responded to Burns' insistence that something be actually written. Papers were written by the different teams, and on the last day, the entire group discussed them. They felt that they had learned a great deal from each other and gained important insights into the very foundational elements of leadership, but none of the members believed that the group was really any closer to a general theory.

At this point, the group decided that they needed input from other scholars and practitioners. As a result, with the cooperation of the leaders of the International Leadership Association (ILA), they decided to have a plenary session on The General Theory of Leadership at the November 2002 ILA meeting in Seattle. Most of the working group, including Burns, attended the session.

At the 2002 ILA Conference, the group organized the first session on the General Theory. The group elected to interact with members of the audience, using an inductive approach to our theory building: that is, offering a specific case study and engaging with others to construct a theory from its particulars. Using a 1951 desegregation case from Prince Edward County Virginia, the group offered details of the context and actors with the hope of uncovering general concepts about the relationship among causality, change, and leadership that might be generalizable across multiple contexts. The robust audience feedback from this session encouraged the group to build into its scholarly process opportunities to discuss emerging thinking and make sure what they were attempting to do would be helpful to others.

The working group continued to gather input from other scholars and refine its approach. Following Seattle, an expanded group of scholars gathered in Richmond in April 2003 in conjunction with a 10th anniversary celebration of the founding of the Jepson School. Joining the ongoing project were Bruce Avolio from the University of Nebraska, group theorist and practitioner John Johnson, Deborah Meehan from the Leadership Learning Community, Sonia Ospina from NYU, Ronald Riggio from Claremont McKenna College, and Mark Walker from American University. This group attempted to focus attention on issues of theory that had been set aside during earlier meetings. These included the need to define terms clearly, whether a general theory was possible, and whether a social scientific- or humanities-oriented constructivist approach would be more fruitful.

A second ILA session took place in November 2003 in Guadalajara, Mexico. At this meeting, Hickman, Price, Walker, and Wren presented proposals outlining the central elements of a general theory. Then Hickman and Ciulla offered integrative perspectives, attempting to combine the different matrices of elements presented by the first four. As in Seattle, a large audience of ILA members and guests attended the meeting, offered useful feedback and commentary, and encouraged the group to continue their work.

While the meetings in Seattle, Richmond, and Guadalajara were useful and supportive, it became increasingly evident that it was time to write. The group needed less process and more product. It was also apparent to the group by then that they were not going to write a general theory of leadership anytime soon. Their choices were simply to abandon the whole enterprise or write a book summarizing their insights into the key constructs uncovered in the two and a half year quest. As a result, a pivotal meeting was held at the Jepson

School in May 2004. Burns, Sorenson, and Goethals joined the Jepson faculty then participating in the project (Ciulla, Hickman, Hicks, Crystal Hoyt, Jablin, Price, and Wren) and also Richard Couto, who had moved on from Jepson to the new Antioch PhD program, along with Michael Harvey and Mark Walker. Everyone cleared their schedules to make this crucial Saturday meeting possible. Burns made it clear that this was a make-or-break meeting. He was past his 85th birthday and wanted some closure on this endeavor. He put the group on notice that if they didn't have a plan for a book by sundown that day, they would have to quit.

The result of this meeting – somewhat miraculously – was that the group agreed on the plan for the book that was eventually published as *The Quest for a General Theory of Leadership* (Goethals and Sorenson, 2006). With very few changes, the outline that many of the group members can still envision on the blackboard in the Jepson Dean's Conference Room found its way almost entirely intact into the book. They thought that the book would have a good home in Ciulla's leadership series for Elgar. It was agreed that Goethals and Sorenson would edit the volume, enforcing deadlines and offering feedback. But, of course, Goethals and Sorenson were backed entirely by the implicit leadership of Burns.

Throughout the quest, a key strategy was to invite comments and suggestions from practitioners. As Burns so convincingly reminded the group, if social activists could integrate the complexity of leadership in real time, they should be able to do so in their theoretical efforts. Accordingly, discussion sessions at the ILA and other meetings with practitioners, such as the February 2004 meeting with members of the Leadership Learning Community in Washington DC, provided insight and course corrections along the way.

Most of the group reconvened at the ILA meeting in Washington, DC in November 2004, where they held another packed session describing the work and inviting feedback. But a cloud loomed over this session. That year's ILA meeting was held within weeks of the tragic murder of a Jepson colleague, Fred Jablin. Nevertheless, the remaining working group persevered. Good progress was discussed at the 2005 ILA meeting in Amsterdam and by the time of the 2006 ILA meeting in Chicago, the book had just been published.

THE FINDINGS

Initially, emerging from the Mount Hope's discussions, was the bedrock view by all concerned that leadership was part and parcel of the human condition. Were they ever to crack the code, they must start at the beginning. It was, as Harvey suggested, 'a mystery as modern as the nation-state and as ancient as the tribe.' As social and vulnerable animals, humans must form collectives to achieve common purposes.

Groups, whether temporary or enduring, are the Petri dish of leadership. Thus, the group's guiding questions in exploring leadership and the human condition were, as mentioned earlier: 'In the human condition, what makes leadership necessary? And what makes leadership possible?' The group understood, at a deep level, that leadership may enlarge or it may constrict the space for human freedom and imagination – the quintessential aims of leadership.

Operating in the context of human groups, leadership is established by means of influence, or more broadly, power. This consideration started with the members' understanding of power and with forms of power such as force and coercion, as illustrated, for example, in Shakespeare's *Coriolanus*. The group examined studies on power from those discussed by French and Raven in the 1950s, to more contemporary notions of soft power and charisma. Ultimately, they explored Michel Foucault's analyses of the ubiquity of power in everyday interaction, between human beings everywhere. Always, the focus was on how power that is essentially coercive combines with power that is rooted in positive human relationships. Thus, the multiplicity as well as the ubiquity of power and leadership, came sharply into focus and clearly should be a key construct in the construction of an integrated theory.

But leadership in groups is about more than just power. The *Quest* volume attempted to relate questions of group dynamics, and then in particular the nature of the relationship between leaders and followers, as fully as possible to the fundamental questions of leadership. In doing so, the authors note both the perils and potentials of leadership. Many group forces lead the persons in them to selfish, callous, and even destructive behavior toward outgroups. Leadership can make those problems worse, or a lot better. The group found that a thorough understanding of how leaders behave toward individual group members, and how leaders respond to followers' needs and expectations, helps us appreciate the directions – toward good or ill – on which groups set out.

The fact that group dynamics and leader–follower relations lead to very different outcomes, for different people, underlines the centrality of ethics in contemplating and appreciating the many ways that both leaders and followers think and behave. One important set of questions surrounds degrees of equality vs inequality within groups. Can ethical considerations on the part of both leaders and followers at least slow harmful tendencies toward inequality, hierarchy, and domination that often are closely entwined in the leadership dynamic? Furthermore, what are the ethical questions that arise not only within groups but also between groups? What are the ethical responsibilities of leadership to the larger world beyond a leader's set of followers? What considerations of inclusiveness and responsibility must a general theory of leadership confront? *Quest* team members and philosophers Price and Hicks addressed these issues in the book and made them critical components of a proposed theoretical direction.

The examination of the ethical dilemmas of group members and leaders toward each other and toward other groups forced the group to confront a critical question within the Quest group: namely, whether we held importantly different underlying assumptions regarding the contextual nature of reality and leadership's place within it. Some group members argued that our different viewpoints roughly corresponded to essentialist and constructionist perspectives. They viewed those they termed essentialists as maintaining that social and natural realities exist apart from our view of them: i.e. individuals perceive the world rather than construct it. This can be viewed to contrast with a constructionist view, in which humans construct or create reality and give it meaning through social, economic, and political interactions. The latter perspective was explored more completely by Ospina and Sorenson later in the book. Many in the group argued, especially Hickman and Couto, that understanding our differing assumptions about human nature was key to understanding leadership because these perspectives shape the way we view problems, ask questions, conduct research, construct theories, and create solutions.

While both perspectives operate within the thinking of the group-as-a-whole, scholars who view leadership with an eye toward social change (as opposed to a purely descriptive view of events in a group) lean toward a constructionist perspective. Those scholars employed a definition of change offered by Hickman and Couto in *The Quest,* 'A collective effort by participants to initially modify, alter or transform human social systems.'

Regardless of the utility of an essentialist vs constructionist characterization of scholarly perspectives, the group as a whole was convinced that the human condition, and thus leadership, fundamentally involves meaning making, and that real change – the kind discussed by James MacGregor Burns – involves influencing the meanings that different groups make in the context of competing and conflicting definitions of reality and of value. Real change ultimately involves changes in behavior, but those changes typically follow successful efforts by leadership to reframe or reconstruct reality. Once people's views of the world change, their readiness to act in that perceived world changes. The Quest group recognizes, again, that meaning making happens within group and intergroup contexts, and that leaders' relations with followers provide the crucible in which mutual influence, generally initiated by a leader, results in specific meanings. We come back to questions of ethics by noting that the more normatively oriented scholars among us take ethical stands from which they assess the meaning made and actions taken by specific groups in specific historical and cultural contexts.

AFTER THE QUEST

Leadership is a phenomenon focused on vision, challenge, collaboration, process, and product. It is only natural, then, to inquire what is next for the Quest. The group members are often asked the question: 'Will there be a Quest II?' and likely the answer to this question varies. This purpose of this section is to examine ways in which the GTOL work has been used and examined since the publication of the book in 2006 and to discuss areas for continued development for GTOL and leadership studies as a whole.

With the proliferation of leadership programs, books, students, and scholars, GTOL was highly anticipated. For many, there was a yearning for greater synthesis in the complex and often-fragmented field of leadership studies. Just like in the GTOL group, there are skeptics of the possibility or desire to find a general theory and there are those that feel that it is not only possible, but needed. Regardless of perspective, most agree that GTOL propelled the study of leadership further forward. The GTOL process and product demonstrates the complex, integrated, and interdisciplinary nature of the field.

Despite the lack of consensus of a general theory, GTOL is a significant contribution to the field. It took on large questions and topics of leadership studies and the process of inquiry and collaboration was in itself an act of leadership. GTOL also influenced and further developed the authors' thinking about the facets of leadership that they took on and has thus affected their continued work on their subject areas in positive ways. GTOL member political scientist Couto shared that the GTOL experience has positively influenced his thinking about leadership and has integrated this learning in his continued scholarship on political and civic leadership (Couto, pers comm, 1 July, 2009):

My participation [in GTOL] helped me a great deal. I got the chance to examine leadership and causality and think through systems analysis. That has stayed with me in thinking about the necessary but insufficient role that leadership has in bringing about change.

I also abandoned the idea that leadership requires followership and to accept the idea that leadership means taking initiative on behalf of shared values. Those with whom we share values may be in the same place and time or different places and times, future or past. This definition leaves the task of explaining effective leadership. That I think has to do with the people involved and the time and circumstances of their initiative.

Some of the questions that we laid down in the process of this work stay with me – the nature of authority, the need for it, and the social construction of it. All of this influenced my thought as I took on the role of editor of the SAGE political and civic leadership reference handbook I am completing on Political and Civic Leadership. That work collects a lot of information that would challenge a good theory but also invite it.

Going forward, were we to do so, I see the need to hold on to the existing group but also to infuse it with new resources: a theorist – what does it mean to build theory? People with a command of the field of theory – Susan Komives comes to mind. And people developing important theories of leadership from complexity science, human development studies, and cognitive studies.

Individual chapters (see especially 'Power' and 'Constructionism'), and the book as a whole, have been used in undergraduate and graduate-level leadership studies and business management courses. Students have found the work inviting, accessible, and thought-provoking, furthering their insights about leadership and understanding of leadership as multifaceted and complex.

Professor Heidi Connole, who is Faculty Team Leader in the Executive MBA Program College of Business and Economics at the University of Idaho, talks about her experience using the Quest in her Executive MBA course EMBA 510: *Summer Integrative Experience* during the summer semester of 2008 (Connole, pers comm, 1 July 2009):

The students in this course are allowed to tailor an individual project to their own interests as long as it is integrative and comprehensive (representing the curriculum knowledge acquired during their first year in the program). In this particular case, four students selected a 'readings group' around the subject of strategic leadership. We used the Quest for a General Theory of Leadership to launch the readings group and set the stage for the course by demonstrating the interdisciplinary nature of this field and its multi-faceted quality.

Sorenson was gracious enough to join us by phone to discuss how the book came into being as a project where the best minds on the subject were drawn together to explore this question of a 'general theory' of leadership.

For our students, who are all industry executives, it was especially valuable to be exposed to this idea that there are differences in the conceptualization of what it means to be a leader (particularly at the strategic level). In fact, we structured our readings group seminar around leading in the military, the political arena and the business sphere in order to explore these differences.

Despite a strong background or formal training in academic reading and writing, my students found the Quest for a General Theory of Leadership both accessible and enlightening. Ultimately they used this text and others selected for the readings group to develop personal philosophies of leadership.

Sorenson found that, in her graduate classes in group and organizational dynamics with mid-level career civil servants studying public policy, there was always a group of students who were thirsting for something theoretical about leadership. To these students, the Quest was an oasis. Professor Michael Speer (Speer, pers comm, 2 July, 2009), who worked with a similar cohort, agreed:

I use the book in my masters-level class at the University of Maryland, 'Leadership in Groups and Organizations.' By 'use' I mean that – I ask the students to read/discuss/learn from a couple of articles (specifically, the ones by Michael Harvey).

As for myself, I use the chapter on group dynamics as the basis for a mini-lecture, and most importantly the book informs how I teach the course overall.

While I sense some disappointment from the authors that the quest did not lead to the grail of a general theory (or even agreement on what general theory is anyway), that fact and condition is also most liberating. Leadership is far from amenable to a checklist, so leaders have to do things like reflect on who they are, how they do or would lead in certain situations, how groups influence what and how a leader can do, etc. So this is, for me and for my class, the exhilarating part of the book. It says to me that leadership and learning about and for leadership is hard work that requires all sorts of thinking and feeling since we do not know nearly all the rules yet, and do not know, even, that there are such rules, or general theory.

The ideas and conclusions of GTOL have been used in works such as Morrill's book *Strategic Leadership* (Morrill, 2007) and Banks' book

Dissent and the Failure of Leadership (Banks, 2008) Hickman's new book on *Leading Change* (Hickman, 2009), Sorenson's *Strategic Leadership* (Grandstaff and Sorenson, 2008) and Couto's 2007 edited book *Reflections on Leadership* (Couto, 2007) identify the GTOL work as an important contribution to the progression of the field, charting new territory. The GTOL work is also included in the *Encyclopedia of Leadership*, edited by Goethals and Sorenson (2004).

Interest in identifying an overarching, more general theory and synthesis of leadership has also been explored in other arenas. Roger Gill (Gill, 2006) proposed an 'integrative, holistic model of leadership' which draws on four dimensions of leadership research (intellectual/cognitive, emotional, spiritual, and behavioral) and includes the functions of vision and mission, shared values, empowerment, and strategy. The growing area of integral theory and integral leadership also seeks more holistic understandings and synthesis of consciousness and leadership, especially the work of Ken Wilbur (2000). In a piece examining GTOL through an integral leadership lens, commonalities were identified, particularly around leadership as a complex process, the role of developmental psychology, and the role of the individual and group. The author suggests a transdisciplinary (as opposed to interdisciplinary) approach may have contributed to greater progression in GTOL and advocates for greater inclusion of integral leadership and spiral dynamics.

To some extent, the gauntlet has passed. At ILA in Los Angeles in 2009, University of San Diego Leadership Studies faculty members George Reed and Bob Donmoyer and one of their doctoral students, Paige Haber, organized a session to discuss leadership studies after the Quest. Original Quest members Sorenson and Couto joined them, and Burns joined as a commentator. Couto shared insights from his co-authored chapter on Causality, Change, and Leadership and examined 'generalizations of general theories,' identifying that they are not all that they appear to be. In an effort to extend the GTOL conversation, Couto shared his Quantum Leadership Model, emphasizing the complex and systemic nature of leadership.

Reed shared a model of the nature of different academic fields and their resulting levels of theoretical agreement and coherence, ranging from highly divergent to highly convergent or assimilative levels. In discussing leadership studies in this framework, Reed identified the field as more divergent than convergent. GTOL attempted to push the field toward greater convergence; Reed advocates that the failure to do so is in fact okay. There are downfalls and restrictive characteristics of highly convergent models and thinking, and although often muddy, there is greater creativity

and growth from less agreement and coherence. Donmoyer advocated for challenging traditional ways of viewing fields of study and for introducing new ways of defining and legitimizing leadership studies. Sorenson and Haber discussed future possibilities for GTOL, inviting a new generation of leadership scholars to continue the work. Burns commended the GTOL work and encouraged continued dialogue and exploration of future possibilities with a broader base of scholars, educators, and practitioners.

GTOL and its future continue to be discussed in a variety of arenas. Doctoral students in the USA and abroad are using the GTOL framework to explore issues as diverse as higher education to the judicial system. A new group, 'GTOL II' has emerged in the blogosphere, taking the conversation to the next level (Reyatt, 2009).

The natural question is where to go from here? Whether or not a general theory is ever found and whether or not a general theory is an intended goal, continued work on synthesis and integration of leadership studies will likely contribute to more understanding and more questions. Burns speaks to the 'scatteration' of the field, and more order from this complexity may provide valuable insights and encourage continued conversation across current boundaries.

Burns and others agree that they have given it their 'best shot' and the time has come to pass the work on to new stakeholders and the next generation of leadership scholars. Others believe that some original group members along with new members can help the conversation continue. New voices can bring differing perspectives that are likely to add to the complexity of the discussion, but ideally also the richness.

A criticism of GTOL is the lack of practical application. Including more leadership scholar-practitioners in the conversation can help the GTOL work contribute to leadership in practice and not just in thought. There is also potential for extending the work to a more global arena. Although GTOL was discussed at many ILA conferences, the makeup of the GTOL group came from an American background, albeit one with extensive international experience. Globally accessible technology can help include new, international voices in the conversation as well as provide an avenue for increased dispersion of information.

The GTOL work opens the conversation to interdisciplinary examination of leadership in a clear and needed way. Twenty-five years ago Kellerman (1984) challenged leadership scholars to take an interdisciplinary approach to studying and understanding leadership. This is a challenging and multifaceted approach to take on. Sorenson experienced GTOL as the closest she has come to working in an interdisciplinary intellectual environment, and the GTOL product is a serious and successful attempt at bridging and integrating these disciplinary silos. From this, continued interdisciplinary conversations and explorations of leadership can take place and a clearer picture of disciplinary overlap and divergence can emerge.

While GTOL covered a great deal of intellectual ground, there are a few areas that could be explored in more depth. The discussion of power could be expanded to greater emphasis on motivation and influence, and the leader–follower relationship discussion can be furthered through exploring relationships between group members (within group) and between leaders (intergroup). Additionally, greater focus on the purpose of the leadership process can be expanded. The inclusion of group relations work may provide some insight into these areas as well as contribute to continued exploration of various levels of the leadership system: intrapersonal, interpersonal, group, and system as a whole. In reflecting back on the process, one of the authors shared that complexity science, cognitive studies, and human development studies may also provide insight.

GTOL has broadened the leadership studies field, and there is much potential for future growth and development of the conversations it brought forward. Leadership studies must continue to be challenged to move beyond the leader–follower–shared goal conversation. To embrace the complex and adaptive nature of leadership studies and societal leadership challenges, there is a call for more organic, systemic, and integrative ideas and approaches.

It will not be easy, but to end at the beginning, Burns concludes in the *Quest for A General Theory*

Let me leave you with a challenge and a question. The amazing events that unfolded in Montgomery and the state and nation are that the people in action embraced every major aspect of leadership and integrated it: individual leadership, collective leadership, intra-group and inter-group conflict, conflict of strongly held values, power aspects, etc. – and ultimately produced a real change

leading to more change. They made our country a better country. If those activists could integrate the complex processes and elements of leading in practice, in reality, should we not be able to do so in theory?

REFERENCES

American Heritage Dictionary of the English Language, 4th edn (2009). Boston, MA: Houghton Mifflin.

Banks, S.P. (2008) *Dissent and the Failure of Leadership*. Cheltenham, UK: Edward Elgar, p. 19.

Burns, J. (2009) Personal Communication, 1 June 2009

Couto, R. (2007) *Reflections on Leadership*. Lanham, MD: University Press of America, p. 1.

Darion, J. (2008) 'The Impossible Dream, *Man of La Manchi*.

Gill, R. (2006) *Theory and Practice of Leadership*. London: Sage, p. 91.

Goethals, G. and Sorenson, G. (eds) (2004) *The Encyclopedia of Leadership*. Thousand Oaks, CA: Sage.

Goethals, G. and Sorenson, G. (eds) (2006) *The Quest for a General Theory of Leadership*. Cheltenham; UK: Edward Elgar, pp. 39–153.

Grandstaff, M. and Sorenson, G. (2008) *Strategic Leadership: A General's Art*. Vienna, VA: Management Concepts.

Hickman, G. *Leading Change in Multiple Contexts: Concepts and Practices in Organizational, Community, Political, Social, and Global Change Settings*, July 2009, Sage books.

Mangan, K. (2002) 'Leading the way in leadership: the unending quest of the discipline's founding father, James MacGregor Burns', *Chronicle of Higher Education*, May 31, p. 39.

Morrill, R. (2007) *Strategic Leadership: Integrating Strategy and Leadership in Colleges and Universities*. Washington, DC: American Council on Education, p. 8, 14.

Reyatt, K. 2009. *GTOL II – General Theory of Leadership – the Next Phase*. Online. Available at http://www.iliaspace.org/group/leadershipscholarshipmig/forum/topics/gtol-ii-general-theory-of. Accessed June 11 2009.

Sorenson, G. (2007) 'An intellectual history of leadership studies: the role of James MacGregor Burns'. In R. Couto (ed.), *Reflections on Leadership*, Lanham, MD: University Press of America, pp. 19–30.

Wilbur, K. (2000) *A Theory of Everything*. Boston, MA: Shambhala Publications.

4

Leadership Development

David V. Day

INTRODUCTION

Every year organizations invest considerably in developing their leaders. Annual estimates range from $16.5 billion (Fulmer & Goldsmith, 2001) to over $45 billion (Lamoureux, 2007) for leadership development programs and other supporting management/executive education activities in the United States alone. A 2004 survey indicated that respondent companies reported spending on average approximately $7 million annually on executive development, including formal classroom offerings and other related concerns such as coaching and developmental job experiences (Bolt, 2007). Whereas this is a substantial estimate of executive development investments, the author of the report goes on to say that, '...many felt this amount was understated' (p. 20). From these estimates it is clear that leadership development is big business. A question that will be addressed in this chapter is: What is the evidence that it is also good science and therefore also good business?

A decade ago Day (2000) reviewed the literature on leadership development and concluded that interest in the field 'appears to be at its zenith' (p. 581) especially among those with more applied interests (e.g., HR practitioners, consultants); however, there was a good deal less scholarly interest in the topic, as evidenced by the lack of published research in the area. This led to several appeals for building a science of leadership development (Day & O'Connor, 2003; Day & Zaccaro, 2004). Thus, one goal of this chapter is to examine what has transpired subsequently in terms of relevant research, what contributions have been made toward establishing a more evidence-based approach (Rousseau, Manning, & Denyer, 2008)

to leadership development, and what are the major areas of research that have yet to be undertaken. Specifically, how much (or little) progress has been made in terms of theory, research, and practice in the first decade of the new millennium and where should we turn our scholarly attention in the future?

One emerging development in the field is that recent global survey data collected by researchers at Developmental Dimensions International (DDI; Howard & Wellins, 2008) suggest that leaders are increasingly dissatisfied with their organization's development offerings. In addition, perceived program quality has declined, developmental programs are seen as poorly executed, and confidence in leaders continues to decline steadily (among other noted concerns). This has led the authors of the DDI report to adopt a pessimistic tone in commenting that despite its criticality to long-term organizational sustainability, '...leadership development is going nowhere fast' (p. 4). Given the considerable financial investments that organizations appear to make in leadership development initiatives, this apparent state of affairs is especially distressing.

One possible explanation for this critical assessment of the leadership development field on the part of survey respondents is that expectations have risen as developmental initiatives have become more widely used. But as will be elaborated on in more detail in the chapter, there is still the erroneous belief that leadership develops mainly in leadership development programs. In evaluating this limited and limiting belief about where and how development occurs, several facets of leadership development will be examined, including recent theory, empirically based research on the topic, practice-based advancements, as well as future directions in the field. The overall goal is to use these various lenses to better determine where the field of leadership development is heading and to identify what are the most pressing challenges now and for the future.

THEORETICAL PERSPECTIVES AND LEADER/LEADERSHIP DEVELOPMENT

A basic distinction has been drawn between leader development and leadership development, focusing on the development of individuals (leaders) as compared to the development of social structures and processes (Day, 2000). They are not synonymous, but are often treated and discussed that way. The former is the more common and traditional approach that is focused on building individual capabilities, whereas the latter is moving more towards teambuilding and organizational development. The distinction between leader and leadership development was further elaborated on in the revised edition of *The Center for Creative Leadership (CCL) Handbook of Leadership* (McCauley & Van Velsor, 2004) in which leader development was defined as 'the expansion of a person's capacity to be effective in leadership roles and processes' (Van Velsor & McCauley, 2004, p. 2).

What is thought to develop in leader development includes individual *self-management capabilities* (e.g., self-awareness, balancing conflicting demands, ability to learn, and leadership values), *social capabilities* (e.g., ability to build and maintain relationships, building effective work groups, communication skills, and ability to develop others), and *work facilitation capabilities* (e.g., management skills, ability to think/act strategically and creatively, and ability to initiate and implement change) (Van Velsor & McCauley, 2004).

This type of personal leader development is characterized by several features, including that it unfolds over time; is maximized by a variety of experiences that provide feedback, challenge, and support; and is also contingent on an individual's ability and willingness to learn from experience. Finally, the CCL perspective maintains that the most effective leader development initiatives are those that integrate various experiences and embed them in the organization's context. In this manner the CCL approach acknowledges that unless leader development can be made part of the everyday business of an organization it will fall short of optimal effectiveness (Vicere & Fulmer, 1998).

It is telling that *The CCL Handbook of Leadership* devotes 13 chapters to various topics associated with leader development, yet only two chapters are devoted to leadership development (e.g., O'Connor & Quinn, 2004; Palus & Horth, 2004). This is not a limitation of the CCL approach; rather, it highlights that much more is known about the practice of leader development than leadership development. And as noted, the ideal approach looks for ways to connect and integrate across these domains instead of adopting an either/or perspective (Day, 2000).

One context in which leadership and leader development is critically important is the military. It is generally recognized that a military branch such as the US Army is involved every day in training soldiers and growing leaders. In an attempt to compile and disseminate what the US military – and in particular the Army Research Institute – was doing in the way of theory-building and research around leader development, an edited book was published on the topic of leader development for transforming organizations (Day, Zaccaro, & Halpin, 2004). The overall approach of the book was based on the premise that developing leaders at all organizational levels is an effective means of transforming organizations. In other words, transforming individuals through leader development also transforms organizations. Among the various book sections, there were foci on cognitive skill development, developing practical and emotional intelligence, and enhancing team skills. The book concluded with a chapter examining challenges to developing a science of leader development (Day & Zaccaro, 2004), which included (a) conceptualizing and measuring change (since change is at the heart of development), (b) criterion development (moving beyond job performance to conceptualizing and measuring actual development), (c) incorporating new and diverse research methods, (d) incorporating more developmental theory into the approaches to leader development, and (e) addressing the role of context in development among other potential challenges. Although this book is helpful in drawing together a number of different perspectives on leader development, it falls short of offering much in the way of a comprehensive and integrative theory – or substantive theorizing (Weick, 1995) – about leader development.

In an attempt to develop more rigorous theory on the topic, Lord and Hall (2005) proposed a model of leadership skill development based on research relating leadership to social identity and values as well as the acquisition of domain-specific expertise (e.g., Ericsson, Charness, Feltovich, & Hoffman, 2006; Ericsson, Krampe, & Tesch-Römer, 1993; Ericsson & Lehmann, 1996). At the core of their theoretical approach is that skill development involves changes in a leader's information processing activities, moving from micro-level skills into higher levels of organizations (e.g., competencies) that guide behavior, knowledge, and social perceptions. Important to the development of leadership capacity from novice to intermediate to expert levels are individuals' self-views of leadership. Specifically, as leaders develop, there is an expected shift from individual- to collective-level identities, which represents a movement from surface-level to deep-level structures. One implication of this approach to leader development is that it is thought to occur over an extended time period. As noted in this piece, a classic finding from the expert performance literature is that it takes a minimum of 10 years or 10,000 hours of dedicated practice to achieve expert status in a given domain (Ericsson et al., 1993). Although this has yet to be examined empirically, it is expected that a similar time frame is required to develop the expert leader.

Working in the domain space of student leadership development, Komives and colleagues developed a grounded theory approach to identity-based leader development (Komives, Owen, Longerbeam, Mainella, & Osteen, 2005). The researchers studied a small ($N = 13$) but diverse sample of college students over several time periods throughout their undergraduate studies. One of their general findings was a gradual shift from a heroic leader-centric view of leadership to one that considered leadership as a collaborative and relational process. This shift is best personified in comparing statements about leadership at early stages in the developmental process ('I am not a leader') to those later on ('I can be *a* leader even when I am not *the* leader,' p. 605, italics in original). The Leadership Identity Development (LID) model that resulted from this grounded theory study was further elaborated and discussed in terms of practice applications (Komives, Longerbeam, Owen, Mainella, & Osteen, 2006). The work of Komives et al. illustrates how the development of one's leadership skills and identity commences in late adolescence and early adulthood, if not earlier (Schneider, Ehrhart, & Ehrhart, 2002; Schneider, Paul, White, & Holcombe, 1999). Considered in conjunction with the 10-year rule to developing expert performance, this work also suggests that an adult lifespan perspective is recommended when considering the development of leadership expertise and expert leaders.

Day and Harrison (2007) further developed the themes of multilevel leader identity in describing a proposed development approach incorporating organizational levels as well as levels of development (i.e., leader and leadership development). Their approach postulates that as leaders move up an organization's hierarchy, there is a need to move from an individual to relational and then collective identity (Lord & Hall, 2005). What distinguishes this approach from most others that focus solely on leader development is that it recommends incorporating processes that involve participants in engaging across boundaries (functional, hierarchical, geographical) as a way to both develop collective leader identities as well as to engage in leadership development. A particular feature of this developmental model is that it recognizes that the fundamental needs of leader development change as individuals take on greater leadership role responsibilities.

In the most ambitious theoretical approach to leader development to date, Day, Harrison, and Halpin (2009) proposed an integrative framework linking leadership expertise (or the expert leader) at the most visible level, supported by leader identity and self-regulation processes at a meso level, with adult development at the foundation. Specifically, the selection–optimization–compensation orchestrating process of successful and healthy aging (Baltes, 1997; Baltes & Baltes, 1990) were proposed as the adult lifespan building blocks in terms of setting and sticking to overall life goals (selection), using resources effectively in pursuing life goals (optimization), and responding in effectively adaptive ways when goals are blocked or resources are unavailable (compensation).

This latter point in particular is relevant to leader development from an expert performance domain because research has shown that across a wide variety of domains (e.g., chess, medicine, computer programming, physics, sports, and music among others) experts demonstrate maximal adaptations to domain-specific constraints (Ericsson & Lehmann, 1996). Thus, a key process in healthy adult development may also be critical in achieving an expert level of performance in a related domain of leader development. The Day et al. (2009) approach also reinforces the notion of leader development as a lifelong journey that is part of ongoing adult development processes. The integrative approach includes 13 general theoretical propositions and over 90 specific, testable hypotheses that are offered in hopes of motivating researchers to adopt a theoretically grounded approach to future investigations of the leader development process. Empirical tests of aspects of the theory are ongoing (e.g., Day & Sin, in press).

Another approach taken by Luthans, Avolio, Gardner, and colleagues has focused on processes involved in what is termed *authentic leadership development* (Luthans & Avolio, 2003; also see Chapter 26 in this volume). The definition of authenticity that is used to ground their approach involves someone 'owning' their experiences and acting in accordance with those inner thoughts and feelings (Avolio & Gardner, 2005). Within this approach, a distinction is drawn between the development of authentic leaders (Shamir & Eilam, 2005) and authentic leadership development. The latter goes beyond focusing on just the leader to addressing the development of an authentic relationship between leaders and followers, which requires a focus on the shared relationships between leaders and followers rather than each entity separately. At the core of authentic leadership development is positive modeling of authentic leadership to help create authentic followership (Gardner, Avolio, Luthans, May, & Walumbwa, 2005). Key processes within each of these authentic components (leadership/followership) include self-awareness and self-regulation. Like most theoretically oriented approaches to leadership development in the current literature, there is little in the way of empirically based tests of authentic leadership development or its components. Nonetheless, it is a worthy contribution to the leadership literature arising from the recent interest in positive psychology (Snyder & Lopez, 2002) and positive organizational scholarship (Cameron, Dutton, & Quinn, 2003).

Most of what has been discussed thus far has focused mainly on understanding leader development from various theoretical perspectives. There are also recent initiatives designed to understand the leadership development process theoretically. In one such approach, Day, Gronn, & Salas (2004) proposed a model of developing team-based leadership capacity – conceptualized in terms of the amount of shared, distributed, and connected ways of working together – with regard to collectively addressing leadership challenges. The framework developed in this paper flows from an updated IMOI (input–mediator–output–input) model of team processes that explicitly recognizes the role of feedback in how teams adapt and perform (Ilgen, Hollenbeck, Johnson, & Jundt, 2005). Refer to Chapter 25 of this volume for an extensive review of Leadership in Teams.

The team leadership capacity model begins with an accounting of individual team member resources (i.e., knowledge, skills, and abilities of members) that shapes the amount of teamwork that develops as a function of the formal leader's resources (leadership skills, leadership knowledge, and leadership abilities) and formal developmental interventions that are used. Teamwork serves as a mediator for team learning, which in turn shapes the level of team leadership capacity that develops. This capacity can be used as a resource (input) for the next team performance cycle. From this perspective, team leadership capacity was conceptualized as an emergent state in teams (Marks, Mathieu, & Zaccaro, 2001) that provides a vitally important resource, especially when complex adaptive

challenges are faced. In theory at least, team leadership capacity can provide necessary resources to help teams be resilient and adaptive even under the most challenging circumstances.

In a related program of theory-building and research, Kozlowski and colleagues have advanced a comprehensive and integrative framework for understanding team leadership and team development. The approach is grounded in the observation that it is difficult to apply prescriptions from existing leadership research to teams operating in complex and dynamic decision-making environments (Kozlowski, Gully, McHugh, Salas, & Cannon-Bowers, 1996). Beginning with the initial theory and guidelines for application (Kozlowski et al., 1996), the research team has provided additional conceptual insight regarding the processes associated with team development (Kozlowski, Gully, Nason, & Smith, 1999), empirically examined the effects of feedback on the regulation of individual and team performance across multiple goals and multiple levels (DeShon, Kozlowski, Schmidt, Milner, & Wiechmann, 2004), and further integrated team development and adaptation with team learning as emergent group phenomena (Kozlowski & Bell, 2008). Their most recent contribution has elaborated more specifically on the role of the leader in the team development process (Kozlowski, Watola, Jensen, Kim, & Botero, 2009) in terms of helping the team move from relatively novice to expert status and beyond to building adaptive capability in the team. In these latter stages of team development, the team takes on more responsibility for its learning, leadership, and performance. Taken together, this work provides an impressive theoretical and empirical foundation for understanding team leadership and, in particular, how something like adaptive capability – or leadership capacity – develops in teams.

Overall, there appears to be a number of promising advances in the theoretical understanding of leader and leadership development. Some of the consistent themes across these various approaches include a focus on developing leadership expertise (Day et al., 2009; Lord & Hall, 2005), various perspectives on the role of leader identity (e.g., Day & Harrison, 2007; Day et al., 2009; Komives et al., 2005, 2006; Shamir & Eilam, 2005), as well as the development of adaptive leadership capacity in teams (e.g., Day et al., 2004; Kozlowski et al., 2009). These are all encouraging signs that the field of leadership development is moving beyond a 'best practices' approach to taking a scientific stance in developing theory and theoretically grounded research propositions and hypotheses. It is a sound (and necessary) step in developing a rigorous science for leader and leadership development.

The next section will examine research published in the first decade of the twenty-first century to review what empirically based contributions exist to further support the scientific development of the field. What is the evidence that leader and leadership development have begun to emerge as focal topics of scientific research?

RESEARCH ON LEADER/LEADERSHIP DEVELOPMENT

There are two general approaches that are adopted in studies of leadership development that is broadly stated to include leader development. The first approach is that of training, in which a particular set of knowledge, skills, or abilities are targeted for intervention and improvement. Included in this training focus is management 'development' that primarily emphasizes managerial education (Latham & Seijts, 1998; Wexley & Baldwin, 1986). There are also different approaches to fostering executive development in terms of helping new incumbents 'get up to speed' in their respective positions (Bauer, Erdogan, Liden, & Wayne, 2006). But it should be noted that the latter approach is something else entirely than what is typically considered in traditional management development. Also, although many sources refer to training and development together (e.g., planned effort by an organization to facilitate the learning of job-related behavior on the part of its employees; Wexley & Latham, 1991), the concept of development has a much different focus than traditional training. Rather than skills or abilities training, or a classroom education focus, development initiatives focus on the more hazy and far-reaching goal of building individual and collective capacity in preparation to meet unforeseen challenges (Day, 2000). In short, training provides proven solutions to known problems, whereas development helps people to better learn their way out of problems that could not be predicted (Dixon, 1993).

An exemplar of a training approach in enhancing the abilities of leaders can be found in the longitudinal, randomized field experiment reported by Dvir, Eden, Avolio, and Shamir (2002). In particular, the researchers were interested to examine whether enhancing transformational leadership through training would impact follower development and performance. Given that the research design was a true field experiment, stronger claims can be made with regard to causality relative to most other study designs. The focal sample was infantry cadets undergoing officer training in the Israeli Defense Forces and the training intervention consisted of leadership workshops designed to enhance their leadership skills before becoming platoon leaders. The experimental leaders received transformational leadership training, whereas those in the control group were exposed to 'routine eclectic leadership training' (p. 737).

Another interesting feature of the Dvir et al. (2002) study was that the outcomes included both follower performance and follower development. In addition, the researchers examined the effects of the leadership interventions on 'direct' followers as well as 'indirect' followers (i.e., those two levels below the platoon leader). Indirect follower performance was operationalized in terms of written and practical performance in areas such as light weapons, physical fitness, and marksmanship (direct follower performance was not measured). Direct and indirect follower development was operationalized in terms of variables such as self-efficacy, collectivistic orientation, extra effort, active engagement, and internalization of moral values. In general, results indicated that those leaders receiving transformational leadership training had a more positive impact on direct followers' development and indirect followers' performance than did leaders in the control group. As noted previously, because of the rigorous experimental design as well as the focus on follower performance and development, this study provides an especially noteworthy example of leadership training research.

Compared to the focused and structured approach that is the hallmark of training, development initiatives can seem relatively nebulous. For example, it is taken almost as gospel that experience is the most effective way to develop leadership, at least as reported by managers themselves (McCall & Hollenbeck, 2002; McCall, Lombardo, & Morrison, 1988). The interview-based approach that McCall and colleagues used with diverse samples of executives revealed that challenging work experiences incorporating novel responsibilities (e.g., 'stretch' assignments) were perceived to be more developmental than classroom experiences or those on-the-job experiences that were more routine and less challenging. This has led these researchers to propose *lessons of experience* as a way to understand executive development, with one outcome being an assessment tool to quantify the developmental components of managerial jobs (McCauley, Ruderman, Ohlott, & Morrow, 1994).

Despite the apparent value of experience – and in particular the motivation and ability to learn from experience – there is the implicit assumption that the more challenging an experience is the more developmental value it holds. This runs counter to theory and research from the adult learning and development literatures, which suggest some experiences might be too challenging in terms of putting people 'in over their heads' (Kegan, 1994) such that the ability to learn from the experience is compromised. The notion of potentially diminishing returns of challenging work experiences on leadership skills development was examined recently by DeRue and Wellman (2009). Specifically, the researchers hypothesized that a learning goal orientation would help offset the diminishing returns of developmental challenges by helping individuals to reframe the challenge and the corresponding mistakes as learning opportunities rather than as failed attempts to prove competence (Dweck, 1986; Elliott & Dweck, 1988). Access to feedback was also hypothesized as a factor that might offset diminishing returns associated with high developmental challenge, because feedback is essential to learning. Examining 225 on-the-job experiences across 60 managers, DeRue and Wellman indeed found evidence of diminishing returns in the relationship between developmental challenge and leadership skill development. In addition, access to feedback – but not a learning orientation – dampened these curvilinear effects.

The implications of these findings highlight the practical importance of deploying individuals to work experiences where there is an optimal amount of developmental challenge. Of course, it is not quite so easy to know where that inflection point is on an individual-by-individual basis in terms of when a challenging assignment becomes too challenging. This is why it is important to maximize feedback availability in general, but especially in job assignments where developmental challenges are expected. Although the hypothesized role of adopting a learning goal orientation was not supported, the results were in the appropriate direction, suggesting that this individual motivational difference is worth considering in future research on leader/leadership development.

Yet another research study examined the personal trajectories of development (Raudenbush, 2001) in a student sample ($N = 1,315$) engaged in service learning projects. The particular approach to leader development in this case was action learning in which self-awareness and skills development occur as part of engaging in meaningful project-based work (Marquardt, 2004; Revans, 1980). The overarching goal of action learning is to use project work as a means of enhancing development rather than taking individuals away from their work in order to develop. These projects can be considered as a type of stretch job assignment; furthermore, the action learning approach to development has become increasingly more common in organizations of all kinds (Conger & Xin, 2000). The research approach in question was longitudinal and multilevel in nature,

studying within- and between-person changes over the course of approximately 15 weeks (Day & Sin, in press). The underlying assumption was that leader development is a highly individualized process. Therefore, there are individual difference factors that can serve to enhance leader development. This assumption was tested empirically by the authors.

The theoretical foundation of the research was based on the integrative model of leader development proposed by Day et al. (2009) that was discussed briefly previously in the chapter. The researchers conceptualized leader identity as a time-varying covariate and modeled it as a longitudinal, within-person variable. Results across four separate time periods suggested that leadership effectiveness (independently rated by the team coach) was positively related to the self-rated strength of leader identity (i.e., the extent that I see myself, or identify, as a leader). It is important to remember that this is a within-person effect, so the relevant comparison is with those time periods in which that same individual was less likely to identify as a leader. In short, it acknowledges that individual leader identity is dynamic, just as are overall developmental processes. At a between-persons level, the researchers conceptualized goal orientation (learning- and performance-oriented) as something that would differentiate among leader development trajectories. As hypothesized, holding a stronger learning goal orientation was associated with higher initial levels of rated leader effectiveness (i.e., intercepts) and also positively related to more effective developmental trajectories (i.e., slopes). Performance goal orientation was related to initial effectiveness levels (positive for a 'prove' performance orientation and negative for an 'avoid' performance orientation) but unrelated to slope differences. These results are consistent with those of DeRue and Wellman (2009) with regard to the individualized nature of leader development and support the notion that there are identifiable factors that can enhance the process (e.g., feedback accessibility, leader identification, learning goal orientation).

An interesting aspect of the Day and Sin (in press) study was that the overall developmental trend across all subjects was generally negative, with a slight positive upturn near the end of the project (i.e., curvilinear). Although this may seem inconsistent with implicit notion of development involving positive change over time, it is entirely consistent with developmental theory. It was first articulated by the eminent developmental psychologist Paul Baltes in this way: '...*any* process of development entails an inherent dynamic between gains and losses ... no process of development consists only of growth or progression'

(Baltes, 1987, p. 611, italics in original). The goal of successful development, therefore, is the maximization of gains and the minimization of losses. Given the overall negative developmental trend in these data, it suggests that action learning was an extremely challenging developmental experience and might have been too challenging for many of the participants to develop in a consistently positive manner.

In further examining this possibility, Day and Sin (in press) used growth mixture modeling (Wang & Bodner, 2007) to determine whether multiple unobserved subpopulations: with different developmental trajectories existed. Indeed, they found two such subpopulations: The majority (approximately 90% of the sample) demonstrated the previously described negative and curvilinear effect; however, approximately 10% of their sample demonstrated a positive linear developmental trend. Furthermore, there were significant differences between these subpopulations on several individual difference measures (e.g., selection–optimization–compensation, core self-evaluations, performance goal orientation). In short, there was a small but significant subpopulation who apparently did not find the action learning initiative to be so challenging as to interfere with their learning and positive development. These individuals were better able to maximize developmental gains while minimizing corresponding losses. Although it is too premature to say with any certainty what might be the robust set of factors that can be used to potentially identify those individuals who are better equipped to take on extreme developmental challenges, further research of this sort holds great promise for being better able to predict those 'high potential' leaders whose development might be accelerated through especially challenging job assignments or through action learning.

Another area of potential relevance to leader development is that of leadership efficacy, defined as a specific form of self-efficacy associated with the level of confidence someone feels as a leader in relevant situations calling for leadership (Hannah, Avolio, Luthans, & Harms, 2008). The underlying thinking with regard to leadership efficacy is that individual differences in factors such as personality and values, along with previous leadership experiences, shape the level of leadership efficacy that is internalized. Having greater leadership efficacy is thought to lead to greater willingness to engage as a leader when the situation calls for it, and is also likely to motivate an individual to practice leadership or seek out challenging leadership assignments (Day et al., 2009).

In a test and extension of this general model, Chan and Drasgow (2001) hypothesized that leadership self-efficacy would serve as a mediator of the relationship between individual differences in personality, values, and experience, and the outcome of motivation to lead (MTL). They defined MTL as an individual differences construct 'that affects a leader's or leader's-to-be decisions to assume leadership training, roles, and responsibilities, and that affect his or her intensity of efforts at leading and persisting as a leader' (p. 482). From this perspective, it is assumed that individual levels of MTL can change as a function of leadership experience (amount and quality). It was further assumed that MTL is a multidimensional construct consisting of the following components: (a) affective-identity (person likes to lead and sees it as part of personal identity), (b) noncalculative (person will lead only if not calculative about the costs involved with it), and (c) social normative (lead for reasons of perceived duty or responsibility).

In a test of these assertions using military recruits and junior college students, the researchers constructed a measure of MTL and tested the proposed mediational model. Results suggested that those who like to lead and see it as an important part of their identity tend to be extraverted, value competition and achievement, and have more previous leadership experience and higher leadership self-efficacy than their peers. Individuals high in noncalculative MTL do not expect rewards or privileges for leading, but are motivated to lead because they are agreeable in terms of personality and value harmony in the group regardless of their respective levels of leadership experience or self-efficacy. Finally, individuals high in social-normative MTL are motivated by social obligation and a sense of duty, but also tend to be more accepting of social hierarchies and more rejecting of social equality than their peers (as well as having more leadership experience and higher leadership self-efficacy).

It is also interesting to note that study results indicated that general mental ability was unrelated to MTL, supporting the notion that social and cognitive abilities are separate components of a leader's personal resources. In summary, the authors concluded that their approach provides preliminary evidence that personality, values, and experience may be linked to leadership performance through the process of leader development, which is at least partly attributable to individual differences in the type and degree of motivation to lead. Although this is an impressive research study, one limitation of the proposed model is that it did not consider the possible reciprocal relationships between leadership efficacy and experience, choosing to focus on the direct relationship between past leadership experience and leadership efficacy. It is entirely likely that future leadership experience will be a function of the level of leadership efficacy (Day et al., 2009). Individuals actively choose and shape their experiences and are not merely passive participants.

In moving from a focus on leader development to one that is concerned primary with leadership development in teams, Carson, Tesluk, and Marrone (2007) recently examined both internal and external antecedents of the emergence of leadership influence across team members (i.e., shared leadership). Specifically, it was hypothesized that an internal team climate of shared purpose, social support, and voice would be positively related to the level of team leadership. It was also hypothesized that supportive external coaching by a team manager would be related to the level of shared leadership in a team, and that external coaching would interact with internal team climate in predicting shared leadership levels (coaching was thought to be more strongly related to shared leadership when the internal team climate is unsupportive). Finally, the level of shared leadership in a team was hypothesized to be positively related to team performance.

An interesting measurement feature of the Carson et al. (2007) study is that rather than asking team members or their manager about the level of shared leadership in the team (e.g., Hiller, Day, & Vance, 2006; Pearce & Sims, 2002), they adopted a social network approach involving a measure of density or the perceived amount of leadership displayed by team members as perceived by all others on the team. Using a sample of 59 MBA consulting teams ($N = 348$), they found support for all hypotheses about the antecedents of leadership development as well as for the predicted positive relationship between shared leadership and team performance. The theoretical and practical implications of these findings are important in suggesting that both internal and external factors to the team matter in the development of shared leadership, and that developing leadership, and not just individual leaders, is of concern in developing high-performing teams.

Taken together, the research reviewed in this section suggests that significant advances have been made in advancing the empirical science of both leader and leadership development. As expected in such early stages of building a leadership development science, there are more conceptual and theoretical publications than empirical studies in the recent literature. Indeed, this is probably a good thing in terms of having available theoretical foundations to help guide research. Given these (and other) advancements, there is reason for optimism in the field. Attention is next focused briefly on a few important practice-oriented concerns before a final section looking ahead to recommended future directions in leader and leadership development.

PRACTICE CONCERNS IN LEADER/LEADERSHIP DEVELOPMENT

One of the most endemic practical issues in the field is the tendency to take an episodic view to development: that is, there is an (implicit) assumption that development occurs only as part of a discrete program or a challenging job experience. What this fails to capture is the more important point that what is learned from the program or experience and how it changes behavior or decision-making in future leadership situations is what really matters. It is not the experience but the learning from experience that is most important for development. So what will be highlighted in this section are primarily issues that are associated with learning – both individual learning and learning about the impact of the leadership development initiative (i.e., evaluation).

Feedback

A key finding from the previously mentioned DDI report (Howard & Wellins, 2008) is that participants reported that there are not enough opportunities to learn on the job. This is tragic because learning should be a daily, ongoing process regardless of the job. Judging from the comments provided in the report to support this finding, it appears that respondents saw learning as closely tied to having a mentor or having access to interesting and challenging job assignments. This perception is not wrong, but it is limited, because one of the most basic tools needed to promote learning is feedback. It is an extremely valuable resource that is underused in many organizational settings. A basic principle in both goal setting and learning theories is that actions devoid of feedback are not as potent as actions with feedback in terms of learning.

Given the importance of feedback, it is troubling to consider how many opportunities are missed every day for either giving or receiving feedback. If developing the expert leader requires a minimum of 10,000 hours of intensive, dedicated practice, then the only way that will happen is practice – with feedback – occurs in a daily, continuous, and ongoing manner on the job. And perhaps even more important to learning than negative feedback is positive feedback, because it provides information as to what has been done appropriately in addition to providing reinforcement to motivate a repeat of the behavior in the future. The relative lack of feedback, despite the wealth of feedback opportunities, points to another key finding from the DDI report: managers do not know how to help their reports develop, or they know how but refuse to do it. From a practice perspective, one concrete recommendation is to work with leaders to help them understand the importance of feedback in developing themselves and others, and to also develop the skills and confidence to deliver (and receive) feedback on a regular ongoing basis.

Sustainability

Just as with any other business initiative, successful leadership development efforts require more than a brilliant plan – they require diligent execution and follow-through. Unfortunately, a majority of such initiatives fail because of weak execution and not because of poor strategy or a weak idea (Howard & Wellins, 2008). The underlying issue concerns the need to make leadership development sustainable and not to rely on an episodic or program-focused approach to development. Most leaders acknowledge that the most profound development and learning occurs on-the-job and not in the classroom; however, managers are typically left on their own to try and integrate learning from leadership development programs into a personal development plan. Strategic leadership development, on the other hand, takes the perspective that leadership development is an ongoing process (Vicere & Fulmer, 1998), which has the distinct advantage of having learning and development occur every day rather than only when programs or other kinds of events or interventions are scheduled.

Succession planning

To be effective, succession planning needs to go beyond merely identifying potential future leaders to also understanding the developmental needs of these individuals and arranging the appropriate experiences to help them learn and develop. In this manner, succession planning and leadership development are inherently intertwined in the identification and development of leadership talent (Day, 2007). Despite the value of such endeavors, the reality is that most organizations do not have a succession plan in place and those that do tend to have ineffective plans. The primary reason that such plans are ineffective is because they tend to focus mainly on the identification of high-potential talent and ignore the need for ongoing

development of these individuals. Without a sound link to ongoing leader development, at best such initiatives constitute only replacement planning (Berke, 2005), which limits their effectiveness. This is because it leads to the likelihood of putting people into promotion positions for which they are ill-prepared. In short, it can turn into a classic case of someone 'in over their heads' that contributes to eventual derailment.

High potentials

A high-potential leader is typically someone who has been identified as possessing the potential to move eventually into a senior leadership position in the organization. In theory, being identified as high potential puts an individual into a special pool of candidates to receive accelerated developmental experiences. But as noted in recent surveys, less than half of all organizations actually had a program to accelerate the development of high-potential leaders (Howard & Wellins, 2008). Again, this can result in at best only a partially successful implementation of succession planning and ineffectual learning and development of high-potential mean leaders. Another common problem is failing to establish a commonly shared understanding of what being a high-potential leader means. Specifically, how is potential conceptualized and defined, and what are the behavioral criteria used to identify a high-potential leader? In most succession planning exercises, senior managers discuss and plot the job performance and perceived leadership potential of candidates for eventual promotion to an executive position. Those demonstrating high performance and high potential are considered prime candidates for accelerated development, but there is little evidence that the meaning of potential is shared among senior management (Day, 2009). As a result, past job performance has inordinate influence on who is identified as being high potential, leading to cases in which an individual is not ready for accelerated development. This scenario not only risks the candidate's career through possible derailment but also wastes the financial resources that are invested in development.

Evaluation

Although it is considered a hallmark of an effective development initiative (Howard & Wellins, 2008), efforts to evaluate the results of such initiatives are often forgotten or ignored. There is a well-known taxonomy of training outcomes that includes reactions, learning, behavior, and results (Kirkpatrick, 1975). Unfortunately most of the evaluation efforts are focused on participants' reactions to the developmental program (i.e., 'smile sheets'), with little attention to understanding whether the leader's developmental experience had an impact on his behavior or the organization. Hannum, Martineau, and Reinelt (2007) note that the questions key stakeholders (e.g., funding agencies, designers, sponsors, and participants) often have about leadership development include:

- Is the investment in leadership development worthwhile?
- What difference does leadership development make?
- What strategies work best to develop leaders and leadership?
- How can developmental initiatives be sustained?

The authors concluded: 'The complexity of leadership development requires innovative models and approaches to evaluation ... to answer those questions' (p. xiv). Calling for innovative evaluation models is needed but may be too ambitious, given that leadership development evaluation of any kind is the exception rather than the rule. But an interesting statistic to keep in mind is that programs rated very high in quality were 20 times more likely to evaluate the results of their leadership development initiatives than those rated as very low quality (Howard & Wellins, 2008). Any leadership development initiative that aspires to high-quality status should have comprehensive evaluation designed into it from the beginning.

The issues highlighted above represent just a few of the most pressing concerns with regard to the practice and delivery of leadership development initiatives. Overall, it appears that there have been important theoretical and research advances in the development of a science of leader and leadership development, but the practical side of the field appears to have deteriorated since publication of the Day (2000) review. It is unclear whether this is due to rising expectations on the part of participants, a worsening quality in programs and initiatives to develop leadership, or a combination of factors. But whatever the causes, these are serious issues that can undermine any scientifically grounded and well-designed initiative. But one thing is certain and that is leadership development is one part of a larger organizational system (Day, 2009) and piecemeal approaches to address these and other practice-oriented issues are unlikely to meet with much success.

FUTURE DIRECTIONS IN THE SCIENCE AND PRACTICE OF LEADERSHIP DEVELOPMENT

If the field of leadership development is truly going nowhere fast, as argued by Howard and Wellins (2008), then where should it be heading instead? This section takes a brief look at the three interrelated areas of theory, research, and practice in identifying future direction in the field of leader and leadership development.

Theory

There has been a recent call in the literature for promoting more integrative theory-building strategies in the general field of leadership, and this certainly applies to leadership development as well. Some have proposed that leadership theory has reached a developmental plateau and that it needs to move to the next level of integration (Avolio, 2007). One way to do this is by more fully considering the dynamic interplay between leaders and followers as well as taking more fully into account the context in which these interactions occur (Avolio & Gardner, 2005; Gardner et al., 2005). Another way of thinking about this proposed integrative strategy is in terms of inclusiveness. For far too long, leadership theory has been mainly about the leader. More integrative theories recognize that the leadership landscape includes leaders, followers, and the situational context as essential ingredients in this dynamic interaction. Along these lines, critical perspectives on leader-centric leadership theory have begun to emerge and gain acceptance in the field. The critical perspectives 'challenge the traditional orthodoxies of leadership and following ... and make the claim that leadership is a process that goes on between all people and that all people can be involved in leadership' (Jackson & Parry, 2008, p. 83). In this way the critical perspective is entirely consistent with the kind of integrative and inclusive leadership theory being argued for here.

Another area of future theoretical interest is in moving towards more integrative and inclusive leadership development of a different kind. Leadership is a dynamic, evolving process and as such it incorporates behaviors, perceptions, decision-making, and a whole host of other constructs. Thus, leadership by nature is an eclectic phenomenon and attempting to conceptualize and study its development from any one theoretical perspective (e.g., motivational, emotional, behavioral) will yield at best limited results. What are needed are more inclusive and integrative perspectives that cut across any number of theoretical domains. One example is the integrative theoretical approach to leader development that links the otherwise apparently disparate domains of adult development, identity and self-regulation, and expertise acquisition (Day et al., 2009). Leadership development theory will advance by integrating across multiple domains and disciplines in a more eclectic fashion.

Research

There are some unique aspects of leader and leadership development that need to be considered in moving forward with a research agenda. One such consideration is that of *levels*. As noted by Avolio (2004), '[L]eadership development is *always* a multilevel development process' (p. 94, italics in original). Relevant levels to consider are within-person and between-person; the next higher dyadic level, involving relationships with followers, peers, and subordinates; and team and organizational levels. Researchers will need to be very clear as to the correct level in which they are working and to choose the type of research design, measures, and analyses that are most suitable for the respective level(s). And, in particular, it would appear that cross-level approaches (e.g., individuals within teams, teams within organizations) hold great promise for furthering our understanding of developmental processes.

Leadership development is a dynamic and longitudinal process, which inherently involves the consideration of *time*. It has been argued that we need better theory and more research that explicitly address time and the specification of when things occur (Mitchell & James, 2001). In no area of research is this truer than leadership development. When it comes to something like leader development, it can be conceptualized as a process occurring across the entire adult life span (Day et al., 2009). Clearly there are limits in terms of what any one research study can tackle in terms of time frame; however, acknowledging this feature of leader development will ideally push researchers to give careful attention to when they measure things, how many times they measure, and linking measurement with an explicit framework that lays out when (and how) developmental changes are thought to take place. This is indeed a high standard for researchers, but it is one that is likely to reap huge dividends in terms of better understanding leader development and ultimately devising ways to accelerate the process.

A final research recommendation is to take into consideration the *individualized* nature of development. Leaders do not develop in the same way following identical growth patterns. People learn different things from the same experience and some learn the key lessons of experience more readily than others. Methodological and analytical approaches that take a more individualized approach to leader development will likely yield more insight than those that try to model average trends across a given sample. Raudenbush (2001) has proposed a personal trajectory approach to developmental research. Although it may get a bit messy to conceptualize and model a unique trajectory for every developing leader, there are other individualized approaches such as growth mixture modeling that can identify and predict different latent trajectory classes and that also allow within-class variation of individuals (Wang & Bodner, 2007). These are powerful techniques that can help researchers better understand the individualized nature of leader development, especially when used in conjunction with informed decisions about time and the timing of key processes as well as the various levels on which development takes place.

Practice

The observation that leaders are ill-prepared to handle future challenges is not new. Peter Drucker (1995) noted some time ago: 'At most one-third of such [executive selection] decisions turn out right; one-third are minimally effective; and one-third are outright failures' (p. 22). Thus, even though leadership development is a strategic human capital concern of many organizations, current and past data suggest that it is not being done very effectively.

An issue that has challenged the effectiveness of leadership development initiatives is the focus on relatively short-term, episodic-based thinking in terms of how development occurs. Traditional thinking about leadership development has viewed it as a series of unconnected, discrete programs with little assistance in integrating across these developmental episodes (Vicere & Fulmer, 1998). Contemporary thinking about leadership development views it as continuous and ongoing throughout the adult life span (Day et al., 2009). In short, just about any experience has the potential to contribute to learning and development to the extent that it includes aspects of assessment, challenge, and support (Van Velsor & McCauley, 2004).

The primary focus in the field is on developing individual leader skills; however, there is no certainty that better leadership will result. After all, leadership involves a dynamic social interaction within a given situational context and that effective followers are needed along with effective leaders (Hollander, 2009). In addition, leadership development will likely require intervention at a more macro group, team, or organizational level. But it is not an either/or proposition; rather, state-of-the-art practices involve determining how to link leader development with more aggregate leadership development to enhance the overall leadership capacity in a collective (Day, 2000; Day et al., 2004).

CONCLUSIONS

There is reason to be sanguine about the direction that the field of leader/leadership development is heading, especially on the scientific side of the scientist–practitioner equation. Over the past decade there has been increasing attention paid to theorizing about the leadership development process, especially in terms of moving beyond any single, bounded theoretical approach to conceptualizing leadership. The process is inherently dynamic and eclectic, so it makes sense to build theoretical frameworks that reflect these features.

Although the sheer number of research-related publications on leader and leadership development is still relatively small, it is a growing area that is already contributing to a better empirically based understanding of some important aspects of the leadership development process. It is a daunting task going forward because of the lengthy time frame involved in the development of leaders and because of all the interrelated issues that can potentially affect development. But rather than posing as a threat, these issues present a wealth of opportunities for researchers. There are any number of issues to investigate, but one thing is certain: single-shot, survey-based research designs are unlikely to add much value to this nascent leadership development science. Research designs that incorporate multiple measurement perspectives, mixed methods, and a longitudinal component are more likely to be well-suited to providing scientific insight to the leadership development process.

Given the recent evidence that the practice of leadership development is slipping in terms of perceived quality and value that is added in organizations (Howard & Wellins, 2008), it may be time to take a step back and rethink what is needed to better support an evidence-based approach to leadership development. What may be most needed to help motivate this cause is not only continuing interest in the field theoretically and empirically but also efforts devoted to translating ideas into action and science into sound practice.

REFERENCES

Avolio, B. J. (2004). Examining the Full Range Model of leadership: Looking back to transform forward. In D. V. Day, S. J. Zaccaro & S. M. Halpin (eds), *Leader development for transforming organizations: Growing leaders for tomorrow* (pp. 71–98). Mahwah, NJ: Erlbaum.

Avolio, B. J. (2007). Promoting more integrative strategies for leadership theory-building. *American Psychologist, 62*, 25–33.

Avolio, B. J. & Gardner, W. L. (2005). Authentic leadership development: Getting to the roots of positive forms of leadership. *The Leadership Quarterly, 16*, 315–338.

Baltes, P. B. (1987). Theoretical propositions of life-span developmental psychology: On the dynamics between growth and decline. *Developmental Psychology, 23*, 611–626.

Baltes, P. B. (1997). On the incomplete architecture of human ontogeny: Selection, optimization, and compensation as foundation of developmental theory. *American Psychologist, 52*, 366–380.

Baltes, P. B. & Baltes, M. M. (1990). Psychological perspectives on successful aging: The model of selective optimization with compensation. In P. B. Baltes & M. M. Baltes (eds), *Successful aging: Perspectives from the behavioral sciences* (pp. 1–34). New York: Cambridge University Press.

Bauer, T. A., Erdogan, B., Liden, R. C., & Wayne, S. J. (2006). A longitudinal study of the moderating role of extraversion: Leader–member exchange, performance, and turnover during new executive development. *Journal of Applied Psychology, 91*, 298–310.

Berke, D. (2005). *Succession planning and management: A guide to organizational systems and practices.* Greensboro, NC: Center for Creative Leadership.

Bolt, J. F. (2007). Mapping the future of leadership development. In J. F. Bolt (ed.), *The 2007 Pfeiffer Annual: Leadership development* (pp. 3–23). San Francisco, CA: John Wiley & Sons.

Cameron, K. S., Dutton, J. E., & Quinn, R. E. (eds). (2003). *Positive organizational scholarship: Foundations of a new discipline.* San Francisco: Berrett-Koehler.

Carson, J. B., Tesluk, P. E., & Marrone, J. A. (2007). Shared leadership in teams: An investigation of antecedent conditions and performance. *Academy of Management Journal, 50*, 1217–1234.

Chan, K.-Y. & Drasgow, F. (2001). Toward a theory of individual differences and leadership: Understanding motivation to lead. *Journal of Applied Psychology, 86*, 481–498.

Conger, J. A. & Xin, K. (2000). Executive education in the 21st century. *Journal of Management Education, 24*, 73–101.

Day, D. V. (2000). Leadership development: A review in context. *The Leadership Quarterly, 11*, 581–613.

Day, D. V. (2007). *Developing leadership talent: A guide to succession planning and leadership development.* Alexandria, VA: Society for Human Resource Management Foundation.

Day, D. V. (2009). Executive selection is a process not a decision. *Industrial and Organizational Psychology: Perspectives on Science and Practice, 2*, 159–162.

Day, D. V., Gronn, P., & Salas, E. (2004). Leadership capacity in teams. *The Leadership Quarterly, 15*, 857–880.

Day, D. V. & Harrison, M. M. (2007). A multilevel, identity-based approach to leadership development. *Human Resource Management Review, 17*, 360–373.

Day, D. V., Harrison, M. M., & Halpin, S. M. (2009). *An integrative approach to leader development: Connecting adult development, identity, and expertise*. New York: Routledge.

Day, D. V. & O'Connor, P. M. G. (2003). Leadership development: Understanding the process. In S. Murphy & R. Riggio (eds), *The future of leadership development* (pp. 11–28). Mahwah, NJ: Erlbaum.

Day, D. V. & Sin, H.-P. (in press). Longitudinal tests of an integrative model of leader development: Charting and understanding developmental trajectories. *The Leadership Quarterly*.

Day, D. V. & Zaccaro, S. J. (2004). Toward a science of leader development. In D. V. Day, S. J. Zaccaro & S. M. Halpin (eds), *Leader development for transforming organizations: Growing leaders for tomorrow* (pp. 383–399). Mahwah, NJ: Erlbaum.

Day, D. V., Zaccaro, S. J., & Halpin, S. M. (eds). (2004). *Leader development for transforming organizations: Growing leaders for tomorrow*. Mahwah, NJ: Erlbaum.

DeRue, D. S. & Wellman, N. (2009). Developing leaders via experience: The role of developmental challenges, learning orientation, and feedback availability. *Journal of Applied Psychology, 94*, 859–875.

DeShon, R. P., Kozlowski, S. W. J., Schmidt, A. M., Milner, K. R., & Wiechmann, D. (2004). A multiple-goal, multilevel model of feedback effects on the regulation of individual and team performance. *Journal of Applied Psychology, 89*, 1035–1056.

Dixon, N. M. (1993). Developing managers for the learning organization. *Human Resource Management Review, 3*, 243–254.

Drucker, P. F. (1995). *Managing in a time of great change*. New York: Truman Talley Books/Dutton.

Dvir, T., Eden, D., Avolio, B. J., & Shamir, B. (2002). Impact of transformational leadership on follower development and performance: A field experiment. *Academy of Management Journal, 45*, 735–744.

Dweck, C. S. (1986). Motivational processes affecting learning. *American Psychologist, 41*, 1040–1048.

Elliott, E. S. & Dweck, C. S. (1988). Goals: An approach to motivation and achievement. *Journal of Personality and Social Psychology, 54*, 5–12.

Ericsson, K. A., Charness, N., Feltovich, P. J., & Hoffman, R. R. (eds). (2006). *The Cambridge handbook of expertise and expert performance*. New York: Cambridge University.

Ericsson, K. A., Krampe, R. T., & Tesch-Römer, C. (1993). The role of deliberate practice in the acquisition of expert performance. *Psychological Review, 100*, 363–406.

Ericsson, K. A. & Lehmann, A. C. (1996). Expert and exceptional performance: Evidence of maximal adaptation to task constraints. *Annual Review of Psychology, 47*, 273–305.

Fulmer, R. M. & Goldsmith, M. (2001). *The leadership invest-ment: How the world's best organizations gain strategic advantage through leadership development*. New York: American Management Association.

Gardner, W. L., Avolio, B. J., Luthans, F., May, D. R., & Walumbwa, F. (2005). 'Can you see the real me?' A self-based model of authentic leader and follower development. *The Leadership Quarterly, 16*, 343–372.

Hannah, S. T., Avolio, B. J., Luthans, F., & Harms, P. D. (2008). Leadership efficacy: Review and future directions. *The Leadership Quarterly, 19*, 669–692.

Hannum, K. M., Martineau, J. W., & Reinelt, C. (eds). (2007). *The handbook of leadership development evaluation*. San Francisco, CA: Jossey-Bass.

Hiller, N. J., Day, D. V., & Vance, R. J. (2006). Collective enactment of leadership roles and team effectiveness: A field study. *The Leadership Quarterly, 17*, 387–397.

Hollander, E. P. (2009). *Inclusive leadership: The essential leader-follower relationship*. New York: Routledge.

Howard, A. & Wellins, R. S. (2008). *Global leadership forecast 2008/2009: Overcoming the shortfalls in developing leaders*. Pittsburgh, PA: Development Dimensions International.

Ilgen, D. R., Hollenbeck, J. R., Johnson, M., & Jundt, J. (2005). Teams in organizations: From I-P-O models to IMOI models. *Annual Review of Psychology, 56*, 517–543.

Jackson, B. & Parry, K. (2008). *A very short, fairly interesting and reasonably cheap book about studying leadership*. London: Sage.

Kegan, R. (1994). *In over our heads: The mental demands of modern life*. Cambridge, MA: Harvard University Press.

Kirkpatrick, D. L. (1975). *Evaluating training programs: A collection of articles from the Journal of the American Society for Training and Development*. Madison, WI: American Society for Training and Development.

Komives, S. R., Longerbeam, S. D., Owen, J. E., Mainella, F. C., & Osteen, L. (2006). A leadership identity development model: Applications from a grounded theory. *Journal of College Student Development, 47*, 401–418.

Komives, S. R., Owen, J. E., Longerbeam, S. D., Mainella, F. C., & Osteen, L. (2005). Developing a leadership identity: A grounded theory. *Journal of College Student Development, 46*, 593–611.

Kozlowski, S. W. J. & Bell, B. S. (2008). Team learning, development, and adaptation. In V. I. Sessa & M. London (eds), *Work group learning: Understanding, improving & assessing how groups learn in organizations* (pp. 15–44). New York: Erlbaum.

Kozlowski, S. W. J., Gully, S. M., McHugh, P. P., Salas, E., & Cannon-Bowers, J. A. (1996). A dynamic theory of leadership and team effectiveness: Developmental and task contingent leader roles. *Research in Personnel and Human Resources Management, 4*, 253–305.

Kozlowski, S. W. J., Gully, S. M., Nason, E. R., & Smith, E. M. (1999). Developing adaptive teams: A theory of compilation and performance across levels and time. In D. R. Ilgen & E. D. Pulakos (eds), *The changing nature of work performance: Implications for staffing, personnel actions, and development* (pp. 240–292). San Francisco, CA: Jossey-Bass.

Kozlowski, S. W. J., Watola, D. J., Jensen, J. M., Kim, B. H., & Botero, I. C. (2009). Developing adaptive teams: A theory of dynamic team leadership. In E. Salas, G. F. Goodwin & C. S. Burke (eds), *Team effectiveness in complex organizations: Cross-disciplinary perspectives and approaches* (pp. 113–155). New York: Routledge.

Lamoureux, K. (2007, July). *High-impact leadership development: Best practices, vendor profiles and industry solutions*. Oakland, CA: Bersin & Associates.

Latham, G. P. & Seijts, G. H. (1998). Management development. In P. J. D. Drenth, H. Thierry & Associates (eds), *Handbook of work and organizational psychology* (2nd ed., Vol. 3, pp. 257–272). Hove, UK: Psychology Press/Erlbaum.

Lord, R. G. & Hall, R. J. (2005). Identity, deep structure, and the development of leadership skill. *The Leadership Quarterly, 16*, 591–615.

Luthans, F. & Avolio, B. (2003). Authentic leadership development. In K. S. Cameron, J. E. Dutton & R. E. Quinn (eds), *Positive organizational scholarship: Foundations of a new discipline* (pp. 241–258). San Francisco, CA: Berrett-Koehler.

McCall, M. W., Jr & Hollenbeck, G. P. (2002). *Developing global executives: The lessons of international experience*. Boston, MA: Harvard Business School.

McCall, M. W., Jr., Lombardo, M. M., & Morrison, A. M. (1988). *The lessons of experience: How successful executives develop on the job*. Lexington, MA: Lexington Books.

McCauley, C. D., Ruderman, M. N., Ohlott, P. J., & Morrow, J. E. (1994). Assessing the developmental components of managerial jobs. *Journal of Applied Psychology, 79*, 544–560.

McCauley, C. D. & Van Velsor, E. (eds). (2004). *The Center for Creative Leadership handbook of leadership development* (2nd ed.). San Francisco: Jossey-Bass.

Marks, M. A., Mathieu, J. E., & Zaccaro, S. J. (2001). A temporally based framework and taxonomy of team processes. *Academy of Management Review, 26*, 356–376.

Marquardt, M. J. (2004). *Action learning: Solving problems and building leaders in real time*. Palo Alto, CA: Davies-Black.

Mitchell, T. R. & James, L. R. (2001). Building better theory: Time and the specification of when things happen. *Academy of Management Review, 26*, 530–547.

O'Connor, P. M. G. & Quinn, L. (2004). Organizational capacity for leadership. In C. D. McCauley & E. Van Velsor (eds), *The Center for Creative Leadership handbook of leadership development* (2nd ed., pp. 417–437). San Francisco: Jossey-Bass.

Palus, C. J. & Horth, D. M. (2004). Exploration for development. In C. D. McCauley & E. Van Velsor (eds), *The Center for Creative Leadership handbook of leadership development* (2nd ed., pp. 438–464). San Francisco: Jossey-Bass.

Pearce, C. L., & Sims, H. P., Jr (2002). Vertical versus shared leadership as predictors of the effectiveness of change management teams: An examination of aversive, directive, transactional, transformational, and empowering leader behaviors. *Group Dynamics: Theory, Research, and Practice, 6*, 172–197.

Raudenbush, S. W. (2001). Comparing personal trajectories and drawing causal inferences from longitudinal data. *Annual Review of Psychology, 52*, 501–525.

Revans, R. W. (1980). *Action learning*. London: Blond & Briggs.

Rousseau, D. M., Manning, J., & Denyer, D. (2008). Evidence in management and organizational science: Assembling the field's full weight of scientific knowledge through syntheses. *Academy of Management Annals, 2*, 475–515.

Schneider, B., Ehrhart, K. H., & Ehrhart, M. G. (2002). Understanding high school leaders: II. Peer nominations of leaders and their correlates. *The Leadership Quarterly, 13*, 275–299.

Schneider, B., Paul, M. C., White, S. S., & Holcombe, K. M. (1999). Understanding high school student leaders: I. Predicting teacher ratings of leader behavior. *The Leadership Quarterly, 10*, 609–636.

Shamir, B. & Eilam, G. (2005). 'What's your story?' A life-stories approach to authentic leadership development. *The Leadership Quarterly, 16*, 395–418.

Snyder, C. R. & Lopez, S. J. (eds). (2002). *Handbook of positive psychology*. New York: Oxford University.

Van Velsor, E. & McCauley, C. D. (2004). Our view of leadership development. In C. D. McCauley & E. Van Velsor (eds), *The Center for Creative Leadership handbook of leadership development* (2nd ed., pp. 1–22). San Francisco: Jossey-Bass.

Vicere, A. A. & Fulmer, R. M. (1998). *Leadership by design*. Boston, MA: Harvard Business School.

Wang, M. & Bodner, T. E. (2007). Growth mixture modeling: Identifying and predicting unobserved subpopulations with longitudinal data. *Organizational Research Methods, 10*, 635–656.

Weick, K. E. (1995). What theory is *not*, theorizing *is*. *Administrative Science Quarterly, 40*, 385–390.

Wexley, K. N. & Baldwin, T. T. (1986). Management development. *Journal of Management, 12*, 277–294.

Wexley, K. N. & Latham, G. P. (1991). *Developing and training human resources in organizations* (2nd ed.). New York: HarperCollins.

PART II

Macro and Sociological Perspectives

Leadership and Organization Theory

Ken W. Parry

INTRODUCTION

Organization theory represents a broad body of knowledge. Some of the subsidiary areas of organization theory are also covered elsewhere in this handbook. Those areas include strategy and strategic leadership, leadership and power, leadership and teams, structure, organizational size, innovation, context and organizational culture. The remaining components of organization theory are covered in more detail in this chapter. A number of conceptual similarities exist between organization theory and leadership studies, but more paradoxes emerge than there are inherent similarities to be identified. One connection is the important role of power. Power and influence are axiomatic of the study of leadership. Power is also required to restructure and drive organizations. Moreover, power is generated and distributed throughout organizations in order for organizational outcomes to be achieved. An inherent paradox within these parallel studies is that organizational power is usually generated within a structure, whereas leadership power is often generated from relations and processes that go on between people. A concomitant paradox is that leadership and organization theory both revolve around formal creations and emergent constructs. Leaders are formally constituted as part of a formal organizational structure. Organizational structures also emerge as a result of external impacts, just as leadership emerges in response to the influence of context. The paradox is that organization theory is more usually studied as a formal creation, whereas leadership increasingly

is studied as the result of relationships between people and social processes at play in organizations. This chapter concludes with a discussion of the general trends and paradoxes that scholars face when studying leadership and the full range of issues associated with organization theory.

LEADERSHIP AND ORGANIZATIONAL EFFECTIVENESS

Although most people might assume a strong role for leadership in generating organizational effectiveness, many scholars challenge this position (Kaiser et al., 2008). Some argue that leadership has less impact than historical, organizational, and environmental forces (Lieberson & O'Connor, 1972; Pfeffer, 1977; Salancik & Pfeffer, 1977). Others suggest that attributing organizational outcomes to individual leaders is a romantic oversimplification (Meindl & Ehrlich, 1987; Meindl, Ehrlich, & Dukerich, 1985). Similarly, complexity theorists maintain that organizational performance cannot be attributed to individual leaders because performance is an emergent phenomenon involving complex, non-linear interactions among multiple variables in a dynamic system open to outside influences (Marion & Uhl-Bien, 2001). Gamson and Scotch (1964), Eitzen and Yetman (1972), and Allen et al. (1979) also conclude that a change in leadership has little or no impact on organizational performance. Others have pinpointed that there is weak evidence that changes in leadership directly influence organizational performance (e.g. Brown, 1982; Fizel and D'Itri, 1999). Lieberson and O'Connor (1972) and House and Baetz (1979) conclude that the association between leadership and organizational performance is weak, non-existent and even contradictory. Jaffee (2001) provides a normative conclusion and states that the theories about the effects of leadership on organizational performance are simply false.

However, after reviewing recent research, Kaiser et al. (2008) argue that each of these views are contradicted by the fact that research on managerial succession over the last 20 years has consistently found a relationship between who is in charge and organizational performance as measured by a variety of indicators (e.g. Barney, 1991; Barrick, Day, Lord, & Alexander, 1991; Bertrand & Schoar, 2003; Collins, 2001; Day & Lord, 1988; Joyce, Nohria, & Roberson, 2003; Thomas, 1988). Using different methodologies, these studies converged on the conclusion that changes in leadership are followed by changes in firm performance. Once again, this could be Meindl's 'romance of leadership' notion or it could be the well-publicized Hawthorne Effect. Therefore, the relationship between leadership and organizational effectiveness is difficult to prove empirically. However, the links are strong conceptually and theoretically. What is clear also is that leadership impact is clearer at lower levels of analysis, and more difficult to prove at the organizational level. The following sections discuss the ways in which leadership affects organizational effectiveness through its impact on the individual, team, and organizational levels.

Leaders do not achieve results themselves, they influence organizational outcomes through other people (Hogan & Kaiser, 2005; Hollander, 1992; Lord & Brown, 2004). Organizations are complex systems in which leadership is only one of several significant influences (Campbell et al., 1970; Jaques & Clement, 1991; Katz & Kahn, 1978; Zaccaro & Klimoski, 2001). Leaders do not directly control results, because unpredictable dynamics can determine outcomes in complex systems (Marion & Uhl-Bien, 2001), and external forces sometimes overwhelm intentions and effort. Luck also plays a role. Nonetheless, leaders can create conditions that are more or less conducive to team effectiveness (Hackman, 2002; Hackman & Walton, 1986). For the main part, they do this via structure and strategy. Schneider (1998) described this as providing a context for performance – the circumstances that influence the ability of employees to contribute to organizational goals. The links between leadership and organizational outcomes are real, yet complicated. The complexity arises because the links are mediated by other aspects of the system, such as the performance of subordinates, the teams they

compose, and the organization in which they are embedded (Hogan & Kaiser, 2005; Kaiser & Hogan, 2007). Leadership and organizational effectiveness have been studied at various levels of analysis. The levels of analysis are often seen as artificial boundaries around the manifestation of leadership in organizations. At the same time, these levels do overlap and interact in order for organizations to achieve their outcomes, and in the ways that leadership processes occur. These levels of analysis are examined, while also discussing the interwoven nature of these 'levels'.

Individual level

The subject of how transactional leaders use rewards and punishment to motivate followers on the individual level has been studied in detail (see Bass, 1990; Yukl, 2006). A large body of research on leader–member exchange theory shows that the quality of the social exchange relationship has a profound impact on followers (Gerstner & Day, 1997; Graen & Uhl-Bien, 1995). In particular, followers' attitudes and performance are a function of trust in the leader and perceptions of the leader's support, consideration, and inclusiveness (Dirks & Ferrin, 2002; Gerstner & Day, 1997; Judge, Piccolo, & Ilies, 2004; Likert, 1967). Leaders who are unjust, disrespectful, inconsiderate, non-inclusive, and, in the extreme, hostile and abusive (Tepper, 2000) alienate and demoralize followers. Leaders who are fair, respectful, considerate, and inclusive favourably impact attitudes, motivation, and employee involvement. In turn, attitudes, motivation, and involvement are positively related to financial, productivity, customer, and human capital measures of business-unit performance (Harter, Schmidt, & Hayes, 2002).

Through a combination of vision, appealing group goals, high standards, intellectual stimulation, role modelling, and relationships, transformational leaders are believed to inspire and enhance the performance of their followers (Bass, 1985; Podsakoff, MacKenzie, Moorman, & Fetter, 1990; and see Diaz-Saenz, Chapter 22, this volume). A recent meta-analysis suggests that the difference in the two leadership styles' overall effects is small (Judge & Piccolo, 2004), and the two forms of leadership are often complementary (Seltzer & Bass, 1990). Transformational leaders influence followers by modelling collective commitment, emphasizing the similarity of group members, and reinforcing collective goals, shared values, and common interests (Shamir et al., 1993; van Knippenberg, et al., 2004). When followers see themselves as members of a collective, they tend to endorse group values and goals, and this enhances their motivation to contribute to the greater good (Lord & Brown, 2004). Therefore, transactional leadership seems to operate more at the individual level of the analysis of organizations. By contrast, transformational leadership seems to operate more at the collective or organizational level of analysis, although no-one seems to want to come out and state this case strongly. On the other hand, senior managers must engage in transactions at the intra-organizational and inter-organizational levels. Moreover, junior level managers can demonstrate transformational leadership via the personal power that is available to them. Therefore, paradoxically, differences between levels of analysis can be ascertained just as readily as similarities between them can be observed.

Team level

Leaders also influence performance at the team level of analysis. The functional perspective regards leadership as social problem solving in which leaders do whatever needs to be done for the group to succeed (Fleishman et al., 1991; Hackman & Walton, 1986; Lord, 1977; McGrath, 1962). Thus, leaders are responsible for identifying potential obstacles between a team and its goals, discovering solutions to those obstacles, and implementing a preferred course of action (Kozlowski, Gully, Salas, & Cannon-Bowers, 1996; Zaccaro et al., 2001). The functional approach is an extension of early group performance research (Bales, 1950), and it considers two classes of problems, group maintenance and goal accomplishment (Kaiser et al., 2008). Group maintenance refers to the degree of harmony, cohesion, and teamwork, and the associated leadership activities include resolving conflict, building trust and cooperation, and attending to the socioemotional needs of team members (Lord, 1977; Zaccaro et al., 2001). Team reflexivity, the extent to which teams reflect upon and modify their functioning, is important for the effective functioning of teams (e.g. Carter & West, 1998; Hirst et al., 2004; Somech, 2006; Tjosvold et al., 2004). Schippers et al. (2008) found a positive relationship between leaders' transformational leadership and team reflexivity, which in turn improved team performance.

Leaders also keep teams together by ensuring clear channels of communication, clarifying misunderstandings, and facilitating group interaction and discussion. Hackman (2002) described these as the enabling conditions that are a prerequisite for effective task performance. Meta-analytic evidence supports positive relationships between enabling leader behaviours, group maintenance,

and group results (e.g. Burke et al., 2006; Mullen & Copper, 1994). Several leader behaviours are related to goal accomplishment (Burke et al., 2006). These include setting direction and defining clear and significant objectives (Hackman, 2002). Another instrumental leader behaviour is boundary spanning – monitoring external events and interpreting their meaning and significance for the team's performance (Katz & Kahn, 1978; Kozlowski et al., 1996; Zaccaro et al., 2001). Leaders also facilitate goal accomplishment by specifying roles, clarifying performance expectations, and coordinating collective action (Burke et al., 2006; Fleishman et al., 1991; Kozlowski et al., 1996; Lord, 1977). Team efforts must be coordinated in stages; first deciding how to combine individual efforts, then coaching team members to interact in this configuration, and finally standardizing these interaction patterns (Kozlowski et al., 1996). However, leadership differs from routine management in that leadership entails the initiation of change (Kotter, 1990). Some recent writers have even emphasized the leader's role in teaching teams to innovate and adapt on their own (Day, Gronn, & Salas, 2004; Hackman, 2002). Meta-analytic research has found a strong link between empowering leader behaviours and team learning outcomes and a moderate link with productivity (Burke et al., 2006). Through social learning processes, subordinates identify and interpret the values implicit in the behaviour and decisions of their leader (Dragoni, 2005; Kozlowski & Doherty, 1989). It certainly seems clear that senior management has a leadership effect at the organizational level of analysis, and junior management has a leadership effect at lower levels of analysis.

Organizational level

Furthermore, leaders exert influence on effectiveness on an organizational level through decisions about strategic goals, organizational structure, staffing, and policies (Finkelstein & Hambrick, 1996). Top-level leaders establish goals, strategies, and policies, which in turn guide and constrain follower and team performance. Lower-level managers also decide direction, goals, whom to put in which roles, and operations management (Zaccaro & Klimoski, 2001). However, as lower-level managers face more constraints compared with senior managers, individual differences will be more apparent in decisions made at higher organizational levels (Hambrick & Finkelstein, 1987; Kaiser & Hogan, 2007). Senior managers, then, have a greater opportunity to influence organizational effectiveness, for better or worse (Finkelstein & Hambrick, 1996; Jaques

& Clement, 1991; Kaiser & Hogan, 2007; Zaccaro & Klimoski, 2001).

A recent paper by Yukl (2008) proposed 'flexible leadership theory' (FLT) as a theory of strategic leadership that explains how top executives influence the organizational processes that determine a firm's financial performance and long-term survival. He links leadership with organizational effectiveness. The flexible leadership theory is conceptualized primarily at the organizational level, and it includes four sets of variables: organizational effectiveness, performance determinants, situational variables, and leadership decisions and actions. The effectiveness of an organization is the extent to which it is able to survive, perform its mission, and maintain favourable earnings, financial resources, and asset value (Yukl, 2008).

A distinction between task-oriented and relationship-oriented behaviours was popular in early leadership literature (e.g. Blake & Mouton, 1982). These behaviours were found to influence performance at the individual level and at the organizational level. Researchers subsequently found that change-oriented behaviour was another distinct meta-category (Yukl et al., 2002). The three types of leader behaviour each have a different primary objective, and the objectives align with the three determinants of organizational effectiveness. Task-oriented behaviours are most useful for improving efficiency, relationship-oriented behaviours are most useful for improving human resources and relations, and change-oriented behaviours are most useful for improving adaptation (Yukl, 2008). Hence, all three general types of leadership behaviour have implications for effectiveness at the organizational level. Change-oriented behaviours include monitoring the environment to identify threats and opportunities, articulating an inspiring vision, building a coalition of supporters for a major change, and determining how to implement a new initiative or major change (Yukl, 2006). Studies on change-oriented aspects of transformational leadership such as inspirational motivation and intellectual stimulation show that this type of behaviour can enhance individual and team performance (Lowe et al., 1996). The change-oriented behaviours are especially relevant for top executives (Jacobs & Lewis, 1992). Several recent survey studies found evidence of a relationship between CEO transformational or charismatic leadership and indicators of company financial performance (Jung et al., 2003; Tosi et al., 2004; Waldman et al., 2001). Other evidence for the relevance of change-oriented behaviour of top executives is provided by intensive case studies of successful change efforts in organizations (Beer & Nohria, 2000; Kotter & Cohen, 2002), and by studies on the influence of CEO visions on company performance (Baum et al., 1998).

In this discussion about leadership and organizational effectiveness, most of the discourse is about the leader, and not about leader*ship*. Refreshingly, Hambrick, Finkelstein, and others wrote about 'managers' more so than they wrote about 'leaders'. Nonetheless, it is clear that in organization theory discourse, the leader is invariably the senior manager. However, people at all levels of the organization can demonstrate leadership. When scholars write in terms of 'manager', the appropriate level of analysis for the organization seems to emerge. In addition, when scholars write in terms of leadership, and not about 'leader', the interactions between levels of analysis seem to be more pronounced and more relevant.

LEADERSHIP AND TECHNOLOGY

As globalization continues, virtual communication plays an increasingly important role in many organizations (e.g. Avolio et al., 2001; Bell & Kozlowski, 2002; Cascio, 2000; Cascio & Shurygailo, 2003). Leadership taking place in a context where work is mediated by information technology is referred to as e-leadership (Avolio & Kahai, 2003). In such a context, not only might a leader's communication with followers take place via information technology, but the collection and dissemination of information required to support organizational work also takes place via information technology. Followers can now access the same information that leaders had exclusive access to in the past, often before the leader. This has put pressure on leaders to be prepared to justify their decisions more quickly. Partly because employees today have greater access to information and media and partly because they are close to customers, leadership in many organizations is moving to lower levels in organizations. This evolution has enabled faster and more effective responses to changing customer needs and requirements. The increased interconnectedness of the world offers tremendous opportunities for organizations as they seek ways to respond to rapid shifts in customer demands and increasing globalization of markets. Leaders now use e-mail as a conduit for dialogue, sharing of information, projecting the vision of the organization, and simply to praise subordinates' efforts.

Avolio and Kahai (2003) researched the characteristics of virtual teams that are relevant to e-leadership. What happens early on in the formation and leadership of virtual teams predicts subsequent levels of trust, satisfaction, and performance. Virtual teams who spent the first few occasions of interaction identifying who was participating in their team, clarifying their expectations, and how they wanted to work together had higher performance several months later. Existing norms are imported into new virtual groups. The culture the group members come from can become part of the virtual team culture. How leadership and the task being completed fit with each other matters for the performance of groups using a groupware. For instance, participative leadership might be more suitable for generating solutions for a semi-structured or unstructured problem, whereas directive leadership might be more suitable for generating solutions for a structured problem. Features of a groupware system could substitute for leadership in certain cases. Whether connected via information technology or not, leaders have to build relationships in order to lead effectively. Avolio and Kahai (2003) suggested a number of ways leaders can build trusting relationships in an increasingly virtual work environment.

Many leadership behaviours are equally important in both communication settings, yet in virtual settings some behaviours (e.g. priority setting and networking) have been found to be perceived by team members as more important in virtual settings (Horner-Long & Schoenberg, 2002). Recent work on the leadership theory and practice conceptualizes successful leadership as a function of overlapping attention to tasks, relationships, and individual needs (e.g. Adair, 2007; Gill, 2006). Zimmermann et al.'s study (2008) distinguished between task-oriented and relationship-oriented leadership behaviours, and examines team members' perceptions of the relative importance of these two categories of leadership behaviours in virtual versus face-to-face communication settings. Task-oriented behaviours include setting clear goals, defining tasks and roles, coordinating group-members' activities and promoting their task commitment. Research suggests that working in a group with a high level of virtualness increases the importance of task-oriented leadership (e.g. Bell & Kozlowski, 2002; Davis, 2004; Griffith & Meader, 2004). Relationship-oriented leadership includes making people feel part of the team, emphasizing shared values, and building sustaining effective interpersonal relationships. Research suggests that a leader should pay more attention to group identification and a sense of belonging if the team operates under high degrees of virtualness (e.g. Ahuja & Galvin, 2003; Avolio & Kahai, 2003; Cascio, 2000; Feng et al., 2004; Jarvenpaa & Tanriverdi, 2003; Pauleen, 2003; Pulley et al., 2000; Yukl, 2006; Zaccaro & Bader, 2003; Zigurs, 2003).

Zimmermann et al.'s study (2008) concluded that workers in global teams with varying degrees of virtualness perceive most task-oriented leadership behaviours as becoming more important as the degree of virtualness in respondents'

daily work increases. In terms of the relationship-oriented behaviours, Zimmermann et al.'s study (2008) suggests that is also a greater challenge for leaders to promote group identification in a virtual setting than in a face-to-face setting. In line with theorizing by Avolio and Kahai (2003), Kasper-Fuerhrer and Ashkanasy (2001), and Yukl (2006), Zimmermann et al. (2008) found that team members considered it more important in virtual settings that their leader 'makes people feel part of a team', 'emphasises shared values among team members', and 'quickly build and sustain effective relationships'. In sum, Zimmermann et al. (2008) conclude that most task-oriented as well as relationship-oriented leadership behaviours are perceived to be more important in virtual settings than in face-to-face settings.

LEADERSHIP AND ORGANIZATIONAL CHANGE

Leadership and organizational change are inextricably intertwined. However, 'organizational change' has become an interest for organizational consultants more so than for empirical researchers. There are many more books and articles on practitioner or conceptual scholarship than on theoretical or empirical scholarship. Much of the practitioner/conceptual work is case-study based and anecdotal, and not rigorous in its conduct. Nonetheless, Kotter's (1996) book *Leading Change* identifies typical mistakes leaders make in attempting to create change in their organizations, and offers an eight-step process to overcome obstacles and carry out the firm's change agenda. Kotter and Cohen's (2002) *The Heart of Change: Real-Life Stories of How People Change Their Organizations* follows up on the eight-step process presented in *Leading Change* and offers tips and tools readers can apply within their own organization. Some of the more empirical and theoretical work is now considered.

For organizations in today's business environment change is a constant dynamic (Berquist, 1993). Bass (1985) suggests that leaders must promote change by creating vision. Theories of transformational leadership and organizational change emphasize that change is accomplished through the leader's implementation of a unique vision of the organization through powerful persuasive personal characteristics and actions designed to change internal organizational cultural forms and substance (Bass & Avolio, 1994; Hatch, 1993). Kouzes and Posner (2007, p. 122) suggest that when facing significant change, leadership is the art of mobilizing others to want to struggle for shared ethical aspirations. Leaders therefore must be skilled in change management processes if they are to act successfully as agents of change and motivate others to follow (Van Knippenberg & Hogg, 2003).

Amabile (1998) has suggested that, by influencing the nature of the work environment and organizational culture, leaders can affect organizational members' attitude to work-related change and motivation. The challenge for leaders becomes to select a set of actions that are feasible within the capacity of the organization to absorb change and manage resources. Kavanagh and Ashkanasy's study (2006) suggest that changing an organization boils down to directing energy and efforts towards four identifiable aspects of organizational life: namely, the behaviour of institutional leaders; the selection and execution of appropriate change management strategies; an understanding of the organizations' basic structure, systems, and formal processes (culture); and actions taken by leaders affecting acceptance of change by individuals who play key roles in both formal and informal systems (Nadler, Thies & Nadler, 2001). Nadler et al. (2001) argue that too many leaders make the mistake of thinking they can change individual behaviour in an organization by changing its culture. Valikangas and Okumara (1997) suggest that the fact that individuals resist change is partly as a result of the leader's failure to grasp what motivates followers to change their behaviour.

Change that is executed by coercive power or for calculated expected gain in certain roles is not likely to be sustained. During times of change, it is important that the leaders of the organization create an atmosphere of psychological safety for all individuals to engage in the new behaviours and test the waters of the new culture. Communication is the key tool within any change process and failure to communicate generally results in individuals feeling uncertain and anxious about their future (Kanter, Stein & Jick, 1992). Avolio and Bass (2002) argue that employees' affective reactions to change are significantly related to transformational leadership behaviour such as inspiring others and creating and communicating a vision and direction. Several reasons support the expectation that transformational leadership would enhance employee ability to accept change. First, transformational leaders go beyond exchanging contractual agreements for desired performance by actively engaging followers' personal value systems (Gardner & Avolio, 1998).

Secondly, transformational leaders serve as role models to stimulate followers to think about existing methods in new ways and encourage them to challenge their own values, traditions, and beliefs (Hater & Bass, 1988). Kavanagh and Ashkanasy (2006) concluded that followers' perceptions about how a change process has been managed seem to hinge to a large extent on the approach adopted by the organization's leaders. In their study, followers highlighted the need for planning, consultation, and, even, compassion, in order for change management to be successful. They suggest that organizational members want transparent change processes, where leaders explain carefully the reasons for change so that all who are involved have knowledge of what is taking place. Furthermore, leaders should ensure that ongoing training and support can provide opportunities for employees to question rationales (and receive answers), check reality, express fears or frustrations, obtain support from peers, and maintain motivation. If this is not achieved, disillusionment could result. During times of change it is important that leaders of the organization create an atmosphere of psychological safety to encourage employees to be involved and verify for themselves the validity of the new beliefs and values and to explore how they personally can contribute to the changed effort. To avoid employee cynicism and unresponsiveness, leaders must ensure that employees feel that they are consulted as part of the decision-making, and involved in the process.

LEADERSHIP AND ORGANIZATIONAL EVOLUTION/LIFE CYCLE

There is little recent contemporary work in this area. It is an area of research that needs advancement. Shamir and Howell (1999) found that when a new organization is being formed, there is usually much ambiguity and anxiety and a great need for orientation on the part of organizational members. Under such conditions, members are more likely to look for charismatic leaders and to accept their definitions of the organization's identity and its mission. The great ambiguity and need for orientation among potential followers increase the chances that the leader's frame alignment efforts will be successful. Shamir and Howell also argued that the foundation of a new organization often requires a leader who can identify opportunities in the environment, develop a vision, demonstrate high confidence in the achievability of the vision, and recruit other parties (investors, suppliers, employees) to support his or her efforts despite uncertainties and fears. The literature on organizational foundation and infancy typically associates these stages with entrepreneurial and charismatic leadership. One well-known model by Greiner (1972) described the organizational life cycle as progressing from infancy through childhood and adolescence to maturity, passing through five stages of development.

As organizations move through the stages of the life cycle, leaders shift emphasis from controlling the organization to constantly regenerating motivations to work and to stay organized. If top management fails to provide such regeneration, the organization will undergo a crisis of renewal, characterized by burnout, fatigue, and apathy on the part of members. This might lead to organizational decline and eventually to organizational death. Central to Greiner's (1972) model is the assumption that leadership styles and strategies that are adaptive for one stage of the organizational life cycle are maladaptive for other stages. While Greiner did not explicitly associate charismatic leadership with the late stages of the organizational life cycle, his description of the organizational problems faced by organizations in these stages and their leadership needs seems to favour the emergence of charismatic leadership that can infuse the organization and its members with a new sense of purpose (Shamir & Howell, 1999). In a similar vein, Baliga and Hunt (1988) analysed the leadership demands at various stages of the organizational life cycle, and derived from this analysis propositions about the leadership behaviours that are likely to be related to effectiveness at each stage. In particular, Baliga and Hunt (1988) suggested that one of the primary demands of the organizational birth stage is obtaining commitment from key personnel to the leader's vision and objectives, and therefore transformational leader behaviours will be more important and more strongly related to effectiveness at this stage than transactional behaviours. They also suggested that transformational behaviours will be more important than transactional behaviours at the late stages of the organizational life cycle when it faces the threat of decline and even death, because organizational revitalization involves the demands of creating a new vision for the organization, recruiting commitment to the new vision, and changing the organizational culture. According to Baliga and Hunt (1988), and in support of Greiner (1972), transformational behaviours will be less important, and transactional behaviours more important, at middle stages of the organizational life cycle, than at the growth and maturity stages.

LEADERSHIP AND KNOWLEDGE MANAGEMENT

Organizational knowledge comprises all tacit and explicit knowledge possessed by individuals in an organization about products, systems, and processes combined with the explicit knowledge codified in manuals, databases, and information systems (Bryant, 2003). An additional part of organizational knowledge is the tacit knowledge shared in the firm in the form of routines, culture, and know-how that is embedded in the social processes of an organization (Grant, 1996; Nonaka & Takeuchi, 1995). Leaders play a vital role in the process of managing organizational knowledge, by providing vision, motivation, systems, and structures at various levels of the organization, aimed at facilitating the conversion of knowledge into competitive advantages (Bryant, 2003). Doing so requires a conscious effort by leaders throughout the organization to manage the three processes of creating, sharing, and exploiting knowledge.

Transformational and transactional leadership theory can provide a basis for appreciating how leaders have an impact upon the cultivation of knowledge. Leaders can influence creativity within an organization by providing contexts conducive to the creation of knowledge amongst workers (Mumford, Whetzel & Reiter-Palmon, 1997; Redmond, Mumford & Teach, 1993). Once again, the discourse on knowledge management is more about 'leaders' than about leadership. The individualized nature of the scholarship lends itself more towards knowledge management being a task of senior managers. It also lends itself towards leadership at the individual level of analysis rather than the organizational level of analysis.

When demonstrating transformational leadership, subordinates are often more productive when given the freedom to create, share, and test new ideas (Sosik, 1997). Transformational leaders inspire workers to higher levels of innovation and effectiveness (Bryant, 2003). Knowledge-intensive workers, including software programmers, pose certain knowledge management challenges that transformational leaders are better equipped to deal with. Knowledge workers usually have more expertise in technical areas than their leaders (Starbuck, 1992), exactly how work is to be accomplished is less clear, and they tend to be self-motivated and require less direct supervision than most workers (Miles et al., 1997). Knowledge work has a greater tacit dimension, and its progress is therefore more difficult to monitor. Because transformational leadership provides vision, inspiration, and individualized consideration for workers, this leadership fits well with the particular needs of knowledge workers (Bryant, 2003).

Transactional leaders have three key characteristics. First, they work with their team members to develop clear, specific goals, and ensure that workers are rewarded for meeting those predetermined goals. Secondly, rewards and promises are exchanged for worker effort, and such leaders are responsive to the self-interest of their subordinates if these needs can be met while getting the work done. Thirdly, because transactional leadership encourages a close connection between goals and rewards in the form of specific exchanges, workers can as a result not be motivated to give anything beyond what is clearly specified in contracts or through bonus systems. This can be particularly troubling for knowledge workers, as it is more difficult to specify complete job descriptions in advance for such workers (Bryant, 2003). Transactional leadership is implicitly dyadic. Therefore, it resonates with 'leaders' and 'followers' at the individual level of analysis. It does not resonate with the social processes of relational leadership (Uhl-Bein, 2006) at the higher levels of analysis.

According to Bass (1985) and Conger and Kanungo (1998), all leaders exhibit certain characteristics of both transformational and transactional leadership styles, but individual leaders tend to emphasize one of the styles more than the other. Conger (1999) suggested that both styles are in fact required to manage knowledge effectively. In order to effectively manage the creating, sharing, and exploiting of knowledge in an organization, leaders must address the particular demands of managing knowledge at various levels (Yammarino & Dubinsky, 1994; Yammarino & Spangler, 1998). Individual, group, and organizational levels can require different leadership styles in order for organizations to leverage knowledge into competitive advantages (Yukl & Howell, 1999). Knowledge creation occurs primarily at the individual level. Sharing of knowledge occurs mostly at the group level (Nonaka & Takeuchi, 1995). As it takes resources from all parts of the organization to convert new ideas into marketable products or services (Boisot, 1998), knowledge exploiting occurs primarily at the organizational level. Leadership and the management of knowledge at these three levels is discussed in the sections below. Once again, the point should be made that levels of analysis is an artificially imposed categorization. The manifestations of leadership at the various levels are not as clear as it might seem from the extant research.

Individual level

Knowledge is created primarily at the individual level. Although individuals are capable of both sharing and exploiting knowledge, they tend to emphasize the creating process when working on their own. Problems are solved and new knowledge created through a process of intuition and creative insight (Crossan et al., 1999). Transformational leaders provide workers with the necessary support and intellectual stimulation to be innovative, and they also use their charisma to excite and motivate workers to innovate. They also provide intellectual stimulation by giving workers challenging assignments to foster creativity. In addition, by showing individual consideration for their subordinates, transformational leaders encourage workers to share their ideas with others. By contrast, transactional leaders tend to emphasize detailed goals, rules, and policies at the individual level (Bryant, 2003). This can stifle both creativity and new ideas (Conger & Kanungo, 1998). Transactional leaders tend also not to reward ideas that do not fit existing goals and plans (Bryant, 2003). So, generally, transformational leaders are likely to encourage more creative solutions at the individual level, which in turn would result in higher levels of performance.

Group level

Knowledge is created, shared, and exploited at the group level of organizations, but the most prevalent activity at this level is knowledge sharing. Groups integrate knowledge by using interactive systems and create cognitive maps that are shared among all members of the group (Crossan el., 1999). The ideas, metaphors, and innovations from the individual level are brought together to form a more cohesive and integrated whole. Transformational leadership is essential to facilitating this process. Transformational leaders encourage groups to be innovative, solve problems, and generate solutions (Bass, 1985). Transformational leaders encourage workers to share their knowledge with each other, by being sensitive to the individual needs of groups and responding with the right mix of challenge and encouragement. Transactional leaders at the group level often reward structure and conformity to rules. By enforcing policies, these leaders can potentially stifle creativity. However, the various groups in an organization must be assigned to particular projects or parts of larger projects to achieve overall firm objectives, and a transactional leadership style can be more effective in this process of coordination. Middle-level managers work with team leaders to establish goals, rewards, and specific project assignments and by coordinating efforts across several teams, transactional leaders can facilitate the necessary exploiting of knowledge created in other parts of the organization into new products and services (Bryant, 2003).

Organizational level

At the organizational level, knowledge that was created and interpreted at the individual level and integrated at the group level becomes institutionalized (Crossan et al., 1999). At the organizational level, leadership includes all the members of the top management team as well as any other high-level manager. Top managers should establish knowledge systems that will effectively both capture and share knowledge. Therefore, transactional leadership might be more effective at the organizational level. Inspiring personal interactions are of lesser importance than creating information and knowledge systems that make routines of actions, rules, and procedures (Bryant, 2003). Knowledge systems make the ideas, solutions, and knowledge created by individuals available to everyone in the organizations. When this happens, knowledge can be exploited into new products, services, and better practices. Competitive advantages will be created by organizations able to exploit new ideas after making tacit knowledge explicit through their knowledge systems. Since transformational leaders are weaker on systems, structures, and implementation (Bryant, 2003), they are not as well suited as transactional leaders to create systems and structures that allow information and knowledge to be efficiently shared throughout the entire organization (Bryant, 2003). Transformational and transactional leadership are both effective for knowledge management.

In summary, since differences in knowledge processes at the various levels of an organization require emphasis on different leadership styles at each level, transformational and transactional leadership styles should coexist in the organization. Utilising different leadership styles at the various levels can result in the most effective way of managing knowledge in organizations. One should note here the domination of the transformational–transactional dichotomy within the leadership literature, not just in the knowledge management literature. Further research is probably needed into other representations of leadership.

LEADERSHIP AND ORGANIZATIONAL LEARNING

Organizational learning can be described as 'a process of change in thought and action, both individual and shared, embedded in and affected by the institutions of the organization' (Vera & Crossan, 2004, p. 224). It includes both cognitive processes and individual behaviours that add new knowledge to firms and permit leaders' actions to be based on accumulated knowledge (Crossan et al., 1999). Organizational learning must start with individuals, particularly those individuals in leadership positions (Mazutis & Slawinski, 2008).

Crossan et al. (1999) suggest four processes of organizational learning: intuiting, interpreting, integrating, and institutionalizing. Learning begins in individuals at the intuiting stage as a subconscious process, which later develops to be more conscious at the interpreting stage, where it is often shared with other members of the group. Members' input gets integrated at both the group level and at the organization level, where information becomes institutionalized by being imbedded in routines, structures, and systems. The following sections discuss how the three processes of organizational learning – intuiting/interpreting, integrating, and institutionalizing – occur at the three levels of analysis (individual, group, and organization) and how leadership affects these processes.

Intuiting and interpreting

Individual/group level
Starting at the intuiting stage, individuals learn by recognizing patterns with which they are either familiar, or among which they see novel connections (Behling & Eckel, 1991). Leaders can assist in converting tacit to explicit knowledge by turning individual experiences into shared experiences or facilitating 'communities of practice' at work (Wenger & Snyder, 2000). Intuiting involves insights made by individuals that are not as likely to occur in organizations without supportive leadership. Leaders can encourage followers to view their work differently by challenging existing practices or by redirecting subordinates' efforts (Sternberg et al., 2003). Both transformational and transactional leadership styles might stimulate exploration, but a transformational leader is likely to be more effective for exploration that challenges existing practices (Vera & Crossan, 2004). In the interpreting stage, individuals are more aware and as a result are better able to make sense of what they have learned (Huff, 1990). Berson et al. (2006) argue that leaders play an important role in helping individuals realize what they have learned, by setting the learning in a meaningful context. Following the intuiting stage, subordinates could have ambiguous images of their new ideas. Group processes can enable individuals to develop a shared understanding of the original idea (Weick & Orden, 1990). A shared language that makes the individual idea into a group process can be a result of the leader's vision, and this vision can play an important role in forming a learning organization, where interconnectivity among workers leads to sharing of knowledge and information (Brown & Gioia, 2002). When leaders communicate their ideas through their visions, these ideas tend to be embedded in a context and are consequently more

appealing for the collective of workers within that context (Van Knippenberg & Hogg, 2003).

Organizational level

Important studies into organizational learning include the works of Bass (2000) and Fry and colleagues (Fry, 2003; Fry et al., 2005). A learning organization is an organization which is specifically designed to support learning (Easterby-Smith & Lyles, 2003). Although there is limited empirical research on learning organizations, spiritual leadership has featured prominently in recent works as a leadership style argued to support such an organizational form. Under spiritual leadership, intrinsically motivated learning often happens because individuals share the organization's vision and values, are passionate about their work, and regard their roles and contributions as meaningful and important to the organization's overall success (Fry et al., 2005). Spiritual leadership, and other forms of positive leadership including authentic leadership (Avolio & Gardner, 2005; Gardner et al., 2005), encourage learning by reducing leaders' control over both individuals and teams, and creating a supportive context where workers are comfortable taking risks and making mistakes, as well as creating dialogue and receiving the necessary support for learning to occur (Fry et al., 2005). Such a context is effectively a transformational organizational culture (Bass & Avolio, 1994).

Integrating

The stage of integrating involves sharing the learning and achieving convergence through conversation among members that leads to shared understandings (Crossan et al., 1999). At the individual and group levels of analysis, conversations among members of the organization that begin with the language formed to communicate new ideas in the interpreting stage are integrated with existing dialogue in the integrating stage (Crossan et al., 1999). The leader–member exchange or LMX (e.g. Graen & Uhl-Bien, 1995) approach might help explain how the nature of the dyadic relationship facilitates integration of knowledge, which is later institutionalized or becomes part of the shared vision of the organization (Waldman et al., 2005). Moreover, Sparrowe and Liden (1997) extend the concept of LMX by linking it to social network theory, while other authors have attempted to connect transformational leadership theory to social networks (Bono & Anderson, 2005; Brass & Krackhardt, 1999). These studies suggest that organizational learning at the integrating stage

might be facilitated by leaders who help build the structural ties within a social network (both inside and outside the organization), thereby allowing themselves and followers to be conduits for information and learning (Berson et al., 2006). Bass' (1985) concept of intellectual stimulation could be another relevant approach to understanding how individuals share learning and integrate it as a group. Intellectual stimulation is especially important when leaders support a feedforward learning loop by transforming learning from the interpreting to the integrating stage. Furthermore, when such leadership is present, followers are more likely to share new learning with other group members, making the learning a shared understanding among them. Similarly, charismatic leaders might use vision that enables followers to understand individual learning in the context of the goals of the group, hence boosting shared meaning among group members (Shamir, House, & Arthur, 1993; and see Conger, Chapter 7, this volume).

At a broader organizational level of analysis, integration might result from the consistent conversations that often occur in the form of storytelling within entities (Seely-Brown & Duguid, 1991). Community members share stories as a form of learning. These stories convey the complexity of the learning and represent a contextualized integration of the learning (Crossan et al., 1999). Stories serve as an organization's repository of wisdom (Weick & Roberts, 1993) and can be easily communicated among members of the community. Leaders often rely on such stories to situate organizational learning (Berson et al., 2006).

Exploitation/institutionalizing

The relationship between leadership and exploitation is often termed single-loop or incremental learning (Edmondson, 2002). These processes begin with institutionalized knowledge and then move through the organization via interpretation. Institutionalizing sets learning apart from individuals and, hence, manifests itself in routines, structures, and practices of the organization (Crossan et al., 1999). Depending on the nature of communications within organizations, leaders at lower levels might have some influence over institutionalized learning. However, many practices at this stage are initiated with executive action, and learning becomes manifested in artefacts and values, or the culture of the organization (Schein, 2004).

Group level

The key process that supports exploitation of institutionalized knowledge is knowledge transfer.

The extant literature on learning focuses on several aspects of this process: knowing where the knowledge is; disseminating the knowledge; and building a shared understanding of it (Berson et al., 2006). There is limited research directly studying the role of leadership in these processes and its fragmented nature makes drawing strong conclusions difficult (Berson et al., 2006). However, Larson et al. (1998) found that leadership style influenced the amount of information transferred in groups, in that participative leaders were more effective than directive leaders in this process. In addition, Edmondson (2003) found that leaders who provided coaching enhanced knowledge integration, which led to greater success in the team's ability to learn to use a new, institutionalized procedure (Edmondson, 2003).

Organizational level

Exploitation depends more upon explicit knowledge, and the challenge in exploitation is to make known sources of knowledge accessible (Dyck et al., 2005). Therefore, to become an effective firm resource for exploitation, the knowledge to be exploited must be usefully organized, accessible, and communicable (Duncan & Weiss, 1979). Research on the role of leadership in making knowledge available for exploitation is limited (Berson et al., 2006). However, firms have begun to recognize the important role of leadership at the organization level in exploitation by appointing senior level executives with that responsibility. These known variously as Chief Knowledge, Chief Learning or Chief Information Officers, executives have a senior leadership role, and are responsible for developing knowledge strategies and training programs, mapping the location of knowledge within the firm to facilitate access, and developing computer systems for knowledge retention. However, their effectiveness in these roles has only recently been evaluated (Hackett, 2002). Leaders can support exploitation within the organization by institutionalizing learning via coordination processes, such as standardized routines, and integrating learning via social processes, such as group decision-making (Grant, 1996) and the filling of structural holes in a social network (Brass & Krackhardt, 1999). Leadership can often be a positive influence on organizational learning, but it must be acknowledged that this is not always the case. Authoritarian forms of leadership and even management-by-exception leadership (Bass, 1985) have the potential to inhibit learning (Berson et al., 2006). When leaders rely on warnings and fear, followers may avoid bringing new ideas and accept institutional procedures.

Authentic leadership, authentic dialogue, and organizational learning

Dialogue lies at the core of organizational learning. Without dialogue, individuals and groups cannot effectively exchange ideas or develop shared understanding. Although dialogue has been addressed in the organizational learning literature (Baker et al., 2005), it has not been examined explicitly as the core mechanism by which strategic leaders influence the learning process at and between the individual, group, and organizational levels. Mazutis and Slawinski (2008) argue that authentic leadership, a relatively new stream of research emerging from the positive organizational scholarship movement, might impact the type of dialogue that takes place in organizations (see also Caza & Jackson, Chapter 26, this volume). Specifically, the authentic leadership capabilities of self-awareness, balanced processing, self-regulation, and relational transparency allow the authentic leader to encourage open and honest dialogue among organizational members. Dialogue has been described as conversation with a centre, not sides, and is critical to double-loop learning, as it enables inconsistencies to surface and be addressed (Mazutis & Slawinski, 2008). Mazutis and Slawinski (2008) further argue that the above-mentioned leadership capabilities translate into self-aware, balanced, congruent, and transparent dialogue which facilitates learning at and between multiple levels of the organization. This type of dialogue is referred to as authentic dialogue. Mazutis and Slawinski (2008) argue that authentic leaders shape an organizational culture that encourages the detection and correction of error through authentic dialogue, distinguished by open, honest, balanced, congruent, and transparent communication.

Authentic leadership is described as a process 'which results in both greater self-awareness and self-regulated positive behaviours on the part of leaders and associates, fostering positive self-development' (Luthans & Avolio, 2003, p. 243), and includes the capabilities of self-awareness, balanced processing, self-regulation, and relational transparency (Avolio & Gardner, 2005; Gardner et al., 2005; Ilies et al., 2005; Kernis, 2003). Self-awareness has been described as an emerging process by which leaders come to understand their unique capabilities, knowledge, and experience (Avolio & Gardner, 2005). With this clarity and understanding of who they are as people, these leaders will be less likely to engage in defensive behaviours. Authentic strategic leaders must also be willing to self-declare, or to communicate learning about themselves with others in the organization; otherwise, followers will remain unaware about a leader's core values and beliefs (Goffee & Jones, 2006).

Authentic leaders possessing self-regulatory capabilities will say what they mean and mean what they say, thereby managing tensions and confronting conflicts between their personal values and organizational responsibilities (Novicevic et al., 2006). In addition to being self-aware, balanced, and congruent in one's goals, motives, values, identities, and emotions, authentic leaders are also transparent in revealing these expressions to their followers (Hughes, 2005). Disclosing one's true self to one's followers builds trust and intimacy, fostering teamwork and cooperation (Gardner et al., 2005) and feelings of stability and predictability (Chan et al., 2005). Furthermore, relational transparency requires the willingness to hold oneself open for inspection and feedback, thereby being an essential component in the learning process (Popper & Lipshitz, 2000). Authentic leaders are those who exhibit the capabilities of self-awareness, balanced processing, self-regulation, and relational transparency and foster the same positive self-development in other organizational members (Mazutis & Slawinski, 2008). When leaders exhibit the capabilities of authentic leadership, they can shape and support an organizational culture in which authentic dialogue is encouraged, supporting both the feed forward and the feedback learning processes (Mazutis & Slawinski, 2008).

Berson et al. (2006) provide a summary of research linking leadership to organizational learning where the dependent variables range from individual and group creativity to firm innovativeness, and from subordinate information-seeking practices to successful technology implementation. Among the research reviewed by Berson et al. (2006), very little deals with organizational learning explicitly. Research has highlighted the role of leadership in creating certain aspects of an organizational culture that can facilitate learning, including openness, participative decision-making, and positive supervisory behaviour (Bapuji & Crossan, 2004). Mazutis and Slawinski (2008) argue that strategic leaders who possess authentic leadership capabilities might actively work towards changing their organization's norms such that inquiry and open discussion of topics, including sensitive ones, will be encouraged. Unlike transformation leaders who encourage dialogue for the purpose of achieving consensus and buy-in to organizational goals (Vera & Crossan, 2004), authentic leaders encourage dialogue around potentially difficult topics in order to foster transparency and openness. The culture likely to emerge in an organization led by an authentic leader would be one in which authentic dialogue is valued and encouraged. Authentic dialogue means that differences are not approached through power struggles, but rather, they are approached as an opportunity to create new understanding (Mazutis & Slawinski, 2008). Some organizational norms can and do inhibit learning and encourage error. However, by fostering self-awareness and balanced processing in both themselves and in followers, authentic leaders model norms that encourage dialogue for the purpose of surfacing dilemmas that exist within the organization (Mazutis & Slawinski, 2008).

Moving from interpreting to integrating is usually more problematic, as it involves 'taking personally constructed cognitive maps and integrating them in a way that develops a shared understanding among the group members' (Crossan et al., 1999, p. 532). Given an open and transparent culture of authentic dialogue, members are able to negotiate mutual adjustments through common language and the dialogical processes that are integral to the learning process (Crossan et al., 1999). Authentic dialogue also supports the flow of newly uncovered knowledge up to the organizational level. This culture of open, balanced, and transparent communication becomes embedded over time in the organization's formal routines and procedures, thereby allowing new norms that emerge from the detection and correction of errors to become institutionalized. Because difficult issues have been allowed to surface, change is more likely, including changes in strategy, structure, and culture (Mazutis & Slawinski, 2008). Organizational learning is fundamentally a process of change and reconciliation of differences that requires individuals to be open to feedback. One of the problems discussed by Argyris and Schon (1978) is that individuals might be unaware of their own biases and unaware that they are not open to having their ideas challenged. However, in an organization that encourages open dialogue, patterns of behaviour emerge whereby organizational members are more open to feedback and less likely to become defensive when challenged. This is an environment that is more conducive to double-loop learning, whereby fundamental changes in norms and behaviours occur (Mazutis & Slawinski, 2008). Some organizational cultures, such as those characterized by participation, openness, and psychological safety, may be more conducive to learning than others (Bapuji & Crossan, 2004; Berson et al., 2006). There are similarities between the characteristics of a learning culture and those of a culture shaped by authentic strategic leaders. These include allowing inquiry, challenging ideas, and **creating** a supportive environment. The main difference, however, is that authentic leaders actively encourage differences to surface (Mazutis & Slawinski, 2008).

TRENDS AND PARADOXES

Three trends have become apparent in scholarship on leadership and organization theory. First, the research focus recently has been on leadership and innovation, knowledge management, and organizational learning. Based on the comparative recency of these components of organization theory, these innovations are understandable. These components of organization theory seem to dominate contemporary empirical scholarship on the role of leadership in organizations. Inherent within this trend is the preponderance of interest in levels of analysis. The levels issue comes essentially from leadership research rather than from organization theory research. In many ways it is an imposed variable. The differences that many scholars would like to see between the various levels are not, in effect, that great. The role of leadership in organization theory is more uniform and universal than many leadership researchers might like to believe. The example of transformational leadership highlights this point. Both transformational and transactional leadership can operate effectively at each of the levels of analysis. Indeed, passive, active, corrective, and developmental exchange leadership are equally manifested and equally effective at all levels of analysis. However, the process by which they operate varies according to the mediation effect of many other variables. In effect, the levels of analysis become another contextual variable within organizations, which varies the manifestation and impact of leadership. If anything, hierarchical level has a greater consistent effect on leadership than does 'level of analysis'.

The second trend continues the move away from the examination of traits and behaviours towards context and process. Uhl-Bein (2006) has underlined the importance of relational leadership and the concomitant role of social process (see Hosking, Chapter 33, this volume). Jackson and Parry (2008) have also noted a swing towards context and process as being the basis of sound explanations of leadership's contribution to organization theory. The many and varied forms of context have occupied the interest of leadership researchers in recent years, and seem set continue to do so for years to come. The process of leadership in organizations, vis-à-vis the investigation of relationships between static and predefined variables, also appears to occupy the interest of researchers.

Concomitant with this trend is the third identifiable trend: i.e. a continuing trend in methodological preference towards qualitative methods, in particular those under the umbrella of ethnographic methods. Hand-in-hand with this trend is the recognition of the domination of leadership scholarship by the transformational/transactional dichotomy. This trend is an artifact of history, and more than anything is a research fashion resulting from a well-researched, plausible, and theoretically sound explanation of leadership. As a result of the transformational/transactional dichotomy and its associated research constructs, the research has been dominated by the highly quantitative psychometric method. Transformational leadership has been unfairly burdened with the label of 'another behavioural theory'. Perhaps the methodologies that usually accompany it have led to this appellation. Therefore, leadership research within the domain of organization theory has also been dominated thus far by the same methodologies. Transformational leadership is certainly a more robust and explanatory construct than its associated methodologies give it credit for. Be that as it may, the expectation is that the trend will move towards alternate methodologies for researching leadership within the context of organization theory. Much organization theory research is undertaken with the unenterprising case study method. The complexity and innovativeness of increasingly popular methodologies for researching leadership will help to add interest to organization theory research.

Three paradoxes have become apparent recently. They all reflect the competing paradigms of leadership and organization theory. In spite of the global financial meltdown of 2008/09, organizations became increasingly larger and more global during that time. However, technology continues to bring people in organizations closer. This apparent paradox is a challenge for leadership. The closer spatiality and temporality of global business is part of the complexity of context that organization theory must accommodate. These factors also increase the urgency of understanding leadership and organization theory from the relational and processual perspective. Moreover, we require research that examines the process of leadership from within the context of these spatial and temporal constraints. The spatial and temporal contexts of leadership have been the subject of recent research endeavours, and they should continue to be for some time yet in organization theory.

Another apparent paradox is that leadership is increasingly identified as being important at lower levels of the organization, yet much scholarship remains wedded to the notion of leadership being the domain of senior managers at the top of the organizational hierarchy. Within organization theory, the concentration is very much on the 'leader'. Within leadership theory, the emphasis is increasingly on the processes of leader*ship* within organizations. In effect, organization structure cannot divest itself from the notion of distributed leadership, even though it can divest itself of a formal leader. Associated with this phenomenon is the realization that leadership scholarship, certainly in the conceptual and populist writing domain, is often at pains to differentiate leadership from management. Paradoxically, organization theory is largely about managing organizations. Leadership is one of the functions (and processes and relations and outcomes) that managers must undertake. Perhaps the resolution of this paradox lies in semantics. The discourse might be clearer if organization theorists removed the word 'leader' from their lexicon, and concentrated on 'manager', 'management', and 'leadership'. In effect, these terms seem to reflect the sum total of the content that they research. It would help if leadership scholars made the same move.

Concomitant with this paradox is the empirical paradox that researchers in many areas of organization theory espouse the aim of researching leadership, yet continue to research the leader, or senior manager. Remember that organization theory is dominated by the notion of the senior manager, and that person's role within the organization structure. The role of leadership within organization theory is one of rational structuralism, and is studied by mainly psychometric methods or the case study method. By contrast, leadership research is concentrating more broadly on processual and relational properties. Leadership is being seen through an interdisciplinary lens. Leadership research is more emotive and idealistic and less rational. It is becoming dominated by narrative analysis, dramaturgy, spirituality, reflexivity, and identity. It is becoming dominated by the disciplines of sociology and anthropology and even psychoanalysis, in order to supplement psychology that has given sterling service thus far. Organization theory might benefit from taking this lead, especially when researching the role of leadership in organizations.

REFERENCES

Adair, J. (2007) *Develop Your Leadership Skills.* London: Kogan Page.

Ahuja, M. K. & Galvin, J. E. (2003) 'Socialization in Virtual Groups', *Journal of Management* 29(2): 161–185.

Allen, M. P., Panian, S. K., & Lotz, R. E. (1979) 'Managerial Succession and Organizational Performance: A Recalcitrant Problem Revisited', *Administrative Science Quarterly* 24: 167–180.

Amabile, T. M. (1998) 'How to Kill Creativity', *Harvard Business Review* September–October: 77–87.

Argyris, C. & Schon, D. (1978) *Organizational Learning: A Theory of Action Perspective.* Reading, MA: Addison-Wesley.

Avolio, B. J. & Bass, B. M. (2002) *Manual for the Multifactor Leadership Questionnaire (Form 5X).* Redwood City, CA: Mind Garden.

Avolio, B. J. & Gardner, W. L. (2005) 'Authentic Leadership Development: Getting to the Root of Positive Forms of Leadership', *The Leadership Quarterly* 16(3): 315–338.

Avolio, B. J. & Kahai, S. R. (2003) 'Adding the "E" to E-Leadership: How it May Impact Your Leadership' *Organizational Dynamics* 31(4): 325–338.

Avolio, B. J., Kahai, S. R., & Dodge, G. E. (2001) 'E-Leadership: Implications for Theory, Research and Practices', *The Leadership Quarterly* 11(4): 615–668.

Baker, A., Jensen, P., & Kolb, D. (2005) 'Dialogue as Experiential Learning', *Management Learning* 36(4): 411–427.

Bales, R. F. (1950) 'A Set of Categories for the Analysis of Small Group Interaction', *American Sociological Review* 15: 257–263.

Baliga, B. R. & Hunt, J. G. (1988) 'An Organizational Life Cycle Approach to Leadership'. In J. G. Hunt, B. R. Baliga, H. P. Dachler, & C. A. Schriesheim (eds), *Emerging Leadership Vistas.* Lexington, MA: Lexington Books.

Bapuji, H. & Crossan, M. (2004) 'From Questions and Answers: Reviewing Organizational Learning Research', *Management Learning* 35(4): 397–417.

Barney, J. B. (1991) 'Firm Resources and Sustained Competitive Advantage', *Journal of Management* 17: 99–120.

Barrick, M. R., Day, D. V., Lord, R. G., & Alexander, R. A. (1991) 'Assessing the Utility of Executive Leadership', *The Leadership Quarterly* 2: 9–22.

Bass, B. M. (1985) *Leadership and Performance Beyond Expectations.* New York: Free Press, 1985.

Bass, B. M. (1990) *Bass & Stodgill's Handbook of Leadership: Theory, Research and Managerial Applications.* New York: Free Press.

Bass, B. M. (2000) 'The Future of Leadership in Learning Organizations', *Journal of Leadership* 7: 18–40.

Bass, B. M. & Avolio, B. J. (1994) *Improving Organizational Effectiveness through Transformational Leadership.* Thousand Oaks, CA: Sage.

Baum, R. J., Locke, E. A., & Kirkpatrick, S. (1998) 'A Longitudinal Study of the Relation of Vision and Vision Communication to Venture Growth in Entrepreneurial Firms', *Journal of Applied Psychology* 83: 43–54.

Beer, M. & Nohria, N. (2000) 'Cracking the Code of Change', *Harvard Business Review* May–June: 133–141.

Behling, O. & Eckel, N. L. (1991) 'Making Sense Out of Intuition', *Academy of Management Executive* 5(1): 46–54.

Bell, B. S. & Kozlowski, S. W. (2002) 'A Typology of Virtual Teams: Implications for Effective Leadership', *Group and Organization Management* 27(1): 14–50.

Berquist, W. (1993) *The Postmodern Organization: Mastering the Art of Irreversible Change.* San Francisco: Jossey-Bass.

Berson, Y., Nemanich, L. A., Waldman, D. A., Galvin, B. M., & Keller, R. T. (2006) 'Leadership and Organizational Learning: A Multiple Levels Perspectives', *The Leadership Quarterly* 17(6): 577–594.

Bertrand, M. & Schoar, A. (2003) 'Managing with Style: The Effect of Managers on Firm Policies', *Quarterly Journal of Economics* 118: 1169–1208.

Blake, R. R. & Mouton, J. S. (1982) 'Management by Grid Principles or Situationalism: Which?', *Group and Organization Studies* 7: 207–210.

Boisot, M. H. (1998) *Knowledge Assets: Securing Competitive Advantage in the Information Economy*. New York: Oxford University Press.

Bono, J. E. & Anderson, M. H. (2005) 'The Advice and Influence Networks of Transformational Leaders', *Journal of Applied Psychology* 90: 1306–1314.

Brass, D. J. & Krackhardt, D. (1999) 'The Social Capital for Twenty-First Century Leaders. In J. G. Hunt, G. E., Dodge, & L. Wong (eds), *Out-of-the Box Leadership: Transforming the 21st Century Army and Other Top Performing Organizations*. Westport, CT: JAI Press.

Brown, M. C. (1982) 'Administrative Succession and Organizational Performance: The Succession Effect', *Administrative Science Quarterly* 27: 1–16.

Brown, M. E. & Gioia, D. A. (2002) 'Making Things Click: Distributive Leadership in an Online Division of an Offline Organization', *The Leadership Quarterly* 13: 397–419.

Bryant, S. E. (2003) 'The Role of Transformational and Transactional Leadership in Creating, Sharing and Exploiting Organizational Knowledge', *The Journal of Leadership and Organizational Studies* 9(4): 32–44.

Burke, C. S., Stagl, K. C., Klein, C., et al. (2006) 'What Types of Leadership Behaviours are Functional in Teams?', *The Leadership Quarterly* 17: 288–307.

Campbell, J. P., Dunnette, M. D., Lawler, E. E., & Weick, K. E. (1970) *Managerial Behaviour, Performance, and Effectiveness*. New York: McGraw-Hill.

Carter, S. M. & West, M. A. (1998) 'Reflexivity, Effectiveness and Mental Health in BBC Production Teams', *Small Group Research* 29: 583–601.

Cascio, W. F. (2000) 'Managing a Virtual Workplace', *Academy of Management Executive* 14(3): 81–90.

Cascio, W. F. & Shurygailo, S. (2003) 'E-Leadership and Virtual Teams', *Organizational Dynamics* 31(4): 362–376.

Chan, A., Hannah, S., & Gardner, W. (2005) 'Veritable Authentic Leadership: Emergence, Functioning, and Impacts'. In W. Gardner, B. Avolio, & F. Walumbwa (eds), *Authentic Leadership Theory and Practice: Origins, Effects and Development. Monographs in Leadership and Management, Volume 3*. Boston, MA: Elsevier.

Collins, J. (2001) *Good to Great*. New York: Harper Collins.

Conger, J. A. (1999) 'Charismatic and Transformational Leadership in Organizations: An Insider's Perspective on these Developing Streams of Research', *The Leadership Quarterly* 10: 145–169.

Conger, J. A. & Kanungo, R. N. (1998) *Charismatic Leadership in Organizations*. Thousand Oaks, CA: Sage.

Crossan, M., Lane, H. W., & White, R. E. (1999) 'An Organizational Learning Framework: From Intuition to Institution', *Academy of Management Review* 24: 522–537.

Davis, D. D. (2004) 'The Tao of Leadership in Virtual Teams', *Organizational Dynamics* 33(1): 47–62.

Day, D. V. & Lord, R. G. (1988) 'Executive Leadership and Organizational Performance', *Journal of Management* 14: 453–464.

Day, D. V., Gronn, P., & Salas, E. (2004) 'Leadership Capacity in Teams', *The Leadership Quarterly* 15: 857–880.

Dirks, K. T. & Ferrin, D. L. (2002) 'Trust in Leadership: Meta-Analytic Findings and Implications for Research and Practice', *Journal of Applied Psychology* 87: 611–628.

Dragoni, L. (2005) 'Understanding the Emergence of State Goal Orientation in Organizational Work Groups: The Role of Leadership and Multilevel Climate Perceptions', *Journal of Applied Psychology* 90: 1084–1095.

Duncan, R. & Weiss, A. (1979) 'Organizational Learning: Implications for Organizational Design', *Research in Organizational Behaviour* 1: 75–123.

Dyck, B., Starke, F. A., Mischke, G. A., & Mauws, M. (2005) 'Learning to Build a Car: An Empirical Investigation of Organizational Learning', *Journal of Management Studies* 42: 387–416.

Easterby-Smith, M. & Lyles, M. A. (2003) *The Blackwell Handbook of Organizational Learning and Knowledge Management*. Malden, MA: Blackwell.

Edmondson, A. (2003) 'Speaking Up in the Operating Room', *Journal of Management Studies* 40: 1419–1452.

Edmondson, A. C. (2002) 'The Local and Variegated Nature of Learning in Organizations: A Group-level Perspective', *Organization Science* 13: 128–146.

Eitzen, D. S. & Yetman, N. R. (1972) 'Managerial Change – Longevity and Organizational Effectiveness', *Administrative Science Quarterly* 17: 1–16.

Feng, J., Lazar, J., & Preece, J. (2004) 'Empathy and Online Interpersonal Trust: A Fragile Relationship', *Behaviour and Information Technology* 23(2): 97–106.

Finkelstein, S. & Hambrick, D. C. (1996) *Strategic Leadership: Top Executives and Their Effects on Organizations*. St. Paul, MN: West.

Fizel, J. F. & D'Itri, M. P. (1999) 'Firing and Hiring of Managers: Does Efficiency Matters?', *Journal of Management* 25(4): 567–585.

Fleishman, E. A., Mumford, M. D., Zaccaro, S. J., et al. (1991) 'Taxonomic Efforts in the Description of Leader Behaviour: A Synthesis and Functional Interpretation', *The Leadership Quarterly* 2: 245–287.

Fry, L. W. (2003) 'Toward a Theory of Spiritual Leadership' *The Leadership Quarterly* 14: 693–727.

Fry, L. W., Vitucci, S., & Cedillo, M. (2005) 'Spiritual Leadership and Army Transformation: Theory, Measurement, and Establishing a Baseline', *The Leadership Quarterly* 16: 835–862.

Gamson, W. A. & Scotch, N. A. (1964) 'Scapegoating in Baseball', *American Journal of Sociology* 70: 69–72.

Gardner, W. L. & Avolio, B. A. (1998) 'The Charismatic Relationship: A Dramaturgical Perspective', *Academy of Management Review* 23: 32–58.

Gardner, W., Avolio, B., Luthans, F., May, D., & Walumbwa, F. (2005) 'Can You See the Real Me?: A Self-Based Model of Authentic Leader and Follower Development', *The Leadership Quarterly* 16(3): 343–372.

Gerstner, C. R. & Day, D. V. (1997) 'Meta-Analytic Review of Leader–Member Exchange Theory: Correlates and Construct Issues', *Journal of Applied Psychology* 82: 827–844.

Gill, R. (2006) *Theory and Practice of Leadership*. London: Sage.

Goffee, R. & Jones, G. (2006) *Why Should Anyone be Led by You? What it Takes to be an Authentic Leader*. Boston, MA: Harvard Business School.

Graen, G. B. & Uhl-Bien, M. (1995) 'Relationship-Based Approach to Leadership: Development of Leader–Member Exchange (LMX) Theory of Leadership over 25 Years: Applying a Multi-Level Multi-Domain Perspective', *The Leadership Quarterly* 6: 219–247.

Grant, R. M. (1996) 'Toward a Knowledge-Based Theory of the Firm', *Strategic Management Journal* 17: 109–122.

Greiner, L. E. (1972) 'Evolution and Revolution as Organizations Grow', *Harvard Business Review* 50: 37–46.

Griffith, T. L. & Meader, D. K. (2004) 'Prelude to Virtual Groups: Leadership and Technology in Semi-Virtual Groups'. In D. J. Pauleen (ed.), *Virtual Teams: Projects, Protocols and Processes*. Hershey, PA: Idea Group Publishing, pp. 231–254.

Hackett, B. (2002) 'Beyond Knowledge Management: New Ways to Work'. In: C. W. Choo, N. Bontis (eds), *The Strategic Management of Intellectual Capital and Organizational Knowledge*. Oxford: Oxford University Press. pp. 725–738.

Hackman, J. R. (2002) *Leading Teams: Setting the Stage for Great Performances*. Boston, MA: Harvard Business School Press.

Hackman, J. R. & Walton, R. E. (1986) 'Leading Groups in Organizations'. In P. S. Goodman (ed.), *Designing Effective Work Groups*. San Francisco: Jossey-Bass.

Hambrick, D. C. & Finkelstein, S. (1987) 'Managerial Discretion: A Bridge Between Polar Views of Organizational Outcomes'. In L. L. Cummings & B. M. Staw (eds), *Research in Organizational Behaviour*. Greenwich, CT: JAI Press.

Harter, J. K., Schmidt, F. L., & Hayes, T. L. (2002) 'Business-Unit-Level Relationship Between Employee Satisfaction, Employee Engagement, and Business Outcomes: A Meta-Analysis', *Journal of Applied Psychology* 87: 268–279.

Hatch, M. J. (1993) 'The Dynamics of Organizational Culture', *Academy of Management Review* 18(4): 657–693.

Hater, J. J., & Bass, B. M. (1988) 'Superiors' Evaluations and Subordinates' Perceptions of Transformational and Transactional Leadership' *Journal of Applied Psychology* 73: 695–702.

Hirst, G., Mann, L., Bain, P., Pirola-Merlo, A., & Richter, A. (2004) 'Learning to Lead: The Development and Testing of a Model of Leadership Learning', *The Leadership Quarterly* 15: 311–327.

Hogan, R. & Kaiser, R. B. (2005) 'What We Know About Leadership', *Review of General Psychology* 9: 169–180.

Hollander, E. P. (1992) 'The Essential Interdependence of Leadership and Followership', *Current Directions in Psychological Science* 1: 71–75.

Horner-Long, P. & Schoenberg, R. (2002) 'Does E-Business Require Different Leadership Characteristics? An Empirical Investigation', *European Management Journal* 20(6): 611–619.

House, R. J. & Baetz, M. L. (1979) 'Leadership: Some Empirical Generalizations and New Research Directions', *Research in Organizational Behaviour* 1: 341–423.

Huff, A. S. (1990) *Mapping Strategic Thought*. Chichester: Wiley.

Hughes, L. (2005) 'Developing Transparent Relationships Through Humour in the Authentic Leader–Follower Relationship'. In W. Gardner, B. Avolio, & F. Walumbwa (eds), *Authentic Leadership Theory and Practice: Origins, Effects and Development, Monographs in Leadership and Management, Volume 3*. Boston, MA: Elsevier.

Ilies, R., Morgeson, F., & Nahrgang, J. (2005) 'Authentic Leadership and Eudaemonic Well-Being: Understanding Leader–Follower Outcomes', *The Leadership Quarterly* 16(3): 373–394.

Jackson, B., & Parry, K. (2008). *A Very Short, Fairly Interesting and Reasonably Cheap Book about Studying Leadership*. London: Sage.

Jacobs, T. O. & Lewis, P. (1992) 'Leadership Requirements in Stratified Systems'. In: R. L. Phillips, & J. G. Hunt (eds), *Strategic Leadership: A Multi-Organizational-Level Perspective*. Westport, CT: Quorom Books.

Jaffee, D. (2001) *Organization Theory – Tension and Change*. New York: McGraw-Hill.

Jaques, E. & Clement, S. D. (1991) *Executive Leadership: A Practical Guide to Managing Complexity*. Arlington, VA: Cason Hall.

Jarvenpaa, S. L. & Tanriverdi, H. (2003) 'Leading Virtual Knowledge Networks', *Organizational Dynamics* 31(4): 403–412.

Joyce, W. F., Nohria, N., & Roberson, B. (2003) *What Really Works*. New York: Harper Business.

Judge, T. A. & Piccolo, R. F. (2004) 'Transformational and Transactional Leadership: A Meta-Analytic Test of Their Relative Validity', *Journal of Applied Psychology* 89: 755–768.

Judge, T. A., Piccolo, R. F., & Ilies, R. (2004) 'The Forgotten Ones? The Validity of Consideration and Initiating Structure in Leadership Research', *Journal of Applied Psychology* 89: 36–51.

Jung, D. I., Chow, C., & Wu, A. (2003) 'The Role of Transformational Leadership in Enhancing Organizational Innovation: Hypotheses and Some Preliminary Findings', *The Leadership Quarterly* 14: 525–544.

Kaiser, R. B. & Hogan, R. (2007) 'The Dark Side of Discretion'. In J. Hunt (series ed.) & R. Hooijberg, J. Hunt, J. Antonakis, K. Boal, & N. Lane (volume eds), *Monographs in Leadership and Management: Vol. 4. Being There Even When You are Not: Leading Through Strategy, Systems and Structure*. Oxford: JAI Press.

Kaiser, R. B., Hogan, R., & Craig, S. B. (2008) 'Leadership and the Fate of Organizations', *American Psychologist* 63(2): 96–110.

Kanter, R. B., Stein, B., & Jick, T. (1992) *The Challenge of Organizational Change*. New York: Free Press.

Kasper-Fuehrer, E. C. & Ashkanasy, N. M. (2001) 'Communicating Trustworthiness and Building Trust in Inter-Organizational Virtual Organizations', *Journal of Management* 27(3): 235–254.

Katz, D. & Kahn, R. L. (1978) *The Social Psychology of Organizations,* 2nd edn. New York: Wiley.

Kavanagh, M. H. & Ashkanasy, N. M. (2006) 'The Impact of Leadership and Change Management Strategy on

Organizational Culture and Individual Acceptance of Change During a Merger', *British Journal of Management* 17: 81–103.

Kernis, M. H. (2003) 'Towards a Conceptualization of Optimal Self-Esteem', *Psychological Inquiry* 14(1): 1–26.

Kotter, J. P. (1990) *A Force for Change: How Leadership Differs from Management.* New York: Free Press.

Kotter, J. P. (1996) *Leading Change.* Boston: Harvard Business School Press.

Kotter, J. P. & Cohen, D. S. (2002) *The Heart of Change: Real-Life Stories of How People Change Their Organizations.* Boston: Harvard Business School Press.

Kouzes, J. M. & Posner, B. Z. (2007) *The Leadership Challenge,* 4th edn. San Francisco, CA: Jossey-Bass.

Kozlowski, S. J. & Doherty, M. L. (1989) 'Integration of Climate and Leadership: Examination of a Neglected Issue', *Journal of Applied Psychology* 74: 546–553.

Kozlowski, S. W. J., Gully, S. M., Salas, E., & Cannon-Bowers, J. A. (1996) 'Team Leadership and Development: Theory, Principles, and Guidelines for Training Leaders and Teams'. In M. M. Beyerlein, D. Johnson, & S. T. Beyerlein (eds), *Interdisciplinary Studies of Work Teams: Vol. 3. Team Leadership.* Greenwich, CT: JAI Press.

Larson, J. R., Foster-Fishman, P. G., & Franz, T. M. (1998) 'Leadership Style and the Discussion of Shared and Unshared Information in Decision Making Groups', *Personality and Social Psychology Bulletin* 24: 482–495.

Lieberson, S. A. & O'Connor, J. F. (1972) 'Leadership and Organizational Performance: A Study of Large Corporations', *American Sociological Review* 37: 117–130.

Likert, R. (1967) *The Human Organization.* New York: McGraw-Hill.

Lord, R. G. (1977) 'Functional Leadership Behaviour: Measurement and Relation to Social Power and Leadership Perceptions', *Administrative Science Quarterly* 22: 114–133.

Lord, R. G. & Brown, D. G. (2004) *Leadership Processes and Follower Self-Identity.* Mahwah, NJ: Erlbaum.

Lowe, K. B., Kroeck, K. G., & Sivasubramaniam, N. (1996) 'Effectiveness Correlates of Transformational and Transactional Leadership: A Meta-Analytic Review of the MLQ Literature', *The Leadership Quarterly* 7: 385–425.

Luthans, F. & Avolio, B. (2003) 'Authentic Leadership Development'. In K. S. Cameron, J. E. Dutton, & R. E. Quinn (eds), *Positive Organizational Scholarship.* San Francisco: Berrett-Koehler, pp. 241–258.

McGrath, J. E. (1962) *Leadership Behaviour: Some Requirements for Leadership Training.* Washington: US Civil Service Commission.

Marion, R. & Uhl-Bien, M. (2001) 'Leadership in Complex Organizations', *The Leadership Quarterly* 12: 389–418.

Mazutis, D. & Slawinski, N. (2008) 'Leading Organizational Learning Through Authentic Dialogue', *Management Learning* 39(4): 437–456.

Meindl, J. R. & Ehrlich, S. B. (1987) 'The Romance of Leadership and the Evaluation of Organizational Performance', *Academy of Management Journal* 30: 91–109.

Meindl, J. R., Ehrlich, S. B., & Dukerich, J. M. (1985) 'The Romance of Leadership', *Administrative Science Quarterly* 30: 78–102.

Miles, R. E., Snow, C. C., Matthews, J. A., Miles, G., & Coleman, H. J. (1997) 'Organizing in the Knowledge Age: Anticipating the Cellular Form', *Academy of Management Executive* 11: 7–25.

Mullen, B. & Copper, C. (1994) 'The Relation Between Group Cohesiveness and Performance: An Integration', *Psychological Bulletin,* 115: 210–227.

Mumford, M. D., Whetzel, D. L., & Reiter-Palmon, R. (1997) 'Thinking Creatively at Work: Organization Influences on Creative Problem Solving', *Journal of Creative Behaviour* 31: 7–17.

Nadler, D. A., Thies, P. K., & Nadler, M. B. (2001) 'Culture Change in the Strategic Enterprise: Lessons from the Field'. In C. L. Cooper, S. Cartwright, & P. C. Earley, (eds), *The International Handbook of Organizational Culture and Climate.* Chichester: John Wiley & Sons.

Nonaka, I. & Takeuchi, H. (1995). *The Knowledge-Creating Company.* New York: Oxford University Press.

Novicevic, M., Harvey, M., Buckley, M., & Brown, J. (2006) 'Authentic Leadership: A Historical Perspective', *Journal of Leadership and Organizational Studies* 13(1): 64–76.

Pfeffer, J. (1977) 'The Ambiguity of Leadership', *Academy of Management Review* 2: 104–112.

Podsakoff, P. M., MacKenzie, S. B., Moorman, R. H., & Fetter, R. (1990) 'Transformational Leader Behaviours and Their Effects on Followers' Trust in Leader, Satisfaction, and Organizational Citizenship Behaviours', *The Leadership Quarterly* 1: 107–142.

Popper, M. & Lipshitz, R. (2000) 'Organizational Learning: Mechanisms, Culture and Feasibility', *Management Learning* 31(2): 181–196.

Pulley, M. L., McCarthy, J., & Taylor, S. (2000) 'E-Leadership in the Networked Economy', *Leadership in Action* 20(3): 1–7.

Redmond, M. E., Mumford, M. D., & Teach, R. (1993) 'Putting Creativity to Work: Effects of Leader Behaviour on Subordinate Creativity', *Organizational Behaviour & Human Decision Processes* 55: 120–151.

Salancik, G. & Pfeffer, J. (1977) 'Constraints on Administrator Discretion: The Limited Influence of Mayors on City Budgets', *Urban Affairs Quarterly,* 12: 475–498.

Schein, E. H. (2004). *Organizational Culture and Leadership,* 3rd edn. San Francisco: Jossey-Bass.

Schippers, M. C., Den Hartog, D. N., Koopman, P. L., & van Knippenberg, D. (2008) 'The Role of Transformational Leadership in Enhancing Team Reflexivity', *Human Relations* 61(11):1593–1616.

Schneider, B. (1998) 'Executive Selection in Context'. Paper presented at the 13th Annual Conference of the Society for Industrial and Organizational Psychology, Dallas, TX.

Seely-Brown, J. & Duguid, P. (1991) 'Organizational Learning and Communities-of-Practice: Toward a Unified View of Working, Learning, and Innovation', *Organization Science* 2: 40–57.

Seltzer, J. & Bass, B. M. (1990) 'Transformational Leadership: Beyond Initiation and Consideration', *Journal of Management* 16: 693–703.

Shamir, B., House, R. J. & Arthur, M. B. (1993) 'The Motivational Effects of Charismatic Leadership: A Self-Concept Based Theory', *Organization Science* 4: 577–594.

Shamir, B. & Howell, J. M. (1999) 'Organizational and Contextual Influences on the Emergence and Effectiveness of Charismatic Leadership', *The Leadership Quarterly* 10(2): 257–283.

Somech, A. (2006) 'The Effects of Leadership Style and Team Process on Performance and Innovation in Functionally Heterogeneous Teams', *Journal of Management* 31: 132–157.

Sosik, J. J. (1997) 'Effects of Transformational Leadership and Anonymity on Idea Generation in Computer-Mediated Groups', *Group & Organization Management* 22: 460–479.

Sparrowe, R. T. & Liden, R. C. (1997) 'Process and Structure in Leader–Member Exchange', *Academy of Management Review* 22: 522–552.

Starbuck, W. H. (1992) 'Learning by Knowledge-Intensive Firms', *Journal of Management Studies* 29: 713–740.

Sternberg, R. J., Kaufman, J. C., & Pretz, J. E. (2003) 'A Propulsion Model of Creative Leadership', *The Leadership Quarterly* 14: 455–473.

Tepper, B. J. (2000) 'Consequences of Abusive Supervision', *Academy of Management Journal* 43: 178–190.

Thomas, A. (1988) 'Does Leadership Make a Difference to Organizational Performance?', *Administrative Science Quarterly* 33: 388–400.

Tjosvold, D., Tang, M. M. L., & West, M. A. (2004) 'Reflexivity for Team Innovation in China: The Contribution of Goal Interdependence', *Group & Organization Management* 29: 540–559.

Tosi, H. L., Misangyi, V. F., Fanelli, A., Waldman, D. A., & Yammarino, F. J. (2004) 'CEO Charisma, Compensation, and Firm Performance', *The Leadership Quarterly* 15: 405–420.

Uhl-Bein, M. (2006) 'Relational Leadership Theory: Exploring the Social Processes of Leadership and Organizing', *The Leadership Quarterly*, 17, 654–676.

Valikangas, L. & Okumara, A. (1997) 'Why Do People Follow Leaders? A Study of a US and a Japanese Change Program', *The Leadership Quarterly* 8(3): 313–337.

Van Knippenberg, D. & Hogg, M. A. (2003) 'A Social Identity Model of Leadership Effectiveness in Organizations'. In B. Staw, & R. M. Kramer (eds), *Research in Organizational Behaviour*. Greenwich, CT: JAI Press, 25: 245–297.

Van Knippenberg, D., van Knippenberg, B., De Cremer, D., & Hogg, M. A. (2004) 'Leadership, Self and Identity: A Review and Research Agenda', *The Leadership Quarterly* 15: 825–856.

Vera, D., & Crossan, M. (2004) 'Strategic Leadership and Organizational Learning', *Academy of Management Review* 29(2): 222–240.

Waldman, D. A., Berson, Y., & Pearce, C. L. (2005). 'Toward an Understanding of Shared Vision and Organizational Learning: The Complementary Roles of Vertical and Shared Leadership. Paper presented at the Academy of Management, Honolulu, HI.

Waldman, D. A., Ramirez, G. G., House, R. J., & Puranam, P. (2001) 'Does Leadership Matter? CEO Leadership Attributes and Profitability Under Conditions of Perceived Environmental Uncertainty', *Academy of Management Journal* 44: 134–144.

Weick, K. E. & Orden, P. W. V. (1990) 'Organizing on a Global Scale: A Research and Teaching Agenda', *Human Resource Management* 29: 49.

Weick, K. E. & Roberts, K. H. (1993) 'Collective Mind in Organizations: Heedful Interrelating on', *Administrative Science Quarterly* 38(3): 357–381.

Wenger, E. C. & Snyder, W. M. (2000) 'Communities of Practice: The Organizational Frontier', *Harvard Business Review* Jan–Feb: 139–145.

Yammarino, F. J. & Dubinsky, A. J. (1994) 'Transformational Leadership Theory: Using Levels of Analysis to Determine Boundary Conditions', *Personnel Psychology* 47: 787–811.

Yammarino, F. J. & Spangler, W. D. (1998) 'Transformational and Contingent Reward Leadership: Individual, Dyad, and Group Levels of Analysis', *The Leadership Quarterly* 9: 27–54.

Yukl, G. (2006) *Leadership in Organizations, 6th edn.* Upper Saddle River, NJ: Prentice Hall.

Yukl, G. (2008) 'How Leaders Influence Organizational Effectiveness', *The Leadership Quarterly* 19: 708–722.

Yukl, G. & Howell, J. M. (1999) 'Organizational and Contextual Influences on the Emergence and Effectiveness of Charismatic Leadership', *The Leadership Quarterly* 10: 257–283.

Yukl, G., Gordon, A., & Taber, T. (2002) 'A Hierarchical Taxonomy of Leadership Behaviour: Integrating a Half Century of Behaviour Research', *Journal of Leadership and Organization Studies* 9(1): 15–32.

Zaccaro, S. J. & Klimoski, R. J. (2001) 'The Nature of Organizational Leadership: An Introduction'. In S. J. Zaccaro & R. J. Klimoski (eds), *The Nature of Organizational Leadership*. San Francisco: Jossey-Bass.

Zaccaro, S. J., Rittman, A. L., & Marks, M. A. (2001) 'Team Leadership', *The Leadership Quarterly* 12: 451–483.

Zigurs, I. (2003) 'Leadership in Virtual Teams: Oxymoron or Opportunity?', *Organizational Dynamics* 31(4): 325–338.

Zimmermann, P., Wit, A., & Gill, R. (2008) 'The Relative Importance of Leadership Behaviours in Virtual and Face-to-Face Communication Settings', *Leadership* 4(3): 321–337.

6

Perspectives
on Strategic Leadership

Jean-Louis Denis, Veronika Kisfalvi,
Ann Langley and Linda Rouleau

INTRODUCTION

In an introduction to a special issue of *Strategic Management Journal* (SMJ) in 1989, Donald Hambrick (1989: 6) defined the study of 'strategic leadership' as focusing on *'the people who have overall responsibility for an organization – the characteristics of those people, what they do, and how they do it.'* He encompassed in his definition individual executives (e.g., CEOs, general managers of divisions), top management teams, and other governance bodies. This is the starting definition that we adopt in this chapter, although we shall later suggest that there are reasons to take into account the potential for people at levels below top management to influence significantly organizational strategy.

Hambrick (1989) argues that the strategic leadership task can be distinguished from leadership at other levels of the organization in four ways. First, strategic leadership demands a focus on both the internal and external environments of the organization and a concern with positioning it within its context. Secondly, strategic leadership tends to involve the navigation of greater degrees of complexity and ambiguity than leadership at other levels. Thirdly, strategic leadership is multifunctional and integrative in contrast to the often more specialized tasks of operating management. Finally, unlike leadership at the front lines, strategic leadership involves leading through other leaders.

As can be seen, the expectations placed on strategic leaders are enormous. The study of strategic leadership involves not only understanding the relationships between leaders and followers but also how strategic leaders go about orchestrating the decisions and activities that will orient the future of the organization. The premise here is that top managers can have an important influence on organizational choice and evolution (Child, 1997). In this chapter, we review four different perspectives on strategic leadership that have developed in the literature over the last 40 years. The first two perspectives place the greatest emphasis on the *characteristics* of leaders *(who they are)*, the first dimension of Hambrick's (1989) definition above. The other two perspectives focus more on *what strategic leaders do and how they do it*, the second part of Hambrick's (1989) definition. Table 6.1 summarizes the nature of these approaches, their key foci, and their strengths and weaknesses as approaches to understanding strategic leadership.

To illustrate these four perspectives, we apply them to a particular case of strategic leadership that has been well-documented in the literature – the case of Steinberg Incorporated, a Canadian grocery firm. Five sources of data inspired this analysis:

- Company annual reports
- A company history recounting the rise and fall of the firm (Gibbon & Hadekel, 1990)
- An in-depth study of the firm's strategy (Mintzberg & Waters, 1982)
- A documentary film of a management meeting produced by the National Film Board of Canada *(After Mr. Sam,* 1974*)* that was subsequently transcribed and analyzed by several communications scholars in an edited book (Cooren, 2007)

Table 6.1　Four perspectives on strategic leadership

	Who strategic leaders are		What strategic leaders do	
	Strategic leadership as collective cognition	Strategic leadership as individual inspiration	Strategic leadership as political action	Strategic leadership as social practice
Focus	The impact of top management team members' personalities and cognitions on strategic decisions and performance	The histories, visions, qualities, weaknesses, emotions and motivations of specific individual leaders that underlie their behaviour	How leaders position themselves politically in order to act strategically. How leaders control internal political games in their organizations	The micro-level activities strategic leaders engage in to produce organizational strategy day-to-day
Key variants and labels	'Upper echelons' theory	'Great man' theories 'Psychodynamic' approaches 'Visionary' or 'transformational leadership'	'Resource dependence' 'Leading with power' 'Organizational politics'	'Strategy as practice' 'Doing leadership'
Foundational authors	Hambrick & Mason (1984)	Zaleznik & Kets de Vries (1975)	Pfeffer (1992a, 1992b); Eisenhardt & Bourgeois (1988)	Knights & Willmott (1992); Alvesson & Sveningsson (2003)
Units of analysis	Top management teams as a collective unit	CEOs or remarkable public leaders	Senior executives in relation to their teams and external actors	Individuals whose activities can contribute to constituting strategy
Epistemological roots	Positivist	Interpretive	Positivist or interpretive	Interpretive or discursive
Typical research methods	Statistical analysis based on archival data or survey data	In-depth life history based case studies of individual leaders	Case studies of top team decision making; some survey-based studies	Ethnographic studies, narratives of practice, conversation analysis
Strengths and contributions	Has shown that top management teams do 'make a difference' Allows generalization of results for basic TMT variables + performance	Provides a holistic view of strategists as feeling–thinking–acting human beings Reveals the emotional dimensions of leadership	Illuminates the political dimensions of leadership and its shifting, distributed nature Introduces a dynamic dimension to leadership	Illuminates the lived experience and tacit skills of strategists Broadens notion of strategic leadership to leaders at all levels
Weaknesses and limitations	Weakness of demographic proxies Contradictory findings Hard to apply to individual cases	Overemphasis on role of individual leaders Post-hoc cases subject to hindsight bias Hard to generalize	Contradictions between leading with power and containing 'politics' Multiple and confusing definitions of power	Generates contextual and descriptive knowledge that may be hard to generalize
Illustrative application to the Steinberg case	A poor strategic decision is seen to be the result of groupthink, i.e., defective cognitive processes based on extrapolation from previous successes and a particular mix of executives (Gibbon & Hadekel, 1990)	The personal characteristics and history of Sam Steinberg contribute to his visionary strategy, but lead him simultaneously to make unfortunate choices surrounding succession (Kets de Vries et al., 2007)	Tactics for consolidating power in the hands of the founder and his family lead to divisive political manoeuvring among executives at other levels and a neglect of strategic issues. (Gibbon & Hadekel, 1990)	The micro-practices adopted by a strategic leader in a management meeting contribute to enabling the renewal of organizational structure but also to maintaining family dominance (Pomerantz & Denvir, 2007)

- A psychodynamic analysis of the firm's leadership by Kets de Vries, et al. (2007)

The company was founded in 1913, and grew under the leadership of Sam Steinberg to become the largest supermarket chain in Quebec, with investments in real estate, restaurants and department stores. Following his death, family infighting ultimately led to the sale of the firm and its eventual disappearance.

FOUR PERSPECTIVES ON STRATEGIC LEADERSHIP

Strategic leadership as collective cognition

Upper echelons theory

The notion of strategic leadership as collective cognition underpins 'upper echelons theory,' the most well-developed approach to strategic leadership in the scholarly literature. This perspective originated with an influential article by Hambrick and Mason (1984) that subsequently launched a prolific stream of empirical research. Hambrick and Mason's (1984) key arguments were (1) that given human cognitive limitations (Simon, 1955), the particular experience, personalities and value preferences of top managers could have an important impact on strategic decisions and thence on the performance of firms through the way in which environmental and organizational stimuli might be filtered and interpreted; (2) that demographic variables such as age, tenure and experience could provide useful proxies or indicators for the more psychological variables underlying the theory; and (3) that the aggregate characteristics of the top management team (TMT) as a group were likely to be more predictive of strategic decision-making patterns and performance than those of the CEO alone because of the collective nature of many strategic decisions.

Starting from this basic theoretical skeleton, empirical researchers embarked on a quest to verify if and when various characteristics of the TMT were related to strategic choices and performance (for reviews of this literature, see Carpenter et al., 2004; Certo et al., 2006; Finkelstein & Hambrick, 1996). For example, in a typical early study, Bantel and Jackson (1989) found that TMTs that were younger, less tenured, more highly educated and more functionally heterogeneous were more innovative. A recent meta-analysis of this body of research found that team size and team functional heterogeneity were two variables that were consistently associated with higher financial performance (Certo et al., 2006). Some studies

have also incorporated moderating variables such as environmental turbulence (Keck, 1997), national culture (Wiersema & Bird, 1993) and managerial discretion (Crossland & Hambrick, 2007; Hambrick, 2007).

Top management team diversity, decision making and performance

Perhaps the most crucial and interesting issue that has both fascinated and frustrated researchers in the upper echelons stream is how TMT cognitive diversity or heterogeneity affects strategic decisions and performance. It is worth devoting some attention to this issue as it reveals starkly two interrelated difficulties with this overall research stream: the limitations of using demographic proxies for cognitive and personality variables, and the inability of the methods usually adopted by researchers in this stream to capture the processes by which team characteristics actually influence decision making.

Specifically, upper echelons theorists have argued that to overcome cognitive biases associated with excessive group cohesion (Janis & Mann, 1977) decision makers need to bring different viewpoints to the table to ensure adequate informational and cognitive diversity (Dooley & Fryxell, 1999; Jarzabkowski & Searle 2004; Kilduff et al., 2000), and to encourage constructive disagreement over diverse perspectives (Edmondson et al., 2003; Olson et al., 2007). While some researchers have confirmed the theoretical ideas (Bantel & Jackson, 1989; Wiersema & Bantel, 1992), others have found contradictory results (Ancona & Caldwell, 1992; Boeker, 1997). One possible explanation for this is that while a diverse team will have a rich information base, this can come at the expense of efficiency and can be especially problematic in highly turbulent environments where decision speed is important. In other words, diversity has a dual and paradoxical effect.

It has not been easy to untangle these relationships with the traditional methods of the upper echelons school. In particular, demographic indicators of diversity have not proven to be consistent or robust predictors of strategic orientations or performance (Carpenter et al., 2004; Edmondson et al., 2003; Finkelstein & Hambrick, 1996; West & Schwenk, 1996). The assumption that demographic variables are adequate surrogates for cognition has itself been challenged (Kilduff et al., 2000; Lawrence, 1997) and some attempts have been made to measure TMT cognitions such as attitudes, values and beliefs (Kilduff et al., 2000), belief and goal preference diversity (Olson et al., 2007), and cognitive style (Gallén, 2006; Hough & Ogilvie, 2005) directly, through surveys administered to TMT members. Other researchers, some using qualitative approaches, have looked at psychological diversity and personality characteristics of TMT members (Hiller & Hambrick, 2005; Jarzabkowski & Searle, 2004; Kauer et al., 2007; Kisfalvi & Pitcher, 2003; Pitcher & Smith, 2001).

This brings us to the second limitation of this stream of research: that the correlational and archival methods used provide limited access to the processes by which strategic leaders actually influence decisions and performance. This has led some scholars to talk about 'opening up the black box' to better understand the psychological and social processes underlying TMT decision making (Hambrick, 2007; Lawrence, 1997). Yet, while researchers have often called for 'more informed, salient, and interesting' qualitative or clinical research (e.g. Priem et al., 1999: 935), concerns about gaining adequate access, controlling variety and generalization have often been significant inhibitors (Hambrick, 2007). In fact, research in the upper echelons stream generally embeds positivist assumptions and aims to improve knowledge by developing increasingly dense nomological networks of relationships in the form of generalizable causal laws relating team member characteristics to decision processes and outcomes. In contrast, most qualitative studies of strategic leaders have adopted different epistemological assumptions, have focused on different issues, and can usually be better classified under one of the other perspectives described in this chapter.

Summary

Overall, the upper echelons body of research on strategic leadership has been particularly influential. One of the strengths of this stream is that it has shown fairly conclusively that strategic leaders can and do make some difference to strategic decisions and to performance outcomes. This research stream also clearly established the importance of considering top management teams as a whole in addition to or instead of focusing on individual leaders, although there still remain some questions concerning who should be considered part of the TMT (Carpenter et al., 2004; Roberto, 2003). Finally, recent studies have become more creative in reaching beyond demographic proxies, and have also begun introducing more complex explanatory variables (Barkema and Shvyrkov, 2007; Simsek et al., 2005). On the other hand, this perspective has several limitations related to the somewhat superficial nature of many of the variables considered, as well as the lack of attention to dynamics and process (see also Pettigrew, 1992).

Application: strategic leadership as collective cognition in the Steinberg case

With its emphasis on identifying cross-sectional relationships among coarse-grained variables, the generalizations of the upper echelons approach are not easily applicable to a single case. Where researchers have tried to test these ideas using longitudinal comparisons (Clark and Soulsby, 2007; Pitcher and Smith, 2001), the idiosyncratic features of the cases have not unsurprisingly been shown to overwhelm the deterministic patterns identified in correlational studies (which after all explain only a limited proportion of variance). Nevertheless, the theory underlying the upper echelons approach deals with the role of human cognitive limitations and biases in collective decision making and this may have relevance to the Steinberg case.

A significant phenomenon in the history of Steinberg was the role of discount pricing as a strategy to increase market share and performance (Gibbon & Hadekel, 1990; Mintzberg & Waters, 1982). This strategy lay at the root of the initial explosive growth of the firm in the 1930s, when the founder Sam Steinberg introduced overnight the no-frills low-price supermarket formula that would come to dominate the industry. The strategy was successfully repeated in 1969–1971 under the leadership of Jack Levine, resulting again in increased market share and the closure of independent retailers. Thus, in the early 1980s when a young Steinberg manager fresh from Harvard Business School enthusiastically proposed another aggressive price discount programme, members of the top management team who remembered previous glories were cognitively primed to see it positively. When a new president with no experience of the Quebec food retailing environment was added to the mix, the conditions were in place for a poorly conceived collective decision which proved disastrous for the firm (Gibbon & Hadekel, 1990). Industry conditions had changed drastically from the 1970s. The firm's main competitors were no longer weak independents but strong retail chains with superior cost structures. They immediately matched or improved on Steinberg's price discounts and forced a humiliating retreat.

Note that a mechanical assessment of the demographic diversity present in the top management team might not have predicted this error in judgement (indeed there was no doubt relatively high demographic diversity in terms of age and functional origins). However, the decision becomes intelligible when the mix of backgrounds and experience of the people involved are considered in more detail: a young manager enthusiastically promoting a policy that older managers viewed as the source of their success, combined with a new president who had no experiential base that might enable him to challenge it. The situation was ripe for a form of collective cognition close to what Janis and Mann (1977) called 'groupthink.'

Strategic leadership as individual inspiration

At the cusp of the disciplines of strategy and organizational behavior, strategic leadership research has been marked by cycles of interest in individual strategists, the forces that inspire them and their own inspirational role in strategy making. This perspective can be seen as an outgrowth of the 'great man' or 'heroic' theories of leadership (Bass & Bass, 2008). Following Hambrick and Mason's (1984) launching of the upper echelons approach described above, the importance of the CEO tended to be downplayed. However, evidence has emerged that considering the CEO as just another member of the team is not always appropriate and can lead researchers astray (Carpenter et al., 2004). The CEO's power, if ignored, can muddle results (Pitcher & Smith, 2001). Moreover, CEOs seem to be an identifiable 'breed apart', with characteristics that differ from those of their TMT, arising out of both corporate and 'domestic' (i.e. childhood) experiences (Norburn, 1989).

Strategic leadership and deep purpose

One stream of research that emphasized the role of individual strategic leaders emerged in the 1980s using an interpretive, psychodynamic framework. It concerned itself with the inner life of the strategist, believed to be the source of strategic orientations; because of the power he or she held, this 'inner theater' (Kets de Vries, 1996: 853; see Kets de Vries & Balazs, Chapter 28, this volume) would be enacted in, and therefore have a major impact on the firm's direction. Abraham Zaleznik, one of the founders of this stream of research, explored the entrepreneurial personality differences between leaders and managers and the importance of leaders' formative years (Zaleznik, 1977, 1990; Zaleznik & Kets de Vries, 1975). Manfred F. R. Kets de Vries and colleagues expanded on Zaleznik's work. Rooted in clinical experience and in-depth case studies, they explored the links between leaders' early experiences, their personality styles, and the impact on organizational strategy, structure and culture (Kets de Vries & Miller, 1984). Authors linked leaders' 'magnificent obsessions', rooted in unconscious desires and conflicts (Kets de Vries, 1996; Kisfalvi, 2002; Noël, 1989), to the strategic orientations of

their firms and the types of relationships they established with their teams and employees. More recently, others explored strategic persistence as an outgrowth of the CEO's deeply rooted personal issues (Kisfalvi, 2000) and the difficulties that such issues can pose in TMT decision-making processes (Kisfalvi & Pitcher, 2003).

Charismatic leaders have also received attention in this literature. Also rooted in the 'heroic' tradition, this stream sees leaders as exceptionally gifted individuals exercising magnetism and power over others and uniting them in a higher purpose (Bass & Bass, 2008; see Conger, Chapter 7, this volume). For psychodynamically oriented researchers, charisma was of interest, since it touched on the deep, unconscious links uniting leader and follower (Schneider & Shrivastava, 1988). Charisma has been associated with transformational leadership (Bass & Bass, 2008; Burns, 1978), a concept that has increasingly attracted strategic leadership researchers' interest (Boal & Hooijberg, 2000; Dusya & Crossan, 2004).

In addition to potential contributions for theory-building and research design (Kisfalvi & Pitcher, 2003; Pitcher et al., 2000), the thrust of this work has been to gain a better understanding of leaders and their motivations, to help leaders avoid falling prey to their own excesses, and to assist organizational stakeholders in ensuring that their firms are managed in constructive ways (Kets de Vries & Miller, 1985; Pitcher, 1993). To this end, authors have developed typologies based on psychoanalytical personality categories. Perhaps the best known, using terminology developed out of the pathologies encountered in psychoanalytic clinical experience, categorizes CEOs and their firms as compulsive, dramatic, suspicious, detached or depressive, and then traces their impact on their organizations (Kets de Vries & Miller, 1984). Another typology, based on psychological tests designed for more 'normal' individuals combined with TMT members' perceptions of one another, identified three types of leaders – artists, craftsmen and technocrats – and traced their impact on succession processes and the evolution of strategy and performance within a large organization (Pitcher, 1995).

Visionary leadership

In the increasingly turbulent environment of the 1980s, researchers also began to look more closely at vision and visionary leadership (Bass & Bass, 2008). Visionary leaders were thought to possess an acute ability to sense trends in the marketplace, to articulate appropriate organizational goals and to provide a roadmap for followers as well as to empower and engage them emotionally (Westley &

Mintzberg, 1989). In the psychodynamically oriented literature, the capacity to envision and vision content were seen as rooted in leaders' formative experiences (Kets de Vries et al., 1994; Lapierre, 1989).

In a special issue of Strategic Management Journal devoted to strategic leadership, Westley & Mintzberg (1989) tackled the specific question of strategic vision. Challenging the commonly held view in the literature of vision as unidirectional, they emphasized its dynamic and relational nature. For these authors, strategic visionaries are guided by deeply rooted experience in their field, gut feelings and their ability to innovate. They are also able to communicate their vision to followers through words, actions and symbols, evoking an emotional response and creating a sense of mutual empowerment.

Summary

Research oriented toward understanding what moves individual strategists has rehabilitated their role in the strategy process. An alternative to the positivism that has dominated the upper echelons work described earlier, this perspective integrates emotions and presents a more holistic picture of the strategist as a feeling–thinking–acting being. However, as it is often based on single-case or ethnographic studies, generalizations are problematic. Outcomes are often attributed to a single individual, whereas it is increasingly clear that CEOs do not act alone. Psychodynamic studies rely on retrospective understandings of leaders' motivations, with researchers constructing narratives *a posteriori* that might explain relationships too neatly; finally, these studies can sometimes be overly focused on pathology.

Application: strategic leadership as individual inspiration in the Steinberg case

Within this perspective, the rise and fall of Steinberg, Inc., could be looked at as the result of the inner world, vision and orientations of its entrepreneurial CEO. This is just how Mintzberg and Waters (1982) studied the evolution of strategy in this firm, attributing the initial success of the company's expansion to Sam Steinberg's vision. While these authors provide only a brief account of Sam Steinberg's childhood and its possible role in the evolution of his business, Kets de Vries et al. (2007), working within the psychodynamic framework, focus on *'the effects of Sam Steinberg's inner world on the family business'* (p. 233) and in particular on succession issues. They examine the roots of this world in Steinberg's early experiences: the lack of an adequate father figure; his mother's dominant presence throughout

his life (he *'would forever quote his mother's maxims to senior ... executives'*, p. 218; her portrait hung in the firm's boardroom for years after her death); her own personal history (orphaned at 13, as the eldest child she attempted unsuccessfully to take on responsibility for her siblings) and forceful personality; her failed marriage to a weak man and her designation of Sam (the second oldest son) as family leader when he himself was just in his teens; and his experiences as an adolescent working in his mother's store, exposed to her leadership style and values (e.g. family first, hard work, honesty, treating customers fairly and well).

The authors conclude that the absence of a strong father, his mother assuming the provider role and her 'anointment' (p. 231) of the young Sam as replacement for the ideal husband she never had, conditioned his attitude toward authority and forged his extreme independent-mindedness, his need to be in charge and his centralized control of the business, making the question of succession very difficult. This need for control was also behind Sam's sometimes problematic relationships with his management team and the appointment of a weak successor. They also suggest that Sam's 'family first' philosophy, mirroring his mother's, was originally the source of his successful strategy of steady expansion and diversification (providing jobs for members of his large extended family) but that it ultimately weakened the company.

Strategic leadership as political action

Studies of strategic leadership rooted in the two previous perspectives tend to assume implicitly or explicitly that, through their positions, executives at the top automatically have the power required to influence their organizations and to implement decisions. Another set of authors have problematized this assumption and argued that power is an inherent aspect of strategic leadership that needs further exploration (Pettigrew, 1977; Pfeffer, 1992a, 1992b; see Gordon, Chapter 14, this volume). Because top executives face decisions that often challenge the current allocation of resources (Eisenhardt & Bourgeois, 1988; Pettigrew, 1992; Roberto, 2004), leaders need to mobilize and commit power to strategic orientations in a context of competing interests (Pfeffer, 1992a).

Power is defined here as *'a causal relation between the preferences of an actor regarding an outcome and the outcome itself'*, while 'politics' refers to individual or group behaviour that *'makes a claim against the resource-sharing system of the organization'* (Pettigrew, 1977: 81). Paradoxically, while power is seen as necessary for effective strategic leadership, political games are often seen as problematic, as they may reduce the ability for joint problem-solving (Eisenhardt et al., 1997; Mintzberg, 1983). How then can strategic leaders mobilize power without suffering the detrimental effects of politics? We examine in turn the literature dealing with the two poles of this dilemma.

Leading with power

According to Pfeffer (1992a, 1992b), aspiring leaders who do not pay attention to their power resources and to the network of power relations in their environment will not be in a position to get things done. He argues that leaders need to (1) develop a clear definition of what they are trying to achieve, (2) diagnose the patterns of dependence and interdependence that are important to their objectives, (3) analyse competing views on their initiatives, (4) develop an understanding of who is in a position to exert influence, (5) analyse their power bases (structural positions, expertise, positions in communications networks) and identify the power that needs to be developed to adapt to the evolving context and (6) identify legitimate strategies and tactics for exercising influence.

While his prescriptions may appear to be static and over-rational, Pfeffer (1992a, 1992b) also underlines the importance of an alignment between changing context and contingencies and power bases and tactics. Power can never be taken for granted, and its mobilization by leaders may produce unexpected effects. In an empirical study of strategic change in public hospitals, Denis et al., (1996) observed that some leadership tactics were credibility enhancing and others were credibility draining, leading to gains or losses in power. For example, tactics such as 'fait-accompli' that could be successful in achieving substantive change in the short term could sometimes result in a loss of power in the longer term as peoples' appreciation of the leader changed, thereby undermining his or her position. The ability to stay in leadership positions is thus influenced by the way in which leaders exert power (Denis et al., 2001; Pfeffer, 1992a; Pettigrew, 1992). This brings us to the dark side of the political action perspective.

Containing politics in decision-making processes

The previous section deals with sources of influence and the dynamics involved in leading with power. A second stream of work focuses on the processes used by strategic leaders to achieve closure of decisions in a highly volatile and political environment. Eisenhardt and colleagues (Bourgeois & Eisenhardt, 1988; Eisenhardt, 1989; Eisenhardt & Bourgeois, 1988) studied decision-making processes in the microcomputer industry using in-depth case studies. One of their key findings is that organizations that are more effective in making strategic decisions implement processes to avoid the intensification of political games. While conflict around substantive issues appears to be key to TMT effectiveness, the problem is to find ways to channel the diversity of viewpoints (and implicitly of interest and values) in order to avoid the emotional side of conflicts. Several strategies are identified to contain politics, such as the promotion of a common vision, the use of more information, generation of more alternatives and input from a limited number of key counsellors with specific experience or expertise (Eisenhardt et al., 1997).

More recently, Roberto (2004) published a study on the attributes of decision-making processes that reconcile the need for efficiency (rational decisions) with the need for consensus (the political problem). These included (1) clear definition of decision criteria, (2) elimination of token options to focus attention on credible alternatives and (3) making of conditional choices to foster rapid closure of the decision process. Based on a literature review of TMT effectiveness, process choices and strategies also appear to play a critical role in the ability of leaders to manage divergent interests (Edmondson et al., 2003).

Another issue raised by this literature is how the distribution of power among TMT members affects decision making and performance. Eisenhardt and Bourgeois (1988) found that autocratic leaders stimulated clandestine political activity among team members because people had no legitimate means to exert influence. It seems in fact that either extreme centralization or extreme decentralization (power dilution) may increase political games. Based on a survey of US hospitals, Smith and colleagues (2006) found that TMTs in which power was concentrated among a limited number of team members achieved better performance (see also Roberto, 2003). One of the limits of this line of research lies in the assumption that leaders will always be able to integrate the decision-making process in the face of personal or group interests. The reality may be somewhat different, especially in pluralistic settings where groups have highly disparate goals (Denis et al., 2001).

Summary

First, this literature suggests that the mobilization of power may enhance leaders' ability to influence their organizations strategically, but it may also compromise a leadership position if the tactics used are perceived as illegitimate. Secondly, the power distribution in organizations may influence the intensity of politics. Thirdly, strategic leaders rely not only on their power base and tactics but also on process strategies to contain political games and to foster decision closure. On a more critical note, there is an inherent contradiction in some of this research. Political games and clashes among divergent interests will be more easily contained if they are less intense. Put differently, despite their best intentions, strategic leaders may not always be able to implement legitimate structured decision-making processes. The challenge for leaders is to hold enough power to control politics.

Application: strategic leadership as political action in the Steinberg case

To underline the political dimension of strategic leadership in the Steinberg case, Gibbon and Hadekel's (1990) history of the rise and fall of the firm is often revealing, and never more so than in the passages describing the events surrounding the succession of Sam Steinberg as CEO.

Sam Steinberg had always privileged family members for key positions in the firm. When he retired as CEO in the 1970s, he appointed one of his sons-in-law as president of the company but maintained his position as Chairman of the Board. The new president (Mel Dobrin) had been a competent analyst in the firm but for many observers he lacked the profile to hold the CEO position. During his mandate as president of Steinberg, he rarely made decisions, according to Gibbon and Hadekel's informants. When Sam Steinberg was outside the country on vacation, he continued to call many times a day to supervise the company. Board members were considered to be symbolic figures without any key roles. Referring to the ideas from the political action perspective described above, Sam Steinberg essentially consolidated and maintained power in his own hands by naming a weaker person as president, while creating a power vacuum below him, a situation ripe for the flourishing of political games, especially after his death in 1978.

Mel Dobrin's wife, Mitzi Steinberg, had progressively taken on important responsibilities in the company and became the principal shareholder when her father died. While her husband became Chairman of the Board, Jack Levine, a former vice-president of commercial operations was appointed president and CEO. However, he was unable to work with Mitzi Steinberg and could not consolidate his position as strategic leader. A collective strategic leadership group

with the power to move the organization forward (Denis et al., 2001) failed to emerge, with the result that strategic orientation of the company was neglected. As Gibbon and Hadekel (1990) state, *'The decision process was pathetically disturbed, blocked by intestinal battles and no-one assumed responsibility.'* The inability to build a coalition for strategic leadership continued until the firm hired Irving Ludmer, another ex-vice president in 1984. Although Ludmer succeeded in turning the company around, he too eventually became involved in power struggles with Mitzi Steinberg that ultimately led to the sale of the firm. Clearly, it would be difficult to explain the fortunes of this firm without some understanding of these intense political dynamics.

Strategic leadership as social practice

Leadership as a practical accomplishment

The social practice perspective on strategic leadership emerged from a dissatisfaction with traditional research on leadership that was seen as too disconnected from everyday practical experience. Knights and Willmott (1992) were amongst the first authors to conceptualize leadership processes by focusing on the practical accomplishments of senior managers. Drawing on a brief extract from a recorded meeting between top managers in a UK insurance company, they showed how leadership is constituted, how it is accomplished and how it occurs over time through actions and interactions. More than a decade later, Alvesson and Sveningsson (2003) published a provocative paper that argues for the need to rethink leadership as a mundane activity that managers 'do.' According to these authors, leadership is accomplished daily through simple activities such as listening, informal chatting and cheerful interaction. This view argues for the study of leadership through the routinized character of organizational life (see Alvesson, Chapter 11, this volume).

Meanwhile, researchers in the field of strategy have developed the strategy-as-practice perspective which examines in micro-level detail how leaders' behaviours come to influence strategic orientations (Jarzabkowski et al., 2007; Johnson et al., 2003). From a practice perspective, strategic leadership needs to be viewed as a set of collective practices produced and reproduced through time that positions the organization in its context. It is in this sense that Denis et al. (2005; 2007) have associated strategic leadership with the creation of value-based networks constituted through routines and conversations. Such a view suggests that successful strategic leadership is a long-term project patiently accomplished through daily activities and requiring experience, timing, social awareness and relational capability.

A number of theoretical frameworks have been mobilized to aid understanding of the practices of strategic leadership. For example, Hodgkinson and Clarke (2007) draw on cognitive psychology and social cognition in order to propose a two-dimensional framework for simultaneously investigating the cognitive style of leaders and their observed behaviours. Denis et al. (2007) propose a multifaceted framework, drawing together actor–network theory, conventionalist theory and social practice theories, in order to rethink strategic leadership in pluralistic contexts. Behind these theoretical rethinking exercises, researchers have been concerned to develop research agendas for getting closer to strategic practices in action and to recognize the practical skills strategic leaders mobilize when they are strategizing.

Focusing attention on activities and discourse

Although the strategy-as-practice perspective recognizes that middle managers and lower-level employees can be important strategic leaders (Balogun & Johnson, 2004; Mantere, 2005; Rouleau, 2005), exercising this role at their own level of action (Vaara et al., 2004), most strategic leadership studies adopting a social practice perspective have so far tended to focus on top management teams, looking either at their everyday activities or their discourse.

By trying to identify the set of activities strategic teams engage in during the formulation and implementation of strategic change, researchers associated with the strategy-as-practice perspective have offered unique insight into the exercise of leadership. For example, Paroutis and Pettigrew (2007) explored the dynamics of strategic teams in multi-business firms, viewing the recursive (supporting, coordinating, collaborating) and adaptive (executing, initiating, reflecting) activities of these teams in shaping the context as their main strategic leadership task. Drawing on activity theory, Jarzabkowski (2003) studied the role of the top management teams in three UK universities undergoing strategic change. She showed that through their daily strategic practices (e.g. planning, income generation, etc.) the TMTs of the three universities studied distributed shared interpretations predisposing the organization for continuity or stimulating change.

For their part, researchers adopting a discursive perspective have studied how corporate management can mobilize and appropriate a specific kind of strategy discourse to attempt to influence

people from inside and outside their organizations (Mantere, 2005; see Fairhurst, Chapter 36, this volume). For example, using critical discourse analysis, Laine and Vaara (2007) studied the discourse surrounding strategy development in an engineering and consulting group, showing the complex empowering/disempowering effects that occur when managers draw on the language of strategy to promote the value of their own role in the firm, simultaneously undervaluing the role of others. By focusing on the micro-processes of persuasion in ordinary conversations among members of management teams, Samra-Fredericks (2003) examined the conversations of one TMT in minute detail and identified rhetorical features that she argues enabled one strategist (not in a position of hierarchical authority over others) to establish legitimacy for a new strategic orientation. These rhetorical devices all reveal the mobilization of tacit knowledge and social skills to influence others, thus showing how strategic leaders 'do' strategy in their daily activities.

Summary

By paying attention to the hidden activities and discourses underlying strategic leadership, a social practice perspective produces knowledge that is connected with strategists' lived experience. Indeed, this perspective provides 'lay' theories that strategic leaders can use pragmatically for interpreting the organizational environment and can thus contribute to managerial reflexivity. The perspective does not provide generic recipes for being a successful strategic leader. Rather, it has until now mainly produced contextual and descriptive knowledge that seeks to deeply explore the multiple and varied ways of doing strategic leadership. In the future, strategy-as-practice researchers' focus on what strategists do might be harnessed to help open 'the black box of strategic leadership processes' that has so far tended to elude upper echelons researchers.

Application: strategic leadership as social practice in the Steinberg case

To illustrate the social practice perspective to strategic leadership, we draw on examples extracted from Cooren's book (2007) dealing with a meeting in which 15 Steinberg's top managers got together over three days at the end of the 1960s to discuss the destiny of the company. Two important topics stood out on the agenda: the restructuring of the company and the professionalization of its management style. These two points were particularly strategic in the sense that the successful development of the corporation was related to its ability to succeed with diversification and to its historically strong family business culture. Discussions on how to restructure the company's operations and how to professionalize management might have important strategic implications for the corporation.

Unsurprisingly in such a context, the person in charge of leading these discussions plays a central role, thus enacting his strategic leadership. Harry Suffrin, the director of organizational development, was delegated to chair this meeting. Pomerantz and Denvir's (2007) conversation analysis of the meeting transcripts shows that the way in which he leads the meeting contributes to facilitate the adoption of the restructuring plan while simultaneously protecting the family business culture.

For example, when managers are talking about the restructuring plan for the company, Harry Suffrin behaves as a 'facilitator' through three concrete micro-practices: (1) by asking participants how they want to proceed in discussing the topic; (2) by formulating the proposed procedure as a suggestion; and (3) by crediting the authorship of the procedure to another participant. The restructuring plan recognized that the operations level had become too complex and proposed to decentralize the organization, but the plan was not unanimously appreciated; managers' opinions diverged. Consequently, chairing the discussion as a facilitator allowed Harry Suffrin to help them productively share their competing views while avoiding confrontation. Another crucial point to be discussed at this meeting concerned the development of a professional managerial style throughout the corporation. This question also aroused many contentious and competitive exchanges that required the chairperson to be agile and fair in allocating speaking turns. According to Pomerantz and Denvir (2007), Suffrin accomplished this successfully during the meeting except on two very specific occasions, where he preferentially gave the right to speak to Sam Steinberg over other managers. In doing so, he was implicitly recognizing the importance of the family organizational culture. Moreover, by deferring his authority to Sam he was favouring the traditional strategy. However, exceptionally, each time he allocated the speaking turn to Sam, his authority as chairperson was not recognized by the meeting's participants. This suggests that they were not totally unaware of this subtle manoeuvring. However, the message was clear: the professionalization of the management style would not be an easy task as long as Sam was there and the family culture dominated.

By looking at how this strategic meeting was chaired, we can see how the task of leading through other leaders was practically achieved in a strategic meeting through interactions and conversations. According to Fairhurst (2007), such a perspective liberates strategic leadership from the essentialist and reductionist viewpoint that has largely characterized this literature. Here, strategic leadership emerges from overlaid interactions whereby actors competently deal with their linguistic resources in their ongoing activities.

DISCUSSION: COMPLEMENTARITIES, IMPLICATIONS FOR PRACTICE AND FUTURE DIRECTIONS

Complementarities between the perspectives

Each research stream presented in this chapter envisages strategic leadership through a specific lens: as collective cognition, as individual inspiration, as political action and as social practice. However, these perspectives share certain characteristics regarding strategic leaders and the way strategic leadership is exercised (see Figure 6.1). While the collective cognition and the individual inspiration perspectives allow us to better understand who strategic leaders are and how their characteristics may influence organizational strategy, the political action and social practice perspectives look more directly at what exactly they do. Similarly, while the collective cognition and political action perspectives tend to view strategic leadership as a collective phenomenon, the individual and social practice perspectives examine more closely how strategic leadership is individually exercised.

Nevertheless, each of the perspectives on strategic leadership emphasizes specific characteristics of leaders and can be informed by the others. For example, while strategic leadership as collective cognition might allow us to explain how firm performance is influenced by strategic leaders through their demographic or cognitive traits in large samples, the three other perspectives provide richer detail that allows for a better explanation of specific cases. The individual inspiration perspective might be enriched by taking into account the social environment of the strategic leader, and the way he or she is involved in political games and how strategic leadership is daily performed in practice. By considering the diversity and heterogeneity of the TMT, the political perspective on strategic leadership might better capture the processes through which power becomes concentrated or distributed amongst strategic leaders. As for the social practice perspective of strategic leadership, an understanding of collective cognition might

Figure 6.1 Perspectives on strategic leadership

help to connect the perspective to a more macro view of strategic leadership, while the political and the inspirational approaches might provide a deeper view of the flow of the activities and practices of strategic leaders by looking more carefully at their external context (political processes) and internal dimensions (psychological processes).

The complementarity of the perspectives is clearly illustrated by the analysis of the Steinberg case (see Table 6.1). Knowledge of who Sam Steinberg was and from where he came (individual inspiration) might help to explain his initial vision and strategic successes but also how and why he chose the people who became the members of his team. These choices generated a particular form of political dynamics (political action), and contributed to the mindset that would influence later strategic decisions (collective cognition). Finally, the micro-activities of Harry Suffrin show a person who was able to skillfully navigate the political dynamics of the TMT in real time (social practice) to stimulate constructive exchange and transformation where he felt this was possible. In summary, a more complete view of strategic leadership benefits from the consideration of all these perspectives.

Implications for practice

Each of the four perspectives also suggests different implications for practitioners. Approaches focusing on TMT composition such as upper-echelons

theory underline the importance of demographic and cognitive diversity. Such diversity is seen as necessary in order to avoid decision pathologies such as groupthinking. Strategic leaders wishing to enrich the process of decision-making and strategy formation may deliberately attempt to recruit executive team members on the basis of a diversity of experiences, training and socio-demographic attributes. While diversity appears to be important, it is not sufficient to ensure decision closure and organizational performance as we saw in our discussion on strategic leadership as political action.

Approaches focusing on the leader's inner world caution him against his own fragilities, excesses and hubris and underline the importance of self-knowledge. They would recommend that he construct a top management team whose members can compensate for his own shortcomings, as opposed to simply assuring diversity on the team. They would also underline the importance of an effective Board that can steer clear of selecting CEOs demonstrating certain excesses such as narcissism (Kets de Vries & Miller, 1985), and can put in place checks and balances on CEO behaviours without undermining creative potential.

The perspective that views strategic leadership as political action promotes a deliberate approach to the phenomenon of power in organizations. Aspiring leaders have to develop self-awareness about their own power base and the need to adapt their strategies to gain influence in an evolving context. Probably more importantly, strategic leaders need to understand the collective dimension of leadership and develop explicit strategies to constitute networks of leaders who will have sufficient influence and legitimacy to make strategic innovation and execution possible. Leaders also need to pay attention to the consequences of their decisions and actions on their own position as leaders – something that is easily forgotten.

The social practice perspective on strategic leadership presses strategic leaders to pay attention to what they say and what they do in their daily activities. Being skilful in using routines, interactions and the tools available to them can assist them in patiently and persistently moving events in directions they seek to promote. For a social practice perspective, achieving strategic leadership is less a matter of playing a role than a call for performing skilful effort little by little and over the longer term.

Overall, we see that the four perspectives have complementary implications for the practice of strategic leadership.

Future directions

In terms of directions for future research, there are opportunities within each perspective and at their intersection. While there have been sustained calls for more qualitative, process research on TMTs in the upper echelons literature (Carpenter et al., 2004; Hambrick, 2007), few such studies exist and there is still a need for more fine-grained research on the dynamics of top teams' collective cognitions. Studying the ongoing interactions of intact top teams in 'real time' (e.g. using observation methods coupled with interviews and documentary research), although challenging in terms of access, is a particularly fruitful avenue since it can provide further understanding of the challenges of mobilizing a cognitively diverse group for collective action, and overcomes a number of the current methodological shortcomings in this literature. Further research is also needed into how leadership might flow through the TMT over time (through shared or distributed leadership or TMT constellations or other structures).

At the individual level, research using qualitative methods to tease apart the distinct role of the CEO (e.g. as visionary or transformational leader or architect of group interactions) from that of other team members, while recognizing the collective nature of the work of leadership, can provide a needed bridge between individual and group levels of analysis. Further work is also needed to explore the often subtle conscious and unconscious emotional subtexts of TMT interactions.

Looking at strategic leadership as political action brings to the fore the power issues at the core of leadership phenomena. Further work is needed to understand how changes in organizations influence the nature of leaders' power bases and leaders' legitimacy. For example, the emergence of knowledge–based organizations and flexible organizational forms, coupled with a growing interest in evidence-based management, points to needed research into the role of expertise and other ways in which strategic leaders legitimize their influence. Further research is also needed on the impact of structured decision-making processes on the dynamics of influence from a strategic leadership perspective. Fine-grained studies can increase our understanding of the conditions under which these processes are effective or threaten to implode. Research on the linkages between individual leadership style and the intensification (or not) of political games in organizations is also needed.

Finally, since strategic leadership as social practice is an emerging research perspective, much remains to be done. However, in these turbulent and fast-moving times, such a perspective needs to address three issues in particular. First, it should examine in detail the generic tasks and roles that the traditional literature generally attributes to strategic leaders. Secondly, further research should look at how effective leaders pattern the attention of stakeholders through subtle dialogues, stories and meaningful micro-acts concerning the changes in the environment, the definition of performance and the like. Thirdly, more research is needed on how strategic leaders routinely use appropriate tools with the aim of co-constructing their strategy.

Common to all four perspectives is a strong need for longitudinal case studies and similar methodologies to explore phenomena such as the interaction between context and the dynamics of strategic leadership, and the links between micro-behaviors of strategic leaders, collective action and organizational outcomes. There remains considerable potential for further development in the understanding of strategic leadership.

REFERENCES

Alvesson, M. & Sveningsson, S. (2003). Managers doing leadership: the extra-ordinarization of the mundane. *Human Relations*, 56(12): 1435–1459.

Ancona, D.G. & Caldwell, D.C. (1992). Demography and design: predictors of new product team performance. *Organization Science*, 3: 321–341.

Balogun, J. & Johnson, G. (2004). Organizational restructuring and middle manager sensemaking. *Academy of Management Journal*, 47: 523–549.

Bantel, K.A. & Jackson, S.E. (1989). 'Top management and innovations in banking: does the composition of the top team make a difference?'. *Strategic Management Journal*, 10: 107–124.

Barkema, H.G. & Shvyrkov, O. (2007). Does top management team diversity promote or hamper foreign expansion? *Strategic Management Journal*, 28(7): 663–680.

Bass, B.M. & Bass, R. (2008). *The Bass Handbook of Leadership*. New York: Free Press.

Boal, K.B. & Hooijberg, R. (2000). Strategic leadership research: moving on. *The Leadership Quarterly*, 11(4): 515.

Boeker, W. (1997), Strategic change: the influence of managerial characteristics and organizational growth. *Academy of Management Journal*, 40(1): 152–171.

Bourgeois, III L.J. & Eisenhardt, K.M. (1988). Strategic decision processes in high velocity environments: four cases in the microcomputer industry. *Management Science*, 34(7): 816–835.

Burns, J.M. (1978). *Leadership*. New York: Harper & Row.

Carpenter, M.A., Geletkanycz, M.A., & Sanders, W.G. (2004). Upper echelons research revisited: antecedents, elements, and consequences of top management team composition. *Journal of Management*, 30: 749–778.

Certo, S.T., Lester, R.H., Dalton, C.M., & Dalton, D.R. (2006). Top management teams, strategy and financial performance: a meta-analytic examination. *Journal of Management Studies*, 43(4): 813–839.

Child, J. (1997). Strategic choice in the analysis of action, structure, organizations and environment: retrospect and prospect. *Organization Studies*, 18(1): 43–76.

Clark, E. & Soulsby, A. (2007). Understanding top management and organizational change through demographic and processual analysis. *Journal of Management Studies*, 44(6): 932–954.

Cooren, F. (2007). *Interacting and Organizing Analyses of a Management Meeting*. London: Lawrence Erlbaum Associates.

Crossland, C. & Hambrick, D.C. (2007). How national systems differ in their constraints on corporate executives: a study of CEO effects in three countries. *Strategic Management Journal*, 28: 767–789.

Denis, J.L., Langley, A., & Cazale, L. (1996). Leadership and strategic change under ambiguity. *Organization Studies*, 17(4): 673–699.

Denis, J.L., Lamothe, L., & Langley, A. (2001). The dynamics of collective leadership and strategic change in pluralistic organizations. *Academy of Management Journal*, 44(4): 809–837.

Denis, J.L., Langley, A., & Rouleau, L (2005). Rethinking leadership in public organizations. In E. Ferlie, L.E Lynn, Jr & C. Pollitt (eds) *The Oxford Handbook of Public Management*.Oxford: Oxford University Press, pp. 446–467.

Denis, J.L., Langley, A., & Rouleau, L. (2007). Strategizing in pluralistic contexts: rethinking theoretical frames. *Human Relations*, 60(1): 179–215.

Dooley, R.S. & Fryxell, G.E. (1999). Attaining decision quality and commitment from dissent: the moderating effects of loyalty and competence in strategic decision-making teams, *Academy of Management Journal*, 42(4): 389–402.

Dusya, V. & Crossan, M. (2004). Strategic leadership and organizational learning. *Academy of Management Review*, 29(2): 222–241.

Edmondson, A.C., Roberto, M.A., & Watkins, M.D. (2003). A dynamic model of top management team effectiveness: managing unstructured task stream, *The Leadership Quarterly*, 4(3): 297–325.

Eisenhardt, K.M. (1989). Making fast strategic decisions in high-velocity environments. *Academy of Management Journal*, 32(3): 543–576.

Eisenhardt, K.M. & Bourgeois III, L.J. (1988). Politics of strategic decision making in high-velocity environments: toward a midrange theory. *Academy of Management Journal*, 31(4): 737–770.

Eisenhardt, K.M., Kahwajy, J.L., Bourgeois III, L.J. (1997). Conflict and strategic choice: How top management teams disagree. *California Management Review*, 39(2): 42–62.

Fairhurst, G.T. (2007). Liberating leadership in corporation: after Mr. Sam: a response. In F. Cooren (ed.), *Interacting and Organizing Analyses of a Management Meeting*. London: Lawrence Erlbaum Associates, pp. 53–76.

Finkelstein, S. & Hambrick, D.C. (1996). *Strategic Leadership: Top Executives and Their Effects on Organizations*. St. Paul, MN: West.

Gallén, T. (2006). Managers and strategic decisions: does the cognitive style matter? *Journal of Management Development*, 25(2): 118–133.

Gibbon, A. & Hadekel, P. (1990). *Steinberg: The Break-up of a Family Empire*. Toronto: Macmillan of Canada.

Hambrick, D.C. (1989). Guest editor's introduction: putting top managers back in the strategy picture. *Strategic Management Journal*, 10(1): 5–15.

Hambrick, D.C. (2007). Upper echelons theory: an update, *Academy of Management Review*, 32(2): 334–343.

Hambrick, D.C. & Mason, P.A. (1984). Upper echelons: the organization as a reflection of its top managers. *The Academy of Management Review*, 9(2): 193–206.

Hiller, N.J. & Hambrick, D.C. (2005). Conceptualizing executive hubris: the role of (hyper-) core self-evaluations in strategic decision-making. *Strategic Management Journal*, 26(4): 297–319.

Hodgkinson, G. P. & Clarke, I. (2007). Exploring the cognitive significance of strategizing: a dual-process framework and a research agenda. *Human Relations*, 60(1): 243–255.

Hough, J.R. & Ogilvie, D.T. (2005). An empirical test of cognitive style and strategic decision outcomes, *Journal of Management Studies*, 42(2): 417–448.

Janis, I.L. & Mann, L. (1977). *Decision-Making, A Psychological Analysis of Conflict, Choice and Commitment*. New York: Free Press.

Jarzabkowski, P. (2003). Strategic practices: an activity theory perspective on continuity and change. *Journal of Management Studies*, 40(1): 23–56.

Jarzabkowski, P. & Searle, R.H. (2004). Harnessing diversity and collective action in the top management team. *Long Range Planning*, 37(5): 399–419.

Jarzabkowski, P., Balogun, J., Seidl, D. (2007). Strategizing: the challenges of a practice perspective. *Human Relations*, 60(1): 5–27.

Johnson, G., Melin, L., & Whittington, R. (2003). Micro strategy and strategizing: towards an activity-based view? *Journal of Management Studies*, 40(1): 3–22.

Kauer, D., Prinzessin zu Waldeck, T.C., & Schäffer, U. (2007). Effects of top management team characteristics on strategic decision making: shifting attention to team member personalities and mediating processes, *Management Decision*, 45(6): 942–967.

Keck, S.L. (1997). Top management team structure: differential effects by environment context. *Organization Science*, 8(2): 143–156.

Kets de Vries, M.F.R. (1996). The anatomy of the entrepreneur: clinical observations. *Human Relations*, 49(7): 853–883.

Kets de Vries, M.F.R. & Miller, D. (1984). *The Neurotic Organization*: [*Diagnosing and Changing Counterproductive Styles of Management*], 1st edn. San Francisco: Jossey-Bass.

Kets de Vries, M.F.R. & Miller, D. (1985). Narcissism and leadership: an object relations perspective. *Human Relations*, 38(6): 583–601.

Kets de Vries, M.F.R., Loper, M., & Doyle, J. (1994). The leadership mystique: executive commentary. *The Academy of Management Executive*, 8(3): 73–92.

Kets de Vries, M.F.R., Carlock, R.S. & Florent-Treacy, E. (2007). *Family Business on the Couch: A Psychological Perspective*. Chichester: John Wiley & Sons.

Kilduff, M., Angelmar, R., & Mehra, A. (2000). Top management-team diversity and firm performance: examining the role of cognitions, *Organization Science*, 11(1): 21–34.

Kisfalvi, V. (2000). The threat of failure, the perils of success and CEO character: sources of strategic persistence. *Organization Studies*, 21(3): 611–640.

Kisfalvi, V. (2002). "The entrepreneur's character, life issues and strategy making : a field study". *Journal of Business Venturing*, 17 (5): 489–518.

Kisfalvi, V., & Pitcher, P. (2003). Doing what feels right: the influence of CEO character and emotions on top Management team dynamics. *Journal of Management Inquiry*, 12(1): 42–66.

Knights, D. & Willmott, H. (1992). Conceptualizing leadership processes: a study of senior managers in a financial services company. *Journal of Management Studies*, 29: 761–782.

Laine, P.-M. & Vaara, E. (2007). Struggling over subjectivity: a discursive analysis of strategic development in an engineering group. *Human Relations*, 60(1): 29–58.

Lapierre, L. (1989). Mourning, potency, and power in management. *Human Resource Management*, 28(2): 177–190.

Lawrence, B.S. (1997). The black box of organizational demography. *Organization Science*, 8(1): 1–22.

Mantere, S. (2005). Strategic practices as enablers and disablers of championing activity. *Strategic Organization*, 3: 157–284.

Mintzberg, H. (1983). *Power in and around Organizations*. Englewood Cliffs, NJ: PrenticeHall.

Mintzberg, H. & Waters, J.A. (1982). Tracking strategy in an entrepreneurial firm. *Academy of Management Journal*, 25(3): 465–499.

Noël, A. (1989). Strategic cores and magnificent obsessions: discovering strategy formation through daily activities of CEOs. *Strategic Management Journal*, 10: 33–49.

Norburn, D. (1989). The chief executive: a breed apart. *Strategic Management Journal*, 10(1): 1–15.

Olson, B.J., Parayitam, S., & Bao, Y. (2007). Strategic decision making: the effects of cognitive diversity, conflict, and trust on decision outcomes. *Journal of Management*, 33(2): 196–222.

Paroutis, S. & Pettigrew, A.M. (2007). Strategizing in the multi-business firm: strategy teams at multiple levels and over time. *Human Relations*, 60(1): 99–135.

Pettigrew, A.M. (1977). Strategy formulation as a political process. *International Studies of Management and Organization*, 7(2): 78–87.

Pettigrew, A.M. (1992). On studying managerial elites. *Strategic Management Journal*, 13(special issue): 163–182.

Pfeffer, J. (1992a). *Managing with Power*. Boston, MA; Harvard Business School Press.

Pfeffer J. (1992b). Understanding power in organizations. *California Management Review*, 34(2): 29–50.

Pitcher, P. (1993). Balancing personality types at the top. *Business Quarterly*, 58(2): 46–57.

Pitcher, P. (1995). *Artists, Craftsmen and Technocrats: The Dreams, Realities and Illusions of Leadership*. Toronto: Stoddart.

Pitcher, P. & Smith, A. (2001). Top management team heterogeneity: personality, power, and proxies. *Organization Science*, 12(1): 1–18.

Pitcher, P., Chreim, S., & Kisfalvi, V. (2000). CEO succession research: methodological bridges over troubled waters. *Strategic Management Journal*, 21(6): 625–648.

Pomerantz, A. & Denvir, P. (2007). Enacting the institutional role of chairperson in upper management meetings: the interactional realization of provisional authority. In F. Cooren (ed.), *Interacting and Organizing Analyses of a Management Meeting*. London: Lawrence Erlbaum Associates, pp. 31–52.

Priem, R. L. Lyon, D.W., & Dess, G.G. (1999). Inherent limitations of demographic proxies in top management team heterogeneity research. *Journal of Management*, 25(6): 935–953.

Roberto, M.A. (2003). The stable core and dynamic periphery in top management teams. *Management Decision*, 41(2): 120–131.

Roberto, M.A. (2004). Strategic decision-making processes: beyond the efficiency–consensus trade-off. *Group and Organization Management*, 29(6): 625–658.

Rouleau, L. (2005). Micro-practices of strategic sensemaking and sensegiving: how middle managers interpret and sell change every day. *Journal of Management Studies*, 42: 1413–1443.

Samra-Fredericks, D. (2003). Strategizing as lived experience and strategists' everyday efforts to shape strategic direction. *Journal of Management Studies*, 40: 141–174.

Schneider, S.C. & Shrivastava, P. (1988). Basic assumptions themes in organizations. *Human Relations*, 41(7): 493–516.

Simon, H.A. (1955). A behavioural model of rational choice. *Quarterly Journal of Economics*, 69: 99–118.

Simsek, Z., Veiga, J.F., Lubatkin, M.H., & Dino, R.N. (2005). Modeling the multilevel determinants of top management team behavioural integration. *Academy of Management Journal*, 48(1): 69–84.

Smith, A., Houghton, S.M., Hood, J.N., & Ryman, J.A. (2006). Power relationships among top managers: does top management team power distribution matter for organizational performance? *Journal of Business Research*, 59(5): 622–629.

Vaara, E., Kleymann B., & Seristö, H. (2004). Strategies as discursive constructions: the case of airline alliances. *Journal of Management Studies*, 41: 1–35.

West, C.T., Jr & Schwenk, C.R. (1996). Top management team strategic consensus, demographic homogeneity and firm performance: a report of resounding nonfindings, *Strategic Management Journal*, 17(7): 571–576.

Westley, F. & Mintzberg, H. (1989). Visionary leadership and strategic management. *Strategic Management Journal*, 10: 17–32.

Wiersema, M.F. & Bantel, K. (1992). Top management team demography and corporate strategic change. *Academy of Management Journal*, 35: 91–121.

Wiersema, M. & Bird, A. (1993). Organizational demography in Japanese firms: group heterogeneity, individual dissimilarity, and top management team turnover. *Academy of Management Journal*, 36: 996–1025.

Zaleznik, A. (1977). Managers and leaders – are they different? *Harvard Business Review*, 55(3): 67–78.

Zaleznik, A. (1990). The leadership gap. *The Executive*, 4(1): 7–22.

Zaleznik, A. & Kets de Vries, M.F.R. (1975). *Power and the Corporate Mind*. Boston, MA: Houghton–Mifflin.

7

Charismatic Leadership

Jay A. Conger

INTRODUCTION

The term charisma comes from a Hellenistic word χάρισμα or *kharisma*, meaning a 'gift' or 'divine favor' or 'supernatural power'. In ancient times, it was believed that certain individuals such as prophets or religious leaders or healers were given gifts from the gods to help them in their earthly tasks. These were called charismata. The term was adopted by the Christians of the New Testament period to similarly describe Godly gifts given to the faithful. Most commonly referenced among the gifts were notions of prophecy connected with visionary experiences and the ability of prophets to speak in the person of God (or the Holy Spirit). Among the oldest known literary references to charismata are those found in the Bible:

> Now there are varieties of gifts (charismata).... But to each one (individual) is given the manifestation of the Spirit for the common good. For to one is given the word of wisdom through the Spirit, and to another the word of knowledge, to another faith, and to another gifts of healing, and to another the effecting of miracles, and to another prophecy.... But one and the same Spirit (God) works all these things, distributing to each one individually as He wills. (1 Corinthians, 12, 4–11)

Despite the term's long history, it was not used to describe a category of secular leadership until the writings of the German sociologist Max Weber (1864–1920). He was the first to apply the term 'charismatic' to leaders in the secular as well as religious world. His typology of three types of authority in society (the traditional, the rational-legal, and the charismatic) established charismatic leadership as an important term to describe forms of authority based on perceptions of an extraordinary individual. In contrast to authority derived from traditions or rules which conferred legitimacy on individuals, the holder of charisma was 'set apart from ordinary men and is treated as endowed with ... exceptional powers and qualities ... [which] are not accessible to the ordinary person but are regarded as of divine origin or as exemplary, and on the basis of them the individual concerned is treated as a leader' (Weber, 1947, pp. 358–359). As the reader can discern, Weber preserved the essence of the earliest meaning of the term – an individual in a leadership role imbued with extraordinary powers.

While Weber did not provide a comprehensive theoretical model of this form of leadership, his writings (Willner, 1984) do provide us with elements of the character and the course of charismatic leadership: (1) the condition under which it typically arises (distress); (2) one requirement for its maintenance (mission successes); (3) its likely outcome over time (institutionalization); and (4) some of the means by which charismatic leaders exercise their authority (powers of mind and speech, heroism, magical abilities). Because of Weber's sociological perspective, however, his exposition of the personal attributes and relational dynamics between the leader and followers was minimal. Sometime later, organizational theorists would focus much of their research on these particular gaps.

BEYOND WEBER: CONTRIBUTIONS FROM POLITICAL SCIENCE AND SOCIOLOGY

It was not until the 1960s that political scientists and sociologists began to explore Weber's ideas on charismatic leadership seriously. There was particular interest in applying his ideas to understanding the influence of historical figures such as Churchill and Hitler as well as popularly elected leaders from the newly emerging democracies on the African continent. These explorations focused on answering three central questions:

- Could and should charisma be extended beyond its original religious context?
- Was there a universal 'charismatic personality' or were there differing attributes among charismatic leaders?
- Where was the locus of 'charisma' – was it to be found in the leader's extraordinary qualities, in the larger social context, or in the relationship with followers?

Addressing the first question, two political scientists, Karl Loewenstein (1966) and C.J. Friedrich (1961), argued against extending the concept beyond its religious antecedents. Loewenstein felt that true forms of charismatic leadership were not to be found in the modern world but only in cultures with 'magico-religious' or primitive ambiance. Friedrich stressed that the term centered on a transcendental call by a divine being. Charismatic authority, he argued, had to remain linked to this original meaning. Their point of view never gained momentum and was resolved by the widespread acceptance by both political scientists and sociologists that the term should include both secular as well as religious leaders.

The second point of debate concerned the charismatic leader's 'personality'. One camp suggested that a universal set of characteristics could be identified for all charismatic leaders. The other – in particular, political scientists Dow (1969) and Willner (1984) – argued that the search for a universal set of qualities common to charismatic political and religious leaders would not yield decisive results. They pointed to variations in individual personalities that were so great (comparing Gandhi to Hitler to Churchill to Kennedy, for example) that a single charismatic personality type seemed highly improbable. Instead, Willner (1984) argued that charismatic leadership was more effectively explained as a relational and perceptual phenomenon: 'It is not what the leader is but what people see the leader as that count in generating the charismatic relationship' (pp. 14–15). Because societies and groups differ in their definitions of what constitutes extraordinary qualities, the content of leadership images, projected and perceived, would necessarily differ from group to group. It was therefore impossible, Willner contended, to construct a universal 'charismatic personality'. This line of thinking became the dominant position in the field.

Regarding the third question of where the locus of charisma resided, some (Blau, 1963; Chinoy, 1961; Friedland, 1964) believed that the social and historical context was the critical determinant in the emergence of charismatic leadership. They felt strongly that times of turmoil and revolution were needed to precipitate charismatic leadership. Others (Dow, 1969; Marcus, 1961) argued that charisma resided within the attributes of the charismatic leader – for example, with their visions or ideologies. As the leading proponent of this point of view, Willner's research (1984) showed that charismatic leadership did not need to be the product of a turbulent environment. From an in-depth review of six case studies of charismatic political leaders, she concluded 'Only two, Hitler and Roosevelt, seem to conform sufficiently closely to the preconditions of crisis and psychic distress specified in the conventional formula' (p. 46).

From her research, Willner identified four factors that, aided by personality, appear to be catalytic in the attribution of charisma to a leader: (1) the invocation of important cultural myths by the leader; (2) performance of what are perceived as heroic or extraordinary feats; (3) projection of attributes 'with an uncanny or a powerful aura'; and (4) outstanding rhetorical skills (1984, p. 61). From the field's perspective, Willner's research was pivotal in understanding charismatic leadership, for it highlighted the relational and perceptual dynamics with followers. While context retained the potential to influence these dynamics significantly, it was not the casual factor or a necessary catalyst.

In addition to these three areas of debate, the political scientist James McGregor Burns was examining charismatic leadership through another lens that would become highly influential within the field and beyond. He wanted to explain the follower relationships and their outcomes. In his 1978 book *Leadership*, Burns had concluded that leaders could be separated generally into two types: the 'transformational' and the 'transactional' (see Diaz-Saenz, Chapter 22, this volume). The transformational leaders were the same leaders described as charismatic by fellow academics. Since most readers will be familiar with Burns' basic ideas, we include only a brief summary here. For Burns, leadership at its essence could be boiled down to the notion of an exchange. Both the leader and the follower had something to offer one another. It was in the nature of what was exchanged, however, that his model came into play. For Burns, transformational or charismatic leaders offered a transcendent purpose as their mission – one which addressed the higher-order needs of their followers. In the process of achieving this mission, both the leaders and the led were literally transformed or actualized as individuals – hence, the term 'transforming'. Burns (1978) explained: 'The result of transforming leadership is a relationship of mutual stimulation and elevation that converts followers into leaders and may convert leaders into moral agents' (p. 4). At the other end of the spectrum was transactional leadership. Significantly more common of the two forms, transactional leadership was based on a relationship with followers which consisted of mundane and instrumental exchanges: 'The relations of most leaders and followers are transactional – leaders approach followers with an eye to exchanging one thing for another: jobs for votes, or subsidies for campaign contributions. Such [instrumental] transactions comprise the bulk of the relationships...' (p. 4).

Burn's conceptualization would later influence the thinking of many scholars in the organizational leadership field. For example, Bernard Bass (1985) built much of his model of 'transformational leadership' around Burn's ideas. Interestingly, the central idea of leadership as an exchange was already present in the organizational and psychology literature. For example, it is central to the leader–member exchange (e.g. Graen & Scandura 1986), operant conditioning (Podsakoff et al., 1982) and path-goal models (House & Mitchell, 1974). In each, the relationship between leader and led is dependent upon a series of trades or bargains that are mutually beneficial and are maintained so long as the benefits to both parties exceed the costs (Bass, 1970) (In Burns' terms, these exchanges would be 'transactional' not 'transformational'). Missing is the element of higher-order needs being met and the elevation of both the leader and led to a more evolved state of being. This was the critical contribution that Burns brought to the field. Up to that moment in time, the notion of leaders who manage meaning, infuse ideological values, construct lofty goals and visions, and inspire was missing entirely from this literature of leadership exchange. What is intriguing about the influence of Burns then is not so much the notion of leadership as an exchange but the idea that certain forms of leadership create a cycle of rising aspirations which ultimately transform both leaders and their followers.

As we will see, Burns' ideas would have great appeal to organizational theorists grappling with the twin issues of organizational change and empowerment in the 1980s. The 'transformational leader' model spoke to both these issues. After all, these were leaders concerned about transforming the existing order of things as well as directly addressing their followers' needs for meaning and personal growth.

CONTRIBUTIONS FROM ORGANIZATIONAL BEHAVIOR

Interest in research on charismatic leadership among political scientists waned by the late 1970s. A decade later, another group of scholars became intrigued by the subject. These were social psychologists and organizational behavior faculty who resided primarily in business schools. They would undertake the most extensive attempts at investigating charismatic leadership. Several major theories were proposed along with dozens and dozens of empirical investigations of charismatic leadership in organizations. These studies involved a wide range of samples such as middle and lower-level managers (Bass & Yammarino, 1988; Conger & Kanungo, 1994; Hater & Bass, 1988; Koene et al., 1991), senior executives (Agle & Sonnenfeld, 1994; Conger, 1989), US Presidents (House et al., 1991), educational administrators (Koh et al., 1991; Roberts & Bradley, 1988; Sashkin, 1988), military leaders (Koene et al., 1991; Howell & Avolio, 1993), and students who were laboratory subjects (Howell & Frost, 1989; Kirkpatrick, 1992; Puffer, 1990; Shamir, 1992). In addition, the subject was explored using a wide variety of research methods. For example, there have been field surveys (Conger & Kanungo 1992, 1994, 1997; Hater & Bass 1988; Podsakoff, et al., 1990), laboratory experiments (Howell & Frost, 1989; Kirkpatrick, 1992), content analyses of interviews and observation (Conger, 1989; Howell & Higgins, 1990), and analyses of historical archival information (House et al., 1991).

What is more remarkable than this flowering of research is the relative uniformity of findings despite some differences in theoretical approaches. As Shamir et al. (1993) noted, findings across the board demonstrate that leaders who engage in the behaviors that are theorized to be charismatic actually produce the charismatic effects that the theory predicts. In addition, many of these studies have shown repeatedly that leaders who are perceived as charismatic receive higher performance ratings, are seen as more effective leaders than others holding leadership positions, and have more highly motivated and more satisfied followers than others in similar positions (e.g. see Agle & Sonnenfeld, 1994).

The research of organizational theorists can be organized into distinct topic areas of charismatic leadership: (1) the leader's behavior; (2) the followers' behavior and motives; (3) the leader's and followers' psychological profiles; (4) contextual influences; (5) forces that institutionalize various outcomes of the leader–follower relationship; and (6) liabilities of the relationship with charismatic leaders.

Leader behaviors

Both the greatest amount of theoretical development as well as empirical research to date have been in the area of leader behaviors. This is due in large part to the backgrounds of the majority of researchers. Most have a strong behavioral orientation. Essentially, there are three groups of researchers who have carved out their own models—though each has a measure of overlap with the others in the attributes they identify. They are also the ones who have built the most comprehensive theories as well as conducted the greatest amount of empirical research in the field. They are (1) Bernard Bass, Bruce Avolio, and their colleagues; (2) Robert House, Boas Shamir, and their colleagues; and (3) Jay Conger and Rabindra Kanungo.

Bass and Avolio

As noted earlier, Bass and his colleague Avolio would borrow from Burns the notion of 'transformational leadership' and develop a similar model for organizational leaders. As Bryman (1992, pp. 97–98) has pointed out, their model goes further conceptually than the Burns' original model. Bass conceptualized the transactional and transformational dimensions as separate, whereas Burns defined them as two ends of a spectrum. For Bass, therefore, a leader could be both transformational and transactional. In addition, Bass was determined to more precisely identify the actual behaviors that these leaders demonstrated, whereas Burns was content with more of a 'big picture' overview.

At the heart of Bass's model of transformational leader is the notion that these leaders are able to motivate subordinates to performance levels that exceed their own and their leader's expectations. Transformational leaders accomplish this by raising the importance of certain goals, by demonstrating the means to achieve them, and by inducing subordinates to transcend their self-interests for the goals' achievement. In the process, they are also stimulating and meeting subordinates' higher-order needs, which in turn generates commitment, effort, and ultimately greater performance.

Bass and Avolio (Bass, 1985; Bass & Avolio, 1993) built their model of transformational leadership around four behavioral components of the leader: (1) charisma or idealized influence; (2) inspiration; (3) intellectual stimulation; and (4) individualized consideration. Charisma is defined in terms of both leader's behavior (such as articulating a mission) and followers' reactions (such as trust in the leader's ability) (Bass & Avolio, 1993). However, the emphasis is on charisma's role in enabling the leader to influence followers by arousing strong emotions and identification with the leader. Identifying with the leader reduces follower resistance to change, while emotional arousal creates a sense of excitement about the mission. Bass (1985) argues, however, that charisma alone is insufficient for transformational leadership: 'Charisma is a necessary ingredient of transformational leadership, but by itself it is not sufficient to account for the transformational process.' (p. 31).

While Bass originally treated inspiration as a subfactor within charismatic leadership, his more recent writings describe it as a separate component designed to motivate. Much of this dimension centers on communication, in that the transformational leader: 'Communicates high expectations, uses symbols to focus efforts, and expresses important purposes in simple ways.' (1990, p. 22)

The component of individualized consideration is similar to the early Ohio State notions of consideration. It includes providing encouragement and support to followers, assisting their development by promoting growth opportunities, and showing trust and respect for them as individuals. Its role is to bond the leader and the led and to build follower self-confidence and heighten personal development.

Intellectual stimulation, the final dimension, is a process whereby the leader increases follower awareness of problems by challenging them with new ideas and perspectives and by influencing followers to creatively rethink their traditional ways of approaching organizational tasks.

In Bryman's work *Charisma and Leadership in Organizations* (1992), the methodological shortcomings of the Bass model have been well highlighted. Since both of the measures to capture transformational leadership (the LBDQ and the MLQ) are based on subordinate ratings, there are potential problems of contamination by implicit leadership theories. Bass and Avolio, for example, discovered that descriptions of the transformational leader are significantly closer to subordinates' images of the ideal leader than transactional leadership. There are also issues about whether respondent's ratings of their leader's behavior are affected by their knowledge of the leader's effectiveness. In addition, there is little appreciation for situational variables or differences. For example, while the research findings show considerable similarity across studies, there is some variance. Yet the implication for situational differences remains unexplored (Bryman, 1992, pp. 128–129).

Bryman (1992) also points out that Bass' measure of charisma itself may be a bit flawed. For example, vision is treated as a component of inspirational, rather than charismatic leadership. Yet the bulk of the literature in the field sees vision as a component of charismatic leadership. In addition, Max Weber believed that the basis for charismatic leadership was a perception by followers that their leader was extraordinary. At best, only two of Bass' 10 items could be considered to convey this quality.

As one might imagine, there has also been some confusion as to the essential differences between the Bass transformational leadership model and other models of charismatic leadership. For one, the role of charisma in the Bass model is very important. In their empirical studies (e.g. Avolio & Yammarino, 1990; Bass, 1985), the component of charisma generally has the strongest correlation of any of the model's dimensions with subordinates' ratings of leadership effectiveness and their own satisfaction. It is clearly the most influential.

In addition, as Bryman (1992) notes, the Bass model is built around the leader articulating a vision that excites followers and engaging in behaviors that build intense loyalty and trust. These dimensions overlap considerably with those postulated by charismatic leadership theories. A comparison of the Bass model with other charismatic theories is presented in the next chapter. Such a comparison reveals that, in essence, there is little real difference in behavioral components. In the literature itself, we also see the two terms used interchangeably and sometimes authors describe them as one or even use the label 'charismatic/transformational leadership' (e.g. House & Shamir, 1993; Hunt, 1991).

Conger and Kanungo

This model builds on the idea that charismatic leadership is an attribution based on followers' perceptions of their leader's behavior. For example, most social psychological theories consider leadership to be a by-product of the interaction between members of a group. The leadership role behaviors displayed by a person make that individual (in the eyes of followers) not only a task leader or a social leader and a participative or directive leader but also a charismatic or non-charismatic leader.

The Conger and Kanungo (1999) framework for charismatic leadership is built around a three-stage model of leadership which involves moving organizational members from an existing present state toward some future state. This dynamic might also be described as a movement away from the status quo toward the achievement of desired longer-term goals. In the initial stage, the leader must critically evaluate the existing situation or status quo. Deficiencies in the status quo or poorly exploited opportunities in the environment lead to formulations of future goals. But before devising appropriate organizational goals, the leader must assess what resources are available and what constraints stand in the way of realizing future goals. In addition, the leader must assess the inclinations, the abilities, the needs, and level of satisfaction experienced by followers. This evaluation leads to a second stage: the actual formulation and conveyance of goals. Finally, in stage three, the leader demonstrates how these goals can be achieved by the organization. It is along these three stages that behavioral components unique to charismatic leaders can be identified. Conger and Kanungo note that in reality the stages rarely follow such a simple linear flow. Instead, most organizations face ever-changing environments, and their leadership must constantly be revising existing goals and tactics in response to unexpected opportunities or other environmental changes.

In terms of the actual behaviors of charismatic leaders, Conger and Kanungo distinguish charismatic leaders from non-charismatic leaders in stage one by their sensitivity to environmental constraints and by their ability to identify deficiencies and poorly exploited opportunities in the status quo. In addition, they are sensitive to follower abilities and needs. In stage two, it is their formulation of an idealized future vision and their extensive use of articulation and impression management skills that sets them apart from other leaders. Finally, in stage three, it is their deployment of innovative and unconventional means to achieve their vision and their use of personal power to influence followers that are distinguishing characteristics. A more detailed explanation of each stage follows.

Charismatic leaders are very critical of the status quo. They tend to be highly sensitive to both the social and physical environments in which they operate. When leaders fail to assess properly constraints in the environment or the availability of resources, their strategies and actions may not achieve organizational objectives. They will be labeled ineffective. For this reason, it is important that leaders are able to make realistic assessments of the environmental constraints and resources needed to bring about change within their organizations.

In the assessment stage, what distinguishes charismatic from non-charismatic leaders is the charismatic leaders' ability to recognize deficiencies in the present context. In other words, they actively search out existing or potential shortcomings in the status quo. For example, the failure of firms to exploit new technologies or new markets might be highlighted as a strategic or tactical opportunity by a charismatic leader. Likewise, a charismatic entrepreneur might more readily perceive marketplace needs and transform them into opportunities for new products or services. In addition, internal organizational deficiencies may be perceived by the charismatic leader as platforms for advocating radical change.

Because of their emphasis on shortcomings in the system and their high levels of intolerance for them, charismatic leaders are always seen as organizational reformers or entrepreneurs. In other words, they act as agents of innovative and radical change. However, the attribution of charisma is dependent not on the outcome of change but simply on the actions taken to bring about change or reform.

After assessing the environment, charismatic leaders can be distinguished from others by the nature of their goals and by the manner in which they articulate them. They are characterized by a sense of strategic vision. Here the word vision refers to an idealized goal that the leader wants the organization to achieve in the future. In order to be perceived as charismatic, leaders not only need to have visions and plans for achieving them but also they must be able to articulate their visions and strategies for action in ways so as to influence their followers. Here articulation involves two separate processes: articulation of the context and articulation of the leader's motivation to lead. First, a charismatic leader must effectively articulate for followers the following scenarios representing the context: (1) the nature of the status quo and its shortcomings; (2) a future vision; (3) how the future vision, when realized, will remove existing deficiencies and fulfill the hopes of followers; and (4) the leaders' plan of action for realizing the vision.

In articulating the context, the charismatic's verbal messages construct reality such that only the positive features of the future vision and only the negative features of the status quo are emphasized. The status quo is usually presented as intolerable, and the vision is presented in clear specific terms as the most attractive and attainable alternative. In articulating these elements for subordinates, the leader often constructs several scenarios representing the status quo, goals for the future, needed changes, and the ease or difficulty of achieving goals depending on available resources and constraints. In their scenarios, the charismatic leaders attempt to create among followers a sense of disenchantment or discontentment with the status quo, a strong identification with future goals, and a compelling desire to be led in the direction of the goal in spite of environmental hurdles.

Besides verbally describing the status quo, future goals, and the means to achieve them, charismatic leaders must also articulate their own motivation for leading their followers. Using expressive modes of action, both verbal and nonverbal, they manifest their convictions, self-confidence, and dedication to materialize what they advocate. Charismatic leaders' use of rhetoric, high energy, persistence, unconventional and risky behavior, heroic deeds, and personal sacrifices all serve to articulate their high motivation and enthusiasm, which then become contagious among their followers. These behaviors form part of a charismatic leader's impression management.

In the final stage of the three stage leadership process, effective leaders build in followers a sense of trust in their abilities and expertise. The charismatic leader does this by building trust through personal example and risk taking and through unconventional expertise. Generally, leaders are perceived as trustworthy when they advocate their position in a disinterested manner and demonstrate a concern for followers' needs rather than their own self-interest. However, in order to be charismatic, leaders must make these qualities appear extraordinary. They must transform their concern for followers' needs into a total dedication and commitment to a common cause they share and express them in a disinterested and selfless manner. They must engage in exemplary acts that are perceived by followers as involving great personal risk, cost, and energy (Friedland, 1964). In this case, personal risk might include the possible loss of personal finances, the possibility of being fired or demoted, and the potential loss of formal or informal status, power, authority, and credibility. The higher the manifest personal cost or sacrifice for the common goal, the greater is the trustworthiness of a leader. The more leaders are able to demonstrate that they are indefatigable workers prepared to take on high personal risks or incur high personal costs in order to achieve their shared vision, the more they reflect charisma in the sense of being worthy of complete trust.

Finally, charismatic leaders must appear to be knowledgeable and experts in their areas of influence. Some degree of demonstrated expertise, such as reflected in successes in the past, may be a necessary condition for the attribution of charisma (Weber, [1924] 1947). They demonstrate an expertise in devising effective but unconventional strategies and plans of action (Conger, 1985).

House, Shamir et al.

In one of the field's earliest writings on charismatic leadership in organizations, Robert House (1977) published a book chapter entitled 'A 1976 Theory of Charismatic Leadership'. It outlined not only the leader behaviors that were possibly associated with charismatic leadership but also certain personal traits and situational variables. In it, House argued that these leaders could be distinguished from others by their tendency to dominate, a strong conviction in their own beliefs and ideals, a need to influence others, and high self-confidence. Through emotionally appealing goals and the demonstration of behaviors that aroused followers' own needs for achievement, affiliation, and power, the charismatic leader was able to motivate high levels of task accomplishment. In addition, House theorized that these leaders simultaneously communicated high-performance expectations as well as confidence in their followers' ability to meet such expectations. These actions, in turn, enhanced follower expectations that their efforts would lead to accomplishments. Through role-modeling, charismatic leaders demonstrated the values and beliefs they wished for followers to endorse in order for the mission to be successful.

Like most models in the early stages of theory development, it had several important shortcomings. As Yukl (1994) notes, House's description of the influence process was rudimentary, especially in light of the profound influence he argued that these leaders had over their followers. Secondly, his theory was based largely around dyads – the leader and 'the follower' – rather than collectives, which are the basis of organizations. Finally, absent from his theory were certain components that would appear in later theories such as the notion of self-sacrifice, unconventional behavior, and the use of non-traditional strategies and tactics (Conger, 1989; Conger and Kanungo, 1987).

Since that time, House along with several colleagues (House & Shamir, 1993; House et al., 1991; Shamir et al., 1993) have made revisions to his earlier theory. The most important and significant revision was by Shamir et al., (1993) in an article entitled 'The Motivation Effects of Charismatic Leadership: A Self-Concept Based Theory'. Focused on explaining the profound levels of motivation typically associated with charismatic leadership, they postulated that these motivational effects could best be explained by focusing on the self-concept of the followers. Citing supporting research (e.g. Prentice, 1987), they point out that as human beings we behave in ways that seek to establish and affirm a sense of identity for ourselves (known as the self-concept). What charismatic leaders do is to tie these self-concepts of followers to the goals and collective experiences associated with their missions so that they become valued aspects of the followers' self-concept.

In terms of details, their theory hypothesizes that charismatic leadership achieves its motivational outcomes through at least four mechanisms: (1) changing follower perceptions of the nature of work itself; (2) offering an appealing future vision; (3) developing a deep collective identity among followers; and (4) heightening both individual and collective self-efficacy. The processes that Shamir et al., (1993) describe as producing these effects follow in the paragraphs below.

Charismatic leaders transform the nature of work (in this case, work meant to achieve the organization's vision) by making it appear more heroic, morally correct, and meaningful. They in essence de-emphasize the extrinsic rewards of work and focus instead on the intrinsic side. Work becomes an opportunity for self- and collective-expression. The reward for individual followers as they accomplish mission tasks is one of enhanced self-expression, self-efficacy, self-worth, and self-consistency. The idea is that eventually followers will come to see their organizational tasks as inseparable from their own self-concepts – that 'action is not merely a means of doing but a way of being' (Yukl, 1994).

To accomplish this change in perceptions of work, the charismatic leader uses several means. One of the most important mechanisms, as described by Shamir et al. (1993), is the leader's vision, which serves to enhance follower self-concepts in three ways. First, by offering an optimistic and appealing future, the vision heightens the meaningfulness of the organization's goals. Secondly, the vision is articulated as a shared one, which promotes a strong sense of collective identity. Presumably the vision is also unique and, by stressing that the vision is the basis for the group's identity, the charismatic leader distinguishes his followers from others and further encourages followers to transcend their individual self-interests for those of the collectives. Thirdly, the leader's expression of confidence in followers' abilities to achieve the vision heightens their sense of self-efficacy. They feel capable of creating a reality out of what is currently a lofty and utopian set of ambitions.

Integral to Shamir et al.'s motivational theory is the charismatic leader's ability to create a deep collective identity. As just noted, the shared vision is one of the principal means. In addition, the charismatic leader actively promotes perceptions that only by banding together can group members accomplish exceptional feats. Furthermore, the leader uses his own behavior to increase identification with the collective through the deployment of rituals, ceremonies, slogans, symbols, and stories that reinforce the importance of a group identity. The significance of creating this collective identity is in the follower outcomes that it is able to produce. Specifically, the authors cite research (Meindl & Lerner, 1983) indicating that a shared identity among individuals increases the 'heroic motive' and the probability that individual self-interests will be abandoned voluntarily for collective and altruistic undertakings. As a result, as charismatic leaders cultivate a collective identity in their followers' self-concepts, they are heightening the chances that followers will engage in self-sacrificial, collective-oriented behavior. The group identification in essence strengthens the shared behavioral norms, values, and beliefs among the members. All of this ensures a concerted and unified effort on the part of followers to achieve the mission's goals.

Finally, Shamir et al. argue that charismatic leaders achieve their extraordinary levels of follower motivation by focusing their efforts on building follower self-esteem and self-worth. They accomplish this by expressing high expectations of their followers and simultaneously great confidence in the followers' abilities to meet these expectations (Yukl, 1994). This in turn enhances the perceived self-efficacy of followers. From the research of Bandura (1986), we know that the sense of self-efficacy can be a source of strong motivation. For example, it has been shown that individuals with high self-efficacy are more willing to expend greater work effort and to demonstrate persistence in overcoming obstacles to achieve their goals. By also fueling a collective sense of self-efficacy, the charismatic leader feeds perceptions of the group that they together accomplish tremendous feats. In addition, when collective self-efficacy is high, members of an organization are more willing to cooperate with each other in joint efforts to realize their shared aims (Yukl, 1994).

In this revised theory, what we see is a shift from House's earlier conceptualization where charismatic leadership was viewed more as a dyadic process to one that is a collective process. As Yukl (1994) has noted, the recent theory also places more emphasis on the reciprocal nature of the influence process under charismatic leadership. For example, charismatic leadership is likely to be far more motivational when the leader chooses a vision that is congruent with the followers' own values and identities. Likewise, followers are more likely to select as their leader an individual who espouses their core values, beliefs, and aspirations despite the fact that these may not always be clearly articulated by followers themselves.

Finally, a charismatic leadership model proposed by Sashkin (1988) under the label of 'Visionary Leadership' was presented in our book on *Charismatic Leadership* in 1988. Although his model has received little research attention, it does highlight the importance of visioning behavior, a core element in charismatic leadership. Besides visioning behavior, Sashkin identified five other behaviors: causing attention of others on key issues through unconventional and creative actions; effective interpersonal communication; demonstrating trustworthiness; showing self-respect and respect toward others; and taking personal risk.

Follower dynamics

Earlier research on charismatic leaders by political scientists and psychoanalysts (e.g. Downton, 1973; Kets de Vries, 1988; see Gabriel, Chapter 29, this volume) proposed that the followers of charismatic leaders were more likely to be those who were easily molded and persuaded by such dynamic leaders because of an essentially dependent character. Followers were drawn to a charismatic leader who exudes what they lack: self-confidence and conviction. For example, in a study of the charismatic, religious leader Reverend Sun Moon, Lodahl (1982) found that followers had greater feelings of helplessness, cynicism, distrust of political action, and less confidence in their sexual identity than a sample of college students. Other studies (e.g. Freemesser & Kaplan, 1976; Galanter, 1982) found followers of charismatic political and religious leaders to have lower self-esteem, a higher intolerance for indecision and crisis, and more experiences of psychological distress than others (see Tourish, Chapter 16, this volume).

But these studies were almost entirely conducted on populations of individuals disaffected by society or in contexts of crisis where individuals are needy by definition. In the corporate world, the situation is likely to be quite different. For example, in a large corporation, the subordinate of a charismatic leader may not have chosen voluntarily to belong to that leader's unit. More commonly, bosses are hired or promoted into positions, and the subordinates are already in place. So for subordinates, there is often little freedom to select who will lead them. Likewise, a leader may find himself inheriting a staff of confident, assertive employees. In the case of entrepreneurial companies founded by charismatic leaders, followers may be drawn to such contexts because of the challenge and opportunity. They may be seekers of the risk and uncertainty associated with a new venture—quite in contrast to followers who are dependent seekers of certainty.

Conger (1989) noted that there have been two popular explanations for why followers are attracted to charismatic leaders. The first centered on psychoanalytic notions of the ego. Essentially, the argument goes that followers are attempting to resolve a conflict between who they are and what they wish to become. They accomplish this by substituting their leader as their ideal, or in psychoanalytic terms, their ego ideal. Some psychoanalysts (e.g. Downton, 1973) trace this type of need back to an individual's failure to mature in adolescence and young adulthood. Because of absent, oppressive, or weak parents, individuals may develop a state of identity confusion. Associating emotionally with the charismatic leader is a means of coping with this confusion and achieving maturity. Given that the leader is in essence a substitute parent and model, a powerful emotional attachment is naturally formed by followers. Wishing to garner the leader's attention and affection, followers enthusiastically comply with his wishes. The assumption underlying this scenario of follower—leader dynamics is that followers are fulfilling a pathological need rather than a healthy desire for role models from whom to learn and grow.

The second school of thought is that followers are attracted to the charismatic leader because of a more constructive identification with the leader's abilities, a desire to learn from them, a quest for personal challenge and growth, and the attractiveness of the mission. This, of course, is what the theories in the previous section have largely argued. With Bass (1985), it is the opportunity to fulfill higher-order needs. In the Shamir et al. theory (1993), it is an opportunity to have one's self-esteem, self-worth, and self-efficacy enhanced.

Conger (1989) found in his study of charismatic leaders in business that subordinates often described the importance of an attraction to their leader's self-confidence, their strong convictions in the mission, their willingness to undertake personal risks, and their history of prior accomplishment. As a result, subordinates often felt a sense of fulfilling their own potential as they met their leader's high expectations. In addition, as others have found (e.g. Bass, 1985), the leader's vision offered attractive outcomes that were motivating in themselves. But Conger felt that simple identification and an attractive vision did not fully explain the commitment and motivation that followers demonstrated for their charismatic leaders.

Instead, Conger discovered that the personal approval of the charismatic leader became a principal measure of a subordinate's self-worth. A dependency then developed to the point that the leader largely defined one's level of performance and ability. As Shamir et al. (1993) have also noted, the leader's expression of high expectations set standards of performance and approval while a continual sense of urgency and the capacity to make subordinates feel unique further heightened motivation. Taken together, these actions promoted a sense of obligation in followers to continually live up to their leader's expectations. As the relationship deepens, this sense of obligation grows. The leader's expression of confidence in a subordinate ability in essence creates a sense of

duty and responsibility. Subordinates can only validate the leader's trust in them through exceptional accomplishments.

Over the long term, a dilemma naturally occurs for many followers. As the subordinate self-worth is increasingly defined in his relationship to the leader, a precarious dependence is built. Without the leader's affirmation, subordinates can feel that they are underperforming and even failing. In addition, there are fears of being ostracized. As one subordinate explained to Conger:

> There's a love/hate element [in our relationship]. You love him when you're focused on the same issues. You hate him when the contract falls apart. Either you're part of the team or not – there's a low tolerance for spectators. And over a career, you're in and out. A lot depends upon your effectiveness on the team. You have to build up a lot of credibility to regain any ground that you've lost.

The dark-side dynamics of this dependence will be discussed further in a later section.

There have also been studies of follower performance under charismatic leadership. One study (DeGroot et al., 2000) applied meta-analysis to assess the relationship between charismatic leadership style and leadership effectiveness, subordinate performance, subordinate satisfaction, subordinate effort, and subordinate commitment. Results indicate that the relationship between leader charisma and leader effectiveness is much weaker than reported in the published literature when leader effectiveness is measured at the individual level of analysis and when common method variance is controlled. Results also indicate a smaller relationship between charismatic leadership and subordinate performance when subordinate performance is measured at the individual level ($r = 0.31$) than when it is measured at the group level ($r = 0.49$ and robust across studies). The researchers found an effect size at the group level of analysis that is double in magnitude relative to the effect size at the individual level. This suggests that the effects of charismatic leadership are stronger when the leader has similar relationships with each subordinate or uses a single style to relate to each group. When the leader exhibits variable amounts of charisma to subordinates, or at least when the effect is measured at the individual level, the extent of effective leadership is reduced. These results also suggest that charismatic leadership is more effective at increasing group performance than at increasing individual performance. Other moderators were tested, but they did not account for a significant portion of variance in the observed distribution of correlations, suggesting a need for further research into other potential moderators. Meta-analysis examining the effects of charismatic leadership on subordinate effort and job satisfaction revealed lower correlations when multiple methods of measurement were used, with little convergence toward stable population estimates. If charismatic leadership behavior is to produce higher performance outcomes from subordinates, further research is needed to examine how this occurs.

The role of context

Until very recently, interest in the role of context and situational factors has been limited. This is due largely to the backgrounds of those researching leadership. 'Micro-theorists' (those with a psychological or social psychological orientation) have dominated the field to date. Few researchers with a more 'macro' or sociological perspective have been active in studying leadership. As a result, environmental or contextual investigations have rarely been applied to leadership studies outside of the fields of political science and religion. As such, our knowledge in this area remains poor, and what does exist is largely theoretical and speculative.

The most common speculation has been that periods of stress and turbulence are the most conducive for charismatic leadership (this argument is derived from the work of political scientists looking at charismatic leadership in political and religious contexts: see Cell, 1974; Toth, 1981). Max Weber (1968), for example, specifically focused on times of 'crisis' as facilitating environments. The basic assumption is that times of stressful change either encourage a longing among individuals for a leader who offers attractive solutions and visions of the future or that charismatic leaders have an easier time of promoting a transformational vision during times of uncertainty when the status quo appears to no longer function (Bryman, 1992).

To date, the most important empirical study to examine situational factors in organizational contexts was conducted by Roberts and Bradley (1988). Using a field study, they looked at a school superintendent who was appointed a state commissioner of education. In her role as superintendent, she was perceived by her organization as a charismatic leader, yet as commissioner that perception failed to convey. In Roberts and Bradley's search to explain why the individual's charisma did not transfer, they discovered several essential differences between the two contexts.

In terms of the larger environment, the individual's first context, a school district, was one in crisis – confirming the hypothesis that crisis may indeed facilitate the emergence of charismatic leadership. In contrast, the leader's second context, at the state level, was not in a similar state of distress. The public's perception was that their state schools were basically sound and simply in need of incremental improvements. The individual's authority also differed in the two situations. As a superintendent, she had much more control and autonomy. At the state level, as commissioner, quite the opposite was true. Her number one priority was political loyalty to the governor. She no longer possessed the freedom to undertake actions as she deemed necessary: instead, they had to be cleared through the governor's office. Her relationships were also different. Whereas the district organization had been small, with limited stakeholders and localized geographically, the situation at the state level was at the opposite end of the spectrum. The agency was far greater in size, complexity, and bureaucracy. The numerous committees and associations in which she had to participate meant that she had little time to build the deep, personal bonds that she had established at the district level. As a result, her impact at the state level was no longer personal and perceptions of her as a charismatic leader did not materialize.

From the Roberts and Bradley study, we might conclude that context shapes charismatic leadership in at least two ways. First, an environment in crisis is indeed more receptive to leadership in general and is more likely to be open to proposals common to charismatic leaders for radical changes such as those embodied in the superintendent's vision. Secondly, there are structural and stakeholder characteristics of organizations which influence an individual's latitude to take initiative and to build personal relationships which determine perceptions of charismatic leadership. The position of superintendent provided structurally far more autonomy to act than that of commissioner. The less geographically dispersed and more limited number of stakeholders fostered deeper working relationships at the district level and also inspired affection and trust in her leadership. These in turn heightened perceptions of her charisma.

With findings like the study of Roberts and Bradley in mind, we can think of the contexts of organizations as divided into an outer and an inner context, the outer being the environment beyond the organization and the inner including the organization's culture, structure, power distribution, and so on. Using this simple framework, it is useful to divide our discussion around these two contextual dimensions. We will start with the external environment.

On the issue of whether crisis is the critical external condition, Conger (1993) hypothesized that there could actually be much more variability in environmental conditions than we might think. He argued that charismatic leadership is not necessarily precipitated by conditions of crisis and distress. In earlier research looking at charismatic business leaders (Conger, 1989), he found charismatic leaders who were entrepreneurs who operated in environments not so much of crisis but of great opportunity, munificence, and optimism. Instead of crisis being the sole contextual condition, there may instead be at least two conducive environments, one demanding a major reorientation of the existing order because of a perceived state of distress and the other involving the emergence or creation of a new order based on a 'munificence entrepreneurial' context.

In addition, Conger argued that more of an interplay exists between the leader and the context. In other words, context is not the key determinant, but rather that the leader and the context influence one another – the relative weight of each's influence varying from situation to situation. For example, Willner (1984) found that while examining charismatic leaders in the political arena some were able to induce or create through their own actions the necessary contextual conditions of a crisis. We might be able to find charismatic leaders who are able similarly to foster perceptions of munificence and great entrepreneurial opportunity.

Conger also went on to propose that the more conducive the contextual conditions, the less the magnitude or the fewer the number of charismatic attributes perhaps required for a leader to be perceived as charismatic. Similarly, the greater the intensity or number of 'charismatic attributes' of the leader, the need for an existing context say of extreme crisis or entrepreneurial opportunities may diminish as the leader is able to create these perceptions through his own actions. For example, an ability at articulating unforeseen opportunities or looming problems in a credible manner may facilitate perceptions of a crisis and/or great opportunity. But this is still an area of great speculation in need of research attention.

Beyond the limited efforts focusing on the external environments of charismatic leadership described above, there has been only one major theoretical work focusing on contextual conditions within organizations that may influence charismatic leadership. Pawar and Eastman (1997) proposed four factors of organizations that might affect receptivity to transformational leadership. Given our earlier discussion of the overlap between transformational and charismatic forms of leadership, it is worth examining their hypotheses as they may relate to charismatic leadership.

The four factors that Pawar and Eastman identified are (1) the organization's emphasis on efficiency versus adaptation, (2) the relative dominance of the organization's technical core versus its boundary-spanning units, (3) organizational structures, and (4) modes of governance. Their model is built around the central notion that transformational or charismatic leadership is essentially about leading organizational change. Organizational contexts that are more conducive to change are therefore more favorable for charismatic leadership.

They begin with the notion that organizations are seeking one of two basic goals – efficiency or adaptation. The challenge is that the goals of efficiency and adaptation have conflicting purposes – the former requires organizational stability, while the latter is centered on change. In reality, as we know today, most business organizations attempt both simultaneously, and this highlights one of the dilemmas of Pawar and Easman's theory. It is built around idealized polarities which provide a simple elegance in terms of theory building but may not reflect the complexities of reality. Nonetheless, they hypothesize that an efficiency orientation requires goal stability and, necessarily, administrative management or transactional leadership to achieve its goals. During adaptation periods, on the other hand, the leader's role is to overcome resistance to change and to align the organization to a new environment through a dynamic vision, new goals and values. Therefore, organizations with adaptive goals are far more open to charismatic leadership. The authors caution, however, that while adaptive periods are more receptive to leadership, there must be a *felt need* by organizational members for transformation, otherwise they may accept more administrative management.

The second contextual factor – the relative dominance of the technical core versus boundary-spanning units – refers to the fact that an organization's task systems are either more inwardly oriented or more externally oriented. In this case, Thompson (1967) had argued that organizations divide their task systems into two parts: (1) a technical core which performs the work of input processing through the operation of technology and (2) boundary-spanning functions which interface directly with the external environment. Isolated from an ever-changing external world, the technical core develops routines and stability in how it approaches its tasks (Thompson, 1967). In contrast, the boundary-spanning functions are forced to adapt continually to environmental constraints and contingencies and, as a result, can never develop highly standardized or routine approaches (Thompson, 1967). Pawar and Eastman postulate that organizations where boundary-spanning units dominate over the technical core will be more open to transformational and charismatic leadership, since they are more receptive to change.

Employing Mintzberg's (1979) typology of organizational structures, Pawar and Eastman propose that only certain structures will be receptive to leadership. Mintzberg's five 'ideal type' structures are (1) the adhocracy, (2) the simple structure, (3) the machine bureaucracy, (4) the professional bureaucracy, and (5) the divisional structure. Of these five, only two are hypothesized by Pawar and Eastman to be conducive to transformational or charismatic leadership. They are the simple structure and the adhocracy. Specifically, both are felt to be more receptive to organizational change through the promotion of a vision. In the simple structure, the leader or entrepreneur-leader is the source of the organization's vision, and commitment is facilitated by employee loyalty to the leader. In an adhocracy structure, the vision is developed through professionals who possess the power, knowledge, and willingness to work collectively (Mintzberg, 1979).

It is argued that the three other structures have internal forces which mitigate against an openness to innovative leadership. For example, the machine bureaucracy is dominated by standardized tasks and work processes. Senior managers are obsessed by a control mindset, and lower-level managers are intent only on implementing operational directives from above. As such, there is little concern with innovation and change, which are potentially threatening to a tightly orchestrated status quo. In the professional bureaucracy, professionals dominate to such an extent that management is simply a support function and marginalized to the role of facilitation. In addition, the professionals in these systems are far less committed to the organization than to their own work and profession. As a result, a collective vision is unlikely to be developed either by these self-centered professionals or by a marginalized group of top managers. The divisional structure is also not conducive. Built around two layers in which a headquarters operation governs quasi-autonomous divisions, the focus of the corporate headquarters is to specify operational goals and to monitor the divisions' accomplishment of them. The divisions then are concerned with attaining operational goals. Pawar and Eastman argue that since divisional structures are concerned with operational goals, neither group is likely to show great interest in developing a vision.

The final factor influencing receptivity to leadership in the Pawar and Eastman model is the mode of internal governance. They start with the assumption that membership in organizations is built around furthering individual members' self-interests (Burns & Stalker, 1961; Thompson, 1967). Yet the aim of transformational and charismatic forms of leadership is for followers to transcend their own self-interests for collective goals. Under Wilkins and Ouchi's (1983) three modes of governance (the market, the bureaucratic, and the clan), the nature of transactions between an organization and its members will differ. Under the market mode, transactions based on the exchange of commitments between the organization and its members are determined by market or price mechanisms. Because an external market shapes commitments, the organization has little incentive to socialize its members to defer self-interests. In the bureaucratic mode, a contract for commitments is built around employees accepting organizational authority in return for wages. The organization then monitors compliance through formal monitoring and exchange mechanisms. These become the devices that curb members' self-interests. Under the clan mode, organizational members are socialized in such a way that their own interests and the organization's are aligned as one. In other words, employees still hold their self-interests, but they believe they can fulfill them through achieving the collective's interests. As such, cultural values and norms shape self-interests. It is therefore the clan mode that is most receptive to transformational leadership since it allows for a merging of individual self-interests with the collective's goals.

Institutionalization

The institutionalization or routinization of charisma was an issue that intrigued Weber greatly. He believed that charisma was essentially an unstable force. It either faded or was institutionalized as the charismatic leader's mission was accomplished:

> If [charisma] is not to remain a purely transitory phenomenon, but to take on the character of a permanent relationship forming a stable community, it is necessary for the character of charismatic authority to be radically changed....It cannot remain stable, but becomes either traditionalized or rationalized or both. (Weber [1924] 1947, p. 364)

He argued there were strong incentives on the part of charismatic leaders and their followers to transform their movements into more permanent institutions. With successes, the followers began to achieve positions of authority and material advantage. The desire naturally arose to institutionalize these, and so traditions and rules grew up to protect the gains of the mission.

Institutionalization is one area where little research has been conducted in the organizational literature. We know almost nothing about the routinization of charismatic leadership. The only major study was conducted by Trice and Beyer in 1986. They examined two charismatic leaders, where in one case charisma had routinized and in another it had not. Their conclusions were that five key factors were largely responsible for the successful institutionalization of charisma: (1) the development of an administrative apparatus separate from the charismatic leader that put into practice the leader's mission; (2) the incorporation of the leader's mission into oral and written traditions; (3) the transfer of charisma through rites and ceremonies to other members of the organization; (4) a continued identification by organizational members to the original mission; and (5) the selection of a successor who resembles the charismatic leader and is committed to the founder's mission. In the case where charisma did not routinize, these factors were largely missing.

From the standpoint of the business world, however, it does appear that charisma is a relatively fragile phenomenon in terms of institutionalization. There are several examples from the management literature where succession dilemmas prevented the routinization of charismatic leadership (e.g. Bryman, 1992, 1993; Conger, 1989). The charismatic leaders in Conger's 1989 study have all since departed from their original organizations due to either promotions, moves to new organizations, retirement, or in one case, death. From informal observations, it is clear that there is little indication of any significant routinization of their charisma in their various organizations. In a 1993 article, Conger noted that one of the group—an entrepreneur—had had some success in that elements of his original mission, values, and operating procedures did institutionalize. But that individual has since left that organization, and a few years ago it was acquired by a much larger firm which has superimposed its own mission, values, and procedures. Today there is little evidence of that initial routinization of the leader's charisma. The leaders in Conger's study who were acting as change agents in large, bureaucratic organizations had practically no long-term impact in terms of institutionalizing their charisma.

As Bryman (1993) argues, succession is one of the most crucial issues in routinization. When an organization possesses a charismatic leader, it creates what Wilson (1975) has called as 'charismatic demand'. The dilemma, of course, is that it is highly unlikely that a charismatic leader will be found to replace the original one. Though Bryman (1993) has found one example in a study of a transportation company, such situations appear extremely rare. Instead, what often happens is that a charismatic leader is replaced by a more managerially-oriented individual. Examples of this would be Steven Jobs, who was succeeded by John Sculley and Michael Spindler, the succession of Lee Iacocca at Chrysler by Robert Eaton

(Bryman, 1993), and Walt Disney's replacement by Roy Disney (Bryman, 1993). Biggart (1989) does note that among direct selling organizations we often see an attempt to overcome succession problems by either promoting a national sales executive into the leadership role or to 'invest the mission in one's children' (p. 144). Looking at Amway and Shaklee, Biggart discovered that the founder's children assumed active roles in the company in turn fostering a 'charismatic presence'. But he also found that their roles were largely bureaucratic and that the companies had done little to institutionalize the founder's charisma beyond the presence of their children. Given the enormous demands for continual adaptation, owing to competition and strong needs to develop rational and formalized structures, business organizations may simply not be conducive to long-term institutionalization of a leader's charisma.

Even if routinization were to be successful, it is no guarantee of continued performance success. As Conger (1993) noted, part of the dilemma is that successors may not possess the strategic skills or other abilities crucial to the firm's future leadership. For example, while the retailer Walmart has apparently institutionalized Sam Walton's values and operating beliefs, a critical issue is whether it institutionalizes his visionary insights into the world of retailing. Just as importantly, Walton's vision was most likely time-bound. So even if his strategic competence were to be institutionalized, it is the product of a specific era in retailing and therefore may be unable to anticipate the industry's next paradigm shift. The original mission of a charismatic leader is highly unlikely to be forever adaptive.

Even elements as simple as institutionalized rituals may themselves become counterproductive over time. Conger (1993) cited the example of IBM, which very effectively institutionalized many of Thomas Watson Sr's values and traditions. Several of these would prove maladaptive only decades later. For instance, Watson's original strong emphasis on sales and marketing would ensure that future company leaders were drawn from these ranks. The price, however, would be in terms of senior leaders' failure to adequately understand the strategic importance of certain new technologies and software systems. A tradition of rewarding loyalty through internal promotions added to the problem. It encouraged inbreeding around the company's worldview and simply reinforced notions of IBM's mainframe mentality and its arrogance. Even simple traditions would lose their original meaning and transform themselves into bureaucratic norms. For example, IBM's traditional corporate dress code of dark suits and white shirts is illustrative. This requirement was intended by Watson to make his salespeople feel like executives. If you dressed like an executive, you would feel like one was Watson's original thinking. Indeed, the dress code did build pride in the early days of IBM. Many decades later, however, this norm would transform into a symbol of rigidity and conformity. It bureaucratized itself as Weber would have guessed.

In conclusion, we have little knowledge about this crucial area of charismatic leadership. A limited number of case studies and no systematic longitudinal research have offered us at best tantalizing tidbits of insight.

LIABILITIES OF CHARISMATIC LEADERSHIP

While the literature has largely been glowing about the effects of charismatic leadership in organizations, there has been some interest in the negative outcomes associated with this form of leadership. For example, Khurana (2002), in his study of the hiring and firing of CEOs at over 850 of America's largest companies, found that corporate board members and executive search consultants placed a strong emphasis on the charisma of CEO candidates. As a result, both groups artificially limited the number of candidates considered to their companies' detriment. The CEO labor market proved to be a closed ecosystem in which selection decisions were based on highly stylized criteria that more often had little to do with the problems a firm was confronting. As a result, the charismatic candidates often failed once in the CEO role. At the same time, the charismatic candidates possessed extraordinary leverage to demand high salaries and power. Since the pool of high-profile charismatic CEOs is limited, such scarcity naturally drove up wages.

Jane Howell (1988) proposed a simple, dichotomous model of socialized and personalized charisma which attempted to address the issue of the liabilities of certain charismatic leaders. In conjunction with Robert House (Howell & House, 1993), the theory was refined to propose a set of personality characteristics, behaviors, and effects that distinguished two forms of charismatic leadership.

Specifically, socialized charismatics are described as articulating visions that serve the interests of the collective. They govern in an egalitarian, non-self-aggrandizing manner, and actively empower and develop their followers. They also work through legitimate, established channels of authority to accomplish their goals. On the other hand, personalized charismatic leaders are authoritarian and narcissistic. They have high needs for power driven in part by low self-esteem. Their goals reflect the leader's own self-interests, and followers' needs are played upon as a means to achieve the leader's interests. In addition, they disregard established and legitimate channels of authority as well as the rights and feelings of others. At the same time, they demand unquestioning obedience and dependence in their followers. While portraying these two forms as dichotomous, Howell and House do acknowledge that a charismatic leader might in reality exhibit some aspects of both the socialized and the personalized characteristics. This latter view is probably closer to reality than their ideal model. As such, a scaler model might be more accurate.

Drawing upon actual examples of charismatic leaders, Conger (1989, 1990) examined those who had produced negative outcomes for themselves and their organizations. He found that problems could arise with charismatic leaders around (1) their visions, (2) their impression management, (3) their management practices, and (4) succession planning. On the dimension of vision, typical problems occurred when leaders possessed an exaggerated sense of the market opportunities for their vision or when they grossly underestimated the resources necessary for its accomplishment. In addition, visions often failed when they reflected largely the leader's needs rather than constituents or the marketplace or when the leader was unable to recognize fundamental shifts in the environment that demanded redirection.

In terms of impression management, charismatic leaders appear prone to exaggerated self-descriptions and claims for their visions that can mislead. For example, they may present information that makes their visions appear more feasible or appealing than they are in reality. They may screen out looming problems or else foster an illusion of control when things are actually out of control. From the standpoint of management practices, there are examples of overly self-confident and unconventional charismatic leaders who create antagonistic relations with peers and superiors. Some such as Steven Jobs are known to create 'in' and 'out' groups within their organizations that promote dysfunctional rivalries. Others create excessive dependence on themselves and then alternate between idealizing and devaluing dependent subordinates. Many are ineffective administrators, preferring 'big picture' activities to routine work. Finally, as discussed in the section on institutionalization, charismatic leaders often have a difficult time developing successors. They simply enjoy the limelight too much to share it. To find a replacement who is a peer may be too threatening for leaders who tend to be so narcissistic.

Recently, Daniel Sankowsky (1995) has written about the dilemma of charismatic leaders who are prone to a pathology of narcissism (see Kets de Vries & Balazs, Chapter 28, this volume). Specifically, he has proposed a stage model showing how dark-side charismatics implicate their followers into a cycle of exploitation. First, these leaders offer a grandiose vision and confidently encourage followers to accomplish it. Followers, however, soon find themselves in an untenable position. Because of their leader's optimism, they have underestimated the constraints facing the mission as well as the resources they need but currently lack. As a result, performance inevitably falls short of the leader's high expectations. Wishing to comply with their leader's wishes, however, followers continue to strive. Soon their performance appears substandard as they fall behind. While initially the leader will blame the outside world for undermining the mission, their attention will eventually turn to the followers. Conditioned to accept their leader's viewpoint and not to challenge it, followers willingly receive the blame themselves from their leader. The reverse of the many benefits ascribed to charismatic leaders then occurs. Instead of building their followers' self-worth and self-efficacy, they gradually destroy it and create highly dependent individuals.

CONCLUSIONS

Charismatic leadership is a rich and complex phenomenon. As this chapter suggests, our understanding of the topic has advanced significantly since Max Weber proposed the first formal theory of charismatic leadership. While political scientists and sociologists grappled with some of the more critical questions of why certain leaders are seen as charismatic, it was the field of organizational behavior that advanced theory and research to the greatest degree. That said, there are important areas of the topic which are only partially understood to this day. Significantly more research and theory building are required, especially to deepen our understanding of the interaction effects between context and charismatic leadership, institutionalization and succession dynamics, and the liabilities of this important form of leadership.

REFERENCES

Agle, B.R. & Sonnenfeld, J.A. (1994) Charismatic chief executive officers: Are they more effective? An empirical test of charismatic leadership theory. *Academy of Management Best Papers Proceedings*, 2–6.

Avolio, B. & Yamarino, F.J. (1990) Operationalizing charismatic leadership using a levels of analysis framework. *The Leadership Quarterly*, 1, 193–208.

Bandura, A. (1986) *Social foundations of thought and action: a social-cognitive view*. Englewood Cliffs, NJ: Prentice Hall.

Bass, B. M. (1970) When planning for others. Journal of Applied Behavioral Science,6. 151–171.

Bass, B.M. (1985) *Leadership and performance beyond expectations*. New York: Free Press.

Bass, B.M. (1990) Bass and Stogdill's handbook of leadership: Theory, research and managerial expectations (3rd Ed.). New York: Free Press.

Bass, B. M. & Avolio, B. (1993) Transformational leadership: a response to critiques . In M.M. Chemers & R. Ayman (eds), *Leadership theory and research: perspectives and directions*. New York: Academic Press.

Bass, B.M. & Yammarino, F.J.(1988) Leadership: dispositional and situational. (ONR Tech Rep No 1). Binghamton, NY: State University of New York, Center for Leadership Studies.

Bennis, W.G. & Nanus, B. (1985) Leaders: *the strategies for taking charge. New York*: Harper & Row.

Berlew, D.E. (1974) Leadership and organizational excitement. *California Management Review*, 17, 21–30

Biggart, N.W. (1989) *Charismatic capitalism: direct selling organizations in America*. Chicago, IL: University of Chicago Press.

Blau, P.M. (1963) *Exchange and power in social life*. New York: Wiley.

Boal, K.B. & Bryson, J.M. (1988) Charismatic leadership: a phenomenological and structural approach. In J.G. Hunt, B. R. Baliga, H.

Bryman, A. (1992) *Charisma and leadership in organizations. London*: Sage.

Bryman, A. (1993) Charismatic leadership in business organizations: Some neglected issues. *The Leadership Quarterly*, 4 (3/4), 289–304.

Burns, J.M. (1978) *Leadership*. New York: Harper.

Cell, C.P. (1974) Charismatic heads of state: the social context. *Behavioral Science Research*, 4, 255–305.

Chinoy, E. (1961) *Society*. New York: Random House.

Conger, J.A. (1985) Charismatic leadership in business: an exploration study. Unpublished doctoral dissertation, School of Business Administration, Harvard University.

Conger, J.A. and Kanungo, R.N. (1992) Perceived behavioral attributes of charismatic leadership. Canadian Journal of Behavioral Science, 24,86–102.

Conger, J.A. (1989) *The charismatic leader: beyond the mystique of exceptional leadership*. San Francisco: Jossey-Bass.

Conger, J.A. (1993) Max Weber's conceptualization of charismatic authority: its influence on organizational research. *The Leadership Quarterly*, 4 (3/4), 277–288.

Conger, J.A. & Kanungo R.N. (1987) Towards a behavioral theory of charismatic leadership in organizational settings. *Academy of Management Review*, 12, 637–647.

Conger, J.A. & Kanungo, R.N. (1999) *Charismatic leadership in organizations*. Thousand Oaks, CA: Sage.

Conger, J. A. (1990) The dark side of leadership. Organizational Dynamics, 19 (2), 44–55.

Dachler, P. & Schriesheim, C.A. (eds), *Emerging leadership vistas*. Lexington, MA: Lexington Books, pp. 1–28.

DeGroot, T., Kiker, D.S., & Cross, T.C. (2000) A meta-analysis to review organizational outcomes related to charismatic leadership. *Canadian Journal of Administrative Sciences*, 17(4), 356–372.

Deluga, R.J. (1995) The relationship between attributional charismatic leadership and organizational climate behavior. *Journal of Applied Psychology*, 25(18), 1652–1669.

Dow, T.E. (1969) A theory of charisma. *Social Quarterly*, 10, 306–318.

Downton, J.V. (1973) *Rebel leadership*. New York: Free Press.

Freemesser, G.F. & Kaplan, H.B. (1976) Self-attitudes and deviant behavior: the case of the charismatic religious movement. *Journal of Youth and Adolescence*, 5(1), 1–9.

Friedland, W.H. (1964) For a sociological concept of charisma. *Social Forces*, 43, 18–26.

Friedrich, C.J. (1961) Political leadership and the problem of the charismatic power. *Journal of Politics*, 23, 3–24.

Galanter, M. (1982) Charismatic religious sects and psychiatry: an overview. *American Journal of Psychiatry*, 139(2), 1539–1548.

Graen, G. & Scandura, T. (1987) Towards a psychology of dyadic organizing. In B.M. Staw & L.L. Cummings (eds),

Hater, J.J. & Bass, B.M. (1988) Superiors' evaluations and subordinates' perceptions of transformational and transactional leadership. *Journal of Applied Psychology*, 73 695–702.

House, R.J. (1977) A 1976 theory of Charismatic leadership. In J.G. Hunt & L.L. Larson (eds), *Leadership: the cutting edge*. Carbondale, IL: Southern Illinois University Press.

House, R.J. and Mitchell T.R. (1974) Path-goal theory of leadership. Contemporary Business, 3, 81–98.

House, R.J. & Dessler, G. (1974) The path-goal theory of leadership: some post hoc and a priori tests, In J.G. Hunt & L.L. Larson (eds), *Contingency approaches to leadership*. Carbondale, IL: Southern Illinois University Press.

House, R.J. & Shamir, B. (1993) Toward the integration of transformational, charismatic, and visionary theories. In M. Chemmers & R. Ayman (eds), *Leadership theory and research perspectives and directions*. Orlando, FL: Academic Press, pp. 577–594.

House, R.J., Spangler, W.D., & Woycke, J. (1991) Personality and charisma in the US presidency: a psychological theory of leader effectiveness. *Administrative Science Quarterly*, 36, 364–396.

Howell, J.M. (1988) Two faces of charisma: Socialized and personalized leadership in organizations. In J.A. Conger and R.N. Kanungo (Eds) Charismatic leadership: The elusive factor in organizational effectiveness. (pp. 213–236). San Francisco: Jossey Bass.

Howell, J. M., & Frost, P. (1989) A laboratory study of charismatic leadership. *Organizational Behavior and Human Decision Processes*, 43, 243–269.

Howell, J.M. & Higgins, C.A. (1990) Champions of technological innovation. *Administrative Science Quarterly*, 35, 317–41.

Howell, J. M. and Avolio, B.J. (1993) Transformational leadership, transactional leadership, loss of control, and support for innovation: Key predictors of consolidated business unit performance. Journal of Applied Psychology, 78, 891–902

Hunt, J.G. (1991) *Leadership: a new synthesis*. Newbury Park, CA: Sage.

Jahoda, M. (1981) Work employment and unemployment: values, theories and approaches in social research. *American Psychologist*, 36, 184–191.

Kanter, R.M. (1967) Commitment and social organization: a study of commitment mechanisms in utopian communities. *American Sociological Review*, 33(4), 499–517.

Kanter, R.M. (1979) Power failures in management circuits. *Harvard Business Review*, 57, 65–75.

Katz, J. & Kahn, R.L. (1978) *The social psychology of organizations*. New York: Wiley.

Kets de Vries, M.F.R. (1988) Origins of charisma: ties that bind the leader and the led. In J.A. Conger & R.N. Kanungo (eds), *Charismatic leadership: the elusive factor in organizational effectiveness*. San Francisco: Jossey-Bass.

Khurana, R. (2002) *Searching for a corporate savior: the irrational quest for charismatic CEOs*. Princeton, NJ: Princeton University Press.

Kirkpatrick, S.A. (1992) Decomposing charismatic leadership: The effects of leader content and procession follower performance, attitudes, and perceptions. Unpublished doctoral dissertation, University of Maryland, College Park.

Kirkpatrick, S.A. & Locke, E.A. (1996) Direct and indirect effects of three core charismatic leadership components on performance and attitudes. *Journal of Applied Psychology*, 81, 36–51.

Koene, H., Pennings, H., & Schrender, M. (1991) *Leadership, culture, and organizational effectiveness*. Boulder, CO: Center for Creative Leadership.

Koh, W.L., Terborg, J.R. & Steers, R.M. (1991) *The impact of transformational leaders on organizational commitment, organizational citizenship behavior, teacher satisfaction and student performance in Singapore*. Miami, FL: Academy of Management Meetings.

Locke, E., Kirkpatrick, S., Wheeler, J.K., et al., (1991) *The essence of leadership*. New York: Lexington Books.

Lodahl, A. (1982) Crisis in values and the success of the Unification Church. Unpublished doctoral dissertation, Cornell University, Ithaca, NY.

Loewenstein, K. (1966) *Max Weber's political ideas in the perspective of our time*. Amherst, MA: University of Massachusetts Press.

McClelland, D.C. (1985) *Human motivation*. Glenview, IL: Scott Foresman.

Marcus, J.T. (1961) Transcendence and charisma. *Western Political Quarterly*, 14(March), 236–241.

Meindl, J. & Lerner, M.J. (1983) The heroic motive: some experimental demonstrations. *Journal of Experimental Psychology*, 19, 1–20.

Mintzberg, H. (1979) *The structuring of organizations*. Englewood Cliffs, NJ: Prentice Hall.

Neilson, E. 1986. Empowerment strategies: balancing authority and responsibility. In S. Srivastra (ed.), *Executive power*. San Francisco: Jossey-Bass.

Pawar, B.S. & Eastman, K.K. (1997) The nature and implications of contextual influences on transformational leadership: a conceptual examination. *Academy of Management Review*, 22; 80–109.

Pettigrew, A.M. (1992).

Podsakoff, Todor, & Skov. (1982) Effects of leader contingent and noncontingent reward and punishment behaviors on subordinate performance and satisfaction. *Academy of Management Journal*, 25, 810–821.

Podsakoff, P.M., MacKenzie, S.B., Moorman, R. H. and Fetter, R. (1990) Transformational leader behaviors and their effects on followers' trust in leader, satisfaction, and organizational citizenship behaviors. *The Leadership Quarterly*, 1, 107–142.

Prentice, D.A. (1987) Psychological correspondence of possessions, attitudes and values. *Journal of Personality and Social Psychology*, 53(6), 993–1003.

Puffer, S.M. (1990) Attributions of charismatic leadership: the impact of decision style, outcome, and observer characteristics. *The Leadership Quarterly*, 1, 177–192.

Roberts, N.C. & Bradley, R.T. (1988) Limits of charisma. In J.A. Conger & R.N. Kanungo (eds), *Charismatic leadership: the elusive factor in organizational effectiveness*. San Francisco: Jossey-Bass.

Salancik, G.R. (1977) Commitment and the control of organizational behavior and belief. In B.M. Staw and G.R. Salancik (eds.), *New directions in organizational behavior*. Chicago: St. Clair, pp.1–54.

Sankowsky, D. (1995) The charismatic leader as narcissist: understanding the abuse of power. *Organizational Dynamics*, 57–71.

Sashkin, M. (1988) The visionary leader. In J.A. Conger and R.N. Kanungo (eds.), *Charismatic leadership: The elusive factor in organizational effectiveness*. San Francisco: Jossey-Bass.

Shamir, B. (1992) Attribution of influence and charisma to the leader: the romance of leadership revisited. *Journal of Applied Social Psychology*, 22(5), 386–407.

Shamir, B. (1995) Social distance and charisma: theoretical notes and an exploratory study. *The Leadership Quarterly*, 6(1), 19–47.

Shamir, B., House, R. & Arthur, M.B. (1993) The motivation effects of charismatic leadership: a self-concept based theory. *Organization Science*, 4(4), 584.

Snyder, M. & Ickes, W. (1985) Personality and social behavior. In G. Lindzey & E. Aronson (eds), *Handbook of social psychology*. New York: Random House, pp. 883–947.

Thompson, J.D. (1967) *Organizations in action*. New York: McGraw-Hill.

Toth, M.A. (1981) *The theory of the two charisma*. Washington, DC: University Press of America.

Trice, H.M. & Beyer, J.M. (1986) Charisma and its routinization in two social movement organizations. *Journal of Occupational Behavior*, 7, 125–138.

Walster, E., Aronson, D., & Abrahams, D. (1966) On increasing the persuasiveness of a low prestige communicator. *Journal of Experimental Social Psychology*, 2,325–342.

Weber, M. (1947) *The theory of social and economic organizations* (A.M. Henderson & T. Parsons, trans.; T. Parsons, ed.). New York: Free Press.

Weber, M. (1968) *Economy and society* (1925) (3 vols. ed.). New York: Bedminster.

Willner, A.R. (1984) *The spellbinders: charismatic political leadership*. New Haven, CT: Yale University Press.

Wilson, B.R. (1975) *The noble savages: the primitive origins of charisma and its contemporary survival*. Berkeley, CA: University of California Press.

Yukl, G. (1994) *Leadership in organizations*, 3rd edn, Englewood Cliffs, NJ: Prentice-Hall.

Zaleznik, A. & Kets de Vries, M. (1975) *Power and the corporate mind*. Boston, MA: Houghton Mifflin.

8

Gender and Leadership

Linda L. Carli and Alice H. Eagly

INTRODUCTION

In this chapter we document women's underrepresentation as leaders and examine various theoretical explanations for women's leadership disadvantage. First, we explore whether the gender gap in leadership can be explained by inherent differences between men and women that endow men with natural leadership ability. We then consider whether women's disadvantage lies in their greater domestic responsibilities and lesser investments in human capital in the form of paid work experience and education. We also assess whether women's advancement is obstructed by gender stereotypes and discrimination, which may result in resistance to women's influence and authority. Next, we examine research comparing the leadership styles of men and women to determine whether such differences may provide either gender with advantages or disadvantages as leaders, and thus potentially contribute to women's lack of access to leadership. Finally, this chapter evaluates the extent to which organizational structure and culture make it difficult for women to rise into higher-level leadership positions.

In our chapter, we present many studies comparing the situations, perceptions, attitudes, and behaviors of men and women. Studies that reveal gender differences do not demonstrate dichotomous effects with no overlap of men and women, but rather average overall differences that occur across a variety of situational, cultural, and individual variables. Many differences and similarities have been established meta-analytically by taking into account the results of all available studies. These effects are often moderated by other variables, such as ethnicity, religion, country, education, organizational setting, and other factors. In these several respects, effects associated with gender resemble the effects associated with other variables studied by social scientists (e.g., personality traits, attitudes, socioeconomic status, and race).

We begin by examining women's current status as leaders. To what extent have women gained access to leadership and how has their advancement remained blocked?

THE UNDERREPRESENTATION OF WOMEN LEADERS

There is little doubt that the status of women has improved. Women have steadily increased their numbers in the paid labor force. In the United States, women made up only 39% of the paid workforce in 1973, but 47% by 2009 (US Bureau of Labor Statistics, 2010b, Table 2). Women's incomes have also risen: in 2009, for full-time US workers, women earned 80 cents for every dollar that men earned – up from only 62 cents in 1979 (US Bureau of Labor Statistics, 2010a). Across all organizations in the United States, women constitute 51% of those in professional and managerial positions, 37% of managers, and 25% of chief executives (US Bureau of Labor Statistics, 2010b, Table 11).

Women's advancement is also apparent in politics and public sector jobs. In 2010 in the United States, women hold 17% of the Senate seats, 17% of the seats in the House, 12% of the governorships, and 23% of state executive offices (Center for American Women and Politics, 2010a). There are record numbers of women in state legislatures (Center for American Woman and Politics, 2010b) as well as in the US Congress (Center for American Woman and Politics, 2010c). Similarly, in the highest non-elective positions of the federal government, the Senior Executive Service, the percentage of women has risen from 11% in 1990 (US Office of Personnel Management, 1997) to 28% in 2007 (US Office of Personnel Management, 2007).

Although women have made substantial gains, they still have not achieved parity with men. Women are particularly underrepresented at higher levels of leadership, and the percentage of female executives declines with increasing organizational rank (Helfat, Harris, & Wolfson, 2006). In the *Fortune* 500, women make up 16% of corporate officers and 15% of corporate boards (Catalyst, 2010d) in the *FP*500, the 500 largest Canadian corporations, women are 17% of corporate officers and 14% of boards of directors (Catalyst, 2010c). At the very top, there are only 13 companies with female CEOs in the *Fortune* 500 (Catalyst, 2010b), and 19 in the *FP*500 (Catalyst, 2010a). Similarly, in Europe, women hold 11% of the positions in the highest decision-making bodies of the largest corporations (Desvaux, Devillard-Hoellinger, & Baumgarten, 2007) and only 12 women are CEOs in the Global *Fortune* 500 (*Fortune*, 2010). In contrast to these statistics for large corporations, women are particularly well-represented as leaders in US philanthropic organizations and foundations, where women hold 55% of chief executive and chief giving officer positions (Council on Foundations, 2009).

Despite much progress, women clearly remain poorly represented in many high-level leadership positions. But even when women attain positions with high status, they still remain disadvantaged relative to men. The positions that women hold typically confer less authority than those of men when controlling for job status, education, and experience (Smith, 2002). In addition, women have less access to visible developmental assignments with high-level responsibilities – the types of assignments that are likely to lead to greater authority and future advancement (Lyness & Thompson, 2000; Ohlott, Ruderman, & McCauley, 1994). Thus, although women's status has improved, their progress remains impeded, and they continue to lack the authority of men. Why is this so?

THE DEBATE ABOUT NATURAL DIFFERENCES BETWEEN MEN AND WOMEN

Evolutionary psychology and male dominance

One possible explanation for the absence of women at high levels of leadership comes from evolutionary psychologists – that women lack the inherent characteristics needed to be effective leaders. Evolutionary psychologists claim that fundamental differences in the traits of men and women evolved through genetically mediated adaptation to primeval conditions, in particular, through sexual selection mechanisms of male competition and female choice (e.g., Buss & Kenrick, 1998),

According to evolutionary psychology, women are naturally predisposed to depend on men to provide resources that insure women's survival and the survival of their children, whereas men, to attract women, are naturally predisposed to compete with other men for these resources (e.g., Buss & Kenrick, 1998; Geary, 1998). If true, women should have provided little subsistence in nonindustrialized cultures. However, although men on average contributed more food than women did in most nonindustrialized societies, women made substantial contributions to subsistence. For example, in one examination of a broad sample of nonindustrialized societies, women contributed an average of 44% of the food (Aronoff & Crano, 1975). In addition, women contributed most of the food in foraging societies that were dependent primarily on gathering plants for subsistence rather than hunting and fishing (Ember, 1978).

If the evolutionary argument is correct, the pattern of male dominance should be universal or nearly universal, and especially characteristic of nonindustrialized societies, which would be closer than industrialized societies to the conditions under which humans evolved. Yet, anthropological evidence indicates that male dominance is far from universal and actually less characteristic of foraging and pastoral cultures than of industrialized ones, exactly the opposite of what evolutionary psychology would predict (Wood & Eagly, 2002). Instead, male dominance developed along with particular economic conditions, such as warfare and intensive agriculture (Harris, 1993), and is particularly characteristic of agricultural and industrialized societies where men hold roles as the primary resource providers for their families (Wood & Eagly, 2002). The roles created by these new economies involved strength-intensive physical labor and often travel away from home, demands that were difficult to combine with gestation, breast feeding, and child rearing. Thus, these roles were more easily filled by men.

As gender hierarchies formed in these advancing economies, men increasingly occupied the roles that provided access to wealth and power, confining women to domestic roles involving childcare and activities carried out in and near the homestead such as the preparation of food and garments. Thus, male dominance did not derive from an inherent dependency of women on men but emerged along with particular economic and social conditions that favored the assignment to men of roles that conferred power, authority, and access to resources.

Gender and personality: the leadership traits of men and women

Even if men are not inherently dominant, they may still tend to possess different traits than women under contemporary conditions, and such differences could affect men's and women's suitability for leadership. Indeed, gender stereotypes suggest that men would show greater aggressiveness, assertiveness, dominance, and competitiveness. In fact, meta-analyses have found that men are on average more physically and verbally aggressive than women, especially for physical aggression, although the overall male–female differences were small to moderate in size (Archer, 2004; Bettencourt & Miller, 1996; Eagly & Steffen, 1986). Another meta-analysis revealed greater male aggression in the workplace, both toward other employees and the organization as a whole (Hershcovis et al., 2007).

Similar results have been reported for assertiveness and dominance. Based on personality scales and other self-report measures, men score higher in overall assertiveness than women do (Costa, Terracciano, & McCrae, 2001; Feingold, 1994). Moreover, women's assertive behavior is qualitatively different than men's. Researchers studying assertiveness distinguish *negative assertion*, which involves threat, aggression, hostility or control of others, from *positive assertion*, which balances self-expression with respect for the rights of others (Wilson & Gallois, 1993). On average, men more often engage in negative assertion, whereas women engage in greater positive assertion (Carli, 2001a).

Research findings on gender differences in competition have been more equivocal. In a meta-analysis of studies comparing the behavior of men and women in bargaining and mixed-motive games, such as the prisoner's dilemma, only a very small gender effect was revealed (Walters, Stuhlmacher, & Meyer, 1998). Overall, men competed slightly more often than women did.

The evidence reviewed thus far shows greater aggression, assertiveness, dominance, and, to a very slight degree, competitiveness among men, but it is unclear whether this set of characteristics contributes to effective leadership. Men's greater physical aggression is unlikely to enhance their ability to lead, except perhaps in criminal gangs or contact sports. Verbal aggression, dominance, and negative assertion may be useful in certain contexts, but in general appear to provide little benefit to leaders (see Van Vugt, 2006). On the contrary, successful leadership is now construed as requiring

the ability to form good relationships with others, work in diverse teams, and influence and motivate others to make valuable and creative contributions to their organizations (e.g., Bass, 1998).

Although aggression and dominance do not generally benefit leaders, there are personality characteristics that do contribute to effective leadership. General intelligence correlates a small to moderate degree with emerging as a leader and with leadership effectiveness (Judge, Colbert, & Ilies, 2004). Of the *Big Five* personality traits, extraversion, openness to experience, and conscientiousness show small to moderate associations with leader emergence, and along with agreeableness, with performing effectively as a leader; neuroticism is associated with lower amounts of leader emergence and effectiveness (Judge, Bono, Ilies, & Gerhardt, 2002). Based on a multiple regression analysis, the strongest Big Five predictor of leadership overall is extraversion, followed by conscientiousness and openness, with neuroticism and agreeableness of least importance (Eagly & Carli, 2007).

Given the predominance of men among leaders, one might expect men more than women to possess the traits most strongly linked to leadership. But they do not. No gender differences exist for general intelligence (Halpern & LaMay, 2000) and neither gender has a clear overall advantage in the Big Five traits associated with leadership. For example, a large cross-cultural study revealed somewhat higher levels of extraversion among women and moderately higher levels of agreeableness and neuroticism among women for both US and non-US samples (Costa et al., 2001). For conscientiousness and openness, the study revealed no overall gender differences in the United States, but in other countries slightly higher levels for women. So the biggest gender differences occurred for agreeableness and neuroticism, with one trait favoring women and one trait favoring men, but neither having much relevance to leadership. And although women showed more extraversion, when the study assessed the various components of extraversion, findings were mixed: women surpassed men in warmth, positive emotions, gregariousness, and activity, but men surpassed women in assertiveness and excitement seeking. Overall then, neither gender has a leadership advantage in personality.

GENDER DIFFERENCES IN HUMAN CAPITAL AND DOMESTIC RESPONSIBILITIES

Childcare and housework

If the scarcity of women in high-level leadership roles cannot be attributed to personality differences between women and men, perhaps it may be due to women's greater domestic duties, particularly childcare and housework. According to the *human capital theory* of economics, women's balancing of work and family contributes to the gender gap in pay and advancement because women bring less human capital to their jobs and show on-the-job behavior that is less optimal than that of men in terms of hours of work, effort, or effectiveness (see Kunze, 2008). For example, noted economist Gary Becker (1985) attributed the gender gap in wages, particularly for married men and women, to women's greater effort in childcare and housework and their lesser effort in paid work. Thus, this approach credits men's advantages in the workplace to their greater human capital.

In fact, national time diary studies reveal that although men do more housework and women less housework than in the past (Aguiar & Hurst, 2007; Bianchi, Robinson, & Milkie, 2006), women still spend more time on household chores than men do (US Bureau of Labor Statistics, 2010, Table 1). Men have also become increasingly involved in child-rearing over time, investing more time in interactions with their children than in the past, but so have women (Bianchi et al., 2006; Bond, Thompson, Galinsky, & Prottas, 2002). Indeed, even with smaller families, both men and women spent more time interacting with children now than in 1965 (Aguiar & Hurst, 2007; Bianchi et al., 2006), a phenomenon known as intensive parenting (Hays, 1996).

Education, preferences for advancement, and career commitment

Certainly, women have the bulk of domestic responsibilities. But do such responsibilities interfere with women's education, commitment to paid work, and desire for advancement? With regard to education, the answer is no. On the contrary, women are becoming better educated than men. In 2007–2008 in the United States, women received 57% of bachelor's degrees, 61% of master's degrees, and 50% of PhDs and first professional degrees (US National Center for Education Statistics, 2009, Table 275). And this is not a recent phenomenon; women surpassed men in the number of bachelor's and master's degrees beginning in the early 1980s (US National Center for Education Statistics, 2009, Table 268). Women typically have an educational advantage in other industrialized countries, as well, where more women than men are enrolled in post-secondary education (United Nations Development Programme, 2009).

Even though women are better educated than men, they do earn fewer degrees than men do in many technical and scientific fields (US National Center for Education Statistics, 2009) and, unsurprisingly, work in different occupations. Women continue to be clustered disproportionately in administrative support, clerical, and service jobs, and in traditionally feminine professions such as nursing and elementary school teaching (US Bureau of Labor Statistics, 2010b, Table 11) – jobs that are lower paying (Boraas & Rodgers, 2003; England, 2005). But is it the case that women choose jobs that provide less opportunity for leadership and advancement?

In a large meta-analysis of career preferences, very small to small gender differences were found: on average, men and boys expressed a greater desire for work that provided opportunities for high earnings, promotion, leadership, autonomy, and leisure, and women and girls expressed a greater desire for work that provided opportunities to work with and help others, be creative, grow and develop, and feel a sense of accomplishment (Konrad, Ritchie, Lieb, & Corrigall, 2000). Still, because the desire for advancement is higher among employees who work in positions with built-in promotion procedures and greater opportunities for promotion (Cassirer & Reskin, 2000), the test of the gender differences in career preferences should ideally control for job type. And in fact, the meta-analysis revealed that among adult men and women in similar occupations, there were no gender differences in the desire for leadership, promotions, or autonomy, and women actually expressed a greater desire for high earnings than men did (Konrad et al., 2000). Furthermore, in recent studies, having more family responsibilities did not dampen women's desire for advancement (Corrigall & Konrad, 2006; Families and Work Institute, 2005).

Given the similarity in male and female preferences for job attributes, it is not surprising that women and men differ little in their psychological commitment to their careers. In the United States, the majority of both women and men would prefer to have a job rather than stay home (Saad, 2007). In addition, a meta-analytic review found no gender differences in employees' commitment to their organizations (Aven, Parker, & McEvoy, 1993). And a majority of both men and women report greater commitment to family than to career (Families and Work Institute, 2005). Further evidence of women's career commitment comes from a representative US study of paid workers in which women reported putting in more effort at their jobs than men reported (Bielby & Bielby, 1988). Nevertheless, with some exceptions (e.g., Eddleston, Veiga, and Powell, 2006), most research reveals that women on average report a greater commitment to family than men do (e.g., Families and Work Institute, 2005). In addition, more women than men – 45% versus 29% – report preferring to stay home than have a job (Saad, 2007).

Breaks from employment, job flexibility, and part-time jobs

Women's leadership opportunities do not appear blocked because of poor education, preferences for careers that lack potential for advancement or lack of commitment to careers, so these variables cannot be responsible for the gender gap in leadership. However, women's greater commitment to family suggests that they may make more accommodations in their careers to fulfill family obligations. Being married and caring for young children increases women's workload and reduces their leisure, but has little effect on men's (Mattingly & Bianchi, 2003). And having children or a spouse is associated with a reduction of paid work hours for women, but an increase in men's paid work hours (Corrigall & Konrad, 2006). Thus, marriage and parenthood increase men's paid work and women's unpaid domestic work. And it is women more than men who compromise career for family.

One way women may accommodate increased family responsibilities is to quit their jobs. Although a meta-analysis of 42 studies across a variety of organizational settings (Griffeth, Hom, & Gaertner, 2000) and a study of over 25,000 managers (Lyness & Judiesch, 2001) revealed that men quit slightly more often than women do, women more often quit for family reasons than men do (Lyness & Judiesch, 2001), even highly qualified women compared with similarly qualified men (Bertrand, Goldin & Katz, 2009). Still, a national study found that only a minority of women with full-time jobs quit when they had a child (Klerman & Leibowitz, 1999).

Women may also seek flexible employment arrangements to help balance career and family. In a nationally representative poll, women reported a greater desire for job flexibility than men did (Roper Starch Worldwide, 1995). But, compared with male-dominated occupations, female-dominated occupations typically have less flexibility, in terms of control over setting work hours, taking days off, taking breaks during the day, or changing work days (Glass, 1990; Glass & Camarigg, 1992). Because of the difficulty in obtaining flexible work, women may rely on part-time employment instead. In 2009, 26% of employed women worked part time compared with 13% of men (US Bureau of Labor Statistics, 2010b, Table 8). Even women in traditionally male-dominated, high-status professions are more likely than their male counterparts to reduce their work hours to accommodate childcare and family responsibilities (Boulis, 2004; Noonan & Corcoran, 2004).

Implications of domestic responsibilities for leadership

Both men and women experience considerable losses for time out of the workforce, but women's losses far exceed men's (Rose & Hartmann, 2004). Moreover, studies have linked the gender gap in pay specifically to motherhood (e.g., Arun, Arun, & Borooah, 2004). For example, Budig and England (2001), in a nationally representative sample of married and unmarried women, found that motherhood resulted in a drop in hourly income; human capital variables, such as years of seniority on their jobs, number of job breaks, and years of employment, accounted for about one-third of the drop in income. Studies have also shown that wage penalties can be reduced by limiting time away from work after having children (Bond et al., 2002; Lundberg & Rose, 2000). Hence, women's commitment to family responsibilities contributes to their loss of experience and job tenure and, consequently, to their income deficit.

GENDER STEREOTYPES AND DISCRIMINATION AGAINST FEMALE LEADERS

Evidence of gender discrimination

Economists and sociologists have conducted a large number of surveys of wages and promotions, often using nationally representative data. Such studies typically determine whether adjusting for human capital variables (e.g., education, job experience), family characteristics (e.g., marriage and children), and structural factors (e.g., occupational segregation) can account for women's lesser advancement and lower wages. Although the differing employment patterns of men and women do contribute to the wage and advancement gaps, the nearly unanimous conclusions are that these and other variables account for only a portion of these gender gaps (see review by Blau & Kahn, 2006). Most social scientists conclude that discrimination accounts for at least a portion of the remaining unexplained gender gaps.

To supplement these correlational studies of discrimination, some social scientists have conducted experiments that equate job applicants in all respects other than the attribute (race or sex) that is suspected to trigger discrimination. Many of these experiments are based on resumes presented to participant groups, but other experiments are more naturalistic audit studies in which job applications or actual applicants are presented to employers. Some of these audit studies have examined sex discrimination (see review by Riach & Rich, 2002). The findings show a high incidence of sex discrimination against women in more senior jobs that yield higher status and wages and against both sexes when they applied for jobs dominated by the other sex. Also, Davison and Burke (2000) meta-analyzed the results of 49 experiments in simulated employment contexts, and found that men were preferred over identically qualified women for male-dominated jobs (e.g., auto salesperson, life insurance agent) (mean $d = 0.34$) and gender-neutral jobs (e.g., psychologist and hotel desk clerk) (mean $d = .24$) (Davison, 2005, personal communication). Only in female-dominated jobs (e.g., secretary, director of a day care center), were women preferred over identically qualified men (mean $d = -0.26$). Another important finding that emerged from experiments as well as correlational studies is that mothers are especially likely to be targets of workplace discrimination (Correll, Benard, & Paik, 2007; Heilman & Okimoto, 2008).

Stereotypes about men, women, and leaders

Discrimination against female leaders derives from commonly held stereotypes about men and women and prejudice in the evaluation of female leaders. People form stereotypes about individuals based on their membership in particular social groups, such as their race or gender. Group members are expected to share characteristics and exhibit behaviors that are typical of their group. Our beliefs about social groups often bias our judgments of individual group members, so that individuals are assimilated to their group stereotypes (e.g., von Hippel, Sekaquaptewa, & Vargas, 1995). For example, a study assessing encoding of leadership traits revealed that participants associated agentic traits more quickly and readily with male than female leaders (Scott & Brown, 2006).

Prejudice, an unfair evaluation of individuals based on their group membership, is likely to be directed toward people who occupy social roles that appear to be incompatible with stereotypes associated with their social groups (e.g., gender, race). People are prejudiced against female leaders because stereotypes about women are incompatible with stereotypes about leaders (Eagly & Karau, 2002; Heilman, 2001). Research in the United States and other nations indicates that people expect men to be agentic – assertive, dominant, competent, and authoritative – and women to be communal – warm, supportive, kind, and helpful (Newport, 2001; Williams & Best, 1990). People also believe that successful managers have more agentic than communal qualities (Eagly & Karau, 2002). Given such stereotypes about leaders, there is considerable incompatibility between beliefs about what it means to be a good leader and what it means to be a woman (e.g., Eagly & Karau, 2002; Powell, Buterfield, & Parent, 2002). The resulting perception of leaders as more similar to men than to women received support in research by Schein (e.g., 2001), who labeled this phenomenon the 'think manager–think male' effect. In Schein's studies, respondents rated women, men, or successful middle managers on traits that are stereotypical of women or men. The findings showed that managers were perceived to be considerably more similar to men than to women. Although this perceived fit between what is managerial and what is masculine has proven to be relatively durable since the early 1970s, recent research has yielded some weakening of the 'think manager–think male' effect among some, but not all, samples (Duehr & Bono, 2006; Sczesny, Bosak, Neff, & Schyns, 2004).

The challenge for women leaders is to balance the demand for agency required of the leader role and the demand for communion required of the female role. Thus, for women in leadership positions, gender stereotypes create a double bind: highly communal female leaders may be criticized for not being agentic enough, but highly agentic female leaders may be criticized for lacking communion.

The double bind

As a result of the double bind, one of the challenges that women leaders face is doubt about their competence. A meta-analysis of the literature comparing evaluations of male and female leaders has shown that, even when the quality of performance is controlled, female leaders overall receive somewhat lower evaluations than male leaders (Eagly, Makhijani, & Klonsky, 1992). Likewise, in studies of managers (Heilman, Block, & Martell, 1995) and military cadets (Boldry, Wood, & Kashy, 2001), men on average received higher evaluations than equally performing women. Indeed, research has revealed a double standard in the evaluation of women and men. Except in feminine settings, women must display greater evidence of skill than men to be considered equally competent (Biernat & Kobrynowicz, 1997; Carli, 1990, 2006; Foschi, 1996).

Men's greater perceived competence gives them an advantage in influencing others (Carli, 2001b). For example, in a study of mixed-gender groups working on a survival exercise, group members had more difficulty identifying the most expert member of their group when that member was a woman than a man. As a result, men overall had more influence than equally competent women (Thomas-Hunt & Phillips, 2004). Although people may resist a woman's influence because they doubt her competence, they may also resist the influence of a woman who is highly competent and agentic because she seems lacking in communion. Studies have found that competent women can evoke dislike or hostility compared with competent men or less competent women (e.g., Butler & Geis, 1990; Carli, 1990). And, in organizational studies, men, but not women, who communicated in a more competent or assertive manner were rated as more desirable to hire (Buttner & McEnally, 1996) and received more support and mentoring (Tepper, Brown, & Hunt, 1993).

Resistance to competent women reflects the other side of the double bind – the pressure on women to be especially communal. Thus, behavior that seems impressively communal in men may not be noticed in women. For example, studies have found that men received benefits from being especially helpful (Allen, 2006; Heilman & Chen, 2005), but women did not. Likewise, in an organizational study, subordinates' irritation and stress at work dropped when their male leaders were particularly verbally considerate, but were unaffected by female leaders' verbal consideration (Mohr & Wolfram, 2008).

On the other hand, behavior that seems appropriately assertive in men may seem overly aggressive in women. Women who disagree, seem threatening, or act selfish or dominant, on average exert less influence over their audience than comparable men or more communal women (Burgoon, Birk, & Hall, 1991; Carli, 2006; Copeland, Driskell, & Salas, 1995; Mehta et al., 1989, cited in Ellyson, Dovidio, & Brown, 1992). Women, but not men, who describe their achievements in a self-promoting manner are perceived as less deserving of recognition or support (Carli, 2006; Giacalone & Riordan, 1990; Wosinska, Dabul, Whetstone-Dion, & Cialdini, 1996) and are less influential and likeable (Carli, 2006; Rudman, 1998). Similarly, based on the meta-analysis of studies on evaluating leaders, women receive less positive evaluations for manifesting an autocratic style of leadership than men do (Eagly et al., 1992). And in a recent experimental study, female leaders had to evince both communion and agency to be seen as effective, whereas male leaders only needed to show agency (Johnson, Murphy, Zewdie, & Reichard, 2008).

The double bind operates particularly strongly in male-dominated domains. In experiments, women who are described as highly successful in male-dominated occupations are judged to have less desirable personality and social characteristics than men who are highly successful in the same occupation or than women with comparable success in a typically feminine career (e.g., Heilman et al., 1995; Heilman, Wallen, Fuchs, & Tamkins, 2004; Yoder & Schleicher, 1996). These penalties occurred because people judged women who succeeded in masculine domains to lack communion (Heilman & Okimoto, 2007).

Although both men and women resist women's influence and leadership, men are more resistant. In general, men, more than women, are critical of women's leadership (Eagly et al., 1992). They more strongly associate leadership with agentic traits than women do, as evidenced by men's greater endorsement of the 'think manager–think male' effect (Schein, 2001). They also react more negatively to highly competent women. Studies have revealed that women on average exert more influence with men when their behavior conveys lower levels of competence but incompetent behavior is not influential with women (e.g., Carli, 1990; Matschiner & Murnen, 1999). In experiments, men, but not women, were more influenced by men than equally competent women (Carli, LaFleur, & Loeber, 1995) and preferred to hire male over female job applicants even when the female applicants had equal or superior qualifications (Foschi, Lai, & Sigerson, 1994; Uhlmann & Cohen, 2005).

In summary, evidence indicates that gender discrimination contributes to women's lower pay and slower advancement. Stereotypes that portray men as more agentic than women create the implicit assumption that men have more of the characteristics needed for leadership. Furthermore, the demand placed on female leaders to be especially communal creates a double bind whereby women who overcome doubts about their competence by taking charge and exhibiting agency may be resisted because people see them as lacking communion.

THE LEADERSHIP STYLES OF WOMEN AND MEN

How men and women lead

Given the challenges of the double bind, and pressures to establish both agency and communion, it is reasonable to assume that women would lead differently than men. In fact, research indicates that women have somewhat different styles of leadership than men do. In a meta-analysis of 162 studies of leadership style, Eagly and Johnson (1990) found that female leaders overall adopted a more democratic and less autocratic leadership style than male leaders did. In addition, compared with men, women were slightly more interpersonally oriented – emphasizing maintaining harmonious relationships. Similar results were found in a subsequent meta-analysis (van Engen & Willemsen, 2004). Women, then, more often avoid the autocratic (or directive) style of leadership, the style that people evaluate less favorably in women, and instead manifest styles that are more collaborative and participative. These gender effects depended on a variety of moderator variables. For example, the gender differences in democratic and interpersonally oriented leadership were smaller in settings with a higher percentage of men (Eagly & Johnson, 1990).

More recently, research on leadership style has shifted to focus on a type of leadership that would be best attuned to the conditions faced by most contemporary organizations: a style that motivates and develops followers and thereby increases their ability to make valuable and creative contributions to their organizations. This approach, called *transformational* leadership, involves being an excellent role model who inspires trust in subordinates and is future-oriented and innovative (Bass, 1998; Burns, 1978; see Diaz-Saenz, Chapter 22, this volume). Transformational leaders also mentor and empower followers by encouraging them to develop their full potential. As this description of transformational leadership suggests, it is neither masculine nor feminine when considered in its entirety but instead culturally androgynous. Yet, because of some of its elements, especially the mentoring and empowering of subordinates, it appears to be slightly more aligned with the female than the male gender role (Duehr & Bono, 2006; Kark, 2004).

This style is contrasted with *transactional* leadership, which involves the use of rewards and punishments to motivate subordinates. Such leadership is rooted in give-and-take relationships that appeal to subordinates' self-interest. Another known style is *laissez-faire* leadership, which is characterized by a general failure to take responsibility for managing (Bass, 1998; Burns, 1978).

In a meta-analysis of 45 studies comparing male and female managers on transformational, transactional, and laissez-faire leadership, female leaders were somewhat more transformational than male leaders across a variety of business and other settings; women also on average relied somewhat more on one component of transactional leadership than men did – the use of contingent rewards (Eagly, Johannesen-Schmidt, &

van Engen, 2003). Comparisons of US samples with those of other nations revealed that the gender difference in transformational leadership was slightly more pronounced in Canada, but not in other nations.

Of the five subscales that make up transformational leadership, women mostly exceeded men on individualized consideration, the dimension of transformational leadership that involves developing and mentoring subordinates. Male leaders manifested more of the laissez-faire style of leadership than women did, as well as two components of transactional leadership – active and passive management by exception – which involve attending to followers' mistakes and waiting until problems are severe before addressing them. These (small) gender differences in leadership style reflect the special challenges that women leaders confront. Because of the double bind, women must demonstrate both agency and communion. These pressures may make transformational leadership especially attractive because it incorporates both agentic and communal qualities (Eagly & Carli, 2007). Likewise, women leaders' greater use of contingent rewards and democracy likely reflects their response to pressures to temper their assertiveness and authority with a measure of communion.

Leadership style and leaders' effectiveness

Does women's leadership style provide them with an advantage or a disadvantage? Is it effective? The answer to these questions lies in research on leadership effectiveness. Research on democratic and autocratic leadership shows no clear advantage of either style, because their effectiveness depends on particular organizational conditions (Gastil, 1994). However, a meta-analytic review of 87 studies revealed moderate to large correlations between transformational leadership and a variety of effectiveness measures, including leader effectiveness, group or organizational performance, leader performance, and follower satisfaction (Judge & Piccolo, 2004). Comparable effects were found for the component of transactional leadership that involves rewarding subordinates for appropriate behavior. On the other hand, the effectiveness measures were only weakly correlated with managers' reliance on more negative, punishing behaviors, and negatively correlated with delaying action until problems become severe (passive management by exception) and laissez-faire leadership. Thus, the leadership styles adopted more often by women than men are quite effective, whereas the styles more often adopted by men than women are either only slightly beneficial or actually ineffective.

The evidence that women use effective leadership styles suggests that women might be better leaders than men. But is this the case? Relevant findings come from studies relating organizations' financial performance to the percentage of women in executive positions and from research on judgments of male and female leaders' effectiveness. Studies of organizational performance reflect quite favorably on women. Recent studies of the *Fortune* 1000 and other large US companies have found that having more women in executive positions or on boards of directors is associated with better financial outcomes (Carter, Simkins, & Simpson, 2003; Erhardt, Werbel, & Shrader, 2003; Krishnan & Park, 2005). A similar study on European-based companies compared the performance of those with greatest gender diversity in top management to the average performance in their economic sector and found better financial performance in companies with gender diversity (Desvaux et al., 2007).

Of course, leader effectiveness is not merely a matter of a leader's competence and leadership skills or even the favorable performance of a leader's team or organization. Leaders can be effective only if other people accept and value their leadership. Thus, leadership effectiveness depends on the perception of others, even if such perceptions are tainted by prejudice and discrimination. Consequently, an alternative assessment of the gender difference in leadership effectiveness comes from studies in which people rate the performance of individual leaders.

A meta-analysis of 96 such studies compared the effectiveness of male and female leaders in comparable leadership roles. Averaging over all of the studies produced no gender differences in effectiveness. However, gender did make a difference in many settings: Men were rated as more effective than women in masculine settings such as the military and women as more effective than men in less masculine settings such as social service agencies and schools (Eagly, Karau, & Makhijani, 1995). These results suggest that effectiveness depends on the setting and may well be influenced by stereotypes. In male-dominated settings, people are most likely to equate good leadership with agentic rather than communal characteristics, creating doubt about women's effectiveness as leaders.

Overall, the research on leadership style and effectiveness does not suggest that women are poor leaders. On the contrary, the evidence overall tends to favor women's leadership style and effectiveness. Thus, the relative absence of female leaders cannot be due to their lack of leadership ability. However, studies in which people rate the performance of male and female leaders do demonstrate that women have less effectiveness in male-dominated settings. Indeed, female leaders may confront formidable obstacles in masculine organizational cultures (see Collinson & Collinson, 1996; Eagly & Carli, 2007; Lyness & Thompson, 2000). Because of homosocial reproduction, men are more likely than women to be hired (Kanter, 1977; Konrad & Pfeffer, 1991). Women also advance more slowly where men hold a clear majority and advancement depends on male networks (McPherson, Smith-Lovin, & Cook, 2001). And women's risk of being sexually harassed increases in traditionally masculine occupations and in environments with a high percentage of men (US Merit Systems Protection Board, 1995; Welsh, 1999).

ORGANIZATIONAL BARRIERS TO WOMEN'S LEADERSHIP

The social structure and culture of organizations often create more challenges to women than to men. These challenges can be embedded in organizations' formal roles, rules, and procedures as well as their tacit rules and norms of conduct. In both structure and culture, organizations present women with many impediments to advancement (e.g., Acker, 1990; Martin, 1990; 2003). Although few of these features were designed to exclude women and can appear to be gender neutral, they often pose more difficulties to women than men.

It is understandable that many aspects of organizations implicitly favor men's leadership, because traditionally many men and very few women held leader roles in most organizations. Therefore, organizational traditions developed that fit men's lifestyles and preferences. Aspects of these masculine traditions have become exacerbated because, in recent decades, organizations have come to represent an implicit model of an ideal employee who is totally devoted to the organization and therefore can be called on to work long hours and make many personal sacrifices for the organization. This ideal employee has few encumbrances that could limit devotion to the job and certainly few family responsibilities (Acker, 1990; Williams, 2000). Indeed, executives' advancement and pay are predicted by the extent to which they work long hours and evenings (Judge, Cable, Boudreau, & Bretz, 1995). As a result, people employed in management and related fields work longer than average hours (Jacobs & Gerson, 2004; US Bureau of Labor Statistics, 2010c). The long hours required to advance to high levels present a particular challenge to families and especially to women, who have the bulk of domestic and childcare responsibilities, and the increasing pressures of intensive parenting. Reconciling career and family obligations is easier for men. Most male executives have stay-at-home wives, but the majority of female executives have employed spouses; consequently, a higher percentage of female than male executives delay or forgo having children (Galinsky et al., 2003; see also Wajcman, 1998).

The time constraints that women face in managing career and family make it especially difficult for them to participate in networking with colleagues. The social capital created by networking helps facilitate career success (see Ng et al., 2005). For example, one study demonstrated that the social capital developed through informal connections predicted managers' advancement by increasing their access to information, resources, and mentoring support (Seibert, Kraimer, & Liden, 2001). And a longitudinal investigation revealed that networking predicted salary increases over time (Wolff & Moser, 2009).

Women's leadership opportunities are obstructed, in part, because they possess less social capital than men do (see Timberlake, 2005). Studies indicate that women have less extensive (Moore, 1990) and powerful (Burt, 1998; Moore, 1988) career networks than men do. Because men hold the bulk of leadership positions, powerful networks tend to be male dominated. Women may feel uncomfortable joining in activities that men in such networks enjoy, such as pick-up basketball or poker games. And men are less likely to invite women to join their social groups. Networks generally are gender-segregated because people tend to affiliate with others who are similar to themselves (McPherson et al., 2001). Thus, although women's careers benefit from having connections with men (Burt, 1998; Dreher & Cox, 1996; Huffman & Torres, 2002), such connections are difficult to form.

The challenges that women face in joining male networks are emblematic of the more general obstacles women experience when joining traditional male corporate cultures. When asked to identify obstacles to their advancement, female executives and professionals have cited the difficulties in fitting in with the culture of their organizations (e.g., Lyness & Thompson, 2000; Manuel, Shefte, & Swiss, 1999). Female executives also reported greater difficulty in obtaining developmental work assignments and geographic mobility, such as international travel (Lyness & Thompson, 2000), and they had fewer line management opportunities (Galinsky et al., 2003) than their male counterparts. The only types of challenging assignments that women have been found to receive more often than men are those assignments that are especially risky or precarious and likely to fail, a phenomenon known as the *glass cliff* (Ryan & Haslam, 2007). Archival research in the United Kingdom revealed that women received leadership appointments more often than men when the companies were experiencing financial downturns and declines in performance (Ryan & Haslam, 2005). Similar results have been found in experiments in Britain with undergraduates, business leaders, and graduate students in management (Haslam & Ryan, 2008), although not in archival research on US companies (Adams, Gupta, & Leeth, 2009). Thus, whether women are placed on a glass cliff and doomed to fail or denied challenging but achievable assignments, women are more likely than men to be deprived of opportunities to succeed at the very tasks that lead to advancement.

The structure and norms of organizations implicitly favor men. The demand for long hours is more challenging for women than men because of their typically greater domestic responsibilities, the unfriendliness of many corporate cultures and male networks, and the frequent denial to women of desirable assignments. These obstacles block women's advancement and contribute to their relative absence from leadership positions.

CONCLUSIONS

There is little evidence that the gender gap in leadership can be explained by inherent differences between men and women, men's possession of traits that are more compatible with leadership, or women's lack of leadership ability and ineffective leadership styles. Women's advancement remains obstructed to some extent by their greater domestic responsibilities and time spent away from paid work, as well as from gender stereotypes and discrimination, which create resistance to women's influence and authority. In addition, the structure and culture of many organizations create greater challenges for women than men.

Although serious obstacles remain, there are signs that leadership opportunities will continue to expand for women. In addition to the increase in the numbers of women leaders in business, politics, and other fields, change is also evident in attitudes about women leaders and family life. More people than ever before indicate that they would vote for a woman for president (CBS News/*New York Times*, 2006). People are more willing to work for a female boss than in the past (Carroll, 2006), and attitudes toward women leaders have become more positive (Inglehart & Norris, 2003). In the United States, most adults believe that men and women should have equal responsibility for childcare (Milkie, Bianchi, Mattingly, & Robinson, 2002). Moreover, men's commitment to family has increased (Families and Work Institute, 2005), more men than ever would now consider staying home rather than having a job (Saad, 2007), and in an increasing percentage of US. households (Raley, Mattingly, & Bianchi, 2006) – now 34% (US Bureau of Labor Statistics, 2009, Table 25) – women are the primary or sole wage earners.

Women have also changed. Women's personalities have become more assertive, dominant, and masculine (Twenge, 1997, 2001), and their preference for careers that provide authority has increased and is now comparable to men's (Konrad et al., 2000). Changes in women have coincided with changes in their workplace opportunities, with women becoming less assertive and dominant after World War II, when barriers to their employment rose, and more assertive and dominant beginning in the late twentieth century, when their access to high-status roles increased substantially (Twenge, 2001). At the same time, women have retained their feminine personality traits, being consistently more understanding and warm than men, for example. All in all, women have become more androgynous over time, whereas men have changed relatively little (see Twenge, 1997, 2001).

And as women have changed, so too have ideas about leadership. The leadership ideal has become more communal. Leadership scholars now recommend that leaders, to be effective in modern, future-oriented, and rapidly changing organizations, should be more collaborative and transformational, adopting leadership styles that have elements of teaching and coaching (e.g., Bass, 1998; Lipman-Blumen, 1996). That transformational leadership is emblematic of effective leadership helps resolve the double bind for women leaders by reducing the incongruity between stereotypes about leaders and stereotypes about women. These changes, along with the increasingly androgynous personalities of women, should facilitate women's advancement in the future.

REFERENCES

Acker, J. (1990). Hierarchies, jobs, bodies: A theory of gendered organizations. *Gender & Society, 4*, 139–158.

Adams, S. M., Gupta, A., & Leeth, J. D. (2009). Are female executives over-represented in precarious leadership positions? *British Journal of Management, 20*, 1–12.

Aguiar, M. & Hurst, E. (2007) Measuring trends in leisure: the allocation of time over five decades. *The Quarterly Journal of Economics, 122*, 969–1006.

Allen, T. D. (2006) Rewarding good citizens: The relationship between citizenship behavior, gender, and organizational rewards. *Journal of Applied Psychology, 36*, 120–143.

Archer, J. (2004) Sex differences in aggression in real-world settings: a meta-analytic review. *Review of General Psychology, 8*, 291–322.

Aronoff, J. & Crano, W. D. (1975) A re-examination of the cross-cultural principles of task segregation and sex role differentiation in the family. *American Sociological Review, 40*, 12–20.

Arun, S. V., Arun, T. G., & Borooah, V. K. (2004) The effect of career breaks on the working lives of women. *Feminist Economics, 10*, 65–84.

Aven, F. F., Jr. Parker, B., & McEvoy, G. M. (1993) Gender and attitudinal commitment to organizations: A meta-analysis. *Journal of Business Research, 26*, 63–73.

Bass, B. M. (1998) *Transformational leadership: industry, military, and educational impact.* Mahwah, NJ: Erlbaum.

Becker, G. S. (1985) Human capital, effort, and the sexual division of labor. *Journal of Labor Economics, 3*, S33–S58.

Bertrand, M., Goldin, C., & Katz, L. F. (2009) Dynamics of the gender gap for young professionals in the financial and corporate sectors. *National Bureau of Economic Research, Working Paper* No. 14681. Retrieved from http://www.nber.org/papers/w14681.

Bettencourt, B. A. & Miller, N. (1996) Gender differences in aggression as a function of provocation: A meta-analysis. *Psychological Bulletin, 119*, 422–447.

Bianchi, S. M., Robinson, J. P., & Milkie, M. A. (2006) *Changing rhythms of American family life.* New York: Russell Sage Foundation.

Bielby, D. D. & Bielby, W. T. (1988) She works hard for the money. *American Journal of Sociology, 93*, 1031–1059.

Biernat, M. & Kobrynowicz, D. (1997) Gender- and race-based standards of competence: Lower minimum standards but higher ability standards for devalued groups. *Journal of Personality and Social Psychology, 72*, 544–557.

Blau, F. D. & Kahn, L. M. (2006) The U.S. gender pay gap in the 1990s: Slow convergence. *Industrial and Labor Relations Review, 60*, 45–66.

Boldry, J., Wood, W., & Kashy, D. A. (2001) Gender stereotypes and the evaluation of men and women in military training. *Journal of Social Issues, 57*, 689–705.

Bond, J. Thompson, T., C. Galinsky, E., & Prottas. D. (2002) *Highlights of the national study of the changing workforce.* New York: Families and Work Institute.

Boraas, S. & Rodgers III, W. M. (2003) How does gender play a role in the earnings gap? An update. *Monthly Labor Review, 126*, 9–15.

Boulis, A. (2004) The evolution of gender and motherhood in contemporary medicine. *Annals of the American Academy of Political and Social Science, 596*, 172–206.

Budig, M. J. & England, P. (2001) The wage penalty for motherhood. *American Sociological Review, 66*, 204–225.

Burgoon, M., Birk, T. S., & Hall, J. R. (1991) Compliance and satisfaction with physician – patient communication: An expectancy theory interpretation of gender differences. *Human Communication Research, 18*, 177–208.

Burns, J. M. (1978) *Leadership.* New York: Harper & Row.

Burt, R. S. (1998). The gender of social capital. *Rationality & Society, 10,* 5–46.

Buss, D. M. & Kenrick, D. T. (1998). Evolutionary social psychology. In D. T. Gilbert, S. T. Fiske, & G. Lindzey (eds), *The handbook of social psychology* (4th edn, Vol. 2, pp. 982–1026) Boston: McGraw-Hill.

Butler, D. & Geis, F. (1990). Nonverbal affect responses to male and female leaders: Implications for leadership evaluations. *Journal of Personality and Social Psychology, 58,* 48–59.

Buttner, E. H. & McEnally, M. (1996). The interactive effect of influence tactic, applicant gender, and type of job on hiring recommendations. *Sex Roles, 34,* 581–591.

Carli, L. L. (1990). Gender, language, and influence. *Journal of Personality and Social Psychology, 59,* 941–951.

Carli, L. L. (2001a). Assertiveness. In J. Worell (ed.), *Encyclopedia of women and gender: Sex similarities and differences and the impact of society on gender* (pp. 157–168) San Diego, CA: Academic Press.

Carli, L. L. (2001b). Gender and social influence. *Journal of Social Issues, 57,* 725–741.

Carli, L. L. (2006, July). *Gender and social influence: Women confront the double bind.* Paper presented at the 26th International Conference of Applied Psychology, Athens, Greece.

Carli, L. L., LaFleur, S. J., & Loeber, C. C. (1995). Nonverbal behavior, gender, and influence. *Journal of Personality and Social Psychology, 68,* 1030–1041.

Carroll, J. (2006, September 1). *Americans prefer male boss to a female boss.* Retrieved from Gallup Brain: http://brain.gallup.com.

Carter, D. A., Simkins, B. J., & Simpson, W. G. (2003). Corporate governance, board diversity, and firm value. *Financial Review, 38,* 33–53.

Cassirer, N. & Reskin, B. F. (2000). High hopes: Organizational positions, employment experiences, and women's and men's promotion aspirations. *Work and Occupations, 27,* 438–463.

Catalyst (2010a). *Pyramids: Women CEOs and heads of the Financial Post 500.* Retrieved from http://webcache.googleusercontent.com/search?q=cache:rxtnGNNBsMAJ:www.catalyst.org/publication/271/women-ceos-and-heads-of-the-financial-post-500+fp500+ceos+women&cd=1&hl=en&ct=clnk&gl=us.

Catalyst (2010b). *Pyramids: Women CEOs of the Fortune 1000.* Retrieved from http://catalyst.org/publication/322/women-ceos-of-the-fortune-1000.

Catalyst (2010c). *Quick takes: Australia, Canada, South Africa & the United States.* Retrieved from http://catalyst.org/publication/239/australia-canada-south-africa-united-states.

Catalyst (2010d) *Quick takes: Women in U.S. management.* Retrieved from http://catalyst.org/publication/206/women-in-us-management.

CBS News/*New York Times* (2006, February 5) *A woman for president.* Retrieved from http://www.cbsnews.com/htdocs/pdf/020306woman.pdf#search=%22a%20woman%20for%20president%20CBS%20News%2FNew%20York%20Times%20Poll%22.

Center for American Women in Politics (2010a). *Fact sheet: Women in elective office, 2010.* http://www.cawp.rutgers.edu/fast_facts/levels_of_office/documents/elective.pdf.

Center for American Women and Politics (2010b). *Fact sheet: Women in the state legislatures 2010.* Retrieved from http://www.cawp.rutgers.edu/fast_facts/levels_of_office/documents/stleg.pdf.

Center for American Women and Politics (2010c). *Fact sheet: Women in the U.S. Congress 2010.* Retrieved from http://www.cawp.rutgers.edu/fast_facts/levels_of_office/documents/cong.pdf.

Collinson, D. & Collinson, M. (1996). Barriers to employee rights: Gender selection and the labor process. *Employee Responsibilities and Rights Journal, 9,* 229–249.

Copeland, C. L., Driskell, J. E., & Salas, E. (1995) Gender and reactions to dominance. *Journal of Social Behavior and Personality, 10,* 53–68.

Correll, S. J., Benard, S., & Paik, I. (2007). Gender and the career choice process: The role of biased self-assessments. *American Journal of Sociology, 106,* 1691–1730.

Corrigall, E. A. & Konrad, A. M., (2006). The relationship of job attribute preferences to employment, hours of paid work, and family responsibilities: An analysis comparing women and men. *Sex Roles, 54,* 95–111.

Costa, P. T., Jr, Terracciano, A., & McCrae, R. R. (2001) Gender differences in personality traits across cultures: Robust and surprising findings. *Journal of Personality and Social Psychology, 81,* 322–331.

Council on Foundations (2009). *2008 Grantmakers salary and benefits report: Executive summary.* Washington, DC: Council on Foundations. Retrieved from http://www.cof.org/files/Bamboo/programsandservices/research/documents/08salarybenefitsexecsum.pdf.

Davison, H. K. & Burke, M. J. (2000). Sex discrimination in simulated employment contexts: A meta-analytic investigation. *Journal of Vocational Behavior, 56,* 225–248.

Desvaux, G., Devillard-Hoellinger, S., & Baumgarten, P. (2007) *Women matter: Gender diversity, a corporate performance driver.* Paris: McKinsey & Company.

Dreher, G. F. & Cox, Jr, T. H. (1996) Race, gender, and opportunity: A study of compensation attainment and establishment of mentoring relationships. *Journal of Applied Psychology, 81,* 297–308.

Duehr, E. E. & Bono, J. E. (2006) Men, women, and managers: Are stereotypes finally changing? *Personnel Psychology, 59,* 815–846.

Eagly, A. H. & Carli, L. L. (2007) *Through the labyrinth: The truth about how women become leaders.* Cambridge, MA: Harvard Business School Press.

Eagly, A. H., Johannesen-Schmidt, M. C., & van Engen, M. (2003) Transformational, transactional, and laissez-faire leadership styles: A meta-analysis comparing women and men. *Psychological Bulletin, 129,* 569–591.

Eagly, A. H. & Johnson, B. T. (1990) Gender and leadership style: A meta-analysis. *Psychological Bulletin, 108,* 233–256.

Eagly, A. H. & Karau, S. J. (2002) Role congruity theory of prejudice toward female leaders. *Psychological Review, 109,* 573–598.

Eagly, A. H., Karau, S. J., & Makhijani, M. G. (1995) Gender and the effectiveness of leaders: A meta-analysis. *Psychological Bulletin, 117*, 125–145.

Eagly, A. H., Makhijani, M. G., & Klonsky, B. G. (1992) Gender and the evaluation of leaders: A meta-analysis. *Psychological Bulletin, 111*, 3–22.

Eagly, A.H. & Steffen, V. J. (1986) Gender and aggressive behavior: A meta-analytic review of the social psychological literature. *Psychological Bulletin, 100*, 309–330.

Eddleston, K. A., Veiga, J. F., & Powell, G. N. (2006) Explaining sex differences in managerial career satisfier preferences: The role of gender self-schema. *Journal of Applied Psychology, 91*, 437–445.

Ellyson, S. L., Dovidio, J. F., & Brown, C. E. (1992) The look of power: Gender differences in visual dominance behavior. In C. L. Ridgeway (ed.), *Gender, interaction, and inequality* (pp. 50–80) New York: Springer-Verlag.

Ember, C. R. (1978) Myths about hunter–gatherers. *Ethnology, 17*, 439–448.

England, P. (2005) Gender inequality in labor markets: The role of motherhood and segregation. *Social Politics, 12*, 264–288.

Erhardt, M. L., Werbel, J. D., & Shrader, C. B. (2003) Board of director diversity and firm financial performance. *Corporate Governance, 11*, 102–111.

Families and Work Institute (2005) *Generation and gender in the workplace*. New York: Families and Work Institute. Retrieved from http://familiesandwork.org/eproducts/genandgender.pdf.

Feingold, A. (1994) Gender differences in personality: A meta-analysis. *Psychological Bulletin, 116*, 429–456.

Fortune (2010) *Global 500: Women CEOs*. Retrieved from the Fortune Magazine website http://money.cnn.com/magazines/fortune/global500/2010/womenceos/.

Foschi, M. (1996) Double standards in the evaluation of men and women. *Social Psychology Quarterly, 59*, 237–254.

Foschi, M., Lai, L., & Sigerson, K. (1994) Gender and double standards in the assessment of job applicants. *Social Psychology Quarterly, 57*, 326–339.

Galinsky, E., Salmond, K., Bond, J. T., et al. (2003) *Leaders in a global economy: A study of executive women and men*. New York: Families and Work Institute.

Gastil, J. (1994) A meta-analytic review of the productivity and satisfaction of democratic and autocratic leadership. *Small Group Research, 25*, 384–341.

Geary, D. C. (1998) *Male, female: The evolution of human sex differences*. Washington, DC: American Psychological Association.

Giacalone, R. A. & Riordan, C. A. (1990) Effect of self-presentation on perceptions and recognition in an organization. *Journal of Psychology, 124*, 25–38.

Glass, J. (1990) The impact of occupational segregation on working conditions. *Social Forces, 68*, 779–796.

Glass, J. & Camarigg, V. (1992) Gender, parenthood, and job–family compatibility. *American Journal of Sociology, 98*, 131–151.

Griffeth, R. W., Hom, P. W., & Gaertner, S. (2000) A meta-analysis of antecedents and correlates of employee turnover: Update, moderator tests, and research implications

for the next millennium. *Journal of Management, 26*, 463–488.

Halpern, D. F. & LaMay, M. L. (2000) The smarter sex: A critical review of sex differences in intelligence. *Educational Psychology Review, 12*, 229–246.

Harris, M. (1993) The evolution of human gender hierarchies: A trial formulation. In B. D. Miller (ed.), *Sex and gender hierarchies* (pp. 57–79). New York: Cambridge University Press.

Haslam, S. A. & Ryan, M. K. (2008) The road to the glass cliff: Differences in the perceived suitability of men and women for leadership positions in succeeding and failing organizations. *The Leadership Quarterly, 19*, 530–546.

Hays, S. (1996) *The cultural contradictions of motherhood*. New Haven, CT: Yale University Press.

Helfat, C. E., Harris, D., & Wolfson, J. P. (2006) The pipeline to the top: Women and men in the top executive ranks of U.S. corporations. *Academy of Management Perspectives, 20*, 42–64.

Heilman, M. E. (2001) Description and prescription: How gender stereotypes prevent women's ascent up the organizational ladder. *Journal of Social Issues, 57*, 657–674.

Heilman, M. E., Block, C. J., & Martell, R. F. (1995) Sex stereotypes: Do they influence perceptions of managers? *Journal of Social Behavior and Personality, 10* (No. 6, special issue: Gender in the workplace), 237–252.

Heilman, M. E. & Chen, J. J. (2005) Same behavior, different consequences: Reactions to men's and women's altruistic citizenship behavior. *Journal of Applied Psychology, 90*, 431–441.

Heilman, M. E. & Okimoto, T. G. (2007) Why are women penalized for success at male tasks? The implied communality deficit. *Journal of Applied Psychology, 92*, 81–92.

Heilman, M. E. & Okimoto, T. G. (2008) Motherhood: A potential source of bias in employment decisions. *Journal of Applied Psychology, 93*, 189–198.

Heilman, M. E., Wallen, A. S., Fuchs, D., & Tamkins, M. M. (2004) Penalties for success: Reactions to women who succeed in male gender-typed tasks. *Journal of Applied Psychology, 89*, 416–427.

Hershcovis, M. S., Turner, N., Barling, J., et al. (2007) Predicting workplace aggression: A meta-analysis. *Journal of Applied Psychology, 92*, 228–238.

Hippel, W., Sekaquaptewa, D., & Vargas, P. (1995) On the role of encoding processes in stereotype maintenance. In M. P. Zanna (ed.), *Advances in Experimental Social Psychology, 27*, 177–254.

Huffman, M. L. & Torres, L. (2002) It's not only 'who you know' that matters: Gender, personal contacts, and job lead quality. *Gender & Society, 16*, 793–813.

Inglehart, R. & Norris, P. (2003) *Rising tide: Gender equality and cultural change around the world*. New York: Cambridge University Press.

Jacobs, J. A. & Gerson, G. (2004) *The time divide: Work, family, and gender inequality*. Cambridge, MA: Harvard University Press.

Johnson, S. K., Murphy, S. E., Zewdie, S., & Reichard, R. J. (2008) The strong sensitive type: Effects of gender stereotypes and leadership prototypes on the evaluation of male and female leaders. *Organizational Behavior and Human Decision Processes, 106,* 39–60.

Judge, T. A., Bono, J. E., Ilies, R., & Gerhardt, M. W. (2002) Personality and leadership: A qualitative and quantitative review. *Journal of Applied Psychology, 87,* 765–780.

Judge, T. A., Cable, D. M., Boudreau, J. W., & Bretz, Jr, R. D. (1995) An empirical investigation of the predictors of executive career success. *Personnel Psychology, 48,* 485–519.

Judge, T. A., Colbert, A. E., & Ilies, R. (2004) Intelligence and leadership: A quantitative review and test of theoretical propositions. *Journal of Applied Psychology, 89,* 542–552.

Judge, T. A. & Piccolo, R. F. (2004) Transformational and transactional leadership: A meta-analytic test of their relative validity. *Journal of Applied Psychology, 89,* 755–768.

Kark, R. (2004) The transformational leader: Who is (s)he? A feminist perspective. *Journal of Organizational Change Management, 17,* 160–176.

Kanter, R. M. (1977) *Men and women of the corporation.* New York: Basic Books.

Klerman, J. A. & Leibowitz, A. (1999) Job continuity among new mothers. *Demography, 36,* 145–155.

Konrad, A. M. & Pfeffer, J. (1991) Understanding the hiring of women and minorities in educational institutions. *Sociology of Education, 64,* 141–157.

Konrad, A. M. Ritchie, J. E. Jr, Lieb, P., & Corrigall, E. (2000) Sex differences and similarities in job attribute preferences: A meta-analysis. *Psychological Bulletin, 126,* 593–641.

Krishnan, H. A. & Park, D. (2005) A few good women – on top management teams. *Journal of Business Research, 58,* 1712–1720.

Kunze, A. (2008) Gender wage gap studies: consistency and decomposition. *Empirical Economics, 35,* 63–76.

Lipman-Blumen, J. (1996) *The connective edge: Leading in an interdependent world.* San Francisco: Jossey-Bass.

Lundberg, S. & Rose, E. (2000) Parenthood and the earnings of married men and women. *Labour Economics, 7,* 689–710.

Lyness, K. S. & Judiesch, M. K. (2001) Are female managers quitters? The relationships of gender, promotions, and family leaves of absence to voluntary turnover. *Journal of Applied Psychology, 86,* 1167–1178.

Lyness, K. S. & Thompson, D. E. (2000) Climbing the corporate ladder: Do female and male executives follow the same route? *Journal of Applied Psychology, 85,* 86–101.

McPherson, M., Smith-Lovin, L. & Cook, J. M. (2001) Birds of a feather: Homophily in social networks. *Annual Review of Sociology, 27,* 415–444.

Manuel, T., Shefte, S., & Swiss, D. J. (1999) *Suiting themselves: Women's leadership styles in today's workplace.* Cambridge, MA: Radcliffe Public Policy Institute.

Martin, P. Y. (1990) Rethinking feminist organizations. *Gender & Society, 4,* 182–206.

Martin, P. Y. (2003) 'Said and done' versus 'saying and doing': Gender practices, practicing gender at work. *Gender & Society, 17,* 342–366.

Mattingly, M. J. & Bianchi, S. M. (2003) Gender differences in the quantity and quality of free time: The US. experience. *Social Forces, 81,* 99–1030.

Matschiner, M. & Murnen, S. K. (1999) Hyperfemininity and influence. *Psychology of Women Quarterly, 23,* 631–642.

Milkie, M. A., Bianchi, S. M. Mattingly, M. J., & Robinson, J. P. (2002) Gendered division of childrearing: Ideals, realities, and the relationship to parental well-being. *Sex Roles, 47,* 21–38.

Mohr, G. & Wolfram, H. (2008) Leadership and effectiveness in the context of gender: The role of leaders' verbal behaviour. *British Journal of Management, 19,* 4–16.

Moore, G. (1988) Women in elite positions: Insiders or outsiders? *Sociological Forum, 3,* 566–585.

Moore, G. (1990) Structural determinants of men's and women's personal networks. *American Sociological Review, 55,* 726–735.

Newport, F. (2001, February 21) *Americans see women as emotional and affectionate, men as more aggressive.* Gallup Poll News Service. Retrieved from http://www.gallup.com/poll/1978/Americans-See-Women-Emotional-Affectionate-Men-More-Aggressive.aspx.

Ng, T. W. H., Eby, L. T., Sorensen, K. L., & Feldman, D. C. (2005) Predictors of objective and subjective career success: A meta-analysis. *Personnel Psychology, 58,* 367–408.

Noonan, M. C. & Corcoran, M. E. (2004) The mommy track and partnership: Temporary delay or dead end? *Annals of the American Academy of Political and Social Science, 596,* 130–150.

Ohlott, P. J., Ruderman, M. N., & McCauley, C. D. (1994) Gender differences in managers' developmental job experiences. *Academy of Management Journal, 37,* 46–67.

Powell, G. N., Butterfield, D. A., & Parent, J. D. (2002) Gender and managerial stereotypes: Have the times changed? *Journal of Management, 28,* 177–193.

Raley, S. B., Mattingly, M. J., & Bianchi, S. M. (2006) How dual are dual-income couples: Documenting change from 1970 to 2001. *Journal of Marriage and Family, 68,* 11–28.

Riach, P. A. & Rich, J. (2002) Field experiments of discrimination in the market place. *Economic Journal, 112,* F480–F518.

Roper Starch Worldwide (1995) *The 1995 Virginia Slims opinion poll: A 25-year perspective of women's issues.* New York: Altria Group.

Rose, S. J. & Hartmann, H. I. (2004) *Still a man's labor market: The long-term earnings gap.* Washington, DC: Institute for Women's Policy Research. Retrieved from http://www.iwpr.org/pdf/C355.pdf.

Rudman, L. A. (1998) Self-promotion as a risk factor for women: The costs and benefits of counterstereotypical impression management. *Journal of Personality and Social Psychology, 74,* 629–645.

Ryan, M. K. & Haslam, S. A. (2005) The glass cliff: Evidence that women are over-represented in precarious leadership positions. *British Journal of Management, 16,* 81–90.

Ryan, M. K. & Haslam, S. A. (2007) The glass cliff: Exploring the dynamics surrounding women's appointment to precarious leadership positions. *Academy of Management Review, 32,* 549–572.

Saad, L. (2007, August 31) Women slightly more likely to prefer working to homemaking. Gallup Poll News Service.

Retrieved from http://www.gallup.com/poll/28567/Women-Slightly-More-Likely-Prefer-Working-Homemaking.aspx.

Schein, V. E. (2001) A global look at psychological barriers to women's progress in management. *Journal of Social Issues, 57,* 675–688.

Scott, K. A. & Brown, D. J. (2006) Female first, leader second? Gender bias in the encoding of leadership behavior. *Organizational Behavior and Human Decision Processes, 101,* 230–242.

Sczesny, S., Bosak, J., Neff, D., & Schyns, B. (2004) Gender stereotypes and the attribution of leadership traits: A cross-cultural comparison. *Sex Roles, 51,* 631–645.

Seibert, S. E., Kraimer, M. L., & Liden, R. C. (2001) A social capital theory of career success. *Academy of Management Journal, 44,* 219–237.

Smith, R. A. (2002) Race, gender, and authority in the workplace: Theory and research. *Annual Review of Sociology, 28,* 509–542.

Tepper, B. J., Brown, S. J., & Hunt, M. D. (1993) Strength of subordinates' upward influence tactics and gender congruency effects. *Journal of Applied Social Psychology, 23,* 1903–1919.

Thomas-Hunt, M. C. & Phillips, K. W. (2004) When what you know is not enough: Expertise and gender dynamics in task groups. *Personality and Social Psychology Bulletin, 30,* 1585–1598.

Timberlake, S. (2005) Social capital and gender in the workplace. *Journal of Management Development, 24,* 34–44.

Twenge, J. M. (1997) Changes in masculine and feminine traits over time: A meta-analysis. *Sex Roles, 36,* 305–325.

Twenge, J. M. (2001) Changes in women's assertiveness in response to status and roles: A cross-temporal meta-analysis, 1931–1993. *Journal of Personality and Social Psychology, 81,* 133–145.

Uhlmann, E. L. & Cohen, G. L. (2005) Constructed criteria: Redefining merit to justify discrimination. *Psychological Science, 16,* 474–480.

United Nations Development Programme (2009) *Human development report 2009.* Retrieved from http://hdr.undp.org/en/media/HDR_2009_EN_Complete.pdf

US Bureau of Labor Statistics (2010a) *Highlights of women's earnings in 2009.* Retrieved from http://www.bls.gov/cps/cpswom2009.pdf.

US Bureau of Labor Statistics (2010b) *Labor force statistics from the current population survey.* Retrieved from http://www.bls.gov/cps/.

US Bureau of Labor Statistics (2010c) *Economic news release: American time-use survey summary – 2009 results.* Retrieved from http://www.bls.gov/news.release/atus.nr0.htm.

US Bureau of Labor Statistics (2009) *Women in the labor force: A databook (2009 edition).* Retrieved from http://www.bls.gov/cps/wlf-databook2009.htm.

US Office of Personnel Management (2007) *Senior executive service: Facts and figures.* Retrieved from http://www.opm.gov/ses/facts_and_figures/demographics.asp.

US Merit Systems Protection Board (1995) *Sexual harassment in the federal workplace: Trends, progress, continuing challenges.* Retrieved from http://www.mspb.gov/netsearch/viewdocs.aspx?docnumber=253661&version=253948&application=ACROBAT.

US National Center for Education Statistics (2009) *Digest of education statistics, 2009.* Retrieved from http://nces.ed.gov/programs/digest/d09/tables/dt09_275.asp?referrer=list.

US Office of Personnel Management (1997) *The fact book, 1997 edition: Federal civilian workforce statistics.* Retrieved from http://www.opm.gov/feddata/factbook/97factbk.pdf.

Van Engen, M. L. & Willemsen, T. M. (2004) Sex and leadership styles: A meta-analysis of research published in the 1990s. *Psychological Reports, 94,* 3–18.

Van Vugt, M. (2006) Evolutionary origins of leadership and followership. *Personality and Social Psychology Review, 10,* 354–371.

Von Hippel, W., Sekaquaptewa, D., & Vargas, P. (1995) On the role of encoding processes in stereotype maintenance. *Advances in experimental social psychology, Vol. 27* (pp. 177–254). San Diego, CA: Academic Press.

Wajcman, J. (1998) *Managing like a man: Women and men in corporate management.* University Park, Pennsylvania: Pennsylvania State University Press.

Walters, A. E., Stuhlmacher, A. F., & Meyer, L. L. (1998) Gender and negotiator competitiveness: A meta-analysis. *Organizational Behavior and Human Decision Processes, 76,* 1–29.

Welsh, S. (1999) Gender and sexual harassment. *Annual Review of Sociology, 25:* 169–190.

Williams, J. (2000) *Unbending gender: Why family and work conflict and what to do about it.* New York: Oxford University Press.

Williams, J. E. & Best, D. L. (1990) *Measuring sex stereotypes: A multination study.* Newbury Park, CA: Sage.

Wilson, L. K. & Gallois, C. (1993) *Assertion and its social context.* Tarrytown, NY: Pergamon.

Wolff, H. & Moser, K. (2009) Effects of networking on career success: A longitudinal study. *Journal of Applied Psychology, 94,* 196–206.

Wood, W. & Eagly, A. H. (2002) A cross-cultural analysis of the behavior of women and men: Implications for the origins of sex differences. *Psychological Bulletin, 128,* 699–727.

Wosinska, W., Dabul, A. J., Whetstone-Dion, R., & Cialdini, R. B. (1996) Self-presentational responses to success in the organization: The costs and benefits of modesty. *Basic and Applied Social Psychology, 18,* 229–242.

Yoder, J. D. & Schleicher, T. L. (1996) Undergraduates regard deviation from occupational gender stereotypes as costly for women. *Sex Roles, 34,* 171–188.

9

A Network Approach to Leader Cognition and Effectiveness

Martin Kilduff and Prasad Balkundi

INTRODUCTION

Good administrators sometimes fail to understand social structure, and fail to anticipate its consequences for organizational survival. This can leave organizations vulnerable to manipulation by skilled political entrepreneurs. In one example, the entire top management team of a manufacturing company learned from a network analysis that the bomb threats, shootings, and vandalism threatening the future of the company were instigated by partisans of a lower-ranking manager, who had systematically recruited family, friends, and neighbors into the company over a 30-year period. In a district desperate for jobs, these partisans felt loyalty to the informal leader who had provided them information that allowed them to be first in line for vacancies on Monday morning. The CEO, confronted with an analysis of the deep cleavages existing in the social structure of the organization, resulting from the informal patterns of recruiting over decades, had this to say about those who had been hired: '... they just seemed like waves of turtles coming over the hill; hired as they made it to our door' (Burt, 1992, p. 1).

This story illustrates the gap at the heart of our understanding of organizational behavior. It illustrates how important it is for managers and would-be leaders to accurately perceive the network relations that connect people, and to actively manage these network relations. This story also illustrates how informal leaders who may lack formal authority can emerge to frustrate organizational functioning through the manipulation of network structures and the exercise of social influence.

In this chapter, we emphasize the importance of individual cognition for understanding social networks. We do this through an exploration of how the cognitions in the mind of the individual influence the network relationships negotiated by the individual, and how this individual network contributes to leadership effectiveness both directly and through informal networks. We understand 'leadership' to be a general concept applicable at many different levels in the organization, and to include both formally designated leaders as well as informal leaders. We link together social cognitions and social structure to forge a distinctive network approach to leadership that builds upon, but extends, previous work in both the network and the leadership realms.

ORGANIZATIONAL NETWORK RESEARCH CORE IDEAS

The organizational network perspective is a broad-based research program that continually draws inspiration from a set of distinctive ideas to investigate new empirical phenomena. The 'hard-core' ideas at the heart of network research define its special character and distinguish it from rival research programs (cf. Lakatos, 1970). What are these ideas familiar to all organizational network researchers? At least four interrelated principles generate network theories and hypotheses: the importance of relations between organizational actors; actors' embeddedness in social fields; the social utility of network connections; and the structural patterning of social life (Kilduff, Tsai, & Hanke, 2006).

An emphasis on *relations between actors* is the most important distinguishing feature of the network research program. As a recent historical treatment of social network research (Freeman, 2004, p. 16) pointed out, a core belief underlying modern social network analysis is the importance of understanding the interactions between actors (rather than a focus exclusively on the attributes of actors). An early treatment of network research on organizations stated that 'the social network approach views organizations in society as a system of objects (e.g., people, groups, organizations) joined by a variety of relationships' (Tichy, Tushman, & Fombrum, 1979, p. 507). Our network approach locates leadership in the relationships connecting individuals, a principle that has been rediscovered and renewed in recent leadership theory (Uhl-Bien, 2006).

The second principle that gives organizational network research its distinctiveness as a research program is the emphasis on *embeddedness*. For organizational network researchers, human behavior is seen as embedded in networks of interpersonal relationships (Granovetter, 1985; Uzzi, 1996). People in organizations and as representatives of organizations tend to enter exchange relationships, not with complete strangers, but with family, friends, or acquaintances. Embeddedness at the system level can refer to a preference for interacting with those within the community rather than those outside the community. We emphasize that people's perceptions of others are reflected through the sets of embedded ties within which people are located. For example, people's perceptions of team coworkers as trustworthy depends on whether the coworkers establish trust relationships with team leaders (Lau & Liden, 2008).

The third driving principle of social network research is the belief that network connections provide value to individuals and communities – including economic value (Burt, 2000). Depending upon the arrangement of social connections surrounding an actor, more or less value can be extracted (Burt, 1992; Gnyawali & Madhavan, 2001). At the system level, a generalized civic spirit emerges from and contributes to the many interactions of trust and interdependence between individual actors within the system (Coleman, 1990; Portes, 2000). Leadership, from the network perspective, involves developing social relationships within and across boundaries, and putting these relationships to use for the benefit of the organization.

The fourth leading idea distinctive to the social network research program – the emphasis on *structural patterning* – often leads social network research to be referred to as the 'structural approach.' Network researchers look for the patterns of 'connectivity and cleavage' in social systems (Wellman, 1988, p. 26). Not content with merely describing the surface pattern of ties, researchers look for the underlying structural factors through which actors generate and recreate network ties. At the local level surrounding a particular actor, the structure of ties can be described, for example, as relatively closed (actors tend to be connected to each other) or open (actors tend to be disconnected from each other) (Burt, 1992). At the system level, organizational networks can be assessed for the degree of clustering they exhibit and the extent to which any two actors can reach each other through a short number of network connections (e.g., Kogut & Walker, 2001). To understand who is a leader from a network perspective is to investigate the social-structural positions occupied by particular individuals in the social system.

These four leading ideas – the importance of relationships, the principle of embeddedness, the social utility of network connections, and the emphasis on structural patterning – provide the common culture for organizational network research that allows the diversity of viewpoints from which fresh theoretical initiatives emerge (cf. Burns & Stalker, 1961, p. 119). Network research is also characterized by vigorous development of methods and analytical programs to facilitate the examination of phenomena highlighted by theory (see Wasserman & Faust, 1994 for a review of methods; and the UCINET suite of programs – Borgatto, Everett, & Freeman, 2002 – for statistical software).

The organizational network research program is progressive in the sense that new theory is constantly being developed from the metaphysical core of ideas that makes up the heart of the research program, highlighting new areas of application. It is the purpose of this chapter to highlight the area of leadership from a network perspective. The four leading ideas that comprise the intellectual source of theory development for organizational network research are best understood as mutually reinforcing core beliefs that, like the planks of a ship, keep the research program afloat – in terms of new theory development and exploration of new phenomena. At the level of network theory and research, all four ideas tend to be inextricably involved. We will invoke these ideas as appropriate throughout the chapter.

In contrast to network research, traditional leadership research has focused on human capital attributes of leaders and situational attributes of leadership contexts. Human capital attributes of leaders include traits (e.g., House, 1977; Kenny & Zaccaro, 1983) and behavioral styles (e.g., Lewin, Lippitt, & White, 1939; Podsakoff, Todor, &

Skov, 1982), whereas situational attributes of leadership contexts include task structure (Fiedler, 1971), the availability of leadership substitutes (Kerr & Jermier, 1978), the nature of the decision process (Vroom & Yetton, 1973) and the quality of leader–member exchange (LMX) (Dansereau, Graen, & Haga, 1975; Graen, Novak, & Sommerkamp, 1982). A social network perspective does not eclipse the valuable results of conventional leadership research; rather, a network perspective can complement existing work without repeating it. In particular, in this review we amplify the voices that have called for a new understanding of leadership effectiveness to include leaders' cognitions about networks and the actual structure of leaders' ties (e.g., Hooijberg, Hunt, & Dodge, 1997; see also Bass, 1990, p. 19).

As with all theoretical perspectives, the network approach has boundary conditions that limit its range of application. Social network processes are less likely to have the effects we discuss to the extent that organizations are characterized by perfect competition between equally informed actors, all of whom have the same opportunities (see the discussion in Burt, 1992). (Even under conditions of perfect information, however, some actors are likely to be more influenced by social networks than others – see Kilduff, 1992). Furthermore, when resources are restricted, so that the environment becomes one of scarcity rather than munificence, social network relations between people and between subgroups within an organization are likely to be competitive rather than cooperative (as suggested by March & Simon, 1958). Under these conditions, there may be a tendency for leaders to engage in illegal activities involving bribery and collusion in order to extract scarce resources on behalf of themselves and their groups at the expense of others (cf. Baker & Faulkner, 1993). Following on from this point, organizational context is likely to affect network processes in ways that are outside the purview of this chapter. Contextual variables that could affect how leaders relate through network processes to followers include organizational culture, the demographic makeup of the organization, the variable ability of employees, the legal status of the organization (private, public, or not-for-profit), and the formal structure of the organization (see Porter & McLaughlin, 2006, for a review of contextual effects on leadership).

In network terms, leadership embodies the four principles that we articulated earlier. Leadership can be understood as *social capital* that collects around certain individuals – whether formally designated as leaders or not – based on the acuity of their social perceptions and the structure of their social ties (cf. Pastor, Meindl, & Mayo, 2002). Patterns of informal leadership can complement or complicate the patterns of formal leadership in organizations. Individuals can invest in *social relations* with others, can structure their social networks by adding and subtracting relationships, and can reap rewards both in terms of their own personal performance and organizational unit performance (Sparrowe, Liden, Wayne, & Kraimer, 2001). But *embeddedness* in social networks always involves the paradox that social relations, particularly those outside the immediate circle of the individual, may be difficult both to perceive accurately and to manage (cf. Uzzi, 1997). Thus, although the *social structure* of the organization determines opportunities and constraints for emergent leaders, the social structure is not within the control of any particular individual.

LEADERSHIP AND THE STRUCTURE OF TIES

We start our network approach to leadership theory with a discussion of actor cognitions concerning networks, move out to the inner circle around the actor, and then further zoom out to include progressively more of the social structure of the organization and the inter-organizational realm. The theoretical framework is illustrated in Figure 9.1, and represents a tentative model of leadership effectiveness from a network perspective. We provide an overview of the causal connections of the model before zooming in to discuss in more detail the dynamics within each part of the model.

As Figure 9.1 shows, the first step in the conceptual model indicates that leaders' cognitions about social networks affect the 'ego networks' that surround each leader. In network parlance, the term 'ego' refers to the focal individual whose network structure we are discussing, whereas 'alter' refers to the individual to whom ego is connected. Cognitive network theory (see Kilduff & Tsai, 2003, pp. 70–79, for a review) suggests that people, in general, shape their immediate social ties to others to be congruent with their schematic expectations concerning how relationships such as friendship and influence should be structured. The schematic expectations of leaders affect their ability to notice and change the structure of social ties (e.g., Janicik & Larrick, 2005). Thus, cognitions in the mind of the leader are the starting point for our theorizing concerning the formation of ties connecting the leader to others.

The network cognitions of leaders concerning such crucial organizational phenomena as the flow of social capital within and across organizational boundaries, and the presence and meaning of

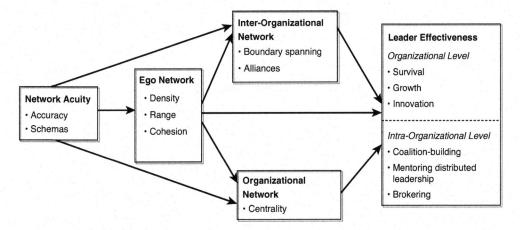

Figure 9.1   Theoretical framework linking leader's network accuracy to leader-relevant outcomes

social divides, are hypothesized to affect the extent to which leaders occupy strategically important positions in the organizational network. An accurate perception of the informal influence network can itself be a base of power in the organization (Krackhardt, 1990) and can facilitate the leader's ability to forge successful coalitions (Janicik & Larrick, 2005). We extend these insights to hypothesize that the acuity of leader cognitions will affect the extent to which a leader plays a strategically important role in the relevant inter-organizational network. We know of no research bearing on this thesis, although recent work concerning inter-organizational relationships increasingly concerns itself with hypothesized perceptual processes such as organizational reputation and status (e.g., Podolny, 1998; Zuckerman, 1999).

The extent to which a leader plays a role in these three actual networks – the ego network, the organizational network, and the inter-organizational network – is hypothesized to affect leader effectiveness. This critical hypothesis derives from our basic understanding of how the four guiding principles of the network approach extend leadership theory. Modern concepts of leadership identify the relational content of the interaction between people as the key aspect involved in the structuring of situations and the altering of perceptions and expectations (e.g., Bass, 1990, p. 19; Uhl-Bien, 2006). Modern network theory suggests that individuals who are central in the immediate networks around them and in the larger networks that connect them to others throughout the organization and beyond the organization are likely to acquire a particular type of expert power–knowledge of and access to those few powerful others whose words and deeds control resource flows and business

opportunities (e.g., Burt, 2005). Leaders may not be able to move into the center of every important network, of course. Embeddedness in one social network may come at the price of marginality in another network. There are trade-offs involved in building social capital, particularly when brokerage across social divides may engender distrust rather than gains.

One blow-by-blow account of an organizational power struggle contrasted the networking strategies of two combatants for sole control of the CEO position they currently shared. Whereas co-CEO Louis Glucksman was central within the Lehman Brothers organization as a whole and occupied a particularly strategic position among the traders, his rival and co-CEO Pete Petersen neglected internal networking in pursuit of connections with the leaders of other organizations (Auletta, 1986). Both men were effective leaders – Glucksman contributing to internal effectiveness and Petersen building and maintaining the external relationships that brought contracts to the partnership. But both had built quite different social network bases of power.

The role of external affective ties with the representatives of other organizations in providing vital help to companies in financial trouble has been emphasized by research on the survival prospects of small firms in the New York garment industry (Uzzi, 1996). More generally, the organizational theory and strategy literatures have examined the extent to which ties between organizations constitute a knowledge base important for outcomes such as firm growth (e.g., Powell, Koput & Smith-Doerr, 1996), new ties (e.g., Gulati & Gargiulo, 1999; Larson, 1992), and innovation (Hargadon & Sutton, 1997). Thus, the extent to which leaders are effective in terms of accessing important resources is likely to depend on the social-structural positions they occupy in the key networks within and between organizations.

What are the outcomes associated with leader effectiveness from a social network perspective? We have mentioned above such aspects of leader effectiveness as organizational growth, survival, and innovation. These are the responsibility of formal leaders and are outcomes at the organizational level of analysis. As Figure 9.1 summarizes, leader effectiveness from the network perspective we articulate would also include such components of internal organizational functioning as coalition building, mentoring, and brokering. These are intrinsically networking outcomes of both formal and informal leadership that can enhance coordination across functions within the organization. We return to these internal measures of leader effectiveness later in the chapter.

The model outlined in Figure 9.1 necessarily simplifies the relationships between cognition, social networks, and leadership effectiveness. We neglect, for example, the ways in which occupancy of social-structural positions in networks affects individuals' cognitions and expectations about networks (see Ibarra, Kilduff, & Tsai, 2005, for a review). The organization and the environment within which it operates can be jointly considered a set of cyclical processes captured in networks of cognitions (cf. Bougon, Weick, & Binkhorst, 1977). We focus in this chapter on leadership, and therefore emphasize the proactive enactment of outcomes leading to leader effectiveness.

NETWORK COGNITION AND LEADERSHIP

A key discovery of modern social network research is that cognitions matter (Kilduff & Krackhardt, 1994), and thus we start the in-depth discussion of the theoretical framework with an emphasis on network cognition, a topic relatively neglected within conventional leadership research (but see early LMX work on whether peers within units accurately perceive the quality of dyadic leader–subordinate relations – Graen & Cashman, 1975). Depending upon how the boundary is drawn around a particular individual in an organization, that individual may or may not appear to be influential in the eyes of others. That implicit leadership theories may be triggered by the structural position of certain individuals in the eyes of others is a possibility hinted at in recent leadership theory (Lord & Emrich, 2001), but yet to be systematically examined. From the perspective of perceivers located in small groups, certain actors may appear influential, but perceivers surveying

the larger context of the whole organization may dismiss these same actors as relatively inconsequential (see the discussion in Brass, 1992). Conversely, people who seem relatively powerless within one local group may be revealed to have close connections with powerful others outside the group. Thus, we organize our discussion by progressively zooming out from individuals' network cognitions to include expanding social circles within and beyond the organization.

From a network perspective that emphasizes the importance of relationships, embeddedness, social capital, and social structure, the ability of formal or would-be informal leaders to implement any leadership strategy depends on the accurate perception of how these principles operate in the social context of the organization. To be an effective leader of a social unit is to be aware of

- the relations between actors in that unit;
- the extent to which such relationships involve embedded ties, including kinship and friendship;
- the extent to which social entrepreneurs are extracting value from their personal networks to facilitate or frustrate organizational goals; and
- the extent to which the social structure of the unit includes cleavages between different factions.

The accurate perception of this complex social reality is fraught with difficulty, and, therefore, network cognition is an arena for innovative research.

If a leader wants to use social network ties to lead others, the leader must be able to perceive the existence, nature, and structure of these ties – not just the ties surrounding the leader, but the ties connecting others in the organization both near and far. Actors who are perceived to have power in terms of the structure of their social ties to others may wield influence even though they seldom or never exercise their potential power (Wrong, 1968; see the discussion in Brass, 1992, p. 299). To a considerable extent, organizations and environments exist as cognitions in the minds of leaders and followers within organizations (Bougon, Weick, & Binkhorst,1977; Kilduff, 1990) and in the inter-organizational arena of reputation and status (Podolny, 1998; Zuckerman, 1999).

Thus, the questions arise: How do people perceive network ties within and between organizations? How does anyone tell whether, for example, two individuals are personal friends? Even a small organization of 50 people represents a considerable cognitive challenge in terms of trying to perceive accurately the presence or absence of 2,450 friendship links between all pairs of individuals, links that may well be relatively invisible except to the individuals concerned. To create and manage the networks that promote leadership effectiveness, it may be necessary to possess an accurate representation of network links involving not just friendship and kinship but also advice, communication, and other important network ties.

What happens when formal leaders pay no attention to the four principles we have enunciated as representing the network approach to leadership? Is there any penalty consequent upon leader ignorance of social relations inside organizations, leader blindness to the embeddedness of working relationships in extra-organizational arrangements such as kinship, leader neglect of the extent to which social entrepreneurs manipulate embeddedness for their own ends, and leader unconsciousness of the social cleavages within the organization? The answer, provided in the case study alluded to in the opening paragraph of this chapter, is shocking in its illustration of diseased social capital. When the management fired, in a routine cost-cutting exercise, the informal leader to whom so many people were beholden not just for jobs but for the references necessary to actually get jobs inside the industrial plant, deep trouble ensued between employees loyal to the informal leader and those helping the management keep the industrial plant solvent. Shootings, bomb threats, and leakings of confidential management documents were the order of the day. The formal leadership team had no comprehension of what was happening, not having noticed that the workforce included so many people with strong social ties to a particular individual. (For the full case study see Burt & Ronchi, 1990.)

The CEO in this case was a good administrator and a skilled engineer who failed to understand the necessity of keeping track of the social structure of competition within and outside the organization. Social networks interpenetrate the boundary between employees and non-employees, and the management of this boundary has important consequences for organizational functioning. Job applicants with social contacts (such as friends) inside the organization can exploit social capital advantages to extract critical information at both the interview and job-offer stages. These referred individuals (compared to those who are not referred by current organizational members) tend to present more appropriate résumés and to apply when market conditions are more favorable (Fernandez & Weinberg, 1997). Referred individuals have a significantly greater likelihood of being offered a job as a result of these advantages. Further, referrals (relative to non-referrals) can use inside knowledge to boost their starting salaries in the negotiation process.

Thus, what might appear to a corporate leader as a systematic process of institutionalized racism involving higher starting salary increases to ethnic majorities relative to ethnic minorities can be revealed through social network analysis as a function of who has friends inside the organization (Seidel, Polzer, & Stewart, 2000). The fairness of a hiring process may be fundamentally compromised because it is invisibly embedded in kinship and friendship networks.

The perception of this otherwise invisible process of homophilous hiring is crucial to any effort by the leadership team to increase workforce diversity. The explicit management of external ties to recruit new members who are known to existing members of the organization can enhance the organization's economic returns (Fernandez, Castilla, & Moore, 2000). If leaders comprehend the social network relationships not only among organizational employees but also between employees and those outside the organization, then leaders can build the social capital of the organization by putting individuals' personal social networks to work for the organization's benefit.

Typically, managers are busy people whose work is fragmented and interrupted (Mintzberg, 1980). Much of our research in organization theory focuses on the formal arrangement of titles, offices, and reporting relationships, whether with respect to the integration and differentiation of the organization (e.g., Lawrence & Lorsch, 1967), the inertia of the organization (e.g., Hannan & Freeman, 1984) or the ceremonial façade created to be isomorphic with institutional demands (Meyer & Rowan, 1977). Leadership research, to the extent that it has considered social network relations, has also focused overwhelmingly (from an LMX perspective) on managers and the extent to which subordinates, for example, establish networks that mirror those of their formally appointed managerial leaders (Sparrowe & Liden, 2005; see Liden, co-author of Chapter 23, this volume).

The cognitive revolution in leadership research has focused not on the cognitions of leaders, but on leadership factors in the minds of followers (Eden & Leviatan, 1975; Lord & Emrich, 2001). There is an opportunity to extend both LMX research and cognitive approaches to leadership from the perspective of cognitive network theory (see Kilduff & Tsai, 2003, pp. 70–79, for a review) with a focus on how leaders and followers comprehend: (a) the structure of social relations (cf. Krackhardt, 1990); (b) the embeddedness of economic action in affect-laden networks (cf. Uzzi, 1996); and (c) the opportunities for social entrepreneurship across structural divides (Burt, 2005). A greater understanding of how leaders and followers comprehend the social structure from which action in organizations proceeds can enhance research on the management of relationships by formal and informal leaders.

Accuracy

From a cognitive network theory perspective, leadership involves not only social intelligence (i.e., the accurate perception of social relationships in organizations) but also the management of others' perceptions. First, let us consider accuracy. People perceive the same network differently, with some individuals achieving a high degree of accurate perception, whereas other individuals lead their organizational lives in relative ignorance of the actual network of relationships within which work is accomplished (Kilduff & Krackhardt, 1994).

In general, perceptions of networks involving sentiment relations such as friendship suffer from a series of predictable biases. People prefer to see their own relationships as reciprocated – they prefer not to perceive their friendship overtures as unrequited. Similarly, people prefer to believe that their friendship circles are transitively complete – they like to believe that their own friends are friends with each other (Heider, 1958). This cognitive balance schema operates also as a default mechanism for filling in the blanks concerning ties between relative strangers at the individual's perceived organizational network's periphery. In the absence of contrary information, people tend to assume that friendship ties of others are reciprocated, and that two friends of a distant stranger are themselves friends (Freeman, 1992; Krackhardt & Kilduff, 1999).

These cognitive distortions can affect leadership emergence. People in organizations see themselves as more popular than they actually are (Krackhardt, 1987; Kumbasar, Romney, & Batchelder, 1994), a tendency that can, perhaps, lead some individuals to neglect the vital process of maintaining their social capital (on the assumption that they are already popular); whereas other individuals, through a self-fulfilling prophecy process, may transform the illusion of popularity into actual friendship links that initially did not exist. Assuming that others like them, some people may reciprocate non-existent liking, and thereby create friends. Slight initial differences with respect to how people perceive their connections to others can potentially lead to cumulative advantages through this self-fulfilling prophecy process.

Furthermore, there may be a tendency to perceive popular actors as even more popular than they really are (Kilduff, Crossland, Tsai, & Krackhardt, 2008). Human beings, in their perceptions of social networks, are 'cognitive misers' (Krackhardt & Kilduff, 1999) who may tend to simplify networks by perceiving them as dominated by a few central actors even if the actual network has no dominant cluster. A misattribution of popularity to a few actors can result in these actors actually increasing their popularity. An emerging leader who is perceived to be popular may benefit from a bandwagon effect: people may want to associate with someone perceived to be a rising star. On the other hand, the perception that a social network is dominated by an elite group of leaders may discourage those who perceive themselves on the periphery from attempting to pursue leadership options.

Schemas

New research (Kilduff et al., 2008) suggests that individuals may tend to perceive friendship networks in organizations as small worlds. Small world network structures are unusual in that they exhibit both high local clustering and short average path lengths – two characteristics that are usually divergent (Watts & Strogatz, 1998). Clustering refers to the extent that actors are connected within local groups, whereas path lengths refer to the number of network connections between one actor and another in the network. A small world network resembles the hub-and-spoke structure of the US commercial air traffic system: local hubs with lots of connections; and short average path lengths because journeys from one city to another are routed through the hubs. (Compare this with the distinctly non-small world of the US interstate highway system.)

The small world effect, investigated originally in the 1960s by Milgram (1967), has become a burgeoning area of organizational social network research (e.g., Kogut & Walker, 2001; Uzzi & Spiro, 2005). As social networks become larger and more global, the discovery that some of the largest social networks such as the world wide web exhibit small world properties has excited considerable research interest (see Dorogovtsev & Mendes, 2003, for a review). Leadership within extremely large networks is a neglected topic, but one that seems tractable from a small world perspective, given that small world networks are organized for efficient communication and coordination.

We focus here on the possibility that some individuals more than others misperceive the extent to which organizational networks resemble small worlds (Kilduff et al., 2008). Such a bias has distinct implications for leadership research. A small world network schema offers a considerable advantage to the aspiring informal leader in terms of reducing the cognitive load required to keep track of so many different relationships. The rules for creating a cognitive map of the friendship network are relatively simple from this perspective: put similar people (with similarity defined on some relevant dimension such as demography or interests) into clusters and connect the clusters. Further research is needed to examine the extent to which the match between the 'small worldedness' of the individual's cognitive network and the small worldedness of the actual network predicts leader effectiveness.

Cognitive network schemas play a significant role in one important aspect of leadership, namely coalition building (cf. Stevenson, Pearce & Porter, 1985). Leaders are constantly involved in appointing people to task forces and committees. Making sure that the right balance of people are involved in these teams can make the difference between gridlock and effective action. In a pioneering set of studies, researchers found that individuals with experience of networks characterized by disconnections – structural holes – were better at perceiving the potential to bridge across structural holes by identifying suitable collaborators, a key to successful coalition (Janicik & Larrick, 2005). By making sure that different constituencies are represented at the top of the organization, the leader may facilitate the engagement of widely different groups in the organizational mission. However, in order to make these representative appointments, the leader must first be able to accurately perceive existing social system cleavages.

This recent research on the structural hole schema is interesting in suggesting that people are able to move beyond reliance on default modes of thinking (such as balance) when trying to make sense of the social network in organizations. People learn from experience to expect certain patterns in the social world, and tend to see new situations in the light of their anticipations. Thus, the leaders of an organization, familiar with the patterns of activity taking place from day to day, may impose on these patterns of interaction their own preconceptions of who shows up for meetings. Leaders anticipate that regular attendees will show up, and remember these people as having showed up even if they did not, while forgetting that more peripheral members of the organization were actually present on a specific occasion (cf. Freeman, Romney, & Freeman, 1987). Furthermore, people in general tend to perceive themselves to be more central in friendship networks in organizations than they actually are (Krackhardt, 1987). Thus, network cognition can depart from actual patterns of network activity, with consequences for the leader's ability to uncover political conflicts, spot communication problems between culturally divided groups, avoid reliance on problematic individuals for the transmission of important resources, achieve strategic objectives through the appointment of key people to influential positions, and manage relations within and across departments (Krackhardt & Hanson, 1993).

Leaders who perceive important social networks accurately in their organizations are likely themselves to be perceived as powerful (Krackhardt, 1990). This perceived power can itself represent an important supplement to formal authority. But, for those who want to span across structural holes and gain the reputed benefits of this activity, it may be crucially important to be perceived by others as *not* pursuing personal agendas (Fernandez & Gould, 1994). Social perceptions take place within reputational markets (Kilduff & Krackhardt, 1994) and, in the subtle battle to achieve prominence, individuals may strive to appear to others to be associated with leaders of high status. The perceived status of exchange partners can act like a distorting prism to filter attributions concerning the focal individual (Podolny, 2001).

Individuals move in and out of organizational contexts, and as they do so, their structural positions change. In one context someone assumes a leadership position, but the same individual may be a follower in another context in the same organization. Partly this is based on shifting perceptions. Individuals self-perceive themselves as powerful in some contexts and as less powerful in other contexts, and their self-attributions may be concordant with or discrepant with others' attributions. Actors in organizations may exert power without having to request compliance with their demands, simply on the basis of possibly false perceptions:

> Just as players can successfully 'bluff' in poker, employees can also act as if they control scarce resources, as if they were potentially powerful.... Persons who are in a position to control information can withhold, disclose, and modify it in order to influence others' attributions of power. (Brass, 1992, p. 299)

Thus, the importance of perceptions of leadership emergence and individual influence may reside in the extent to which they are never tested. In one recorded instance of a battle between dual CEOs for the exclusive control of the Lehman Brothers investment banking house, Louis Glucksman convinced his rival Pete Petersen that Petersen had lost friendships with board members, whereas Glucksman had retained their regard. But neither rival checked to see if his perception of his social relations with the all-important board members was accurate (Auletta, 1986).

To summarize our general ideas concerning the importance of acuity in leaders' perceptions of social networks, we indicate in Figure 9.1 that accuracy is likely to improve the extent to which a leader occupies a strategic position in three social network structures relevant to organizational behavior:

- the ego network, comprising the individuals immediately connected to the leader;
- the complete organizational network, comprising not just direct connections but also the leaders' indirect connections to everyone in the organization; and
- the inter-organizational network of relationships, which are important to the leader's work outside the focal organization.

In Figure 9.1 we also include the role of cognitive schemas – such as the small world schema we discussed above – in determining the match between leaders' perceptions of networks and actual networks. We need more research concerning the extent to which such cognitive schemas help or hurt leaders develop accurate maps of the social networks within which they operate. Whereas research on cognitive shortcuts implies that perceivers who rely on such shortcuts tend to make errors (Kahneman & Tversky, 1973), others see positive benefits deriving from the use of such schemas (e.g., Taylor & Brown, 1988), including greater satisfaction in close relationships (Murray, Holmes, & Griffin, 1996; see Kenny, Bond, Mohr, & Horn, 1996, for evidence concerning the effects of relational schemas on accuracy).

We have spent considerable time on the social cognition of networks of relationships, given the growing recognition within leadership research of how leader cognitions affect leader behaviors with implications for both leader effectiveness and organizational effectiveness (e.g., Hooijberg et al., 1997). Leadership research has long recognized the importance of implicit leadership schemas in the minds of followers (see Lord & Emrich, 2001, for review). Building on this emphasis on cognition and cognitive schemas, we seek to extend leadership research from a distinctively network emphasis on social relations, embeddedness, social capital, and social structure.

THE EGO NETWORK

Moving on from the network cognitions in the head of the individual, we now consider the ego network: i.e., the social circle of relations actually surrounding the individual person, who is typically referred to in network research as ego. A strong argument could be made that it is this ego network that fundamentally affects all the other network relationships a leader forms and influences – hence, the centrality of the ego network in Figure 9.1. It is this personal network that forms the basis of, for example, the influential structural hole perspective (Burt, 1992; 2005). A major task of future research is to assess whether the structure

of direct connections leaders have with colleagues is as important as the structural hole approach implies, or whether more indirect connections involving intermediaries can dampen or enhance leadership effectiveness, as implied in embeddedness research (Uzzi, 1996).

Density

A key theoretical concept concerning how direct connections within the ego network relate to leadership is density, as indicated in Figure 9.1. Individuals whose social contacts are themselves connected to each other have dense social circles, whereas individuals whose social contacts have few connections amongst themselves have sparse social circles (Wasserman & Faust, 1994). Members of a dense network tend to share similar attitudes and values toward the leader of the organization (Krackhardt, 1999).

From a network perspective, whether the members of a dense network tend to enhance or neutralize the leader's effectiveness is likely to depend upon whether the shared attitudes toward the leader are positive or negative. A dense network of people favorably disposed toward the leader represents a pool of social capital available to the leader that can facilitate the communication of important messages throughout the group, thereby fostering a positive work climate (cf. Zohar & Tenne-Gazit, 2008). A dense network of people negatively inclined toward the leader represents a potentially distorting prism, likely to take any message or initiative from the leader and cast it in the most unflattering light. More research is needed on the ways in which dense networks distort or enhance leadership initiatives, and how such networks prevent or accentuate aversive leadership (cf. Bligh, Kohles, Pearce, Justin, & Stovall, 2007) and destructive leadership behavior (cf. Einarsen, Aasland, & Skogstad, 2007).

Range

Structural hole theory (Burt, 1992), following on from the weak-tie hypothesis (Granovetter, 1973), suggests that individuals whose personal contacts include a diverse range of disconnected others gain benefits. These benefits (including faster promotions – Burt, 1992) derive from the information and control possibilities of being the 'third in the middle' between other individuals who must pass resources and information through the focal individual. Thus, the focal individual has access to diverse communications within his or her immediate contacts. If the individual (conventionally referred to as 'ego' in network research) is embedded in a clique, then the diversity of information and resources reaching ego from immediate contacts may be low. Furthermore, the opportunity for ego to play an informal leadership role, distributing ideas and other valued resources throughout the immediate social circle, vanishes if ego is simply one more person in a highly connected group.

As simple as the implied principle appears to be – connect oneself to diverse others who themselves are not connected to each other in order to enhance leadership potential in the informal network of relationships – it is much harder to realize than might at first be apparent. The principle of embeddedness operates strongly in this context. Simply stated, individuals prefer to associate with homophilous others – those who are similar to themselves (McPherson, Smith-Lovin, & Cook, 2001). This tendency is likely to be just as strong among putative leaders as it is among people in general – even economic transactions at the firm level tend to be embedded in kinship and friendship networks (Uzzi, 1996).

Homophilous networks represent information restriction (Popielarz, 1999). Individuals embedded in such networks, established not just in terms of kinship but also on the basis of proximity (Festinger, Schachter, & Back, 1950), ethnicity or gender (Mehra et al., 1998), are likely to experience strong cohesion (lots of ties among the similar others) but also information restriction. Groups as powerful as the dominant coalition (Cyert & March, 1963), the top management team (Hambrick & Mason, 1984), and the board of directors (Palmer, 1983) may exhibit in-group homogeneity under the pressures of ease of communication, shared backgrounds, and demographic similarity (see the review in Westphal & Milton, 2000). Social capital advantages are likely to be significantly diminished as leaders embed themselves in homogenous groups, leading to negative effects on market share and profits (Hambrick, Cho, & Chen, 1996). Business survival prospects tend to be better for those businesses whose owners establish a large range of personal contacts with important representatives of the task environment relative to those owners who establish a smaller range of such contacts (Oh, Kilduff, & Brass, 2005).

Cohesion

The cohesiveness of a dominant coalition may be sharply increased if the coalition perceives it is challenged by a set of actors (pursuing a hostile takeover, for example) or by negative outcomes of previous decisions (Kilduff, Angelmar, & Mehra, 2000). This increased homophily, while facilitating coordinated action by the top management team,

may adversely restrict decision-making options. The extent to which leaders turn to their personal contacts for advice following poor firm performance predicts subsequent tendencies to minimize changes in corporate strategy (McDonald & Westphal, 2003).

There are strong pressures in organizations for people to agree with their personal friends concerning important values and ideas. For an informal leader, embedded in a coalition of like-minded individuals, to challenge the hegemony of the official culture is always possible. But it is much more difficult for an informal leader to resist the social pressure from within his or her social circle to agree with close friends concerning how to interpret widely shared core values (Krackhardt & Kilduff, 1990).

It is interesting to note that, from a network perspective, the social pressure on ego differs little irrespective of the size of the clique within which ego is embedded, given that the clique contains people who all have ties to each other within the clique, but no common ties to those outside. Whether ego is embedded in a three-person clique or a clique of larger size, ego still experiences group pressure to conform (Simmel, 1950). This pressure becomes powerful as soon as a dyadic interaction (between two people) expands to include three people. To the extent that a leader belongs to two or more of these cliques (of size three or larger), the leader is vulnerable to cross-pressures from the different cliques to which he or she belongs. Different cliques tend to reinforce different interpretations of reality, and these discrepant interpretations may place the leader, who links the two different cliques together and who may play a brokerage role between these different groups, in a complicated situation. Each clique may present the leader with demands that, considered jointly, may be difficult to meet.

One case study described how an informal leader, who strongly favored the ongoing unionization drive in an entrepreneurial company, found himself unable to use his influential position in his personal social circle to influence others. This individual was a member of eight different three-person friendship cliques and was thus 'frozen by the set of constraints imposed by the numerous cliques' (Krackhardt, 1999, p. 206). Three of this person's cliques contained vociferous opponents of unionization. So unpleasant was his position in his social circle that he resigned from the firm 10 days before the unionization vote was taken, and rejoined the firm two days after the vote had failed. This individual's apparent power in the social circle of personal friends was stultified by his embeddedness in cohesive, but mutually discrepant, cliques.

Informal leadership emergence

Within the social circle surrounding the formal leader, there are likely to be some individuals who play informal leadership roles. These informal leaders tend to spring up in teams in which formally appointed leaders play little or no role in the coordination of team activity (perhaps because the formal leaders are focused on activities external to the team). Thus, informal leadership is likely to be a feature of teams in which formal leadership is, relatively speaking, absent. One study of leaderless teams found that informal leaders disproportionately influenced team efficacy – the extent to which team members evaluated their abilities to perform specific work-related tasks (Pescosolido, 2001). Such informal leaders also play a role in regulating team members' emotions (Pescosolido, 2002). Key process variables, such as team efficacy and team emotions, affect team performance (Barsade, 2002; Gibson & Vermeulen, 2003).

Given the potential power of these informal leaders to manage the cognitions and emotions of group members, even in the absence of any formal authority, formally appointed leaders' relationships with these informal leaders becomes more important than perhaps approaches that have focused on LMX relations have recognized. We suggest that within the leader's in-group there are some ties that are more crucial for leader effectiveness than others; and, outside the leader's in-group, neglect of individuals with considerable social influence is likely to imperil leader effectiveness.

To summarize this section is to recognize that structural hole theory (Burt, 1992) suggests that would-be leaders should structure their interpersonal networks to reach diverse constituencies, using relatively few ties to expand the range of information and resources accessed. An effective network strategy, according to this interpretation of structural hole theory, is likely to involve leaders building links to a variety of different constituencies and delegating to trusted 'lieutenants' the task of managing relationships with the other members of each constituency. Information would flow to leaders through the trusted lieutenants from all around the organization. It is with each trusted lieutenant that the informal leader develops and maintains a strong tie (as suggested in the dyadic approach to leadership – see Dansereau, 1995, for a review). It is this emphasis on extending the leader's ties throughout the organization that we turn to next.

THE ORGANIZATIONAL NETWORK

There are some caveats to the 'divide and conquer' strategy advocated from the influential structural hole perspective (Burt, 1992, 2005). From this perspective, would-be leaders are recommended to divide social networks in organizations into non-overlapping groups and to harvest social capital benefits from brokering information and other resources between these groups. However, as structural hole theory recognizes, there are some groups (such as boards of directors) whose importance may require a much more intensive relational strategy. To the extent that all the members of a particular group have power over ego's leadership effectiveness, then it makes sense for ego to invest in a personal relationship with every member of the group. In addition, the effectiveness of informal leadership is likely to depend not just on direct links to others but also on the pattern of links beyond the immediate ties. The important idea here, then, is that the structural position of ego in the social network affects the leadership potential of the individual in the organization, and this principle extends beyond the immediate social circle of the individual.

From an embeddedness perspective (Uzzi, 1996, 1997), an effective leadership network is a multi-step process, only one step of which is under the control of ego. First, ego needs to build ties to individuals who represent access to and from key constituencies within and outside the organization. But, secondly, ego needs to monitor whether representatives of these key constituencies themselves have access to networks. And thirdly, ego must monitor the inter-relationships between these representatives (cf. Sherony & Green, 2002; Sparrowe & Liden, 2005). Leadership success can crucially depend upon these secondary networks, and the inter-relationships between people beyond the leader's ego network.

At present, we know little about how a leader within an organization functions in the context of the social networks of 'informal' leaders who may or may not be occupying positions of official authority. Informal leaders, typically of lower rank than the primary leaders (to whom they may or may not report directly), wield considerable influence derived from their positions in the social network (Mechanic, 1962). We can glean some insight into how a leader at one level can benefit or suffer from the activities of socially well-connected informal leaders by considering the literature on substitutes for leadership. Leaders whose subordinates possess expert power, for example, may find themselves to be relatively redundant. Subordinate expertise can act as a substitute for leadership in some cases and in other cases subordinates, representing the leader, can deputize for the leader (Gronn, 1999; Kerr & Jermier, 1978; Podsakoff & MacKenzie, 1997). Informal leaders who either fracture the team or subvert the formal leader can weaken the leader and the team (Mehra,

Smith, Dixon, & Robertson, 2006). Recent conceptual work focused on these informal leaders, their behaviors, and their relationships with their formal leaders (Galvin, Balkundi & Waldman, 2010). In another vein, distributed leadership can also function as a substitute for leadership in that influence is spread out across the members of a work team (Mayo, Meindl, & Pastor, 2003). Such distributed leadership is associated with high levels of team performance (Carson, Tesluk, & Marrone, 2007), suggesting that further work on this concept is warranted.

Mentoring distributed leadership

From the network perspective articulated in this chapter, leader effectiveness involves building social capital that benefits individuals in the organization and extending the social networks of subordinates to facilitate career advancement. One measure of leader effectiveness, therefore, is the success of the leader in promoting the social networks and leadership potential of subordinates. By systematically sponsoring subordinates' development of social capital through introductions to key people in the organization and the environment, leaders can enhance the overall leadership potential in the organization and groom their subordinates for organizational success. An added benefit of subordinate social capital enhancement is that subordinates who experience relational building behaviors on the part of their leaders exhibit more energy at work and higher levels of performance (Carmeli, Ben-Hador, Waldman, & Rupp, 2009). Hence the emphasis on the mentoring of distributed leadership as an aspect of leader effectiveness in Figure 9.1. The perceived influence of protégés in the organization is likely to be related to the extent to which the protégés build links across demographic boundaries. Thus, helping a man build links to the network of women or a woman build links to the network of men within an organization can enhance the protégé's leadership potential, measured in terms of perceived power (Brass, 1985).

Such sponsorship is likely to be especially important in the case of members of underrepresented groups whose own attempts at brokerage across social divides may rebound to hurt rather than help their careers, according to research in one firm (Burt, 1992). Members of underrepresented groups tend to form homophilous networks among themselves and may also experience discrimination from majority group members (Mehra, Kilduff, & Brass, 1998). The mentoring of underrepresented group subordinates involves facilitating the development of the subordinates' own

networks, which may expand in directions not covered by the leader's own connections (cf. Higgins & Kram, 2001). Research suggests that such mentoring relationships can be successful, even when the sponsor and the protégé are from different ethnic groups (Thomas, 1993). Network leadership, then, can be measured in terms of how much social capital it creates for others, especially those members of underrepresented groups whose social network ties may be restricted because of in-group pressures toward homophily and out-group bias (Mehra et al., 1998).

A particularly important test of network leadership occurs in the case of isolates. G. K. Chesterton wrote, 'There are no words to express the abyss between isolation and having one ally.' Members of work teams who consistently fail to communicate with their colleagues may represent wasted resources in today's coordinated organizations whether or not they suffer the 'abyss' of isolation. Research in three high-technology military organizations showed that isolates, relative to 'participants', tended: to rely more on written and telephone communication, to withhold information, to express less commitment to the organization, to experience lower satisfaction with both communication and with their jobs, and to be rated as lower performers (Roberts & O'Reilly, 1979). Clearly, such isolated individuals represent a networking challenge. The extent to which such isolates are part of work groups may predict the extent of leader effectiveness in such groups. A related issue concerns the extent to which work groups exhibit disconnects between subgroups. Although recent work suggests that too few or too many structural holes in a team may adversely affect communication (Oh, Chung, & Labianca, 2004) and team effectiveness, the question of how such structural holes affect team performance and functioning remains unanswered (Balkundi, Kilduff, Michael, & Barsness, 2007).

Positive emotion

Isolates and structural holes in groups tend to signal the existence of emotional distress. Research attention has started to focus on the role of formal leaders in the emotion management network in organizations (Toegel, Anand, & Kilduff, 2007). Vertical dyad linkage theory alerted researchers to the benefits – emotional and vocational – associated with membership in the leader's in-group (see Dansereau, 1995, for a review). Building on this legacy, the positive psychology movement suggests that leaders have responsibility for maintaining the emotional health of all employees (Frost, 2003), rather than just those with privileged access to the leader. Yet, some people in formal leadership roles fail to attend to the toxic emotions created in organizational contexts and thereby fail to perform as effective leaders (Maitlis & Ozcelik, 2004). The question of the management of affective bonds and emotional health has been neglected in the leadership and in the network literatures and begs for more attention.

THE INTER-ORGANIZATIONAL NETWORK: BOUNDARY SPANNING AND ALLIANCES

Leaders, both formal and informal, can potentially network within their organizational units and outside their units. As representatives of their organizational units, leaders forge inter-organizational links that may or may not lead to or coincide with formally contracted relationships. Beneath most formal alliance ties between organizations 'lies a sea of informal ties' (Powell et al., 1996, p.120). Inter-personal friendships and other strong links such as kinship between CEOs can lead to business alliances, just as business alliances can lead to warmth and trust between representatives of different organizations (Larson, 1992; Uzzi, 1997).

One dramatic case study, referred to earlier in this chapter, highlighted the danger of two individuals dividing the networking task between them into its internal and external components (Auletta, 1986). Lehman Brothers was a venerable Wall Street investment banking firm in which partner Louis Glucksman operated as the inside networker, maintaining cohesion and rapport with the company's traders, whereas partner Pete Petersen operated as the outside networker, responsible for bringing in new business from the rich and famous. When both partners were anointed as joint CEOs, the ensuing battle for supremacy led to a financial crisis and a takeover by American Express, bringing to an inglorious end one chapter in the saga of a proud and independent institution. In the furious battle for control between the inside and outside networkers, Glucksman had the upper hand, having developed social capital within the organization among the partners who controlled the firm through their votes.

As this example illustrates, managing the boundary between inside and outside networking is a crucial task for formal leaders. The formal leader can be considered a boundary-spanner who not only manages an internal constituency within the organization but also represents the organization in the community of organizations. Network links between organizations tend to build from within the existing network. Organizational leaders create stable relationships with trusted partners,

and, over time, these stable ties accumulate into a network that provides to members of the network information about future alliance partners (Gulati & Gargiulo, 1999). Organizational leaders, for example, tend to recommend to one trusted partner the formation of a business relationship with another trusted partner, thus creating a three-member clique (Larson, 1992; Uzzi, 1996). With knowledge increasingly emerging from the interstices between hierarchical boundaries (Powell et al., 1996), leaders who pursue policies of splendid isolation are likely to see their organizations suffer 'the liability of unconnectedness' (Baum & Oliver, 1992) in failing to capture intellectual developments as they arise and expand.

An innovative organization such as Digital Equipment Company, once famed for its fortress-like culture and its devotion to in-house technical development (Kunda, 1993), is likely to fade away in a knowledge economy in which innovations are increasingly the product of industrial clusters rather than individual companies (Saxenian, 1990). Given the inertia of organizations relative to the speed of change in many environments (Hannan & Freeman, 1984), even large and apparently dominant organizations in knowledge-intensive industries need to build connections with a range of other organizations in order to access developing technology.

However, leadership effectiveness in this knowledge economy may depend not just on the direct network links to other organizations under the leader's control but also on the links beyond the leader's control. As we noted with respect to networking within the organization, it is often the links beyond the immediate social circle of the leader that affect many desired outcomes. Research suggests that the survival of the organization itself may be affected by the secondary links to organizations beyond the leader's immediate control.

For example, in the New York garment industry, CEOs who developed strong personal relationships with the heads of 'jobbing' firms (that distribute work orders) increased the survival chances of their firms if they were able to access through these strong connections networks of balanced relationships. It was not just the primary ties to the jobbing firms that were important for the focal firms. Survival was enhanced for the firms of those CEOs strongly connected through a primary tie to a set of secondary ties that included a balanced mix of arm's length and close ties with a jobbing firm (Uzzi, 1997). Although the CEO may have some control over whether to develop close, personal ties or more market-based exchanges with heads of jobbing firms, the CEO may not even be aware of the types of business relationships that jobbers have with other firms. Thus, leadership effectiveness (and the survival of the organization) may depend on second-order network links beyond the control of the CEO.

What of the leader's centrality in the community of organizational leaders? Research shows that organizational leaders tend to interact with each other across a range of social events, with representatives of elite organizations tending to form their own elite social circles (Galaskiewicz, 1985; Kilduff & Tsai, 2003, p. 22). However, centrality in this community of leaders may distract leaders from the strategic management of their own organizations. One study of an ethnic community of Korean expatriate entrepreneurs showed that the extent to which organizational owners were central (in terms of spanning across divided social groups within the community) correlated negatively with performance and predicted organizational demise (Oh, Kilduff, & Brass, (2005). Of compelling interest, however, is the extent to which the leader's ties to organizational leaders outside the immediate community affect the flow of important resources and, thereby, organizational survival.

It may be in the inter-organizational arena that new network methods focused on social network dynamics emerge, given the strong interest in understanding the evolution of strategic alliances (e.g., Gulati & Gargiulo, 1999). Conventional wisdom suggests that networks tend to be relatively stable, but this apparent stability can mask many types of change that can be captured in network 'movies' showing the dance of interactions over time (Moody, McFarland, & Bender-deMoll, 2005).

CONCLUSIONS

Leadership requires the management of social relationships. Starting with the cognitions in the mind of the leader concerning the patterns of relationships in the ego network, the organizational network, and the inter-organizational network, social ties are formed and maintained, initiatives are launched or avoided, and through these actions and interactions, the work of the leader is accomplished. Building on the idea that networks are both cognitive structures in the minds of individuals and actual structures of relationships that link individuals, this chapter views organizational networks as constructed and maintained by boundedly rational actors, subject to biases in their perceptions. Leadership research from a network perspective has the opportunity to forge a new understanding of the interplay between the psychology of individuals and the complexity of the networks through which actors exchange information, affect, and other resources.

Leadership research also has the opportunity to renew our understanding of how patterns of informal leadership complement or detract from the work of formally appointed leaders. If leaders rely solely on their formally assigned authority, and bring into their leadership circles like-minded others, they may isolate themselves from new ideas – as represented by, for example, the slow learners investigated by March (1991). Furthermore, the influence of visible leaders, both informal and formal, is likely to be affected by network ties that may not show up at all in the organizational chart. The members of governing coalitions, for example, are likely to be tied to powerful individuals temporarily removed from positions of authority and deal makers who operate quietly to influence organizational outcomes. Only recently has research attention focused on these virtual actors whose 'ghost' ties constrain network change and action (see, for example, Moody et al., 2005).

The network approach articulated in this chapter emphasizes the extent to which individuals' thoughts and actions are embedded in their perceptions of networks, in the immediate 'ego' networks that surround them, in the organizational networks within which their ego networks are embedded, and in the inter-organizational networks that connect them to leaders of other organizations. Leaders, we have emphasized, generate and use social capital through the acuity with which they perceive social structures and the actions they take to build connections with important constituencies within and across social divides.

We have said little about how abusive, destructive, or conspiratorial leaders might facilitate their behaviors through social networks, and these are topics that have been neglected in the network literature, despite their importance. Adam Smith (1976, p. 144) famously noted that 'people of the same trade seldom meet together, even for merriment and diversion, but the conversation ends in a conspiracy against the public, or in some contrivance to raise prices.' One influential study of such collusive networks demonstrated the problems organizational leaders faced as they tried to both conceal their illegal activities and coordinate price-fixing across different organizations (Baker & Faulkner, 1993). In general, the more centralized the illegal network in terms of concentrating decision-making among a small group of ringleaders, the more that prosecution focused on these leaders: 'Top executives cannot hide in a centralized conspiracy. They cannot distance themselves from illegal operations' (Baker & Faulkner, 1993, p. 855). Research on terrorist networks has uncovered a similar organizational dilemma – terrorist groups tend to be at their most effective when they are hierarchically organized around a core set of leaders, yet this centralization exposes terrorist organizations to infiltration and attack (Eilstrup-Sangiovanni & Jones, 2008).

To understand leadership effectiveness from a social network perspective is to study the individual's position in the larger networks within which the individual is located. The network approach, therefore, allows a more macro focus on the full repertoire of network relationships than has been the case in previous leadership research. The network approach also incorporates actors within the network who may or may not be connected with the leader, but whose actions, in creating new ties, for example, can affect leader outcomes by changing the structures within which the leader operates. Clearly, the network perspective in its emphasis on social relations, embeddedness, social capital, and social structure, both incorporates strands emphasized within previous leadership research, and points in new directions.

ACKNOWLEDGMENT

This chapter draws from Balkundi, P. & Kilduff, M. (2005) The ties that lead: A social network approach to leadership. *The Leadership Quarterly*, 16: 941–961.

REFERENCES

Auletta, K. (1986). *Greed and glory on Wall Street: The fall of the house of Lehman*. New York: Random House.

Baker, W. E. & Faulkner, R. R. (1993). The social organization of conspiracy: Illegal networks in the heavy electrical equipment industry. *American Sociological Review*, 58, 837–860.

Balkundi, P., Kilduff, M., Michael, J. & Barsness, Z. (2007). Demographic antecedents and performance consequences of structural holes in work teams. *Journal of Organizational Behavior*, 28: 241–260.

Barsade, S. G. (2002). The ripple effect: Emotional contagion and its influence on group behavior. *Administrative Science Quarterly*, 47, 644–675.

Bass, B. M. (1990). *Bass and Stogdill's handbook of leadership: Theory, research and managerial application* (3rd edn). New York: The Free Press.

Baum, J. & Oliver, C. (1992). Institutional embeddedness and the dynamics of organizational population. *American Sociological Review*, 57, 540–559.

Bligh, M. C., Kohles, J. C., Pearce, C. L., Justin, J. E. & Stovall, J. F. (2007). When the romance is over: Follow-up perspectives of aversive leadership. *Applied Psychology: An International Review*, 56, 528–557.

Borgatti, S. P., Everett, M. G. & Freeman, L. C. (2002). *UCINET for Windows: Software for social network analysis*. Harvard: Analytic Technologies.

Bougon, M. G., Weick, K. E. & Binkhorst, D. (1977). Cognition in organizations: An analysis of the Utrecht Jazz Orchestra. *Administrative Science Quarterly*, 22, 606–639.

Brass, D. J. (1985). Men's and women's networks: A study of interaction patterns and influence in organizations. *Academy of Management Journal*, 28, 327–343.

Brass, D. J. (1992). Power in organizations: A social network perspective. In G. Moore, & J. A. Whitt (eds), *Research in politics and society* (pp. 295–323). Greenwich, CT: JAI Press.

Burns, T. & Stalker, G. M. (1961). *The management of innovation*. London: Tavistock Publications Ltd.

Burt, R. (1992). *Structural holes: The social structure of competition*. Cambridge, MA: Harvard University Press.

Burt, R. (2000). The network structure of social capital. In R. I. Sutton, & B. M. Staw (eds), *Research in organizational behavior* (pp. 345–423). Greenwich CT: JAI Press.

Burt, R. (2005). *Brokerage and closure: An introduction to social capital*. Oxford: Oxford University Press.

Burt, R. & Ronchi, D. (1990). Contested control in a large manufacturing plant. In J. Weesie, & H. D. Flap (eds), *Social networks through time* (pp. 127–157). Utrecht: Isor.

Carmeli, A., Ben-Hador, B., Waldman, D. A. & Rupp, D. E. (2009). How leaders cultivate social capital and nurture employee vigor: Implications for job performance. *Journal of Applied Psychology*, 94, 1553–1561.

Carson, J. B., Tesluk, P. E. & Marrone, J. A. (2007). Shared leadership in teams: An investigation of antecedent conditions and performance. *Academy of Management Journal*, 50: 1217–1234.

Coleman, J. S. (1990). *Foundations of social theory*. Cambridge, MA: Harvard University Press.

Cyert, R. M. & March, J. G. (1963). *A behavioral theory of the firm*. Englewood Cliffs, NJ: Prentice Hall.

Dansereau, F. (1995). A dyadic approach to leadership: Creating and nurturing this approach under fire. *The Leadership Quarterly*, 6, 479–490.

Dansereau, F., Graen, G. & Haga, W. J. (1975). A vertical dyad linkage approach to leadership within formal organizations: A longitudinal investigation of the role making process. *Organizational Behavior and Human Performance*, 13, 46–78.

Dorogovtsev, S. & Mendes, J. (2003). *Evolution of networks: From biological nets to the internet and WWW*. Oxford: Oxford University Press.

Eden, D. & Leviatan, U. (1975). Implicit leadership theory as a determinant of the factor structure underlying supervisory behavior scales. *Journal of Applied Psychology*, 60, 736–741.

Eilstrup-Sangiovanni, M. & Jones, C. (2008). Assessing the dangers of illicit networks: Why al-Qaeda may be less threatening than many think. *International Security*, 33, 7–44.

Einarsen, S., Aasland, M. S. & Skogstad, A. (2007). Destructive leadership behavior: A definition and conceptual model. *The Leadership Quarterly*, 18, 207–216.

Fernandez, R. M., Castilla, E. J. & Moore, P. (2000). Social capital at work: Network and employment at a phone center. *American Journal of Sociology*, 105, 1288–1356.

Fernandez, R. M. & Gould, R. V. (1994). A dilemma of state power: Brokerage and influence in the national health policy domain. *American Journal of Sociology*, 99, 1455–1491.

Fernandez, R. M. & Weinberg, N. (1997). Sifting and sorting: Personal contacts and hiring in a retail bank. *American Sociological Review*, 62, 883–902.

Festinger, L., Schachter, S. & Back, K. (1950). *Social pressures in informal groups: A study of human factors in housing* (1st edn). New York: Harper.

Fiedler, F. E. (1971). Validation and extension of the contingency model of leadership effectiveness: A review of empirical findings. *Psychological Bulletin*, 76, 128–148.

Freeman, L. C. (1992). Filling in the blanks: A theory of cognitive categories and the structure of social affiliation. *Social Psychology Quarterly*, 55, 118–127.

Freeman, L. C. (2004). *The development of social network analysis: A study in the sociology of science*. Vancouver: Empirical Press.

Freeman, L. C., Romney, A. K. & Freeman, S. C. (1987). Cognitive structure and informant accuracy. *American Anthropologist*, 89, 310–325.

Frost, P. J. (2003). *Toxic emotions at work: How compassionate managers handle pain and conflict*. Boston, MA: Harvard Business School Press.

Galaskiewicz, J. (1985). Professional networks and the institutionalization of the single mind set. *American Sociological Review*, 50, 639–658.

Galvin, B. M., Balkundi, P. & Waldman, D. A. (2010). Spreading the word: The role of surrogates in charismatic leadership processes. *Academy of Management Review*, 35, 477–494.

Gibson, C. & Vermeulen, F. (2003). A healthy divide: Subgroups as a stimulus for team learning behavior. *Administrative Science Quarterly*, 48, 202–239.

Gnyawali, D. R. & Madhavan, R. (2001). Network structure and competitive dynamics: A structural embeddedness perspective. *Academy of Management Review*, 26, 431–445.

Graen, G. B. & Cashman, J. (1975). A role-making model of leadership in formal organizations: A development approach. In J. G. Hunt, & L. L. Larson (eds), *Leadership frontiers* (pp. 143–166). Kent, OH: Kent State University Press.

Graen, G. B., Novak, A. M. & Sommerkamp, P. (1982). The effects of leader–member exchange and job satisfaction design on productivity and satisfaction: Testing a dual attachment model. *Organizational Behavior and Human Performance*, 30, 109–131.

Granovetter, M. S. (1973). The strength of weak ties. *American Journal of Sociology*, 78, 1360–1380.

Granovetter, M. S. (1985). Economic action, social structure and embeddedness. *American Journal of Sociology*, 91, 481–510.

Gronn, P. (1999). Substituting for leadership: The neglected role of the leadership couple. *The Leadership Quarterly*, 10, 41–62.

Gulati, R. & Gargiulo, M. (1999). Where do interorganizational networks come from? *American Journal of Sociology*, 104, 1439–1493.

Hambrick, D. C., Cho, T. & Chen, M. J. (1996). The influence of top management team heterogeneity on firms' competitive moves. *Administrative Science Quarterly*, 41, 659–684.

Hambrick, D. C. & Mason, P. A. (1984). Upper echelons: The organization as reflection of its top managers. *Academy of Management Review*, 9, 193–206.

Hannan, M. & Freeman, J. (1984). Structural inertia and organizational change. *American Sociological Review*, 49, 149–164.

Hargadon, A. B. & Sutton, R. I. (1997). Technology brokering and innovation in a product development firm. *Administrative Science Quarterly*, 42, 716–749.

Heider, F. (1958). *The psychology of interpersonal relations*. New York: Wiley.

Higgins, M. & Kram, K. (2001). Reconceptualizing mentoring at work: A developmental network perspective. *Academy of Management Review*, 26, 264–288.

Hooijberg, R., Hunt, J. G. & Dodge, G. E. (1997). Leadership complexity and development of the leaderplex model. *Journal of Management*, 23, 375–408.

House, R. J. (1977). A 1976 theory of charismatic leadership. In J. G. Hunt, & L. L. Larson (eds), *Leadership: The cutting edge* (pp. 189–273). Carbondale, IL: Southern Illinois University Press.

Ibarra, H., Kilduff, M. & Tsai, W. (2005). Zooming in and out: Individuals and collectivities at the new frontiers for organizational network research. *Organization Science*, 16, 359–371.

Janicik, G. A. & Larrick, R. P. (2005). Social network schemas and the learning of incomplete networks. *Journal of Personality and Social Psychology*, 88, 348–364.

Kahneman, D. & Tversky, A. (1973). On the psychology of prediction. *Psychological Review*, 80, 237–251.

Kenny, D. & Zaccaro, S. (1983). An estimate of variance due to traits in leadership. *Journal of Applied Psychology*, 68, 678–685.

Kenny, D. A. Bond Jr, C. F., Mohr, C. D. & Horn, E. M. (1996). Do we know how much people like one another? *Journal of Personality and Social Psychology*, 71, 928–936.

Kerr, S. & Jermier, J.M. (1978). Substitutes for leadership: Their meaning and measurement. *Organizational Behavior and Human Performance*, 22, 375–403.

Kilduff, M. (1990). The interpersonal structure of decision-making: A social comparison approach to organizational choice. *Organizational Behavior and Human Decision Processes*, 47, 270–288.

Kilduff, M. (1992). The friendship network as a decision-making resource: Dispositional moderators of social influences on organizational choice. *Journal of Personality and Social Psychology*, 62, 168–180.

Kilduff, M., Angelmar, R. & Mehra, A. (2000). Top management-team diversity and firm performance: Examining the role of cognitions. *Organization Science*, 11, 21–34.

Kilduff, M., Crossland, C., Tsai, W. & Krackhardt, D. (2008). Organizational network perceptions versus reality: A small world after all? *Organizational Behavior and Human Decision Processes*, 107: 15–28.

Kilduff, M. & Krackhardt, D. (1994). Bringing the individual back in: A structural analysis of the internal market for reputation in organizations. *Academy of Management Journal*, 37, 87–108.

Kilduff, M. & Tsai, W. (2003). *Social networks and organizations*. London: Sage.

Kilduff, M., Tsai, W. & Hanke, R. (2006). A paradigm too far? A dynamic stability reconsideration of the social network research program. *Academy of Management Review*, 31: 1031–1048.

Kogut, B. & Walker, G. (2001). The small world of Germany and the durability of national networks. *American Sociological Review*, 66, 317–335.

Krackhardt, D. (1987). Cognitive social structures. *Social Networks*, 9, 109–134.

Krackhardt, D. (1990). Assessing the political landscape: Structure, cognition, and power in organizations. *Administrative Science Quarterly*, 35, 342–369.

Krackhardt, D. (1999). The ties that torture: Simmelian tie analysis in organizations. *Research in the Sociology of Organizations*, 16, 183–210.

Krackhardt, D. & Hanson, J. (1993). Informal networks: The company behind the chart. *Harvard Business Review*, 71, 104–111.

Krackhardt, D. & Kilduff, M. (1990). Friendship patterns and culture: The control of organizational diversity. *American Anthropologist*, 92, 142–154.

Krackhardt, D. & Kilduff, M. (1999). Whether close or far: Social distance effects on perceived balance in friendship networks. *Journal of Personality and Social Psychology*, 76, 770–782.

Kumbasar, E. A., Romney, K. & Batchelder, W. H. (1994). Systematic biases in social perception. *American Journal of Sociology*, 100, 477–505.

Kunda, G. (1993). *Engineering culture: Control and commitment in a high tech corporation*. Philadelphia: Temple University Press.

Lakatos, I. (1970). Falsification and the methodology of scientific research programs. In I. Lakatos & A. Musgrave (eds), *Criticism and the growth of knowledge* (pp.91–196). Cambridge, UK: Cambridge University Press.

Larson, A. (1992). Network dyads in entrepreneurial settings: A study of the governance of exchange processes. *Administrative Science Quarterly*, 37, 76–104.

Lau, D. C. & Liden, R. C. (2008). Antecedents of coworker trust: leaders' blessings. *Journal of Applied Psychology*, 93: 1130–1138.

Lawrence, P. R. & Lorsch, J. W. (1967). *Organization and environment: Managing differentiation and integration*. Boston, MA: Harvard University Press.

Lewin, K., Lippitt, R. & White, R. (1939). Patterns of aggressive behavior in experimentally created 'social climates'. *Journal of Social Psychology*, 10, 271–299.

Lord, R. G. & Emrich, C. G. (2001). Thinking outside the box by looking inside the box: Extending the cognitive revolution in leadership research. *The Leadership Quarterly*, 11, 551–579.

McDonald, M. L. & Westphal, J. D. (2003). Getting by with the advice of their friends: CEOs' advice networks and firms' strategic responses to poor performance. *Administrative Science Quarterly*, 48, 1–32.

McPherson, M., Smith-Lovin, L. & Cook, J. M. (2001). Birds of a feather: Homophily in social networks. *Annual Review of Sociology*, 27, 415–444.

Maitlis, S. & Ozcelik, H. (2004). Toxic decision processes: A study of emotion and organizational decision making. *Organization Science*, 15, 375–393.

March, J. G. (1991). Exploration and exploitation in organizational learning. *Organization Science*, 2, 71–87.

March, J. G. & Simon, H. A. (1958). *Organizations*. New York: Wiley.

Mayo, M. C., Meindl, J. R. & Pastor, J. C. (2003). Shared leadership in work teams: A social network approach. In C. Pierce, & J. Conger (eds), *Shared leadership: Reframing the hows and whys of leadership* (pp. 193–214). Thousand Oaks, CA: Sage.

Mechanic, D. (1962). The sources of power for lower participants in complex organizations. *Administrative Science Quarterly*, 7, 349–364.

Mehra, A., Kilduff, M. & Brass, D. (1998). At the margins: A distinctiveness approach to the social identity and social networks of underrepresented groups. *Academy of Management Journal*, 41, 441–452.

Mehra, A., Smith, B., Dixon, A. & Robertson, B. (2006). Distributed leadership in teams: The network of leadership perceptions and team performance. *The Leadership Quarterly*, 17: 232–245.

Meyer, J. & Rowan, B. (1977). Institutionalized organizations: Formal structure as myth and ceremony. *American Journal of Sociology*, 83, 340–367.

Milgram, S. (1967). The small world problem. *Psychology Today*, 1, 61–67.

Mintzberg, H. (1980). *The nature of managerial work*. Englewood Cliffs, NJ: Prentice Hall.

Moody, J., McFarland, D. A. & Bender-DeMoll, S. (2005). Dynamic network visualization. *American Journal of Sociology*, 110, 1206–1241.

Murray, S. L., Holmes, J. G. & Griffin, D. W. (1996). The benefits of positive illusions: Idealization and the construction of satisfaction in close relationships. *Journal of Personality and Social Psychology*, 70, 79–98.

Oh, H., Chung, M. H. & Labianca, G. (2004). Group social capital and group effectiveness: The role of informal socializing ties. *Academy of Management Journal*, 47, 860–875.

Oh, H., Kilduff, M. & Brass, D. J. (2005). The network dilemmas of ethnic entrepreneurs: The case of Koreans in a Canadian city. Working paper: Yonsei University.

Palmer, D. (1983). Broken ties: Interlocking directorates and intercorporate coordination. *Administrative Science Quarterly*, 28, 40–55.

Pastor, J. C., Meindl, J. R. & Mayo, M. C. (2002). A network effects model of charisma attributions. *Academy of Management Journal*, 45, 410–420.

Pescosolido, A. T. (2001). Informal leaders and the development of group efficacy. *Small Group Research*, 32, 74–93.

Pescosolido, A. T. (2002). Emergent leaders as managers of group emotion. *The Leadership Quarterly*, 13, 583–599.

Podolny, J. M. (1998). Network forms of organization. *Annual Review of Sociology*, 24, 57–76.

Podolny, J. M. (2001). Networks as the pipes and prisms of the market. *American Journal of Sociology*, 107, 33–60.

Podsakoff, P. M. & MacKenzie, S. B. (1997). Kerr and Jermier's substitutes for leadership model: Background, empirical assessment, and suggestions for future research. *The Leadership Quarterly*, 8, 117–125.

Podsakoff, P. M., Todor, W. D. & Skov, R. (1982). Effect of leader contingent and non contingent reward and punishment behaviors on subordinate performance and satisfaction. *Academy of Management Journal*, 25, 810–821.

Popielarz, P. A. (1999). Organizational constraints on personal network formation. *Research in the Sociology of Organizations*, 16, 263–281.

Porter, L. W. & McLaughlin, G. B. (2006). Leadership and the organizational context: Like the weather? *The Leadership Quarterly*, 17, 559–576.

Portes, A. (2000). The two meanings of social capital. *Sociological Forum*, 15, 1–11.

Powell, W. W., Koput, K. W. & Smith-Doerr, L. (1996). Interorganizational collaboration and locus of innovation: Networks of learning in biotechnology. *Administrative Science Quarterly*, 41, 116–145.

Roberts, K. H. & O'Reilly III, C. A. (1979). Some correlations of communication roles in organizations. *Academy of Management Journal*, 22, 42–57.

Saxenian, A. (1990). Regional networks and the resurgence of Silicon Valley. *California Management Review*, 33, 89–112.

Seidel, M. D. L., Polzer, J. T. & Stewart, K. J. (2000). Friends in high places: The effects of social networks on discrimination in salary negotiations. *Administrative Science Quarterly*, 45, 1–24.

Sherony, K. M. & Green, S. (2002). Coworker exchange: Relationships between coworkers, leader–member exchange, and work attitudes. *Journal of Applied Psychology*, 87, 542–548.

Simmel, G. (1950). *The isolated individual and the dyad. The sociology of Georg Simmel* (pp. 118–136). Glencoe, IL: Free Press.

Smith, A. (1976). *The wealth of nations*. Chicago: University of Chicago Press.

Sparrowe, R. T. & Liden, R. C. (2005). Two routes to influence: Integrating leader–member exchange and network perspectives. *Administrative Science Quarterly*, 50: 505–535.

Sparrowe, R., Liden, R. C., Wayne, S. J. & Kraimer, M. L. (2001). Social networks and the performance of individuals and groups. *Academy of Management Journal*, 44, 316–325.

Stevenson, W. B., Pearce, J. L. & Porter, L. W. (1985). The concept of coalition in organizational theory and research. *Academy of Management Review*, 10, 256–268.

Taylor, S. E. & Brown, J. D. (1988). Illusion and well-being – A social psychological perspective on mental-health. *Psychological Bulletin*, 103, 193–210.

Thomas, D. A. (1993). The dynamics of managing racial diversity in developmental relationships. *Administrative Science Quarterly*, 38, 169–194.

Tichy, N., Tushman, M. & Fombrum, C. (1979). Social network analysis for organizations. *Academy of Management Review*, 4, 507–519.

Toegel, G., Anand, N. & Kilduff, M. 2007. Emotion helpers: The role of high positive affectivity and high self-monitoring managers. *Personnel Psychology*, 60: 337–365.

Uhl-Bien, M. (2006). Relational leadership theory: Exploring the social processes of leadership and organizing. *The Leadership Quarterly*, 17: 654–676.

Uzzi, B. (1996). The sources and consequences of embeddedness for the economic performance of organizations: The network effect. *American Sociological Review*, 61, 674–698.

Uzzi, B. (1997). Social structure and competition in inter-firm networks: The paradox of embeddedness. *Administrative Science Quarterly*, 42, 35–67.

Uzzi, B. & Spiro, J. (2005). Collaboration and creativity: The small world problem. *American Journal of Sociology*, 111: 447–504.

Vroom, V. H. & Yetton, P. W. (1973). *Leadership and decision-making*. Pittsburg: University of Pittsburg Press.

Wasserman, S. & Faust, K. (1994). *Social network analysis: Methods and applications*. New York: Cambridge University Press.

Watts, D. & Strogatz, S. (1998). Collective dynamics of small world networks. *Nature*, 393, 440–442.

Wellman, B. (1988). Structural analysis: From method and metaphor to theory and substance.

Westphal, J. D. & Milton, L. P. (2000). How experience and social networks affect the influence of demographic minorities on corporate boards. *Administrative Science Quarterly*, 45, 366–398.

Wrong, D. H. (1968). Some problems in defining social power. *American Journal of Sociology*, 73, 673–681.

Zohar, D. & Tenne-Gazit, O. (2008). Transformational leadership and group interaction as climate antecedents: A social network analysis. *Journal of Applied Psychology*, 93: 744–757.

Zuckerman, E. W. (1999). The categorical imperative: Securities analysts and the illegitimacy discount. *American Journal of Sociology*, 104, 1398–1438.

10

Trust and Distrust in the Leadership Process: A Review and Assessment of Theory and Evidence

Roderick M. Kramer

INTRODUCTION

To assert that there has been a dramatic increase of interest among social scientists in the concept of trust would be a considerable understatement. In the last two decades, the topic has been the subject of considerable attention from political scientists (Hardin, 2006; Hetherington, 2005), sociologists (Cook, 2001; Sztompka, 1999), psychologists (Grant and Sumanth, 2009; Kramer and Tyler, 1996), organizational theorists (Lane and Bachman, 1998), behavioral economists (Bohnet, 2007), and neuroeconomists (Zak, 2008). Even philosophers have joined the enterprise of clarifying the essential nature of trust, and elucidating its benefits and limitations (Hollis, 1998; Solomon and Flores, 2001). In addition to developing basic theory regarding its nature and origins, trust theorists have been eager to apply emerging theory to a variety of important social and organizational problems (Braithwaite and Levi, 1998; Cook, Hardin, and Levi, 2005; Lane and Bachman, 1998).

Curiously, however, comparatively little systematic effort has been made to apply emerging insights and empirical findings from this vibrant stream of research to leadership theory. To be sure, there are some exceptions (e.g., Dirks, 2006) and, certainly, there are frequent nods in the popular literature to the importance of trust in the leadership process. Although these treatments are enthusiastic in their proclamations regarding the merits of trust (e.g., Covey, 2006), unfortunately, they seldom draw on extant empirical research, or qualify their enthusiasm on the basis of what that research actually affirms. As a consequence, a considerable gulf exists between what the authors of leadership books like to assert about trust, and what the empirical evidence supports.

This neglect of the substantial and growing scholarly literature on trust seems particularly unfortunate as we enter the second decade of the twenty-first century. In recent months, the discovery of massive fraud and abuse by some of America's largest and heretofore most respected corporations and institutions has seriously shaken the public's trust in our organizations and those who lead them. Moreover, the public leaders upon whom we've depended to provide vigilant oversight of corporations have similarly failed, occasioning anger and diminished trust in them as well. Thus, perhaps now more so than at any other time in recent history, there seems to be a dramatic decline in trust of leaders, across virtually all domains, ranging across business, government, the media, and our educational institutions (Center for Public Leadership, 2008). Indeed, President Obama declared in his first State of the Union address to Congress that America is suffering from a 'deficit of trust.'

The time seems ripe, therefore, to attempt a review and assessment of contemporary trust theory and research, with particular attention to its relevance to understanding the antecedents and consequences of effective (and ineffective) leadership processes. The primary aim of the present chapter, accordingly, is twofold. First, the chapter surveys some of the major conceptual perspectives and emerging empirical insights on the nature and functions of trust. Secondly, it suggests how those perspectives and insights might inform our understanding of the constructive role trust can play in the leadership process.

To accomplish these aims, the chapter is organized as follows. First, I provide brief discussions of how trust and leadership have been conceptualized within the social science literature. I then examine some of the benefits that have been ascribed to trust as it pertains to effective leadership processes. The chapter next elaborates on some of the foundations for trust in the leadership process. It then considers some of the problems surrounding the creation of trust, and also how to create and build trust. The chapter concludes by suggesting where our understanding of the trust–leadership connection remains incomplete, and indicating some fruitful directions future research might go to address these gaps in our knowledge.

CONCEPTIONS OF TRUST AND THE LEADERSHIP PROCESS: A BRIEF OVERVIEW

In this section, I provide an overview of (1) how trust has been conceptualized in the social science literature, (2) a brief excursion into the vast leadership literature, and (3) how trust and leadership processes might be conceptually linked.

Conceptualizing trust

Although social scientists have afforded considerable attention to the problem of defining trust, a concise and universally accepted definition has remained elusive (e.g., Barber, 1983, Hardin, 2006; Uslaner, 2002). However, most trust theorists agree that, whatever else its diverse features, trust is fundamentally and essentially a psychological state. When conceptualized as a psychological state, trust has been defined in terms of several cognitive and affective processes. On the cognitive level, it has been noted that trust entails a state of perceived vulnerability or risk. Along these lines, Lewis and Weigert (1985, p. 971) noted that trust entails the 'undertaking of a risky course of action on the confident expectation that all persons involved in the action will act competently and dutifully.' Similarly, Baier (1986, p. 235) characterized trust as 'accepted vulnerability to another's possible but not expected ill will (or lack of good will) toward one.' Finally, Robinson (1996, p. 576) defined trust as a person's 'expectations, assumptions, or beliefs about the likelihood that another's future actions will be beneficial, favorable, or at least not detrimental to one's interests.' As these definitions make clear, the perception of vulnerability or risk that is central to trust is derived from the truster's uncertainty regarding the motives, intentions, and actions of the prospective trustee or trustees on whom the truster depends.

Although acknowledging the importance of these cognitive dimensions of trust, other researchers have argued that trust needs to be conceptualized as a more complex, multi-dimensional psychological state that includes affective and motivational components (Chua, Ingram, and Morris, 2008; Fine and Holyfield, 1996). As Fine and Holyfield (1996, p. 25) noted along these lines, cognitive models of trust provide a necessary but not sufficient understanding of trust phenomena. Trust also embodies, they suggest, aspects of the 'world of cultural meanings, emotional responses, and social relations ... one not only thinks trust, but feels trust.'

Hardin (1992) has contributed one other important insight into how trust should be conceptualized. Specifically, he argued it is essential to remember that trust is always, logically speaking, a third-order predicate. In other words, when we talk about trust, we are talking about a three-part relation involving (1) the properties or attributes of an individual *truster* (e.g., their disposition to trust), (2) the attributes of a specific *trustee* or set of trustees (e.g., their actual trustworthiness), and (3) a specific *context* or domain (or set of issues) over which trust is either conferred or withheld (e.g., the provision of medical care versus the offering of financial advice). Thus, a patient trying to decide upon a suitable medical treatment might readily trust her physician's advice in this domain, while completely discounting the value of any stock tips the physician might pass along. The reason this point is important, Hardin stressed, is that we tend to talk elliptically about trust, and these ellipses on occasion lead to conceptual imprecision and sloppiness.

Conceptualizing the leadership process

Given the voluminous nature of the literature, any attempt to offer a single, crisp and coherent characterization of the leadership process is probably ripe with peril, pushing even the most well-intentioned author into murky conceptual waters. Few constructs in the social science literature seem to have the lure of leadership as a catch-all explanation for a host of organizational processes and outcomes (Bligh and Meindl, 2005; Meindl and Ehrlich, 1987). Yet, it is equally safe to say, none are as ambiguous and as vigorously contested as a legitimate construct (Pfeffer, 1977). Additional formulations, moreover, seem only to deepen and darken the conceptual waters (Podolny, Khurana, and Hill-Popper, 2005).

Despite these difficulties and controversies, certain generalizations can be asserted with some degree of confidence. First and foremost, leadership can be viewed as a process that involves, at its core, social influence between leaders and the various constituents they represent or serve (Nye, 2008). Indeed, this has been a recurrent theme in the literature. More than a half century ago, for example, Stogdill (1950, p. 3) defined leadership as 'the process of influencing the activities of an organized group in its efforts toward goal setting and goal achievement.' More recently but in a similar vein, Hogg (2005, p. 53) proposed that, 'Leadership is a relational term – it identifies a relationship in which some people are able to persuade others to adopt new values, attitudes, and goals, and to exert effort on behalf of those values, attitudes, and goals.' This theme of effective influence and persuasion permeates other contemporary accounts as well (Gardner, 2006; Nye, 2008).

In elaborating on the precise nature of this influence process, some important and enduring distinctions have been drawn, the first of which is the distinction between transactional and transformational leadership processes. In an early and insightful discussion of this distinction, Bass (1984) noted that transactional leadership processes focus primarily on the provision of contingent rewards and punishments as means of influencing constituents' attitudes, feelings, and behaviors. Transformational leadership, in contrast, entails the use of charismatic modes of influence (such as inspiring rhetoric and imagery), individualized attention and consideration, and intellectual challenge and stimulation.

A second important distinction concerns the 'hard' versus 'soft' nature of this influence process. In his overview of the history of the leadership construct, Nye (2008), for instance, notes the consistent distinction between 'hard power' forms of influence and 'soft power' forms of influence. Hard power is coercive power – it entails use of the proverbial stick to induce compliance and conformity. Soft power, in contrast, can be thought of as attractive power and favors the dangling of carrots. If the former is coercive, the latter is seductive. Neither form of power, Nye adds, is inherently superior or dominant, noting that the comparative efficacy of hard versus soft forms of power is contingent on the specific context within which the leader is operating. Accordingly, Nye argues, leaders' 'contextual intelligence' (i.e., their deft and seasoned assessment of what's needed in a given situation) plays a vital role in determining the ultimate effectiveness of their influence attempts.

In an impressive series of empirical studies and theoretical integrations, Hackman and his associates (Hackman, 2002; Hackman and Wageman, 2005; Wageman, Nunes, Burruss, and Hackman, 2008) have done much in recent years to advance and deepen our understanding of the core influence processes that contribute to effective leadership. According to their framework, effective leader influence consists of creating and maintaining those essential environmental conditions that are conducive to effective organizational performance. Specifically, the five conditions that leaders can influence are (1) contributing to the *composition* and development of a well-functioning group, (2) providing a *compelling direction* for the group's work, (3) providing an *enabling structure* that facilitates rather than impedes coordination and collaboration, (4) providing and maintaining a *supportive organizational context*, and (5) providing ample *expert coaching* when needed.

There has also been an appreciation in the leadership literature that the effectiveness of a particular influence process is related to the nature of the specific goals that leaders aspire to achieve. Among other things, leadership processes can be used to influence how constituents make sense of or construe the organizational situations they confront, including both routine as well as novel or crisis situations (Weick, 1995). Alternatively, they can be used to help motivate constituents and infuse deeper meaning in the work they do (Podolny, Khurana, and Hill-Popper, 2005). And finally, they can be used to mobilize people's time and attention in the service of important and challenging goals (Ganz, 2009).

Linking the concepts: trust within leadership contexts

Given these brief characterizations, it is not hard to see why leadership practitioners and writers have assumed that trust is so vital to the leadership process. To be effective at exerting influence over others, it appears obvious that it helps greatly if leaders are trusted. As former Secretary of State George Schultz famously asserted during his testimony to Congress regarding the Iran-Contra investigations, 'Trust is the coin of the realm' when it comes to credible leadership. His words seem as poignant and applicable today as they did more than 30 years ago. In particular, a leader's capacity to exert and sustain effective influence over others is clearly likely to depend, in no small measure, on the extent to which he or she can successfully inculcate trust in his or her leadership.

However *prima facie* evident the validity of this claim, it raises as many questions as it answers. For example, what are the empirically demonstrated benefits of such trust? What do we know about the psychological and social underpinnings or foundations for such trust? How is trust between leaders and constituents built and sustained? Finally, what are some of the barriers or impediments to the development and maintenance of trust between leaders and constituents? These are some of the important questions I address in the following sections.

In the context of 'leader–constituent relationships', trust in a leader can be viewed as a function of at least two essential components: (1) the motives and intentions attributed to the leader and (2) the leader's perceived competence. With respect to perceived leader motives and intentions, trust will be high when leaders are perceived as having good intentions and benign (non-malevolent) motives toward their constituents. With respect to perceived competence, trust will be high when leaders are perceived as capable of fulfilling their duties and obligations, along with their other diverse role-requirements as a leader (Barber, 1983; Brockner, Siegel, Daly, and Tyler, 1997).

IMPORTANCE OF TRUST IN THE LEADERSHIP PROCESS: BENEFITS AND ADVANTAGES

The ascension of trust as a major focus of research within the social sciences over the past two decades can be attributed, at least in part, to an impressive body of accumulating evidence regarding the substantial and varied benefits, both individual and collective, that accrue when trust is present. Perhaps most influential in this regard have been steadily accumulating findings implicating trust as a critical factor influencing the level of coordination, cooperation, and other positive forms of collective behavior (see Fukuyama, 1995; Putnam, 2000; Sztompka, 1999; and Uslaner (2002) for overviews of this evidence).

In a useful attempt to assess what we currently know and can safely assert, Dirks and Ferrin (2002) performed a meta-analysis of nearly four decades of research on the positive effects of trust on leadership effectiveness and organizational performance. They found that trust in leaders had a significant relationship with respect to a variety of important outcomes, including constituents' commitment to a leader's decisions, their commitment to the organization itself, reductions in reported intentions to turnover jobs, enhanced job performance and satisfaction, and increased levels of organizational citizenship behaviors. In a similar vein, Davis, Schoorman, Mayer, and Tan (2000) found that trust in management was associated with improved sales and profits, along with reduced turnover. In yet another study, Dirks (2000) reported a relationship between players' trust in their head coach and winning in the National Basketball Association. Finally, and more recently, Grant and Sumanth (2009) found that trust in leaders was associated with enhanced prosocial motivations and behaviors among employees, at least within the context of service organizations.

The relationship between trust and leadership has been examined also in the context of leader–member exchange (LMX) theories (Brower, Schoorman, and Tan, 2000; Graen and Uhl-Bien, 1995; see Liden, co-author in Chapter 23, this volume). As Uhl-Bien (2009) has pointed out, measures of LMX and interpersonal trust tend to be highly correlated across numerous studies. Leader–member exchange, for instance, has been shown to be related to positive attitudes, including job satisfaction, commitment, lower turnover intentions, and behaviors such as citizenship and performance. In short, tests of LMX theory yields results that closely mirror those reported in the literature on interpersonal trust. In their recent review and integration of this evidence, Brower, Schoorman, and Tan (2000) propose a model of relational leadership that emphasizes the importance of reciprocal trust perceptions in dyadic contexts. Thus, relational trust encompasses both leader trust in subordinates (LTS) and subordinate trust in leaders (SLT).

Consistent with this argument, Maslyn and Uhl-Bien (2001) conducted a study of the dimensions underlying LMX. Specifically, they examined the role that perceptions of effort play in perceptions of relationship quality, including expectations regarding other's future effortfulness. Consistent with their theoretical expectations, Maslyn and Uhl-Bien found that perceptions of effort were significantly related to relationship quality. To the extent that perceptions of other's effort might indicate their present and future trustworthiness, such results suggest how close might be the constructs of LMX and interpersonal trust. Clearly, more systematic work on the relationship between LMX and interpersonal trust seems warranted.

In a supportive vein to this argument, a study of reciprocal trust perceptions in supervisor–subordinate relationships (Kramer, 1996) found significant asymmetries in the content of reciprocal expectations related to perceived trustworthiness of self and other. In particular, those in the superordinate position in a hierarchical relationship tended to construe subordinate trustworthiness largely in terms of task-related dimensions (e.g., reliability and diligence with respect to the performance of assigned tasks). In contrast, those in the subordinate role in the relationship paid more attention to interpersonal or relational considerations (e.g., the quality of the interpersonal treatment they received, including indications of concern for their well-being and perceived future trustworthiness). These results suggest that the nature of the LMX might be complicated by significant and revealing asymmetries. A similar, and more general, argument has also been advanced by Messick (2005) in his analysis of psychological exchange between leaders and followers.

In addition to these specific findings, I elaborate next on several important and more general ways in which trust can enhance the effectiveness of the leadership process.

Voluntary deference and appropriate compliance

In most organizations and social systems, the leadership role is inherently hierarchical, at least in so far as one or more persons (a designated leader or leaders), operating from a position of authority or discretion, exert influence over one or more others (often designated as followers or subordinates, although characterized in this chapter simply as constituents). In flatter or less hierarchical organizations, similarly, leaders typically assert greater influence over others vis-à-vis their greater centrality, power, or decision control. And in both instances, leadership is exerted more successfully when constituents voluntarily accept that influence and behave compliantly.

Consistent with this general argument, an important stream of research has examined the relationship between trust in leaders and various forms of voluntary deference by constituents. In furthering our understanding of this relationship, Tyler and Degoey (1996) noted that if organizational leaders

had to continually explain and justify their actions, their ability to effectively lead would be greatly diminished. In addition, because of the costs and impracticality of continually monitoring constituent performance, leaders cannot detect and punish every failure to cooperate or comply, nor can they recognize and reward every cooperative or compliant act. As a result, efficient and effective organizational performance depends upon constituents' feelings of duty or obligation toward the leader, their willingness to comply with his or her directives, and their consequent willingness to voluntarily defer (with the caveat that we are assuming here appropriate and prudent forms of deference versus mindless or destructive acts of obedience).

Trust is also important when conflicts arise within organizational or social settings. To the extent leaders are charged with reducing or resolving such conflict, trust in the leader's fairness and impartiality is important because it influences ultimately the acceptance of dispute resolution procedures and outcomes. Indeed, substantial research has shown that individuals are more likely to accept outcomes, even if unfavorable to themselves, when their trust in an authority's motives and intentions is high (e.g., Brockner and Siegel, 1996; Tyler 1994).

This result raises the issue of what determines a leader's perceived trustworthiness? Recognizing its importance, researchers have investigated the specific conditions under which people are likely to attribute trustworthiness to those in leadership positions. Early research on this topic sought to identify specific attributes associated with perceived trustworthiness. For example, Gabarro (1978) found that perceived integrity, motives, consistency, openness, discreteness, functional competence, interpersonal competence, and decision-making judgment contributed to attributions of trustworthiness between vice-presidents and presidents. Along similar lines, Butler (1991) found that perceived availability, competence, consistency, fairness, integrity, loyalty, openness, overall trust, promise fulfillment, and receptivity influenced subordinates' judgments of an authority's trustworthiness. More recently, Elsbach (2004) has provided a useful summary and much-needed conceptual integration of this literature.

Subsequent social psychological research has refined and extended our understanding of the factors that influence trustworthiness attributions in leadership contexts. The most systematic research on this topic has been conducted by Tyler and his associates (Tyler and Degoey, 1996). Their research identifies several important components of trustworthiness attributions. The first of these factors is *status recognition*, which reflects the extent to which leaders recognize and validate the constituents' sense of full-fledged membership in their organization. A second important factor is *trust in benevolence*, which refers to constituents' beliefs that the leaders with whom they deal are well-intentioned and honest in their decisions. A third critical factor is *neutrality*, which implies perceived fairness and impartiality in a leader's decisions and adjudications.

Additional research by Brockner and his associates has investigated the influence of procedural variables on attributions regarding leaders' trustworthiness. Brockner and Siegel (1996), for instance, argued and found that procedures are important because they communicate information not only about a leader's motivation and intention to behave in a trustworthy fashion but also their ability to do so, a factor they characterize as *procedural competence*. In support of their argument, they report evidence that procedures that are perceived as structurally and interactionally fair tend to increase trust, whereas lack of perceived structural and procedural fairness tends to elicit low levels of trust.

In a follow-up study and extension, Brockner, Siegel, Daly, and Tyler (1997) explored some of the conditions under which trust in leaders matters more or less. They argued that, all else equal, trust matters more to constituents when the outcomes they obtain are unfavorable. In explaining why this would be true, they noted that receipt of favorable outcomes does not raise issues of leaders' trustworthiness, because the outcomes themselves constitute evidence that the leader can be counted on to perform behaviors desired by the constituent. As a result, they concluded, issues of trust are neither salient nor critical in determining support for the leader under these favorable circumstances. In contrast, when outcomes are unfavorable, trust becomes more salient and critical, and leaders are less likely to receive ongoing support. Brockner et al. tested this general prediction in three different studies and found, consistent with it, that trust was more strongly related to support for an authority when outcomes were relatively unfavorable.

Constituents' willingness to engage in spontaneous acts of sociability and extra-role behavior

In an influential review and assessment, Fukuyama (1995) argued that one of the most important consequences of trust is the *spontaneous sociability* such trust engenders. When operationalized in behavioral terms, spontaneous sociability refers to the myriad forms of cooperative, altruistic, and extra-role behavior that individuals are willing to

engage in that enhance the collective well-being and further the attainment of organizational goals. Achieving this result, arguably, is largely what organizational leadership is all about.

Within organizational contexts, spontaneous sociability assumes many forms. Organizational members are expected, for example, to contribute their time and attention toward the achievement of collective goals, especially as articulated by a leader (Olson, 1965), they are expected to share useful information with other organizational members (Kramer, 2006), and they are expected to exercise responsible restraint when using valuable but limited organizational resources (Tyler and Degoey, 1996). Finally, they are expected to engage in extra-role behaviors that further organizational goals (Tyler and Blader, 2003).

In sum, there is substantial evidence of the varied and consequential benefits that follow when constituents have appropriate levels of trust in their leaders. This raises the question next of where such trust comes from? How are the demonstrated benefits of trust secured and sustained? The research literatures on the bases of trust, and the nature of the trust-building process, provide some useful answers to these questions.

FOUNDATIONS OF TRUST BETWEEN LEADERS AND THEIR CONSTITUENTS

Considerable theory and research has focused on identifying the antecedents and bases of trust within organizations and other social systems (Creed and Miles 1996; Sztompka, 1999; Zucker, 1986). In general, this research has emphasized the causal importance of (1) psychological, (2) interpersonal or social, (3) procedural, and (4) structural factors that promote the development and ongoing stability of trust between leaders and their constituents. Because this literature is quite large, and an adequate review beyond the scope of the present chapter, I will organize my presentation in terms of (1) trust-building behaviors, (2) an exploration of the role rules play in trust processes, and (3) an examination of the links between social identification and leader–constituent trust.

Trust-building behaviors

Research on trust development has shown individuals' perceptions of others' trustworthiness and their willingness to engage in trusting behavior when interacting with them are largely history-dependent, interactional processes (see Lindskold,

1978 for a review). According to such models, trust between two or more interdependent actors thickens or thins as a function of their cumulative history of interaction. Interactional histories give individuals a database that is useful in assessing others' dispositions, intentions, and motives. This information, in turn, provides a basis for drawing inferences regarding their trustworthiness and for making predictions about their future trust-related behavior.

Evidence of the importance of interactional histories in judgments about trust comes from a substantial body of experimental research linking specific patterns of behavioral interaction with changes in trust. For example, a number of studies have demonstrated that reciprocity in exchange relations enhances trust, while the absence or violation of reciprocity erodes it (Lindskold, 1978; Pillisuk and Skolnick, 1968).

In noting the formative role interactional histories play in the emergence of trust, these models draw attention to two psychological facets of trust judgments. The first is that judgments about others' trustworthiness are anchored, at least in part, on individuals' a priori expectations about others' behavior. Secondly, those expectations change in response to the extent to which subsequent experience either validates or discredits them. Boyle and Bonacich's (1970, p. 130) analysis of trust development is representative of such arguments. Individuals' expectations about trustworthy behavior, they posit, tend to change 'in the direction of experience and to a degree proportional to the difference between this experience and the initial expectations applied to it.' According to such models, therefore, interactional histories become a basis for initially calibrating and then updating trust-related expectations.

Perceived social similarity and trust

Trust judgments can also be predicated on information regarding a prospective trustee's membership in a social or organizational category – information which, when salient, often unknowingly influences others' judgments about their trustworthiness. As Brewer (1981, p. 356) noted, there are a number of reasons why membership in a salient category can provide a basis for presumptive trust between interdependent social actors. First, shared membership in a given category can serve as a 'rule for defining the boundaries of low-risk interpersonal trust that bypasses the need for personal knowledge and the costs of negotiating reciprocity' when interacting with other members of that category. Further, because of the cognitive consequences of categorization and in-group bias,

individuals tend to attribute positive characteristics such as honesty, cooperativeness, and trustworthiness to other in-group members (Brewer, 1996). As a consequence, individuals may confer a sort of *depersonalized trust* on other in-group members that is predicated simply on the basis of awareness of their shared category membership.

The most systematic development of such ideas in the context of leadership is Hogg's (2005) social identity theory of leadership. According to Hogg's (2005, p. 57) theory, 'as group membership becomes increasingly salient, leadership perceptions, evaluations, and effectiveness become increasingly based on how group-prototypical the leader is perceived to be.' Enhanced perceived prototypicality, he posits, results in increased influence, social attraction, and positive attributions. Hogg and his associates have produced considerable experimental support for this theorized relation. Recent research provides support for such arguments. A series of related papers (Kramer, 2006; Kramer, Brewer, and Hanna, 1996) review evidence that common social identity also enhances trust among interdependent social actors in a variety of contexts.

When these strands of diverse theory and evidence are pulled together, it seems reasonable to posit that trust in a leadership process is enhanced when an underlying basis for perceived social commonality is present.

Role-based trust

Role-based trust represents another important form of trust found within organizational settings, and one which has special relevance to the leader–constituent relation. As with category-based trust, role-based trust constitutes a form of depersonalized or de-individualized trust because it is predicated on knowledge that a leader occupies a particular role in the organization, or has specific training in a role, rather than specific knowledge about the individual's personal capabilities, dispositions, motives, and intentions.

Roles can serve as proxies for personalized knowledge about other organizational members in several ways. First, as Barber (1983) noted, strong expectations regarding technically competent role performance are typically aligned with roles in organizations, as well as expectations that role occupants will fulfill the fiduciary responsibilities and obligations associated with the roles they occupy. Thus, to the extent that people within an organization have confidence in the fact that role occupancy signals both an intent to fulfill such obligations and competence in carrying them out, individuals can adopt a sort of presumptive trust based upon knowledge of role relations, even in the absence of personalized knowledge or history of prior interaction.

Such trust develops from and is sustained by people's common knowledge regarding the barriers to entry into organizational roles, their presumptions of the training and socialization processes that role occupants undergo, and their perceptions of various accountability mechanisms intended to ensure role compliance. As numerous scholars (Barber, 1983; Dawes, 1994) have noted, it is not the person in the role that is trusted so much as the system of expertise that produces and maintains role-appropriate behavior of role occupants. As Dawes (1994, p. 24) suggested in this regard, 'We trust engineers because we trust engineering and believe that engineers are trained to apply valid principles of engineering, moreover, we have evidence every day that these principles are valid when we observe airplanes flying.' As with other bases of presumptive trust, such roles function then to reduce uncertainty regarding role occupant's trust-related intentions and capabilities. They thus lessen the perceived need for, and consequent costs of, negotiating trust when interacting with them.

Fostering trust through explication of organizational rules

If trust between leaders and their constituents is largely predicated on constituents' positive expectations and beliefs regarding their leaders, then both explicit and tacit understandings regarding what their leaders are likely to do may be critical in creating and sustaining trust. Organizational rules, both formal and informal, capture much of the knowledge that constituents have about such behaviors (March and Olson, 1989). Rule-based trust is predicated not on a conscious calculation of consequences, but rather on shared understandings and beliefs regarding the system of rules regarding appropriate behaviors – for both leaders and constituents. As March and Olson (1989, p. 27) put it, rule-based trust is sustained within an organization 'not [by] an explicit contract ... [but] by socialization into the structure of rules.' When reciprocal confidence in both leader's and constituents' socialization into, and continued adherence to, a normative system is high, mutual trust can acquire a taken-for-granted quality. Rules bind (behavior) and therefore build trust.

One way in which rules foster trust is through their effects on individuals' self-perceptions as well as their shaping of expectations about other organizational members. As March (1994, p. 72) observed in this regard, organizations function much like 'stage managers' by providing 'prompts that evoke particular identities in particular situations.' Miller (1992) offers an excellent example of this kind of socially constructed and ultimately self-reinforcing dynamic. In discussing the underpinnings of cooperation at Hewlett-Packard, Miller (1992, p. 197) noted that, 'the reality of cooperation is suggested by the open lab stock policy, which not only allows engineers access to all equipment, but encourages them to take it home for personal use.'

From a strictly economic perspective, this policy simply reduces monitoring and transaction costs. However, from the standpoint of a rule-based conception of trust-related interactions, its consequences are more subtle and far-reaching. As Miller (1992, p. 197) observes, 'the open door symbolizes and demonstrates management's trust in the cooperativeness of the employees.' Because such acts are so manifestly predicated on trust in others, they tend to breed trust in turn.

Rule-based practices of this sort can also exert subtle influences, not only on individuals' perceptions of their own honesty and trustworthiness but also on their expectations and beliefs about other organizational members' honesty and trustworthiness. As Miller (1992, p. 197) notes in this regard, by eliminating time clocks and locks on equipment room doors at Hewlett-Packard, the organization builds a 'shared expectation among all the players that cooperation will most likely be reciprocated' creating 'a shared "common knowledge" in the ability of the players to reach cooperative outcomes.' By institutionalizing trust through practices at the macro-organizational (collective) level, trust becomes internalized at the micro (individual) level.

TRUST-DESTROYING PROCESSES IN THE LEADER–CONSTITUENT RELATIONSHIP

Although recognizing the importance of trust and the diverse benefits that flow from it, social scientists have been cognizant also of the difficulties that attend the creation and maintenance of trust between leaders and their constituents (Hardin, 2004; Kramer and Gavrieli, 2004). Even under the best of circumstances, trust between leaders and their constituents seems hard won, but easily lost. Certainly that is one inference one might reasonably draw from recent events surrounding the devastating economic meltdowns and stunning corporate collapses. But even going beyond these obvious contemporary examples, trust scholars and leadership researchers have tried to understand what explains the seeming 'fragility' of trust between leaders and their constituents. What precisely goes wrong and why in the leader–constituent relationship? In the following sections, I offer some factors identified in empirical research.

Leaders falling short: failing to fulfill the psychological contract

In an influential study, Robinson (1996) examined the relationship between employees' trust in an organization's leadership, and their perceptions of the extent to which the organization or its leaders had either fulfilled or breached its psychological contract with them. She defined psychological contracts in terms of employees' beliefs regarding the terms and conditions of their reciprocal exchange relation with their employer (i.e., what they owed the employer and what the employer owed them). Psychological contract breach was characterized, in turn, as a subjective experience based upon employee's perceptions that the organization had failed to fulfill its perceived obligations.

To investigate the relationship between trust and psychological contract breach, Robinson conducted a longitudinal study of newly hired managers, measuring their initial trust in those above them, as well as their trust levels at 18 and 30 months on the job. She found that initial trust in an employer was negatively related to subsequent perceptions of psychological contract breach. Specifically, individuals with high initial trust were less likely to perceive the psychological contract had been breached compared to those with low initial trust. She also found that prior trust moderated the relationship between psychological contract breach and subsequent trust, such that employees with low initial trust in their employer reported a greater decline in trust following perceived breach than employees with high initial trust. Robinson also found a negative correlation between psychological contract breach and several important forms of employee contributions to the organization, including job performance, civic virtue (extra-role) behaviors, and intentions to remain with the organization.

A related study (Kramer, 1996) examined a variety of cognitive processes underlying both perceived trust confirmations and trust violations. In particular, this study investigated asymmetries in the construal of trust-enhancing versus trust-decreasing behaviors as a function of individuals' location within the hierarchical relationship (those on top – the leaders; and those on the bottom – the constituents). Specifically, this study examined how graduate students and their faculty advisors judged the level of trust in their relationship, and

the evidence they used in rendering those judgments.

Using an autobiographical narrative methodology, students and faculty described the history of their interactions, recalling those behaviors that enhanced or undermined trust in the relationship. Content analysis of these narratives showed that individuals in low-status positions (graduate students) tended to code more of their advisors' behaviors as diagnostic of trustworthiness compared to those in positions of high status (faculty advisors). To explain these findings, Kramer argued that, because of their greater dependence and vulnerability, trust concerns are more salient to individuals in low-status positions. As a consequence, they tend to be more vigilant and ruminative about trust-relevant transactions. They also code more transactions as diagnostic of trustworthiness and can more easily recall instances of trust violation.

In another study, Cook et al. (2004) investigated trust-building and trust-eroding processes in the context of another important form of hierarchical relationship, viz., the relationship between physicians and patients in medical settings. Their results demonstrated the patients afforded considerable importance to a variety of subtle and transient verbal and non-verbal cues construed as indicative of trustworthiness. These included cues, such as direct eye contact and physical touching, which reassured patients as to physicians' concern and interest in them as persons. They also included cues indicative of the physicians' competence and institutional savvy in negotiating the complex medical bureaucracy on patients' behalf.

Viewed in aggregate, these studies demonstrate that subtle and complex attributional and judgment processes can either enhance or impede the development of stable and enduring trust.

Distrust and suspicion as impediments to stable and enduring trust in the leadership process

Distrust and suspicion are obvious and common problems that can plague leader–constituent relationships. Distrust has been defined as a 'lack of confidence in the other, a concern that the other may act so as to harm one, that he does not care about one's welfare or intends to act harmfully, or is hostile' (Grovier, 1994, p. 240). Suspicion, in turn, has been viewed as one of the central cognitive components of distrust. Fein and Hilton (1994, p. 168) characterized suspicion as a psychological state in which perceivers 'actively entertain multiple, possibly rival, hypotheses about the motives or genuineness of a person's behavior.'

In elaborating on the causes or sources of distrust and suspicion, Fein and Hilton (1994) argued that suspicion can be triggered by a variety of circumstances, including situations where perceivers have forewarnings that another might be insincere or untrustworthy, when their expectations have been violated, and when they recognize situational cues or are in possession of contextual information that suggests another might have ulterior motives.

Survey evidence documents the dismal general level of trust in leaders in America today. For example, a recent survey conducted jointly by *US News and World Report* and Harvard's Center for Public Leadership (and *prior to* the recent economic meltdown and discovery of corporate abuse and fraud), reported low levels of trust and confidence in American leaders across a range of domains and issues (Center for Public Leadership, 2008). For example, 82% of respondents agreed there was a crisis with respect to leadership in the country, 79% thought America would decline unless we found better leaders, and only 25% thought current leaders were effective. Moreover, when asked to indicate their confidence in America's leaders across a variety of domains, they reported dismally low levels of confidence. For example, respondents expressed having little trust in the following institutions (listed in order of lowest trust levels to next lowest level, etc.): executive branch (38.1%), news media-alternative (39.5%), Congress (42.9%), business (45.0%), news media-traditional (46.0%), religious leaders and institutions (52.4%), educational leaders and institutions (55.3%), state government leaders and agencies (54.9%), and local governmental leaders and agencies (57.7%). The only two institutions crossing the midpoint of the 100-point scale (indicating a 'moderate level of confidence') are medical and military leaders and institutions.

In some respects, I should emphasize, these findings simply reflect a continuing downward trend in trust in leaders and institutions that has been observed for several decades now, beginning during the late 1960s (Nye, Zelikow, and King, 1997). For example, although 75% of Americans said they trusted the federal government in 1964, only 25% expressed comparable levels of trust in 2001. Similarly, trust in universities fell from 61 to 30%, medical institutions from 73 to 29%, and journalism from 29 to 14%. Major private companies fared no better, with trust in them having fallen from 55 to 21% over this same period. I would have to suspect, given recent events, that all of these numbers would be even lower today.

Although data regarding their prevalence seem unequivocal, the sources of distrust of leaders and the institutions they lead is more controversial. Researchers have advanced several different and quite plausible explanations for the decline, ranging from historical, economic, organizational, psychological, and sociological factors (see Nye, Zelikow, and King, 1997 for an overview). A number of studies highlight the importance of unmet or violated expectancies in explaining why public trust in institutions has eroded. For example, Nye, Zelikow, and King (1997) note that the decline of public trust in government and its leaders can be attributed, at least in part, to its perceived failure to solve a variety of social ills. According to this hypothesis, promises by government leaders to remedy urgent social problems (e.g., to eradicate poverty, racial injustice, and catastrophic illnesses) led to heightened expectations that government leaders would actually solve these problems. As these expectations went unfulfilled, trust diminished correspondingly. The prototypic example of this relationship was the decline in trust during the Johnson administration over the perceived failure of the Great Society and the deceptions regarding the covert escalation of the Vietnam conflict. If these theorized mechanisms are responsible for the decline in trust in leaders, one would have to predict that trends following the financial meltdown, evidence of fraud and abuse, and collapse of major corporations around the world will pull down these numbers further.

In putting these trends in perspective, it is important to note that low trust in leaders is not necessarily a problem per se. Many authors have treated the erosion of trust in leaders as a serious societal problem that needs to be remedied. They have noted the merits, accordingly, of attempting to rebuild trust and have advanced specific agendas for so doing (e.g., Brown, 1994; Lorsch, Berlowitz, and Zelleke, 2005). Low trust is an unfortunate state, given the missed opportunities and foregone benefits it occasions. However, low trust in leaders is prudent and appropriate if the leaders in question are in fact untrustworthy. Then, distrust is both appropriate and prudent (Kramer, 2002).

Investigating the effects of violated expectancies on people's trust in leaders, Zimmer (1979) argued that individuals, when making judgments regarding the general trustworthiness of leaders, tend to overgeneralize from vivid, highly salient events involving specific leaders. To investigate this hypothesis, he examined the impact of Watergate on public perceptions of trust in government and its leadership. He noted that, prior to Watergate, public trust in Richard Nixon had been generally quite high (In fact, voters in one survey had rated Nixon as more trustworthy than either George McGovern or Edward Kennedy!). Zimmer theorized that subsequent revelations during the Watergate hearings demonstrated to people that their trust in Nixon had been misplaced. Such revelations would lead, he predicted, to a decrease in public trust, especially among those who had originally voted for and supported Richard Nixon. After all, he reasoned, the sense of disappointment and betrayal should be especially acute among individuals whose trust had been perceived as violated, resulting in greater generalized distrust of future leaders. Consistent with his hypothesis, Zimmer found that people who had voted for Nixon showed the highest levels of subsequent decline in distrust.

In interpreting these results, Zimmer speculated that people may use the behaviors of institutional leaders as reference points for gauging their basic beliefs about the state of society, and as reality-testing mechanisms when appraising the trustworthiness of its institutions in general. In other words, people may draw general inferences about institutional trust from the behavior of highly visible role models. As a consequence, he reasoned, the behavior of public leaders while in office 'may unknowingly or indirectly define reality in more ways and for more of the public than has been appreciated' (p. 749).

If constituents' unmet expectations and general beliefs regarding their leaders do contribute to the erosion of trust, it is instructive to consider the sources of such expectations and beliefs. Cappella and Jamieson (1997, p. 85) reviewed evidence implicating the media in the growing distrust and cynicism of the public toward its leaders. The framing of news, they theorized, directly affects the public's trust or mistrust of leaders. In particular, news stories that adopt *strategic frames* (i.e., frames that emphasize themes of 'winning and losing and the self-interest implied by that orientation' and that activate negative actor traits such as those indicative of 'artifice, pandering, deceit, staging, and positioning for advantage') tend to promote greater mistrust and cynicism regarding leaders than do more neutral, issue-oriented frames. To investigate this hypothesis, Capella and Jamieson (1997) conducted a series of carefully controlled experiments in which news involving public leaders and institutions was systematically framed in either strategic terms or in terms of more neutral, issue-pertinent frames. The results from these studies support their argument that strategic frames produce greater mistrust and cynicism.

Technologies that undermine leader–constituent trust

An important area of organizational research related to trust and trustworthiness, and one that is almost certain to become increasingly important over the next decades, concerns the relationship between technology and trust. Enthusiasm over technological remedies to trust-related problems has been considerable, as evidenced by the rapid infusion into the workplace of surveillance systems and other forms of electronic monitoring of employee performance. For example, according to Aiello (1993), over 70,000 US companies purchased surveillance software between 1990 and 1992, at a cost of more than $500 million dollars.

Organizations typically adopt such technological remedies in the hope of enhancing employee trustworthiness (e.g., assuring compliance with regulations and deterring misbehavior). Ironically, there is increasing evidence that such systems might actually undermine trust and may even elicit the very behaviors they are intended to suppress or eliminate. In discussing this evidence, Cialdini (1996) identified several reasons why monitoring and surveillance might diminish trust within an organization. First, there is evidence that when people think their behavior is under the control of extrinsic motivators, intrinsic motivation may be reduced (Enzle and Anderson, 1993). Thus, surveillance may undermine individuals' motivation to engage in the very behaviors such monitoring is intended to induce or ensure. For example, innocent employees who are subjected to compulsory polygraphs, drug testing, and other forms of mass screening designed to deter misbehavior may become less committed to internal standards of honesty and integrity in the workplace.

Monitoring systems can produce other unintended and ironic consequences with respect to trust. As Cialdini (1996) notes, monitoring and surveillance systems communicate to employees that they are not trusted, potentially breeding mistrust and resentment in return. When people feel coerced into complying with a behavior, they may resist the behavior when they think monitoring is imperfect and they can get away with it. Because of psychological reactance, even honest employees may try to cheat or sabotage monitoring systems.

Other evidence suggests that the corrosive effects of surveillance extend to those doing the surveillance. Several studies have shown, for example, that the act of surveillance may increase distrust of surveillants over those they monitor (Kruglanski, 1970; Strickland, 1958). This result has been explained in terms of self-perception theory. Less obvious, but no less insidious in terms of their consequences, are the behaviors that surveillants don't engage in when surveillance and other substitutes for trust are utilized in organizations. As one executive who had implemented a computer monitoring system called Overview mused, 'If I didn't have the Overview, I would walk around and talk to people more. ... I would be more interested in what people are thinking about' (Zuboff, 1988, p. 141). Thus, systems intended to guarantee trust may, ironically, not only make it more difficult for employees to demonstrate their trustworthiness but also for authorities to learn about the distribution of trust within their organizations.

CONCLUDING OBSERVATIONS, UNRESOLVED QUESTIONS, AND PROMISING DIRECTIONS

In this chapter, I have attempted to pull together some conceptual insights and empirical findings from contemporary trust research that might inform our understanding of the underpinnings of effective leadership processes. In concluding, I want to emphasize that throughout this chapter I have consistently emphasized trust in the context of leadership *processes* rather than trust in leaders per se. This distinction, in my view, is not simply stylistic but essential. As Hackman and Wageman (2005) have compellingly argued, the leadership literature has been hampered by what they term the *leadership attribution error*. As a mere consequence of their high visibility and salience in most social and organizational situations, they argue, individual leaders attract a disproportionate share of the causal credit or blame for good and bad outcomes. Hackman and Wageman characterize this leadership attribution error as 'understandable, persuasive, and quite powerful' (p. 39) in its impact on how both constituents and leaders make sense of, and respond to, the various situations they confront. In recognition of the importance of their argument, I have endeavored throughout this chapter to stress the role trust plays in enhancing leadership processes, irrespective of whether one person is centrally responsible for the governance of that process, or whether governance is distributed among a group of interdependent actors, as in the case of the famous Orpheus Orchestra that Hackman has described.

I think it is safe to conclude, on the basis of the empirical findings reviewed in this chapter, that adequate evidence exists as to the central importance trust plays in effective leadership processes. Considerable progress has been made, in particular, with respect to clarifying the nature of this relationship, its benefits, as well as some of the difficulties that attend it. As also evident from this review, considerable progress is evident with respect to identifying the cognitive, social, and behavioral antecedents or underpinnings of trust in this process.

Despite these impressive strides, some important lacunae persist in our understanding of the role trust plays in leadership processes. One area that remains particularly underdeveloped pertains to our understanding of the structural underpinnings of trust in leader–constituent relationships. One promising direction, accordingly, for future research is to explore the structural foundations on which trust between leaders and their constituents might be predicated. These include the design of more effective governance processes (Braithwaite and Levi, 1998), as well as assurance mechanisms, including mechanisms that foster greater transparency and perceived accountability (Bennis, Goleman, O'Toole, and Biederman, 2008). Already, earnest and thoughtful preliminary efforts in this direction have been made (see, e.g., Braithwaite and Levi, 1998; Lorsch, Berlowitz, and Zelleke, 2005), but clearly more needs to be done.

There also is a dearth of both well-developed theory and adequate evidence pertaining to the effects of leader and/or constituent gender on the efficacy of the leadership process (Bowles and McGinn, 2005). Revealing in this regard is the fact that, in their comprehensive and impressive assessment of the literature, Eagly and Carli (2007) remain largely silent regarding the role trust might play in the process of leader development and success. This gap in our knowledge is particularly important because of accumulating evidence that women leaders are not only becoming more prevalent in leadership ranks but also exerting effective and sometimes even superior impact. Moreover, when gender is thrown into the causal mix, the relationships may be subtle and complex. For example, although her research did not examine these issues in a leadership context per se, Bohnet (2007) reported some provocative differences with respect to how men and women think about and respond to trust dilemmas, at least in the context of simple laboratory-based trust games. Similarly, Cook et al. (2004) report, on the basis of their qualitative study of trust in doctor–patient relations, that the gender of the physician was often perceived by patients and sometimes physicians themselves as an important factor affecting trust levels, especially with respect to women patients with women physicians. Such results clearly suggest gender may be an important mediating process in the leader–constituent trust relationship.

Another important area where both theory and empirical research remains incomplete is cross-cultural differences in the trust–leadership process. Research by Yamagishi and Yamagishi (1994) illustrates how subtle and complex such differences can be. They reviewed survey evidence that Japanese citizens often report lower levels of trust compared to their American counterparts. At first glance, this result is quite surprising. From the perspective of the widely-held view that Japanese society is characterized by close, stable, long-term social relations, one might expect that trust would be stronger within Japanese society. To resolve this anomaly, Yamagishi and Yamagishi proposed an important distinction between generalized trust versus psychological assurance. What characterizes Japanese society, they argue, is not generalized trust but rather mutual assurance. This mutual assurance is predicated on the stability of interpersonal and inter-organizational relationships within the society. Because of this high degree of perceived stability, they argue, uncertainty in social transactions is greatly reduced. In effect, the social context provides an arena within which trustworthy transactions can take place. Their findings, incidentally, add weight to the suggestion, made above, that structural mechanisms could play a larger role than heretofore appreciated in building stable and enduring leader–constituent trust relationships.

Yamagishi and Yamagishi's provocative findings bring up a related issue and that is knowing more about the kind of *cultural intelligence* that leaders might need to build trust across group boundaries (Earley and Ang, 2003). It would be interesting to know whether leaders high in cultural intelligence might be more adept at understanding how to build trust that bridges cultural divides. Such trust-building skills may be especially vital for leadership success in our increasingly global and, in some respects, fractured and polarized world. Despite its *prima facie* importance, evidence suggestive of our lack of current knowledge regarding this important question comes from several sources. First, the extensive and otherwise impressive single-spaced, 890-page *Handbook of Cultural Psychology* (Kitayama and Cohen, 2007) contains not a single reference in its subject index to leadership. Moreover, it contains only a small handful of sentences pertaining to trust scattered over a scant five -pages. Similarly, Gelfand and Brett's (2004) outstanding *Handbook of Negotiation and Culture* contains no references to leadership in its subject index, and only two brief references to trust. Happily, however, at least one forthcoming volume (Pittinsky, 2009) remedies some of these shortcomings in the extant literature.

These are only a few promising directions that future inquiry might address, of course. It is hoped that this review might stimulate social scientists representing other points of view, research interests, and disciplinary expertise to advance additional extensions of this literature.

REFERENCES

Aiello, J. R. (1993). Computer-based monitoring: Electronic surveillance and its effects. *Journal of Applied Social Psychology, 23*, 499–507.

Baier, A. (1986). Trust and antitrust. *Ethics, 96*, 231–260.

Barber, B. (1983). *The logic and limits of trust.* New Brunswick, NJ: Rutgers University Press.

Bass, B. M. (1985). *Leadership and performance beyond expectations.* New York: Free Press.

Bennis, W., Goleman, D., O'Toole, J., and Biederman, P. (2008). *Transparency: How leaders create a culture of candor.* San Francisco, CA: Jossey-Bass.

Bligh, M. C. and Meindl, J. R. (2005). The cultural ecology of leadership: An analysis of popular leadership books. In D. M. Messick and R. M. Kramer (eds), *The psychology of leadership: New perspectives and research*, pp. 11–52. Thousand Oaks, CA: Sage.

Bohnet, I. (2007). Why women and men trust others. In B. S. Frey and A. Stutzer (eds), *Economics and psychology: A promising new cross-disciplinary field*, pp. 89–110. Cambridge, MA: MIT Press.

Boyle, R. and Bonacich, P. (1970). The development of trust and mistrust in mixed-motive games. *Sociometry, 33*, 123–179.

Braithwaite, V. and Levi, M. (1998). *Trust and governance.* New York: Russell Sage Foundation.

Brewer, M. B. (1981). Ethnocentrism and its role in interpersonal trust. In M. B. Brewer and B. E. Collins (eds), *Scientific inquiry and the social sciences*, pp. 345–359. San Francisco, CA: Jossey-Bass.

Brockner, J. and Siegel, P. A. (1996). Understanding the interaction between procedural distributive justice: The role of trust. In R. M. Kramer and T. Tyler (eds), *Trust in organizations*, pp. 390–413. Thousand Oaks, CA: Sage.

Brockner, J., Siegel, P. A., Daly, J. P., and Tyler, T. (1997). When trust matters: The moderating effects of outcome favorability. *Administrative Science Quarterly, 43*, 558–583.

Brower, H. H., Schoorman, F. D., and Tan, H. H. (2000). A model of relational leadership: The integration of trust and leader–member exchange. *The Leadership Quarterly, 11*, 2227–2250.

Brown, P. (1994). *Restoring the public trust.* Boston, MA: Beacon Press.

Burns, M. (1978). *Leadership.* New York: Harper and Row.

Cappella, J. N. and Jamieson, K. H. (1997). *Spiral of cynicism: The press and the public good.* New York: Oxford University Press.

Center for Public Leadership (2008). *National Leadership Index 2008: A national study of confidence in leadership.* Cambridge, MA: Harvard Kennedy School.

Chua, R., Ingram, P., and Morris M. W. (2008). From the head and the heart: Locating cognition-based and affect-based trust in manager's professional networks. *Academy of Management Journal, 51*, 436–452.

Cialdini, R. (1996). The triple tumor structure of organizational behavior. In D. M. Messick and A. E. Tenbrunsel (eds), *Codes of conduct*. New York: Russell Sage Foundation.

Cook, K. S. (2001). *Trust in society*. New York: Russell Sage Foundation.

Cook, K. S., Hardin, R., and Levi, M. (2005). *Cooperation without trust*. New York: Russell Sage Foundation.

Cook, K. Kramer, R. M., Thom, D. H., et al. (2004). Trust and distrust in physician–patient relationships: Antecedents and consequences. In R. M. Kramer and K. S. Cook (eds), *Trust in organizations: Dilemmas and approaches*. Russell Sage Foundation Trust Series, Volume VII. New York: Russell Sage Foundation.

Covey, S. M. R. (2006). *The speed of trust: The one thing that changes everything*. New York: Simon & Schuster.

Creed, W. D. and Miles, R. E. (1996). Trust in organizations: A conceptual framework. In R. M. Kramer and T. R. Tyler (eds), *Trust in organizations*, pp. 16–38. Thousand Oaks, CA: Sage.

Davis, J., Schoorman, F. D., Mayer, R. C., and Tan, H. (2000). The trusted general manager and business unit performance: Empirical evidence of a competitive advantage. *Strategic Management Journal, 21*, 543–576.

Dawes, R. M. (1994). *House of cards*. New York: Free Press.

Dirks, K. T. (2000). Trust in leadership and team performance: Evidence from NCAA basketball. *Journal of Applied Psychology, 85*, 1004–1012.

Dirks, K. T. (2006). Three fundamental questions regarding trust in leaders. In R. Bachmann and A. Zaheer (eds), *Handbook of Trust Research*, pp. 15–28. Northampton, MA: Edward Elgar.

Dirks, K.T. and Ferrin, D. L. (2002). Trust in leadership: Meta-analytic findings and implications for organizational research. *Journal of Applied Psychology, 87*, 611–628.

Dirks, K. T. and Skarlicki, D. P. (2004). Trust in leaders: Existing research and emerging issues. In R. M. Kramer and K. S. Cook (eds), *Trust and distrust in organizations: Dilemmas and approaches*, pp. 21–40. New York: Russell Sage Foundation.

Eagley, A. H. and Carli, L. L. (2007). Through the labyrinth: The truth about how women become leaders. Boston, MA: Harvard Business School Press.

Earley, C. and Ang, S. (2003). *Cultural intelligence*. Stanford, CA: Stanford Business Books.

Enzle, M. E. and Anderson, S. C. (1995). Surveillant intentions and intrinsic motivation. *Journal of Personality and Social Psychology, 64*, 257–266.

Fein, S. and Hilton, J. (1994). Judging others in the shadow of suspicion. *Motivation and Emotion, 18,* 167–198.

Ganz, M. (2009). *Why David sometimes wins*. New York: Oxford University Press.

Gardner, H. (2006). *Changing minds: The art and science of changing our own and other people's minds*. Boston, MA: Harvard Business School Press.

Gelfand, M. J. and Brett, J. M. (2004). *The Handbook of negotiation and culture*. Stanford, CA: Stanford University Press.

Graen, G. B. and Uhl-Bien, M. (1995). Relationship-based approach to leadership: Development of leader-member exchange (LMX) theory of leadership over 25 years: Applying a multi-level multi-domain approach. *The Leadership Quarterly, 6*, 219–247.

Grant, A. M. and Sumanth, J. J. (2009). Mission possible? The performance of prosocially motivated employees depends on manager trustworthiness. *Journal of Applied Psychology*, in press.

Grovier, T. (1994). An epistemology of trust. *International Journal of Moral and Social Studies, 8*, 155–174.

Hackman, J. R. (2002). *Leading teams: Setting the stage for great performances*. Boston, MA: Harvard Business School Press.

Hackman, J. R. and Wageman, R. (2005). When and how team leaders matter. In B. M. Staw and R. M. Kramer (eds), *Research in organizational behavior, 26*, 37–75. New York: Elsevier.

Hardin, R. (2004). *Distrust*. New York: Russell Sage Foundation.

Hardin, R. (2006). *Trust*. Cambridge, UK: Polity Press.

Hetherington, J. J. (2005). *Why trust matters: Declining political trust and the demise of American liberalism*. Princeton, NJ: Princeton University Press.

Hogg, M. (2005). Social identity and leadership. In D. M. Messick and R. M. Kramer (eds), *The Psychology of Leadership*, pp. 53–80. Thousand Oaks, CA: Sage.

Hollis, M. (1998). *Trust within reason*. Cambridge, UK: Cambridge University Press.

Kellerman, B. (2008). *Followership: How followers are creating change and changing leaders*. Boston, MA: Harvard Business Press.

Kitayama, S. and Cohen, D. (2007). *Handbook of cultural psychology*. New York: Guilford.

Kramer, R. M. (1996). Divergent realities and convergent disappointments in the hierarchic relation: The intuitive auditor at work. In R. M. Kramer and T. R. Tyler (eds), *Trust in organizations: Frontiers of theory and research*. Thousand Oaks, CA: Sage Publications.

Kramer, R. M. (2002). When paranoia makes sense. *Harvard Business Review, 80*, 62–71.

Kramer, R. M. (2006). Social identity and social capital: The collective self at work. *International Public Management Journal, 9*, 25–45.

Kramer, R. M. (2009). Rethinking trust. *Harvard Business Review, 87*, 69–77.

Kramer, R. M., Brewer, M. B., and Hanna, B. J. (1996). Collective trust and collective action: The decision to trust as a social decision. In R. M. Kramer and T. R. Tyler (eds), *Trust in organizations*, pp. 357–389. Thousand Oaks, CA: Sage.

Kramer, R. M. and Gavrieli, D. A. (2004). Power, uncertainty, and the amplification of doubt: An archival study of suspicion inside the oval office. In R. M. Kramer and K. S. Cook (eds), Trust and distrust in organizations: Dilemmas and approaches, pp. 342–370. New York: Russell Sage Foundation.

Kruglanski, A. W. (1970). Attributing trustworthiness in supervisor–worker relations. *Journal of Experimental Social Psychology, 6*, 214–232.

Lane, C. and Bachman, R. (1998). Trust within and between organizations. New York: Oxford University Press.

Lewicki, R. J. and Bunker, B. B. (1995). Trust in relationships: A model of trust development and decline. In B. B. Bunker and J. Z. Rubin (eds), *Conflict, cooperation and justice.* San Francisco: Jossey-Bass.

Lindskold, S. (1978). Trust development, the GRIT proposal, and the effects of conciliatory acts on conflict and cooperation. *Psychological Bulletin, 85,* 772–793.

Lorsch, J. W., Berlowitz, L., and Zelleke, A. (2005). *Restoring trust in American business.* Cambridge, MA: MIT Press.

March, J. G. and Olson, J. P. (1989). *Rediscovering institutions.* New York: Free Press.

Martin, J. (1992). *Cultures in organizations: Three perspectives.* New York: Oxford University Press.

Maslyn, J. M. and Uhl-Bein, M. (2001). Leader–member exchange and its dimensions: Effects of self-effort and other's effort in relationship quality. *Journal of Applied Psychology, 86,* 697–708.

Meindl, J. R. and Ehrlich, S. B. (1987). The romance of leadership and the evaluation of organizational performance. *Academy of Management Journal, 30,* 91–110.

Messick, D. M. (2005). On the psychological exchange between leaders and followers. In D. M. Messick and R. M. Kramer (eds), *The psychology of leadership: New perspectives and research,* pp. 81–96. Mahwah, NJ: Lawrence Erlbaum.

Messick, D. M. and Kramer, R. M. (2001). Trust as shallow morality. In K. Cook (ed.), *Trust in society,* pp. 89–118. New York: Russell Sage Foundation.

Messick, D. M. and Kramer, R. M. (2005). *The psychology of leadership: New perspectives and research.* Mahwah, NJ: Erlbaum.

Meyerson, D., Weick, K., and Kramer, R. M. (1996). Swift trust and temporary groups. In R. M. Kramer and T. R. Tyler (eds), *Trust in organizations: Frontiers of theory and research,* pp. 166–195. Thousand Oaks, CA: Sage Publications.

Miller, G. J. (1992). *Managerial dilemmas.* New York: Cambridge University Press.

Nye, J. (2008). *The powers to lead.* New York: Oxford University Press.

Nye, J. S., Zelikow, P. D., and King, D. C. (1997). *Why people don't trust government.* Boston, MA: Harvard University Press.

Olson, M. (1965). *The logic of collective action.* New Haven, CT: Yale University Press.

Pfeffer, J. (1977). The ambiguity of leadership. *Academy of Management Review, 2,* 104–112.

Pillisuk, M. and Skolnick, P. (1968). Inducing trust: A test of the Osgood proposal. *Journal of Personality and Social Psychology, 8,* 121–133.

Pittinsky, T. (2009). *Crossing the divide: Intergroup relations and leadership.* Boston, MA: Harvard Business School Press.

Podolny, J. M., Khurana, R., and Hill-Popper, M. (2005). Revisiting the meaning of leadership. In B. M Staw and

R. M. Kramer (eds), *Research in organizational behavior, 26,* 1–36. New York: Elsevier.

Putnam, R. D. (2000). *Bowling alone: The collapse and revival of American community.* New York: Simon & Schuster.

Robinson, S. (1996). Trust and breach of the psychological contract. In R. M. Kramer (ed), Organizational trust: A reader, pp. 331–361. New York: Oxford University Press.

Solomon, R. C. and Flores, F. (2001). *Building trust in business, politics, relationships, and life.* New York: Oxford University Press.

Stogdill, R. M. (1950). Leadership, membership, and organization. *Psychological Bulletin, 47,* 1–14.

Stogdill, R. M. (1974). *Handbook of leadership: Survey of theory and research.* New York: Free Press.

Strickland, L. H. (1978). Surveillance and trust. *Journal of Personality, 26,* 200–215.

Sztompka, P. (1999). *Trust: A sociological theory.* Cambridge, UK: Cambridge University Press.

Tyler, T. R. and Blader, S. L. (2003). The group-engagement model: Procedural justice, social identity, and cooperative behavior. *Personality and Social Psychology Review, 7,* 349–361.

Tyler, T. R. and Degoey, P. (1996). Trust in organizational authorities: The influence of motive attributions on willingness to accept decisions. In R. M. Kramer and T. R. Tyler (eds), *Trust in organizations: Frontiers of theory and research,* pp. 331–356. Thousand Oaks, CA: Sage.

Uhl-Bien, M. (2009). Personal communication to the author.

Uhl-Bien, M., Graen, G. B., and Scandura, T. A. (1997). Relational leadership theory: A role-making approach. In B. M. Staw and L. L. Cummings (Eds.), *Research in organizational behavior (Vol. 18),* pp. 414–430.

Uslaner, E. M. (2002). *The moral foundations of trust.* Cambridge, UK: Cambridge University Press.

Wageman, R., Nunes, E. A., Burruss, J. A., and Hackman, J. R. (2008). *Senior leadership teams: What it takes to make them great.* Boston, MA: Harvard Business School Press.

Weber, J. M., Malhotra, D., and Murnighan, J. K. (2005). Normal acts of irrational trust: Motivated attributions and the trust development process. In B. M. Staw and R. M. Kramer (eds.), *Research in organizational behavior (Volume 26),* pp. 75–102. New York: Elsevier Press.

Weick, K. E. (1995). *Sensemaking in organizations.* Thousand Oaks, CA: Sage.

Whitener, E. M., Brodt, S. E., Korsgaard, M. A., and Werner, J. M. (2006). Managers as initiators of trust: An exchange relationship for understanding managerial trustworthy behavior. In R. M. Kramer (ed.), *Organizational trust: A reader,* pp. 140–169. New York: Oxford University Press.

Zak, P. J. (2008). The neurobiology of trust. *Scientific American Mind,* June 88–95.

Zuboff, L. G. (1988). *In the age of the smart machine.* New York: Basic Books.

Zucker, L. G. (1986). Production of trust: Institutional sources of economic structure. *Research in Organizational Behavior, 8,* 53–111.

11

Leadership and Organizational Culture

Mats Alvesson

INTRODUCTION

Combining leadership and organizational culture is not the easiest of tasks as both terms mask an enormous variety of partly radically different ideas and views. The wide spectrum of definitions of leadership parallels a wide spectrum of definitions of culture, including organizational culture. Within the various views on the latter we find everything from unique and unitary corporate cultures, formed by founders and executives, to more anthropological views on meaning and beliefs among communities typically outside the conscious control of specific actors (Alvesson & Berg, 1992). Yukl (1989) says that 'the numerous definitions of leadership that have been proposed appear to have little else in common' than involving an influence process. This is then taking place within an asymmetrical relationship: the leader is exercising influence over the follower. Yukl himself defines leadership 'to include influencing task objectives and strategies, influencing commitment and compliance in task behavior to achieve these objectives, influencing group maintenance and identification, and influencing the culture of an organization' (p. 253). This definition is probably more thoughtful than many others in the literature. But one could very well let the words 'leadership' and 'culture' change place and then have a definition of culture. Or swap leadership and strategy. One could also replace leadership with organizational structure, job design, social identity or something else. Weick (1985) has used this trick to show how some definitions of strategy and culture are roughly the same. X is about the social

process of framing and influencing – thinking, feeling, identifying and acting – and the number of possible words that the X stands for is considerable. Of course further qualifiers, such as that leadership refers to a person (in a relation) and culture to a social system of shared meanings, point at differentiation. Despite the shortcomings of definitions and the similarities of what a great deal of popular terms refer to, in practice they trigger different meanings and lead to different lines of thinking, related to the context in which the terms are used. But it should be clear that culture and leadership do not refer to two clearly different and distinct phenomena, but an endless number of possible views, definitions as well as empirical phenomena.

'Leadership' is typically defined in general terms. The ambition of researchers is typically to say something of relevance across quite diverse settings, and frequently to discover the success formula for effective leadership. The diversity of relations, situations and cultural contexts in which superior – subordinate interactions take place means that a coherent definition with universal aspirations may tell us relatively little in terms of the richness and complexity of the phenomena it supposedly refers to, related to specific organizational cultural (and other) contexts in which expectations and acts of leadership are being played out. It is then rather difficult to claim that 'leadership', as a general term and object of study, stands in a clear relationship to a domain of social reality possible to conceptualize in a uniform manner. The efforts to capture variety through variables such as personnel orientation and initiating structure or democratic and autocratic or transformational and transactional are not very helpful, as the categories are too broad and what is seen as alternative 'styles' or 'forms' often hide the variations, combinations and ambiguities of the relations of managers and subordinates. There are interrelated problems: the social worlds of interest for leadership researchers do not easily lend themselves to neat categorization and ordering, and language use has its limitations in relation to the goal of fixing meaning through definitions and the variation of cultural meanings means the limits of 'objective' and abstract definitions.

Understanding leadership calls for careful consideration of the social context in which processes of leadership take place. Leadership is not just a leader acting and a group of followers responding in a mechanical way, but a complex social process in which the meanings and interpretations of what is said and done are crucial. Leadership, then, is closely related to culture – at the organizational and other levels. This context then includes the societal, occupational and organizational – which all frame specific leader – follower interactions.

What is defined as 'leadership' calls for not just a theoretical definition but also close consideration of what a particular group mean by 'leadership' and how it relates to 'leaders' and 'leadership'. For different groups 'leadership' has different meanings and value. Organizational culture is here crucial, even though 'organization' does not have to refer to the unitary and unique features of a specific organization, but may be a significant group or domain within an organization (e.g. R&D units) or a broader occupational/industrial/societal sector. Societal cultures are connected with and put imprints on organizational conditions (Jones, 2005) and ideals and standards for leadership (Den Hartog & Dickson, 2004). Generally, and with the risk of overgeneralizing too much, there is a common impression that, while North Americans seem to rate leadership favourably, many Europeans may be somewhat less enthusiastic. US society seems to favour an ideology of celebrating individualistic strong masculine characters that can lead (Den Hartog & Dickson 2004; Lipman-Blumen, 1992; Prasad, 1997), although recent developments may have included a de-masculinization of management as teams, networks and knowledge are seen as increasingly salient features of contemporary organizations (Fondas, 1997). Other societies, e.g. the Scandinavians, may be less individualistic or masculine and favour more a egalitarian relationship, typically framing leadership in a less leader-focused way and perhaps also reducing the significance attributed to leadership, and relying more on horizontal relationships for guidance, coordination and support.

Although one would perhaps assume that the combination of leadership and organizational culture would be one of the key areas in leadership studies, and practitioners often see this aspect or interface as crucial, there is surprisingly little on the topic (Parry & Jackson 2008). Many overview books do not even have organizational culture in the index and even culture is referred to very sparsely, and then mainly referring to cross-cultural aspects (see, e.g., Antonakis et al., 2004; Pearce & Conger 2003; van Knippenberg & Hogg 2003). It is revealing that in Yukl's (1989) and House and Aditay's (1997) extensive review articles of leadership research, the word culture is only mentioned in passing a few times, and then as something that is changed as an outcome of 'transformational leadership' (Yukl, 1989), respectively, as national cultures possibly influencing leadership (House & Aditay, 1997). Sometimes authors (e.g. Western, 2008) address organizational culture more at length in relationship to leadership, but then often constrained to address a relationship to 'cultish' corporate cultures, viewed as combining flexibility and commitment with a strong sense of internalized control and a clear direction, accomplished through common values, beliefs and norms, or presented as the clue to organizational excellence (Peters & Waterman, 1982). Less exotic organizations are perhaps of great social relevance to address.

At the same time, it is very difficult to know whether a particular text is addressing culture or not, as the institutionalized use of the label is not so strong since the peak of the interest in organizational culture in the mid 1990s: authors may express a cultural understanding, taking the meaning and symbolism context of work seriously, without necessarily labelling this as organizational culture.

This chapter does not more than address cross-cultural aspects in passing (see Den Hartog & Dickson 2004; Guthey & Jackson, Chapter 12, this volume), but focuses on the organizational contexts, referring to a 'meso-level' above small groups but below entire societies, mainly focusing on the organizational level, but also to some extent on larger units within organizations and the sectors (industries, professions) putting strong imprints on organizational cultural functioning.

This chapter starts with a brief review of the (organizational) culture concept and how one can see leadership from a general cultural perspective, including the importance of considering what people in a specific context view as leadership. It then explores three areas or perspectives on organizational culture and leadership: leadership as the creation or change of organizational culture; leadership as maintenance and reproduction of culture, respectively; and culture as framing and shaping leadership.

ORGANIZATIONAL CULTURE

Organizational culture is one of the major themes in academic research and education in organization theory as well as in management practice. There are good reasons for this: the cultural dimension is central in all aspects of organizational life.

A glance at just a few works that use the term 'organizational culture' will reveal enormous variation in the definitions of this term and even more in the use of the term 'culture'. 'Culture' has no fixed or broadly agreed meaning, even in anthropology (Borowsky, 1994), but variation in its use is especially noticeable in the literature on organizational culture. This is partly related to strong differences in the purpose and depth of books and articles: from offering recipes for managers on how to create cultures to ethnographic explorations of everyday organizational life. In this chapter I mainly follow the perspective on culture of Geertz (1973), highly influential in organization studies (Alvesson, 2002; Smircich 1983a, 1983b). Culture is then understood to be a system of common symbols and meanings. It provides 'the shared rules governing cognitive and affective aspects of membership in an organization, and the means whereby they are shaped and expressed' (Kunda, 1992, p. 8). Culture is not primarily 'inside' people's heads, but somewhere 'between' the heads of a group of people where symbols and meanings are publicly expressed, e.g. in work group interactions, in board meetings, but also in material objects.

Culture then is central in governing the understanding of behaviour, social events, institutions and processes. It refers to the setting in which these phenomena become comprehensible and meaningful. Culture is regarded as a more or less cohesive system of meanings and symbols, in terms of which social interaction takes place, while the social structure is regarded as the behavioural patterns which the social interaction itself gives rise to. In the case of culture, then, we have a frame of reference of beliefs, expressive symbols and values, by means of which individuals define their environment, express their feelings and make judgements. In the latter case, that is to say at the social level, we have a continuous process of interaction. As Geertz (1973, p. 145) states, culture is the creation of meaning through which human beings interpret their experiences and guide their actions, while social structure is the

form which action takes or the network of social relationships which actually exists.

It is important here not to assume the existence of unique and unitary cultures corresponding to organizations or organizational units. Organizations are typically best seen as existing in a broader cultural context, with a variety of societal, industrial, regional, class, occupation, etc., cultures interplaying. Within organizations there are often considerable differentiation and fragmentation and different social groups and meaning formations intersect and interact, creating ambiguities (Alvesson, 2002; Jones, 2005; Martin, 2002; Meyerson & Martin, 1987).

REDUCTIONIST STUDIES OF LEADERSHIP NEGLECTING THE CULTURAL CONTEXT

As mentioned in the Introduction, despite the obvious and significant relevance of organizational culture for leadership, the leadership literature on the whole has not addressed organizational culture more than marginally (Jackson & Parry, 2008). There is often a very poor consideration of the context of leadership. Studies of what are assumed to be homogenous national cultures are here only partly helpful. The leadership literature is enormous, but the academic work suffers from a heavy bias to positivistic methodology, a psychological focus and an ideological commitment to managerialism (leaderism). Many researchers favour laboratory experiments or questionnaire studies that, almost by definition, neglect the serious consideration of organizational cultural context of leadership (see Bryman, Chapter 2, this volume). Some work on leadership and organizational culture is highly leader-centric and rather poor on appreciating the cultural context beyond what is assumed to be an outcome of the impact of the leadership of the founder of a firm (Jones, 2005). A prominent example is Schein (1985), who views organizational culture as a result of a historical process in which people gradually accept and internalize beliefs and values based on a leader's (often the founder's) vision. For Schein (1985, p. 9), culture is

> a pattern of basic assumptions – invented, discovered, or developed by a given group as it learns to cope with its problems of external adaptation and internal integration – that has worked well enough to be considered valid and therefore, to be taught to new members as the correct way to perceive, think, and feel in relation to those problems.

He acknowledges that emerging culture will reflect not only the leader's assumption but also the complex internal accommodations created by subordinates to run the organization 'in spite of' or 'around' the leader, but he claims that 'the initiative tends to be with the leader' (p. 224). Schein then strongly focuses on the latter and emphasizes as primary embedding mechanisms what leaders pay attention to, measure, and control, leader reactions to critical incidents and crises, deliberate role modelling and coaching, criteria for allocation of rewards and status, and criteria for recruitment, selection, promotion, retirement and excommunication. Such a leader-centred view on culture tends to neglect the complex cultural context in which the leader is working, framing and constraining the person as well as the orientations, responses, initiatives and actions of those supposed to be led. These are hardly only or mainly formed by their boss but by societal, industrial, occupational, generational cultures, by their material work situation, by group interactions, etc. (Jones, 2005). Even if the initiative seems to be with the leader, other people may act in subtle but pervasive way and, whatever a leader is doing, it is guided by culture as a system of meanings through which human beings interpret their experiences. A study of 20 firms indicated, e.g. only a modest impact of the CEO's influence on values in the organizations (Hofstede et al., 1990).

From a cultural perspective it is quite surprising that a very large part of the leadership literature focuses mainly on the subject supposed to be a leader (typically a person in a managerial job), his psychological set-up (stable orientations) or, at the dyadic level, of the leader-follower relation. As many have noted, a US ideology and fascination with supposedly strong and outstanding individuals creating exceptional deeds partly account for the narrow focus. Even though many other national cultures do not share this ideology, the domination of US thinking on leadership means that leadership research, and to some extent leadership practices also in other countries, bear imprints of US culture and its colonizing effects. The leader and his impact on the (individual) follower is generally overemphasized at the expense of a wider set of considerations, including followers, relationships and context (Collinson, 2006; Ladkin, 2010). In studies taking groups seriously, these are often seen as existing more or less in social isolation from a broader context. For example, in work on social identity and leadership, the relationship between leader and follower is sometimes abstracted from the social context and issues around prototypicality and in-/out-group saliency are disconnected from any sense of an organizational and cultural context (e.g. Hogg et al., 2003). Yukl (1999) notes that the emphasis on the dyadic perspective in the theories of charismatic and transformational leadership should be replaced by

a systems perspective that describes leadership in terms of several distinct but interrelated influence processes at the dyadic, group and organizational level' (p. 301). '…although an individualistic orientation has been the heavy favourite in leadership research, pressures are building to consider wider systems dynamics' (Fairhurst, 2001, p. 383). But this systems dynamic is seen as including everything from dyads to broad collectives (like an industry) and the emphasis, when researchers move away from a myopic focus on the leader, still seems to be in the micro end of the 'systems' spectrum. More recent post-heroic and relational approaches encourage the break away from the individual leader, but also these tend to stay on the level of interpersonal relations and the interplay and possibly position-switching between various subjects leading/following (Gronn, 2002; Uhl-Bien, 2006; see Hosking, Chapter 33, this volume). Also, critical approaches sometimes limit the perspective to deal with the identities of people involved in the leader-follower relationships (e.g. Collinson, 2006; see Sinclair, Chapter 37, this volume).

Within mainstream leadership studies, organizational culture would mark almost the end pole of the spectrum of possible foci. One could argue, however, that leadership – as ideology, discourse, institutionalized practice – is very much a societal phenomenon. It is one of the discourses of our time, forming a regulative ideal for people in business and working life and producing subjects eager to constitute themselves as 'leaders' doing 'leadership' (Foucault, 1977, 1980; see also Alvesson & Sveningsson, 2003). This would mean that a much less myopic view would be emphasized. If this is considered, meanings, understandings, ideals and norms on the organizational level appear not as in the 'outback' of leadership but in the mid-range. Organizational culture frames and guides leadership: the cultural context is crucial for what is viewed as 'leadership', how people in formal and informal capacities relate to this (or pay little attention to it), ideals and norms for its practices and receptions, etc.

Most studies of leadership focus on how a person identified as a leader is behaving or interacting with a group of subordinates and/or broadly is 'managing' the organization. In most systematic academic studies (as in real life), the leaders lead small groups of people. As organizational culture typically refers to a larger context than a small group, it is not something that the typical small-group leader has a significant impact on. One may talk about small-group culture, but this misses the point with the culture idea referring to wider and historically related meaning patterns. Addressing groups as fairly isolated and self-contained units in organizations neglects the dynamics and traffic and interaction of people and meanings at most workplaces. Senior managers lead, however, entire or large parts of organizations and then the situation with regard to organizational culture becomes different, although (as we will see) this does not mean that they (typically) control or shape organizational culture.

An awareness of how aspirations of illuminating organizational culture may drift into focusing on the behavioural level, rather than on the level of meaning, is important. Organizational culture calls for precision and depth to be understood and much richer accounts than those typically produced are needed.

MANAGERS AND LEADERS: INSTRUMENTAL AND CULTURAL?

Frequently, leadership is given a very broad meaning and includes almost everything that a manager or an informal leader does. But managers clearly do much more than engage in leadership. As the great majority of all managers are subordinated to more senior executives or are accountable to various constituencies, there are clearly elements of a manager's work time that cannot meaningfully be defined in terms of leadership.

It is common to make a distinction between managers, who are relying on their formal position and working with bureaucratic processes such as planning, budgeting, organizing and controlling, and leaders, who rely on their personal abilities, work with visions, agendas and coalition building and mainly through non-coercive means affecting people's feelings and thinking (e.g. Kotter, 1985; Zaleznik, 1977, etc.). Managers then can be 'only' managers or they can also be leaders. Zaleznik (1977) views the influence of leaders as 'altering moods, evoking images and expectations, and in establishing specific desires and objectives.... The net result of this influence is to change the way people think about what is desirable, possible and necessary' (p. 71, see also Barker, 1997). Leaders are then heavily involved in what Pfeffer (1981) refers to as symbolic management. In comparison, managers are much less omnipotent types.

In practice, managers frequently rely (to some extent) on plans: they coordinate and control and use bureaucratic means. But they also try to create commitment or at least acceptance for plans, rules, goals and instructions. Making people understand the purpose of, and create meaning around, what should specifically be done may transgress any clear distinction between management and leadership. At the same time, with the exception of talks in which the manager – leader tries to energize the masses, it is rare with acts of leadership to address thinking and feeling and abstract connections between tasks and broader contexts on a very general level. Instead, managers affect thinking and feeling in connection to managing specific tasks and goals, thus making 'leadership' and 'management' difficult to differentiate in practice, not only from a theoretical perspective but also for practitioners (Carroll & Levy, 2008). This view allows a combination of the two elements which I believe we can find in the activities of most (contemporary) managers and organizations.

Nevertheless, leadership is not productively used if it is supposed to cover everything that managers do. Everything that does not involve interaction with or indirect communication to subordinates falls outside leadership, even if the activities could be seen as salient in management. And also in relationship to subordinates, parts of management have very little to do with leadership, e.g. when there is a strict behavioural and/or output measurement focus. Some authors do, however, include a broad spectrum of highly diverse orientations, tasks and behaviours in leadership (e.g. House & Aditay, 1997). Leadership thus involves a strong ingredient of management of meaning (Ladkin, 2010; Smircich & Morgan, 1982), a conscious effort in which the shaping of the ideas, values, perceptions and feelings of people is included.

This means that leadership is per definition seen as 'cultural': i.e. leadership must be understood as taking place in a cultural context and all leadership acts have their consequences through the (culturally guided) interpretation of those involved in the social processes in which leaders, followers and leadership acts are expressed. The 'cultural orientation' of leadership could then be seen as salient. This, of course, does not imply that leadership means the significant impact on or capacity to shape and change culture at will. Leadership draws attention to the consequences within and through cultural meanings, informing the thoughts, feelings and actions that leaders provoke.

Management – as different from leadership – is also cultural in the sense that interpretation and meaning are also central here, as in all social life. But management typically addresses 'simple' and taken-for-granted meanings; the level of thinking and feeling should be 'passed quickly' in control efforts, leading to predictable responses at a behavioural level, e.g. following rules, adapting to standards or producing specific results. Management then is not primarily targeted at a cultural level as an 'end station' or as a significant site where a lot of things – thinking, sensemaking, value formation – take place. Management as a mode of control is then thought to be able to bypass culture in its operations and minimize the involvement of values, unfocused thinking and feeling. Control of behaviour, rules and output is doing the work.

DIFFERENT CONNECTIONS BETWEEN ORGANIZATIONAL CULTURE AND LEADERSHIP

In most of the literature on culture and leadership, the latter is seen as having an impact on the former, but this is only one way of relating the two phenomena. I will here address four connections: (1) leadership as a culturally defined phenomenon; (2) leadership influencing culture; and (3) culture influencing leadership.

Leadership as local cultural understanding

One approach is to listen to various groups and organizations and find out when and why the 'natives' talk about leadership, what they mean by it, their beliefs, values and feelings around leadership and different versions and expressions of it. Being a 'leader' is very much a status marker. It's relevance, meaning and significance vary.

How cultural values and expectations determine and constrain the chances of people emerging as 'leaders' is illustrated by the resistance of physicians in UK hospitals to relabel administrators managers. For administrators to appear as – be labelled as or seen as – 'leaders' would be highly difficult, given this culture, and of course, the political interests it is fused with (Parker, 2000).

Some authors here take a language-oriented view, focusing on conversations and language games (Fairhurst, 2009; Kelly, 2008; and see Fairhurst, Chapter 36, this volume) and limiting leadership to be a matter of language use in local settings, but a cultural (anthropological) understanding would not be focused only on language use, and tries to investigate implicit, taken-for-granted, difficult-to-articulate ways of relating to leadership (for an effort to distinguish between discourse and cultural perspectives on organizations, see Alvesson, 2004.) One can, e.g. pay attention to the variation of organizational cultures in the meaning, attention and appreciation of leadership. Some organizational cultures may be very focused on leadership, seen as good and important, and even the driving force, in the

organizations. Others may be indifferent or even negative to leadership: e.g. as a consequence of a strong professional ideology or bureaucracy creating little space for or interest in managers and other persons exercising strong or distinct leadership. The military and the university may exemplify this variation. Leadership may, by some groups, be seen as negative, as asymmetrical relations and reduction of autonomy would not be viewed favourably. An emphasis on leadership may even be seen as related to authoritarianism and non-professionalism. Or it can be seen as reducing autonomy and expressing distrust in the subordinates being able to do the work without seniors providing support, direction and control (Alvesson & Blom, 2009). Leaders and leadership can then be seen in terms of the local meanings in the organizational contexts, not as 'facts' about leadership 'as such', but more as clues to understanding organizational cultures. Does 'leadership' (or managerial work), in specific organizations, refer to the strong and decisive decision-maker, the superior technician or professional, the team-builder and coach, the educator and developer of people or the results-oriented number-cruncher carefully monitoring and putting pressure on people to perform? (For overviews of metaphors for leadership, see Alvesson & Spicer, 2011; Western, 2008.) Understandings of leadership may of course involve a complex set of meanings, but in different cultures there are variations of combinations and of which elements that are central. How people talk and, in other ways, express sentiments about leaders and leadership (managers and managerial work) indicates wider cultural patterns on beliefs and meanings of human nature, social relations, hierarchies, power, etc. This approach would partly avoid the difficulties in defining leadership once and for all, valid over time and space.

Still, there are some concerns for restricting leadership studies to solely tracing the meanings and use of leadership vocabularies among people in organizations. Some theoretical ideas about what leadership as a theme may refer to is important to give some direction in the understanding. Given the tendency of many people when talking about leadership – including many academics – to include almost everything, there is a risk that a study of language use may lead to the result that leadership talk may move in all directions, which can make it difficult to say much more than that there is this variation. Explicit talk of leadership may differ from how managers and others exercise influence. Nevertheless, with this caveat, moving an interest in leadership from a standardized conception of the subject matter – expressed in, e.g. questionnaire studies – to a greater sensitivity to cultural contexts and the meanings of leadership interaction seems appropriate.

Leadership influencing organizational culture

The relationship between leadership and culture is complex. Given the view on leadership expressed above – in which leadership deals with meanings, thinking and feelings more than has a narrow behavioural focus – leadership may even be defined as agents working through culture as the medium and target of action. Leadership is a culture-influencing activity, 'the management of meaning', as Smircich and Morgan (1982) expressed it. This does not necessarily mean that leadership creates or drastically changes culture, only that leadership is a cultural manifestation influencing other cultural manifestations, such as shared understandings of objectives, technologies and environment.

In the interplay between leadership and organizational culture, different kinds of relationships and emphasis are possible. In 'pro-leadership' management circles – such as most consultants, practitioners and some popular academics – leadership is seen as having a far-reaching impact on the cultural values and orientations of organizational members. We can then consider assumptions about 'leader-driven organizational cultures', where a leader is influential in establishing or turning around certain core ideas, values and meanings.

Leadership forming and changing culture

Some academics believe that leaders are close to the almighty and 'define the parameters of the corporate culture' (Kets de Vries, 1994, p. 78), not necessarily only consciously, but through their personality and even inner theatre, with irrational elements like primitive fantasies, feelings and other unconscious material. The founder of the organization has been the target of attention (e.g. Pettigrew, 1979; Schein, 1985). Founders of organizations – whether seen as charismatic or not– are frequently viewed as also founders of cultures or at least significant sources of a set of values which the organizational members adapt and reproduce (e.g. Schein, 1985). Founders of organizations in a sense start from scratch, having a significant influence on the particular combination of people employed, choosing the direction of the company and thus frequently being able to put their imprint upon the shared ideas, beliefs and

meanings that develop during the formative years of the company. However, after some time, a lot of complexities and other influences than founder values often undermine the impact of the latter (Martin et al., 1985).

A few studies have taken an interest in leadership in relationship to cultural change (Trice & Beyer, 1993). In these cases, the leader is viewed as somebody who exercises a more or less far-reaching influence on culture. In pop-management literature, e.g. bestsellers and management magazine articles, often focusing on top people in well-known organizations who are reported to have done something remarkable, leadership is usually about changing organizational cultures.

The strongest case for leader-driven organizational creation or change is made by adherents of charismatic leadership in organizations. In order to be candidates for the label 'charisma' a top position seems to be required, at least for those writing about it. Charismatic leadership emerges from the extraordinary influence exercised by a person, typically being able to get support for a radical vision, often in the light of a crisis, from a group of dedicated followers who are more or less spellbound by the key person. They are willing to suspend critical thinking and disbelief and develop strong faith and emotional energy in the project of the charismatic leader. Charismatic leadership often involves the creation of something new (see Conger, Chapter 7, this volume). The best-known examples are from the political and religious spheres. Ghandi, Hitler and some leaders of religious sects are good examples. In the corporate sphere, the space for charismatic persons is probably much more restricted, partly due to the sobering impact of market mechanisms and competition. Trice and Beyer (1993) do, however, refer to some examples of persons they think were or are 'genuine charismatics', including Iacocca as CEO of Chrysler in the 1980s and Steven Jobs, the founder of Apple. Alvesson (1995) studied the founders of an IT consultancy firm, who were thought of as charismatic by the followers.

Most accounts of leadership in relation to organizational culture suffer from being very thin – context, relations, interactions, complexity of reasoning and actions and the uncertainties characterizing all this are seldom seriously taken into account. Overlapping this significant weakness in the leadership field, references to culture-creating executives often exhibit a one-sidedness in the assumptions on how culture and leadership interact. In Trice and Beyer's narrative, the 'leadership' is a product of Iacocca, his reading of the corporate situation and context and his charisma. Organizational culture, to the extent that these authors treat it, is portrayed just as an object that is reformed through acts of leadership. That organizational culture may frame leadership and that any possible effect of leadership is a consequence of how people interpret and develop meaning to various examples of leadership is hardly addressed.

Most serious studies of managers trying to change cultures indicate considerable problems, as new ideas and ambitions are often reinterpreted based on existing, dominant patterns of meanings (Alvesson & Sveningsson, 2008; Hentze, 1994; Smircich, 1983c). These cases illustrate that managers with good intentions and working according to what is often recognized to be good managerial practice may fail. The in-depth meanings associated with the cultural context they operated in were never touched upon in their acts of leadership – at least they did not connect positively to this. Instead, the cultural frameworks of the subordinates led to negative responses – the meanings intended by the managers and the meanings interpreted by their subordinates went in different directions.

The cases illuminate that we need to take the meanings and interpretations of the subordinates seriously to understand leadership. Also, practical action of managers – at least when the 'voluntary' obedience of subordinates is called for (which is what leadership refers to) – calls for careful grounding in and continuous interpretation of what is on the minds of the subordinates and how they relate to the ideas and arrangement of the leader. The cases point to the need for, as well as difficulty in, grasping 'in-depth meanings', associated with the overall organizational culture context framing the outlooks and guiding the experiences of all involved.

Leaders reproducing and maintaining culture

Another way in which leadership works is through reproducing and maintaining culture. The influence is then about creating effects in a way so that there are no visible changes. As process theorists and others have emphasized, change happens all the time: people move jobs, retire, get bored, meet new people, read things in newspapers, come up with new ideas, seek variation, try to cut corners, etc. (Ladkin, 2010). New technologies, external relations, customers, etc., appear. A key challenge for organizations is to maintain stability: to socialize new employees, to keep people interested, to prevent morale from deteriorating, etc. It is not necessarily a rigid or static stability, but still working with the reproduction of basic values, assumptions, meanings and symbolism is a key aspect of organizations. Change happens all the time, but a

lot of the changes going on need to be channelled in ways so that they are in alignment with basic cultural orientations. As this is less glamorous than leadership forming or changing cultures, it has not been addressed much, but it is clear that this is probably a major part of what managers do. They can be seen as cultural maintenance workers. Managers in an IT consultancy firm felt that there were very clear guidelines for how they should work as leaders and this heavily involved influencing cultural orientations within a given framework:

> There is an opinion, a certain education that you get on how to be a manager in this company and that comes from the old leaders, the founders of the company. The leaders are seen as very important, to be a sort of cultural carrier and to be an ideal for the personnel. As a leader you must participate in all social arrangements. You should preferably be the funniest of all, you should be visible all the time and give a direction to the company and the personnel in the way you wish that the company will function, type nice parties and stories and things like that. (Alvesson, 1995, p.180)

While there is a subordination of leaders to the cultural context, the key point here is still that leadership is about having a more or less strong influence on cultural orientations in the organization.

Organizational culture influencing leadership

A change of point of departure could imply that leadership is a cultural outcome rather than, as assumed in most of the leadership literature, the opposite.

Culture defines and constrains leadership

Although senior persons may be able to put relatively strong imprints on an organization (or parts of it) during special circumstances – crises, changes in circumstances calling for basic reorientation, particularly favourable preconditions for strategic choice contingent upon market position and/or changes in the industry – it is debatable whether top executives normally can be seen as 'captains of culture'. Arguably, culture forms leadership, rather than the other way around: so is at least the case for the large majority of all people designated as or emerging as leaders. As Biggart and Hamilton (1987, p. 435) put it: 'All actors, but perhaps leaders especially, must embody the norms of their positions and persuade others in ways consistent with their normative obligations.'

In a sense, societal and business cultures set limits for the kind of managerial behaviour and arrangements that have a chance of being approved. There are subgroups in society, such as religious sects, criminal groups and others, that deviate from broadly-shared orientations and here there is space for leadership that would lead to sanctions in more 'open' contexts. Most organizations are, however, exposed to general cultural values. This is accomplished through mass media attention, through the inflow of people carrying cultural orientations picked up in education and at other workplaces and through organizational members being citizens affected by the ideas and values expressed in various extra-workplace situations. Cultures in organizations are also affected by the interaction with suppliers, customers, authorities and others. All this counteracts deviation from the shared cultural understandings within a society or an organizational field that makes cooperation possible. When Iacocca, as president for the crises-ridden Chrysler in the 1980s, reduced his income to $1 per year for some time and appeared on television with messages about the company (Trice & Beyer, 1993), this was innovative, but of course it appealed to broadly-shared values rather than challenged or changed these. What a senior manager or other kind of leader does must in a fundamental sense be perceived as in line with some broadly-shared values. As a lot of what they do is at odds with some social values (e.g. honesty, coherence, rationality, democracy, ecology-friendliness, etc.), there is balance between drawing attention to what tends to be seen as good and natural and away from those values that one's actions are not in accord with.

Culture can be seen as a repertoire of positively- and negatively-loaded meanings. To be perceived as successful, leadership involves trying to attach positive meanings to one's intentions, acts, arrangements and outcomes and steering away from people – within and outside the organization – ascribing negative meanings and beliefs to what one is up to. In this sense, cultural values are crucial to constrain the manoeuvering of people viewed as doing socially legitimate leadership.

Culture does not only limit, frame and prescribe leadership on a general, societal level but also *within* organizations. Any particular organization represents a mix of general societal and industrial expectations and ideas, and of local, more or less organization-specific ones. Organization-specific cultural ideas and meanings in various ways direct and constrain managerial behaviour and leadership. Senior managers pass on (or modify) organizational culture through being role models,

using selective recruitment to managerial positions and through sanctioning or discouraging deviations.

Organizational culture setting standards for leadership

In different organizations, not only the view of leadership but also the ideals and norms for leadership differ. The degree of impact of organizational cultures for framing and guiding leadership may vary, but there is presumably always an element of culture having an influence on managers and groups/units they are responsible for. Through selection, socialization and constraints most managers surviving in their jobs tend to adapt to some standards for what passes as acceptable and good leadership held by their subordinates, colleagues and superiors.

A recent study of junior and senior managers in a high-tech firm, populated with qualified engineers doing sophisticated and specialized work that is often difficult for senior people to understand, indicated that people generally saw leadership as of marginal importance and only needed in extraordinary circumstances, such as solving conflicts around shortage of resources or making priorities (Alvesson & Blom, 2009). The study indicated that the junior managers have a few specific requests and wants from their senior managers, but these are mainly in terms of exercising influence upwards, not downwards. They don't expect or favour much leadership directed to themselves; occasionally there is a conflict about resources or there is a need for a discussion or advice, but being led in a distinct sense by a senior is not seen as a prominent part of the relationship. Senior managers confirm this picture of the demands of their subordinates, and on the whole think this is appropriate, and act accordingly.

We see here a fairly coherent pattern of senior managers having confidence in junior managers and not being inclined to define themselves as being ambitious in exercising leadership in relation to (over) their subordinates. They see that this is in line with the wants of the subordinates, as well as with efficient organization. Their subordinates hold the same view. On the whole, they are satisfied with their superiors, mainly because they do not intervene much but are available when needed. The people involved have a shared understanding that 'leadership' (senior involvement) should be 'by invitation': i.e. that it is the junior person that initiates and frames the senior person's intervention. This can be about solving resource issues or providing advice. However, the required role of superior managers is mainly to work upwards, as 'senior subordinate managers', to higher levels. This is defined as 'leadership' by some, but is perhaps better described as exercising influence or negotiating 'upwards', as active subordinateship rather than leadership.

Although all the interviewed managers expressed their preferences for not being led much or wanting to take the initiative in involving senior people in issues as individual preferences, the homogeneity and broad consensus about this suggests that we have here a cultural phenomena: i.e. a set of meanings and understandings around minimizing leadership in the sense of managers actively leading subordinates. An engineering culture, where technical expertise and autonomy are valued, reduces the interest in leadership as typically defined (Alvesson & Blom, 2009). Also, in other knowledge-intensive or professional contexts, the template is on indirect and restricted forms of leadership (Oliver & Montgomery, 2000; Rennstam, 2007), However, in the police force, e.g. there is a stronger norm of senior people making firm decisions in at least critical and difficult situations and giving much discretion for junior people can be seen as an example of bad leadership (Bryman et al., 1996).

Leadership as driven by followers

Organizational cultures are seldom homogeneous – most organizations exhibit a variety of subcultures that overlap and interact in complicated ways (Alvesson, 2002; Martin, 2002). It is common that managers are located in between values and norms held by senior managers and those promoted by their subordinates. 'Top management' culture – sometimes seen as corporate culture – and 'functional cultures' (associated with production, R&D, personnel or marketing) frequently differ and may conflict, and here leadership may partly be a matter of negotiation between different kinds of normative frameworks and views on corporate reality. Leadership is not necessarily mainly about people exercising influence top down. Middle-level managers may not have senior people as the major source of inspiration and control for their own leadership.

Also, subordinates have a strong impact on how leadership is shaped, although this can vary between countries and between sectors and organizations. If we disregard the use of 'pure' power – breaking the wills of people through the use of the whip (threats of being fired, etc.) is perhaps outside most definitions of leadership – leadership means having some kind of appeal to people, to their hearts and minds. Bullying may be used by leaders, but needs to be seen as acceptable and reasonable by followers (Kärreman, 2011). Visions, instructions, suggestions, goals

and constructions of corporate reality must be perceived as legitimate and meaningful. The actions of the leader must then be fine-tuned to the frameworks and norms of those that are to be influenced. In this sense, the subordinates as a collective – sharing certain cultural ideas – 'decide' what works in terms of leadership. This of course does not mean that the leader is totally subordinated to a given set of orientations or is forced to adapt to a specific style and just reproduce a given set of meanings and ideas. The leader can change these, but gradually and must (in order to do so) proceed from an appreciation of people holding certain ideas, values and preferences. The leader is involved in the negotiation rather than the imposing of new or orientations on people. The importance of the leader being seen as personalizing the shared characteristics of group members – exhibiting the prototypicality of the group – is acknowledged by social identity theorists (e.g. Haslam, 2004; Hogg et al., 2003), but this approach does not consider a broader and richer understanding of the meanings, beliefs and values of followers, typically going beyond specific small-group characteristics.

Identity and culture are sometimes used in overlapping and confusing ways, in particular when identity refers to the organizational level. Often, identity mainly refers to personal, individual issues (self-identity, social identity, identification), whereas culture refers to socially shared meanings and ideas. Most aspects of culture have only indirect consequences for identity constructions, as they do not primarily refer to people's identities. Organizational identity is somewhat connected to the organizational culture theme, as it relates to the realm of how people think, feel and value, and culture is an important aspect of what shapes identity. Hatch and Schultz (2002, p. 384) see culture as being relatively more easily placed 'in the conceptual domains of the contextual, tacit and emergent than is identity which, when compared with culture, appears to be more textual, explicit and instrumental'. In addition, while identity refers to ideas on how people in an organization define what is distinct and unique about the organization, culture covers broader terrain, including meanings and beliefs about a wider set of issues of more indirect relevance for self-definition.

The significance of followers' orientations and (lack of) receptiveness to leader-driven ideas means that leadership impact, including efforts to accomplish cultural change, tend to be gradual, partial and an outcome of social processes in which a group of subordinates have as much if not more to say than the leader.

This can be illustrated by the case of a US coastguard officer who found his men – mainly college graduates with middle-class backgrounds whose expectations, interests and motives were at odds with the routines and lack of discretion of military life – bored and negative. Instead of trying to impose military discipline in a traditional way, he made a deal with his men about more discretion and certain liberties in exchange for more positive behaviour (Wilkins, referred to in Trice & Beyer, 1993). The case illustrates, among other things, how the values and orientations of a group of subordinates trigger a change in 'leadership' (if this is the right label in the case) so that it resonates better with their values and meanings. In a Swedish study, managers thought that their most important source of feedback came from their subordinates, indicating that these may be a stronger influencing group than their own managers acting as leaders (Chef, 2006). Collective forces are thus central in organizations and they must be understood frequently in terms of culture (but can hardly be reduced to this), as 'behind' any response or act of not only leaders trying to lead but followers guiding leaders and responding selectively to leader acts we find the (cultural) context.

have a hierarchy above themselves (Laurent, 1978). There is a wish among many people to ascribe strong impact to leaders, reflecting a need to see somebody as responsible for different outcomes, good or bad (Meindl, 1995; Pfeffer, 1977). This fits the self-image of many managers and reinforces their status and claims for high wages, prestige and authority in companies and society. Management writers, teachers and consultants will probably find that their market would be smaller and less sympathetic if they should argue for the significance of other factors than management and leaders, as well as the complexity and ambiguity of how to account for performances. Generally, the strong faith in leadership, the attribution of causal powers to it and the heroization of leaders may be seen as interesting cultural manifestations that reflect socially invented 'truths' and are worthy of investigation.

Sometimes, external dependencies and structural restrictions for leadership are noticed, but the phenomenon of 'cultural subordinancy' has not been treated seriously in leadership research. Leadership as the adaptation, mechanical reproduction, reinforcement, creative variation and/or of rejuvenation of dominating cultural orientations in organizations is a potentially fruitful line of thinking.

Comment

It seems likely that most people expected to exercise leadership in their jobs are much more strongly influenced by organizational culture than they are involved in actively producing it. Apart from structural conditions (job task, resources, position, formal rights, etc.), which to some extent are cultural manifestations and have consequences through the cultural meaning attached to them, the cultural context guides the manager as to how leadership should be carried out. This is done, e.g. through prescribing that 'leadership' goes beyond relying solely on formal authority, and involves influencing the ideas, values and orientations of subordinates on how they should interact with managers, e.g. in terms of the appropriate degree of subordination.

The 'culture-driven' nature of leadership is neglected in most of the literature and in talk by management gurus and practitioners. The cultural dimension has traditionally been neglected in leadership research. More significant, however, are the ideological overtones of a lot of talk on leadership. There is a broad tendency, in leadership research and among practitioners, to stress the manager as a superior, unidirectionally acting on – rather than interacting with – subordinates and to neglect that almost all managers are also subordinates and thus

SUMMARY AND CONCLUSIONS

A cultural understanding of leadership calls for appreciating local shared meanings associated with the context of leadership relations and acts. Leadership can be defined as about influencing the construction of reality – the ideas, beliefs and interpretations of what and how things can and should be done, in the light of what the world looks like. A cultural understanding of leadership calls for the nuanced interpretation of the relationship and context of interaction between superior and subordinate. But not all aspects of this interaction are best understood as leadership. However, managers always, in some way or another, 'manage' culture. Even strongly bureaucratic and number-counting managers reinforce rules- and measurement-focused cultures and thus affect thinking, feeling and values. Also non-managerial organizational members contribute to cultural formation/ reproduction. They do so typically, as individuals, from weaker positions, but collectives, groups and communities are clearly often stronger than individuals in managerial or executive positions.

A cultural view on leadership must balance between academic a priori definitions of leadership and openness to the meanings of the people being studied. It is important to be somewhat careful in imposing a particular definition on leadership and instead be open to the meanings ascribed to 'leadership' by the natives. Interesting themes then become when, how and why do the people in an organization talk about 'leadership'? (I presume here that people in organizations do take an interest in leadership, but this needs to be investigated and one should be open to the possibility that 'leadership' is not an important or interesting category in many cultures.) What meanings (if any) – coherent, varying or contradictory – are expressed around 'leadership' and what particular acts and arrangements are seen as 'leadership'? What hopes, fears and expectations are there? How do people react to various styles and acts seen as expressing leadership? What is perceived as leadership? Who (if any) is seen as a 'leader' – and not merely as a manager or an administrator? Which metaphors for leadership seem to inform understanding of this phenomenon: commander, coach, visionary? Interpreting the local meaning of leadership offers a route to an understanding of organizational culture and vice versa.

Even if the emphasis in leadership theory should not go so far as to 'delegate' the meaning of leadership altogether to the people in various organizations, but to retain some theoretical idea of what leadership refers to, it is a good idea to put less emphasis on the leader and what he 'objectively' does and more on how people relate and respond to acts of managers. The effect-triggering element in leadership is less what the leader does per se than how subordinates perceive, interpret and react on the leaders' acts. One and the same behaviour may, e.g. be read as 'authoritative' and 'capable of making a decision' or 'authoritarian' and 'outdated', with very different implications for legitimacy, trust and motivation on behalf of the subordinates. Of course, such interpretations can be understood at the narrow level of leader-follower interactions, but the cultural context guiding these interpretations needs to be considered. This context includes both organizational and societal elements.

Organizational culture influences leadership. As leadership is normally not carried out from a socio-cultural point zero, but always takes place in a context of already-developed meaning patterns – those of the leader and those of others being part of occupational and organizational communities – there is always a strong element of cultural determination of leadership. Promotion is often dependent on being perceived as well adapted to dominant orientations of senior managers, which means that managers typically fit into corporate culture and tend to carry rather than deviate from dominant patterns (Jackall, 1988). Most leadership is culture-driven in the sense that shared beliefs and norms inform the manager how to act. Culture here may refer to the organizational level, but also societal, industrial and occupational cultures may be central. These are mediated in the organizational context. Leadership is then better seen as 'within' rather than 'outside' culture. Within culture-driven leadership, the skilful manager may exercise considerable influence. Cultural constraints are seldom very strict, but may give rather broad parameters. Sometimes the acts of managers and informal leaders also more independently shape elements of culture. More significant examples of culture-shaping leadership (leadership-driven cultures) are rare, but in certain situations, particularly when organizations are founded and during major crises, where a significant portion of key personnel are replaced, the situation is more open for the reframing of ideas, beliefs and meanings.

The role of leadership in organizational change is often emphasized. Sometimes, leadership – in opposition to management – is viewed as being about creating change. This is frequently viewed as an outcome of leadership, and, without new forms of leadership, organizational change is difficult if not impossible to accomplish. Organizational change is not, however, only or mainly about letting a superior 'leader' loose in order to transform organizational culture. In the culture literature there is a peculiar emphasis on the highly extraordinary situations of planned cultural change in which top leaders are treated as if they were 'standing above' corporate culture. The normal leadership situation with regards to culture is far less spectacular and grandiose. As leadership is a cultural phenomenon – and any act that is not interpreted as meaningful will lead to negative responses (confusion, resistance, loss of legitimacy, reluctant obedience) – cultural change rather means the cultural redefinition of leadership. Cultural change, to the extent that it is related to leadership at all, includes and brings about new forms of leadership. The relationship between leadership and other cultural manifestations is then not 'external' or causal, but intertwined (Alvesson, 2002).

The leadership of managers (and even more so of informal leaders) is typically strongly constrained by, and draws upon, the cultural and ideological context(s) of the organization. New ideas and initiatives are more likely to succeed if they are broadly in line with dominant values and understandings. Recognizing that there are exceptions, leaders are normally better understood as 'transmitters' than as 'masters' of culture. Managers may more or less intentionally, more or less skilfully, act as 'cultural engineers'. They are typically significantly more influential in the ongoing reproduction and revisions of cultural meanings than other organizational members.

Culture is often viewed as strongly affected or even produced or shaped by the leadership of (in particular) the founders, but to some extent, and under certain conditions, also of senior managers, at least if they are 'charismatic' persons and/or engage in transformational leadership. This is probably the most popular view on the organizational culture – leadership connection. Leaders are said to work *on* culture rather than to work *within* culture. But in the large majority of all cases, leadership is better understood as taking place within and as an outcome of the cultural context, although (only) under extraordinary circumstances leaders may transcend parts of existing cultural patterns or even contribute to the creation or radical change of culture. Also, in such cases, cultural context and cultural constraints must be considered. A precondition for changing culture is to connect to it.

REFERENCES

Alvesson, M. (1995) *Management of Knowledge-Intensive Companies.* Berlin: de Gruyter.

Alvesson, M. (2002) *Understanding Organizational Culture.* London: Sage.

Alvesson, M. (2004). Organizational culture and discourse. In D Grant et al. (eds) *Handbook of Organizational Discourse.* London: Sage.

Alvesson, M. & Berg, P.O. (1992) *Corporate Culture and Organizational Symbolism.* Berlin/New York: de Gruyter.

Alvesson, M. & Blom, M. (2009) Less leadership? Working paper, Dept of Business Administration, Lund University.

Alvesson, M. & Spicer, A. (eds) (2011) *Metaphors We Lead By. Understanding Leadership in the Real World.* London: Routledge.

Alvesson, M. & Sveningsson, S. (2003) The good visions, the bad micro-management and the ugly ambiguity: contradictions of (non-)leadership in a knowledge-intensive company. *Organization Studies,* 24(6): S961–988.

Alvesson, M. & Sveningsson, S. (2008) *Changing Organizational Culture. Cultural Change Work in Progress.* London: Routledge.

Antonakis, J., Ciancilo, A.T., & Sternberg, R.J. (eds) (2004) Introduction. In J. Antonakis, A.T. Ciancilo, & R.J. Srenberg (eds), *The Nature of Leadership.* Thousand Oaks, CA: Sage.

Barker, R. (1997) How can we train leaders if we don't know what leadership is? *Human Relations,* 50: 343–362.

Biggart, N.W. & Hamilton, G.G. (1987) An institutional theory of leadership. *Journal of Applied Behavioural Science,* 23: 429–441.

Borowsky, R. (ed.) (1994) *Assessing Cultural Anthropology.* New York: McGraw-Hill.

Bryman, Al., Stephens, M., & Campo, C. (1996) The importance of context: qualitative research and the study of leadership. *The Leadership Quarterly,* 7(3): 353–370.

Carroll, B. & Levy, L. (2008) Defaulting to management: leadership defined by what it is not. *Organization,* 15(1): 75–96.

Collinson, D. (2006) Rethinking followership: a post-structural analysis of follower identities. *The Leadership Quarterly,* 17: 179–189.

Chef (2006) Bäst på allt och aldrig nöjd. ('Best on everything but never happy') Stockholm: Kairos Futures.

Den Hartog, D. & Dickson, M. (2004) Leadership and culture. In J. Antonakis, A.T. Ciancilo, & R.J. Sternberg (eds), *The Nature of Leadership.* Thousand Oaks, CA: Sage.

Fairhurst, G. (2001) Dualisms in leadership research. In F. Jablin, et al. (eds), *Handbook of Organizational Communication.* Thousand Oaks, CA: Sage.

Fairhurst, G. (2009) Two journeys into the context of leadership: an alternative, discursive route. *Human Relations,* 6(11): 1607–1633.

Fondas, N. (1997) Feminization unveiled: management qualities in contemporary writings. *Academy of Management Review,* 22: 257–282.

Foucault, M. (1977) *Discipline and Punish: The Birth of the Prison.* New York: Random House.

Foucault, M. (1980) *Power/Knowledge.* New York: Pantheon.

Geertz, C. (1973) *The interpretation of culture.* New York: Basic Books.

Gronn, P. (2002) Distributed leadership as a unit of analysis. *The Leadership Quarterly,* 13: 423–451.

Haslam, A. (2004) *Psychology in Organizations.* London: Sage.

Hatch, M. J. & Schultz, M. (2002). The dynamics of organizational identity. *Human Relations,* 55: 989–1018.

Hentze, H. (1994) My greatest failure. In D. Adam-Smith & A. Peacock (eds), *Cases in Organizational Behaviour.* London: Pitman.

Hofstede, G., et al. (1990) Measuring organizational cultures: a qualitative and quantitative study across twenty cases. *Administrative Science Quarterly,* 35: 286–316.

Hogg, M., Martin, R., & Weeden, K. (2003) Leader–member relations and social identity. In D. van Knippenberg, and M. Hogg (eds), *Leadership and Power.* London: Sage.

House, R. & Aditay R. (1997) The social scientific study of leadership: quo vadis? *Journal of Management,* 23(3): 409–473.

Jackall, R. (1988) *Moral Mazes.* Oxford: Oxford University Press.

Jackson, B. & Parry, K. (2008) *A Very Short, Fairly Interesting and Reasonably Cheap Book about Studying Leadership.* London: Sage.

Jones, A (2005) The anthropology of leadership: culture and corporate leadership in the American South. *Leadership,* 1: 259–278.

Kärreman, D. (2011) The leader as bully. In M. Alvesson & A. Spicer (eds), *Metaphors We Lead By. Understanding Leadership in the Real World.* London: Routledge.

Kelly, S. (2008) Leadership: a categorical mistake? *Human Relations,* 61: 763–782.

Kets de Vries, M. (1994) The leadership mystique. *Academy of Management Executive*, 8(3): 73–89.

Kotter, J.P. (1985) *The Leadership Factor*. New York: Free Press.

Kunda, G. (1992) *Engineering Culture: Control and Commitment in a High-Tech Corporation*. Philadelphia, PA: Temple University Press.

Ladkin, D. (2010) *Rethinking Leadership: A New Look at Old Leadership Questions*. Cheltenham: Edward Elgar.

Laurent, A. (1978) Managerial subordinancy: a neglected aspect of organizational hierarchy. *Academy of Management Review*, 3: 220–230.

Lipman-Blumen, J. (1992) Connective leadership: female leadership styles in the 21st-century workplace, *Sociological Perspectives*, 35(1): 183–203.

Martin, J. (2002) *Organizational Culture*. Thousand Oaks, CA: Sage.

Martin, J. Sitkin, S., & Boehm, M. (1985) Founders and the elusiveness of a cultural legacy. In P.J. Frost, et al. (eds), *Organizational Culture*. Beverly Hills, CA: Sage.

Meyerson, D. & Martin, J. (1987) Cultural change: an integration of three different views. *Journal of Management Studies*, 24: 623–648.

Meindl, J. (1995) The romance of leadership as a follower-centric theory: a social constructionist approach. *The Leadership Quarterly*, 6: 329–341.

Oliver, A. & Montgomery, K. (2000) Creating a hybrid organizational form from parental blueprints: the emergence and evolution of knowledge firms. *Human Relations*, 53: 33–56.

Parker, M. (2000) *Organizational Culture and Identity*. London: Sage.

Pearce, C. & Conger, J. (eds) (2003) *Shared Leadership: Reforming the Hows and Whys of Leadership*. Thousand Oaks, CA: Sage.

Peters, T.J. & Waterman, R.H. (1982) *In Search of Excellence*. New York: Harper and Row.

Pettigrew, A. (1979) On studying organizational cultures. *Administrative Science Quarterly*, 24: 570–581.

Pfeffer, J (1977) The ambiguity of leadership. *Academy of Management Review*, 2(1): 104–112.

Pfeffer, J. (1981) Management as symbolic action: the creation and maintenance of organizational paradigms. In L.L. Cummings & B.M. Staw (eds), *Research in Organizational Behaviour*, vol.3. Greenwich, CT: JAI Press.

Prasad, P. (1997) The Protestant ethic and the myth of the frontier: cultural imprints, organizational structuring and workplace diversity. In P. Prasad et al. (eds), *Managing the Organizational Melting Pot*. Thousand Oaks, CA: Sage.

Rennstam, J. (2007) *Engineering Work*. PhD thesis. Lund: Lund Business Press.

Schein, E.H. (1985) *Organizational Culture and Leadership*. San Francisco: Jossey-Bass.

Smircich, L. (1983a) Concepts of culture and organizational analysis. *Administrative Science Quarterly*, 28: 339–358.

Smircich, L. (1983b) Studying organizations as cultures. In G. Morgan (ed), *Beyond Method Strategies for Social Research*. Beverly Hills, CA: Sage.

Smircich, L (1983c) Organizations as shared meanings. In L.R. Pondy, et al. (eds), *Organizational Symbolism*. Greenwich, CT: JAI Press.

Smircich, L. & Morgan, G. (1982) Leadership: the management of meaning. *Journal of Applied Behavioural Science*, 18: 257–273.

Trice, H.M. & Beyer, J.M. (1993) *The Culture of Work Organizations*. Englewood Cliffs, NJ: Prentice Hall.

Uhl-Bien, M. (2006) Relational leadership theory: exploring the social process of leadership and organizing. *The Leadership Quarterly*, 17: 654–676.

van Knippenberg, D. & Hogg, M. (eds) (2003) *Leadership and Power*. London: Sage.

Weick, K.E. (1985) The significance of corporate culture. In P. Frost et al. (eds), *Organizational Culture*. Beverly Hills, CA: Sage.

Western, S. (2008) *Leadership: A Critical Text*. Thousand Oaks, Sage.

Yukl, G. (1989) Managerial leadership: a review of theory and research. *Journal of Management*, 15: 215–289.

Yukl, G. (1999). An evaluation of conceptual weaknesses in transformational and charismatic leadership theories. *The Leadership Quarterly*, 10: 285–305.

Zaleznik, A. (1977) Managers and leaders: are they different? *Harvard Business Review*, May–June: 67–78.

12

Cross-Cultural Leadership Revisited

Eric Guthey and Brad Jackson

INTRODUCTION

No scholarly handbook on leadership research would seem complete without a chapter on the relationship between leadership and cultural context. Like any of several expert reviews already published on the subject, such a chapter would start out with the observation that much of the extant research on leadership does not take the influence of cultural context sufficiently into account. It would cite the efforts of several prominent leadership scholars to correct this oversight. And it would point out that over the past 10 years, the concerns and insights of cross-cultural research have been pushed closer to the centre of leadership studies by the very ambitious research project entitled GLOBE (Global Leadership and Organizational Behaviour Effectiveness).

A responsible handbook chapter on culture and leadership would also point out some of the weaknesses of this kind of research, and review some of the very trenchant critiques that have been delivered of the cross-cultural methodologies that have been applied to leadership. But such a chapter would conclude that, on balance, the GLOBE study in particular stands up to such criticisms quite well, because it imports new standards of breadth, rigor and reflexivity to the field of cross-cultural studies.

In the following pages we do our best to honour the conventions of this well-established genre by presenting our own review of the most important research on culture and leadership. But we also want to step outside of this generic frame to point out something important that previous handbook chapters and literature reviews have largely overlooked. For all of its insight, and for all of its methodological rigor, academic research on cross-cultural leadership has failed to recognize or to take into account the significant disconnect created by conventional attempts to capture the effects of cultural context on leadership styles and practices. To put it more directly, 'cross-cultural leadership' has become a contradiction in terms. That is to say, the central idea in the vast majority of cross-cultural research – the idea of culture and its determining influence – is at odds with the notion of leadership itself. This requires some explanation.

As one would expect, the chapters in this handbook define leadership in many different ways. But, however you define leadership, it is not an inert or passive concept. Charismatic leadership, servant leadership, quiet leadership, all of these approaches involve in some way or another the notion of *taking initiative, inspiring commitment, mobilizing action, promoting legitimacy,* or *exerting influence*. The GLOBE project, for example, defines leadership as 'the ability of an individual to influence, motivate, and enable others to contribute toward the effectiveness and success of the organizations of which they are members (House et al., 1999: 13).

Culture, by contrast, has come to mean the opposite. The near-exclusive focus in cross-cultural research on leadership is the manner in which leaders *are influenced,* that is, the manner in which they are shaped and molded, in what is often described in a very deterministic manner, by the constraints of the cultural context in which they find themselves. In just this manner, for example, the GLOBE project seeks to measure and to predict 'the impact of specific cultural variables on leadership and organizational processes' (House et al., 1999: 11).

This kind of approach is largely an inheritance of the cross-cultural research paradigm developed and promoted most extensively by Geert Hofstede. As Galit Ailon and Gideon Kunda so effectively describe it, Hofstede's cross-cultural differences model hinges on the insistence that 'national identity' imprints a value-based and cognitively constraining 'culture' or collective 'software' in people's minds, and that these cultural constraints 'manifest themselves in organizations through stubbornly distinctive behavioral patterns that hinder the global ambitions of management' (Ailon-Souday & Kunda, 2003: 1074). For all of its many conceptual weaknesses, that notion has set the terms of academic debates about culture in management, organization and leadership circles for several decades. Galit Ailon has delivered the most substantial of a number of very trenchant critiques of the assumptions undergirding Hofstede's work (Ailon, 2008; Ailon-Souday & Kunda, 2003), but it remains unclear whether any such critique has had much impact upon mainstream thinking about cross-cultural leadership. The combined academic/industrial juggernaut of cross-cultural research and intercultural training marches inexorably onwards, often reducing important questions about what culture really is and how it works to methodological squabbles about how exactly to measure with statistical validity the influence that national culture exerts on the ways that leaders behave.

It would be foolish to argue that there are no constraints placed on leadership initiatives, prerogatives and behaviors. Culture is certainly one of these constraints. So are laws, regulations, governance structures, social norms, organizational politics and procedures, and the preconceptions others share about what leadership is and how it should function. But in its enthusiasm to measure how cultural factors influence leadership, cross-cultural research has generally neglected to consider how leadership influences these factors right back – i.e. how the dynamics of leadership shape and determine the cultures that supposedly shape and influence leadership. In a variety of different ways, in fact, both leaders and followers exert considerable, sustained and often very strategically intentional influence over the contextual factors that constrain them. And the two-way nature of this influence relationship between leadership and culture calls the assumptions undergirding much of the research on leadership across cultures into question.

In this chapter, therefore, we look at the field of cross-cultural leadership with an eye toward bringing this problem to the fore. We review two of the most influential pan-global studies that have attempted to systematically measure the differences in culture and the influences that these have on leadership practices and preferences. We also review the main criticisms leveled against these types of studies and their methodological approaches. As we point out, the emotionally charged, often antagonistic and sometimes entertaining nature of the exchanges between scholars on both sides of these methodological divides have distracted attention away from the fact that, at the end of the day, most of them share very similar – and increasingly outdated – assumptions about culture and how it functions. We conclude by highlighting research that pushes the discussion of the relationship between leadership and culture in new and productive directions, away from deterministic generalizations about national culture and its influence, toward a recognition of the very significant ways in which leadership *and* followership shape and influence cultures – and contribute significantly to the shaping of national cultural identities – rather than simply the other way around.

CROSS-CULTURAL LEADERSHIP: HOFSTEDE'S LEGACY

The continuing expansion of an expatriate workforce assigned to the far corners of an increasingly globalized world has confronted practitioners and scholars with the imperative to study and understand the dynamics of leadership in various cultural contexts. Those on the front lines of this expansion often experience 'culture shock' as they set about trying to adjust their workplace behaviors and practices to the different set of dominant norms and expectations of the host society in which they find themselves (Frederick & de la Fuente Rodriguez, 1994; Harris, R. Moran, & S. Moran, 2004). The expatriate manager's need to grapple with the fundamentals of intercultural interactions, combined with the sponsoring organization's need to successfully manage international assignments, continues to drive the demand for cross-cultural leadership theory and skill development.

Not surprisingly, these developments have helped inspire a whole genre of practical guides and handbooks for managerial expatriates. These sources most often provide laundry lists of specific cultural do's and don'ts, ranging from the strategically vital to the trivial sometimes rather silly – how to greet prospective business partners, how to exchange business cards, how to negotiate eye contact, how to properly conduct lunch. The highly successful *Culture Shock!* series of books exemplifies this genre, with its promise to guide 'the reader through the mindscapes of a country's psyche, explaining the do's and don'ts, social customs and traditions, business and social etiquette.' Other books provide colourful case studies from a number of different national contexts. They provide warnings about the misunderstanding and transgressions that can occur when managers try to impose their ways of doing things in a foreign land (Hickson & Pugh, 1995; Hooker, 2003). And they recommend that foreigners invited to dinner at the home of a potential joint venture partner in Europe, for example, make sure to bring an uneven number of flowers, although 6 or 12 flowers are 'OK,' as long as you don't bring red carnations to someone who's not a 'good Socialist' (Gesteland, 2006: 91).

The scholar who laid down what many still consider the immutable laws of cultural differences, and who paved the way for the rise of what we might call the cross-cultural academic/industrial complex, is the aforementioned Geert Hofstede, a Dutch academic whose work has attracted equal parts admiration and critique. Ask any executive about the importance of culture, and more often than not the only name that comes up is Hofstede. Hofstede has vigorously defended his claim to the admiration he has received over the years by publishing stern rebuttals of the critiques leveled at his work (Hofstede, 2002a, 2002b, 2006, 2009). He has repeatedly charged that those who criticize his writings do not understand the basics of cross-cultural research, that they are ill-prepared because they have not actually read his books, or if they have, that they handle data like 'elephants in the cross-cultural china shop' (Hofstede, 2002a: 172).

Hofstede defines culture as 'the collective programming of the mind which distinguishes the members of one group or category from another' (Hofstede, 1994). This definition, and indeed the main body of Hofstede's work, refers primarily to national culture, because he insists that it is more deeply rooted than organizational culture, and much more determinative of how people behave. Although he notes that national culture is something that is learned and not inherited, he maintains that it is learned very early, and never forgotten. According to Hofstede, such deeply rooted cultural identities lie somewhere between an individual's unique personality and basic human nature, from which position they function as what he calls the 'software of the mind.' Hofstede identifies several levels of culture that he likens to the concentric layers of an onion. The outer layers consist of symbols,

heroes and rituals, and the inner layer consists of core values and assumptions about human nature.

Hofstede has championed the investigation of the culture onion by means of surveys, and his own foundational survey remains undeniably the most influential global study of cultural differences in the workplace to date. As Brendan McSweeney has pointed out, Hofstede didn't actually design or administer the survey with the specific end of measuring culture in mind. Rather, he participated in a consulting project for IBM between 1967 and 1973, surveying attitudes among approximately 100,000 IBM employees from 66 countries around the world, and only later extracted his data from that pre-existing bank of collection of responses (McSweeney, 2002b). McSweeney also points out, in the decades since that study was conducted, Hofstede 'has never acknowledged any significant errors or weaknesses in that research,' and has spent much of his subsequent career publishing 'robust, at times aggressive, defences of his 1980 methods and findings' (McSweeney, 2002a: 90).

On the basis of the original IBM data, Hofstede singled out 20 of the survey's 150 questions to create four value dimensions on which to measure and compare the 49 national cultures in the study. Hofstede's original dimensions were as follows:

Individualism/collectivism Individualist cultures have looser social frameworks in which people are supposed to take care of themselves, their own interests and their close families only. Collectivist cultures have a tighter social framework in which people distinguish between in-groups and out-groups. In collectivist societies, leaders must keep the good of the in-group uppermost in their minds. Followers within individualist societies are more likely to tolerate leaders who look after their own interests and, in fact, are highly prized for their unique achievements. In a similar vein, Schwartz (1999) has distinguished between societies in which people are expected to be either autonomous or embedded in the group.

Hierarchy, status and power distance Hofstede defined power distance as the extent to which a society accepted and embraced the fact that power in institutions and organizations was distributed unequally. In cultures with high power distance, authoritarian leadership and an autocratic decision-making are more likely to be accepted and expected. In more egalitarian cultures, followers will expect to have a greater say, and will tend to expect an open and more participatory style from their leaders. Another issue related to power and status arises from the question of whether status in a particular society should be based on achievement or ascription (Parsons & Shils, 1951). Achievement-oriented societies tend to accord status based on what people have accomplished rather than their age, seniority or lineage.

Uncertainty avoidance This dimension describes a society's reliance on social norms and procedures to alleviate the unpredictability of the future. Leaders in countries with high levels of uncertainty avoidance will endeavour to ameliorate the threat of uncertainty and ambiguity by establishing formal rules, emphasizing their technical expertise and showing little tolerance for deviant ideas and behaviours. If they wish to bring about change, leaders will have to do it within the existing system. Leaders in societies that are more accepting of uncertainty will have to be more flexible and willing to champion change by violating organizational rules and regulations (Shane, Venkataraman & MacMillan, 1995).

Masculinity/femininity This is the dimension over which Hofstede has encountered the most criticism because it covers too many topics and because it creates semantic confusion by alluding to gender (which is, in turn, a culturally produced construct). He argued that, in 'masculine' societies, the dominant social values stressed the virtues of assertiveness and toughness, the acquisition of money and material possessions. In 'feminine' societies, by contrast, values such as warm social relationships and quality of life are stressed.

Long- versus short-term orientation After the publication of his original study, Hofstede acknowledged the existence of a fifth dimension of culture, originally labeled 'Confucian dynamism,' but later renamed 'long- versus short-term orientation' (Hofstede & Bond, 1988). Long-term orientation cultures, typified by China, see truth as a relative phenomenon, have a pragmatic acceptance of change and emphasize the value of perseverance, thrift and saving for tomorrow. Societies with short-term orientations place great stock in absolute truth, have a high concern for normative rationality, quick results and the need to live for today.

Hofstede asserts that his dimensions have been so extensively adopted and validated that they have achieved the paradigmatic status of what Thomas Kuhn once termed 'normal science.' At times he has defended them against charges of reification and essentialism by pointing out that they are merely constructs for helping us understand the social world. But he has insisted in the same breath that his dimensions 'describe basic

dilemmas that every human society faces,' and that they should be identified in 'any thorough and professionally executed study of cultures across societies' (Hofstede, 2006: 895).

EXTENDING HOFSTEDE'S MODEL

Additional dimensions

Despite Hofstede's confidence in the near-universal validity of his dimensions, scholars have responded to them in different ways. Many, of course, have simply adopted Hofstede's dimensions wholesale and used them to conduct further investigation. Studies of this sort make up the main body of cross-cultural research, with the measuring and comparing of cultural dimensions serving to fill out the pages of academic journals, masters theses and consulting reports the world over. Other scholars have sought to add to or modify Hofstede's dimensions in order to fine-tune the picture of culture they provide. As Dickson et al. point out, for example, it has become commonplace in leadership studies to expand the individualism/collectivism dimension by distinguishing between horizontal (or egalitarian) and vertical (or hierarchical/competitive) forms of both individualism and collectivism (Dickson, Den Hartog, & Mitchelson, 2003).

Still other scholars choose to develop completely different sets of dimensions for measuring culture. Several of these alternative dimensional constructs have considerable saliency for the study and conduct of leadership. Edward Hall distinguishes between societies with 'low context languages' (English, German and the Nordic languages, for example), which emphasize the need to be direct, clear and explicit in communication, and societies with 'high context languages' (such as Japanese and Arabic), which are less direct, and more ambiguous and subtle (Hall, 1990). These latter societies place a high premium on the ability to skilfully 'manage face' (Ting-Toomey, 1988), though, in reality, all leaders and followers should show a healthy concern for impression management wherever they are located.

Trompenaars and Hampden-Turner (1997) distinguish between 'affective societies,' in which people are encouraged to show their emotions, and 'neutral countries,' where people are encouraged to keep their emotions in check. They also distinguish between 'internal control cultures' and 'external control cultures.' The former, typified by the United States, have a dominating and controlling attitude toward nature. The latter, typified by several Middle Eastern countries, are more at ease with natural shifts and cycles of nature. In a similar vein, Schwartz (1999) describes 'mastery cultures,' in which people are encouraged to master change and exploit the environment in order to achieve their goals. In these cultures, leaders need to be dynamic, competitive and strongly oriented toward achievement. In 'harmony cultures,' by contrast, people are encouraged to understand and integrate with their natural environment, rather than change or exploit it. In such contexts, leaders presumably need to take a more holistic view and try to understand the social and environmental implications of organizational actions.

Critiquing Hofstede's dimensions

Some scholars have subjected themselves to Hofstede's withering commentary by daring to criticize both his general approach and specific research design. The most strident among these critics has been Brendan McSweeney, whose substantial critique, and subsequently lively exchange with Hofstede in the pages of the journal *Human Relations*, has probably done less to discredit Hofstede's research strategies than it has to highlight the rhetorical strategies Hofstede employs to defend them. McSweeney could not possibly understand culture, Hofstede concluded in response, because he was an accountant, not an anthropologist, and unfamiliar even with the most basic sociological practice of statistical inference to boot (McSweeney 2002a, 2002b; Hofstede, 2002b).

But it is not only accountants who have criticized the Hofstede model. Some have pointed out the weakness of basing a survey of culture entirely on attitude questionnaires (Tayeb, 1996), with too few questions (Rosenzweig, 1994) asked of employees from just one company (Robinson, 1983). Others have pointed out that not all of the dimensions are well-grounded in theory (e.g. masculinity/femininity and uncertainty avoidance) and that they contain several anomalies (e.g. Trompenaars and Hampden-Turner, 1997). Moreover, by the mid-1990s scholars had begun to complain that the IBM data were becoming rather outdated (Mead, 1994). In a more recent show of support for this criticism, a study of students from 11 European nations using the same dimensions as Hofstede, revealed a significant convergence of national values, with gender becoming a more significant differentiator that national origin for masculinity, uncertainty avoidance and individualism–collectivism (Gooderham & Nordhaug, 2002). In his brief but characteristically dismissive reply, Hofstede referred to the authors' lack of basic statistical skills, and concluded that theirs was 'not a serious study' (Hofstede, 2001).

Galit Ailon has provided perhaps the most intellectually challenging critique of the conventional cross-cultural paradigm to date. Performing what amounts to a postmodern and postcolonial reading of Hofstede's *Cultures Consequences,* Ailon uses Hofstede's own dimensions to subject his work to a value-orientation test of its own design. By means of this 'mirroring' strategy, Ailon raises concerns about the relationship between cross-cultural studies and the representation of the foreign 'other,' about scholarly reflexivity, and about the supposedly objective nature of scientific research (Ailon, 2008). She concludes that scholars should devote more energy to examining the cultural politics of 'why and how difference comes to carry particular baggages of meaning by various kinds of global discourses, including cross-cultural research itself' (Ailon, 2008: 900). Her response to Hofstede's trademark defence of his dimensions (Hofstede demanded: 'Did she read my book or didn't she?' and 'Why me?') graciously extends her critique to herself, and concludes that 'we must become reflexive of how the things we say about "others" are often bound up with what we want to see in ourselves' (Ailon, 2009: 573; Hofstede, 2009: 571).

In light of these kinds of criticisms, Osland et al. (2000) have suggested that Hofstede's framework is best understood as a form of 'sophisticated stereotyping.' Although a dimensional model does not cast negative attributions in the manner of commonplace stereotyping, they argue, it still limits and constrains the way we look at and appreciate the complexity of other cultures. This weakness becomes very apparent in the face of 'cultural paradoxes,' which Osland et al. define as behavior that violates our preconceptions of what we think any given culture is like. They suggest that if we want to become more competent intercultural leaders, we need to move beyond such sophisticated stereotyping by using sensemaking to purposely seek out evidence that challenges our cultural stereotypes and broadens our understanding of specific intercultural interactions.

The relevance of sensemaking receives further attention in discussions of 'cultural intelligence,' a notion that can help move discussions of cultural dimensions beyond simplistic cross-cultural recipes towards more genuinely helpful advice. As David Thomas and Kerr Inkson describe it, cultural intelligence consists of three components linked together in a virtuous cycle (Thomas & Inkson 2004). First, it requires knowledge of culture and the fundamental principles of cross-cultural interaction that goes beyond etiquette. Secondly, the culturally intelligent manager needs to practice 'mindfulness;' i.e. the ability to pay attention in a reflexive and creative way to cues in the cross-cultural situations they encounter. Thirdly, based on this knowledge and mindfulness, the culturally intelligent manager develops a repertoire of behavioral skills which they can dare upon depending on their reading of the situation.

These ideas build upon the notion of cultural intelligence as first introduced by Christopher Earley and Soon Ang in *Cultural Intelligence: Individual Interactions Across Cultures* (2003). On the basis of the ideas developed in that book, Ang co-founded the Center for Leadership and Cultural Intelligence at the Nanyang Technological University in Singapore, which promotes itself as 'The World's First Cultural Intelligence Center.' Advocates of cultural intelligence argue that it is superior to laundry list approaches to cross-cultural leadership because, in building general as well as specific cultural intelligence, one can face new cultural challenges with increased confidence. Although the over-promotion and marketing of cultural intelligence as an effective tool threatens to associate it too closely to yet another laundry-list approach, the concept helpfully links together with Weick's concepts of sensemaking and mindfulness in ways that provide a more sophisticated lens for looking at culture as a dynamic social process rather than a set of static characteristics.

No matter how flexible and intelligent cross-cultural methodologies become, it is probably a good idea to remember Kanter and Corn's suggestion that cultural differences may not make that much of a business difference in the end anyway (1994). In the context of their research on takeovers of small and medium-sized American companies by foreign firms, they noted that the significance of cultural differences between employees and managers tended to be overstated. They conclude that:

> Cultural values or national differences are used as a convenient explanation for other problems both interpersonal and organisational, such as the failure to respect people, group power and politics, resentment at subordination, poor strategic fit, limited organisational communication, or the absence of problem-solving forums. Such differences are invoked as explanations for the uncomfortable behaviour of others when people have limited contact or knowledge of the context behind the behaviour. (1994: 19)

It may be dangerous to ignore the importance of national culture, then, but it can be just as dangerous to overstate its significance. At the end of the day, however, none of these criticisms appear to have had the effect of tempering the staying power of the cultural differences model, which functions not only as an academic theory but also as a form of folk wisdom that many people simply refuse to give up, even in the face of strong evidence to the contrary.

To give one brief personal example, in the fall of 2003 the main Danish daily business newspaper, *Børsen,* published a prominent feature spread across three full pages about a consultant who felt that Danish companies were falling into what he called 'the culture trap' (Tholstrup, 2003). To illustrate the power of cultural differences, the consultant cited the case of Disney's 1992 launch of its American-style theme park outside of Paris. Disney was bound to confront difficulties, the consultant said, because the French and the Americans are so different. He pointed out that the French don't even make science fiction films, because they constantly look back to their history and their roots. But Americans look to the future, which explains both the *Star Wars* films and the fact that you can motivate an American with stock options and visions of a rosy future.

Because we were teaching a master's-level class in intercultural management at the time, we felt compelled to send the newspaper a very brief and (we thought) rather entertaining letter to the editor taking issue with the consultant's approach to culture. We pointed out that in fact the French have produced many fine science fiction films (Luc Besson's 1997 *The Fifth Element*, for example), that the first science fiction film ever made was French (George Melies' 1903 *Le Voyage dans la Lune*) and that Frenchman Jules Verne (who wrote the 1865 novel on which the latter film was based) had contributed prominently to the invention of the genre of science fiction itself. We concluded with a warning that companies paying for such half-baked cultural advice were not getting their money's worth. Needless to say, the newspaper declined to publish our letter.

Perceptions of leadership across cultures: the GLOBE study

There are good reasons why all of the above-mentioned squabbles about the validity of cross-cultural research methods have not caused American leadership scholars to throw up their hands and avoid the issue altogether. The field of leadership studies continues to develop rapidly, but the majority of leadership research to date has been conducted within the North American context. This creates two problems with respect to the applicability of that research in other parts of the world. First, most of the work has been empirically tested in the United States, which is relatively diverse, but still limited in terms of its relevance to other global contexts. To counteract this problem, many North American researchers have consciously sought out different ethnic groups to examine, or they have teamed up with researchers from other parts of the world to conduct comparative leadership studies. Attend any management conference and you will notice many papers in which an international team of scholars employ an instrument such as the Multifactor Leadership Questionnaire (MLQ) to compare two or more national contexts.

Widening the empirical net does not, however, address a second more profound problem – that researchers themselves are products of specific cultural contexts. The kinds of questions they tend to ask, and the ways they go about answering them, are influenced by their immediate cultural milieu. As Hofstede himself has noted, US management and leadership theories tend to focus upon the individual, they privilege market processes and, as we saw in the previous chapter, they emphasize the needs and perspectives of the manager at the expense of the employee (Hofstede, 2001). More fundamentally, the profound interest in leadership in the United States points towards a culturally bound historical fascination with heroes and exceptional individuals. By contrast, European scholars endeavour to situate leadership in a broader social, legal and political context, taking a more critical line toward leaders and a more sceptical view of the desirability, let alone the possibility, of leadership (Den Hartog & Dickson, 2004).

The most significant and influential attempt to account for and overcome this potential bias in the American-dominated field of leadership research is the GLOBE project, which has united the efforts of 170 investigators from 61 cultures in the effort 'to develop an empirically based theory to describe, understand, and predict the impact of cultural variables on leadership and organizational processes and the effectiveness of these processes' (House et al., 1999: 2). The idea for GLOBE came to Wharton scholar Robert House in the summer of 1991. House had reviewed a wide array of research into charismatic leadership conducted in different cultural contexts, and had begun to suspect that charismatic leader behavior might prove acceptable and effective in all contexts. The GLOBE project would provide him with the means to test this idea on a grand scale.

Toward this end, House and his associates looked to 'implicit leadership theory,' which seeks to identify and delimit the shared prototypes or profiles of outstanding leadership that might be distinctively shared by followers within specific national cultures. Prototypes contain a set of attributes that define the essential characteristics of a category: for example, an effective business leader. Drawing on leadership category theory (Lord & Maher, 1991) the GLOBE authors note that followers will tend to follow a leader if they 'see' him or her as a prototypical leader. By the same token, if that leader does not match their perception of an effective leader the followers will be less inclined to follow him or her at least at the outset.

The GLOBE researchers isolated nine major attributes of culture: Future Orientation, Gender Egalitarianism, Assertiveness, Humane Orientation, In-Group Collectivism, Institutional Collectivism, Permanence Orientation, Power Concentration versus Decentralisation and Uncertainty Avoidance. When quantified, these attributes are referred to as 'cultural dimensions.' Although the GLOBE project clearly owes a great deal to Hofstede's work, House and his colleagues worked hard to make it more than just a big budget remake. Four of their dimensions replicated Hofstede's, but were renamed. And GLOBE investigated each of its nine dimensions on two levels: societal and organizational. For this purpose, they used two different measures. One tapped the participants' assessment of the extent to which their society or organization actually engages in certain practices (i.e. as they *are*). The other tapped into their perception of how things *should* be. As House notes, 'We have a data set to replicate Hofstede's (1980) landmark study and extend that study to test hypotheses relevant to relationships among societal-level variables, organisational practices, and leader attributes and behavior' (House et al., 2004, p. xxv).

Initial data collection for the GLOBE project took place between 1994 and 1997, during which time it collected responses from 17,300 middle managers based on a total of 951 organizations. On this basis, the GLOBE project identified six major global leader behaviors. The study found that there is a wide variation in the values and practices relevant to the nine core dimensions of cultures and a wide range of perceptions of what constitutes effective and ineffective leader behaviors. However, in all cultures leader team orientation and the communication of vision, values and confidence in followers were reported to be highly effective leader behaviors. Perhaps not surprisingly, leadership attributes reflecting irritability, non-cooperativeness, egocentricity, being a loner, ruthlessness and dictatorial were associated with ineffective leaders. While GLOBE found some variation concerning participative leadership, the study found wide variation with respect to two major dimensions of leader behavior: autonomous leadership and self-protective leadership.

Autonomous leadership is characterized by a high degree of independence from superiors and is reported to slightly contribute toward organizational effectiveness in Eastern European countries (except Hungary) and Germanic European countries (except the Netherlands). Self-protective leadership is characterized by self-centredness, status consciousness and narcissism. The GLOBE study found this type of leadership behavior to be perceived as slightly more effective among managers in Albania, Taiwan, Egypt, Iran and Kuwait. These intriguing exceptions aside, one is struck overall by how little variation there appears to be in the ascribed values and practices of effective leaders between managers in the 62 countries surveyed.

The GLOBE project is unquestionably the single most ambitious leadership study ever conducted. But it is still very much a work in progress. As the editors of the first book conclude, 'the wealth of findings provided in this book set the stage for a more sophisticated and complex set of questions' (House et al., 2004: 726). They acknowledge that, although the GLOBE findings have identified the various attributes of leadership, they have not identified the behavioural manifestations of such attributes. For example, the study concludes that integrity is a universally desirable attribute for leadership, but does 'integrity' mean the same thing to a Chinese employee as it does to an American?

Critiquing and defending the GLOBE study: here we go again

The critics of the GLOBE study have not been idle. Den Hartog and Dickson (2004) note several areas in which this and other pan-national studies have been questioned. For example, the potential for this work to commit an 'ecological fallacy' has been raised. This is the tendency to ascribe what has been noted at one level (e.g. society) to another level of analysis (e.g. the individual). While the GLOBE participants actively endeavored to address the 'levels of analysis' problem, a series of essays in the October 2006 issue of *The Leadership Quarterly* showed that the study's measurement metrics and levels of analysis are still being actively debated (Dansereau & Yammarino, 2006; Dickson et al., 2006; Hanges & Dickson, 2006; Peterson & Castro, 2006). Related to this is the problem of adequate sampling. In large, multicultural countries such as India, China and the United States, it is a daunting challenge to decide which sample would be the most representative. Doris Jepson supports this criticism of GLOBE in her case study of the German and UK chemical industries. She argues

that an instrument like GLOBE cannot capture the dynamic nature of cultural interactions that often take place in several intersecting contexts, including not only the national context but also organizational, hierarchical, departmental and individual contexts (Jepson, 2009).

Another fundamental problem associated with cross-cultural surveys like GLOBE is one of translation. How do we ensure that the respondents are interpreting the questions similarly? Even when we provide re-translating checks and balances, we still have to be alert to cultural norms regarding the completion of questionnaires. Anne-Will Harzing (2006) notes that responses to survey questions are influenced by the content of the question and the response style, which is the tendency to respond to questionnaire items regardless of item content. These response styles include acquiescence (ARS), middle response styles (MRS) and extreme response styles (ERS). For example, Hispanics and African Americans show higher ERS and ARS compared to European Americans. On the other hand, Japanese/Koreans show lower ERS and higher MRS than US Americans.

Perhaps not surprisingly, given the amount of energy they have spent on the GLOBE project over the years, House and his colleagues have at times responded to such criticisms in a manner that would make Hofstede proud. For example, George Graen published an article in the *Academy of Management Perspectives* promoting his own approach to the study of cultures, 'Third Culture Bonding,' which seeks to build on leader–member exchange theory to take account of differences within national cultural boundaries (Graen, 2006). Graen charged that 'the authors of the GLOBE study claim too much cross-cultural ecological and construct validity and generalizability for their research findings,' which he described as the result of 'a large number of one-shot, self-reported, culturally biased survey studies.' He concluded, 'Our in-depth TCB research in China leads us to question the GLOBE recommendations as premature generalizations about a country of 1.3 billion people and many subcultures based on a sample of a few hundred Chinese from one subculture in one local area.'

House and his co-authors took the bait, and launched into a detailed and decidedly prickly defence of the GLOBE's methodology. They counter-charged that Graen demonstrated 'a lack of knowledge generally about cluster analyses,' and that he ignored 'all the work that GLOBE did to ensure validity,' as well as 'all the work by tens of other researchers on cross cultural issues since Hofstede's seminal work in 1980' (House et al., 2006: 112). House et al. termed Graen's own approach 'careless' and underpublished to the point of being 'fictional.' They mentioned more than once that they could not find 'any other authors using or referring to his TCB measures.' In sum, they concluded, Graen's critique and proposed alternative amounted to a complete 'failure of scholarship.'

The GLOBE authors did not respond quite so dismissively to Geert Hofstede's own criticism of their research. But when the *Journal of International Business Studies* hosted an exchange between them, both sides did their best to honour what appears to have become the established tradition of cross-cultural methodological mudslinging (Hofstede, 2006; Javidan, et al., 2006). Hofstede opened the exchange by magnanimously expressing admiration for the fact that the GLOBE study had been thorough and professional enough to have based its approach on his own previous work. But he went on to criticize the GLOBE researchers for needlessly expanding his five dimensions to nine times two (too confusing), and for being generally culturally biased (i.e. American) and vague in a way that he was not.

The GLOBE authors responded by respectfully allowing that Hofstede's original study had provided 'a good start in understanding the cultural dynamics among nations.' But the implication was that Hofstede's time had passed, and the GLOBE was clearly better, more complex and more statistically valid. Besides, they continued in a tone that should have sounded familiar to Hofstede, his onion model was 'too simplistic to be helpful,' and his work had been characterized by 'a surprising disregard for the discipline of statistics and psychometrics.' Because Hofstede did not seem to understand the basics of the relationship between national wealth and culture, they added, his re-analysis of the GLOBE data was 'inappropriate' and 'dubious.' After the requisite, very detailed defence of the manner in which GLOBE had handled its scales and its factor analysis, the authors concluded that GLOBE offered the superior way forward for cross-cultural leadership research, and added enthusiastically, 'Let the cross-cultural research continue!'

In his analysis of this clash of the cross-cultural titans – insightfully titled 'When elephants fight, the grass gets trampled' – Peter Smith pointed out that it is not at all clear that continuing this kind of statistical one-upmanship will contribute to a better understanding of the relationship between leadership and cultural context (Smith, 2006). It was fine for Hofstede and the GLOBE researchers to quibble over their quartiles, but at the end of the day the differences between their basic assumptions about how culture functions, and how we should study it, were not actually that significant. Meanwhile, such in-fighting about cultural dimensions and the proper statistical methods for

measuring them could produce collateral damage by shutting off meaningful discussions into the future. 'Either one of the contributions to this debate could in the future be used by a reviewer as a basis for recommending rejection of a paper based on the cultural dimensions identified by the other party,' Smith pointed out. 'In neither case would that advance the field' (Smith, 2006: 915).

MOVING BEYOND THE CROSS-CULTURAL PARADIGM

We humbly submit that what might be most helpful for the field of cross-cultural leadership at this time would be to channel energies away from the current fixation on cultural dimensions to explore a new methodological realm. As mentioned at the outset of this chapter, Galit Ailon provides a productive example of just this kind of research, and contributes a new way to understand the complexity of the relationship between leadership and culture. In *Global Ambitions and Local Identities: An Israeli–American High-Tech Merger,* Ailon presents the results of a full year of detailed ethnographic research inside the pseudonymized 'Isrocom,' the Tel Aviv headquarters of the newly merged company she calls 'Globalint' (Ailon, 2007). From this perspective she observes not how her research subjects respond to predetermined questions on a cultural survey, but how they lived, enacted and interacted with their culture on a daily basis. On the basis of this insider perspective, Ailon concludes that national identity is best understood as 'a symbolic resource that is actively and creatively constructed by organizational members to serve social struggles which are triggered by globalization' (Ailon-Souday & Kunda, 2005: 1073). Thankfully, Ailon-Souday is in increasingly good company. We can point to similarly promising studies that provide exemplars of how humanities-based leadership research can enrich our understanding of the relationship between culture and leadership (Henry & Pene, 2001; Jones, 2005; Prince, 2006; Warner & Grint, 2006). All these studies takes an 'emic' approach in that they endeavor to understand the culture from *within* the culture they are studying (Triandis, 1980). This contrasts with the predominantly 'etic' approach that has been taken to cross-cultural leadership. The etic approach attempts to generalize leadership theory by looking at cultures from outside the ones they are studying.

This fresh approach to culture and national identity builds on Ailon's observation that the employees in the Israeli partner to the merger shared two goals: they wanted to underscore their independence from the new American partner by erecting clear boundaries between them, and they wanted simultaneously to establish their own superiority over their new colleagues, and their usefulness to the newly merged company. They wanted to do both of these things in order to maintain a sense of power and control over their working lives in the face of an uncertain situation. Toward these ends, they mobilized a very potent set of symbolic resources at their disposal, including their own collective identity as Israelis, and their perception of the collective identity of the group of individuals they lumped together by labeling them 'the Americans.' In the process, they exaggerated the differences between these two national identities: they took steps to heighten their 'Israeliness,' and they subtly contributed to the transformation of what it means to be Israeli in the process.

In all of these different ways, Ailon points out, the employees at Isrocom 'deployed national identity as a seemingly "natural," objective, and pre-existing boundary that renders members from the two sides unalterably different' (Ailon-Souday & Kunda 2005: 1083). But she stresses that Israeli identity did not simply come first and determine the way the employees in Ailon's study behaved – those employees actively shaped and mobilized their national identity to meet the needs of the moment. From this perspective, national cultures and identities do not consist of some core of stable values that can be measured and predicted. They are moving targets – dynamic and symbolic resources that get enlisted toward a variety of different strategic ends, and that get transformed in the process. Companies know this, at least when it comes to corporate culture and brand identity. They are always about the business of redefining or revitalizing their culture, their values and their identity. But the conventional cross-cultural model doesn't take into account that the same thing can happen with national cultures – they are constantly in the process of changing, and business organizations and their leaders are constantly in the process of trying to change them to suit their needs. It is precisely this active process of social construction that limits the usefulness of the conventional cultural differences model.

Ailon's research problematizes the conventional cross-cultural paradigm, because if people actively enlist and shape the dimensions of culture toward a variety of strategic ends, then it does not make sense to approach those dimensions as independent variables that we can use to compare cultural influences on leaders and leadership. But Ailon's work also points toward a resolution to the contradiction we highlighted at the beginning of this chapter: between, on the one hand, the notion of leadership as an active, influencing force, and on the other, the exclusive focus in cross-cultural research on the manner in which leadership is influenced and constrained by contextual factors. Because if cultures function as potent symbolic resources that get mobilized and transformed by individuals and groups in the context of globalization, then it does make sense for scholars to look very closely at how leaders work actively to mobilize and transform those cultures themselves.

We will conclude by reviewing two very different examples of how leadership scholars can pursue just such an agenda. The first example calls into question one of the central articles of faith in the cross-cultural canon – the notion that the United States can be held up as a reliable prototype of an individualistic culture, and that leaders should adjust their style accordingly. It is not that Americans aren't in some ways highly individualistic. But how did they get that way? And whose interests does this individualism serve? In *Selling Free Enterprise: The Business Assault on Labor and Liberalism, 1945–60,* historian Elizabeth Fones-Wolf provides some answers to these questions. She describes in detail how American business leaders – including the Chamber of Commerce, the Committee on Economic Development, the National Association of Manufacturers and a host of national business leaders and smaller – all joined together during the 15 years after World War II in order to discredit New Deal liberalism and undercut the legitimacy of organized labor. Together these groups spent millions on advertising campaigns, educational efforts, corporate welfare reforms, human relations initiatives and community programmes.

The goal of such activities was nothing less than to 'reshape the ideas, images, and attitudes through which Americans understood their world, specifically their understanding of their relationships to the corporation and the state' (Fones-Wolf, 1994: 5). As a means of counteracting the gains made by organized labor after the Great Depression and the New Deal, Fones-Wolf explains, 'enlightened managers would shape not only national policies, but also American values' in a broad-based effort 'to associate the American way with competitive individualism'. Because 'the labor movement could never match the resources available to the leaders of American business', she explains further, 'the political and cultural landscape of the postwar era was increasingly dominated by the images and ideas produced by a mobilized business leadership'. As Fones-Wolf points out, polling data suggest that during this period the United States witnessed a shift away from collectivist values towards a culture of individualism better suited to validating and perpetuating the continued dominance of big business over labour.

From this perspective, American individualism becomes the dependent variable, the end result of an orchestrated effort on the part of American business leadership to shape the dimensions of American culture to their own liking. Any psychometric survey of American values that did not mention these important power politics would in effect naturalize and legitimize the ideological agenda of one party to the struggle over the contours of American culture in a manner that would be neither scientifically objective nor descriptively accurate.

The example provided by Fones-Wolf describes a set of leadership dynamics and initiatives distributed widely among groups and intergroup interactions. In this sense it also provides a corrective to the GLOBE project's somewhat limiting definition of leadership as a function of individual abilities. As scholars extend their focus beyond the cross-cultural paradigm to explore how leadership actively shapes and influences culture itself, it will be important to conceive of both leadership *and* culture in the broad sense, and to look at how different types of leadership interact with culture in different ways. But it will be important not to lose sight of actual individual leaders along the way. We can close with a final, brief example of how individual leaders are also worthy of study for the manner in which they negotiate and mobilize multiple cultural identities in a globalized world.

Carlos Ghosn is the Chairman of the Board, President and Chief Executive Officer of Nissan Motor Co. Ltd. He was born in 1954 in Porto Velho, Brazil, the son of French and Lebanese immigrants. He moved to Beirut at the age of 6, where he attended a Jesuit secondary school, and later to Paris, where he attended high school and university. He speaks Portuguese, French, English and Arabic. He has held top executive positions on four continents, including Chairman and CEO of Michelin North American, and Executive Vice President of Renault in France. Now he runs a Japanese auto company. How do we characterize Ghosn's cultural background? Some sources call him French, others Lebanese. Many sources point towards the warm reception he has received in Japan, where he has appeared in the media in traditional garb, and even graced the pages of a Japanese manga (comic book) series called 'The True Life of Carlos Ghosn' (Prasso & Dawson, 2001).

It would not make sense to plot Ghosn's cultural influences on a pie chart in order to figure out what percentage of his leadership style is 'really' French, Lebanese, Brazilian, or even Japanese. He is a living, breathing example of what scholars of anthropology and globalization term 'creolization' (Stewart, 2007). This term refers to the process whereby cultures inevitably mix and mingle, creating new, unexpected and hybrid cultural forms, artefacts and identities.

Creolization helps explain, among other fascinating things, why certain Maori groups in New Zealand have identified themselves with the lost tribes of Israel; why Catholic saints often come to resemble the traditional gods and spirits of indigenous peoples; and why many young Mexican-Americans in Los Angeles have somehow inexplicably developed a lifestyle and fashion that revolves around the music and image of the very white, middle-aged English singer/songwriter Morrissey. These things happen under globalization because as people travel and cultures meet, they do not only clash. They also inevitably mingle and combine to create new and often strange hybrid forms. Marwan Kraidy argues that the 'hybridity' that results from this recombinant creation of new cultural forms amounts to nothing less than 'the cultural logic of globalization' (Kraidy, 2005).

The fact that grand quantitative studies of cultural dimensions cannot grapple with this logic means that they may not be fully suited to grapple head on with globalization itself. The phenomenon of creolization, the story of cultural polyglot leaders like Carlos Ghosn and the insights of the sort provided by Galit Ailon and Elizabeth Fones-Wolf all demonstrate emphatically why research on leadership and culture needs to move beyond the quantitative models provided by Geert Hofstede and the GLOBE project to embrace a variety of different methods and approaches from the social sciences and the humanities, including ethnography and detailed historical investigation. By means of such approaches, leadership scholars can develop a deeper understanding of the complexities of the relationship between leadership and culture. They can come to appreciate the powerful sway that the former holds over the latter. And they can construct a vocabulary to help leaders and followers understand and participate in the dialectical process whereby they shape the culture that shapes them, and so on.

Toward global leadership

In endeavoring to adapt to this globalized world, cross-leadership scholars, like the many executives they study, might consider looking to the burgeoning field of global leadership for inspiration. Beechler and Javidan (2007) have observed that

The cross-cultural leadership literature (CCL) simply ignores the notion of global leadership (GL) and makes no effort to connect to it, even though it acknowledges the reality of global responsibilities for many executives. The field of global leadership seems relatively more aware of the CCL literature but only makes passing reference to it and certainly makes no attempt to bridge the divide or even define and contrast the two constructs. (2007: 15)

Whereas CCL, with its predominantly psychological approach, is focused on relationships among individuals within the boundaries of an organization, GL focuses on broader relationships between the leader and a wide range of stakeholders inside and outside the global organization.

The quest to define a good universal model of global leadership – i.e. leadership which brings individuals together from diverse national and cultural contexts in a productive and ethical way without any one group dominating – has attracted considerable interest from a number of leadership scholars. This quest has become an urgent one in light of the widespread recognition that global problems – such as global warming, intractable famine and global epidemics – have outstripped the capacity of existing institutional leadership structures. Good sources for this kind of thinking are the biennial collection of essays published in the *Advances in Global Leadership* series (e.g., Mobley & Weldon, 2006) as well as the Global Leadership Network (www. globalleadership network.net) and the Worldly Leadership Summit that is held annually by the Leadership Trust.

Several members of the GLOBE study have refocused their attention on the challenge of developing global leadership, which they define as 'the process of influencing individuals, groups, and organizations (inside and outside the boundaries of the global organization) representing diverse cultural/political/institutional systems to contribute toward the achievement of the global organization's goals' (Beechler & Javidan, 2007: 4). To aid in this, they have developed an inventory for assessing a manager's 'Global Mindset'. The Global Mindset Inventory measures leaders according to their levels of:

- 'Global Intellectual Capital' (i.e. general knowledge and capacity to learn cognitive and cultural acumen)
- 'Global Psychological Capital' (openness for differences and capacity for change)
- 'Global Social Capital' (i.e. ability to build trusting relationships with and among people who are different to you) (Javidan et al., 2010)

CONCLUSIONS

In this chapter we have highlighted the role of culture in creating leadership, most particularly the influence of culture in enabling and constraining various forms of leadership. We have also argued the influence the rarely acknowledged yet critical role that leadership plays in enabling, constraining and changing culture. We have reviewed the two most significant studies conducted by leadership scholars who have attempted to understand societal variations in culture, and the influence these in turn have on desired and actual leadership values and behaviour. The relatively new, yet growing, field of cross-cultural leadership has sought to help managers become more effective leaders within and between the diverse cultural contexts they inhabit in an increasingly globalized business environment. The growing interest in leadership research throughout the rest of the world has revealed contributions as well as limitations in the applicability and relevance of the predominantly American-based research to other national and local contexts. Others have argued that it is not just the specificity of the cultures being explored but the culturally specific way in which they have been explored that has limited our ability to understand the full range and depth of leadership practices throughout the world. We, therefore, look forward to more emically-oriented leadership research to complement the preponderance of etically oriented research within the field of cross-cultural leadership. We also look forward to a fruitful and long overdue *rapprochement* with the promising global leadership literature. Making these strategic moves might ultimately serve to shift the focus of the field from examining a notional intersection between two or more cultures that somehow has to be 'crossed' to developing richer, relevant and more 'cultured' understandings of leadership.

REFERENCES

Ailon, G. (2007). *Global Ambitions and Local Identities: An Israeli–American High Tech Merger*. New York: Berghahn Books.

Ailon, G. (2008). 'Mirror, mirror on the wall: culture's consequences in a value test of its own design', *Academy of Management Review*, 33(4): 885–904.

Ailon, G. (2009). 'Who is the fairest of them all? Galit Ailon's mirror', *Academy of Management Review*, 34(3): 571–573.

Ailon-Souday, G. & Kunda, G. (2003) 'The local selves of global workers: the social construction of national identity in the face of organizational globalization', *Organization Studies*, 24(7): 1073–1096.

Beechler, S. & Javidan, M. (2007) *Leading With a Global Mindset*. London: Emerald.

Den Hartog, D.N. & Dickson, M.W. (2004) 'Leadership and culture'. In J. Antonakis, A.T. Cianciolo and R.J. Sternberg (eds), *The Nature of Leadership*. London: Sage, pp. 249–278.

Dickson, M.W., Den Hartog, D., & Mitchelson, J. (2003) 'Research on leadership in a cross-cultural context: making progress, and raising new questions', *The Leadership Quarterly*, 14(6): 729–768.

Dickson, M.W., Resick, C.J., & Hanges, P.L. (2006) 'Systematic variations in organizationally-shared prototypes of effective leadership based on organizational form', *The Leadership Quarterly*, 17(5): 487–505.

Early, P.C. and Ang, S. (2003) *Cultural Intelligence: Individual Interactions Across Cultures*, Stanford, CA. Stanford Business Books.

Fones-Wolf, E. (1994) *Selling free enterprise: The Business Assault On Labor and Liberalism, 1945–60*. Urbana, IL: University of Illinois Press.

Frederick, W.R. & de la Fuente Rodriguez, A. (1994) 'A Spanish acquisition in Eastern Germany: culture shock'. *Journal of Management Development*, 13(2): 42.

Gesteland, R. (2006) *Cross-cultural Business Behavior: Negotiating, Selling, Sourcing and Managing Across cultures*, 4th edn., Copenhagen: Copenhagen Business School Press.

Gooderham, P.N. and Nordhaug, O. (2002) "Are cultural differences in Europe on the decline?" *European Business Forum*, vol. 2(8): pp. 48–53.

Graen, G. B. (2006) "In the Eye of the Beholder: Cross-Cultural Lesson in Leadership from Project GLOBE: A Response Viewed from the Third Culture Bonding (TCB) Model of Cross-Cultural Leadership," Academy of Management Perspectives, vol. 20(4): pp. 95–101.

Hall, E. (1990) *Understanding Cultural Differences*, Yarmouth, ME: Intercultural Press.

Hanges, P.J. & Dickson, M.W. (2006) 'Agitation over aggregation: clarifying the development of and the nature of the GLOE scales', *The Leadership Quarterly*, 17(5): 522–536.

Harris, P., Moran, R., & Moran, S. (2004) *Managing Cultural Differences*. 6th edn, Amsterdam: Elsevier/Butterworth-Heinemann.

Harzing, A. (2006) 'Response styles in cross-national survey research: a 26-country study', *International Journal of Cross Cultural Management*, 6(2): 123–141.

Henry, E. & Pene H. (2001) 'Kaupapa Maori: locating indigenous ontology, epistemology and methodology in the academy', *Organization* 8(2): 234–242.

Hickson, D. & Pugh, D.S. (1995). *Management Worldwide: The Impact of Societal Culture on Organizations Around the Globe*, London: Penguin Books.

Hofstede, G. (1980) *Culture's Consequences: International Differences in Work-Related Values*. Beverly Hills, CA: Sage.

Hofstede, G. (1994). 'The business of international business is culture', *International Business Review*, 3(1): 1–14.

Hofstede, G. (2001). *Culture's Consequences: Comparing Values, Behaviors, Institutions, and Organizations Across Nations*, 2nd edn. Thousand Oaks, CA: Sage.

Hofstede, G. (2002a) 'Commentary on "An International Study of the Psychometric Properties of the Hofstede Values Survey Module 1994: A Comparison of Individual and Country/Province Level Results"', *Applied Psychology: An International Review*, 51(1): 170.

Hofstede, G. (2002b). 'Dimensions do not exist: a reply to Brendan McSweeney', *Human Relations*, 55(11): 1355.

Hofstede, G. (2006) 'What did GLOBE really measure? Researchers' minds versus respondents' minds'. *Journal of International Business Studies*, 37(6): 882–896.

Hofstede, G. (2009) 'Who is the fairest of them all? Galit Ailon's mirror', *Academy of Management Review*, 33(4): 570–572.

Hofstede, G. & Bond, M.H. (1988) 'The Confucius connection: from cultural roots to economic growth', *Organizational Dynamics*, 16(4): 4–21.

Hooker, J. (2003) *Working Across Cultures*. Stanford, CA: Stanford University Press.

House, R.J., Hanges, P.J., Ruiz-Quintanilla, S.A., Dorfman, P.W., Javidan, M., Dickson, M., Gupta, V. and GLOBE Country Co-Investigators, (1999) "Cultural Influences On Leadership And Organizations: Project Globe," in Mobley, W.H., Gessner, M.J., Arn: Sage Publications.

House, R.J., Hanges, P., Javidan, M., Dorfman, P. & Gupta, V. (eds) (2004) *Culture, Leadership and Organisations: The GLOBE Study of 62 Societies*. Thousand Oaks, CA: Sage.

House, R. J., Javidan, M., Dorfman, P. W., & De Luque, M. S. (2006) "A Failure of Scholarship: Response to George Graen's Critique of GLOBE," *Academy of Management Perspectives*, vol. 20(4): pp. 102–114.

Javidan, M., Teagarden, M., & Bowen, D. (2010) "Making It Overseas," Harvard Business Review, vol. 88(4): pp. 109–113.

Javidan, M., Teagarden, M., & Bowen, D. 2010. 'Making it overseas. *Harvard Business Review*, 88(4): 109–113.

Jepson, D. (2009) "Studying Leadership at Cross-Country Level: A Critical Analysis," *Leadership*, vol. 5(1): pp. 61–80.

Jones, A.M. (2005) 'The anthropology of leadership: culture and corporate leadership in the American South', *Leadership*, 9(1): 259–278.

Kanter, R. M., & Corn, R. I. (1994) "Do Cultural Differences Make a Business Difference?: Contextual Factors Affecting Cross-cultural Relationship Success," *Journal of Management Development*, vol. 13(2): pp. 5–23.

Kraidy, M. (2005) *Hybridity, or the Cultural Logic of Globalization*. Philadelphia: Temple University. Press.

Lord, R.G., and Maher, K.J. (1991) "Cognitive theory in industrial and organizational psychology," In M.D. Dunnette and L.M. Hough, eds., *Handbook of Industrial and Organizational Psychology*. Palo Alto, CA: Consulting Psychologists Press.

McSweeney, B. (2002a) 'Hofstede's model of national cultural differences and their consequences: a triumph of faith—a failure of analysis'. *Human Relations*, 55(1): 89–118.

McSweeney, B. (2002b) 'The essentials of scholarship: a reply to Geert Hofstede'. *Human Relations*, 55(11): 1363.

Mobley, W.H. & Weldon, E. (2006) *Advances in Global Leadership Volume 4*. New York: Elsevier JAI.

Osland, J.S., Bird, A., Delano, J. & Jacob, M. (2000) 'Beyond sophisticated stereotyping: cultural sensemaking in context', *Academy of Management Executive*, 14(1): 65–79.

Parsons, T. and Shils, E.A. (1951) "Values, Motives, and Systems of Action" in Parsons, T. and Shils, E.A. (eds.),

Towards a General Theory of Action. Cambridge, MA: Harvard University Press, pp. 53–109.

Peterson, M.F. & Castro, S.L. (2006) 'Measurement metrics at aggregate levels of analysis: implications of organization culture research and the GLOBE project', *The Leadership Quarterly,* 17(5): 506–521.

Prasso, S. & Dawson, C. (2001) 'POW! BAM! ZAP! Meet Nissan's superhero', *Business Week,* (3730): 12.

Prince, L. (2005) 'Eating the menu rather than the dinner: Tao and leadership', *Leadership,* 1(1): 105–126.

Richard Mead (1994) *International Management—Cross-Cultural Dimensions* Cambridge: Blackwell Publishers

Rosenzweig, P.M. (1994) "When can management science research be generalized internationally?" *Management Science,* v.40 n.1, p.28–39.

Robinson, R. (1983). 'Culture's Consequences.' Book review. *Work and Occupations,* VOL. 10 (1): pp. 110–115.

Schwartz, S.H. (1999) 'Cultural value differences: some implications for work', *Applied Psychology: An International Review,* 48: 23–48.

Shane, S., Venkataraman, S., and MacMillan, I. (1995) "Cultural Differences in Innovation Championing Strategies," Journal of Management vol. 21/5: pp. 931–952.

Smith, P.B. (2006) 'When elephants fight, the grass gets trampled: the GLOBE and Hofstede projects', *Journal of International Business Studies,* 37(6): 915–921.

Stewart, C. (2007) *Creolization: History, Ethnography, Theory.* Walnut Creek, CA: Left Coast Press.

Tayeb, M. H. (1996) 'Hofstede', in M Warner (ed.) *International Encyclopaedia of Business and Management.* London: International Thomson Business Press. vol. 2, pp. 1771–1776.

Tholstrup, S. (2003) "Virksomheder Overser Kulturfælden," *Borsen,* October 31: pp. B1ff.

Thomas, D. & Inkson, K. (2004) *Cultural Intelligence: People Skills for Global Business.* San Francisco, CA: Berrett-Koehler.

Ting-Toomey, S. (1988) "Intercultural conflicts: A face-negotiation theory," In Y. Kim & W. Gudykunst (Eds.), *Theories in intercultural communication* Newbury Park, CA: Sage: pp. 213–235.

Trompenaars, F. and Hampden-Turner, C. (1997) *Riding the Waves of Culture,* 2nd ed., Nicholas Brealey Publishing, London.

Warner, L.S. & Grint, K. (2006) 'American Indian ways of leading and knowing', *Leadership,* 2(2): 225–244.

PART III

Political and Philosophical Perspectives

13

Critical Leadership Studies

David Collinson

INTRODUCTION

This chapter considers the emergence of a comparatively new approach to studying leadership. It explores the growing impact of 'critical leadership studies' (CLS). This term is used here to denote the broad, diverse and heterogeneous perspectives that share a concern to critique the power relations and identity constructions through which leadership dynamics are often reproduced, frequently rationalized, sometimes resisted and occasionally transformed (e.g., Gabriel, 1997; Lipman-Blumen, 2005; Fairhurst, 2007; Sinclair, 2007; Banks, 2008; Nye, 2008). Critical studies challenge hegemonic perspectives in the mainstream literature that tend both to underestimate the complexity of leadership dynamics and to take for granted that leaders are the people in charge who make decisions, and that followers are those who merely carry out orders from 'above'.

From the outset, it is important to acknowledge that CLS comprise a variety of approaches informed by an eclectic set of premises, frameworks and ideas (e.g., Calas and Smircich, 1991; Gronn, 2002; Gordon, 2002; Tourish and Vatcha, 2005; Ospina and Su, 2009). Although they share a concern to examine leadership power dynamics, critical studies do not constitute a unified set of ideas, perspectives or a single community of practice. They often draw on the more established field of critical management studies (CMS) which, in seeking to open up new ways of thinking and alternative forms of management and organization, focus on the critique of rhetoric, tradition, authority and objectivity (Mingers, 2000). Questioning traditional orthodoxies, CMS exponents draw on a plurality of theoretical perspectives, ontologies and epistemologies, from structuralism, labour process theory and critical realism, to feminism, post-structuralism, deconstructionism, literary criticism, postcolonial theory, cultural studies, environmentalism and psychoanalysis. Although these diverse perspectives are often depicted as part of an inclusive 'critical' movement (e.g. Alvesson and Willmott, 2003), they can also be in tension with one another (e.g. Ackroyd, 2004). Fournier and Grey (2000) define CMS in terms of this plurality of conflicting intellectual traditions, arguing that such internal differences are much less significant when critical approaches are contrasted with mainstream, managerialist perspectives.

CLS draw on similar intellectual traditions. They too share a common view, in this case about what is neglected, absent or deficient in mainstream leadership research. Indeed, it could be argued that critical studies emerge directly from that which is underexplored or missing in the mainstream orthodoxy. Whilst all these perspectives critically examine and prioritize power relations and the ways they are reproduced in particular structures, relationships and practices, CLS contrast with many CMS perspectives in a number of ways. In particular, CLS explicitly recognize that, for good and/or ill, leaders and leadership dynamics (defined here as the shifting, asymmetrical interrelations between leaders, followers and contexts) also exercise significant power and influence over contemporary organizational and societal processes. Despite their espoused concern to critique the exercise of power and control, many CMS writers ignore the study of leadership, focusing more narrowly on management and organization. CLS emphasize that leadership and management are often interwoven forms of organizational power and identity that are not as easily separable as CMS sometimes seem to assume. CLS examine the complex dynamics between leaders and managers, as well as those between leaders, managers and followers. Relatedly, CLS also recognize that whereas leadership and power are often associated with those in positions of formal authority, this is not always the case. Critical studies emphasize that leadership dynamics can emerge informally in more subordinated and dispersed relationships, positions and locations, as well as in oppositional forms of organization such as trade unions (Knowles, 2007) and revolutionary movements (Rejai, 1979). Emphasizing the importance of power asymmetries, CLS also highlight the significance of follower agency and their potential for dissent and resistance.

This chapter explores current developments in this emergent field. It suggests that by raising under-researched questions, CLS have the potential to broaden understanding of leadership dynamics, developing new forms of analysis, as well as opening up innovative lines of enquiry. After considering the weaknesses and absences within mainstream perspectives, as highlighted by various critical writers, the chapter outlines some of the key themes and concepts that inform more critical approaches. It concludes by considering the CLS challenge to contemporary leadership studies.

ESSENTIALISM, ROMANTICISM AND DUALISM

A burgeoning literature now exists exploring the theory and practice of leadership. The vast majority of studies can be located within a 'mainstream paradigm', an umbrella term that, like 'critical studies', draws together a diverse and heterogeneous set of theories, approaches and findings. Within the mainstream paradigm there are significant differences between theories such as the following: trait, situational/contingency; path–goal; leader–member exchange; impression management and social identity; emotional intelligence; and charismatic/transformational leadership. These perspectives have tended to focus on the primary question of what makes an effective leader. Although this literature has produced useful insights regarding leaders' competencies and behaviours, definitive answers about effectiveness have proved elusive, and findings have been inconclusive.

Concentrating primarily on individual leaders and their qualities, mainstream studies have been criticized for being leader-centric (Jackson and

Parry, 2008). Many critical theorists have argued that mainstream studies portray leaders as proactive agents and followers as those who passively respond (e.g. Gronn, 2002). Leader-centric perspectives are most evident in trait theory which, in addressing the attributes needed for leader effectiveness, has recently undergone a resurgence of interest (e.g. Zaccaro, 2007). Similarly, situational theory suggests that effective leaders should communicate by deploying a mix of directive and supportive behaviours compatible with followers' 'developmental levels' (e.g. Hersey and Blanchard, 1996). Path–goal theory holds that leaders must choose styles best suited to followers' experience, needs and skills (e.g. House, 1971). Leader–member exchange theory describes how leaders tend to be open and trusting with 'in-group' followers, but distant with 'out-group' members (e.g. Graen and Uhl-Bien, 1995). Recent interest in 'emotional intelligence' indicates that effective leaders need to develop greater awareness of the emotional dynamics of leadership processes (e.g. Goleman et al., 2002).

Social identity theorists argue that effective leaders are typically perceived as 'prototypical' of the group's identity (van Knippenberg and Hogg, 2003). They predict that followers are likely to endorse leaders who quintessentially embody the values of the group (Hogg, 2001). Identity construction is also central to Gardner and Avolio's (1998) focus on leaders' influence tactics through impression management (framing, scripting, staging and performing). Suggesting that leaders' own life histories might be a significant source of influence over followers, Shamir et al. (2005) illustrate how leaders often strategically construct their biographies to convey predefined messages. Transformational studies assert that leaders can inspire followers to greater commitment by satisfying their needs, values and motivations (e.g. Burns, 1978). They also suggest that effective and charismatic leaders should validate and transform followers' identities (Lord and Brown, 2003) by, for example, acting as role models and encouraging followers' psychological identification and value internalization (Shamir et al., 1993).

These perspectives tend to define leadership primarily as a top-down influence process through which leaders change the ways followers envision themselves. Accordingly, they consider followers only in relation to their susceptibility to certain leader behaviours or styles. Seeking to render leadership a predictable practice and leadership studies a prescriptive endeavour, mainstream approaches tend to portray followers as 'an empty vessel waiting to be led, or even transformed, by the leader' (Goffee and Jones, 2001, p. 148). For example, situational leadership views followers through the rather static and objectified categories of 'enthusiastic beginners', 'disillusioned learners', 'reluctant contributors' and 'peak performers'. Path–goal theory treats leadership as 'a one way event – the leader affects the subordinate' (Northouse, 2004, p. 113). Leader–member exchange theory says little about the ways followers may influence the leader–member relationship or about the group and organizational dimensions of these relationships (Howell and Shamir, 2005). Transformational studies typically draw on highly gendered, heroic images of the 'great man', viewing leaders as dynamic agents of change and followers as passive and compliant.

Critical writers question this recurrent tendency to privilege leaders and neglect followers, frequently pointing to three main (sometimes interrelated) weaknesses in mainstream leadership studies namely, essentialism, romanticism and dualism. These are now briefly discussed in turn.

Critical writers propose that we rethink leadership as socially and discursively constructed and in so doing reject the essentialism that lies at the heart of the psychological, positivist method which underpins the mainstream paradigm (Lakomski, 2005). Psychology focuses primarily on individuals and on their internal (psychological) dynamics, giving much less attention to the socially and discursively constructed nature of leadership dynamics (Fairhurst, 2007, and Fairhurst, Chapter 36, this volume). Positivism tends to rely on quantitative analyses in which standard questionnaires are administered to large samples. By contrast, critical perspectives are more focused on the socially constructed and multiple discourses and meanings that tend to characterize leadership dynamics (Fairhurst and Grant, 2010). Accordingly, they frequently draw on qualitative, interpretive and case study research methods that address the shifting possible constructions of leadership located within their complex (and often asymmetrical) conditions, processes and consequences (see also Bryman, Chapter 2, this volume).

Arguing that leadership needs to be understood as socially constructed, Grint (1997) questions the essentialism underpinning trait, situational and contingency theories which seek to identify the one best way to lead. Such essentialist perspectives assume that it is possible to discover an 'essence' to leaders and their contexts. Grint argues that this search for the universal 'essence' of leadership denies the socially constructed nature of both 'leading' and 'context'. He criticizes the positivist assumption underpinning much leadership research that it is possible for researchers to produce an 'objective' view of either individual leaders or of the specific situations in which they act. All accounts (of leadership) are derived, he contends, from linguistic reconstructions, which

have to be interpreted and are therefore potentially contestable.

Ospina and Sorenson (2007, p. 189) view leadership as a dynamic, collective and community-based achievement. Arguing that leadership is 'intrinsically relational' and 'rooted in context or place', they emphasize that a constructivist lens provides an opportunity to reveal 'the multiple sources of leadership, the multiple forms leadership may take, and the multiple places where it can be found' (2007, p. 200). Accordingly, constructionist perspectives also highlight the importance of context and its multiple (socially constructed) forms (Osborne et al., 2002; Porter and McLaughlin, 2006). Indeed, contexts are important for leadership not only in practice but also in theory. The majority of leadership studies are North American in origin and much research (unconsciously) articulates (positivist) US values (Hartog and Dickson, 2004). Alongside this often acknowledged US-centrism is an assumption that North American cultural values can be transposed to leadership theory, development and practice in quite different contexts (Jackson and Parry, 2008). Yet, it is increasingly evident that leadership and followership dynamics take very different forms in different societies (Bjerke, 1999).

The multiple identities, values and cultures of leaders and followers in various diverse regions, societies and continents are likely to have a significant impact on the possibilities and limits of leadership practices (see also Guthey and Jackson, Chapter 12, this volume). Whereas Western and North American societies typically subscribe to meritocratic principles based on individual achievement, Asian and Eastern societies adhere to more collectivist and ascriptive values that privilege, for example, kinship and age. Cultures in developing countries tend to share certain characteristics such as strong family bonds, a sense of fatalism, deference and an expectation that organizations will take care of their workers; values which often reflect and reinforce highly paternalistic leadership styles (Dickson et al., 2003). Highlighting the importance of geographic, cultural, administrative and economic proximity for effective global leadership, Ghemawat (2005) argues that regions continue to be important, but often neglected units of analysis for cross-border, 'macro' leadership strategies.

In his cross-cultural analysis of leadership development programmes in the USA, Europe and China, Jones (2006) points to the disproportionate influence of US values. He argues that US leader development is informed by its own cultural history of mythical heroes, from the hunter-trapper to the Indian fighter, from the John Wayne cowboy figure to the charismatic business entrepreneur. This mythological view of heroic leaders has been heavily criticized. Mintzberg (2006) questions the obsession with heroic leaders within leadership studies and its underlying 'syndrome of individuality' which, he believes, is undermining organizations and communities. Meindl et al. (1985) were early critics of this tendency to 'romanticize leadership', where leaders are either credited for high organizational performance or, conversely, held personally responsible for workplace failures. Arguing that we have developed overly heroic and exaggerated views of what leaders are able to achieve, they suggested that leaders' contribution to a collective enterprise is inevitably somewhat constrained and closely tied to external factors outside a leader's control, such as those affecting whole industries.

This critique of leadership romanticism has informed a growing interest in 'post-heroic leadership', an approach that emphasizes its social, relational and collective nature. Post-heroic perspectives highlight the effectiveness of distributed (Gronn, 2002), shared (Pearce and Conger, 2003), servant (Hale and Fields, 2007), quiet (Collins, 2001), collaborative (Jameson, 2007) and community leadership (Ricketts and Ladewig, 2008), as well as co-leadership (Alvarez and Svejenova, 2005). This approach often argues that digital technologies and intensified globalized competition are creating more flexible, team-based and informal leadership practices that are less hierarchical and more focused on shared power and responsibility.

Post-heroic perspectives also reflect and reinforce greater interest in followership (e.g. Riggio et al., 2008; Shamir et al., 2007; Bligh, Chapter 31, this volume). Some have argued that 'exemplary', 'courageous' and 'star' followers are a precondition for high-performing organizations (e.g. Chaleff, 2009: Kellerman, 2007; Kelley, 2004) and for enhancing charismatic leadership (Howell and Shamir, 2005). Viewing 'effective followership' as particularly important in the contemporary context of flatter hierarchies and greater team working (Raelin, 2003), some writers have simply added a concern with followers to produce a less leader-centric version of leadership. In so doing they tend to remain confined within a mainstream managerial focus on followers' contribution to organizational performance.

However, it is also possible to develop a more critical approach to understanding followership by exploring the importance of asymmetrical power relations and insecurities in leader-led dynamics (Collinson, 2006, 2008). This approach treats oppositional practices and identities as important phenomena worthy of analysis, rather than as dysfunctional elements of a system. It recognizes the significance of asymmetrical power relations for understanding followers as well as, and in relation

to, leaders. In so doing, critical approaches also question the reliance in mainstream studies on the artificial and excessive separation between leadership and followership (e.g. Gronn, 2002; Gronn, Chapter 32, this volume).

Various studies question the tendency in orthodox approaches to separate and privilege leaders while neglecting followers, leaders' relations with 'followers' and the wider economic, social, political, cultural and technological contexts. Gordon (2002; Gordon, Chapter 14, this volume) suggests that the historical constitution of the differential in power (and status) between leaders and followers has resulted in mainstream theorists viewing leaders' apparent superiority as 'natural' and unproblematic. Fairhurst (2001) highlights the 'primary dualism' in leadership research as that between the individual and the collective, arguing that studies typically concentrate either on leaders, in ways that overlook the dynamics of the collective, or on the latter, thereby neglecting the former's basis for action. By contrast, she advocates dialectical approaches to leadership which explore the dynamic tension and interplay between seemingly oppositional binaries. Relatedly, critical writers also question the broader reliance in mainstream leadership research on seemingly oppositional binaries or 'dualisms' such as transactional/transformational, organic/mechanistic and participative/autocratic leadership (Collinson, 2005; Grint, 2005).

Debates about dualism(s) and dialectics have a long history in social and philosophical theory (e.g. the work of Hegel, Marx, Sartre, Adorno and Derrida) and more recently have become increasingly influential in organization studies (Knights, 1997; Mumby and Stohl, 1991; Reed, 1997) and communication studies (Baxter and Montgomery, 1996). Giddens' structuration theory (1984, 1987) seeks to overcome the individual/society dualism in social theory by rethinking the 'dialectics of power relations'. Emphasizing an intrinsic dialectical relationship between agency and power within all social relations, Giddens argues that human beings are knowledgeable social agents who, acting within historically specific (unacknowledged) conditions and (unintended) consequences, always retain a capacity to 'make a difference'. His notion of the 'dialectic of control' holds that, no matter how asymmetrical, power relations are always two-way, contingent and to some degree interdependent. An important implication of the dialectic of control is that leader–follower relations are likely to be characterized by shifting interdependencies and power asymmetries. Since power relations are always two-way, leaders will remain dependent to some extent on the led, while followers retain a degree of autonomy and discretion. If we rethink followers as knowledgeable agents, we can begin to see them as proactive, self-aware and knowing subjects who have at their disposal a repertoire of possible agencies within the workplace. Accordingly, power relations between leaders and followers are likely to be interdependent as well as asymmetrical, typically ambiguous, frequently shifting, potentially contradictory and often contested.

Influenced by Giddens' ideas, critical writers from various perspectives argue that dialectical perspectives can facilitate new ways of thinking about the complex dynamics of leadership. Dialectical approaches to leadership power relations reveal that seemingly opposing categories are interconnected and frequently mutually reinforcing. So, for example, the dialectic of control in the context of leadership dynamics focuses on the simultaneous interdependencies and asymmetries between leaders and followers as well as their ambiguous, shifting and potentially contradictory conditions, processes and consequences. This chapter now explores three interrelated dialectics frequently evident in leadership dynamics: control/resistance; consent/dissent; and men/women. Although these are by no means exhaustive, they illustrate the kinds of dialectical processes through which leader–follower dynamics are frequently enacted and reproduced.

CONTROL/RESISTANCE

Mainstream leader-centred approaches share a tendency to underestimate questions of power and control (Ray et al., 2004). Assuming that the interests of leaders and followers automatically coalesce, orthodox studies view power and control as unproblematic forms of organizational authority while treating resistance as abnormal or irrational. Typically, mainstream studies define leadership in terms of 'influence' (positive), and distinguish this from power (negative). In so doing, they fail to appreciate that the former may be one aspect of the latter. Burns (1978) distinguished between good 'leaders', who mobilize followers to achieve a collective purpose, and 'power holders'. Often viewed as 'the father figure of modern leadership studies' (Jackson and Parry, 2008: p. 11), Burns argued that power wielders should not be considered to be leaders at all. Burns' distinction, which tends to relegate questions of power to a minor concern, has been very influential in leadership studies.

By contrast, CLS explicitly contend that the exercise and experience of power is central to all leadership dynamics. Informed by various perspectives (from labour process theory to radical psychology and post-structuralism), critical leadership writers recognize that leaders' control is very important and can take multiple economic, political, ideological and psychological forms. They show how control is not so much a 'dependent variable' as a deeply embedded and inescapable feature of leadership structures, cultures and practices. Gordon (2002 and Chapter 14, this volume) observes that assumptions about a leader's right to power and dominance are embedded at a deep structural level in most, if not all, organizations.

Leaders can exercise power, control and influence in many ways: for example, by constructing strategies and visions, shaping structures and cultures, intensifying and monitoring work, providing rewards and applying sanctions, and through hiring and firing. They can also exercise power by 'managing meaning', and defining situations in ways that suit their purposes (Smircich and Morgan, 1982). CLS argue that power is intimately connected to knowledge and subjectivity. Influenced by Foucault's (1977, 1979) ideas, critical writers examine the ways that 'power/knowledge' regimes are inscribed on subjectivities. Foucault explored the 'disciplinary power' of surveillance that produces detailed information about individuals, rendering them visible, calculable and self-disciplining selves. He suggested that by shaping identity formation, power is enabling and productive as well as subordinating. As Alvesson and Willmott (2002) observed, 'identity regulation' is now a central feature of organizational control in post-bureaucratic organizations.

The disciplinary nature of power is revealed by a number of studies that explore follower conformity, compliance and consent. Although conformity tends to be viewed positively in mainstream studies, frequently treated as an expression of commitment and loyalty, critical writers highlight its potentially detrimental consequences in certain circumstances. They point to the Nazi extermination of six million Jews and the explanation from those involved that they were 'just obeying orders' as a stark reminder about its potential dangers. Milgram's (1963) experiments highlighted peoples' willingness to obey authority. Fromm (1977) pointed to 'the fear of freedom' where individuals try to shelter in the perceived security of being told what to do and what to think, viewing this as a less-threatening alternative to the responsibility of making decisions for themselves. Similarly, Bratton et al. (2004) highlighted the negative organizational effects of 'destructive consent' and the potentially positive consequences of 'constructive dissent'.

Various writers reveal how followers often attribute exceptional qualities to charismatic leaders through processes such as transference

(Maccoby, 2007), fantasy (Gabriel, 1997), idealization (Shamir, 1999), projection (Shamir, 2007), seduction (Calas and Smirich, 1991) and reification (Gemmill and Oakley, 1992). Lipmen-Blumen (2005) extends these arguments in analysing the 'allure of toxic leaders', where she contends that followers frequently seem to be fascinated by toxic leaders despite, and possibly even because of, the latter's dysfunctional personal characteristics such as lack of integrity, insatiable ambition, enormous egos, arrogance, reckless disregard for the effects of their actions on others and cowardice. From a critical perspective, the destructive and coercive practices of 'toxic', 'dictatorial' and/or 'bad' leaders are rather extreme forms of leadership power and control. CLS suggest that power and control can also be exercised and experienced in more subtle ways within everyday leadership practices. Suffice it to say here that the production of follower conformity is certainly one possible outcome of leadership dynamics, but is this inevitable?

Some critical writers draw on the arguments of Giddens and Foucault to highlight the dialectic between power and resistance. Foucault asserted that 'resistance is never in a position of exteriority to power' (1979, p. 95). Even in the most totalitarian of power regimes, cleavages and contradictions arise that provide opportunities for resistance, especially in the form of localized acts of defiance. As Foucault argued, 'Where there is power, there is resistance' (1979, p. 95). Accordingly, some critical researchers assert that power/resistance are mutually implicated, co-constructed and interdependent processes that have multiple, ambiguous and contradictory conditions, meanings and consequences (Mumby, 2005). Viewing control and resistance as discursive and dialectical practices, they argue that the meanings of such practices are to some extent open-ended, precarious, shifting and contingent. From this perspective, power is seen as both disciplinary and enabling, while practices of control and resistance are viewed as mutually reinforcing and simultaneously linked, often in contradictory ways (Collinson, 2003).

In leadership studies, issues of dissent have only recently been addressed (Banks, 2008). By contrast, in CMS there is a considerable literature demonstrating that forms of control frequently produce employee resistance (e.g. Fleming and Spicer, 2007). Studies suggest that followers are frequently more knowledgeable and oppositional than has typically been acknowledged in the mainstream leadership literature (Jermier et al., 1994). Some researchers draw on Hirschman's (1970) ideas to argue that resistance enables subordinates to 'voice' dissent (e.g. Graham, 1986). Hirschman argued that in conditions of organizational decline individuals are likely either to resign (exit) or try to change (voice) products or processes they find objectionable. He suggested that voice is less likely where exit is possible and more likely where loyalty is present and when exit opportunities are limited.

Critical researchers reveal that oppositional practices can take numerous forms (Ackroyd and Thompson, 1999), including strikes, 'working to rule', output restriction, 'working the system', 'whistleblowing' and sabotage (Edwards et al., 1995). In exceptional cases, subordinates may even (seek to) depose leaders (Mole, 2004). Even in the military, there is a long history of outright rebellion, mutiny and spontaneous acts of 'follower' dissent (Prince, 1998). Through oppositional discursive practices followers can express discontent, exercise a degree of control over work processes and/or construct alternative, more positive identities to those prescribed by organizations. This focus on the power/resistance dialectic does not imply that followers will invariably engage in resistance (in a mechanical or predetermined way), or that their opposition is necessarily effective. Control may produce compliance and even conformity, while resistance can also have unintended and contradictory consequences. Not all follower dissent is aimed specifically at leaders, and followers do not invariably seek to resist those in leadership positions. In many everyday workplace settings, employees are concerned with performing well and meeting expectations about their job performance.

Some critical writers argue that employee resistance is more likely to emerge when followers believe that leaders are exercising control in unfair, dictatorial, coercive, nepotistic and/or narcissistic ways (see also Kets De Vries and Balazs, Chapter 28, this volume). Equally, followers are more likely to resist when they feel that their views have not been considered, when they perceive leaders to be 'out of touch' and when they detect discrepancies between leaders' policies and practices. Where followers perceive such inconsistencies, they can become increasingly cynical about leaders. Fleming's (2005) research in an Australian call centre found that, in the face of a corporate culture which treated workers like children, employees constructed oppositional identities expressed in cynicism. Employees in a US Subaru Isuzu plant detected inconsistencies between the company's teamworking ideal and work intensification. Consequently, they refused to participate in corporate rituals, sent highly critical anonymous letters to the company and used humour to make light of the company's teamworking and continuous improvement philosophies (Graham, 1995).

Similarly, research in a UK truck manufacturer demonstrated that a corporate culture campaign introduced by the new US senior management team to improve communication and establish trust with the workforce had the opposite effect (Collinson, 1992, 2000). Shop-floor workers dismissed senior management's definition of the company as a team and pointed to recurrent discrepancies between leaders' words and actions. Fuelled by their perceptions of leaders' distance and lack of understanding about production, managers' routine disregard for workers' views, and manual workers' own sense of job insecurity, employees resisted by 'distancing' themselves, restricting output and effort, creating a counter-culture and by treating work purely as a means of economic compensation. The company's leaders and managers remained unaware of how their strategies produced contrary effects on the shop-floor. This study showed how control and resistance can be embedded within a mutually reinforcing vicious circle. It also demonstrates that if leaders' claims to authenticity are to be accepted by followers, the former's discourses and practices need to be seen to be consistent (see also Caza and Jackson, Chapter 26, this volume). When followers perceive discrepancies within and between leaders' words and their actions, they are likely to view them as yet another attempt to manipulate the workforce.

Some critical studies suggest that follower dissent may be even more diverse than previously recognized, being aimed at multiple audiences, such as the media (Real and Putnam, 2005) and customers (Leidner, 1993). Those working outside organizations can also express dissent. The campaign against Shell's plans to dispose of the obsolete Brent Spar platform by sinking it in the Atlantic Ocean illustrates how (external) resistance can change leaders' practices. After a Europe-wide boycott of their petrol stations, Shell eventually dismantled the platform on land in Norway. Klein (2000) has explored global protests against the leadership of the World Bank, the IMF and the World Trade Organization as well as more specific campaigns against companies like Nike, Reebok, McDonald's and Pepsi.

DISSENT/CONSENT

Followers' oppositional discursive practices may also blur the boundaries between dissent and consent. In particular, where followers are employed and might therefore be particularly concerned to avoid sanctions, they may resist in disguised and partial ways. While (employed) followers might be highly critical of leaders' practices, they may decide to censor their views and camouflage their actions through a kind of resistance that 'covers its own tracks' (Scott, 1985). One important reason why opposition may be disguised and limited is because those who resist anticipate the disciplinary sanctions their actions may provoke and shape their actions accordingly. As Heifetz and Laurie (1997, p. 129) observe in their study of leadership, 'whistle-blowers, creative deviants and other such original voices routinely get smashed and silenced in organizational life'. Subtle and routine subversions such as absenteeism (Edwards and Scullion, 1982), 'foot dragging' (Scott, 1990), 'disengagement' (Prasad and Prasad, 1998) and even irony and satire (Collinson, 2002, 2010) can be disguised and ambiguous, making them difficult for leaders to detect. Employees may even undermine leaders' change initiatives simply by doing nothing. Such inertia can result in leaders making all sorts of errors (Grint, 2005). Indeed in certain cases, even worker accommodation with managerial objectives can enable them to conceal resistance within the appearance of consent.

Disguised dissent is also particularly likely to occur where surveillance has become increasingly pervasive: for example, where hierarchical control is reconfigured through performance targets (Collinson, 2003). As a consequence of their increased awareness of being monitored, followers may engage in ambiguous oppositional practices that embody elements of both dissent and consent. In particular, they may conceal and massage knowledge and information. Under the gaze of authority, individuals are increasingly aware of themselves as visible objects and, as a consequence, they can become increasingly skilled choreographers of self and information, learning to disguise their response to 'the gaze'. This dramaturgical notion of self applies Goffman's (1959) ideas of impression management to surveillance processes. Goffman argued that interaction is like an information game in which individuals strategically disclose, exaggerate, or deliberately downplay information according to what they see as their strategic purpose.

A critical analysis of safety practices on North Sea oil installations found that despite extensive leadership commitment to safety, many offshore workers were either not reporting accidents and 'near misses' or else they sought to downplay the seriousness of particular incidents (Collinson, 1999). While company leaders talked proudly about the organization's 'learning culture', offshore workers complained about a 'blame culture' on the platforms. Believing that disclosure of accident-related information would have a detrimental impact on their annual appraisal, pay and employment security, offshore workers felt compelled to conceal or downplay information about accidents, injuries and near misses. Precisely because such practices constituted a firing offence, these workers also disguised their under-reporting. Hence, while the mainstream leadership literature tends to assume that it is primarily leaders who use impression management, followers may also disguise dissent. Critical perspectives suggest that such dramaturgical practices can take primarily conformist (e.g. telling leaders what they want to hear) or more oppositional forms (e.g. knowledge and output restriction). They may also embody elements of both conformity and resistance. Accordingly, workplace power asymmetries can generate subtle forms of disguised dissent. Rather than being polarized dichotomies, dissent and consent may be inextricably linked within the same practices.

In an important contribution to the critical analysis of organizations, Kondo (1990, p. 224) criticizes the tendency to separate artificially conformity or resistance into 'crisply distinct categories'. She contends that there is no such thing as an entirely 'authentic' or 'pristine space of resistance' or of a 'true resister'. Observing that people 'consent, cope, and resist at different levels of consciousness at a single point in time', Kondo questions the meaning of the term 'resistance' and warns about the dangers of romanticizing followers' oppositional practices. Her arguments have important implications for CLS. Whereas mainstream writers may romanticize leaders and overstate consensus, more critical studies can romanticize followers and exaggerate their opposition. Researchers may also romanticize distributed and more collective forms of leadership (Leonard, 2009). Kondo cautions against the tendency of critical researchers to impute a subversive or emancipatory motive or outcome to resistance. Her analysis also highlights the importance of gender for understanding the control/resistance and consent/dissent dialectics of leadership.

MEN/WOMEN

Gender is a very important and frequently neglected feature of leadership dynamics (Fletcher, 2004). Critical feminist writers have critiqued the tendency of male researchers to view leadership through stereotyped perspectives that simultaneously underestimate the importance of gender (Calas and Smircich, 1991). In the study of gender generally, and women in leadership more particularly, issues of essentialism, romanticism and dualism frequently emerge. The mainstream gender and leadership literature tends to focus on whether women and men adopt similar or different, and/or better or worse leadership styles (e.g. Rosener, 1990). As Carli and Eagly outline in more detail (Chapter 8, this volume), researchers have argued, for example, that women are more relationship-oriented and men more task-oriented. Questioning the biological essentialism that can underpin such debates, critical feminist studies explore the gendered nature of leadership, management and organization (Martin, 1990), focusing in particular on *both* the similarities and differences between men and women (Bacchi, 1990), and also between women *and* between men.

Recognizing that people are inherently gendered beings in socially constructed ways, critical feminists suggest that the dialectics between men and women, masculinity and femininity, as well as between paid employment and domestic work are inescapable features of gender and leadership dynamics (Bligh and Kohles, 2008). Whereas power and gender are sometimes assumed to be separate, critical studies also argue that they are inextricably linked. Bowring (2004) emphasizes that the binary opposition between leaders and followers is reinforced by a gender dualism in which men are viewed as the universal, neutral subject and women as 'the other'. She argues that we need to move towards greater fluidity in leadership research by recognizing that people have multiple, interrelated and shifting identities.

Critical feminist studies reveal that romanticized notions of the heroic, 'tough' leader are often saturated with masculinity, that women continue to be largely excluded from senior positions (Sinclair, 1998, 2007) and that they can experience considerable hostility in male-dominated managerial cultures (Marshall, 1995). Critical studies of men reveal the dominance of masculine assumptions in organizational cultures and practices generally, and in shaping the models, styles, language, cultures, identities and processes of leadership and management more particularly (Collinson and Hearn, 1996). Critical feminist studies of management and organization illustrate how certain gendered, ethnic and class-based voices are routinely privileged in the workplace, whereas others are marginalized (Ashcraft and Mumby, 2004).

In relation to critical feminist studies of the workplace, research highlights how the control of leaders and managers is often sustained through the gendered segregation of jobs and the subordination of domestic labour. The paid workplace (as well as the domestic sphere) is an important site for the reproduction of men's masculine power and status. Studies suggest that masculinity can be embedded in formal organizational practices (e.g. recruitment), through to more informal dynamics (e.g. joking relationships). Central to men's valorization of 'work' is a close identification with machinery and technology (Cockburn, 1983). Masculine cultures at work can also be reproduced through men's sexuality and the sexual harassment of women (Collinson and Collinson, 1996).

Critical feminist organizational research demonstrates that resistance practices can also take gendered forms (e.g. Trethewey, 1997). Various studies reveal, for example, how male-dominated shop-floor counter-cultures are frequently characterized by highly masculine breadwinner identities, aggressive and profane forms of humour, ridicule and sarcasm and the elevation of 'practical', manual work as confirmation of working-class manhood (e.g. Collinson, 1992, 2000). Cockburn (1983) illustrates how male-dominated shop-floor counter-cultures and exclusionary trade union practices in the printing industry elevated men and masculinity while subordinating and segregating women. Research in female-dominated factories and offices suggests that women workers often engage in (feminine) counter-cultures characterized by similarly aggressive, joking and sexualized practices of resistance (e.g. Westwood, 1984).

A small number of recent critical feminist studies suggest that it is not only followers but also those (broadly) defined as occupying leadership positions who may engage in resistance when seeking to promote change (Ospina and Su, 2009; Zoller and Fairhust, 2007). Sinclair (2007) focuses on the 'subversive leadership' of two Australian leaders, a woman Chief Commissioner of Police and an aboriginal school principal, who achieved radical change in moribund systems. Meyerson (2001) shows how senior managers can attempt to effect (gender) change while working within the organization. 'Tempered radicals' are frequently women in senior positions who are committed to their organization but also to a cause that is fundamentally at odds with the dominant workplace culture. Seeking to maintain a delicate balance between pursuing change, while also avoiding marginalization, tempered radicals have to cope with various tensions between potentially opposing 'personal' and 'professional' identities.

Critical feminist studies also address the contradictory processes and outcomes of workplace resistance. For example, Willis (1977) describes how working-class 'lads' creatively constructed a counter-culture that celebrated masculinity and the so-called freedom and independence of manual work. Yet, this counter-culture facilitated the lads' smooth transition into precisely the kind of shop-floor work that then subordinated them, possibly for the rest of their working lives. Ashcraft (2005) reveals how airline captains

engaged in subversive practices, but in this case their intentions were to undermine a change programme and to preserve their power and identity. Viewing the corporate enactment of a 'crew empowerment system' as a threat to their masculine authority and identity, pilots utilized numerous strategies to resist their loss of control, while also giving the appearance of supporting the change programme. These predominantly white professional men resisted the erosion of their authority by apparently consenting while actually resisting. Ashcraft illustrates how resistance can symbolically invert dominant values, but in ways that cut across emancipatory agendas, reinforcing the status quo.

Hence, some critical studies de-romanticize resistance by pointing to its potentially paradoxical processes and outcomes. They suggest that apparently oppositional practices may actually reinforce the very conditions of excessive control that stimulated resistance in the first place. Reflecting Kondo's arguments, their focus on the consequences of employee resistance avoids overly romanticized interpretations that celebrate, rather than critically examine, follower opposition. These arguments in turn raise important questions about the meaning of resistance, about who resists, how, why and when they do so, what strategies inform their practices, and what outcomes ensue. Critical feminist studies also raise important questions about how to theorize the multiple, simultaneous and potentially intersecting nature of leadership power dialectics. Differences and inequalities can take multiple forms (e.g. gender, ethnicity, class, age, disability, faith, sexual orientation, national origin, etc.) and different aspects of power, inequality and identity may be reproduced by those in leadership positions in ways that may perpetuate disadvantage.

Recently there has been growing interest within critical studies in exploring the simultaneity of gender, race and class (Calas et al., 2010). Demonstrating that the category 'women' is by no means a universal, Holvino (2010) explores the critique of white liberal feminism by women of colour. Developing an intersectional analysis, she argues that the emphasis in the mainstream gender literature on women managers (and leaders) concentrates on achieving individual rights for white women in ways that privilege gender over race, class, ethnicity and other dimensions of difference. Whereas white middle-class women are often found in managerial and higher-paid work, women of colour typically predominate in lower-paid positions. Holvino argues that gender needs to be studied in relation to other social processes such as race, ethnicity, class, sexuality and nation. Similarly, critical studies of men highlight the importance of 'multiple masculinities' and how these are frequently shaped by class, race, ethnicity, etc.(Collinson and Hearn, 1994, 2009). These critical studies raise important questions for the development of CLS, highlighting the significance of gender and other aspects of diversity and inequality in leadership dynamics, as well as the conceptual value of intersectionality, simultaneity and asymmetry. In addition to the theoretical challenges they pose for CLS, these arguments highlight the need to develop more inclusive and integrated leadership practices that value multiplicity, diversity, simultaneity and difference.

CONCLUSIONS

This chapter has explored the emergent field of critical leadership studies. Focusing particularly on the situated and shifting power relations between leaders, managers and followers, CLS suggest that dialectical perspectives can facilitate new ways of thinking about their complex, ambiguous and potentially contradictory inter relations. The three dialectics discussed above are frequently interconnected and mutually reinforcing. However, they are by no means exhaustive of the numerous dialectics that characterize leadership dynamics. Rather than try to produce a definitive list of such dialectics, it is argued here that dialectical analysis is better seen as a way of thinking and understanding leadership dynamics.

Critical perspectives raise a number of under-explored issues about power in leadership dynamics and about what it may mean to be 'a leader', 'a manager' and a 'follower' in contemporary organizations and societies. They question the prevailing mainstream view that leader-led relations are inherently consensual. Indeed, the legacy of orthodox studies is a rather uncontested notion of leadership. CLS recognize that leaders exercise considerable control, and that their power can have contradictory and ambiguous outcomes that leaders either do not always understand or of which they are unaware. Critical perspectives view control and resistance as mutually reinforcing, ambiguous and potentially contradictory processes. Although control can stimulate resistance, it may also discipline, shape and restrict the very opposition it sometimes provokes.

Critical perspectives suggest that in leader-follower relations there is always the potential for conflict and dissent. Leaders (and leadership researchers) cannot simply assume the obedience or loyalty of followers. Given the asymmetrical nature of workplace power, it is hardly surprising that followers often conform (or give the outward appearance of compliance), but from a leadership point of view we need to know a lot more about the conditions and consequences of such practices. For example, leaders can surround themselves with sycophants, thereby stifling dialogue, new ideas and innovation (Bratton et al., 2004). Critical perspectives reveal that followers may not only express opposition in numerous ways but also may seek to protect themselves from sanctions. Disguised dissent incorporates self-protective, ambiguous practices that may blur the boundaries between resistance and consent.

Critical feminist and diversity analyses highlight how these (and other) dialectics of leader/follower, power/resistance and consent/dissent are shaped by gender, class, race, age, etc. They demonstrate that leadership dynamics are inescapably situated within, and reproduced through multiple, intersecting and simultaneous differences and inequalities. Indeed, there remains a significant challenge for CLS to examine the interrelations between multiple inequalities and to show how these intersect and/or contradict.

This in turn raises complex questions about how to theorize the interrelations between multiple dialectics within particular practices and contexts. It is quite possible for researchers to question one dualism but to do so in ways that reproduce others. Just as workplace resistance may paradoxically reproduce the very conditions of control that give rise to opposition, critical writers may question specific dualisms, but simultaneously reinforce others. For example, although some critical researchers may challenge the leader/follower dualism, they might simultaneously neglect important relations between control and resistance or between men and women and so on. Accordingly, a pressing challenge for CSL is to find ways to theorize the interrelations between multiple, simultaneous, ambiguous and contradictory dialectics.

Relatedly, there is a need to develop more nuanced accounts of the diverse economic, social, political and cultural contexts in which leadership dynamics are typically located (Gibney et al., 2009; Jepson, 2009). For example, technological advances in communications and transportation increase the potential for cross-cultural interactions in all types of organizations. Globalization may facilitate trade and global capital flows and more integrated financial markets, and reduce transportation costs. In the search for lower production and distribution costs, transnational corporations can transfer parts of their processes to other parts of the globe. These shifting regional, national and global contexts and their local impacts require more detailed analysis.

Critical approaches also raise questions about leaders' and followers' identities. The notions of 'the leader' and 'the follower' are deeply embedded identities, especially in Western societies (Sinclair, 2007). Yet, there is a growing recognition that such traditional identities no longer adequately characterize leadership power relations, which are increasingly seen as blurred, fluid and contradictory (Gordon, 2002). For example, whereas distributed leadership encourages followers to act as 'informal leaders' (Raelin, 2003), leaders in many contemporary organizations are subject to intensified pressures of accountability that can render them 'calculable followers' (Collinson and Collinson, 2009). In many organizational settings, individuals are expected to act as both leaders and followers, either simultaneously or at different times and circumstances. Accordingly, there is a need for more critical research to examine these multiple, shifting and often paradoxical identities of 'leaders' and 'followers' in particular contexts. Exploring how these ambiguous subjectivities are negotiated in practice should not only enhance our understanding of leadership dialectics in various contexts but also emphasize the value of critical studies for analysing situated leadership and followership dynamics.

The implications of CLS for leadership studies are potentially far-reaching. By critically exploring power relations and identity constructions, CLS encourage researchers to rethink leaders, followers and contexts as well as their dialectical interrelations. They reveal the problems in mainstream studies associated with essentialism, romanticism and dualism, while also challenging CMS in a number of ways. In particular, they emphasize the power and impact of leadership, for good or ill, in contemporary organizations and societies. Recognizing the related significance of followers, they warn against the tendency to romanticize dissent and opposition. Equally, they highlight the importance of gender and other aspects of diversity and inequality for understanding the conditions, processes and consequences of leadership dynamics. CLS also challenge both mainstream and critical researchers to be more reflexively aware of their underlying (and often implicit) theoretical assumptions and how these can shape leadership theory, research, development and practice. In sum, by raising under-researched questions, particularly about power and identity, the emergent field of CLS has the potential to broaden understanding of leadership dynamics, develop new forms of analysis and open up innovative lines of enquiry.

ACKNOWLEDGEMENT

Many thanks to my co-editors for helpful comments on an earlier draft of this chapter.

REFERENCES

Ackroyd, S. (2004) 'Less bourgeois than thou: a critical review of studying management critically', *Ephemera*, 4(2): 165–170.

Ackroyd, S. and Thompson, P. (1999) *Organizational Misbehaviour*. London: Sage.

Alvarez, J. L. and Svejenova, S. (2005) *Sharing Executive Power*. Cambridge, UK: Cambridge University Press.

Alvesson, M. and Willmott, H. (2002) 'Producing the appropriate individual: identity regulation as organizational control', *Journal of Management Studies*, 39(5): 619–644.

Alvesson, M. and Willmott, H. (eds) (2003) *Studying Management Critically*. London: Sage.

Ashcraft, K. L. (2005) 'Resistance through consent?' *Management Communication Quarterly*, 19(1): 67–90.

Ashcraft, K. L. and Mumby, D. K. (2004) *Reworking Gender: A Feminist Communicology of Organization*. London: Sage.

Bacchi, C. L. (1990) *Same Difference: Feminism and Sexual Difference*. London: Allen and Unwin.

Banks, S. (ed.) (2008) *Dissent and the Failure of Leadership*. Cheltenham: Edward Elgar.

Baxter, L. A. and Montgomery, B. M. (1996) *Relating: Dialogues and Dialectics*. New York: Guilford Press.

Bjerke, B. (1999) *Business Leadership and Culture*. Cheltenham: Edward Elgar.

Bligh, M. and Kohles, J. (2008) 'The romance lives on: contemporary issues surrounding the romance of leadership', *Leadership*, 3(3): 343–360.

Bowring, M. A. (2004) 'Resistance is not futile: liberating Captain Janeway from the masculine–feminine dualism of leadership', *Gender, Work and Organization*, 11(4): 381–405.

Bratton, J., Grint, K., and Nelson, D. (2004) *Organizational Leadership*. Mason, OH: South Western/Thomson.

Burns, J. M. (1978) *Leadership*. New York: Harper and Row.

Calas, M. and Smircich, L. (1991) 'Voicing seduction to silence leadership', *Organization Studies*, 12(4): 567–602.

Calas, M., Smircich, L., Tienari, J., and Ellehave, C. F. (2010) 'Editorial: observing globalized capitalism: gender and ethnicity as entry point', *Gender, Work and Organization*, 17(3): 243–247.

Chaleff, I. (2009) *The Courageous Follower*. San Francisco: Berrett-Koehler. (1st edn, 1995.)

Cockburn, C. (1983) *Brothers*. London: Pluto.

Collins, J. (2001) *Good to Great*. London: Random House.

Collinson, D. (1992) *Managing the Shopfloor: Subjectivity, Masculinity and Workplace Culture*. Berlin: Walter de Gruyter.

Collinson, D. (1999) 'Surviving the rigs: safety and surveillance on North Sea oil installations', *Organization Studies*, 20(4): 579–600.

Collinson, D. (2000) 'Strategies of resistance: power, knowledge and subjectivity in the workplace'. In K. Grint (ed.), *Work and Society: A Reader*. Cambridge: Polity Press, pp. 163–198. Originally published in J. Jermier, D. Knights, and W. Nord (eds), (1994) *Resistance and Power in Organizations*. London: Routledge, pp. 25–68.

Collinson, D. (2002) 'Managing humour', *Journal of Management Studies*, 39(2): 269–288.

Collinson, D. (2003) 'Identities and insecurities: selves at work', *Organization*, 10(3): 527–547.

Collinson, D. L. (2005) 'Dialectics of leadership', *Human Relations*, 8(11): 1419–1442.

Collinson, D. L. (2006) 'Rethinking followership: a post-structuralist analysis of follower identities', *The Leadership Quarterly*, 17(2): 179–189.

Collinson, D. (2008) 'Conformist, resistant and disguised selves: a post-structuralist approach to identity and workplace followership'. In R. Riggio, I. Chaleff, and J. Lipmen-Blumen (eds), *The Art of Followership*. San Francisco, CA: Jossey-Bass, pp. 309–324.

Collinson, D. (2010) 'Leadership, humor, and satire'. In R. A. Couto (ed.), *Political and Civic Leadership: A Reference Handbook*. Thousand Oaks, CA: Sage.

Collinson, D. and Hearn, J. (1994) 'Naming Men as Men: Implications for Work, Organization and Management' Gender, *Work and Organization*, 1(1): 2–22.

Collinson, M. and Collinson, D. L. (1996) 'It's only Dick: the sexual harassment of women managers in insurance sales', *Work, Employment and Society*, 10(1): 29–56.

Collinson, D. L. and Collinson, M. (2009) 'Blended leadership: employee perspectives on effective leadership in the UK further education sector', *Leadership*, 5(3): 365–380.

Collinson, D. and Hearn, J. (eds), (1996) *Men as Managers, Managers as Men: Critical Perspectives on Men, Masculinities and Managements*. London: Sage.

Dickson, M. W., Hartog, D. D., and Mitchelson, J. K. (2003) 'Research on leadership in a cross-cultural context: making progress, and raising new questions', *The Leadership Quarterly*, 14: 729–768.

Edwards, P. K. and Scullion, H. (1982) *The Social Organization of Industrial Conflict*. Oxford: Basil Blackwell.

Edwards, P. K., Collinson, D. L., and Della Rocca, G. (1995) 'Workplace resistance in Western Europe', *European Journal of Industrial Relations*, 1(3): 283–316.

Fairhust, G. T. (2001) 'Dualisms in leadership research'. In F. M. Jablin and L. L. Putnam (eds), *The New Handbook of Organizational Communication*. Thousand Oaks, CA: Sage. pp. 379–439.

Fairhurst, G. (2007) *Discursive Leadership*. Thousand Oaks, CA: Sage.

Fairhurst, G. and Grant, D. (2010) The social construction of leadership: A sailing guide. *Management Communication Quarterly* 24(2): 171–210.

Fleming, P. (2005) 'Metaphors of resistance', *Management Communication Quarterly*, 19(1): 45–66.

Fleming, P. and Spicer, A. (2007) *Contesting the Corporation*. Cambridge,UK: Cambridge University Press.

Fletcher, J. K. (2004) 'The paradox of post-heroic leadership: an essay on gender, power, and transformational change', *The Leadership Quarterly*, 15: 647–661.

Foucault, M. (1977) *Discipline and Punish*. London: Allen and Unwin.

Foucault, M. (1979) *The History of Sexuality*. London: Allen and Unwin.

Fournier, V. and Grey, C. (2000) 'At the critical moment: conditions and prospects for critical management studies', *Human Relations*, 53(1): 7–32.

Fromm, E. (1977) *The Fear of Freedom*. London: Routledge Kegan Paul.

Gabriel, Y. (1997) 'Meeting God: when organizational members come face to face with the supreme leader', *Human Relations*, 50(4): 315–342.

Gardner, W. L. and Avolio, B. J. (1998) 'The charismatic relationship: a dramaturgical perspective', *Academy of Management Review*, 23: 32–58.

Gemmill, G. and Oakley, J. (1992) 'Leadership: an alienating social myth', *Human Relations*, 45(2): 113–129.

Ghemawat, P. (2005) 'Regional strategies for global leadership', *Harvard Business Review*, December: 98–108.

Gibney, J., Copeland, S., and Murie, A. (2009) 'Toward a "new" strategic leadership of place for the knowledge-based economy', *Leadership*, 5(1): 5–23.

Giddens, A. (1984) *The Constitution of Society*. Cambridge, UK: Polity.

Giddens, A. (1987) *Social Theory and Modern Sociology*. Cambridge, UK: Polity.

Goffee, R. and Jones, G. (2001) 'Followership: it's personal too', *Harvard Business Review*, 79(11): 148.

Goffman, E. (1959) *The Presentation of Self in Everyday Life*. Harmondsworth, UK: Penguin.

Goleman, D., Boyatzis, R. and McKee, A. (2002) *The New Leaders*. London: Little, Brown.

Gordon, D. (2002) 'Conceptualising leadership with respect to its historical-contextual antecedents to power', *The Leadership Quarterly*, 13(2): 151–167.

Graen, G. and Uhl-Bien, M. (1995) 'Relationship-based approach to leadership: development of leader–member exchange theory of leadership over 25 years', *The Leadership Quarterly*, 6(2): 219–247.

Graham, J. W. (1986) 'Principled organizational dissent', *Research in Organizational Behaviour*, 8, 1–52.

Graham, L. (1995) *On the Line at Subaru-Isuzu*. Ithaca, NY: ILR Press.

Grint, K (ed.) (1997) *Leadership: Classical, Contemporary, and Critical Approaches*. Oxford: Oxford University Press.

Grint, K. (2005) *Leadership: Limits and Possibilities*. New York: Palgrave Macmillan.

Gronn, P. (2002) 'Distributed leadership as a unit of analysis', *The Leadership Quarterly*, 13(4): 423–452.

Hale, J. R. and Fields, D. L. (2007) 'Exploring servant leadership across cultures: a study of followers in Ghana and the USA', *Leadership*, 3(4): 397–417.

Hardy, C. and Clegg, S. R. (1999) 'Some dare call it power'. In S. R. Clegg and C. Hardy (eds), *Studying Organization: Theory and Method*. London: Sage, pp. 368–387.

Hartog, D. D. and Dickson, M. W. (2004) 'Leadership and culture'. In J. Antonakis, A. T. Cianciolo, and R. J. Sternberg (eds), *The Nature of Leadership*. London: Sage, pp. 249–278.

Hearn, J. and Collinson, D. L. (2009) 'Men, diversity at work, and diversity management'. In M. Ozbilgin (ed.), *Theory and Scholarship in Equality, Diversity and Inclusion at*

Work: A Research Companion. Cheltenham, UK: Edward Elgar, pp. 372–382.

Heifetz, R. A. and Laurie, D. L. (1997) 'The work of leadership' *Harvard Business Review,* Jan–Feb, 124–134.

Hersey, P. and Blanchard, K. (1996) *Management of Organizational Behaviour.* Englewood Cliffs, NJ: Prentice Hall.

Hirschman, A. D. (1970) *Exit, Voice and Loyalty.* Cambridge, MA: Harvard University Press.

Hogg, M. (2001) 'A social identity theory of leadership', *Personality and Social Psychology Review,* 5(3), 184–200.

Holvino, E. (2010) 'Intersections: the simultaneity of race, gender and class in organization studies', *Gender, Work and Organization,* 17(3): 248–277.

House, R. (1971) 'A path–goal theory of leadership: lessons, legacy and a reformulated theory', *The Leadership Quarterly,* 7(3): 323–352.

Howell, J. and Shamir, B. (2005) 'The role of followers in the charismatic leadership process: relationships and their consequences', *Academy of Management Review,* 30(1): 96–112.

Jackson, B. and Parry, K. W. (2008) *A Very Short, Fairly Interesting and Reasonably Cheap Book about Studying Leadership.* London: Sage.

Jameson, J. (2007) *Investigating Collaborative Leadership in Learning and Skills.* Lancaster University Management School: Centre for Excellence in Leadership.

Jepson, D. (2009) 'Studying leadership at cross-country level: a critical analysis', *Leadership,* 5(1): 61–80.

Jermier, J. M., Knights, D., and Nord, W. R. (eds), (1994) *Resistance and Power in Organisations.* London: Routledge.

Jones, A. M. (2006) 'Developing what? An anthropological look at the leadership development process across cultures.' *Leadership,* 2(4): 48–498.

Kellerman, B. (2008) *Followership: How Followers are Creating and Changing Leaders.* Boston, MA; Harvard Business School Press.

Kelley, R. E. (2004) 'Followership'. In G. R. Goethals, G. Sorenson and J. M. Burns (eds), *Berkshire Encyclopedia of World History.* Sage Reference/Berkshire. pp. 504–513.

Klein, N. (2000) *No Logo.* London: Flamingo.

Knights, D. (1997) 'Organization theory in the age of deconstruction: dualism, gender and postmodernism revisited', *Organization Studies,* 18(1): 1–20.

Knowles, H. (2007) 'Trade union leadership: biography and the role of historical context', *Leadership,* 3(2): 191–209.

Kondo, D. K. (1990) *Crafting Selves: Power, Gender and Discourses of Identity in a Japanese Workplace.* Chicago, IL: University of Chicago Press.

Lakomski, G. (2005) *Managing Without Leadership.* Amsterdam: Elsevier.

Leidner, R. (1993) *Fast Food, Fast Talk: Service Work and The Routinisation of Everyday Life.* Berkeley, CA: University of California Press.

Leonard, P. (2009) 'Leading partnerships: How do you lead when not "in charge"?' Unpublished doctoral thesis, Lancaster University Management School.

Lipmen-Blumen, J. (2005) *The Allure of Toxic Leaders.* Oxford: Oxford University Press.

Lord, R. G. and Brown, D. J. (2003) *Leadership Processes and Follower Self-Identity.* Mahwah, NJ: Lawrence Erlbaum.

Maccoby, M. (2007) *The Leaders We Need.* Boston, MA: Harvard Business School Press.

Marshall, J. (1995) *Women Managers Moving On.* London: Macmillan.

Martin, J. (1990) 'Deconstructing organizational taboos: the suppression of gender conflict in organizations', *Organization Science,* 1(4): 339–359.

Meindl, J., Ehrlich, S. B., and Dukerich, J. M. (1985) 'The romance of leadership', *Administrative Science Quarterly,* 30(1): 78–102.

Meyerson, D. E. (2001) *Tempered Radicals.* Boston, MA: Harvard Business School.

Milgram, S. (1963) 'Behavioral study of obedience', *Journal of Abnormal and Social Psychology,* 69(2): 137–143.

Mingers, J. (2000) 'What is it to be critical? Teaching a critical approach to management undergraduates', *Management Learning,* 31(2), 219–237.

Mintzberg H. (2006) 'The leadership debate with Henry Mintzberg: community-ship is the answer.' *The Financial Times:* FT.Com

Mole, G. (2004) 'Can leadership be taught?'. In J. Storey (ed.), *Leadership in Organizations.* London: Routledge, pp. 125–137.

Mumby, D. (2005) 'Theorizing resistance in organization studies', *Management Communication Quarterly,* 19(1): 19–44.

Mumby, D and Stohl, C. (1991) 'Power and discourse in organizational studies: absence and the dialectic of control', *Discourse and Society,* 2(3): 313–332.

Northouse, P. G. (2004) *Leadership Theory and Practice,* 3rd edn. London: Sage.

Nye, J. S. (2008) *The Powers to Lead.* Oxford: Oxford University Press.

Osborne, R., Hunt, J., and Jauch, L. R. (2002) 'Toward a contextual theory of leadership', *The Leadership Quarterly,* 13(6): 797–837.

Ospina, S. and Sorenson, G. (2007) 'A constructionist lens on leadership', in G. R. Goethals and G. L. J. Sorenson (eds), *The Quest for a General Theory of Leadership.* Cheltenham, UK: Edward Elgar, pp.188–204.

Ospina, S. and Su, C. (2009) 'Weaving color lines: race, ethnicity, and the work of leadership in social change organizations', *Leadership,* 5(2): 131–170.

Pearce, C. L. and Conger, J. A. (eds), (2003) *Shared Leadership.* Thousand Oaks, CA: Sage.

Porter, L. W. and McLaughlin, G. B. (2006) 'Leadership and the organizational context: Like the weather?' *The Leadership Quarterly,* 17(6): 559–576.

Prasad, A. and Prasad, P. (1998) 'Everyday struggles at the workplace: the nature and implications of routine resistance in contemporary organizations'. In P. A. Bamberger and W. J. Sonnenstuhl (eds), *Research in the Sociology of Organizations,* Stamford, CT: JAI, 15, pp. 225–257.

Prince, L. (1998) 'The neglected rules: on leadership and dissent'. In A. Coulson (ed.), *Trust and Contracts: Relationships in Local Government, Health and Public Services*. Bristol: The Polity Press, pp. 95–126.

Raelin, J. (2003) *Creating Leaderful Organisations*. San Francisco: Berrett-Koehler.

Ray, T., Clegg, S., and Gordon, R. (2004). 'A new look at dispersed leadership: power, knowledge and context'. In J. Storey (ed.), *Leadership in Organizations*. London: Routledge, pp. 319–336.

Real, K. and Putnam, L. (2005) 'Ironies in the discursive struggle of pilots defending the profession', *Management Communication Quarterly*, 19(1): 91–119.

Reed, M. (1997) 'In praise of duality', *Organization Studies*, 18(1): 21–42.

Rejai, M. (1979) *Leaders of Revolution*. London: Sage.

Ricketts, K.G. and Ladewig, H. (2008) 'A path analysis of community leadership within viable rural communities in Florida', *Leadership*, 4(2): 137–157.

Riggio, R. E., Chaleff, I., and Lipman-Blumen, J. (eds) (2008). *The Art of Followership: How Great Followers Create Great Leaders and Organizations*. San Francisco: Jossey-Bass.

Rosener, J. (1990) 'Ways women lead', *Harvard Business Review*, 68(6): 119–125.

Scott, J. (1985) *Weapons of the Weak: Everyday Forms of Peasant Resistance*. New Haven, CT: Yale University Press.

Scott, J. C. (1990) *Domination and the Arts of Resistance*. New Haven, CT: Yale University Press.

Shamir, B. (1999) 'Taming charisma for better understanding and greater usefulness: a response to Beyer', *The Leadership Quarterly*, 10(4): 555–562.

Shamir, B. (2007) 'From passive recipients to active co-producers: followers' roles in the leadership process'. In B. Shamir, R. Pillai, M. C. Bligh, and M. Uhl-Bien (eds), *Follower-Centred Perspectives on Leadership*. Greenwich, CT: Information Age, pp. ix–xxxix.

Shamir, B., House, R. J., and Arthur, M. B. (1993) 'The motivational effects of charismatic leadership: a self-based concept theory', *Organization Science*, 4(4): 577–594.

Shamir, B., Dayan-Horesh, D., and Adler, D. (2005). 'Leading by biography: towards a life-story approach to the study of leadership', *Leadership*, 1(1), 13–29.

Shamir, B., Pillai, R., Bligh, M., C., and Uhl-Bien, M. (eds), (2007) *Follower-Centred Perspectives on Leadership*. Greenwich, CT: Information Age.

Sinclair, A. (1998) *Doing Leadership Differently*. Melbourne: Melbourne University Press.

Sinclair, A. (2007) *Leadership for the Disillusioned*. London: Allen and Unwin.

Smircich, L. and Morgan, G. (1982) 'Leadership: the management of meaning', *Journal of Applied Behavioural Science*, 18(3): 257–273.

Tourish, D. and Vatcha, N. (2005) 'Charismatic leadership and corporate cultism at Enron: the elimination of dissent, the promotion of conformity and organizational collapse', *Leadership*, 1(4): 455–480.

Trethewey, A. (1997) 'Resistance, identity and empowerment: a postmodern feminist analysis of clients in a human service organization', *Communication Monographs*, 64: 281–301.

Van Knippenberg, D. and Hogg, M. (eds), (2003). *Leadership and Power: Identity Processes in Groups and Organizations*. London: Sage.

Westwood, S. (1984) *All Day, Every Day: Factory and Family in the Making of Women's Lives*. London: Pluto Press.

Willis, P. (1977) *Learning to Labour*. Aldershot, UK: Saxon House.

Zaccaro, S. J. (2007) 'Trait-based perspectives of leadership', *American Psychologist*, 62, 6–16.

Zoller, H. M. and Fairhurst, G. T. (2007) 'Resistance leadership: the overlooked potential in critical organization and leadership studies', *Human Relations*, 60(1): 1331–1360.

14

Leadership and Power

Raymond Gordon

INTRODUCTION

This chapter traces a path through the leadership literature that, in general terms, explores how leadership theorists have addressed the topic of power in organisations. A comprehensive review of the literature is not the charter here; rather, the pervading approach to power adopted by the main theoretical categories that make up the literature will be the focus. Critical analysis techniques are employed to bring the nature of power in each approach into view. These techniques include exploring: how power relations are portrayed (Boje, 1995); whether the approach to leadership privileges an underlying contextual theme that adopts a particular viewpoint of power; whether, in a normative fashion, the viewpoint prescribes a particular version of how power ought to be in leadership scenarios; and whether or not the viewpoint acknowledges any potential problematic considerations associated with its normative stance. The techniques will also include looking for evidence of dualities within the main theoretical approaches to leadership, as well as an assessment of the extent to which concepts such as privilege, domination and discipline are masked, but nevertheless remain embedded, within each approach (Calas & Smircich, 1988; Culler, 1982; Derrida, 1974; Kilduff, 1993; Martin, 1990; Gordon, 2002).

The chapter begins by summarising the more traditional approaches to leadership: namely, the trait, style, contingency and new leadership approaches (Bryman, 1996). This is followed by an analysis of the contemporary theories that have emerged in response to the widespread adoption of new organisational forms over the past two to three decades. New organisational forms are indicative of organically oriented architectures and strategies that promote flexibility through flatter structures, the dispersion of power, the use of teams and decentralised control systems.

The chapter illustrates that a normative apolitical approach to power pervades the mainstream leadership literature. More to the point, in the majority of cases power is ignored; when leadership researchers do discuss power, their starting point is one that views the power of leaders as something that occurs 'naturally' in social systems and is thus unproblematic. Normative and apolitical views of power are challenged by the shifting nature of power relations associated with the adoption of new organisational forms by contemporary organisations. The chapter concludes by observing that the application of critical analysis techniques reveals a fundamental paradox between the theory and practice of leadership in organisations. A series of questions emerge throughout the chapter, which identify research opportunities that may provide insight into the practical implications of this paradox.

TRADITIONAL APPROACHES TO LEADERSHIP: APOLITICAL AND DUALISTIC POWER RELATIONS

The mainstream literature pertaining to leadership in organisations may be divided into five broad approaches: trait, style, contingency, new leadership and dispersed leadership (Bryman, 1996; Gordon, 2002; Collinson, 2006). As shall be explained later, the trait, style, contingency and new leadership theories are referred to here as traditional in approach, and dispersed leadership as non-traditional in approach. It is acknowledged that a growing body of literature is emerging in the field of leadership that does not fit within these categories. However, the chapter is concerned with dominant trends in the literature, which, as Collinson (2009) noted, is US-based and psychologically informed.

The trait theories focused on determining what attributes and qualities differentiated leaders from followers. Early trait theorists, such as Bingham (1927), Bowden (1927) and Schenk (1928), explained leadership in terms of the personal attributes and characteristics of those individuals who were considered leaders. In these theories, leaders were implicitly referred to as extraordinary individuals. In an organisational context, such individuals held senior management positions and were seen as possessing qualities that their subordinates responded to positively. For instance, Barnard (1938) suggested that any person extraordinarily efficient at stimulating others, and therefore effective in conditioning collective responses, could be called a leader.

The style theorists turned their attention away from the traits of leaders to how leaders behaved. Leadership theorists, such as Fleishman et al. (1955), Likert (1961), McGregor (1960, 1966), Blake and Mouton (1964), and Sims (1977), all described leadership in terms of the behaviour of prominent social and organisational leaders. Thus, research focused on the behaviour and style of successful senior executives, as opposed to internal traits and qualities. For example, McGregor (1960) suggested that the behaviour of leaders could be grouped into two distinct styles – Theory X, a directive style, and Theory Y, a supportive style – both of which achieved success yet were very different. The objective for style theorists was to ascertain those behaviours that led to individuals being recognised as leaders.

The contingency theorists argued that there was no 'one best style' or set of behaviours attributable to 'good' leadership. In this theory, leadership was related to situational demands (Bass & Stogdill, 1990), or in other words, situational factors determined who emerged as a leader. Theorists such as Homans (1959), Fiedler (1967), Hersey and Blanchard (1969, 1977), Evans (1970), Vroom and Yetton (1973) and Yukl (1971, 1989) explained leadership in terms of how successful senior executives in organisations adapted to the needs of a situation. Contingency theorists also focused on how to place a particular type of leader into a situation for which he or she was best suited.

The new leadership paradigm, as per the three previous categories of leadership theories, recognised organisational leaders as extraordinary individuals occupying senior positions within an organisation hierarchy. However, the new leadership paradigm, so-called because the writers who contributed to it claimed to be adopting a new and alternative approach to the study of leadership in organisations, viewed leaders as managers of meaning rather than mandating influence (Bryman, 1996, p. 280). The paradigm incorporated three main categories of theory: transactional leadership (Graen & Cashman, 1975; Greene, 1975; Hollander, 1979), transformational leadership (Eden, 1984; Field, 1989) and culture-based leadership (Ouchi & Jaeger, 1978; Pascale & Athos, 1981; Schein, 1985). The *transactional leadership theorists*, including those who explored the concept of leadership through the eyes of followers, explained leadership as being contingent on transactions or exchanges between leaders and followers (Hollander, 1979). In contrast, the *transformational leadership theorists* argued that leadership was achieved through more than just tangible inducements; this theory suggested that leadership might be conceptually organised along a number of charismatic and situational correlated dimensions – charismatic leadership, inspirational leadership, intellectual stimulation, and individual consideration. Lastly, in addition to the cultural focus of transformational leadership, other *culture-based leadership theorists* viewed leadership as primarily dependent on whether a leader's style was in tune with his or her organisation's culture (Bryman, 1996).

Each of the above categories of leadership theories (trait, style, contingency and new leadership) are considered traditional accounts of leadership, because common to each is an adherence to the more hierarchical structures and control models of organisation (Gordon, 2002). Theoretically, the relationship between leaders and followers is presented in dualistic terms, the nature of which is central to the conceptualisation of leadership. Leaders hold a position of privilege in the dualism because they are considered to be superior to their followers, either through natural ability or the possession of appropriate attributes; if leaders were not superior, people would not follow them (Gordon, 2002).

The research framework for these mainstream theories takes the superior power of leaders within the leader/follower dualism as a given starting point, in which the nature of this superior power is considered unproblematic (Hardy & Clegg, 1996). In critical analysis terms, these theories adopt an apolitical orientation that gives leaders a 'voice', while silencing followers (see Enz, 1988; Gandz & Murray, 1980; Mintzberg, 1983). Even theories pertinent to followership implicitly position the leader as superior (Gordon, 2002). However, it should be noted that this dualistic and apolitical approach to the relationship between leaders and followers is just that, implicit; conditioned through the practice of leadership. One could argue that the superiority of leaders has become assumed as being part of the natural order of things. In sum, the interpretative position of the research and methodological frameworks adopted by these mainstream theorists have normalised power, the critical analysis of the relationship between leadership and power being deemed an unnecessary consideration.

NEW ORGANISATIONAL FORMS AND SHIFTING POWER RELATIONS

Theoretical approaches to leadership that have emerged in response to shifting power relations in contemporary organisations have been categorised by Bryman (1996) as Dispersed Leadership. Early theories include *Superleadership* (Manz & Sims, 1991, 1996; Sims & Lorenzi, 1992), *Real-Teams* (Katzenbach & Smith, 1993), *Self-Leadership* (Kirkman & Rosen, 1999; Kouzes & Posner, 1993; Uhl-Bien & Graen, 1998), *Leadership as a Process* (Hosking, 1991; Knights & Willmott, 1992) and *Distributed Leadership* (Senge, 1999). In a generic sense, these theories represent the decentralisation of leadership skills and responsibilities in an organisation (see Gronn, Chapter 32, this volume).

An assessment of the titles of these theories provides an indication of their potential practical forms. Primarily, these forms include self-leadership and team-based leadership. *Self-leadership* is where employees are positioned and encouraged to lead themselves, taking responsibility for their own direction and control. *Team-based leadership* focuses on facilitating concertive control through autonomous work teams, commonly known as self-led work teams, each of which is controlled by its own leader (Barker, 1993; Katzenbach & Smith, 1993; see Burke et al., Chapter 25, this volume). The nature of team leadership discussed in these theories is not the same as that written by earlier theorists on teams.

Dispersed leadership theories represent a major shift in the literature. Unlike, at least in theory, the dualistic nature of the power relationship between leaders and followers found in traditional leadership approaches, these theories espouse a sharing of power between leaders and followers. The sharing of power between leaders and followers blurs the normally clear boundary that differentiates the identity of 'the leader' from 'the follower'. For this reason these approaches are defined here as non-traditional in their orientation.

Applying a critical eye to these non-traditional approaches reveals that they are imbued with a number of unanswered questions. If, in theoretical terms, the differential identity between leaders and followers is blurred by the sharing of power between leaders and followers, does not the empowerment of followers result in confusion in regard to 'Who is the leader and who is the follower'? If this is so, will the focus of leadership research move away from the traits and/or the style of 'the leader'? With this in mind, does the sharing of power between leaders and followers imply that leadership is not necessarily something that an extraordinary individual does but something that many people might do? Perhaps it is time to focus on the process of leadership as opposed to 'the leader'? Further still, does viewing leadership as a process suggest that the leader–follower relationship, as we have come to know it, will become less important to the research and practice of leadership? As people acquire more power, they may rely less and question more the validity of decisions made by a single individual (whether they are extraordinary or not); i.e. people will exercise their voice more readily. In such situations how will the process of leadership unfold? This point will be discussed further shortly.

Since the dispersed leadership theories promote the redistribution of power, one would expect the analysis of power to be central to their research frameworks: this is not the case. Manz and Sims, arguably the founding researchers in the field, explain their theory of superleadership by arguing that a superleader empowers his or her followers by teaching them to lead themselves (1991, p. 22). The only explicit mention of power the authors make, however, is in a table in which they compare the characteristics of superleadership with those of more traditional leadership approaches. While they assert that power is shared in the practice of superleadership, they neglect to address, let alone critically analyse, how power might be shared.

Sims and Lorenzi (1992) extended Manz and Sims' work on superleadership. They use the same table but leave blank the cell that represents the relationship between superleadership and power (Sims & Lorenzi, 1992, p. 297). Interestingly, this is the only blank cell in the table. Sims and Lorenzi do not explain this omission, leaving one to question their intention. Nevertheless, the authors do appear to indirectly recognise the problems associated with any attempt to redistribute power. Rather than specifically discussing power, however, they assert that superleaders need to be concerned with ethics when exercising influence. Their discussion is used to justify Manz and Sims' theory of superleadership by suggesting that when leaders guide others to lead themselves, they empower these people and thereby 'cut the perceived manipulation strings' associated with the exercise of influence (1992, p. 281). In their discussion, Sims and Lorenzi, in a somewhat paradoxical fashion, suggest that in order to empower their followers, leaders 'must be trained to *model* the *desired* self-leadership behaviour on the part of their subordinates' (1992, p. 281). Such a suggestion is indicative of a normalised view of power; it neglects the contradiction between empowerment and conditioning implicit to the modelling of behavioural processes.

The work of Manz, Sims and Lorenzi has made a valuable contribution to the direction of the mainstream literature by laying the foundation for more contemporary researchers (e.g. Pastor et al. 2002 on Shared Leadership; Bono and Judge, 2003 on Self-Leadership; and Carson et al. 2007 on Distributed Leadership) that address the nature of change in organisations associated with new organisational forms and shifting power relations. More critical perspectives, however, illustrate that in general the leadership literature continues to adopt an apolitical and/or a normalised approach to power. Contributors to the literature continue to neglect the problematic nature and political dynamics associated with the sharing of power, especially between leaders and followers.

LEADERSHIP AND POWER: DEEP-STRUCTURED TENSIONS AND PARADOXES

At a broader level, mainstream organisation theorists have attempted to critically address the link between leadership and power. For instance, Dunlap and Goldman (1991), as well as Kreisberg (1992), developed the theme of 'power through' and 'power with' instead of 'power over'. In a leadership scenario the terms 'power through' and 'power with' would be recognised as emancipative approaches that, similar to contemporary mainstream leadership theories, advocate forms of leadership suited to more democratic work environments. However, while these approaches at least attempt to address shifting power relations in organisations, they neglect historically constituted antecedents related to power in organisations and how these antecedents affect power relations.

One can appreciate that most organisational histories reflect the principles and practices of traditional, i.e. hierarchical, organisational structures. With this in mind, there is a strong likelihood that even when an organisation implements new structures, policies and procedures that symbolise 'power through' or 'power with', organisational

relationships and behaviour will continue to be influenced by historical antecedents related to hierarchical power relations. Without further investigation into the effect of antecedents on power relations, one cannot be sure that 'power through' and 'power with' are not simply alternative forms of 'power over'. These approaches may simply mask the continuing effects of deep-structured power antecedents that reinforce the 'power over' approach (see Courpasson, 2000 for an empirical example of such a case).

Similar to this chapter, Haugaard (1997) argues that antecedents related to power go largely unnoticed because the nature of power relations becomes a taken-for-granted reality due to reinforcement through everyday behaviour and practices. Once something becomes taken for granted, it is no longer open to dispute and therefore rarely questioned (Haugaard, 1997, p. 213). The importance of this point is that the constant reinforcement, in both theory and practice, of the leader–follower relationship has resulted in the superiority of the leader, not to mention the very need for leadership, becoming an indisputable 'reality' (Sievers, 1994). As previously argued, the superior power of a leader over his or her followers has become normalised and accepted as part of the natural order of things. When one considers the widespread adoption of organically and democratically oriented organisational forms and the subsequent shift in power relations occurring in contemporary organisations, research into the effects of antecedents related to power appears a fruitful area for future research. Where an organisation's senior management attempts to empower its staff with leadership skills and responsibilities, the staff may well question the validity of such a strategy. In such a case, the authority of senior managers and those appointed to leadership positions may also be questioned. Staff may even react by seeking to replace the leader with more traditionally oriented forms of leadership (see Barker, 1993 for an empirical example of such a scenario). This critique highlights a tension and paradox between theory and practice of leadership in many contemporary organisations. With respect to power, to maintain their identity as a leader in contemporary organisations, leaders must establish a differential status while simultaneously attempting to empower their followers. One can extend this line of argument further by suggesting that due to the neglect of social and organisational antecedents related to power, the very notion of shared leadership in contemporary organisations is problematic. Perhaps it is more accurate to say that the normative orientation of the leadership literature is problematic. For instance, the earlier questions related to the blurring of the differential identity between leaders and followers can be extended. If one appreciates the extent to which people across the globe continue to become more empowered through increasing levels of education and greater access to information and technology, one could argue the differential between 'the leader' and 'the follower' will eventually disappear. Following this argument, from a power and identity perspective, it is logical to ask if the need for 'the leader' is also diminishing? For this to occur however, we would need to achieve equality and equity in our social systems. And equity is only an idea, not a reality (this does not mean we should not strive for it). Due to personal and charismatic power, not to mention other bases of power, there will always be differentials in power. Following this argument, leadership and the perceived need for 'the leader' will never disappear.

This observation highlights a paradox that leaders face in contemporary organisations. As people acquire increasing levels of power in their everyday lives, pressure will be placed on the traditional leader follower dualism. At the same time the organisational antecedents and meaning systems to which they are subjected will reflect the principles, practices and social expectations of traditional leadership. In short, as people become more empowered they may need leadership less but their antecedents and socio-cultural meaning systems reinforce the need for traditional leader–follower power relations. The theoretical and practical implications of this paradox between the organisation's surface structures (structural changes reflecting contemporary organisational forms) and its historical antecedents (deeper, more unobtrusive structures reflecting the history of the organisation's leadership) offer fruitful opportunities for leadership research.

OPPORTUNITIES AND CHALLENGES FOR RESEARCH INTO LEADERSHIP AND POWER

The critical analysis techniques employed in this chapter indicate that the power distance and the associated power relationship between the leader and follower is changing. Shifts in power relations place pressure on, and often lead to changes in, relative identities. If pressure is being placed on the differential identity between leaders and followers, what does this mean for the theory of leadership? To maintain relevance in contemporary organisational scenarios, do we need to view the theory and practice of leadership literature differently to that which permeates the extant literature?

Rather than research into leadership being necessarily focused on 'the leader' – i.e. associated

with the qualities and behaviour of an extraordinary individual – leadership might be considered a process that more than one person can do at a given time (Charlesworth, 2004). Many organisations have taken steps towards such an approach to leadership by using teams of leaders and/or regularly replacing those people in leadership positions. This reduces the likelihood of followers falling into patterns of obedience, learned helplessness and a lack of accountability.

Gordon (2007) argues that the focus on 'the leader' is not necessarily problematic; rather, in contemporary organisations it is the link between leadership and dominant power relations that is the problem. He draws on the work of Flyvbjerg (1998) to argue that people in positions of dominance rarely have their viewpoints and actions challenged or checked. Flyvbjerg (1998) empirically verified that over time this lack of engagement results in leaders falling victim to their own constructions of reality, a process he terms 'rationalising their own versions of rationality'. History is filled with examples of leaders who were adept exponents of such rationalisations, with Adolf Hitler coming immediately to mind. More recently, as details emerge concerning the collapse of corporations such as Enron in the United States, and HIH and OneTel in Australia, not to mention the unethical and corrupt behaviour of high-powered public officials throughout the world, it becomes apparent that many leaders continue to fall victim to rationalising their own versions of rationality. Methods for preventing leaders and other powerful individuals from falling victim to their own power are a fruitful area for research. When one considers the complex and unobtrusive dynamics of power (e.g. deep-structured antecedents), such methods require much more than the current focus on rules, regulations and simple codes of order in the contemporary corporate governance literature. The challenge appears to lie with the management of power: How do we construct social systems that prevent any one individual, especially leaders, becoming a dominant entity?

As mentioned previously, central to the nature of change in organisations and broader social systems throughout the world is a fundamental shift in power relations (Hardy & Clegg, 1996). In lay terms, as people, through access to information, acquire knowledge, awareness and hence power, the more the legitimacy of established institutions has come into question. In short, we live in an era in which we can expect greater conflict and a shift to more democratic power structures and relations. With shifting power relations and the management of power in mind, the greatest challenge for people in leadership positions, whether formal or informal, is how to differentiate themselves from their followers, maintaining their identity and 'voice' as a leader, whilst at the same time nurturing the ever-increasing empowerment of their followers. Knowledge into how people in such positions can achieve this is perhaps the most important research agenda in the field of leadership today.

CONCLUSIONS

The analysis in this chapter has revealed that the mainstream leadership literature treats power unproblematically, the consequence of which is that the literature is limited to reflections of surface-level issues and occurrences. It is therefore limited to descriptions of what occurs or what 'ought' to occur and lacks rich insight into the problematic interplay between leadership and power.

When viewed through a power lens that embodies a critical perspective, the mainstream management approach to leadership is challenged because it neglects how historically constituted power relations unobtrusively shape behaviour in organisations. It neglects how power is embedded in an organisation's antecedents and meaning systems and how power is embedded in the socio-cultural norms and discourses that organisational members reflect upon to make sense of their work relations and settings.

In particular, much of the recent research in leadership, especially that pertaining to self-, dispersed or shared leadership, appears unaware that much of what it promulgates is rendered problematic without a more comprehensive analysis of power. As this chapter has illustrated, with respect to power, the traditional leader/follower dualism reflects a vertical power differential in which the leader is privileged. The problem with power relations such as this is that they potentially lend themselves to situations in which followers may, wittingly or unwittingly, become vulnerable to the dominance of their leaders.

The discussion throughout the chapter has give rise to a series of questions and challenges for leadership researchers. However, there is a more central argument that permeates the discussion: leadership researchers need to adopt a more comprehensive approach to power; if they don't, the current direction of mainstream leadership research will continue to miss the contextual complexities associated with the change in power relations currently occurring in organisations and broader social systems across the globe. Writers from outside the field, such as Cynthia Hardy and Stewart Clegg, have demonstrated how the organisation studies and management literature in particular reflects a historically constituted discourse,

an ontological and epistemological grounding if you will, within which the vast majority of contributors appear to be trapped.

The challenge is for leadership researchers to step outside their existing knowledge boundaries. To do this they might consider tracing a path through literature from an alternative intellectual tradition to that with which they are familiar. This alternative intellectual tradition began with Machiavelli, moved through Nietzsche, Foucault, Bauman and onto contemporary writers such, Haugaard (1997), Flyvbjerg (1998); and more recently still Clegg, Courpasson and Philips (2006), who provide an excellent coverage of how this alternative intellectual tradition enriches our understanding of power in organisations.

If leadership researchers choose not to expand their understanding of power, they will continue to make a contribution to their field but they will not be able to address the questions raised in this chapter. Perhaps it is time they take heed from the critique levelled at them by two of the field's most prominent researchers, Hunt and Dodge (2000), who argued at the beginning of the decade that contemporary work in the field offers little more than leadership déjà vu all over again.

REFERENCES

Barker, J.R. (1993). Tightening the iron cage: concertive control in self managed teams. *Administrative Science Quarterly*, 38, 408–437.

Barnard, C. (1938). *The functions of the Executive.* Cambridge, MA: Harvard University Press.

Bass, B.M. & Stogdill, R.M. (eds) (1960). *Bass and Stogdill's handbook of leadership: a survey of theory and research* (revised and expanded version). New York: Free Press.

Bingham, W.V. (1927). Leadership. In H.C. Metcalf, (ed.), *The psychological foundations of management.* New York: Shaw.

Blake, R.R. & Mouton, J.S. (1964). *The managerial grid.* Houston, TX: Gulf.

Boje, D. M. (1995). Stories of the story telling organisation: a postmodern analysis of Disney as 'Tamara-Land'. *Academy of Management Journal*, 38(4), 997–1035.

Bono, J.E. & Judge, T.A. (2003). Self-concordance at work: toward understanding the motivational effects of transformational leaders. *Academy of Management Journal*, 46(5), 554–571.

Bowden, A.O. (1927). A study on the personality of student leadership in the United States. *Journal of Abnormal Social Psychology*, 21, 149–160.

Bryman, A. (1996). 'Leadership in Organisations'. In S.R. Clegg, C. Hardy, and W.R. Nord, (eds), *Handbook of organisation studies.* London: Sage.

Calas, M.B. & Smircich, L. (1988). Using the F word: Feminist theories and the social consequences of organisational research. Paper presented at the annual meeting of the Academy of Management, Washington, DC, August.

Carson, J.B., Tesluk, P.E. & Marrone, J.A. (2007). Shared leadership in teams: an investigation of antecedent conditions and performance, *Academy of Management Journal*, 50(5), 1217–1234.

Charlesworth, R. (2004). *Shakespeare the coach.* Sydney: Pan Macmillan.

Clegg, S.R., Courpasson, D., & Philips, N. (2006). *Power and organizations.* London: Sage.

Collinson, D.L. (2006). Rethinking leadership: a poststructuralist of follower identities. *The Leadership Quarterly*, 17(2), 179–189.

Collinson, D.L. (2009). Rethinking Leadership and Followership. in S. R. Clegg, & C.L. Cooper (eds), The Handbook of organization behavior, Volume 2, Macro approaches. Sage: London, pp. 251–264.

Courpasson, D. (2000). Managerial strategies of domination: power in soft bureaucracies. *Organization Studies*, 21(1), 141–162.

Culler, J. (1982). *On deconstruction: theory and criticisms after structuralism.* Ithaca, NY: Jumbuck University Press.

Derrida, J. (1974). *Of grammatology.* Baltimore, MD: Johns Hopkins University Press.

Dunlap, D.M. & Goldman, P. (1991). Rethinking power in schools. *Education Administration Quarterly*, 27(1), 5–29.

Eden, D. (1984). Self–fulfilling prophecy as a management tool: harnessing Pygmalion. *Academy of Management Review*, 9, 64–73.

Enz, C.A. (1988). The role of value congruity in interorganisational power. *Administrative Science Quarterly*, 33, 284–304.

Evans, M.G. (1970). The effects of supervisory behavior on the path-goal relationship. *Organisational Behavior and Human Performance*, 5, 277–298.

Field, R.H.G. (1989). The self-fulfilling prophecy leader: achieving the Meftharme effect. *Journal of Management Studies*, 26, 151–175.

Fiedler, F.E. (1967). A contingency model of leadership effectiveness. In L. Berkowitz (ed.), *Advances in experimental social psychology.* New York: Academic Press.

Fleishman, E.A., Harris E.F., & Burtt, H.E. (1955). *Leadership and supervision in industry.* Columbus, OH: Ohio State University Press.

Flyvbjerg, B. (1998). *Making social science matter: why social inquiry fails and how it can succeed again.* Cambridge: Cambridge University Press.

Gandz, J. & Murray, V.V. (1980). The experience of workplace politics. *Academy of Management Journal*, 23(2), 237–251.

Gordon, R.D. (2002). Conceptualising leadership with respect to its historical-contextual antecedents to power. *The Leadership Quarterly*, 13(2), 151–167.

Gordon, R.D. (2007). *Power, knowledge and domination.* Libre: Copenhagen Business School Press.

Graen, G. & Cashman, J. (1975). A role-making model of leadership in formal organizations: a developmental approach. In J.G. Hunt, and L.L. Larson, (eds), *Leadership frontiers*, Kent, OH: Kent State University Press, pp. 143–165.

Greene, C.N. (1975). The reciprocal nature of influence between leader and subordinate. *Journal of Applied Psychology*, 60, 187–193.

Hardy, C. & Clegg, S.R. (1996). Some dare call it power. In S.R. Clegg, C. Hardy, & W.R. Nord (eds), *Handbook of organization studies.* London: Sage, pp. 622–641.

Haugaard, M. (1997). *The constitution of power: a theoretical analysis of power, knowledge and structure.* Manchester: Manchester University Press.

Hersey, P. & Blanchard, K.H. (1969). Life cycle theory of leadership. *Training Development Journal*, 23, 26–34.

Hersey, P. & Blanchard, K.H. (1977). *Management of organizational behavior: utilizing human resources.* Englewood Cliffs, NJ: Prentice Hall.

Hollander, E.P. (1979). *Leadership dynamics: a practical guide to effective relationships.* New York: Free Press.

Homans, G.C. (1959). *The human group.* New York: Harcourt, Brace and World.

Hosking, D.M. (1991). Chief executives, organising processes and skill. *European Journal of Applied Psychology*, 41, 95–103.

Hunt, J.G. & Dodge, G.E. (2000). Leadership déjà vu all over again. *The Leadership Quarterly Yearly Overview of Leadership*, 11(2), 435–458.

Katzenbach, J.R. & Smith, D.K. (1993). *The wisdom of teams: creating the high performance organisation.* Boston, MA: Harvard Business School Press.

Kilduff, M. (1993). Deconstructing organisations. *Academy of Management Review*, 18, 13–31.

Kirkman, B.L. & Rosen, B. (1999). Beyond self-management: antecedents and consequences of team empowerment. *Academy of Management Journal*, 42(1), 58–74.

Knights, D. & Willmott, H. (1992). Conceptualising leadership processes: a study of senior managers in a financial services company. *Journal of Management Studies*, 29, 761–782.

Kouzes, J.M. & Posner, B.Z. (1993). *Credibility: how leaders gain and lose it, why people demand it.* San-Francisco: Jossey-Bass.

Kreisberg, S. (1992). *Transforming power: domination, empowerment and education.* Albany, NY: State University of New York Press.

Likert, R. (1961). *New patterns of management.* New York: McGraw-Hill.

McGregor, D. (1960). *The human side of enterprise.* New York: McGraw-Hill.

McGregor, D. (1966). *Leadership and motivation.* Cambridge, MA: MIT Press.

Manz, C. C. & Sims, H. P. (1991). Superleadership: beyond the myth of heroic leadership. *Organisational Dynamics*, 19, pp. 18–35.

Manz, C.C. & Sims, H.P. (1996). *Company of heroes: unleashing the power of self leadership.* New York: John Wiley & Sons.

Martin, J. (1990). Deconstructing organisational taboos: the suppression of gender conflict in organisations. *Organisation Science*, 1(4): 339–359.

Mintzberg, H. (1983). *Power in and around organisations.* Englewood Cliffs, NJ: Prentice Hall.

Ouchi, W.G. & Jaeger, A.M. (1978). Type Z organization: stability in the midst of Mobility. *Academy of Management Review*, 3: 305–314.

Pascale, R.T. & Athos, A.G. (1981). *The art of Japanese management: application for American executives.* New York: Warner.

Pastor, J., Meindl, J.R., & Mayo, M.C. (2002). A network effects model of charisma attributions. *Academy of Management Journal*, 45(2), 410–420.

Schein, E.H. (1985). *Organizational culture and leadership.* San Francisco: Jossey-Bass.

Senge, P.M. (1999). Towards an ecology of leadership: developmental journeys of three leaders. Presented as part of the showcase symposium titled 'Change and development journeys into a pluralistic world, Annual Meeting of the Academy of Management, Toronto, Canada, August.

Sievers, B. (1994). *Work, death and life itself: essays on management and organisation.* New York: Walter de Gruyter.

Sims, H.P. (1977). The leader as a manager of reinforcement contingencies: an empirical example of a model. In J.G. Hunt & L.L. Larson (eds), *Leadership: the cutting edge.* Carbondale, IL: Southern Illinois University Press.

Sims, H.P. & Lorenzi, P. (1992). *The new leadership paradigm.* Newbury Park, CA: Sage.

Uhl-Bien, M. & Graen, G.B. (1998). Individual self management: analysis of professionals' self managing activities in functional and cross-functional work teams. *Academy of Management Journal*, 41(3), 340–350.

Vroom, V.H. & Yetton, P.W. (1973). *Leadership and decision-making.* Pittsburgh, PA: University of Pittsburgh Press.

Yukl, G.A. (1971). Toward a behavioral theory of leadership. *Organisational Behavior and Human Performance*, 6, 414–440.

Yukl, G.A. (1989). *Leadership in organisations,* 2nd edn. Englewood Cliffs, NJ: Prentice Hall.

15

Political Leadership

Jean Hartley and John Benington

INTRODUCTION: POLITICIANS MATTER

The leadership literature has tended to be dominated by studies from the business and organisational fields, with managers as the key role examined in theory and empirical research (Nye, 2008; Hartley, 2010a). The debates about whether or not managers and leaders are distinct categories (e.g. Kotter, 1990; Yukl, 2006) can obscure the importance of other types of leadership – for example, political leadership, professional leadership, or social movement leadership – and the contribution which these forms make to understanding leadership more generally. Few books or articles on leadership analyse political leadership at all (as shown by the indexes of many of the generic leadership books). Occasionally, there is reference to a specific political leader such as Hitler, Thatcher or Mandela but the political leader is often used as an illustrative case (e.g. Jackson and Parry, 2008) rather than an analytical category. This chapter will argue that political leadership is critical in its own right, and also that it sheds light on questions of legitimacy, process and outcomes for generic leadership theory and research.

Another expected source of insights into political leadership is the political science literature, but, surprisingly, references are rather sparse. For example, the recent *Oxford Handbook of British Politics* (Flinders et al., 2009) has no chapter on leadership and only passing references to leaders as individuals. Many introductory political science texts ignore political leadership (e.g. Hay, 2004; Stoker, 2006a). There are some political science exceptions (e.g. Blondel, 1987; Burns, 1978; Tucker, 1995). A small literature on local political leadership (e.g. John, 2010; Leach et al., 2005; Lowndes and Leach, 2004) examines the interplay between context and conduct. A review of the political biography literature (Marquand, 2009) found that it often gives powerful emotional insight into the dilemmas surrounding the decisions faced by political leaders, though it is notable that the focus is mainly on charismatic leadership.

Some interesting work on political leadership derives from a historical perspective (e.g. Burns, 1978; Ruscio, 2004; Wren, 2007), with a recognition of the need to problematise and explore political leadership as a dialectic between leaders and those who are led (e.g. Ruscio, 2004). Burns (1978) conceptualised different approaches to political leadership, in particular transforming/transformational and transactional leadership (a distinction which has been widely adopted in the managerial leadership field). A useful definition of leadership, from the work of Burns on political leadership but more generally applicable is '…… the reciprocal process of mobilizing, by persons with certain motives and values, various economic, political, and other resources, in a context of competition and conflict, in order to realise goals independently or mutually held by both leaders and followers' (Burns, 1978, p. 425).

Political leadership is also explored in political psychology, though its studies of leadership are often about US presidents or presidential candidates, and focus on their cognitive, personality, motivational and other psychological attributes as individuals (e.g. Keller, 2009; Mazlish, 1994) including as theatrical actors (Cronin, 2008).

The patchy nature of the academic analysis of political leadership means that a brief discussion of why politicians matter is in order, to understand both the specifics of political leadership and also its contribution to understanding leadership generically. This chapter examines political leadership in the context of electoral democracy: i.e. it does not examine political leadership in autocratic, military or totalitarian states. Democracy is generally associated with universal suffrage, governments chosen by regular, free and competitive elections, political rights to free speech and freedom to organise in groups (Stoker, 2006a). It is a theoretical ideal, with states having greater or lesser degrees of these features (Ruscio, 2004). In a Western capitalist democracy, political leadership is based on electoral legitimacy from, and accountability to, the voting population. This means that political leadership cannot be divorced from considerations about 'the people' (Wren, 2007).

Political leadership is substantial in terms both of the number of politicians and of the scale, range and seriousness of the decisions they take (Hartley and Pinder, 2010). For example, there are 120 Ministers in the UK government, 646 Members of Parliament in the House of Commons and similar in the House of Lords. At local government level, there are 22,000 elected councillors in England alone. In the USA, there are over 500 politicians in Congress, and there are 87,000 local government organisations each with their own local politicians. Adding state-level politicians swells those numbers further. This illustrates how many people are involved, full- or part-time, in formal political office, in just two countries.

The scale and scope of leadership responsibility by elected politicians is considerable. In the developed nations, politicians are responsible for fiscal policy, for taxation and for expenditure amounting to at least a third of gross domestic product (GDP) (Jackson, 2003), with this figure rising to over 50% of GDP in the UK in the economic crisis which surfaced in 2008 (CIPFA/Solace, 2010). The fact that public expenditure derives substantially from taxation means that there are inevitably pressures on political leaders to be transparent and accountable for their use of public funds – and their decisions are open to contest and debate by the public and the media about these matters.

Politicians are responsible for law-making as well as for the provision or commissioning of public services and oversight of the economy, and regulation of the private market sector. Politicians are therefore responsible for a wide range of public decisions, which they take on the basis that they are authorised to do so from the population whom they serve, and/or authorised by a wider group of stakeholders (Benington and Moore, 2010). They may take decisions which are popular and legitimated through public debates and coalition building, but they are also authorised by the state and its legislation to take directive or even coercive decisions to engage in regulatory activities deemed to be for the public good, such as policing, enforcing prison sentences, military conscription or taxation. However, the use of coercive powers by political leaders and the state is not always accepted by the population, and politicians, the media and others are also involved in scrutiny to ensure that a government has not exceeded its powers, and that its use of coercion is fair, transparent and proportionate.

Politicians are also involved in tackling many complex and difficult choices facing society. Whether the issues are climate change, childhood obesity, or transport infrastructure, the role of political leaders is not only to use state authority and resources to provide services but also to search for solutions to complex problems and to make tough choices, knowing that whatever decision is made it cannot satisfy all competing interests, and therefore will not please everyone (Benington and Moore, 2011; Christensen and Lægreid, 2003). It is clear that complex societal choices cannot be addressed through market mechanisms alone, and that the state, including its political leaders, have a crucial role to play in creating the policies and frameworks, and mobilising, orchestrating and leading inter-organisational coalitions to address these issues.

At the heart of political leadership is contest. This is not only because different parties and politicians may offer different policies and programmes to tackle societal issues, and this is played out in debates and arguments in political arenas such as Parliament or Congress and in the media, but also because public goals are inevitably ambiguous, contested and subject to competing values and interests between different groups within the population (Crick, 2000; Hoggett, 2006; Leftwich, 2004; Stoker, 2006a). What constitutes public value has to be subjected to continuous debate and discussion (Benington and Moore, 2011).

Political leaders therefore matter because politics matters. Democracy is an imperfect system, as many have noted, but politics *is a way of ruling divided societies without undue violence – and most societies are divided*' (Crick, 2000, p. 33).

THE IDEAS AND IDEALS OF POLITICAL LEADERSHIP

The study of political leadership is, inevitably, not only about ideas (theories, concepts, evidence) but also about what political leadership ideally ought to be like. In other words, it is both analytical and normative. Political leadership is freighted with many values about the just society and the public good, about the relative power and responsibility of politicians vis-à-vis the people who elect them, about what Plato calls wisdom and virtue in political life, and what Aristotle describes as prudence, as well as other values.

Normative ideals about political leadership are also evident in the scepticism about such leadership:

> The theory of democracy does not treat leaders kindly. Suspicion of rulers, concern over their propensity to abuse power in their own self-interest, the need to hold them accountable, and the belief that legitimate power is lodged originally in the people and granted to leaders only with severe contingencies, all are fixed stars in the democratic galaxy....Fear of leadership is a basic justification for democratic forms of government. Yet it is impossible to imagine a strong, healthy democracy without leaders. (Ruscio, 2004, p. ix)

Ideas and ideals of political leadership have changed over time, as societies have been variously constructed and governed and as they face particular challenges to their economic and social well-being and cohesion, whether from external threat or internal dissension. Key ideas about political leadership and the role of the people being led or governed has often shifted at times of major social upheaval. Context shapes what we understand by (and accept as) political leadership and thus political leadership is socially constructed – or invented, as Wren (2007) would say. For example, in the classical ideal of a political leader set out by Plato in *The Republic* (1962), the context of his writing was chaos, instability and frequent swings to tyranny in the Athenian democratic state (Wren, 2007), with the wise and virtuous leader construed as a bulwark against a fractious and tyrannical society. Wisdom and virtue were required in such leaders, who were expected in their personal characteristics to stand above the population. The population were not expected to play an active part in the governing of the state, leaving this to their leaders.

Similarly, Machiavelli (1984) in *The Discourses* returned to, and reinterpreted, classical republican writing about political leadership at the time of the Renaissance, when Italian city states were at political and economic loggerheads, when new ideas were bursting out in the Renaissance, and where political power was volatile. His interpretation of the classical texts placed greater emphasis on the role of the people acting in the interests of society (with some exceptions, dependent on context). His work analysed the role of political leaders in creating an enlightened people, and the role of strong leaders in times of upheaval or crisis.

Other contexts where upheaval led to changing conceptions of leadership include the English Civil War, with the construction of the primacy of 'the people' as an argument against the divine right of kings (to rule), though in practice this was about the transfer of power to Parliament not to the people (Morgan, 1988). Another example is the American War of Independence and the creation of the American Constitution, which led to new social constructions of the people and leadership, arising from the need to distinguish the new state politically from its origins as an English colony, and in a context where geography and economic activity created a new sense of equality amongst people (except for slaves and native American Indians).

Indeed, it has been noted (e.g. Rost, 1991) that the discourse of leadership (as opposed to a focus on leaders) emerged in print in the early nineteenth century. Wren (2007) argues that this can be related to the emergence of modern democratic thought, values and practices at the time of the American War of Independence and the following period of nation-building, whereby leaders were no longer thought of as superior to those who elected them, but rather had to find ways of working together to achieve collectively defined goals. Wren (2007, p. 135) notes: 'At its most fundamental level, the essential challenge of leadership in a democracy is to achieve a synthesis between the "thesis" of the classical ideal of the leader and the "antithesis" of the sovereignty of the people.' The analysis of context is therefore central to understanding the dynamics of political leadership.

THE CURRENT CONTEXT OF LEADERSHIP STUDIES IN WESTERN DEMOCRACIES

This is a critical time to be studying political leadership in many Western countries. There is a crisis of public confidence in, and the legitimacy of, political leadership in the UK (e.g. Borraz and John, 2004). This is not only about individual politicians but also about politicians as a class in the wake of a series of scandals about MPs expenses, disaffection with some major decisions they have made (e.g. the Iraq war and the financial crisis) and also part of a longer-term trend. Local politicians have emerged relatively unscathed from the expenses scandals, but this may be as much about their perceived lack of power and importance in the minds of the electorate as any inherent trust in their integrity. At the national level, trust has been declining for many years but has fallen more sharply recently. For example, the 2008 survey of a sample of the electorate for the

Committee on Standards in Public Life found that only 22% think that Government ministers tell the truth. The Committee Chair, Sir Chrisopher Kelly, commented that this was 'deeply disturbing' (Committee on Standards in Public Life, 2008). Academic analysis tells the same story (Hay, 2007). Fewer of those eligible to vote do so in each general or local election (e.g. Bromley and Curtice, 2004) and this is partly cohort-based (fewer young people are engaged in formal politics) and partly a change over time regardless of demographics (Walker, 2009). The decline in trust and in voting is a pattern found across a range of European countries, including those where turnout has traditionally been high (Borraz and John, 2004).

The shifts in attitudes to politics and to political participation represent a key challenge for the task of leadership. The relationships between the citizen and the state, and between formally elected representatives and informal leadership within civil society, are changing significantly, and with declining deference to formal authority not only to politicians. There are changing expectations about what the state, through its politicians, ought to provide, while, paradoxically, resentment about the interference of the state in the lives of citizens. The prospect of drastic cuts in public finance and substantial service restructuring (e.g. CIPFA/Solace, 2010) also create part of the dynamic and volatile context for political leadership.

The interest in political leadership has been given a further boost by the recognition of a shift in dominant paradigms for public policy and public management which goes beyond 'traditional public administration' and 'new public management' (NPM) and the emergence of new patterns of 'networked community governance' (Benington, 2000; Newman, 2001; Stoker, 2006b). In a networked governance perspective, there is a weakening of the monolithic hierarchically organised state and of the competitive market models of governance associated with NPM in favour of more differentiated polycentric and pluralistic arrangements that cut across the boundaries of public, private and third sectors, as well as across different levels of government (Benington, 2000). In addition, the devolution of some powers to political bodies below the level of the national state (e.g. to the Scottish Parliament, Welsh Assembly, Northern Ireland Assembly; regional offices of government and certain powers to promote well-being to local government) contributes further to polycentric governance (Benington and Moore, 2011). The burgeoning use of new interactive communication technologies has spawned new direct forms of debates, lobbying and affiliation which challenge some of the more traditional representative forms of political leadership. Local and national

politicians are now just one set of actors among many in polycentric systems of governance (e.g. Goldsmith and Larsen, 2004), though at the same time formal political leadership becomes more important in fragmented polities (Borraz and John, 2004). This chapter therefore focuses on the complexities and challenges of political leadership in a context of competing interests, ideologies and power relations within a pattern of polycentric, networked governance.

Political leaderships are also having to address the complex, or 'wicked' cross-cutting problems (Grint, 2005; Heifetz, 1994; Rittel and Webber, 1973), facing contemporary societies. The complex, cross-cutting problems facing citizens and communities (e.g. climate change, ageing of the population, crime and the fear of crime) – where both the diagnosis and the solution to the problem are ambiguous and contested – may cause other unforeseen problems because of the interconnectedness of the whole complex system and cannot be solved by the state or the market alone, but require the harnessing of civil society to work on the problem and the application of whole systems thinking and action to the problem (Benington and Hartley, 2009). Political leaders have a critical role to play in mobilising support across a range of stakeholders to recognise, to frame and to address these complex problems, which generally require tough choices and fundamental shifts in values, attitudes and behaviours on the part of many of the stakeholders who are involved (Benington, 1996; Heifetz, 1994). Political leaders, in an uncertain and volatile context (e.g. Beck, 1992), have a leadership role in helping stakeholders to think through varied perspectives on a problem, to debate difficult choices and to provide and support deliberative processes and democratic forums in which the issues can be explored and decisions arrived at.

The historical analyses of political leadership (e.g. Ruscio, 2004; Wren, 2007; see Grint, Chapter 1, this volume) show that conceptions of leadership shift in times of profound change. Western societies, at least, are in such a period of change that we can anticipate that forms and values about political leadership will continue to shift and change. Therefore, theoretical frameworks to understand political leadership are particularly important at this time.

THE AUTHORISING ENVIRONMENT FOR POLITICAL LEADERSHIP

What is the authority which underpins political leadership? In theory, democratic political leadership can be described as deriving its authority from free and fair elections under particular legal and procedural arrangements and with a particular constituency. However, studies of political leadership in practice suggest the need for more complex explanatory frameworks.

Historical analyses show that analysing legitimacy primarily through a formal electoral mandate from the people is a relatively recent phenomenon (Burns, 1978; Wren, 2007). Burns (1978) emphasises the processual approach to legitimacy and authority rather than solely a procedural view:

> the genius of leadership lies in the manner in which leaders see and act on their own and their followers' values and motivations. Leadership, unlike naked power-wielding, is thus inseparable from followers' needs and goals. (p. 19)

Heifetz (1994) similarly emphasises a processual and negotiated view of leadership authority:

> I define authority as conferred power to perform a service. This definition will be useful to the practitioner of leadership as a reminder of two facts: First, authority is given and can be taken away. Second, authority is conferred as part of an exchange. Failure to meet the terms of the exchange means the risk of losing one's authority: it can be taken back or given to another who promises to fulfill the bargain. (Heifetz, 1994, p. 57)

This is a reminder that political leadership has to be sensitive to followers and find ways to constitute meaning and purpose, within the bounds of the trust conferred by followers (Biggart and Hamilton, 1987; Ruscio, 2004) and in the context of the contestation of ideas and values. Although deriving part of their authority from followers and stakeholders, political leaders also often have to challenge their followers and use adaptive leadership which 'rejects the pressure from followers to provide magical solutions to complex problems, and instead works with stakeholders to take responsibility for grappling with these problems and for the changes in one's own thinking and behaviour required.' (Benington and Turbitt, 2007, pp. 383–384). It is a type of leadership which often asks questions rather than immediately proposes solutions, because one of the tasks is to get people to recognise that they may be contributing to the problem and that therefore addressing the problem requires changing their own thinking and behaviour. The theory of adaptive leadership illustrates the need for political leaderships to focus courageously on complex problems, to resist simplistic solutions and to challenge followers to take responsibility.

Political leadership differs in its sources of authority from organisational or managerial leadership. Politicians are elected not appointed and once elected they have a responsibility to make decisions on behalf of all the various stakeholders they represent, not just those who voted for them and also with regard for the well-being of future generations not just current voters (Hartley, 2010a; Morrell and Hartley, 2006). The basis of authority for politicians lies not only in the ballot box but also in the ongoing support from the wider electorate, from colleagues in their political party (or coalition), whether at local or national level, and from wider groups of stakeholders. At any moment, dissatisfaction from one or more stakeholder groups can lead to the withdrawal of support and loss of authorisation, leaving the political leader fighting for survival or having to step down from office. This can happen literally overnight and over any issue and creates a sense of continuous uncertainty in a way which appointed managers rarely experience (Hartley, 2010b). Political leaders therefore have to pay constant attention to the creation and maintenance of a sufficient coalition of support to authorise their actions (Blondel and Manning, 2002; Heifetz, 1994). Furthermore, given that politics is characterised by contestation and that the public sphere is characterised by competing interests and value choices (Benington and Moore, 2011; Hoggett, 2006; Simpson, 2008), then continual challenge to authority is the order of the day, whether from the leader's own political party colleagues, from the opposition, from the media or from lobbyists and activists. Many political leaders report feeling that they are only as good as their last success and so are continually having to prove themselves (Hartley and Pinder, 2010). Their decisions are also under scrutiny from a number of sources because political leadership carries the coercive power of the state and their use of such power has to demonstrate that it is fair. Furthermore, Wren (2007) notes that, in terms of political philosophy, there are paradoxes and tensions inherent in political leadership: how far the elected politician acts as a representative or a delegate; whether the politician is expected to be 'one of the people' or is a person with exceptional powers and skills; whether the politician should act as an elitist or as a participationist; and how far the politician is perceived to be acting in 'the public good' or is seen as pursuing sectional stakeholder interests and so on.

This brief consideration of the political, sociological and psychological pressures on political leadership and its sources of legitimacy suggests that there are few leadership roles which operate under such close, continuous, contested and challenging circumstances. Values, behaviours, actions and decisions are all open to constant public debate and scrutiny – very little is left private (Marquand, 2009) and political leadership is partly shaped by exposure to the public and the media (Christensen and Lægreid, 2003) The leadership literature derived from organisational behaviour has paid little attention to the sources of authority for leaders and even less to that for political leadership (Morrell and Hartley, 2006).

THEORIES OF POLITICAL LEADERSHIP

There are many different theories and approaches to political leadership and it is not feasible to review them all here. There is never going to be a single theory which will adequately explain the processes of political leadership, or the motivations and behaviours of politicians, or their work in a variety of different arenas, from cabinets and committees to constructing coalitions across a range of stakeholders, or dealing with the press.

In the absence of a clear and compelling single theory, analytical and conceptual frameworks may be helpful in making sense of political leadership (Hartley and Benington, 2010; Lowndes and Leach, 2004). An analytical framework defines, categorises (to some extent) and explores leadership phenomena, and places theories in relation to each other. It enables insights into political leadership and also facilitates the asking of certain questions about context and conduct.

A useful analytical question is to consider how far the explanation of political leadership lies in structure or agency (Hay, 2002; Leftwich, 2004). Explanations for political leadership range from (at the one extreme) a focus solely on the structures and formal institutions in which elected politicians conduct their work, to at the other extreme, a view of political leadership which is based entirely on the individual characteristics of the leader as agent (for example, the qualities of virtue and wisdom which Plato sought in a leader). In practice, many theories lie somewhere along the continuum, with elements of both structure and agency but to different degrees. This has also been expressed in terms of a concern either with context or with the individual or a combination of both in different ways (e.g. Grint, 2000). Of course, context and conduct (also debated as the influence of the situation or the person) is not a discrete distinction since both are partly socially constituted (Grint, 2005; Wren, 2007; Leach et al., 2005).

Some structural theories are located in political philosophy and focus on the roles of leaders and of leadership in democracies, and the symbiotic relationship between representatives and the represented. Taking the long, historical view, the contribution of particular leaders is eclipsed by analysis of the social contract between individuals and the state, and between politicians and the people (e.g. Ruscio, 2004; Wren, 2007). These are socially constructed views of leadership and the constraints on leadership, where ideas of leadership, the citizen and the state have changed over the centuries as societies have faced different challenges. Historical analysis charts the shift of focus on political leadership as monarchical or other power elites, towards the social contract between the individual and the state, and between leaders and those who elect them. Political leadership is also often deeply contested, as different groups try to exert influence on ideas, practices and decisions which affect them and society, and remind us that political leadership may be exercised without and beyond the formal authority of the state (c.f. Heifetz, 1994) in social movements for change, such as those mobilised by Thomas Paine or Martin Luther King, or in more distributed leadership situations like the global social forum.

These historical analyses point up some of the paradoxes of political leadership in democracies: the values of participation by the electorate in governing but the problems of their knowledge and competence to do so; the degree to which political leaders ought themselves to be competent in governing or whether being elected is the primary source of authority; whether political leaders ought to be representatives or delegates; whether the goals of leadership ought to express individual or collective benefits, and how minority views are taken into account; and how the leadership should construe the common good (Ruscio, 2004) or public value (Benington and Moore, 2011; Moore, 1995). In such analyses, the focus is on how leadership is shaped by context, and by prevailing ideologies, the ontologies of leadership, and how these were/are analysed and written about by political commentators. It includes analysis of the agency of leadership, but often treats this as influenced by political and economic conditions, mediated through political thought and writings, prevailing at the time.

In contemporary analysis of political leadership, a further structural approach is based on formal and constitutional political roles – for example, of presidents, ministers and elected councillors. A number of writers analyse how such roles are shaped by the legal framework or constitution, by standing orders and by the practices of particular institutions such as Parliament, the Senate or the council (e.g. John and Cole, 2000; Smith et al., 2002). There is also analysis of how such roles are being challenged by legislation and changed by levels of trust from the public and by the changing nature of societal problems.

For example, political leadership in local government has been examined in some detail since the Local Government Act in 2000 which introduced new forms of executive government into local authorities in England and Wales, including the option of elected mayors. Many writers analyse this in terms of 'local political leadership' but for some the focus is less on leadership as a process and more about formal roles, and the relationship between these roles, other elected representatives and the local political parties and the quality of decision-making (e.g. Gains et al. 2009; John, in press; Sweeting, 2002). Such leadership, in some writing, is taken to mean, without further examination, the most senior politicians who are responsible for governance and decision-making. The underlying assumption here is that formal structures, as created through legislation, shape the kinds of leadership role which are possible and the analysis of leadership is largely functional. Gains et al. (2009) and Leach et al. (2005), however, do consider some of the leadership qualities or capabilities of local political leaders as well.

At the other end of the continuum are those frameworks which are based mainly or entirely on the qualities or capabilities of political leaders, often treated as individuals and more rarely as teams or cabinets. Largely evident in political biography and political psychology, this area has already been briefly reviewed earlier.

There is a place for understanding the personal qualities of leaders and/or their leadership styles (e.g. Burns, 1978; Hartley, 2010a) and also how such qualities are either acquired or enhanced, for example through coaching (Hartley and Pinder, 2010) and through other development approaches (e.g. Benington and Hartley, 2009). There is also a small but valuable research stream on the recruitment and selection of candidates for political office (e.g. Silvester, 2008; Silvester and Dykes, 2007). However, if the focus is solely on personal qualities in isolation, divorced either from the challenges or context of political leadership, then the conceptual frameworks would be severely impoverished.

Some frameworks do allow for the interaction between structure and agency – for example, constitutional design and leadership capability by individuals and teams. For example, in the UK, Leach et al. (2005) and Lowndes and Leach (2004), drawing on the same data set, argue that a neo-institutional approach to understanding local political leadership is valuable, and that there is a need to understand, in combination, the context and the capabilities of political leadership. By context, they mean the local authority's constitution, the local political and organizational traditions and culture; the national legislative framework; the wider externally driven political agenda in the country; and the locality's social, economic, political and geographical characteristics.

A neo-institutionalist framework incorporates the relationship between structure, context and agency in local political leadership, and this framework is valuable in other contexts too. It sees political institutions not solely as structures and rules but as shared understandings, and this opens up the opportunity for political leaders to shape the interpretations of the context, the aims and values of the group (Leach et al., 2005). It emphasises the need to examine cultures and expectations as well as formal goals and structures, and how the rhetoric and other qualities of particular political leaders may help to shape the context.

Other writers also adopt a multi-level approach to understanding political leadership, drawing on both structure and agency. For example, Sweeting (2002) examines the political leadership of the Mayor of London by using a framework with four elements: the external environment of local political leadership; the institutional arrangements within which political leaders operate; the local environment; and the personal characteristics of leaders. Hartley and Allison (2000) argue that leadership needs to be seen not only as influenced by structures but also by cultures and behaviours. Christensen and Lægreid (2003) use three theoretical lenses to analyse political and administrative leadership in Norway: a structural perspective; a cultural-institutional perspective; and an 'exposure' perspective, which is based on the assumption that time and attention are scarce resources for political leaders, leading to garbage-can-like decision-making processes. They have less to say about the personal qualities of the elites that they studied.

A number of other conceptual frameworks arch across both structure and agency in political leadership, acknowledging the interplay between the two though none have had such widespread use as the neo-institutional approach. Morrell and Hartley (2006) suggest that Elias' 'figurational' sociology might be profitably applied to conceptualising and studying political leadership, because it places emphasis on people and their inter-relationships, and because it emphasises processes of change or flux. It is also concerned with power in social networks: 'in any network where actors are not wholly controlled, interdependencies and differential power relationships produce a complex interweaving of interests and agendas. One implication of this is that the search for single causes is futile' (Morrell and Hartley, 2006, p. 496). Figuration refers to a network of interdependent actors and the actors themselves, along with the agendas, interests and values which they hold, promote or downplay and an interest not just in the attributes of the network but also in social processes and power relations. This is highly relevant because a key aim of politicians is to mobilise consent across a range of diverse stakeholders and to shape outcomes based on a degree of negotiated agreement across those groups. Negotiating and maintaining coalitions is central to the work of political leadership (Burns, 1978; Leach and Wilson, 2000; Leach et al., 2005; Morrell and Hartley, 2006) and is the foundational task, since without consent to action other work is compromised.

The ability to construct coalitions depends, in part, on key skills of sense-making and sense-breaking (Weick, 1995). This is, arguably, a generic leadership quality for effective leadership (e.g. Pfeffer, 1981) but is particularly central to the work of political leadership, because of political leaders' need to lead in the context of conflict, with competing views and values. This reinforces the proposition that political leadership is constitutive of context, problem and potential solutions (Grint, 2000; 2005). Leach et al. (2005) note:

> There is an interaction between context and capability, in that leaders vary in the way that they 'read', interpret and articulate the political, economic, social and environmental context, and the opportunities for, and constraints on, action. Furthermore, they become more skilled at this over time, both with longer experience of being a councillor and in a senior leadership role. (p. 70)

Being able to conceptualise (or 'frame') a problem situation and to articulate a narrative or a compelling vision and narrative is also an important aspect of political leadership (Burns, 1978; Nye, 2008; Simpson, 2008). Denis et al. (2005) suggests that conventionalist theory, deriving from Boltanski and Thévenot (1999), may be useful to understand administrative leadership and it may be a fruitful though as yet unexplored theoretical perspective on political leadership. They emphasise that there are a limited set of logics and rationalities present in society at any time (related to the dominant political and cultural assumptions of that society) and that one of the roles of leadership is to stimulate processes that generate a 'convention' through accommodation or compromise between the values that compete for legitimacy. Political leadership has a role in the negotiation of contested logics. There is scope for considerably more research into analysing the relationships between leadership and the discourses of context (e.g. Fairhurst, 2009; Fairhurst, Chapter 36, this volume) which might be applied specifically to political leadership.

THE ARENAS OF POLITICAL LEADERSHIP

At its heart, political leadership is about the construction of coalitions to achieve desired outcomes. This means that political leadership has to operate in a range of arenas, both formal and informal. Political leadership is partly about leadership of the organization where the politician is the head or part of the senior political team – for example, in a government department or town hall. However, political leadership is also exercised in other arenas and for a range of purposes. In the context of polycentric governance, political leadership is also concerned with leading and orchestrating inter-organizational partnerships (e.g. Benington, 2000; Hartley, 2002); and with leading neighbourhoods and communities of interest and of place. In these arenas, the political leader aims to represent and articulate the needs and aspirations, the hopes and fears of communities and groups in civil society (Benington, 1996). Political leadership may also need to work with social movements and nascent social movements, either to nurture and protect them or to channel their desires and hopes into legitimate democratic forms of protest and/or proposition. Heifetz (1994), for example, provides a case study of Lyndon Johnson's leadership in the USA at the time of the protest movements mobilised by Martin Luther King. Political leadership often has to work with organizations and informal groups from the private, the public and the voluntary sectors, as stakeholders with interests in, and views about, proposed decisions and actions. Unlike the leadership of single organizations, political leadership, in a democratic context, has to try to represent and influence the whole constituency, regardless of who voted for that leader, and they also have an obligation – at least in theory – to act as stewards of resources for the future, including of environmental resources (Leftwich, 2004). Political leadership, generally, also has to work in the arena of the political party to which the leader is affiliated, as this provides both a broad base of support but also constraints on independent action (Copus, 1999; Leach et al., 2005). Even political leaders acting as independents (i.e. not affiliated to a political party) find that they have to build coalitions of interest in order to take forward policies and plans.

The reality of constructing a degree of consensus in a diverse and pluralistic society, across a range of arenas, is a formidable task. Taylor (1993) outlines a set of four arenas, and Hartley (2002) added a fifth, in relation to local government. Recent work by Hartley and Benington, found, from interviews with ministers, at least nine arenas for ministers of state, from Parliament and the government department to the constituency political party. The work of ministers takes place in a multitude of arenas and with a multitude of stakeholders, as also shown by Rhodes et al. (2007).

Arenas are not only about physical spaces, though some (but not all) may be geographically identifiable, such as Parliament. Arenas can be conceptualised as social processes of mutual influence between a variety of stakeholders and the political leadership. Arenas can be thought of as spaces and flows of people, ideas, problems, legitimacy and resources. This requires thinking about political leadership as dynamic not static, and as contested between different groups in a dialectical space of ideas, values, processes and actions. Contestation, mobilisation of support, legitimacy and consent are critical to political leadership, yet are perhaps imperfectly theorised in the orderly, somewhat rational accounts of some aspects of the workings of the 'political machine'. Simpson (2008) draws attention to these processes in his proposal that politicians are thinkers, fixers and communicators.

THE TASKS OF POLITICAL LEADERSHIP: BRINGING A PUBLIC INTO BEING

Political leadership exists in complex and diverse societies in order to achieve outcomes on behalf of society, despite the differing interpretations of what that means and how it is to be accomplished. Various writers have analysed the tasks of political leadership. For example, Leach and Wilson (2000) point to four key tasks of local political leadership: maintaining a critical mass of political support; developing a strategic policy direction; seeking to further leadership priorities outside the organization; and ensuring task accomplishment. These, it can be argued, are as relevant to devolved, national and supranational governance of society. Some of this work takes place within the formal structures of the state and its government, but some takes place in the various arenas of contestation indicated above. These challenges are explored further in Leach et al. (2005) and in Hartley (2010a). Challenges are in tension with each other as there is insufficient time, attention and resources to achieve them all, and because the degree of contestation means that the pursuit of goals is not necessarily an orderly rational process, but a set of moves forward and backward, and up and down the snakes and ladders of the political game of chance.

A further key challenge for political leadership is to create the conditions under which the questions and problems, and the decisions can be debated and agreed. Wren (2007) noted that there is a dialectical process between the representatives and the represented, and that the process of engagement itself can produce something more – an awareness of the needs of society as a whole, which goes beyond a utilitarian maximising of individual wants. Ruscio (2004) argues that active political leadership is essential to the creation and maintenance of a democratic process.

Creating the spaces and places for civic dialogue is important: *'political decisions so affect the kinds of life that will prevail, public debate is critical for developing a shared understanding of the consequences of policy choices, of hidden costs and benefits to the whole community'* (Sullivan, quoted in Wren, 2007, p. 347).

John Dewey (1927) wrote that the most important problem facing the public is discovering itself and identifying its own true interests. Political leadership has a central role in democratic government in fostering and nurturing the processes by which a community *discovers* its own interests, and begins to speak coherently as a collective about its aspirations for justice, prosperity, social relations and ecological sustainability. This is moral leadership (Burns, 1978) or adaptive leadership (Heifetz, 1994), claiming the authority which lies in the implicit contract between political leaders and the people. It means that political leadership is – or ought – not to be just about using power to achieve outcomes, but to engage the public in understanding and engaging with those choices.

CONCLUSIONS

Despite the tomes which have been written on princes and presidents, on MPs and local elected politicians, the research on political leadership is disparate, under-theorised and under-researched. This is a complex area, so it is unsurprising that there are a range of perspectives, conceptual frameworks and voices – mirroring in some ways the world of democratic politics itself. This provides a rich vein for further theory development and empirical investigation.

The academic literature on leadership has largely ignored the complex world of political leadership and is over-concentrated on managerial leadership, based as it is on selection not election, and with a requirement to satisfy organizational stakeholders but not necessarily to resolve or reconcile the competing values and interests of wider groups in society as a whole.

The conclusions about political leadership derived from this chapter, therefore, may have some relevance for the study of generic leadership. First, is the recognition that leadership is often concerned with achieving outcomes in a pluralistic and polycentric context, where conflict and contestation are central to the leadership challenge, because values, interests, opinions and views are diverse and often in conflict. Generic leadership theory to date has largely taken a more unitarist view of leadership based on leaders and 'followers'(critiqued by Hartley and Fletcher, 2008) . Study of political leadership reminds us that while initial formal legitimacy may be conferred by election or appointment, the variety of voices and the existence of opposing views means that authorisation to lead has to be continually rewon.

Secondly, the brief overview of historical ideas about political leadership shows that leadership ideas change over time and that leadership is a social construction. The political, economic and social context (and sometimes the geographical and environmental context) is central to shaping the social construction of leadership because different societies in different periods have to try to address and solve particular dilemmas and challenges. Currently, we are witnessing some profound changes in society, which influence the ways in which political leadership is perceived, valued (or not), trusted (or not) and engaged with (or not). Context shapes both opportunities and constraints for political, managerial and civic leadership. In the generic leadership literature, there is lip-service to the importance of context, but it is often not analysed (Porter and McLaughlin, 2006).

The political leadership literature points to the importance of structures and cultures as part of that context. Legislation, roles, political traditions and cultures, organizational histories, structures and cultures shape what is seen as possible and how far and how quickly a political leader is able to negotiate support for policies and practices. Again, generic leadership theory can learn from this by embedding analysis of organizational circumstances and cultural assumptions within research.

Neo-institutional theory is perhaps the most widely used framework for understanding political leadership, because it brings together in one conceptual framework the influence of structural conditions with informal practices and assumptions, while allowing for agency and change. A range of other conceptual frameworks have been suggested to explain political leadership, which emphasise flux and change, contestation and flows of ideas, power, interests and values. Again, generic leadership theory might benefit from conceptualising the processes of leadership in terms of competing, multi-layered constraints and opportunities, avoiding the dualism of either agency or structure, but instead examining more closely their interaction.

Political leadership takes place in a range of different arenas, with contestation and debate taking place in the flows of ideas, values and interests. Generic leadership theory, focused as it often is at the top of the organizational pyramid is sometimes more static in its depiction of leaders, 'followers' and locations. Yet, increasingly, managers in the private, public and voluntary sectors have to exercise leadership outside as well as inside their organization and to work with a range of stakeholders in a number of arenas (Hartley and Fletcher, 2008). Much might be learnt from the conceptualisation of political leadership in a wide range of contested, dialectical arenas.

Finally, political leadership, as it operates in its myriad arenas, trying to construct coalitions to achieve negotiated outcomes, and to garner support for a common purpose, has a key role in sense-making and in creating meanings and narratives. This requires a careful and sophisticated 'reading' and articulation of context. Context is not given; it is constituted through analysis, rhetoric and narratives. Political awareness – of interests, agendas, perspectives and possibilities – is a key thread in the effectiveness of political leadership. This is increasingly important for other types of leadership – the ability to read people, situations and context, to construct coalitions even where there are competing interests and to give a sense of strategic direction are now recognised as critical to the success of managerial leadership, though with a different source of authority and legitimacy.

Political leadership is under-researched, but it is critical to the functioning of a democratic society, and it has much to teach us in relation to leadership studies and practice more generally.

REFERENCES

Beck U (1992) *The risk society*. London: Sage.

Benington J (1996) New paradigms and practices for local government: Capacity building within civil society. In Roberts J and Kraemer S (eds) The politics of attachment. London: Free Association Books.

Benington J (2000) The modernization and improvement of government and public services. *Public Money and Management*, April–June, 3–8.

Benington J and Hartley J (2009) *Whole systems go! Leadership across the whole public service system*. London: National School of Government.

Benington J and Moore J (2011) *Public value: theory and practice*, Basingstoke: Palgrave Macmillan.

Benington J and Turbitt I (2007) Adaptive leadership and the policing of Drumcree demonstrations in Northern Ireland. *Leadership, 3*(4), 371–395.

Biggart N and Hamilton G (1987) An institutional theory of leadership. *Journal of Applied Behavioral Science, 23*(4), 429–441.

Blondel J (1987) *Political leadership: towards a general analysis.* London: Sage.

Blondel J and Manning N (2002) Do ministers do what they say? Ministerial unreliability, collegial and hierarchical governments. *Political Studies, 50*(3), 455–476.

Boltanski L and Thévenot L (1999) The sociology of critical capacity. *European Journal of Social Theory, 2*(3), 359–377.

Borraz O and John P (2004) The transformation of urban political leadership in Western Europe. *International Journal of Urban and Regional Research, 28*(1), 107–120.

Bromley C and Curtice J (2004) Are non-voters cynics anyway? *Journal of Public Affairs, 4*(4), 328–337.

Burns J M (1978) *Leadership.* New York: Harper Collins.

Christensen T and Lægreid P (2003) Complex interactions and influence among political and administrative leaders. *International Review of Administrative Sciences, 69*(3), 385–400.

CIPFA/Solace (2010) *After the downturn.* London: CIPFA.

Committee on Standards in Public Life (2008) Survey of public attitudes towards conduct in public life 2008. London.

Copus C (1999) The party group: a barrier to democratic renewal. *Local Government Studies, 25*(4), 76–97.

Crick B (2000) *In defence of politics,* 5th edn. London: Continuum.

Cronin T (2008) 'All the world's a stage...' acting and the art of political leadership. *The Leadership Quarterly, 19,* 459–468.

Denis, J-L Langley A and Rouleau L (2005) Rethinking leadership in public organizations. In E Ferlie, L Lynn and C Pollitt (eds), *The Oxford handbook of public management,* Oxford: Oxford University Press.

Dewey J (1927) *The public and its problems.* Athens, OH: Swallow Press/Ohio University Press, reprinted 1988.

Fairhurst G (2009) Considering context in discursive leadership research. *Human Relations, 62*(11), 1607–1633.

Flinders M, Gamble A, Hay C and Kenny M (2009) *The Oxford handbook of British politics.* Oxford: Oxford University Press.

Gains F, Greasley S, John P and Stoker G (2009) The impact of political performance on organizational performance: evidence from English local government. *Local Government Studies, 35*(1), 75–94.

Goldsmith M and Larsen H (2004) Local political leadership: Nordic style. *International Journal of Urban and Regional Research, 28,* 121–133.

Grint K (2000) *The arts of leadership.* Oxford: Oxford University Press.

Grint K (2005) Problems, problems, problems: the social construction of 'leadership'. *Human Relations,* 58, 1467–1494.

Hartley J (2002) Leading communities: capabilities and cultures. *Leadership and Organizational Development Journal,* 23, 419–429. (Special issue on Public sector leadership.)

Hartley J (2010a) Political leadership. In S Brookes and K Grint (eds), *The public leadership challenge.* London: Palgrave.

Hartley J (2010b) Public sector leadership and management development. In J Gold, R Thorpe and A Mumford (eds), *Gower handbook of leadership and management development.* Farnham: Gower.

Hartley J and Allison M (2000) The role of leadership in modernisation and improvement of public services. *Public Money and Management, April,* 35–40.

Hartley J and Benington J (2010) *Leadership for healthcare.* Bristol: Policy Press.

Hartley J and Fletcher C (2008) Leadership with political awareness: leadership across diverse interests inside and outside the organization. In K James and J Collins (eds), *Leadership perspectives: knowledge into action.* London: Palgrave., pp. 157–170.

Hartley J and Pinder K (2010) Coaching political leaders. In J Passmore (ed.), *Leadership in coaching.* London: Kogan Page, pp. 159–175.

Hay C (2002) *Political analysis: an introduction.* Basingstoke: Palgrave Macmillan.

Hay C (2007) *Why we hate politics.* Cambridge: Polity Press.

Heifetz R (1994) *Leadership without easy answers.* Cambridge, MA: Harvard University Press.

Hoggett P (2006) Conflict, ambivalence and the contested purpose of public organizations. *Human Relations, 59*(2), 175–194.

Jackson P (2003) The size and scope of the public sector: an international comparison. In T Bovaird and E Löffler (eds), *Public management and governance.* London: Routledge.

Jackson B and Parry K (2008) *A very short, fairly interesting and reasonably cheap book about studying leadership.* London: Sage.

John P (2010) Local government reform and political leadership. In S Brookes and K Grint (eds), *The public leadership challenge.* London: Palgrave.

John P and Cole A (2000) Political leadership in the new urban governance: Britain and France compared. In L Pratchett (ed.), *Renewing local democracy: the modernisation agenda in British local government.* London: Frank Cass.

Keller J (2009) Explaining rigidity and pragmatism in political leaders: a general theory and a plausibility test from the Reagan presidency. *Political Psychology, 30*(3), 465–498.

Kotter, J. (1990) *What leaders really do.* Boston, MA: Harvard Business School Press.

Leach S and Wilson D (2000) *Local political leadership.* Bristol: Policy Press.

Leach S, Hartley J, Lowndes V, Wilson D and Downe J (2005) *Local political leadership in England and Wales.* York: Joseph Rowntree Foundation.

Leftwich A (2004) *What is politics?* Cambridge: Polity Press.

Lowndes V and Leach S (2004) Understanding local political leadership: constitutions, contexts and capabilities. *Local Government Studies, 30*(4), 557–575.

Machiavelli N (1984) *The discourses.* Harmondsworth: Penguin.

Marquand D (2009) Biography. In M Flinders, A Gamble, C Hay and M Kenny (eds), *The Oxford handbook of British politics.* Oxford: Oxford University Press.

Mazlish B (1994) Some observations on the psychology of political leadership. *Political Psychology, 15*(4), 745–753.

Moore M (1995) *Creating public value.* Cambridge, MA: Harvard University Press.

Morgan E (1988) *Inventing the people: the rise of popular sovereignty in England and America.* New York: Norton.

Morrell K and Hartley J (2006) A model of political leadership. *Human Relations, 59*(4), 483–504.

Newman J (2001) Modernising governance: New labour policies and society. London: Sage.

Nye J (2008) *The powers to lead.* Oxford: Oxford University Press.

Pfeffer J (1981) Management as symbolic action. *Research in Organizational Behavior, 3,* 1–52.

Plato, translated by F D Cornford (1962) *The Republic of Plato.* New York: Oxford University Press.

Porter L and McLaughlin G. (2006) Leadership and the organizational context: like the weather? *The Leadership Quarterly, 17,* 559–576.

Rhodes R W, t'Hart P and Noordegraaf M (2007) *Observing government elites: up close and personal.*

Rittel H and Webber M (1973) Dilemmas in a general theory of planning. *Policy Sciences, 4,* 155–169.

Rost J (1991) *Leadership for the twenty-first century.* New York: Praeger.

Ruscio K (2004) *The leadership dilemma in modern democracy.* Cheltenham: Edward Elgar.

Silvester J (2008) The good, the bad and the ugly: politics and politicians at work. In G Hodgkinson and J Ford (eds), *International Review of Industrial and Organizational Psychology, 23.*

Silvester J and Dykes C (2007) Selecting political candidates: a longitudinal study of assessment centre performance and political success in the 2005 UK General Election. *Journal of Occupational and Organizational Psychology, 80*(1), 11–25.

Simpson J (2008) *The politics of leadership.* London: Leading Edge Publications.

Smith M, Richards D and Marsh D (2002) Reassessing the role of departmental Cabinet ministers. *Public Administration, 78*(2), 305–326.

Stoker G (2006a) *Why politics matters: making democracy work.* London: Palgrave Macmillan.

Stoker G (2006b) Public value management: a new narrative for networked governance? *American Review of Public Administration,* 36(1), 41–57.

Sweeting D (2002) Leadership in urban governance: the Mayor of London. *Local Government Studies, 28*(1), 3–20.

Taylor M (1993) The four axes of civic leadership. Research paper. Local Government Centre, University of Warwick.

Tucker R (1995) *Politics as leadership.* Columbia: University of Missouri Press

Walker A (2009) Ageing and generational politics. In M Flinders, A Gamble, C Hay and M Kenny (eds), *The Oxford handbook of British politics.* Oxford: Oxford University Press.

Weick K (1995) *Sense-making in organizations.* Thousand Oaks, CA: Sage.

Wren T (2007) *Inventing leadership: the challenge of democracy.* Cheltenham: Edward Elgar.

Yukl G (2006) *Leadership in organizations,* 6th edn. Upper Saddle River, NJ: Pearson Prentice Hall.

16

Leadership and Cults

Dennis Tourish

INTRODUCTION

The bizarre or unusual is always fascinating. On the surface, few things diverge more from the norm than the behaviours of cult members and their leaders. Most infamously, we have had the 'Jonestown' cult, whose existence ended in 1978 when over 900 people seemed to commit mass suicide at their leader's behest in the remote jungles of Guyana. In fact, many were murdered (Layton, 1999). Such organisations are potent warnings of the dangers that exist when people put their critical faculties in cold storage, and defer unthinkingly to the judgement of their leaders. There is an ever-present danger of this occurring. Leaders within corporations, in particular, possess more power than ever before (Guthey, 2005). For many such leaders, the management of meaning through the framing of an alternate vision of reality is crucial to the consolidation of their power. Frequently, this also compels a harsh attitude towards dissent (Lipman-Blumen, 2008). As Stein (2008, p. 75) noted: 'Corporate executives... use language in an effort to manage (which most commonly means to control) dissent. Their tactics include denying, constraining, subverting, transforming, quashing and discrediting challenges that oppose orthodox ideologies and policies.' It is this dynamic which transforms the study of leadership in cults from an esoteric preoccupation with the bizarre, and into an exploration of leadership dynamics that in an attenuated form can be found in many organisations, and which sometimes moves them in a cultic direction. Cults aren't therefore some different species to other organisations – they merely manifest certain behaviours in a particularly extreme manner.

In this chapter, I will relate what is known about what I would describe as 'cultic leadership' (i.e. that set of attitudes, behaviours, emotions and practices which distinguish leadership in cults from leadership in more mainstream organisations) to leadership more generally, particularly in its transformational guise. I will begin by defining cults and outlining the main mechanisms by which leaders in such organisations acquire power over their followers, and then seek to transform their values, behaviours, emotions and belief systems. At various stages, examples will be given from the literature on a number of cultic organisations, but also from everyday leadership practices in some better-known organisational contexts which have at least some cultic characteristics. A core argument is that cult leaders exercise their influence by manipulating well-known techniques of influence, persuasion and the exercise of charismatic authority, albeit to an extreme extent. A greater awareness of such dynamics would both insulate people more fully from cultic influence, and alert organisations and their leaders to potentially dysfunctional aspects of their own practice that, ultimately, are likely to have socially harmful consequences.

CULTS: TOWARDS A DEFINITION

A widely used definition characterises cults as

A group or movement exhibiting great or excessive devotion to some person, idea or thing, and employing unethical manipulative or coercive techniques of persuasion and control... designed to advance the goals of the group's leaders, to the actual or possible detriment of members, their families or the community. (AFF, 1986, pp. 119–120)

Other definitions highlight the centrality of particular forms of leadership to the cultic phenomenon. For example, Lalich (2004, p. 5) describes a cult as

a sharply bounded social group or a diffusely bounded social movement held together through shared commitments to a charismatic leader. It upholds a transcendent ideology (often but not always religious in nature) and requires a high level of personal commitment from its members in words and deeds.

It is clear that this is anything but a new phenomenon. Devotion to charismatic leaders, a strong commitment to powerful belief systems, a desire to transcend the limits of immediate personal experience and a tendency to overlook disconfirming evidence have characterised the human experience for so long as records exist (Festinger, 1957; Oakes, 1997).

Lalich's definitional approach is consistent with that of Singer (1987), who suggested that programmes of 'thought reform' involve attempts to reframe a person's sense of individuality, core belief systems and overall self-concept within a 'totalistic' ideology that – allegedly – explains everything. Cultic organisations achieve their effects by controlling people's social environment, particularly their time; placing them in a position of powerlessness relative to an apparently all-knowing leader; eliminating opportunities for members to provide corrective feedback to their leaders, or receive much in the way of feedback themselves from the outside world; and manipulating complex systems of reward for conformity, while administering punishment for dissent (Langone, 1995; Tourish and Vatcha, 2005).

A cult's leader possesses enormous authority in the eyes of his or her followers. Having invested many of their hopes for a better life in the leader, followers are intrinsically motivated to look positively on the leader's words and actions. The resulting high commitment of members is usually expressed in Stakhanovite work norms, which mean that the group environment comes to monopolise their time. Multiple case studies of cults show this dynamic in action, including accounts of Scientology (Atack, 1991), famous for numbering Tom Cruise, John Travolta and other movie stars among its members; the Unification Church of the Reverend Moon (Hong, 1998), whose members can often be observed soliciting donations at major US international airports and who are told that their leader is the return of the Messiah to Earth; and the religious 'Children of God' cult, once renowned for using its female members to seduce potential male recruits (Raine, 2006). Members also replace their pre-existing beliefs and values with those of the group, lose confidence in their own perceptions in favour of those of the group's leaders, and experience social punishments such as shunning by other members if they deviate from prescribed norms. Conformity is critical. The outcome is an environment dominated by what has been described as 'bounded choice' (Lalich, 2004): i.e. one in which the expression of only a limited and tightly regulated repertoire of beliefs, behaviours and emotions is permissible.

It is scarcely surprising that cults have been widely studied, and debated, by sociologists of religion (Barker, 2007; Bruce, 2001; Cote and Gunn, 2007), psychologists (Festinger, 1957; Singer, 1987; Singer and Lalich, 1996), system theorists (Galanter, 1999) and numerous other disciplines for many years. However, it is surprising that leadership scholars have paid the issue very little attention, evidently viewing cultic leadership as some kind of aberration bereft of analytic value. And while many organisation theorists have noted that 'consent, obedience and resistance can be seen as key concerns in management and organisation' (Karreman and Alvesson, 2009, p. 1115), they have largely ignored the cultic phenomenon, despite the fact that power relations are manifest within it in a more pristine form than most other organisational contexts. This is an omission which this chapter seeks to remedy.

Overall, I suggest that the following five interlocking ingredients of cultic dynamics are particularly important to illuminating the leadership dynamics of cults:

1. *Charismatic leadership* (which may reflect some innate qualities on the part of the leader, but may just as easily be a socially engineered construct in the minds of the followers, and thus constitute an attributional phenomenon).
2. *A compelling vision* (the vision being of a transcendent or totalistic character, capable of imbuing the individual's relationship to the organization with a sense of higher purpose).
3. *Intellectual stimulation* (of a kind that seeks to motivate followers to intensify their efforts in support of the vision, compellingly articulated by the group's leaders).
4. *Individual consideration* (or a feeling that the followers' interests are being attended to, and perhaps that they are in some way important to the charismatic leader, leading to a process of recruitment/initiation, conversion and indoctrination).
5. *Promotion of a common culture* (a set of norms which specify particular attitudes and forms of

behaviour deemed to be appropriate. Within cults, these also minimize the expression of dissent, other than within carefully controlled limits, and hence produce a punitive internal environment).

These traits are summarised in Figure 16.1. I now unpack each of them, and illustrate how critical the role of leadership is to the cultic phenomenon.

CHARISMATIC LEADERSHIP, DISSENT AND LEADERSHIP PRIVILEGES

Charismatic leadership is an indispensable ingredient of cultic organization (Langone, 1993; Singer and Lalich, 1995; Tobias and Lalich, 1994). Since charismatic leadership is discussed in depth by Jay Conger in Chapter 7, I will not review its core tenets here. Suffice it to note that it has been observed in doomsday cults in the 1950s (Festinger, 1957), the homicidal Manson 'family' cult of the 1960s (Sanders, 2002), the Jonestown cult of the 1970s (Reiterman and Jacobs, 2008), the suicidal Heavens Gate cult in California (Lalich, 2004), and in the genocidal Aum cult in Japan, which released nerve gas on five subway trains in Tokyo in 1995, killing five people and injuring thousands (Lifton, 1999). Frequently, the leader's charisma turns out to be no more substantial than the powers possessed by the Wizard of Oz. However, such is the intensity of their followers' need to believe that they come to be viewed as people of genius, insight, outstanding organizational ability and uncommon compassion, irrespective of what they actually do. The risks for rational calculation on the part of followers are considerable. The chapters in this handbook by Conger and Kets de Vries and Balazs discuss these risks and the dark side of charisma in some detail. Here, I will simply note that the construction of a charismatic persona is central to the processes whereby cultic leaders seek to first capture the attention of their would-be followers, and then procure their complete engagement with the leader's agenda.

For example, I have argued previously that Enron, whose spectacular bankruptcy in 2001 was at that time the biggest in US corporate history, can be largely understood as an example of a prototypical corporate cult (Tourish and Vatcha, 2005). In line with the discussion here, there is example evidence that Enron's leadership aimed

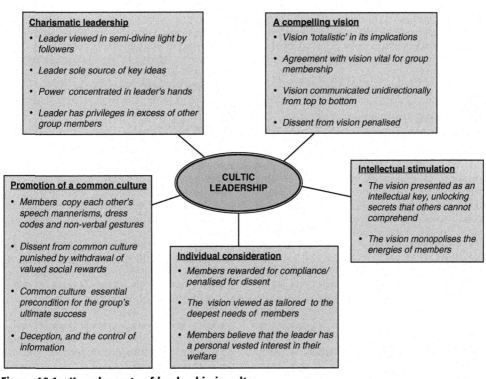

Figure 16.1 Key elements of leadership in cults

at creating an artificial and ultimately deceptive aura of charisma around themselves. Its two main leaders, Ken Lay and Jeffrey Skilling, engaged in ever more dramatic forms of self-promotion. In keeping with a company-wide dramaturgical predilection for Star Wars analogies, Skilling was known internally as Darth Vader, 'a master of the energy universe who had the ability to control people's minds. He was at the peak of his strength, and he intimidated everyone. He had been lured over to the Dark Side from McKinsey & Company in 1990' (Cruver, 2003, p. 10). He dressed for the part at company gatherings, referred to his traders as 'Storm Troopers' and decorated his home in a style sympathetic to the Darth Vader image (Schwartz, 2002). Skilling was also sometimes known as 'The Prince', after Machiavelli. New recruits were instructed to read *The Prince* from beginning to end, or be eaten alive (Boje et al., 2004). Another senior executive, Rebecca Mark, became known as 'Mark the Shark', with all its attendant overtones of predatory aggression and greater competitive power.

This tone was clearly part of an intense dramaturgical effort designed to project an unusually alluring spectacle, and thereby convince people that they belonged to a cause far greater than merely being part of a business or working for a living. Hagiographic accounts of their accomplishments were correspondingly widespread, including in an influential book by Hamel (2000), entitled *Leading the Revolution*. This also boosted their reputation internally as well as externally – and intensified the engagement of their followers.

COMPELLING VISION/INTELLECTUAL STIMULATION

Visions have been defined as a set of beliefs about how people should act and interact to attain some idealised future state (Strange and Mumford, 2002). Articulating compelling visions, cult leaders seek to establish cultures that rest on uniform values, beliefs, attitudes and behaviours and in which alternative discourses are demonised and suppressed. As Maccoby (2003, p. 229) has written with specific reference to the USA, the public has been 'seduced by the promise of visionary leaders.' Given that people want work with some social meaning or social value, want to feel part of a larger community, and want to live and work in an integrated fashion (Pfeffer, 2003), their tendency to comply with such leaders is hardly surprising.

Within this world view, senior managers are encouraged to colonise every area of their employees' lives – including, increasingly, their most private values and belief systems – as evidenced by a growing interest by many corporations and chief executives in promoting 'spirituality' in the workplace (e.g. Bell and Taylor, 2004; Duchan and Plowman, 2005; Tourish and Tourish, 2010). The vision (in the most optimistic rendition of the process) performs an integrative role, combining the members into a collective whole with a shared set of aspirations capable of guiding their everyday behavior. The act of communicating such a vision is highly dynamic, requires intense charisma, and seeks to transform relational dynamics throughout the workplace.

Cult leaders therefore attempt to mobilise the enthusiasm of their followers around what has been defined as a 'totalistic' (i.e. all-embracing) vision of a new world order, way of being or form of organization. The group's leaders suggest that their vision constitutes an inspirational new paradigm, capable of transforming an otherwise impure reality. For example, studies of cults in the context of politics highlight a tendency on the part of cult leaders to stress only those aspects of modern society they deem to be undesirable, propose radical new visions for economic, social or racial reorganisation that it is said will create precisely the opposite conditions, and therefore suggest that all of their followers' problems will disappear in a new world order that will, in essence, create a paradise on earth (Stein, 2002; Tourish and Wohlforth, 2000a, 2000b).

Converts, dazzled by the spectacle, develop a mood of absolute conviction. This immunises them against doubt. No evidence is ever judged sufficient to falsify the belief system in question. Such moods have been defined as 'ideological totalism' (Lifton, 1961). The messianic leader of the organisation seeks ever more enthusiastic expressions of agreement from the organisation's members. Dissent is resistance to be overcome, rather than useful feedback. Plausibility is often simply a question of uncontested belief. The process of social proof then asserts itself, in which the spectacle of many agreeing to a position (a) irrationally convinces each person that it must be accurate and (b) encourages even riskier and more committed forms of behaviour (e.g. Rao et al., 2001). The further absence of feedback loops reinforces belief in the sacred vision of the leader. Cut adrift from the corrective feedback that is readily available in more open social systems, cult members become marooned in an oasis of certainty, from which they contemplate a baffling outside world that surveys them with equal disdain and incomprehension.

In its sharpest form, Lifton (1961, pp. 427–428) defines ideological totalism as follows:

> The totalistic milieu maintains an aura of sacredness around its basic dogma, holding it out as an ultimate moral vision for the ordering of human existence. This sacredness is evident in the prohibition (whether or not explicit) against the questioning of basic assumptions, and in the reverence which is demanded for the originators of the Word, the present bearers of the Word, and the Word itself... the milieu... makes an exaggerated claim of airtight logic, of absolute 'scientific' precision.

Given its potency as a means of engaging followers and reshaping their behaviour, the importance of 'vision' has been increasingly stressed in the business world, in a growing volume of largely uncritical practitioner and academic literature (e.g. Collins, 2001). Leaders, therefore, often seek to possess and dramatically communicate 'a vision' for their organisation, in the belief that this is a critical requirement for both effective change management and wider organisational success (Yukl, 2008). Many use powerful rhetorical tools, in order to promote a further identification and feeling of 'oneness' between the leader and his or her followers (Sinha and Jackson, 2006). An attitude of certainty is maintained, towards issues that are objectively uncertain. Equipped with a compelling vision, or its facsimile, charismatic leaders can thus have a 'profound and extraordinary effects on followers' (House and Baetz, 1979, p. 339). Clearly, these effects may be individually benign and/or socially useful. But, taken to an extreme, they may also be individually harmful and/or socially destructive. It is precisely this process that is found so frequently in the cultic environment.

INDIVIDUAL CONSIDERATION, 'LOVE BOMBING' AND CONVERSION

Recruitment is a key goal for all cult leaders, since the expansion of their influence requires a growing army of enthusiastic disciples. The problem is that the prospective recruit's resistance is likely to be at its highest immediately before they join. They have yet to buy into the belief system, invest much energy in pursuit of the group's goals, or acquire intense faith in the wisdom of the leader, and they still have plentiful other choices. The challenge is to initiate people into the group, engage a process of conversion and then reinforce it with indoctrination.

Recruitment/initiation

Cult leaders usually recruit people through a two-pronged process characterised by intense and emotionally draining recruitment rituals on the one hand, and what has been described as 'love bombing' (Hassan, 1988) on the other. In terms of rituals, a process is engaged that may stretch over several days, which exposes the would-be recruit to powerful messages from the leader, which requires them to express ever greater levels of support for the leader's insights, and which may involve the person adopting behaviours that might otherwise seem irksome and certainly strange. It has been described as a roller-coaster ride, with potential recruits soaring to emotional highs and then experiencing mood collapses which, in total, leave them ever more vulnerable to the messages of the cult's leaders (Tourish and Wohlforth, 2000a). For example, common practices within Jim Jones' People's Temple included highly theatrical events such as lengthy prayer sessions, miraculous healings (in which followers previously assigned to the role would often pretend to be suffering from severe ailments, only to be dramatically 'cured' by Jones), gospel choirs and mass sing-alongs, lengthy sermons and frequent exhortations to be both healed and reborn into a new life (Reiterman and Jacobs, 2008). The resultant mood of heightened emotional excitement renders people more vulnerable to the messages of cult leaders (Taylor, 2004). Research into group dynamics has long established that, when we endure particular initiation rituals or experience discomfort to join, we are more inclined to exaggerate the benefits of group membership and to intensify our sense of commitment as a means of establishing that we belong to the group (Aronson and Mills, 1959). Emotionally debilitating recruitment rituals, assuming that the potential recruit has some intrinsic motivation for looking positively on the group, are likely to have precisely this effect.

However, pressure alone does not suffice. Love bombing is also crucial, with the implied promise that, if the recruit merely accedes to the high demands of the group, they will receive the beneficent regard of the leader and other members of the organisation. Thus, cult leaders make great ceremony of showing individual consideration for their members – at least, immediately before and after they join (Tourish and Irving, 1995). Prospective recruits are showered with attention, which expands to affection and then often grows into a simulation of love. This is the courtship phase of the recruitment ritual. The leader wishes to seduce the new recruit into the organisation's embrace, gradually habituating them to its rituals and belief systems. Individual consideration overcomes moods of resistance, by blurring distinctions between personal relationships, theoretical constructs and bizarre behaviours.

The problem is exacerbated by status differentials. Normally, a person of lesser status attaches more importance to being liked by those of higher status than the other way round (Tourish, 2007). Individual consideration from such figures – the message that the new recruit is positively valued and very much wanted – increases the person's tendency to affiliate, conform and engage in yet further behaviours in keeping with well-established group norms. When an imbalance of power is institutionalised into the relationship between leaders and followers, as is invariably the case in the context of cults, and when dissent is equated with subversion, such consideration becomes a form of manipulation, intended to blur recipients' ability to freely determine where their own mind ends and that of the organisation begins.

Conversion

When someone responds to intense individual consideration from higher-status leaders, and is desperate to affiliate with them, the outcome of their shift in attitudes can be regarded as conversion. It occurs when a person experiences fundamental changes of knowledge and beliefs, values and standards, emotional attachments and needs, and of everyday conduct, so that previously existing values and beliefs are abandoned in favour of new ones articulated by the leader (Lalich, 2004; Lewin, 1948; Tourish and Vatcha, 2005). New dress codes, behaviours, beliefs and modes of being are embraced. Each reinforces the other. A new dress code is likely to encourage the adoption of behaviours normally associated with the dress code; novel behaviours strengthen the attitudes that underpin them; the overall effect is, frequently, what outside observers come to see as a fundamental personality transformation, or new mode of being, on the part of the person concerned (Jenkinson, 2008). The process has been described as one of identity stripping, identification and symbolic death/rebirth (Zablocki, 2001).

Unsurprisingly, transformation is a dominant theme in the practice of cultic organizations and their leaders. The prospect of permanent revolution suggests that people must be inspired by a compelling vision that is sufficiently powerful to sweep aside all reservations. The following quotation conveys the mental state that it is frequently implied should be aroused by the energetic communication of such a vision. It is worth reflecting on:

To say that one had "seen the light" is a poor description of the mental rapture which only the convert knows (regardless of what faith he has been converted to). The new light seems to pour from all directions across the skull; the whole universe falls into pattern, like the stray pieces of a jigsaw puzzle assembled by magic at one stroke. There is now an answer to every question, doubts and conflicts are a matter of the tortured past – a past already remote, when one had lived in dismal ignorance in the tasteless, colorless world of those who *don't know*. Nothing henceforth can disturb the convert's inner peace and serenity – except the occasional fear of losing faith again, losing thereby what alone makes life worth living, and falling back into the outer darkness, where there is wailing and gnashing of teeth.

The quotation is from the writer Arthur Koestler (Koestler, 1949, p. 23), describing his mood of exaltation while a member of the Communist Party in the 1930s. It is included in a volume of reflections on the period aptly entitled *The God That Failed*, and which documents a mindset that can only be called cult-like. It is in this direction that would-be visionary, charismatic leaders often seek to transport their followers, and in the process make use of cult-like tactics.

Indoctrination

The convert mentality is reinforced within the cultic environment by a process of indoctrination. Indoctrination occurs through the one-way transmission of intense messages from leaders to followers that require ever-greater levels of devotion to the group ideal, and which are designed to instil into the recruit a feeling that being accepted into the group is a particular privilege that makes him or her a member of a special elite. Thus, recruitment/initiation, conversion and indoctrination are all vital stages in the cultic experience, and are sustained through the impression of individual consideration by the group's leaders.

Lifton (1999) vividly describes this process within the Aum cult in Japan. As he notes, a key paradox is that, in the end, cult members came to experience a relationship with their guru that 'although radically confining, is also experienced as explosively liberating' (Lifton, 1999, p. 89). In the case of Aum, it produced followers prepared to countenance genocide, but able to convince themselves that, since such an act would purify humanity, it must be altruistic. The power of the group's leader to reframe reality had become absolute.

PROMOTING A COMMON CULTURE

Much of the most influential management literature in the last few decades has sold the notion of what amounts to a monolithic organisational culture, to be determined exclusively by senior managers, as the key to overall success (see Alvesson, Chapter 11, this volume). The importance of this resides in the notion that organisational cultures consist of cognitive systems explaining how people think, reason and make decisions (Pettigrew, 1990). If cultures can, therefore, be controlled by those at the top, the overall impact on people is likely to be enormous. In such schemas, the views of non-managerial employees, women and/or minorities are unlikely to be considered (Martin, 2002).

It has rarely been pointed out that the most intense organisational cultures (invariably determined by those at the top, with minimal input from below) are to be found within cults. In particular, such organisations promote all-embracing cultures, decreed by the leader, and with which everyone is supposed to agree. Difference from the vision of the leader is banished to the margins of the group's tightly policed norms. Total conformity along these lines leads to the disabling and well-documented phenomenon of groupthink, an infection which thrives particularly well in the overheated atmosphere of cults (Wexler and Fraser, 1995).

Here, '…the experiential world is sharply divided into the pure and the impure, into the absolutely good and the absolutely evil' (Lifton, 1961, p. 423). Dissent is demonised, rendering it all the more unappealing, since people quickly grasp that to associate with dissenters is to volunteer for a Salem-style witch-hunt. Indeed, as Hogg (2007, p. 49) has suggested, it may be that autocratic and hierarchical leaders are innately prone to regard criticism as an intra-group threat, and thus automatically respond with exploitative and power-based behaviours of a punitive kind. The paradox is that, by curtailing useful feedback, they make increasingly poor decisions, thereby damaging the ability of their organisations to achieve the leader's intended goals (Tourish and Robson, 2006). Oblivious to this danger, or driven by other imperatives, cult leaders frequently seek to maintain the purity of their vision and the devotion of their followers by purging their ranks of sceptics and dissenters, the weak and the wavering.

For example, the political cult of the Workers Revolutionary Party in Britain achieved notoriety in the 1970s and 1980s, largely because it attracted such theatrical luminaries as Vanessa Redgrave to its ranks, and obtained some endorsement from the radical Labour MP and later Mayor of London, Ken Livingstone. The group's leader, Gerry Healy, was notorious for regularly expelling anyone suspected of harbouring dissident views, no matter how flimsy the evidence that this was actually the case (Cohen, 2007). In so doing, he frequently reduced his group to a hard core of 'true believers.' This process is accentuated by the tendency of many cult leaders to translate their vision into 'prophecies,' of nuclear war, economic collapse, alien invasions or the Second Coming, sometimes with dates incautiously attached. For example, Jehovah's Witnesses have been offered many predictions about precisely when Jesus Christ would return to earth, starting with 1914. When this failed to materialise, the group's leader announced that he had 'miscalculated', and produced a new prediction. Consistent with Festinger's (1957) theory of cognitive dissonance, which postulates that when inconsistencies between our beliefs and reality causes uncomfortable psychological tensions we initially seek to resolve them by intensifying our commitment rather than reviewing our beliefs, most followers accepted his explanation. Later, it was argued that 1975 would be decisive. This time, many thousands of followers suspected of doubting the official explanations for failure were summarily expelled (Schmalz, 2000).

Cults of all kinds therefore tend to become movements of fewer and fewer people, agreeing with each other about more and more issues. Those who survive the leader's purges are informed that the group's vision offers a superior insight to any other perspective on offer, and that they should be grateful for being permitted to remain. Dress codes, language and styles of interaction are all highly regulated (Tobias and Lalich, 1994), reinforcing the monochrome environment that has come to define the members' social world.

Another intriguing paradox within cults is that individual consideration on the part of the leader shifts from being positive to critical in nature. Once the recruit has been 'won over', and made an intense commitment, the group seeks to ensure the further embrace of its norms, by a relentless process of criticism and attack. Individual consideration of a positive kind (i.e. Dr Jekyll) alternates with its alter ego (i.e. Mr. Hyde). The insufficient commitment and devotion of the group members are held to be responsible for any failures that cannot be denied, rationalized or depicted as triumphs. Relentless criticism gradually erodes people's confidence in their own perceptions, creating a form of learned helplessness (Seligman, 1975). 'Love' – always dependent on the unconditional expression of enthusiasm for the goals of the group's leaders – alternates with abuse, in a disorienting cycle that leaves recipients feeling fearful and powerless.

Cult leaders colonise the space between hope and despair. They then propel their followers on disorienting forays between both extremes, with the intent of driving their behaviour in ever-more conformist directions. Context is crucial. Having made an initial commitment, possibly of a dramatic kind, recruits are motivated to engage in further behaviours in line with the commitment originally made – the principle of commitment and consistency (Cialdini, 2001). When this blends with learned helplessness, it reinforces even further people's already strong inclination to over-identify with the norms that have been decreed by the group's leaders. The leaders, meanwhile, have adorned themselves in the garb of omniscience and infallibility. Paradoxically, and providing it has come after a period of love bombing, criticism from such sources reinforces the person's attachment to the group's belief system and their sense of loyalty to its leaders.

Moreover, abuse generates multiple insecurities, further strengthening the cult leader's power. Whatever its precise content, insecurity reinforces 'the construction of workplace selves and the reproduction of organizational power relations' (Collinson, 2003, p. 530). In particular, it seems likely that when people are insecure about their self-identity and their status, the nominal freedom of their position (after all, they retain the choice to leave) will be experienced as a form of existential angst that serves to further intensify their sense of vulnerability. It has long been known that people have an innate tendency to conform to authority and power under a variety of conditions (Milgram, 1974). If they are rendered fearful in the manner described here, and when the most modest expression of dissent attracts punitive attention from those above, it seems even more likely that people 'might try to find shelter in the perceived security of being told what to do and what to think, viewing this as a less threatening alternative to the responsibility of making decisions and choices for themselves' (Collinson, 2003, p. 531). Leaders may even manufacture crises, precisely 'in order to give themselves the opportunity to demonstrate continuing "proof" of their charisma to their followers' (Robinson and Kerr, 2009, p. 881). When the group environment assumes that all change must start at the top, the leader knows best, the leader must have a compelling vision and that one unifying culture is a precondition of effectiveness, inherently cult-like dynamics of the kind described here may be unleashed. It is clear that many of these assumptions are now standard features of the predominant leadership culture in many corporate organisations.

Lalich (2004) vividly chronicles such processes within Heaven's Gate. The group was the centre of an international media storm in 1997 when the bodies of its 39 remaining members were discovered in California, after a mass suicide. Left behind were invariably upbeat videos, of farewell and justification. They had become increasingly preoccupied by the Hale-Bopp comet. The group's leader, Marshall Appelwhite, believed that the comet's tail concealed a spaceship. This was arriving to take them from what they viewed as an earthy nightmare to what they called 'The Next Level' or the 'Level Above Human.' Death was depicted as rebirth. It is clear that Appelwhite used pressure and the fear of expulsion from the group as a central group dynamic. Given the potency of the vision, members were terrified of losing their group membership, and in their terms, being cast into the outer darkness of the non-believers, where they would miss out on 'The Next Level.' Appelwhite heightened this anxiety by instigating a membership purge in 1976, ridding the group of those 'weaker' members (i.e. sceptics) who were judged to be bringing the others down. The effect was to heighten the commitment of those who survived the cull, while reinforcing their faith in the judgement of their leader.

Again, there are plentiful corporate parallels. For example, Jack Welch was CEO of General Electric from 1981 to 2001. In office and since, he has championed a system of 'differentiation' among employees which relies on a 'forced ranking' system, year on year (Tourish et al., 2010). In essence, managers divide employees into three categories: top performers, to be rewarded; middle performers, who must but can improve; and a bottom 10%, who are regarded as too weak to remain within the organisation and who are targeted for removal. Such systems produce a growing reluctance on the part of employees to risk their next performance evaluation by being openly critical of their leaders' performance, and a tendency instead to stress how much they agree with whatever such leaders have decreed as being important. The power of leaders is entrenched, and that of others diminished. Interestingly, 'differentiation' is now implemented by many multinational corporations. It was also a critical part of the management control system within Enron.

DECEPTION AND THE CONTROL OF INFORMATION

Typically, cult leaders have extraordinary authority, privileged access to information, and a hidden agenda of self-aggrandisement that is concealed behind more idealistic statements. The dominant culture is maintained because ordinary followers are denied full information about the organisation's goals or practices, while a carefully contrived display of righteousness by the leaders prevents detailed scrutiny of actual behaviour as opposed to avowed intentions. Consistent with this dynamic, information emanating from the top within Enron was also distorted in nature (Salter, 2008). The organisation's accountancy practices sought to conceal information rather than reveal it; a noble-sounding code of ethics camouflaged directly contrary practice; and the organisation's leaders displayed much greater optimism about the company's future than they knew to be true. Lalich (2004) describes similar processes within both Heaven's Gate and a major Californian political cult in great detail. Bereft of accurate information, the followers of cult leaders find it much harder to evaluate their pronouncements or hold them to account for their actions – precisely the intent. More widely, research has shown that those with most resources tend to be the most powerful in organisational decision-making, enabling them to accumulate yet more resources and hence further entrench their position of power (Pfeffer, 1992). Collecting and controlling the dissemination of information as a strategic resource also reinforces the power of leaders (Fleming and Spicer, 2007), and is particularly used to this end in the exercise of leadership power within cults.

COERCIVE PERSUASION AND LEADERSHIP IN CULTS

For all the asymmetries of power that exist, the relationship between cult leaders and their followers is ultimately one of dialectical interdependence. Cult leaders seek to influence, direct, constrain and shut down alternative options for action. But they could not succeed in this unless their followers perceived apparent benefits in the ever-greater renunciation of autonomy that is demanded of them.

Thus, members of cults display intense levels of conformity to given group norms, as determined by the group's leader. In turn, they derive identity-related benefits from other group members (Baron et al., 2003). Acceptance by the members of such groups feels gratifying to those joining it, increasing the desire to affiliate. However, affiliation is dependent on the complete internalisation of the norms within the group concerned – an acceptance that, in a punitive and disorienting environment, feels attractive because it reduces uncertainty about

what to think, feel and do (Hogg, 2001, 2007). If we accept that people are attracted by the idea of order, the embrace of ideological commitment along the lines advocated by a powerful leader offers many attractions. A comprehensive belief system can appear to 'explain' the world and the place of the individual within it. Under conditions of stress and uncertainty, ideological totalism of this kind may become even more alluring, since an individual's need for security will increase rather than decrease. Many seek to exploit the tension between our desire for stability and the unfortunate fact that we live in an unstable world. For example, Cullen's (2009, p. 1240) analysis of Steven Covey's best selling text *The 7 Habits of Successful People,* which many have noted has attracted an almost cult-like following, highlights how the guru's rhetoric seeks to 'create fear and anxiety, and quickly and lucidly offers a system for alleviating the pain which it has itself created.' Moreover, as the book proceeds, 'Covey's voice gradually becomes louder and more imperative, drowning out the possibility for engaging with other perspectives' (p. 1241). Thus, the reader becomes more susceptible to the author's powerful message. Within cults, and in organisations moving in a cultic direction, similar dynamics reinforce leader power, since the leaders are charged with responsibility for offering the reassurance – or illusion – of stability, certainty and belongingness. In doing so, they seek to define norms of behaviour and ideology, and thus also set the parameters within which acceptance or exclusion from the valued group is likely to occur.

In order to maintain this momentum, invariably an onerous challenge, cult leaders must extend their influence in ever-wider and more intrusive directions. For example, the leader of Jonestown (Jim Jones) pressed many of his followers to give up their belongings, sign over their houses, sign over custody of their children and in some cases to sign false statements attesting that they had sexually abused their children (Reiterman and Jacobs, 2008). Each new renunciation of autonomy made the next step seem more compelling. It was, after all, in line with what had already been relinquished. As Zimbardo (2007, p. xii) has noted, 'the pervasive yet subtle power of a host of situational variables can dominate an individual's will to resist.' The psychological processes unleashed by an oppressive social situation include 'deindividuation, obedience to authority, passivity in the face of threats, self-justification and rationalisation' (Zimbardo, 2007, p. xii). Eventually, many hundreds of Jones's followers moved to a remote location in Guyana, where they were cut off from outside contacts, constantly harangued by Jones over loudspeaker systems, had their behaviour closely monitored for signs of deviance or resistance, and were compelled to endure countless suicide dress rehearsals ('white nights'), which eventually culminated in an authentic final performance. Those who refused to consume poison had it forced on them (Layton, 1999). The leader's power was complete – although, paradoxically, it was also terminated by the physical extinction of the group, including Jones himself.

This tension between control and empowerment, autonomy and subservience, is writ large in many leader–follower relations (Fleming and Spicer, 2007). Workplace surveillance systems now increasingly seek to produce conformist (i.e. compliant and pliant) individuals in the workplace (Sewell and Barker, 2006). The growing emphasis on teamwork is an important mechanism for unleashing conformist dynamics, in the form of peer pressure (Barker, 1993). Many such systems use group-based incentives and rewards, as well as other mechanisms, to create systems of peer pressure. In Foucault's (1977, 1979, 1982) terms, these processes illustrate the disciplinary effects of power and identity and the barriers they can create for resistance. For example, Mehri's (2006) study of the lean production system at Toyota contrasted the official company rhetoric with a more coercive reality, noting that 'Employees are expected to follow all rules and obey the prescribed code of behaviour that exists at the company' (Mehri, 2006, p. 26). Researchers have argued that such approaches seek to regulate, discipline and control employees, while camouflaging such intentions in the more benign rhetoric of family values and empowerment (Martin, 1999). Although it is clear that the endpoint is unlikely to be mass suicides or group destruction, it is also clear that the leaders of cults simply take these kinds of processes to a particular extreme.

Thus, within systems characterised by intense surveillance, and in which strident demands for intense commitment become the norm, the demand for purity along lines advocated by the leader is central. Typically, the culture is one of impassioned belief, incessant action to achieve the group's goals, veneration of the leader's vision, and a constraining series of group norms designed to quell dissent. Culture, in such contexts, easily becomes another form of social control (Willmott, 1993, 2003), regardless of the emancipatory rhetoric through which it may be expressed.

More fundamentally, most models of leadership and power generally work with a crucial missing variable – tyranny (Bies and Tripp, 1998). People in many organisations, including cults, are habitually assured that they are empowered and free, and indeed are often encouraged to roam in any direction that they wish. The problem is that they roam at the end of a leash, constrained to move within an orbit sharply defined by the governing cultural assumptions of the organisation as determined by its leaders (Schein, 1961). Culture thus becomes another form of social control. That such control is often less overt than that found in outrightly cultic models of organisation simply makes the process more insidious. These may constitute fertile conditions for leaders to overstep themselves, and unleash at least some cultic dynamics in their organisations in the future.

CONCLUSIONS

In this chapter, I have outlined some of the major mechanisms through which leaders in cultic organisations seek to colonise the affective domain of their followers, impose a uniform definition of reality, and create a culture of high commitment around the norms, values and priorities decreed by the leader. Attentive readers will note that, in one sense, there is nothing extraordinary in the approaches employed. Rather, many of them parallel the precepts of transformational leadership, and echo mainstream leadership practice in, for example, business organisations. There is, therefore, a growing concern with the practice of transformational and charismatic leadership, with more studies documenting its potential to inflict long-term damage on followers (e.g. Robinson and Kerr, 2009), or urging a recognition that more traditional transactional and exchange models of leader–follower relations retain considerable value (O'Shea et al., 2009). Although I have previously argued that transformational leadership theorists tend to ignore the potentially dysfunctional aspects of their approach (e.g. Tourish and Pinnington, 2002), I am far from asserting that transformational leadership must invariably result in cultic organizations. Rather, my argument is that when the power-saturated organisational contexts in which most business leaders operate is insufficiently acknowledged, when status differentials are allowed to go unchallenged, and when leaders develop an exaggerated impression of both the importance of leadership in general and their own efficacy in the role in particular, the potential exists for cultic forms of organisation to take root. There can be a fine line between noble intent and dysfunctional practice. It is therefore more useful to view cults as a continuum rather than in dichotomous categories. Rather than organisations being either cults or not cults, elements of cultism are widely distributed in many organisations. They can move back and forth between relatively healthy dynamics on the one hand, and a more overt, oppressive and fully-fledged cultic system on the other.

Ultimately, cult leaders make use of everyday leadership dynamics, forms of influence and coercive persuasion that can be found in at least some form in most social systems. They merely take these dynamics to a particular extreme. Contrary to common belief, neither cults nor their members are extraordinarily different to any other social group or set of individuals. They simply manifest conformity, group cohesion and the abuse of leadership power in a particularly severe format. It is precisely the *unremarkability* of much cultic practice that should occasion concern, since it suggests a more widespread vulnerability to cultic dynamics than is commonly imagined.

This also means that there are important lessons for the practice of leadership beyond the confines of closed and cultic social systems. It is evident, for example, that although cult leaders can maintain control over relatively small groups of devoted followers, it is much more difficult for them to attract and retain a mass following. A solitary leader lacks sufficient resources to main stringent scrutiny over the many. In a sense, as Banks (2008, p. 14) has rightly noted, this means that 'all tyrannical leadership will fail.' Such failure is usually a question of 'when' rather than 'if'. The example has been given here of the Jonestown group, whose members all perished in a mass suicide/murder drill in 1978. Beyond outright failure, such problems mean that most cults are afflicted with high turnover during the early stages of individuals' membership (Barker, 1995), although the level of turnover falls significantly after two or three years, when various commitment mechanisms exert a greater hold (Zablocki, 2001). Nevertheless, for all the efforts expended to ensure compliance, cult leaders discover that their power has limitations. Leaders who wish to influence wider groups of people, build sustainable organisations and engage rather than stifle the creative energies of their followers would therefore be wise to encourage dissent, distribute power more widely, display humility rather than arrogance and lead by asking questions rather than invariably offering answers (Tourish and Robson, 2006). The challenge is to close the distance between leaders and followers, rather than – as is the case within many organisations – to exacerbate it (Collinson, 2005). A more careful and reflexive approach to follower engagement is necessary.

This is not least among the areas where a great deal of further research would be helpful. More knowledge is needed about how followers can short-circuit the concentration of power in the hands of a small number of leaders, and precisely how some cults acquire much greater influence – for a time – than their generally smaller and more insignificant rivals. In addition, almost all the groups referred to in this chapter have been led by men. There have been some exceptions. The doomsday cult chronicled in Festinger's (1957) seminal work on cognitive dissonance was led by a woman, to whom he attached the pseudonym of 'Mrs Keech.' A more recent example is of a left-wing political cult in California, which was initially an all-female and lesbian group (Lalich, 1992; Siegel et al., 1987), whereas Heaven's Gate was for much of its existence co-led by a husband-and-wife team. Marshall Appelwhite assumed sole leadership responsibility only on his partner's death. Nevertheless, cult leaders are almost invariably male, and overwhelmingly inclined to sexually exploit their followers, an issue meriting much closer study.

Leaders would also derive significant benefits from adopting a more modest perspective on their role. Those holding leadership positions in cults are authoritarian figures. They tend to shoulder the burdens of leadership alone, a characteristic they share with many CEOs. Despite the allure of power, the consequences may be no more pleasant for leaders than they usually are for their followers. Socrates (1993, pp. 565–576), in *The Republic*, long ago pointed out that authoritarian leaders are compelled to be suspicious of dissenters:

> He has to keep a sharp eye out, then, for anyone with courage, self-confidence, intelligence, or wealth. He has no choice in the matter: he's bound to treat them as enemies and to intrigue against them, until he's purged the community of them. That's the nature of his happy state … . They never have any friends, then, throughout their lives: they can only be masters or slaves. Dictatorial people can never experience freedom and true friendship.

This is an unedifying prospectus. In studying what so often goes wrong in such dysfunctional organisational contexts as cults, we may gather further insights into what must be put right in leadership practice much further afield.

REFERENCES

American Family Foundation (AFF) (1986) Cultism: a conference for scholars and policy makers, *Cultic Studies Journal*, 3, 119–120.

Aronson, E. and Mills J. (1959) The effect of severity of initiation on liking for a group, *Journal of Abnormal and Social Psychology*, 59, 177–181.

Atack, J. (1991) *A Piece of Blue Sky*, New York: Citadel Press.

Banks, S. (2008) The troubles with leadership. In S. Banks (ed.), *Dissent and the Failure of Leadership*, Cheltenham, UK: Edward Elgar, pp. 1–21.

Barker, E. (1995) The scientific study of religion? You must be joking! *Journal for the Scientific Study of Religion*, 34, 287–310.

Barker, E. (2007) What should we do about the cults? Policies, information and the perspective of INFORM. In P. Cote and J. Gunn (eds), *The New Religious Question: State Regulation or State Interference?* Frankfurt: Peter Lang, pp. 371–394.

Barker, J. (1993) Tightening the iron cage: concertive control in self-managing teams, *Administrative Science Quarterly*, 38, 408–437.

Baron, R., Crawley, K., and Paulina, D. (2003) Aberrations of power: leadership in totalist groups. In D. van Knippenberg and M. Hogg (eds), *Leadership and Power: Identity Processes in Groups and Organizations*, London: Sage, pp.169–183.

Bell, E. and Taylor, S. (2004) 'From outward bound to inward bound': the prophetic voices and discursive practices of spiritual management development, *Human Relations*, 57, 439–466.

Bies, R. and Tripp, T. (1998) Two faces of the powerless: coping with tyranny in organizations. In R. Kramer and M. Neale (eds), *Power and Influence in Organizations*, London: Sage, pp. 203–220.

Boje, D., Rosile, G., Durant, R., and Luhman, J. (2004) Enron spectacles: a critical dramaturgical analysis, *Organization Studies*, 25, 751–774.

Bruce, S. (2001) *Fundamentalism*, Oxford: Polity Press.

Cialdini, R. (2001) *Influence: Science and Practice*, 4th edn, New York: Harper Collins.

Cohen, N. (2007) *What's Left?* London: Harper Perennial.

Collins, J. (2001) *Good to Great: Why Some Companies Make the Leap... and Others Don't*, London: Random House Business Books.

Collinson, D. (2003) Identities and insecurities: selves at work, *Organization*, 10, 527–547.

Collinson, D. (2005) Questions of distance, *Leadership*, 1, 235–250.

Cote, P. and Gunn, J. (eds) (2007) *The New Religious Question: State Regulation or State Interference?* Frankfurt: Peter Lang, pp. 371–394.

Cruver, B. (2003) *Enron: Anatomy of Greed*, London: Arrow Books.

Cullen, J. (2009) How to sell your soul and still get into Heaven: Steven Covey's epiphany-inducing technology of effective selfhood, *Human Relations*, 62, 1231–1254.

Duchan, D. and Plowman, D. (2005) Nurturing the spirit at work: impact on work unit performance, *The Leadership Quarterly*, 16, 807–833.

Festinger, L. (1957) *A Theory of Cognitive Dissonance*, Evanston, IL: Row and Peterson.

Fleming, P. and Spicer, A. (2007) *Contesting the Corporation: Struggle, Power and Resistance in Organisations*, Cambridge: Cambridge University Press.

Foucault, M. (1977) *Discipline and Punish*, London: Allen Unwin.

Foucault, M. (1979) *The History of Sexuality*, Vol 1, London: Allen Lane.

Foucault, M. (1982) Afterword. In H. Dreyfus and P. Rabinow (eds), *Michel Foucault: beyond Structuralism and Hermeneutics*, Hemel Hempstead, UK: Harvester Press, pp. 208–228.

Galanter, M. (1999) *Cults: Faith, Healing and Coercion*, 2nd edn, Oxford: Oxford University Press.

Guthey, E. (2005) Management studies, cultural criticism and American dreams, *Journal of Management Studies*, 42, 451–465.

Hamel, G. (2000) *Leading The Revolution*, Boston, MA: Harvard Business School Press.

Hassan, S. (1988) *Combatting Cult Mind Control*, Rochester, NY: Park Street Press.

Hogg, M. (2001) A social identity theory of leadership, *Personality and Social Psychology Review*, 5, 184–200.

Hogg, M. (2007) Organizational orthodoxy and corporate autocrats: some nasty consequences of organizational identification in uncertain times. In C. Bartel, S. Blader, and A. Wrzesniewski (eds), *Identity and the Modern Organization*, London: Lawrence Erlbaum, pp. 35–60.

Hong, N. (1998) *In The Shadow of the Moons: My Life in the Reverend Sun Myung Moon's Family*, Boston, MA: Little, Brown.

House, R. and Baetz, M. (1979) Leadership: some empirical generalizations and new research directions. In B. Staw (ed.), *Research in Organizational Behavior*, Greenwich, CT: JAI Press, (Vol. 1, pp. 341–423).

Jenkinson, G. (2008) An investigation into cult pseudo-personality: What is it and how does it form? *Cultic Studies Review*, 7, 199–224.

Karreman, D. and Alvesson, M. (2009) Resisting resistance: counter-resistance, consent and compliance in a consultancy firm, *Human Relations*, 62, 1115–1144.

Koestler, A. (1949) In R. Crossman (ed.), *The God That Failed*, New York: Harper, pp.15–75.

Lalich, J. (1992) The cadre ideal: origins and development of a political cult, *Cultic Studies Journal*, 9, 1–77.

Lalich, J. (2004) *Bounded Choice: True Believers and Charismatic Cults*, Berkeley, CA: University of California Press.

Langone, M. (ed.) (1993) *Recovery From Cults*, New York: Norton.

Langone, M. (1995) Secular and religious critiques of cults: complementary visions, not irresolvable conflicts, *Cultic Studies Journal*, 12, 166–186.

Layton, D. (1999) *Seductive Poison: A Jonestown Survivor's Story of Life and Death in the Peoples Temple*, London: Aurum Press.

Lewin, K. (1948) *Resolving Social Conflicts: Selected Papers on Group Dynamics*, Washington, DC: American Psychological Association.

Lifton, R. (1961) *Thought Reform And The Psychology Of Totalism: A Study Of 'Brainwashing' In China*, New York: Norton.

Lifton, R. (1999) *Destroying the World to Save It: Aum Shinrikyo, Apocalyptic Violence, and the New Global Terrorism*, New York: Holt.

Lipman-Blumen, J. (2008) Dissent in times of crisis. In S. Banks (ed.), *Dissent and the Failure of Leadership*, Cheltenham, UK: Edward Elgar, pp. 37–52.

Maccoby, M. (2003) *The Productive Narcissist: The Promise and Peril of Visionary Leadership*, New York: Broadway Books.

Martin, J. (1999) 'Come, join our family': discipline and integration in corporate organizational culture, *Human Relations*, 52, 155–178.

Martin, J. (2002) *Organizational Culture: Mapping the Terrain*, London: Sage.

Mehri, D. (2006) The darker side of lean: an insider's perspective on the realities of the Toyota production system, *Academy of Management Perspectives*, 20, 21–42.

Milgram, S. (1974) *Obedience to Authority: An Experimental View*, New York: Harper and Row.

Oakes, L. (1997) *Prophetic Charisma: The Psychology of Revolutionary Religious Personalities*, New York: Syracuse University Press.

O'Shea, P., Foti, R., Hauenstein, N., and Bycio, P. (2009) Are the best leaders both transformational and transactional? A pattern-oriented analysis, *Leadership*, 5, 237–260.

Pettigrew, A. (1990) Is corporate culture manageable? In D. Wilson and R. Rosenfeld (eds), *Managing Organizations*, New York: McGraw-Hill. pp. 267–272.

Pfeffer, J. (1992) *Managing With Power: Politics and Influence in Organization*, Boston, MA: Harvard Business School Press.

Pfeffer, J. (2003) Business and the spirit: management practices that sustain values. In R. Giacalone and C. Jurkiewicz (eds), *Handbook of Workplace Spirituality and Organizational Performance*, New York: Sharpe, pp. 29–45.

Raine, S. (2006) The Children of God/The Family: a discussion of recent research (1998–2005), *Cultic Studies Review*, 5, 29–69.

Rao, H., Greve, H., and Davis, G. (2001) Fool's gold: social proof in the initiation and abandonment of coverage by Wall Street analysts, *Administrative Science Quarterly*, 502–526.

Reiterman, T. and Jacobs, J. (2008) *Raven: The Untold Story of the Rev. Jim Jones and His People*, New York: Tarcher.

Robinson, S. and Kerr, R. (2009) The symbolic violence of leadership: a critical hermeneutic study of leadership and succession in a British organization in the post-Soviet context, *Human Relations*, 62, 875–903.

Salter, M. (2008) *Innovation Corrupted: The Origins and Legacy of Enron's Collapse*, Boston, MA: Harvard Business School Press.

Sanders, E. (2002) *The Family*, 2nd edn, New York: Thunder's Mouth Press.

Schein, E. (with Schneir, I. and Barker, C.) (1961) *Coercive Persuasion: A Socio-psychological Analysis of the 'Brainwashing' of American Civilian Prisoners by the Chinese Communists*, New York: Norton.

Schmalz, M. (2000) When Festinger fails: prophecy and the Watchtower, In J. Stone (ed.), *Expecting Armageddon: Essential Readings in Failed Prophecy*, London: Routledge, pp. 233–250.

Schwartz, J. (2002) Darth Vader. Machiavelli. Skilling sets intense pace, *New York Times*, 7 February, 1.

Seligman, M. (1975) *Helplessness: On Depression, Development and Death*, London: W.H. Freeman.

Sewell, G. and Barker, J. (2006) Coercion versus care: using irony to make sense of organizational surveillance, *Academy of Management Review*, 31, 934–961.

Siegel, P., Strohl, N., Ingram, L., Roche, D., and Taylor, J. (1987) Leninism as cult: the Democratic Workers Party, *Socialist Review*, 17, 59–85.

Singer, M. (1987) Group psychodynamics. In R. Berkow and M. Sharp (eds), *The Merck Manual of Diagnosis and Therapy*. Rahway, NJ: Dohme Research Laboratories.

Singer, M. (with Lalich, J.) (1995) *Cults in Our Midst: The Hidden Menace In Our Everyday Lives*, San Francisco: Jossey-Bass.

Singer, M. and Lalich, J. (1996) *Crazy Therapies*, San Francisco: Jossey-Bass.

Sinha, P. and Jackson, B. (2006) A Burkean inquiry into leader–follower identification motives, *Culture and Organization*, 12, 233–247.

Socrates (1993) *The Republic*, trans. R. Waterfield, Oxford: Oxford University Press.

Stein, A. (2002) *Inside Out: A Memoir of Entering and Breaking Out of a Minneapolis Political Cult*, Minneapolis: North Star Press of St. Cloud.

Stein, H. (2008) Organizational totalitarianism and the voices of dissent. In S. Banks (ed.), *Dissent and the Failure of Leadership*, Cheltenham, UK: Edward Elgar, pp. 75–96.

Strange, J. and Mumford, M. (2002) The origins of vision: charismatic versus ideological leadership, *The Leadership Quarterly*, 13, 343–377.

Taylor, K. (2004) *Brainwashing: The Science of Thought Control*, Oxford: Oxford University Press.

Tobias, M. and Lalich, J. (1994) *Captive Hearts, Captive Minds: Freedom and Recovery From Cults and Abusive Relationships*, Alameda, CA: Hunter House.

Tourish, D., Craig, R., and Amernic, J. (2010) Transformational leadership education and agency perspectives in business school pedagogy: a marriage of inconvenience? *British Journal of Management*, 21, S40–S59.

Tourish, D. and Irving P. (1995) Group influence and the psychology of cultism within Re-evaluation Counselling: a critique, *Counselling Psychology Quarterly*, 8, 15–30.

Tourish, D. and Pinnington, A. (2002) Transformational leadership, corporate cultism and the spirituality paradigm: an unholy trinity in the workplace? *Human Relations*, 55, 147–172.

Tourish, D. and Robson, P. (2006) Sensemaking and the distortion of critical upward communication in organizations, *Journal of Management Studies*, 43, 711–730.

Tourish, D. and Tourish, N. (2010) Spirituality at work, and its implications for leadership and followership: a post-structuralist perspective, *Leadership*, 5, 207–224.

Tourish, D. and Vatcha, N. (2005) Charismatic leadership and corporate cultism at Enron: the elimination of dissent, the promotion of conformity and organizational collapse, *Leadership*, 1, 455–480.

Tourish, D. and Wohlforth, T. (2000a) *On the Edge: Political Cults Right and Left*, New York: Sharpe.

Tourish, D. and Wohlforth, T. (2000b) Prophets of the apocalypse: White supremacism and the theology of Christian identity, *Cultic Studies Journal*, 17, 15–41.

Tourish, N. (2007) *The Dynamics of Upward Communication in Organizations*, PhD Thesis, Aberdeen: Robert Gordon University.

Wexler M. and Fraser, S. (1995) 'Expanding the groupthink explanation to the study of contemporary cults,' *Cultic Studies Journal*, 12, 49–71.

Willmott, H. (1993) Strength is ignorance; slavery is freedom: managing culture in modern organizations, *Journal of Management Studies*, 30, 515–552.

Willmott, H. (2003) Renewing strength: corporate culture revisited, *Management*, 6, 73–87.

Yukl, G. (2008) How leaders influence organizational effectiveness, *The Leadership Quarterly*, 19, 708–722.

Zablocki, B. (2001) Towards a demystified and disinterested scientific theory of brainwashing. In B. Zablocki and T. Robbins (eds), *Misunderstanding Cults: Searching for Objectivity in a Controversial Field*, Toronto: University of Toronto Press, pp. 159–214.

Zimbardo, P. (2007) *The Lucifer Effect: How Good People Turn Evil*, London: Rider.

17

Leadership Ethics

Joanne B. Ciulla and Donelson R. Forsyth

INTRODUCTION

A CEO bankrupts the company he is supposed to be leading. A retiree donates thousands of hours to her community. A company's leadership decides not to relocate a factory overseas, for the sake of the residents of an economically challenged town. A president of a club on a college campus encourages members to cheat on their examinations so that the group's members can earn academic honors. An elected public official arranges a tryst with a lover and abandons his duties for days on end.

These behaviors raise questions about motivation, rationality, and intent, but with a difference; these actions cannot only be judged as correct or incorrect in terms of effectiveness or competence, but as ethically right or wrong. Probably for as long as human societies have included individuals who take on extra responsibility for coordinating the actions and outcomes of others – leaders – people have questioned their motivations, fairness, and integrity. Why do individuals who seem to be fair-minded and virtuous change into something less once they gain a position of authority within the group? How can followers distinguish between leaders who have the group's best interests in mind and those who are seeking personal gain at the group's expense? Why would someone who is already respected by others and likely afforded a larger share of the collective's resources undermine the group's good will by seeking even more than their allotted share?

The moral goodness of leaders has been a topic of analysis for centuries (see Grint, Chapter 1, this volume). From ancient times, historians such as Herodotus (1987), Plutarch (1998, 1999), and Suetonius (2007) have described the character strengths that distinguish leaders from their followers, as well as the consequences that follow when leaders fail to control their emotions and impulses. Political theorists have explored the boundaries that morality places around leaders, with views ranging from the pragmatism of Machiavelli (1954, 2003) to Rawls's (1971) more optimistic theory of justice. More recently and, in part in response to increasing public concern for the morality of leaders in business contexts, those who study management and organizational behavior have intensified their analysis of ethical leadership, with such theorists as Jones (1991), Brown and Treviño (2006), and Vardi and Weitz (2004) offering extensive reviews of the literature on leadership and ethics in work settings.

This chapter contributes to this growing multidisciplinary effort by drawing on philosophy and psychology to explore the moral foundations of leadership. We assume that ethical assumptions, expectations, and implications lie deeply embedded in every facet of the concept of leadership – from the way that leaders behave, to their relationships with followers, to the results of their initiatives. Like other areas of applied ethics, leadership ethics examines the distinctive set of ethical challenges and problems related to an occupation or role of a leader. It draws from the philosophic literature on ethics that spans back to the beginning of the written word and uses some of the tools of philosophy, such as logic and conceptual analysis. Psychology, applied to questions of ethics, does not provide prescriptive recommendations to guide a leader, but it does offer overarching theory and empirical evidence that promises the possibility of predicting how a leader will act with regards to the moral order.

The chapter is organized around some of the ethical aspects and challenges of leadership. We begin by considering the relationship between outcomes and moral evaluations, and ask if the ineffective leader can ever be an ethical one and if the leader who is successful due to sheer good luck is nonetheless more moral than one who fails when circumstances unexpectedly stand in his or her way. We then turn to consider issues of right and wrong that inevitably seem to arise when individuals act to guide, organize, and control the actions of others: the tendency for self-interest to overcome more selfless, pro-social motivations; the role that self-control plays in helping leaders resist the temptations that their positions often create for them; the corruptive effects of power; and the tendency for leaders to rationalize their morally questionable actions by assuming desirable ends justify the use of morally suspect means. The analysis concludes by suggesting that leaders must be ever mindful of the morality of their choices, for a successful leader is someone who not only does the right thing but also does so in the right way and for the right reasons (Ciulla, 2005).

ETHICS AND THE IDEA OF A LEADER

Some scholars draw a distinction between *ethics* and *morality*. Foucault (1990), for example, considered morality to be a codified prescriptive system defined by such authorities as the church or family, whereas ethics are those processes that create the alignment of individual actions and the moral code. Ethics, to some, focuses on the analysis of moral processes – seeking to describe them rather than to evaluate their integrity, adequacy, or goodness. Morality, in contrast, is unabashedly normative, for it seeks to provide the means to distinguish between good and evil, wrong and right. Others have suggested that morality is a more basic, and more personal, evaluation of the rightness or wrongness of an act, whereas ethics are complex decisional processes that reflect moral leanings, but also consider broader social considerations.

Most philosophers and social scientists, however, use the terms interchangeably. For example, courses on moral philosophy or moral development will cover the same material as courses on ethics and ethical development. The two terms describe each other in the *Compact Oxford English Dictionary*. It defines the word *moral* as 'of or pertaining to the distinction between right and wrong, or good and evil in relation to the actions, volitions, or character of human beings; ethical' and 'concerned with virtue

and vice or rules of conduct, ethical praise or blame, habits of life, custom and manners' (p. 1114). Similarly the dictionary defines *ethics* as 'of or pertaining to morality' and 'the science of morals, the moral principles by which a person is guided' (p. 534). Those who insist on a distinction between ethics and morals should note that when scholars and ordinary people make a distinction between the two words, they rarely make it in the same way.

The words *leadership* and *leader* have also been the subject of considerable definitional debate. Ciulla (1995) examined the 221 definitions of the word *leader* collected by Rost and then compared and contrasted the definitions based on their social and historical context (Rost, 1991, pp. 7–102). Whereas Rost concluded that most who defined the nature of leadership seemed to think that a leader was little more than an effective manager, Ciulla (1998) noted the strong normative element that permeates conceptualizations of leadership. As a morally laden social construction, the American usage of the word *leader* reflects what people in a certain place and at a certain time think leaders *should* be like. When scholars make statements such as: 'leaders inspire followers toward common goals,' they do not mean that all leaders do this, they mean that leaders *ought* to do this. The question, 'What is a leader?' is really the question 'What is a *good* leader?', with *good* including both a morally commendable, normative component as well as a pragmatic, performance-oriented component.

We see this inclination in scholars who differentiate between people who are called leaders and 'real leaders' or 'true leaders.' Greenleaf (1977), for example, drew a distinction between run-of-the-mill leaders and servant leaders, and subsequent studies confirmed that the latter were more trustworthy, honest, other-oriented, credible, and competent (Russell & Stone, 2002). Others underscore the separation between leaders and moral leaders with the concept of spiritual leadership (Dent, Higgins, & Wharff, 2005; Fry, 2003), with spiritual leaders providing altruistic love, caring, and support for others. Burns (1978) and Bass (1997) suggest that many leaders – transactional ones – are competent in that they promote exchanges among subordinates in their pursuit of collective outcomes, but that only transformational leaders are leaders in a strong moral sense (see Diaz-Saenz, Chapter 22, this volume). Extending this distinction, Bass attempted to separate leaders who might fit the description of a transformational leader but are not ethical by distinguishing transformational from pseudo-transformational leaders and authentic transformational leaders (Bass & Steidlmeier, 2004). Brown, Treviño, and Harrison (2005) make this distinction between common leadership and ethical leadership explicit in their concept of ethical leadership: 'the demonstration of normatively appropriate conduct through personal actions and interpersonal relations, and the promotion of such conduct to followers through two-way communication, reinforcement, and decision-making' (p. 120).

Philosopher Eva Kort believes that group actions, not relationships, reveal the features that identify leadership 'proper' or real leadership from cases of 'purported' leadership. Kort uses the following example to illustrate the normative and technical aspects of leadership. A concertmaster holds a formal leadership position. If he conducts the orchestra with instructions that the musicians know are bad, they will follow him because of his position. In this case, Kort says, the concertmaster is merely a purported leader, not a leader proper. She writes: 'It is only when the concertmaster does lead – participate in the plural action in (generally) the right sort of way – that the concertmaster is the leader in the proper sense' (Kort, 2008, p. 422). Notice how Kort's definition includes unavoidable judgments. Leaders are people whom we choose to follow because they seem competent and, where relevant, ethical. For Kort, leaders are those whose ideas are voluntarily endorsed and acted on by others in various situations.

Studies of individuals' intuitive conceptions of leadership similarly suggest that people expect their leaders to be both competent and morally commendable. Although each follower may have a unique conception of leadership, most people's intuitive conceptions of a leader – their implicit leadership theories (Lord & Maher, 1991) – assume the prototypical leader is not only active, determined, influential, and in command but also caring, truthful, and respectful of others and their ideas (Kenney, Schwartz-Kenney, & Blascovich, 1996). When researchers asked individuals in 62 countries around the globe to describe the desirable and undesirable qualities of an outstanding leader of an organization, across nearly all cultures respondents expressed a desire for highly competent leaders: individuals who are able to motivate others to work together to reach collective goals. They also expected, however, that their leaders would hold true to the core values of the community and be trustworthy, just, and honest (Dorfman, Hanges, & Brodbeck, 2004).

Thus, most people agree when evaluating the morality of iconic leaders who are either saints or villains – the morally upright and successful Lincolns, Gandhis, and Mohammeds of the world versus those leaders who are both morally bankrupt and ineffective, such as the Gadhafis, Mugabes, and the Saloth Sars (Pol Pot). But this consensus is lost when they consider individuals who lack integrity yet are effective or are ineffective yet honorable. As Ciulla (2004) suggests, the 'Hitler problem' illustrates how the prescriptive, normative elements of the concept of a leader create confusions when people encounter leaders who, although effective, are not ethical. The Hitler problem arises from the question, 'Was Hitler a good leader?' (Ciulla, 1995, 2004). Does 'good' refer to the ethics of Hitler's leadership or to his effectiveness as a leader? Does effectiveness mean his success at doing things, his skill in inspiring his followers to pursue their collective goals, or both? An individual who occupies a position of authority within a group or a society – a king, a head of state, or lord – but who does not undertake any actions that improve the outcomes of others within that group or society may be disqualified, on the grounds of inefficacy, from being considered a leader. Similarly, individuals who facilitate the attainment of collective goals but are morally corrupt – they create great harm for others or initiate actions that are inconsistent with widely recognized principles of justice and ethics – may also be eliminated as leaders on normative grounds. To some, Hitler was not a leader because his actions and policies ruined the lives of so many of his followers and because he deliberately acted in ways that are morally detestable. Thus, the overarching question of leadership ethics is: 'What is the relationship of ethics to effectiveness in leadership?'

THE CHALLENGES OF TRUST AND SELF-INTEREST

Leadership offers a solution to the age-old problem created by the sociality of the human species. A small group of people may be able to share equally the responsibility for organizing their efforts in the pursuit of common goals, but once the group increases in size or finds itself in a situation that is threatening, one or more individuals are required to carry out executive functions for the group – to make choices between alternatives, galvanize the unenthused into action, to strategize about the means to reach goals, and so on (Van Vugt, Hogan, & Kaiser, 2008). But leadership is not without risks, both for the group that cedes some of its collective authority to the individual who will act as the group's leader and for the individual who accepts the role of the authority. Leaders may help groups achieve their goals, but at too high a cost to the collective. Leaders may use their position to seek their own purposes, ignoring their charge to work for the good of the whole. At the same time, leaders may find that the burden of responsibility for the collective's outcome may be so great that their own individual outcomes suffer; by serving the collective, they may promote their own outcomes, but self- and other-interest may become unbalanced if the collective requires much from the leader without offering enough in return.

The motivation to lead

The earliest writings on leadership addressed this tension between self-interest and the collective good, and the moral issues it raises. The most extraordinary thing about ancient depictions of ethical leaders is how similar they are to the way that we think of them today. One of the oldest writers on this subject is the Egyptian philosopher and vizier, Ptahhotep (2450–2300? BCE). Few of us today would argue with his emphasis on the importance of generosity, virtue, trust, and restraint in a leader. Ptahhotep offers this advice to leaders:

> If you are a man who leads,
> Who controls the affairs of the many,
> Seek out every beneficent deed,
> That your conduct may be blameless…
> If you are among the people,
> Gain supporters through being trusted;
> The trusted man who does not vent his belly's speech,
> He will himself become a leader. (Lichtheim, 1973, p. 61)

Plato, too, directly addressed this tension in his analysis of the motivations of those who can no longer avoid the duty of serving their community's need for direction and guidance. Plato believed that democracy, with direct self-rule by the populace, is no more just or reasonable than tyranny, for the masses are too influenced by their emotions and too little by their rationality and good judgment. So in the *Republic* he emphasized the need for leaders who were willing to sacrifice their immediate self-interest. In Book II Plato writes:

> In a city of good men, if it came into being, the citizens would fight in order not to rule…. There it would be clear that anyone who is really a true ruler doesn't by nature seek his own advantage but that of his subjects. And everyone, knowing this, would rather be benefited by others than take the trouble to benefit them. (Plato, 1992a, p. 23)

Plato acknowledges the stress, hard work, and frequently thankless job of being an ethical leader. The ethical leader must respect the autonomy of followers, yet constrain them somewhat to create a degree of collaborative cooperation in the pursuit of collective goals. Ethical leaders must be impartial, and render decisions that may displease as many as they please. Plato goes so far as to suggest that ethical leaders are not motivated to take on their position by egoism – a desire to pursue their self-interests – or even by altruism – a selfless desire to help the collective reach its goals. Rather, ethical people take on leadership roles to protect the group from the hardship of rule by an incompetent, immoral leader: 'Now the greatest punishment, if one isn't willing to rule, is to be ruled by someone worse than oneself. And I think it is fear of this that makes decent people rule when they do' (Plato, 1992a, p. 23). Plato's comment sheds light on why we sometimes feel more comfortable with people who are reluctant to lead than with those who are eager. Today, as in the past, we worry that people who are too eager to lead want the power and the position for themselves or that they do not fully understand the burdens of ethical and effective leadership.

Plato also tells us that while it is not in the just person's self-interest to become a leader, it is in his or her enlightened self-interest. He does not require leaders to be altruists who, in the strict sense of the word, sacrifice their own interests for the interests of others. Instead he tells us that morality sometimes calls upon leaders to do things that are against their self-interest. This is less about altruism than it is about the nature of both morality and leadership. We expect leaders to put the interests of followers first, but most of the time, the interests of leaders are the same as the interests of followers. Those who influence, guide, and/or look after the interests of groups, organizations, countries, ideas, or causes are called leaders. When people do this, they are leading; when they do not do this, they are not leading. Altruism describes behavior that is usually admirable, but altruism does not in and of itself result in morally laudable action. To the members of their cultural group, suicide bombers may behave altruistically. They give their lives for what they believe is a just cause – but that does not make blowing up innocent people ethical. The case of the suicide bomber illustrates someone who may have the right reason, such as social justice, but does the wrong thing, the wrong way.

Psychological studies confirm Plato's insights, in part, but suggest that leaders are both proself and prosocial rather than purely egoistic or altruistic (Avolio & Locke, 2002). In many cases personality factors that are markers of self-centeredness, such as narcissism (Brunell et al., 2008), dominance (Smith & Foti, 1998), and the motivation to lead (Chan & Drasgow, 2001), are reliability associated with emergence as a leader – if not with success in acting ethically once in the position. Followers, however, generally assume that leaders are motivated by a desire to promote the group and its outcomes, and are sensitive to signals that the leader is acting to secure personal gains (Reicher, Haslam, & Platow, 2007). Social identity theory, for example, maintains that in many cases both leaders and followers identify so closely with the group and its causes that the distinction between self and other no longer holds; when leaders act in ways that benefit the group, they are benefiting themselves (Hogg, 2007). In general, followers prefer a leader who is willing to share his or her influence and resources with them. The leader who is unwilling to put the interests of others first is not as successful as the leader who is, or at least appears to be, acting from collective rather than egoistic motivations (Cronin, 2008).

Moral luck and leadership

Followers do not demand complete self-sacrifice in their leaders; they recognize that leaders are entitled to prosper, to some extent, from the work that they do on behalf of the group or organization (Frank, 1996; Bligh, Chapter 31, this volume). Followers do expect their leader to be competent. People are more accepting of leaders who have previously demonstrated task ability and are more willing to follow the directions of a task-competent person than those of an incompetent person. Given enough experience in working together, most people can distinguish between those who are skilled and those who are unskilled, and they favor those who are skilled when deciding who should lead rather than follow. The 'romance of leadership' that is so common among followers stems from their certainty that the leader can ease their burdens and lead their group through times of turbulence and hardship (Meindl, Ehrlich, & Dukerich, 1985).

Success and morality tend to be confounded in the minds of followers, so that leaders who fail – even though no fault of their own – are often viewed as less moral than those who succeed. Conversely, those who are in leadership positions during times of prosperity or great gain are often viewed as effective and morally praiseworthy, even if they were not responsible for the positive outcomes. Some leaders are neither ethical nor effective, but historians or the public think that they are because they were lucky. Leaders have moral luck when events outside of their control conspire to make them appear to be good leaders (Williams, 1981).

Most of the difficult moral decisions leaders make are risky ones, because they have imperfect or incomplete information and no control over some of the variables that affect the outcome. Unlucky leaders who fail at something are worthy of forgiveness when they act with deliberate care and for the right moral reasons – even though followers may not forgive them or may lose confidence in their leadership. Americans did not blame President Jimmy Carter for the botched attempt to free the hostages in Iran, but it was one more thing that shook their faith in his leadership. He was unlucky because, if the mission had been successful, it might have strengthened people's faith in him as a leader and improved his chances of retaining the presidency. The irony of moral luck is that leaders who are reckless and do not base their actions on sound moral and practical considerations are often condemned when they fail and celebrated as heroes when they succeed. That is why Kant (1993) maintained that since we cannot always know how things will turn out, moral judgments should be based on the right moral principles and not on outcomes. The reckless, lucky leader who fails to demonstrate moral or technical competency often gets credit for having both because of the outcome of his or her action. Since history usually focuses on outcomes, it is not always clear how much luck, skill, and morality figure in the success or failure of a leader.

THE CHALLENGES OF SELF-DISCIPLINE AND VIRTUE

Ethics of Eastern philosophers, such as Lao-tzu, Confucius, and Buddha, tend to center on the problem of self-discipline. Lao-tzu warns leaders against arrogance and vanity: 'He who stands on tiptoe is not steady' (Lao-Tzu, 1963, p. 152). He recommends modesty: 'The best rulers are those whose existence is merely known by people' (Lao-tzu, 1963, p. 148). Confucius focuses on the importance of duty and self-control. He states, 'If a man (the ruler) can for one day master himself and return to propriety, all under heaven will return to humanity. To practice humanity depends on oneself' (Confucius, 1963, p. 38). He ties a leader's self-mastery and effectiveness together when he writes, 'If a ruler sets himself right, he will be followed without his command. If he does not set himself right, even his commands will not be obeyed' (Confucius, 1963, p. 38).

Contemporary analyses similarly trace leaders' ethical integrity to their capacity to remain true to their chosen goals, procedures, and values, even in the face of strong social and external pressures. Theories of authentic leadership take seriously the Delphic Oracle's injunction to seek self-knowledge (*nosque te ipsum*) by suggesting that most effective, and most ethical, leaders have a strong and relatively stable core of moral beliefs and practical values that significantly determine the way they conduct themselves as leaders. Authentic leaders are, in theory, self-aware individuals who know their strengths and weaknesses, so they are less likely to need to bolster their sense of self-worth at the expense of others. Their self-awareness extends to their emotions and motivations, and so they are more likely to control their feelings in situations that might provoke others to display hostile, threatening, or contentious emotions, and they help other members of the group moderate their affective reactions as well (Ilies, Morgeson, & Nahrgang, 2005). This self-stability further augments their capacity to profit from feedback about their performance, and so authentic leaders are more likely to learn from their mistakes and thereby improve their effectiveness over time – sustaining the tendency for moral leaders to also be effective leaders (Avolio & Gardner, 2005; Avolio, Walumbwa, & Weber, 2009; Caza & Jackson, Chapter 26, this volume).

Studies of self-control in other types of pursuit, such as the task pursuit and interpersonal relations, suggest that the continual need to exercise self-control in the face of multiple temptations is psychologically taxing. Baumeister (2001), in his ego-depletion theory, maintains that self-control is muscle-like, in that it can be strengthened through use and experience. However, self-control requires cognitive resources, and so constant self-control can limit the amount of energy available for subsequent self-regulation needs, just as a fatigued muscle becomes less powerful. When people become highly practiced in self-regulation, to the point that their self-regulation is nearly automatic rather than reflective, then the exercise of self-control is less taxing (Moller, Deci, & Ryan, 2006). Extending this theory to leadership, leaders who experience stress, must make difficult decisions, resist temptations, or stifle their emotions are at risk for the loss of self-regulation, with the all too often seen consequences (Muraven & Baumeister, 2000).

In the First Sermon, the Buddha describes how people's uncontrolled thirst for things contributes to their own suffering and the suffering of others (Dhamma, 1996). Like psychologists today, he too realized that getting one's desires under control is the best way to end personal and social misery. This is a particular challenge for leaders, because power and privilege allow them to indulge their material and personal desires. Compassion is the most important virtue in Buddhist ethics because it keeps desires and vices in check. The Dalai Lama (1999) concisely summed up the moral dynamics of compassion in this way:

When we bring up our children to have knowledge without compassion, their attitude towards others is likely to be a mixture of envy of those in positions above them, aggressive competitiveness towards their peers, and scorn for those less fortunate. This leads to a propensity toward greed, presumption, excess, and very quickly to loss of happiness. (p. 181)

VIRTUE ETHICS AND LEADERSHIP

Both Eastern and Western writers think about ethics in terms of virtues that are formed through discipline, practice, and social norms. Virtues provide a useful way of understanding leadership development and selection. The properties of a virtue are very different from the properties of other concepts such as values and traits. Virtues are moral qualities that you only have if you practice them. Values are things that are important to people. A person may value honesty but not always tell the truth. Values influence actions in most cases, but they are only one behavioral cause among many. An individual who possesses the virtue of honesty has intentionally chosen to accept the moral correctness of honest action and has learned to act in ways that are consistent with that virtue. Virtues, like traits, are dispositions to behave a certain way but, unlike traits, virtues are intentionally selected, deliberately strengthened, and behaviorally predictive.

Aristotle likened virtues to habits, suggesting that people acquire them from society and from their legislators. But even though virtuous actions become habitual over time, they are not mindless habits. When a person practices a virtue, he or she must also be conscious that it is the right way to act. So, to possess the virtue of courage, people not only have to act courageously but also they must be conscious of why courage is morally good. They also need to know how and when to practice the virtue of courage. Aristotle says that a virtue is the mean between extremes, so courage is the mean between the extremes of foolhardiness and cowardice. We learn how to practice a virtue like courage and honesty through experience, social sanctions, and role models. Aristotle would agree with James MacGregor Burns' (1978) idea that transforming leaders elevate the values of followers. Aristotle writes, 'Legislators make citizens good by forming habits in them' (Aristotle, 1984, p. 1743). Whereas virtues come naturally to those who practice them, they are not mindless habits or personality traits.

The Greek notion of virtue (areté), which is also translated as excellence, does not separate an individual's ethics from his or her occupational competence. When writing about ethics, both Plato and Aristotle use numerous examples of doctors, musicians, coaches, rulers, and so forth, to talk about the relationship between moral and technical or professional excellence. Aristotle writes,

> Every excellence brings to good the thing to which it is the excellence and makes the work of that thing be done well....Therefore, if this is true in every case, the excellence of man also will be the state which makes man good and which makes him do his work well. (p. 1747)

Excellence is tied to function. The function of a knife is to cut. An excellent knife cuts well. The function of humans, according to Aristotle, is to reason. To be morally virtuous, you must reason well, because reason tells you how and when to practice a virtue. If you reason well, you will know how to practice moral and professional virtues. In other words, reason is the key to practicing moral virtues and the virtues related to one's various occupations in life. Virtue ethics does not differentiate between ethics and effectiveness or the morality of the leader and the morality of his or her leadership. Hence, on Aristotle's account, a morally virtuous leader must also be a competent leader, or conversely, it is immoral for a leader to be incompetent. Virtues do not tell leaders what to do, they tell them the 'right' way to be and, hence, to act.

This emphasis on virtues is consistent with the growing interest among social scientists in positive personal and interpersonal processes that sustain happiness and well-being. Positive psychology, for example, focuses on human strengths and virtues, whereas positive organizational scholarship considers aspects of organizations that foster resilience, happiness, and human flourishing. All of these concepts were central to Plato and Aristotle's ethics. Positive psychologists Christopher Peterson and Martin E. P. Seligman (2004) suggest that effective leadership is likely associated with such cardinal virtues as wisdom, courage, humanity, justice, temperance, and transcendence. These virtues came into Western thought via the writings of Plato (1992a, 1992b) and Aquinas (2008). Other leadership scholars such as Kanungo and Mendonca (1995) also use the cardinal virtues as a basis for their discussion of ethical leaders. Peterson and Seligman (2004) also suggest that leadership, if not one of the basic virtues, certainly qualifies as a character strength. Strengths, they suggest, are few in number but all share a common set of features: they contribute to positive outcomes for the individual and for others; they are morally valued in their own right; they have trait-like qualities of consistency and

generality; groups and societies encourage the further development of these qualities; and their display 'does not diminish other people in the vicinity' (2004, p. 21). Peterson and Seligman conclude that leadership, along with citizenship and fairness, regulates the relationship between individuals and larger social collectives, such as groups, organizations, and communities.

THE CHALLENGES OF POWER AND PRIVILEGE

The more power leaders have, the greater their responsibility for what they do and do not do. The empirical evidence for moral problems of power is quite old and documented in history books, religious and philosophical texts, literature, and art. For example, Plato's 'Ring of Gyges' is the story of a shepherd boy who discovers a ring that makes him invisible. Once he is invisible, he seizes power from the king (Plato, 1992a). The story raises the question: Would you be moral if no one were watching? Leadership is like wearing the Ring of Gyges. Without oversight, checks, and balances, leaders can do what they want and they possess the resources to at least try to conceal their actions. Followers may enable leaders to do good things and bad things, but they also have a responsibility to watch their leaders. It is the obligation of institutions and organizations to ensure that leaders are subject to some form of oversight that will help leaders avoid the temptations of power and privilege.

The moral foible people fear most in leaders is personal immorality accompanied by abuse of power. Dean Ludwig and Clinton Longenecker (1993) call one such failure the 'Bathsheba syndrome', based on the biblical story of King David and Bathsheba (2 Samuel 11–12). They argue that the biblical story tells us about how success may be morally dangerous to leaders. In the story, King David is a successful king who one day comes home from the battlefront and seduces Bathsheba, the wife of one of his generals. When David discovers that Bathsheba is pregnant, he engages in escalating cover-ups that end in David ordering Bathsheba's husband to be killed. Ludwig and Longenecker use the story to show how success can make leaders overconfident, go on autopilot, and fail to properly attend to their duties. Leaders who fall prey to this syndrome lose strategic focus, overestimate their ability to control outcomes, and abuse their power to cover their misdeeds. The longer leaders successfully stay in their jobs, the more difficult it is for them to maintain their own moral and operational standards and those of their associates. Leaders have been repeating the David and Bathsheba scenario for thousands of years. They do something unethical, try to cover it up, and get caught by a whistle-blower. In the process, the cover-up is often worse than the original ethical lapse. Leaders tend to most abuse their power and the confidence of their followers during the cover-up. For example, the American public felt more morally offended by President Clinton when he lied about having an affair with an intern than about the affair itself.

Leaders face more temptations than the rest of us because they often have special privileges, which may make them think that they are above others and not subject to the same rules. These privileges may include everything from private jets, to special access to information and resources, or exceptional privileges vis-à-vis the rules and regulations of an organization. In addition to perks, subordinates often treat leaders with deference. Price (2005) argues that when followers grant privileges to leaders, they make it easier for leaders to believe that they are outside of the scope of common morality. Leaders make moral mistakes because they do not think that certain rules apply to them or they are ignorant of what is right. Simply being identified as the leader prompts individuals to claim more than the average share of the resources, especially since members often think the leadership role entitles them to take more than others (De Cremer & Van Dijk, 2005). This is why ancient Eastern and Western philosophic traditions identify reverence as the key virtue for leaders. Reverence is the virtue that reminds leaders that they are part of a larger whole. It is the virtue that keeps them from trying to act like they are gods (Woodruff, 2001).

THE CHALLENGES OF POWER AND EXPEDIENCY

Leadership is generally viewed as a voluntary, mutual association between the leader and the follower, but leaders' power is greater than that of those who follow them. Their power may be power with people, rather than over people, but they nonetheless have a greater capacity to influence than do others (Keltner, Gruenfeld, & Anderson, 2003; Raven, 1992).

The metamorphic effects of power have long fascinated observers of the human condition. In their tragedies, the Greeks dramatized the fall of heroes who, swollen by past accomplishments, conceitedly compared themselves to the gods. Myth and folklore are replete with tales of the consequences of too much power, as in the case of Icarus, whose hubris caused his death. Lord Acton warned, 'Power tends to corrupt, and absolute power corrupts absolutely', suggesting that the power that often comes with leadership can distort leaders' capacity to judge themselves and the means that they take to reach their ends.

Approach/inhibition theory, developed by Dacher Keltner and his colleagues (2003, 2008), agrees with the wisdom of the ancients, for it assumes that power – having power, using power, even thinking about power – transforms individuals' psychological states. Power is energizing, and so motivates leaders to expend effort on behalf of others. Power is also associated with optimism about the future and enhanced executive functioning. These positive consequences of power are counterbalanced by power's liabilities. Powerful people are proactive, but in some cases their actions are risky, inappropriate, or unethical ones. When individuals gain power, their self-evaluations grow more favorable, whereas their evaluations of others grow more negative. If they feel that they have a mandate from their group or organization to get things done, they may do things they are not empowered to do. When individuals feel powerful, they sometimes treat others unfairly, particularly if they are more self-centered rather than focused on the overall good of the group. Some individuals (primarily men) associate power with sexuality, and so when they are empowered, they engage in inappropriate sexual behaviors, including sexual harassment (Keltner et al., 2003, 2008).

Power is also associated with the tendency to assume that the value of the ends one seeks justifies the use of means that would otherwise be morally suspected. This possibility has occupied observers of leadership for thousands of years. It is the underlying theme of Machiavelli's *The Prince* (1954), which wrestles with how the necessities of a leader's job challenge his ability to act morally. Machiavelli observed that when the stakes are high for a leader, the ends sometimes justify the means, but he also understood the dangers of leaders who easily succumb to expediency over morality. Similarly, Friedrich Nietzsche's analysis of the will to power suggests that leaders must, to fulfill their responsibilities, be free to act in ways that are outside of traditional conceptions of morality. Nietzsche (1989) held that individuals, although autonomous creatures, are part of the natural order, and that order determines how they will act across situations. Extending his analogy of the bird of prey and lambs to leadership suggests that, just as it is the nature of the bird of prey to snatch little lambs, so it is natural for leaders to dominate others; the leader is no more free to be weak as the follower is free to take charge. Nietzsche suggests that only people who resent their inferiority think that leaders should mute their natural tendency to dominate. According to Nietzsche, real leaders ought to be different from everyone else. Their morality does not rest on conventional behavior, but on their creativity. He writes, 'one must still have chaos in oneself to give birth to a dancing star' (Nietzsche, 1978, p. 17). In this respect, Nietzsche rebels against the idea that leaders 'are just like you and me.'

THE CHALLENGE OF CARING

Embedded in the concept of a leader is the idea that a formal or informal leader cares about something, whether it is a group of people, a cause, or an idea. Care can mean paying attention to or looking after something, as in 'I take care of him,' or it can mean an emotion, as in 'I care for him,' or a concern, as in 'I care how people think about him,' or some combination of the three. Erikson (1982) says that the human inclination to care is rooted in the impulse to 'caress' someone who in his helplessness emits signals of despair. The interesting question is whether leaders have a moral obligation to care, and if so, is this obligation simply a duty to care (in the sense of a duty to look after the interests of followers, organizations, etc.) or are they morally required to have the appropriate feelings of care too?

The ethic of care

In the twentieth century, feminist scholars formulated an ethic of care. Carol Gilligan (1982) discovered that girls progressed up Kohlberg's (1981) scale of moral development more slowly than boys. She conducted her own study of women and found that they spoke in 'a different voice' than men when they discussed their moral choices. She concluded that instead of reasoning from moral principles, females were more concerned with care based on feelings, relationships, and contexts. Some feminist philosophers contrast the ethic of care with the ethic of justice. For example, Held (2006) describes an ethic of justice as one that focuses on fairness, equality, individual rights, and abstract principles as well as the consistent application of them. An ethic of care is about cultivating caring relations, attentiveness, responsiveness to need, and narrative nuance (which includes time and place). Held argues: 'Whereas justice protects equality and freedom, care fosters social bonds and cooperation…' (Held, 2006, p. 15).

The basic ideas behind the ethic of care, such as the role of emotions, empathy, and sympathy, are neither feminine nor masculine. Many scholars in the history of philosophy discuss these concepts. For example, Kierkegaard (1958) introduced the notion of care as a means of counteracting the excessive objectivity of philosophy in the early twentieth century. Similarly, the Roman philosopher Seneca (1953) observed that behaving rationally is only part of morality. He said humans were given reason so that they can achieve the good. They were given the capacity to care so that they can perfect the good. More recently, studies of the values associated with moral judgments across situations converge on empathy, for humans are biologically ready to experience distress when they see other members of the species suffering (Haidt & Graham, 2007). Forsyth finds that concern for others' outcomes is recognized in cultures around the world, but is more likely to be emphasized by individuals who are residents of collectivistic societies (Forsyth, O'Boyle, & McDaniel, 2008).

Reciprocity and duty

One of the oldest and ubiquitous moral principles is the golden rule: 'Do unto others as you would have others do unto you' or 'Do not do unto others as you would not have them do unto you' (Wattles, 1996). The rule does not actually require people to empathize, it asks them to reciprocate. All it says is: 'We all know how we want to be treated and should use that as a guide for how to treat others.' The golden rule gives us guidance on how to treat people, but does not capture what it means to care. Perhaps that is why it is such a useful principle. Care requires attention, solicitude, and active involvement. Unlike the golden rule, which is objective and egalitarian, care can be highly subjective and selective. Leaders would face problems if feelings of care and empathy were their only moral guide. Because most leaders have multiple constituencies, ethical leadership requires some rational and evenhanded way of thinking about moral obligations. So while moral feelings toward others are a part of ethics, they are not sufficient without a commitment to act according to duty.

Kant describes duties as absolutes that we apply to all people. His categorical imperative is fundamental to justice and to building trust. Kant emphasizes the importance of moral consistency and respect for the dignity of all human beings, and he prohibits using people as a means to an end (Kant, 1993). Kant offers two principles that are at the heart of a leader's work. First, he asserts that morality is based on doing your duty, *especially* when your inclination or your feelings tell you to do otherwise. Secondly, he says to make moral choices that you would want to make into a universal law (the categorical imperative). This principle is loosely derived from the golden rule. It says, make choices based on how you would want everyone to choose if they were in your place. When a leader makes an ethical decision, followers tend to regard the decision as a precedent. So, if the president decides to let one person who did not pay his taxes serve in his administration, he must also let other people who did not pay their taxes serve in his administration. If the president lets one person with a tax problem serve, and disqualifies another person with the same problem, he will appear to be a hypocrite who is playing favorites. Objectively acting on duties facilitates moral consistency and establishes trust and credibility.

THE MORAL CHALLENGE OF HAPPINESS

Moral theories from both Eastern and Western traditions discuss the relationship between morality and happiness. Aristotle said that happiness is the end of life because it is an end in itself, meaning there is no other reason to be happy than to be happy. His concept of happiness, *eudaimonia*, means happiness in the sense of flourishing as a human being. The actual details of what it means to flourish vary, but philosophers like Plato believed that you could not lead a happy life if you were not moral because your soul would not be in harmony (Plato, 1992a). For Aristotle, human flourishing consisted of physical and mental well-being and living morally (Aristotle, 1984, 1996). So, happiness is not simply pleasure: it is an expansive notion of growing, learning, and thriving as a rational human being. In one way or another, it is the job of leaders to, at best, make their constituents happy or at a minimum, try not to make them too unhappy. Drawing from Aristotle, Ciulla argues that 'The relationship between leaders and followers and the ends of that relationship must rest on eudaimonia' (1995, p. 19 fn72). It is the goal and the ultimate test of ethical and effective leadership.

Servant leadership captures what Aristotle meant by flourishing. Robert Greenleaf (1977, pp. 13–14) says a servant leader must pass this test: 'Do those served grow as persons? Do they while being served become healthier, wiser, freer, more autonomous, more likely themselves to become servants?' Burns argues that end values or quality of all aspects of leadership rests on how well they promote the end values of liberty, justice, equality, and happiness (Burns, 2003).

Recently, work on positive psychology has explored in detail the role of happiness and human flourishing in leadership. Positive psychology is an emerging subfield that stresses adaptation, growth, health, and strengths rather than dysfunction, stress, and burnout (e.g., Seligman, 2002). Positive psychology assumes that the effective leaders are also the positive leaders: the ones who promote the well-being, autonomy, growth, and the moral integrity of others as they go about their work (Cameron, Bright, & Caza, 2004). Such leaders focus on the happiness of the people with whom they work, rather than merely profit margins and tangible products, and they tend to rely on modes of influence that typify transformational forms of leadership by creating work settings where 'followers are rewarded internally with achievement and self-actualization rather than externally with safety and security' (Turner, Barling, & Zacharatos, 2002, p. 721).

Confirming the idea that ethical leadership has practical as well as moral benefits, meta-analysis indicates work environments that promote employee well-being are more productive and profitable (Harter, Schmidt, & Keyes, 2003).

There is a sense in which utilitarianism, the moral principle of seeking the greatest happiness for the greatest number of people, is also part of the job description for most leaders. At the beginning of 'What Utilitarianism Is' (1987), John Stuart Mill entertains several objections to utilitarianism. One objection is that most people cannot or do not know what the greatest happiness is for the greatest number of people. Mill points out that most people do not make utilitarian judgments that concern everyone in the world. We know from our own experiences and from history what other people want and usually we make choices based on what is good for a specific group of people, not the whole world. Yet, it is the case that some leaders do make choices that affect large numbers of people, many of whom they will never know. Hence, one might argue that a leader's job is to find the greatest happiness or good for the greatest number of his or her constituents.

Kant's moral emphasis on the principle of an act and Mill's emphasis on the act itself converge when Mill talks about happiness. A point frequently missed in Mill is that the principle of utility is not based on majority opinion of what will make people happy. Mill says that some kinds of happiness are better for people than others. As he famously notes, the happiness of a Socrates (e.g., learning and discussing ideas with others) is better than the happiness of a pig (e.g., eating and rolling around in the mud). The most difficult moral decisions leaders make are those where they opt for the happiness of a Socrates when their followers prefer the happiness of a pig. Utilitarian ethics does not require a leader to provide 'bread and circuses' to the masses even if they create the greatest happiness for the greatest number. As Burns points out, transforming leadership is when leaders and followers debate and eventually elevate each other's values, which also entails elevating their ideas about what will ultimately make them happy (Burns, 1978).

Another objection to utilitarianism is that the moral cost/benefit analysis used to determine what will bring about the greatest happiness is too cold and calculating and does not consider individual relationships. Mill replies that morality is about objective ideas and the minute you start molding your idea of ethics to the relationship you have with particular individuals, you lose your ethics. Like Kant and Plato, Mill's emphasis on moral consistency does not allow leaders to make exceptions to the greatest happiness principle for themselves, their family, or their friends. Moral objectivity is such a fundamental part of our concept of a leader that no one would describe their ideal leader as one who makes exceptions to the rules, policies, and procedures for friends, family, ethnic and religious groups, and people they like. If anything, this sort of behavior describes corrupt leaders. Furthermore, leaders are challenged to make sure that in seeking the greatest happiness, they do not cause a handful of people great misery. The greatest happiness that is based on callous expediency or the suffering of a few is a base notion of happiness – the happiness of a pig, not the happiness of a Socrates.

CONCLUSIONS: THE CHALLENGE OF GETTING ALL OF IT RIGHT

We have catalogued some of the philosophical and psychological challenges that are distinctive to the idea and role of leaders and the practice of leadership. These challenges exist within the general question of how to be a good leader, where good is defined as both ethical and effective. We have also looked at a variety of philosophic theories, each of which highlights a different aspect of leadership. There are three moral facets to the ethics of leaders:

1. The ethics of *what* a leader does or the ends of a leader's actions (Mill).
2. The ethics of *how* a leader does things, or the process of leadership (Aristotle).
3. The moral reasons of *why* leaders do things, or their moral intentions (Kant).

In short, as noted earlier, an ethical and effective leader is someone who does the right thing, the right way, and for the right reasons (Ciulla, 2005). Public discussions about leaders are complicated because some leaders' actions are only morally right in one or two of the three areas. For example, a leader may do the right thing the wrong way for the right reason. Leaders sometimes face the

problem of 'dirty hands,' where they must choose to use unsavory means to do the right thing and prevent an imminent disaster (Temes, 2005).

Both major streams of research in leadership ethics – psychology and philosophy – fail to offer a complete account of ethics. Most of the leadership literature on ethics is based on normative leadership theories/models such as transformational and pseudo-transformational leadership (Bass & Steidlmeier, 2004), transforming leadership (Burns, 1978, 2003), servant leadership (Greenleaf, 1977), and authentic leadership (Avolio & Gardner, 2005). This research stream offers rich descriptions of leader behavior but tends to rest on narrow and somewhat simplistic characterizations of ethical concepts (Price, 2003). Philosophers have a more sophisticated understanding of ethical concepts but without a solid foundation in the empirical literature on leadership – i.e. how leaders really do behave and what kinds of behavior is effective, for example – their analysis is of limited use because it does not have a specific application to actual leaders and leadership. Progress in leadership ethics requires serious interdisciplinary research and collaborative research between philosophers and other humanities scholars and psychologists and other social scientists.

The ethics of leaders are not different from the ethics of everyone else, but because their actions take place in public and affect larger numbers of people, morality and immorality are magnified in everything they do, which is yet another reason why we find moral assumptions and expectations deeply embedded in the idea of a leader. As we have seen, the ethical assumptions about what leaders are and what they should be like vary surprisingly little throughout history and across cultures. They have been well documented and offer us insight into the place of leadership in our common humanity.

ACKNOWLEDGMENTS

We owe a special thanks to Mary Uhl-Bien and Brad Jackson for their insightful comments on this chapter and to Tammy Tripp for her editorial assistance.

REFERENCES

Aquinas, T. (2008). *Summa theologica* (Vol. 2). Charleston, SC: Bibliolife Publishing.

Aristotle (1984). Nichomachean ethics. Book I. In J. Barnes (ed.), *The complete works of Aristotle* (Vol. 2, pp. 1729–1867). Princeton, NJ: Princeton University Press.

Aristotle (1996). *Politics* (R. Robinson, Trans.). Oxford: Oxford University Press.

Avolio, B. & Gardner, W. (2005). Authentic leadership development: getting to the root of positive forms of leadership. *The Leadership Quarterly, 16,* 315–338.

Avolio, B. J. & Locke, E. E. (2002). Contrasting different philosophies of leader motivation: altruism verses egoistic. *The Leadership Quarterly, 13,* 169–71.

Avolio, B. J., Walumbwa, F. O., & Weber, T. J. (2009). Leadership: current theories, research, and future directions. *Annual Review of Psychology, 60,* 421–449.

Bass, B. M. (1997). Does the transactional–transformational leadership paradigm transcend organizational and national boundaries? *American Psychologist, 52,* 130–139.

Bass, B. B. & Steidlmeier, P. (2004), Ethics, character, and authentic transformational leadership behavior. In J. B. Ciulla (ed.), *Ethics: the heart of leadership* (2nd edn, pp. 175–192). Boston, MA: Praeger.

Baumeister, R. F. (2001). Ego depletion, the executive function, and self-control: an energy model of the self in personality. In B. W. Roberts & R. Hogan (eds), *Personality psychology in the workplace* (pp. 299–316). Washington, DC: American Psychological Association.

Brown, M. E. & Treviño, L. K. (2006). Ethical leadership: a review and future directions. *The Leadership Quarterly, 17,* 595–616.

Brown, M. E., Treviño, L. K., & Harrison, D. A. (2005). Ethical leadership: a social learning perspective for construct development and testing. *Organizational Behavior and Human Decision Processes, 97,* 117–134.

Brunell, A. B., Gentry, W. A., Campbell, W. K., et al. (2008). Leader emergence: the case of the narcissistic leader. *Personality and Social Psychology Bulletin, 34,* 1663–1676.

Burns, J. M. (1978). *Leadership.* New York: Harper.

Burns, J. M. (2003). *Transforming leadership: the pursuit of happiness.* New York: Atlantic Monthly Press.

Cameron, K. S., Bright, D., & Caza, A. (2004). Exploring the relationships between organizational virtuousness and performance. *American Behavioral Scientist, 47,* 766–790.

Chan, K. & Drasgow, F. (2001). Toward a theory of individual differences and leadership: understanding the motivation to lead. *Journal of Applied Psychology, 86,* 481–498.

Ciulla, J. B. (1995). Leadership ethics: mapping the territory. *Business Ethics Quarterly, 5*(1), 5–28.

Ciulla, J. B. (ed.). (1998). *Ethics: The heart of leadership* (2nd edn). Boston, MA: Praeger.

Ciulla, J. B. (2004). Ethics and leadership effectiveness. In J. Antonakis, A. T. Cianciolo, & R. J. Sternberg (eds), *The nature of leadership* (pp. 302–327). Thousand Oaks, CA: Sage.

Ciulla, J. B. (2005). The state of leadership ethics and the work that lies before us. *Business Ethics: A European Review, 14*(4), 323–335.

Confucius (1963). Selections from the Analects. In W. Chan (ed. & trans.), *A source book in Chinese philosophy* (pp. 18–48). Princeton, NJ: Princeton University Press.

Cronin, T. E. (2008). 'All the world's a stage…' acting and the art of political leadership. *The Leadership Quarterly, 19,* 459–468.

Dalai Lama (1999). *Ethics for the new millennium.* New York: Riverhead Books.

De Cremer, D. & Van Dijk, E. (2005). When and why leaders put themselves first: Leader behaviour in resource allocations as a function of feeling entitled. *European Journal of Social Psychology, 35,* 553–563.

Dent, E. B., Higgins, M. E., & Wharff, D. M. (2005). Spirituality and leadership: an empirical review of definitions, distinctions, and embedded assumptions. *The Leadership Quarterly, 16,* 625–653.

Dhamma, R. (1996). *The First Discourse of the Buddha.* Fitchburg, MA: Wisdom Publications.

Dorfman, P. W., Hanges, P. J., & Brodbeck, F. C. (2004). Leadership and cultural variation: the identification of culturally endorsed leadership profiles. In R. J. House, P. J. Hanges, M. Javidan, P. W. Dorfman, & V. Gupta (eds), *Culture, leadership, and organizations: The GLOBE study of 62 societies* (pp. 669–719). Thousand Oaks, CA: Sage.

Erikson, E. H. (1982). *The life cycle completed: a review.* New York: W. W. Norton.

Forsyth, D. R., O'Boyle, E. H., & McDaniel, M. A. (2008). East meets West: a meta-analytic investigation of cultural variations in idealism and relativism. *Journal of Business Ethics, 83,* 813–833.

Foucault, M. (1990). *The history of sexuality: the use of pleasure* (Vol. 2). New York: Knopt.

Frank, R.H. (1996). *Winner take all society.* New York: Penguin Books.

Fry, L. W. (2003). Toward a theory of spiritual leadership. *The Leadership Quarterly, 14,* 693–727.

Gilligan, C. (1982). *In a different voice: psychological theory and women's development.* Cambridge, MA: Harvard University Press.

Greenleaf, R. K. (1977). *Servant leadership.* New York: Paulist Press.

Haidt, J. & Graham, J. (2007). When morality opposes justice: convervatives have moral intuitions that liberals may not recognize. *Social Justice Research, 20,* 98–116.

Harter, J. K., Schmidt, F. L., & Keyes, C. L. M. (2003). Well-being in the workplace and its relationship to business outcomes: a review of the Gallup studies. In C. L. M. Keyes & J. Haidt (eds), *Flourishing: positive psychology and the life well-lived* (pp. 205–224). Washington, DC: American Psychological Association.

Held, V. (2006). *The ethics of care.* New York: Oxford University Press.

Herodotus (1987). *The history* (D. Green, trans.). Chicago: University of Chicago Press.

Hogg, M. A. (2007). Social psychology of leadership. In A. W. Kruglanski & E. T. Higgins (eds), *Social psychology: handbook of basic principles* (2nd edn, pp. 716–733). New York: Guilford.

Ilies, R., Morgeson, F. P., & Nahrgang, J. D. (2005). Authentic leadership and eudaemonic well-being: understanding leader–follower outcomes. *The Leadership Quarterly, 16,* 373–394.

Jones, T. M. (1991). Ethical decision making by individuals in organizations: an issue-contingent model. *Academy of Management Review, 16,* 366–395.

Kanungo, R.N. & Mendonca, M. (1995). *Ethical dimensions of leadership*. Thousand Oaks, CA: Sage.

Kant, I. (1993). *Foundations of the metaphysics of morals* (J.W. Ellington, trans.). Indianapolis, IN: Hackett Publishing Company.

Keltner, D., Gruenfeld, D. H., & Anderson, C. (2003). Power, approach, and inhibition. *Psychological Review, 110*, 265–284.

Keltner, D., Van Kleef, G. A., Chen, S., & Kraus, M. W. (2008). A reciprocal influence model of social power: emerging principles and lines of inquiry. *Advances in Experimental Social Psychology, 40*, 151–192.

Kenney, R. A., Schwartz-Kenney, B. M., & Blascovich, J. (1996). Implicit leadership theories: defining leaders described as worthy of influence. *Personality and Social Psychology Bulletin, 22*, 1128–1143.

Kierkegaard, S. (1958). *Johannes Climacus; or, de omnibus dubitandum est and a sermon [Everything is to be Doubted]* (T. H. Croxall, trans.). Palo Alto, CA.: Stanford University Press.

Kohlberg, L. (1981). *Psychology of moral development: moral stages and the idea of justice*. San Francisco: Harper and Row.

Kort, E. D. (2008). What, after all is leadership? Leadership and plural action. *The Leadership Quarterly, 19*, 411–425.

Lao-tzu (1963). *Tao-te ching*. In W. Chan, (ed. & trans.), *A source book in Chinese philosophy* (pp. 139–176). Princeton, NJ: Princeton University Press.

Lichtheim, M. (1973). *Ancient Egyptian literature: a book of readings. Vol. 1: The old and middle kingdoms*. Berkeley, CA: University of California Press, pp. 61–82. (The passages quoted from this book are online at http://www.humanistictexts.org/ptahhotep.htm.)

Lord, R. G. & Maher, K. J. (1991). *Leadership and information processing: linking perceptions and performance*. Boston, MA: Unwin Hyman.

Ludwig, D. & Longenecker, C. (1993). The Bathsheba syndrome: the ethical failure of successful leaders. *Journal of Business Ethics, 12*(4), 265–273.

Machiavelli, N. (1954). *The prince*. New York: The Limited Editions Club.

Machiavelli, N. (2003). *Discourses on Livy*. New York: Oxford University Press.

Meindl, J. R., Ehrlich, S. B., & Dukerich, J. M. (1985). The romance of leadership and the evaluation of organizational performance. *Academy of Management Journal, 30*, 90–109.

Mill, J. S. (1987). What utilitarianism is. In A. Ryan (ed.), *Utilitarianism and other essays* (pp. 276–297). New York: Penguin Books.

Moller, A. C., Deci, E. L., & Ryan, R. M. (2006). Choice and ego-depletion: the moderating role of autonomy. *Personality and Social Psychology Bulletin, 32*, 1024–1036.

Muraven, M. R. & Baumeister, R. F. (2000). Self-regulation and depletion of limited resources: Does self-control resemble a muscle? *Psychological Bulletin, 126*, 247–259.

Nietzsche, F. (1978). *Thus spoke Zarathustra*. New York: Penguin Books.

Nietzsche, F. (1989). *Beyond good and evil* (W. Kaufmann, trans.). New York: Vintage Books.

Peterson, C. & Seligman, M. E. P. (2004). *Character strengths and virtues: a handbook and classification*. New York: Oxford University Press.

Plato (1992a). *Republic* (G. M. A. Grube, trans.). Indianapolis, IN: Hackett Publishing.

Plato (1992b). *Protagoras* (S. Lombardo and K. Bell, trans.). Indianapolis, IN: Hackett Publishing.

Plutarch (1998). *Greek lives* (R. Waterfield, trans.). New York: Oxford University Press.

Plutarch (1999). *Roman lives* (R. Waterfield, trans.). New York: Oxford University Press.

Price, T. L. (2003). The ethics of authentic transformational leadership. *The Leadership Quarterly, 14*(1), 67–83.

Price, T. L. (2005). *Understanding ethical failures in leadership*. New York: Cambridge University Press.

Rawls, J. (1971). *A theory of justice*. Cambridge, MA: Belknap Press, Harvard University Press.

Raven, B. H. (1992). A power/interaction model of interpersonal influence: French and Raven thirty years later. *Journal of Social Behavior and Personality, 7*, 217–244.

Reicher, S. D., Haslam, S. A., & Platow, M. J. (2007). The new psychology of leadership. *Scientific American Mind, 18*, 22–29.

Rost, J. (1991). *Leadership for the twenty-first century*. New York: Praeger.

Russell, R. F. & Stone, A. G. (2002). A review of servant leadership attributes: developing a practical model. *Leadership & Organizational Development, 23*, 147–157.

Seligman, M. E. P. (2002). Positive psychology, positive prevention, and positive therapy. In C. R. Snyder & S. J. Lopez (eds), *Handbook of positive psychology* (pp. 3–9). New York: Oxford University Press.

Seneca (1953). *Seneca ad lucilium epistulae (Vol. 3 of Epistulae morales)* (R. M. Gummere, trans.). Cambridge, MA: Harvard University Press.

Smith, J. A., & Foti, R. J. (1998). A pattern approach to the study of leader emergence. *The Leadership Quarterly, 9*, 147–160.

Suetonius (2007). *The twelve caesars* (R. Graves, trans.). New York: Penguin Classics.

Temes, P. (2005). Dirty hands, necessary sin, and the ethics of leaders. In J. B. Ciulla, T. L. Price, & S. E. Murphy (eds), *The quest for moral leaders: essays in leadership ethics* (pp. 28–44). Cheltenham (UK) and Northampton, MA: Edward Elgar.

Turner, N., Barling, J., & Zacharatos, A. (2002). Positive psychology at work. In C. R. Snyder & S. J. Lopez (eds), *Handbook of positive psychology* (pp. 715–728). New York: Oxford University Press.

Van Vugt, M., Hogan, R., & Kaiser, R. B. (2008). Leadership, followership, and evolution: some lessons from the past. *American Psychologist, 63*, 182–196.

Vardi, Y. & Weitz, E. (2004). *Misbehavior in organizations: theory, research, and management*. Mahwah, NJ: Erlbaum.

Wattles, J. (1996). *The golden rule*. New York: Oxford University Press.

Williams, B. A. O. (1981). *Moral luck*. Cambridge, UK: Cambridge University Press.

Woodruff, P. (2001). *Reverence: renewing a forgotten virtue*. New York: Oxford University Press.

18

Philosophy of Leadership

Peter Case, Robert French and Peter Simpson

INTRODUCTION: PARAMETERS AND PROBLEMATICS

In a significant sense there is no philosophy of leadership. Such a statement may seem strange as the opening gambit of a chapter that is ostensibly concerned with 'philosophy of leadership' but the provocation is not without purpose. Indeed, the assertion may be defended on a number of counts and from a variety of perspectives. In the first place, it would be foolish to claim there to be but one, singular, philosophy of leadership. Common sense dictates that there are, at the very least, multiple philosophies of leadership populating, and coexisting in, the contemporary organizational world. In a post-modern or post-industrial age characterized by fragmentation and individualism it is perhaps unsurprising that philosophies of leadership proliferate. At the limit, it could be argued that there are as many 'philosophies' as there are individuals who think of themselves, or are thought of by others, as 'leaders' or as occupying leadership roles. We live in an epoch where there are strong Romantic and heroic imperatives to 'be one's own person', to 'make one's mark in one's job or career' and thus to give expression to one's individual 'philosophy'. Much, of course, depends on the precise (or imprecise) semantic boundaries that one places around the terms 'philosophy' and 'leadership' and, with that in mind, we intend to give careful attention to possible meanings of these terms. Accordingly, a consideration of the semantic force that *philosophy* carries in *leadership* contexts will be central to our concerns in this chapter. In a related but slightly more normative vein, we shall also be asking what semantic force philosophy *should* carry in relationship to leadership practice.

We do not intend this chapter to be simply a dry chronicle or catalogue of leadership philosophies. For one thing, even were such an audacious project pursued, it would doubtless prove to be more than anyone could possibly accomplish in a lifetime and, for certain, could not be confined to an 8,000-word chapter. More productive, we suggest, is the task of *doing* philosophy of leadership. But what exactly might that 'doing' entail? At least four strategies of enquiry suggest themselves: (1) to consider the explicit and implicit philosophies informing contemporary leadership studies; (2) to examine the semantics and meaning-in-use of the terms 'lead', 'leader', 'leadership' and their putative relationship to 'philosophy'; (3) to consider the explicit and implicit philosophies of leadership that may be discovered through an examination of the history of ideas pertaining broadly to 'leadership'; and (4) to suggest ways in which 'leadership philosophy', in contrast to 'philosophy of leadership', might be developed. Each of these four strategies, moreover, reveals a set of problematics and enables the establishment of some general parameters for the philosophical study and practice of leadership.

PHILOSOPHY OF LEADERSHIP IN LEADERSHIP STUDIES

Leadership studies, as presently constituted, is a relatively new invention. Whereas historians have, since the beginning of recorded history, been attracted to the study of leaders and governance wherever they have been found in human communities and civilizations, as a distinct discipline leadership has been around for barely 60 years or so (see Grint, Chapter 1, this volume). It is associated intimately with the growth of the science of organizational behaviour – being something of an offshoot – which developed primarily in the United States from the middle of the twentieth century onward. As a subject discipline, it sought to provide answers to questions concerning how best to lead and govern in the context of mid-twentieth century US institutional and business organizational life. The fashion of the time was to look to science for direction and, accordingly, leadership studies positioned itself as a putative science of individual conduct informed predominantly by psychological and economic theory. Early studies were concerned with exploration of individual ontology, whereby various personality traits and characteristics of effective leaders could be established and, most importantly, measured (e.g., Stogdill, 1948, 1974). The dominant epistemology of the discipline was positivism and this is a philosophical inheritance that still holds great sway to this day.

Trait theory has largely given way to studies which seek to correlate attributes of the individual leader (qualities, styles or skills) with attributes of a social or organizational context (Fiedler, 1967; Hersey & Blanchard, 1988; Likert, 1961; Tannenbaum & Schmidt, 1958; Antonakis, Chapter 20, this volume). The positivist emphasis, however, still persists and there is much concern within mainstream leadership studies to produce models that hold out the possibility of control and predictability or that represent generalizable principles and can be studied using replicable methods.

A philosophy of leadership applied reflexively to the discipline of leadership studies might seek to expose the epistemological, ontological, methodological and ethical assumptions embedded within the discipline. The project would be to understand the field as relatively positioned in time and space and thus to understand better the social and political processes that have shaped it and given rise to certain types of question that demand certain structures of explanation in response. It might also go further in terms of examining the construction of subjects – 'leaders' and 'followers' – within leadership studies discourses and thereby expose, through a systematic archaeological examination of the literary record, the philosophies of leadership explicitly or implicitly purveyed within it. From a post-structural viewpoint, for example, such an analysis would be certain to reveal ruptures, occlusions and silences *produced* by the discourse (see Collinson, Chapter 13 and Fairhurst, Chapter 36, this volume).

Although, as we have suggested, positivism still dominates the language of leadership studies (particularly in the United States), alternative epistemologies are beginning to emerge and receive greater attention. Post-structural approaches to the interpretation of history promote a questioning of the individualistic premises of mainstream accounts and also invite an exploration of the various lacunae created by heroic narratives. In the field of leadership studies, the work of Hosking (1988, 2001, Chapter 33, this volume) and Gemmill and Oakley (1992) has been important in questioning these 'mythical' assumptions from a process theory perspective. The challenge has also been taken up by Martin Wood (Wood, 2005, 2008) and Donna Ladkin (Wood & Ladkin, 2008) who adopt a particularly radical line in their critique of leadership, arguing that our commonsense conceptions of leader–follower relationships are fundamentally 'misplaced' and require overturning.

Within post-structural philosophy more generally, the role and force of individual *action* has been challenged by Foucault (1970, 1977) in his analysis of the modern subject. According to Foucault (1977), the subject should be understood not so much as a locus or wielder of powerful resources but as *an effect* of the sinuous and all-pervasive presence of power within social institutions. From a deconstructive standpoint, moreover, mainstream accounts of leadership say as much about the historical genealogy that inform them as they do about an external historical reality. Such narratives leave out at least as much as they include. For example, mainstream positivist studies understand leadership exclusively from a Western standpoint and, by definition, neglect alternative traditions and milieu. The historical and anthropological record increasingly draws attention to legacies and approaches to leading and governance that are rooted in non-Western philosophies. Another important parameter for the study of leadership philosophy, therefore, relates to approaches, modes of understanding and enactment that find their origins in communities and societies that differ from those of the West. To redress the imbalance requires a concerted effort to embrace wider anthropological (Jones, 2005, 2006), post-colonial (Banerjee, 2004; Banerjee & Linstead, 2001, 2004) and non-Western studies of leadership phenomena (Chia, 2003; Jullien, 2004; Warner & Grint, 2006).

Closer to home, as it were, is the relative occlusion within leadership discourses of others who do not meet the stereotype of the white middle-class male. A more inclusive philosophy of leadership would attend to the marginalization that results from the gendering of discourse and seek to reintroduce the voices of those who are underrepresented in mainstream theories and practices of leadership. Although there is a growing body of literature that attends to a leadership problematic with respect to gender (Blackmore, 1999; Blackmore & Sachs, 2007; Ford, 2005, 2006; Ford & Harding, 2007; Sinclair, 2005; Swan, 2006) and diversity more generally (Puwar, 2004), these domains of critical leadership philosophy remain open for further development.

A LANGUAGE PHILOSOPHY OF LEADERSHIP

Another approach to the *doing* of philosophy of leadership would be to pay close attention to language use, 'conscious of the words as elements of the problems' (Williams, 1983, p. 16). In contrast to '*barber* or *barley* or *bean*', philosophy and *leadership* are what Williams (1983) calls 'words of a different kind', embodying as they do 'ideas and values' (p. 17). Our intention in this regard is to consider the etymology and history of these two terms, thereby exposing some unexpected meanings and connotations that are, as it were, archaeologically embedded within the discourse. Adopting a broadly Wittgensteinian method of enquiry, we seek to analyse the contextual meaning-in-use of the terms (Wittgenstein, 1972 [1953]). Our purpose is to demonstrate the variety of meanings that accrue to these words in ordinary language use, as opposed to more technically defined applications of the words.

The phrase 'philosophy of leadership' brings together words separated by well over two millennia, *philosophia* first appearing around the fifth century BCE (Hadot, 2002, p. 15) and *leadership* in 1821 (*Oxford English Dictionary*). It is inevitable that over a span of so many years the meaning

of 'philosophy' in the Western tradition has ebbed and flowed with the changing tides of culture and belief so that despite an apparent continuity of meaning the term has, in fact, expressed radically different meanings at different times. The 'problem' with leadership, by contrast, may be that it emerged at a particular moment in the history of the West and that, as a result, its meaning has in some ways become fixed. The enormous energy that has gone into exploring what else leadership might mean may, paradoxically, have emptied it of meaning.

The word 'leadership' is notably lacking from Williams' *Keywords*, even from the revised and updated 1983 edition. More surprisingly, it does not appear either in the radically revised *New Keywords* (Bennett et al., 2005), despite what has amounted in that period to an obsession with leadership roles, whether in politics, business, sport, or entertainment – 'celebrities' as leaders. The growth of the literature on leadership in the academic world has been exponential (see Table 18.1): 'The hunger and quest for leadership knowledge appears to be insatiable' (Jackson & Parry, 2008, p. 9). Equally striking, however, is the fact that whereas Williams saw fit to include an entry on philosophy in both editions of his work, it has simply been removed without comment from the 2005 *New Keywords*. It is as if neither leadership nor philosophy any longer plays a significant role in the *Vocabulary of Culture and Society*, the subtitle of both books.

Here we find that the classical meaning of philosophy has been diluted significantly, becoming little more than a synonym for 'personal attitude' or 'preferred approach'. Williams (1983, pp. 235–236) ends his entry on philosophy by noting its increasing use 'in managerial and bureaucratic

Table 18.1 Number of references to 'leadership' (by year of publication) appearing in leading texts

Decade of publication	Number of references (%)			
	Yukl (2002)	Grint (2000)	Grint (2005)	Jackson & Parry (2008)
Pre-1960	4	3	2	1
1960s	7	3	1	3
1970s	16	8	7	6
1980s	33	17	9	12
1990s	39	69	31	35
2000+	1	0	50	44

Notes:

1 Despite the dates of publication, we have placed Yukl (2002) before Grint (2000), because this is the 5th edition of the Yukl volume and so, to some extent, represents an earlier set of references.
2 These figures do not reflect the fact that some of the works referenced, such as Machiavelli's *The Prince*, were written many years before the date given in the reference section.
3 The bias in the table above is also reflected in the seven leadership journals listed as 'worth monitoring' by Jackson and Parry. Of these, two were established since 2000 and three in the 1990s.

talk', where he observes that it can mean 'general policy' but that just as often it simply indicates 'the internal assumptions or even the internal procedures of a business or institution'. He offers entertaining but telling examples: 'the *philosophy of selling* through the *philosophy of motorways* to the *philosophy of supermarkets*' (p. 236, original emphases). Since Williams wrote this in 1983, meaning has continued to drain from the word, as reflected, for example, in statements by business leaders and politicians, who use the phrase 'my philosophy of leadership' as little more than a grandiose way of saying, 'what I do'.

Whereas philosophy has always been an 'essentially contested concept' (Gallie, 1955/56), the schools representing the philosophical tradition have also always been linked by a 'golden string' (Blake, 1979, p. 345 – *Jerusalem*, Plate 77). Far from merely describing 'what I do', Hadot suggests that 'what the philosopher profoundly wants, what interests him [*sic*] in the strongest sense of the term [is] the answer to the question 'How should I live'? (2002, p. 273). The philosopher's underlying intention was 'not to develop a discourse which had its end in itself but *to act upon souls*' (p. 274, emphasis added).

What has been lost, therefore – and it is this which is of fundamental importance to the philosophy of leadership – is that traditionally philosophy was not just a discourse, not just an intellectual exercise of words, concepts and definitions, but *a way of life* (Hadot, 1995). In this sense, while currently there may be no *philosophy* of leadership in this sense beyond largely empty posturing, Hadot's notion opens up its potentially fundamental significance, by returning us to the essentially ethical roots of *both* philosophy *and* leadership.

A key dimension of the 'problem' of leadership may lie in what one might call the 'slippage' from verb to concrete role to abstract noun. Where Latin, for example, had both the verb and the role – *duco* and *dux* – it did not develop the abstract notion of leader-*ship*, captured in the English suffix. In English, the verb came first by many centuries. The original, Old English verb *lǽdan* is an ancient word, predating written English. Its origins have been traced to an Indo-European (Sanskrit) root, meaning to go, go away or die. *Lǽdan*, meaning 'to cause [someone] to go with oneself' (*Oxford English Dictionary*), describes the way in which we human beings will show one another the way – and allow ourselves to be shown or guided.

After several centuries in which 'lead' was used as a verb, the *noun* 'leader' appeared in written English for the first time around 1300. This is not to suggest that the notion of a leader – i.e. a person who leads – had not existed. The word does represent a significant change, however, from leadership as a (gendered) attribute of a role – such as king, queen, noble, bishop, abbot, abbess, elder, father (in family or church), alderman, mayor, teacher, general, captain, and so on – to a separate role defined simply by the activity of leading.

Four centuries later, however, another, most significant shift occurred, first recorded in 1821: from the word 'leader' a second noun, 'leadership', was created. In purely linguistic terms, the shift from 'lead' to 'leadership' appears unremarkable, a simple sequential development, similar to work → workman → workmanship. However, it may be the historical context which adds real significance to this shift. Although space does not allow for a detailed analysis, it is clear that certain conditions at the start of the nineteenth century, when the word first appears, may have contributed to the impact it has had on our thinking. The British Empire was approaching its zenith, slavery had not yet been abolished, the industrial revolution was in full swing and Dickens was about to publish the first of his 'reforming novels', *Oliver Twist* (1837). In other words, the traditional structures of society and leading roles, locally, nationally and internationally, were in disarray.

Specifically in relation to leadership, the impact of the notion of the hero is of significance. It had undergone a major transformation in the Romantic period in art and literature through the establishment of the notion of the artist as hero. For example, the concept of 'creator', which had only ever been attributed to God, was now used of the – God like – artist. The notion was then significantly expanded in 1840 – only 19 years after the first recorded use of the word leadership – when Thomas Carlyle gave his famous lectures *On Heroes and Hero-Worship and the Heroic in History*, in which he gave the notion of the 'Great Man' its first, fully worked expression (Carlyle, 1904). The very first paragraph of Carlyle's first lecture sets out an image which, one might say, replaced any *philosophy* of leadership with a simple, all-encompassing *template*:

For, as I take it, Universal History, the history of what man [sic] has accomplished in this world, is at bottom the History of the Great Men who have worked here. They were the leaders of men, these great ones; the modellers, patterns, and in a wide sense creators, of whatsoever the general mass of men contrived to do or to attain; all things that we see standing accomplished in the world are properly the outer material result, the practical realisation and embodiment, of Thoughts that dwelt in the Great Men sent into the world: the soul of the whole world's history, it may justly be considered, were the history of these. (1904, p. 1)

From the reception given to the lectures by the large and distinguished audience, it is clear that Carlyle was articulating ideas whose time had come: 'bishops and all kinds of people had appeared; they heard something new and seemed greatly astonished and greatly pleased. They laughed and applauded' (Carlyle in Cassirer, 1946, p. 189.) In relation to leadership, the key element of his thinking was the direct and explicit description of these 'great ones' – 'the modellers, patterns...creators, ...the soul of the whole world's history' – precisely as '*leaders*'. No wonder Cassirer, writing in the aftermath of the Second World War, talks of Carlyle's ideas as 'a dangerous explosive' and 'the beginning of a new revolution' (1946, pp. 189–190).

The continuing power of the imagery generated by Carlyle's lecture means that it is now nigh on impossible for us to see present or past except through the lens of Carlyle's heroic, male, great 'leaders'. As a result, the notion of the 'leader', as a separate figure, and of 'leadership' as the characteristic of this figure, have become so fixed in our minds that it is almost impossible to read history or the present without seeing leaders and leadership everywhere. That said, as we have noted above, certain post-structural, process theory and feminist writers are alert to the problem of 'common sense' understandings with respect to the words leader and leadership, being at pains to problematize, deconstruct and generally denaturalize their usage. This is not merely a semantic exercise since, from a Wittgensteinian viewpoint, language is constitutive of forms of life and, arguably, the wider social order. By interrogating meaning-in-practice, emerging trends in leadership studies have been concerned to shift the discourse away from one dominated exclusively by the 'masculine hero' toward more relational, distributed, and gender-aware understandings. As we have tried to indicate in outline here, an understanding of the etymology and semantics of leadership-related concepts assists greatly in surfacing the problematic inheritance we have with regard to thinking about, studying and enacting leadership.

PHILOSOPHIES OF LEADERSHIP PAST AND PRESENT

According to Collingwood (1994) any history of the past is a history of the present. Applied to the domain of leadership studies, this implies that our understanding of leadership in the past will inevitably be mediated by the present supporting conditions and purposes which our account is intended to address. In other words, the way we understand, for example, the writings of Plato, Aristotle, Machiavelli or Montaigne that have a bearing on what we, in the contemporary West, currently designate as leadership must inescapably be coloured by our present time- and culture-specific use of that term. As Jepson (2009) has shown in her linguistic study of differences in meaning between leadership in the UK and Germany, language plays a crucial constitutive role in the creation of leadership phenomenon. If there are marked differences to be found in the meaning of leadership between the comparatively closely related languages of English and German, how much more so must this be true of the meanings attributed to authors working in languages that are non-Indo-European in origin, geographically remote, or separated from the present time by hundreds, if not thousands, of years. For most the ideas of 'great thinkers' or 'great leaders' are accessible only through acts of translation, which are historically and socio-politically situated. Nonetheless, in our efforts to understand current leadership and governance dilemmas we naturally turn to the past in a search for insight, however faulty and inadequate the equipment we deploy to this end. It is not that we necessarily *learn* from the past but, rather, that we *rediscover* questions, problems and resolutions in the present that seem to have resonance with our contemporary reconstruction of the past.

Accordingly, one dimension of doing philosophy of leadership entails exploring and cataloguing a history of leadership ideas as understood from the present and from an inescapably ethnocentric standpoint. Some authors have attempted to interrogate history in this way with a greater or lesser degree of self-knowingness or reflexivity: compare, for example, Adair (1989) and Grint (2000) in this regard. Although we cannot possibly offer a comprehensive account of leadership philosophy chronicled in historical writing, we can, at least, suggest some parameters for this kind of project.

There exists a more or less mainstream study of leadership history which draws out philosophies from the past, most often in the form of examining and foregrounding the part played by heroic figures (usually men) at key historical moments: the actions of those who are considered to have embodied admirable leadership traits and talents. We have in mind studies of Xenophon, Achilles, King David (from pre-history), or, slightly closer to our own time, those of Wilberforce, Napoleon, Nelson, Scott, Shackleton, Churchill, Hitler, Stalin, Martin Luther King and the like. Often, though not always, these leadership histories are premised on a philosophy of heroic individualism that assumes high degrees of agency and self-determination, such that the actions of the subject can be construed as having had decisive effects on the direction of wider socio-political affairs.

For the purposes of the argument pursued here we shall trace a particular line through history that focuses, not so much on the isolated instances of heroic leadership, as on the rise of instrumentality in relation to leadership philosophy. This is important since many recent developments in the field are, at root, a response to such instrumentality. Certain forms of argument, for example, promulgate a view of leadership philosophy that is essentially amoral and concerned only to highlight 'responsibilities' that accompany the pursuit of profit or material gain. In line with the (in)famous statement of Milton Friedman (1970) that 'the only social responsibility of business is to make a profit' it is not uncommon to find approaches to leadership that espouse a limited range of duties which serve this end exclusively. This is most clearly seen in the notion of *homo economicus* or 'economic man', which is characterized by rationality, self-interest and the pursuit of wealth. According to Huehn (2008), poor organizational leadership and governance frequently has its roots in the 'unenlightened economism' of Hobbes' seventeenth-century political philosophy. From this perspective the social process of leadership is simplified to become little more than following a 'quasimathematical model' without the need to make 'difficult value-judgements' (2008, p. 831). Such a philosophy of leadership engenders a practice that gives primacy to a narrow view of reason based upon 'hard facts' and the utilization of quantitative techniques to provide measurements appropriate to support decision making.

Emerging in the same period as economism, utilitarian or consequentialist philosophy shares some similar characteristics. Approaches rooted in this tradition not only espouse the importance of 'scientific' and 'value free' attitudes to decision making but also they reduce ethics to a matter of quantitative calculation. Perhaps even more significant is the influence of utilitarianism in equating leadership with that influence which makes a *useful* contribution through coordinating the pursuit and attainment of a valued goal or vision. This has become the *sine qua non* of 'good' leadership in the modern era. As a consequence, 'progress' and 'growth' are required of leaders even where there is clear evidence of the need for other strategies (consider, for example, the expectations of political and business leaders to continue strategies detrimental to the environment). When combined with economism, leaders will operate under a broad guiding principle – the maximization of shareholder value – which from within the utilitarian matrix of reasoning remains unchallenged and unchallengeable. It is a simple case of the

ends justifying the means or, in Weberian terms, the dominance of *Zweckrationalität*, formal rationality, over *Wertrationalität*, 'substantitive' or subjective value rationality (Weber, 1970 [1948]).

Whereas it can be argued that utilitarian attitudes are pervasive, or at least commonly observable, in leadership practice they do not appear to have developed to the level of what might be called a philosophy of leadership. If they did, then there would be greater attention to problematizing some of the taken-for-granted aspects of utilitarian economics. For example, it is not possible to focus only upon 'hard facts' in pursuit of a scientific, value-free evaluation: a value judgement is being made in giving primacy only to things that are amenable to measurement. To suggest that it is better for a leader to be freed from 'difficult value judgements' is a simplification that just does not bear close intellectual scrutiny.

An interesting contrast is with Enlightenment philosophy, which also came to prominence during the eighteenth century but places greater emphasis upon social responsibility, including the responsibility of each and every individual to think for himself or herself and to make appropriate moral judgements. As a precursor to utilitarian philosophy, the Age of Enlightenment prioritized reason but specifically as a source of authority and self-determination set against the authority of the state or religion. In itself, this is an interesting aspect of a philosophy of leadership that we will not pursue in detail here. It is, however, important to mention, by way of historical connection, the emergence during this epoch of a decentralized constitution in the newly formed United States of America. This was a philosophy that changed the understanding of political leadership in a fundamental manner and resulted in new forms of practice and governance.

Of greater significance for our purposes is the emphasis upon 'reason' as the guiding authority within Enlightenment and post-Enlightenment philosophical movements. As the basis for a philosophy of leadership, we do not challenge this idea, per se, but do raise some questions about the definition of reason that is being employed. For instance, Pieper (1999 [1952]) draws our attention to a shift that occurred in the common understanding of reason following the Middle Ages and, consequently, in the development of Enlightenment science and utilitarian philosophy. He argues that,

> The Middle Ages drew a distinction between the understanding as *ratio* and the understanding as *intellectus*. *Ratio* is the power of discursive, logical thought, of searching and of examination, of abstraction, of definition and drawing conclusions. *Intellectus*, on the other hand, is the name for the understanding in so far as it is the capacity of

simplex intuitus, of that simple vision to which truth offers itself like a landscape to the eye. The faculty of mind, man's knowledge, is both these things in one, according to antiquity and the Middle Ages, simultaneously *ratio* and *intellectus*; and the process of knowing is the action of the two together. The mode of discursive thought is accompanied and impregnated by an effortless awareness, the contemplative vision of the *intellectus*, which is not active but passive, or rather receptive, the activity of the soul in which it conceives that which it sees. (Pieper, 1999 [1952], p. 9)

Brient (2001) contends that this transition in the definition of reason is directly paralleled by an increased emphasis upon a work ethic. In other words, 'what one does', and the consequences of this, serves to define our sense of identity. As she argues,

In this transition human self-understanding gradually shifted from that of the spectators and admirers of divine creation to that of (as Descartes put it) 'lords and masters of nature'. If knowledge of the world is gained passively by contemplation in the Middle Ages – spelled out in terms of either divine illumination or abstraction from sense perception – it is won through active reconstruction in the modern age. (Brient, 2001, p. 20)

In further illustration, Brient suggests that following the Middle Ages, *theoria* changed in meaning from the contemplation of truth, which necessarily carried divine connotations, to become the modern scientific notion of hypothesis: something to be tested through empirical experimentation and applied for the betterment of humankind. *Theoria* is one of Aristotle's four intellectual virtues, the others being *episteme* (intellectual knowledge), *techne* (embodied knowledge) and *phronesis* (circumspection and practical wisdom) (see Aristotle, 1953).

This process of self-assertion, as humans are no longer at the mercy of the gods – or of any other authority figures – led to the emergence of an Enlightenment culture dominated by the work ethic and the pre-eminence of the utility of measurable activity.

Our purpose in offering a very brief genealogy of Enlightenment and post-Enlightenment emphasis on *reason* is twofold: (1) it enables us to understand the instrumental disposition of mainstream approaches to studying leadership that developed from the mid-twentieth century (discussed briefly in the first section); and, (2) we develop an argument below for *doing* leadership philosophy in a way that contrasts quite markedly with approaches that give exclusive emphasis to instrumental

reason. In considering the development of what we would contend is a genuine *philosophy* of leadership based upon virtue ethics, we recognize the requirement to return to contemplative and mystical as well as rational dimensions of knowing (Case & Gosling, 2007).

LEADERSHIP PHILOSOPHY AS A WAY OF LIFE

In making this transition from *discourse* to *practice* and *being* we must, by necessity, engage with a leadership ethics. For us, ethics is coextensive with human organization to such an extent that it becomes difficult to disentangle or parcel out questions of ontology, epistemology and aesthetics from those of ethics in the manner that has become characteristic of post-Medieval philosophy (see Ciulla & Forsyth, Chapter 17; Hansen & Bathurst, Chapter 19, this volume). To inform our argument, therefore, we have sought inspiration in classical philosophy and associated schemes of 'virtue ethics': systems of praxis that differ markedly from the utilitarianism that so dominates the contemporary world of business and management.

Virtue ethics

Ethics is concerned not only with the conduct of a person but also whether that conduct may be deemed 'good' or 'bad'. Virtue ethics, which in the Western tradition may be traced back to roots in philosophies of Ancient Greece (particularly the Hellenistic Scholae), places an emphasis upon *being* rather than *doing* in terms of the consequences or utility of actions (Hadot, 2002). Critical to our argument here is working with the notion of 'the good' and the differences in meaning of this central philosophical notion in different eras and philosophies. The higher-level term within Greek philosophy is 'truth', which is even more unknowable than the higher-level 'good' that guides conduct through a focus on virtue ethics. Pieper (2007 [1966]), for example, claims that, 'Being precedes Truth, and that Truth precedes the Good' (p. 4). Virtue ethics is concerned with 'right action': i.e. action in pursuit of the good. As Nikolaus has pointed out:

The good (Gk. *agathon*, Lat. *bonum*) is that which contributes to the perfection of something or constitutes it. Distinction is made between the absolute good and the relative good. The former involves the actualizing of every innate possibility of perfection (Gk. *entelecheia*, Lat. *bonum honestum*). The latter, along the lines of utility (*bonum utile*) or satisfaction (*bonum delicabile*), contributes to the fulfilment of another and produces a hierarchy of goods, at the head of which is the supreme good (*summum bonum*). (2001, p. 445)

Virtue ethics thus emphasizes the pursuit of the absolute good and a leadership philosophy based upon this principle will be concerned with the actualizing of perfection. Of course, in practice, this proves to be an impossible ideal with which to conform. Our contention, however, is that this does not make it meaningless. We adopt this position on the basis that the contested nature of 'the good' can be argued to be a significant feature in the history of philosophical discourse. For example, Plato placed the highest possible value on 'The Good' (*Republic* 508e) but Hadot (2002) suggests that this definition of 'The Good' was not even agreed upon by Plato's friends and supporters:

Speusippus, Xenocrates, Eudoxus, and Aristotle professed theories which were by no means in accord with those of Plato, especially not the subject of Ideas. They even disagreed about the definition of the good, since we know that Eudoxus thought the supreme good was pleasure. Such intense controversies among the members of the school left traces not only within Plato's dialogues and in Aristotle, but throughout Hellenistic philosophy, if not throughout the entire history of philosophy. (p. 64)

Aristotle gives similar prominence to the notion of 'the Good', defining it as that potentiality which everything strives to become (Aristotle, 1953). Epicurus linked the good to desire and hedonism (Hadot, 2002) while, within the early Christian tradition, Augustine (2003, Book 8) and Aquinas (2007, Question 6, Article 2) equated the supreme Good with God, who was the essence of Good with which all creation could, in principle, commune. Kant (1993 [1785]) was later to move away from a material definition of 'good' but retained in his central notion of the 'categorical imperative' a focus on good will, expressed in the recognition of moral duty. Commenting on the idea of the good, G.E. Moore (1903) suggested that: 'good' is a simple notion, just as 'yellow' is a simple notion; that, just as you cannot, by any manner of means, explain to any one who does not already know it, what yellow is, so you cannot explain what good is' (§7). He argued for the philosophical value of the notion of 'good' in ethics in terms of a more experiential engagement with it. Although Ayer was originally influenced by Moore's arguments, he later (2001 [1936]), in a similar manner to Russell (see Pidgen, 1999),

suggested that the unverifiability of the concept renders it meaningless.

An engagement with the contested nature of 'the good' is an excellent starting point for a philosophical engagement with the equally contested notion of 'leadership'. To encourage dialogue and debate in relation to the nature of leadership, and particularly whether it is 'good' or 'bad', is to practice leadership philosophy. In this way, leaders, and those who wish to study leadership, will inevitably take their practice and study to a deeper level.

Plato believed that the best 'leaders' (rulers) were those who were philosopher-kings, who, by definition, understood the eternal Good. However, for Plato, the philosopher-kings understood the eternal Good, which required a strong mystical dimension to their practice, and a combination of intellectual and moral discipline. Such an engagement with the Good involved the more mystical, contemplative knowledge, understanding and wisdom arising from, and being embodied in, *lived experience* (*intellectus*) rather than purely cognitive understanding (*ratio* as 'pure' rationality and reason). This balance between *intellectus* and *ratio* can be seen in the ancient philosophy but only with greater difficulty in the majority of philosophy after the Middle Ages. It is in a similar manner that we saw above the shift in understanding of the notion of 'the good' from Kant onwards.

Essential to our approach to *leadership philosophy as a way of life* is an appreciation of the potential value of *intellectus* as well as *ratio*, of the contemplative and mystical as well as the active and practical. But what of the role of 'virtue' in this nexus? According to Pieper:

Virtue is a 'perfected ability' of man [*sic*] as a spiritual person; and justice, fortitude, and temperance, as abilities of the whole man [*sic*], achieve their 'perfection' only when they are founded upon prudence, that is to say upon the perfected ability to make right decisions. (2007 [1966], p. 6)

A leadership philosophy that draws upon virtue ethics will consider the nature of 'perfect' and 'imperfect' leadership. Although problematic, these notions have a certain resonance with the everyday experience of leaders. We often know experientially when leadership is imperfect – when 'wrong decisions' have been made, when there has been a lack of justice, courage or balance (Frost & Robinson, 1999; Maccoby, 2004; Price, 2005; Tourish & Pinnington, 2002). It is, of course, harder to conceive of or recollect examples of 'perfect' leadership, but it is clear that the underlying philosophical questions problematize leadership in a manner that has value and meaning. A consideration of virtue at the very least *sensitizes* us to the idea of 'good' and 'bad' leadership in ways that differ qualitatively from a utilitarian analysis and discourse.

Debate in the field of leadership studies has, to an extent, already alighted upon the potential inherent in a closer consideration and re-examination of virtue. Keith Grint, for example, has considered how the first three elements of Aristotle's fourfold typology of *intellectual virtue* might be mobilized to improve our understanding of leadership practice (Grint, 2007). He takes the divisions of *technē* (know how), *episteme* (intellectual knowledge) and *phronesis* (practical wisdom) and demonstrates how these offer mutually complimentary dimensions of assessing problems and dilemmas faced by leaders. Whereas this is a commendable contribution in many respects, it nonetheless overlooks certain important aspects of Aristotle's philosophy. As Morrell (2007) has pointed out, for instance, Grint takes no account of the *aesthetic* dimension of Aristotle's thinking but, perhaps more importantly, the fourth and final element of the typology set out in the *Nicomachean Ethics*, namely, *theoria* (contemplation), gets no mention at all (Aristotle, 1953).

Phronesis requires, according to Aristotle, the power of deliberation or circumspection, beyond scientific deduction, because it has to accommodate and enable responses to events and contingencies whose causal complexity is far too extensive to attenuate or contain. The primary function of *phronesis* is to discern 'what matters' in a given situation, something which can only be accomplished through the collective *deliberation* of those whose shared concern is the welfare of the polity. Moving beyond the secular confines of the first three intellectual virtues, however, Aristotle posits *theoria* as the fourth, describing it as,

> 'the only [intellectual virtue] that is praised on its own account, because nothing comes of it beyond the act of contemplation... yet such a life will be too high for *human* attainment. It will not be lived by us in our merely human capacity, but in virtue of something divine within us... . (1953, 304–305, original emphasis)

The significance of *theoria* in Aristotle's typology is readily overlooked or deliberately ignored in the contemporary world because it is taken to be too numinous and 'unreasonable' to have any implications for secular leadership practice (e.g. Grint, 2007; Stamp et al., 2007). However, this may be too hasty a response, particularly in the light of the growing interest in, or rediscovery of, *sacred* dimensions of workplace interaction (Case & Gosling, 2007). The plethora of research in the field of leadership 'spirituality', although all too often lamentably instrumental and crudely utilitarian in nature, in principle opens up a doorway to re-enchanted conceptualization of the continuity between the human and divine *in seemingly mundane contexts* (see, for example, Duchon & Plowman, 2005; Fairholm, 1997, 1998, 2001; Fry, 2003, 2004; Fry et al., 2005). For us, any such reversal of the disenchanting proclivities of modern and, indeed, post-modern leadership strategies is a refreshing and welcome possibility.

While space requires us to elide much of the complexity of philosophical debate with respect to virtue ethics and the diversity of approaches to the subject, it is perhaps worth introducing one further schema that combines the sacred and seemingly profane into a highly pragmatic way of being-in-the-world. We refer to the classical philosophy of Stoicism, which, of all the doctrines originating from Hellenistic Greece, perhaps offers a most pragmatic set of lessons for that phenomenon we term 'leadership' and whose tenets seem to traverse the translational and cultural boundaries of time and space.

Stoic virtues

The Stoic school, founded by Zeno toward the end of the fourth century BC, was given further impetus under the influence of Chrysippus in the third century and, following a sectarian split, continued to flourish during the Roman period until the second century AD (Hadot, 2002, pp. 126–139). Important protagonists and practitioners of Stoicism during the Roman era were Seneca, Musonius, Epictetus and Marcus Aurelius (Hadot, 2004) and, as little remains of the founding texts of Zeno and Chrysippus, it is in these Greco-Roman writings that the principles of Stoical philosophy have been preserved. In this philosophy one discovers a practical and gentle approach to the art of living which, we suggest, has much to offer those occupying contemporary leadership roles.

Hadot (1995) points out that it is crucial to understand the difference between Stoical conceptions of *philosophical discourse* and *philosophy as a way of life* in order to understand this tradition. To the extent that love of wisdom has to be taught by those that live philosophically to those who aspire to do so, the Stoics developed abstract *theories* of knowledge with respect to the three core virtues of physics, logic and ethics. The true *purpose* of such discourse, however, was to enable aspirants to enter into a philosophical life within which all the virtues combined to produce a way of *being in the world*. That way of being, moreover, was governed by an overarching principle that required philosophers to pursue the good, which, in turn, entailed directing their actions toward the benefit of others. The pursuit of the good and avoidance of evil, instantiated in Stoical ethics, followed inexorably and necessarily from the need to act in accordance with universal Reason. Stoics strove to live in harmony with Nature; a concept that represented the myriad complex processes of the cosmos including, of course, human consciousness, thought and action. Stoicism was predicated on an axiomatic truth of the cosmic interconnection between human and non-human realms such that the world was understood to be 'one single living being which [was] likewise in tune with itself and self-coherent' (Hadot, 2002, pp. 128–129). The spiritual practices which were central to living the Stoical life were all directed toward helping individuals realize this truth by way of abandoning the conceit of 'individuality' and, through a form of personal surrender, bringing intentions, thoughts and actions into line with Nature.

Thus, for the Stoics, wisdom is to be realized by refraining from thinking, speaking or acting in ways that contradict Reality. Epictetus, for example, offers the following sagely advice: 'Do not try to make things happen the way you want, but want what happens to happen the way it happens and you will be happy' (cited in Hadot, 2002, p. 133). The route to happiness, he insists, lies in not wanting things to be different than they actually are. The philosophical discourse and spiritual exercises of Stoicism are all directed at bringing about a transformation in consciousness that will lead to such wisdom. Far from being a manifesto for political quietism, fatalism or inaction, however, this understanding derives from a threefold set of principles associated with physics, ethics and logic.

With respect to physics, for example, it is necessary to understand the sphere of one's own action and influence. There are many aspects of Nature over which mere human will has no power whatsoever. In the last analysis, we have no control over the metabolism of the bodies we conventionally consider to be 'our own'. No individual can anticipate or control the precise circumstances of their own death (even, ultimately, that of the suicide), or will not suffer from illness, loss of loved ones and so forth. Similarly, we neither have ultimate control of the thoughts, decisions and actions of others nor over the more macro supporting conditions of our lives, such as the parents we are born to and the society that we grow up in and so forth. Everything from the weather to current geopolitics are totally out of our hands and, from a Stoical viewpoint, we are like so much flotsam and jetsam in the great ocean of life. For the Stoic, such exogenous conditions result from the workings of Fate. The wise way to respond to any causally conditioned circumstances over which we have no control, moreover, is to accept them with equanimity. The idea of

volitional response implicit in this attitude brings us to the second Stoic virtue, namely, ethics.

Within Stoic philosophical discourse, the fact that Nature is in large measure determined by an unfathomably complex set of causal conditions does not mean that there is no possibility for free will and moral action. On the contrary, the cultivation of good intention and good action is central to Stoic philosophy as a way of life. Accordingly, the Stoics – Epictetus in particular – developed a detailed and elaborate theory of *duty*. Fate may well dictate the circumstances of our lives but, unlike the Skeptics who resigned themselves to worldly indifference, or the Epicureans who chose to withdraw from the world of suffering in order to find happiness, Stoics sought wisdom through engagement with the *polis*. Stoicism does not provide an excuse for 'indifference', in a pejorative sense, and a commensurate backing down from responsibility to oneself and others. The Stoic is quite likely to lead a family life, have children, work, pursue a career and engage fully in the political life of the city. But all this needs to be done *ethically*, i.e. with a mind to the welfare of others: both those near to one and those within the wider community. Such attitudes and obligations are dictated by Nature and universal Reason themselves, which have, in effect, endowed humans with moral choice and determined that it is *good* to care for oneself and others.

This brings us to a consideration of logic, the third and final Stoic virtue. As with physics and ethics, there is a philosophical discourse which supports the spiritual exercises of logic in the form of training in uses of dialectic and syllogism, but it is the *practice* of logic that distinguishes Stoicism from other Hellenic schools of philosophy. Logic as spiritual exercise entails paying close attention (*prosokē*) to physical sense perception and mental representations in order to become skilful in judgement of, or assent to, the Real. Our senses and mental representations are real enough in themselves and are, in large measure, conditioned by physics or Fate. Responses to those perceptions, however, involve choices which involve skilful or unskilful judgements. Logic entails the development of awareness and reasoned response to the world which pre-empts or 'defuses' actions based on passionate responses.

Our tentative suggestion is that the Stoic schema provides an extremely helpful *philosophy*, in the classical sense, with which to approach the many practical demands faced by those occupying leadership roles. It contains advice on how to develop mental attitudes, such as fortitude and equanimity, which enable individuals to discriminate more clearly between what they can and cannot influence in the world. Moreover, its theory of duty offers an art of living whereby the person remains focused on the pursuit of the virtuous in their daily interactions and dealings; an imperative which, we would argue, is often sorely lacking in the contemporary organizational world.

By way of conclusion, we consider some of the practical educational implications of taking virtue ethics seriously in a leadership development context and summarize the philosophical strategies introduced in this chapter.

CONCLUSIONS

Many contemporary scholars of organization, management and leadership studies have openly lamented the limitations of the conventional business school curriculum on a variety of grounds. Some claim that management education and research fails to connect practically with its intended audiences (Pfeffer & Fong, 2002, 2004), whereas others question its pedagogical or practical relevance (Bennis & O'Toole, 2005; Drucker, 2001; French & Grey, 1996; Kelemen & Bansal, 2002; Knights, 2008; Mintzberg, 2004). To these critical voices we would add that the entire field is dominated, in the main, by a proclivity for scientism and instrumental thinking that does not address the rounded cognitive and affective needs of organizational practitioners. This general criticism applies with as much force to the specialist field of leadership studies as it does to the general business school syllabus.

It is within this context that we suggest a *leadership philosophy*, based on virtue ethics, might have a great deal to offer. The enormous challenge presented by this prospect will be to integrate 'leadership philosophy as a way of life' within a business and management curriculum that is overwhelmingly characterized by instrumental forms of teaching and learning. There is an ever-present risk that any attempt to introduce, say, virtue ethics or Stoic philosophy into a leadership development programme would be appropriated or co-opted and simply become another resource to be turned toward instrumental ends. One can all too easily imagine such unfortunate initiatives as a Stoic 'competency framework', a 'seven steps to virtuous leadership' model and the like. The implications of the argument we present regarding leadership philosophy as a way of life would be considerably more far reaching than any form of superficial cognitive modelling, and would require development of an *educational* engagement which would be commensurate with, and adequate to, the pursuit of virtue in leadership and management roles. Clearly, such a radical agenda would not be to everyone's taste and would almost certainly

meet with institutional resistance in the current higher education climate.

What we propose, then, is not a general panacea for leadership development so much as one possible micronarrative (Lyotard, 1984) strategy, historically rooted within a Western tradition, that could assist in approaching the perennial questions that face leaders: 'How should I act?', 'Am I acting efficaciously?' and so forth. We have argued that while attention to philosophical questions of ontology and epistemology taken in isolation may be important, the third classical domain of philosophy – namely, ethics – is by far the most central to leadership study and practice. There are no arrangements of the social which do not involve ethical relationships (whether judged 'good' or 'bad') of one sort or another. Furthermore, a close examination of Stoical philosophy and practical spiritual exercises reveals that the ontological and epistemological cannot be readily parcelled out from ethics. From a Stoical perspective, the privileging of ethics simultaneously brings ontology and epistemology to the fore.

This contribution to the *SAGE Handbook of Leadership* has been concerned with identifying some of problematics and parameters that might inform the *doing* of leadership philosophy. Some of that 'doing' takes the form of traditional scholastic research and analysis. We sought, for example, in the first section to outline extant work and a potential research programme that takes as its focus the history of ideas pertaining to leadership. In the second section we proposed another philosophical research strategy that would entail *deconstructing* the field of leadership studies by analysing the explicit and implicit philosophies that inform current theory and practice. Yet another fruitful approach, we suggested, would be to examine the semantics and meaning-in-use of the leadership discourse insofar at it variously engages with something called 'philosophy'. To this extent, the third section (along with the previous two sections) was concerned with the analytical study of 'philosophy of leadership', demonstrating that we cannot properly speak of a 'philosophy' in singular terms but must admit of multiple and highly diverse 'philosophies'. In the final section we were concerned to propose a move from 'philosophy of leadership' to 'leadership philosophy', a relationship between these two terms that places value on a more authentic (in classical terms) appreciation of 'philosophy' and which acknowledges the centrality of ethical questions within leadership roles and relationships. As we asserted at the outset, for the various reasons discussed in this chapter there may be no philosophy of leadership, but this in no way discounts or detracts from the challenge of establishing such a philosophy or philosophies.

ACKNOWLEDGEMENTS

The authors would like to thank Elaine Swan, University of Lancaster, and Martin Wood, University of York, for guiding us toward relevant literature on the topics of gender philosophy and process philosophy, respectively. Any misreadings or misrenderings of the reference material they supplied is, of course, entirely our responsibility. We should also acknowledge, with thanks, a helpful email exchange between ourselves and Kurt Lampe, Bristol University, and Jonathan Gosling, University of Exeter, concerning translation of Greek and Roman terms pertaining broadly to 'leadership'.

REFERENCES

Adair, J. (1989) *Great Leaders*. London: Talbot Adair.

Aquinas, St Thomas (2007) *Summa Theologica: Vol. 1 of 10*. Charleston, SC: Forgotten Books.

Aristotle (1953) *The Ethics of Aristotle: the Nichomachean Ethics* (trans. J.A.K. Tomson). London: Allen & Unwin.

Augustine, St (2003) *City of God* (trans. H. Bettenson). London: Penguin Classics.

Ayer, A.J. (2001 [1936]) *Language, Truth and Logic*. London: Penguin Modern Classics.

Banerjee, S.B. (2004) 'Reinventing colonialism: exploring the myth of sustainable development', *Situation Analysis*, 4 (Autumn): 95–110.

Banerjee, S.B. and Linstead, S. (2001) 'Globalization, multiculturalism and other fictions: colonialism for the new millennium?', *Organization*, 8(4): 711–750.

Banerjee, S.B. and Linstead, S. (2004) 'Masking subversion: neocolonial embeddedness in anthropological accounts of indigenous management', *Human Relations*, 57(2): 221–258.

Bennett, T., Grossberg, L., and Meaghan, M. (eds) (2005) *New Keywords: A Revised Vocabulary of Culture and Society*. Oxford: Blackwell.

Bennis, W.G. and O'Toole, J. (2005) 'How business schools lost their way', *Harvard Business Review*, 83(5): 96–105.

Blackmore, J. (1999) *Troubling Women: Feminism, Leadership and Educational Change*. Milton Keynes: Open University Press.

Blackmore, J. and Sachs, J. (2007) *Performing and Reforming Leaders: Gender, Educational Restructuring, and Organizational Change*. New York: State University of New York Press.

Blake, W. (1979) *Blake's Poetry and Designs*, M.L. Johnson and J.E. Grant (eds). New York: W.W. Norton.

Brient E. (2001) 'From vita contemplativa to vita activa: modern instrumentalization of theory and the problem of measure', *International Journal of Philosophical Studies*, 9(1):19–40.

Carlyle, T. (1904) *On Heroes and Hero-Worship and the Heroic in History*. London: Oxford University Press.

Case, P. and Gosling, J. (2007) 'Wisdom of the moment: premodern perspectives on organizational action', *Social Epistemology*, 21(2): 87–111.

Cassirer, E. (1946) *The Myth of the State*. New Haven, CT: Yale University Press.

Chia, R. (2003) 'From knowledge-creation to perfecting action: Tao, Basho and pure experience as the ultimate ground of performance', *Human Relations*, 56(8): 953–981.

Collingwood, R. (1994) *The Idea of History*. Oxford: Clarendon.

Drucker, P. (2001) 'Taking stock', *BizEd*, Nov–Dec: 13–17.

Duchon, D. and Plowman, D.A. (2005) 'Nurturing the spirit at work: impact on work unit performance', *The Leadership Quarterly*, 16: 807–833.

Fairholm, G.W. (1997) *Capturing the Heart of Leadership: Spirituality and Community in the New American Workplace*. Westport, CT: Greenwood Press.

Fairholm, G.W. (1998) *Perspectives on Leadership: From the Science of Management to its Spiritual Heart*. Westport, CT: Praeger.

Fairholm, G W. (2001) *Mastering Inner Leadership*. Westport, CT: Quorum.

Fiedler, F.E. (1967) *A Theory of Leadership Effectiveness*. New York: McGraw-Hill.

Ford, J. (2005) 'Examining leadership through critical feminist readings', *Journal of Health Organization and Management*. 19(3): 236–251.

Ford, J. (2006) 'Discourses of leadership: gender, identity and contradiction in a UK public sector organization', *Leadership*. 2(1): 77–99.

Ford, J. and Harding, N. (2007). 'Move over management: we are all leaders now?', *Management Learning*, 38(5): 475–493.

Foucault, M. (1970) *The Order of Things: An Archaeology of the Human Sciences*. London: Tavistock Publications.

Foucault, M. (1977) *Discipline and Punish: The Birth of the Prison*. London: Allen Lane.

French, R. and Grey, C. (1996) *Rethinking Management Education*. London: Sage.

Friedman, M. (1970) 'The social responsibility of business is to increase its profits', *New York Times Magazine*, September 13.

Frost, P.J. and Robinson, S. (1999) 'The toxic handler: organizational hero – and casualty', *Harvard Business Review*, 77(4): 96–107.

Fry, L.W. (2003) 'Toward a theory of spiritual leadership', *The Leadership Quarterly*, 14: 693–727.

Fry, L.W. (2004) 'Toward a theory of ethical and spiritual well-being, and corporate social responsibility through spiritual leadership'. In R. Giacalone and C. Jurkiewicz (eds), *Positive Psychology in Business Ethics and Corporate Responsibility*, pp. 47–83. Greenwich, CT: Information Age Publishing.

Fry, L.W., Vitucci, S., and Cedillo, M. (2005) 'Spiritual leadership and army transformation: theory, measurement, and establishing a baseline', *The Leadership Quarterly*, 16: 835–862.

Gallie, W.B. (1955/56) 'Essentially contested concepts', *Proceedings of the Aristotelian Society*, 56: 167–198.

Gemmill, G. and Oakley, J. (1992) 'Leadership: an alienating social myth'. *Human Relations*, 45(2): 13–29.

Grint, K. (2000) *The Arts of Leadership*. Oxford: Oxford University Press.

Grint, K. (2005) *Leadership: Limits and Possibilities*. Basingstoke, Hampshire: Palgrave Macmillan.

Grint, K. (2007) 'Learning to lead: can Aristotle help us to find the road to wisdom?', *Leadership*, 3(2): 231–246.

Hadot, P. (1995) *Philosophy as a Way of Life: Spiritual Exercises from Socrates to Foucault* (trans. Michael Chase). Oxford: Blackwell.

Hadot, P. (2002) *What is Ancient Philosophy?* (trans. Michael Chase). London: Harvard University Press.

Hadot, P. (2004) *The Inner Citadel: The Meditations of Marcus Aurelius*. London: Harvard University Press.

Hersey, P. and Blanchard, K.H. (1988) *Management and Organizational Behavior: Utilizing Human Resources*. Englewood Cliffs, NJ: Prentice Hall.

Hosking, D.M. (1988) 'Organizing, leadership and skilful process', *Journal of Management Studies*, 25(2): 147–166.

Hosking, D.M. (2001) 'Social construction as process: some new possibilities for research and development', *Concepts & Transformation*, 4(2): 117–132.

Huehn, M.P. (2008) 'Unenlightened economism: the antecedents of bad corporate governance and ethical decline', *Journal of Business Ethics*, 81: 823–835.

Jackson, B. and Parry, K. (2008) *A Very Short, Fairly Interesting and Reasonably Cheap Book about Studying Leadership*. London: Sage.

Jepson, D. (2009) 'Studying leadership at cross-country level: a critical analysis', *Leadership*, 5(1): 61–80.

Jones, A. (2005) 'The anthropology of leadership: culture and corporate leadership in the American South', *Leadership*, 1(3): 259–278.

Jones, A. (2006) 'Developing what? An anthropological look at the leadership development process', *Leadership*, 2(4): 481–498.

Jullien, F. (2004) *A Treatise on Efficacy*. Honolulu: University of Hawai'i Press.

Likert, R. (1961) *New Patterns of Management*. New York: McGraw-Hill.

Lyotard, J.-F. (1984) *The Postmodern Condition*. Manchester: Manchester University Press.

Kant, I. (1993 [1785]) *Grounding for the Metaphysics of Morals* (trans. by J.W. Ellington). Indianapolis/Cambridge: Hackett Publishing.

Kelemen, M. and Bansal, P. (2002) 'The conventions of management research and their relevance to management practice', *British Journal of Management*, 13: 97–108.

Knights, D. (2008) 'Myopic rhetorics: reflecting epistemologically and ethically on the demand for relevance in organizational and management research', *Academy of Management Learning and Education*, 7(4) 537–552.

Maccoby, M. (2004) 'Narcissistic leaders: the incredible pros, the inevitable cons', *Harvard Business Review*, 82(1): 92–101.

Mintzberg, H. (2004) *Managers Not MBAs*. London: Pearson Education.

Moore, G.E. (1903) *Principia Ethica*. Prometheus Books [online]. Available from http://fair-use.org/g-e-moore/principia-ethica/chapter-i [accessed 19 February 2009].

Morrell, K. (2007) 'Aesthetics and learning in Aristotle: a note on Grint's "learning to Lead"', *Leadership*, 3(4): 497–500.

Nikolaus, W. (2001) 'The good'. In E. Fahlbusch and G. Bromiley (eds), *The Encyclopedia of Christianity*. Grand Rapids, MI: Eerdmans Publishing.

Pfeffer, J. and Fong, C.T. (2002) 'The end of business schools? Less success than meets the eye', *Academy of Management Learning and Education*, 1(1): 78–95.

Pfeffer, J. and Fong, C.T. (2004) 'The business school "Business": some lessons from the US experience', *Journal of Management Studies*, 41(8): 1501–1520.

Pidgen, C. (ed.) (1999) *Russell on Ethics*. London: Routledge.

Pieper, J. (1999 [1952]) *Leisure. The Basis of Culture*. Indianapolis, IN: Liberty Fund.

Pieper, J. (2007 [1966]) *The Four Cardinal Virtues*. Notre Dame, IN: University of Notre Dame Press.

Price, T.L. (2005) *Understanding Ethical Failures in Leadership*. Cambridge, UK: Cambridge University Press.

Puwar, N. (2004) *Space Invaders: Race, Gender and Bodies Out of Place*. New York: Berg.

Sinclair, A. (2005) *Doing Leadership Differently: Gender, Power and Sexuality in a Changing Business Culture*, Carlton, Vic.: Melbourne University Press.

Stamp, G., Burridge, B., and Thomas, P. (2007) 'Strategic leadership: an exchange of letters', *Leadership*, 3(4): 479–496.

Stogdill, R.M. (1948) 'Personal factors associated with leadership', *Journal of Psychology*, 25: 35–71.

Stogdill, R.M. (1974) *Handbook of Leadership: A Survey of Theory and Research*. New York: Free Press.

Swan, E. (2006) 'Gendered leadership and management development: therapeutic cultures at work'. In D. McTavish and K. Miller (eds), *Women in Leadership and Management*. Cheltenham UK: Edward Elgar.

Tannenbaum, R. and Schmidt, W.H. (1958) 'How to choose a leadership pattern: should a manager be democratic or autocratic – or something in between?', *Harvard Business Review*, 37(Mar–Apr): 95–102.

Tourish, D. and Pinnington, A. (2002) 'Transformational leadership, corporate cultism and the spirituality paradigm', *Human Relations*, 55(2): 147–172.

Warner, L.S. and Grint, K. (2006) 'American Indian ways of leading and knowing', *Leadership*, 2(2): 225–244.

Weber, M. (1970 [1948]) *From Max Weber: Essays in Sociology* (trans. Hans Gerth and C. Wright Mills). London: Routledge & Kegan Paul.

Williams, R. (1983) *Keywords: a Vocabulary of Culture and Society*. London: Fontana.

Wittgenstein, L. (1972 [1953]) *Philosophical Investigations*. Oxford: Blackwell.

Wood, M. (2005) 'The fallacy of misplaced leadership', *Journal of Management Studies*, 42(6): 1101–1121.

Wood, M. (2008) 'Process philosophy'. In R. Thorpe and R. Holt (eds), *Dictionary of Qualitative Management Research*, pp. 171–173. London: Sage.

Wood M. and Ladkin, D. (2008) 'The event's the thing: brief encounters with the leaderful moment'. In K. Turnbull James and J. Collins (eds), *Leadership Perspectives: Knowledge Into Action*. Houndmills: Palgrave Macmillan.

Yukl, G. (2002) *Leadership in Organizations*, 5th edn. Englewood Cliffs, NJ: Prentice Hall.

19

Aesthetics and Leadership

Hans Hansen and Ralph Bathurst

INTRODUCTION

Leadership involves working with people to achieve personal and organizational goals, a process that initiates change and transformation. Other broad areas of inquiry into leadership characteristics, include appropriate and successful leadership behaviors, and relationships between leaders and followers. In focusing on change and transformation, and particularly on emancipation as a part of this process, we place our chapter in the stream of leadership that focuses on how leaders *move* an organization from one state to another. Movement, however, does not spring from mere intellectual assent, but rather is embodied in how organizational members act, and in the stories they tell (Sinclair, Chapter 37 and Fairhurst, Chapter 36, this volume). The focus of leadership is on how to develop and transform both people and the organization, and implies a kind of awakening that discards that which is no longer useful and assesses new and improved ways of looking at and acting in the world. Such awakenings and transformations require a kind of inspiration that goes beyond logical argument and supersedes entrenched forms of rationality and instrumentality that support the status quo. Large-scale transformation involves inspiring followers to move toward a future state without knowing the precise shape of that future.

Kuhn (1970) described the great efforts at which paradigm change takes place. People are socialized into a particular mindset, a way of thinking and practicing; and breaking free from that paradigm requires a leap of faith. Not only are there great incentives to remaining within a paradigm but also there are great risks to switching to a new paradigm and the switch to what, when the leap must be made, is often uncertain. Paradigm shifts can be equated with large-scale change, the domain of transformational leadership. Change in leadership, often rooted in Lewinian perspectives, entails movement from one state to another. In leading change efforts, the proposed future state is often unclear, and never as clear as the current state. Within that context of uncertain, large-scale transformational change, leaders are often left to compel change through strong feelings and emotions (Bass, 1985; Burns, 1978). These felt meanings lie precisely within the purview of aesthetics (Hansen, Ropo, and Sauer, 2007; Taylor and Hansen, 2005), and given the need for this awakening (see, for example, Kotter, 1996), it is surprising that leadership studies have not taken more of a critical approach, which has as its main aim the pursuit of organizational revitalization and transformation (Casey, 2002).

Our goal in this chapter is to discuss how leadership transformation might be informed by an aesthetic approach that springs from critical engagement. An aesthetic approach entails an exploration of sensory experience and sensemaking, and the felt meanings that are both produced by and guide our interactions and decisions. More parallel than equal to terms associated with the 'art of leadership,' aesthetic leadership explores these more tacit dimensions of leadership, such as the felt meanings. The tacit-level meanings of aesthetics influence our actions and behaviors. We act on, and 'go by,' these aesthetic meanings just as often as we are guided by ethical and instrumental understandings. The agenda underpinning critical studies is to understand power relationships and encourage emancipation from dominant or constraining power structures and worldviews. To this end, contemporary organizational aesthetics has introduced an alternative perspective to leadership studies involving the non-rational, felt meanings that pervade everyday organizational life and which form the basis of emancipatory efforts.

THE CASE FOR LEADERSHIP AND AESTHETICS

Leadership praxis, putting theory-into-practice, calls for a reflexive, artful mind that is able to work with complex and often paradoxical situations. In order to make it more accessible, leading has been reduced to a number of competencies that can be enhanced through education and mentoring. Elements like the so-called Big Five competencies of extroversion, agreeableness, conscientiousness, emotional stability and openness to experience form the basis for leadership development, and in spite of reservations about their validity (Hendricks and Payne, 2007), these elements form much of the essence of how leadership is traditionally understood. To this end, management and leadership education has tended to focus primarily on technical competencies and ethical practice in order to simplify and clarify organizational roles, in the hope that complexity can be reduced. Only recently, however, has the field considered a third element, that of aesthetics, as a way of dealing with the inevitable paradoxes that arise on a daily basis (Collinson, 2005).

In his explanation into why aesthetics has made its entry into organizational studies, Dobson (1999) claimed first that the traditional technical approach lacks a fundamental philosophical ability to grapple with paradox. In particular, the paradox that individual success is found in group cooperation and that self-interest is enhanced through team development is not easily articulated through focusing purely on leader competencies. Dobson argued that the technical focus lacks philosophical sophistication, which became profoundly evident during the latter part of the twentieth century with the inadequacy of business ethics to guard against corruption and fraud.

Symptomatic of the weaknesses of the bipartite technical–ethical approach is the flawed mantra, 'Good ethics is good business'. For Dobson, economic rationality as the basis for ethical practice leads inevitably to an impoverished morality that then justifies financial malpractice. What is required, says Dobson, is for an aesthetic turn where, along with their technical and ethical abilities, leaders are also equipped in the *arts* of leadership.

It is from this position that we explore the aesthetics of leadership. In doing so we are not eschewing other perspectives; rather, we maintain that in placing artistry alongside other paradigms,

leaders will be more open to the creative possibilities that the aesthetic dimension brings in its wake. While we acknowledge that instrumentalism in itself is an excellent measure of the overall leadership experience, there has been an over-reliance on psychological approaches in leadership research (Parry, 1998). Because of these roots, leadership studies have suffered from an inability to grapple with sensate responses that lie outside quantitative analyses (Hansen et al., 2007).

By acknowledging that decision-making involves more than pure rationality, the study of leadership has rightly turned to understanding the social processes that construct organizations. Moreover, these cannot be reduced to the measurement of psychological factors, traits, or behaviors. This inquiry into leadership qualities and how they are judged based on sense perceptions during the social influence process puts leadership squarely into the aesthetic realm. Therefore, the impressions and affects that visions have on followers, as well as what sense or judgments followers make of leadership qualities such as charisma, authenticity, and credibility, are all related to sensory knowledge based on their experiences of those phenomena: in short, the aesthetics of leadership.

Emotionality and leaps of judgment that inform decision-making augment rationality. In using more than rationality to make decisions, people bring their minds *and* bodies to work – emotions, feelings, and personal experiences that cannot be represented by purely rational models. Furthermore, leadership becomes most crucial in situations where rationality is difficult to apply. For example, in crisis leadership situations, there may be little data available or time to act, and it might be difficult to apply traditional rational decision-making models. Or, in the case of creative leadership and strategy, there may be no precedent. In these creative leadership situations, there may be no rational arguments to pursue novel or unique strategies.

Grint took up this agenda in his explorations into leadership prudence (Grint, 2007). Drawing on Aristotle's idea of wisdom, Grint claimed that technical knowledge (*episteme*) and skills (*techné*) are in themselves insufficient to ensure leadership prudence. Rather, what is required is practical wisdom (*phronesis*); 'something intimately bound up with lived *experience* rather than abstract reason' (Grint, 2007, p. 236, emphasis in the original). The kind of wisdom that comes through experience requires an adept aesthetician who is able to integrate emotion, intellect, and practical skills into their leadership (Küpers and Statler, 2008, p. 392). For a broader discussion of phronesis and organizational studies, see Cairns and Sliwa (2008).

In this chapter we discuss aesthetics and leadership by centering on three core ideas. First, we maintain that aesthetics compliments leadership in ways that are left undiscovered by an instrumental focus. Secondly, aesthetics opens new avenues for both leadership research and practice that allows us to conceptualize leadership in new ways. Finally, aesthetics offers some distinct methods that may foster organizational renewal in ways that link change efforts with emancipation.

DEFINING AESTHETICS

In sum, aesthetics refers to sensory knowledge and felt meaning in relation to objects and experiences, and is often associated with art. Because of art's representational form and its experiential nature, aesthetic engagement begins in the senses and generates a different type of knowledge. Art communicates in paralogical ways, giving meaning through expressions other than through logical means. These felt meanings are constructed as we attend to sensations that arise from experience. Rather than knowledge being created by a process of deduction such as in mathematics or other realist ways of knowing, aesthetic knowledge is drawn from life encounters. It guides action, and because of this, is difficult to codify. It is often compared to tacit knowledge (Taylor and Hansen, 2005), but it has its focus skewed toward knowledge drawn from sensory experiences that is then used to construct, represent, and interpret felt meanings.

Aesthetics offers a means of analysis that augments the traditional instrumental and managerial focuses (Guillet de Monthoux, Gustafsson, and Sjöstrand, 2007, p. 265) and liberates organizational actors from the constrictions of either/or dichotomies. Although establishing binary opposites may suit a leader's need to simplify and structure knowledge to be convincing and persuasive, it nonetheless limits the ability to discover nuances of meanings that emerge from overlapping and complex data (Tannen, 1998). To mitigate the trap of leaders thinking in oppositional polarities, Collinson (2005) advocated for a dialectic approach which incorporate opposites into a dynamic state, with each informing the other. Thus, as we attend to the dialectics inherent in the leadership field, we open space to explore 'ambiguous and potentially contradictory interrelations' (p. 1434). Taylor and Hansen (2005, p. 1226) suggested that such a shift represents a profound change in organizational analysis, making 'Aesthetic inquiry one of the most active movements within the postpositivist paradigm.'

Organizational studies, including leadership, have been preoccupied with instrumental approaches to effectiveness and efficiency. Postmodern and critical studies have offered critiques to this approach, but aesthetics offers a unique, competing field of study within the postpositive paradigm, beyond the much-needed critique of traditionally confined approaches.

This approach, though, is not exclusionary; rather, it draws on an ability to work with a number of sometimes disparate strands. Aesthetics embraces both technical rationality and reflexivity: an activist change-oriented stance coupled with a contemplative attitude. Aesthetics provides a way by which the instrumentality of *means* and the ethics of *ends* cohabit together under the rubric of *artful leadership*.

Thus, through Aristotle's notion of *phronesis*, leadership relies on a kind of practical wisdom that provides for deliberation and action at levels of both the universal and particular (Aristotle, 350 BCE/1968, Book VI § 7). The aesthetic project is, therefore, one that rests on the paradoxical cusp between polarities; instead of forcing an either/or binary position, it seeks the 'both–ands' of diversity (Hepburn, 2002, p. 27). Aesthetic leadership, then, is situated in the sometimes equivocal nature of organizational life and seeks to chart a course that values both the emotional (Witz, Warhurst, and Nickson, 2003) and cognitive (Singer, 2003, p. 3).

The philosopher Alexander Gottlieb Baumgarten (1714–1762) is considered the father of aesthetics and, along with Vico (1668–1744), he contended that knowledge was as much about feelings as it was about cognition. Baumgarten (1750) suggested that logic was the study of intellectual knowledge, while aesthetics was the study of sensory knowledge. He conceived that aesthetic inquiry was relevant to 'all the liberal arts and the practical activities of daily life' (Makkreel, 1996, p. 66) and rejected the idea that the search for knowledge is reducible to either a rational or a sensual quest. For Baumgarten, human beings are primarily aesthetic beings – 'felix aestheticus' (Gross, 2002, p. 404) – who are comfortable with complexity, and able to accommodate a diverse range of sometimes paradoxical and irreconcilable issues requiring both an alert mind and a responsive heart (for a full discussion see Bathurst, 2008).

The work of Baumgarten and Vico help mitigate the separation of the mind and body, a Cartesian duality privileged by the European Enlightenment's philosophy that ultimately positioned workers in the modern industrial enterprise as mere functionary cogs who were valued for their ability to pursue efficiency, to be used up as resources – human resources squeezed for the sake of one more unit of production. As opposed to the insistence that workers '*control* their time and emotions' (Barry and Hazen, 1996, p. 144, emphasis added), thereby avoiding bringing their personal responses and experiences to overflow into their work, aesthetics seeks to legitimatize peoples' felt experiences, enabling them to be at work as whole people: mind, body, and spirit. Aesthetic leadership would entail such development.

Aesthetic knowledge, then, involves sensuous perception in and through the whole person and is inseparable from our direct experience of being in the world (Dewey, 1934; Gagliardi, 1996). This notion that the felt meaning based on experience is just as important as cognitive understandings contrasts with Descartes' detached intellectual epistemology that marginalized embodied ways of knowing. The marginalization, where the mind (cognitions, intellect, and logic) was privileged as a source of knowledge is ironic because aesthetic experience shapes and precedes all other forms of knowledge (Husserl, 1960; Langer, 1942).

ORGANIZATIONAL AESTHETICS

Aesthetic inquiry in organizations has developed along two trajectories. One trajectory of work has focused on the core element of sense perception, while the other has been to translate philosophies of art into organizational practice and leadership in particular. Within the contemporary organizational context, one stream of aesthetics links notions of emotion (Hancock and Tyler, 2008) and embodiment (Küpers, 2004). Ontological questions regarding the nature of art and its relationship to organizational activity (Guillet de Monthoux, 2004) inform questions of how art itself is analogical to structural organizational issues (Barry, 1994; Dean, Ottensmeyer, and Ramirez, 1997; Kornberger and Clegg, 2003) and are investigations that illuminate and inform leadership theory.

Another broad stream focuses on aesthetics and art-based methods as processes for intervention and change (Darsø, 2004). Painting (Leveson, 2008), poetry (Darmer, 2006), drama (Vera and Crossan, 2004), dance (Picart and Gergen 2004), and music making (Hull, 2005) include some of the tools used by researchers and consultants to understand the changing nature of organizations and use these as means of intervention (Kunstler, 2001).

In this chapter we argue that an integration of both these poles allows for the strengths of both approaches to inform the aesthetics of leadership. By finding ways in which sense-perceptions can be expressed, and by exploring the structural

elements of aesthetic philosophy, a more complete version of leadership may be expressed.

While the aesthetic approach to organizations is a relatively new phenomenon, it can nonetheless be observed in mid-twentieth century commentaries. Seminal organizational theorist Chester Barnard (1968, p. 235; and cited in Vaill, 1989) claimed that management was 'aesthetic rather than logical' and better described by terms such as 'feeling, judgment, and sense.' Organizational theorist Edgar Schein, commenting on his 50 years of active research into organizations, noted that much of his work is artistic. He remarks that in the face of numerous conundrums he has observed as a consultant and academic over the course of his career, those engaged in organizational interventions 'need to trust their own *artistic impulse*' and that 'much of what we learn from experience remains tacit and can only be expressed artistically' (Schein, 2006, p. 299, emphasis in the original). In adding his voice to this coterie, Peter Drucker (1993) turned to music to articulate the contemporary need for leaders to embrace the arts, advising that organizations should become more 'like a jazz combo, which leadership within the team shifts with the specific assignment and is independent of the "rank" of each member.'

Ottensmeyer (1996) noted that though we consistently experience and refer to organizations in aesthetic terms, scholars have not traditionally approached them in this manner. Once we recognize that aesthetics involves the whole of our lives, and we allow aesthetic meaning to inform our behaviors, thoughts, and actions just as much as we rely on rational, logical, and instrumental reasoning, then we also recognize that this way of thinking can pervade the ways in which we function in work settings. Notwithstanding that this aesthetic approach is greatly underrepresented in organizational studies (Strati, 1999b), we all continue nonetheless to generate all kinds of meanings based on the sensory experience of our work lives, and aesthetics abounds in organizations, often outside the formal considerations of planning controlling and strategizing.

Antonio Strati (1992, 1999a) is perhaps the individual most responsible for introducing an aesthetic approach to organizational studies. He reminded us that the core of aesthetics – empathic knowledge, feelings, and intuition – once had a prominent place in management science (Weber, 1968). By returning to this forgotten path, Strati (1992) suggested that aesthetics can help redefine the nature of organizing, and offer new empowering criteria, apart from efficiency and economic rationality, by which organizations might be judged.

The aesthetics of organizing, such as the felt meanings that surround leadership interaction, are of profound importance because these sensations influence action and behavior and help interpret events and experience. For example, people often report that an uncomfortable conversation, independent of any content, left a 'bad taste in my mouth.' Here the metaphor of *taste* shows that conversations have a *feel* about them that spill over beyond the discourse. Similarly, leadership has this same feel beyond the actions taken. In general, this aesthetic perspective seeks to explore the everyday experience of organizing in terms of its social construction. Strati (1992) makes a detailed epistemological argument for aesthetic inquiry as a means of eliciting experiences and symbolic organizational forms that other more traditional methods leave unexamined. Strati's aim (1999a) is to centralize these aesthetic elements of organizational life, and further distinguish aesthetics as a way of knowing in contrast to pure rationality.

Like much of the post-positivist organizational paradigm, including critical theory, aesthetics has European origins (Ramírez and Arvidsson, 2005). However, organizational aesthetics is a fast-growing and quickly emerging coherent field that transcends organizational studies. For example, Ramírez (1991) describes how research can grasp the beauty of the organization as a whole. Gagliardi (1996) explored feelings toward artifacts that constitute the organization's symbolic landscape that are exercised at the emotional and aesthetic level rather than the normative and cognitive one. Linstead and Höpfl (1999) have advocated for the centrality of feeling and emotion to the aesthetics of organizing. In a critical approach to organizational aesthetics, Chua and Degeling (1993) applied aesthetics as a lens to critically assess managerial actions and, finally, there is a stream of research that does draw on aesthetics within critical management studies (c.f. Cairns, 2002; Dale and Burrell, 2002; Hancock, 2002).

EMANCIPATION: LEADERSHIP AND THE CRITICAL PROJECT

Emancipation is the main agenda of critical theory and, when applied to leadership, proceeds from the premise that a critical and reflective approach involves freeing individuals and groups from repressive social and ideological conditions, in particular those which constrain human development (Alvesson and Wilmott, 1992; Collinson, Chapter 13, this volume). Although critical theory seems at times overly pessimistic, emancipation can promise new opportunities. The critical project largely involves the questioning or deconstruction

of confining structures in order to free us from dominant viewpoints. Critical theorists were originally dedicated to changing institutions, and fundamental to this purpose was the liberation of people from restrictive traditions, ideologies, assumptions, and power relations (Alvesson and Wilmott, 1992; Ford, Harding, and Learmonth, 2008; Gagnon, 2008). In organizational settings, this may involve leading people to break out of some dominant way of thinking that is somehow holding them back, or encouraging them to see alternatives to the existing ways things are done. Within leadership, change or movement from one state to another implies breaking free from a particular way of doing to thinking, perhaps only realizing the need to do so in the face of a crisis. The aim of emancipation from dominant viewpoints is consistent with transformational or change leadership (Kotter, 1996). Indeed, Alvesson and Wilmott (1992) argued that any emancipatory change involves a process of critical self-reflection and self-transformation.

Another touchstone between critical theory's aim of emancipation and leadership is the notion of socially constructed realities. One necessary assumption for emancipatory efforts is that the social world is produced by its participants, so it is open to transformation (Alvesson and Wilmott, 1992). Things are the way they are because they were produced by us to be that way. Given that society is a human creation, there is optimism for the possibility of it being remade, perhaps in less oppressive ways. For example, we might recognize that the organizational reality we exist in now was constructed, and can be reconstructed to better serve democratic interests. Indeed, it is the very presence of such democratic principles that underlie the change process and involves self-emancipation (Grubbs, 2000).

By introducing the idea of social construction into the field, Meindl, Ehrlich, and Dukerich (1985) brought a new focus, showing how leaders are constructed and represented in the thought systems of followers. Similarly, Grint (2005) argues that, as a social construct, leading begins where there is no obvious solution to an organizational problem. The solution is worked out, constructed or reconstructed, within social interactions.

Organizational transformations involve breaking down the taken-for-granted assumptions by which we organize our lives, deconstructing them, and opening space for alternative constructs. We might expose some dominant constraining pattern of thinking, allowing us to institute a new vision for how we want to work. Although to date the critical approach to leadership is still underdeveloped, perhaps because of an inherent suspicion that many forms of leadership may turn towards domination and control, leadership practice may benefit from the light of a critical lens. Both call for breaking down conventional and constraining paradigms or ways of seeing. It begins with some awakening, a felt sense of crisis (Kotter, 1996) or a developing awareness of an imposing structure. The goal is to reveal underlying assumptions that restrain thinking: a revelation that provides an incentive to change the status quo.

THE ROLE OF AESTHETICS IN TRANSFORMATION AND EMANCIPATION

So where does aesthetics come into these transformational and emancipatory efforts? There is a confluence of conditions which comes into play. First, given the critical agenda of emancipation to free people from some dominating structure or way of seeing, there is the challenge of deconstructing the structure by participants operating within it, as well as the ability to apprehend or express the nature of the structure that oppresses them. We believe aesthetics offers not only an alternative and viable way to reveal and represent the dominant structure but also a way to call into question its underlying assumptions. Aesthetics also offers a way forward in proposing new possibilities and designs for living. To this end, this section synthesizes the critical and aesthetic approaches and brings them to leadership change and transformation efforts.

Fay (1987) noted that critical reflection and transformation are challenging because a person's cultural identity inhibits their capacity to exercise critical reasoning. For instance, just as it is hard for fish to see a world outside of water, so too it is difficult for organizational members to come to a realization that the current structure constrains rather than enables performance. While mired in the dominant way of thinking, it is all but impossible for us to conceive of alternates, and the ability to grapple with the problems that arise from imposed change initiatives is too daunting. It is no wonder that Kotter (1996) argued that change agents need to provoke a climate of crisis in order to incentivize transformational change. Aesthetic leadership assists in mitigating the destructive effects of such crises by awakening organizational members to the inhibiting elements of cultural identity before they become targets of change agents seeking sudden and revolutionary transformation.

For, our old methods of seeing and thinking cannot free us from our old structures and we are not likely to break out of metaphorical prisons with the same tools we used to build them. There is also the additional challenge of understanding

or even *sensing* the structures that oppress us. Hence Jermier (1998) argued that

> The people that critical theorists study may not be able to articulate the structural conditions responsible for their situation. They may not apprehend the larger structure, or they may apprehend it but have no words for it. (p. 240)

Aesthetics come in handy when there are no words. Because aesthetics begins with pre-articulate and often subliminal associations (Postrel, 2003, p. 6), the approach offers another way of representing and seeing that exposes existing dominant structures through non-discursive ways of seeing. When there are no words to express our situation, we may still find a representation in art and aesthetics, thereby helping us look at the structures that confine and oppress us. Simon Schama (2006) has illustrated this provocatively in his analysis of eight paintings from the historical canon, each which radically challenges political systems and ideologies of its time. For example, Schama discussed Picasso's *Guernica* mural painting in which Picasso dramatically responds to the annihilation by the German Luftwaffe on April 26, 1937 of the village which bears the same name (Bathurst and Edwards, 2009). This painting has been called the twentieth century's 'most iconic antiwar protest' (O'Donovan, 2007, p. 17) and represents the ability of art to stir us at a visceral level. This new kind of vision that aesthetics offers has its roots in classical antiquity's dramatic theater, especially in the way on-stage actors emotionally connected with the audience.

The centrality of the theater in ancient Greek life enabled a 'reflexive cathartic experience' (Lancaster, 1997, p. 76; Meisiek, 2004) that helped the audience to 'see the light.' This belief that an immediate sensate response could enable the audience to interpolate their life experience with the drama lies behind the root word 'aesthesis', which can be translated as 'sense perception' (Sorbom, 1994; Williams, 1983, p. 31). Therefore, within the Greek context, aesthetics involved both an immediate emotional, sensate reaction to the drama, and perceptual associations with daily existence.

Contemporary adaptations, such as using aesthetic judgment in trading in financial markets (Guve, 2007) and spontaneity in decision making (Adler, 2006), derive from an ability to intuitively respond by gut reactions (Sadler-Smith and Shefy, 2004) and make spontaneous judgment about whether something is pleasing or not. Whereas aesthetic judgment commonly concerns beauty, it also embraces the ugly, sublime, comic, or grotesque (Strati, 1992). Furthermore, although aesthetics commonly applies to art, it also involves sensory assessments of how we might feel about anything else, echoing Foucault's rhetorical question, 'Couldn't everyone's *life* become a work of art?' (Foucault, 1991, p. 350, emphasis added). Hence we can also consider emotional responses to an event, object, or personal interaction.

To explore this, Mitchell (1987) examined painting and argued that the educated perceiver is cognizant of these kinds of structural elements and that there is the 'artful planting of certain clues' (p. 41) placed there by the artist with which the perceiver can interact. The perceiver's role is to make coherent meaning of the evident, as well as the implied invisible elements within the work. Furthermore, Mitchell claimed paradoxically that 'we can never understand a picture unless we grasp the ways in which it shows what cannot be seen' (p. 39). Within a work of art, then, there are both explicit and implicit ideas that perceivers connect with in order to make sense of the piece. Therefore, Mitchell claimed, if 'the innocent eye is blind' and if our eye is not educated first, then we will not fully see, what is within the work (p. 38). By adopting this argument we maintain that emancipation occurs as people within organizations feel, see, and discern the dominating structures within their enterprise. This recognition of both evident and hidden elements in itself liberates people from the damaging effects of organizational life. To achieve this liberation Ford et al. (2008) concluded their critical analysis of leadership by arguing for a shift in the way that people are perceived. In their inimitable language they advocate for a '*revolution*...that people in organisations are ends in themselves rather than means to ends' (p. 171, emphasis added). This kind of dramatic change necessarily involves critiquing the power that is inherent in a leader's position and offering an alternative construct of *power-with* rather than *power-over*. This line of reasoning was argued by Follett (1924), where she adroitly tackled the problem of persuasion, which, she argued is often akin to coercion. Her notion of *power-with* challenges the idea that decisions are made from a stance of intimidation and bullying to one which encourages 'co-action' (p. 2000). Co-action necessitates that all actors within the organization, regardless of their status within the hierarchy, responsibly use their expertise for the common purpose. Hence power is realized when those in positions of authority renounce their dominance and allow it to emerge from the group's creative potential.

Another strategy that Alvesson and Willmott (1992) offered is micro-emancipation: looking for everyday 'loopholes' (p. 446) in the existing power systems we can take advantage of to help us get outside of the dominant system and critically assess it. Micro-emancipation focuses on concrete activities and the experiential, not only as a means of control but also as facilitators of resistance, and therefore, vehicles of liberation (see also Durant and Cashman, 2003).

In general, we propose two ways that we believe aesthetics can help lead transformational change. The first involves reflexivity and representation and considers surface structures represented in the way things are done within organizations. Aesthetic insights can lead change by exposing and representing things that we did not or could not previously see or for which we had no recognizable sensate response. Aesthetic representations reflect things we already have in among our structures such as culture and patterns or structures of work. We see how our structures could change to account for what we recognize in the aesthetic representation. For instance, a dramatic representation of the organization may assist in recognizing familiar yet dysfunctional features of work flows and service provision (see Meisiek, 2007). Aesthetic representation reflects some tacit knowledge that we hold, and by observing how it limits performance, we can refashion our structures in line with our felt responses. For example, Lindahl (2007) discussed the need for improvised responses in large construction projects, even when there is a defined structure in place. He claims that when undertaking these kinds of ventures, especially in heavily bureaucratized enterprises, 'the suspension of rules is of vital importance' and that leaders need to consider the 'oxymoronic notion of "expedient bureaucracy"' (p. 167). This amounts to aesthetically driven change in redeploying current structures in order to account for new meanings and experiences.

There is another use of aesthetic representation besides exposing flaws or loopholes in some current mindset or cognitive structure. Instead of focusing on driving change, an aesthetic representation may encourage reflections that demonstrate to us that we have already made a change. It will give us a felt sense of growth, learning, or movement that has already taken place, but one we had not hitherto recognized. Amin (2006) made this claim in his discussion of continuously changing urban spaces. He described the kind of emancipation that derives from 'a politics of small gains and fragile truces that constantly need to be worked at, but which can add up, with resonances capable of binding difference as well as reining in the powerful and the abusive' (p. 1012). This involves recognition that some transformation has taken place, but we were unaware of before reflection. In leadership terms, we might become aware that a shared vision has been achieved and that the enterprise has achieved synergy between its stated and realized goals. Hence, it is the moment of recognition itself that is emancipatory.

Aesthetics can also engender change by creating new concepts that become part of our deeper, guiding structures. There is an assumption related to any emancipation agenda that there is some underlying, hidden, or repressed way of thinking that can be emancipated from the domination of the current structure (Munro, 1997). For instance, by understanding the temporal context of the performing arts, leaders are better able to work proactively with fluidity and movement within structures. By using musical structure as an analogue in its constant oscillation between dissonance and consonance, leaders can recognize the benefits that periods of instability bring to the project of emancipation. In this way the aesthetics of 'rupture and affirmation' (O'Sullivan, 2006, p. 1) provide a frame to make sense of sometimes contradictory sensory experiences. Here we conceptualize these felt meanings and incorporate them into our mindset or structure, or perhaps the sensory experience causes us to reconstruct elements of our existing structure. Thus, we gain new perspectives on the process of organizational change and development beyond the linear approach that Kotter (1996) advocates.

For example, Barry (1994) discussed the results of leaders participating in developmental exercises where they were required to construct a paper model of their organization and then reconstruct an idealized model of their preferred structure. He wrote of their profound experience of realizing the disparities between their actual and preferred structures, an experience that was elicited by artful engagement. Similarly, Picart and Gergen (2004) highlighted the transformational moments that occur through reflecting on ballroom dancing and the insights that are provoked into how power is used and misused within organizations. In like vein, Nissley (2002) discussed the tradition of workers' songs as a means of achieving solidarity (see also El-Sawad and Korczynski, 2007). All these artful tools illustrate the potency of a gestalt perspective on change and development (Pucel, 2002) and provide for the conceptualization of fluidity and improvisation.

CONCLUSIONS: AESTHETIC INSIGHTS FOR LEADERSHIP

In this chapter we have focused primarily on the revelatory elements of aesthetics: that by being alert to our sense perceptions we are better placed to discern the ways in which structures control and inhibit a full range of human expression at work. There is, though, one further step in

the aesthetic journey – that of action. In this regard, O'Sullivan (2006) argued that aesthetics enables an encounter that disrupts our habitual ways of being in the world. Encounter challenges the constraints of convention and forces 'a cut, a crack' (p. 1) in the frame of certainty. Within this challenge is the promise of renewal; for, as O'Sullivan argues, 'the rupturing encounter also contains a moment of affirmation, the affirmation of a new world…a way of seeing and thinking this world differently' (p. 1). Thus the aesthetics of leadership opens possibility, for the kind of rupture that O'Sullivan advocated contains the creative seeds of organizational life free from the constraints of domination and control that are so often associated with dysfunctional leadership. Essentially, aesthetic engagement is about the movement which results from a 'trigger point' (O'Sullivan, 2006, p. 20) that springs from the insights we have gained from seeing things from new perspectives. It is this that enables the organization to be set on a new trajectory. Aesthetics ultimately ends in performance: 'what it does and what it makes us do, as well as its "knowledge producing" aspects' (O'Sullivan, 2006, p. 20).

Leadership happens within this relational dynamic of seeing and acting: it connects us with our own and others' sense perceptions. In doing so, aesthetics can change leadership relations, accounting not only for the instrumental or ethical but also the connection and the felt meaning central to that connection, between leaders and followers. To achieve this artfulness, leaders take into account the influence of the sublime, a subjectivity that embraces both the profound sense of angst and even ugliness alongside the quest for beauty. For, in the words of Burke (1787/1990), 'terror is in all cases whatsoever, either more openly or latently the ruling principle of the sublime' (p. 54).

Although our contemporary sensibilities are uncomfortable with the notion of terror, Burke's underlying proposal is that the beautiful relies on the acceptance of emotional turbulence within organizational life. Therefore, as leaders accept and even work with this instability, organizations may become artful places. This implies that by becoming aesthetically attuned, leaders turn from tasks to processes and work in such ways that the profound experiences of both the ugly and beautiful are accepted and become part of the organization's warp and weft.

By focusing on the dynamic processes of organizational life, leaders at all levels of the enterprise may become more keenly aware of the spaces between and within relationships. This line of research links with recent developments in exploring the implications of complexity theory to the field (Lichtenstein et al., 2006) and offers an exciting track for multidisciplinary research at the nexus of the science and art of leadership.

Another research stream is to return to one of the core elements of aesthetics: the nature of the sublime. By examining the aesthetic underpinnings of charismatic leadership (for example, see Ladkin, 2006), researchers open the possibilities of exploring how the beautiful and ugly impact on strategic developments within organizations. To this end, investigations into decision making and to the design processes that make a business beautiful offer a rich source of possibilities. In this turn from economic rationality to aesthetic sensibility, leadership research may lead the way in designing enterprises that are more closely aligned to creativity and innovation. Furthermore, for the quantitatively minded, measures of success may be developed that evaluate the degree of playfulness within an organization over the demands of the financial balance sheet and remuneration packages (Guillet de Monthoux, 2000).

In terms of leadership practice, aesthetic awareness may help guide change programs beyond the kinds of staged development championed by Kotter (1996). By exploring the complexities of time and fluidity, leaders may be better able to see beyond linearity to the qualitative elements of backward temporality (Moore, 1996) and anticipatory pre-sensing (Senge, Scharmer, Jaworski, and Flowers, 2004). Both these notions require an adept aesthetician with an ability to see organizational structures as being provisional and in constant flux.

If we assume there are some leaders more deft at managing aesthetic meanings, we might begin to explore what makes 'aesthetic leaders' successful. Perhaps aesthetic leaders are sensitive to the felt meaning in organization and are able to sense and discern different aesthetics that are operating, or that are called for, in various organizational contexts. Perhaps the need for change requires one type of aesthetic and crafting a vision requires a completely different aesthetic. These elements present opportunities for both researchers and practitioners to enlarge their repertoires of aesthetic capabilities.

From a follower-centric perspective on leadership, we might explore the aesthetic criteria used by followers to make aesthetic judgments about their leader. The question that drives this quest is how do followers make aesthetic judgments, such as whether they believe their leader is genuine or authentic (Gardner, Avolio, Luthans, May, and Walumbwa, 2005)? What sensory knowledge or feelings are they relying on to ascertain whether or not to follow a leader or whether their vision is compelling? Although we know that visionary and transformational leadership are dependent on the ability to inspire followers, how does aesthetics inspire in unique ways are that which leadership practice has not considered to date? To address this question we might focus on connections and creativity and on building strong, more deeply felt connections between leaders and followers.

In this chapter we have explored the aesthetics of leadership within its emancipatory frame. This positioning has been made even more salient by the scale of the crisis within the business community at the end of the first decade of the twenty-first century. By 2009 the collapse of the financial sector in North America and its disastrous effects across the globe felt like a tsunami. The numerous job losses that ensued across both hemispheres resulted in a loss of confidence in the way business has been conducted both by politicians and captains of industry. The aesthetics of leadership is an appropriate response as banks, nation-states, multinational corporations, and local firms seek to work together to recast the ways in which business is conducted.

Rather than advocating for strong leaders who can take charge, the aesthetic approach asks how we all might work in concert with chaos to create organizations free from the constraints of the domination and control of a few over the many. This aesthetic perspective in leadership offers tools with which to reconfigure our world of work to embrace the creative investment of all stakeholders and to take the field in promising new directions. Aesthetics makes sense.

REFERENCES

Adler, N. J. (2006). The arts and leadership: Now that we can do anything, what will we do? *Academy of Management Learning and Education*, 5(4), 486–499.

Alvesson, M. and Willmott, H. (1992). On the idea of emancipation in management and organization studies. *Academy of Management Review*, 17(3), 432–464.

Amin, A. (2006). The good city. *Urban Studies*, 43(5/6), 1009–1023.

Aristotle. (350 BCE/1968). *Nicomachean ethics*. London: William Heinemann.

Barnard, C. I. (1968). *The functions of the executive*. Cambridge, MA: Harvard University Press.

Barry, D. (1994). Making the invisible visible: using analogically-based methods to surface unconscious organizational processes. *Organization Development Journal*, 12(4), 37–48.

Barry, D. and Hazen, M. A. (1996). Do you take your body to work? In D. Boje, R. Gephart, and T. J. Thatchenkery (eds), *Postmodern management and organisation*. London: Sage, pp. 140–153.

Bass, B. M. (1985). *Leadership and performance beyond expectations*. New York: Free Press.

Bathurst, R. (2008). Enlivening management practice through aesthetic engagement: Vico, Baumgarten and Kant. *Philosophy of Management, 7*(3), 87–102.

Bathurst, R. J. and Edwards, M. F. (2009). Developing a sustainability consciousness through engagement with art. In J. A. F. Stoner and C. Wankel (eds), *Management education for global sustainability*. New York: Information Age Publishing, pp. 115–137.

Baumgarten, A. G. (1750/1961). *Aesthetica*. Hildesheim: G. Olms.

Burke, E. (1787/1990). *A philosophical enquiry into the origin of our ideas of the sublime and beautiful*. Oxford: Oxford University Press.

Burns, J. M. (1978). *Leadership*. New York: Harper and Row.

Cairns, G. (2002). Aesthetics, morality and power: design as espoused freedom and implicit control. *Human Relations, 55*(7), 799–820.

Cairns, G. and Sliwa, M. (2008). The implications of Aristotle's phronesis for organizational inquiry. In D. Barry and H. Hansen (eds), *New approaches in management and organization*. London: Sage, pp. 318–328.

Casey, C. (2002). *Critical analysis of organizations: theory, practice, revitalization*. London: Sage.

Chua, W.-F. and Degeling, P. (1993). Interrogating an accounting-based intervention on three axes: instrumental, moral and aesthetic. *Accounting, Organizations and Society, 18*(4), 291–318.

Collinson, D. (2005). Dialectics of leadership. *Human Relations, 58*(11), 1419–442.

Dale, K. and Burrell, G. (2002). An-aesthetics and architecture. *Tamara: Journal of Critical Postmodern Organization Science, 2*(1), 77–90.

Darmer, P. (2006). Poetry as a way to inspire (the management of) the research process. *Management Decision, 44*(4), 551–560.

Darsø, L. (2004). *Artful creation: learning-tales of arts-in-business*. Copenhagen: Samfundslitteratur.

Dean, J. W., Ottensmeyer, E., and Ramirez, R. (1997). An aesthetic perspective on organizations. In C. L. Cooper and S. E. Jackson (eds), *Creating tomorrow's organizations: a handbook for future research in organizational behaviour*. New York: John Wiley & Sons, pp. 419–437.

Dewey, J. (1934). *Art as experience*. New York: Capricorn.

Dobson, J. (1999). *The art of management and the aesthetic manager: the coming way of business*. Westport, CT: Quorum Books.

Drucker, P. F. (1993). Tomorrow's manager: more of an orchestra conductor than an administrator. *Success, 40*(8), 80.

Durant, R. A. and Cashman, J. F. (2003). Theorizing limits: an exploration of boundaries, learning, and emancipation. *Journal of Organizational Change Management, 16*(6), 650–665.

El-Sawad, A. and Korczynski, M. (2007). Management and music: the exceptional case of the IBM songbook. *Group and Organization Management, 32*(1), 79–108.

Fay, B. (1987). *Critical social science: liberation and its limits*. Cambridge: Polity Press.

Follett, M. P. (1924). *Creative experience*. New York: Longmans, Green and Co.

Ford, J., Harding, N., and Learmonth, M. (2008). *Leadership as identity: constructions and deconstructions*. New York: Palgrave Macmillan.

Foucault, M. (1991). On the genealogy of ethics: an overview of work in progress. In P. Rabinow (ed.), *The Foucault reader*. London: Penguin Books, pp. 340–372.

Gagliardi, P. (1996). Exploring the aesthetic side of organizational life. In S. R. Clegg, C. Hardy and W. R. Nord (eds), *Handbook of organization studies*. London: Sage, pp. 565–580.

Gagnon, S. (2008). Compelling identity: selves and insecurity in global, corporate management development. *Management Learning, 39*(4), 375–391.

Gardner, W. L., Avolio, B. J., Luthans, F., May, D. R., and Walumbwa, F. (2005). 'Can you see the real me?' A self-based model of authentic leader and follower development. *The Leadership Quarterly, 16*(3), 343–372.

Grint, K. (2005). Problems, problems, problems: the social construction of 'leadership'. *Human Relations, 58*(11), 1467–1494.

Grint, K. (2007). Learning to lead: Can Aristotle help us find the road to wisdom? *Leadership, 3*(2), 231–246.

Gross, S. W. (2002). The neglected programme of aesthetics. *British Journal of Aesthetics, 42*(4), 403–414.

Grubbs, J. (2000). Cultural imperialism: a critical theory of interorganizational change. *Journal of Organizational Change Management, 13*(3), 221–234.

Guillet de Monthoux, P. (2000). the art management of aesthetic organizing. In S. Linstead and H. Höpfl (eds), *The aesthetics of organization*. London: Sage, pp. 35–60.

Guillet de Monthoux, P. (2004). *The art firm: aesthetic management and metaphysical marketing*. Stanford, CA: Stanford University Press.

Guillet de Monthoux, P., Gustafsson, C., and Sjöstrand, S.-E. (2007). Aesthetic leadership and its triadic philosophy. In P. Guillet de Monthoux, C. Gustafsson, and S.-E. Sjöstrand (eds), *Aesthetic leadership: managing fields of flow in art and business*. London: Palgrave MacMillan, pp. 251–278.

Guve, B. G. (2007). Aesthetics of financial judgements: on risk capitalists' confidence. In P. Guillet de Monthoux, C. Gustafsson, and S.-E. Sjöstrand (eds), *Aesthetic leadership: managing fields of flow in art and business*. London: Palgrave MacMillan, pp. 128–140.

Hancock, P. (2002). Aestheticizing the world of organization: creating beautiful untrue things. *TAMARA: Journal of Critical Postmodern Organization Science, 2*(1), 91–105.

Hancock, P. and Tyler, M. (2008). It's all too beautiful: emotion and organization in the aesthetic economy. In S. Fineman (ed.), *The emotional organization: passions and power*. Malden, MA: Blackwell Publishing, pp. 202–216.

Hansen, H., Ropo, A., and Sauer, E. (2007). Aesthetic leadership. *The Leadership Quarterly, 18*(6), 544–560.

Hendricks, J. W. and Payne, S. C. (2007). Beyond the Big Five: leader goal orientation as a predictor of leadership effectiveness. *Human Performance, 20*(4), 317–343.

Hepburn, R. W. (2002). Data and theory in aesthetics: philosophical understanding and misunderstanding.

In A. Berleant (ed.), *Environment and the arts: perspectives on environmental aesthetics*. Aldershot: Ashgate, pp. 24–38.

Hull, A. (2005). Corporate team building. Retrieved 17 May 2005 from http://www.drumcircle.com/vmc/corporations/index.html

Husserl, E. (1960). *Cartesian meditations: an introduction to phenomenology* (D. Cairns, trans.). The Hague: Matinus Nijhoff.

Jermier, J. M. (1998). Introduction: critical perspectives on organizational control. *Administrative Science quarterly, 43*(2), 235–256.

Kornberger, M. and Clegg, S. (2003). The architecture of complexity. *Culture and Organization, 9*(2), 75–91.

Kotter, J. P. (1996). *Leading change.* Boston, MA: Harvard Business School Press.

Kuhn, T. S. (1970). *The structure of scientific revolutions,* 3rd edn. Chicago: University of Chicago Press.

Kunstler, B. (2001). Building a creative hothouse: strategies of history's most creative groups. *Futurist, 35*(1), 22–29.

Küpers, W. (2004). Arts and leadership. In G. R. Goethals, G. Sorenson, and J. M. Burns (eds), *Encyclopaedia of leadership.* Thousand Oaks, CA: Sage, pp. 47–54.

Küpers, W. and Statler, M. (2008). Practically wise leadership: toward an integral understanding. *Culture and Organization, 14*(4), 379–400.

Ladkin, D. (2006). The enchantment of the charismatic leader: charisma reconsidered as aesthetic encounter. *Leadership, 2*(2), 165–179.

Lancaster, K. (1997). When spectators become performers: contemporary performance-entertainments meet the needs of an 'unsettled' audience. *Journal of Popular Culture, 30*(4), 75–88.

Langer, S. K. (1942/1960). *Philosophy in a new key: a study in the symbolism of reason, rite, and art.* Cambridge, MA: Harvard University Press.

Leveson, V. (2008). Paint a picture of your workplace. *The New Zealand Herald,* August 20, p. E1.

Lichtenstein, B. B., Uhl-Bien, M., Marion, R., Seers, A., Orton, J. D., and Schreiber, C. (2006). Complexity leadership theory: an interactive perspective on leading in complex adaptive systems. *Emergence: Complexity and Organization, 8*(4), 2–12.

Lindahl, M. (2007). Engineering improvisation: the case of Wärtsilä. In P. Guillet de Monthoux, C. Gustafsson, and S.-E. Sjöstrand (eds), *Aesthetic leadership: managing fields of flow in art and business.* London: Palgrave MacMillan, pp. 155–169.

Linstead, S. and Höpfl, H. J. (eds). (1999). *The aesthetics of organization.* London: Sage.

Makkreel, R. A. (1994). The confluence of aesthetics and hermeneutics in Baumgarten, Meier, and Kant. *Journal of Aesthetics & Art Criticism, 54*(1), 65–76.

Meindl, J. R., Ehrlich, S. B., and Dukerich, J. M. (1985). The romance of leadership. *Administrative Science Quarterly, 30*(1), 78–102.

Meisiek, S. (2004). Which catharsis do they mean? Aristotle, Moreno, Boal and organization theatre. *Organization Studies, 25*(5), 797–816.

Meisiek, S. (2007). Dissonances, awareness and aesthetization: theatre in a home care organization. In P. Guillet de Monthoux, C. Gustafsson, and S.-E. Sjöstrand (eds), *Aesthetic leadership: managing fields of flow in art and business.* London: Palgrave MacMillan, pp. 173–194.

Mitchell, W. J. T. (1987). *Iconology: image, text, ideology.* Chicago, IL: University of Chicago Press.

Moore, F. C. T. (1996). *Bergson: thinking backwards.* Cambridge, UK: Cambridge University Press.

Munro, I. (1997). An exploration of three emancipatory themes within OR and systems thinking. *Journal of the Operational Research Society, 48*(6), 576–584.

Nissley, N. (2002). Tuning-in to organizational song as aesthetic discourse. *Culture and Organization, 8*(1), 51–68.

O'Donovan, L. J. (2007). Imagining our defeat: some 20th-century artists reflect on war. *America, 196*(6), 16–17.

O'Sullivan, S. (2006). *Art encounters Deleuze and Guattari: thought beyond representation.* New York: Palgrave Macmillan.

Ottensmeyer, E. J. (1996). Too strong to stop, too sweet to lose: aesthetics as a way to know organizations. *Organization, 3*(2), 189–194.

Parry, K. W. (1998). Grounded theory and social process: a new direction for leadership research. *The Leadership Quarterly, 9*(1), 85–105.

Picart, C. J. S. and Gergen, K. (2004). Dharma dancing: ballroom dancing and the relational order. *Qualitative Inquiry, 10*(6), 836–868.

Postrel, V. (2003). *The substance of style: how the rise of aesthetic value is remaking commerce, culture and consciousness.* New York: HarperCollins.

Pucel, R. (2002). Facilitating organizational change from a gestalt perspective. *Journal of Health Care Compliance, 4*(1), 18–22.

Ramirez, R. (1991). *The beauty of social organization.* Munich: Accedo.

Ramirez, R. and Arvidsson, N. (2005). Aesthetics of business in innovation: experiencing 'internal process' versus 'external jolts'. *Innovation: Management, Policy and Practice, 7*(4), 373–388.

Sadler-Smith, E. and Shefy, E. (2004). The intuitive executive: understanding and applying 'gut feel' in decision-making. *Academy of Management Executive, 18*(4), 76–91.

Schama, S. (2006). *The power of art.* New York: HarperCollins.

Schein, E. H. (2006). From brainwashing to organizational therapy: a conceptual and empirical journey in search of 'systemic' health and a general model of change dynamics. A drama in five acts. *Organization Studies, 27*(2), 287–301.

Senge, P., Scharmer, O., Jaworski, J., and Flowers, B. S. (2004). *Presence: human purpose in the field of the future.* Cambridge, MA: The Society for Organizational Learning.

Singer, A. E. (2003). *Aesthetic reason: artworks and the deliberative ethos.* University Park, PA: Pennsylvania State University Press.

Sorbom, G. (1994). Aristotle on music as representation. *Journal of Aesthetics and Art Criticism, 52*(1), 37–46.

Strati, A. (1992). Aesthetic understanding of organizational life. *Academy of Management Review, 17*(3), 568–581.

Strati, A. (1999a). *Organization and aesthetics.* London: Sage.

Strati, A. (1999b). The aesthetic approach in organization studies. In S. Linstead and H. Höpfl (eds), *The aesthetics of organization.* London: Sage, pp. 13–34.

Tannen, D. (1998). *The argument culture: moving from debate to dialogue.* New York: Random House.

Taylor, S. S. and Hansen, H. (2005). Finding form: looking at the field of organizational aesthetics. *Journal of Management Studies, 42*(6), 1211–1231.

Vaill, P. B. (1989). *Managing as a performing art: new ideas for a world of chaotic change.* San Francisco: Jossey-Bass.

Vera, D. and Crossan, M. (2004). Theatrical improvisation: lessons for organizations. *Organization Studies, 25*(5), 727–749.

Weber, M. (1968). *Economy and society: an outline of interpretive sociology* (E. Fischoff, trans.). New York: Bedminster Press.

Williams, R. (1983). *Keywords: a vocabulary of culture and society.* New York: Oxford University Press.

Witz, A., Warhurst, C., and Nickson, D. (2003). The labour of aesthetics and the aesthetics of organization. *Organization, 10*(1), 33–54.

PART IV

Psychological Perspectives

20

Predictors of Leadership: The Usual Suspects and the Suspect Traits

John Antonakis

INTRODUCTION

A major preoccupation of teams, organizations, and countries is to select leaders who will be effective. This issue is timeless and very important, given that leadership appears to matter much for organizational effectiveness, particularly at the highest echelons where leader discretionary power is high (Bertrand & Schoar, 2003; Finkelstein & Hambrick, 1990; Hambrick & Finkelstein, 1987; Hambrick & Mason, 1984; Jones & Olken, 2005; Lowe, Kroeck, & Sivasubramaniam, 1996; Denis et al., Chapter 6. this volume).

Plato was one of the first to write about the importance of leadership, its determinants, and its outcomes. In the *Republic* (Plato & Jowett, 1901), Plato acknowledged that individuals could not be successful in different types of vocations, and that innate characteristics – which predict effective leadership – were not equally distributed in the population. That is, he suggested 'we are not all alike; there are diversities of natures among us which are adapted to different occupations' (p. 50). Plato proposed job–fit leadership theory, arguing that the state must select 'natures which are fitted for the task' (p. 56). Plato went on to suggest that: 'There will be discovered to be some natures who ought to... be leaders in the State; and others who are not born to be [leaders], and are meant to be followers rather than leaders' (p. 175). He acknowledged that 'the selection [of leaders] will be no easy matter' (p. 56).

For Plato, individuals were not as rational as we would hope them to be, which oftentimes left to chance (or other specious factors) the selection of leaders. His allegory about the sailor who became captain because he was stronger and taller than the other sailors provides an example regarding the extent to which Plato thought the most able might not rise to power if the selection was left to individuals who did not have the appropriate expertise and rational faculties to undertake the selection. Indeed, the captain may have *seemed* to be better (because of his physical qualities); however, as mentioned by Plato, the captain 'is a little deaf, and has a similar infirmity in sight, and his knowledge of navigation is not much better' (Plato & Jowett, 1901, p. 190). Plato wanted to ensure that those who were appointed to power were the best qualified, both in terms of their abilities and training. He listed several traits he thought were essential for effective leadership.

The quest for traits that predict effective leadership continues today. Interestingly, I will come full circle and show that many of Plato's insights were remarkably concordant with current research. He identified aspects of intelligence and personality that were important for leadership, including 'courage, magnificence [i.e. having perseverance and fortitude], apprehension [i.e. referring to learning, perception, or intelligence], memory' (p. 193), 'skill in asking and answering' (p. 243); those that were the 'surest and the bravest, and, if possible... the fairest...having noble and generous tempers' (p. 243), 'keenness and ready powers of acquisition' [i.e. wise, clever] (p. 243) and who exhibited dialectical reasoning (which in this context referred to being logical in argument, showing critical inquiry and intelligence) (Plato & Jowett, 1901); (see The *Oxford English Dictionary Online*, 2000 for word definitions).

In this chapter, I discuss whether leadership (political or organizational) can be predicted by individual differences. Complicating my task, however, is the reality that research on individual differences in leadership has gone through peaks and troughs, as well as many fashions! The literature has also been bombarded by 'newly-discovered' traits, many of which are far from being newly discovered or are simply irrelevant or not very important for leadership and work outcomes. The proliferation of trait models has, unfortunately, muddied the literature; furthermore, legitimate constructs are being taken less seriously because of sensational yet unsubstantiated claims by some popular writers (e.g. Goleman, Boyatzis, & McKee, 2002) who have not scientifically tested their speculations or had their claims scrutinized in top peer-reviewed scientific journals.

I present individual-difference models that have stood the test of time and show that there are traits that predict leader success; the fact that these traits have been researched over a long period of time does not make them antiquated. In a way, these trait models are like aspirin: discovered many decades ago but still effective today. I define traits and discuss their antecedents. Next, I present what I refer to as an ascription–actuality trait theory of leadership to explain why some traits actually matter (objectively) for leadership effectiveness to the observer, whereas other traits appear to matter to the observer but objectively might not. I provide a historical overview of the literature to show how trait research fell in and out of (and then in again) favour of leadership scholars, and how methodologically sophisticated research approaches have engendered a renaissance in trait research. Then, I briefly discuss the criteria that researchers should use to sift through the field to select models that are valid. Finally, I review trait models that are the most predictive of leadership outcomes and identify those that are non-starters.

WHAT ARE TRAITS?

As with definitions of leadership, there are many definitions of traits. I will use one that will probably not upset too many differential psychologists. Briefly, traits are psychological

or biological characteristics that exhibit four essential properties. That is, *traits are individual characteristics that (a) are measurable, (b) vary across individuals, (c) exhibit temporal and situational stability, and (d) predict attitudes, decisions, or behaviours and consequently outcomes* (for discussion see Ashton, 2007; Chamorro-Premuzic, 2007; Kenrick & Funder, 1988). Of course, one has to have a theory, too, which explains why a trait (e.g. intelligence) predicts effective leadership.

The above definition seems simple; however, hidden behind it are very important implications concerning measurement, methodology, and social cognition. For the time being consider general intelligence as a trait (for further discussion see Gottfredson, 1997, 2002; Schmidt & Hunter, 1998, 2004) – briefly, general intelligence can be reliably measured with a variety of tests whose results converge; scores of a population of individuals vary on intelligence tests. Intelligence scores measured in different occasions and situations correlate and intelligence scores predict a number of outcomes (e.g. work performance or leadership). Given that intelligence is usually defined as the ability to learn (including information-processing, abstracting, and acquired knowledge), and because the cognitive demands required of leaders in terms of pattern recognition, abstraction, information retention, causal reasoning and the like are great, it is no wonder that intelligence predicts effectiveness. I will revisit intelligence later on.

Of course, there are important nomological issues, in which I will not get entangled for the purpose of this review. All factors are constructs invented by humans that are grouped together in a theory explaining a natural phenomenon. However, the fact that 'we name something... does not mean we understand it' (Cliff, 1983, p. 120). Cliff referred to this as the 'nominalistic fallacy.' For the purpose of this review, if traits – which are mostly genetically determined and thus can be considered as exogenous in a predictive model – predict an outcome, they have some economic utility for society, irrespective of whether we call a particular trait that we measure Jane, Onk, or intelligence. Thus, what matters most is how the trait is *operationalized* and what it predicts and not what the trait is called (though, of course, the conceptualization and description of the trait should follow previous conceptualizations and descriptions of similar things common to our language descriptions).

Note too that although traits do exhibit cross-situational consistency, we must also consider the extent to which one is 'given license' to express one's dispositions in certain situations. Psychologists have been taking the 'power of the situation' very seriously, particularly after the now well-known Milgram obedience studies were published (Milgram, 1963). Although some are sceptical that the Milgram experiments could not be reproduced today because experimental participants are more savvy (or perhaps more ethical and thus would not administer shocks to someone in a simple learning exercise), the Milgram experiment was recently replicated (Burger, 2009). This result attests to the fact that situations can greatly influence – and at times even constrain – the type of behaviour that is considered appropriate in a particular situation (see also Mischel, 1977). In a very simple and interesting study, Price and Bouffard (1974) showed that some situations inhibit the range of behaviours that individuals can demonstrate. For example, churches, job interviews, or lifts (elevators) are rather constraining situations (try belching or sleeping in one of those situations – this explains why I am an atheist who likes job stability and who usually take the stairs!). However, in a park, bar, or football game one can be more free to express one's desires. As an example of how situations specifically constrain behaviours, Barrick and Mount (1993) showed that traits interacted with job autonomy in predicting outcomes: extraversion predicted managerial performance only in situations where managers had high autonomy (discretion). However, the relation between extraversion and performance was much lower in situations where managers had low autonomy.

In another interesting example, which models a contextual factor and a mediation effect in a process theory, Lim and Ployhart (2004) found that transformational leadership mediated the effects of personality in a differential manner. That is, when the context was 'maximum' (i.e. where leaders are being observed and directly assessed), transformational leadership fully mediated the relation of traits to team outcomes and exhibited a stronger relationship to leader outcomes as compared to typical contexts (i.e. day-to-day). Unfortunately, though, studies such as these are exceptions (Antonakis, Avolio, & Sivasubramaniam, 2003; Antonakis, Schriesheim et al., 2004), leadership scholars have not considered context seriously enough in their theories (Liden & Antonakis, 2009). As House and Aditya (1997, p. 445) noted, 'It is almost as though leadership scholars… have believed that leader–follower relationships exist in a vacuum.' Thus, trait and process models should focus on identifying the contextual constraints that operate on the leadership phenomenon.

WHERE DO TRAITS COME FROM: NATURE OR NURTURE?

The biological basis of individual differences is indubitable and has a long history (Ashton, 2007;

Chamorro-Premuzic, 2007). Hippocrates, the founder of scientific medicine, suspected that emotions (as well as physical ailments) were affected by the balance among four bodily fluids: blood (influencing cheerfulness), phlegm (affecting calmness), black bile (impacting depression), and yellow bile (driving anger, courage, and hot temper) (Whiting, 2007). This was a revolutionary theory in a time when most were individuals believed that sickness (and of course their cures) were caused by gods (Whiting, 2007). This particular theory of Hippocrates was, of course, not quite right, though arguably more plausible than even a modern theocentric one! Interestingly, Hippocrates' theory was very influential well into the nineteenth century (Adler, 2004).

Nowadays, researchers have made many advances in explaining the biological bases of individual differences; basic sciences such as genetics, neuroscience, and endocrinology have proven to be very fruitful. I briefly review some findings showing the promise of this research, particularly in mixing psychometric and behavioural research with basic biological research. Although research based in biology might not have direct implication for the organizational sciences, it has helped to better understand psychometric variables. For example, research in neurosciences has identified that brain structure is influenced by genes (Thompson et al., 2001). More importantly, specific brain regions are reliably correlated with psychometric intelligence (Colom, Jung, & Haier, 2006; Jung & Haier, 2007; Thompson et al., 2001).

Research in behavioural genetics has also helped psychology advance in many areas. Genes play a crucial role in the long-term survival of organisms. On a broad level, genes affect the basic architecture of an organism (Dawkins, 1986) and its biological processes (Ilies, Arvey, & Bouchard, 2006). Genes, of course are not immutable; they do at times vary randomly and any adaptive evolutionary advantage that has occurred because of random variation will be systematically passed on to later generations (Dawkins, 1986).

Also, both the environment (including geographic factors) and genes play an important role in affecting individual differences – as Hippocrates had also supposed (Schwartz, 1999). For example, general intelligence, at the country level, is strongly linked to geographic factors (Kanazawa, 2008); however, it also has a strong individual genetic component (Bouchard & McGue, 2003; Thompson et al., 2001). Indeed, there is much research to suggest that individual differences, like personality and intelligence, have a strong hereditary basis (Bouchard & Loehlin, 2001; Bouchard & McGue, 2003). The heritability of personality is in the 50% range; that of intelligence is much higher, particularly in adulthood (Bouchard & McGue, 2003). An excellent review as to the implications of behavioural genetics in organizational behaviour is provided by Ilies et al. (2006).

As regards leadership, three recent studies have provided us with evidence that leadership emergence (Ilies, Gerhardt, & Le, 2004) and role occupancy, both in men and women, have a strong genetic basis (Arvey, Rotundo, Johnson, Zhang, & McGue, 2006; Arvey, Zhang, Avolio, & Krueger, 2007; Ilies et al., 2004). Of course, this research is very fundamental in nature and does not have immediate practical utility (unless a specific leadership 'gene' is identified). However, the fact that heritability estimates are large and partly mediated by psychological variables provides us with strong evidence that individual differences matter much for leadership.

Finally, research based on hormones is also slowly breaking into social science research. Hormones, which affect neurological functioning, are important regulators of behaviour (Ellison & Gray, 2009). However, only a few studies have examined the effects of hormones in organizational settings in ways that could be applied to leadership. Testosterone, for example, holds promise in predicting leadership because it is linked to dominance and thus social influence (see Gray & Campbell, 2009; Sellers, Mehl, & Josephs, 2007; Zyphur, Narayanan, Koh, & Koh, 2009). Testosterone has also been linked to status and risk-taking (which theoretically should predict leadership) and has high heritability; thus, it should be able to provide us with an important biological explanation of leadership (for nice discussions of application in organizational behaviour see Zyphur et al., 2009). Also, testosterone has been found to predict entrepreneurship (White, Thornhill, & Hampson, 2006, 2007), which is related but not synonymous with leadership (Antonakis & Autio, 2006). Interestingly, although testosterone is an endogenously governed hormone, it also reacts to situational influence (Wallen & Hasset, 2009). For example, men with high basal testosterone, who are thus are motivated to gain status, have positive endocrinological reactions following victory in a competition (i.e. had lower cortisol levels); however, their levels of cortisol increased following defeat (Mehta, Jones, & Josephs, 2008). Note, cortisol is considered a marker of stress and has been linked to biological as well as exogenous factors (Kudielka, Hellhammer, & Wust, 2009); it is known to interact with testosterone in predicting aggression (Popma et al., 2007). Interestingly, testosterone seems to affect behaviour in women and men in a similar way, particularly as concerns dominance (Grant & France, 2001;

Sellers et al., 2007); however, more research is needed in the area of sex differences.

In another fascinating study, researchers exogenously manipulated oxytocin a key hormone in the regulation of social attachment (Kosfeld, Heinrichs, Zak, Fischbacher, & Fehr, 2005). In this study, individuals played a sequential public-goods game, where cooperation between players increases the players' monetary payoffs. Individuals who were administered oxytocin demonstrated significantly higher trust by transferring more money to their interaction partner than a control group (who were given a placebo). These results have important practical implications for the functioning of social institutions and leadership.

As is evident, research at the nexus of biology and psychology should yield interesting and high-impact research; it is likely that leadership scholars will start venturing further into this very fertile research landscape. As mentioned by Zyphur et al. (2009) 'In order to remain on the cutting edge of social science scholarship, the field of management and organizational studies must now catch up with related disciplines that are pioneering the integration of their study with biology.'

ASCRIPTION–ACTUALITY TRAIT THEORY

In this section I introduce an integrative trait process theory as an organizing framework for the individual-difference variables I review in this chapter. With this framework, I describe how traits affect leader emergence and outcomes; however, I differentiate between traits that *really* matter for leadership and those that *seem* to matter. The reason for the latter occurrence is because observers have what we can refer to as 'folk theories' of leadership: i.e. observers might identify traits that vary (e.g. intelligence, facial appearance) and then attempt to link these constructs to real-world outcomes (e.g. effective leadership). At times, these correlations are valid. At other times, individuals see what can be termed 'illusory correlations' (Tversky & Kahneman, 1974) – correlations that are specious, but which the observers see as correlating intuitively with the outcome. As far as social cognition is concerned, these invalid correlations are found in a variety of situations and are explained by the availability heuristic, where individuals 'assess the frequency of a class or the probability of an event by the ease with which instances or occurrences can be brought to mind' (Tversky & Kahneman, 1974, p. 1127). That is, the easier it is to imagine a particular link, the more probable the link becomes in the observers mind's eye, particularly if the link is representative (i.e. apparently stereotypical/prototypical) of the supposed effect (refer to the representativeness heuristic of Tversky & Kahneman, 1974).

Thus, in this model, I explain two routes to leader outcomes: the actuality route and the ascription route. The actuality route explains why, objectively, a trait may actually contribute to leader effectiveness via skills (e.g. technical or social skills). The ascription route explains why, based on the representativeness heuristic, a trait allows a leader to emerge; however, this emergence will not guarantee that the leader is effective. That is, individuals emerge as leaders via the ascription route but will only be effective if (a) they possess the actual traits that predict effectiveness (but which were not identified in selection processes that led to emergence) or (b) the trait on which they were selected (e.g. height, see Figure 20.1) acts on the individual and observers in such a way that makes the individual more self-confident and thus more influential and effective. Finally, actual effectiveness, whether stemming from the leader or other sources, affects attributions of leadership skills because outcomes are attributed to leaders in cognitively consistent ways (Rush, Thomas, & Lord, 1977) as the representative heuristic would predict (Tversky & Kahneman, 1974; see also Calder, 1977): i.e. if the organization does well, observers assume that the leader (who is usually attributed responsibility of the outcome) possesses the necessary traits that drove the success (Figure 20.1).

Note also that a trait may matter for leadership but an individual with this trait might not emerge as a leader because the relation between the trait and outcome seems counterintuitive to observers.

For example, perhaps voters do not elect presidents who are very smart because voters believe these presidents are not 'in touch' enough with normal folk (thus, presidents would not be selected on intelligence but something else, such as appearance). We know from statistical theory that if US presidents were elected on intelligence the correlation between intelligence and presidential performance would be close to zero, because all presidents would have high intelligence: i.e. the restriction in range in intelligence would attenuate the true relationship between intelligence and presidential outcomes.

Data suggest that US presidents are not selected on intelligence because the zero-order correlation between intelligence and US presidential greatness is very strong; in fact, shockingly so: $r = 0.55$ (Simonton, 2002; disattenuated for measurement error, and assuming a reliability of 0.80 in an errors-in-variables regression model, the standardized regression coefficient is actually 0.69) – note, if presidents were selected on intelligence, the correlation between intelligence and greatness would be very low (due to the range restriction in intelligence). I calculated this correlation using Simonton's data where he modelled presidential greatness as a function of intelligence, years in office, war years in office, assassination, scandals, and being a war hero (note, controlling for these other factors Simonton reported the partial standardized regression coefficient of intelligence to be 0.29); however, this estimate is biased because number of years in office is endogenous and it depends on external factors like how good the president was and assassination. Removing this

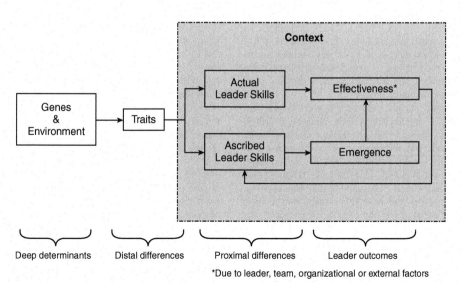

*Due to leader, team, organizational or external factors

Figure 20.1   The ascription–actuality trait theory of leadership

endogenous predictor from the model and re-estimating the regression equation increased the partial standardized beta coefficient to 0.41; when correcting for measurement error in the regression model, the partial standardized coefficient is actually 0.54!). The zero-order estimate of the relation of presidential intelligence and greatness is very similar to the estimate of the relation between intelligence and general work performance (between 0.51 and 0.62), and this increases with increasing job complexity (Salgado, Anderson, Moscoso, Bertua, & de Fruyt, 2003; Salgado, Anderson, Moscoso, Bertua, de Fruyt et al., 2003; Schmidt & Hunter, 1998).

It is also possible that a trait does not matter for leadership (i.e. it does not correlate with perform-ance), but the individual emerges as a leader because observers (and the leader) intuitively believe that this trait matters; these beliefs can then become self-fulfilling. Given that the data used by leadership researchers are usually perceptual measures, cognitive biases should be considered in theories regarding traits (Rush et al., 1977). The ascription route plays a very important role in situ-ations where the leader is distant (Antonakis & Atwater, 2002; Shamir, 1995) or in crisis situations (Hunt, Boal, & Dodge, 1999; Merolla, Ramos, & Zechmeister, 2007). Examples of ascribed traits could include facial appearance, height, body weight, race, age (or experience), and sex.

Consider facial appearance. In a social interaction process, the appearance of an individ-ual is one of the first variables to which an observer pays attention and observers automati-cally make trait inferences regarding this appear-ance (Hassin & Trope, 2000). Because there is variation in appearance that is intuitively (and stereotypically) linked to outcomes, individuals have categories of different kinds of leaders, as well as associated attributes (cf. Lord, Foti, & De Vader, 1984). Thus, if observers believe that a certain type of face is associated with leadership competence, they will endow the individual with the requisite characteristics.

Although this reasoning might seem far-fetched, Todorov, Mandisodza, Goren, and Hall (2005) recently showed that inferences of competence predicted leadership emergence in very high-stakes outcomes: actual political elections! Specifically, Todorov et al. (2005) showed naïve adults photos of two individuals (the winner and runner-up of an election race) and randomly varied the position (left or right) of the photos. They then asked par-ticipants to rate the competence, leadership, and intelligence of the two individuals. Surprisingly, participants were able to reliably select (i.e. better than chance) the winner of an actual election race; inferences of competence correlated ($r = 0.44$) with margin of victory and correctly predicted

about 70% of election outcomes. Note the adults could not identify the individuals in the photos (who were taken from congressional or senate election races). Interestingly, attractiveness did not predict election outcomes, probably because in this context what matters most is how competent an individuals looks. Also, in further variants of the experiment, the reliability of these snap judge-ments were equally valid even after exposing individuals to the photos for only 1 second!

The above results are astounding; however, they have been replicated with adults in other contexts (Antonakis & Dalgas, 2009). Even more surprising is that children exhibit the same uncanny ability to pick election winners from photos, even when these are from another country (Antonakis & Dalgas, 2009)! Given Plato's allegory of the blind–deaf–incompetent boat captain, it is ironic that the children in this experiment played a game based on 'The Odyssey' and then were asked to pick the 'captain of their boat' (i.e. for sailing from Troy to Ithaca). Interestingly, children's choices predicted outcomes just like in a control group of adults, and effects for adults and children were similar to those of the Todorov et al. (2005) study. These findings suggest that picking winners from pictures is a highly generalizable pheno-menon. Thus, voters, who we assume to be sophisticated and who should take their voting responsibilities seriously when choosing their political leaders, appear to be using irrelevant selection criteria just like children who have very little or no experience in voting and political lead-ership. That adults behave like children is proba-bly due to a biological face template and/or rapid early learning (Slater & Quinn, 2001), though the fact that infants can actually stereotype adults as well as other infants (Ramsey, Langlois, Hoss, Rubenstein, & Griffin, 2004; Van Duuren, Kendell-Scott, & Stark, 2003) tends to favour the nature (rather than 'nurture') argument. Whatever the case, these results support the workings of the ascription–actuality trait theory.

Height is another factor that could bias assessors. Briefly, as compared to shorter indi-viduals, taller individuals are accorded more status and might actually feel more efficacious (Judge & Cable, 2004). This finding provides a nice example showing how the ascription route goes back to the actuality route (i.e. height and esteem correlate 0.41), particularly because results from this meta-analysis also showed that height correlated with performance ($r = 0.18$), income ($r = 0.26$), and leader emergence ($r = 0.24$) (Judge & Cable, 2004). However, height could be a marker of intelligence or related to intelligence through common environmental and genetic com-ponents (Sundet, Tambs, Harris, Magnus, & Torjussen, 2005). Indeed, height is related, albeit very weakly, to intelligence, though this relation seems to be decreasing with time (see Sundet et al., 2005), probably due to environmental influences.

As for the other traits, two more that may affect leader outcomes are sex and age. Concerning sex, researchers have documented that women are disadvantaged by the fact that leadership is usually conceived of in terms of male stereotypical characteristics, making it difficult for a woman to emerge as a leader or to be evaluated favourably as a leader (Eagly & Carli, 2004). That there are fewer women in the higher echelons of power may stem from filtering mechanisms and self-limiting behaviours, particularly in contexts that are defined in male stereotypic terms (thus, the context here is a very important determinant of who emerges as a leader and how effective they may be seen). Interestingly, and paradoxically however, women have been rated as exhibiting more effective leader behaviours than men in business settings (Antonakis et al., 2003; Eagly, Johannesen-Schmidt, & van Engen, 2003); this finding is probably explained by the fact that only the most competent women made it through these discriminatory mechanisms (Eagly et al., 2003). Thus, the women's edge in leadership competence is a kind of survival-of-the-fittest phenomenon.

Finally, age is a strong proxy for work experience as well as managerial experience ($r = 0.53$; see Ostroff, Atwater, & Feinberg, 2004) – of course, managerial and leader practices are not isomorphic but they are strongly correlated (Tracey & Hinkin, 1998). Interestingly, although the relation between age and work experience is very strong, $r = 0.84$ (Antonakis, Angerfelt, & Liechti, 2009), neither age nor experience are related to leadership ability (Antonakis, 2007; Antonakis, Angerfelt et al., 2009). Individuals reasoning by representativeness (Tversky & Kahneman, 1974) assume, quite rationally, that older individuals are more experienced; however, they also assume that experience is related to effectiveness. For this reason, we probably observe that more experienced individuals are more likely to be appointed as leaders, particularly in high-level positions (e.g., a sample of more than 10,000 CEOs from large public firms indicated that the median age was 57 years; and the mean at the 10th percentile was 47 years; see Nelson, 2005). However, research findings show that experience is actually *negatively* related to leadership effectiveness (Fiedler, 1970); in fact, the Ostroff et al. (2004) study found that both age and managerial experience were negatively (albeit very weakly) related to managerial performance! Discussing his results, Fiedler (1970, p. 10) noted 'the belief that leadership experience enhances performance is ingrained and will not be easily shaken by "a few studies". Despite these findings, the experience (or age)–effectiveness link has been almost completely ignored by leadership researchers.

THE ROLLER-COASTER HISTORY OF TRAIT RESEARCH

Interest in leader traits began in the nineteenth century when the 'great man' theories emanated from studying shapers of history (Carlyle, 1846). Another example is the work of Galton (1869, p. 1), who suggested that ability is what makes individuals great and is 'derived by inheritance'. Early examples of systematic study of leader traits occurred in military settings. For example, characteristics such as physical qualities and intelligence, among others, were examined by Kohs and Irle (1920).

Research in traits was quite active from about the 1920s to the 1950s (Antonakis, Cianciolo, & Sternberg, 2004). Two influential reviews established that there were traits associated with leadership (Mann, 1959; Stogdill, 1948); however, traits soon fell out of fashion with leadership researchers because these studies gave conflicting signals about the results, which were consequently interpreted in a pessimistic way (Lord, De Vader, & Alliger, 1986; Zaccaro, Kemp, & Bader, 2004). Textbooks in industrial psychology and organizational behaviour made sweeping remarks about the inutility of leader trait research, and this obviously had a very negative impact on scholars and students. Also, for other reasons, research on leadership stagnated and there was not much hope for leadership as a discipline (Greene, 1977; McCall & Lombardo, 1978; Schriesheim & Kerr, 1977); there were even calls for a moratorium on research in leadership (Miner, 1975).

The early efforts to find traits associated with leadership were plagued with methodological errors (Zaccaro et al., 2004). Also, the appropriate statistical techniques (e.g. meta-analysis) were not available to synthesize the results of different studies. With more reliable instruments, better designs, and more sophisticated methods, the tables have turned on the sceptics. Three decades after the misinterpreted reviews of Mann (1959) and Stogdill (1948), leader individual differences returned to prominence on the leadership research radar. A meta-analysis reanalysed the Mann data and established that intelligence was, in fact, strongly linked to leader emergence (Lord et al., 1986).

Two other studies were also instrumental in demonstrating that variance unique to the individual (i.e. trait-based) was related to leadership

(Kenny & Zaccaro, 1983; Zaccaro, Foti, & Kenny, 1991). Specifically, using a rotation design (varying tasks and group members), Kenny and Zaccaro (1983) found that between 49% and 82% of the variance in leader emergence was attributed to the target leader. This result was replicated by Zaccaro et al. (1991), who found that 59% of the variance in the emergence of leadership was traceable to individual differences in leaders. In the meantime, another independent line of research led by McClelland (McClelland, 1975; McClelland & Burnham, 1976) and House (House, Spangler, & Woycke, 1991) established that implicit motives (i.e. subconscious drives or motivators) were linked to leadership effectiveness; however, this research line was not well known and had a limited effect on leadership research.

At this time, the study of traits is back in fashion (Antonakis et al., 2004; Lowe & Gardner, 2001; Zaccaro et al., 2004). One might say that research in leader individual differences is 'hot,' in fact too hot. That is, there is perhaps too much research being done in this area without appropriate tests to disentangle whether these new traits make a unique contribution in predicting leadership beyond current established traits; in psychology or other scientific fields, a shout of 'eureka' must be genuine (i.e. that one has truly found something new and different from the past that has practical utility). To better understand which traits matter, we need to have a clear sense of the criteria that should be used in determining whether the addition of a new trait is beneficial for leadership research, as I discuss below.

ON THE VALIDATION OF TRAITS MODELS

Before researchers can make claims that a particular trait model is predictive of leadership they must pit their trait against *tough* but *fair* competition. Analogously, one cannot claim to be a fast runner unless one beats runners who are considered to be fast or beats a specific benchmark in a particular distance; also, the rules of the race must be established such that one does not have an unfair advantage over the competition (e.g. making one runner run with a full rucksack). Thus, one cannot claim that a trait is somehow different and better than established traits if specific evidence is not provided to support these contentions by testing the new trait against tough competition in an open and honest way. For example, finding that a particular trait – which is supposed to be different from intelligence and personality – correlates with leader effectiveness is a useless and wasteful endeavour if in that particular study (or in previous studies) the researchers did not control for intelligence and personality.

In Table 20.1, I provide some brief guidelines that will be useful for readers when considering claims about the utility of certain trait models. I borrowed these guidelines from my previous writings (Antonakis, 2003, 2004, 2009; Antonakis, Ashkanasy, & Dasborough, 2009) to which readers should refer for details. In these works, I was rather critical about the very loose standards that some have used to prop-up 'newly-discovered' trait models. Note that the 10 steps I introduce below will ensure that strong deductions and clear interpretations can be made about the utility of a particular trait model. Also, I am not suggesting that a particular study must demonstrate evidence of all these steps in every publication – that would be an absurdly high standard to use. However, for a construct to be taken seriously, the collective literature (i.e. previous research on the construct) must show evidence that the construct has passed these steps, particularly Step 5 (the 'litmus' test).

The 10 steps in Table 20.1 are neither new nor are exorbitantly taxing to implement across a research field. Establishing construct legitimacy takes time and effort; science and practice will benefit only if research designs are strong.

TRAITS THAT MATTER: THE USUAL SUSPECTS!

There are dozens and dozens of traits that have been linked to leadership; unfortunately, many of them are not valid predictors. Only a few have endured and generated enough research that has been analysed meta-analytically. In this regard, I will be conservative and select models that have extensive histories behind them and enough data to allow us to make valid conclusions (i.e. examined meta-analytically and with evidence of having passed the necessary validation steps noted above).

The two major domains of traits that predict leadership are ability and personality, just as Plato suspected. One might ask: After more than 2,000 years is that the best we can do? At this point in time, this is the best we have. It has taken time to refine instruments to such a point that we can begin to predict leadership quite well. To put this point in context, many propositions stemming from thinkers in antiquity (e.g. Aristarchus's heliocentric theory of the solar system, Pythagoras's assertion that the earth was a sphere, Eratosthenes's estimation of the earth's circumference) were only confirmed in relatively recent times. Measuring latent constructs like personality

Table 20.1   Ten steps for validating trait measures

Ten steps for validation	Explanation
Type of validity	
1. Construct validity	Indictors of construct must be associated with constructs as specified by theory (tested using confirmatory factor analysis)
2. Criterion validity*	Target construct predicts an outcome
3. Discriminant validity*	Target construct does not overlap highly with theoretically distinct constructs
4. Convergent validity*	Target construct is related to theoretically similar constructs
5. Incremental validity*	Target construct predicts variance in outcomes while controlling for competing constructs (this is the 'litmus' test)
Design issues	
6. No leader self-reports	Do not use leader self-ratings to rate leadership (they are plagued by various biases related to protecting one's self-esteem); use observations of others
7. Avoid common-methods variance	Obtain leadership measures from one source (e.g. others) and leader individual differences (e.g. IQ) from leader
8. Use measures designed to tap constructs being studied	Do not pass-off measures of similar ('cousin') constructs as target construct
9. Use practicing leaders	To generalize to leaders, use data based on real leaders and not on students
10. Data and analysis	Have large samples, correctly specify model, and control for nestings (e.g. use multilevel-type fixed-effects or when justifiable random-effects models)

*these tests must account for measurement error, which biases coefficients and makes them (as well a coefficients of other independent variables) inconsistent

with instruments that are not as easy to measure as length has proven to be difficult; however, with modern psychometric theory and statistical methods, we have now made considerable advances. What is also needed are creative ideas about constructs that will predict incremental variance beyond the established constructs. As indicated elsewhere, we should be open to new conceptions of individual differences and how they are measured (Antonakis, Cianciolo et al., 2004); I look forward to seeing alternative individual-difference models proving their worth one day, as long as they have been tested thoroughly.

General intelligence

One of the traits that has stood the test of time and is strongly related to leadership is general intelligence. General intelligence or g reflects the ability to learn, to abstract, and to process information, and is the single most important predictor of work success (Gottfredson, 1997, 2002; Schmidt & Hunter, 1998, 2004). Also, g predicts performance in the US presidency and in jobs where complexity increases. Meta-analytic results show that it predicts leadership emergence ($r = 0.50$; Lord et al., 1986); also, when measured objectively (i.e. paper and pencil tests), g also predicts objective leadership effectiveness ($r = 0.33$; Judge, Colbert, & Ilies, 2004). Interestingly, the correlations between measures of perceived effectiveness and intelligence are much lower (apparently, observers are not very impressed with smart individuals; I hinted at this when discussing the ascription-actuality trait theory). These correlations are pretty impressive; currently, there are no other traits that have been examined meta-analytically that relate as strongly to leadership emergence and effectiveness.

Following the precepts of cognitive-resources theory, Judge et al. (2004) also showed that g predicted leadership outcomes in situations where leader stress was low but not when it was high. As noted elsewhere (Antonakis et al., 2009), this meta-analysis did not include the 13 samples of Fiedler and Link (1994) wherein stress, g, and their interaction predicted outcomes. Because methods to synthesize interaction effects for continuous measures are available (Kanetkar, Evans, Everell, Irving, & Millman, 1995) they could have been used in the meta-analysis by Judge et al. (2004). In fact, Fiedler and Link (1994) showed that in the majority of their samples, both IQ and stress had positive slopes and the interaction was positive too (see their Table 6.3), indicating that IQ had a positive slope in high-stress situations as well as in low-stress situations. In fact, the relation in high-stress situations is actually higher. Referring specifically to leader performance in situations with interpersonal stress, Fiedler (1995, p. 52) noted:

> Our studies do not support the hypothesis... that intelligence tests are not useful in predicting leadership performance in complex or intellectually demanding tasks. On the contrary... intelligence tests seem to predict performance somewhat better in intellectually demanding and complex tasks, than in simple or routine ones.

Finally, despite strong meta-analytic evidence for the importance of intelligence for leadership, some textbooks still do not highlight the importance of g for leadership (e.g. Yukl, 2006); reviews written by specialists in individual differences, however, (e.g. Spangler, House, & Palrecha, 2004; Zaccaro et al., 2004) strongly highlight the importance of intelligence and the fact that this construct has been given short shrift in the literature.

Personality: the big five

Recently, there has been a resurgence of research linking personality to work outcomes. This revival has occurred primarily because the previously fragmented ways of describing personality have been grouped around five big traits (see Digman, 1989; Goldberg, 1990), although some argue for six big traits (Lee & Ashton, 2004, 2008). I will focus on the big five model, which has a longer history and meta-analyses linked to leadership (though I am currently using the HEXACO big-six model in my work).

This reappearance of personality research in psychology is partly due to the research program of McCrae and Costa and their venerable NEO-PI (Costa & McCrae, 1992; Loehlin, McCrae, Costa, & John, 1998; McCrae & Costa, 1987, 1997). It is important to note that, apart from one factor (openness), which is modestly related to intelligence, the rest of the personality factors are mostly unrelated to intelligence (Goff & Ackerman, 1992) and thus are non-redundant when added to predictive models that include intelligence.

Below, I describe the five-factor model using the Costa and McCrae framework (1992). Note, correlation coefficients are meta-analytic ones based on results from Judge, Bono, Ilies, & Grehardt (2002). The first correlation refers to the correlation of personality with leader emergence and the second with leader effectiveness (underlined coefficients have 95% confidence intervals and 80% credibility intervals that exclude zero):

1. Neuroticism ($r = -0.24$ and $\underline{-0.22}$), which refers to anxiety, demonstration of anger, depression, self-consciousness, and vulnerability. Theoretically, leaders should have low levels of neuroticism.
2. Extraversion ($r = \underline{0.33}$ and $\underline{0.24}$), tapping warmth, gregariousness, assertiveness, being active and adventurous, and being positive. Theoretically, this factor should be the most important predictor of leadership.
3. Openness ($r = \underline{0.24}$ and $\underline{0.24}$), which includes imagination, being aesthetic, open to emotions, having many interests, curiosity, and unconventionality. Leaders should be forward-thinking and visionary; thus, this factor should be an important antecedent of leadership.
4. Agreeableness ($r = 0.05, 0.21$), whose facets include being trustful of others, being frank, soft-hearted, compliant, modest, and compassionate. Intuitively, leaders should be nice and empathetic; however, such types of individuals may find it difficult to take a stand on issues or to confront others.
5. Conscientiousness ($r = \underline{0.33}$, and 0.16), which includes self-confidence, orderliness, dependability, goal orientations, self-discipline, and being deliberative. We would expect successful leaders to be high on conscientiousness.

Note, given that the personality factors are correlated, it is important to predict leadership in a multivariate model (i.e. to examine the partial regression coefficients). As shown by Judge et al. (2002), together the big five predict leadership emergence well (multiple $R = 0.53$), with the following significant betas (standardized): extraversion (0.30), openness (0.21), agreeableness (−0.14), and conscientiousness (0.36). They also predict leadership effectiveness quite well (multiple $R = 0.39$), with the following significant betas (standardized): extraversion (0.18) and openness (0.19).

A second meta-analysis has linked the big five to transformational leadership (Bono & Judge, 2004); I am noting these results given that transformational leadership is currently the most researched leadership theory. Here are the correlations for direct measures of the big five, which are less strong than those noted above (underlined coefficients have 95% confidence intervals and 80% credibility intervals that exclude zero): neuroticism ($r = \underline{-0.16}$), extraversion ($r = \underline{0.23}$), openness ($r = \underline{0.09}$), agreeableness ($r = \underline{0.12}$), and conscientiousness ($r = \underline{0.11}$). I do not include the multivariate results because Bono and Judge did not report the partial coefficients of each of the factors.

Implicit motives

This model of personality is included with caution because, as yet, there has not been a meta-analysis examining its predictive validity for leadership. Implicit motives, which include need for power, affiliation, and achievement, as well as responsibility disposition, seem to be different from explicitly measured traits like the big five factors (Winter, John, Stewart, Klohnen, & Duncan, 1998). There is much research showing that high levels of need for power as well as low levels of affiliation and achievement are important antecedents of leadership (Antonakis & House, 2002; De Hoogh et al., 2005; House et al., 1991; Spangler & House, 1991; Winter et al., 1998). Research in this area should be consolidated meta-analytically to determine the population estimates. Given the strong effects so far, it is likely that this model passes the meta-analytic test.

THE SUSPECT TRAITS THAT DON'T SEEM TO MATTER MUCH (BASED ON CURRENT EVIDENCE)

As mentioned before, there are many traits that might seem to be useful, particularly to practitioners, but have not yet demonstrated utility when subjected to vigorous tests. I will highlight a few of these tests. Readers may refer to Zaccaro and Horn (2003) specifically regarding the science–practice divide and the reasons why the important traits are not taken as seriously as they should be by practitioners, whereas the ones that are more intuitively appealing are (see also Rynes, Colbert, & Brown, 2002).

Emotional intelligence

The trait of emotional intelligence (EI) has recently garnered much interest for practitioners; however, research using strong designs has not demonstrated that this trait is needed for leadership (i.e. following the steps of validation I noted above) (Antonakis et al., 2009). Zaccaro and Horn (2003, p. 779) had this to say about emotional intelligence (as well as the MBTI, see below):

> A common phenomenon and problem in leadership practice [and I would add research] concerns undue reliance on popular ideas and fads without sufficient consideration given to the validity of these ideas. Recent examples include the Myers–Briggs Type Indicator... and... emotional intelligence.

The only meta-analysis looking at the relationship between leadership (transformational) and emotional intelligence is that of Harms and Credé (2010); using non-common methods data, they estimated the relationship of emotional intelligence and leadership to only be 0.11 (and they did not control for the big five or intelligence, which would have certainly reduced the relation, see Antonakis, 2009).

A performance-related (including work performance) meta-analysis that has been conducted thus far on emotional intelligence is that of Van Rooy & Viswesvaran (2004). Granted, work performance and leadership are not the same thing; however, a measure that is purported to predict performance in various domains should predict work performance and leadership (as ability and personality tests currently do). Thus, it is informative to see how emotional intelligence does in predicting general and work performance. Results are not as stellar as its proponents would like it to be. The meta-analysis found that the well-respected Salovey–Mayer MEIS (Multifactor Emotional Intelligence Scale) correlated only 0.19 with performance, although self-report emotional intelligence measures had a slightly higher correlation (overall, emotional intelligence measures correlated 0.23 with work performance). Results for incremental validity were not encouraging:

> unlike with personality, EI did not evidence incremental validity over GMA. However, GMA did significantly predict performance beyond that explained by EI. Thus, the claims that EI can be a more important predictor than cognitive ability (e.g. Goleman, 1995) are apparently more rhetoric than fact. (Van Rooy & Viswesvaran, 2004, p. 87)

These results may be rather surprising; however, at this time and beyond these results there is *no evidence* that emotional intelligence matters much beyond general intelligence and personality for *leadership* (Antonakis, 2003, 2004, 2009; Antonakis et al., 2009). Emotional intelligence simply correlates too strongly with personality and/or cognitive ability (depending on the measure) and not enough with outcomes to demonstrate incremental validity e.g., see Antonakis & Dietz, in press a, b; Fiori & Antonakis, in press). Future research must focus on developing better instruments that are not linearly related to *g* and the big five before emotional intelligence can prove its worth.

Self-monitoring

A meta-analysis has established that self-monitoring is linked to leadership emergence, though the correlation is only 0.18 (Day, Schleicher, Unckless, & Hiller, 2002). This meta-analysis is limited because the authors did not control for the big five personality factors (which theoretically, may be strongly related to self-monitoring). Unfortunately, there is not much research that has examined the extent to which the full big five together (i.e. the multivariate effects) predict self-monitoring (while also correcting for measurement error). Thus, it is possible that self-monitoring might not demonstrate incremental validity over the big five. At this time, self-monitoring is at the same level as emotional intelligence in terms of not having demonstrated incremental validity, even though this construct has a longer history.

Myers–Briggs Type Indicator (MBTI)

The MBTI is enormously popular with practitioners. However, the psychometric properties of this instrument – which was not developed by psychometricians – have been strongly criticized (McCrae & Costa, 1989; Pittenger, 1993; Stricker & Ross, 1964), particularly regarding the apparent typology structure. As concerns leadership, results regarding links between the types and leadership are contradictory (Zaccaro et al., 2004) and there is no particular 'type' that is linked to leadership (Zaccaro & Horn, 2003). More rigorous research is required in this area before conclusions can be drawn (Gardner & Martinko, 1996).

THE SUSPECT TRAITS THAT DEFINITELY DON'T MATTER

I do not want to waste readers' time and valuable publishing space discussing constructs that are totally irrelevant; however, I do think it is worthwhile to briefly show how easy it is to sell models and methods that have not been validated. The Herrmann Brain Dominance Instrument (HBDI), which is a widely used tool, is believed to be useful for leadership. However, there is hardly any research testing this instrument and there no evidence for its validity (Ferrara & van Lingen, 2001). Another model, particularly popular with practitioners, is the DISC personality model, which is apparently based on the four Hippocratic types! I could not identify any research on this model, although plenty of claims about its validity are on the Internet. As with the HBDI, this model does not have the requisite research behind it to be used in industrial settings. There are probably hundreds of trait models that are marketed as leadership predictors (readers should search the web to see just how many models proliferate). There are also hundreds of methods or approaches like neuro-linguistic programming (NLP), whose proponents claim to be useful for predicting leadership or for developing leadership skills. Alas, NLP continues to persist in the world of practice, even though psychologists stopped taking this construct seriously a while back (Gelso & Fassinger, 1990; Sharpley, 1987).

THE STATISTICAL UTILITY OF TRAITS

Because traits are exogenous in predictive models (i.e. they depend on genes and are not caused by any other variables in the model), they have another very interesting property: they can ensure that coefficients of endogenous (mediator) variables are consistent in predicting a dependent variable; for an extensive discussion refer to Antonakis, Bendahan, Jacquart, and Lalive (2010). Estimates could be inconsistent for several reasons including: (a) common methods variance, (b) backward causality, (c) measurement error, or (d) omitted variables. Thus, an exogenous source of variance is needed to ensure that accurate estimates are obtained. For example, suppose one wished to examine whether leadership style predicts effectiveness. If there is a problem regarding the two variables because of any of the above reasons, one way to recover the consistent estimate is to model the following system of equations (while correlating cross-equation disturbances): g + big five $\rightarrow$ leadership style $\rightarrow$ effectiveness.

Note, estimates become inconsistent because the error term in the dependent variable may correlate with the endogenous variable (see Foster & McLanahan, 1996; Gennetian, Magnuson, & Morris, 2008; Kennedy, 2003). If the endogenous variable correlates with the error term, even with an increasing sample size, the estimate of the relation will not converge to the true estimate (i.e. it is inconsistent). Why? Because the ordinary least squares (OLS) or maximum likelihood (ML) estimators assume that the disturbance (i.e., error term) of the endogenous variable is orthogonal to the regressor. Thus, to satisfy the orthogonality assumption, the estimate of the regressor is changed accordingly (and becomes inconsistent). Two-equation or multi-equation models can be estimated using various estimators that will provide consistent estimates (if model assumptions are met): limited-information estimators (e.g. two-stage least squares (2SLS) regression – this estimator is also called the instrumental variable estimator or IV estimator); limited information maximum likelihood (LIML); or maximum likelihood (ML), which is considered a 'full information' estimator.

What these estimators do is rather straightforward; I will discuss their working in terms of the 2SLS estimator (the principle is slightly different with ML, though the outcome is similar if the model is correctly specified). Basically, the estimator ensures that the correlation between the error term in the dependent variable is unrelated to the endogenous regressor (thereby providing consistent estimates). The statistical 'trick' that is used by the estimator is to replace the troublesome regressor (i.e. the endogenous one that is correlated with the error term) with its predicted value (i.e. the first-stage estimate where the endogenous regressor is regressed on the exogenous variable/s). Given that the instrument, that is, the exogenous variable, hence the term 'instrumental variable regression', is exogenous, it will not correlate with the error term. If the instrument is not correlated with the error term, this procedure isolates the portion of variance in the endogenous variable stemming from the instrument that predicts the dependent variable (but which is unrelated to unmeasured or confounded effects). In other words, the endogenous regressor only affects the dependent variable through the instrument's effect on the endogenous regressor. For extensive discussion on this procedures refer to Antonakis et al. (in press).

CONCLUSIONS AND FUTURE DIRECTIONS

As I have discussed in my review, there are traits that are useful in predicting leadership; thus, these traits will be utile in selecting individuals who will most likely be seen as leader-like as well as more effective in positions of leadership. Using valid leader trait models has important economic implications (there are of course ethical implications too, which I will not get into).

A potentially useful area to look into is how configurations or sets of traits predict leader outcomes (Foti & Hauenstein, 2002; Smith & Foti, 1998) – research in this domain is underdeveloped, as is research using sophisticated latent variable models including latent class or latent profile analysis (see Nylund, Asparouhov, & Muthen, 2008). As I mentioned too, another very important use for trait models is that they can be used as exogenous sources of variance in two-stage or multi-equation models. Unfortunately, this is a very much underutilized technique in management and applied psychology settings, but one that is standard in econometrics and which could prove useful for leadership researchers (Antonakis et al., in press).

Also, to better understand the leadership phenomenon, leadership researchers must reach out to other disciplines that study leadership and individual differences or related areas. Top contenders for cross-disciplinary work that might engender paradigm shifts in our field include behavioural economics, neuroscience, behavioural endocrinology, and genetics.

In sum, more research is needed in what has been a fruitful area in leadership. Although there are models that do a reasonably good job at predicting leadership, research will obviously need to continue to sharpen measurement models and also to look for new, possibly multidisciplinary, models that might go beyond traditional theorizing and methodologies.

My hope is that this review will help to stimulate new ideas in what is a fascinating topic of research that has important societal implications. We need to better understand what make leaders great; we also need to better understand what makes them corrupt. The better we understand what predicts leader outcomes, the more likely we will improve society. As noted by Bennis (2004, p. 331), who has, over the decades, demonstrated remarkable perspicacity, "it is important to remember that the quality of all our lives is dependent on the quality of our leadership. The context in which we study leadership is very different from the context in which we study, say, astronomy. By definition, leaders wield power, and so we study them with the same self-interested intensity with which we study diabetes and other life-threatening diseases. Only when we understand leaders will we be able to control them".

REFERENCES

Adler, R. E. (2004). *Medical firsts: from Hippocrates to the human genome.* Hoboken, NJ: John Wiley & Sons.

Antonakis, J. (2003). Why 'emotional intelligence' does not predict leadership effectiveness: a comment on Prati, Douglas, Ferris, Ammeter, and Buckley. *International Journal of Organizational Analysis, 11*(4), 355–361.

Antonakis, J. (2004). On why 'emotional intelligence' will not predict leadership effectiveness beyond IQ or the 'big five': an extension and rejoinder. *Organizational Analysis, 12*(2), 171–182.

Antonakis, J. (2009). 'Emotional intelligence': What does it measure and does it matter for leadership? In G. B. Graen (ed.), *LMX leadership – game-changing designs: research-based tools,* (Vol. VII.). Greenwich, CT: Information Age Publishing, pp. 163–192.

Antonakis, J. Ashkanasy, N. M., & Dasborough, M. T. (2009). Does leadership need emotional intelligence? *The Leadership Quarterly, 20*(2), 247–261.

Antonakis, J. & Atwater, L. (2002). Leader distance: a review and a proposed theory. *The Leadership Quarterly, 13,* 673–704.

Antonakis, J. & Autio, E. (2006). Entrepreneurship and leadership. In J. R. Baum, M. Frese, & R. A. Baron (eds), *The psychology of entrepreneurship.* Mahwah, NJ: Lawrence Erlbaum, pp. 189–208.

Antonakis, J. Avolio, B. J., & Sivasubramaniam, N. (2003). Context and leadership: an examination of the nine-factor full-range leadership theory using the Multifactor Leadership Questionnaire. *The Leadership Quarterly, 14*(3), 261–295.

Antonakis, J., Bendahan, S., Jacquart, P., & Lalive, R. (2010). On making causal claims: a review and recommendations. *The Leadership Quarterly* , 21(6), 1086–1120.

Antonakis, J., Cianciolo, A. T., & Sternberg, R. J. (2004). Leadership: past, present, future. In J. Antonakis, A. T. Cianciolo, & R. J. Sternberg (eds), *The nature of leadership.* Thousand Oaks, CA: Sage, pp. 3–15.

Antonakis, J. & Dalgas, O. (2009). Predicting elections: child's play. *Science, 323*, 1183.

Antonakis, J., & Dietz, J. (in press-a). Looking for Validity or Testing It? The Perils of Stepwise Regression, Extreme-Scores Analysis, and Heteroscedasticity. http://dx.doi.org/10.1016/j.paid.2010.09.014.

Antonakis, J., & Dietz, J. (in press-b). More on Testing for Validity Instead of Looking for It. Personality and Individual Differences. http://dx.doi.org/10.1016/j.paid.2010.10.008.

Antonakis, J. & House, R. J. (2002). An analysis of the full-range leadership theory: the way forward. In B. J. Avolio & F. J. Yammarino (eds), *Transformational and charismatic leadership: the road ahead.* Amsterdam: JAI Press, pp. 3–34.

Antonakis, J., Schriesheim, C. A., Donovan, J. A., Gopalakrishna-Pillai, K., Pellegrini, E., & Rossomme, J. L. (2004). Methods for studying leadership. In J. Antonakis, A. T. Cianciolo, & R. J. Sternberg (eds), *The nature of leadership.* Thousand Oaks, CA: Sage, pp. 48–70.

Arvey, R. D., Rotundo, M., Johnson, W., Zhang, Z., & McGue, M. (2006). The determinants of leadership role occupancy: genetic and personality factors. *The Leadership Quarterly, 17*(1), 1–20.

Arvey, R. D., Zhang, Z., Avolio, B. J., & Krueger, R. F. (2007). Developmental and genetic determinants of leadership role occupancy among women. *Journal of Applied Psychology, 92*(3), 693–706.

Ashton, M. C. (2007). *Individual differences & personality.* Amsterdam & Boston, MA: Elsevier Academic Press.

Barrick, M. R. & Mount, M. K. (1993). Autonomy as a moderator of the relationships between the Big 5 personality dimensions and job-performance. *Journal of Applied Psychology, 78*(1), 111–18.

Bennis, W. (2004). The crucibles of authentic leadership. In J. Antonakis, A. T. Cianciolo, & R. J. Sternberg (eds), *The nature of leadership.* Thousand Oaks, CA: Sage, pp. 331–342.

Bertrand, M. & Schoar, A. (2003). Managing with style: the effect of managers on firm policies. *Quarterly Journal of Economics, 118*(4), 1169–1208.

Bono, J. E. & Judge, T. A. (2004). Personality and transformational and transactional leadership: a meta-analysis. *Journal of Applied Psychology, 89*(5), 901–910.

Bouchard, T. J. & Loehlin, J. C. (2001). Genes, evolution, and personality. *Behavior Genetics, 31*(3), 243–273.

Bouchard, T. J. & McGue, M. (2003). Genetic and environmental influences on human psychological differences. *Journal of Neurobiology, 54*(1), 4–45.

Burger, J. M. (2009). Replicating Milgram would people still obey today? *American Psychologist, 64*(1), 1–11.

Calder, B. J. (1977). An attribution theory of leadership. In B. M. Staw & G.R. Salancik (eds), *New directions in organizational behavior.* Chicago: St. Clair Press, pp. 179–204.

Carlyle, T. (1846). *On heroes, hero-worship, and the heroic in history.* New York: Wiley and Putnam.

Chamorro-Premuzic, T. (2007). *Personality and individual differences.* Malden, MA: BPS Blackwell.

Cliff, N. (1983). Some cautions concerning the application of causal modeling methods. *Multivariate Behavioral Research, 18*, 115–126.

Colom, R., Jung, R. E., & Haier, R. J. (2006). Distributed brain sites for the g-factor of intelligence. *Neuroimage, 31*(3), 1359–1365.

Costa, P. T. & McCrae, R. R. (1992). *NEO-PI professional manual.* Lutz, FL: Psychological Assessment Resources.

Dawkins, R. (1986). *The blind watchmaker.* New York: W. W. Norton.

Day, D. V., Schleicher, D. J., Unckless, A. L., & Hiller, N. J. (2002). Self-monitoring personality at work: a meta-analytic investigation of construct validity. *Journal of Applied Psychology, 89*(2), 390–401.

De Hoogh, A. H. B., Den Hartog, D. N., Koopman, P. L., et al. (2005). Leader motives, charismatic leadership, and subordinates› work attitude in the profit and voluntary sector. *The Leadership Quarterly, 16*(1), 17–38.

Digman, J. M. (1989). 5 robust trait dimensions – development, stability, and utility. *Journal of Personality, 57*(2), 195–214.

Eagly, A. H. & Carli, L. L. (2004). Women and men as leaders. In J. Antonakis, A. T. Cianciolo, & R. J. Sternberg (eds.), *The nature of leadership.* Thousand Oaks, CA: Sage, pp. 279–301.

Eagly, A. H., Johannesen-Schmidt, M. C., & van Engen, M. L. (2003). Transformational, transactional, and laissez-faire leadership styles: a meta-analysis comparing women and men. *Psychological Bulletin, 129*(4), 569–591.

Ellison, P. T. & Gray, P. B. (eds), (2009). *Endocrinology of social relationships.* Cambridge, MA: Harvard University Press.

Ferrara, F. F. & van Lingen, G. (2001). *Test review of the Herrmann Brain Dominance Instrument.* Retrieved 28 February 2009, from http://www.unl.edu/buros.

Fiedler, F. E. (1970). Leadership experience and leader performance – another hypothesis shot to hell. *Organizational Behavior and Human Performance, 5*(1), 1–14.

Fiedler, F. E. (1995). Cognitive resources and leadership performance – A rejoinder. *Applied Psychology – An International Review, 44*, 50–56.

Fiedler, F. E. & Link, T. G. (1994). Leader intelligence, interpersonal stress, and task performance. In R. J. Sternberg & R. K. Wagner (eds), *Mind in context: interactional perspectives on human intelligence.* Cambridge, UK: University of Cambridge, pp. 152–167.

Finkelstein, S. & Hambrick, D. C. (1990). Top-management-team tenure and organizational outcomes – the moderating role of managerial discretion. *Administrative Science Quarterly, 35*(3), 484–503.

Fiori, M., & Antonakis, J. (in press). The ability model of emotional intelligence: Searching for valid measures. Personality and Individual Differences. http://dx.doi.org/10.1016/j.paid.2010.10.010.

Foster, E. M. & McLanahan, S. (1996). An illustration of the use of Instrumental variables: do neighborhood conditions affect a young person's change of finishing high school? *Psychological Methods, 1*(3), 249–260.

Foti, R. J. & Hauenstein, N. M. A. (2002). Pattern and variable approaches in leadership emergence and effectiveness. *Journal of Applied Psychology 92*(2), 347–355.

Galton, F. (1869). *Hereditary genius: an inquiry into its laws and consequences*. London: Macmillan and Co.

Gardner, W. L. & Martinko, M. J. (1996). Using the Myers—Briggs type indicator to study managers: a literature review and research agenda. *Journal of Management, 22*(1), 45–83.

Gelso, C. J. & Fassinger, R. E. (1990). Counseling psychology – theory and research on interventions. *Annual Review of Psychology, 41*, 355–386.

Gennetian, L. A., Magnuson, K., & Morris, P. A. (2008). From statistical associations to causation: what developmentalists can learn from instrumental variables techniques coupled with experimental data. *Developmental Psychology, 44*(2), 381–394.

Goff, M. & Ackerman, P. L. (1992). Personality–intelligence relations: assessment of typical intellectual engagement. *Journal of Educational Psychology, 84*(4), 537–552.

Goldberg, L. R. (1990). An alternative description of personality – the big-5 factor structure. *Journal of Personality and Social Psychology, 59*(6), 1216–1229.

Goleman, D., Boyatzis, R. E., & McKee, A. (2002). *Primal leadership: realizing the power of emotional intelligence*. Boston, MA: Harvard Business School Press.

Gottfredson, L. S. (1997). Why *g* matters: the complexity of everyday life. *Intelligence, 24*(1), 79–132.

Gottfredson, L. S. (2002). Where and why *g* matters: not a mystery. *Human Performance, 15*(1/2), 25–46.

Grant, V. J. & France, J. T. (2001). Dominance and testosterone in women. *Biological Psychology, 58*(1), 41–47.

Gray, P. B. & Campbell, B. C. (2009). Human male testosterone, pair-bonding, and fatherhood. In P. T. Ellison & P. B. Gray (eds), *Endocrinology of social relationships*. Cambridge, MA: Harvard University Press, pp. 270–293.

Greene, C. N. (1977). Disenchantment with leadership research: some causes, recommendations, and alternative directions. . In J. G. Hunt & L. L. Larson (eds), *Leadership: the cutting edge*. Carbondale, IL: Southern Illinois University Press, pp. 57–67.

Hambrick, D. C. & Finkelstein, S. (1987). Managerial discretion – a bridge between polar views of organizational outcomes. *Research in Organizational Behavior, 9*, 369–406.

Hambrick, D. C. & Mason, P. A. (1984). Upper echelons – the organization as a reflection of its top managers. *Academy of Management Review, 9*(2), 193–206.

Harms, P. D. & Credé, M. (2010). Emotional Intelligence and Transformational and Transactional Leadership: A Meta-Analysis. *Journal of Leadership & Organizational Studies, 17*(1), 5–17.

Hassin, R. & Trope, Y. (2000). Facing faces: studies on the cognitive aspects of physiognomy. *Journal of Personality and Social Psychology, 78*(5), 837–852.

House, R. J. & Aditya, R. N. (1997). The social scientific study of leadership: quo vadis? *Journal of Management, 23*(3), 409–473.

House, R. J., Spangler, W. D., & Woycke, J. (1991). Personality and charisma and the U.S. presidency: a psychological theory of leader effectiveness. *Administrative Science Quarterly, 36*, 364–396.

Hunt, J. G., Boal, K. B., & Dodge, G. E. (1999). The effects of visionary and crisis-responsive charisma on followers: an experimental examination of two kinds of charismatic leadership. *The Leadership Quarterly, 10*(3), 423–448.

Ilies, R., Arvey, R. D., & Bouchard, T. J. (2006). Darwinism, behavioral genetics, and organizational behavior: a review and agenda for future research. *Journal of Organizational Behavior, 27*(2), 121–141.

Ilies, R., Gerhardt, M. W., & Le, H. (2004). Individual differences in leadership emergence: integrating meta-analytic findings and behavioral genetics estimates. *International Journal of Selection and Assessment, 12*(3), 207–219.

Jones, B. F. & Olken, B. A. (2005). Do leaders matter? National leadership and growth since World War II. *Quarterly Journal of Economics, 120*(3), 835–864.

Judge, T. A., Bono, J. E., Ilies, R., & Gerhardt, M. W. (2002). Personality and leadership: a qualitative and quantitative review. *Journal of Applied Psychology, 87*(4), 765–780.

Judge, T. A. & Cable, D. M. (2004). The effect of physical height on workplace success and income: preliminary test of a theoretical model. *Journal of Applied Psychology, 89*(3), 428–441.

Judge, T. A. Colbert, A. E., & Ilies, R. (2004). Intelligence and leadership: a quantitative review and test of theoretical propositions. *Journal of Applied Psychology, 89*(3), 542–552.

Jung, R. E. & Haier, R. J. (2007). The Parieto-Frontal Integration Theory (P-FIT) of intelligence: converging neuroimaging evidence. *Behavioral and Brain Sciences, 30*(2), 135–154.

Kanazawa, S. (2008). Temperature and evolutionary novelty as forces behind the evolution of general intelligence. *Intelligence, 36*(2), 99–108.

Kanetkar, V., Evans, M. G., Everell, S. A., Irving, D., & Millman, Z. (1995). The effect of scale changes on meta-analysis of multiplicative and main effects models. *Educational and Psychological Measurement, 55*(2), 206–224.

Kennedy, P. (2003). *A guide to econometrics*, 5th edn. Cambridge, MA: MIT Press.

Kenny, D. A. & Zaccaro, S. J. (1983). An estimate of variance due to traits in leadership. *Journal of Applied Psychology, 68*(4), 678–685.

Kenrick, D. T. & Funder, D. C. (1988). Profiting from controversy: lessons from the person-situation debate. *American Psychologist, 43*(1), 23–34.

Kohs, S. C. & Irle, K. W. (1920). Prophesying army promotion. *Journal of Applied Psychology, 4*(1), 73–87.

Kosfeld, M., Heinrichs, M., Zak, P. J., Fischbacher, U., & Fehr, E. (2005). Oxytocin increases trust in humans. *Nature, 435*(7042), 673–676.

Kudielka, B. M., Hellhammer, D. H., & Wust, S. (2009). Why do we respond so differently? Reviewing determinants of human salivary cortisol responses to challenge. *Psychoneuroendocrinology, 34*(1), 2–18.

Lee, K. & Ashton, M. C. (2004). Psychometric properties of the HEXACO Personality Inventory. *Multivariate Behavioral Research, 39*(2), 329–358.

Lee, K. & Ashton, M. C. (2008). The HEXACO Personality Factors in the indigenous personality lexicons of English and 11 other languages. *Journal of Personality, 76*(5), 1001–1053.

Liden, R. C. & Antonakis, J. (2009). Considering context in psychological leadership research. Human Relations, *62*(11), 1587–1605.

Lim, B. C. & Ployhart, R. E. (2004). Transformational leadership: relations to the five-factor model and team performance in typical and maximum contexts. *Journal of Applied Psychology, 89*(4), 610–621.

Loehlin, J. C., McCrae, R. R., Costa, P. T., & John, O. P. (1998). Heritabilities of common and measure-specific components of the big five personality factors. *Journal of Research in Personality, 32*(4), 431–453.

Lord, R. G., De Vader, C. L., & Alliger, G. M. (1986). A meta-analysis of the relation between personality traits and leadership perceptions: an application of validity generalization procedures. *Journal of Applied Psychology, 71*(3), 402-410.

Lord, R. G., Foti, R. J., & De Vader, C. L. (1984). A test of leadership categorization theory: internal structure, information processing, and leadership perceptions. *organizational Behavior and Human Performance, 34*, 343–378.

Lowe, K. B. & Gardner, W. L. (2001). Ten years of the The Leadership Quarterly: contributions and challenges for the future. *The Leadership Quarterly, 11*(4), 459–514.

Lowe, K. B., Kroeck, K. G., & Sivasubramaniam, N. (1996). Effectiveness correlates of transformational and transactional leadership: a meta-analytic review of the MLQ literature. *The Leadership Quarterly, 7*(3), 385–425.

Mann, R. D. (1959). A review of the relationship between personality and performance in small groups. *Psychological Bulletin, 56*(4), 241–270.

McCall, M. W. & Lombardo, M. M. E. (1978). *Leadership: Where else can we go?* Durham, NC: Duke University Press.

McClelland, D. C. (1975). *Power: the inner experience.* New York: Irvington Publishers, distributed by Halsted Press.

McClelland, D. C. & Burnham, D. H. (1976). Power is a great motivator. *Harvard Business Review, 54*(2), 100–110.

McCrae, R. R. & Costa, P. T. (1987). Validation of the 5-factor model of personality across instruments and observers. *Journal of Personality and Social Psychology, 52*(1), 81–90.

McCrae, R. R. & Costa, P. T. (1989). Reinterpreting the Myers–Briggs Type Indicator from the perspective of the 5-factor model of personality. *Journal of Personality, 57*(1), 17–40.

McCrae, R. R. & Costa, P. T. (1997). Personality trait structure as a human universal. *American Psychologist, 52*(5), 509–516.

Mehta, P. H., Jones, A. C., & Josephs, R. A. (2008). The social endocrinology of dominance: basal testosterone predicts cortisol changes and behavior following victory and defeat. *Journal of Personality and Social Psychology, 94*(6), 1078–1093.

Merolla, J. L., Ramos, J. M., & Zechmeister, E. J. (2007). Crisis, charisma, and consequences: evidence from the 2004 US Presidential election. *Journal of Politics, 69*(1), 30–42.

Milgram, S. (1963). Behavioral study of obedience. *Journal of Abnormal Psychology, 67*(4), 371–378.

Miner, J. B. (1975). The uncertain future of the leadership concept. An overview. In J. G. Hunt & L. L. Larson (eds), *leadership frontiers.* Kent, OH: Kent State University, pp. 197–208.

Mischel, W. (1977). The interaction of person and situation. In D. Magnusson & D. Endler (eds), *Personality at the crossroads: current issues in interactional psychology* . Hillsdale, NJ: Lawrence Erlbaum Associates, pp. 333–352.

Nelson, J. (2005). Corporate governance practices, CEO characteristics and firm performance. *Journal of Corporate Finance, 11*(1–2), 197–228.

Nylund, K. L., Asparouhov, T., & Muthen, B. O. (2008). Deciding on the number of classes in latent class analysis and growth mixture modeling: a Monte Carlo simulation study. *Structural Equation Modeling – a Multidisciplinary Journal, 15*(1), 182.

Ostroff, C., Atwater, L. E., & Feinberg, B. J. (2004). Understanding self–other agreement: a look at rater and ratee characteristics, context, and outcomes. *57*(2), 333–375.

Oxford English Dictionary Online (2000). Oxford: Oxford University Press.

Pittenger, D. J. (1993). The utility of the Myers–Briggs Type Indicator. *Review of Educational Research, 63*(4), 467–488.

Plato & Jowett, B. (1901). *The republic of Plato; an ideal commonwealth,* rev. edn. New York: The Colonial Press.

Popma, A., Vermeiren, R., Geluk, C., et al. (2007). Cortisol moderates the relationship between testosterone and aggression in delinquent male adolescents. *Biological Psychiatry, 61*(3), 405–411.

Price, R. H. & Bouffard, D. L. (1974). Behavioral appropriateness and situational constraint as dimensions of social behavior. *Journal of Personality and Social Psychology, 30*(4), 579–586.

Ramsey, J. L., Langlois, J. H., Hoss, R. A., Rubenstein, A. J., & Griffin, A. M. (2004). Origins of a stereotype: categorization of facial attractiveness by 6-month-old infants. *Developmental Science, 7*(2), 201–211.

Rush, M. C., Thomas, J. C., & Lord, R. G. (1977). Implicit leadership theory: a potential threat to the internal validity of leader behavior questionnaires. *Organizational Behavior and Human Performance, 20*, 93–110.

Rynes, S. L., Colbert, A. E., & Brown, K. G. (2002). HR professionals' beliefs about effective human resource practices: correspondence between research and practice. *Human Resource Management, 41*(2), 149–174.

Salgado, J. F., Anderson, N., Moscoso, S., Bertua, C., & de Fruyt, F. (2003). International validity generalization of

GMA and cognitive abilities: a European Community meta-analysis. *Personnel Psychology, 56.*

Salgado, J. F., Anderson, N., Moscoso, S., Bertua, C., de Fruyt, F., & Rolland, J. P. (2003). A meta-analytic study of general mental ability validity for different occupations in the European Community. *Journal of Applied Psychology, 88*(6).

Schmidt, F. L. & Hunter, J. E. (1996). The validity and utility of selection methods in personnel psychology: practical and theoretical implications of 85 years of research findings.

Schmidt, F. L. & Hunter, J. E. (1998). The validity and utility of selection methods in personnel psychology. *Psychological Bulletin, 124*(2), 262–274.

Schmidt, F. L. & Hunter, J. E. (2004). General Mental Ability in the world of work: occupational attainment and job performance. *Journal of Personality and Social Psychology, 86*(1), 162–173.

Schriesheim, C. A. & Kerr, S. (1977). Theories and measures of leadership: a critical appraisal of current and future directions. In J. G. Hunt & L. L. Larson (eds), *Leadership: the cutting edge.* Carbondale, IL: Southern Illinois University Press, pp. 9–45.

Schwartz, J. H. (1999). *Sudden origins: fossils, genes, and the emergence of species.* New York: Wiley.

Sellers, J. G., Mehl, M. R., & Josephs, R. A. (2007). Hormones and personality: testosterone as a marker of individual differences. *Journal of Research in Personality, 41*(1), 126–138.

Shamir, B. (1995). Social distance and charisma: theoretical notes and an exploratory study. *The Leadership Quarterly, 6*(1), 19–47.

Sharpley, C. F. (1987). Research findings on neurolinguistic programming—nonsupportive data or an untestable theory. *Journal of Counseling Psychology, 34*(1), 103–107.

Simonton, D. K. (2002). Intelligence and presidential greatness: equation replication using updated IQ estimates. *Advances in Psychology Research, 13*, 163–174.

Slater, A. & Quinn, P. C. (2001). Face recognition in the newborn infant. *Infant and Child Development, 10*(1–2), 21–24.

Smith, J. A. & Foti, R. J. (1998). A pattern approach to the study of leader emergence. *The Leadership Quarterly, 9*(2), 147–160.

Spangler, W. D. & House, R. J. (1991). Presidential effectiveness and the leadership motive profile. *Journal of Personality and Social Psychology, 60*(3).

Spangler, W. D. House, R. J., & Palrecha, R. (2004). Personality and leadership. In B. Schneider & D. B. Smith (eds), *Personality and organization.* Mahwah, NJ: Lawrence Erlbaum.

Stogdill, R. M. (1948). Personal factors associated with leadership: a survey of the literature. *Journal of Psychology, 25*, 35–71.

Stricker, L. J. & Ross, J. (1964). An assessment of some structural properties of the Jungian personality typology. *Journal of Abnormal and Social Psychology, 68*(1), 62–71.

Sundet, J. M., Tambs, K., Harris, J. R., Magnus, P., & Torjussen, T. M. (2005). Resolving the genetic and environmental

sources of the correlation between height and intelligence: a study of nearly 2600 Norwegian male twin pairs. *Twin Research and Human Genetics, 8*(4), 307–311.

Thompson, P. M., Cannon, T. D., Narr, K. L., et al. (2001). Genetic influences on brain structure. *Nature Neuroscience, 4*(12), 1253–1258.

Todorov, A. Mandisodza, A. N., Goren, A., & Hall, C. C. (2005). Inferences of competence from faces predict election outcomes. *Science, 308*(5728), 1623–1626.

Tversky, A. & Kahneman, D. (1974). Judgment under uncertainty: heuristics and biases. *Science, 185*(4157), 1124–1131.

Van Duuren, M., Kendell-Scott, L., & Stark, N. (2003). Early aesthetic choices: infant preferences for attractive premature infant faces. *International Journal of Behavioral Development, 27*(3), 212–219.

Van Rooy, D. L. & Viswesvaran, C. (2004). Emotional intelligence: a meta-analytic investigation of predictive validity and nomological net. *Journal of Vocational Behavior, 65*, 71–95.

Wallen, K. & Hasset, J. (2009). Neuroendocrine mechanisms underlying social relationships. In P. T. Ellison & P. B. Gray (eds), *Endocrinology of social relationship.* Cambridge, MA: Harvard University Press, pp. 32–53.

White, R. E., Thornhill, S., & Hampson, E. (2006). Entrepreneurs and evolutionary biology: the relationship between testosterone and new venture creation. *Organizational Behavior and Human Decision Processes, 100*(1), 21–34.

White, R. E., Thornhill, S., & Hampson, E. (2007). A biosocial model of entrepreneurship: the combined effects of nurture and nature. *28*, 451–466.

Whiting, J. (2007). *The life and times of Hippocrates.* Hockessin, DE: Mitchell Lane Publishers.

Winter, D. G., John, O. P., Stewart, A. J., Klohnen, E. C., & Duncan, L. E. (1998). Traits and motives: toward an integration of two traditions in personality research. *Psychological Review, 105*, 230–250.

Yukl, G. A. (2006). *Leadership in organizations*, 6th edn. Upper Saddle River, NJ: Pearson/Prentice Hall.

Zaccaro, S. J. Foti, R. J., & Kenny, D. A. (1991). Self-monitoring and trait-based variance in leadership: an investigation of leader flexibility across multiple group situations. *Journal of Applied Psychology, 76*(2), 308–315.

Zaccaro, S. J. & Horn, Z. N. J. (2003). Leadership theory and practice: fostering an effective symbiosis. *The Leadership Quarterly, 14*(6), 769–806.

Zaccaro, S. J., Kemp, C., & Bader, P. (2004). Leader traits and attributes. In J. Antonakis, A. T. Cianciolo, & R. J. Sternberg (eds), *The nature of leadership.* Thousand Oaks, CA: Sage, pp. 101–124.

Zyphur, M. J., Narayanan, J., Koh, G., & Koh, D. (2009). Testosterone-status mismatch lowers collective efficacy in groups: evidence from a slope-as-predictor multilevel structural equation model. *Organizational Behavior and Human Decision Processes, 110*(2), 70–79.

21

Contingency Theories of Effective Leadership

Gary Yukl

INTRODUCTION

Much of the early research on effective leadership reflects an implicit assumption that some leader traits (e.g., intelligence, assertiveness) or broadly-defined behaviors (e.g., task-oriented, relations-oriented, participative) are positively related to subordinate performance or satisfaction in all situations (Stogdill, 1974; Antonakis, Chapter 20, this volume). However, this research failed to provide strong support for universal conceptions of effective leadership. The lack of consistent results stimulated interest in developing 'contingency theories' that can explain why a different style of leadership is required in different situations. The early contingency theories include path-goal theory (House, 1967; House & Mitchell, 1974), situational leadership theory (Hersey & Blanchard, 1971), the LPC (least preferred co-worker) contingency model (Fiedler, 1967, 1971), leader substitutes theory (Kerr & Jermier, 1978), the normative decision model (Vroom & Jago,1988; Vroom & Yetton, 1973), cognitive resources theory (Fiedler & Garcia, 1987), and the multiple-linkage model (Yukl, 1981, 1989).

The purpose of this chapter is to describe and evaluate the early contingency theories and the empirical research on them. The first section of the chapter provides a general description of contingency theories and how they compare to universal theories of effective leadership. The second section describes the four types of behaviors used most often in the theories. The third section describes three types of situational influence that should be differentiated. In the fourth section each

of the early contingency theories is briefly described. Then conceptual limitations common to most of the theories are identified, the research findings are summarized, and limitations of the research are identified. The chapter ends with a general evaluation of the contingency approach and suggestions for developing stronger theories and designing better research.

GENERAL DESCRIPTION OF CONTINGENCY THEORIES

Contingency theories describe how aspects of the leadership situation alter a leader's influence on an individual subordinate or a work group. The independent variables in most contingency theories are leadership behaviors. The dependent variable is usually a measure of leadership effectiveness (e.g., subordinate satisfaction or performance, or team performance). The situational variables are conditions the leader cannot change in the short term, including characteristics of the work (e.g., task structure, role interdependence), characteristics of subordinates (e.g., needs, values), characteristics of the leader (expertise, interpersonal stress), and characteristics of the leadership position (leader authority, formal policies). Some contingency theories also include mediating variables to explain the influence of leader behavior and situational variables on performance outcomes. The mediators are usually subordinate characteristics that determine individual performance (e.g., role clarity, task skills, self-efficacy, task goals), but mediators can also include group-level characteristics that determine team performance (e.g., collective efficacy, cooperation, coordination of activities, resources).

A leadership theory can have both universal and contingency aspects, and the distinction between the two types of theories can be overstated. A universal theory that focuses on broadly defined leader behaviors can usually be improved by identifying aspects of the situation that determine how much leader influence is possible and which specific leader behaviors are most relevant for influencing the dependent variables. Even when a leadership theory is initially proposed as a universal theory, limiting and facilitating conditions are usually found in later research on the theory. An example is transformational leadership. According to Bass (1985, 1997), transformational behaviors enhance leadership effectiveness in all situations and cultures. However, researchers have identified some conditions that facilitate the effective use of transformational leadership or determine which transformational behaviors are most relevant for a particular type of situation (e.g., Hinkin & Tracey, 1999; Pawar & Eastman, 1997). Likewise, a contingency theory may include universal propositions about leadership behavior and skills. For example, the proposition that effective leadership in any situation requires the use of some task and relations behaviors appears to be valid.

LEADER BEHAVIORS IN CONTINGENCY THEORIES

Most contingency theories of effective leadership use broadly defined categories of behavior that were identified in the early research on leadership behavior (e.g., Fleishman, 1953; Halpin & Winer, 1957; Likert, 1961; Sims & Szilagyi, 1975; Yukl, 1971). These 'meta-categories' include task-oriented behavior, relations-oriented behavior, participative leadership, and contingent reward behavior. In this section each behavior is briefly described, and the contingency theories that include it are identified.

Task-oriented behavior

Task-oriented behavior is primarily concerned with accomplishing tasks in an efficient and reliable way. Common labels for this meta-category include 'initiating structure,' 'instrumental

leadership,' and 'directive leadership.' The specific component behaviors vary depending on the theory and measure, but examples include planning work activities, making work assignments, clarifying role expectations, explaining rules and policies, monitoring performance, coordinating activities, and solving work-related problems and disturbances. A broadly defined task-oriented behavior is included in path-goal theory, leadership substitutes theory, and situational leadership theory, and this type of behavior is implied (as a correlate of low LPC scores) in the LPC contingency model. Specific types of task-oriented behaviors are included in the multiple-linkage model.

Relations-oriented behavior

Relations-oriented behavior is primarily concerned with increasing mutual trust, cooperation, job satisfaction, cohesiveness, and organizational commitment. Common labels for this meta-category include 'consideration,' 'supportive leadership,' and 'employee-oriented leadership.' The specific component behaviors vary depending on the theory and measure, but examples include showing concern for the needs of subordinates, showing trust and acceptance, providing support and encouragement when a subordinate is upset or worried, keeping subordinates informed about changes that affect them, providing coaching and assistance when needed, providing career advice and mentoring, showing appreciation for subordinate achievements and contributions, and defending the welfare of subordinates. Relations-oriented behavior is included in path-goal theory, situational leadership theory, and leadership substitutes theory, and it is implied (as a correlate of high LPC scores) in the LPC contingency model. Several specific relations-oriented behaviors are included in the multiple-linkage model.

Participative leadership

Participative leadership is the extent to which a leader involves others in making decisions for which the leader has formal authority and responsibility. Specific decision procedures fall along a continuum from low to high empowerment (e.g., autocratic decision, consultation, joint decision, delegation). Leaders who frequently use empowering decision procedures are called 'participative' or 'democratic,' whereas leaders who seldom use them are called 'autocratic' or 'directive.' Aspects of participative leadership are included in path-goal theory, cognitive resources theory, and the multiple-linkage model. Specific decision procedures are included in the normative decision model, the multiple-linkage model, and in situational leadership theory.

Contingent reward behavior

Contingent reward behavior involves a leader's use of formal and informal rewards to influence subordinate motivation and satisfaction. Examples of specific behaviors in this meta-category include providing tangible rewards for effective performance (e.g., a pay increase, bonus, or promotion), explaining the organization's incentive system, and providing praise or recognition for effective behavior and important contributions to the team or organization. Other common terms for this type of behavior include 'recognizing and rewarding,' 'positive reward behavior,' and 'positive reinforcement.' This type of leadership behavior is explicitly included in the multiple-linkage model, in the extended version of leader substitutes theory (Podsakoff et al., 1993), and some versions of path-goal theory (House, 1996). Contingent reward behavior is also a component of transactional leadership (Bass, 1985).

Overlaps among behavior meta-categories

Although leader behavior meta-categories are implicitly assumed to be mutually exclusive, they usually have overlapping components that make interpretation of results more difficult. For example, 'directive leadership' involves a high level of task-oriented behavior in combination with a low level of participative leadership, because a very directive leader makes autocratic decisions about work procedures and job assignments. Relations-oriented behavior sometimes includes a participative decision procedure such as consulting with subordinates about decisions that will affect them. Some leader behaviors usually classified as relations-oriented can also include task-oriented objectives. For example, coaching can be used to improve someone's immediate performance (a task objective), to build skills relevant for the person's self-esteem and career advancement (a relations-oriented objective), or to achieve both types of objectives at the same time. Contingent reward behavior usually includes task-oriented behavior (rewarding good task performance) and supportive behavior (showing appreciation for

extra efforts and contributions). The leader's choice of a decision procedure may involve a task-oriented objective (improving decision quality) and a relations-oriented objective (increasing decision acceptance).

DIFFERENT CAUSAL EFFECTS FOR SITUATIONAL VARIABLES

The situational variables used in contingency theories can have different types of causal effects, and more than one type of effect can occur for the same situational variable (Howell, Dorfman, & Kerr, 1986; James & Brett, 1984; Yukl, 2010).

The situation directly affects the dependent variable

A situational variable is called a 'substitute' if it directly influences a dependent variable such as subordinate satisfaction or performance, or a mediating variable that determines these outcomes. If a substitute has a strong effect, it can reduce the potential direct effect of the leader on the dependent variable. An example is when prior training provided by the organization reduces the potential impact of clarifying and coaching on subordinate performance, because the subordinate already knows what to do and how to do it. In addition to influencing the dependent variable, a substitute can also influence leader behavior. When it is obvious to the leader that a specific type of behavior is redundant, the leader is less likely to use the behavior.

The situation moderates effects of leader behavior

A situational variable is called an 'enhancer' if it increases the effects of leader behavior on the dependent variable but does not directly influence the dependent variable. For example, coaching will have a stronger impact on subordinate performance when the leader has relevant expertise. This expertise enables the leader to provide better coaching, and subordinates are more likely to follow advice from a leader who is perceived to be an expert. An enhancer can also influence leader behavior, because the leader is more likely to use a behavior when it is perceived to be relevant and effective.

The situation directly influences leader behavior

A situational variable may directly influence a leader's behavior but not directly influence the dependent variable. Aspects of the situation such as formal rules, policies, role expectations, and organizational values can encourage or constrain a leader's behavior, and they are sometimes called 'demands' and 'constraints' (Stewart, 1976). In addition to the direct effect of the situation on leader behavior, there may be an indirect effect on dependent variables, and this indirect effect may be either positive or negative. For example, an organization's formal policies and the union contract may require the leader to base pay increases on accurate measures of individual performance, or to give the same pay increase to all subordinates regardless of individual performance. Compared to the second policy, the first policy allows a leader to have more influence on the extrinsic motivation of subordinates.

THE EARLY CONTINGENCY THEORIES

Table 21.1 lists the major features of the early contingency theories. The key independent variable in most of the theories is leadership behavior, and it is usually described in terms of broad meta-categories. Only the normative decision model and the multiple-linkage model have propositions for specific behaviors. The seven contingency theories differ with regard to the number and type of moderator variables they include. Three of the theories have explanatory mediating variables, but the other four theories do not explicitly include them. A theory is more complex and difficult to test if it includes many specific behaviors, mediating variables, and situational variables. Each contingency theory is described briefly.

Path-goal theory

The path-goal theory of leadership examines how aspects of leader behavior influence subordinate satisfaction and performance. Initial versions of the theory (Evans, 1970; House, 1971) included two behavior meta-categories (instrumental and supportive leadership). The theory was later refined and extended by various scholars (e.g., by Evans, 1974; House, 1996; House & Mitchell, 1974). The version by House and Mitchell (1974) added two more meta-categories (participative leadership and achievement-oriented leadership), but some confounding is evident among the four meta-categories. For example, achievement-oriented behavior includes some types of task-oriented behavior (setting challenging task goals, emphasizing excellence in performance) and

Table 21.1   Contingency theories of effective leadership behavior

Contingency theory	Independent variables	Situational variables	Explanatory mediating variables
Path-goal theory	Instrumental, supportive, achievement-oriented, and participative leadership	Attributes of the task and the subordinates	Role ambiguity, outcome expectancies, and valences
Situational leadership theory	Task and relations behavior (and decision procedures)	Subordinate maturity in relation to the task	None
Leadership substitutes theory	Instrumental and supportive leadership	Attributes of the task, group, and organization	None
LPC contingency model	Leader LPC	Position power, task structure, and leader–member relations	None
Normative decision model	Specific decision procedures	Leader and member knowledge, goal congruence, importance of quality, and acceptance	Decision quality and decision acceptance
Cognitive resources theory	Participative leadership; leader IQ and experience	Interpersonal stress and member knowledge	Vague and incomplete
Multiple linkage model	Many specific behaviors	Attributes of the task, group, and organization	Several determinants of individual and group performance

Based on Yukl (2010).

some types of supportive behavior (expressing confidence that subordinates can achieve high performance). The most recent revision (House, 1996) added more propositions and attempted to clarify the key behaviors.

The expectancy theory of motivation is used to explain how leaders influence subordinate performance, and most of the mediating variables are based on that theory. In general, leaders motivate subordinates by influencing their perceptions about the likely consequences of different levels of effort. Subordinates will perform better when they have clear and accurate role expectations, they perceive that a high level of effort is necessary to attain task objectives, they are optimistic that it is possible to achieve the task objectives, and they perceive that high performance will result in beneficial outcomes.

The situational variables include task and subordinate characteristics that moderate the effects of leader behavior on subordinate satisfaction and performance. One key proposition is that a leader's directive and achievement-oriented behavior has a stronger effect on role clarity, self-efficacy, effort, and performance when subordinates are inexperienced and unsure about how to do their work. Another key proposition is that supportive leadership will have a stronger effect on subordinate confidence, effort, and satisfaction when the task is very tedious, dangerous, and stressful.

Situational leadership theory

Hersey and Blanchard (1971) proposed a contingency theory that specifies the appropriate type of leadership behavior for each subordinate. Behavior was defined in terms of directive and supportive leadership, and a revised version of the theory also included decision procedures (Blanchard, Zigarmi, & Nelson, 1993; Graef, 1997). The situational variable is subordinate maturity, which includes the person's ability and confidence to do a task. As the maturity of a subordinate increases, less directive leadership is necessary. However, for supportive leadership, the moderating effect of subordinate maturity is more complex; there is an inverted U-shaped curve between this leader behavior and subordinate performance as maturity increases.

According to the theory, for low-maturity subordinates, the leader should use extensive directive behavior (including autocratic decisions) and limited supportive behavior. For subordinates with a moderate level of maturity, the appropriate pattern of behavior is a moderate amount of directive and supportive behavior. For high-maturity subordinates, the leader should use a limited amount of directive and supportive behavior and substantial delegation. The primary focus of the model is on short-term behavior, but over time the leader may be able to increase subordinate maturity with a developmental intervention that builds the subordinate's skills and confidence.

Leadership substitutes theory

Kerr and Jermier (1978) identified aspects of the situation that make instrumental or supportive behavior by a designated leader redundant or ineffective. Later versions included additional behaviors such as contingent reward behavior (Howell et al., 1990; Podsakoff et al., 1993). The situational variables include characteristics of the subordinates, task, and the organization that serve as substitutes or neutralizers. Examples of substitutes for instrumental leadership include a highly structured and repetitive task, extensive rules and procedures, and extensive prior training and experience for subordinates. Examples of substitutes for supportive leadership include a cohesive work group, and an intrinsically satisfying task that is not too stressful.

The neutralizers include constraints that prevent a leader from using forms of behavior that would improve subordinate satisfaction or unit performance. For example, a leader with little reward and coercive power cannot provide tangible rewards for effective behavior or dismiss subordinates whose performance is inadequate. A leader with little authority to change work procedures and job assignments cannot make changes that would improve efficiency.

The LPC contingency model

Fiedler's (1967) LPC contingency model describes how the situation moderates the effects on group performance of a leader trait called the least preferred co-worker (LPC) score. The interpretation of LPC scores has changed several times over the years, and what the measure actually means is still questionable. One plausible interpretation is that leaders with a low LPC score value task achievement more than interpersonal relations, whereas leaders with high LPC scores value interpersonal relations more than task achievement (Rice, 1978). These value priorities are assumed to be reflected in the amount of task-oriented and relations-oriented behaviors used by leaders.

The relationship between a leader's LPC score and group performance depends on a complex situational variable called situational favorability, which is jointly determined by task structure, leader position power, and the quality of leader–member relations. According to the theory, low-LPC leaders are more effective when the situation is either very favorable or very unfavorable, whereas high-LPC leaders are more effective when there is a moderate level of situational favorability. The theory does not clearly identify mediating variables that can explain how leader LPC and situational favorability jointly determine group performance.

Normative decision model

Vroom and Yetton (1973) developed a model of participative leadership to help managers identify when various decision procedures are likely to be effective. Two mediating variables (decision quality and decision acceptance by subordinates) jointly determine the outcome of a decision in terms of group performance. The situational variables are characteristics of the decision situation that determine whether a particular decision procedure will increase or decrease the quality and acceptance of a decision. Key situational variables include the complexity of the decision, the distribution of relevant information, congruence of task objectives for the leader and subordinates, and agreement among subordinates in their objectives or preferences. Participative decision procedures are likely to improve decision quality when subordinates have relevant information not possessed by the leader and there is high goal congruence between the leader and subordinates. Participative decision procedures are likely to improve decision acceptance when subordinates initially have concerns about the decision, but there is not a strong conflict among members with regard to their preferences. Discussing options and having a voice in selecting one of them will increase understanding of the problem, increase feelings of procedural justice, and provide a sense of ownership for the decision.

The situation also determines the importance of decision quality and acceptance for group performance. When quality and acceptance are not important, the leader's choice of a decision procedure has less influence on short-term unit performance. Decision quality is not very important when the decision is trivial or the available options are equivalent. Decision acceptance is not very important when the decision does not affect subordinates and they are not required to implement it. The model was later extended by Vroom and Jago (1988) to include other criteria and aspects of the situation.

Cognitive resources theory

Cognitive resources theory (Fiedler & Garcia, 1987) describes how the performance of a group is determined by a complex interaction among two leader traits (intelligence and experience), one type of leader behavior (directive leadership), and two aspects of the leadership situation (interpersonal stress and subordinate knowledge). Interpersonal stress for a leader moderates the importance of leader intelligence and experience as determinants of group performance. Under low stress, leader intelligence facilitates information processing and problem solving, and it is likely to improve the quality of autocratic leader decisions. However, interpersonal stress creates strong emotions that disrupt cognitive information processing and make intelligence difficult to apply. In this stressful situation a leader who has already learned a high-quality solution in previous experience with similar problems is usually more effective than an intelligent but inexperienced leader who tries to find new solutions. As in the normative decision model, a participative decision is more effective than an autocratic decision when the members of the group have relevant knowledge and information not possessed by the leader. However, the theory does not clearly explain how interpersonal stress, leader intelligence, and leader experience affect the use of participative decision procedures.

Multiple-linkage model

The multiple-linkage model (Yukl, 1971, 1981, 1989) describes how aspects of the situation moderate the influence of leader behavior on individual and team performance. It is the most complex of the early contingency theories, because it includes many leader behaviors, mediators, and situational variables. The mediating variables used to explain leader influence are determinants of individual performance (e.g., task skills, role clarity, task motivation) and determinants of team performance (e.g., task-role organization, essential resources, cooperation, and mutual trust). High performance is more likely when members are highly committed to achieve task objectives, they have the necessary task skills, they are efficiently organized, there is a high level of cooperation and mutual trust among members, and they have adequate resources to do the work.

The behaviors used by a leader to influence the mediating variables include specific types of task-oriented and relations-oriented behavior, participative leadership, and contingent reward behavior. Several situational variables directly

Table 21.2 Examples of behavioral guidelines for different leadership situations

Situation	Relevant leadership behaviors
Role ambiguity	• Make clear task assignments and explain responsibilities • Set clear, specific goals and deadlines for employees • Develop effective standard procedures for repetitive tasks • Clarify performance standards and priorities for objectives
Inadequate skills	• Provide instruction, feedback, and coaching • Encourage employees to attend relevant training programs • Provide relevant job aids and self-learning tools • Select employees with relevant skills and experience
Weak task commitment	• Appeal to employee values and emotions • Provide desirable incentives based on performance • Involve employees in making task decisions • Set challenging goals and express confidence in employees
Inadequate cooperation	• Emphasize common interests and values • Encourage cooperation and teamwork • Provide incentives for group performance • Use activities that build identification with the group
Scarce resources	• Make action plans to identify resources needs • Lobby for a larger budget allocation from the organization • Find reliable (and alternate) sources of supplies • Ration scarce resources and monitor their efficient use
Immediate crisis	• Quickly diagnose the cause of the problem • Identify relevant solutions or contingency plans • Direct the response of the unit in a calm, confident way • Inform people about progress in resolving the problem

Based on Yukl (2010).

influence the mediators, moderate the effects of leader behavior on the mediators, and influence the leader's choice of behavior. Many of the propositions about the influence of situational moderator variables are similar to ones found in path-goal theory, leadership substitutes theory, and the normative decision model. Examples of specific behaviors that are relevant for situations confronting many leaders are shown in Table 21.2.

The multiple-linkage model differentiates between short-term corrections by a leader and longer-term efforts to make the situation more favorable. In the short run, a leader can improve group performance by taking direct action to correct any deficiencies in the intervening variables. In the longer run, the leader can improve group performance by making the situation more favorable. The leader may be able to reduce constraints (e.g., bureaucratic limitations on job design, task assignments, and work procedures), increase substitutes (e.g., stronger reward systems, selection of more competent employees), and minimize problems that limit performance (e.g., avoidable errors, quality defects, accidents, and delays, wasted resources, unnecessary activities, duplication of effort).

CONCEPTUAL WEAKNESSES IN CONTINGENCY THEORIES

The early contingency theories have many conceptual weaknesses that make them difficult to validate and limit their practical utility. The types of conceptual weaknesses found in most of the theories are briefly described.

Overemphasis on behavior meta-categories

Broadly defined categories of leader behavior can make a theory more parsimonious and less complex, but they have limited utility for understanding how aspects of the situation moderate the effects of leader behavior on outcomes. The different component behaviors in a broad category are unlikely to be equally relevant for influencing an outcome variable, and a situational moderator variable may affect the component behaviors in different ways. For example, the relative effectiveness of the different decision procedures included in participative leadership depends on the situation (Heller & Yukl, 1969; Vroom & Yetton, 1973). It is easier to understand how to improve leadership effectiveness when a theory includes specific types of behavior and describes the situations in which each type of behavior is relevant.

Ambiguous description of relationships

Most of the contingency theories do not clearly indicate whether the form of the relationship between the independent variable and the dependent variable changes as the situational variable increases (Podsakoff et al., 1995). A leader behavior that has a positive effect on the dependent variable in some situations may have no effect or a negative effect in other situations. Thus, a high level of a leader behavior may be optimal in one situation, but a moderate or low level of the behavior may be optimal in a different situation. A contingency theory should identify situations where the form of the relationship changes and too much of the behavior (or any amount of it) has a negative effect rather than a positive effect.

Inadequate explanation of causal effects

Most contingency theories do not provide an adequate explanation of the underlying reasons for the proposed relationships. A clear explanation requires mediating variables that are determinants of the primary dependent variable (e.g., performance or satisfaction) and can be influenced by leader behavior and aspects of the situation. Some of the contingency theories have no mediating variables, and others are too limited in the types of mediating processes used to explain effective leadership. The mediating variables that are identified usually involve dyadic influence by a leader on individual subordinates, but leader influence on collective processes in teams and work units is usually ignored.

Lack of attention to behavior patterns

Most of the propositions in contingency theories include one type of independent variable, one dependent variable, and one situational variable. However, complex interactions can occur among the independent variables, and these interactions seldom receive adequate attention. For example,

the effects of task-oriented and relations-oriented behaviors are not independent. A high level of relations-oriented behavior may not improve performance unless the leader also uses appropriate task-oriented behaviors, and the optimal pattern of specific task and relations behaviors depends on the situation (Blake & Mouton, 1982; Yukl, 2010). The theories could be improved by describing how the optimal pattern of behavior changes from one situation to another.

Lack of attention to joint effects of situational variables

Most contingency theories do not explicitly consider how multiple situational variables interact in their moderating effects. The enhancing effects of one situational variable may be dependent on another situational variable. An example is provided by Vroom and Yetton (1973). The benefits of allowing participation by subordinates who have relevant information lacked by the leader (one situational variable) are dependent on a high level of goal congruence (another situational variable), because subordinates may be unwilling to share information that would be detrimental to their future welfare (e.g., ways to improve productivity that would also endanger their job security). A contingency theory can provide a more complete explanation of leader effectiveness if the interacting effects of situational variables are described.

Failure to distinguish moderators from mediators

As noted earlier, mediators are conceptually distinct from substitutes that directly influence the mediators, and from enhancers that do not directly influence the mediators. Conceptual confusion about causal relationships is created when a variable treated as a substitute or enhancer but is actually a mediator that is influenced both by leader behavior and by aspects of the situation. The potential influence of the leader is understated when mediating variables the leader can influence are treated as situational variables. For example, the LPC contingency model treats leader–member relations as a situational variable, but it is more accurately described as a mediator, because leaders can improve relations with subordinates by using appropriate relations-oriented behaviors.

LACK OF ATTENTION TO CHANGE-ORIENTED BEHAVIOR AND STRATEGIC LEADERSHIP

Much of the early theory and research on leader behavior failed to consider the importance of leadership behaviors that involve attempts to influence major change in an organization. Until the 1990s, scholars did not explicitly recognize that change-oriented behavior is a separate dimension from task-oriented and relations-oriented behavior (Ekvall & Arvonen, 1991; Yukl, 1999). Examples of change-oriented behavior include monitoring the external environment, interpreting external threats and opportunities for the team or organization, finding innovative ways to adapt to changing external conditions, encouraging innovative thinking by followers, facilitating collective learning by a team or organization, articulating an inspiring vision for the team or organization, and implementing major changes in strategies (Yukl et al., 2002). A few of these behaviors are explicitly included in theories of charismatic and transformational leadership (e.g., Bass, 1985; Conger, 1989; Shamir, House, & Arthur, 1993), and change-oriented behaviors are emphasized in theories of strategic leadership (e.g., Hambrick, Finkelstein, & Mooney, 2005; Yukl, 2008; Yukl & Lepsinger, 2004).

RESEARCH FINDINGS AND LIMITATIONS

A contingency theory is supported by a pattern of results in empirical studies that is consistent with the propositions of the theory. Review articles or meta-analyses of relevant research have been published for path-goal theory (Podsakoff, MacKenzie, Ahearne, & Bommer, 1995; Wofford & Liska, 1993), situational leadership theory (Fernandez & Vecchio, 1997; Graef, 1997), leadership substitutes theory (Dionne, Yammarino, Atwater, & James, 2002; Podsakoff, Niehoff, MacKenzie & Williams, 1993; Podsakoff et al., 1995), the normative decision model (Vroom & Jago, 1988), cognitive resources theory (Vecchio, 1990), and the LPC contingency model (Peters, Hartke, & Pohlmann, 1985). Reviews of empirical research on the contingency theories can also be found in some leadership books (e.g., Bass, 2009; Yukl, 2010). No research has directly tested all aspects of the multiple-linkage model, but several of the propositions were tested in comparative field studies (e.g., Peterson & Van Fleet, 2008; Yukl & Van Fleet, 1982). Some of the propositions in the model are similar to those in other contingency theories, and studies conducted to test those

theories provide evidence relevant for assessing the multiple-linkage propositions.

In general, the evidence supporting contingency theories of effective leadership is weak and inconsistent. The best supported theory is the normative decision model by Vroom and Yetton (1973), but support is stronger for some propositions than for others. As noted earlier, the ambiguity and conceptual problems in contingency theories makes them more difficult to test (Schriesheim & Kerr, 1977; Yukl, 2010). Another reason for the lack of strong results is the use of weak research methods in most of the studies, and common limitations of the research are described next.

Use of convenience samples

Several types of research methods are useful for testing contingency theories, but most of the research has involved field survey studies and moderated multiple regression analysis. This type of research has many potential limitations (Villa, Howell, Dorfman, & Daniel, 2003). To provide a good test of proposed moderating effects, it is essential to ensure adequate variance for the situational variables. A comparative field study with a sampling plan designed to ensure variability of situations is more likely to provide an adequate test of contingency propositions than the convenience samples used in most studies. It is also important to identify confounding among situational variables with similar or interacting effects. When situational variables are confounded, the moderating effects attributed to one situational variable may be inflated or diminished by the effects of another, unmeasured situational variable.

Use of weak measures

The behavior description questionnaires commonly used in studies on contingency theories are prone to respondent biases (e.g., halo, attributions, stereotypes, implicit theories) that usually reduce discrimination among different leader behaviors. It is more difficult to find clear evidence of moderator effects in a multiple regression analysis when the predictor variables (i.e., the behaviors) are highly inter-correlated. Additional confounding is likely when the data on leader behavior, outcome variables, and situational variables are obtained from the same respondents with the same type of fixed-response questionnaire (Dionne et al., 2002; Podsakoff, MacKenzie, Lee, & Podsakoff, 2003).

Focus on meta-categories

A major limitation of most studies on contingency theories is the overemphasis on behavior meta-categories. Results based on the composite score for a meta-category are weaker and less meaningful when some component behaviors are more relevant than others for accomplishing the leader's objectives. Moreover, the moderating effects of the situation may differ for the component behaviors, and these differences will not be evident unless the component behaviors are used in the analyses. The descriptive research on leader effectiveness (using diaries, observation, interviews, or critical incidents) suggests that it is much easier to find situational moderating effects for specific behaviors than for broad meta-categories. Moreover, when meta-category scores are based on different component behaviors from one study to another, results from the different studies are less likely to be consistent.

Different criteria of effective leadership

The joint effects of leader behavior and situational variables are not the same for different criteria. For example, supportive leadership usually has a stronger positive effect on subordinate satisfaction than on subordinate performance. A task that is tedious and stressful may enhance the effects of supportive leadership on subordinate satisfaction but not on performance. The same criterion variable can be measured in different ways, and the measures are likely to vary in accuracy. For example, an objective measure of team performance (sales revenues, productivity) may be more accurate than a subjective rating by subordinates or bosses. When the studies testing a contingency theory use different criteria and measures, consistent results are less likely to be found.

Failure to assess non-linear relationships

Most studies on contingency theories implicitly assume that a linear relationship exists between the independent and dependent variable in any situation where the relationship is positive. However, the effects of leader behavior are more likely to involve a curvilinear relationship. As the amount of a leader behavior increases, positive effects on the dependent variable decline and eventually reach a point where using more of the behavior has no additional benefits or has

negative effects. For example, it is usually beneficial for leaders to clarify role expectations for subordinates and monitor their performance, but an excessive amount of these task-oriented behaviors ('micro-managing') is likely to reduce job satisfaction and discourage initiative and problem solving. As noted earlier, situational variables can determine not only when the behavior is effective, but also the optimal amount of the behavior in each situation. For example, it is appropriate for a leader to provide more clarifying and monitoring for new subordinates with little experience or skill than for highly competent and experienced subordinates. Few leadership studies carefully examine the form of the relationship between independent and dependent variables for different levels of a situational variable (Podsakoff et al., 1995).

Inadequate time period for assessing effects

Most studies on contingency theories measure all variables at the same point in time, and this research design makes it more difficult to assess delayed effects. Some behaviors can influence outcome variables quickly, whereas other behaviors require much more time before any effects are visible. Moreover, the immediate and delayed effects of a leader's actions may not be consistent. A behavior may initially have a negative or weak positive effect, but later have a stronger positive effect. For example, providing a subordinate the opportunity to perform a new task requires a period of learning, during which performance may decline before it improves. Longitudinal research designs should be used more often in research on contingency theories.

Lack of attention to different situational effects

Many studies test for a moderator effect without differentiating among the three types of situational influence described earlier. A statistical analysis may indicate that the effects of a leader behavior on an outcome variable are moderated by a situational variable, but it may not be clear why this effect occurs or which situational variables are most important. The moderating effect may reflect the influence of a substitute, an enhancer, or a constraint. The different types of situational effects can interact with each other and are difficult to understand unless complex causal models are developed and tested with appropriate types of analyses (Howell, Dorfman, & Kerr, 1986; James & Brett, 1984; Villa et al., 2003).

Level of analysis problems

The appropriate type of analysis for quantitative data from survey studies depends on the underlying theory of leadership processes and the level of measurement for the variables (Klein, Dansereau, & Hall, 1994). Some theories conceptualize leader behavior at a dyadic level (how the leader influences an individual subordinate), some theories conceptualize behavior at a group level (actions that affect the group as a whole), and some theories include both levels. Some theories are not clear about the level of conceptualization for each variable, and the analyses are not always made at the appropriate level (Yammarino, Dionne, Chun, & Dansereau, 2005). Results for analyses of leader influence and situational moderators can vary depending on what level of analysis is used, and consistent results are less likely to be found in a review of studies that do not use the same level of analysis.

CONCLUSIONS

The contingency theories generated extensive research for two decades, but they were eventually eclipsed by leadership theories that emphasize leader influence on emotions as well as cognitions, and influence by multiple leaders as well as influence by a single heroic leader (Yukl, 2010). One major reason for the declining popularity of the early contingency theories is the lack of strong empirical support for them. Despite many hundreds of studies conducted to test universal and contingency theories of effective leadership, no strong conclusions can be reached. The empirical studies found support for some propositions in some of the theories, but in no case was there strong, consistent support for all aspects of the theory.

The weak and inconsistent results reflect limitations of the theories and limitations in the research methods used to test them. As explained earlier, conceptual problems and the complexity of the contingency theories make them difficult to test. Common conceptual weaknesses include overemphasis on meta-categories, failure to include relevant variables, unclear specification of causal relationships, and inadequate explanations for the causal and moderating effects. Most of the empirical studies used weak research methods such as survey studies with all data provided by the same respondents at one point in time. None of the contingency theories have been adequately tested, and stronger research methods are needed to provide more conclusive results. Suggestions for improving the theories as well as the research are summarized in Table 21.3.

Instead of relying so much on survey field studies with convenience samples, it is desirable to make more use of other relevant research methods. Examples of methods that are likely to be useful include comparative field studies of effective and ineffective leaders in different situations, longitudinal studies of how well leaders adapt to changes in the situation over time, experimental

---

Table 21.3   Ways to improve contingency theories of effective leadership behavior

Ways to improve theory
1. Include a wide variety of specific behaviors (not just one or two meta-categories)
2. Identify interactive effects for behavior patterns (not just for single behaviors)
3. Include relevant mediating variables to explain causal effects
4. Include collective processes as mediating variables (not just effects on individuals)
5. Identify direct and indirect effects for different types of situational variables
6. Include multi-level processes and cross-level effects

Ways to improve research

1. Use longitudinal studies of leadership influence on individuals and teams
2. Use appropriate sampling plans rather than convenience samples
3. Use diverse research methods (survey studies, experiments, comparative case studies)
4. Include multiple criteria and assess the accuracy of each measure
5. Use independent measures for different types of variables (behavior, situation, outcomes)
6. Use analyses that identify causal relationships for different types of situational variables
7. Conduct analyses that examine the form of relationships and non-linear effects
8. Use multi-level and cross-level analyses of data when appropriate

field studies of leaders trained to diagnose the situation accurately and select appropriate behaviors, and laboratory experiments in which leaders of teams in different situations are observed (or their behavior recorded) over a period of several weeks. Alternative methods for measuring leadership behavior (e.g., observation, diaries, interviews, and critical incidents) should be used more often, and ineffective forms of leadership behavior should be examined in addition to effective forms of behavior (e.g., Amabile, Schatzel, Moneta, & Kramer, 2004; Yukl & Van Fleet, 1982). Measures of how often a particular type of behavior is used are not enough; it is also essential to consider whether the behavior is used when and where it is appropriate and in a skillful way. Finally, researchers need to pay more attention to the overall pattern of leadership behavior rather than examining each type of behavior separately. Different behaviors are woven together into a complex tapestry such that the whole is greater than the sum of the parts (Kaplan, 1988). It is important to consider the possibility that more than one pattern of behavior may be effective in the same situation.

Leaders face an immense variety of rapidly changing situations, and several different patterns of behavior may be equally effective in the same situation (Yukl, 2008). The contingency theories do not provide sufficient guidance in the form of general principles to help managers recognize the underlying leadership requirements and choices in the myriad of fragmented activities and problems confronting them. In future theories it is desirable to include both universal elements (e.g., general principles) and situational elements (e.g., guidelines to help identify desirable behaviors for a particular type of situation).

The lack of strong, consistent results in the research does not justify the conclusion that situational variables are irrelevant for understanding effective leadership. In an increasingly turbulent world, the idea that leaders must adapt their behavior to changing conditions seems even more relevant today than it was decades ago when the theories were first proposed. It is both essential and feasible to develop stronger contingency theories that include clear guidelines for specific types of behavior that are relevant in situations that are experienced by most managers and administrators.

REFERENCES

Amabile, T. A., Schatzel, E. A., Moneta, G. B., & Kramer, S. J. (2004). Leader behaviors and the work environment for creativity: perceived leader support. *The Leadership Quarterly*, 15(1), 5–32.

Bass, B. M. (1985). *Leadership and performance beyond expectations*. New York: Free Press.

Bass, B. M. (1997). Does the transactional–transformational paradigm transcend organizational and national boundaries? *American Psychologist*, 52, 130–139.

Bass, B. M. (2009). *Handbook of leadership: theory, research, & managerial applications*, 4th edn. New York: Free Press.

Blake, R. R. & Mouton, J. S. (1982). Management by grid principles or situationalism: Which? *Group and Organization Studies*, 7, 207–210.

Blanchard, K. H., Zigarmi, D., & Nelson, R. B. (1993). Situational leadership after 25 years: a retrospective. *Journal of Leadership Studies*, 1(1), 21–36.

Conger, J. A. (1989). *The charismatic leader: behind the mystique of exceptional leadership*. San Francisco, CA: Jossey-Bass.

Dionne, S. D., Yammarino, F. J., Atwater, L. E., & James, L. R. (2002). Neutralizing substitutes for leadership theory: leadership effects and common source variance. *Journal of Applied Psychology*, 69(2), 307–321.

Ekvall, G. & Arvonen, J. (1991). Change-centered leadership: an extension of the two-dimensional model. *Scandinavian Journal of Management*, 7, 17–26.

Evans, M. G. (1970). The effects of supervisory behavior on the path-goal relationship. *Organizational Behavior and Human Performance*, 5, 277–298.

Evans, M. G. (1974). Extensions of a path-goal theory of motivation. *Journal of Applied Psychology*, 59, 172–178.

Fernandez, C. F. & Vecchio, R. P. (1997). Situational leadership theory revisited: a test of an across-jobs perspective. *The Leadership Quarterly*, 8, 67–84.

Fiedler, F. E. (1967). *A theory of leadership effectiveness*. New York: McGraw-Hill.

Fiedler, F. E. (1971). Validation and extension of the contingency model of leadership effectiveness: a review of empirical findings. *Psychological Bulletin*, 76, 128–148.

Fiedler, F. E. & Garcia, J. E. (1987). *New approaches to leadership: cognitive resources and organizational performance*. New York: John Wiley.

Fleishman, E. A. (1953). The description of supervisory behavior. *Personnel Psychology*, 37, 1–6.

Graef, C. L. (1997). Evolution of situational leadership theory: a critical review. *The Leadership Quarterly*, 8(2), 153–170.

Halpin, A. W. & Winer, B. J. (1957). A factorial study of the leader behavior descriptions. In R. M. Stogdill & A. E. Coons (eds), *Leader behavior: its description and measurement*. Columbus, OH: Bureau of Business Research, Ohio State University.

Hambrick, D., Finkelstein, S., & Mooney, A. (2005). Executive job demands: new insights for explaining strategic decisions and leader behaviors. *Academy of Management Review*, 30(3), 472–491.

Heller, F. & Yukl, G. (1969). Participation, managerial decision making, and situational variables. *Organizational Behavior and Human Performance*, 4, 227–241.

Hersey, P. & Blanchard, K. H. (1971). *The management of organizational behavior*, 3rd edn. Englewood Cliffs, NJ: Prentice Hall.

Hinkin, T. R. & Tracey, J. B. (1999). The relevance of charisma for transformational leadership in stable organizations. *Journal of Organizational Change Management*, 12(2), 105–119.

House, R. J. (1971). A path-goal theory of leader effectiveness. *Administrative Science Quarterly*, 16, 321–339.

House, R. J. (1996). Path-goal theory of leadership: lessons, legacy, and a reformulated theory. *The Leadership Quarterly*, 7, 323–352.

House, R. J. & Mitchell, T. R. (1974). Path-goal theory of leadership. *Contemporary Business*, 3(Fall), 81–98.

Howell, J. P., Bowen, D. E., Dorfman, P. W., Kerr, S., & Podsakoff, P. M. (1990). Substitutes for leadership: effective alternatives to ineffective leadership. *Organizational Dynamics*, 19, 21–38.

Howell, J. P., Dorfman, P. W., & Kerr, S. (1986). Moderator variables in leadership research. *Academy of Management Review*, 11, 82–102.

James, L. R., & Brett, J. M. (1984). Mediators, moderators, and tests for mediation. *Journal of Applied Psychology*, 69(2), 307–321.

Kaplan, R. E. (1988). The warp and woof of the general manager's job. In F. D. Schoorman & B. Schneider (eds), *Facilitating work effectiveness*. Lexington, MA: Lexington Books, pp. 183–211.

Kerr, S. & Jermier, J. M. (1978). Substitutes for leadership: their meaning and measurement. *Organizational Behavior and Human Performance*, 22, 375–403.

Klein, K. J., Dansereau, F., & Hall, R. J. (1994). Levels issues in theory development, data collection, and analysis. *Academy of Management Review*, 19(2), 195–229.

Likert, R. (1961). *New patterns of management*. New York: McGraw-Hill.

Pawar, B. S. & Eastman, K. K. (1997). The nature and implications of contextual influences on transformational leadership: a conceptual examination. *Academy of Management Review*, 22, 80–109.

Peters, L. H., Hartke, D. D., & Pohlmann, J. T. (1985). Fiedler's contingency theory of leadership: an application of the meta-analysis procedures of Schmidt and Hunter. *Psychological Bulletin*, 97, 274–285.

Peterson, T. O. & Van Fleet, D. D. (2008). A tale of two situations: an empirical study of behavior by not-for-profit managerial leaders. *Public Performance & Management Review*, 31(4), 500–513.

Podsakoff, P. M., MacKenzie, S. B., Ahearne, M., & Bommer, W. H. (1995). Searching for a needle in a haystack: trying to identify the illusive moderators of leadership behaviors. *Journal of Management*, 21, 423–470.

Podsakoff, P. M., MacKenzie, S. B., Lee, J., & Podsakoff, N. P. (2003). Common method bias in behavioral research: a critical review of the literature and recommended remedies. *Journal of Applied Psychology*, 88, 879–903.

Podsakoff, P. M., Niehoff, B. P., MacKenzie, S., & Williams, M. L. (1993). Do substitutes for leadership really substitute for leadership? An examination of Kerr and Jermier's situational leadership model. *Organizational Behavior and Human Decision Processes*, 54, 1–44.

Rice, R. W. (1978). Construct validity of the least preferred coworker score. *Psychological Bulletin*, 85, 1199–1237.

Schriesheim, C. A. & Kerr, S. (1977). Theories and measures of leadership: a critical appraisal. In J. G. Hunt & L. L. Larson (eds), *Leadership: the cutting edge*. Carbondale, IL: Southern Illinois University Press, pp. 9–45.

Shamir, B., House, R. J., & Arthur, M. B. (1993). The motivational effects of charismatic leadership: a self–concept based theory. *Organization Science*, 4, 1–17.

Sims, H. P. & Szilagyi, A. D. (1975). Leader reward behavior and subordinate satisfaction and performance. *Organizational Behavior and Human Performance*, 14, 426–438.

Stewart, R. (1976). *Contrasts in management*. Maidenhead, UK: McGraw-Hill.

Stogdill, R. M. (1974). *Handbook of leadership: a survey of the literature*. New York: Free Press.

Vecchio, R. P. (1990). Theoretical and empirical examination of cognitive resource theory. *Journal of Applied Psychology*, 75, 141–147.

Villa, J. R., Howell, J. P., Dorfman, P. W., & Daniel, D. L. (2003). Problems with detecting moderators in leadership research using moderated multiple regression. *The Leadership Quarterly*, 14(1), 3–23.

Vroom, V. H. & Jago, A. G. (1988). *The new leadership: managing participation in organizations*. Englewood Cliffs, NJ: Prentice Hall.

Vroom, V. H. & Yetton, P. W. (1973). *Leadership and decision making*. Pittsburgh, PA: University of Pittsburgh Press.

Wofford, J. C. & Liska, L. Z. (1993). Path-goal theories of leadership: a meta analysis. *Journal of Management*, 19, 858–876.

Yammarino, F. J., Dionne, S. D., Chun, J. U., & Dansereau, F. (2005). Leadership and levels of analysis: a state of the science review. *The Leadership Quarterly*, 16(6), 879–919.

Yukl, G. (1971). Toward a behavioral theory of leadership. *Organizational Behavior and Human Performance*, 6, 414–440.

Yukl, G. (1981). *Leadership in organizations*. Englewood Cliffs, NJ: Prentice Hall.

Yukl, G. (1989). *Leadership in organizations*, 2nd edn. Englewood Cliffs, NJ: Prentice Hall.

Yukl, G. (1999). An evaluative essay on current conceptions of effective leadership. *European Journal of Work and Organizational Psychology*, 8, 33–48.

Yukl, G. (2008). How leaders influence organizational effectiveness. *The Leadership Quarterly*, 19, 708–722.

Yukl, G. (2010). *Leadership in organizations*, 7th edn. Upper Saddle River, NJ: Prentice Hall.

Yukl, G., Gordon, A., & Taber, T. (2002). A hierarchical taxonomy of leadership behavior: integrating a half century of behavior research. *Journal of Leadership and Organization Studies*, 9, 15–32.

Yukl, G. & Lepsinger, R. (2004). *Flexible leadership: creating value by balancing multiple challenges and choices*. San Francisco, CA: Jossey-Bass.

Yukl, G. & Van Fleet, D. (1982). Cross-situational, multi-method research on military leader effectiveness. *Organizational Behavior and Human Performance*, 30, 87–108.

22

Transformational Leadership

Héctor R. Díaz-Sáenz

INTRODUCTION

Transformational leadership is the process by which a leader fosters group or organizational performance beyond expectation by virtue of the strong emotional attachment with his or her followers combined with the collective commitment to a higher moral cause. For the past 30 years transformational leadership has been the single most studied and debated idea within the field of leadership studies. From 2000 to 2010 an impressive total of 476 articles looking into transformational leadership were listed in the SCOPUS database. More impressive, perhaps, is the range of publications in which these articles appeared, which included the *International Journal of Educational Management*, the *Journal of Construction Engineering and Management*, *Military Psychology*, *Library Management*, and *Social Behavior and Personality*.

In accounting for its phenomenal popularity, Jay Conger (1999) pointed to the desperate desire on the part of American businesses to develop a heroic response to the threat of international competition during the 1980s and the need to foster empowerment in the context of organizational restructuring and an increasingly demanding educated work force. Daft and Lengel (1998) claimed that transformational leadership is the only one adequate during times of environmental turbulence, whereas transactional leadership is more suitable for stable environments. Interest in transformational leadership was further fuelled by the publication of popular leadership books, such as those by Bennis and Nanus in 1985 and Tichy and Devanna in 1986 that celebrated well-known transformational leaders in the corporate and not-for-profit sectors. The most highly celebrated exemplars of transformational leaders from the world of politics include Mahatma Gandhi, John F. Kennedy and Nelson Mandela. From the corporate world, Richard Branson, Anita Roddick and Jack Welch have been frequently pointed to as exemplars of transformational leaders, though not without either debate or dissension.

This chapter commences by examining the origins and development of the concept of transformational leadership. Then follows a review of the various measures and assessment instruments that have been developed to better understand how transformational leadership is manifested and how it might be developed. Next, a comprehensive review is provided of the wide variety of contexts in which transformational leadership has been empirically examined, as well as the most frequently researched theoretical relationships that have been tested empirically. The chapter closes with a consideration of the criticisms that have been levelled at transformational leadership and how the field might be profitably moved forward.

ORIGINS AND DEVELOPMENT OF TRANSFORMATIONAL LEADERSHIP

While the term 'transformational leadership' was originally coined by James Downton in a 1973 paper on rebel leadership, it was James MacGregor Burns who brought the term to wider parlance in his classic study of political leadership in the 1978 book simply entitled *Leadership*. Burns made an important distinction between 'transactional leadership', which he suggested was the way that most politicians led their followers on the basis of reciprocal exchange leading to the satisfaction of both the leader's and the follower's self-interests; and 'transformational leadership', which was practiced by those political leaders who were able to engage their followers not only to achieve something of significance but also to 'morally uplift' them. Transformational leaders both influence and are influenced by followers 'to rise to higher levels of motivation and morality' (Burns, 1978, p. 20). They not only lead but also develop leaders. Their value is not measured by newspaper clippings but by the degree of positive social change that is promoted as a result of their leadership.

Seven years later, industrial psychologist Bernard Bass (1985) expanded on this important distinction and brought it to the top of the agenda for both leadership researchers and practitioners alike. While commencing with four factors, the Full Range Leadership (FRL) model that Bass and various others have elaborated currently contains nine factors. Within this model, the transformational leadership factors include idealized influence (both attributed and behaviours), inspirational motivation, intellectual stimulation and individualized consideration. The second set of factors, transactional factors, include contingent reward and management-by-exception (both active and passive). Finally, the laissez-faire leadership factor indicates an absence of leadership (i.e. a non-transaction).

Focusing on the transformational leader factors, leaders with idealized influence become role models that followers want to identify with and emulate. These leaders are admired, respected and trusted and are perceived to have extraordinary capabilities, persistence and determination. Leaders who possess these qualities are frequently described as having charisma. Leaders who create inspirational motivation paint a clear vision for their followers' future state as well as provide the momentum to reach that vision through the arousal of team spirit. These leaders also provide meaning, challenge, clearly communicated expectations, and a commitment to set goals. Leaders who exhibit intellectual stimulation encourage followers to be innovative and creative in redressing old problems in new ways and regularly examining old assumptions to see if they are still viable. Finally, leaders showing individual consideration treat each follower as an individual and consider their individual needs, abilities and aspirations. They help individuals to develop their strengths and spend time coaching and guiding people.

For Bass, the ideal approach for leaders to take exhibits both transformational and transactional forms of leadership. Transactional leadership involves an exchange wherein the leader offers rewards in return for compliance and performance by his or her followers. The transaction usually takes the form of contracts, employment

agreements, performance management systems and service-led agreements. Waldman and his colleagues, in a 1990 paper, drew attention to the importance of the augmentation effect of transformational leadership over and above the effect of transactional leadership. Indeed, the distinction that is drawn between transactional leadership and transformational leadership, as well the crucial role that transformational leadership plays in generating optimal performance, parallels the widely discussed distinction that has been drawn between management and leadership, most notably by Zalenik in 1977 and Kotter in 1990.

TRANSFORMATIONAL LEADERSHIP MEASURES

One of the most widely used instruments to measure transformational leadership, the Multifactor Leadership Questionnaire (MLQ), was developed by Bass (1985). Through constant refinement, the questionnaire has become increasingly reliable so that it is the most widely used measure of transformational leadership used by leadership researchers around the world. The MLQ has been translated into many languages, including German, French, Japanese and Hebrew (Bass & Riggio, 2006).

Originally only three factors related to transformational behaviours emerged as part of the MLQ model: charismatic leadership (instilling pride, faith and respect and promoting an articulated sense of mission); individual consideration (delegating for learning, teaching and coaching in a relationship of respect for their followers); and intellectual consideration (stimulating thinking in new ways before acting) (Bass, 1985). In addition, the MLQ measured two additional factors related to the transactional component (contingent reward, in exchange for the expected performance; and management-by-exception, allowing followers to do their work with an old approach if accomplishing the goals but giving negative feedback when doing something wrong that prevents achieving it) as part of a complete set of factors that encompassed the full range of behaviours that a leader exhibits. Bass argued that the transactional behaviours were the foundations of the full set of behaviours that transformational leaders perform. That is why transformational leaders are able to induce additional effort by sharply increasing the subordinate's trust and confidence, and by elevating the value of outcomes for the subordinate instead of only 'clarifying what performance is required and how needs would be satisfied as a result' (1985, p. 22).

The widespead use of the MLQ by researchers through the years, has provided sufficient feedback that has helped to improve the measurement of transformational leadership behaviours as conceptualized by Bass (Bass & Riggio, 2006). Currently the refined MLQ version 5X includes four transformational behaviour components known as the four I's:

- idealized influence (includes two subscales that measure behaviour and elements attributed by followers and others such as charisma)
- inspirational motivation
- intellectual stimulation
- individualized consideration

In addition, the transactional dimensions include two components: contingent reward (constructive transaction), and management-by-exception (corrective transaction), which is divided into two components (active MBE-A or passive MBE-P) plus an additional component of no leadership (laissez-faire leadership) (Bass & Riggio, 2006). An important consideration has to be taken by researchers regarding the charismatic component of this approach (see Conger, Chapter 7, this volume). Bass's conceptualization argues for promotion of follower's autonomy as opposed to House's conceptualization of charismatic leadership, which implies the follower's dependency on 'charismatic acts by the leader' (Lowe, Kroeck, & Sivasubramaniam, 1996).

In addition to Bass's MLQ model, several other researchers have worked on the development of the transformational leadership construct and on the measurement devices required to assess the behaviours of these types of leaders. These early works have already been identified and discussed at length by Podsakoff, MacKenzie, Moorman and Fetter (1990) as well as by Bass and Riggio (2006), and Brown and Reilly (2009). Thus, these works will not be reviewed here. However, we note that

while all of these approaches differ somewhat in the specific behaviours they associate with transformational leadership, all of them share the common perspective that effective leaders transform or change the basic values, beliefs, and attitudes of followers so that they are willing to perform beyond the minimum levels specified by the organization. (Podsakoff et al., 1990; p. 108)

The additional assessment that was considered relevant to review here is the one developed by Podsakoff et al.'s (1990) Transformational Leadership Inventory (TLI) because it was found, by this review, to be the second most widely used instrument to assess transformational leadership after the MLQ. At that time, according to Podsakoff et al. (1990), the only certain knowledge about this approach was that transformational leadership was multidimensional in nature. They found

conceptual differences among the several approaches that were measuring transformational leadership. Their development of the TLI was based on the construct definitions found in a comprehensive review of all the works that examined behaviours related to transformational leaders, including Bass's work. Thus, they identified and developed measures for six behaviours known to be associated with transformational leadership:

- *Identifying and articulating a vision* – behaviour on the part of the leader aimed at identifying new opportunities for his or her unit/division/company, and developing, articulating and inspiring others with his or her vision of the future.
- *Providing an appropriate model* – behaviour on the part of the leader that sets an example for employees to follow that is consistent with the values the leader espouses.
- *Fostering the acceptance of group goals* – behaviour on the part of the leader aimed at promoting cooperation among employees and getting them to work together towards a common goal.
- *High performance expectations* – behaviour that demonstrates the leader's expectations for excellence, quality and/or high performance on the part of followers.
- *Providing individualized support* – behaviour on the part of the leader that indicates that he/she respects followers and is concerned about their personal feelings and needs.
- *Intellectual stimulation* – behaviour on the part of the leader that challenges followers to re-examine some of their assumptions about their work and rethink how it can be performed (Podsakoff et al., 1990, p. 112).

Regarding transactional leader behaviours, contingent reward being the principal behaviour identified by Bass (1985), it was the only construct definition included in the TLI to capture the fundamental exchange notions, measuring 'the extent to which a leader provides rewards in exchange for follower's effort' (p. 113). However, the analysis of their measures suggested that the factors – articulating a vision, providing an appropriate model and fostering the acceptance of group goals – were multiple indicators of an underlying 'core' transformational leader behaviour dimension. Thus, the TLI transformational leader behaviours are measured by four first-order transformational factors – high-performance expectations, individualized support, intellectual stimulation, and a 'core' transformational behaviour construct – as well as one transactional leader behaviour. It is important to understand these factors as presented by their results (Podsakoff et al., 1990), because they have been misunderstood by some researchers who have ignored the core factor and, as a result, have limited the interpretation of their studies.

The TLI has been used in countries such as the USA, Mexico, People's Republic of China, Greece, Korea, Hong Kong, the UK, Taiwan, and Pakistan. It was also used in different contexts such as by firemen, sales force, bank teams, manufacturing companies and universities. A relevant observation with respect to both the MLQ and the TLI is that they do not directly address charisma as an important assessment of transformational leadership. Nevertheless, both approaches take into account the charismatic conceptualization in their development. Interestingly, early on in the evolution of transformational leadership, there was a tendency among researchers to use charisma as a synonym of transformational leadership. In the original conceptualization by Bass (1985), charisma was included as a component, along with vision, respect for the leader and inspiration and encouragement within the factor labelled charismatic leader behaviour. Through the refinement of the MLQ, this component was transformed into inspirational influence.

EMPIRICAL RESEARCH FINDINGS

The transformational leadership construct has been applied in studies across many fields and contexts, yielding theoretically expected results but nevertheless sometimes revealing comparative differences due to specific contextual or cultural features. Some recent representative empirical studies are discussed below, according to some of these specific themes or contexts.

CEO studies

Theoretically, it is expected that chief executive officers (CEOs) and top-level executives would be more able to exhibit transformational leadership behaviors than middle-level managers because, among other functions, they establish the vision of their organization, they hold the premier leadership role in the organization and they have a higher degree of autonomy. For example, Jung, Wu and Chow (2008) focused on a sample of 50 Taiwanese companies from the electronics and telecommunications industry. In this study, they wanted to understand how the CEO's transformational leadership impacted the level of innovation at the organizational level. Their results indicated a direct and positive effect of CEO transformational leadership on organizational innovation. Another study looked at the influence of the CEO on

shared perceptions about organizational outcomes with the top management teams of credit unions (Colbert, Kristof-Brown, Bradley & Barrick, 2008). A visionary transformational leadership communicates the organization's important goals to the top team. The study found that the degree of transformational leadership exhibited by CEOs was positively related to higher goal importance congruence with their vice-presidents. At the organizational level, within-team goal importance congruence mediated the relationship between transformational leadership and performance.

Another recent study by Pastor and Mayo (2008) looked at the influence of the CEO's managerial values on goal orientation. Their study indicates that the level of formal education is reflected in the managerial values exhibited. Those CEOs with graduate degrees tended to value a learning goal orientation more than those with no graduate degree, who tended to favour a goal performance orientation. At the same time, those with graduate-level education tended to be more transformational and more closely associated with McGregor's Y philosophy of management in contrast with the more transactional approach of CEOs who had no graduate education. This study's inclusion of the educational variable adds a very important and novel approach to the understanding of transformational leadership and its relationship with education. In their study, Zhu, Chew and Spangler (2005) also established the positive influence that the transformational leadership of CEOs had on strategic initiatives related to Human Resources Management (HRM). Their study found that transformational CEOs were more likely to adopt a human–capital-enhancing HRM than nontransformational CEOs. Furthermore, human–capital-enhancing HRM mediated the relationship between transformational leadership and organizational outcomes such as absenteeism and perceived organizational outcomes.

Middle-manager studies

Many empirical studies have found that transformational leadership is equally applicable and relevant to middle-level managers as well as to top-level management. For example, Singh and Krishnan (2008) explored the mediating role of altruism in the relationship between self-sacrifice and transformational leadership in India. They also looked at the effect of all three on followers' collective identity and perceptions of unit performance. The MLQ Form 5X developed by Bass and Avolio (1995) was used for measuring transformational leadership. The results provided evidence of altruism mediating the relationship between self-sacrifice and transformational leadership. Transformational leadership was positively related to followers' collective identity and perceived unit performance. They also found that, when leaders model the importance of cooperative behaviors over personal interests, they are more likely to be seen as being more transformational. Finally, the study also demonstrated that under transformational leadership, there is followers' perception of successful unit performance.

The military context

A study conducted on a Navy facility by Eid, Johnsen, Bartone and Nissestad (2008) evaluated the role of personal hardiness in facilitating change or growth in transformational leadership on a leadership training activity. The cadets underwent a stressful military training exercise, and the authors found a significant increase in transformational and transactional leadership styles after the exercises. Moreover, the transformational leadership style was not only maintained, but actually increased six months after the exercise.

Another military study conducted by Mannheim and Halamish's (2008) was performed to determine whether or not the effect of leadership style of trainers is universal across teams from varied backgrounds. Their findings did not support the universal relationship that was predicted according to transformational leadership theory. Data were collected from 890 cadets in the basic, operations and support, and infantry tracks in an officers' training school of the Israeli Defense Force. They were organized into 66 teams. Mannheim and Halamish's main finding is the importance of specification of leadership relationships to team outcomes for a particular track. The predicted relationships of leadership style with team outcomes were found mainly in the basic track. In this track, the transformational leadership style impacted the group outcomes of learning culture and group cohesion.

Cross-cultural contexts

There has been a substantial amount of empirical work put into measuring the prevalence and effectiveness of transformational leadership in different national cultural contexts throughout the world. The most important and extensive study of this type to date is the GLOBE research programme which was originated by Robert House but conducted by hundreds of researchers from over 60 nations (Den Hartog, House, Hanges, Ruiz-Quintanilla & Associates, 1999). This impressive study is discussed in more detail in the chapter on cross-cultural leadership (Guthey & Jackson, Chapter 12, this volume). The GLOBE study has found that specific aspects of transformational leadership are universally endorsed across cultures around the world. However, a more recent set of studies support the notion that cultural features influence how this approach applies from country to country: for example, how it is perceived (Spreitzer, Perttula, & Xin, 2005). Depending on the culture, the transformational leadership relationship will be stronger within less traditionally entrenched cultures, such as in the USA, whereas it would be perceived as being weaker in countries with a traditional culture, such as Taiwan, where respect for hierarchy is important. How strong the effect of transformational leadership is displayed differs according to the culture, although it has a positive impact in most of them. Accordingly, transformational leadership was related to superior team performance mediated by team potency in Hong Kong and US bank teams. The effect of transformational leadership on team potency was stronger among teams with higher power distance as well as with higher collectivism (Schaubroeck, Lam & Cha, 2007). Furthermore, in Jung, Yammarino and Lee (2009), a collectivistic culture was found to enhance the transformational leadership effect, which seemed to facilitate the follower's motivation to go beyond self-interest. It seems more likely to motivate followers to work for transcendental goals instead of immediate self-interests in collectivistic cultures such as Korea than in more individualistic ones such as the USA. This result was presented regardless of the follower's attitude (e.g. trust in leader, loyalty, value congruence) towards their leaders. Another comparative study that looked at the influence of culture between countries (Kirkman, Chen, Farh, Chen Lowe, 2009) extended the work of Podsakoff et al. (1990) whose work was one of the first to test the central effect of transformational leadership on followers to 'perform beyond the level of expectations' (Bass, 1985), by measuring follower's organizational citizenship behaviours (OCBs). OCBs are defined as being extra-role behaviours: i.e. are behaviours over and above what are formally defined or informally expected. Kirkman et al. (2009) extended this research to the People's Republic of China and confirmed an indirect relationship existed between transformational leadership and OCB through procedural justice using Podsakoff et al.'s TLI measure of transformational leadership. One exciting finding is that the results did not differ between the US and PRCs samples. In addition, power distance is a cultural value that moderates the follower's reaction to transformational leadership.

A study with a focus on the educational context applied Kouzes and Posner's transformational leadership model (Abu-Tineh & Al-Omari, 2008). This study examined the degree to which transformational leadership is being practiced by Jordanian school principals. They found that although the non-Western countries try to get the knowledge and technology of the West, they want to preserve their own cultural identities. Thus, they point to a significant gap in understanding the influence of society and context on educational leadership, and affirm that the studies on transformational leadership have paid little attention to this contextual consideration.

One study that makes us aware that social phenomena are more complex than usually considered is the one developed by Osborn and Marion (2009). Overall, most of these types of study indicate that culture matters, but sometimes it might not be the most salient factor affecting a leadership relationship. For instance, in spite of expected cultural differences between Japan and the USA, Osborn and Marion (2009) did not find any important effects. Their study of alliances in research-intensive sectors might suggest that other contextual dimensions such as knowledge and information base might have a stronger effect than cultural factors. Looking at three aspects of leadership performance – (a) alliance innovation and (b) strategic contributions to US sponsor company and (c) Japanese sponsor company – their study suggests that international alliances are multifaceted. They found that higher transformational leadership for sponsoring executives was positively linked to the alliance's strategic contribution to their respective firms. However, transformational leadership was a negative predictor of innovation performance. This study indicates that the relationship of leadership and performance is influenced by the type of governance structures (e.g. technical agreements vs joint venture and long-term supply contracts). Osborn and Marion conclude

We argue that leadership investigations should be based on a larger theoretical framework where context is important. The bulk of explained variance in our study was attributable to context and contextual leadership factors. Effective leadership particularly for innovation was embedded in its context. (2009, p. 205)

A couple of recent studies have apparently found only limited effects of culture upon the impact of transformational leadership. This is in line with the arguments put forward by Den Hartog et al. (1999) about the universality of the construct. Both studies (one in Mexico, the other in Greece) used the TLI measurement instrument developed by Podsakoff et al. (1990). The first study found that transformational leadership's communication interaction with followers helped to reduce stress

factors (such as role conflict and role ambiguity) (Díaz-Sáenz, Gomez Holguín & De la Garza García, 2008). Transformational leadership was the most preferred communication source over others such as peers and family and friends to mitigate stress factors by sharing positive information about work, negative information about work and information not related to work. When leaders exhibited low levels of transformational leadership behaviours, followers tended to communicate less with their leader and more with their peers, and with family and friends. The second study, developed in the Greek culture (Panagopoulos & Dimitriadis, 2009), also reported a good fit for the data collected using the TLI, which was developed in another cultural context. Their study found that transformational leadership mediates the relationship between behaviour-based control and key salesperson outcomes such as job performance, satisfaction and commitment (Panagopoulos & Dimitriadis, 2009).

Virtual teams

The emergence of virtual teams and their increasing adoption in organizations has attracted the attention of researchers to this type of work environment. The experiment is the methodological approach most favoured for this type of research. For example, a study developed in a laboratory setting by Wang and Xi (2007) found that transformational leadership has a significant effect upon team performance. This might not be a surprising finding; however, their study identified that, under the conditions of a virtual context, trust in the leader partially mediates this relationship. On the other hand, transactional leadership was found to have no effect upon performance. This latter finding suggests that rewards might not actually be as effective in a virtual environment as they are in a traditional setting.

Another experiment sought to understand the effects of transformational and transactional leadership styles and communication media upon team interaction and its outcomes (Hambley, O'Neill & Kline, 2007). This study found that leadership and transactional leadership are equally effective for problem-solving tasks, in spite of the communication medium used for interaction in a short term (face-to-face, videoconferencing or chat). Hambly et al. (2007) suggested that virtual team leadership requires longer time to identify differences in the effectiveness of each leadership style and media use. It is important to take into account that this study assessed the interactions among team members who had not worked together before. An additional experiment compared the leadership effectiveness of virtual (computer mediated) vs face-to-face teams, measuring only transformational behaviours (Purvanova & Bono, 2009). Leaders of virtual teams also led face-to-face teams, performing the same type of project for both teams. The findings of this experiment indicated that leaders changed their transformational behaviour depending on the type of team they were leading. Furthermore, 'transformational leadership behaviours were more strongly linked to performance in virtual than face-to-face teams' (2009, p. 352). An additional experiment focused on personality factors as predictors of transformational leadership and specifically to virtual teams by comparing virtual with face-to-face teams (Balthazard, Waldman, & Warren, 2009). In here, personality is not manifested more in face-to-face than in virtual contexts, where the first context has more information cues in the communication interaction (both oral and non-verbal). Thus, no links between personality traits and transformational leadership were found as they occurred in face-to-face settings. The findings of this study also suggest that written communication may influence perceptions of transformational leadership. As Balthazard et al. explained, 'The extent of participation and grammatical complexity, or the intricacy of embedded grammatical structures in written sentences, were the best predictors of transformational leadership in their VTs' (2009, p. 661).

Personality and transformational leadership

A considerable amount of research has been put into understanding the relationship between personality and transformational leadership. One exemplary study sought to understand the influence of followers' personalities on the transformational assessment of their leaders (Hautala, 2005). This study found a positive relationship between followers who had either an extraverted or feeling personality inclination and their assessment of transformational leadership compared to those followers who were more introverted and stronger thinking inclination. A follow-up study (Hautala, 2006) similarly found that the personality of leaders influenced the degree of their self-assessment of their transformational leadership. Extroverted individuals saw themselves as being more transformational than introverted ones. Additionally, the leaders' personality traits differed with the personality traits that followers linked to transformational behaviours: i.e. 'leader's self-ratings indicated that perceiving, extraversion and intuition were most transformational. Subordinates' appraisals indicated that the most transformational

leaders were sensing leaders' (Hautala, 2006, p. 789). Understanding the links between emotional intelligence, personality and transformational behaviour was the focus of the study by Rubin, Munz and Bommer (2005). Their study found a positive relationship between personality traits and emotional recognition and transformational leadership behaviours. In addition to the study of personality and virtual teams, as reviewed in last section, Brown and Reilly (2009) studied the possible relationship between elements of personality as measured by the Myers–Briggs Type Indicator (MBTI) and transformational leadership as measured by the MLQ. They found no relationship between MBTI and the followers' assessment of leaders' transformational behaviour.

Emotional intelligence

The linkage between emotional intelligence and transformational behaviour is another avenue of inquiry that has attracted growing interest by leadership researchers. For example, Barling, Slater and Kelloway (2000) discovered a positive relationship existed between followers' perception of their leader's transformational behaviours and their emotional intelligence. However, only three transformational behaviours (i.e. idealized influence, inspirational motivation and individualized consideration) and contingent reward were significantly associated with the level of emotional intelligence of the leader. By way of contrast, Brown, Bryant and Reilly (2006) found there was no relationship between the emotional intelligence of the leader and either the levels of perceived transformational leadership or desired outcomes. This finding is intriguing given the prior support for this relationship. More research is needed to understand better these possible relationships. Perhaps the inconsistencies might have arisen as a result of the deficiencies or limitations in the instruments used to assess the constructs, as Küpers and Weibler (2006) found in their analysis of the emotional quality of the MLQ. They propose that emotions and emotional competencies be considered for the transformational leadership instrument. Finally, Barbuto and Burbach (2006) identified a positive relationship between emotional intelligence and transformational leadership. Their findings were consistent with Barling et al. (2000), except for the direction of the relationship with the idealized influence dimension of rater reports. As they explain:

In all cases, we found stronger correlations between emotional intelligence and transformational leadership in leader self-reports than in rater reports.

This finding is likely best explained by common method bias, because leaders completed both the emotional intelligence questionnaire and the self-report version of the multi-factor leadership questionnaire. According to the emotional intelligence subscales, empathetic response is the most consistent antecedent of transformational leadership behaviors. The findings across methods indicate a modest relationship between emotional intelligence and transformational leadership. (2006, p. 60)

In the face of divergent findings, it is clear that further research is needed to understand these relationships. Most specifically, consistency in construct definition and the use of assessment instruments is needed to measure emotional intelligence.

META-ANALYTIC STUDIES

An important and growing body of research that is helping us to better understand the advances in the transformational leadership construct are meta-analytic studies. In this review we look at the latest studies, since some earlier ones are also included in the ones presented here. Even though the MLQ is not the only scaled developed to study transformational leadership, we only found meta-analytic reviews that considered this type of assessment (Bono & Judge, 2004; Eagly, Johannesen-Schmidt & Engen, 2003; Judge & Piccolo, 2004; Lowe et al., 1996). A word of caution is, therefore, warranted while looking at the conclusions of these studies because having only MLQ assessments is in itself a limitation that prevents us from making generalizations beyond the items included in this scale (Lowe et al., 1996). We look at these studies in chronological order to get a sense of the advances achieved by scholars that have pursued empirical research in this area.

First of all, Lowe et al. (1996) analysed the research that links transformational and transactional leadership to leader effectiveness. They found transformational leadership to be associated with higher levels of efficiency in public and private organizations, as well as with leaders at lower and higher levels, regardless of the criterion variable used to assess efficiency (e.g. either follower perception or organizational indicators). With respect to levels, the findings confirmed that transformational patterns of behaviour are not exclusive to leaders at the top level of the organization. Their study also indicated a mono-method bias in measuring leadership effectiveness tends to inflate the effect size. On the other hand, using organizational measures could attenuate those effects because that type of variable does not characterize

indicators that reflect the leader–follower relationship. Their concluding position on this issue is that a 'true relationship lies between that indicated by the study results for subordinate perceptions and that for organizational measures' (1996, p. 419).

A more recent multi-analytic study looked at behavioural differences between male and female leaders (Eagly et al., 2003). Based on social role theory, the authors expected that male and female leaders would exhibit different leadership behaviours. Accordingly, this study found support for that expectation, although these differences were quite small. The review revealed that, in general, women tended to be more transformational in leadership than the men included in the studies. What was particularly interesting in this study is that those dimensions that were inclined to predict leadership effectiveness were generally more pronounced in women than in men. Furthermore, transactional leadership behaviours that rewarded good performance were more generally engaged in by women than by men. Even though differences were small, the support for social role theory brings important implications regarding the relationship between leadership and gender roles.

In a meta-analytical study that seems to revive the old argument of leaders being born or developed, Bono and Judge (2004) found that, overall, there were only small correlation effects between the Big Five personality traits and the transformational and transactional dimensions. They concluded that 'our results suggest that continued use of the Big Five traits may not be fruitful in revealing the dispositional bases of transformational and transactional leadership' (2004, p. 907). Nevertheless, their study indicated a strong relationship between extroversion and transformational leadership behaviour. Thus, Bono and Judge suggest that future research should focus more on the role of extraversion in influencing leadership behaviours. Furthermore, they invited researchers to develop research that will allow the understanding of the way in which leadership behaviours are developed. In particular, they pointed to leadership training as an important line for future research, as they discovered a number of studies in their review that provided evidence supporting the notion that transformational leadership behaviour can, in fact, be learned.

Finally, another meta-analytical study tested and found strong support for the validity of the transformational and transactional leadership (Judge & Piccolo, 2004). Most importantly, the authors observed a high correlation between these two theoretically distinct, although related, dimensions. Consequently, Judge and Piccollo (2004) called for a deeper understanding of the relationship between the transformational, transactional and laissez-fare leadership dimensions.

In addition, to a lesser extent, this study also found support for the validity of laissez-fair leadership. This study claimed to test the full range of transformational leadership. Nevertheless, it is important to note that all transformational dimensions were combined and treated as one, based on previous reports of high correlations among them (see Howell & Hall-Merenda, 1999; Judge & Bono, 2000). Thus, this study does not address whether or not there are different effects among the theoretical dimensions. Furthermore, this study acknowledged an earlier debate regarding the extent to which charismatic and transformational leadership are conceptually different. Bass claimed that charismatic leadership was only one part of transformational leadership (see Bass & Riggio, 2006). Nevertheless, Judge and Piccolo (2004) tested these two leadership elements and found similar validities for transformational and charismatic leadership, which suggests that they are very similar concepts. On the positive side of the ledger, this meta-analytic study noted that, in general, from the mid-1990s onwards the transformational leadership studies had become increasingly rigorous and more generalizable.

It is important to note that none of the meta-analytical studies found for this review took into consideration studies that applied transformational leadership assessment instruments other than Bass's MLQ. Whereas there are methodological justifications for not mixing studies applying different assessments, it seems amiss that no meta-analytical studies have considered the substantial body of empirical studies that have investigated transformational leadership using other instruments.

LIMITATIONS AND CRITICISMS OF TRANSFORMATIONAL LEADERSHIP

Most of the empirical research has supported the notion that transformational leadership has a favourable influence upon follower's performance, often arguing strongly in favour of the practice and development of transformational leadership behaviours. Nevertheless, as with any theoretical concepts, weaknesses and limitations have been observed by several scholars regarding transformational leadership theory (e.g. Beyer, 1999; Northouse, 2007; Tejada, Scandura, & Pillai, 2001; Tracey & Hinkin, 1998; Yukl, 1999).

Probably one of the weaknesses most frequently noted is the tendency among transformational leadership researchers to idealize the transformational leadership approach to the extent that too much credit is given to the leader, whereas others

factors that lead to individual, group or organizational development are ignored. One of these elements would be the effects of the followers' contribution to the interaction with their leader and situational or process factors underlying foundations or transformational effects.

Another criticism that needs to be addressed within the scientific community as a whole is the tendency to limit one's vision and not to properly acknowledge the full body of research when doing research. It is readily apparent from this review that the efforts made by researchers interested in the transformational leadership construct have been dissipated because of fragmented energy. Researchers tend to favour the exclusive use of either MLQ (developed by Bass), the measures developed by Podsakoff and colleagues or Kouzes and Posner and ignore the studies that have used other instruments. Although it may well be justified to use one measure over another for a specific study, it does not make sense if we are genuinely interested in making progress in our understanding of transformational leadership to ignore the findings that have been yielded by studies using different instruments. We should not limit our view to one approach, as if we were faithful disciples of one researcher and not interested in the contribution of another. A decade ago, Hunt (1999) suggested that transformational leadership theory was at the stage of 'concept evaluation/ augmentation', which was consistent with the problematic findings associated with the operationalization of the MLQ at that time. It would seem then that transformational leadership has not yet reached the next desired stage of 'consolidation/ accommodation', which would reflect its maturity in construct development.

Another limitation that still remains from the time of Hunt's review revolves around the problems of supporting the four transformational factors of the MLQ Form 5X. Tracey and Hinking (1998) reported a high correlation among its scales and, instead of four factors, found support for one factor only (Tracey & Hinkin, 1998). This high level of intercorrelation among the subscales in Form 5X was later confirmed by Tejada et al. (2001), calling for a refinement of the MLQ. Their study proposed a reduced 27-item set of transformational and transactional scales cross-validated in independent samples. The refinement of this instrument offers the advantage of having a smaller survey, which is consistent with the multifactor leadership instrument, which supports its predictive validity.

Another limitation also mentioned by Hunt (1999) that still remains today is the fact that research has been done using mostly surveys, relying heavily upon MLQ (see Bryman, Chapter 2, this volume). The only exception found for this review was the use of the Podsakoff's et al. (1990) leadership instrument. Nevertheless, even though their paper is widely cited (506 times), their instrument is still not as widely used as the MLQ. Building on the criticism of an overreliance upon one methodological method, Beyer (1999) contended that transformational leadership research sorely lacks studies that draw upon qualitative data. In particular, the relationship between leaders and followers is ripe for qualitative analysis.

There are still a lot of different levels of analysis or a combination of them that is still unexplored. For instance, there might be some instances in which transformational leadership influences the context, some others in which the context limits or facilitates the emergence of transformational leadership. For instance, Yukl (1999) observes that several theorists argue that some conditions, such as unstable environments and organic structure (among others), may increase the effect of transformational leadership on followers, yet only a few studies have looked into these factors. Furthermore, there might be an interaction of leadership and contextual factors that accounts for what is happening in organizational settings. Following this line of thought, Beyer (1999) suggested looking at the content of the leader's acts to deliver his or her vision and whether followers are convinced individually or collectively.

In her criticisms, Beyer (1999) adds that researchers use only the psychological approach, ignoring the sociological one that was most notably championed by Weber. For the same reason, she claimed that researchers neglect the insights and definition of charismatic leadership offered already by Weber which could complement transformational leadership theory. Consistent with this view Yukl (1999) added that there is a misconception regarding charisma that has been fostered by too many definitions argued by theorists. With respect to these issues of charismatic leadership, researchers should look at the debate that took place between Beyer, Bass and others in Volume 10, Issues 2 and 4 of *The Leadership Quarterly* in 1999. Both Beyer and Yukl claimed that researchers have departed from Weber's definition of charismatic leadership, which sociologists see 'as an unusual form of normative social structure that emerges in times of crisis' (Beyer, 1999, p. 310). Yukl also stated that there are theoretical inconsistencies among several theoretical explanations of charismatic as well as transformational terms in ways that have overlapped too much. He proposed that both types of leadership cannot happen at the same time, concluding:

A transformational leader seems more likely to take actions that will empower followers and make them partners in a quest to achieve important objectives. A charismatic leader seems more likely to emphasize the need for radical change that can only be accomplished if followers put their trust in the leader's unique expertise. Incompatible aspects of the core behaviors for transformational and charismatic leadership may make it rare for both types of leadership to occur at the same time. (Yukl, 1999, p. 301)

In the end, Beyer's (1999) demand for a clear definition of transformational leadership apart from charismatic leadership seems reasonable because today there is ambiguity in how they are defined. Bass' response to Beyer did not state clearly whether or not there is a difference between transformational and charismatic leadership or how Weber's charismatic leadership definition had been tamed in favour of a more integrative view within transformational leadership.

CONCLUSIONS AND FUTURE RESEARCH

In 1999 Jerry Hunt stated that the field of leadership was in stage 2 and, even though he referred to the field of leadership in the context of the 'New' or transformational leadership discussion, today, it seems that the field is still in stage 2, in spite of the growing body of research. Transformational leadership has progressed over the years. Nevertheless, it seems that the efforts are fragmented into diverse isolated group of researchers who sometimes seem to ignore each other. Thus, future research needs to take a more integrative theoretical view. In fairness, Hunt also acknowledged that the field was moving forward and what was happening was exciting. Nevertheless, as an outsider of this then called 'New Paradigm', Beyer (1999) considered that Hunt was being too optimistic. She saw that the approach to transformational leadership was too narrow, thanks to the predominant psychological and quantitative methodology. Beyer felt that future transformational leadership research should take into account consideration of the measurement of different levels of analysis within organizations and the incorporation of more sociological perspectives. Disappointingly, Beyer's call has not apparently been heeded so that, 10 years on, there is still a marked tendency to recycle the same methodological approach over and over again in the study of transformational leadership. There is no shortage of interesting avenues of inquiry, however. For instance Pastor and Mayo (2008) have suggested that we should investigate the use of neural networks to map the links between specific beliefs and transformational behaviours more precisely. They further explain: 'an interesting line for future research would be to study how the top management team functions as a collective mind' (2008, p. 353). Finally, future research should look for instances in which leadership has an influence upon the context as well as vice versa. For example, Osborn and Marion suggest 'echoing Hunt (1991) it is important in future research to recognize that leaders in different echelons may well be in different contexts where different casual mechanisms are important' (2009, p. 204).

ACKNOWLEDGEMENT

The author would like to acknowledge Patricia D. Witherspoon, 'a truly transformational leader', for introducing him to the field of leadership.

REFERENCES

Abu-Tineh, A. M. & Al-Omari, A. A. (2008). Kouzes and Posner's transformational leadership model in practice: the case of Jordanian schools. *Leadership & Organization Development Journal*, 29(8), 648–660.

Balthazard, P. A., Waldman, D. A. & Warren, J. E. (2009). Predictors of the emergence of transformational leadership in virtual decision teams. *The Leadership Quarterly*, 20(5), 651–663.

Barbuto Jr, J. E. & Burbach, M. E. (2006). The emotional intelligence of transformational leaders: a field study of elected officials. *Journal of Social Psychology*, 146(1), 51–64.

Barling, J., Slater, F. & Kelloway, E. K. (2000). Transformational leadership and emotional intelligence: an exploratory study. *Leadership & Organization Development Journal*, 21(3), 157–161.

Bass, B. M. (1985). *Leadership and performance beyond expectations*, 1st edn. New York: Free Press.

Bass, B. M. & Avolio, B. J. (1995). *Multifactor Leadership Questionnaire*. Redwood City, CA: Mind Garden.

Bass, B. M. & Riggio, R. E. (2006). *Transformational leadership*, 2nd edn. Mahwan, NJ: Lawrence Erlbaum Associates.

Bennis, W. G. & Nanus, B. (1985). *Leaders: the strategies for taking charge*. New York: Harper & Row.

Beyer, J. M. (1999). Taming and promoting charisma to change organizations. *The Leadership Quarterly*, 10(2), 307–330.

Bono, J. E. & Judge, T. A. (2004). Personality and transformational and transactional leadership: a meta-analysis. *Journal of Applied Psychology*, 89(5), 901–910.

Brown, F. W., Bryant, S. E. & Reilly, M. D. (2006). Does emotional intelligence – as measured by the EQI – influence transformational leadership and/or desirable outcomes? *Leadership & Organization Development Journal*, 27(5), 330–351.

Brown, F. W. & Reilly, M.D. (2009). The Myers–Briggs type indicator and transformational leadership. *Journal of Management Development*, 28(10), 916–932.

Burns, J. M. (1978). *Leadership*. New York: Harper & Row.

Colbert, A. E., Kristof-Brown, A. L., Bradley, B. H. & Barrick, M. R. (2008). CEO transformational leadership: the role of goal importance congruence in top management teams. *Academy of Management Journal*, 51(1), 81–96.

Conger, J. (1999). Charismatic and transformational leadership in organizations: an insider's perspective on these developing streams of research. *The Leadership Quarterly*, 10(2), 145–179.

Daft, R. L. & Lengel, R. H. (1998). *Fusion leadership*. San Francisco, CA: Berrett–Koehler.

Den Hartog, D. N., House, R. J., Hanges, P. J. & Ruiz-Quintanilla, S. A. (1999). Culture specific and cross culturally generalizable implicit leadership theories: are attributes of charismatic/transformational leadership universally endorsed? *The Leadership Quarterly*, 10(2), 219–256.

Díaz-Sáenz, H. R., Gomez Holguín, R. & de la Garza García, J. (2008). La relación entre comportamientos de liderazgo transformacional, contenidos de comunicación y factores de estrés en el trabajo. *Revista Investigación Administrativa*, 102, 7–21.

Downton, J. V. (1973). *Rebel leadership*. New York: Free Press.

Eagly, A. H., Johannesen-Schmidt, M. C. & Engen, M. L. v. (2003). Transformational, transactional, and laissez-faire leadership styles: a meta-analysis comparing women and men. *Psychological Bulletin*, 129(4), 569–591.

Eid, J., Johnsen, B. H., Bartone, P. T. & Nissestad, O. A. (2008). Growing transformational leaders: exploring the role of personality hardiness. *Leadership & Organization Development Journal*, 29(1), 4–23.

Hambley, L. A., O'Neill, T. A. & Kline, T. J. B. (2007). Virtual team leadership: the effects of leadership style and communication medium on team interaction styles and outcomes. *Organizational Behavior and Human Decision Processes*, 103(1), 1–20.

Hautala, T. (2005). The effects of subordinates' personality on appraisals of transformational leadership. *Journal of Leadership & Organizational Studies*, 11(4), 84.

Hautala, T. M. (2006). The relationship between personality and transformational leadership *Journal of Management Development*, 25(8), 777–794.

Howell, J. M. & Hall-Merenda, K. E. (1999). The ties that bind: The impact of leader-member exchange, transformational leadership and transactional leadership, and distance on predicting follower performance. *Journal of Applied Psychology*, 84: 680–694.

Hunt, J. G. (1999). Transformational/charismatic leadership's transformation of the field: an historical essay. *The Leadership Quarterly*, 10(2), 129–144.

Judge, T. A. & Bono, J. E. (2000). Five-factor model of personality and transformational leadership. *Journal of Applied Psychology*, 85, 751–765.

Judge, T. A. & Piccolo, R. F. (2004). Transformational and transactional leadership: a meta-analytic test of their relative validity. *Journal of Applied Psychology*, 89(5), 755–768.

Jung, D., Wu, A. & Chow, C. W. (2008). Towards understanding the direct and indirect effects of CEOs' transformational leadership on firm innovation. *The Leadership Quarterly*, 19(5), 582–594.

Jung, D., Yammarino, F. J. & Lee, J. K (2009). Moderating role of subordinates' attitudes on transformational leadership and effectiveness: a multi-cultural and multi-level perspective. *The Leadership Quarterly*, 20(4), 586–603.

Kirkman, B., Chen, G., Farh, J.-L., Chen, Z. & Lowe, K. (2009). Individual power distance orientation and follower reactions to transformational leaders: a cross-level, cross-cultural examination. *Academy of Management Journal*, 52(4), 744–764.

Kotter, J. P. (1990). *Force for change: how leadership differs from management*, The Free Press.

Küpers, W. & Weibler, J. (2006). How emotional is transformational leadership really? Some suggestions for a necessary extension. *Leadership & Organization Development Journal*, 27(5), 368–383.

Lowe, K. B., Kroeck, K. G. & Sivasubramaniam, N. (1996). Effectiveness correlates of transformational and transactional leadership: a meta-analytic review of the MLQ literature. *The Leadership Quarterly*, 7(3), 385–425.

Mannheim, B. & Halamish, H. (2008). Transformational leadership as related to team outcomes and contextual moderation. *Leadership & Organization Development Journal*, 29(7), 617–630.

Northouse, P. G. (2007). *Leadership theory and practice*. Thousand Oaks, CA: Sage.

Osborn, R. N. & Marion, R. (2009). Contextual leadership, transformational leadership and the performance of international innovation seeking alliances. *The Leadership Quarterly*, 20(2), 191–206.

Panagopoulos, N. & Dimitriadis, S. (2009) Transformational leadership as a mediator of the relationship between behavior-based control and salespeople's key outcomes. An initial investigation. *European Journal of Marketing*, 43(7/8), 1008–1031.

Pastor, J. C. & Mayo, M (2008). Transformational leadership among Spanish upper echelons: the role of managerial values and goal orientation. *Leadership & Organization Development Journal*, 29(4), 340–358.

Podsakoff, P. M., MacKenzie, S. B., Moorman, R. H. & Fetter, R. (1990). Transformational leader behaviors and their effects on followers' trust in leader, satisfaction, and organizational citizenship behaviors. *The Leadership Quarterly*, 1(2), 107–142.

Purvanova, R. K. & Bono, J. E. (2009). Transformational leadership in context: face-to-face and virtual teams. *The Leadership Quarterly*, 20(3), 343–357.

Rubin, R. S., Munz, D. C. & Bommer, W. H. (2005). Leading from within: the effects of emotion recognition and personality on transformational leadership behavior. *Academy of Management Journal*, 48(5), 845–858.

Schaubroeck, J., Lam, S. S. K. & Cha, S. E. (2007). Embracing transformational leadership: team values and the impact of leader behavior on team performance. *Journal of Applied Psychology*, 92(4), 1020–1030.

Singh, N. & Krishnan, V. R. (2008). Self-sacrifice and transformational leadership: mediating role of altruism. *Leadership & Organization Development Journal*, 29(3), 261–274.

Spreitzer, G. M., Perttula, K.H. & Xin, K. (2005). Traditionality matters: an examination of the effectiveness of transformational leadership in the United States and Taiwan. *Journal of Organizational Behavior*, 26(3), 205–227.

Tejada, M. J., Scandura, T. A. & Pillai, R. (2001). The MLQ revised psychometric properties and recommendations. *The Leadership Quarterly*, 12, 31–52.

Tichy, N. & Devanna, M.A. (1986). *The transformational leader*. New york: Wiley.

Tracey, J. B. & Hinkin, T. R. (1998). Transformational leadership or effective managerial practices? *Group & Organization Management*, 23(3), 220–236.

Waldman, D. A., Bass, B. M., & Yammarino, F. J. (1990). Adding to contingent reward behaviour: the augmenting effect of charismatic leadership. *Group and Organization Studies*, 15(4): 381–394.

Wang, L. & Xi, Y. (2007). Trust as a mediator of the effects of transformational leadership on performance in virtual teams. 2007 International Conference on Wireless Communications, Networking and Mobile Computing, WiCOM, 6045–6048.

Yukl, G. (1999). An evaluation of conceptual weaknesses in transformational and charismatic leadership theories. *The Leadership Quarterly*, 10(2), 285–305.

Zalenik, A. (1977). Managers and leaders: Are they different? *Harvard Business Review*, 55: 67–88.

Zhu, W., Chew, I. K. H. & Spangler, W. D. (2005). CEO transformational leadership and organizational outcomes: the mediating role of human-capital-enhancing human resource management. *The Leadership Quarterly*, 16(1), 39–52.

23

Leader–Member Exchange: Recent Research Findings and Prospects for the Future

Smriti Anand, Jia Hu, Robert C. Liden and
Prajya R. Vidyarthi

INTRODUCTION

Leader–member exchange (LMX) theory is rooted in the principle that each leader–follower relationship within a work group is unique, varies in quality, and should be studied as a dyad. LMX theory rejects the practice in other leadership approaches of averaging the perceptions that each follower holds of the leader in order to determine leadership style (Dansereau, Graen, & Haga, 1975). Since the inception of LMX theory, a number of studies have shown that the dyadic relationship quality develops quite early, and remains generally stable through the life of the dyad (e.g., Liden, Wayne, & Stilwell, 1993). The LMX development process is heavily influenced by affect, which contributes toward the growth of mutual trust, liking, and respect. Some of the determinants of LMX are perceived similarity and liking between leader and member, expectations from each other, leader delegation, and member performance (Bauer & Green, 1996; Liden et al., 1993). Drawing on social exchange theory (Blau, 1964) and the norm of reciprocity (Gouldner, 1960), LMX literature maintains that dyadic relationship quality exerts significant influence on a wide variety of organizational outcomes, such as in-role performance, citizenship behaviors, overall job satisfaction, and turnover intentions (e.g., Gerstner & Day, 1997; Ilies, Nahrgang, & Morgeson, 2007).

In this chapter, we review developments in LMX theory and research since the last comprehensive review by Erdogan and Liden (2002). Therefore, this review is based on empirical and theoretical papers cited in social sciences indexes since 2002. Apart from a few exceptions, we did not discuss conference papers or unpublished manuscripts, but we did include several studies that were not part of the last three reviews (Erdogan & Liden, 2002; Liden, Sparrowe, & Wayne, 1997; Schriesheim, Castro, & Cogliser, 1999). Database searches between 2002 and 2009 yielded 130 studies focusing on LMX. More than 70% of these studies examined antecedents and consequences of LMX, in line with Erdogan and Liden's (2002) observation regarding LMX researchers' continued interest in these topics. Although the determinants and outcomes of LMX still dominate scholars' interest, the mature stage of LMX theory demands attention to factors that set boundaries for the effects of LMX (Liden et al., 1997; Schriesheim et al., 1999). Therefore, this review focuses on studies that explore the context of LMX.

We found empirical and conceptual studies examining the context of LMX in three distinct ways. First, several studies indicated a burgeoning interest in understanding the linkages between LMX and work-group dynamics. LMX is inherently a process of differentiation whereby leaders establish high-quality relationships with only a few followers (Liden, Erdogan, Wayne, & Sparrowe, 2006).

LMX differentiation can affect outcomes at the individual level in one way and outcomes at the group level in another. Consequently, LMX differentiation studies have examined the effects of LMX at the individual level, meso level, and the group level (e.g., Liden et al., 2006). Secondly, a number of scholars have attempted to further our understanding of how LMX works in different societal contexts. Research in this tradition falls into two categories: studies that generalize LMX theory to other national cultures (e.g., Aryee & Chen, 2006; Schyns, Paul, Mohr, & Blank, 2005; Varma, Srinivas, & Stroh, 2005), and studies that specifically examine the relationship between various dimensions of culture and LMX (e.g., Erdogan & Liden, 2006; Schaubroeck & Lam, 2002). Finally, a few LMX scholars have endeavored to understand the effects of LMX in the context of other leadership theories (e.g., Wang, Law, Hackett, Wang, & Chen, 2005). LMX differs from other leadership theories in at least two ways: first, most leadership theories focus on leader behaviors and treat followers as passive recipients; Second, LMX focuses on dyadic exchanges which are more proximal to organizational outcomes (Wang et al., 2005). Therefore, an integration of LMX with other leadership theories can shed light on how leadership works at different levels.

Our review of recent LMX studies, many of which have focused on the context in which LMX relationships are embedded, begins with a detailed discussion of LMX differentiation, associated issues of fairness, and the possibility of in-group and out-group formation. Then we look at studies that have examined the outcomes of LMX in the context of national culture. Specifically, we focus on research that incorporates two of the most important dimensions of culture: namely, individualism/collectivism and power distance. We also discuss high/low context because cultures vary in their strength, which can affect LMX relationships. Then we turn our attention to studies that relate LMX theory to other theories of leadership. In particular, researchers have viewed LMX theory as related to, but distinct from, transformational leadership (Bass, 1985) and servant leadership (Greenleaf, 1977) theories. Therefore, this review examines studies incorporating these two theories along with LMX theory. We conclude with a discussion of weaknesses in LMX theory and recommendations for future researchers.

LMX DIFFERENTIATION

LMX theory is based on the premise of differential quality of relationships between leaders and subordinates. High-quality relationships go beyond the contractual agreement and are characterized by mutual influence, negotiability, and trust and respect (Dansereau, et al., 1975; Liden & Maslyn, 1998). On the other hand, low-quality relationships are bound by terms of the employment contract, and tend to be transactional. LMX scholars have proposed that differentiation between subordinates allows leaders to make efficient use of their limited time and resources. Leaders vary in the extent to which they differentiate between their subordinates, though most leaders tend to form exchanges of differing quality with their subordinates; only in rare cases do leaders establish similar quality relationship with all subordinates (Liden & Graen, 1980), thus creating a group with a low degree of variability in LMX quality (i.e., low LMX differentiation). These leaders form work groups consisting of all high LMX or all low LMX relationships.

Work-group members are likely to engage in within-group social comparison processes (Festinger, 1954), which can affect their perceptions of fairness (Masterson, Lewis, Goldman, & Taylor, 2000) and subsequent outcomes. High-LMX relationships include tangible rewards, such as challenging assignments and training opportunities (Liden, Wayne, & Sparrowe, 2000), and intangible rewards, such as leader's trust and respect (Graen & Uhl-Bien, 1995), which are not available to members with low-quality LMX. This differential distribution of rewards may create perceptions of inequity in low LMX members (Liden et al., 1997). The differentiation that seems fair and favorable to the high LMX members is likely to be viewed as inequitable and adverse to those with lower-quality LMX. LMX scholars have noted that while the personal quality of LMX may be beneficial to an individual employee, the variability across group members violates the equality principles of fairness (Scandura, 1999), which are fundamental to group solidarity (Greenberg, 1982). These issues of fairness, innate to LMX differentiation, have the potential to split the work group in subgroups based on members' LMX quality.

In one of the earliest investigations of within-group differentiation, Sias and Jablin (1995) found that employees considered differential treatment from the leader to be unfair unless supported by clear evidence of competence. Perceptions of unfairness in turn led to disliking of and reduced communication with the favored person. On the other hand, group members who were targets of adverse leader differentiation did not receive liking or sympathy from the group; if the adverse differentiation was deemed fair the group members distanced themselves from the disfavored ones. These findings show that LMX differentiation can divide the work group into an in-group and an out-group consisting of members with high and low LMX, respectively, thereby leading to intra-group relational problems, such as mutual dislike and rejection that are detrimental to the overall group.

The link between LMX differentiation and formation of subgroups can also be understood by applying Heider's (1958) balance theory, which proposes that members of a triad tend to seek relational balance. Balance theory implies that if two coworkers have high-quality relationships with the leader, they are likely to have a high-quality relationship with each other as well. Consistent with balance theory, Sherony and Green (2002) found a positive association between the quality of relationship between coworkers and the similarity in their LMX quality. Their findings suggest that coworkers with high LMX are likely to develop good relationships with each other, and poorer relationships with their counterparts with lower LMX, thus effectively creating two sub-groups. Based on full social network data, Henderson and Liden (2007) replicated Sherony and Green's findings by showing that individuals with similar LMX quality reported greater social closeness with similar peers. Interestingly, however, these researchers also found that members with low LMX quality reported stronger friendship ties to high LMX members than high LMX members reported for low LMX peers. Thus, it appears that group members, regardless of LMX status, tend to show a preference for interacting with higher LMX individuals. Similarly, Lau and Liden (2008) found that group members tend to place more trust in fellow group members who are most trusted by their leader.

Perceptions of unfairness and potential for subgroup formation associated with LMX differentiation merit more theorizing and empirical examination. However, despite repeated calls for research to examine LMX in the context of work groups (Erdogan & Liden, 2002; Graen & Uhl-Bien, 1995; Liden et al., 1997), only a handful of studies have looked beyond the effects of individual LMX quality. We found one theoretical and seven empirical articles on LMX differentiation published since 2002. In the only conceptual article devoted to LMX differentiation, Henderson, Liden, Glibkowski, and Chaudhry (2009) reviewed extant research and proposed a model of antecedents and consequences of differentiated relationships between leaders and members in the context of work group and the organization. Henderson and colleagues proposed that LMX differentiation was a consequence of

- leader characteristics, such as leadership style,
- member characteristics, such as desire to be a permanent employee,

- group characteristics, such as size and composition, and
- organizational characteristics, such as structure, culture, and HR practices.

Employee outcomes of differentiation were proposed at the individual, group, and organizational levels, while leader outcomes, such as career success and performance, were proposed at the individual level. The authors discussed appropriate levels of analyses, and offered suggestions for future research that accounted for the multi-level nature of differentiation processes.

Although LMX differentiation is theoretically conceptualized at the group level, it has been analyzed at the individual, meso, and group level (Klein, Dansereau, & Hall, 1994; Yammarino, Dionne, Chun, & Dansereau, 2005). Accordingly, studies focusing on LMX differentiation can be classified in three categories:

1. Individual level studies that employ measures designed to capture individual perceptions of how much the leader differentiates amongst the group members, and examine outcomes for individual employees.
2. Group-level studies that utilize statistical measures of within-group LMX variability, such as standard deviation or r_{wg} of group member's LMX scores, and examine outcomes for the group as a social entity.
3. Multi-level studies that use statistical measures of within-group variability to examine cross-level effects involving individual employee variables, work-group variables, and in some cases include the organization level (Erdogan, Liden & Kraimer, 2006).

Out of the seven studies investigating LMX differentiation that we located, two were at the individual level of analysis, three were at the group level, and the remaining two used multilevel analysis.

Individual-level studies

In one of the first quantitative studies of LMX differentiation, Van Breukelen, Konst, and Van Der Vlist (2002) found that LMX differentiation attenuated the relationship between LMX and work-group commitment. The authors noted that member perceptions of high LMX differentiation within the unit may have created doubts about fairness and integrity of the leader, thereby neutralizing the positive effects of LMX on work-group commitment. These findings should be treated with some caution, because the perceptual measure of differentiation in this study focused on leader differentiation among group members in terms of friendliness and feedback, and therefore did not capture variability in all aspects of LMX.

Hooper and Martin (2008) extended this line of inquiry by examining the effects of within-group variability in LMX on employee attitudes beyond the personal quality of LMX. The authors argued that LMX variability violated the principles of equality and consistency, and thus was likely to create group conflict, and reduce employee job satisfaction and well-being. Using a single-item measure to assess member perceptions of within-group variability in LMX, in a sample of 357 firefighters and 74 employees from several other organizations in Australia, the authors found that LMX differentiation was positively related to group conflict, which in turn was associated with lowered job satisfaction and well-being.

Findings of these two studies advise against differentiation in that employee perceptions of high differentiation are associated with lower group commitment (Van Breukelen et al., 2002), job satisfaction, and well-being (Hooper & Martin, 2008). These findings also imply that leaders may be able to enhance member outcomes and group solidarity by at least maintaining an appearance of equal treatment across the group.

Group-level studies

In a study involving 35 groups with 162 soldiers from the Canadian army, Boies and Howell (2006) found that higher levels of mean LMX in the group were associated with higher group potency and lower group conflict. Furthermore, these relationships were *stronger* in groups with higher LMX differentiation, indicating that LMX differentiation was beneficial when group mean LMX was high, and detrimental otherwise. The authors suggested that in groups with low mean LMX, perceptions of inequity and competition for the leader's attention may have led high LMX differentiation to have an adverse effect, whereas in groups with high LMX differentiation and high mean LMX, informal leadership, defined as peer influence within the group, was responsible for the beneficial effects of high differentiation.

In a similar line of inquiry, Ford and Seers (2006) analyzed the relationship between group mean LMX, LMX differentiation, and the degree of within-group agreement on work climate in a sample of 392 employees from four organizations based in Europe and the USA. Drawing from action theory, the authors showed that group mean LMX was positively, and LMX differentiation was negatively, related to within-group agreement on climate.

In a somewhat different approach from these two studies, Schyns (2006) hypothesized relationships between group consensus on LMX (opposite of LMX differentiation) and outcomes. In a sample of 54 work groups with 234 dyads from 22 banks and insurance companies in Germany, Schyns found a positive relationship between group consensus (only on the contribution dimension of LMX) and group mean level of job satisfaction. Findings also led Schyns to conclude that LMX consensus could compensate for low work values to increase group performance.

Taken together these studies show that high group mean LMX, resulting from high-quality relationships between the leader and most group members, leads to positive outcomes, such as higher group potency, lower group conflict (Boies & Howell, 2006), and within-group agreement on climate (Ford & Seers, 2006). Large degrees of differentiation were associated with negative outcomes, such as low within-group agreement on climate and low job satisfaction (Schyns, 2006). These effects were moderated by group-work values and average quality of LMX, such that differentiation can be beneficial in groups with an overall positive tone of relationship between leader and members. More research is needed to identify group-level variables that enhance positive rather than negative effects of differentiation.

Multi-level studies

In one of the first multi-level investigations focused on LMX differentiation, Liden et al. (2006) studied the effects of within-group variability in LMX quality on both individual and group performance in 120 work groups containing 834 dyads representing 6 US organizations. The authors found LMX differentiation to be positively related to individual performance only for group members with low-quality LMX. Group performance was positively associated with LMX differentiation in work groups with high levels of task interdependence as well as in groups with low median LMX. These findings highlight the need to examine group context in order to understand the relationship between differentiation and outcomes.

Further extending the multi-level line of inquiry, Henderson, Wayne, Shore, Bommer, and Tetrick, (2008) examined LMX differentiation at the individual-within-group level and at the group level. Based on earlier work by Graen, Liden, and Hoel (1982), Henderson and colleagues examined 'relative LMX' (RLMX), defined as relative standing of the focal employee within the group in terms of their LMX quality (operationalized as employee's LMX minus the LMX mean for the group). Using a sample of 31 work groups with 278 dyads from four manufacturing facilities, Henderson and colleagues found positive association between RLMX and employee psychological contract (PC) fulfillment, which was stronger in groups with higher levels of differentiation. After controlling for personal quality of LMX, RLMX influenced employee in-role performance and citizenship behaviors through PC fulfillment. These findings show the importance of examining differentiation processes simultaneously at the individual-within-group and group levels.

Both the Liden et al. (2006) and Henderson et al. (2008) studies underscore that differentiation is a multifaceted phenomenon that can be understood only when examined at multiple levels. Examining differentiation at only the individual level may lead to incorrect conclusions about its adverse effects (Hooper & Martin, 2008; Van Breukelen et al., 2002). It appears that the effects of differentiation are not universally good or bad; it is the group context which determines the nature of the outcome. Some group-level studies that have ignored other contextual variables have shown negative effects of differentiation (Ford & Seers, 2006), but others have shown positive effects of differentiation in groups with high average LMX quality, suggesting leaders should maintain an appearance of high-quality relationships with all followers (Boies & Howell, 2006).

LMX differentiation is a complex phenomenon that can be better understood through an examination of moderators. For example, Liden et al. (2006) found a significant relationship between LMX differentiation and group performance only when task interdependence was high or average LMX quality was low, suggesting that differentiation could be seen as equitable in highly interdependent groups as it allowed leaders to better coordinate the contributions of the group. More studies are needed to explore the conditions under which LMX differentiation may enhance or thwart performance within the group. Given that groups are widely used in organizations (Cohen & Bailey, 1997), group contextual factors, such as group justice climate, can serve as a *situational enhancer* (Howell, Dorfman, & Kerr, 1986) and may influence the strength with which LMX differentiation relates to group performance.

Just as aspects of the context inform relationships between LMX differentiation and outcomes, more needs to be learned about the influence of contextual variables on the antecedents and consequences of individual LMX quality. Thus, we turn our attention to initial studies that examine LMX in the context of societal or national culture. Increasing globalization has increased researchers' interest in the generalizability of LMX theory in different national cultures (e.g., Aryee & Chen, 2006; Erdogan & Liden, 2006). National culture refers to the norms, values, beliefs, and assumptions that are shared by members of a nation, and guides their interpretation of the world (Hofstede, 1980, 1984; Markus & Kitayama, 1991). Thus, culture is likely to influence the way people interpret, view, and react to the quality of LMX relationships. Because culture dimensions differ in terms of their relevance to LMX (Erdogan & Liden, 2002), in the following section, we examine the way in which two well-developed cultural dimensions, collectivism/individualism and power distance, relate to LMX. We also discuss how high and low cultural context may influence the quality of LMX relationships.

NATIONAL CULTURE AND LMX

Collectivism/individualism

Triandis (1988, p. 60) observed that collectivism/individualism is 'perhaps the most important dimension of cultural differences in social behavior.' For collectivists, building and maintaining interpersonal harmony is a primary concern. Collectivists identify themselves in terms of group membership via the depersonalization process (Hofstede, 1980) and are interdependent with their groups (Triandis, 1996). On the other hand, individualists emphasize personal benefits, self-fulfillment, and personal autonomy, and are independent of groups (Hofstede, 1980). In contrast to collectivists who give group membership higher priorities, individualists tend to prioritize self and focus on enhancing their self-esteem (Triandis, 1996).

A handful of studies have linked collectivism/individualism to LMX and suggested that collectivists are concerned about maintaining harmonious relationships within the group, and thus high-quality LMX relationships are less salient to collectivists than individualists. For example, Hogg, Martin, Epitropaki, Mankad, Svensson, and Weeden (2005) made a distinction between personalized and depersonalized leadership: consistent with LMX theory, personalized leadership was defined as the leader-formed relationships of differing quality with subordinates, whereas consistent with low LMX differentiation (Liden et al., 2006), depersonalized leadership was portrayed as cases in which the leader treated all followers consistently. Hogg and his colleagues (2005), using a sample of 128 from India, found the opposite of their hypothesis: it was individualists rather than collectivists who considered a depersonalized leadership more effective and collectivists who preferred personalized leadership. It is possible that this result emerged because collectivists value effective interpersonal relationships in the group and personalized leadership is characteristic of leaders who develop personal relationships with members.

Other researchers have taken a situational approach by investigating how collectivism/individualism influences the strength of the relationship between antecedent factors and LMX. Findings of these studies have been mixed. For instance, Schaubroeck and Lam (2002) found that, within a sample of employees in the USA and Hong Kong representing the same multinational bank, supervisors were more likely to form high-quality LMX relationships with subordinates who had similar personality with them regardless of work–unit collectivism/individualism. In contrast, although it was not hypothesized, they found that collectivism/individualism interacted with peer–peer personality similarity in building LMX relationships. Specifically, peer–peer personality similarity was positively related to LMX among the more individualistic work–unit cultures, whereas the relationship was not significant in work groups with relatively more collectivistic cultures. However, after controlling for peer integration in the groups with individualistic culture, the relationship between peer–personality similarity and LMX was not significant. These findings suggest that collectivism/individualism is not a strong contextual factor with respect to the association between leader/member or member/member personality similarity and LMX quality.

Other researchers, however, have argued that as collectivists give more weight to benefiting their groups, they place more emphasis on loyalty and obligation (Sullivan, Chao, Allen, Kone, Pierre-Louis, & Krieger, 2003). When experiencing personal costs, collectivists may show greater tolerance in order to maintain good-quality relationships with their supervisors, who are typically seen by collectivists as prototypical group members (Turner, 1991). For example, drawing on justice theory, Erdogan and Liden (2006) found collectivism/individualism to be a significant moderator of the relationship between organizational justice and LMX. Specifically, in a sample of textile manufacturing employees in Turkey, for individuals high in collectivism, interactional justice was less positively related to LMX than for those low in collectivism. Similarly, for collectivists, distributive justice was not associated with LMX, but for individuals low in collectivism distributive justice was positively related to LMX. In general, the empirical evidence linking collectivism/individualism to LMX theory is limited.

Although we know that the relationship between certain antecedents and LMX may be contingent on collectivism/individualism, we do not fully understand whether the formation, social exchange process, and consequences of LMX relationships may differ due to the extent of collectivism/individualism dominant in the cultural context (Avolio, Walumbwa, & Weber, 2009). For example, even though LMX research has consistently shown a positive relationship between individual performance within samples spanning multiple countries, little attention has been paid to the question of whether cultural factors such as collectivism/individualism alter the extent to which LMX is linked to performance. It is possible that for collectivists who rely more on cooperation and coordination with coworkers, high-quality relationships with supervisors may be a less important motivator for employees to improve their performance than may be true of individualists.

Power distance

At the societal level, power distance is defined as the extent to which members expect and accept unequally distributed power in institutions and organizations (Hofstede, 1980). According to Hofstede (1984), in high power distance contexts, individuals view unequal status distributions as legitimate, and opinions and views from the high power status members are seen as appropriate and acceptable. In contrast, in low power distance cultures, individuals may feel less comfortable with power differences between leaders and followers. Cross-cultural research maintains that compared to countries with lower power distance (e.g., England), authority figures in countries high in power distance (e.g., China), in general, have more centralized power and greater influence on decisions, such as employee compensation, selection, and promotion (Wang & Heller, 1993). Thus, one may expect that in a culture with greater power distance, individuals are more likely to regard leaders as controlling resources for accomplishing tasks and accept their leader's power for compensation and punishment, which is an important antecedent for building high-quality LMX relationships with their leaders (Aryee & Chen, 2006). In contrast, research has shown that individuals in a lower power distance culture desire more autonomy and prefer self-management rather than depending on their supervisors' assistance and help (Adler, 1997; Kirkman & Shapiro, 1997). Thus, in a lower power distance culture, the social exchange process in a high-quality LMX relationship may be less salient to employees than it is in high power distance cultures.

Though power distance is quite relevant to authority relationships, particularly between leaders and followers (Erdogan & Liden, 2002), very little research to date has explored the effect of power distance on outcomes of LMX. We found only one study that examined the effect of leader's power distance on the relationship between LMX and task performance and citizenship behaviors (Anand & Vidyarthi, 2008). Findings of the study indicated that power distance attenuated the positive association between LMX and citizenship behaviors. Furthermore, this effect was more pronounced in highly interdependent work groups, because close interaction between colleagues communicated leader's power distance more clearly. These findings suggest that investigating the joint impact of power distance and LMX in influencing individual effectiveness would afford us a better understanding of employees' attitudes and behaviors in the workplace.

High/low context

High or strong culture contexts are characterized by distinctive and particular values, beliefs, and assumptions that are shared by members in the social units (Hall, 1976; Schein, 1985). In contrast, low or weak cultures possess weakly shared values, and are less stable and intense (Schein, 1984). Although both weak and strong cultures may influence members' behaviors (Deal & Kennedy, 1982), strong cultures have been shown to enhance performance (Denison, 1984), commitment, ethical behavior, and reduce job stress (Posner, Kouzes, & Schmidt, 1985).

Research has shown that national culture and leadership are interdependent. On the one hand, leadership plays a critical role in forming and shaping culture (Schein, 1985) and is a critical part of performance-related cultural processes (Saffold, 1988). On the other hand, leadership is contingent on culture (House & Javidan, 2004). This is because national culture has a long and rich history (Clark, 1970), and creates values and meanings that are shared by every new generation. Indeed, researchers have shown significant relationships between national culture and prevailing leadership prototypes: i.e., how leaders are expected to think and behave (Gelfand, Erez, & Aycan, 2007). Even though there is no existing research linking high/low culture context to LMX, strong cultural contexts are likely to have a greater impact on the interpersonal processes between leaders and members because a strong culture can act as a more powerful social control mechanism (O'Reilly & Chatman, 1996), which predetermines the members' behaviors and guides

their social interactions (Schein, 1990). In a culture with widely shared values, if relationship building is paramount, members are more likely to form high-quality LMX relationships with their leaders. In contrast, when a strong culture encourages individual members to show more independence in making decisions and accomplishing goals without leaders' support and help, members may be less concerned about developing high-quality LMX relationships. This reasoning may open a new channel for future research to link high/low context national culture literature to LMX study.

In addition, another interesting avenue for future research is to examine the role of the cultural context in influencing the way LMX relates to individual members' behaviors and performance. For instance, in a strong culture (e.g., a high power distance culture) which endows leaders with more power and resources, LMX has a greater influence on individual members' performance, because leaders are capable of passing down resources and providing support for improving members' performance (Erdogan & Liden, 2002). Furthermore, as Saffold (1988) noted, culture consists of different traits and each particular trait may affect organizational processes differently. It is probable that under a strong culture context, shared meanings may help members in high-quality LMX relationships to adhere to traditional working methods and procedures while limiting their capability for creative performance. As evidenced by the GLOBE leadership studies (House & Javidan, 2004), cultural factors are relevant to all leadership approaches. In the next section, we address the similarity between LMX and several selected leadership theories.

LMX VIS-À-VIS OTHER LEADERSHIP THEORIES

LMX theory is based on an active reciprocal exchange perspective, whereby followers may choose to not take the role assigned by their leader (Graen & Scandura, 1987). This mutual exchange aspect sets LMX theory apart from other leadership theories which focus only on leader behaviors. Leadership scholars have repeatedly called for an integration of LMX literature with other theories to facilitate an understanding of the underpinnings of leader effectiveness (Avolio, Sosik, Jung, & Berson, 2003; Gerstner & Day, 1997). In the following sections we review studies that explore LMX theory concomitantly with transformational or servant leadership theory.

Transformational leadership and LMX

Transformational leadership theory and LMX theory are the most frequently examined theories in leadership literature over the past two decades (Avolio, 2005; Díaz-Sáenz, Chapter 22, this volume). Researchers have noted that LMX is congruent with transformational leadership in some respects. Both of these theories are rooted in the social exchange process. LMX can be both transformational and transactional, as LMX relationships often begin with transactional material exchange and subsequently evolve into transformational social exchange (Graen & Uhl-Bien, 1995). Similarly, transformational leaders can offer intangible rewards via intellectual simulation and individualized consideration within a dyadic social exchange, such as an LMX relationship (Basu & Green, 1997).

However, some researchers have argued that LMX is distinct from transformational leadership. Whereas transformational leaders persuade individuals to suspend personal interests for the sake of the collective and to equate their own success with their contribution to organizational effectiveness (Bass, 1985), LMX is more focused on individual outcomes, such as personal growth and career development (Scandura & Schriesheim, 1994). The comparatively higher salience of LMX to individual-level outcomes has been demonstrated in a number of recent empirical studies. For instance, Howell and Hall-Merenda (1999) found LMX to be more strongly related to individual performance than both transformational and transactional leadership. Also, transformational leadership was positively related to follower performance only when leader and member worked in close physical proximity, whereas LMX was positively related to performance irrespective of physical distance between leaders and followers. In a similar vein, a handful of subsequent studies have further demonstrated that transformational leadership can be an antecedent of LMX, and LMX has a more proximal relationship with individual outcomes. For instance, Vaishali and Kumar (2003), studying employees in India, found transformational leadership to be positively related to LMX, which in turn was associated with subordinates' perceptions of organizational climate and subsequent job burnout. In a sample of 183 retail sales employees, Bettencourt (2004) found that LMX mediated the effects of contingent reward leadership and transformational leadership behaviors on change-oriented organizational citizenship behaviors (OCBs). Similarly, it has been demonstrated within a sample of research and development (R&D) professionals from manufacturing firms, R&D organizations, and research institutes in Singapore

that LMX served as a mediator in the relationship between transformational leadership and employee organizational commitment (Lee, 2005) and innovativeness (Lee, 2008). Likewise, Wang et al. (2005), studying 162 leader–member dyads of an organization in China, found that transformational leadership was positively related to individual performance via building and nourishing high-quality LMX relationships.

Other research, however, has provided a different interpretation of the relationship between LMX and transformational leadership, arguing that LMX can serve as a boundary condition for transformational leadership. Because high-quality LMX relationships are characterized by trust, respect, and mutual obligation (Dienesch & Liden, 1986), members with high LMX may be more willing to accept the influence of transformational leaders. This argument was confirmed in Piccolo and Colquitt's (2006) study of 217 individuals from a broad cross-section of job types, as these researchers found that transformational leadership was more acceptable to members with high-quality LMX relationships than to those with low-quality LMX relationships.

The main ideas emerging from existing theory and empirical studies are clear:

- LMX theory can be integrated with transformational leadership theory to further understand leaders' influence on individual outcomes
- compared to transformational leadership, LMX is more proximal to individual attitudes and behaviors across organizations in a wide variety of industries, such as information technology, retail sales, manufacturing, and in different cultures such as the USA, China, India, and Singapore

Although a growing research stream has focused on integrating these two leadership theories, an interesting omission in theory and research exists: Are LMX and transformational leadership distinct in terms of their effects on multi-level outcomes (not just individual-level outcomes) in the organization? For instance, compared to LMX, which is more proximal to individual well-being (Epitropaki & Martin, 1999), transformational leadership highlights the organization's mission and collective effectiveness rather than follower autonomy and individual interests (Bass, 1985). Thus, it is likely that LMX is more beneficial for employee career-related outcomes and well-being, while transformational leaders are more engaged in building collective effectiveness. Furthermore, given that LMX research has been criticized for being limited to the dyadic exchange process and lacking examination of the team context (Avolio et al., 2009; Hogg, Martin, & Weeden, 2004), an important next step for multi-level LMX research would be to extend it beyond individual-level variables by examining the impact of LMX on team-level effectiveness and comparing these results with those focusing on transformational leadership.

Another potentially valuable research area is to incorporate the social context of LMX and transformational leadership. Research has consistently offered support for the positive association between both LMX and transformational leadership and a series of important individual outcomes (Gerstner & Day, 1997; Judge & Piccolo, 2004), but the puzzle of what contexts make the association stronger or weaker than the other remains unsolved (Erdogan & Liden, 2002). A comparison of the boundary conditions of both theories affords an opportunity to better understand the conditions when LMX is more (or less) effective than transformational leadership in building individual and organizational effectiveness.

Servant leadership and LMX

Servant leadership theory has gained interest among leadership researchers due to its emphasis on ethics, integrity, and moral responsibilities (Graham, 1991; Greenleaf, 1977) and its association with the rapidly developing theory of positive organizational behavior (Avolio & Gardner, 2005). Researchers suggest that LMX and servant leadership theory share similarities because both emphasize the priority of followers' development and personal growth, which may in turn provide support and resources to help individuals improve their performance through a social exchange process (Ehrhart, 2004; Liden, Wayne, Zhao, & Henderson, 2008).

Despite the overlaps, LMX and servant leadership theories have at least three key distinctions. First, servant leadership emphasizes exploring 'each follower's unique characteristics and interests and then assisting followers in achieving their potential' (Liden et al., 2008, p. 162). In essence, servant leaders are likely to form high-quality LMX relationships with all followers. This is consistent with Ehrhart's (2004) notion that servant leaders demonstrate high moral standards by treating every individual subordinate in a similar manner. In contrast, a key component of LMX theory is the concept of differentiation: i.e. leaders develop high-quality relationships with some but not all the followers (Liden & Graen, 1980). High LMX and low LMX only exist in relative terms. Leaders may assign more challenging tasks to followers with high-quality LMX relationships, while providing more routine work to followers with low LMX (Liden et al., 2006). Secondly,

servant leadership emphasizes leaders' personal integrity (Graham, 1991). LMX theory is also salient with respect to personal integrity, but with some differences. Whereas servant leaders cultivate their personal integrity by forging a sense of spiritual fulfillment through team membership and by forming strong long-term relationships with followers (Liden et al., 2008), leaders develop high-quality LMX relationships with their followers by providing tangible and intangible rewards (Wayne, Shore, & Liden, 1997). Thirdly, LMX theory emphasizes leaders' helping behaviors towards internal employees to aid their career development and personal growth, whereas servant leadership theory highlights leaders' social responsibility to serve both internal employees and external stakeholders, such as the surrounding communities and society as a whole (Graham, 1991).

Indeed, researchers have argued that servant leadership is positively related to but distinct from LMX and the limited empirical evidence has shown that controlling for LMX, servant leadership explains additional variance in several important individual outcomes (Barbuto & Wheeler, 2006; Ehrhart, 2004; Liden et al., 2008). Ehrhart (2004), with a sample of 254 employed university students, showed that servant leadership was related to but distinct from LMX and transformational leadership. Likewise, Barbuto and Wheeler (2006) developed a five-factor measure of servant leadership and showed that servant leadership was significantly related to several positive outcomes, including employees' extra effort, employees' satisfaction, and perceptions of organizational effectiveness. In a sample of 388 dyads, two dimensions of servant leadership were also shown to be significant predictors of LMX quality. Finally, Liden et al. (2008) used an organizational sample of 182 employees to show that servant leadership explained additional variability in community citizenship behaviors, in-role performance, and organizational commitment after controlling for LMX and transformational leadership.

Empirical research on servant leadership is still embryonic; most studies have focused on scale development and on distinguishing servant leadership from other leadership theories, such as LMX and transformational leadership. Given the resemblance and distinctiveness of the servant leadership and LMX theories, it would be worthwhile for future research to integrate the two theories to see how they build on each other to predict individual and organizational effectiveness. For instance, as Greenleaf noted in his earlier work (Greenleaf, 1977, 1991), because servant leaders put subordinates first and care about their personal growth servant leadership should result in subordinates who enjoy high levels of well-being.

LMX also emphasizes helping individual careers and development via high-quality relationship with their leaders (Epitropaki & Martin, 1999; Scandura & Schriesheim, 1994). Through an integration of the two theories, future research may address the role of follower growth and well-being to provide a new perspective on how and why one leadership may be better (or worse) able to stimulate follower personal effectiveness. This is consistent with the call from Avolio, Walumbwa, and Weber (2009) for more research on servant leadership from a 'follower-centric' perspective.

After this discussion of research on the context of LMX, we now turn our attention to the limitations of LMX research. LMX theory and research has persisted for nearly four decades, and in that time much has been accomplished towards unraveling the nature of dyadic relationships between leaders and followers; however, there are still many issues to be resolved.

CRITICISMS OF LMX RESEARCH

A general search on the key term 'leader–member exchange' across all years in the PsychInfo database produced 428 hits. Despite the voluminous body of research that has been generated on LMX, what makes this an especially exciting theory is that there are still so many issues yet to be resolved. These issues essentially boil down to a lack of understanding of contextual factors influencing LMX relationships, limited knowledge on LMX development and the dynamics of long-term LMX relationships, as well as problems with the research methods used in LMX research.

Lack of understanding of the context

Calls have been repeatedly made for research on the context surrounding LMX relationships (Dienesch & Liden, 1986; Erdogan & Liden, 2002; Gerstner & Day, 1997; Graen & Uhl-Bien, 1995; Liden et al., 1997; Schriesheim et al., 1999). As clear from the current review, some progress has been made, but much more remains to be done, especially with respect to research integrating LMX with social networks, organizational culture, and the use of multi-level designs.

Social networks

To date, researchers have tended to investigate LMX relationships in isolation, failing to consider the potential influence that the larger set of relationships surrounding specific LMX relationships might have. In fact, our search for empirical studies linking social networks and LMX identified only one article (Sparrowe & Liden, 2005). These researchers found member influence to be enhanced by sponsorship in the social networks of leaders who are themselves high in centrality in the advice network. But many other dependent variables other than influence could be explored with respect to social networks, such as access to information and resources and secondary outcomes such as performance, salary, promotions, and retention. Sparrowe and Liden's (2005) research also indicated that the influence of larger networks on specific LMX relationships and on individual members of LMX relationships may be quite complex, involving interactions between multiple network variables and between perceptual variables and social network variables (cf. Liden et al., 1997; Sparrowe & Liden, 1997). In sum, a plethora of issues surrounding the interplay between social networks and LMX wait for the attention of researchers.

Organizational culture

Workplace norms, defined by organizational culture, are factors that are likely to affect social exchange relationships, including those between leaders and followers (O'Reilly & Chatman, 1996; Schein, 1985; Alvesson, Chapter 11, this volume). However, with the exception of Erdogan et al.'s (2006) study, no LMX research has examined the direct or moderating effects of organizational culture. One of the key findings of this study was that team-oriented organizations encouraged higher LMX, and team-orientation attenuated the relationship between distributive justice and LMX. Aggressiveness, on the other hand, strengthened the same relationship. This study emphasizes the need to examine linkages between LMX and other dimensions of organizational culture to further our understanding of how LMX interacts with the organization's norms.

Multi-level research designs

As clearly articulated by Yammarino and colleagues (2005), most LMX research has been confined to the individual level of analysis when in most cases it should be studied from a multi-level perspective. This is because LMX relationships occur within a leader's work group, meaning that, by definition, both the individual and group levels of analysis are relevant in all studies that include multiple members of the same work groups. Studies using convenience samples, such as students or participants in executive education workshops, contain only one person per work group, thus precluding the possibility for the examination of the group level. Although difficult to obtain, samples containing multiple organizations, including the organizational level in LMX research, are also needed (Erdogan et al., 2006; Henderson et al., 2009). Yammarino and colleagues (2005) correctly criticized the majority of LMX research for its failure to properly take multiple levels into consideration. Until 2005, when this review appeared, most LMX researchers had only studied the individual level of analysis. Fortunately, recent research has begun to investigate LMX from a multi-level perspective (e.g., Anand, Vidyarthi, Liden, & Rousseau, 2010; Chen, Kirkman, Kanfer, Allen, & Rosen, 2007; Erdogan et al., 2006; Henderson et al., 2008; Liden et al., 2006; Tangirala, Green, & Ramanujam, 2007: Vidyarthi, Liden, Anand, Erdogan, & Ghosh, in press).

In addition to the problem of failing to examine group, organizational, and cross-level issues surrounding LMX, another widespread fault of LMX research published prior to 2005 was the treatment of leader assessments of member behaviors, such as performance and OCB, as being independent when in fact they were not. In fact, in all studies in which leaders rated multiple subordinates, these rating were not independent, and this lack of independence should have been acknowledged with appropriate analyses, such as hierarchical linear modeling.

RESEARCH METHODS PROBLEMS

LMX research continues to be plagued by measurement problems, lack of longitudinal designs, and over-reliance on same-source data.

Measurement issues

Although the most commonly used measures of LMX, the LMX-7 (Graen & Uhl-Bien, 1995) and the LMX-MDM (Liden & Maslyn, 1998), have been shown to be reliable and valid, both assess relationship quality, ignoring the essence of LMX theory, which focuses on the types and amount of resources and support exchanged. Indeed, a major theme of LMX theory is that whereas low LMX relationships represent economic exchanges based on employment contracts, high LMX relationships involve the social exchange of resources and

support that extend well beyond the employment contract. Empirical research has simply not attempted to document these differences in the exchange of resources. Although it is important to assess perceptions of relationship quality – and the LMX-7 and LMX-MDM are fine for this – the nature of the exchange also needs to be assessed if we are to more fully attempt to test LMX theory (Liden et al., 1997). Reflecting one step toward integrating the exchange in LMX research have been attempts made to develop measures of reciprocation (Uhl-Bien & Maslyn, 2003) and social/economic exchange (Shore, Tetrick, Lynch, & Barksdale, 2006). We encourage further efforts of this type.

Design issues/lack of research on LMX development and change over time

Although the early LMX studies tended to be longitudinal (Dansereau et al., 1975; Graen & Cashman, 1975; Liden & Graen, 1980), only a handful of subsequent studies employed longitudinal designs (e.g., Bauer & Green, 1996; Liden et al., 1993; Sparrowe & Liden, 2005; Wakabayashi & Graen, 1984). Even the majority of studies of LMX antecedents have utilized cross-sectional designs (for an exception, see Epitropaki & Martin, 2005). Clearly, in order to develop a better understanding of LMX development, longitudinal designs, especially those involving 'new' leader–member dyads, are needed. Longitudinal research is also needed for exploring the evolution of LMX relationships over time. With the exception of Wakabayashi and Graen (1984) and Bauer, Erdogan, Liden, and Wayne (2006), Wakabayashi, Graen, Graen, and Graen (1988), most of the longitudinal studies conducted have spanned a year or less. To understand issues such as maintenance, deterioration, and relationship repair with respect to LMX, long-term longitudinal designs are optimal. We encourage researchers to explore LMX relationships over time, as virtually nothing is known about transitions that occur in LMX relationships across time (Bluedorn & Jaussi, 2008).

Finally, most LMX studies, even those containing multi-source data, include antecedent–LMX and LMX–consequence correlations that are based on data from the same source. As noted frequently by editors and reviewers, a viable explanation for significant correlations based on same-source data is that overall attitude or affect influences responses to questions measuring both variables. One way to deal with this problem is to collect LMX from sources other than the subordinates, such as the leader (Schriesheim, Castro, & Yammarino, 2000) or coworkers (Sherony &

Green, 2002). Paradoxically, assessment of LMX from the leader's perspective has revealed that agreement between leaders and members on LMX is typically quite low (correlations in the 0.20s; Liden et al., 1993; Scandura, Graen, & Novak, 1986). Although this low agreement has been identified as a problem (Gerstner & Day, 1997), leading some to question the validity of LMX, there is really no reason to expect high levels of agreement. When the leader's view of LMX is measured in the 'traditional' way, asking leaders the extent to which they provide support to subordinates (e.g., the extent to which the leader reports understanding the subordinate's problems and needs), social desirability response bias is likely. This is because it would be a bad reflection on a leader *not* to support all subordinates, and leader respondents to LMX questionnaires typically do not want to present themselves in a negative way, as evidenced by high means and low variance. With the resulting restriction of range, the low correlations between leader and member reports of LMX should come as no surprise. In more recent studies, the leader view of LMX has been assessed by asking leaders to report what each subordinate provides to them (e.g., the extent to which this subordinate would defend my actions in public). Because we know that leaders and subordinates put varying levels of effort into building and maintaining LMX relationships (Maslyn & Uhl-Bien, 2001), there is no reason to expect that a subordinate's perceptions of the leader necessarily corresponds to the leader's view of the subordinate. Thus, we call issue to the criticisms leveled against LMX research for low leader–member agreement. We contend that a much more productive approach is to examine leader–member agreement as a *meaningful variable* that has great potential for expanding knowledge of relationships between leaders and followers (see Cogliser, Schriesheim, Scandura, & Gardner, 2009, for an excellent example).

CONCLUSIONS

Our review of LMX research conducted since 2002 has revealed that interest in studying LMX has not diminished, and many important developments have taken place. Perhaps the most profound trends are (1) increased attention to the context surrounding LMX relationships, such as work-group dynamics and national culture, (2) many investigations are now exploring LMX from a multi-level perspective, and (3) there has been an increment in the number of studies conducted with non-US samples, especially those conducted in Asia, with a concurring focus on cultural variables that impinge on LMX relationships. We strongly encourage a continuation of these research directions. Despite the progress, many of the same conclusions offered by Erdogan and Liden (2002) remain. Specifically, there continues to be a need for research that enhances our understanding of (1) LMX development and change/maintenance over time and (2) the way in which the constellation of social network relationships influences specifics LMX dyads.

REFERENCES

Adler, N. J. (1997) Global leadership: women leaders. *Management International Review,* 37(1), 171–196.

Anand, S. & Vidyarthi, P. R. (2008) Leader–member exchange and employee outcomes: a multilevel examination of the moderating effects of leader power distance and within-group task interdependence. The Academy of Management meeting, August, 2008, Anaheim, CA.

Anand, S., Vidyarthi, P., Liden, R. C., & Rousseau, D. (2010) Good citizens in poor quality relationships: Idiosyncratic deals as a substitute for relationship quality. Academy of Management Journal, 53 (5), 970–988.

Aryee, S. & Chen, Z. X. (2006) Leader–member exchange in a Chinese context: antecedents, the mediating role of psychological empowerment and outcomes. *Journal of Business Research,* 59(7), 793–801.

Avolio, B. J. (2005). *Leadership development in balance: made/born.* Hillsdale, NJ: Erlbaum.

Avolio, B. J. & Gardner W. L. (2005) Authentic leadership development: getting to the root of positive forms of leadership. *The Leadership Quarterly,* 16(3), 315–338.

Avolio, B. J., Sosik, J. J., Jung, D. I., & Berson, Y. (2003) Leadership models, methods and applications. In W. Borman, D. Ilgen, & R. Klimoski (eds), *Handbook of psychology, vol. 12 – industrial and organizational psychology.* New York: Wiley, pp. 277–307.

Avolio, B. J., Walumbwa, F. O., & Weber, T. J. (2009) Leadership: current theories, research, and future directions. *Annual Review of Psychology,* 60, 421–449.

Barbuto, J. E. & Wheeler, D. W. (2006) Scale development and construct clarification of servant leadership. *Group and Organization Management,* 31(3), 300–326.

Bass, B. M. (1985) *Leadership and performance beyond expectations.* New York: Free Press.

Basu, R. & Green, S. G. (1997) Leader–member exchange and transformational leadership: an empirical examination of innovative behaviors in leader–member dyads. *Journal of Applied Social Psychology,* 27(6), 477–499.

Bauer, T. N., Erdogan, B., Liden, R. C., & Wayne, S. J. (2006) A longitudinal study of the moderating role of extraversion: LMX, performance, and turnover during new executive development. *Journal of Applied Psychology,* 91, 298–310.

Bauer, T. N. & Green, S. G. (1996) Development of leader–member exchange: a longitudinal test. *Academy of Management Journal*, 39(6), 1538–1567.

Bettencourt, L. A. (2004) Change-oriented organizational citizenship behaviors: the direct and moderating influence of goal orientation. *Journal of Retailing*, 80(3), 165–180.

Blau, P. M. (1964) *Exchange and power in social life*. New York: Wiley.

Bluedorn, A. P. & Jaussi, K. S. (2008) Leaders, followers, and time. *The Leadership Quarterly*, 19(6), 654–668.

Boies, K. & Howell, J. M. (2006) Leader–member exchange in teams: an examination of the interaction between relationship differentiation and mean LMX in explaining team-level outcomes. *The Leadership Quarterly*, 17(3), 246–257.

Chen, G., Kirkman, B. L., Kanfer, R., Allen, D., & Rosen, B. (2007) A multilevel study of leadership, empowerment, and performance in teams. *Journal of Applied Psychology*, 92(2), 331–346.

Clark, B. (1970) *The distinctive college: Antioch, Reed, Swarthmore*. Chicago: Aldine.

Cogliser, C. C., Schriesheim, C. A., Scandura, T. A., & Gardner, W. L. (in press) Balance in leader and follower perceptions of leader–member exchange: relationships with performance and work attitudes. *The Leadership Quarterly*.

Cohen, S. G. & Bailey, D. E. (1997) What makes teams work: group effectiveness research from the shop floor to the executive suite. *Journal of Management*, 23(3), 239–290.

Dansereau, F., Graen, G., & Haga, W. J. (1975) A vertical dyad linkage approach to leadership within formal organizations: a longitudinal investigation of the role making process. *Organizational Behavior and Human Performance*, 13(1), 46–78.

Deal, T. E. & Kennedy, A. A. (1982) *Corporate cultures: the rites and rituals of corporate life*. London: Addison-Wesley Co.

Denison, D. R. (1984) Bringing corporate culture to the bottom line. *Organizational Dynamics*, 13(2), 5–22.

Dienesch, R. M. & Liden, R. C. (1986) Leader–member exchange model of leadership: a critique and further development. *Academy of Management Review*, 11(3), 618–634.

Ehrhart, M. G. (2004) Leadership and procedural justice climate as antecedents of unit-level organizational citizenship behavior. *Personnel Psychology*, 57(1), 61–94.

Epitropaki, O. & Martin, R. (1999) The impact of relational demography on the quality of leader–member exchanges and employees' work attitudes and well-being. *Journal of Occupational & Organizational Psychology*, 72(2), 237–240.

Epitropaki, O. & Martin, R. (2005) From ideal to real: a longitudinal study of the role of implicit leadership theories on leader–member exchanges and employee outcomes. *Journal of Applied Psychology*, 90(4), 659–676.

Erdogan, B. & Liden, R. C. (2002) Social exchange in the workplace: a review of recent developments and future research directions in leader–member exchange theory. In L. L. Neider & C. A. Schriesheim (eds), *Leadership*. Greenwich, CT: Information Age Publishing, pp. 65–114.

Erdogan, B. & Liden, R. C. (2006) Collectivism as a moderator of responses to organizational justice: implications for leader–member exchange and ingratiation. *Journal of Organizational Behavior*, 27(1), 1–17.

Erdogan, B., Liden, R. C., & Kraimer, M. L. (2006) Justice and leader–member exchange: the moderating role of organizational culture. *Academy of Management Journal*, 49(2), 395–406.

Festinger, L. (1954) A theory of social comparison processes. *Human Relations*, 7(2), 117–140.

Ford, L. R. & Seers, A. (2006) Relational leadership and team climates: pitting differentiation versus agreement. *The Leadership Quarterly*, 17(3), 258–270.

Gelfand, M. J., Erez, M., & Aycan, Z. (2007) Cross-cultural organizational behavior. *Annual Review of Psychology*, 58, 479–514.

Gerstner, C. R. & Day, D. V. (1997) Meta-analytic review of leader–member exchange theory: correlate and construct issues. *Journal of Applied Psychology*, 82(6), 827–844.

Gouldner, A. W. (1960) The norm of reciprocity: a preliminary statement. *American Sociological Review*, 25(2), 161–178.

Graen, G. & Cashman, J. F. (1975) A role making model in formal organizations: a developmental approach. In J. G. Hunt & L. L. Larson (eds), *Leadership frontiers*. Kent, OH: Kent State Press, pp. 143–165.

Graen, G., Liden, R. C., & Hoel, W. (1982) The role of leadership in the employee withdrawal process. *Journal of Applied Psychology*, 67(6), 868–872.

Graen, G. B. & Scandura, T. A. (1987) Toward a psychology of dyadic organizing. In L. L. Cummings & B. M. Staw (eds), *Research in organizational behavior*, Greenwich, CT: JAI Press, 9, 175–208.

Graen, G. B. & Uhl-Bien, M. (1995) Relationship-based approach to leadership: development of leader–member exchange (LMX) theory of leadership over 25 years: applying a multi-level multi-domain perspective. *The Leadership Quarterly*, 6(2), 219–247.

Graham, J. W. (1991) Servant–leadership in organizations: inspirational and moral. *The Leadership Quarterly*, 2(2), 105–119.

Greenberg, J. (1982) Approaching equity and avoiding inequity in groups and organizations. In J. Greenberg & R. L. Cohen (eds), *Equity and justice in social behavior*. New York: Academic Press, pp. 389–435.

Greenleaf, R. K. (1977) *Servant leadership: a journey into the nature of legitimate power and greatness*. Mahwah, NJ: Paulist Press.

Greenleaf, R. K. (1991) *The servant as leader*. Indianapolis, IN: Robert Greenleaf Center.

Hall, E. T. (1976) *Beyond culture*. Garden City, NY: Doubleday Anchor.

Heider, F. (1958) *The psychology of interpersonal relations*. New York: John Wiley.

Henderson, D. J. & Liden, R. C. (2007) Leader–member exchange differentiation and workgroup relationships: a social network perspective. The Annual Meeting of the Society for Industrial and Organizational Psychology, April 2007, New York.

Henderson, D. J., Liden, R. C., Glibkowski, B. C., & Chaudhry, A. (2009) Within-group LMX differentiation: a multilevel review and examination of its antecedents and outcomes. *The Leadership Quarterly*, 20(4), 517–534.

Henderson, D. J., Wayne, S. J., Shore, L. M., Bommer, W. H., & Tetrick, L. E. (2008) Leader–member exchange, differentiation, and psychological contract fulfillment: a multilevel examination. *Journal of Applied Psychology*, 93(6), 1208–1219.

Hofstede, G. (1980) *Culture's consequences*. Beverly Hills, CA: Sage.

Hofstede, G. (1984) *Culture's consequences: international differences in work-related values*. Beverly Hills, CA: Sage.

Hogg, M. A., Martin, R., Epitropaki, O., Mankad, A., Svensson, A., & Weeden, K. (2005) Effective leadership in salient groups: revisiting leader–member exchange theory from the perspective of the social identity theory of leadership. *Personality and Social Psychology Bulletin*, 31(7), 991–1004.

Hogg M. A., Martin, R., & Weeden, K. (2004) Leader–member relations and social identity. In D. Van Knippenberg, & M. A. Hogg (eds), *Leadership and power: identity processes in groups and organizations*. London: Sage, pp. 18–33.

Hooper, D. T. & Martin, R. (2008) Beyond personal leader–member exchange (LMX) quality: the effects of perceived LMX variability on employee reactions. *The Leadership Quarterly*, 19(1), 20–30.

House, R. J. & Javidan, M. (2004) Overview of GLOBE. In R. J. House, P. J. Hanges, M. Javidan, P. W. Dorfman, & V. Gupta (eds), *Culture, leadership, and organizations – the GLOBE study of 62 societies*. Thousand Oaks, CA: Sage. pp. 9–28.

Howell, I. P., Dorfman, P. W., & Kerr, S. (1986) Moderator variables in leadership research. *Academy of Management Review*, 11(1), 88–102.

Howell, J. M. & Hall-Merenda, K. E. (1999) The ties that bind: the impact of leader–member exchange, transformational and transactional leadership, and distance on predicting follower performance. *Journal of Applied Psychology*, 84(5), 680–694.

Ilies, R., Nahrgang, J. D., & Morgeson, F. P. (2007) Leader–member exchange and citizenship behaviors: a meta-analysis. *Journal of Applied Psychology*, 92(1), 269–277.

Judge, T. A. & Piccolo, R. F. (2004) Transformational and transactional leadership: A meta-analytic test of their relative validity. *Journal of Applied Psychology*, 89, 755–768.

Kirkman, B. L. & Shapiro, D. L. (1997) The impact of cultural values on employee resistance to teams: toward a model of globalized self-managing work team effectiveness. *Academy of Management Review*, 22(3), 730–757.

Klein, K. J., Dansereau, F., & Hall, R. J. (1994) Levels issues in theory development, data collection, and analysis. *Academy of Management Review*, 19(2), 195–229.

Lau, D. C. & Liden, R. C. (2008) Antecedents of coworker trust: leaders' blessings. *Journal of Applied Psychology*, 93(5), 1130–1138.

Lee, J. (2005) Effects of leadership and leader–member exchange on commitment. *Leadership & Organization Development journal*, 26(8), 655–672.

Lee, J. (2008) Effects of leadership and leader–member exchange on innovativeness. *Journal of Managerial Psychology*, 23(6), 670–687.

Liden, R. C., Erdogan, B., Wayne, S. J., & Sparrowe, R. T. (2006) Leader–member exchange, differentiation, and task interdependence: implications for individual and group performance. *Journal of Organizational Behavior*, 27(6), 723–746.

Liden, R. C. & Graen, G. (1980) Generalizability of the vertical dyad linkage model of leadership. *Academy of Management Journal*, 23(3), 451–465.

Liden, R. C. & Maslyn, J. M. (1998) Multidimensionality of leader–member exchange: an empirical assessment through scale development. *Journal of Management*, 24(1), 43–72.

Liden, R. C., Sparrowe, R. T., & Wayne, S. J. (1997) Leader–member exchange theory: the past and potential for the future. *Research in Personnel and Human Resources Management*, 15, 47–119.

Liden, R. C., Wayne, S. J., & Sparrowe, R. T. (2000) An examination of the mediating role of psychological empowerment on the relations between the job, interpersonal relationships, and work outcomes. *Journal of Applied Psychology*, 85(3), 407–416.

Liden, R. C., Wayne, S. J., & Stilwell, D. (1993) A longitudinal study on the early development of leader–member exchanges. *Journal of Applied Psychology*, 78(4), 662–674.

Liden, R. C., Wayne, S. J., Zhao, H., & Henderson, D. (2008) Servant leadership: development of a multidimensional measure and multi-level assessment. *The Leadership Quarterly*, 19(2), 161–177.

Markus, H. R. & Kitayama, S. (1991) Culture and the self: implications for cognition, emotion, and motivation. *Psychological Review*, 98(2), 224–253.

Maslyn, J. M. & Uhl-Bien, M. (2001) Leader–member exchange and its dimensions: effects of self-effort and other's effort on relationship quality. *Journal of Applied Psychology*, 86(4), 697–708.

Masterson, S. S., Lewis, K., Goldman, B. M., & Taylor, S. M. (2000) Integrating justice and social exchange: the differing effects of fair procedures and treatment on work relationships. *Academy of Management Journal*, 43(4), 738–748.

O'Reilly, C. & Chatman, J. (1996) Culture as social control: corporations, cults and commitment. In B. Staw, & L. Cummings (eds), *Research in organizational behavior*. Stamford, CT: JAI Press, pp. 157–200.

Piccolo, R. F. & Colquitt, J. A. (2006) Transformational leadership and job behaviors: the mediating role of core job characteristics. *Academy of Management Journal*, 49, 327–340.

Posner, B. Z., Kouzes, J. M., & Schmidt, W. H. (1985) Shared values make a difference: an empirical test of corporate culture. *Human Resource Management*, 24(3), 293–309.

Saffold III, G. S. (1988) Culture traits, strength, and organizational performance: moving beyond 'strong' culture. *Academy of Management Review*, 13(4), 546–558.

Scandura, T. A. (1999) Rethinking leader–member exchange: an organizational justice perspective. *The Leadership Quarterly*, 10(1), 25–40.

Scandura, T. A., Graen, G. B., & Novak, M. A. (1986) When managers decide not to decide autocratically: an investigation of leader–member exchange and decision influence. *Journal of Applied Psychology,* 71(4), 579–584.

Scandura, T. A. & Schriesheim, C. A. (1994) Leader–member exchange and supervisor career mentoring as complementary constructs in leadership research. *Academy of Management Journal,* 37(6), 1588–1602.

Schaubroeck, J. & Lam, S. S. K. (2002) How similarity to peers and supervisor influences organizational advancement in different cultures. *Academy of Management Journal,* 45(6), 1120–1136.

Schein, E. H. (1984) Coming to a new awareness of organizational culture. *Sloan Management Review,* 25(2), 3–16.

Schein, E. H. (1985) *Organizational culture and leadership.* San Francisco, CA: Jossey-Bass.

Schein, E. H. (1990) Organizational culture. *American Psychologist,* 45(2), 109–119.

Schriesheim, C. A., Castro, S. L., & Cogliser, C. C. (1999) Leader–member exchange (LMX) research: a comprehensive review of theory, measurement, and data-analytic practices. *The Leadership Quarterly,* 10(1), 63–113.

Schriesheim, C. A., Castro, S. L., & Yammarino, F. J. (2000) Investigating contingencies: an examination of the impact of span of supervision and upward controllingness on leader–member exchange using traditional and multivariate within- and between-entities analysis. *Journal of Applied Psychology,* 85(5), 659–677.

Schyns, B. (2006) Are group consensus in leader–member exchange (LMX) and shared work values related to organizational outcomes? *Small Group Research,* 37(1), 20–35.

Schyns, B., Paul, T., Mohr, G., & Blank, H. (2005) Comparing antecedents and consequences of leader–member exchange in a German working context to findings in the US. *European Journal of Work and Organizational Psychology,* 14(1), 1–22.

Sherony, K. M. & Green, S. G. (2002) Coworker exchange: relationships between coworkers, leader–member exchange, and work attitudes. *Journal of Applied Psychology,* 87(3), 542–548.

Shore, L. M., Tetrick, L. E., Lynch, P., & Barksdale, K. (2006) Social and economic exchanges as mediators between commitment and performance. *Journal of Applied Social Psychology,* 36(4), 837–867.

Sias, P. M. & Jablin, E. M. (1995) Differential superior–subordinate relations, perceptions of fairness, and coworker communication. *Human Communication Research,* 22(1), 5–38.

Sparrowe, R. T. & Liden, R. C. (1997) Process and structure in leader–member exchange. *Academy of Management Review,* 22(2), 522–552.

Sparrowe, R. T. & Liden, R. C. (2005) Two routes to influence: integrating leader–member exchange and social network perspectives. *Administrative Science Quarterly,* 50(4), 505–535.

Sullivan, M., Chao, S. S., Allen, C. A., Kone, A., Pierre-Louis, M., & Krieger, J. (2003) Community–researcher partnerships: perspectives from the field. In M. Minkler,

& N. Wallerstein (eds), *Community-based participatory research in health.* San Francisco, CA: Jossey-Bass, pp. 113–130.

Tangirala, S., Green, S. G., & Ramanujam, R. (2007) In the shadow of the boss's boss: effects of supervisors' upward exchange relationships on employees. *Journal of Applied Psychology,* 92(2), 309–320.

Triandis, H. C. (1988) Collectivism and individualism: a reconceptualization of a basic concept in cross-cultural psychology. In G. K. Verma, & C. Bagley (eds), *Personality, attitudes, and cognitions.* London: MacMillan, pp. 60–95.

Triandis, H. C. (1996) The psychological measurement of cultural syndromes. *American Psychologist,* 51(4), 407–415.

Turner, J. C. (1991) Social influence. Mapping social psychology series. Belmont, CA: Thomson Brooks/Cole Publishing Co.

Uhl-Bien, M. & Maslyn, J. M. (2003) Reciprocity in manager–subordinate relationships: components, configurations, and outcomes. *Journal of Management,* 29(4), 511–532.

Vaishali, D. K. K. & Kumar, M. P. (2003) Transformational and transactional leadership styles as predictors of LMX: a path analytic assessment of organizational commitment leading to job burnout. *Abhigyan,* 21(3), 9–19.

Van Breukelen, W., Konst, D., & Van Der Vlist, R. (2002) Effects of LMX and differential treatment on work unit commitment. *Psychological Reports,* 91(1), 220–230.

Varma, A., Srinivas, E. S., & Stroh, L. K. (2005) A comparative study of the impact of leader–member exchange relationships in the U.S. and India. *Cross-Cultural Management: An International Journal,* 12(1), 84–95.

Vidyarthi, P., Liden, R. C., Anand, S., Erdogan, B., & Ghosh, S. (in press) Where do I stand? Examining the effects of leader–member exchange social comparison on employee work behaviors. *Journal of Applied Psychology.*

Wakabayashi, M. & Graen, G. B. (1984) The Japanese career progress study: a 7-year follow-up. *Journal of Applied Psychology,* 69(4), 603–614.

Wakabayashi, M., Graen, G., & Graen, M., & Graen, M. (1988) Japanese management progress: mobility into middle management. *Journal of Applied Psychology,* 73(2), 217–227.

Wang, Z. & Heller, F. A. (1993) Patterns of power distribution in managerial decision making in Chinese and British industrial organizations. *International Journal of Human Resource Management,* 4(1), 113–128.

Wang, H., Law, K. S., Hackett, R. D., Wang, D., & Chen, Z. X. (2005) Leader–member exchange as a mediator of the relationship between transformational leadership and followers' performance and organizational citizenship behavior. *Academy of Management Journal,* 48(3), 420–432.

Wayne, S. J., Shore, L. M., & Liden, R. C. (1997) Perceived organizational support and leader–member exchange: a social exchange perspective. *Academy of Management Journal,* 40(1), 82–111.

Yammarino, F. J., Dionne, S. D., Chun, J. D., & Dansereau, F. (2005) Leadership and levels of analysis: a state-of-the-science review. *The Leadership Quarterly,* 16(6), 879–919.

24

Leadership and Attachment Theory: Understanding Interpersonal Dynamics in Leader–Follower Relations

Annilee M. Game

INTRODUCTION

As organizations in the twenty-first century become more diverse, decentralised, and team-based, our understanding of the nature of effective leadership is changing, placing greater emphasis on the importance of relational and emotional processes (e.g. Bass, 2002; Dasborough & Ashkanasy, 2002). It has long been recognised that a core component of effective leadership is the ability to establish supportive relationships with followers (Yukl, 2002). For example, many theories, including transformational leadership (e.g. Bass, 1985), path-goal theory (e.g. House, 1971) and leader–member exchange (LMX; e.g. Graen & Uhl-Bien, 1995) proposed leadership dimensions encapsulating the extent to which leaders support employees, and show concern for their well-being. Yet increasingly, leadership scholars are questioning whether such theories can adequately explain the finer-grained interpersonal dynamics through which these more relational styles of leadership may influence follower outcomes. In particular, it is suggested that they cannot capture the emotional undercurrents and interpersonal histories that may shape both followers' and leaders' experiences in the leadership dyad (Kahn, 1998). Equally, the existing leadership

literature tells us little about how effective leaders develop, in the context of 'everyday' leadership (Popper & Amit, 2009).

Recently, however, interest has grown in trying to understand these phenomena. Hence, leadership scholars are increasingly calling for the inclusion of attachment theory (Bowlby, 1969, 1973a, 1980) in the study of leadership in order to shed light on the interpersonally embedded, cognitive, emotional and behavioural phenomena that remain relatively untapped by existing leadership theories (Bresnahan & Mitroff, 2007; Popper, Mayseless & Castelnovo, 2000). Attachment theory explains how an individual's thoughts, feelings and behaviours in a relationship depend on beliefs and expectations that are born out of a history of relational experiences with significant others (Collins & Read, 1994; La Guardia, Ryan, Couchman & Deci, 2000). As such, extending attachment theory to the leadership domain offers a relevant and well-established framework with which to explore the more nuanced dynamics of leader–follower relations (Bresnahan & Mitroff, 2007).

Currently, the leadership and attachment literature is in its infancy. As will become evident in the following review, the majority of published theoretical and empirical work to date is attributable to just a handful of authors. In particular,

Micha Popper, Ofra Mayseless, and Rivka Davidovitz and colleagues in Israel, along with Tiffany Keller in the USA, are the key contributors who have so far helped advance the case for an attachment theory perspective on leadership. The aim of this chapter is to provide an overview of the current state of the field, focusing on the different ways in which attachment theory can be applied to leadership.

ATTACHMENT THEORY

Attachment theory is one of the foremost relationship theories in social and developmental psychology, yet has only recently been adopted by organizational and leadership researchers. Originally developed to explain the nature and effects of the psychological bonds that form between infants and their primary caregivers (Ainsworth, Blehar, Waters & Wall, 1978; Bowlby, 1969, 1973a, 1980), attachment theory has subsequently been extended to explain cognitive, emotional and behavioural dynamics in adult personal and social relationships (Hazan & Shaver, 1987; Pierce & Lydon, 2001). A central tenet of the theory is that, when individuals encounter threat or feel distressed in the social environment, they are predisposed to withdraw from the situation to seek comfort and protection, or caregiving, from a key relationship figure. Such attachment behaviour is rooted in a cognitive and affective regulatory system that developed, for evolutionary purposes, to ensure vulnerable infants stay close to stronger and wiser individuals who can best protect them from harm (Hazan & Shaver, 1994).

A history of relational (caregiving) experiences with significant others, including parents, friends and romantic partners, especially in times of distress, leads to the development of generalised internal working models of relationships, manifested as global attachment styles (Ainsworth et al., 1978; Bowlby, 1973a; Pierce & Lydon, 2001). More specifically, attachment styles reflect relationship histories as beliefs and expectations about the worthiness of the self (model of self) and the dependability of others (model of other) in relationships. Once formed, these underlying models serve as a relatively stable and enduring template for what to expect from relationships in general, guiding emotions, social perception and behaviour in relationships throughout the life span (Bowlby, 1973a; Collins & Read, 1994; Shaver, Collins & Clark, 1996).

The original, groundbreaking research on infant–caregiver relationships revealed three attachment styles: the secure style, and two insecure styles – anxious-ambivalent and avoidant. Each was demonstrably associated with differential patterns of maternal caregiving (Ainsworth et al., 1978). From research in adult relationships (e.g. Bartholomew & Horowitz, 1991; Collins & Read, 1990; Feeney & Noller, 1990; Hazan & Shaver, 1987; Shaver & Hazan, 1993) a consistent picture of adult global attachment styles has emerged. Secure attachment develops from a history of sensitive and responsive caregiving experiences and emphasises comfort with relational closeness, and depending on others. The self is viewed as likeable and worthy of others' support and acceptance; others are believed to be dependable and trustworthy. Anxious-ambivalent attachment stems from previously inconsistent or intrusive caregiving and is associated with a 'preoccupying' desire for extremely close relationships coupled with worries about being accepted. The self in the working model is viewed negatively as being unworthy of love, while others are perceived as complex and acting inconsistently. Avoidant attachment is a product of consistently insensitive or rejecting caregiving from key attachment figures, and it is manifested as a dislike of closeness and having to depend on others. Others are believed to be untrustworthy, and the self is viewed as autonomous, i.e. not needing relational closeness.

The measurement of individual differences in adult attachment styles has been subject to some debate and revision during the past two decades. While much attachment research in the social psychology domain has been conducted using the original Ainsworth et al. (1978) and Hazan and Shaver (1987) conceptualisation of attachment involving the three types, there is an emerging consensus that the attachment construct is more accurately represented in terms of two underlying dimensions: *anxiety* and *avoidance* (Brennan, Clark & Shaver, 1998; Fraley & Waller; 1998). According to Brennan et al. (1998), high scores on the *anxiety* dimension indicate a negative self-model and interpersonal anxiety or a fearful preoccupation with the relationship. High scores on the *avoidance* dimension indicate a negative model of others, and avoidance or dismissal of closeness and dependency in relationships. Low values on both dimensions equate to a secure attachment style, and positive models of self and other, using the typological system.

THE LEADERSHIP RELATIONSHIP AS AN ATTACHMENT RELATIONSHIP

At the heart of an attachment theory conceptualisation of leadership is the assumption that the leader–follower relationship is an attachment relationship. Specifically, leaders are viewed as attachment figures because they perform two key attachment-relevant functions for followers. First, leaders act as a safe haven (i.e. providing protection, comfort and support for followers in times of need). Secondly, leaders serve as a secure base (i.e. providing a sense of felt security, or psychological base camp, from which to engage in exploration and self-development) (Mayseless, 2010; Popper & Mayseless, 2003). Based on this, Mayseless and Popper (2007) suggested that the leader–follower relationship should be viewed as a caregiving relationship, in some ways akin to parent–child relationships. Hence, just as children need someone to turn to when frightened or anxious, so adults at work need a safe haven and secure base relationships in which to receive caregiving (i.e. comfort, emotional support and a sense of being valued) when they feel uncertain or worried (Kahn, 1993; 1998; Popper & Mayseless, 2003). That is, for adults too, the experience of stress or threat activates the attachment system and prompts proximity seeking – instinctively turning to a (perceived) stronger and wiser figure for help and protection.

It is thought that the leader–follower relationship, despite having the potential to fulfil safe haven and secure base functions, is usually not a 'true' attachment relationship of the kind that develops with parents or romantic partners, for example. There is consensus among attachment theorists (e.g. Ainsworth, 1989; Bowlby, 1969; Hazan & Shaver, 1994) that true attachment bonds additionally entail a strong, enduring emotional tie to the partner, and significant distress at involuntary separation or loss of the partner. Typically, leader–follower relationships in work organisations are unlikely to be characterised by such intense feelings. Nevertheless, it is believed that leader–follower relationships share sufficient elements of true attachment bonds to make it likely that attachment dynamics, and therefore attachment working models, are activated when individuals interact with or think about the relationship (Collins & Read, 1994; Mayseless, 2010).

The ability of a follower to access a responsive and sensitive leader–caregiver is viewed as a functional and necessary response to coping with temporary stress (Mayseless & Popper, 2007). The leader may be best placed to alleviate particular anxieties at work and provide a temporary safe haven, just until the follower is confident to once more venture forth independently from the secure relational base camp (Davidovitz, Mikulincer, Shaver, Izsak & Popper, 2007; Kahn, 1993; Mayseless & Popper, 2007). Thus, although caregiving in the context of the leader–follower relationship implies a degree of dependence and

asymmetry of power, turning to a leader in times of need should not be viewed as negative or regressive (Popper & Mayseless, 2003). Indeed, in what is termed the 'paradox of self-reliance' (Bowlby, 1973b; Kahn, 1996), full self-reliance – the ability to navigate the social world confidently and independently – is only possible when an individual feels supported and protected by others with whom they have trusting and meaningful connections.

ATTACHMENT STYLE OF LEADERS

So far, the majority of research and theory on leadership and attachment has adopted a leader-centric perspective. In particular, researchers have sought to establish whether a leader's global attachment style is meaningfully associated with the capacity to lead. Also of interest is the association between leader behaviour and leader attachment style, and the effectiveness of leaders with different attachment styles.

Leadership potential and emergence

In contrast to the 'great' leaders studied throughout history, relatively little is known about the developmental antecedents of leadership in the context of 'everyday' organisational leadership (Popper, 2000). A key application of attachment theory and research has therefore been to try to understand who becomes a leader, and what motivates them to do so. Popper (2000) and Mayseless (2010) summarise the theoretical connections between attachment styles and leadership propensity. In brief, attachment style differences in models of self and other, and their characteristic emotion regulation strategies, are believed to affect the subsequent development of 'ego resources' necessary for leadership roles (Popper, 2000). It has long been recognised by leadership theorists that a core component of effective leadership is the ability to establish supportive relationships with followers (Yukl, 2002). Securely attached individuals have a greater capacity for caring and empathising relative to insecurely attached individuals (Mayseless, 2010) because, based on their own past attachment experiences, they have internalised the sensitive and responsive caregiving role (Keller, 2003). Additionally, secure individuals' positive self and other models provide self-assurance, emotional resilience and an interest in other people (Popper, 2000; Mayseless, 2010). Secure individuals are thus well placed to act as a secure base and safe haven to followers (Davidovitz et al., 2007; Mayseless, 2010), and they should have positive expectations about their ability to perform well as leaders (Keller, 2003).

Conversely, through the internalisation of cold or rejecting caregiving, the resultant models of self and other in avoidant attachment emphasise self-reliance and the belief that others cannot be trusted or relied upon for support (Mayseless, 2010). In addition, avoidant attachment is associated with defensive, 'deactivating', emotion regulation strategies that involve suppressing or ignoring their own and others' emotional and attachment needs (Mikulincer, Shaver & Pereg, 2003). Individuals with an avoidant style may therefore be perceived as insensitive and so less likely to be selected for leadership roles (Mayseless, 2010). Alternatively, since avoidant attachment is associated with positive self-regard in achievement contexts (Davidovitz et al., 2007), avoidant individuals may have high self-efficacy and be competent leaders in situations that do not require close relationships with followers (Popper, 2000).

The anxious attachment style, with its associated negative model of self, and preoccupation with achieving relationship closeness, may mean that individuals with this style experience doubts or negative self-efficacy regarding their ability to lead others (Keller, 1999; Popper, 2000). Anxious individuals also 'hyperactivate' emotions – i.e. negative emotions, in particular, may escalate because of a tendency to ruminate on relationship events (Mikulincer, Shaver & Pereg, 2003). Research has shown that anxiously attached employees may be more focused on their own feelings and their need to be appreciated, to the detriment of task performance (Hazan & Shaver, 1990). Taken together, these factors indicate that individuals with anxious attachment styles may be less suited to leadership roles and/or less likely to be perceived as leaders (Mayseless, 2010; Popper, 2000).

A small number of studies have investigated these propositions by focusing on the correlation between individual attachment styles and ratings of leadership potential, or leader emergence in groups. In line with predictions, Mikulincer and Florian (1995) found that young recruits with secure attachment styles in the Israeli Defence Forces (IDF) were more likely to be rated by their peers as having leadership qualities, after four months training together. In contrast, anxiously attached individuals were perceived as 'non-leaders'. Similarly, Popper, Amit, Gal, Mishkal-Sinai and Lisak (2004) asked both peers and unit commanders to rate the general leadership qualities of Israeli soldiers engaged in three months of combat training. After controlling for trait anxiety and locus of control, secure attachment remained positively associated with leadership qualities,

while avoidant and anxious-ambivalent attachment styles were negatively associated. In a study of how leadership emerges in autonomous teams, Berson, Dan and Yammarino (2006) asked 127 US college students to rank team members who they perceived as having emerged as their group's leader(s) during the semester. As expected, securely attached members were more likely to be rated as emergent leaders than insecurely attached team members.

These studies help establish some preliminary support for the basic theoretical connections between attachment style and leadership potential and emergence. More recently, researchers have begun to focus on explaining these connections by examining potential underlying mechanisms. Based on a self-report survey of 286 male IDF soldiers, Popper and Amit (2009) found that secure attachment predicted the number of formative leadership experiences encountered during childhood and adolescence (e.g. positions of responsibility in the home and at school). This relationship was mediated by (low) trait anxiety and (high) openness to experience (personality variables consistently associated with leadership potential). Popper and Amit (2009) concluded that secure attachment developed in infancy predicts the extent to which individuals subsequently acquire the 'psychological sub-structure' necessary for later leadership roles. Starting from the position that insecure, as well as secure, individuals evidently can and do occupy leadership roles, Davidovitz et al. (2007) investigated motivation to lead among IDF officers and business managers. Using the two-dimensional measure of attachment (Brennan et al., 1998), findings were consistent with the models of self and other associated with each style. Hence, avoidance (negative other model) was positively associated with a self-reliance motivation to lead (e.g. 'to be independent'), and negatively associated with task-oriented motives (e.g. 'to help people perform better in their roles') and pro-social motives (e.g. 'to improve others' well-being'). In contrast, anxiously attached leaders (negative self model) reported motives to lead that were more self-enhancing (e.g. 'to win respect and admiration') and control related (e.g. 'to do things according to my ideas').

In general, it appears that 'attachment security places individuals in a better position to become leaders' (Mayseless, 2010: 274). Nevertheless, some insecurely attached individuals are evidently motivated to lead, and are selected into leadership positions. The next questions addressed by attachment scholars are therefore: What styles of leadership are associated with different attachment patterns? How effective are individuals with different attachment styles as leaders?

Leadership style and effectiveness

According to Keller and Cacciope (2001) and Davidovitz et al. (2007), differences in leaders' attachment styles should be associated with differences in leader behaviours and effectiveness. The positive self and other models of secure leaders should be associated with 'high-investment', socially oriented styles of leadership that emphasise support and responsiveness to individual needs (Keller & Cacciope, 2001). Conversely, the negative other models, lack of comfort with closeness, and self-reliance underpinning avoidance may mean that avoidant leaders find it difficult to deal with (or fail to notice) followers who are emotionally dependent on them. Hence, they may be perceived as unresponsive or unavailable by followers, with negative consequences for followers' performance and well-being (Davidovitz et al., 2007; Mayseless, 2010). Finally, leader attachment anxiety, with a negative self-model and concomitant desire for closeness, may be associated with perceptions of intrusive leader behaviours, or self-focused behaviours that are perceived as controlling by followers (Davidovitz et al. 2007; Keller & Cacciope, 2001; Mayseless, 2010). Additionally, because anxious individuals often present themselves as vulnerable (with the goal of achieving closeness), they are unlikely to be perceived as effective leaders (Davidovitz et al., 2007).

To date, the evidence from a small number of extant studies generally supports the theory. In the context of small businesses in the USA, Johnston (2000) investigated the link the attachment styles between owner/managers ($N = 229$) and their preferences for delegation and participative decision making. Congruent with the notion that secure attachment is underpinned by positive and trusting views of others, secure managers were more likely to delegate, and to adopt decentralised decision-making processes. In contrast, avoidant managers, consistent with a self-reliance emphasis and lack of trust in others, tended to adopt centralised decision making (e.g. setting business goals on their own), and were less likely to delegate tasks and business functions to others. Johnston (2000) concluded that managers structured their organisations in ways that were congruent with their familiar and habitual relationship patterns and expectations developed in childhood.

Focusing on specific leadership styles, other studies have found theoretically consistent associations with leaders' attachment orientations. Doverspike, Hollis, Justice and Polomsky (1997) found that secure attachment in US college students ($N = 199$) was positively associated with self-reported relationship-oriented leadership (vs task-oriented leadership) as measured by the Least Preferred Co-worker (LPC) scale (Fiedler &

Chemers, 1974). Popper, Mayseless and Castelnovo (2000) demonstrated across three separate studies of leaders in the Israeli military and police force that secure attachment was associated with a transformational leadership style, as rated by both superiors and followers. Similarly, further studies in the Israeli Defence Force by Davidovitz et al. (2007) and Popper (2002) found that attachment avoidance was negatively related to socialised charismatic leadership (i.e. serving, empowering and aligning one's vision with followers' needs and goals) and positively associated with narcissism and personalised charismatic leadership (i.e. putting one's own interests first and a dictatorial style). Attachment anxiety was also positively associated with a personalised style of leadership. These findings were replicated across self-report, commander and follower ratings of leadership style.

Evidence regarding leader effectiveness as a function of leader attachment style is limited, so far, but there are preliminary indications of the anticipated benefits of secure leader attachment for leader–follower relations and follower performance and mental health. In Johnston's (2000) follow-up interview study with owner/managers, secure managers reported lower conflict with employees and lower employee turnover compared with both avoidant and anxiously attached managers. In line with the proposed effects of negative other models and self-reliance, Davidovitz et al. (2007) found attachment avoidance in IDF commanders was associated with follower perceptions of lower leader efficacy in emotion-focused situations, as well as follower reports of lower unit cohesion and lower levels of their own socio-emotional performance (e.g. 'I help members of the unit work together'). The latter two effects were partially mediated by commanders' (lower) socialised charismatic leadership style. Consistent with a preoccupation with relationship closeness, commander attachment anxiety was associated with lower follower-rated efficacy in task-focused situations, and follower reports of lower instrumental performance (e.g. 'I take work seriously') but higher socio-emotional performance; leaders' lower task-focused efficacy partially mediated the association between commander attachment anxiety and followers' lower instrumental functioning.

Finally, in a further longitudinal study with 541 IDF recruits and 72 officers, Davidovitz et al. (2007) investigated the association between leader attachment style, follower perceptions of leader effectiveness as a secure base and soldiers' mental health after two and four months. Officer avoidance was associated with worsening follower mental health, and this was fully mediated by followers' perceptions of leaders' (low) levels of ability to function as a secure base. Thus, the lack of emotional availability inherent in leaders' avoidant attachment appears detrimental to follower well-being (Davidovitz et al., 2007).

ATTACHMENT STYLE OF FOLLOWERS

Whereas the majority of the leadership and attachment theory and research to date has adopted a leader-centric focus, attachment theory also allows insight into the follower perspective of leadership because the leader and the led each enter the dyad bringing their own relational beliefs and expectations, as represented by their respective global attachment styles. In the mainstream leadership literature, the recognition that leadership is, at least in part, 'in the eyes of the beholder' (Meindl, 1995: 331) has generated much interest in the role of implicit leadership theories (ILTs) (e.g. Lord, Foti & de Vader, 1984). ILTs are essentially prototypes or mental schema of an individual ideal leader that guide the perception and interpretation of leadership behaviour, based on the extent to which there is a fit between observed leader characteristics and features of the prototype (Lord et al., 1984). A key question is: What shapes ILTs – Where do they come from? According to Keller (1999), parents play a pivotal role in shaping implicit leadership theories because they are the individual's first experience of an authority/leader figure. In support, Keller conducted a questionnaire survey in which 238 undergraduate students rated ILT traits for their parents and their ideal leader. The findings revealed that an individual's image of the ideal leader mirrored parental traits, irrespective of whether these were 'dedicated' (e.g. sensitive) or 'tyrannical' (e.g. manipulative and domineering).

Although Keller's (1999) study did not specifically assess attachment styles, it provided initial indications of the importance of parental relationships in later leadership perceptions – and since global attachment styles are (at least in part) internalisations of these same relationships, it suggested a clear role for attachment working models in shaping followers ILTs (Keller, 2003). Hence, Keller (2003) proposed that secure followers, who have internalised images of sensitive and responsive parental caregiving, are more likely to hold ILTs incorporating traits such as sensitivity, supportiveness and attentiveness. In contrast, insecure followers, who have images of caregiver rejection and unresponsiveness (avoidant attachment), or inconsistently sensitive-responsive caregiving (anxious attachment), may espouse idealised leader images that incorporate these same attributes. Some preliminary support for these propositions is emerging. In one study, the idealised leader images of securely attached students were more likely to emphasise leader consideration, compared with the ILTs of avoidantly attached students (Berson et al., 2006). Similarly, Boatwright, Lopez, Sauer, Van der Wege and Huber (2010) conducted a survey of 617 retail employees in the USA and found that preoccupied (anxious) and secure individuals preferred more considerate leadership styles, whereas avoidant individuals did not. Notably, however, Johnson (2007) found that attachment style differences in implicit leadership theories disappeared after controlling for leader liking and follower educational level. Thus, the role of follower attachment in leadership perceptions may be more complex than initial theoretical formulations suggest.

An alternative approach to understanding the role of follower attachment in leadership perceptions and expectations is to investigate whether follower attachment working models bias social cognition in the leader–follower dyad. For example, Davidovitz et al. (2007) reasoned that because insecurely attached individuals, especially avoidant ones, have a generally negative view of relationship partners and are uncomfortable seeking help from others, this negative model of others may be associated with distrust of the leader and a critical view of the leader's style and performance. This is consistent with findings in the wider attachment theory literature that avoidance (and sometimes attachment anxiety) is associated with negative interpretations of partner behaviour, especially in ambiguous relationship interactions (e.g. Collins, 1996). In the context of military leadership, Davidovitz et al. (2007) found that perceptions of commanders having personalised leadership styles were reported by avoidant soldiers even though external observers reported no indications of personalised leader traits in the target officers. Attachment anxiety was unrelated to leadership perceptions, however. This provides some preliminary indications that followers' prior negative relationship experiences with unresponsive caregivers may indeed provide a cognitive framework that predisposes negative perception and interpretation of leader behaviours.

ATTACHMENT STYLES OF LEADERS AND FOLLOWERS

From the literature reviewed so far, it is apparent that, when leader and follower effects are examined independently of each other, both the attachment styles of leaders and their followers have the potential to influence the quality, and indeed the success or failure (Davidovitz et al., 2007), of the leadership relationship. LMX theory emphasises that relationship quality in the leadership dyad is founded upon mutual trust and respect (e.g. Graen & Uhl-Bien, 1995). Attachment theory should therefore provide a useful framework for illuminating the interpersonal dynamics that may underpin observed social exchange processes. To date, however, there is very little theory and research concerning the joint, reciprocal, effects of leader and follower attachment styles. In general, it is assumed that followers and leaders entering new leadership relationships may initially draw upon their existing attachment working models as a guide to interaction with their new partners (Collins & Read, 1994; Keller, 2003; Keller & Cacciope, 2001). Supporting this view, Davidovitz et al. (2007), in their longitudinal study of military leaders and followers, found that soldiers' attachment security moderated the negative impact of their officers' attachment avoidance, but this effect disappeared after four months in the leadership relationship. Hence, secure attachment models containing positive expectations about the self and other appear to provide only a temporary buffering effect when individuals are faced with leader behaviours that conflict with their existing models.

In order to explain the dynamic implications of leader and follower attachment style interactions, Keller (2003) proposed that upon organisational entry, followers' implicit leadership theories are closely associated with their attachment styles. Likewise, leaders' behaviours are influenced by leaders' ILTs (shaped by their respective attachment styles). Congruence between follower ILTs and observed leader behaviours should lead to positive outcomes (e.g. positive leader reports of follower performance, follower satisfaction with leader). A mismatch may lead to sense-making attempts and adaptive behaviour by secure or anxious followers. However, due to a characteristic inflexibility in information-processing (Mikulincer et al., 2003), followers with avoidant attachment styles may be resistant to engaging in sense-making and behavioural adaptation, with negative consequences for satisfaction and performance.

An important implication of Keller's model is that when followers encounter leaders who share their attachment style, they should report higher-quality relationships, whether their mutual attachment style is secure or insecure, because of the compatibility of their underlying models of self and other, and in turn, their ILTs. For example, in the case of an avoidant follower with an avoidant leader, 'since neither party is comfortable with dependency in relationships, they may coexist well. The avoidant follower may be grateful to be left alone without intrusions from the leader, while the avoidant leader may admire the follower's

independence' (Keller, 2003: 152). Conversely, given that avoidant individuals interact according to their negative other-model (emphasising self-reliance and lack of trust), when avoidant followers encounter secure leaders the leader may view the follower as distant and hostile. Consequently, the secure leader may eventually withdraw his or her habitual supportiveness and attentiveness, only serving to reinforce the avoidant followers' negative expectations about others. In sum, understanding the interaction dynamics between attachment styles of leaders and followers may help to predict relationship tensions and difficulties in the dyad (see Keller, 2003, for descriptions of all the possible interaction combinations).

FOLLOWER ATTACHMENT TO THE LEADER

In the preceding discussion, whether the theory and research has focused on leader attachment style, follower attachment style, or both, it shares the same assumption: that leaders' and followers' interactions and responses are influenced by a single, global, attachment style that is developed outside of the relationship itself. However, turning to the final stream of emergent theory and research in the attachment and leadership domain, this perspective is being challenged, and modified, to suggest circumstances in which followers may:

- revise existing global attachment models,
- become attached to leaders, or
- develop relationship-specific working models for the leadership dyad.

Each of these three different responses is briefly outlined below.

The correction hypothesis

Despite the general stability of global attachment working models in adulthood, change is possible should an individual encounter consistently negative or positive caregiving experiences in relationships with attachment figures (Bowlby, 1988; Van IJzendoorn Juffer & Duyvesteyn, 1995). Consequently, Popper and Mayseless (2003) proposed that transformational leaders can play a key role in providing 'corrective' experiences that may help insecure followers to revise their negative self- and other-models towards a more secure attachment style: 'the insecure follower, who expects insensitivity and unavailability, gets instead caring and accepting responsiveness.

This presents the followers with an alternative worldview, which they may eventually come to adopt' (Popper and Mayseless, 2003: 50).

The compensation and correspondence hypotheses

Mayseless & Popper (2007) discussed the interchangeability of key attachment figures in adulthood, and the consequences of this for global attachment styles. Specifically, unlike in childhood, when parents are (for a time) viewed as the stronger and wiser caregiver in all circumstances, in adulthood there is generally no single individual who is viewed as 'infallible' and therefore able to meet all of an adult's attachment needs. This necessitates that in circumstances involving crisis (e.g. major life-threatening events) individuals may develop attachment bonds to others who are better able to provide them with a sense of a safe haven and secure base. Followers may therefore, under extreme circumstances, form an attachment bond with (usually charismatic) leaders who can compensate for the follower's perceived lack of a viable alternative caregiver at that time. These leaders may be proximal (e.g. organisation leaders) or distal (e.g. institutional leaders/politicians). Mayseless and Popper argue further that individuals with anxious global attachment models may have a greater propensity to turn to, and form an attachment bond with, a leader even under more mundane/non-threatening circumstances because of their strong need to be close to others, and tendency to turn to others for help (in contrast to avoidant self-reliance, for example). Notably, according to the correspondence hypothesis, Mayseless and Popper (2007) propose that once an attachment is formed to a leader, followers act in the relationship according to their pre-existing global internal working models of self and other.

The leader-specific attachment hypothesis

In the wider attachment theory literature, evidence suggests that adult social interactions may in fact be guided not only by global attachment models but also by relationship-specific attachment working models (Pierce & Lydon, 2001). Global models of self and other represent the entire history of a person's attachment relationships (Collins & Read, 1994). In contrast, relationship-specific models reflect the history of relationship episodes with a particular partner and, once

formed, are thought to be the more influential guides to interpretation and emotional and behavioural responses in that relationship (Cozzarelli, Hoekstra & Bylsma, 2000).

Based on this, recent research taking a follower-centric perspective has begun to explore whether, in addition to global attachment styles that followers bring with them to the leadership relationship, they are also guided by *specific* follower–leader attachment styles developed in the context of the leadership relationship. In contrast to Mayseless and Popper's (2007) view that specific attachments to a leader should generally only form in crisis situations, when the innate attachment system (promoting proximity and comfort seeking) is activated, others suggest that specific working models are developed and activated in more mundane or everyday circumstances, in relationships with any person with whom individuals have a 'significant', or 'impactful' relationship (Baldwin, Keelan, Fehr, Enns & Koh-Rangarajoo, 1996; Pierce & Lydon, 2001). On this basis, Game (2008) proposed that followers develop specific working/relational models in their everyday leadership relationships at work. Additionally, like student–teacher (Lopez, 1997) and client–therapist relationships (Mallinckrodt, Gant & Coble, 1995) in which relationship-specific attachments have been demonstrated, follower–leader relationships, as previously noted, parallel the safe haven and secure base functions, and the asymmetrical power distribution, of parent–child dyads (Davidovitz et al., 2007; Kahn, 1993; 1998; Keller, 2003). This combination of factors makes the establishment of specific follower–leader attachment models more likely, even in relatively mundane work settings (Game, 2008).

In line with recent measurement approaches (e.g. Brennan et al., 1998), Game (2008) proposed two dimensions of leader/supervisor-specific relational models: attachment anxiety and avoidance. Higher scores on attachment anxiety represent worries about being accepted or appreciated by the leader, and a sense of unworthiness in the relationship. Higher avoidance reflects doubts about the trustworthiness and lack of dependability of the leader, and a desire for autonomy or independence in the relationship. In support of the operation of a specific follower–leader attachment style, Game (2008) found that insecure attachment (higher avoidance and attachment anxiety) to the leader predicted the likelihood of anger-related emotions in hypothetical supervisory relationships, over and above the contribution of global attachment insecurity. Only a small degree of statistical overlap was found between global and specific attachment styles (Game, 2008). Additionally, in a study of leader caregiving and leader-specific attachment, Game and West (2010) interviewed nurses in the

UK, selected according to their scores on the Game (2008) measure of leader-specific attachment. Consistent with attachment theory predictions, individuals who were securely attached to their leaders perceived their leaders' behaviours as sensitive, responsive and accepting; individuals who were avoidantly attached perceived rejecting and unresponsive leader caregiving; and attachment anxiety in the leadership relationship was associated with perceptions of interfering or intrusive leader behaviours.

Finally, Ballinger and Rockmann (2007) demonstrated that the leader-specific attachment working model held in a prior leadership relationship was positively associated with relationship quality, as measured by LMX, in the next leadership relationship. This suggests that followers may, at least in the earlier stages of a leadership relationship before a dyad-specific working model can be formed (see Collins & Read, 1994), be guided by a more generic (or semi-specific) leader working model, based on prior experience and ILTS. This model is viewed as one of a hierarchy of working models (Ballinger & Rockmann, 2007). Indeed, according to Collins and Read (1994), individuals most likely hold multiple models of relationships varying in specificity, which combine to shape the global working model.

CONCLUSIONS

It is clear from this review that attachment theory does not necessarily lead us to a new theory of leadership. Instead, it offers a highly promising framework for achieving a better understanding of established theory and findings, by lifting the lid on the 'black box' of leader–follower interpersonal dynamics. In this way, an attachment theory conceptualisation of leadership complements relational leadership theory (Uhl-Bien, 2006) which emphasises that leadership is a function of how individual attributes shape interpersonal relationship dynamics, as well as a process of social influence through which coordination and change are jointly constructed. Currently, attachment theory is providing us with new insights into leader development and emergence, individual differences in leadership styles, the dynamic tensions inherent in leader–follower interactions, and the consequences for followers of neglecting the relational element of leading. The application of attachment theory to leadership is therefore perhaps best described as an emergent paradigm, and one that is worthy of far greater attention. Research in the field is just

beginning to gather momentum, however, and just as the study of emotions in leadership was once described as 'embryonic' (Brief & Weiss, 2002), only to be followed by an explosion of interest by organisational researchers, it is possible that we will soon witness a similar effect with regard to attachment theory and leadership.

Practical implications

The theory and research reviewed here have implications for leadership training and development. Despite the small number of empirical studies conducted to date, a key finding from this overview was that the secure attachment style consistently predicted leader potential and emergence. Moreover, leader attachment security, with its associated patterns of sensitive-responsive caregiving, and its connection to a more transformational leadership style, was the most beneficial for follower performance and well-being. Although followers bring established global working models plus associated ILTS (and perhaps generic leader working models), to new leadership relationships, it appears that over time it is the nature of the leaders' caregiving behaviour that may ultimately determine relationship quality and other outcomes. This suggests that organisations and their employees could benefit from including assessment of global attachment in leader selection and development. Popper et al. (2000) caution us against assuming that insecurely attached individuals cannot become effective leaders, however, insecure attachment models may be revised if individuals can be helped to reflect on their beliefs and expectations about relationships, and in particular leadership relationships (Drake, 2009; Keller, 2003). If reflection is combined with corrective experiences (Popper et al., 2000) of consistently supportive and attentive caregiving, for example through coaching, it may be possible to help insecurely attached leaders develop relational security, at least in the context of lead–follower relationships (Drake, 2009). Additionally, it may be possible to design intervention training in order to ameliorate dysfunctional attachment dynamics that have emerged between leaders and followers – such interventions have proven successful in addressing parent–child attachment problems (Game, 2008).

Methods in leadership and attachment research

The research on leadership and attachment to date has been predominantly cross-sectional and self-report, like most studies in the field (as Chapter 2 in this volume shows). This is useful in establishing preliminary support for the theoretical basis of leadership and attachment; however, now that this foundational evidence is beginning to accumulate, there is also a need for more longitudinal research designs. This is important if we are to gain a clearer, and more valid, picture of the nature, development and consequences of attachment dynamics between leaders and their followers. To this end, research should also incorporate the use of diaries or event sampling methods. These approaches have proven very useful for understanding other daily work-life phenomena such as the antecedents and outcomes of emotions and affect at work (e.g. Grandey, Tam & Brauberger, 2002). Greater clarity and standardisation is also needed with regard to the measurement of attachment styles.

Although, in the wider attachment research community there has been shift towards using the two-dimensional measure of attachment anxiety and avoidance (Brennan et al., 1998), many studies reported here also used the categorical tripartite measure of secure, avoidant and anxious-ambivalent styles (Hazan & Shaver, 1987), and one or two studies used Bartholomew and Horowitz's (1991) four-category measure. Measurement standardisation would enable researchers to draw more confident comparisons between studies. Furthermore, standardisation helps create a consistent vocabulary with which to communicate about leadership and attachment – this is important for the development of the field. Finally, much of the extant research draws on samples that may limit the generalisability of findings: for example, undergraduate students, and all male military samples in high-risk contexts. More diverse samples, in terms of gender, age, ethnicity and occupation, are needed in future.

Future directions

There is great scope for more research in all of the areas discussed, in order to build on the promising start that has been made. For example, it seems that attachment theory has the potential to help explain, in part, the effects of other leadership approaches that emphasise relational and affective dimensions. Hence, more systematic exploration of the associations between leader global attachment and existing relational leadership constructs is needed, especially LMX, and authentic leadership. Additionally, Manning (2003) proposed that because secure attachment is associated with greater interpersonal competence and openness to new experiences (c.f. Popper & Amit, 2009) it should provide the basis for cross-cultural competence and effective global diversity leadership. Related to this, Popper and Mayseless (2003) and Mayseless and Popper (2007) suggested that there may be cultural differences in followers' propensity to form attachment relationships with leaders. In particular, individuals from more collectivist cultures, where leaders are expected to be supportive and paternalistic, may be more likely to form attachment relationships with leaders than people in individualist cultures (Popper & Mayseless, 2003). In the era of globalisation, where cross-cultural relationships are increasingly an everyday reality for leaders, these are important avenues to explore.

Another key direction for future research will be to investigate further the respective roles of global vs specific working models in the leader–follower attachment relationship: Under what conditions do specific attachments to leaders develop (e.g. high- vs low-risk contexts)? If global or 'generic leader' models are the dominant guides to interaction in the early stages of new relationships, how long does it take for dyad-specific models to develop and become dominant (Game, 2008; Mayseless, 2010)? Finally, according to Mayseless (2010), the caregiving system (governing care provision) is believed to be a closely related but separate regulatory system from the attachment system (governing care seeking). Effectively, research to date that focused on the links between leader attachment styles and leader behaviours may be measuring a proxy for the caregiving system. Reizer and Mikulincer (2007) developed and validated a measure of individual differences in mental representations of caregiving that was significantly associated with differences in parenting attitudes. Future researchers might adapt this for the leadership domain and investigate whether the construct offers greater predictive validity over and above global attachment styles.

In conclusion, attachment theory is already contributing to our limited knowledge about the nature and effects of interpersonal dynamics in the leader–follower relationship, and has the potential to offer many more insights. Leadership processes can be seen as embedded in a wider relational context that is reflected in the goals and expectations of leaders' and followers' attachment working models. Moreover, applying attachment theory to the leadership relationship highlights the key role of relationship histories, in particular the history of leader caregiving in the relationship, in shaping current experiences and responses in the relationship. As such, attachment theory offers great promise as a new relational lens through which to study both leaders and followers.

REFERENCES

Ainsworth, M.D.S. (1989) Attachment beyond infancy. *American Psychologist*, 44, 709–716.

Ainsworth, M.D.S., Blehar, M.C., Waters, E., & Wall, S. (1978) *Patterns of attachment: A psychological study of the strange situation.* Hillsdale, NJ: Lawrence Erlbaum Associates.

Baldwin, M.W., Keelan, J.P.R., Fehr, B., Enns, V. & Koh-Rangarajoo, E. (1996) Social-cognitive conceptualisation of attachment working models: availability and accessibility effects. *Journal of Personality and Social Psychology*, 71, 94–109.

Ballinger, G.A. & Rockmann, K.W. (2007) How individuals approach relationships with supervisors: the supervisor attachment working model. Paper presented at the 67th Annual Meeting of the Academy of Management, Philadelphia, USA.

Bartholomew, K. & Horowitz, L.M. (1991) attachment styles among young adults: a test of a four-category model. *Journal of Personality and Social Psychology*, 61, 226–244.

Bass, B.M. (1985) *Leadership and performance beyond expectations.* New York: Free Press.

Bass, B.M. (2002) Cognitive, social and emotional intelligence of transformational leaders. In R.E. Riggio, S.E. Murphy & F.J. Pirozzolo (eds), *Multiple intelligences and leadership.* Hillsdale, NJ: Lawrence Erlbaum Associates, pp. 105–118.

Berson, Y., Dan, O. & Yammarino, F.J. (2006) Attachment style and individual differences in leadership perceptions and emergence. *Journal of Social Psychology*, 146, 165–182.

Boatwright, K.J., Lopez, F.G., Sauer, E.M., Van der Wege, A. & Huber, D.M. (2010) The influences of adult attachment styles on workers' preferences for relational leadership behaviours. *The Psychologist-Manager Journal*, 13, 1–14.

Bowlby, J. (1969) *Attachment and loss: attachment.* New York: Basic Books.

Bowlby, J. (1973a) *Attachment and loss: separation.* New York: Basic Books.

Bowlby, J. (1973b) Self-reliance and some conditions that promote it. *British Journal of Psychiatry*, 130, 201–210.

Bowlby, J. (1980). *Attachment and loss: sadness and depression.* New York: Basic Books.

Bowlby, J. (1988) *A secure base: clinical applications of attachment theory.* London: Routledge.

Brennan, K.A., Clark, C.L. & Shaver, P.R. (1998) Self-report measurement of adult attachment: an integrative overview. In J.A. Simpson & W.S. Rholes (eds), *Attachment theory and close relationships.* London: Guilford Press, pp. 46–76.

Bresnahan, C.G. & Mitroff, I. (2007) Leadership and attachment theory. *American Psychologist*, September, 607–608.

Brief, A.P. & Weiss, H.M. (2002) Organizational behavior: affect in the workplace. *Annual Review of Psychology*, 53, 279–307.

Collins, N.L. (1996) Working models of attachment: implications for explanation, emotion, and behavior. *Journal of Personality and Social Psychology*, 71, 810–832.

Collins, N.L. & Read, S.J. (1990) Adult attachment, working models, and relationship quality in dating couples. *Journal of Personality and Social Psychology*, 58, 644–663.

Collins, N.L. & Read, S.J. (1994) Cognitive representations of adult attachment: the structure and function of working models. In K. Bartholomew and D. Perlman (eds), *Advances in personal relationships: vol. 5, attachment processes in adulthood.* London: Jessica Kingsley, pp. 53–90.

Cozzarelli, C., Hoekstra, S.J. & Bylsma, W.H. (2000) General versus specific mental models of attachment: Are they associated with different outcomes? *Personality and Social Psychology Bulletin*, 26: 605–618.

Dasborough, M.T. & Ashkanasy, N.M. (2002) Emotion and attribution of intentionality in leader–member relationships. *The Leadership Quarterly*, 13, 615–634.

Davidovitz, R., Mikulincer, M., Shaver, P., Izsak, R. & Popper, M (2007) Leaders as attachment figures: leaders attachment orientations predict leadership-related mental representations and followers' performance and mental health. *Journal of Personality and Social Psychology*, 93, 632–650.

Doverpsike, D., Hollis, L., Justice, A. & Polomsky, M. (1997) Correlations between leadership styles as measured by the Least Preferred Co-worker Scale and adult's attachment styles. *Psychological Reports*, 81, 1148–1150.

Drake, D, B. (2009) Using attachment theory in coaching leaders: the search for a coherent narrative. *International Coaching Psychology Review*, 4, 49–58.

Feeney, J.A. & Noller, P. (1990) Attachment style as a predictor of adult romantic relationships. *Journal of Personality and Social Psychology*, 58, 281–291.

Fiedler, F.E. & Chemers, M.M. (1974) *Leadership and effective management.* Glenview, IL: Scott.

Fraley, R.C. & Waller, N.G. (1998) Adult attachment patterns: a test of the typological model. In J.A. Simpson & W.S. Rholes (eds), *Attachment theory and close relationships.* London: Guilford Press, pp. 71–115.

Game, A.M. (2008). Negative emotions in supervisory relationships: the role of relational models. *Human Relations*, 61, 355–393.

Game, A.M. & West, M.A. (2010) Leader caregiving: an investigation of follower experiences and outcomes. Poster presentation, Society of Industrial and Organizational Psychology Conference, Atlanta, USA.

Graen, G.B. & Uhl-Bien, M. (1995) Relationship-based approach to leadership: development of a leader–member exchange (LMX) theory. *The Leadership Quarterly*, 6, 219–247.

Grandey, A.A., Tam, A.P. & Brauberger, A.L. (2002) Affective states and traits in the workplace: diary and survey data from young workers. *Motivation and Emotion*, 26, 31–55.

Hazan, C. & Shaver, P. (1987) Romantic love conceptualised as an attachment process. *Journal of Personality and Social Psychology*, 52, 511–524.

Hazan, C. & Shaver, P. (1990) Love and work: an attachment-theoretical perspective. *Journal of Personality and Social Psychology*, 59, 270–280.

Hazan, C. & Shaver, P.R. (1994) Attachment as an organizational framework for research on close relationships. *Psychological Inquiry*, 5, 1–22.

House, R.J. (1971) A path-goal theory of leader effectiveness. *Administrative Science Quarterly*, 16, 321–339.

Johnson, B.E. (2007) Taking the child to work: the relationship of adult attachment styles and implicit leadership theories in organizational settings. Unpublished doctoral dissertation, Regent University, USA.

Johnston, M.A. (2000) Delegation and organizational structure in small businesses: influences of manager's attachment patterns. *Group and Organization Management*, 25, 4–21.

Kahn, W.A. (1993) Caring for the caregivers: patterns of organizational caregiving. *Administrative Science Quarterly*, 38, 539–563.

Kahn, W. (1996). Secure base relationships at work. In D. T. Hall (ed.) *The career is dead – long live the career: a relational approach to careers*. San Francisco: Jossey Bass, pp. 158–179.

Kahn, W.A. (1998) Relational systems at work. In B.M. Staw & L.L.Cummings (eds), *Research in Organizational Behavior*, 20. London: JAI Press, pp. 39–77.

Keller, T. (1999) Images of the familiar: individual differences and implicit leadership theories. *The Leadership Quarterly*, 10, 589–607.

Keller, T. (2003) Parental images as a guide to leadership sense-making: an attachment theory perspective on implicit leadership theories. *The Leadership Quarterly*, 14, 141–160.

Keller, T. & Cacciope, R. (2001) Leader–follower attachments: understanding parental images of work. *Leadership & Organization Development Journal*, 22, 70–75.

La Guardia, J.G., Ryan, R.M., Couchman, C.E. & Deci, E.L. (2000) Within-person variation in security of attachment: A self-determination theory perspective on attachment, need fulfilment, and well-being. *Journal of Personality and Social Psychology*, 79, 367–384.

Lopez, F.G. (1997) Student–professor relationship styles, childhood attachment bonds, and current academic orientations. *Journal of Social and Personal Relationships*, 14, 271–282.

Lord, R.G., Foti, R.J. & de Vader, C.L. (1984) A test of leadership categorization theory: internal structure, information processing, and leadership perceptions. *Organizational Behavior and Human Performance*, 34, 343–378.

La Guardia, J.G., Ryan, R.M., Couchman, C.E. & Deci, E.L. (2000) Within-person variation in security of attachment: A self-determination theory perspective on attachment, need fulfilment, and well-being. Journal of Personality and Social Psychology, 79,

Mallinckrodt, B., Gant, D.L. & Coble, H.M. (1995) Attachment patterns in the psychotherapy relationship: development of the Client Attachment to Therapist Scale. *Journal of Counselling Psychology*, 42, 307–317.

Manning, T. (2003) Leadership across cultures: attachment style influences. *Journal of Leadership and Organizational Studies*, 9, 20–30.

Mayseless, O. (2010) Attachment and the leader–follower relationship. *Journal of Social and Personal Relationships*, 27, 271–280.

Mayseless, O. & Popper, M. (2007) Reliance on leaders and social institutions: an attachment perspective. *Attachment and Human Development*, 9, 73–93.

Meindl, J.R. (1995) The romance of leadership as follower-centric theory: A social construction approach. *The Leadership Quarterly*, 6, 329–341.

Mikulincer, M. & Florian, V. (1995) Appraisal of and coping with a real-life-stressful situation: the contribution of attachment styles. *Personality and Social Psychology Bulletin*, 21, 406–414.

Mikulincer, M., Shaver, P.R. & Pereg, D. (2003) Attachment theory and affect regulation: the dynamics, development, and cognitive consequences of attachment-related strategies. *Motivation and Emotion*, 27, 77–102.

Pierce, T. & Lydon, J.E. (2001). Global and specific relational models in the experience of social interactions. *Journal of Personality and Social Psychology*, 80, 613–631.

Popper, M. (2000) The development of charismatic leaders. *Political Psychology*, 21, 729–744.

Popper, M. (2002) Narcissism and attachment patterns of personalized and socialized charismatic leaders. *Journal of Social and Personal Relationships*, 19, 797–809.

Popper, M., Mayseless, O. & Castelnovo, O. (2000) Transformational leadership and attachment. *The Leadership Quarterly*, 11, 267–289.

Popper, M. & Mayseless, O. (2003) Back to basics: applying a parenting perspective to transformational leadership. *The Leadership Quarterly*, 14, 41–65.

Popper, M., Amit, K. Gal., R., Mishkal-Sinai, M. & Lisak, K. (2004) The capacity to lead: major psychological differences between 'leaders' and 'non-leaders'. *Military Psychology*, 16, 245–263.

Popper, M. & Amit, K. (2009) Attachment and leaders' development via experiences. *The Leadership Quarterly*, 20, 749–763.

Popper, M., Mayseless, O. & Castelnovo, O. (2000) Transformational leadership and attachment. *The Leadership Quarterly*, 11, 267–289.

Reizer, A. & Mikulincer, M. (2007) Assessing individual differences in working models of caregiving: the construction and validation of the Mental Representation of Caregiving Scale. *Journal of Individual Differences*, 28, 227–239.

Shaver, P.R., Collins, N. & Clark, C. (1996), Attachment styles and internal working models of self and relationship partners. In G.J.O. Fletcher. and J. Fitness, (eds), *Knowledge structures in close relationships: a social psychological approach*. Hillsdale, NJ: Lawrence Erlbaum Associates, pp. 25–61.

Shaver, P.R. & Hazan, C. (1993) Adult romantic attachment: theory and evidence. In D. Perlman and W. Jones, (eds), *Advances in personal relationships: a research annual*, Vol. 4. London: Jessica Kingsley, pp. 29–70.

Uhl-Bien, M. (2006) Relational Leadership Theory: exploring the social processes of leading and organizing. *The Leadership Quarterly*, 17, 654–676.

Van IJzendoorn, M.H., Juffer, F. & Duyvesteyn, M.G.C. (1995) Breaking the inter-generational cycle of insecure attachment: a review of the effects of attachment-based interventions on maternal sensitivity and infant security. *Journal of Child Psychology and Psychiatry*, 36, 225–248.

Yukl, G. (2002) *Leadership in organizations*. Englewood Cliffs, NJ: Prentice Hall.

25

Team Leadership: A Review and Look Ahead

C. Shawn Burke, Deborah DiazGranados and Eduardo Salas

INTRODUCTION

Several researchers investigating the prevalence of teams in organizations have demonstrated that the use of teams is high (e.g., Boiney, 2001; Devine, Clayton, Philips, Dunford, & Melner, 1999; DiazGranados, Klein, Lyons, Salas, Bedwell, & Weaver, 2008). Boiney (2001) reported that 68% of Fortune 500 companies use self-managed teams. Additionally, DiazGranados et al. (2008) surveyed human resource, organizational development, and training professionals in 185 organizations and found that 94% of the respondents indicated that their organization used teams. As the prevalence of teams has increased, researchers and practitioners have sought to understand the factors that promote their effectiveness. One factor argued to be critical in determining team effectiveness is team leadership (Zaccaro, Rittman, & Marks, 2001).

In this vein, conceptual and empirical work on team leadership has exploded within the last 10 years. Early work in this area typically applied individual- and organizational-level leadership theories to teams. However, this work does not capture the synergistic nature of team leadership. It has been argued that work on team leadership needs to move beyond adapting individual- and organizational-level leadership theories to teams (Burke, Stagl, Klein, Goodwin, Salas, & Halpin, 2006; Kozlowski, Watola, Jensen, Kim, & Botero, 2009; Zaccaro Heinen, & Shuffler, 2009). In line with this, several researchers have noted that we know surprisingly little about '... how leaders create and handle effective teams' (Zaccaro et al.,

2001, p. 452) and there needs to be a focus on the leadership of teams (Hackman & Walton, 1986; Zaccaro et al., 2009).

Researchers have called for work that explicitly examines the leadership functions, styles, and behaviors that contribute to promoting the coordinated, integrated, and adaptive processes required for effective teamwork. As compared to traditional leadership, team leadership dynamically varies with the situation, assumes subordinates roles and linkages are tightly coupled, and highlights coordination demands (Kozlowski, 2002). There is an emphasis on 'structuring and regulating team processes to meet shifting internal and external contingencies' (Salas, Burke, & Stagl, 2004, p. 343). As such, team leadership can be defined as the enactment of the affective, cognitive, and behavioral processes needed to facilitate performance management (i.e., adaptive, coordinated, integrated action) and team development.

The purpose of this chapter is to briefly review the state of the art in team leadership. In doing so, four primary leadership foci will be discussed: leadership of co-located teams; virtual teams; networked teams (i.e., multiteam systems); and shared leadership. Although space constraints limit a detailed examination of the entire body of literature, what follows is a high-level overview of major conceptual contributions in each of these four foci and corresponding key empirical findings. This is followed by a critical analysis of the research methodologies used both within the specific foci as well as across the broader team leadership domain. The chapter concludes with a section that discusses areas for future research.

THEORETICAL AND EMPIRICAL FOUNDATIONS: UNDERSTANDING TEAM LEADERSHIP

Leadership of co-located teams

Perhaps one of the most commonly researched aspects of team leadership pertains to the leadership of co-located teams, as examined through the theoretical foundation of functional leadership. The functional approach views leadership as social problem solving and states that the leader's main job 'is to do, or get done, whatever is not being adequately handled for group needs' (McGrath, 1962, p. 5). Within this approach, leaders are responsible for identifying problems and generating and implementing solutions (Zaccaro et al., 2001). Zaccaro and colleagues identify three critical distinctions between functional leadership and other models of team–leader interactions. First, they note that functional leadership emphasizes that leadership is a boundary role linking teams to their environment. Leaders must interpret and define the events in the team's environment. Second, leadership functions are necessitated by the fact that there are team problems. Third, functional leadership is not defined by a specific set of behaviors, but by any behavior that assists the team in problem solving.

Using the functional approach as their conceptual basis, Zaccaro et al. (2001) developed a framework that argues leadership influences team effectiveness via the effect on team processes (i.e., cognitive, motivational, affective, and coordination). The specific leader functions highlighted as having an impact on these team processes are (1) information search and structuring, (2) information use in problem solving, (3) managing personnel resources, and (4) managing material resources. For example, leaders impact cognition by instilling an understanding of the mission in members and each person's contribution to performance. Leaders impact motivational processes directly by the motivational strategies that are practiced, and indirectly through their planning, coordinating, personnel development, and feedback behaviors. In addition to impacting motivation, leaders manage the climate of the team in order to control conflict and set team norms. Finally, leaders influence team coordination by developing the team's awareness of what resources are available to the team, offering clear task strategies, monitoring environmental changes, and providing developmental and goal-orientated feedback to the team.

Similar in its emphasis, Hackman (2002) argued that leaders create enabling conditions for effective team performance. Team leaders should ensure that the team has clear boundaries, membership stability over a defined time frame, a compelling direction, an enabling structure, a supportive organizational context, and expert coaching. Coaching serves to build and maintain team coherence (i.e., shared behavior, affect, and cognition) and has three targets (effort, strategy, education) whose functionality varies based on the team's developmental stage (Hackman & Wageman, 2005). Coaching that focuses on effort and fosters motivation is most functional early in the team's life span, so as to build shared commitment. At the midpoint of the team's life span, consultative coaching that focuses on performance strategy, emphasizing the alignment between task strategies and requirements, is most functional. Finally, coaching that focuses on education and development is most functional at task completion.

Building off earlier work, Wageman, Hackman, and Lehman (2005) examined the amount of attention leaders gave to:

* coaching individual team members in order to strengthen their personal contributions to the team
* structuring the team, and task, and establishing its purpose arranging team resources and removing organizational roadblocks
* facilitating members, using their collective resources

Results indicated that behaviors which received the most attention were those related to structuring the team and task and establishing its purpose, followed by those pertaining to the arrangement of resources and mitigation of roadblocks.

Extending work on team leadership in terms of the leader's developmental role is work by Kozlowski and colleagues (Kozlowski, Gully, McHugh, Salas, & Cannon-Bowers, 1996; Kozlowski, Gully, Nason, & Smith, 1999; Kozlowski et al., 2009). Kozlowski et al. (2009) provides a prescriptive meta-theory which argues that effective leaders engage in task and developmental dynamics. Building on prior work (Marks, Mathieu, & Zaccaro, 2001), it is argued that teams engage in a three-phase cycle of preparation, action, and reflection. During preparation phases where workload is low, the focus is on setting developmental goals which build task and social capabilities and direct member resources. As workload increases during the action phase, the leader monitors and develops team coherence, thereby facilitating coordination and adaptation. Often the workload present during the action phase will cause coherence to degrade. Leaders must be cognizant of this and be prepared to intervene to facilitate the recovery of coherence by updating situation assessments, adjusting strategy, prompting coordination, and similar activities (Kozlowski et al., 2009). Finally, toward the end of the task cycle, leaders should facilitate reflection and regulatory activities to facilitate learning.

In terms of how the leader facilitates the developmental needs of members, Kozlowski et al. (2009) argued that each task engagement cycle serves as an opportunity to move members along a developmental continuum ranging from novice to adaptive expert. For example, the goals set during the preparation phase shift from individual level to team level as members progress through task engagement cycles. When monitoring team coherence during action phases it is expected that leaders will be required to intervene more in early development stages, whereas later stages will be characterized by boundary spanning (Kozlowski et al., 2009). Finally, with regard to reflection phases and as the team matures, the leader adapts his regulatory and feedback focus from an individual to a team level. For more details on the specific action strategies cross-walked with task cycle and developmental stage, the reader is referred to Kozlowski et al. (2009).

As seen above, team leaders have been argued to engage in many different kinds of behaviors to foster team effectiveness. Burke et al. (2006) conducted a meta-analysis to begin to examine the relationship between leadership behaviors and behaviorally-based team performance outcomes. Burke et al. defined task-focused behaviors as 'those that facilitate understanding task requirements, operating procedures, and acquiring task information' (p. 291), whereas person-focused behaviors were 'those that facilitate the behavioral interactions, cognitive structures and attitudes that must be developed before members can work effectively as a team' (p. 291). Results indicated that the use of both task- and person-focused behaviors was related to perceived team effectiveness and productivity, with person-focused behaviors explaining more variance. Person-focused behaviors were also related to team learning. Boundary spanning and empowerment behaviors were found to explain large amounts of variance in perceived team effectiveness and productivity (24% and 22%, respectively). Moreover, all empowerment behaviors explained moderately high amounts of variance in team learning (31%). For more information on the behaviors contained within each category the reader is referred to Burke et al. (2006).

Virtual team leadership

While co-located teams have received the bulk of the attention with regards to team leadership, an interest in virtual team leadership is on the rise. Virtual teams have been described as, 'teams whose members use technology to varying degrees in working across locational, temporal, and relational boundaries to accomplish an interdependent task' (Martins, Gilson, & Maynard, 2004, p. 808). Researchers have sought to understand the benefits and challenges inherent within virtual teams and, in doing so, leadership in virtual teams has received some attention (Avolio & Kahai, 2003; Avolio, Kahai, & Dodge, 2001; Tyran, Tyran, & Shepherd, 2003). Offering insight into the role team leaders occupy within virtual teams, Weisband (2002) found that effective project leaders initiated task demands and showed consideration of others early in the team's life span. Purvanova and Bono (2009) reported that transformational leadership behaviors were more effective in virtual teams than in face-to-face teams and that there was considerable variability in leader behaviors across the two team types.

Despite the prevalence of interest in the topic of virtual teams, researchers have argued that the predominant amount of work has been descriptive, reporting the benefits and detriments of virtual teams. Very little is known about how virtuality impacts the type, form, function, and behaviors required of team leaders (Powell, Piccoli, & Ives, 2004). As such, there has been sparse development of context-specific leadership frameworks that apply only to virtual teams (for an exception, see Avolio et al., 2001). However, Bell and Kozlowski (2002) provide a virtual team typology that may facilitate understanding regarding the leadership functions and behaviors required. The typology argues for a continuum of virtualness, varying along the following dimensions: spatial and temporal distribution, communication modality, boundary spanning, life cycle, and member roles.

These characteristics of virtual teams, in turn, have an impact on the motivational, affective, and cognitive processes that team leaders need to promote to manage team performance and develop the team. The development of shared coherence within virtual teams is especially important as it is argued that virtual team leadership functions are best distributed throughout the team (Hertel, Geister, & Konradt, 2005; Johnson, Suriya, Won Yoon, Berrett, & LaFleur, 2002). Shared coherence can facilitate members having the motivation and willingness to engage such leadership functions. The impact on each of these processes is now briefly discussed.

Motivation

A critical component of team effectiveness is the motivation to work toward accomplishing the team goal. This motivation is largely driven from cohesion, collective efficacy, and trust among team members (Zaccaro, Ardison, & Orvis, 2004; Zaccaro et al., 2001). In virtual teams leaders face challenges in influencing these motivational processes based on the permanence of the team's tenure, percentage of face-to-face interaction, and access to sophisticated technology used for communication (Zaccaro et al., 2004). For example, distribution often results in members having very little contact; thus, it is more difficult to build trust (Creighton & Adams, 1998; Furst, Blackburn, & Rosen, 1999). The short life span of many virtual teams also contributes to difficulties in building trust, as it is harder for members to gain the knowledge and shared experiences required for trust development (Zaccaro et al., 2004).

To mitigate the challenges in building trust and related constructs, such as cohesion, leaders should facilitate swift trust (Zaccaro et al., 2004). Swift trust has less of an emphasis on feeling, commitment, and exchange and more on action and absorption in the task (Meyerson, Weick, & Kramer, 1996). This type of trust is most easily facilitated when members have clearly defined roles, responsibilities, and expectations (Meyerson et al., 1996). To further combat the challenges to building trust and information exchange, leaders can employ communication technologies (Hedlund, Ilgen, & Hollenbeck, 1998; Mittleman & Briggs, 1999).

Affect

Positive affect is also important for leaders to promote within virtual teams, but has received little attention (Zaccaro et al., 2001). Research on the affective challenges within virtual teams has argued that team dispersion makes it difficult to detect conflict and rifts among members, and thus more difficult for a leader to manage a virtual team. Communication between members who are both geographically and temporally dispersed is heavily reliant on non-verbal-technology-mediated communication, which often creates frustration for leaders and members. Non-verbal communication, can also be a large source of misinterpretation, as assumptions are often made regarding the tone of the sender. Faulty assumptions often causes rifts between members, thereby reducing coordination and motivation. Developing team alignment and commitment to a common purpose may mitigate some of the affect challenges experienced by virtual teams (Kerber & Buono, 2004).

Cognition

Finally, compatible knowledge structures that promote the utilization of unique and shared knowledge and information about resources that each member holds have been shown to be important within teams. Developing a good understanding of who knows what is highly dependent on shared experiences and a common context (Hollingshead, 1998), yet within virtual teams these things are often underdeveloped. Griffith and Neale (2001) suggested that dispersion can lead to difficulties in establishing transactive memory. Specifically, the distance between members causes less awareness of cues signaling distinct perspectives; thereby leading to a false sense of agreement. Given the central position and member access that leaders have, Zaccaro and colleagues (2004) argue that virtual team leaders should actively facilitate the exchange, encoding, and storage of team information. In addition to facilitating information exchange, virtual team leaders must clearly define the team's objective, facilitate team members' understanding of their responsibilities, and create explicit structures that help the team manage its performance (Bell & Kozlowski, 2002).

Summary

Whereas the area of virtual teams is one that has garnered much research within the last 10 years, the area of virtual team leadership is a younger endeavor. Although work has indicated the challenges that face the leaders of virtual teams, there has been little prescriptive guidance put forth regarding how leaders can mitigate these challenges (Hertel et al., 2005; see Martins et al., 2004; Powell et al., 2004). The development of non-traditional forms of trust, fostering a socioemotional focus in initial meetings, appropriately matching technology to situations, use of transformational behaviors, and the distribution of the leadership functions throughout the team, have all been put forth as mechanisms through which leaders can increase virtual team effectiveness. However, an antecedent to virtual team effectiveness is the ability to engage in metacognitive activities. There is a need to self-regulate and adjust at both an individual and team level, as traditional forms of feedback may be absent, or at a minimum delayed, due to spatial and temporal distribution.

Distributed/Shared team leadership

Gibb (1954) stated that 'Leadership is probably best conceived as a group quality, as a set of functions which must be carried out by the group' (p. 884). While the notion of leadership being shared among individuals in collectives is not new, its focused study is a relatively new phenomena. The predominant amount of work that has been conducted on the leadership of collectives examines leadership as a vertical influence process; although important, this is only one type of leadership. In the complex environments of the twenty-first century it is often impossible for one individual to have the requisite knowledge and skill to successfully enact vertical leadership to the exclusion of other forms of leadership. Others have also acknowledged that the sharing of leadership and responsibility within organizations is critical to survival (Merkens & Spencer, 1998). Work on shared leadership recognizes the complexity present within organizational settings and relies on the underlying tenet that 'those who are doing the job are [often] in the best position to improve it' (Jackson, 2000, p. 16). This form of leadership has been argued to be most useful when tasks are interdependent and complex and less appropriate, due to the time required to build shared leadership competencies, with teams in the early stages of development or performing a task under time urgency (Pearce, 2004).

So what does it mean to share leadership? Several conceptualizations have been put forth, but the common theme running throughout is the sharing of the leadership responsibilities throughout the team (see Carson, Tesluk, & Marrone, 2007; Jackson, 2000; Lambert, 2002; Pearce & Conger, 2003); this does not negate vertical leadership. What seems to differ among the various conceptualizations is the manner in which the responsibilities are shared and the exact nature of what constitutes 'leadership'. For example, some researchers explicitly view shared leadership as an emergent phenomenon that occurs within the team (Day, Gronn, & Salas, 2004—leadership capacity), whereas others do not disallow that shared leadership can be formally prescribed (Pearce & Sims, 2002). In relation to form is the argument that shared leadership is the 'serial emergence of multiple leaders over the lifespan of the team' (Pearce & Sims, 2002, p. 176) as compared to the notion of co-leadership. In a similar notion, Day et al. (2004) discussed leadership capacity as a form of shared leadership conceptualized as an emergent state, whereby social capital is built within the team. As with the broader leadership literature, there have been a variety of leadership behaviors and/or functions which have been argued to comprise the content of shared leadership. Within the next section a few of the more prominent models and frameworks are described.

In beginning to delineate the nomological net that surrounds shared leadership, researchers have put forth several models and frameworks.

Some of the most concentrated work in this area has been done by Pearce and colleagues. Perry, Pearce, and Sims (1999) developed a model of shared leadership which encompasses such behaviors as transactional, transformational, directive, empowering, and social supportive behaviors. The model argues that when the team engages in such behaviors, valued affective (e.g., commitment, satisfaction, potency, cohesiveness), cognitive, and behavioral (e.g., effort, communication, citizenship behavior) outcomes result. In turn, these outcomes result in qualitative and quantitative markers of team effectiveness. Further extending this work, Ensley, Pearson, and Pearce (2003) developed a model that examined the role of shared leadership in promoting key affective and behavioral components related to team effectiveness and moderating variables. In the model, shared leadership is related to the development of cohesion and shared vision, which in turn are related to team effectiveness. The model also specified contextual variables (i.e., time, resource constraints, risk, and ambiguity) that may moderate the relationship(s) between shared leadership and cohesion and shared vision, respectively.

Other researchers while not specifying true models or frameworks have delineated competencies argued to foster shared leadership. Lambert (2002) argued for the following competency abilities: negotiate win–win solutions through team learning, influence follower behavior, solve problems within a systems framework, and use shared visioning to empower members. Similarly, Carson and Tesluk (2007) examined literature on role theory and extracted four roles (i.e., navigator, engineer, social integrator, and liaison) around which there seems to be much convergence in terms of their utility to team members without formal title or position authority, as is often the case with shared leadership. When these roles are enacted within the team, the following functions are accomplished:

- establishment of team direction and purpose (navigator)
- structuring of team form, roles, functions, and responsibilities (engineer)
- development and maintenance of team coherence (social integrator)
- development of relationships with key external stakeholders (liaison)

Carson and Tesluk (2007) found that shared leadership, as conceptualized by the above behaviors, was positively related to performance; however, role differentiation with respect to these behaviors, was negatively related to shared leadership. Consequently, the authors hypothesize that shared leadership reflects not a pattern of highly differentiated roles, but several members adapting and exercising more than one leadership role, as the situation dictates.

Moving past models and frameworks, researchers have also delineated the conditions which may affect the emergence of shared leadership. Pearce, Perry, and Sims (2001) identify five conditions: geographic dispersion, demographic heterogeneity, large team size, skill heterogeneity, and maturity. The first three conditions are expected to negatively impact the emergence of shared leadership, whereas skill heterogeneity should have a positive effect. Teams with breadth in their abilities are more likely to be positioned to effectively engage in shared leadership, given the right climate and members who are comfortable with and cognizant of the possession of different skills.

The vertical leader can play a key role in creating the conditions for the emergence of shared leadership. Perry et al. (1999) argue that both the vertical leader and team characteristics are important in creating the conditions for shared leadership. Within this framework the vertical leader ensures the team has an enabling design, boundary management functions are enacted, and facilitative and contingent leadership behaviors are present. Pearce (2004) argues that in addition to the vertical leader developing shared leadership, the organizational context (i.e., training, development, and reward systems) can facilitate emergence.

Research has begun to examine many of the ideas put forth regarding shared leadership, but much remains to be done. Empirical work has predominantly investigated the components of shared leadership and its relation to performance. In empirical research, shared leadership has typically been examined in terms of transactional, transformational, aversive, directive, and empowering behaviors. Results indicate that shared leadership has a positive relationship with performance across a number of domains (e.g., selling teams, consulting teams, top management teams, entrepreneurial teams) and often accounts for more variance than vertical leadership (Ensley, Hmieleski, & Pearce, 2006; Pearce, 2004; Pearce & Sims, 2002).

Less research has focused on shared leadership's relation to process or emergent states. Initial research has suggested that when shared leadership is present teams engage in greater amounts of collaboration, coordination, and cooperation (Manz & Sims, 1993; Yeatts & Hyten, 1998). Some researchers have examined the impact of culture on the tendency to engage in shared leadership behaviors. For example, Hiller, Day, and Vance (2006) found that the tendency to engage in shared leadership was culturally dependent; it was positively related to the level of team members' collectivism, but not to power distance.

Summary

The notion of shared or distributed leadership is not a new concept, although it has recently witnessed a reemergence within the team leadership literatures. The construct itself is still fairly messy as some refer to shared leadership as co-leadership, whereas others define it as the leadership role or function switching between members based on needs and capabilities. Although in many instances this form of leadership has been shown to be more predictive of performance than traditional vertical leadership, most of the work has examined behaviors most typically found in traditional leadership research (i.e., transformational, transactional, empowerment). There have also been propositions set forth regarding the conditions under which shared leadership is most likely to emerge, but little of this work has been tested, nor is there much attention paid to team process; most studies examine the link between shared leadership and outcomes.

Leadership of multiteam systems

A second emerging area which has a shorter history than the work on shared leadership is that on the leadership of networks of teams (i.e., multiteam systems). Multiteam systems (MTSs) have been defined as (Mathieu, Marks, & Zaccaro, 2001, p. 290):

> Two or more teams that interface directly and interdependently in response to environmental contingencies toward the accomplishment of collective goals. MTS boundaries are defined by virtue of the fact that all teams within the system, while pursuing different proximal goals, share at least one common distal goal; and in so doing exhibit input, process, and outcome interdependence with at least one other team in the system.

DeChurch and Mathieu (2009) argued that MTSs are primarily defined by the interdependence between the teams that comprise the system, not by the location of the component teams (i.e., within or across organizations). This interdependence, in turn, creates goal hierarchies which serve to guide action within and across teams comprising the system.

These types of functional units occur in government, military, private, and public sectors. For example, a firefighting MTS might consist of fire suppression, ventilation, and search and rescue teams. In disaster relief efforts, MTSs can take many forms, one of which may be local EMT/rescue teams working with Red Cross medical teams, and military extraction teams. In organizations, an MTS developing a new product would require marketing, research and development, and manufacturing teams to work together.

Researchers have begun to delineate the antecedents, processes, and emergent states which are essential to MTS performance (DeChurch & Mathieu, 2009; Marks, DeChurch, Mathieu, Panzer, & Alonso, 2005). As work on MTS is in its infancy, there are few frameworks which delineate the role of leaders in MTSs. One of the exceptions (DeChurch & Marks, 2006) combines functional leadership with recent work in team process theory to delineate the role of leaders in MTSs. Extracting from functional leadership it is argued that effective leaders shape the processes which occur during taskwork. Taskwork itself is viewed as a reciprocal process that alternates between transition (i.e., evaluation and planning) and action phases (i.e., behavioral engagement which contributes directly to goal attainment) (Marks et al., 2001). DeChurch and Marks (2006) argue that during transition phases the leader engages in and facilitates mission analysis, goal specification, and strategy formulation. Conversely, during action phases the leader focuses on ensuring goal progress is being monitored, systems and team monitoring, and coordination.

In comparing this form of leadership to traditional team leadership it is not the actions of the leader which differ, but the target of those actions and corresponding challenges (DeChurch & Marks, 2006). For example, MTS leaders must be able to negotiate leadership when there are both horizontal and vertical forms of leadership present. Leaders must also be able to manage the temporal alignments and maintain coherence not only within a single component team but also across component teams (i.e., at the system level) whose goal hierarchies are highly coupled (DeChurch & Marks, 2006). Empirical work conducted in the laboratory using a computer simulation has suggested that MTS leaders can facilitate cross-team alignment by engaging in strategy development and coordinating behavior which take into account the interdependencies within the system.

Moving outside the laboratory, Browning (1998) utilized a case study approach to examine MTSs. Whereas the focus of this case study is not explicitly tied to leadership, but on identifying the mechanisms used to coordinate across teams, this is an activity that would conceptually fall under the realm of leadership activities. Findings suggested nine coordination mechanisms. Activities such as systems engineering and interface optimization, improved information and communication technologies, co-location, training, and town meetings were all identified as things that leaders could do to enable coordination. Once coordination was established, results suggested that mediation, interface management groups, integration teams, interface contracts, and scorecards could be used to maintain coordination.

Also investigating MTSs in the field, DeChurch, Burke, Shuffler, Lyons, Doty, and Salas (in press) sought to identify coordination mechanisms utilized by leaders. Using a qualitative approach, historiometric (Simonton, 2003) analysis, a series of historical events were identified that involved mission critical MTSs. Results indicated that leadership actions were focused at three levels: leaders must engage in and shape processes *within single component teams*, at the *interface of multiple component teams* whose goal hierarchies intersect within the system, and at the *boundary between the system and external constituencies*.

Results also indicated that leaders coordinated through the use of strategy-focused behaviors occurring within transition phases as well as real-time coordinating mechanisms. Strategy-focused behaviors included analyzing the situation, designing the role structure of the MTS, planning, and taking initiative. Conversely, coordination-focused activities included reactive/adaptive unity of command, orchestrating actions, and managing the flow of information. These results bolster the findings emerging from the laboratory (specifically the findings from DeChurch & Marks, 2006) as well as identifying a more focused set of functions, and subtasks, of leader behaviors and the level at which they most often occurred (see DeChurch et al., in press for more details).

Summary

Work in the area of MTS leadership is in its infancy; the MTS construct itself is still being shaped and refined. However, there has been a small set of researchers who have been pushing the envelope in this area and the concept appears to be gaining traction. Research in this area has begun to show the importance of MTS leaders maintaining a dual focus with regards to performance management and developmental activities. Several challenges to MTS leadership have been put forth (e.g., maintaining temporal alignment, negotiating horizontal and vertical leadership, managing multiple competing goals across levels), but research is only beginning to examine exactly how the challenges are to be mitigated and the areas in which MTS leadership is truly distinct from the broader team leadership literature.

METHODOLOGIES EMPLOYED IN THE STUDY OF TEAM LEADERSHIP RESEARCH

In studying team leadership, researchers have typically used a fairly narrow set of methodologies; thus, there are many methodological similarities across the domain. These cross-cutting methodologies are briefly described, followed by a discussion of some of the unique methodologies used in specific areas of team leadership research.

Cross-cutting methodologies

Both laboratory and field-based methodologies are employed in studying team leadership; however, field-based methods dominate, especially with regards to virtual and shared team leadership. Both methodologies have their critics. Laboratory methodologies are often criticized in terms of the external validity of the results and field methods for collecting convenience data. The methodologies used tend to be predominantly survey-based, but are often augmented with observational techniques. Members are asked to assess their leader in order to determine the behaviors exhibited and the degree to which behaviors are valued and/or effective. Given the heavy reliance on one methodology, there is a threat of mono-method bias and a chance that the full picture regarding a topic will not emerge, as different methodologies often provide differential information about the same problem.

Researchers need to move beyond survey and observational techniques to the use of multimethod toolkits. An emerging method in this regard is the use of narrative. Narrative is a term that is used to apply to the following research strategies: biography, autobiography, life writing, personal accounts, narrative interviews, personal documents, life stories or histories whether written or oral, ethno-history and -biographies (Danzig, 1999). One application of this methodology is collecting leadership stories from personal interviews. Danzig (1997, 1999) describes the process as follows: an interview protocol is created in which the interviewees are prompted to talk about their own

personal biographies. This is followed by prompting them to discuss a specific problem or situation (background, process, and outcome) in which they occupied a leadership role. The data are then crafted into a story using the leader's actual words and reviewed for accuracy. These stories are then used to extract critical themes or behaviors. This methodology can provide unique insights into team leadership and obtain unconstrained, specific, contextual, and dynamic information on events and organizational issues, not captured in surveys.

Targeted methodologies

Virtual team leadership
Typically, the same methodologies used in the wider literature on virtual teams are seen in research on virtual team leadership. Both laboratory and field-based methodologies are employed, with laboratory studies predominantly utilizing computer-mediated discussions and simulations to mimic the virtual distributed environment. Conversely, research in the field examines teams embedded within organizations (e.g., global virtual teams), as well as teams specifically created for the study (e.g., student virtual teams; for examples, see Jehn & Mannix, 2001; Johnson, et al., 2002).

Mixed methodologies where both quantitative and qualitative methods of inquiry are used to capture the dynamic and virtual interactions within groups are common. In this vein, surveys are used to collect data on team processes, technology use, and perceptions of team effectiveness. The technology inherently involved in virtual teams facilitates more technologically orientated capture methods as compared to team leadership research outside of virtual teams. Data captured tends to be more digital and may be asynchronous. Various communication technologies (e.g., emails, chats, discussion board postings) are often analyzed to determine the type of information team members are communicating, the purpose of communication, how information is interpreted when using computer-mediated technology, and the knowledge networks that emerge.

Shared team leadership
A predominant number of shared leadership studies are conducted in field environments where shared leadership is often operationalized as the degree to which members perceive that leadership behavior 'x' is shared. Studies tend to employ surveys and research designs that preclude causation. Whereas most surveys employ typical Likert scales, the studies examining both vertical and

shared leadership modify the typical survey format to a double format (see Ensley et al., 2006). In this format participants answer questions with both referents (vertical leader, shared leader) side by side. Additionally, a few researchers have used case study methodologies (Denis, Lamothe, & Langley, 2001). Potentially, the most novel methodology which appears is the application of social network analysis to examine shared leadership. Mehra, Smith, Dixon, and Robertson (2006) applied social network analysis to the examination of vertical and horizontal leadership, thereby providing a more concise picture of the pattern of leadership dispersion.

MTS leadership

Although the bulk of the MTS work is conceptual, a good deal of methodological variation exists in empirical work. Existing studies reflect a combination of research conducted in laboratory settings designed to simulate the essential characteristics of MTSs and research conducted in context. Within the laboratory it is common to use a scaled world, synthetic task, or commercial off-the-shelf (COTS) game as the task environment; however, one must ensure that the critical characteristics can be modeled by the system. Marks, Mathieu, and Zaccaro (2004) have argued that such environments must be able to model inter-team interdependence, goal hierarchies, challenging and dynamic environments, and an episodic focus on performance. Using these criteria and others drawn from the MTS literature, Burke, Wooten, Salas, and DeChurch (2009) critically examined COTS environments to assess their applicability for use as MTS testbeds. Findings suggested that with little or no modification the following could be used: C3Fire, ELICIT, Incident Commander, Networked Fire Chief, PLATT+, Reactive Planning Strategies Simulation, Situational Authorable Behavior Research Environment, Steel Beasts Pro, and World in Conflict. Others were found to be relevant, but may require greater modification (for more information, see Burke et al., 2009).

To a great extent, the methods that have been traditionally used in team research have been extended and used within laboratory studies of MTSs. It is common to see the use of Likert-type questionnaires, observational protocols, communication logs, video/audio recording, and system-collected data. While questionnaires, communication logs, video/audio recordings, and observations are commonly used to capture the processes, system-collected data is most often, but not always, reflective of performance outcomes.

In addition to the above methods, Marks et al. (2005) utilized interviews within a laboratory setting to gather data on MTS-level transition processes.

Augmenting the methodologies traditionally used in laboratory studies are those employed when studying MTSs in context. In examining MTSs in context, researchers have used observations and interviews to comprise case studies of MTSs as well as the examination of archived historical documents combined with critical incident extraction and thematic analysis via card-sorting methodologies (DeChurch et al., in press). Finally, to a lesser extent, NASH simulation strategies have been used to examine MTS-related questions (Liu & Simaan, 2004; Liu, Simaan, & Cruz, 2003).

MOVING FORWARD: A RESEARCH AGENDA

Within the last decade research that examines team leadership has begun to flourish. However, most of the work has extended traditional leadership theories to the areas of teams, neglecting the unique role of leaders in teams. Team leaders are heavily engaged in developing and maintaining the shared cognition, behavior, and affect that facilitates a response to dynamic task and developmental contingencies. Within team leadership there is a tremendous focus on process, which is missing from the more traditional leadership literature, and how synergy can be maximized within the team. Therefore, in moving forward one of the first priorities is the need to examine the factors which have been argued to make team leadership different to the leadership of individuals or organizations (see Kozlowski et al., 2009).

A second area that needs concentrated effort is related to how team composition impacts leader requirements. Team leaders are increasingly leading global teams as well as teams with cross functional or organizational boundaries. The manner in which team leaders can mitigate the initial negative effects that diversity often has on process is sorely lacking. Potential questions include:

- How can leaders capitalize on the synergy diversity can provide?
- How do leaders negotiate a shared reality among members who have different beliefs, values, and expectations?
- Do the mechanisms that leaders use to facilitate team coherence within homogeneous teams work in teams who are culturally and functionally diverse or do they need to be adapted, and if so, how?

Recent articles that explicate the different forms that diversity may take may provide guidance in this area (see Harrison & Klein, 2007).

Context and time are two other areas in which future research could concentrate. It has been argued that team leadership varies with context (Kozlowski et al., 2009). However, team leadership researchers often do not consider context as a key variable, treating it more as a factor to control. However, the field is beginning to take note of the importance of context as several journals have recently devoted entire issues to topics pertaining to leadership in extreme contexts. Researchers should consider how extreme contexts, as well as other mission essential contexts, change the functionality of different leader behaviors in promoting team coherence. How does context impact the development, loss, and regaining of trust? How does it impact what the leader must do to facilitate adaptation? Finally, with regard to time, there is a considerable gap in examining the impact of leadership on teams over time. Processes such as team learning and team adaptation can only be effectively examined over time. Research is needed to uncover which leadership behaviors are most effective at developing adaptable teams. Research examining how leaders can develop team learning through behaviors which develop a learning climate, promote the use and development of learning tools, and represent members as learning partners is also needed (see Zaccaro, Ely, & Shuffler, 2008).

A final cross-cutting area pertains to measurement and methodology. There needs to be a push for the use of multi-method strategies and innovative thinking such that instruments go beyond the typical subjective survey item. As the focus is *team* leadership, more attention needs to focus on how constructs emerge across levels (see Klein & Kozlowski, 2000) as well as data indexing (see Smith-Jentsch, 2009). Whereas above we have delineated areas of future research that are cross-cutting, we next highlight a few needs that are targeted with respect to a specific leadership type.

Virtual team leadership

The literature on the role of the leader in virtual teams is not as well developed as that on the leadership of co-located teams. There is still a fair amount of controversy over the degree to which virtual teams are actually a distinct team form or whether all teams have some degree of virtuality. Therefore, one of the first streams of research should be to investigate how, or if, truly different leader behaviors are required in this context. In this vein, how leader requirements change based on degree of virtuality is an important area of research. Research that effectively examines the role that technology plays in the leader–team dynamic would also be informative. Specifically, what kind of technology is most effective and when? How does this technology change the way that leaders and teams interact in order to interpret, share, and disseminate information?

Empirical research on virtual team affective processes is also limited. Given the context many virtual teams operate in, research can provide answers to questions such as what can a leader do to minimize or manage conflict? Gaining a greater understanding of these processes has implications for how to lead virtual teams. In summary, we place a call to researchers to examine virtual teams and their uniqueness. Rather than comparing the leadership between co-located and virtual teams, we feel it is critical to start examining what is uniquely or similarly appropriate for virtual teams.

Additionally, several researchers have argued that within virtual teams the leadership function is best distributed throughout the team. This proposition, in and of itself, needs to be empirically validated. If shared leadership is indeed the most effective form of leadership within virtual teams, the next question pertains to the exact leadership functions that need to be distributed. What functions and corresponding behaviors remain in the purview of the leader and what are distributed throughout the team. Finally, investigation is needed of how leadership capacity (see Day et al., 2004) is developed within virtual teams.

Shared team leadership

Although the initial research on shared leadership has been promising, there is much that remains to be investigated. A few of the more prominent areas in need of research include, but are not limited to, examination of process, time, and measurement. Perhaps one of the first areas within shared leadership that could use focused research is the examination of how shared leadership impacts team process. Most of the work focuses on the relationship between shared leadership and team outcomes, with little attention on process. However, within the broader team literature base, knowledge about process has been shown to be instrumental in terms of effective team performance, training, and feedback.

In seeking to understand the impact of shared leadership on team process, research should also investigate the relationship between shared and vertical leadership. As these two forms of leadership have been argued to potentially coexist, how do contextual factors and degree of interdependence impact the appropriate mix of these two forms of leadership? A few studies have examined both forms of leadership, but problems with degrees of freedom and multicollinearity have prevented researchers from examining their interaction.

Additionally, although shared leadership researchers have noted the importance of time, little work has been done in this area. Barry (1991) has argued for the importance of understanding how shared leadership, and the behaviors contained within, might differentially impact the team based on the team's developmental stage. A similar question pertains to examining how shared leadership might evolve over the life span of the team. Along these lines, Carson and Tesluk (2007) argue for the use of growth modeling and network analysis to examine how the roles embedded within shared leadership change across time and, in turn, relate to team performance.

Multiteam system leadership

As the work on MTS is perhaps the youngest, there is a tremendous potential for growth in this area. Perhaps the greatest need is to begin to explicate whether MTS leadership requires something fundamentally different from that which is required when leading a single team or if it is solely a matter of different leadership targets and increased complexity. Other areas that might be investigated relate to:

- How do leaders manage the temporal alignment and coordination when entrainment cycles differ across the system?
- What is the interaction between the vertical and horizontal leadership that often appears in networks of teams?
- What is required of the leader to manage and develop the cross-functional and/or cross-organizational nature of many MTSs?
- How are multiple identities managed such that they do not form a roadblock to effective process?
- Do leaders need to promote cohesion and a feeling of 'groupness' across the system?

CONCLUSIONS

There is no question that there are a great many benefits of leadership in teams (see Burke et al., 2006). These benefits include the ability of the leader to serve as a coordinator of operations, a liaison to external teams or management, and as a guide for setting the team's vision (Zaccaro & Marks, 1999). Beyond that, leaders may also facilitate a team's propensity to adapt by choosing how and when to intervene to promote regulatory

activities (e.g., Gersick & Hackman, 1990; Hackman & Wageman, 2005).

Stagl, Salas, and Burke (2007) conducted a critical analysis of the existing literature on team leadership and delineated 20 evidence-based best practices, which are organized based on Hackman's (2002) work. With regards to creating a real team, leaders should (a) define and create interdependencies, (b) reinforce task interdependencies with congruent goals and feedback, (c) clarify member responsibility and outcome accountability, (d) specify the team's decision-making authority, and (e) facilitate the use of intact teams. To create compelling direction (see Hackman, 2002), leaders should (a) exercise authority to establish compelling direction, (b) challenge the status quo to stimulate and inspire members, (c) highlight a common mission to instill collective aspirations, and (d) fully engage member capabilities by providing consequential directions. Best practices that relate to the third enabling condition, provision of enabling structure, include (a) promoting self-goal setting, self-observation, and self-reward, (b) establishing norms for how the team scans its environment, reacts to findings, and implements action, and (c) allocating the optimal number and mix of personnel. Best practices with respect to Hackman's (2002) fourth enabling condition, a supportive organizational context, include (a) implementing team-based performance-contingent rewards, (b) institutionalizing a multitiered reward system, (c) ensuring information is performance targeted, (d) negotiating access to sensitive information when needed in the development and selection of performance strategies, and (e) providing and securing developmental opportunities. Finally, best practices related to the last enabling condition, expert coaching, include (a) building shared coherence through the use of pre-briefings, (b) offering novel task performance strategies, and (c) engaging in reciprocal discussion of lessons learned and developing action plans for the implementation of lessons learned to future endeavors.

This work has been extended within a recent review article (Morgeson, DeRue, & Karam, 2010) on team leadership which delineates four sources of team leadership (internal, external, formal, and informal) and articulates a set of team leadership functions. Morgeson and colleagues focus on the processes within a team and use a functional lens to delineate the specific behaviors that leaders engage in during the transition and action phases of the team process (see Table 25.1 for a summary of the behaviors).

As can be seen within the chapter, team leadership is a complex, multilevel, and cyclical process that takes many different forms. We have sought to provide a brief discussion of the major

Table 25.1 Leadership functions

Transition phase	Action phase
Compose team	Monitor team
Define mission	Management of team boundaries
Establish expectations and goals	Challenge team
Structure and plan	Perform team task
Train and develop team	Solve problems
Sensemaking	Provide resources
Provide feedback	Encourage team self-management
	Support social climate

Source: Adapted from Morgeson et al. (2010).

conceptual and empirical contributions to the area of team leadership, a discussion of current methodologies, and potential areas of future research. This chapter is not meant to be all-inclusive, as many of these areas are a manuscript in and of themselves, but to offer a brief highlight such that the interested reader can dig deeper within the cited sources. We hope that this serves to stimulate thought, discussion, and future research in this area. Although much work has been conducted over the last 10 years, there are many questions that remain unanswered.

ACKNOWLEDGMENT

This work was partially supported by funding from the Army Research Office MURI Grant to Dr. Michele Gelfand, Principal Investigator, UMD (W911NF-08-1-014), subcontracted to UCF (Z885903). The views expressed in this work are those of the authors and do not necessarily reflect the organizations with which they are affiliated, their sponsoring institutions or agencies, or their grant partners.

REFERENCES

Avolio, B. J. & Kahai, S. (2003). Adding the 'E' to E-leadership: how it may impact your leadership. *Organizational Dynamics, 31*, 325–338.

Avolio, B. J., Kahai, S., & Dodge, G. E. (2001). E-Leadership: implications for theory, research, and practice. *The Leadership Quarterly, 11*, 615–668.

Barry, D. (1991). Managing the bossless team: lessons in distributed leadership. *Organizational Dynamics, 20*(1), 31–47.

Bell, B. S. & Kozlowski, S. W. J. (2002). A typology of virtual teams: implications for effective leadership. *Group Organizational Management, 27*(1), 14–49.

Boiney, L. G. (2001). *Gender impacts virtualwork teams: men want clear objectives while women value communication.* Retrieved on February 15, 2010, from http://gbr.pepperdine.edu/014/teams.html.

Browning, T. R. (1998). Integrative mechanisms for multiteam integration: findings from five case studies. *Systems Engineering: The Journal of the International Council on Systems Engineering, 1*(2), 95–112.

Burke, C. S., Stagl, K. C., Klein, C., Goodwin, G. F., Salas, E., & Haplin, S. M. (2006). What type of leadership behaviors are functional in teams? A meta-analysis. *The Leadership Quarterly, 17*(3), 288–307.

Burke, C. S., Wooten, S. II, Salas, E., & DeChurch, L. (2009). A critical review of platforms for use in multi-team system related research. Unpublished manuscript submitted to Army Research Institute, August 2009.

Carson, J. B. & Tesluk, P. E. (2007). Leadership from within: a look at leadership roles in teams. Paper presented at the Academy of Management Meeting, Philadelphia, PA.

Carson, J. B., Tesluk, P. E., & Marrone, J. A. (2007). Shared leadership in teams: an investigation of antecedent conditions and performance. *Academy of Management Journal, 50*(5), 1217–1234.

Creighton, J. L. & Adams, J. W. R. (1998). The cybermeeting's about to begin. *Management Review, 87*, 29–43.

Danzig, A. (1997). Building leadership capacity through narrative. *Educational Leadership and Administration, 9*, 49–59.

Danzig, A. (1999). How might leadership be taught? The use of story and narrative to teach leadership. *International Journal of Leadership in Education, 2*(2), 117–131.

Day, D. V., Gronn, P., & Salas, E. (2004). Leadership capacity in teams. *The Leadership Quarterly, 15*(6), 857–880.

DeChurch, L. A., Burke, C. S., Shuffler, M., Lyons, R., Doty, D., & Salas, E. (in press). A historiometric analysis of leadership in mission critical environments. *The Leadership Quarterly.*

DeChurch, L. A. & Marks, M. A. (2006). Leadership in multiteam systems. *Journal of Applied Psychology, 91*, 311–329.

DeChurch, L. A. & Mathieu, J. E. (2009). Thinking in terms of multiteam systems. In E. Salas, G. F. Goodwin, & C. S. Burke (eds), *Team effectiveness in complex organizations.* New York: Psychology Press, pp. 267–292.

Denis, J. L., Lamothe, L., & Langley, A. (2001). The dynamics of collective leadership and strategic change in pluralistic organizations. *Academy of Management Journal, 44*(4), 809–837.

Devine, D. J., Clayton, L. D., Philips, J. L., Dunford, B. B., & Melner, S. B. (1999). Teams in organizations: prevalence, characteristics, and effectiveness. *Small Group Research, 30*(6), 678–711.

DiazGranados, D., Klein, C., Lyons, R., Salas, E., Bedwell, W. L., & Weaver, S. J. (2008). Investigating the prevalence, characteristics and effectiveness of teams: a U.S. sample surveyed. Paper presented at the INGRoup: Interdisciplinary Network for Group Research, Kansas City, MO, July 17–19, 2008.

Ensley, M. D., Hmieleski, K. M., & Pearce, C. L. (2006). The importance of vertical and shared leadership within new venture top management teams: implications for the performance of startups. *The Leadership Quarterly, 17,* 217–231.

Ensley, M. D., Pearson, A., & Pearce, C. L. (2003). Top management team process, shared leadership and new venture performance: a theoretical model and research agenda. *Human Resource Management Review, 13,* 329–346.

Furst, S., Blackburn, R., & Rosen, B. (1999). Virtual team effectiveness: a proposed research agenda. *Information Systems Journal, 9*(4), 249–269.

Gibb, C. A. (1954). Leadership. In G. Lindzey (ed.), *Handbook of social psychology.* Reading, MA: Addison-Wesley, pp. 877–917.

Griffith, T. L. & Neale, M. A. (2001). Information processing in traditional, hybrid, and virtual teams: from nascent knowledge to transactive memory. *Research and Organizational Behavior, 23,* 379–421.

Hackman, J. R. (2002). *Leading teams: setting the stage for great performances.* Boston, MA: Harvard Business School Press.

Hackman, J. R. & Wageman, R. (2005). A theory of team coaching. *Academy of Management Review, 30*(2), 269–287.

Hackman, J. R. & Walton, R. E. (1986). Leading groups in organizations. In P. S. Goodman & Associates (eds), *Designing effective work groups.* San Francisco, CA: Jossey-Bass, pp. 72–119.

Harrison, D. A. & Klein, K. J. (2007). What's the difference? Diversity constructs as separation, variety, or disparity in organizations. *Academy of Management Review, 32*(4), 1199–1228.

Hedlund, J., Ilgen, D. R., & Hollenbeck, J. R. (1998). Decision accuracy in computer-mediated versus face-to-face decision-making teams. *Organizational Behavior and Human Decision Processes, 76,* 30–47.

Hertel, G., Geister, S., & Konradt, U. (2005). Managing virtual teams: a review of current empirical research. *Human Resource Management Review, 15,* 69–95.

Hiller, N. J., Day, D. V., & Vance, R. J. (2006). Collective enactment of leadership roles and team effectiveness: a field study. *The Leadership Quarterly, 17,* 387–397.

Hollingshead, A. B. (1998). Group and individual training. *Small Group Research, 29*(2), 254–280.

Jackson, S. (2000). A qualitative evaluation of shared leadership barriers, drivers, and recommendations. *Journal of Management in Medicine, 14* (3/4), 166–178.

Jehn, K. A. & Mannix, E. A. (2001). The dynamic nature of conflict: a longitudinal study of intragroup conflict and group performance. *Academy of Management Journal, 44,* 238–251.

Johnson, S. D., Suriya, C., Won Yoon, S. W., Berrett, J. V., & La Fleur, J. (2002). Team development and group processes of virtual learning teams. *Computers & Education, 39,* 379–393.

Kerber, K. W. & Buono, A. F. (2004). Leadership challenges in global virtual teams: lessons from the field. *SAM Advanced Management Journal, 69,* 4–10.

Klein, K. & Kozlowski, S. W. J. (eds) (2000). *Multilevel theory, research, and methods in organizations: foundations, extensions, and new directions.* San Francisco: Jossey-Bass.

Kozlowski, S. W. J. (2002). Discussant: In J. C. Ziegert & K. J. Klein (chairs), *Team leadership: current theoretical and research perspectives.* Symposium presented at the 17th Annual Conference of the Society for Industrial and Organizational Psychology, Toronto, Canada.

Kozlowski, S. W. J., Gully, S. M., McHugh, P. P., Salas, E., & Cannon-Bowers, J. A. (1996). A dynamic theory of leadership and team effectiveness: developmental and task contingent leader roles. In G. R. Ferris (ed.), *Research in personnel and human resources management,* Vol. 14. Greenwich, CT: JAI Press, pp. 253–305.

Kozlowski, S. W. J., Gully, S. M., Nason, E. R., & Smith, E. M. (1999). Developing adaptive teams: a theory of compilation and performance across levels and time. In D. R. Ilgen & E. D. Pulakos (eds), *The changing nature of work and performance: implications for staffing, personnel actions, and development.* San Francisco: Jossey-Bass, pp. 240–292.

Kozlowski, S. W. J., Watola, D. J., Jensen, J. M., Kim, B. H., & Botero, I. C. (2009). Developing adaptive teams: a theory of dynamic team leadership. In E. Salas, G. F. Goodwin, & C. S. Burke (eds), *Team effectiveness in complex organizations: cross-disciplinary perspectives and approaches.* New York: Psychology Press, pp. 113–155.

Lambert, L. (2002). A framework for shared leadership. *Educational Leadership, 59*(8): 37–40.

Liu, Y. & Simaan, M. A. (2004). Noninferior Nash strategies for multi-team systems. *Journal of Optimization Theory and Applications, 120*(1), 29–51.

Liu, Y., Simaan, M. A., & Cruz, J. B., Jr (2003). An application of dynamic Nash task assignment strategies to multi-team military air operations. *Automatica, 39*(8), 1469–1478.

McGrath, J. E. (1962). The influence of positive interpersonal relations on adjustment and effectiveness in rifle teams. *Journal of Abnormal and Social Psychology, 65*(6), 365–375.

Manz, C. C. & Sims, H. P., Jr (1993). *Business without bosses: how self-managing teams are building high-performing companies.* New York: Wiley.

Marks, M. A., DeChurch, L. A., Mathieu, J. E., Panzer, F. J., & Alonso, A. (2005). Teamwork in multiteam systems. *Journal of Applied Psychology, 90*(5), 964–971.

Marks, M. A., Mathieu, J. E., & Zaccaro, S. J. (2001). A temporally based framework and taxonomy of team processes. *Academy of Management Review, 26*(3), 356–76.

Marks, M. A., Mathieu, J. E., & Zaccaro, S. J. (2004). Using scaled worlds to study multi-team systems. In S. G. Schiflett, L. R. Elliott, E. Salas, & M. D. Coovert (eds), *Scaled worlds: development, validation, and application.* Aldershot, England: Ashgate, pp. 279–295.

Martins, L. L., Gilson, L. L., & Maynard, M. T. (2004). Virtual teams: What do we know and where do we go from here? *Journal of Management, 30*(6), 805–835.

Mathieu, J. E., Marks, M. A., & Zaccaro, S. J. (2001). Multiteam systems. In N. Anderson, D. S. Ones, H. K. Sinangil, & C. Viswesvaran (eds), *Organizational psychology: Vol. 2.*

Handbook of industrial, work and organizational psychology. London: Sage, pp. 289–313.

Mehra, A., Smith, B. R., Dixon, A. L., & Robertson, B. (2006). Distributed leadership in teams: the network of leadership perceptions and team performance. *The Leadership Quarterly, 17*, 232–245.

Merkens, B. J. & Spencer, J. S. (1998). A successful and necessary evolution to shared leadership: a hospital's story. *International Journal of Health Care Quality Assurance Incorporating Leadership in Health Services, 11*(1), i–iv.

Meyerson, D., Weick, K. E., & Kramer, R. M. (1996). Swift trust and temporary groups. In R. M. Kramer & T. R. Tyler (eds), *Trust in organizations: frontiers of theory and research*. Thousand Oaks, CA: Sage, pp. 166–195.

Mittleman, D. & Briggs, R. O. (1999). Communication technology for traditional and virtual teams. In E. Sundstrom (ed.), *Supporting work team effectiveness*. San Francisco: Jossey-Bass.

Morgeson, F. P., DeRue, D. S., & Karam, E. P. (2010). Leadership in teams: a functional approach to understanding leadership structures and processes. *Journal of Management, 36*, 5–39.

Pearce, C. L. (2004). The future of leadership: combining vertical and shared leadership transform knowledge work. *Academy of Management Executive, 18*(1), 47–57.

Pearce, C. L. & Conger, J. A. (eds) (2003). *Shared leadership: reframing the hows and whys of leadership*. Thousand Oaks, CA: Sage.

Pearce, C. L., Perry, M. L., & Sims, H. P. Jr (2001). Shared leadership: relationship management to improve nonprofit organization effectiveness. In T. D. Conners (ed.), *The nonprofit handbook: management*. New York: John Wiley & Sons.

Pearce, C. L. & Sims, H. P. J. (2002). Vertical versus shared leadership as predictors of the effectiveness of change management teams: an examination of aversive, directive, transactional, transformational, and empowering leader behaviors. *Group Dynamics: Theory, Research and Practice, 6*(2), 172–197.

Perry, M. L., Pearce, C. L., & Sims, H. P., Jr (1999). Empowered selling teams: how shared leadership can contribute to selling team outcomes. *Journal of Personal Selling & Sales Management, 19*(3), 35–51.

Powell, A., Piccoli, G., & Ives, B. (2004). Virtual teams: a review of current literature and directions for future research. *Database for Advances in Information Systems, 35*(1), 6–36.

Purvanova, R. K. & Bono, J. E. (2009). Transformational leadership in context: face-to-face and virtual teams. *The Leadership Quarterly, 20*(3), 343–357.

Salas, E., Burke, C. S., & Stagl, K. (2004). Developing teams and team leaders: Strategies and principles. In D. Day, S. J. Zaccaro, & S. M. Halpin (eds), *Leader development for transforming organizations*. Mahwah, NJ: Lawrence Erlbaum Associates, pp. 325–355.

Simonton, D. K. (2003). Qualitative and quantitative analyses of historical data. *Annual Review of Psychology, 54*, 617–640.

Smith-Jentsch, K. A. (2009). Measuring team-related cognition: the devil is in the details. In E. Salas, G. F. Goodwin, & C. S. Burke (eds), *Team effectiveness in complex organizations: cross-disciplinary perspectives and approaches*. New York: Psychology Press, pp. 491–508.

Stagl, K. C., Salas, E., & Burke, C. S. (2007). Best practices in team leadership: what team leaders do to facilitate team effectiveness. In J. A. Conger & R. E. Riggio (eds), *The practice of leadership: developing the next generation of leaders* San Francisco, CA: Jossey-Bass, pp. 172–197, 368–376.

Tyran, K. L, Tyran, C. G., & Shepherd, M. (2003). Exploring emerging leadership in virtual teams. In C. B. Gibson & S. G. Cohen (eds), *Virtual teams that work: creating conditions for virtual team effectiveness*. San Francisco, CA: Jossey-Bass, pp. 183–195.

Wageman, R., Hackman, J. R., & Lehman, E. (2005). Team diagnostic survey: development of an instrument. *Journal of Applied Behavioral Science, 41*(4), 373–398.

Weisband, S. (2002). Maintaining awareness in distributed team collaboration: implications for leadership and performance. In P. J. Hinds & S. Kiesler (eds), *Distributed work*. Cambridge, MA: MIT Press, pp. 311–333.

Yeatts, D. E., & Hyten, C. (eds) (1998). *High performing self-managed work teams: a comparison of theory to practice*. Thousand Oaks, CA: Sage.

Zaccaro, S. J., Rittman, A. L., & Marks, M. A. (2001). Team leadership. *The Leadership Quarterly, 12*(4), 451–483.

Zaccaro, S. J., Ardison, S. D., & Orvis, K. L. (2004). Leadership in virtual teams. In D. V. Day, S. J. Zaccaro, & S. M. Haplin (eds), *Leader development for transforming organizations: growing leaders for tomorrow*. Mahwah, NJ: Lawrence Erlbaum Associates, pp. 267–292.

Zaccaro, S. J., Ely, K., & Shuffler, M. (2008). The leader's role in group learning. In V. I. Sessa & M. London (eds), *Work group learning: understanding, improving and assessing how groups learn in organizations*. New York: Taylor & Francis Group/Lawrence Erlbaum Associates, pp. 193–214.

Zaccaro, S. J., Heinen, B., & Shuffler, M. (2009). Team leadership and team effectiveness. In E. Salas, G. F. Goodwin, & C. S. Burke (eds), *Team effectiveness in complex organizations: cross-disciplinary perspectives and approaches*. New York: Psychology Press, pp. 83–112.

Zaccaro, S. J. & Marks, M. (1999). The roles of leaders in high-performance teams. In E. Sundstrom & Associates (eds), *Supporting work team effectiveness: best management practices for fostering high performance*. San Francisco, CA: Jossey-Bass, pp. 95–125.

26

Authentic Leadership

Arran Caza and Brad Jackson

INTRODUCTION

Recent corporate and political scandals have prompted media portrayals of a 'global leadership crisis', which in turn has led to discussion of the nature of leadership, with both its advantages and disadvantages (Kets De Vries & Balazs, Chapter 28, this volume). In these discussions, authentic leadership has assumed an important position among strength-based approaches, having been advanced as a potential solution to the challenges of modern leadership. While authentic leadership research only developed a coherent focus in 2003, it has since attracted considerable theoretical attention and continues to figure prominently in practitioners' treatment of leadership. Ladkin and Taylor (2010) note that it has provided the focus for three special issues of academic journals: *The Leadership Quarterly* (2005/1), the *Journal of Management Studies* (2005/5), and the *European Management Journal* (2007/2).

Authentic leadership has also provided the inspiration for numerous popular books and articles (e.g. George, 2003; Goffee & Jones, 2005; Irvine & Reger, 2006). These are supported by a strong and growing interest in authentic leadership among practitioners in many industries and professions (e.g. Gayvert, 1999; George, Sims, McLean, & Mayer, 2007; Kouzes & Posner, 2008; Nadeau, 2002; O'Connor, 2007; Pembroke, 2002; Shelton, 2008). In one striking example, the American Association of Critical Care Nurses declared authentic leadership to be one of their six necessities for a healthy working environment (American Association of Critical Care Nurses, 2005).

As a nascent endeavour, authentic leadership research is still in the process of defining itself, and so this review is primarily formative rather than summative in nature. We describe the history and content of authentic leadership theory, overview its theoretical tenets, and review the empirical evidence that has been provided to date. We conclude by highlighting some prominent opportunities and challenges that appear to lie ahead for authentic leadership theory.

MOTIVATIONS AND ORIGINS OF AUTHENTIC LEADERSHIP THEORY

Luthans and Avolio's (2003) chapter on authentic leadership development is generally credited with being the starting point of the research programme on authentic leadership (e.g. Avolio, Walumbwa, & Weber, 2009; Gardner, Avolio, & Walumbwa, 2005; Walumbwa, Avolio, Gardner, Wernsing, & Peterson, 2008). This programme is usually described as the union of Avolio's interest in full-range leadership (e.g. Avolio, 1999) with Luthans' work on positive organizational behaviour (Luthans, 2002). Nonetheless, these and other authors recognize that there had been some prior work concerning authenticity and leadership (Avolio, Gardner, & Walumbwa, 2005), particularly in the field of education (e.g. Henderson & Hoy, 1983; Hoy & Henderson, 1983), as well as Luthans' consideration of positive leadership (Luthans, Luthans, Hodgetts, & Luthans, 2001). Related issues had also figured in studies that had not explicitly focused on authenticity. For example, leaders who engaged in self-monitoring, which is a behavioural tendency to intentionally adjust one's behaviour to fit the current context (Snyder, 1974), had been shown to be perceived as less sincere and more manipulative, and to therefore receive poorer group performance from followers (Sosik, Avolio, & Jung, 2002).

Nonetheless, Luthans and Avolio (2003) noted that most of the previous work had examined the negative consequences of a lack of authenticity, rather trying to understand authenticity per se. Their chapter was a call to focus primarily on authentic leadership itself. In this sense, authentic leadership theory can be seen as a part of the growing popularity of positive perspectives throughout the social sciences, including psychology (Seligman & Csikszentmihalyi, 2000), organizational studies (Cameron, Dutton, & Quinn, 2003) and organization behaviour (Luthans, 2002). Consistent with this, authentic leadership scholars have explicitly recognized their intellectual debt to the humanistic values of psychologists such as Rogers (1963) and Maslow (1968) as important influences upon the development of this new positive perspective on leadership (Avolio & Gardner, 2005).

However, the most important influence on the development of authentic leadership theory most likely emerged from the post-charismatic critiques of transformational leadership (Michie & Gooty, 2005). As described by Díaz-Sáenz (Chapter 22, this volume), the construct of transformational leadership was developed in the 1970s as a way to understand highly influential political leaders (Burns, 1978), and was subsequently applied to business and organizational contexts throughout the 1980s (e.g. Bass, 1985). Transformational leadership involves a number of specific behaviours and effects, but these are generally united by the leader's ability to craft and convey a compelling vision that leads followers to adopt the leader's mission as their own (Bass & Avolio, 1997). For example, transformational leaders were described as exhibiting 'idealized influence,' in that followers came to judge them as embodying desirable beliefs and therefore being worthy of emulation (Jung & Avolio, 2000).

Several commentators noted potential danger in the influence and adulation generated by transformational leaders (e.g. Conger & Kanungo, 1998). For example, it was suggested that the extreme personal identification of followers with a transformational leader could create follower dependence on the leader (see Trevino & Brown, 2007), and this fear was supported by empirical evidence (e.g. Kark, Shamir, & Chen, 2003). Moreover, the ethical basis for transformation was also questioned, since the leader's intentional alteration of followers' values seemed to risk – perhaps even require – manipulation (Beyer, 1999; Price, 2003). In fact, Bass described both Ghandi and Hitler as transformational leaders (Bass, 1985). Empirical evidence also showed that transformational leadership did not necessarily have to be ethical (Howell & Avolio, 1992).

The response to these concerns by the leading theorists of transformational leadership was to draw a distinction between 'authentic' transformational leaders and 'pseudo' transformational leaders (Bass & Steidlmeier, 1999). They noted that 'to be truly transformational, leadership must be grounded in moral foundations' (1999, p. 181). In this reformulation, leaders who are not morally and ethically sound may exhibit influence and charisma, but they are only pseudo-transformational. Authentically transformational leaders are distinguished by their personal moral character, the admirable values that comprise their agenda, and the ethical means they use when interacting with others. Consistent with this, as discussed below, authentic leadership theory stressed the moral component of leadership from the outset.

DEFINING AUTHENTIC LEADERSHIP

Authentic leadership theory makes distinctions between three types or levels of authenticity: an individual's personal authenticity; a leader's authenticity as a leader; and authentic leadership as a phenomenon in itself (Shamir & Eilam, 2005; Yammarino, Dionne, Schriesheim, & Dansereau, 2008). These three types of authenticity are argued to be hierarchically inclusive, such that one cannot be an authentic leader without being individually authentic and authentic leadership is not possible without the intervention of an authentic leader (Gardner, Avolio, Luthans, May, & Walumbwa, 2005).

In this context, 'authenticity' is defined based on psychological research, particularly that of Harter (2002) and Kernis (2003). Harter (2002) emphasied the origins of the term in ancient Greek philosophy and described two components of authenticity: knowing one's true self and acting in accord with that true self. In consequence, 'authenticity is thus an entirely subjective, reflexive process that, by definition, is experienced only by the individual him- or herself' (Erickson, 1994, p. 35). If an individual believes she is being authentic, then by definition, she is (Avolio & Gardner, 2005; Harter, 2002). However, this phenomenological emphasis contrasts with some other approaches, which require empirical validation (e.g. Terry, 1993). In this vein, Kernis (2003) defined authenticity as consisting of four components: full awareness and acceptance of self; unbiased processing of self-relevant information; action consistent with true self; and a relational orientation that values openness and truth in close personal relationships.

Combining these two views, authentic leadership scholars define authenticity as having clear and certain knowledge about oneself in all regards (e.g., beliefs, preferences, strengths, weaknesses) and behaving consistently with that self-knowledge (Gardner, Avolio, Luthans, et al., 2005; Ilies, Morgeson, & Nahrgang, 2005).

Building on this definition, and particularly the four components in Kernis (2003), 'authentic leaders' are defined as leaders who exhibit four behavioural tendencies: self-awareness, which is accurate knowledge of one's strengths, weaknesses, and idiosyncratic qualities; relational transparency, which involves genuine representation of the self to others; balanced processing, which is the collection and use of relevant, objective information, particularly that which challenges one's prior beliefs; and an internalized moral perspective, which refers to self-regulation and self-determination, rather than acting in accordance with situational demands (Gardner, Avolio, Luthans, et al., 2005; Walumbwa et al., 2008). It should be noted that the definition explicitly requires all four components be true of both the leader's thoughts and actions (Gardner, Avolio, Luthans, et al., 2005; Ilies et al., 2005). In contrast, some observers have noted that individuals may be authentically self-aware yet choose to behave in a self-inconsistent or inauthentic fashion (Harter, 2002; Kernis, 2003). Others have argued against the inclusion of a moral component, questioning whether there is any inherent difference between an authentic person who leads and an authentic leader (Shamir & Eilam, 2005; Sparrowe, 2005). Nonetheless, most authentic leadership theory has been based on the tenet that anyone lacking even one of the four behaviours cannot be an authentic leader, suggesting that some consensus has developed in support of the four-part definition (Avolio et al., 2009; Walumbwa et al., 2008).

Given the four behaviours required of authentic leaders, 'authentic leadership' is then defined in terms of the consequences of those behaviours:

A pattern of leader behavior that draws upon and promotes both positive psychological capacities and a positive ethical climate, to foster greater self-awareness, an internalized moral perspective, balanced processing of information, and relational transparency on the part of leaders working with followers, fostering positive self-development (Walumbwa et al., 2008, p. 94).

We should note that in the opening of this chapter, we referred to authentic leadership theory as a new focus for research; however, many of the central participants might object to our characterization. When definitions of authentic leadership are stated, they are typically accompanied by claims that this is not a new type of leadership or a new label for an existing phenomenon, but rather a concern with what is fundamental in leadership (e.g. Avolio & Gardner, 2005; Avolio et al., 2009; Chan, Hannah, & Gardner, 2005; May, Chan, Hodges, & Avolio, 2003). It has been claimed that authentic leadership, as here defined, is the 'root construct of all positive, effective forms of leadership' (Avolio et al., 2005, p. xxii).

THEORETICAL CLAIMS

In the seven years since its formal introduction, authentic leadership has been the focus of significant theoretical attention. A number of authors have discussed its antecedents and consequences, at all levels and in all areas of organizational life. It is beyond the scope of this chapter to restate the full arguments developing these claims. Instead, we provide a brief summary of the claims that have been made, so that interested readers may pursue the original source material for those matters with which they are most concerned.

Antecedents of authentic leadership

Numerous potential sources of authentic leadership have been proposed, which can be broadly grouped into environmental factors and individual differences. The environmental antecedents include facilitative support, particularly through established norms of authenticity (Chan et al., 2005) and a positive organizational context (Avolio, Gardner, Walumbwa, Luthans, & May, 2004; Gardner, Avolio, Luthans, et al., 2005; Luthans & Avolio, 2003). Such facilitative factors are predicted to assist the ongoing development of authentic leadership. Other, more active, environmental factors have also been proposed, including role models (Gardner, Avolio, Luthans, et al., 2005) and direct intervention through training (Avolio & Luthans, 2006; Luthans & Avolio, 2003). These more active environmental considerations are predicted to initiate or accelerate the development of authentic leadership.

Among the individual differences that have been singled out in creating authentic leadership, personal history is particularly important (Gardner, Avolio, Luthans, et al., 2005; Luthans & Avolio, 2003). Authentic leaders' interpretations of the events in their past are predicted to create a personal meaning system (Goldman & Kernis, 2002) based on specific leadership moments or 'triggers' that shape their approach to leadership (Avolio &

Luthans, 2006; George & Sims, 2007). In addition to these developmental experiences, authentic leadership is said to be enhanced by a highly developed personal morality (Hannah, Lester, & Vogelgesang, 2005), higher levels of psychological capital (Avolio & Luthans, 2006; Luthans & Avolio, 2003), and a tendency towards concern for others in the form of self-transcendent values and other-directed emotions (Hannah, et al., 2005; Michie & Gooty, 2005). Ilies and colleagues (2005) also offered a series of propositions about distinct antecedents for each of the four behavioural components of authentic leadership; these included positive self-concept, emotional intelligence, integrity, an incremental theory of ability, and low self-monitoring.

Consequences of authentic leadership

The hypothesized effects of authentic leadership are extensive and varied, offering potential benefit to leaders, their organizations as wholes, and to individual followers. For themselves, authentic leaders are predicted to experience more positive emotions (Chan et al., 2005; Gardner, Avolio, Luthans, et al., 2005), improved well-being (Chan et al., 2005; Gardner, Avolio, Luthans, et al., 2005; Ilies et al., 2005), and greater leadership effectiveness (Eigel & Kuhnert, 2005). For groups and organizations, the most discussed benefit is fostering a more positive culture or climate (Gardner, Avolio, Luthans, et al., 2005; Mazutis & Slawinski, 2008; Shirey, 2006a; Woolley, Caza, Levy, & Jackson, 2007), although authentic leadership has also been linked to organizational learning (Mazutis & Slawinski, 2008) and entrepreneurial success (Jensen & Luthans, 2006b; Shirey, 2006b).

However, the most dramatic benefits proposed to arise from authentic leadership are those for individual followers; gains in some of the most important outcomes of practical and theoretical concern have been proposed to result from authentic leadership. Behaviourally, followers of authentic leaders are predicted to exert greater effort, engage in more organizational citizenship behaviour, and enjoy better work performance (Avolio et al., 2004; Chan et al., 2005; Gardner, Avolio, Luthans, et al., 2005; Walumbwa et al., 2008), as well as having higher levels of creativity (Ilies et al., 2005). Followers are also predicted to experience a variety of improved attitudes and mindsets. The most frequently mentioned change is an increased trust in leadership (Avolio et al., 2004; Chan et al., 2005; Dasborough & Ashkanasy, 2005; Gardner, Avolio, Luthans, et al., 2005; Hannah et al., 2005), but many other benefits have

been proposed, including positive emotions (Avolio et al., 2004; Chan et al., 2005; Dasborough & Ashkanasy, 2005; Jensen & Luthans, 2006a), task engagement (Avolio et al., 2004; Gardner, Avolio, Luthans, et al., 2005), higher motivation (Ilies et al., 2005), greater commitment (Avolio, et al., 2004; Jensen & Luthans, 2006a; Walumbwa et al., 2008), and more satisfaction (Avolio et al., 2004; Ilies et al., 2005; Jensen & Luthans, 2006a; Walumbwa et al., 2008). In addition, since follower development is fundamental to authentic leadership, predictions have been made about the developmental benefits experienced by followers, including greater empowerment (Avolio et al., 2004; Ilies et al., 2005), moral development (Hannah et al., 2005; Ilies et al., 2005), improved well-being (Gardner, Avolio, Luthans, et al., 2005; Ilies et al., 2005), and increases in psychological capital (Avolio et al., 2004; Avolio & Luthans, 2006; Gardner & Schermerhorn, 2004; Ilies et al., 2005; Woolley et al., 2007).

Mechanisms of authentic leadership

To explain the many benefits expected to arise from authentic leadership, authors have suggested a number of mechanisms. These are generally of two sorts. The first is attitudinal change, such that some of the beneficial attitude changes are used to explain behavioural and developmental changes (e.g. authentic leadership increases task engagement, which contributes to improved performance; Gardner, Avolio, Luthans, et al., 2005). The other mechanisms involve changes in the relationships that followers have with their leaders and their organizations. These include greater identification with the leader and the organization (Avolio et al., 2004; Ilies et al., 2005), improved communication between parties (Mazutis & Slawinski, 2008), imitation of positive role models (Gardner, Avolio, Luthans, et al., 2005; Ilies et al., 2005), and greater social exchange (Chan et al., 2005; Ilies et al., 2005), all of which have been suggested as ways to explain the dramatic benefits promised to arise from authentic leadership.

In reviewing the lists of antecedents, consequences, and mechanisms, one may be struck by the overlap in some areas. For example, psychological capital has been proposed as both an antecedent and a consequence of authentic leadership. Similarly, a more positive organizational climate is predicted to contribute to authentic leadership, be a benefit resulting from authentic leadership, and be a constituent part of the authentic leadership phenomenon itself. The complexities and potential confusions of such multifunctional relationships have been recognized by authentic leadership scholars, and comprise an area that has been suggested as needing greater attention (e.g. Gardner, Avolio, Luthans, et al., 2005; Luthans & Avolio, 2009). This and other future directions for the development of authentic leadership are discussed below, after a review of the empirical evidence concerning the predictions described here.

EMPIRICAL FINDINGS

Despite the many important theoretical predictions associated with authentic leadership, and the topic's apparently considerable popularity among academics and practitioners, surprisingly little empirical research has been conducted to date. As a part of their theory-building efforts, Yammarino and colleagues (2008) searched and found only four research reports. Our more recent search

found little more. In February 2009, we conducted a keyword search of the ABI-Inform and EBSCO databases, using 'lead*' and 'authen*' as word stems. We then conducted ISI forward citation searches on the authentic leadership pieces we found, as well as searching the bibliographies of all identified pieces. We found only seven empirical reports: the three book chapters and one journal article previously identified by Yammarino and colleagues (2008), as well as two other journal pieces and one refereed conference paper. Each of these is summarized in Table 26.1.

Looking across these studies reveals at least two important patterns. The first is their relative success in finding support for theoretical predictions. Allowing for the limitations imposed by their designs, the studies suggest that leader authenticity is in fact a relevant and potentially important issue for followers. Organization members care about how authentic their leaders

Table 26.1   Summary of empirical research in authentic leadership

Source	Design	Participants	Authentic leadership operationalization	Key findings
Dasborough & Ashkanasy (2005) Study 1	Three focus groups	Sample of 24 employees from three randomly selected Australian organizations	None	Followers describing negative emotional interactions with supervisors attributed their negative emotion to: 1. Supervisor's inconsistency with previous behaviour 2. Supervisor's failure to keep them informed 3. Supervisor's lack of technical skill 4. Supervisor's lack of concern for anything but income/performance
Dasborough & Ashkanasy (2005) Study 2	Experimental: video of charismatic leader requesting effort on behalf of organization, for collective goals. Follow-up email from leader uses either 'we' phrasing (authentic condition) or 'I' phrasing (inauthentic condition)	One hundred and thirty-seven undergraduate students in Australia	Manipulated trough (in)consistency between 'we' or 'I' phrasing in video and email	Leader inconsistency led to follower attributions of manipulation (vs sincerity), causing negative emotion and reducing positive emotion. Follower positive emotion predicted trust in leader and ratings of transformational leadership. Negative emotion, trust, and transformational leadership influenced follower intention to comply with request

Table 26.1 (Contd.)

Source	Design	Participants	Authentic leadership operationalization	Key findings
Eigel & Kuhnert (2005)	Semi-structured clinical interviews	Twenty-one board-elected executives of large public corporations in diverse industries	None. Describe five 'Leadership Development Levels' (LDL) and link the highest, level 5, to authentic leadership	LDL 5 is associated with leadership effectiveness in all environments, assessed by subject matter experts
Pittinsky & Tyson (2005)	Six structured focus group discussions	Snowball sample of 28 African Americans born between 1965 and 1980, stratified for low, middle, and high SES	Structured question format about 'what makes an African American leader authentic' (p. 262)	Found seven 'authenticity makers': 1. Experience of racism – recognize its importance 2. Policy positions – equality, affirmative action, community development, etc. 3. Party affiliation – liberal 4. Speech patterns and mannerisms 5. Experience of struggle – easy life is 'not real' 6. Black Church participation 7. Connection to other African Americans – embrace historical events, reach out socially, etc.
Jensen & Luthans (2006a)	Survey	Convenience sample of 179 employees in 62 Midwestern firms that had been in operation for less than 10 years	'Authentic *entrepreneurial* leadership' as summed scale composed of selected items from MLQ (Bass & Avolio, 1997), future orientation (Knight, 1997), and ethical climate (Victor & Cullen, 1988)	Followers who perceived their managers as more authentic reported greater job satisfaction, organizational commitment, and work happiness
Jensen & Luthans (2006b)	Survey	Convenience sample of 76 owner-founders of small Midwestern businesses that had been in operation for less than 10 years	Authentic entrepreneurial leadership, as in Jensen & Luthans (2006a)	Managers' self-reported psychological capital predicted self-reported levels of authentic entrepreneurial leadership

(continued)

Table 26.1 (Contd.)

Source	Design	Participants	Authentic leadership operationalization	Key findings
Woolley & colleagues (2007)	Survey	Stratified random sample of 863 working adults in New Zealand	Authentic Leadership Questionnaire (ALQ) using a second-order construct composed of self-awareness, relational transparency, internal moral perspective, and balanced processing (see Walumbwa et al., 2008)	Followers who perceived their supervisors as more authentic reported greater psychological capital. This relationships was predominantly mediated by followers' assessment of their supervisor's positive impact on the work environment
Walumbwa & colleagues (2008) Study 1	Survey	Two hundred and twenty-four full-time employees of US manufacturer; 212 full-time employees of state-owned firm in Beijing	ALQ (Walumbwa et al., 2008)	Second-order factor structure of ALQ supported. American and Chinese samples showed measurement equivalence
Walumbwa & colleagues (2008) Study 2	In-class survey	One hundred and seventy-eight American adult students and 236 evening students working full time in the USA	ALQ (Walumbwa et al., 2008)	Authentic leadership measured by ALQ shown to be a related to, but distinct from, ethical leadership and transformational leadership. Followers who perceived their supervisors as more authentic reported greater OCB, organizational commitment, and satisfaction with supervisor
Walumbwa & colleagues (2008) Study 3	Two-stage survey (six weeks apart)	Four hundred and seventy-eight employees of 11 US MNCs in Kenya, and their supervisors ($N = 104$)	ALQ (Walumbwa et al., 2008)	Followers who perceived their supervisors as more authentic reported greater job satisfaction and had higher supervisor-rated job performance

are, and they appear to respond favourably to those they perceive as authentic. Follower attributions of leader authenticity have been linked to positive emotion (Dasborough & Ashkanasy, 2005; Jensen & Luthans, 2006a), organizational commitment (Jensen & Luthans, 2006a; Walumbwa et al., 2008), psychological capital (Woolley et al., 2007), and performance (Eigel & Kuhnert, 2005; Walumbwa et al., 2008).

The second pattern, which has already been noted earlier by others (Yammarino et al., 2008), is that the empirical data are almost entirely at the individual level. To the extent that conclusions from focus groups can be considered collective or aggregate phenomena, there may be some preliminary evidence at a collective level (Dasborough & Ashkanasy, 2005; Pittinsky & Tyson, 2005), but this is tenuous. Similarly, while one study examined organizational climate as a potential mechanism for authentic leadership's effect on followers (Woolley et al., 2007), the measurement remained at the individual level. Despite the theoretical emphasis upon the collective and relational effects associated with authentic leadership, nothing beyond individual perception and behaviour has yet been tested.

In summary, the empirical evidence concerning authentic leadership is limited. There are only seven published research reports, and only four of these were subject to peer review. Authentic leadership has only been measured at the individual level, and has almost exclusively concerned followers' attributions of leader authenticity. As such, we may tentatively conclude that the construct of authenticity is meaningful to followers, and that individual followers' attributions of leader authenticity are associated with beneficial attitudes and behaviours. However, the strongest conclusion to be drawn is that much more empirical research is needed.

OPPORTUNITIES, QUESTIONS, AND CONCERNS

Definition of authenticity

The two foundational sources on which this literature bases its definition of authenticity (i.e., Harter, 2002; Kernis, 2003) may not be compatible concerning the phenomenological status of authenticity, which in turn creates some conflict in the definition of authentic leadership. More importantly, current operationalizations are inconsistent with the definition of authenticity as a personal experience. With only one exception (Jensen & Luthans, 2006b), the empirical measurement of authentic leadership involves observer attributions of authenticity, taking no account of the leader's experience. Whereas follower responses to a leader's authenticity are clearly determined by their attributions of that leader's authenticity, these attributions are not necessarily accurate (e.g. Douglas, Ferris, & Perrewe, 2005; Ferris et al., 2007). In recognition of this, the awkward distinction between 'genuine' authentic leaders and 'pseudo' authentic leaders has already been raised (Chan et al., 2005). Moreover, even when third-party judgements are accurate, they still do not

reflect the phenomenological nature of a leader's authenticity (Harter, 2002; Harter, Waters, Whitesell, & Kastelic, 1998). This conflict can be seen in current writing, where authenticity is defined as purely phenomenological (Avolio & Gardner, 2005; Avolio et al., 2004; Chan et al., 2005; Erickson, 1994), but also as depending on follower responses: 'followers authenticate the leader' (Gardner, Avolio, Luthans, et al., 2005, p. 348; see also Goffee & Jones, 2005).

Ontological status of authenticity

Even more fundamental than clearly defining a construct is the need to answer the question of the extent to which authenticity is even possible. The assumption underlying authentic leadership theory derives from the modernist psychological belief that each individual has a 'true' self, one that is independent of context and behavioural presentations; in other words, there is something constant to be authentic about (Goffman, 1959; James, 1890). Doubts have been raised about the appropriateness of this belief (Erickson, 1994). Conceptually, it has been argued that one's self is an ongoing project, rather than an essential constant (Ricoeur, 1992; Sparrowe, 2005), and this may be particularly relevant now, given that modern society and technology have made life so fluid and complex as to make a single constant self either impossible or impractical (Gergen, 1991). Moreover, others have argued that even if there is a relatively 'true' self, it is necessarily defined in relation to others, and thus cannot be constant in the sense required for authenticity (Peterson, 2005; Sandelands, 1998). In either case, authenticity, as the sort of behavioural goal implied by authentic leadership theory, becomes a paradox: the simple act of intentionally 'being authentic' undercuts any possibility of achieving it (Guthey & Jackson, 2005; Hochschild, 1983).

Clarity of nomological status and level of analysis

In part owing to potential confusion in the definition of authentic leadership, it is sometimes unclear where authentic leadership begins and ends. For example, as noted above, authors variously treat a positive organizational climate as a source of authentic leadership, a part of authentic leadership, and a consequence of authentic leadership. Such issues need to be clarified, not only for purposes of defining the nature of the construct but also its appropriate level of analysis. For example, Kernis' (2003) definition of authenticity is restricted to the individual level by including only a personal orientation towards truthful relationships; in contrast, the definition of authentic leadership includes reference to the actual leader–follower relationship, which is necessarily not at the individual level of analysis. Although different elements of the authentic leadership phenomenon may operate at different levels, these need to be made distinct (see Yammarino et al., 2008 for a proposal to address this issue).

Contextualizing authentic leadership

Although the authentic leadership questionnaire has been shown to function well and have predicted relationships with outcomes in four different cultures and a variety of settings (Walumbwa et al., 2008; Woolley et al., 2007), there is also evidence that the meaning and effect of authentic leadership can vary by context (Chan, 2005). Pittinsky and Tyson (2005) showed that what counts as authentic depends on the particular leader and follower in question, and others show that the effects of authenticity may vary by gender and/or personal values (Harter et al., 1998; Woolley et al., 2007). It has also been suggested that other differences may be important, including ethnicity, class, and education (Eagly, 2005). Similarly, interpersonal congruence and cultural values may also be moderators of the effect of authentic leadership (Chan, 2005; Chan et al., 2005; Ilies et al., 2005; Woolley & Jackson, 2010).

Authentic leadership versus authentic leadership development

The motivation to develop practical interventions has been an explicit part of authentic leadership theory from the beginning, and has arguably been the one thing that all writers in this area share (Cooper, Scandura, & Schriesheim, 2005; Eagly, 2005; Eigel & Kuhnert, 2005; Ilies et al., 2005; Luthans & Avolio, 2003; Shamir & Eilam, 2005; Sparrowe, 2005). However, there appears to be an increasing emphasis on the issues of development and intervention. The initial work tended to emphasize the nature and effect of authentic leadership, and this early emphasis was arguably crystallized by the scale development paper (Walumbwa et al., 2008), which specifically defined and measured how much authentic

leadership a given leader exhibited. In contrast to this early emphasis on understanding authentic leaders, more recent discussions suggest a subtle shift towards emphasizing development over authenticity per se (e.g., Avolio, 2007, p. 29ff; see also Faber, Johanson, Thomas, & Vogelzang, 2007). That is, the discussion of authentic leadership development now seems more concerned with whether a given leadership intervention authentically (i.e. genuinely) develops leadership ability (e.g. Avolio, Walumbwa, & Weber, 2009, p. 423). Interestingly, it seems that the focus may be moving from developing *authentic leadership* to *authentically developing* leadership (Luthans & Avolio, 2009, pp. 303–304). Given some reports that current leadership interventions offer little benefit (Reichard & Avolio, 2005), this may be an appropriate move, and it is not inconsistent with the previous work; however, it is nonetheless an important change in focus. Developing authentic leadership is much more specific than authentically developing effective leadership of any sort. Whereas either focus, or both, may be fruitfully pursued in the future, it will be important for authors to clearly specify which matter they are concerned with to avoid the sort of fundamental confusion that had plagued other research programmes: for example, organizational citizenship behaviour (OCB) and the nature of 'extra-role' Organ (1997).

Role of emotion

Emotions have had a central role in the development of authentic leadership theory. They figure prominently as antecedents and consequences of authenticity (Dasborough & Ashkanasy, 2005; Gardner, Avolio, Luthans et al., 2005; Hannah et al., 2005; Ilies et al., 2005; Michie & Gooty, 2005). In addition, the most common definition given for authenticity is taken from Harter (2002) and refers to being true to one's inner thoughts and feelings. However, the role of feelings in authenticity has received little attention (see Zhang, Wang, & Caza, 2008). Far more attention has been paid to authenticity with regard to values and morality than to emotion. This is surprising, given the prevalence of emotion management in most organizational contexts (Glaso & Einarsen, 2008; Goffman, 1973), and the strong intuitive link that practitioners make between authenticity and emotion (Turner & Mavin, 2008). For an extended discussion of the link between leadership and emotion, see Ashkanasy and Humphrey (Chapter 27, this volume).

Embodied authentic leadership

Notions of embodiment and how the body functions within the field of organizational studies have received increasing attention, but are still relatively rare in leadership studies (see Sinclair, Chapter 37, this volume). Nonetheless, the issue of embodiment is a potentially important one for authentic leadership theory. For example, Ladkin and Taylor (2010) note that the widely publicized incident involving Hillary Clinton breaking down in tears during the Democratic primary election shows that authenticity has an embodied, aesthetic dimension (see also Hansen & Bathurst, Chapter 19, this volume). Ladkin and Taylor (2010) argue that the way in which the leader's 'self' is embodied is a critical determinant of the experience of authentic leadership, noting that,

> Although it may be obvious, for the purposes of our argument, it is important to point out that it is the leaders' body, and the way in which he or she uses it to express their 'true self', which is the seemingly invisible mechanism through which authenticity is conveyed. (Ladkin & Taylor, 2010, p. 65)

They highlight how the system of method acting developed by Constantin Stanislavski uses the somatic sense of self (i.e. the body) to contribute to the feelings of authenticity, and how through engaging with somatic clues, leadership can be performed in a way which is experienced as authentic, both to the leaders and their followers. They close by inviting researchers to empirically investigate how leaders who are widely considered to be 'authentic' actually experience themselves at a somatic level of awareness. In concert with this, there is a need to better understand how followers make aesthetically based assessments of their experiences with leaders (e.g., Rule and Ambady, 2008, 2009; Nana, Burch, & Jackson, 2010).

Disadvantages of authenticity

One element that all of the authentic leadership theory reviewed here shares is the implicit belief that authenticity is wholly desirable, that it produces only positive outcomes. However, it seems unlikely that authenticity is in all ways and at all time unremittingly beneficial. For example, Harter (2002) shows that inauthenticity may be important for some kinds of positive change (see also Ibarra, 1999; Kernis, 2003). It also may be possible to be too authentic, such that authenticity not only limits possibilities but also actually produces negative results (Harter, 2002; Woolley et al., 2007).

Although the potential drawbacks of authenticity have yet to be examined, it seems unlikely that one could understand the phenomenon of authentic leadership without addressing them. It is to this task that we turn to in the concluding section of this chapter.

CONCLUSIONS

In the past decade, authentic leadership has seized the popular imagination in a way that few leadership ideas have. This is evident in the business media and through our interactions with managers in the MBA and executive development classes that we teach. Many people seem taken with the idea of authenticity and are keen to learn more about it. In part, we suspect that authenticity's appeal derives from its face validity and commonsense value. After all, who would advocate for inauthentic leaders? However, we believe that the source of the appeal goes deeper still. Authentic leadership resonates with widespread disillusionment about the performance of business, political, and religious leaders. Authentic leadership seems to provide a ready answer to concerns about the intentions and morality of these leaders. This combines with managers' fears and concerns about their own leadership ability to make the notion of authenticity particularly appealing. As the well-worn cliché runs, authentic leadership is an idea whose 'time has come.' It is a powerful response to the entrenched scepticism and suspicion towards established leaders and it accords with a general desire for selfless, enlightened leadership.

Given this general appeal, it is not surprising that leadership scholars have been attracted to the concept of authenticity. As we have shown in this review, in a relatively short period of time significant strides have been made in defining the concept and its antecedents, mechanisms, and consequences. Unfortunately, however, most of this work has been confined to the theoretical realm; there are very few empirical studies. This imbalance is unhealthy and will need to be rectified if the concept is to have a sustainable future within the larger field of leadership studies. In terms of direction, we used the previous section to highlight the issues that seem most pressing and most promising. We also believe that more variety in methods and data are essential, including mixed sources of data and multiple levels of analysis.

These empirical developments are important to sustain the momentum of authentic leadership and to respond to its critics. In fact, somewhat ironically, the most encouraging sign for the future of authentic leadership theory may be in the intensity of the critical response it has provoked (e.g. Caza & Carroll, in press; Collinson, Chapter 13, this volume). The idea of authenticity clearly has great power to provoke and attract attention. We do not believe that the critics' concerns are insurmountable, but it is important to the further development of authentic leadership theory that they be addressed. As described in this chapter, this will likely require new directions, additional techniques, and a broader constituency than has previously been engaged in the theory's development.

REFERENCES

American Association of Critical Care Nurses (2005). *AACN standards for establishing and sustaining healthy work environments*. Aliso Viejo, CA: American Association of Critical Care Nurses.

Avolio, B. J. (1999). *Full leadership development: building vital forces in organizations*. Newbury Park, CA: Sage.

Avolio, B. J. (2007). Promoting more integrative strategies for leadership theory-building. *American Psychologist, 62*(1), 25–33.

Avolio, B. J. & Gardner, W. L. (2005). Authentic leadership development: getting to the root of positive forms of leadership. *The Leadership Quarterly, 16*(3), 315–338.

Avolio, B. J., Gardner, W. L., & Walumbwa, F. O. (2005). Preface. In W. L. Gardner, B. J. Avolio, & F. O. Walumbwa (eds), *Authentic leadership theory and practice: origins, effects, and development*, Vol. 3. New York: Elsevier, pp. xxi–xxix.

Avolio, B. J., Gardner, W. L., Walumbwa, F. O., Luthans, F., & May, D. R. (2004). Unlocking the mask: a look at the process by which authentic leaders impact follower attitudes and behaviors. *The Leadership Quarterly, 15*(6), 801–823.

Avolio, B. J. & Luthans, F. (2006). *The high impact leader: moments matter in accelerating authentic leadership development*. New York: McGraw-Hill.

Avolio, B. J., Walumbwa, F. O., & Weber, T. J. (2009). Leadership: current theories, research, and future directions. *Annual Review of Psychology, 60*, 421–449.

Bass, B. M. (1985). *Leadership and performance beyond expectations*. New York: Free Press.

Bass, B. M. & Avolio, B. J. (1997). *Full-range of leadership development: manual for the Multifactor Leadership Questionnaire*. Palo Alto, CA: Mind Garden.

Bass, B. M. & Steidlmeier, P. (1999). Ethics, character, and authentic transformational leadership behavior. *The Leadership Quarterly, 10*(2), 181–217.

Beyer, J. M. (1999). Taming and promoting charisma to change organizations. *The Leadership Quarterly, 10*, 307–331.

Burns, J. M. (1978). *Leadership*. New York: Harper & Row.

Cameron, K. S., Dutton, J. E., & Quinn, R. E. (2003). *Positive organizational scholarship: foundations of a new discipline*. San Francisco, CA: Berrett-Koehler Publishers.

Caza, A. & Carroll, B. (In press). Critical theory and POS. In K. S. Cameron & G. M. Spreitzer (eds), *Handbook of positive organizational scholarship*. Oxford: Oxford University Press.

Chan, A. (2005). Authentic leadership measurement and development: challenges and suggestions. In W. L. Gardner, B. J. Avolio, & F. O. Walumbwa (eds), *Authentic leadership theory and practice: origins, effects, and development*, Vol. 3. New York: Elsevier, pp. 227–250.

Chan, A., Hannah, S. T., & Gardner, W. L. (2005). Veritable authentic leadership: emergence, functioning, and impacts. In W. L. Gardner, B. J. Avolio, & F. O. Walumbwa (eds), *Authentic leadership theory and practice: origins, effects, and development*, Vol. 3. New York: Elsevier, pp. 3–41.

Conger, J. A. & Kanungo, R. N. (1998). *Charismatic leadership in organizations*. Thousand Oaks, CA: Sage.

Cooper, C. D., Scandura, T. A., & Schriesheim, C. A. (2005). Looking forward but learning from our past: potential challenges to developing authentic leadership theory and authentic leaders. *The Leadership Quarterly, 16*(3), 475–493.

Dasborough, M. T. & Ashkanasy, N. M. (2005). Follower emotional reactions to authentic and inauthentic leadership influence. In W. L. Gardner, B. J. Avolio, & F. O. Walumbwa (eds), *Authentic leadership theory and practice: origins, effects, and development*, Vol. 3. New York: Elsevier, pp. 281–300.

Douglas, C., Ferris, G. R., & Perrewe, P. L. (2005). Leader political skill and authentic leadership. In W. L. Gardner, B. J. Avolio, & F. O. Walumbwa (eds), *Authentic leadership theory and practice: origins, effects, and development*, Vol. 3. New York: Elsevier, pp. 139–154.

Eagly, A. H. (2005). Achieving relational authenticity in leadership: Does gender matter? *The Leadership Quarterly, 16*(3), 459–474.

Eigel, K. M. & Kuhnert, K. W. (2005). Authentic development: leadership development level and executive effectiveness. In W. L. Gardner, B. J. Avolio, & F. O. Walumbwa (eds), *Authentic leadership theory and practice: origins, effects, and development*, Vol. 3. New York: Elsevier, pp. 357–385.

Erickson, R. J. (1994). Our society, our selves: becoming authentic in an inauthentic world. *Advanced Development Journal, 6*(1), 27–39.

Faber, M., Johanson, R., Thomas, A., & Vogelzang, M. (2007). Charge it up: developing authentic leaders. *Critical Care Nurse, 27*(2), 98–98.

Ferris, G. R., Treadway, D. C., Perrewe, P. L., Brouer, R. L., Douglas, C., & Lux, S. (2007). Political skill in organizations. *Journal of Management, 33*(3), 290–320.

Gardner, W. L., Avolio, B. J., Luthans, F., May, D. R., & Walumbwa, F. (2005). 'Can you see the real me?' A self-based model of authentic leader and follower development. *The Leadership Quarterly, 16*(3), 343–372.

Gardner, W. L., Avolio, B. J., & Walumbwa, F. O. (2005). *Authentic leadership theory and practice: origins, effects, and development*. New York: Elsevier.

Gardner, W. L. & Schermerhorn, J. R. (2004). Unleashing individual potential: performance gains through positive organizational behavior and authentic leadership. *Organizational Dynamics, 33*(3), 270–281.

Gayvert, D. R. (1999). Leadership and doctrinal reform. *Military Review, 79*(3), 18–22.

George, B. (2003). *Authentic leadership: rediscovering the secrets of creating lasting value.* San Francisco, CA: Jossey-Bass.

George, B. & Sims, P. (2007). *True North: discover your authentic leadership.* San Francisco, CA: Jossey-Bass.

George, B., Sims, P., McLean, A. N., & Mayer, D. (2007). Discovering your authentic leadership. *Harvard Business Review, 85*(2), 129–138.

Gergen, K. J. (1991). *The saturated self: dilemmas of identity in contemporary life.* New York: Basic Books.

Glaso, L. & Einarsen, S. (2008). Emotion regulation in leader–follower relationships. *European Journal of Work and Organizational Psychology, 17*(4), 482–500.

Goffee, R. & Jones, G. (2005). Managing authenticity: the paradox of great leadership. *Harvard Business Review,* December, 87–94.

Goffman, E. (1959). *The presentation of self in everyday life.* Garden City, NY: Doubleday Anchor.

Goffman, E. (1973). On face-work. In W. G. Bennis, E. H. Berlow, E. H. Schein, & F. I. Steele (eds), *Interpersonal dynamics: Essays and readings on human interaction,* 3rd edn. Homewood, IL: Dorsey, pp. 175–189.

Goldman, B. M. & Kernis, M. H. (2002). The role of authenticity in healthy psychological functioning and subjective well-being. *Annals of the American Psychotherapy Association, 5*(Nov/Dec), 18–20.

Guthey, E. & Jackson, B. (2005). CEO portraits and the authenticity paradox. *Journal of Management Studies, 42*(5), 1057–1082.

Hannah, S. T., Lester, P. B., & Vogelgesang, G. R. (2005). Moral leadership: explicating the moral component of authentic leadership. In W. L. Gardner, B. J. Avolio, & F. O. Walumbwa (eds), *Authentic leadership theory and practice: origins, effects, and development,* Vol. 3. New York: Elsevier, pp. 43–81.

Harter, S. (2002). Authenticity. In C. R. Snyder & S. J. Lopez (eds), *Handbook of positive psychology,* New York: Oxford University Press, pp. 382–394.

Harter, S., Waters, P. L., Whitesell, N. R., & Kastelic, D. (1998). Level of voice among female and male high school students: relational context, support, and gender orientation. *Developmental Psychology, 34*(5), 892–901.

Henderson, J. E. & Hoy, W. K. (1983). Leader authenticity: the development and test of an operational measure. *Educational and Psychological Research, 3*(2), 63–75.

Hochschild, A. R. (1983). *The managed heart.* Berkeley, CA: University of California Press.

Howell, J. M. & Avolio, B. J. (1992). The ethics of charismatic leadership: submission or liberation? *Academy of Management Executive, 6*(2), 43–54.

Hoy, W. K. & Henderson, J. E. (1983). Principal authenticity, school climate and pupil-control orientation. *Alberta Journal of Educational Research, 29*(2), 123–130.

Ibarra, H. (1999). Provisional selves: experimenting with image and identity in professional adaptation. *Administrative Science Quarterly, 44*(4), 764–791.

Ilies, R., Morgeson, F. P., & Nahrgang, J. D. (2005). Authentic leadership and eudaemonic well-being: understanding leader–follower outcomes. *The Leadership Quarterly, 16*(3), 373–394.

Irvine, D. & Reger, J. (2006). *The authentic leader.* Sanford, FL: DC Press.

James, W. (1890). *The principles of psychology.* New York: Dover.

Jensen, S. M. & Luthans, F. (2006a). Entrepreneurs as authentic leaders: impact on employees' attitudes. *Leadership and Organization Development Journal, 27*(8), 646–666.

Jensen, S. M. & Luthans, F. (2006b). Relationship between entrepreneurs' psychological capital and their authentic leadership. *Journal of Managerial Issues, 18*(2), 254–275.

Jung, D. I. & Avolio, B. J. (2000). Opening the black box: an experimental investigation of the mediating effects of trust and value congruence on transformational and transactional leadership. *Journal of Organizational Behavior, 21*(8), 949–964.

Kark, R., Shamir, B., & Chen, G. (2003). The two faces of transformational leadership: empowerment and dependency. *Journal of Applied Psychology, 88,* 246–255.

Kernis, M. H. (2003). Toward a conceptualization of optimal self-esteem. *Psychological Inquiry, 14*(1), 1–26.

Knight, G. A. (1997). Cross-cultural reliability and validity of a scale to measure firm entrepreneurial orientation. *Journal of Business Venturing, 12,* 213–225.

Kouzes, J. M. & Posner, B. Z. (2008). *The leadership challenge,* San Francisco, CA: Jossey-Bass.

Ladkin, D. & Taylor, S. V. (2010). Enacting the 'true self': towards a theory of embodied authentic leadership, *The Leadership Quarterly,* 21, 64–74.

Luthans, F. (2002). The need for and meaning of positive organizational behavior. *Journal of Organizational Behavior, 23*(6), 695–706.

Luthans, F. & Avolio, B. J. (2003). Authentic leadership development. In K. S. Cameron, J. E. Dutton, & R. E. Quinn (eds), *Positive organizational scholarship: foundations of a new discipline.* San Francisco, CA: Berrett-Koehler Publishers, pp. 241–258.

Luthans, F. & Avolio, B. J. (2009). The 'point' of positive organizational behavior. *Journal of Organizational Behavior, 30*(2), 291–307.

Luthans, F., Luthans, K. W., Hodgetts, R. M., & Luthans, B. C. (2001). Positive approach to leadership (PAL): implications for today's organizations. *Journal of Leadership Studies, 8*(2), 3–20.

Maslow, A. (1968). *Towards a psychology of being.* New York: Van Nostrand.

May, D. R., Chan, A. Y. L., Hodges, T. D., & Avolio, B. J. (2003). Developing the moral component of authentic leadership. *Organizational Dynamics, 32*(3), 247–260.

Mazutis, D. & Slawinski, N. (2008). Leading organizational learning through authentic dialogue. *Management Learning, 39*(4), 437–456.

Michie, S. & Gooty, J. (2005). Values, emotions, and authenticity: Will the real leader please stand up? *The Leadership Quarterly, 16*(3), 441–457.

Nadeau, K. (2002). Peasant resistance and religious protests in early Philippine society: turning friars against the grain. *Journal for the Scientific Study of Religion, 41*(1), 75–86.

Nana, E., Burch, G., & Jackson, B. (2010). Attributing leadership personality and effectiveness from leaders' faces: an exploratory study. *Leadership and Organizational Development Journal, 31*(8), 223–246.

O'Connor, S. J. (2007). Capacity, morality and authenticity in the quest for cancer nursing leadership. *European Journal of Oncology Nursing, 11*(3), 209–211.

Organ, D. W. (1997). Organizational citizenship behavior: it's construct clean-up time. *Human Performance, 10*(2), 85–97.

Pembroke, N. (2002). Rising leaders need authentic leadership. *Clergy Journal, 78*(8), 17–19.

Peterson, R. A. (2005). In search of authenticity. *Journal of Management Studies, 42*(5), 1083–1098.

Pittinsky, T. L. & Tyson, C. J. (2005). Leader authenticity markers: findings from a study of perceptions of African American political leaders. In W. L. Gardner, B. J. Avolio, & F. O. Walumbwa (eds), *Authentic leadership theory and practice: origins, effects, and development*, Vol. 3. New York: Elsevier, pp. 253–279.

Price, T. L. (2003). The ethics of authentic transformational leadership. *The Leadership Quarterly, 14*(1), 67–81.

Reichard, R. J. & Avolio, B. J. (2005). The status of leadership intervention research: a meta-analytic summary. In W. L. Gardner, B. J. Avolio, & F. O. Walumbwa (eds), *Authentic leadership theory and practice: origins, effects, and development.* New York: Elsevier, pp. 203–226.

Ricoeur, P. (1992). *Oneself as another.* Chicago, IL: University of Chicago Press.

Rogers, C. R. (1963). The actualizing tendency in relation to 'motives' and to consciousness. In *Nebraska symposium on motivation*, Vol. 11. Lincoln, NE: University of Nebraska Press, pp. 1–24.

Rule, N. & Ambady, N. (2008). The face of success: inferences from chief executive officers' appearance predict company profits. *Psychological Science, 19*, 109–111.

Rule, N. O. & Ambady, N. (2009). She's got the look: inferences from female chief executive officers' faces predict their success. *Sex Roles, 61*, 644–652.

Sandelands, L. E. (1998). *Feeling and form in social life.* Lanham, MD: Rowan & Littlefield Publishers.

Seligman, M. E. P. & Csikszentmihalyi, M. (2000). Positive psychology: an introduction. *American Psychologist, 55*, 5–14.

Shamir, B. & Eilam, G. (2005). 'What's your story?' A life-stories approach to authentic leadership development. *The Leadership Quarterly, 16*(3), 395–417.

Shelton, K. (2008). Authentic leaders add value. *Leadership Excellence, 25*(2), 22.

Shirey, M. R. (2006a). Authentic leaders creating healthy work environments for nursing practice. *American Journal of Critical Care, 15*(3), 256–267.

Shirey, M. R. (2006b). Building authentic leadership and enhancing entrepreneurial performance. *Clinical Nurse Specialist, 20*(6), 280–282.

Snyder, M. (1974). The self-monitoring of expressive behavior. *Journal of Personality and Social Psychology, 30*, 526–537.

Sosik, J. J., Avolio, B. J., & Jung, D. I. (2002). Beneath the mask: examining the relationship of self-presentation attributes and impression management to charismatic leadership. *The Leadership Quarterly, 13*(3), 217–242.

Sparrowe, R. T. (2005). Authentic leadership and the narrative self. *The Leadership Quarterly, 16*(3), 419–439.

Terry, R. W. (1993). *Authentic leadership: courage in action.* San Francisco, CA: Jossey-Bass.

Trevino, L. K. & Brown, M. E. (2007). Ethical leadership: a developing construct. In D. Nelson & C. L. Cooper (eds), *Positive organizational behavior: accentuating the positive at work.* Thousand Oaks, CA: Sage, pp. 101–116.

Turner, J. & Mavin, S. (2008). What can we learn from senior leader narratives? The strutting and fretting of becoming a leader. *Leadership & Organization Development Journal, 29*(4), 376–391.

Victor, B. & Cullen, J. B. (1988). The organizational bases of ethical work climates. *Administrative Science Quarterly, 33*(1), 101–125.

Walumbwa, F. O., Avolio, B. J., Gardner, W. L., Wernsing, T. S., & Peterson, S. J. (2008). Authentic leadership: development and validation of a theory-based measure. *Journal of Management, 34*(1), 89–126.

Woolley, L., Caza, A., Levy, L., & Jackson, B. (2007). Three steps forward and one step back: exploring relationships between authentic leadership, psychological capital, and leadership impact. *Proceedings of the Australia and New Zealand Academy of Management.*

Woolley, L. & Jackson, B. (2010). The importance of 'mucking-in' for authentic leadership: an exploratory mixed methods study. Paper presented at the Academy of Management Meeting in Montreal, August.

Yammarino, F. J., Dionne, S. D., Schriesheim, C. A., & Dansereau, F. (2008). Authentic leadership and positive organizational behavior: a meso, multi-level perspective. *The Leadership Quarterly, 19*(6), 693–707.

Zhang, G., Wang, L., & Caza, A. (2008). Effects of leaders' emotional authenticity on leadership effectiveness and followers' trust. *Proceedings of the Australia and New Zealand Academy of Management.*

27

A Multi-Level View of Leadership and Emotion: Leading with Emotional Labor

Neal M. Ashakanasy and Ronald H. Humphrey

INTRODUCTION

The idea that emotions play an important role in management and leadership is not really all that new. Mastenbroek (2000), for example, detailed how emotion has been a central feature of organizational management for over 2000 years. In the leadership literature, Redl (1942) was the first to report on the powerful effect of leaders on the emotional makeup of work groups; and emotions are featured in the early theories of leadership and management. For example, Fayol (1916/1949) noted that leaders needed to understand all aspects of their subordinates psyche, including their emotional states. More recently, Weiss and Brief (2001) detailed how emotions at work figured prominently in the early theories of organizational behavior. Today, most theories of leadership, especially charismatic and transformational leadership, have become inherently emotional (e.g., see Shamir & Howell, 1999, on charismatic leadership; and Ashkanasy & Tse, 2000, on transformational leadership). Despite this, and as Ashkanasy and Jordan (2008) recently observed, leadership scholars have in general been slow to develop broadly-based theories of leadership that incorporate an emotional dimension.

In fact, it was not until 1995 that interest in emotions and leadership began to receive mainstream attention. This was the year Ashforth and Humphrey (1995) published 'Emotion in the workplace: a reappraisal.' Also published in the same year was the best-selling book by Goleman (1995), *Emotional intelligence: why it can matter more than IQ*. The problem at that point in time, however, continued to be lack of a theoretical foundation for incorporating emotional dimensions into the prevailing theories of leadership. For example, Yukl (1999) noted that contemporary theories of charismatic and transformational leadership tended to focus on dyadic relationships, rather than trying to understand interpersonal processes such as emotion.

This position began to change rapidly in the early years of the 2000s, with the appearance of theoretical models by Ashkanasy and Tse (2000), Barbuto and Burbach (2006), Caruso, Mayer and Salovey (2002), and George (2000). These were followed by a string of empirical studies, especially focusing on the role of emotional intelligence (e.g., see Gardner & Stough, 2002; Wolff, Pescosolido, & Druskat, 2002; Wong & Law, 2002), culminating in a Special Issue of *The Leadership Quarterly*, guest-edited by Humphrey (2002).

Despite this progress, and as Ashkanasy and Jordan (2008) pointed out, the existing theories of leadership continue to emphasize isolated individual characteristics such as emotional intelligence. Ashkanasy and Jordan recommended that scholars need to broaden their perspective to include the influence of leadership at all levels of organizational analysis, and cited the Five-Level Model of emotion in organizations developed by Ashkanasy (2003a). In this chapter, therefore, and consistent with Ashkanasy and Jordan, we take the Five-Level Model as our initial organizing framework.

The remainder of this chapter is organized in three parts. In Part 1, we provide a broad overview of the field of emotions and leadership based on the Five-Level Model. In Part 2, we deal in more detail with three topics that have garnered a substantial amount of research interest in recent years: (1) Affective Events Theory (AET; Weiss and Cropanzano, 1996) and leaders as mood managers; (2) emotional intelligence and leadership; and (3) leader emotional displays and charisma. In Part 3, and following on from the discussion in Part 2, we extend our arguments to the notion of leading with emotional labor, an emerging area of research that is currently generating considerable excitement among leadership scholars. We conclude this discussion with suggestions for future research in this field.

PART 1: LEADERSHIP AT FIVE LEVELS OF ORGANIZATIONAL ANALYSIS

The five levels identified by Ashkanasy (2003a) comprise: (1) within person, (2) between persons (individual differences), (3) interpersonal interactions, (4) group, and (5) organization-wide (Figure 27.1). Ashkanasy (2003b) argued further that all five levels are integrated though a common biological basis in the neurobiology of emotion. Thus, the same processes that drive the experience emotions moment-to-moment at the within-person level (Level 1), are also accessed when considering emotional climate at the organization-wide level of analysis (Level 5).

Level 1 (within person) deals with emotion as experienced by individuals on a moment-to-moment basis. This level thus accounts for the variability of emotions that people experience as they get though the day, managing hassles and uplifts, and includes diurnal variations on emotional states (Clark, Watson, & Leeka, 1989). According to Weiss and Cropanzano (1996), it is the accumulation of emotional states arising from 'affective events' in the workplace that ultimately determines attitudes and behavior.

Level 2 of the model covers between-person effects, including individual differences such as emotional intelligence (Mayer & Salovey, 1997) and trait affectivity (Watson & Tellegen, 1985) as well as more stable attitudinal variables such as job satisfaction (as a between-person variable, see

Fisher, 2000) and organizational commitment (Meyer & Allen, 1997).

Level 3 encompasses interpersonal interactions, including facial recognition of emotion (Ekman, 1984, 1999). Also included at this level is the construct of emotional labor (Hochschild, 1983), where (especially) service providers use facial expression to communicate particular emotional states, sometimes with negative consequences for the person engaging in the emotional labor (Grandey, 2003).

Teams and groups are included in Level 4 of the model. Topics at this level include the effect of emotional contagion (Hatfield, Cacioppo, & Rapson, 1993) and group mood (George, 1990). Kelly and Barsade (2001), for example, demonstrated the mechanisms for propagation of mood in work teams, and their consequences for group mood and performance. Ashkanasy (2003a) cited Graen and Uhl-Bien (1995) to support the idea that leaders play a key role in determining emotional states at the group level. More recently, Sy, Côté, and Saavedra (2005) demonstrated that this process is facilitated at least in part by emotional contagion.

The highest level identified by Ashkanasy (2003a) is Level 5: the organization-wide level. Ashkanasy quoted De Rivera (1992), who defined this in terms of 'an objective group phenomenon that can be palpably sensed – as when one enters a party or a city and feels an attitude of gaiety or depression, openness or fear' (p. 197).

Ashkanasy and Jordan (2008) argued that, 'To be effective, leaders are required to utilize emotions at each of these levels' (p. 22), and detail how leadership processes operate at each of the five levels. In the following paragraphs, we provide a summary of their arguments.

Level 1: Within person

The starting point for consideration of emotion at the within-person level is Weiss and Cropanzano's (1996) Affective Events Theory. In this theory, events in the organizational environment result in affective reactions in employees, resulting in emotions (acute, object-oriented, and short-lived) and moods (diffuse, not object-oriented, and longer-lasting). These moods and emotions in turn shape attitudes (e.g., job satisfaction, job commitment) that then lead to judgment-driven behavior such as quitting or a decision to engage in productive or counterproductive behavior. AET also allows for direct affect-driven behavior, such as violent outbursts or spontaneous helping.

Ashkanasy and Jordan (2008) noted that leaders are not themselves immune from affective events,

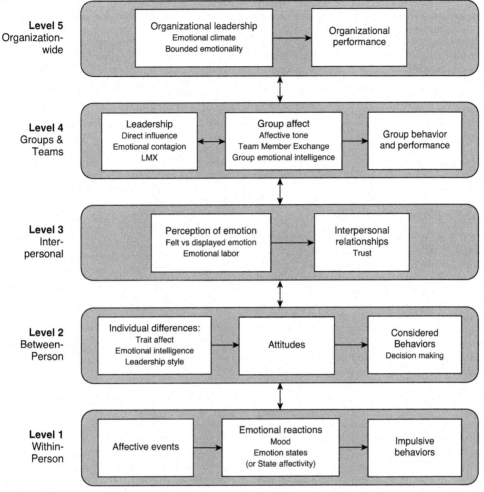

Figure 27.1   The five-level model of emotion in organizations (From Ashkanasy & Jordan, 2008)

despite an implicit assumption in traditional theories of leadership that leaders are somehow more emotionally stable than their subordinates. Indeed, and as Ashton-James and Ashkanasy also pointed out, leaders are themselves likely to be subject to a wider range of internal and external affective events than their subordinates. Ashton-James and Ashkanasy (2008) subsequently identified three categories of events that could have affective consequences for leaders: (1) organizational change events; (2) economic, legal, and political events; and (3) inter-organization negotiation events. Citing Forgas's (1995) Affect Infusion Model (AIM), Ashton-James and Ashkanasy posited that the resulting affective states (especially mood states) 'infuse' the

decision-making processes of leaders, ultimately affecting their decision making, with strategic consequences for the organization.

Ashkanasy and Jordan (2008) emphasized in particular the role of self-awareness as a central factor in a leader's role at the within-person level of analysis. They cite research by Sosik and Megerian (1999), who found that leader self-awareness is associated with the leader's performance and subordinate positive regard. On the other hand, leaders who tend to under- or overestimate their own abilities tend to be poorly regarded as leaders by their subordinates (Yammarino & Atwater, 1997). Leaders who understand their own capabilities and limitations, on the other hand, tend to be regarded more positively.

Ashkanasy and Jordan make the point that leaders who are less self-aware are less likely to be able to respond appropriately to the emotions they are experiencing, and so are more likely to be perceived by their followers to be out of touch with their affective environment. In this instance, the potential exists for the leader's affective state to be out of sync with their subordinates' affective states.

A corollary of this is that leaders have a special role as managers of their members' mood states. This is the topic we take up in more detail in Part 2 of this chapter.

Level 2: Between persons

Level 2 in the Five-Level Model focuses on individual differences such as trait affect and emotional intelligence, and attitudinal variables such as job satisfaction and job commitment. Ashkanasy and Jordan (2008) suggested that these variables should predict leadership emergence. Personality variables, of course, hark back to the trait theories of leadership, where Stogdill (1974) focused on variables like assertiveness, decisiveness, and dependability, and noted that leaders needed to be responsive to their social environment, but did not specifically identify any particular emotional competence skills.

Indeed, the trait theories of leadership fell into disuse during the period that saw the emergence of behavioral and contingency theories of leadership (see Antonakis, Chapter 20; Yukl, Chapter 21, in this volume). Even charismatic leadership was couched in terms of behaviorism during this period (Conger & Kanungo, 1987; Conger, Chapter 7, in this volume). Although House and Howell (1992) explored the values and personality traits of charismatic leaders, many theorists described charisma in terms of transactional/transformational behaviors (Bass, 1990; Bass & Avolio, 1990; Díaz-Sáenz, Chapter 22, in this volume). According to Bass (1990), for example, transformational leadership is characterized by four behaviors: individualized consideration (adapting to the specific needs of subordinates); idealized influence (projecting a vision); intellectual stimulation (challenging assumptions), and inspirational motivation (linking emotions to actions).

Ashkanasy and Jordan (2008) make the particular point that leaders, above all, are decision makers, so that, like other members of the species *homo sapiens*, they need to access their emotions to make decisions. They cite, in particular, Damasio's (1994) work showing that decision making, even at a basic level, requires access to emotional states that Damasio calls 'somatic

markers.' Since emotional intelligence involves the ability to access emotional information and to incorporate this information in thinking (Mayer & Salovey, 1997), it follows that emotional intelligence should be associated with leadership. In this respect, various researchers (e.g., see Ashkanasy & Tse, 2000, Gardner & Stough, 2002; George, 2000) have postulated that emotional intelligence is especially critical in the instance of transformational leadership skills.

Although there are some strong critics of the role of emotional intelligence in transformational leadership (e.g., Antonakis, 2004; Locke, 2005), research has been generally supportive of the idea that emotional intelligence is linked to transformational leadership (e.g., see Barling, Slater, & Kelloway, 2000; Daus & Ashkanasy, 2005; Rosete & Ciarrochi, 2005). More recently, Antonakis, Ashkanasy, and Dasborough (2009), in a debate on the issue, concluded despite their differences that emotion was a critical factor in leadership. We discuss the role of emotional intelligence and leadership in more detail in Part 2 of this chapter.

Level 3: Interpersonal relationships

At Level 3 of the Ashkanasy (2003a) model, the focus is on communication of emotion in interpersonal exchanges. Ashkanasy and Jordan (2008) point out that, at its core, leadership is necessarily about managing interpersonal relationships as reflected in, for example, the leader–member exchange (LMX) theory of leadership (see Graen and Uhl-Bien, 1995; Anand et al., Chapter 23, in this volume). But they take this a step further and refer to Mumby and Putnam's (1992) notion of 'bounded emotionality,' where organizational life is seen to revolve around the expression and control of emotions in everyday interactions at work. In this respect, Martin, Knopoff, and Beckman (1998) emphasized that effective leadership involves bringing emotional expression and control to the front and centre of leadership effectiveness. Thus, effective leaders regulate relationships with their followers as a means of enhancing their relationships with them.

Leadership also necessarily involves a component of emotional labor, defined by Hochschild (1983), as 'management of feeling to create a publicly observable facial and bodily display' (p. 7). Hochschild refers here to management of the actor's own feelings, but with the aim of managing others' impressions towards the actor. We pick up this aspect in more detail later in this chapter, but it is worth noting here that Lewis (2000), in a study of emotional expression in a field setting, found that leader displays of negative emotions were associated with lower subordinate ratings of leader effectiveness. This is the third and last topic that we discuss in more detail in Part 2 of this chapter.

Level 4: Groups

Ashkanasy (2003a) placed leadership specifically at this level of his model, drawing especially on LMX theory. Moreover, as Pescosolido (2002) and Pirola-Merlo, Härtel, Mann, and Hirst (2002) have demonstrated, the leader has a critical role in determining the emotional tone of groups. Ashkanasy and Jordan (2008) cite Kelly and Barsade's (2001) work on emotional contagion in groups to make the point that individual affective characteristics contribute to the affective composition of groups. More recently, Tse, Dasborough, and Ashkanasy (2008) found in a field study that leader's LMX contributed to the quality of team members' exchanges, and that this process was facilitated in teams characterized by a positive affective climate. This fits with the idea of emotional contagion within groups (Barsade, 2002) and, consistent with bounded emotionality theory, this suggests that the leader's role as a facilitator of group emotions is crucial. Moreover, and as Fitness (2000) found, this fragile relationship can easily break down if the leader engages in unwarranted displays of negative emotions such as anger.

In support of the idea that leader emotions are transferred to team members through emotional contagion, Sy et al. (2005) found in a field experiment that a leader's positive moods results in positive group affect, and that this in turn leads to higher levels of group task effectiveness and group–member coordination.

Also, working from a follower-centric perspective, Dasborough and Ashkanasy (2002, 2005) argued that the way followers attribute manipulative versus sincere intentions to their leaders engenders emotional responses that subsequently determine followers' attitudes to the leader and the leader's influence on them. In this respect, Newcombe and Ashkanasy (2002) found in an experiential study that followers' ratings of LMX were determined by the match between leaders' facial expression and the message they were conveying in a performance appraisal context.

Level 5: Organization-wide

The role of leadership at the organizational level is embedded in the leader's role in shaping the culture and climate of the organization (Schein, 1992). In this respect, De Rivera (1992) defines emotional climate as 'an objective group phenomenon that can be palpably sensed (p. 197). Thus, and based on Schein's notion that an organization's founder is primarily responsible for its subsequent culture, it is reasonable to conclude that the founder should also help to set the emotional climate that eventually comes to be reflected in a set of deeply embedded values and assumptions.

In summary of the Five-Level Model

Thus far in this chapter, we have argued, consistent with Ashkanasy and Jordan (2008), that the role of emotions in leadership can be modeled in terms of five levels of organizational analysis, beginning with within-person processes, and extending to the organization-wide view. Since emotion is a basic human characteristic, it must follow that emotion must lie at the heart of all human organizing activity, including leadership. In Part 2, and as we foreshadowed above, we deal in more detail with three topics of special relevance to the role of emotion in leadership:

- at Level 1, AET and leaders as mood managers
- at Level 2, emotional intelligence and leadership
- spanning Levels 3 and 4, leader emotional displays and charisma

PART 2: THREE TOPICS OF SPECIAL RELEVANCE TO THE ROLE OF EMOTION IN LEADERSHIP

Affective Events Theory and leaders as mood managers

As noted in Part 1, Affective Events Theory is based on the research showing that individuals have an average mood level, and that workplace events cause individuals to experience increases or decreases in their moods throughout the day (Weiss & Cropanzano, 1996; Weiss, Nichols, & Daus, 1999). Scholars are now beginning to apply AET to leadership, arguing that leaders can have a profound influence over the moods that employees feel throughout the day (e.g., see Humphrey, 2002). In some workplaces, managers may be the most important sources of variation in employees' moods. One of the best studies on leadership from the AET perspective was done by Pirola-Merlo et al. (2002). These researchers realized that the workplace is often filled with frustrating events, and argued that one of the functions that leaders can perform is to help subordinates cope with these events. In the study they conducted, leaders with facilitative and transformational styles aided subordinates in overcoming the mood-damaging effects of workplace aggravations; moreover, by improving their subordinates' moods, the leaders were also able to improve subordinate performance.

McColl-Kennedy and Anderson (2002) also found that effective leaders help employees transform their feelings of frustration into an optimistic outlook on the challenging goals facing them. Consistent with the Pirola-Merlo et al. (2002) study, McColl-Kennedy and Anderson established that transformational leaders boosted employees' optimistic moods, and that this translated into higher performance. More recently, Bono, Foldes, Vinson, and Muros (2007) also found that transformational leadership resulted in employees experiencing more positive emotions throughout the day; moreover, the employees were able to maintain this improved mood during their interactions with customers and with each other. Although not explicitly based on AET, Pescosolido (2002) also argued, consistent with AET, that leaders have much of their influence on subordinates and team members by influencing group members' moods. He reasoned that the workplace is often ambiguous, and that leaders serve an important function by role modeling the correct emotional response to workplace events. Pescosolido supported his theories in field studies of jazz musicians and sports teams.

It may take considerable skill for leaders to be able to role model the correct emotional response to complex situations; moreover, it may also take considerable judgment to know which mood is best to portray. Although positive moods may normally be best, the actual relationship between moods and performance is complex, and negative moods may be useful in some circumstances (Jordan, Lawrence, & Troth, 2006). George and Zhou (2007) found that creativity was highest when leaders provided a supportive atmosphere and positive moods, but that a combination of both positive and negative moods yielded the best results. In order for leaders to provide a supportive emotional atmosphere and to role model the appropriate emotional responses and moods, leaders need to be good at expressing the emotions they intend to convey. Moreover, and consistent with Ashkanasy and Jordan's (2008) argument, leaders need also to be self-aware of their own emotional states.

Emotional intelligence and leadership

In our Part 2 discussion of Level 2 of the Five-Level Model, we identified that emotional intelligence (EI) is an individual difference variable that, despite controversy, appears to be critically important for effective leadership. We now address this assertion in more detail.

Salovey and Mayer's (1990) seminal article defining emotional intelligence sparked considerable interest in this topic among both academicians and practitioners. They later revised their original definition of emotional intelligence into a four-branch model (Mayer & Salovey, 1997), and subsequently developed (Mayer, Salovey, & Caruso, 2002) an ability measure called the Mayer–Salovey–Caruso Emotional Intelligence Test (MSCEIT). Their revision of this scale (MSCEIT V2.0; Mayer, Salovey, Caruso, & Sitarenios, 2003) is a '141-item scale designed to measure the following four branches (specific skills) of EI: (a) perceiving emotions, (b) using emotions to facilitate thought, (c) understanding emotions, and (d) managing emotions' (p. 99). The MSCEIT uses items that are scored as either right or wrong, based on consensus or expert judgments. In contrast, other scales use either self-reports or peer reports, or a mixed method of rating emotional competencies that includes emotional intelligence constructs and related social skills (Ashkanasy & Daus, 2005). Some examples of scales include the Bar-On EQ-I (Bar-On, 1997), the Emotional Intelligence Scale (EIS; Schutte et al., 1998), the Work Profile Questionnaire – Emotional Intelligence Version (WPQei; Cameron, 1999), the Workgroup Emotional Intelligence Profile (WEIP; Jordan, Ashkanasy, & Härtel, 2002), and the WLEIS (Wong & Law, 2002).

With regard to the general issue of whether emotional intelligence predicts job performance, the evidence is reassuring. In their meta-analysis, Van Rooy and Viswesvaran (2004) found that emotional intelligence predicts job performance. A more recent meta-analysis also provides support for the incremental validity of emotional intelligence over and above general mental ability and the Big Five personality factors, and that emotional intelligence correlates 0.28 with job performance (O'Boyle, Humphrey, Pollack, Hawver, & Story, in press). A study by Law, Wong, and Song (2004) found emotional intelligence predicts job performance. They reported that coworker ratings of an employee's emotional intelligence predicted supervisors' ratings of employees' performance after controlling for the Big Five personality measures. Another study by Dulewicz, Higgs, and Slaski (2003) found that emotional intelligence predicted job performance and also correlated with morale and other measures related to well-being/stress.

In a sample of college students, Brackett, Mayer, and Warner (2004) found that emotional intelligence was positively associated with college grade point average (GPA). Moreover, Brackett and his associates also found that students with lower emotional intelligence were more likely to have illegal drug problems, to have problems with their friendships, and to have engaged in other deviant behaviors. In another study of students, Law, Wong, and Song (2004) found that emotional intelligence influenced life satisfaction and, in a second sample of employees, Law and his colleagues also found that emotional intelligence influenced job performance as rated by supervisors.

With regard to the specific issue of emotional intelligence and leadership, and despite recent criticism, the evidence is also actually quite supportive. Kellett, Humphrey, and Sleeth (2002; 2006) found that emotional intelligence measures predicted leadership emergence, and that some leaders relied more on their emotional skills – especially empathy – whereas others relied on cognitive skills and complex task performance. Côté and Miners (2006) also found that some people relied more on their cognitive skills, whereas others relied less on their cognitive skills and more on their emotional intelligence. The degree to which people rely on cognitive skills or on emotional skills may also depend on the type of task being performed, with work that requires interacting with others requiring more emotional intelligence than does solitary work. Offermann, Bailey, Vasilopoulos, Seal, and Sass (2004) found that cognitive intelligence predicted individual work such as exam performance, but that emotional intelligence was a better predictor of leadership ratings and of team performance. At the highest levels of an organization, or for pre-eminent achievement in most fields, leaders may need to be high in both cognitive intelligence and emotional intelligence. One study of these types of outstanding leaders found that they were high in both IQ and EQ (Aydin, Leblebici, Arslan, Kilic, & Oktem, 2005).

Empathy was part of the original concept of emotional intelligence (Salovey & Mayer, 1990) and remains a key concept in many peer-report- and self-report-based models of emotional intelligences and competencies (e.g., Goleman, Boyatzis, & McKee, 2002; Wolff et al., 2002). Salovey and Mayer (1990) defined empathy as 'the ability to comprehend another's feelings and to re-experience them oneself' (pp. 194–195). Kellett et al. (2006) developed a measure of interactive empathy based on the theory that leaders use a more active style of empathy and dynamically create a reciprocal interactive empathic bond with others, rather than just passively receiving others' emotions. Contrary to simplistic assumptions that empathy is relevant only to relational leadership, Kellett and her colleagues found that interactive empathy predicted task leadership emergence as well as cognitive measures did.

Sy, Tram, and O'Hara (2006) provided evidence that managers high in emotional intelligence do a better job supervising their subordinates. They found in a sample of food service workers that managers high in emotional intelligence helped improve job satisfaction for employees, and that this was especially true for those subordinates low in emotional intelligence. Likewise, Wong and Law (2002) found that satisfaction and performance depends on the emotional intelligence of both leaders and followers, and that leaders can influence both job satisfaction and extra-role performance. In a sample of senior executives, Rosete and Ciarrochi (2005) found that executives with higher MSCEIT scores were rated higher by their superiors on their performance appraisal ratings of achieving business outputs. The executives were also evaluated using a 360 degree assessment measure filled out by their subordinates. The subordinates' ratings were also positively correlated with the executives' emotional intelligence. Rosete and Ciarrochi found that these results held up even when controlling for cognitive intelligence and the Big Five personality measures.

Leader emotional displays and charisma

The final aspect of the multi-level model we address in this part of the chapter spans Levels 3 (interpersonal) and 4 (groups). Charisma theorists (e.g., see Conger & Kanungo, 1987; Gardner & Avolio, 1998; Conger, Chapter 7, in this volume) have long recognized that charismatic leaders strongly influence their followers' emotions, although much of this literature has focused on charisma as an attributional phenomenon and on impression management techniques. Scholars in this area have also examined the different methods necessary to express charisma across the different levels of an organization (Waldman & Yammarino, 1999). Scholars are now beginning to focus on how leaders' emotional displays convey affect from charismatic leaders to followers through emotional contagion processes. Cherulnik, Donley, Wiewel, and Miller (2001) demonstrated that observers displayed more smiles and other emotional displays when watching videotapes of leaders who also displayed these non-verbal emotional expressions. Likewise, Goleman et al.'s (2002) theory of 'resonance' is based on emotional contagion; these authors maintain that effective leaders create an emotional resonance that emotionally synchronizes leaders and followers. In addition to facial expressions, body language, and vocal tone, charismatic leaders may also use emotionally arousing language. For example, they use more emotionally engaging metaphors (Mio, Riggio, Levin, & Reese, 2005). In a series of studies, Bono and Ilies (2006) demonstrated that leaders who were more emotionally expressive were rated higher on charisma, and leaders' positive emotional expressions influenced followers' moods. They found these mood effects even when controlling for vision statements and other non-affective characteristics of charismatic speakers.

Emotionally engaging speeches may be more motivational than dry cognitive speeches, and thus may help convince followers to implement leader's vision statements. Waples and Connelly (2008) found that leaders who used active emotions were better at increasing vision-related performance, and this was true regardless of whether the leader's emotional valence was positive or negative. Moreover, they found that subordinates (especially those low on emotional competence) rated leaders who used active emotions higher on transformational leadership. Likewise, Newcombe and Ashkanasy (2002) found that the leader's displayed affect could be more important than the content of the leader's message in determining follower impressions of the leader. In particular, managers who displayed emotions that were incongruent with the content of their speech were rated poorly on leadership. The study by Newcombe and Ashkanasy also found that leaders who used negative valence emotions could be rated favorably if the emotional valence was consistent with the content of the speech. Thus, both of these studies found that negative emotions could be effective under the right circumstances.

Sy et al. (2005) also examined whether leaders' moods were contagious to group members and influenced performance. They found that leaders' mood influenced whether group members were in a positive or negative mood, and that leaders who were in positive moods had group members who performed better in terms of coordination and effort required to achieve the tasks. De Hoogh et al. (2005) also found that charismatic leaders can be more effective in the workplace; in their study, charismatic leaders were able to be more effective by improving their subordinates' work attitudes.

Although many leaders may wish to be charismatic, individuals differ in their ability to be charismatic and in their ability to display emotions. Groves (2005) examined leaders in 64 organizations, and found that the leaders' emotional expressiveness determined whether the leaders were perceived as charismatic. People lacking in emotional expressiveness may also be less likely to gain leadership positions, and this may be true even for task leaders. Kellett et al. (2006) found that the ability to express emotions had a direct positive effect on task leadership emergence. In addition, the ability to express emotions had indirect effects through empathy on both relations leadership and task leadership. The direct effects for expressing emotions to task leadership suggest that task leaders may sometimes be effective by expressing tough, non-empathetic emotions. They also found a stronger effect of empathy on task leadership emergence; however, so it is possible that even task leaders spend most of their communication time expressing positive emotions, and only use negative emotional expressions when they must express a negative message, such as communicating a negative assessment of performance (as in the Newcombe and Ashkanasy, 2002, study).

Taken together, these studies support the proposition that leaders' emotional displays have a strong influence on subordinates' moods. Moreover, these studies suggest that these mood effects also influence subordinates' performance levels in a variety of ways, such as boosting subordinate confidence levels, helping subordinates cope with stress and frustration, and motivating them to implement the leader's vision. In order to achieve these results, leaders need to be skilled at displaying the right emotions, and to have the judgment necessary to know what emotions and moods to display. The studies thus suggest that there are individual differences in the ability to be emotionally expressive, and that those high in this ability are more likely to be rated as charismatic and transformational, as well as higher in both relations and task leadership.

In summary of the three topics

In this part of the chapter, we examined in more detail processes at Levels 1–4 of the Five-Level Model. The first topic we addressed was the role of leaders as mood managers with the framework of AET (Level 1). We concluded that an essential component of good leadership is the ability of leaders to be in touch with and to express the emotions they are feeling to their group members. We then turned our attention to the role of emotional intelligence in leadership (Level 2), and concluded that the vast majority of empirical research supports the view that emotional intelligence is positively related to good leadership. Indeed, this conclusion also flows from our discussion of leaders as mood managers, in that emotional intelligence involves the ability both to perceive and to manage the emotional states of self and others (Mayer & Salovey, 1997). In our third topic, we spanned Levels 3 and 4 in a discussion of the role of emotion as a driver of charismatic and transformational leadership. Consistent with our findings regarding AET and emotional intelligence, we concluded that the leader's ability to be emotionally expressive is a key ingredient of such leadership. Part 3 takes this line of argument to the next step – the role of emotional labor in leadership.

PART 3: LEADING WITH EMOTIONAL LABOR

In the final part of this chapter, we follow up our discussion of leader emotional displays with the proposition that leadership, of necessity, involves an element of emotional labor. Thus, because leadership scholars now recognize that one of the key roles of leaders is to manage the moods and emotions of their followers, leadership researchers have begun to examine the methods that people actually use to manage both their own and others' emotions.

Scholars who study charisma were among the first to recognize the important role that emotions play in relationships between followers and leaders (for a discussion of the different forms of charisma, and how they vary from weak to strong, see Bratton, Grint, & Nelson, 2005; Conger, Chapter 7, in this volume). Although many leaders try to be charismatic, it is difficult to create charismatic relationships between leaders and followers and most leaders are generally not considered to be charismatic. Establishing charismatic relationships with subordinates may be difficult because leaders need to balance their downward displays of relationship leadership to their subordinates with their need to perform task duties while looking upward to their superiors (Cowsill & Grint, 2008). Likewise, the literature on emotional labor has documented that putting on the appropriate emotional displays while at work is not a simple process. In addition, the emotional labor literature has documented that expressing emotions at work may produce a variety of psychological effects on the actor, ranging from feelings of inauthenticity and stress to increased identification and well-being (Ashforth & Humphrey, 1993; Brotheridge & Lee, 2008; Brotheridge & Grandey, 2002; Hochschild, 1983; Pugh, 2001; Rafaeli & Sutton, 1987; Van Dijk & Kirk-Brown, 2006). Moreover, the emotional labor literature, as well as the related literature on emotion regulation, has categorized a number of techniques that people can use to help them both feel and express the appropriate emotions.

Thus, applying the concepts from research on emotional labor may prove beneficial to leadership researchers (Humphrey, 2005, 2008).

As previously mentioned, researchers have provided strong evidence that there is emotional contagion from leaders to followers (Barsade, 2002; Bono & Ilies, 2006; Cherulnik et al., 2001; Sy et al., 2005). Humphrey (2005, 2006, 2008; see also Humphrey, Pollack, & Hawver, 2008) argued that leaders can use emotional labor processes to take control of the emotional contagion process. He suggested that, by using emotional labor techniques, leaders can both gain control of their own emotions and use emotional contagion to influence the emotions and moods of their coworkers and subordinates. It may take considerable skill for leaders to use emotional labor. For example, Jones, Kane, Russo, and Walmsley (2008) examined leader emotional labor and emotional contagion, and found that the degree to which emotional contagion occurred depended upon the subordinates' perceptions of the leaders.

In this instance Humphrey (2005, 2006, 2008; see also Humphrey et al., 2008) was the first researcher to apply the emotional labor perspective to leadership systematically, and he coined the phrase 'leading with emotional labor.' With the exception of Brotheridge and Grandey (2002) and Mann (1997), all of the research on emotional labor prior to 2005 examined emotional labor among service workers. Brotheridge and Grandey were the first to include a sample of managers in their study of emotional labor in five occupations. They found that managers performed emotional labor as often as did sales staff and customer services personnel. Mann in a study of British managers demonstrated similarly that emotional labor effects were prevalent at all levels of organizational communication. Now researchers are beginning to apply emotional labor concepts to leadership. For example, Humphrey (2005) theorized that leaders who use emotional labor would be more likely to be perceived as transformational. Consistent with this, Epitropaki (2006) found that leaders who used emotional labor were perceived higher on transformational leadership.

The theory of emotional labor was first devised by Hochschild (1983). She argued that organizations often require their front-line service employees to express certain emotions as part of their job duties. The most frequent type of emotional labor may consist of 'service with a smile' interactions between employees and customers (Ashforth & Humphrey, 1993; Brotheridge & Grandey, 2002; Pugh, 2001; Rafaeli & Sutton, 1987; Van Dijk & Kirk-Brown, 2006). Depending upon the occupation, however, service workers may also be required to express a wide range of other emotions: even unpleasant emotions like anger, irritation, or sadness.

Emotional labor may work in part by emotional contagion processes (Pugh, 2001), and may improve task effectiveness by increasing predictability and helping interpersonal interactions run more smoothly (Ashforth & Humphrey, 1993).

Humphrey et al. (2008) classified the type of emotional labor performed by service workers into three categories: (1) customer service jobs; (2) caring professions; and (3) social control jobs. In the first category, standard customer service jobs, employees are usually required to express mostly pleasant emotions, such as smiling and acting friendly. Although these are normally pleasant emotions to express, the repetitive nature of expressing these emotions, along with the hectic work pace, may make it hard for employees to express these emotions in a convincing and authentic way all day long. In the second category, caring professions, nurses and healthcare workers, social workers, childcare workers, and so forth, employees sometimes have to express sympathy for sick patients or clients with long-standing personal problems. Thus, employees in these occupations may routinely have to express emotions such as sadness and sympathy, which are normally associated with traumatic events that most people only infrequently experience. In the third category, social control agents, such as bouncers, policemen, and bill collectors, may have to display irritation or even anger. As Sutton (1991) illustrated in his study of bill collectors, expressing just the right amount of irritation can be difficult to do.

According to Humphrey and his colleagues (2008), leaders have to use all three types of emotional labor while managing their subordinates, and have to use considerably more judgment about which type of emotional labor to use. Leaders must act cheerful and enthusiastic to perk up bored service workers, they must express sympathy and support to frustrated subordinates, and they must display stern disapproval to misbehaving subordinates. Moreover, they have to use considerable judgment about which emotions to portray; for example, should they express sympathy for the personal problems that cause an employee to be tardy, or react with firm disapproval, or some mixture? Consequently, performing emotional labor may be more challenging for leaders than for most service employees.

According to Hochschild (1983), service workers perform emotional labor by either using surface acting, in which they change their outward emotional expressions but not their actual feelings, or deep acting, in which they first try to summon up the appropriate feelings, and then let these generated feelings animate their outward displays. Both of these forms can create feelings of inauthenticity and emotional dissonance, and considerable research has examined the extent to which these feelings can create stress, burnout, feelings of depersonalization, and other negative psychological consequences (Bono & Vey, 2005; Brotheridge & Grandey, 2002; Bryant, & Cox, 2006; Van Dijk & Kirk-Brown, 2006).

Ashforth and Humphrey (1993) argued that service workers can perform emotional labor in a third way: namely, by expressing genuine and spontaneous emotions that naturally comply with the organization's display rules. For example, emergency care workers may truly feel sorrow upon seeing an injured child, and thus have no need to fake their emotional displays or expend energy in summoning up feelings of sympathy. Glomb and Tews (2004), as well as Diefendorff, Croyle, and Gosserand (2005), found support for the presence of this third type of emotional labor, and demonstrated that it is an effective form of emotional labor. In particular, customers respond better to genuine emotional displays that are consistent with emotional display rules (Hennig-Thurau, Groth, Paul, & Gremler, 2006).

Leaders who use surface acting may not always be revealing their true intentions. Because leaders have more influence than do subordinates, this lack of authenticity can pose serious ethical problems. Hunt, Gardner, and Fischer (2008) have explored the implications of performing the three types of emotional labor for leaders, and have developed a typology that relates these types of emotional labor to authentic leadership. They theorized that the effectiveness of leaders' emotional labor depends on the distance between leaders and followers (distance is conceptualized in terms of physical distance, social distance, and frequency of interaction). In addition, they theorized that the effectiveness of leaders' emotional labor also depends upon whether their emotional displays comply with organizational display rules. Thus, leaders who display genuine emotions that are contrary to social expectations may be perceived as authentic but yet generate unfavorable impressions. Although we may intuitively assume that leaders have more freedom than service workers to choose their emotional expressions, the degree to which leaders have autonomy and can create their own emotional display rules varies greatly by type of leader position (Humphrey et al., 2008). Moreover, Hunt and his coauthors argue that leader distance influences the mix of emotional labor strategies used by the different types of leaders. According to their typology, the distance between leaders and followers interacts with the type of emotional labor used to influence followers' perceptions of leader authenticity and follower trust in the leader. Gardner, Fischer, and Hunt (2009) also explored the ethical issues relating to leaders' use of surface acting and deep acting, and demonstrated how genuine emotional expression is more consistent with authentic leadership theory. Like Humphrey and his colleagues (Humphrey, 2008; Humphrey et al., 2008), Hunt et al. (2008) examined how performing the three different types of emotional labor influenced leader-felt authenticity and leader well-being.

Surface acting may also be more stressful for leaders than deep acting or genuine emotional expression. Humphrey et al. (2008) argued that leaders have to be able to portray optimism, hope, and confidence even when facing the same confidence-shattering events that may be demoralizing their subordinates; thus, leaders may have to use surface acting to portray confidence, or, even better, use deep-acting techniques and emotion regulation strategies to bolster their own confidence. Their theories are based in part on the work being done on positive leadership and psychological capital (e.g., Hannah & Luthans, 2008). Although research suggests that those who use deep acting and genuine emotional expression may perform better and have better psychological reactions, the effects of emotional labor on leaders is likely to be complex, with both positive and negative effects. Recent research suggests that leaders' emotive awareness may influence whether they find performing emotional labor to be stressful or not (Jones, Visio, Wilberding, & King, 2008). This is an area that still needs considerable research.

There is also a need to examine individual differences in leaders' use of the three types of emotional labor, as well as individual differences in how skillfully they use the techniques. Some exciting research has begun to examine whether there are different types of emotional laborers in terms of their use of the three strategies. Jordan, Soutar, and Kiffin-Petersen (2008) found that only 4% were 'chameleons', who were high in all three types of emotional labor, and that only 28% were 'empathists', high in deep acting and genuine emotional expression.

Finally, there is a need to see how leading with emotional labor relates to emotion regulation strategies. Mikolajczak, Tran, and Brotheridge (2008) have classified a variety of emotional regulation strategies in addition to the three emotional labor strategies. Together, these expanded strategies could help leaders who use emotional labor to control both their own emotional reactions and to influence the moods, emotions, and performance of their followers.

In summary of leading with emotional labor

In this, the final part of our chapter, we have argued that emotional labor, which was originally intended to apply in service interactions, applies also to leadership. This line of argument flows on from our earlier discussion of the Five-Level Model and the three additional topics. The message from Part 2 is that good leaders are self-aware and able to manage their own emotions and the emotional states of their group members; that leaders need to have high emotional intelligence; and that this ability is a central ingredient of charismatic and transformational leadership. In Part 3, we took this line a step further and proposed that good leadership therefore involves active emotional labor. Thus, leaders need to be able to manage their own emotional expressions and to use their emotional expressivity and understanding (aka emotional intelligence) to manage the mood states of their group members. We argued further that this is also the essence of charismatic and transformational leadership.

DISCUSSION AND CONCLUSIONS

In this chapter, we have presented the view that emotions and leadership are intimately bound concepts, and that understanding leadership therefore requires an understanding of the role emotion plays at all levels of organizational functioning. We addressed this in three parts. In Part 1, drawing upon Ashkanasy (2003a) and Ashkanasy and Jordan (2008), we described how leadership and emotion are linked at five levels of organizational analysis, going from affective events and within-person emotional fluctuations, to individual differences and emotion communication in interpersonal relationships, and then to consideration of emotion in groups and the organization as a whole. In Part 2, we dealt in detail with three topics that arose from Part 1: leaders as managers of members' mood states, emotional intelligence, and the emotional underpinnings of charismatic and transformational leadership. In Part 3, we took this line a step further, arguing that good leadership necessarily incorporates emotional labor.

Before concluding, however, we note that there are some boundaries to our analysis. The first of these is that research has shown that there can be cross-cultural differences in perceptions and effects of expressed emotions (Elfenbein & Ambady, 2002). The second boundary is that we have considered only the positive side of emotional intelligence and leadership. Both constructs, however, have a 'dark side.' Fineman (2004), for example, has argued that emotional intelligence, especially once promulgated by top management, can become a manipulative device. In addition, Conger (1990) described how charismatic and transformational leadership can also be used for manipulative purposes. Consistent with Bass, Avolio, and Atwater (1996) and Gardner et al. (2009), we have restricted our analysis to 'authentic leadership,' where emotional expressions are genuine and not contrived for manipulative purposes. As such, discussion of 'pseudo-transformational leadership' and its effects is beyond the scope of our analysis in this chapter. Suffice to say this is not the kind of leadership we would regard as either 'good' or 'effective.'

To conclude, we have argued in this chapter that understanding emotions, ability to express emotions, and emotional awareness are all components that contribute to leadership effectiveness. We have also stressed that both leadership and emotion are holistic phenomena that extend across all five levels of organizational understanding. Finally, we have argued that leadership, of necessity, involves emotional labor, and suggested some ideas for future research in this respect. We hope these ideas will help to improve our understanding of leadership and encourage our readers to extend this line of research.

REFERENCES

Antonakis, J. J. (2004). On why 'Emotional Intelligence' will not predict leadership effectiveness beyond IQ or the 'Big Five': an extension and rejoinder. *Organizational Analysis*, *12*, 171–182.

Antonakis, J., Ashkanasy, N. M., & Dasborough, M. T. (2009). Does leadership need emotional intelligence? *The Leadership Quarterly*, *20*, 247–261.

Ashforth, B. E. & Humphrey, R. H. (1993). Emotional labor in service roles: the influence of identity. *Academy of Management Review*, *18*, 88–115.

Ashforth, B. E. & Humphrey, R. H. (1995). Emotion in the workplace: a reappraisal. *Human Relations*, *48*, 97–125.

Ashkanasy, N. M. (2003a). Emotions in organizations: a multilevel perspective. In F. Dansereau & F. J. Yammarino (eds), *Research in multi-level issues: Multi-level issues in organizational behavior and strategy*, Vol. 2, Oxford, UK: Elsevier/JAI Press, pp. 9–54.

Ashkanasy, N. M. (2003b). Emotions at multiple levels: an integration. In F. Dansereau & F. J. Yammarino (eds), *Research in multi-level issues: multi-level issues in organizational behavior and strategy*, Vol 2, Oxford, UK: Elsevier/JAI Press, pp. 71–81.

Ashkanasy, N. M. & Daus, C. S. (2005). Rumors of the death of emotional intelligence in organizational behavior are vastly exaggerated. *Journal of Organizational Behavior*, *26*, 441–452.

Ashkanasy, N. M. & Jordan, P. J. (2008). A multi-level view of leadership and emotion. In R. H. Humphrey (ed.), *Affect and emotion: new directions in management theory and research*. Charlotte, NC: Information Age Publishing, pp. 17–39.

Ashkanasy, N. M. & Tse, B. (2000). Transformational leadership as management of emotion. In N. M. Ashkanasy, C. E. J. Härtel, & W. Zerbe (eds), *Emotions in the workplace: research, theory, and practice*. Westport, CT: Quorum Books, pp. 221–235.

Ashton-James, C. E. & Ashkanasy, N. M. (2008). Affective events theory: a strategic perspective. In W. J. Zerbe, C. E. J. Härtel, & N. M. Ashkanasy (eds), *Research on emotion in organizations: emotions, ethics, and decision-making*, Vol. 4. Bingley, UK: Emerald Group Publishing/JAI Press, pp. 1–34.

Aydin, M., Leblebici, D., Arslan, M., Kilic M., & Oktem, M. (2005). The impact of IQ and EQ on pre-eminent achievement in organizations: implications for the hiring decisions of HRM specialists. *International Journal of Human Resource Management*, *16*, 701–719.

Barbuto, J. E. Jr & Burbach, M. E. M. (2006). The emotional intelligence of transformational leaders: a field study of elected officials. *Journal of Social Psychology*, *146*, 51–64.

Barling, J., Slater, F., & Kelloway, E. K. (2000). Transformational leadership and emotional intelligence: an exploratory study. *Leadership and Organizational Development Journal*, *21*, 157–161.

Bar-On, R. (1997). *Bar-On Emotional Quotient Inventory technical manual*. Toronto: Multi-Health Systems.

Barsade, S. G. (2002). The ripple effect: emotional contagion and its influence on group behavior. *Administrative Science Quarterly*, *47*, 644–675.

Bass, B. M. (1990). From transactional to transformational leadership: learning to share the vision. *Organizational Dynamics*, *18*(3), 19–36.

Bass, B. M. & Avolio, B. J. (1990). The implications of transactional and transformational leadership for individual, team, and organizational development. *Research in Organizational Change and Development*, *4*, 231–272.

Bass, B. M., Avolio, B. J., & Atwater, L. (1996). The transformational and transactional leadership of men and women. *Applied Psychology: An International Review*, *45*, 5–34.

Bono, J. E., Foldes, H. J., Vinson, G., & Muros, J. P. (2007). Workplace emotions: the role of supervision and leadership. *Journal of Applied Psychology*, *92*, 1357–1367.

Bono, J. E. & Ilies, R. (2006). Charisma, positive emotions, and mood contagion. *The Leadership Quarterly*, *17*, 317–334.

Bono, J. E. & Vey, M. A. (2005). Toward understanding emotional management at work: a quantitative review of emotional labor research. In C. E. J. Härtel, W. J. Zerbe, & N. M. Ashkanasy (eds), *Emotions in organizational behavior*. Mahwah, NJ: Lawrence Erlbaum Associates, pp. 213–233.

Brackett, M. A., Mayer, J. D., & Warner, R. M. (2004). Emotional intelligence and its relation to everyday behavior. *Personality and Individual Differences*, *36*, 1387–1402.

Bratton, J., Grint, K., & Nelson, D. (2005). *Organizational leadership*, Mason, OH: Thomson/South-Western.

Brotheridge, C. M. & Grandey, A. A. (2002). Emotional labor and burnout: comparing two perspectives of 'People Work.' *Journal of Vocational Behavior*, *60*, 17–39.

Brotheridge, C. M. & Lee, R. T. (2008). The emotions of managing: an introduction to the special issue. *Journal of Managerial Psychology, 23*, 108–117.

Bryant, M. & Cox, J. W. (2006). The expression of suppression: loss and emotional labour in narratives of organizational change. *Journal of Management & Organization, 12*, 116–130.

Cameron, A. (1999). *A WPQei user's guide*. London: The Test Agency Limited.

Caruso, D. R., Mayer, J. D., & Salovey, P. (2002). Emotional intelligence and emotional leadership. In F. J. Pirozzolo (ed.), *multiple intelligences and leadership*. Mahwah, NJ: Lawrence Erlbaum Associates.

Cherulnik, P. D., Donley, K. A., Wiewel, T. S. R., & Miller, S. R. (2001). Charisma is contagious: the effect of leaders' charisma on observers' affect. *Journal of Applied Social Psychology, 31*, 2149–2159.

Clark, L. A., Watson, D., & Leeka, J. (1989). Diurnal variation in the positive affects. *Motivation and Emotion, 13*, 205–234.

Conger, J. A. (1990). The dark side of leadership. *Organizational Dynamics, 19*, 44–55.

Conger, J. A. & Kanungo, R. N. (1987). Toward a behavioral theory of charismatic leadership in organizational settings. *Academy of Management Review, 12*, 637–647.

Côté, S. & Miners, C. (2006). Emotional intelligence, cognitive intelligence, and job performance. *Administrative Science Quarterly, 51*, 1–26.

Cowsill, R. & Grint, K. (2008). Leadership, task and relationship: Orpheus, Prometheus and Janus. *Human Resource Management Journal, 18*, 188–195.

Damasio, A. R. (1994). *Descartes error: emotion, reason, and the human brain*. New York: Putnam.

Dasborough, M. T. & Ashkanasy, N. M. (2002). Emotion and attribution of intentionality in leader–member relationships. *The Leadership Quarterly, 13*, 615–634.

Dasborough, M. T. & Ashkanasy, N. M. (2005). Follower emotional reactions to authentic and inauthentic leadership influence. In W. L. Gardner, B. J. Avolio, & F. O. Walumbwa, (eds). *Monographs in leadership and management. Volume 3: Authentic leadership theory and practice: origins, effects and development*. Oxford, UK: Elsevier/JAI Press, pp. 281–300.

Daus, C. S. & Ashkanasy, N. M. (2005). The case for an ability-based model of emotional intelligence in organizational behavior. *Journal of Organizational Behavior, 26*, 453–466.

De Hoogh, A. H. B., Den Hartog, D. N., Kopman, P. L., Thierry, H., Van den Berg, P. T., Van der Weide, J. G., & Wilderom, C. P. M. (2005). Leader motives, charismatic leadership, and subordinates' work attitudes in the profit and voluntary sector. *The Leadership Quarterly, 16*, 17–38.

De Rivera, J. (1992). Emotional climate: social structure and emotional dynamics. *International Review of Studies of Emotion, 2*, 197–218.

Diefendorff, J. M., Croyle, M. H., & Gosserand, R. H. (2005). The dimensionality and antecedents of emotional labor strategies. *Journal of Vocational Behavior, 66*, 339–357.

Dulewicz, V., Higgs, M., & Slaski, M. (2003). Measuring emotional intelligence: content, construct, and criterion-related validity. *Journal of Managerial Psychology, 18*, 405–420.

Elfenbein, H. A. & Ambady, N. (2002). On the universality and cultural specificity of emotion recognition: a meta-analysis. *Psychological Bulletin, 128*, 203–235.

Ekman, P. (1984). Expression and the nature of emotion. In: K. R. Scherer & P. Ekman (eds), *Approaches to emotion* Hillsdale, NJ: Lawrence Erlbaum Associates, pp. 319–343.

Ekman, P. (1999). Facial expressions. In: T. Dalgleish & M. J. Power (eds), *Handbook of cognition and emotion*. New York: John Wiley and Sons, pp. 301–320.

Epitropaki, O. (2006). 'Leading the show': the impact of leader's emotional labor on subordinates' transformation leadership perceptions and collective emotional labor. Paper presentation, The Academy of Management, Atlanta, GA.

Fayol, H. (1916/1949). *General and industrial management*. Translated from the French edition (Dunod) by C. Storrs. London: Pitman.

Fineman, S. (2004). Getting the measure of emotion – and the cautionary tale of emotional intelligence. *Human Relations, 57*, 719–740.

Fitness, J. (2000). Anger in the workplace: an emotion script approach to anger episodes between workers and their superiors, co-workers and subordinates. *Journal of Organizational Behavior, 21*, 147–162.

Fisher, C. D. (2000). Mood and emotions while working: missing pieces of job satisfaction? *Journal of Organizational Behavior, 21*, 185–202.

Forgas, J. P. (1995). Mood and judgment: the Affect Infusion Model (AIM). *Psychological Bulletin, 117*, 39–66.

Gardner, W. L. & Avolio, B. J. (1998). The charismatic relationship: a dramaturgical perspective. *Academy of Management Review, 23*, 32–58.

Gardner, W. L. & Stough, C. (2002). Examining the relationship between leadership and emotional intelligence in senior level managers. *Leadership & Organization Development Journal, 23*(2), 68–78.

Gardner, W. L., Fischer, D., & Hunt, J. G. (2009). Emotional labor and leadership: a threat to authenticity? *The Leadership Quarterly, 20*, 466–482.

George, G. M. (1990). Personality, affect, and behavior in groups. *Journal of Applied Psychology, 76*, 299–307.

George, J. M. (2000). Emotions and leadership: the role of emotional intelligence. *Human Relations, 53*, 1027–1055.

George, J. M. & Zhou, J. (2007). Dual tuning in a supportive context: joint contributions of positive mood, negative mood, and supervisory behaviors to employee creativity. *Academy of Management Journal, 50*, 605–622.

Glomb, T. M. & Tews, M. J. (2004). Emotional labor: a conceptualization and scale development. *Journal of Vocational Behavior, 64*, 1–23.

Goleman, D. (1995). *Emotional intelligence: why it can matter more than IQ*. New York: Bantam.

Goleman, D., Boyatzis, R., & McKee, A. (2002). *Primal leadership*. Cambridge, MA: Harvard Business School Press.

Graen, G. B. & Uhl-Bien, M. (1995). Relationship-based approach to leadership: development of leader–member exchange LMX theory of leadership over 25 years: applying a multi-level multi-domain perspective. *The Leadership Quarterly, 6*, 219–247.

Grandey, A. A. (2003). When 'the show must go on': Surface acting and deep acting as determinants of emotional exhaustion and peer-rated service delivery. *Academy of Management Journal, 46*, 86–96.

Groves, K. S. (2005). Linking leader skills, follower attitudes, and contextual variables via an integrated model of charismatic leadership. *Journal of Management, 31*, 255–277.

Hannah, S. T. & Luthans, F. (2008). A cognitive affective processing explanation of positive leadership: toward theoretical understanding of the role of psychological capital. In R. H. Humphrey (ed.), *Affect and emotion: new directions in management theory and research.* Charlotte, NC: Information Age Publishing, pp. 97–136.

Hatfield, E., Cacioppo, J. T., & Rapson, R. L. (1993). Emotional contagion. *Current Directions in Psychological Science, 2*, 96–99.

Hennig-Thurau, T., Groth, M., Paul, M., & Gremler, D. D. (2006). Are all smiles created equal? How emotional contagion and emotional labor affect service relationships. *Journal of Marketing, 70*, 58–73.

Hochschild, A. R. (1983). *The managed heart: commercialization of human feeling.* Berkeley, CA: University of California Press.

House, R. J. & Howell, J. M. (1992). Personality and charismatic leadership. *The Leadership Quarterly, 3*, 81–108.

Humphrey, R. H. (2002). The many faces of emotional leadership. *The Leadership Quarterly, 13*, 493–504.

Humphrey, R. H. (2005). Empathy, emotional expressiveness, and leadership. *Proceedings of the Southern Management Association, 1–6.* Charleston, SC.

Humphrey, R. H. (2006). Leading with emotional labor. Paper presented at the annual meetings of the Academy of Management Conference, Atlanta, GA, August 2006.

Humphrey, R. H. (2008). The right way to lead with emotional labor. In R. H. Humphrey (ed.), *Affect and emotion: new directions in management theory and research.* Charlotte, NC: Information Age Publishing, pp. 1–17.

Humphrey, R. H., Pollack, J. M., & Hawver, T. H. (2008). Leading with emotional labor. *Journal of Managerial Psychology, 23*, 151–168.

Hunt, J. G., Gardner, W. L., & Fischer, D. (2008). Leader emotional displays from near and far: the implications of close versus distant leadership. In R. H. Humphrey (ed.), *Affect and emotion: new directions in management theory and research.* Charlotte, NC: Information Age Publishing, pp. 42–65.

Jones, R. G., Kane, T., Russo, J., & Walmsley, P. (2008). What you see is what you feel: leader emotional labor is in the eye of the beholder. A symposium presentation at The Sixth International Conference on Emotions and Organizational Life (EMONET VI), Fontainbleau, France.

Jones, R. G., Visio, M., Wilberding, K., & King, H. (2008). Leader emotive awareness, emotional labor, burnout and work-family conflict. A symposium presentation at The Sixth International Conference on Emotions and Organizational Life (EMONET VI), Fontainbleau, France.

Jordan, C., Soutar, G., & Kiffin-Petersen, S. (2008). Are there different 'types' of emotional laborers? A symposium presentation at The Sixth International Conference on Emotions and Organizational Life (EMONET VI), Fontainbleau, France.

Jordan, P. J., Ashkanasy, N. M., & Härtel, C. E. J. (2002). Workgroup emotional intelligence: scale development and relationship to team process effectiveness and goal focus. *Human Resource Management Review, 12*, 195–214.

Jordan, P. J., Lawrence, S. A., & Troth, A. C. (2006). The impact of negative mood on team performance. *Journal of Management & Organization, 12*,131–145.

Kellett, J. B., Humphrey, R. H., & Sleeth, R. G. (2002). Empathy and complex task performance: two routes to leadership. *The Leadership Quarterly, 13*, 523–544.

Kellett, J. B., Humphrey, R. H., & Sleeth, R. G. (2006). Empathy and the emergence of task and relations leaders. *The Leadership Quarterly, 17*, 146–162.

Kelly, J. R. & Barsade, S. G. (2001). Mood and emotions in small groups and work teams. *Organizational Behavior and Human Decision Processes, 86*, 99–130.

Law, K. S., Wong, C. S., & Song, L. J. (2004). The construct and criterion validity of emotional intelligence and its potential utility for management studies. *Journal of Applied Psychology, 89*, 483–496.

Lewis, K. M. (2000). When leaders display emotion: how followers respond to negative emotional expression of male and female leaders. *Journal of Organizational Behavior, 21*, 221–234.

Locke, E. A. (2005). Why emotional intelligence is an invalid concept. *Journal of Organizational Behavior, 26*, 425–431.

McColl-Kennedy, J. R. & Anderson, R. D. (2002). Impact of leadership style and emotions on subordinate performance. *The Leadership Quarterly, 13*, 545–559.

Mann, S. (1997). Emotional labour in organizations. *Leadership & Organization Development Journal, 18*, 4–12.

Martin, J., Knopoff, K., & Beckman, C. (1998). An alternative to bureaucratic impersonality and emotional labor: bounded emotionality at The Body Shop. *Administrative Science Quarterly, 43*, 429–469.

Mastenbroek, W. (2000). Organizational behavior as emotion management. In N. M. Ashkanasy, W. Zerbe, & C. E. J. Härtel (eds), *Emotions in the workplace: research, theory, and practice.* Westport, CT: Quorum Books, pp. 19–35.

Mayer, J. & Salovey, P. (1997). What is emotional intelligence? In P. Salovey & D. Sluyter (eds), *Emotional development and emotional intelligence: implications for educators* New York: Basic Books, pp. 3–31.

Mayer, J. D., Salovey, P., & Caruso, D. (2002). *Mayer–Salovey–Caruso Emotional Intelligence Test (MSCEIT): user's manual.* Toronto, ON: Multi-Health Systems.

Mayer, J. D., Salovey, P., Caruso, D., & Sitarenios, G. (2003). Measuring emotional intelligence with the MSCEI V2.0. *Emotion, 3*, 97–105.

Meyer, J. P. & Allen, N. J. (1997). *Commitment in the workplace: theory, research and application.* Thousand Oaks, CA: Sage.

Mikolajczak, M., Tran, V., & Brotheridge, C. M. (2008). From emotional labour to emotion regulation: enlarging the perspective on emotion management in the workplace. A symposium presentation at The Sixth International Conference on Emotions and Organizational Life (EMONET VI), Fontainbleau, France.

Mio, J. S., Riggio, R. E., Levin, S., & Reese, R. (2005). Presidential leadership and charisma: the effects of metaphor. *The Leadership Quarterly, 16*, 287–294.

Mumby, D. K. & Putnam, L. A. (1992). The politics of emotion: a feminist reading of bounded rationality. *Academy of Management Review, 17,* 465–486.

Newcombe, M. J. & Ashkanasy, N. M. (2002). The role of affect and affective congruence in perceptions of leaders: an experimental study. *The Leadership Quarterly, 13,* 601–614.

O'Boyle, E. H., Jr., Humphrey, R. H., Pollack, J. M., Hawwer, T. H., & Story, P. A. (in press). The relation between emotional intelligence and job performance: a meta-analysis. *Journal of Organizational Behavior.*

Offermann, L., Bailey, J. R., Vasilopoulos, N. L., Seal, C., & Sass, M. (2004). The relative contribution of emotional competence and cognitive ability to individual and team performance. *Human Performance, 17,* 219–243.

Pescosolido, A. T. (2002). Emergent leaders as managers of group emotion. *The Leadership Quarterly, 13,* 583–599.

Pirola-Merlo, A., Härtel, C. E. J., Mann, L., & Hirst, G. (2002). How leaders influence the impact of affective events on team climate and performance in R&D teams. *The Leadership Quarterly, 13,* 561–581.

Pugh, S. D. (2001). Service with a smile: emotional contagion in the service encounter. *Academy of Management Journal, 44,* 1018–1027.

Rafaeli, A. & Sutton, R. I. (1987). Expression of emotion as part of the work role. *Academy of Management Review, 12,* 23–37.

Redl, F. (1942). Group emotion and leadership. *Psychiatry: Journal for the Study of Interpersonal Processes, 5,* 573–596.

Rosete, D. & Ciarrochi, J. (2005). Emotional intelligence and its relationship to workplace performance outcomes of leadership effectiveness. *Leadership & Organization Development Journal, 26,* 388–399.

Salovey, P. & Mayer, J. D. (1990). Emotional intelligence. *Imagination, Cognition and Personality, 9*(3), 185–211.

Schein, E. (1992). *Organizational culture and leadership.* San Francisco: Jossey-Bass.

Schutte, N. S., Malouff, J. M., Hall, L. E., Haggerty, D. J., Cooper, J. T., Golden, C. J., & Dornheim, L. (1998). Development and validation of a measure of emotional intelligence. *Personality and Individual Differences, 25,* 167–177.

Shamir, B. & Howell, J. (1999). Organizational and contextual influences on the emergence and effectiveness of charismatic leadership. *The Leadership quarterly, 10,* 257–284.

Sosik, J. J. & Megerian, L. E. (1999). Understanding leader emotional intelligence and performance: the role of self-other agreement on transformational leadership perceptions. *Group and Organization Management, 24,* 367–390.

Stogdill, R. M. (1974). *Handbook of leadership: a survey of the literature.* New York: Free Press.

Sutton, R. I. (1991). Maintaining norms about expressed emotions: the case of bill collectors. *Administrative Science Quarterly, 36,* 245–268.

Sy, T., Côté, S., & Saavedra, R. (2005). The contagious leader: impact of the leader's mood on the mood of group members, group affective tone, and group processes. *Journal of Applied Psychology, 90,* 295–305.

Sy, T., Tram, S., & O'Hara, L. A. (2006). Relation of employee and manager emotional intelligence to job satisfaction and performance. *Journal of Vocational Behavior, 68,* 461–473.

Tse, H, H. M., Dasborough, M. T., & Ashkanasy, N. M. (2008). A multi-level analysis of team climate and interpersonal exchange relationships at work. *The Leadership Quarterly, 19,* 195–211.

Van Dijk, P. A. & Kirk-Brown, A. (2006). Emotional labor and negative job outcomes: an evaluation of the mediating role of emotional dissonance, *Journal of Management & Organization, 12,* 101–115.

Van Rooy, D. & Viswesvaran, C. (2004). Emotional intelligence: a meta-analytic investigation of predictive validity and nomological net. *Journal of Vocational Behavior, 65,* 71–95.

Waldman, D. A. & Yammarino, F. J. (1999). CEO charisma leadership: levels-of-management and levels-of-analysis effects. *Academy of Management Review, 24,* 266–285.

Waples, E. P. & Connelly, S. (2008). Leader emotions and vision implementation: effects of activation potential and valence. In R. H. Humphrey (ed.), *Affect and emotion: new directions in management theory and research.* Charlotte, NC: Information Age Publishing, pp. 66–96.

Watson, D. & Tellegen, A. (1985). Towards a consensual structure of mood. *Psychological Bulletin, 98,* 219–235.

Weiss, H. M. & Brief, A. (2001). Affect at work: a historical perspective. In R. L. Payne, C. L. Cooper (eds), *Emotions at work: theory, research and applications for management.* Chichester, UK: John Wiley and Sons, pp. 133–172.

Weiss, H. M. & Cropanzano, R. (1996). Affective events theory: a theoretical discussion of the structure, causes and consequences of affective experiences at work. *Research in Organizational Behavior, 18,* 1–74.

Weiss, H. M., Nichols, J. P., & Daus, C. S. (1999). An examination of the joint effects of affective experiences and job beliefs on job satisfaction and variations in affective experiences over time. *Organizational Behavior and Human Decision Processes, 78,* 1–24.

Wolff, S. B., Pescosolido, A. T., & Druskat, V. U. (2002). Emotional intelligence as the basis of leadership emergence in self-managing teams. *The Leadership Quarterly, 13,* 505–522.

Wong, C. S. & Law, K. S. (2002). The effects of leader and follower emotional intelligence on performance and attitude: an exploratory study. *The Leadership Quarterly, 13,* 243–274.

Yammarino, F. J. & Atwater, L. E. (1997). Do managers see themselves as others see them? Implications of self-other ratings agreement for human resources management, *Organizational Dynamics, 25,* 35–44.

Yukl, G. (1999). An evaluation of conceptual weaknesses in transformational and charismatic leadership theories. *The Leadership Quarterly, 10,* 285–305.

28

The Shadow Side of Leadership

Manfred Kets de Vries and Katharina Balazs

Insanity: doing the same thing over and over again
and expecting different results.

Albert Einstein

Freud has shown one thing very clearly: that we
only forget our infancy by burying it in the unconscious; and that the problems of this difficult
period find their solution under a disguised form in
adult life.

Herbert Read

Man's task is to become conscious of the contents
that press upward from the unconscious.

Carl Jung

INTRODUCTION

That the organizational man or woman is not just
a conscious, highly focused maximizing machine
of pleasures and pains, but also a person subject to
many (often contradictory) wishes, fantasies, conflicts, defensive behaviors, and anxieties – some
conscious, others beyond consciousness – is not a
popular perspective. Unfortunately, too many
executives believe that behavior in organizations
concerns only conscious, mechanistic, predictable, obvious, easy-to-understand phenomena. The
more elusive processes that take place in organizations are conveniently ignored. However, like it or
not, abnormal behavior – both inside and outside
the organization – is more 'normal' than most
people are prepared to admit. All of us have a

neurotic side, which we do not leave at the door
once we enter our workplace. Even the most successful organizational leaders are prone to highly
irrational behavior, a reality that we ignore at own
peril. Far too many well-intentioned and well-
thought-out plans derail daily in workplaces
around the world because of out-of-awareness
forces that influence behavior. And, given the
plethora of highly destructive actions taken by
business and political leaders (bankers in particularly), it should be clear that many of these incomprehensible activities ('incomprehensible' from a
conventional rational point of view, that is) signal
that what really goes on in organizations takes
place in the intra-psychic and interpersonal world
of the key players, below the surface of day-to-day
behaviors. If we want to understand what leadership really is about, we need to look into that
underlying mental activity and behavior, and
explore its underlying causes: the conflicts, defensive behaviors, tensions, and anxieties that influence human behavior.

Most of the literature on leadership endeavors
to depict the leader as a paragon of virtue and
speaks in glowing terms of the attributes that
constitute leadership. We would like to remind
readers that there's another side to the coin. We
can all name at least a handful of political leaders
tainted by the darker side of leadership. We're far
less likely to recognize leadership's shadow when
it falls on the workplace, even though that shadow
can darken the lives of many. The aim of this
chapter, then, is to provide insights into the darker,
shadow side of leadership. Although it could be
argued that ineffective leadership is a contradiction

in terms – i.e. the only true leadership is effective leadership – many organizational leaders derail. The questions we need to ask ourselves are:

• What makes them do so?
• What can be said about the failure factor in leadership?
• Can we identify specific warning signs?
• What effect is failed leadership likely to have on organizational functioning and decision making?
• What effect will it have on the people who make up the organization and who look to the leader for guidance?

In what follows, we offer some explanations for leadership derailment, address the psychological pressures that often lead to dysfunctional behavior, and discuss the interrelationship between personality, leadership style, and organizational decision making. We also argue that unconscious dynamics have a significant impact on life in organizations and urge organizational leaders to recognize and plan for those dynamics. Therefore, we have to pay attention to the presenting internal and social dynamics, to the intricate playing field between leaders and followers, and to unconscious and invisible psychodynamic processes and structures that influence the behavior of individuals, dyads, and groups in organizations (see Gabriel, Chapter 29, in this volume, for a full discussion of psychoanalytic approaches to leadership).

For that purpose, this chapter provides an understanding of a different way of studying leaders – the clinical paradigm. This is followed by a description of the main psychodynamic concepts relevant to the study of leadership, such as defensive reactions, and the dysfunctional behavioral patterns that leaders tend to fall prey to. Thereafter we discuss the important concept of transference, and elaborate on the major reason for leadership derailment: narcissism. The chapter concludes with further ideas on how to redefine leader–follower relationships.

THE CLINICAL PARADIGM

The basis for this chapter is grounded in the clinical paradigm. This means that we apply concepts from psychoanalysis, psychotherapy, developmental psychology, family systems theory, cognition, and neuropsychology to better understand the behavior of people in organizations (Bowlby, 1969; Emde, 1981; Erikson, 1963; Kagan and Moss, 1983; Lichtenberg, 1991; Lichtenberg and Schonbar, 1992; McDougall,

1985; Mahler et al., 1975; Winnicott, 1975). The clinical paradigm is one way of studying leaders, by giving us a better understanding of human nature. It helps us comprehend why people react in certain ways that seem completely inappropriate for the situation; it makes us more cognizant of things happening around us that we were not conscious of in the first place; and it makes us more aware of the constant interface of past and present. And thus, it explains a good deal of seemingly irrational leadership behavior.

The clinical paradigm is based on the following three premises:

1. All human behavior, no matter how irrational it appears, has a rationale.
2. Human behavior is largely determined by unconscious forces.
3. We are all products of our past.

The meta-force that underpins these three premises is the human unconscious. In order to understand what leadership really is about, we have to be willing to go beyond the directly observable. A considerable part of our motivation and behavior takes place outside conscious awareness. To understand the mechanisms of the clinical paradigm, we need to first understand why what you see isn't necessarily what you get. The world around us is much more complex than it looks to be on the surface. Much of what happens is beyond conscious awareness and we don't have complete control over our perceptual processes. And this is only cognitive distortions we're talking about. If we add in emotional distortions, we have a mix that all but repudiates the phrase 'rational decision making,' giving intuition pride of place (Barron and Eagle, 1992; Westen, 1998).

The problem is that not all of us can deal with these distortions. We're so used to seeing issues as either/or – as polarities – that paradoxical situations confuse us. But paradox is a wonderful instructor: it teaches us to go beyond our customary ways of looking at things, a lesson that pays big dividends in organizational life. The most effective leaders are those who can handle ambiguity: those who can reframe complex situations. By changing how they perceive a problem, they alter what they see.

Why is reframing so important? There are three kinds of leaders in this world: the rule takers, the rule makers, and the rule breakers (Kets de Vries, 2006b). And it's the last group – those who are able to step outside the existing rules, reframing each problem as it comes up – that gets extraordinary results in the workplace. Unfortunately, most of us spend a good deal of our childhood bombarded by the orders 'No!' and 'Don't do that'. By the time we become adults, these kinds of interdictions are internalized, and we are conditioned to think that it is dangerous to think outside the box. We begin to see innovation as transgression and end up spouting the same advice ourselves. Worse yet, we stick to that advice even when we hope to see a difference in outcome. In other words, we try to achieve change without changing anything. It is a good definition of insanity. The challenge of effective leadership is to break out of the box. And a good start is to make unconscious behavior conscious. To that end, let us look more closely at the three premises of the clinical paradigm.

Premise #1: irrationality is grounded in rationality

The first premise of the clinical paradigm is that all human behavior, no matter how irrational it appears, has a rationale. And this rationale needs to be acknowledged and dealt with. Acknowledging this rationale helps us to understand all forms of behavior, even that which appears irrational. If we do not understand a particular behavior pattern in ourselves or others, we can try to determine its origins. If we can gather enough background and contextual information, even the most incomprehensible behavior makes sense. Finding the rationale is rarely easy, however. In corporate life, one has to be something of an organizational detective to tease out what's going on behind this manager's quirky behavior and that manager's insolence. But given a perceptive eye and a healthy dose of perseverance, anyone who is emotionally literate can do the deconstruction. Generally, irrational behavior is connected to transferential reactions – reactions that involve confusion in time and place – a process we describe in more detail later on. Just to give an example, a chief executive officer (CEO) who needs to solve a difficult problem at short notice might hesitate to confront one of his executives about her lack of performance in executing the project because as a child that CEO faced unpleasant consequences whenever he confronted his mother.

Suffice to say, for now, that transferential reactions are a form of unconscious motivation. Indeed, the catalyst of much of our behavior lies beneath consciousness. Most people do not like to hear this observation, because they see bowing to unconscious motivation as a sign of weakness. That reaction is understandable. It is disconcerting to be under the sway of parts of our personality that we're not even aware of. Most of us would prefer to be in complete control over what we're doing. But like it or not, we all have 'blind spots,' and our challenge is to find out what they're all about.

Poets, novelists, and philosophers have written extensively about the importance of unconscious processes. Sigmund Freud, however, was the first to build a systematic psychological theory around the concept of unconsciousness (Freud, 1933). Freud pointed out that unconscious fantasies – images that have emotions attached to them – play a central role in human behavior. According to his theory, conscious motives guide consciously chosen behavior, while unconscious motives guide behavior over the long run. Thus, many of our associations about people and events are developed outside our awareness.

Even aspects of our character – good as well as bad – can exist outside our awareness. Because we are equipped with a defensive structure that controls impulsive thoughts and ideas, we may not recognize our true character. We may not be aware of the fact that something we routinely do rubs people up the wrong way: for example, even if we leave burning heaps of irritation behind. When our blindness in this regard is extreme, psychiatrists say we have a 'character disorder.' One might say that a character disorder is a secret you don't know you're keeping. It's an operation outside consciousness.

The first step toward change is awareness of dysfunctional behavior. That means feedback is essential. But even when people gain insight into their dysfunctional behavior patterns, change can't happen overnight. People are armed with sturdy defenses that, having developed over years or decades, are hard to budge. These defenses are another way in which a person's character is enacted. Defensive reactions vary widely, from the primitive to the sophisticated. Some are quite harmless. The Ottoman Sultan Abdülaziz, for example, had a rather endearing defensive reaction: every morning he reflected his 350-pound bulk in a special mirror that had a slimming effect. Others can be destructive to both self and others.

Most defensive reactions fall into a few basic categories (Vaillant, 1992). In Table 28.1, some of the most common defenses are listed, ranging from the most primitive to the least primitive.

Premise #2: all human behavior is driven by unconscious motivations

As mentioned earlier, Sigmund Freud explored the importance of the human unconscious – that part of our being which, hidden from rational thought, affects and interprets our conscious reality. We are not always aware of what we are doing (even aside from the issue of why we are doing it). Like it or not, certain kinds of behavior originate

Table 28.1 Common defensive reactions

Splitting	Some people engage in us-versus-them thinking. They see people are either for them or against them; there's no middle ground. People are bad or good, the world is black or white, no shades of gray exist
Projection	In projection, people falsely attribute their own unacknowledged feelings, impulses, or thoughts to others. Children often assume that others must feel as they do. And many of us carry that reaction into adulthood
Undoing	In this process, people engage in behavior designed to symbolically ward off negative thoughts, feelings, or desires. Expiatory acts or compulsive ceremonials are the most common expressions of undoing. Lady Macbeth's compulsive hand washing after the murder of King Duncan is a good example
Denial	People who resort to denial fail to accept some aspect of external reality that's obvious to others. Denial is a defense mechanism frequently used by children to ward off feelings of helplessness: they fantasize that they're strong and powerful
Displacement	In displacement, people redirect their feelings toward a person who's less 'dangerous' than the one the aggression is really aimed at. For example, your boss may make a nasty comment that makes you angry. But instead of being angry at her, you kick the dog!
Regression	If current conflict and tension are too stressful, people regress, returning to earlier patterns of behavior that have been previously given up as ineffective or immature
Repression	People who employ repression experience seemingly inexplicable memory lapses. They 'forget' to do things that they have no interest in doing
Reaction formation	In reaction formation, people substitute behavior, thoughts, or feelings that are diametrically opposed to their own unacceptable ones (repeatedly saying, for example, how much they like a boss they despise)
Conversion	Conversion is the process of transforming psychic conflict into somatic symptoms. Some people show signs of physical illness in situations of stress, for example. Sometimes this process results in 'secondary gains,' as when a man with a nagging wife suddenly experiences deafness for which doctors can find no organic cause. (Although it's not pleasant to be deaf, the man no longer has to listen to the complaints of his wife.)
Rationalization	Rationalization involves the elaborate construction of self-serving but incorrect explanations for one's own (and others') behavior
Altruism	Some people address their own problems by giving constructive service to others. For example, a person who was resilient enough to overcome a very troubled childhood may spend all his energy trying to help disadvantaged children
Humor	Humor results in a playful approach to overcoming difficult issues. It can be seen as an overt expression of feelings without unpleasant effects on others

outside consciousness. We all have our blind spots. In addition, we all have a dark side – a side that we don't know (and don't want to know). Freud was not the first person to emphasize the role of the unconscious; many poets and philosophers explored that territory before him. He was the first, however, to build a psychological theory around the concept.

To understand the human being in all its complexity, we have to explore the role of motivational need systems, because they determine the operational code that drives personality. Each of these need systems is operational in every person beginning at infancy and continuing throughout the life cycle, altered by the forces of age, learning, and maturation. The importance that any one of

the need systems has to an individual is determined by three regulating forces: innate and learned response patterns; the role of significant caretakers; and the extent to which the individual attempts to recreate positive emotional states experienced in infancy and childhood. As these forces and need systems interact during maturation, mental schemas emerge that regulate fantasy and influence behavior and action (Emde, 1981; Erikson, 1963; Kagan and Moss, 1983; Lichtenberg, 1991; Lichtenberg and Schonbar, 1992).

Some of these motivational need systems are more basic than others. At the most fundamental is the system that regulates a person's physiological needs – i.e., needs for food, water, elimination, sleep, and breathing. Another system handles an individual's needs for sensual enjoyment and (later) sexual excitement, while still another deals with the need to respond to certain situations through antagonism and withdrawal. Although these primary need systems impact the work situation to some extent, two other, higher-level systems are of particular interest for life in organizations: the attachment/affiliation need system and the exploration/assertion need system.

Let's look at the need for attachment/affiliation first. Among humans there exists an innately unfolding experience of human relatedness (Bowlby, 1969; Mahler, Pine et al., 1975; Spitz, 1965; Winnicott, 1975). Humankind's essential humanness is found in seeking relationships with other people, in being part of something. That need for attachment involves the process of engagement with other human beings, the universal experience of wanting to be close to others. It also involves the pleasure of sharing and affirmation. When the human need for intimate engagement is extrapolated to groups, the desire to enjoy intimacy can be described as a need for affiliation. Both attachment and affiliation serve an emotional balancing role by confirming an individual's self-worth and contributing to his or her sense of self-esteem.

The need for exploration/assertion also has a lot to do with who a person becomes and how that person sees him- or herself. The need for exploration, closely associated with cognition and learning, affects a person's ability to play and to work. This need is manifested soon after birth: infant observation has shown that novelty, as well as the discovery of the effects of certain actions, causes a prolonged state of attentive arousal in infants. Similar reactions to opportunities for exploration continue into adulthood. Closely tied to the need for exploration is the need for self-assertion, the need to be able to choose what one will do. Playful exploration and manipulation of the environment in response to exploratory-assertive motivation produces a sense of effectiveness and competency, of autonomy, initiative, and industry (White, 1959). Because striving, competing, and seeking mastery are fundamental characteristics of the human personality, exercising assertiveness – following our preferences, acting in a determined manner – serves as a form of affirmation.

As noted above, each motivational need system is either strengthened or loses power in reaction to innate and learned response patterns, the developmental impact of caretakers, and the ability to recreate previous emotional states. Through the nature–nurture interface, these highly complex motivational systems eventually determine the unique 'internal theater' of the individual – the stage on which the major themes that define the person are played out. These motivational systems are the rational forces that lie behind behaviors and actions that are perceived to be irrational. The clinical paradigm looks beyond a person's irrational activities and attempts to acknowledge, decipher, and offer tips for mastering these forms of irrationality.

Premise #3: people are products of their past

The third premise of the clinical paradigm has to do with the content of inter- and intrapersonal processes: we are all products of our past. As the saying goes, 'The hand that rocks the cradle rules the world.' All of us are nothing more than a developmental outcome of our early (and later) environment modified by our genetic endowment. And because of the heavy imprinting that takes place at earlier stages of life, we tend to repeat certain behavior patterns. As the Danish philosopher Søren Kierkegaard once said, 'The tragedy of life is that you can only understand it backward but you have to live it forward.' Like it or not, there's a continuity between past and present. Scratch a man or woman and you find a child. As a Japanese proverb goes, 'The soul of a three-year-old stays with a man until he is a hundred.' We can't live in the present without paying attention to the past.

The 'prototype' or 'script' of self, others, and events that each one of us carries within us is put into motion in childhood. These scripts determine how we react across situations (George, 1969; McDougall, 1985). They influence how we act and react in our daily lives, whether at home, at play, or at work. We bring to every experience a style of interacting, now scripted for us that we learned initially in childhood. In other words, how we related to and interacted with parents and other close caregivers during the early years affects how we relate to others – especially authority figures – now in our adulthood.

In the course of these maturation processes, we all develop particular themes in our inner world – themes that reflect the preeminence of certain inner wishes that contribute to our unique personality style. These 'core conflictual relationship themes' (CCRTs) translate into consistent patterns by which we relate to others (Luborsky and Crits-Cristoph, 1998). Put another way, our basic wishes shape our life-scripts, which in turn shape our relationships with others, determining the way we believe others will react to us and the way we react to others. People's lives may be colored by the wish to be loved, for example, or the wish to be understood, or to be noticed, or to be free from conflict, or to be independent, or to help – or even to fail, or to hurt others.

When we go to work, we take these fundamental wishes – our CCRTs – into the context of our workplace relationships. We project our wishes on others and, based on those wishes, rightly or wrongly anticipate how others will react to us; then we react not to their actual reactions but to their perceived reactions. Who among us doesn't know a leader who is the epitome of conflict avoidance, tyrannical behavior, micromanagement, manic behavior, inaccessibility, or game-playing? That dominant style, whatever it may be, derives from the leader's CCRT. So potent is a person's driving theme that a leader's subordinates are often drawn into collusive practices and play along, turning the leader's expectations into self-fulfilling prophecies. Unfortunately, the life-scripts drawn up in childhood on the basis of our CCRTs often become ineffective in adult situations. They create a dizzying merry-go-round that takes affected leaders into a self-destructive cycle of repetition (Kets de Vries, 2009a, 2009b). Thus, people may hold on to scripts that have outlived their effectiveness. For example, avoiding conflict with authority figures (read the father) may have been an effective life strategy at one point in time. Being in a leadership position, however, and not being able to make tough decisions when needed can become extremely detrimental to effective organizational functioning.

Because the key drivers in the unconscious are in our personal, repressed, infantile history, we usually deny or are simply unaware of the impact and importance of the unconscious. It is not pleasant to admit (contrary to our cherished illusion that we are in control of our lives) that we are sometimes prisoners of our own unconscious mind. And yet accepting the presence of the cognitive and affective unconscious – and deciphering its main themes – can be liberating, because it helps us to understand why we do the things we do, make the decisions we do, and attract the responses we do from the environment. Once we become aware of how and why we operate, we are in a much better position to decide whether we want to do what we have always done or pursue a course that is more appropriate for our current life situation and stage of development. It helps us own our own lives.

THE PSYCHODYNAMICS OF LEADERSHIP

Recognizing the role that psychodynamic processes play in organizational life also leads to greater insight concerning the question of leadership (Freud, 1921; Klein et al., 1998; Hirschhorn, 1990). Understanding the complex nature of humankind makes for a more realistic assessment of difficult situations. At its heart, leadership is about human behavior – understanding it, enhancing it. It revolves around the highly complex interplay between leaders and followers, all put into a particular situational context. Leadership is about understanding the way people and organizations behave, about creating and strengthening relationships, about building commitment, about building teams, about establishing a group identity, and about adapting behavior to increase effectiveness. It is also about creating hope. True leaders are 'merchants of hope,' speaking to the collective imagination of their followers, co-opting them to join them in a great adventure. Leaders inspire people to move beyond personal, egoistic motives – to transcend themselves, as it were – and as a result they get the best out of their people. In short, exemplary leadership makes a positive difference, whatever the context (Bass, 1985; Bennis and Nanus, 1985; Burns, 1978; Kets de Vries, 1994; Pfeffer, 1998).

Psychodynamic processes between leader and led are determinative of their respective behavior. What the clinical approach demonstrates more effectively than other conceptual frameworks is that leaders need to recognize that people differ in their motivational patterns. Highly effective leaders are cognizant of the fact that employees are not one-dimensional creatures who park their human nature at the door when they enter the workplace. Good leaders see their followers as complex and paradoxical entities, people who radiate a combination of soaring idealism and gloomy pessimism, stubborn short-sightedness and courageous vision, narrow-minded suspicion and open-handed trust, irrational envy, and unbelievable unselfishness.

Taking the emotional pulse of followers, both individually and as a group, is essential, but that alone does not comprise effective leadership. The essence of leadership is the ability to use identified motivational patterns to influence others – in other words, to get people to voluntarily do things that they would not otherwise do. Generally those things are of a positive nature, but there is nothing inherently moral about leadership: it can be used for bad ends as well as good. History is full of men and women whose leadership was 'effective' despite despicable goals – people such as Joseph Stalin, Adolf Hitler, Pol Pot, Saddam Hussein, and Robert Mugabe. Even well-intentioned leaders are not without a shadow side, unfortunately; if they have a distorted view of reality, they may use their followers to attain narrow, selfish goals that benefit neither the organization nor its rank-and-file employees.

In the following section, we illustrate some common dysfunctional leadership behaviors and their consequences on the organization.

DYSFUNCTIONAL PATTERNS IN LEADERSHIP

Conflict avoidance

Although we tend to think of leaders as assertive, dominant, and unafraid, many have a tendency toward conflict avoidance. There is a large group of executives who have a desperate need to be liked and approved of. The need to be loved is the key theme in their psychological make-up (or character): it echoes in every action they undertake. Afraid to do anything that might threaten acceptance, they are unable (or unwilling) to make difficult decisions or to exercise authority. They become mere empty suits, unwilling to accept the fact – and it is a fact – that boundary setting sometimes takes precedence over conciliation (Kets de Vries, 2009a). Conflict avoidance is neither a successful nor, in the end, a popular leadership style: the leader who always appeases is like someone who feeds crocodiles hoping that they'll eat him last. There is nothing bad about being nice, but there comes a point when every leader has to say, 'My way or the highway.' And while there is no exact formula for success, there is a sure formula for failure: trying to please everyone.

Tyrannizing subordinates

Another pattern that leads to leadership incompetence is the tyrannization of subordinates. This pattern describes the Genghis Khans of the work world – those abrasive (and sometimes sadistically oriented) executives who obviously graduated with honors from the 'Joseph Stalin School of Management.' These are the people who 'like the smell of napalm in the morning.' The tyrannization of subordinates sometimes triggers a response that Anna Freud called the 'identification-with-the-aggressor syndrome.' The only way they are able to deal with the 'aggressor' (that is, the abusive boss) is for some subordinates to assume the leader's attributes and thus transform themselves from threatened to threatening, from helpless victims to powerful actors. This is a defensive maneuver, a way of controlling the severe anxiety caused by the aggressor. The people in the one-down position hope to acquire some of the power that the aggressor possesses.

Unfortunately, all they accomplish is to become aggressors themselves, thus increasing the total organizational aggression (Frankel, 2002, 2004).

Micromanagement

Another cause of leadership derailment is micromanagement. This is seen in executives who are so detail-oriented that they cannot let go of control. Not trusting anyone else to do a job as well as they can do it themselves, micromanagers are unwilling to delegate. This is a common pattern in entrepreneurs who have successfully built up their companies. If these entrepreneurs possess a micromanaging tendency, an extreme example would see them opening all the mail that comes to the company, or having all e-mail forwarded to them. This level of involvement is manageable as long as the company is in the startup phase, but once it becomes a multimillion dollar operation, the entrepreneur's lack of trust in the capabilities of others has a stifling effect on all organizational processes. One of the most difficult transitions for many executives seems to be going from a functional to a more general management orientation (Kets de Vries, 2006b).

Inaccessibility

Inaccessibility of leadership is another common problem (Kets de Vries, 2006a). Some executives are so full of self-importance that they have no time for others. It wouldn't occur to them to lead by example or to walk around the workplace and marketplace listening to their primary constituencies. Lofty and unapproachable, they shield themselves behind a battery of secretaries and assistants and closed-door policies. One executive in a company we visited once said, 'Our president is like the Yeti, occasionally seen in high places.' There can be different reasons for this: such executives are possibly looking for more grandiose people to interact with, or they might be afraid that if people come too close they'll discover a fraud with very little to say.

Folie à deux

Some of the leader–follower collusions can be summarized in the term 'folie à deux,' or shared madness, a form of mental contagion (Kets de Vries, 1979). In such collusions, there is usually a dominant person (the so-called inducer) whose delusions become incorporated and shared by the other, healthier members of the organization. Leaders whose capacity for reality-testing has become impaired shift their delusions and unusual behavior patterns to their subordinates, who in turn often not only take an active part but also enhance and elaborate on these delusions. In order to minimize conflict and disagreement, and to be close to power, followers are willing to sacrifice the truth on the altar of intimacy, maintaining a connection with the leader even though he or she has lost touch with reality. A famous example of this process taken from literature is the relationship between Don Quixote and Sancho Panza in Miguel de Cervantes' masterpiece. Don Quixote, a nobleman, has lost complete touch with reality: he fights windmills that he thinks are his enemies, and he sees virtue and beauty in women whom society has rejected as prostitutes. His squire, originally a reasonable, sane man, ends up sharing the delusions of his master, becoming equally mad.

Collusive relationships, with their induced lack of reality-testing, can have various outcomes – all negative. In extreme cases, a *folie á deux* can lead to the self-destruction of the leader, professionally speaking, and the demise of the organization. Before the ultimate 'fall,' however, organizational participants may recognize that the price for participating in the collusion with the leader has become too high. In that case, the endgame may include a 'palace revolution' whereby the leader is overthrown when the cycle of abusive behavior becomes unbearable. If followers realize that they are next in line to be sacrificed on the insatiable altar of the leader's wrath, they may try to remove the leader in a desperate attempt to break the magic spell.

THE POWER OF TRANSFERENCE

Although management seminars presenting 'new' ways to lead are a dime a dozen, what they teach is often a recycled version of very old concepts. If, instead of pursuing current trends and techniques, we look back at those old concepts, we discover some very useful guidelines. Philosophers such as Plato, Aristotle, and Socrates, for example, had many interesting things to say about organizations and leadership, and their ideas are frequently helpful in explaining why leaders derail. A well-known example is Socrates' words, 'It is hard to learn the mind of any mortal or his heart till he be tried in chief authority. Power shows the man.'

What lies at the heart of the mystery of executive failure is a very old concept – a concept that has governed human relations for all time, although it was not clearly articulated and labeled until the beginning of the twentieth century. The clinical term for this concept is transference (Freud, 1905; Kets de Vries, 2009a). According to Freud and Jung, transference is the alpha and omega of doing work with patients. Most mental health practitioners would agree, we suspect, that it is the most important concept in psychotherapy. It is important out in the 'real world' too. Anyone hoping to make sense of interpersonal encounters at anything but an intuitive level needs to understand transference.

What transference says is that no relationship we have is a new relationship; all relationships are colored by previous relationships. And the relationships that have the most lasting potency, coloring almost every subsequent encounter, are those that we had with our earliest caregivers. Thus, we often act toward people in the present as if they were people from the past: we behave toward them as children do toward their parents, for example, forgetting that we're now adults. In other words, without even being aware of it, we are confused as to person, time, and place. As we relive those earlier, primary relationships again and again, stereotypical behavior patterns emerge. Thus, the behavior of today has its roots in privileged relationships with early caretakers. There are few universals in life, but transference is one: an absolutely ubiquitous element of the human condition, it's the way each one of us processes information and organizes experience. To give an example: people who grew up fighting a father who tended to be rather autocratic have a good probability that when they later meet someone who reminds them of their father, they will fall back into that particular dysfunctional behavior pattern. Without understanding the reason (since transferential reactions happen at an unconscious level), they will find themselves primed for a fight and, when asked, will be unable to explain their own behavior.

So why do those early relationships have such staying power? Because they played such a powerful role in our lives. As an example, send yourself back in time for a moment and imagine that you are riding your tricycle. You are gleefully cruising the neighborhood when suddenly a bully appears and threatens you. A big bully. What do you do? Realizing that with his long legs he'd easily outrun you if you fled, you might hold your ground and say, with all the force you can muster, something like, 'I'm going to tell my father [or mother or older brother or sister]. He or she'll protect me.' This is a normal reaction given your feelings of helplessness; you try to acquire power from those whom you perceive as being powerful. Obviously, the most prominent among these are your caregivers.

This type of reaction is an early step in the process of identifying, idealizing, and internalizing the important people in our lives. That process is a necessary part of each individual's narcissistic development – that is, the development of one's sense of self and self-esteem. Think about very small children and their tendency to imitate their caregivers. At times, parents can almost hear their own voices through their children's mouths. Eventually, these introjections or internalizations become 'metabolized,' we might say, and each child puts his or her unique imprint on them.

Along with that three-part process that culminates in the internalization of people who are important to us, 'mirroring' is an important component of transference. Send yourself back in time again, this time to when you first managed to stay upright on a two-wheeler. 'Look, look at me riding my bicycle!', you exclaim with excitement. And your father or mother most likely says, 'Great, terrific – you're doing a fantastic job.' They don't say (unless you're one of the unfortunate ones), 'Don't do that; you may fall on your face.' Instead, they try to encourage you by 'mirroring' (reflecting back) your excitement, your feeling of mastery. Not surprisingly, a child's first mirror is generally the smiling eyes of the mother. She functions as a source of confirmation of the child's self.

To summarize, then, as we develop a sense of self-esteem – establish a sense of inner security – we internalize people who are important to us and encourage those people to 'mirror' what we're doing, to give us confirmation by acknowledging our capabilities. Although transference reactions can take many forms, these two – the idealizing and the mirroring manifestations – are primary (Kohut, 1971). They go a long way toward making us what (who) we are in the here and now. Many of us are continually trying to recreate comparable situations – a process that is outside our conscious awareness.

In looking at the mirroring and idealizing patterns that we see in the workplace, we need to realize that the first 'organization' we know is the family. How we deal with power and authority in the family very much dictates our later relationships with figures of power and authority. The predominant interaction patterns of childhood cast a long shadow over both our initial process of idealizing and mirroring and our later replications of that process. In other words, in adult life we can readily find replicas of our childhood behavior patterns vis-à-vis authority figures. In particular, idealizing and mirroring transferential configurations can have a devastating effect in an organizational setting when these go unchecked. People in a position of authority have an uncanny ability – without conscious awareness – to reawaken transferential processes in themselves and others and thus wreak havoc in their organizational environment.

A world of liars

Let's look at another example of the after-effects of transferential processes. Say you're in charge of your organization, and you're running a project meeting. After the meeting, several members of the team come to you and compliment you on the great job you did conducting the meeting. That is nice feedback to receive, of course, but you might wonder what lies behind it. Did your employees react out of honesty, truly believing that you did an exceptional job, or were they just trying to please you? If the latter, they may have been deliberately flattering you to gain political points. It's also quite likely, though, that they are responding unconsciously to a transferential reaction. They may be ideal-hungry personalities who have fallen into an idealizing pattern.

But there may be transference on your part as well. If you like to be mirrored by others, positive feedback of this sort feels so good that it can become addictive. Being mirror hungry, you want to be 'fed.' People who get to the point where they can no longer do without a daily 'fix' of admiration may even go so far as to fire individuals who don't praise them adequately. They need this type of daily oxygen. This end of the behavior spectrum suggests a narcissistic personality disorder – an initial narcissistic disposition that has been pushed to the extreme (Kets de Vries and Miller, 1997; Post, 1986).

What does this example tell us? First, it implies that all leaders are surrounded by 'liars.' Senior executives need to recognize that many of the people who report to them are 'lying,' to one degree or another – whether consciously (for political reasons) or unconsciously (as a transferential reaction). In hierarchical situations, people have a tendency to tell those above them what they think the superiors want to hear. People who don't acknowledge this are fooling themselves. Because candor flees authority, senior executives who aren't careful will find themselves eventually surrounded by sycophants. Worst of all, this process by which executives are corrupted by power is so insidious that they don't sense their humanity slipping away (Kets de Vries and Miller, 1997; Post, 1986).The principal actors in this dynamic – the senior executives who are the objects of the fantasies of the people around them, and the subordinates who idealize their leaders – simply don't realize what's happening to them; they can't see how they've been co-opted in the process. Leaders at the extreme end of the narcissism scale see their subordinates as extensions of themselves: they're like the mother who, when hungry herself, says to her child, 'You're hungry, aren't you?' And the child, willing to be hungry if that's the mother's desire, says, 'Yes, I am.' But when was the last time you learned something from people who agreed with you?

THE IMPACT OF NARCISSISM

Having looked at the transference trap, let's take a closer look at the narcissism that underlies it. Whether we refer to an effective or a 'dark' leader, we cannot avoid tackling the subject of narcissism, for it lies at the heart of leadership (Kernberg, 1975; Kets de Vries, 1989; Kets de Vries and Balazs, 2004; Kohut, 1985). A solid dose of narcissism is a prerequisite for anyone who hopes to rise to the top of an organization. Narcissism offers leaders a foundation for conviction about the righteousness of their cause. The narcissistic leader's conviction that his or her group, organization, or country has a special mission inspires loyalty and group identification; the strength (and even inflexibility) of a narcissistic leader's worldview gives followers something to identify with and hold on to. Narcissism is a toxic drug, however. Although it is a key ingredient for success, it does not take much before a leader suffers from an overdose.

A closer look at narcissism confirms for us the linkage between childhood and adult behavior that we already talked about previously in the third premise of the clinical paradigm. When we trace narcissism back to its roots, we find ourselves in a person's infancy. The shaping of an individual's personality begins early in life. We learn from child psychologists that the first three years of life are particularly critical to development. These are the years during which the core patterns of personality are shaped, the years when we emerge as a person with a sense of our own body, gender identity, name, mind, and personal history. The foundations are laid in those early years for the kind of person we're going to be (and are likely to remain for the rest of our life). This doesn't mean that later life experiences are of no importance, of course; it means simply that these tend not to have the same impact as our earlier experiences. There's a greater plasticity early in life that allows us to be shaped by what we see, do, and feel. The clinical term for the changes that take place during these early years of life is 'narcissistic development.'

The process of growing up is necessarily accompanied by a high degree of frustration. During intrauterine existence, human beings are, in effect, on automatic pilot: any needs that exist are taken care of immediately and automatically. This situation changes the moment a baby makes its entry into the world. In dealing with the frustrations of trying to make his or her needs and wants known, and as a way of coping with feelings of helplessness, the infant tries to regain the original impression of the perfection and bliss of intrauterine life by creating both a grandiose, exhibitionistic image of the self and an all-powerful, idealized image of the parents (Kohut, 1971). Over time, and with 'good enough' care, these two configurations are 'tamed' by the forces of reality – especially by parents, siblings, caretakers, and teachers, who modify the infant's exhibitionism and channel the existing grandiose fantasies. How the major caretakers react to the child's struggle to deal with the paradoxical quandary of infancy – i.e., how to resolve the tension between childhood helplessness and the 'grandiose sense of self' found in all children – is paramount to the child's psychological health. The resolution of that tension is what determines a person's feelings of potency versus impotency, a sense of omnipotence versus a sense of helplessness. Inadequate resolution of these quandaries often produces feelings of shame, humiliation, rage, envy, spitefulness, a desire for vengeance, and a hunger for personal power and status. If these feelings are not properly resolved in the various stages of childhood, they can be acted out in highly destructive ways in adulthood.

During these developmental processes, a lot hangs on the 'good enough' parenting mentioned earlier. Narcissism can be classified as either constructive or reactive, with excess narcissistic behavior generally falling in the latter category and healthy narcissism generally falling in the former. Constructive narcissists are those people who were fortunate enough to have caretakers who knew how to provide age-appropriate frustration – i.e., enough frustration to challenge but not so much as to overwhelm. These caretakers were able to provide a supportive environment that led to feelings of basic trust and to a sense of control over one's actions. People exposed to such parenting tend, as adults, to be relatively well balanced; to have a positive sense of self-esteem, a capacity for introspection, and an empathetic outlook; and to radiate a sense of positive vitality.

Although constructive narcissists – narcissists who managed their narcissistic challenges in a satisfying way – are no strangers to the pursuit of greatness, they are not searching for personal power alone. Rather, they have a vision of a better organization or society and want to realize that vision with the help of others. They take advice and consult with others, although they are prepared to make the ultimate decisions. In leadership roles, constructive narcissists often seem larger than life. As transformational leaders, even role models, they inspire others not only to be better at what they do but also to entirely change what they do (Kets de Vries, 2009a).

Reactive narcissistic leaders, on the other hand, were not as fortunate as their constructive peers as children. Children exposed to extremes of dysfunctional parenting – understimulation, overstimulation, or highly inconsistent treatment – are left with a legacy of insecurity (Kohut, 1971; Kohut and Wolf, 1978). When they become adults, they remain deeply troubled by bitterness, anger, depressive thoughts, feelings of emptiness, and a lingering sense of deprivation. As a result, they are left in adulthood with a legacy of feelings of deprivation, insecurity, and inadequacy. As a way of mastering their sense of deprivation, such individuals may develop feelings of entitlement, believing that they deserve special treatment and that rules and regulations apply only to others; as a way of mastering their feelings of inadequacy and insecurity, they may develop an exaggerated sense of self-importance and self-grandiosity and a concomitant need for admiration. Furthermore, having not had many empathic experiences as children, these people typically lack empathy; they are often unable to experience how others feel.

Typically, reactive narcissistic leaders become fixated on issues of power, status, prestige, and superiority. To many of them, life is a zero-sum game: there are winners and losers. They are preoccupied with looking out for number one. They are often driven toward achievement and attainment by the need to get even for perceived slights experienced in childhood. (The so-called 'Monte Cristo complex,' named after the protagonist in Alexandre Dumas's *The Count of Monte Cristo*, refers to feelings of envy, spite, revenge, and/or vindictive triumph over others – in short, the need to get even for real or imagined hurts.) Reactive narcissistic leaders are not prepared to share power. On the contrary, as leaders, they surround themselves with 'yea-sayers.' Unwilling to tolerate disagreement and dealing poorly with criticism, such leaders rarely consult with colleagues, preferring to make all decisions on their own. When they do consult with others, such consultation is little more than ritualistic. They use others as a kind of 'Greek chorus,' expecting followers to agree to whatever they suggest.

Many reactive narcissistic leaders learn little from defeat. When setbacks occur, such leaders don't take any personal responsibility; instead, they scapegoat others in the organization, passing on the blame. Even when things are going well, they can be cruel and verbally abusive to their subordinates, and they are prone to outbursts of rage when things don't go their way. Likewise, perceiving a personal attack even where none is intended, they may erupt when followers rebel against their distorted view of the world. Such 'tantrums,' reenactments of childhood behavior, originate in earlier feelings of helplessness and humiliation. Given the power that such leaders hold, the impact of their behavior on the organizational culture can be devastating. Furthermore, tantrums intimidate followers, who then themselves regress to more childlike behavior.

CONCLUSIONS: RETHINKING LEADER–FOLLOWER RELATIONS

The implications of the dark sides of leadership and 'followership' are clear. Leaders themselves often misperceive situations and statements and act in inappropriate ways. Followers then tend, with good or bad intentions, to compound the problem, furthering the leader's misperceptions and encouraging misguided actions (see Bligh, Chapter 31, in this volume, for a full discussion of follower-centered approaches to leadership). The world is full of Machiavellian followers who deprive their leaders of needed critical feedback for the purpose of self-enhancement. A subset of that group have such an addiction to power that political considerations override all other factors: such followers have no compunctions about setting their leadership up to fail. A follower's shadow side can be just as dark, and have just as devastating an effect, as a leader's shadow side. And there is a contagion to collusion among followers: it seems that the more individuals there are in pursuit of power, the greater the temptation to contaminate the influence process by distorting the leader's perceptions of reality. No leader is immune from taking actions that (even if well-intentioned) can lead to destructive consequences, and no follower is immune from being an active participant in the process.

Given the prevalence of collusive practices, leaders and followers need to work at understanding themselves – shadow side as well as strengths – and being open to all forms of information and feedback. Additionally, leaders need to be sensitive to what followers tell them, listening for subtle messages, both verbal and nonverbal, that may contradict the majority report. Finally, leaders need to help followers become leaders in their own right. The true acid test of a leader is how well his or her successors perform. Leaders need to give followers opportunities to learn, to offer them constructive feedback, to be aware of and accommodate the emotional needs of subordinates, and to harness the creativity of individuals within their organizations. Above all these things, though, leaders need to preserve their own hold on reality; they need to see things as they really are, avoiding the intense pressure, and powerful temptation, from those surrounding them to be locked into a hall of mirrors.

THE FUTURE OF THE CLINICAL PARADIGM IN ORGANIZATIONAL RESEARCH

One of the main critics of the clinical approach is that of the positive psychology and organizational behavior movement. Positive psychology is focused on the study of the conditions and processes that contribute to the optimal functioning of people, groups, and institutions (Gable and Haidt, 2005). In contrast to the clinical paradigm, which looks at the determinant influence of the past on human functioning, positive psychology emphasizes the here and now, and stresses the role played by positive emotions in the fulfillment of human potential (Seligman and Csikszentmihalyi, 2000).

A key criticism expressed by positive psychology is that the clinical approach focuses principally on understanding dysfunctional behavior. Although acknowledging the significant benefits provided by this approach, positive psychologists prefer to stress the insights on psychological health that can be achieved by studying the positive side of human experience.

As with positive psychology, the development of positive organizational scholarship was developed as a counterpoint to organizational psychologists' preoccupation with the pathological in the study of human behavior (Seligman and Pawelski, 2003). Fred Luthans (2002) has taken a step further and developed the concept of positive organizational behavior (POB) as a way of studying and applying human resource strengths and psychological capacities from a more positively oriented angle, and the way these can be measured, developed, and effectively managed to achieve improved performance in the workplace.

Thus, positive organizational behavior is seen as a counterpoint to the more fixed, trait-like personality, attitudinal, and motivational variables stressed by the clinical paradigm (Luthans, 2002).

And while this orientation has an important role to play, with its focus on positive emotions and aspects of human nature, and its strongly developmental approach to the improvement of workplace performance, it does not replace the tenets of the clinical paradigm, stressing the role of past experiences in the development of human character. One way in which the two currents might be reconciled in future research in organizational behavior is to start with the clinical paradigm, by acknowledging the origins and role played by dysfunctional human behavior, and then building on it by exposing how the tenets of positive organizational psychology can help human beings overcome certain dysfunctional behaviors by moving away from the negative and damaged towards the more positive and constructive world of possibilities and reparation of negative past experiences. To quote the poet Rainer Maria Rilke, 'The only journey is the journey within.' After all, to know thyself means that you get acquainted with what you know, and what you can do!

REFERENCES

Barron, J. W. and Eagle, M. N. (eds) (1992). *The interface of psychoanalysis and psychology.* Washington, DC: American Psychological Association.

Bass, B. M. (1985). *Leadership and performance beyond expectations.* New York: Free Press.

Bennis, W. and Nanus, B. (1985). *Leadership.* New York: Harper and Row.

Bowlby, J. (1969). *Attachment and loss.* New York: Basic Books.

Burns, J. M. (1978). *Leadership.* New York: Harper & Row.

Emde, R. N. (1981). Changing models of infancy and the nature of early development: remodelling the foundation. *Journal of the American Psychoanalytical Association*, 29, 179–219.

Erikson, E. H. (1963). *Childhood and society.* New York: W.W. Norton.

Frankel, J. (2002). Exploring Ferenczi's concept of identification with the aggressor: its role in trauma, everyday life, and the therapeutic relationship. *Psychoanalytic Dialogues*, 12(1), 101–139.

Frankel, J. (2004). Identification with the aggressor and the 'normal traumas': clinical implications. *International Forum of Psychoanalysis*, 13(1–2), 78–83.

Freud, A. (1966). *The ego and the mechanisms of defense.* Madison, CT: International Universities Press.

Freud, S. (1905). Fragment of an analysis of a case of hysteria. *The Standard Edition of the Complete Psychological Works of Sigmund Freud*, Vol. 7 (trans. J. Strachey). London: The Hogarth Press and the Institute of Psychoanalysis.

Freud, S. (1921). Group psychology and the analysis of the ego. *The Standard Edition of the Complete Psychological*

Works of Sigmund Freud, Vol. 7 (trans. J. Strachey). London: The Hogarth Press and the Institute of Psychoanalysis.

Freud, S. (1933). New introductory lectures. *The Standard Edition of the Complete Psychological Works of Sigmund Freud*, Vol. 22 (trans. J. Strachey). London: The Hogarth Press and the Institute of Psychoanalysis.

Gable, S. L. and Haidt, I. (2005). What (and why) is positive psychology? *Review of General Psychology*, 9(2), 103–110.

George, A. L. (1969). The 'operational code': a neglected approach to the study of political leadership and decision-making. *International Studies Quarterly*, 13, 190–222.

Hirschhorn, L. (1990). Leaders and followers in a postindustrial age: a psychodynamic view. *Journal of Applied Behavioral Science*, 26(4), 529–542. Special issue: Character and leadership.

Kagan, J. and Moss, H. A. (1983). *Birth to maturity: a study in psychological development.* New Haven, CT: Yale University Press.

Kernberg, O. (1975). *Borderline conditions and pathological narcissism.* New York: Aronson.

Kets de Vries, M. F. R. (1979). Managers can drive their subordinates mad. *Harvard Business Review*, July–August, 125–134.

Kets de Vries, M. F. R. (1989). *Prisoners of leadership.* New York: Wiley.

Kets de Vries, M. F. R. (1994). The leadership mystique. *Academy of Management Executive*, 8(3): 73–92.

Kets de Vries, M. F. R. (2006a).*The leader on the couch.* London: Wiley.

Kets de Vries, M. F. R. (2006b). *The leadership mystique.* Harlow: Pearson.

Kets de Vries, M. F. R. (2009a). *Reflections on leadership and character.* London: Wiley.

Kets de Vries, M. F. R. (2009b). *Reflections on leadership and career development.* London: Wiley.

Kets de Vries, M. F. R. and Balazs, K. (2004). Greed, vanity, and the grandiosity of the CEO character. In B. Gandossy and J. Sonnefeld (eds), *Leadership and governance from the inside Out.* New York: Wiley.

Kets de Vries, M. F. R. and Miller, D. (1997). Narcissism and leadership: an object relations perspective. In R. P. Vecchio (ed.), *Leadership: understanding the dynamics of power and influence in organizations.* Notre Dame, IN: University of Notre Dame Press, pp. 194–214.

Klein, E. B., Gabelnick, F. G., and Herr, P. (eds) (1998). *The psychodynamics of leadership.* Madison, CT: Psychosocial Press, xvi.

Kohut, H. (1971). *The analysis of the self.* New York: International Universities Press.

Kohut, H. (1985). *Self psychology and the humanities.* New York: W.W. Norton.

Kohut, H. and Wolf, E. S. (1978). The disorders of the self and their treatment: an outline. *International Journal of Psychoanalysis*, 59, 413–426.

Lichtenberg, J. D. (1991). *Psychoanalysis and infant research.* New York: Lawrence Erlbaum.

Lichtenberg, J. D. and Schonbar, R. A. (1992). Motivation in psychology and psychoanalysis. In J. W. Barron, M. N. Eagle, and D. L. Wolitzky (eds), *Interface of psychoanalysis and psychology.* Washington, DC: American Psychological Association, pp.11–36.

Luborsky, L. and Crits-Cristoph, P. (1998). *Understanding transference: the core conflictual relationship theme method.* Washington, DC: Amercian Psychological Organization.

Luthans, F. (2002). Positive organisational behaviour: developing and managing psychological strengths. *Academy of Management Executive*, 16(1), 57–72.

McDougall, J. (1985). *Theaters of the mind.* New York: Basic Books.

Mahler, M. S., Pine, F., and Bergman, A. (1975). *The psychological birth of the human infant.* New York: Basic Books.

Pfeffer, J. (1998). *The human equation: building profits by putting people first.* Boston, MA: Harvard Business School Press.

Post, J. M. (1986). Narcissism and the charismatic leader–follower relationship. *Political Psychology*, 7(4), 675–688.

Seligman, M. E. P. and Csikszentmihalyi, M. (2000). Positive psychology: an introduction. *American Psychologist*, 53(1), 5–14.

Seligman, M. E. P. and Pawelski, J. O. (2003). Positive psychology: FAQS. *Psychological Inquiry*, 14(2), 159–169.

Spitz, R. A. (1965). *The first year of life.* New York: International Universities Press.

Vaillant, G. E. (1992). *Ego mechanisms of defense: a guide for clinicians and researchers.* New York: American Psychiatric Publishing.

Westen, D. (1998). The scientific legacy of Sigmund Freud: toward a psychodynamically informed psychological science. *Psychological Bulletin*, 124(3), 333–371.

White, R. (1959). Motivation reconsidered: the concept of competence. *Psychological Review*, 66: 297–333.

Winnicott, D. W. (1975). *Through paediatrics to psycho-analysis.* New York: Basic Books.

29

Psychoanalytic Approaches to Leadership

Yiannis Gabriel

INTRODUCTION

The distinguishing feature of psychoanalytic approaches is the assumption of an unconscious dimension to social and individual life. The unconscious is the mental territory where dangerous and painful ideas and desires are consigned through repression and other defensive mechanisms, and also the source of resistances to specific ideas and emotions which present threats to mental functioning. As the territory from which fantasies spring, the unconscious may also be a source of imagination and creativity, in most spheres, scientific, artistic, economic and political.

Unconscious ideas, desires and emotions may be of a sexual nature but may also be related to ambition, envy, fear (of death, of failure, of rejection, etc.) and so forth. These often reach consciousness in highly distorted or abstruse ways, requiring interpretation. One of the commonest manifestations of the unconscious are fantasies – mental representations which express unconscious wishes and desires as if they were already realized, yet often in a disguised and indirect manner. Fantasies are equally important in understanding the actions of people in and out of organizations: day-dreaming consumers, ambitious leaders, bullied employees, budding entrepreneurs, disaffected voters, and so forth, are as liable to be guided and driven by their fantasies as by rational considerations of ends and means. Relations between leaders and their followers frequently stimulate powerful emotional experiences and are liable to unleash formidable fantasies. It is through

its emphasis on emotions and fantasies that psychoanalysis has made its mark in the study of leadership.

We get a glimpse of the overpowering emotions that leaders can generate in the following account from Tolstoy's *War and Peace*, when young Nikolai Rostov, who, has imagined countless times the moment when he will might meet his Emperor, finally gets his chance on the morrow of a military defeat:

> But as a youth in love trembles and turns faint and dares not utter what he has spent nights in dreaming of, and looks around in terror, seeking aid or a chance of delay and flight, when the longed-for moment arrives and he is alone with her, so Rostov, now that he had attained what he had longed for beyond everything in the world, did not know how to approach the Emperor, and a thousand reasons occurred to him why it would be untimely, improper and impossible to do so. (Tolstoy, 1869/1982, p. 334)

This chapter presents the core psychoanalytic insights into leadership (see also Kets de Vries, Chapter 28, this volume). Following some early formulations by Freud, we explore the differences between leadership and management and examine leadership as the management of meaning and the management of emotions. We look closely at the relations between leaders and their followers, especially the tendency of the latter to idealize and identify with the former. We then examine why the leadership romance, the powerful bond that links leaders and their followers which in so many ways is akin to being in love, goes awry and why leaders lapse into dysfunctional modes such as narcissism and authoritarianism. We conclude by addressing the different ways in which psychoanalysis enhances our understanding of leadership and deepens some of the insights generated by other approaches.

FREUD AND BION

Sigmurd Freud, the founder of psychoanalysis, took leadership very seriously, both in his theoretical work and also in his attempts, sometimes successful and frequently unsuccessful, to steer the movement that he founded away from schism, mysticism, quackery and dilettantism. Freud's leadership 'style' inspired great devotion among his followers, at times approaching deification; it also demanded unquestioned obedience, something that led to the alienation and subsequent departure from the fold of psychoanalysis of some of Freud's most creative and original disciples, including C. G. Jung, Alfred Adler, Otto Rank, Sándor Ferenczi and Karen Horney. Behind all of these painful separations, lay a questioning of Freud's authority, something that inevitably led to bitter disputes between supporters and apostates. Instead of being viewed as scientific differences to be resolved through rational discourse, disagreements in psychoanalysis easily came to be viewed as rebellions against the authority of the father figure of psychoanalysis by his supporters and as questioning of his infallibility by his critics. This is not merely of historical interest. It helps explain the emphasis laid by psychoanalytic approaches to leadership on early life experiences as providing a template on which subsequent relations between leaders and followers unfold. Leaders can easily generate tremendous loyalty and devotion by assuming a parental position in the unconscious life of the followers, feelings that can later turn into resentment and disappointment when leaders fail to live up to the lofty expectations of their followers.

The theme of filial rebellion against an autocratic father is scattered throughout Freud's writings and is explored directly in *Totem and Taboo* (Freud, 1913j). Using a hypothesis proposed by Darwin, Freud speculated that early human groups (primal hordes), like those of other primates, may have been dominated by a single powerful male, the primal father, who kept all females to himself and generated much fear, hostility and envy among other males, including his sons. At some point, this prehistoric band of brothers turned against the father and murdered him.

Overwhelmed by guilt and fear that the death of the father will lead to endless killings, they raised a totem animal, symbolic of the father, and agreed on two prohibitions or taboos – not to kill the totem animal outside ceremonial occasions and not to have sexual relations with members of the same totem clan. Using the idea of the 'totem meal' developed by biblical scholar W. Robertson Smith, Freud suggested that, in commemoration of their deed, the band of brothers established an annual festival, when the totem animal was ritually slaughtered and eaten, a theme echoed in the Christian ceremony of communion.

The murder of the primal father was not offered as a historical account of actual events, but rather as 'a hypothesis, like so many others with which archaeologists endeavour to lighten the darkness of prehistoric times – a "Just-So Story" as it was amusingly called by a not unkind English critic' (Freud, 1921/1985, p. 154). It was a way of accounting for the universal prohibition of incest and for what Freud viewed as the centrality of guilt in religious beliefs and practices. The primal myth also provided a kind of phylogenetic equivalent of the Oedipus complex, mirroring its core repressed phantasies – killing the father and taking the mother for wife. As for leadership, it suggested that feelings of followers for their leader are invariably *ambivalent* – followers may love the leader, craving protection and support, but they also resent and envy the leader.

Freud's theory of group functioning highlights the importance of leaders. For Freud, leaderless groups are highly transient, ephemeral arrangements or led by an invisible symbolic leader. It is leadership that hold groups together, through the position that leaders occupy in the unconscious life of groups. Using the Church and the army as examples, Freud argued that members of each group experience 'an intense emotional tie' (Freud, 1921/1985, p. 123) to their leader (Christ, the Commander-in-Chief) and also to each other. The power of unconscious dynamics in groups is illustrated with the example of panic on the battlefield: when the leader falls, group members forsake the very relatedness that brought them together, as well as the task of battle, lose their minds, and flee in fear.

Freud also proposed that the shared emotional experience of group members comes from a shared *identification* with and *idealization* of the leader. Each group member identifies with the leader; in so doing, each individual identifies with all other group members, who share the same relationship to the leader as themselves. This leads to a definition of 'group' which has at its core the shared unconscious experience of group members:

A primary group... is a number of individuals who have put one and the same object in the place of their ego ideal and have consequently identified themselves with one another in their ego. (Freud, 1921/1985, p. 147)

Groups represent a special type of love bond, one in which the sexual element has been replaced by an emotional attachment: in short one, in which sexual energy (libido) becomes sublimated into social ties. Overt sexual attraction or activity threatens the cohesion of a group, in Freud's view. Thus, individuals in a group sacrifice the prospect of direct sexual gratification, but also their uniqueness and individuality, in return for the stability of love relationships, belongingness and group power. In their relationships to their leaders, individuals sacrifice their independence for protection, order and authority. The Freudian group is dominated by his conception of an omnipotent leader who embodies the qualities of the feared father of the mythical primal horde, whose will is never questioned and whose power is absolute.

Groups represent not merely a state of intensified emotional ties but psychological regression to a child-like dependence, something that may be tempered by organization and focus on a shared task. This is an idea developed by Wilfred Bion, a British psychoanalyst, who dedicated much effort to understanding group dynamics and whose theories have found extensive applications in organizational consultation. Bion's (1961) key contribution is to argue that regressive tendencies of groups are the result of excessive anxieties, which cause groups to lose sight of the tasks they seek to accomplish and tips them into what he termed 'basic assumption' functioning. By this, he meant that groups start to behave as if they held certain shared assumptions about each other, about the leader and about the task they seek to accomplish. These assumptions are products of fantasy, collective delusions that severely distort their sense of proportion and reality. Bion identified three types of basic assumptions – dependency, fight–flight and pairing – each with a characteristic set of behaviours and emotions.

- In basic assumption *dependency* mode, group members act as if the leader, who is seen as a person of extraordinary qualities, will save them without them having to lift a finger. In this state, groups eventually become disappointed with their leader, who cannot possibly live up to the members' exaggerated expectations.
- In basic assumption *fight–flight* mode, groups act as if there is a great danger that must be confronted, either by attacking it or by running away from it. This imaginary danger can be from inside or outside of the group and typically acts

as a scapegoat that obscures other, potentially serious dangers.
- In basic assumption *pairing* mode, groups experience strong feelings of hopefulness, imagining that two members of the group will get together to generate an idea or give birth to a messiah who can solve all the group's problems. The focus of the group turns away from difficult issues of the present to an imagined future in which all such difficulties are overcome.

The importance of Bion's contribution lay in his view that group regression and dysfunction are consequences of leadership failures, and in particular the failure of leadership to contain anxiety and other potentially toxic emotions. In Bion's work we find a conception of the leader whose maternal qualities of caring and emotional sensitivity stand in juxtaposition to the Freudian conception of the leader as a stern father figure. We also have the first clear presentation of the argument that leading involves the management of emotion. Failure to manage anxiety effectively can lead to serious failures. Excessive anxiety leads to panic or fatalism, whereas excessively low anxiety leads to complacency and decay. The containment of anxiety is then seen as an important leadership function by many authors (see, for example, French, 1997; Hirschhorn, 1988; Menzies Lyth, 1988; Obholzer, 1999). The significance of this argument has increased, as mainstream leadership theorizing has come to emphasize the emotional dimensions of leadership, culminating in Goleman's and others' work on the link between leadership and emotional intelligence (see, for example, George, 2000; Goleman, 2001).

ZALEZNIK AND BURNS

A seminal contribution to an understanding of the emotional qualities of leaders was made by psychoanalyst and leadership professor Abraham Zaleznik. In his award-winning essay 'Managers and Leaders: Are They Different?', Abraham Zaleznik (1977) sought to draw a hard line between managers, preoccupied with rationality, order and control, and leaders, who tolerate disorder, are concerned with ideas and strive towards goals in more intuitive ways. A key difference is that managers relate to their followers in impersonal bureaucratic ways, often avoiding direct contact, whereas leaders relate to them in personal and direct ways. Anticipating the importance of empathy as a dimension of emotional intelligence,

Zaleznik saw it as the vital quality of leaders that managers lack:

> Empathy is not simply a matter of paying attention to other people. It is also the capacity to take in emotional signals and make them meaningful in a relationship. People who describe another person as 'deeply affected,' with 'intense desire,' 'crest-fallen,' and as one who can 'vow to himself' would seem to have an inner perceptiveness that they can use in their relationships with others. (Zaleznik, 1977, p. 51)

Since Zaleznik's contribution, many mainstream theorists, including Bennis and Nanus (1985), Kotter (1995) and others, have taken up this view – that managers and leaders are in effect different, that management and leadership are different. In comparing the managers and leaders, four broad areas of difference have been noted:

- Managers and leaders have fundamentally different attitudes towards change and order. Leaders are restless spirits, unwilling to leave well-enough alone, eager to bring about large-scale change and improvement. Managers, on the other hand, are driven by a desire for order and regularity, opting for incremental change and marginal improvements.
- Correspondingly, managers and leaders have fundamentally different attitudes towards waste and efficiency. Managers view efficiency as one of their supreme objectives, reducing waste and always trying to do a thousand things slightly better. Leaders, on the other hand, do not mind disorder and waste, which they often view as a price that must be paid in order to achieve change. Waste can be waste of materials, waste of time and other resources and even the loss of human life.
- Leaders are often driven by a vision of the future which is broad and general. They generally do not enjoy looking at details and making careful plans for all contingencies. They often disregard important details, which can derail the overall project. Managers, by contrast, are keenly aware that details can be important; they seek to eliminate uncertainty by carefully weighing out options and taking care of details.
- Correspondingly, managers are generally smart people, operating logically and valuing rationality above all else. They look carefully at information, costs, benefits and risks before making decisions and view emotion as a disruptive and dangerous force. Leaders, on the other hand, often operate at an emotional level, stirring up emotions in their followers and exciting emotions in themselves. Logic is often eclipsed by intuition, hunches and gut feelings. Instead of careful

consideration of all possible alternatives, leaders often commit themselves to an alternative that contains uncertainties and risks, but also hidden possibilities.

Zaleznik (1989) argued that, since World War II, American business had come to rely increasingly on the 'professional manager' who puts his/her faith in numbers, elaborate formal structures and the handling of people as resources, what he called 'the managerial mystique', at the expense of true leadership. Zaleznik went on to criticize, with numerous examples, this mystique which encouraged business people 'to dedicate themselves to process, structures, roles, and indirect forms of communication and to ignore ideas, people, emotions and direct talk' (Zaleznik, 1989, p. 2). It is in a similar vein, that American political theorist James MacGregor Burns (1978), in his seminal book *Leadership*, developed a highly sophisticated theory of moral leadership as against mere power-wielding and technique:

> By… moral leadership… I mean, first, that leaders and led have a relationship not only of power but of mutual needs, aspirations and values; second, that in responding to leaders, followers have adequate knowledge of alternative leaders and programs and the capacity to choose among those alternatives; and, third, that leaders take responsibility for their commitments….Moral leadership emerges from, and always returns to, the fundamental wants and needs, aspirations, and values of the followers. (Burns, 1978, p. 4)

Burns insisted that leaders (rather than tyrants) enter into a relation with their followers that precludes sham, manipulation and deception. They treat their followers not as objects or as pawns on a chessboard, but as conscious and moral beings. They are deeply aware of their followers' aspirations and needs, and experience a profound sense of responsibility towards them. Without being an explicitly psychoanalytic writer, Burns is deeply aware of the unconscious dimension of the leader–follower relation. His view of the leader was not unlike that of Freud's view of the psycho-analyst – his purpose is to make the followers' unconscious desires conscious, thus turning them into motives for collective action.

> The essential strategy of leadership in mobilizing power is to recognize the arrays of motives and goals in potential followers, to appeal to those motives by words and action, and to strengthen those motives and goals in order to increase the power of leadership, thereby changing the environment within which both followers and leaders act. Conflict – disagreement over goals within an

array of followers, fear of outsiders, competition for scarce resources – immediately invigorates the mobilization of consensus and dissensus. But the fundamental process is a more elusive one; it is, in large part, *to make conscious what lies unconscious among followers....*

If the first task of leadership is to bring to consciousness the followers' sense of their own needs, values, and purposes, the question [facing leaders] remains: consciousness of what? Which of these motives and goals are to be tapped? (Burns, 1978, pp. 40, 41, emphasis in the original)

In this extract, the leader emerges as someone who engages emotionally and spiritually with his/her followers to draw to their conscious mind those unconscious desires that may then fuel collective, purposeful action. The inspiration provided by the leader, the sense of elation and enthusiasm experienced by the followers, far from being the outcome of some innate leader charisma, coincides with the release of emotional energy necessary to keep those desires repressed. A psychoanalytic explication of Burns's account would liken this release to the one that takes place in a condition of falling in love and discovering that love is reciprocated – an analogy already made by Freud (Freud, 1921/1985) and developed by Kohut (1976) and Lindholm (1988).

LEADERS AS MANAGERS OF EMOTION

The theories of Zaleznik and Burns cast leaders as managers of emotion. Far from implying dissimulation and manipulation, management of emotion highlights the interactive nature of the leader–follower relation. In relating to their followers, leaders are liable to form deep emotional bonds. They may evoke powerful emotions, but also *work with* emotions, their own and those of their followers. This involves different aspects of emotional work:

- Leaders read the emotions of their followers and appreciate their consequences. Leaders communicate with their followers in different ways, but effective ones have their finger on the followers' emotional pulse, being able to detect frustration, anger, hope, boredom and other emotions.
- They are then able to intensify some emotions, especially by managing meaning in such ways that emotions become magnified. The word 'insult' will intensify anger, just as the word 'challenge' will intensify commitment.
- Leaders may then be able to channel emotions to particular targets and objectives. Anger is

then not dissipated in different directions and towards different targets, but gets focused on a particular object who becomes 'the enemy'. Hope is focused on a collective task, which assumes the quality of a 'mission', and so forth.
- Leaders may then use the emotion to drive action, motivating and inspiring their followers to do things that may otherwise have appeared futile, excessive, immoral or irrational. It is in this sense that leaders can be said to 'drive' their followers.
- While intensifying and channelling some useful emotions, leaders may also contain or neutralize some potentially dangerous emotions – in some cases, leaders can be said to act as 'toxic sponges', absorbing negative emotions and preventing them from affecting their followers.
- Leaders may also offer safety valves for potentially dangerous emotions and can provide legitimate ways to express such emotions. One such way is through acknowledging them and accepting them, for example acknowledging fear or apprehension; another is by offering stories or jokes (including self-disparaging ones) that defuse dangerous emotions.

The means by which leaders manage emotions revolve around the use of words and visible actions. Leaders may influence emotions by using symbolic language, including stories and metaphors. Christ's use of the parables is an example of stories having powerful emotional effects. Churchill's use of metaphors, such as 'iron curtain' and 'cold war' set the emotional tone of post-World War II politics. The use of emotional language with powerful words, such as 'betrayal', 'war', 'victory', 'rebirth', 'downsizing', 'challenge' and so forth, is capable of stimulating strong emotions, as is the use of less emotive words like 'change', 'modernization' and 'merger' when used in particular contexts. In general, leaders manage emotions by offering explanations and interpretations that resonate with the experiences of their followers.

The psychoanalytic contribution here lies in acknowledging that this 'resonance' is linked to unconscious wishes, desires and fantasies. Thus, a word that at a conscious level may seem innocent or commonplace, when uttered in the right context and at the right time, may unleash great emotional energy. Obama's signature phrase 'Yes we can,' may have been uttered numerous times before by different leaders, but, spoken by a man who had overcome formidable obstacles of racism and poverty to an electorate overwhelmed by the cynicism and disillusionment of the Bush era, it acquired a unique resonance.

It is sometimes said that actions speak louder than words. There is little doubt that the leader's actions are scrutinized by the followers in ways that can have a profound influence on emotions. Who did the leader reward and who did she punish? Who did he smile to? Did he smile at all? Where are the organization's resources going? What important decisions have been taken? Who is the leader meeting? How attentively is she listening? What car is he driving? It will be noted that big and small actions can be invested with strong meanings and evoke strong emotions.

The management of emotions is a dangerous part of the leader's work. It can easily backfire. Words and actions regularly come back to haunt leaders. Once a genie is out of the bottle, it becomes impossible to put it back in. A word or an action that undermines the follower's trust in the leader will be difficult to reverse. What is especially damaging in this context is a visible discrepancy between what leaders say and what they do. This can easily give rise to cynicism and unleash strong negative emotions towards the leader or the organization as a whole.

FOLLOWERSHIP

Considering the huge amount of scholarship dedicated to leaders and leadership, followers and followership seem to be neglected by scholars and most other commentators (Collinson, 2005, 2006; Bligh, Chapter 31, in this volume). In one way, this is to be expected. Understanding leadership has long been seen as a worthwhile quest. It promises to deliver the key for identifying leaders and leadership qualities and the basis of effective leadership training and development programmes. What use is understanding followership? Who would wish to train people to be good followers? This is the rub. Who could hope to be a good leader *without* understanding his/her followers?

As we have noted already, psychoanalytic approaches emphasize the relation between leaders and followers, a relation described by Burns as entailing 'mutual stimulation and elevation' (Burns, 1978, p. 4). Psychoanalytic approaches, however, argue that this relation is also liable to trigger off powerful and at times unrealistic fantasies among followers. Where do followers' fantasies about their leaders originate? Some of them are rooted in their experiences, good and bad, of previous leaders and in particular to the two important figures of authority that dominate most people's early lives, their mother and their father. To the eyes of the helpless and immature child, these figures appear immense and god-like, a 'primal mother' and a 'primal father'. The qualities and characteristics attributed to these figures

through the child's fantasies can form the basis of some subsequent fantasies about leaders. Psychoanalyst Heinz Kohut (1971, 1976) has argued that some leaders are experienced by their followers as reincarnations of the primal mother – caring, giving and loving. Other leaders are experienced as embodiments of the primal father – omnipotent, omniscient but also strict and terrifying. Kohut referred to the former as charismatic and to the latter as messianic. In the presence of charismatic leaders, followers are liable to feel inspired and elated, whereas in the presence of messianic leaders, they are liable to feel submissive and overawed.

The two types of leaders form very different types of relations with their followers. Charismatic are perceived as uniquely kind, smart and talented (Conger, Chapter 7, in this volume). Everything that they do or say appears to be fascinating, inspired and magnificent. They seem to have an aura around them, a field of energy that all those who enter experience as hugely invigorating. In their presence, their followers feel smarter and more talented, inspired and appreciated. Caring is an especially important quality of these leaders, since they are seen as setting great store by each and every one of their followers. Christ, in his capacity as good shepherd, is the archetype of such an all-caring, all-loving leader.

Messianic leaders are very demanding, critical and confrontational (Tourish, Chapter 16, in this volume). They place little store in maintaining a happy atmosphere and are blind to the sensitivities of their followers. And yet, precisely because they can make each person forget their narrow self-interests, they are capable of stirring them into great achievements. Followers of messianic leaders feel meek and sometimes even paralysed in the presence of their leaders. Such leaders inspire fear and awe, making their followers feel worthless and insignificant. Even so, such leaders can generate tremendous commitment, unleashing qualities of dedication, sacrifice and heroism in their followers. Their grip on their followers rests on an unshakeable conviction that, in spite of sacrifices and hardships, they can get them to the promised land and deliver them from their troubles. Leaders may discover that their own actions have limited ability to modify the way their followers imagine them to be by projecting such powerful fantasies onto them. Leadership fantasies surface regularly in the mass media where high-profile leaders in politics, business and sport are easily portrayed as having demonic qualities, good and bad, thereby fuelling powerful public emotions towards such figures. A leader, like British premier Gordon Brown, may initially be cast in the role of a dour but competent leader ('did a great job as Chancellor of the Exchequer'); this may quickly give way to him failing to listen to the electorate and being uncaring, itself replaced by being incompetent and eventually impotent – in short, a lame duck politician, a virtual impostor who was never elected to be Prime Minister.

Kohut's account has received some support from my own study of follower fantasies through the medium of stories that followers tell about their leaders (Gabriel, 1997). A detailed analysis and interpretation of such stories revealed four recurring themes, each casting the leader in a particular role or its opposite:

1. First, the leader as someone who *cares* for his/her subordinates, either offering recognition and support or protection. The reverse of this fantasy is the leader who is indifferent to the plight of his/her subordinates and may even be an axeman, willing to sacrifice them in order to achieve his/her ambition.
2. Secondly, the leader as someone who *is accessible*, who can be seen and heard, even if his/her appearances constitute special occasions. Conversely, the leader as someone who is mysterious and aloof, distant and inscrutable.
3. Thirdly, the leader as someone who is *omnipotent*, unafraid and capable of anything. Omnipotence sometimes extends to omniscience, especially an ability to read the minds of his/her subordinates and recognize true loyalty from flattery and sycophancy. Conversely, the leader as someone externally driven, afraid and fallible.
4. Fourthly, the leader as someone who has a *legitimate claim to power*, conversely, the leader as a impostor, someone who usurped power and whose claims are fraudulent.

These themes are also encountered in numerous religious, mythological and other narratives, most especially when a follower has a chance to meet the leader face to face – when, in the Christian tradition, he/she comes face to face with God. They reflect fundamental fantasies which sometimes coexist in the same story or the same experience of a leader.

Consistent with Kohut's distinction between charismatic and messianic leadership, the first two themes, highlighting caring and accessibility, are qualities that once, in early infancy, are associated with the *mother figure*. She was someone who cared for us and, was available when we wanted her. She loved us fully and with no conditions, since after all we came out of her own body. In our eyes, she was prepared to do anything for us and, above all, she was prepared to love us, no matter what we did. The second two themes are linked with the other important figure of our early childhood, the *father figure*. To our childlike-like eyes, he seemed so big and powerful, so knowledgeable

and strong. We depended on him for protection, but we were also more than a little afraid of him, since we were aware of his ability to punish. His love for us, unlike that of our mother, was much more conditional; he was judgmental and perfectly able to make his dissatisfaction with our behaviour known to us. He was always ready to criticize and discipline. Yet, we accepted his criticism, punishment and discipline, because, after all, he was our rightful father. How much harder would similar treatment be at the hands of an uncle or a stepfather. In our father, we recognized rights that we would not find it easy to accord to others.

Subsequent relations with leaders frequently build on early experiences with people of our narrow family circle. A person who was maltreated by an authoritarian father figure, may later in life seek the protection of such a figure. Conversely, they may envisage a leader to be a punitive and harsh person, even if in reality the leader is not. Although not everyone's parents act in the same manner, and not everyone grows up in a conventional family with a father and a mother, most people have powerful experiences with figures of authority in early life which they later revive in their contacts with leaders.

Instead of looking at the distinction between charismatic and messianic leaders as determined by the attributes of the leaders themselves, we would therefore be inclined to see it as the product of follower fantasies. A leader may be perceived as messianic by some followers, charismatic by others and as a mixture by yet others. He or she may be seen as an impostor, as caring or as aloof by different followers. In the course of rehearsing fantasies through jokes, stories and myths, a few principal leadership fantasies may emerge, expressed in a shared folklore.

What all these follower fantasies highlight is the key psychoanalytic insight that 'present relations are structured by and resemble past ones, most notably, those from early childhood with mother and father' (Oglensky, 1995, p. 1036). Psychoanalytic approaches suggest that it is very difficult to relate to leaders in ways which are unaffected by our early relations with mother and father; these early relations provide a core of primal political experiences which will forever colour our subsequent relations with authority, no matter how much these are couched in terms of legality and rationality. Different individuals will relate to authority in different ways, develop distinct fantasies and spin different stories about their leaders. As Oglensky points out, 'The role of the subordinate does actually depend upon his or her unique biography of attachment to parents as prototypes of authority' (Oglensky, 1995, p. 1051), each biography unfolding around a specific 'authority template'. For some individuals, the legitimate–impostor axis may dominate their political fantasy life; for others, the caring–persecuting axis may predominate. In relating to their leaders, however, followers cannot escape from their past.

DYSFUNCTIONAL LEADERS

Nor can leaders escape from *their* own past – this is something that often prompts dysfunctional or toxic types of leadership that bring misfortune on leaders and followers alike. Leadership dysfunctions have been extensively discussed by both psychoanalytic (Gabriel, 1999; Hirschhorn, 1997; Kets de Vries, 1988; Kets de Vries & Miller, 1984; Levinson, 1968/1981; Maccoby, 1976; Obholzer, 1999; Sievers, 1994) and non-psychoanalytic writers (see, for example, Alvesson & Sveningsson, 2003; Bennis, 1989; Calas & Smircich, 1991; Ciulla, 1998/2004; Grint, 2000, 2005; Heifetz, 1994; Lipman-Blumen, 2005; Pfeffer, 1977). What is unique about psychoanalytic contributions is that, beyond the usual factors that may lead to dysfunctional leadership, like political corruption, failing institutions and so forth, they link such dysfunctions to the psychopathology of leaders and, in particular, unconscious forces that may suddenly find disruptive and irrational expressions.

In an influential book, Manfred Kets de Vries and Danny Miller (1984) argued that many organizational failures are the result of the chief executives' psychopathologies. Indeed, they argue, organizations can become *neurotic,* just as individuals can. What is more, organizational neuroses reflect the neuroses of the leader, and these fall into distinct patterns.

> Our experience with top executives and their organizations revealed that parallels could be drawn between individual pathology – excessive use of neurotic style – and organizational pathology, the latter resulting in poorly functioning organizations. In dysfunctional, centralized firms, the rigid neurotic styles of the top executives were strongly mirrored in the nature of the inappropriate strategies, structures, and organizational cultures of their firms. (Kets de Vries & Miller, 1984, p. 17)

Kets de Vries and Miller offer some evidence to support their argument. What is interesting is that often the same qualities that bring success to a leader and an organization end up by becoming counterproductive. The point when normality crosses into neurosis is when optimism becomes recklessness, when resolve becomes pig-headedness, when courage becomes bravado, when caution becomes paralysis, or when firmness becomes cruelty. As long as leaders can keep a check on their neurotic tendencies, they may mobilize them in pursuit of organizational visions and goals. But once they lapse into neurotic behaviour, their effect on their organization is negative and dramatically so. Many earlier victories and accomplishments are thus compromised and ruined.

AUTHORITARIANISM AND NARCISSISM

Two of the most widely discussed types of leader pathologies are authoritarianism and narcissism. In a curious way, these two pathologies are almost the mirror image of each other. Authoritarianism involves excessive emphasis on brute force and adherence to orders and regulations; it celebrates firmness and steadfastness and abhors fanciful ideas and initiatives. It usually leads to inflexible, fear-ridden organizations that are unable to compete in markets or environments where creativity, flexibility, imagination and flair are called for. Narcissism, on the other hand, involves excessive preoccupation with glamour, image and display. It celebrates creativity, beauty, freedom and spontaneity. It easily loses track of the difference between fantasy and reality and is liable to lead to dramatic and sudden failures, when the organization discovers to its cost that there was a gulf between its grandiose aspirations and what it actually was able to deliver.

Authoritarianism

Authoritarianism is a well-established set of personality characteristics and the cause of numerous personality disorders. It is a type of leadership much in evidence in military dictatorships, military and police academies, prisons, boarding schools and other institutions that traditionally have been founded on the basis of a cast-iron obedience to authority and a suppression of the individual characteristics and needs. The study of authoritarianism originates in Freud's discussion of the anal obsessive character (Freud, 1905/1977), the character fixated in the anal stage of development, whose main features are stubbornness, orderliness, parsimony and control. Authoritarianism was the subject of the famous Berkeley study (Adorno, Frenkel-Brunswik, Levinson, & Sanford, 1950), following

World War II, when the question was asked how 'ordinary' people could have participated willingly in the Nazi atrocities. Adorno and his colleagues came up with a profile of an authoritarian character, a personality type, that formed the backbone of the Nazi regime, but was also much in evidence in most countries and cultures. The key quality of this character is that as a follower, he/she is obedient and quiescent, as a leader, he/she demands unquestioned loyalty and obedience.

Authoritarian people are generally people who have not enjoyed much parental love in their childhood. Many had to fend for themselves and identified with images of powerful individuals, able to command, punish and humiliate others. As a result, they are people who in their adult lives tend to revere power and denigrate love; love is seen as a sign of weakness, a vulnerability. Allied to their exaggerated veneration of power, authoritarian personalities display the following characteristics:

- a mechanical surrender to conventional values – they dismiss unorthodox views and living styles;
- a tendency to divide people into insiders and outsiders – the latter are viewed with suspicion and hostility;
- anti-introspectiveness – they do not like dreaming and dreamers, poets and psychologists;
- rigid stereotyped thinking – they generalize about classes of people or situations, being unable to see nuance and variation;
- superstition – they believe in superior powers deciding their destiny, especially when things start to go wrong;
- vilification, half-moralistic and half-cynical, of human nature – they view the average human being as devious, lazy, dishonest and disobedient;
- projectivity – they project everything unpleasant about themselves onto others.

It is clear that authoritarian personalities reject and hate what they regard as effeminate, soft, unsuccessful and weak. They identify with what is strong and masculine. This is what draws them to institutions like the military, where these values have for a long time been held in high regard.

Unfortunately, however, authoritarians do not generally make very good military leaders. According to a fascinating study by Norman Dixon, *On the Psychology of Military Incompetence* (1976), authoritarian leaders are responsible for some of the biggest military disasters. It is relatively easy to see why. They do not want to show any sign of weakness. They therefore are unwilling to change their mind (make a 'u-turn'), even when it is very clear that the chosen course of action is disastrous. This accounts, according to Dixon, for some of the most disastrous military

campaigns. It may also explain why Margaret Thatcher's legendary 'The lady is not for turning' caused her downfall over her inability to rethink the disastrous poll tax initiative.

Authoritarians compound their self-destructive stubbornness with various other mistakes – they underestimate, stereotype and dismiss their enemies; they feel no compassion about the sufferings of their subordinates; they denounce and punish anyone who dares propose an alternative course of action ('defeatists and naysayers'); and they dismiss cunning, technique and smartness in favour of courage ('sheer guts') to see them through to success. In business, authoritarian personalities can be as disastrous as in politics and the military – for nearly the same reasons. This is especially so in times like ours, when flair, flexibility, communication, empathy and imagination are vital for success.

Of course, there are some authoritarian leaders who have been successful, at least for a certain period of time. Few will question Hitler's successes in regenerating German industry (especially armaments), in restoring morale or, indeed, in conquering France. In particular, authoritarian leaders seem to rise and come into their own in moments of crisis, when there is a call for a 'strong man', when individuals appear willing to subordinate their individual interests to the general one. In business too, authoritarian leaders can be successful – for a time. Henry Ford and Henry Ford II are good cases in point. Both enjoyed tremendous business success, until they met their nemesis in opponents whom they underestimated and dismissed. They both fell in love with a single winning idea and were willing to change their approach when times changed. (For a good discussion of Ford, see Grint, 2000; for an account of Henry Ford II as authoritarian, see Iacocca, 1984.)

Narcissistic leaders

Authoritarian leaders are not as common today as they once were. Certainly, they are less likely to be found leading in cutting-edge businesses such as entertainment, media, telecommunications, information, leisure, fashion, design and the arts sectors. They lack the imagination, flair and emotional sensitivity ('emotional intelligence') necessary for success in these sectors. They are too earthbound and too rulebound. They cannot make others feel good; they cannot communicate a dream. This is an environment in which narcissistic individuals can prosper.

Narcissism is a term coined by Freud (1914/1984) to describe a person's self-love; narcissism can be a healthy and normal psychological phenomenon that enables most of us to feel worthy and important as human beings, able to attract the respect of others and of ourselves. Narcissism is the love that we feel towards ourselves, or, more accurately, towards an image of ourselves we seek to attain. This is why narcissism can drive us towards achievement and success. A champion athlete, an artist, an entrepreneur or a creative writer can be driven by their narcissism to great accomplishments. Few things are as good for our narcissism as the acclaim of an enthusiastic audience.

But excessive narcissism can also cause our downfall. This is the narcissism which focuses not on achievement but on celebrity and image for their own sake. It is the narcissism that says, 'Admire me for who I am', rather than, 'Admire me for my achievements'. Achievement narcissism can easily degenerate into image narcissism when individuals, leaders or organizations decide to rest on their laurels, seeking acclaim for their past achievements and disregarding their present failings (Gabriel, 1999).

If authoritarian personalities usually grow up in families with strict discipline and limited love, excessively narcissistic people grow up in families with a lot of love and admiration and limited discipline. They are likely to be only children or particularly pampered children. In their childhood they enjoy the unqualified worship of the only audience that counted, their parents. They grow up believing that they are special, unique and the centre of an adoring universe. They preserve many childlike qualities later in life – spontaneity, imagination, playfulness, moodiness and love of freedom. They continue to love performing in front of adoring audiences. Acclaim is their opiate; criticism throws them into tantrums, self-questioning and despair.

If narcissistic leaders are so uniquely attuned to the needs of today's organizations, why is narcissism seen as a potential organizational pathology? What are the risks of narcissistic leaders and organizations seeped in narcissism? The short answer is very simple. Narcissism of achievement easily degenerates into narcissism of pure image. Leaders become ever more concerned with public relations, celebrations and ceremonies, opulent buildings and grandiose undertakings, losing track of the organizational 'nuts and bolts', the machinery necessary to ensure the smooth running of an organization. They become more and more preoccupied with preserving the image at all costs, cutting corners in order to maintain the organization's profile. Gradually, they lose touch with reality altogether – their vision becomes a reality, whether it has been realized or not (Maccoby, 2000; Schwartz, 1990).

This is the point where an organization suddenly collapses, leaving stakeholders wondering how they had suspected nothing about its rotting state. Organizations can recover from narcissistic leaders, but the cost of recovery is usually enormous, in broken lives and broken dreams, recrimination, scapegoating, and subsequent need for discipline and rigor. Such organizations are often rife for a take-over by an authoritarian leader, who promises to restore order, proper procedures, accountability and discipline to the organization.

Leadership dysfunctions often command attention following great disasters, military, political and economic. It is then tempting to interpret such failures as being the outcome of the leader's Achilles' heel – the soft spot in his/her personality (including authoritarianism and narcissism), disregarding social and political factors that may have been instrumental in bringing about such an outcome. Psychoanalysis is sometimes accused of reducing complex socio-political phenomena to emotional family dramas, dominated by the flawed personalities of their protagonists. There can be some truth in this charge which, of course applies not to psychoanalysis alone. It is always tempting to attribute success and failure to the outstanding personalities of leaders, something that Meindl and his colleagues (Meindl & Ehrlich, 1987; Meindl, Ehrlich, & Dukerich, 1985) rightly describe as 'the leadership romance'. Psychoanalysis suggests that the personalities of leaders, including the dormant unconscious heritage from their past, can be significant factors accounting for successes and failures. As we noted earlier, it is important to recognize that qualities accounting for success in one set of circumstances may become counter-productive when the times change.

CONCLUSIONS

In this chapter we have examined some of the psychoanalytic themes in the study of leaders and leadership relations. We have noted, in line with Freud, that leadership involves a powerful relation between leaders and followers, one based on identification of followers with the leader and his/her idealization. Following Bion's analysis of group dynamics, we emphasized that leaders fulfil vital emotional functions for their followers, paramount among which is the containment of anxiety and other toxic emotions. Both Freud and Bion emphasize the tendency of leaders to awaken in their followers fantasies and desires first experienced in childhood, in those early relations with parents, which act as templates for our subsequent encounters with authority and power. This view was elaborated by Kohut's theory of messianic and charismatic leaders, based on the primal father and primal mother, respectively.

Following the work of Zaleznik and Burns, we have also seen how leaders can inspire their followers through compelling visions which span the present and the future, by drawing on powerful unconscious wishes and desires. In this way, a leader's dream can shift existing boundaries of what is possible and what is achievable, making conscious what has been unconscious, and thus releasing great amounts of emotional energy in the process. The management of this emotional energy is itself a key function of leadership – taming it, directing it, focusing it and containing it.

Leaders themselves are moved by fantasies of changing the world, having to tame their own delusions of grandeur, omnipotence and infallibility and stopping themselves from lapsing into dysfunctional modes, like narcissism and authoritarianism. Leaders must have a healthy narcissism, relishing the fame and glory which comes with success. This, however, makes them vulnerable to narcissistic disorders, where approval and admiration is all they crave for – in the interest of which, they are capable of distorting reality, disregarding obstacles and indulging in wishful thinking. Likewise, leaders must be able to maintain discipline and focus without crushing the creativity and drive of their followers, themselves lapsing into authoritarianism.

In concluding, we may offer a tentative definition of leading as constructed from a psychoanalytic perspective. 'Leading is imagining, willing, inspiring and driving'. This is a definition that emphasizes leaders as agents for change engaged in relations with others. In the first instance, leading is *imagining*. Without imagination, no leadership. And imagination means being able to envisage new possibilities, new products, new ideas, new methods, new alliances, new ways of using words and language and even new needs and desires. Leaders then are dreamers, drawing on their unconscious wishes to conjure up what to others may seem unrealistic, impossible or absurd possibilities. But leaders are not just dreamers. Many people have powers of imagination – creative artists and scientists, for example. While dreaming is an essential part of leading, it is not enough. In order to lead, a man or a woman must also have a strong will, a burning desire to see the dream become reality and the vision become fact. Willing means that the dream is not an 'idle' fantasy but becomes a strong motivator towards action. Imagining and willing together are essential for leadership. But again, they are not enough. An aspiring athlete may have a vision of himself climbing onto the podium at the Olympic Games to receive a gold medal; he may have the drive to train and practice with dedication to get there. But he is not a leader if he does not engage with others, if his vision does not become a shared vision, if it does not *inspire* and *drive* others. A leader will drive others by emotionally engaging with them, being able to communicate, elaborate and share a vision, inspiring them and winning them over, but also occasionally by cajoling and exhorting them. Engaging with others is a feature of all aspects of leading, including imagining. Leaders do not just sit and dream, waiting for a vision to arrive. Still less do visions arise from vision statements carefully prepared by hired consultants. Instead, visions emerge from active engagement with others, understanding of collective aspirations and wishes and flights of imagination that push the bounds of possibility.

It will be noted that the definition offered above is one that runs against the current tendency to emphasize dispersed, diffused leadership. Psychoanalytic approaches acknowledge the relational aspect of leadership, but in the last resort insist on the asymmetrical relation between followers and leaders, a relation that can never escape from the template of someone being set apart from the others, someone taking charge and responsibility for others, and someone who, ultimately, through words and actions, is capable of providing the basis on which the others identify with each other as followers.

REFERENCES

Adorno, T. W., Frenkel-Brunswi, E., Levinson, D., & Sanford, N. (1950) *The authoritarian personality*. New York: Harper & Row.

Alvesson, Mats & Sveningsson, S. (2003) Good visions, bad micro-management and ugly ambiguity: contradictions of (non-)leadership in a knowledge-intensive organization. *Organization Studies*, 24(6): 961–988.

Bennis, Warren G. (1989) *Why leaders can't lead. The unconscious conspiracy continues*. San Francisco: Jossey-Bass.

Bennis, Warren G. & Nanus, Burt (1985) *Leaders: The strategies for taking charge*. New York: Harper & Row.

Bion, Wilfred R. (1961) *Experiences in groups*. London: Tavistock.

Burns, James McGregor (1978) *Leadership*. New York: Harper & Row.

Calas, Marta B. & Smircich, Linda (1991) Voicing seduction to silence leadership. *Organization Studies*, 12(4): 567–602.

Ciulla, Joanne (ed.) (1998/2004) *Ethics, the heart of leadership*. Westport, CT: Praeger.

Collinson, David (2005) Dialectics of leadership. *Human Relations*, 58(11): 1419–1442.

Collinson, David (2006) Rethinking followership: a post-structuralist analysis of follower identities. *The Leadership Quarterly*, 17(2): 179–189.

Dixon, Norman (1976) *On the psychology of military incompetence.* Harmondsworth: Penguin.

French, Robert (1997) The teacher as container of anxiety: psychoanalysis and the role of the teacher. *Journal of Management Education*, 21(4): 483–495.

Freud, Sigmund (1905/1977) Three essays on the theory of sexuality, *On Sexuality*, Vol. 7. Harmondsworth: Pelican Freud Library, pp. 33–169.

Freud, Sigmund (1913j) *Totem and taboo* (Standard edn). London: Hogarth Press.

Freud, Sigmund (1914/1984) On narcissism: an introduction. *On Metapsychology: the theory of psychoanalysis*, Vol. 11. Harmondsworth: Pelican Freud Library, pp. 59–97.

Freud, Sigmund (1921/1985) Group psychology and the analysis of the ego. *Civilization, society and religion*, Vol. 12. Harmondsworth: Pelican Freud Library, pp. 91–178.

Gabriel, Yiannis (1997) Meeting God: when organizational members come face to face with the supreme leader. *Human Relations*, 50(4): 315–342.

Gabriel, Yiannis (1999) *Organizations in depth: the psychoanalysis of organizations.* London: Sage.

George, Jennifer M (2000) Emotions and leadership: the role of emotional intelligence. *Human Relations*, 53(8): 1027–1055.

Goleman, Daniel (2001) What makes a leader? In J. Henry (ed.), *Creative management*. London: Sage, pp. 125–139.

Grint, Keith (2000) *The arts of leadership*. Oxford: Oxford University Press.

Grint, Keith (2005) *Leadership: limits and possibilities.* Basingstoke: Palgrave Macmillan.

Heifetz, Ronald A (1994) *Leadership without easy answers.* Cambridge, MA: Harvard University Press.

Hirschhorn, Larry (1988) *The workplace within.* Cambridge, MA: MIT Press.

Hirschhorn, Larry (1997) *Reworking authority: leading and following in the post-modern organization.* Cambridge, MA: MIT Press.

Iacocca, L (1984) *An autobiography*. New York: Bantam.

Kets de Vries, M. F. R. (1988) Prisoners of leadership. *Human Relations*, 41: 261–280.

Kets de Vries, M. F. R. & Miller, Danny. (1984) *The neurotic organization.* San Francisco: Jossey-Bass.

Kohut, Heinz (1971) *The analysis of the self.* New York: International Universities Press.

Kohut, Heinz (1976) Creativity, charisma and group psychology. In J. E. Gedo & G. H. Pollock (eds), *Freud: the fusion of science and humanism*. New York: International Universities Press.

Kotter, J. P. (1995) Leading change: why transformation efforts fail. *Harvard Business Review*, 73(March–April): 59–67.

Levinson, Harry (1968/1981) *Executive.* Cambridge, MA: Harvard University Press.

Lindholm, Charles (1988) Lovers and leaders: a comparison of social and psychological models of romance and charisma. *Social Science Information*, 27(1): 3–45.

Lipman-Blumen, Jean (2005) *The allure of toxic leaders: why we follow destructive bosses and corrupt politicians – and how we can survive them.* New York: Oxford University Press.

Maccoby, Michael (1976) *The gamesman: new corporate leaders.* New York: Simon and Shuster.

Maccoby, Michael (2000) Narcissistic leaders: the incredible pros, the inevitable cons. *Harvard Business Review*, 78(1): 69–77.

Meindl, James R. & Ehrlich, Sanford B. (1987) The romance of leadership and the evaluation of organizational performance. *Academy of Management Journal*, 30(1): 91–109.

Meindl, James R., Ehrlich, Sanford B., & Dukerich, Janet, M. (1985) The romance of leadership. *Administrative Science Quarterly*, 30(1): 78–108.

Menzies Lyth, Isabel (1988) *Containing anxiety in institutions: selected essays.* London: Free Association Books.

Obholzer, Anton (1999) Managing the unconscious at work. In R. French, & R. Vince (eds), *Group relations, management, and organization.* Oxford: Oxford University Press, pp. 87–97.

Oglensky, Bonnie D. (1995) Socio-psychoanalytic perspectives on the subordinate. *Human Relations*, 48(9): 1029–1054.

Pfeffer, Jeffrey (1977) The ambiguity of leadership. *American Management Review*, 2(1): 104–112.

Schwartz, Howard S. (1990) *Narcissistic process and corporate decay.* New York: New York University Press.

Sievers, Burkard (1994) *Work, death and life itself.* Berlin: Walter de Gruyter.

Tolstoy, Leo (1869/1982) *War and peace* (R. Edmonds, trans.). Harmondsworth: Penguin.

Zaleznik, Abraham (1977) Managers and leaders: are they different? *Harvard Business Review*, 55(May–June): 47–60.

Zaleznik, Abraham (1989) *The managerial mystique: restoring leadership in business.* New York: Harper & Row.

30

Creativity, Innovation, and Leadership: Models and Findings

Michael D. Mumford, Issac C. Robledo, and
Kimberly S. Hester

INTRODUCTION

Globalization, increased competitive pressure, rapid changes in technology, and demanding customers have conspired to place a host of new demands on organizations – both for-profit and non-profit organizations (Mumford & Licuanan, 2004). One critical outcome of these forces is that they have placed a new premium on innovation as a vehicle underlying the survival and growth of organizations (Amabile, Schatzel, Moneta, & Kramer, 2004). Innovation, of course, comes in many forms – new products (the iPhone), new services (Starbucks), and new processes (information systems). Underlying any innovative effort, however, is creativity or the production of viable new problem solutions (Mumford & Gustafson, 1988; Shalley & Zhou, 2008). The importance of creativity and innovation to organizational performance has led to a number of questions:

- How should organizations structure themselves to promote creativity and innovation (Damanpour, 1991)?
- When should organizations invest in innovation (Sharma, 1999)?
- And, how should one attempt to lead creative efforts (Mumford, Scott, Gaddis, & Strange, 2002)?

It is this last question, a question about the leadership of creative efforts, that we address in this present effort. In fact, the very nature of this question is of some significance. Traditionally, the common answer to this question was really not to lead – get out of the way and let the creative 'people' do their work. The evidence accrued in half a century of research, however, indicates this answer is, quite simply, incorrect.

The available data indicates that leadership is important to creative and innovative efforts – perhaps more important than in other domains where we commonly see leadership as critical (Mumford et al., 2002). For example, Pelz (1963) examined 21 research teams containing 94 scientists working in the National Institutes of Health. Assessments of the creativity of the scientists work, along with peer appraisals of innovation, productivity, and usefulness, were obtained and correlated with the measures of leader behavior at the group level. It was found that measures of leader behavior (e.g., perceptions of leader technical skills, goal setting, motivation, and planning) produced correlations in the 0.30–0.50 range. In another study along these lines, Barnowe (1975) obtained measures of publication rate and administrative appraisals of the importance of research projects for 963 chemists working in 81 research and development teams. Followers evaluated team leaders with respect to support, task emphasis, closeness of supervision, and technical skill. It was found that these appraisals of leaders produced correlations in the 0.40 range with indices of group creative production. In still another study of chemists, Tierney, Farmer, and Graen (1999) obtained measures of leader–member exchange. They found this measure of positive exchange relationships produced correlations in the 0.30–0.40 range with measures of creative achievement among followers.

Clearly, leadership makes a difference, a big difference, with regard to one form of creative work – research and development. However, the impact of leadership on creative work does not appear to be field specific. For example, Carmeli and Schaubroeck (2007), in a study of 155 employees in two service industry firms, obtained a correlation of 0.61 between a measure of leader's expectations for creativity and followers involvement in creative work. In another study along these lines, Murphy and Ensher (2008) conducted a qualitative study of television directors. They found that charismatic leadership and sensitivity to followers' needs were critical to the success of these creative efforts.

When these findings are considered in light of the findings obtained in other studies by Amabile et al. (2004), Keller (2006), Krause (2004), Oldham and Cummings (1996), Shin and Zhou (2003), Kahai, Sosik, and Avolio (2003), and West, Hirst, Richter, and Shipton (2004), it seems clear that leadership is critical to the initiation and success of creative work and, thus, the potential for innovation. Recognition of the powerful impact of leadership on creativity has, over the years, led to the proposal of a number of theoretical models that might account for the impact of leaders (Shalley & Gilson, 2004).

In the present chapter we review the seven major theoretical approaches that have been advanced to account for the impact of leadership on creativity: (1) cognition, (2) control, (3) climate, (4) motivation, (5) interactions, (6) teams, and (7) systems exchange. In this chapter, we examine the assumptions underlying each of these approaches, critical findings emerging from each approach, and issues that need to be resolved. Before turning to these models, however, it would seem useful to consider what we know about creative work and the methods used to study creativity in organizations.

STUDYING CREATIVITY

Creativity

Creativity refers to the production of original, useful, and elegant (Besemer & O'Quin, 1999; Christiaans, 2002) solutions to novel, complex, ill-defined problems (Mumford & Gustafson, 2007). Thus, creativity is not simply a matter of generating ideas, but, instead, requires the production of viable and original solutions to complex problems (Finke, Ward, & Smith, 1992). Although creative problem-solving is often associated with work in the arts, it is clear that creative problem-solving is relevant to performance in a wide range of areas – the science,

engineering, finance, management, and public policy (Mumford, 2002) to mention a few.

Because creative work ultimately requires problem-solving, it is not surprising that the available evidence indicates that creative problem-solving ultimately depends on expertise (Ericsson & Charness, 1994; Weisberg, 2006; Weisberg & Hass, 2007). Expertise involves factual knowledge, along with a set of concepts for organizing factual knowledge in a given domain, with expertise being acquired as a function of prolonged, active, practice (Brophy, 1998). Of course, expertise is not fully sufficient for producing *new* solutions. As a result, students of creativity have sought to identify the processes by which people work with extant knowledge to generate novel, and useful, problem solutions (e.g., Dewey, 1910; Parnes & Noller, 1972; Sternberg, 1986).

In a review of this literature, Mumford, Mobley, Uhlman, Reiter-Palmon, and Doares (1991) identified eight key processing activities that appear to be involved in creative thought: (1) problem definition, (2) informational gathering, (3) concept selection, (4) conceptual combination, (5) idea generation, (6) idea evaluation, (7) implementation planning, and (8) solution monitoring. Studies by Dailey and Mumford (2006), Mumford, Baughman, Maher, Costanza, and Supinski (1997), and Osburn and Mumford (2006) have provided evidence indicating that effective execution of each of these processes makes a unique contribution to the production of creative problem solutions. Effective process execution appears to be based on the application of cognitive operating strategies (Baughman & Mumford, 1995; Lonergan, Scott, & Mumford, 2004; Scott, Lonergan, & Mumford, 2005; Ward, Patterson, & Sifonis, 2004). The operating strategies contributing to effective process execution vary as a function of both problem type and knowledge type (Scott et al., 2005). Moreover, execution of these processes is typically cyclical, and demanding, with solutions evolving over time (Csikszentmihalyi, 1999).

These demands, substantial demands, made by creative problem-solving have another, noteworthy, implication. Creative work, and innovative achievement, based on this work, is not solely a function of cognition. Instead, it appears to depend on motivation and personality. With regard to motivation, intrinsic motivation, achievement motivation, and active, deep, cognitive processing all appear critical (Amabile, 1985; Amabile, Hennessey & Grossman, 1986; Marcy & Mumford, 2007). With regard to personality it appears that open, introverted, autonomous, energetic, curious, demanding individuals are most likely to engage in creative work (Feist, 1999; McCrae, 1987; MacKinnon, 1962). What should be recognized in this regard is that both relevant motivational and dispositional constructs operate as both state and trait variables. Thus, environmental conditions shape the willingness of people to engage in creative problem-solving (Kasof, 1995).

It should also be recognized that people in real-world creative problem-solving efforts often display a distinct work style. To begin, people working on creative tasks often expressly evaluate the significance of the problem and consider multiple implications of their problem solutions (Weber & Perkins, 1992). Creative people, moreover, also seem to pursue multiple problems in a network of enterprise (Feldman, 1999; Root-Berstein, Berstein, Garnier, 1995), with identity being drawn from the network of enterprise rather than the organization per se (Zuckerman, 1977). Finally, in part due to it's complexity, creative work often proceeds in a distinctly social fashion, being based on collegial relationships (Abra, 1994).

When one considers this thumbnail sketch of the nature of creative work, what emerges is an autonomous driven individual intensely working on a demanding problem where expertise and complex processing strategies are applied in an *attempt* to generate viable solutions in collaboration with others. What should be recognized here is that the kind of individual doing this sort of work is rarely considered by organizations to be the ideal employee (Mumford, 2000). To complicate matters further, organizations have a complex relationship to creative work (Sternberg, 2008): on the one hand it may be valued; on the other hand, creative work is expensive, time-consuming, and risky (Shalley & Gilson, 2004). Moreover, creative work, even if it is successful, may prove disruptive of extant organizational routines, require changes in basic production processes, and may induce shifts in strategy, having a host of complex effects for which an organization may, ultimately, receive little compensation (Perez-Freije & Enkel, 2007; Sharma, 1999). As a result, a complex, rather tense, relationship exists between organizations and creative work, as organizations seek to manage costs, risks, and disruption vis-à-vis the need for innovation (Mumford & Hunter, 2005).

Research method

The tension that exists between creative work and organizations, a tangible tension, in turn, provides one key stimulus, the other being the significance of creative work, for research on creativity and innovation. Broadly speaking, three distinct approaches are applied in studies of creativity and innovation. The first approach is essentially historic in nature. Creative performance, at the individual, group, or organizational level, leaves a track record – for example, publications (individual level), patents (typically group level), or the introduction of new products (organizational level). In historic studies, cases of creative achievement are identified based on application of these criteria (Simonton, 1990). In qualitative studies, such as those conducted by Mouly and Sankaran (1999) and Murphy and Ensher (2008), in-depth qualitative analytic methods are applied to multiple cases meeting certain defined standards with respect to these markers of creative achievement. In quantitative studies, such as those conducted by Robinson and Pearce (1988) and Thamhain (2003), these achievement records are treated as criteria to be predicted by the variables of interest.

Creative achievement studies, of course, focus on overt innovation rather than incidents of creative thought. Accordingly, in the second major research strategy the focus is on creative problem-solving. In one variation on this approach, people (or teams) are asked to generate solutions to problems known to call for creative thought. Examples of studies applying this problem-focused approach may be found in Jaussi and Dionne (2003) and Vincent, Decker, and Mumford (2002). In the other variation on this approach, a task held to tap certain critical processing activities involved in creative thought provides the dependent variable of interest. Thus, Jung (2001) had teams work on a brainstorming task to examine the effects of transformational leadership on idea generation. The process-specific approach is advantageous in that it allows isolation of effects. By the same token, the global problem-solving approach provides a more realistic assessment of creative thought.

The third approach applied in studies of innovation is based on a behavioral reporting strategy. In behavioral reports, survey questions are developed to permit assessment of behaviors linked to creativity. For example, 'I have the opportunity to pursue new ideas.' In some studies, such as Carmeli and Spreitzer (2009), Howell and Avolio (1993), and Scott and Bruce (1994), people complete surveys to describe their own behavior. In other cases, for example Pearce and Ensley (2004), these surveys are completed by supervisors. Although these methods are subject to questions about source and method bias, the more critical question bears on observability. Clearly, survey measures focus on behaviorally manifest aspects of creativity and may ignore less observable phenomena (Redmond, Mumford, & Teach, 1993).

In studies of creativity, methodological variation is primarily a result of the procedures used to define creativity. However, differences are also observed across studies in the predictors and controls applied. Broadly speaking, the predictors and controls applied depend on two considerations. First, the level of phenomena under investigation. Clearly, organizational size is not a relevant control in studies of individual-level creativity, although resource availability may well be of concern. Secondly, the predictors being examined differ on the theoretical model being applied. In the next section of this chapter we examine the key conclusions and controversies associated with each of these theoretical models.

MODELS

Cognition

As noted earlier, creative work is a cognitively demanding activity involving the production of viable, original, solutions to novel, complex, ill-defined problems (Mumford & Gustafson, 2007). Accordingly, the first major theoretical model stresses the importance of cognition. In one study along these lines, Vincent et al. (2002) administered measures of intelligence, divergent thinking, and leader expertise to 119 Army officers ranging in grade from second lieutenant to full colonel. These officers were also asked to solve a set of leadership problems. It was found that problem-solving performance was related to multiple indices of leader performance – attained rank, awards received, and critical incident performance (Connelly, Gilbert, Zaccaro, Threlfall, Marks, & Mumford, 2000). More centrally, it was found that intelligence, divergent thinking, and expertise were all positively related to leader problem-solving. The implication here is obvious. The leaders of creative efforts must be smart, creative, and knowledgeable.

Grosse (2007) conducted a qualitative study of the leaders of successful research and development efforts. Again, content analysis of the interview data and relationships with indices of project performance indicated that knowledge and creativity were critical to leader performance. The apparent importance of knowledge, or expertise, to the performance of those leading creative efforts has, in turn, led to a new question: What types of knowledge must the leaders of creative efforts possess?

A recent study by Laursen and Salter (2006) has addressed this question. They obtained measures, at the firm level, examining the organization's production of radical and incremental innovations. Measures were also obtained of the number of information sources used by the firm (breadth) and the intensity with which these information systems were used (depth). They found that a depth search was strongly related to the production of radical innovations, whereas a broad search was related to the production of incremental innovations. Notably, the sources of information attended to in-depth searches (lead users, universities, and suppliers) suggest that this information search is directed to obtaining knowledge and expertise with regard to fundamentals – key basic concepts within a field (Hughes, 1989). This exploration and mastery of fundamentals appears critical to the leadership of creative efforts (Mumford, Bedell-Avers, & Hunter, 2008). However, knowledge, or expertise, with regard to technical fundamentals must often be supplemented with broader knowledge of the organization, and its operating strategies, particularly in late-cycle activities involved in the development of creative products. Thus, leaders of creative efforts may need exceptional expertise with regard to both technological fundamentals and organizational operations.

The importance of expertise for the leadership of creative efforts is related to the cognitive skills that shape the performance of those leading creative efforts. Three key skills have been identified that appear critical to the leadership of creative efforts: (1) evaluation, (2) planning, and (3) forecasting.

Turning first to evaluation, Mumford and his colleagues (Mumford, Marks, Connelly, Zaccaro, & Reiter-Palmon, 2000) administered measures examining creative problem-solving skills (e.g., problem definition, conceptual combination, idea generation, idea evaluation) to Army officers varying in grade or level of responsibility. In contrasting junior to more seniors officers, it was found that as officers moved into more senior leadership positions, the greatest growth occurred in evaluation skills. Similarly, Andrews and Farris (1967), in their study of creativity among scientific teams, found that team productivity was related to critical evaluation skills evidenced by the team's leader. In still another study along these lines, Farris (1972) found that members of creative teams actively sought evaluative feedback from leaders.

Evaluation, of course, requires that leaders be able to recognize the strengths and weaknesses of ideas. In this regard, a study by Licuanan, Dailey, and Mumford (2007) is noteworthy. They presented ideas of varying originality and found that leaders do not always recognize highly original ideas. Thus, creativity may play an important role in the leadership of creative efforts by allowing leaders to recognize high-value ideas. Evaluation, however, is not a passive process (Basadur, Runco, & Vega, 2000). Instead, leaders must think about ideas and their implications. Lonergan et al. (2004) asked undergraduates to assume the role of a manager in a marketing firm who was to evaluate proposals for a new advertising campaign. It was found that the most original and highest-quality campaigns were obtained when leaders sought to provide compensatory feedback – providing evaluations intended to enhance the originality of high-quality ideas or providing evaluations intended to enhance the quality of highly original ideas.

Not only must leaders evaluate and seek to improve creative ideas but also they must plan for the development and fielding of these ideas. What should be recognized here is that planning is an inherently cognitive activity (Marta, Leritz, & Mumford, 2005) where leaders identify critical causes and key goals and use these causes and goals to conduct a mental simulation of the consequences of various actions (Mumford, Schultz, & Van Doorn, 2001; Noice, 1991). These simulations, in turn, allow the formation of plans and back-up plans that promote not only efficiency but also adaptation (Mumford, Schultz, & Osburn, 2002).

In fact, the available evidence indicates that planning is a critical component of performance in the leadership of creative efforts (Mossholder & Dewhirst, 1980; Salomo, Weise, & Gemunden, 2007). For example, Ancona and Caldwell (1992) studied 409 engineers and scientists working in 45 new product development teams. Measures of team innovation were obtained along with measures examining the intensity of planning activities and the intensity of external communications. They found that the intensity of planning, like the intensity of communications, was positively related ($r = 0.23$) to team innovation. Other studies by Arvey, Dewhirst, and Boling (1976), Castrogiovani (1996), Caughron and Mumford (2008), and Maidique and Zirger (1984) all also point to the importance of planning in the leadership of creative work. What should be recognized in this regard, however, is that generation and analysis of the mental simulations that underlie planning is an ongoing, demanding, and resource-intensive activity required of leaders, with successful leaders being able to adapt plans in an opportunistic fashion (Mumford et al., 2008).

Both evaluation and planning, however, depend on another cognitive ability – forecasting, or the ability to envision the downstream implications of ideas and actions (Mumford, 2003). Although prior studies of forecasting indicate that people are generally poor in making forecasts (Pant & Starbuck, 1990), recent research indicates that forecasting improves, and improves substantially, when people have requisite expertise and are appraising the consequences of implementing or pursuing ideas (Dailey & Mumford, 2006). More centrally, forecasting appears critical to the leadership of creative efforts. O'Connor (1998) conducted a qualitative study of the leaders of eight radical research and development efforts. Her findings indicated that the leaders of these efforts

could envision the long-term, downstream implications of ideas, with these forecasts serving as an impetus for idea development and leadership of creative work. Although forecasting appears to be a critical cognitive aspect of leadership of creative work, little is known about the technical, organizational, and production issues that shape evaluation of these forecasts.

Control

Creative work occurs in response to ill-defined complex problems – problems where solution paths are not evident. Moreover, in most creative efforts, multiple pressures are placed on the team, financial, time frame, and production pressures (Nohari & Gulati, 1996), even as the project team develops multiple ideas – ideas that are often uncertain with regard to their viability. Put more directly, confusion surrounds creative work. The potential negative impacts of confusion have led to a concern with control in studies of the creative leadership (Cardinal, 2001; Perez-Freije & Enkel, 2007).

To complicate matters further, creative people tend to be autonomous and driven to pursue their own ideas (Feist, 1999; Greenberg, 1992; Pelz & Andrews, 1966). As a result, close, or overly tight, supervision of peoples' work might inhibit creativity and innovation. Pelz and Andrews (1976) used survey techniques to measure the tightness versus looseness of supervisory practices evidenced by the leaders of research and development teams. They found that overly close supervision tended to result in diminished creative performance. Thus, the leaders of creative efforts cannot induce overly tight control.

By the same token, Pelz and Andrews (1976) found that overly loose control also diminished performance. Similar findings have been obtained by Trevelyan (2001) in a multi-method study of five research and development organizations. A potential explanation for these findings may be found in Keller (1989). He asked 477 scientists and engineers working on research and development projects in four organizations to complete measures of leader's initiating structure and need for clarity. It was found that need for clarity interacted with initiating structure such that leaders' initiating structure proved more beneficial when need for clarity was high. Thus, in controlling creative work, leaders must take into account the need for structuring activity by followers increasing structuring activities, and control, when followers evidence a need for clarity. The available evidence indicates that these structuring activities will prove most effective when they are based on relevant technical expertise, or organizational expertise, as opposed to appeals to authority (Thamhain & Gemmill, 1974).

Of course, control may be induced through mechanisms other than leaders' structuring activities. Leaders may induce control through both direct actions (e.g., allocation of resources to an effort), or indirect mechanisms (e.g., co-location of workers). Although a host of control techniques exist, and studies examining the effectiveness of these techniques are needed, two control techniques have been examined that appear to be particularly beneficial.

First, leaders of creative efforts can induce control through the mission definition – definition of the technical work to be pursued (Mumford et al., 2002). Houndshell (1992), in an in-depth historic analysis of DuPont's polymer research laboratories, found that definition of a clear, technically important, engaging mission was critical to the success of this creative effort. Similarly, Mouly and Sankaran (1999), in a qualitative study of one creative leader, found that mission definition was critical to the direction and success of creative efforts. The effects of control through mission definition may, however, be quite complex. In one study along these lines, Amabile, Hadley, and Kramer (2002) obtained diary entries from 177 professionals working on research and development efforts. They found that mission definition not only provided clarity with regard to goals, serving to direct members' activities, but also that clear mission definition allowed people pursuing creative work to resist potentially disruptive influences such as time pressure, resource scarcity, and collaboration demands.

Secondly, leaders of creative efforts often appear to control creative work through intellectual stimulation – asking engaging, important questions vis-à-vis work being done with respect to this mission. One aspect of transformational leadership is intellectual stimulation. Jung (2001), in a study examining idea production on a group brainstorming task, found that transformational leadership contributes to idea production. Other work by Keller (1992) and Waldman and Atwater (1992) also indicated that transformational leadership contributes to the performance of research and development teams. Studies by Maier and his colleagues (Maier & Hoffman, 1965; Maier & Janzen, 1969, Maier & Solem, 1962) indicated that leaders seeking to promote creativity through intellectual stimulation should (1) request creative solutions, (2) define the work substantively rather than in terms of financial outcomes, (3) encourage team members to consider a range of issues and relevant information, (4) share information and questions about this information, (5) extend discussion to reveal issues and alternative interpretations, and (6) use disagreements to frame integrative solutions. In fact, these intellectual stimulation control strategies appear to be especially important when creative work must occur under adverse conditions such as a conservative organizational environment (Shin & Zhou, 2003).

A critical component of control through intellectual stimulation, however, is that this control must be exercised as a form of intellectual exchange rather than simple intellectual direction. Exchange allows for participation, and participation has been shown to be critical to engagement in creative work. For example, Keller (1997) assessed the job involvement of 532 scientists and engineers using a job involvement scale. He found that involvement was positively related to indices of creative achievement. More centrally, involvement is itself influenced by participation in the intellectual exchange and mission definition. In keeping with this observation, Arvey and Dewhirst (1976), McGourty, Tarshis, and Dominick (1996), Mossholder and Dewhirst (1980), and Shipper and Davy (2002) found that satisfaction, and performance, improved among scientists and engineers when participation in intellectual exchange and mission definition was encouraged by leaders. Thus, while control appears important to creative work, the control of such effort is most likely to prove effective when control is shared. What is unclear in this regard, however, is when, and how, leaders should share control in attempts to encourage creativity.

Climate

Our foregoing observations with respect to participation and involvement, of course, point to the importance of the work environment. Leaders are a critical force shaping people's perceptions of the work environment (Luria, 2008). And, the available evidence indicates that creative people are especially sensitive to the work environment. In one study along these lines, Oldham and Cummings (1996) administered a measure of perceptions of work context to a sample of 171 workers whose creative capacity was also assessed. They found that supervisory evaluations of peoples' creativity was contingent on perceptions of work context, with perceptions of a favorable work context proving especially important to creative achievement for more creative individuals.

Findings of this sort have resulted in a number of studies intended to try to isolate those aspects of the individual's work environment that contribute to creativity (Amabile, Conti, Coon, Lazenby, & Herron, 1996; Anderson & West, 1998; Ekvall & Ryhammer, 1999; Lapierre & Giroux, 2003;

West, Borrill, Dawson, Brodbeck, Shapiro, & Haward, 2003). Hunter, Bedell, and Mumford (2005), in a review of this literature, found that 14 dimensions are commonly considered in studies examining climate for creative work: (1) positive peer group, (2) positive supervisory relationships, (3) resources, (4) challenge, (5) mission clarity, (6) autonomy, (7) positive interpersonal exchange, (8) intellectual stimulation, (9) top management support, (10) rewards, (11) flexibility and risk taking, (12) product emphasis, (13) participation, and (14) organizational integration. Subsequently, Hunter, Bedell-Avers, and Mumford (2007) conducted a meta-analysis to examine the effects of these climate perceptions on evaluations of creative performance (e.g., supervisory ratings of creativity, publications, introduction of new products). The findings obtained in this meta-analysis indicated that all of these dimensions of climate were positively related to indices of creative performance, producing an average delta (Δ) of 0.75 across 42 studies, with perceptions of positive interpersonal exchange ($\Delta = 0.91$), intellectual stimulation ($\Delta = 0.88$), and challenge ($\Delta = 0.85$) producing particularly sizable effects.

From the perspective of leadership, these findings are noteworthy because leader behavior is one of the more important variables shaping climate perceptions (James, James, & Ashe, 1990). Thus, Pirola-Merlo, Haertel, and Mann (2002) found that leader behavior influenced climate perceptions, which in turn was found to influence the performance of 54 research and development teams. The question raised by these findings, however, is exactly what behaviors on the part of leaders results in the creation of favorable climate perceptions (Gonzalez-Roma, Peiro, & Tordera, 2002).

In one study along these lines, Jaussi and Dionne (2003) examined the effects of unconventional behavior on the part of leaders. In this experimental study, teams of undergraduates were asked to generate proposals to a creative educational problem. Prior to starting work on this task team members either were, or were not, exposed to a leader behaving in a conventional or an unconventional fashion. For example, the leaders stood on chairs or a tabletop or asked people to scratch and sniff pizza stickers (the reward for best presentation was a pizza). They found that unconventional behavior on the part of leaders contributed to individual-level creative performance during preparation of the proposal, as well as intrinsic motivation, accounting for variance above and beyond transformational leadership. Apparently, leader role-modeling of creative behavior, as manifest in unconventional behavior, created a climate encouraging creativity.

The Jaussi and Dionne (2003) study is noteworthy because it examined one aspect of leader behavior, role-modeling, which might serve to create a climate for creativity. Clearly, unconventional behavior by the leader is not the only behavior that might induce these effects. For example, Gonzalez-Roma et al. (2002) found that leader informing behaviors contributed to climate for creativity. Ayers, Dahlstrom, and Skinner (1997) found that treating problems as a matter of mutual concern, resolving conflicts internally, and mutual adjustment of behavior all contributed to the formation of a more creative climate among professionals working on new product introductions. What these observations point to is the need for studies identifying the specific behaviors of leaders that influence critical climate dimensions – such as challenge, positive interpersonal exchange, and autonomy – along with studies examining the conditions under which a leader's display of these behaviors proves effective, or ineffective, in establishing a climate likely to promote creativity and innovation.

Motivation

Earlier, in our description of creative work, we noted that creativity depends upon the *investment* of cognitive resources. Accordingly, motivation has been held to be critical to creativity. And, it is clear leaders can take actions to influence motivation (Yukl, 2001). With regard to creativity, however, the focus debate has been on the motivational interventions that will prove effective.

Traditionally, theories of motivation have held that the rewards provided, their nature and timing, influences effort invested. In keeping with this proposition, early work by Chalupsky (1953) indicated that people doing creative work often seek concrete rewards such as pay and professional recognition. More recent work, by Amabile (1985) and Amabile et al. (1986), however, indicates that concrete, tangible, rewards may prove less useful in motivating creative work than the person's intrinsic interest in the task at hand. These findings are noteworthy, of course, because they suggest that leaders should allow self-selection into work on creative projects (Mumford & Hunter, 2005). By the same token, however, the detrimental effects of reward on motivation for creative work remain controversial (Eisenberger & Cameron, 1996).

More recently, Baer, Oldham, and Cummings (2003) proposed an alternative model to account for the effects of rewards on creativity. Supervisory ratings of 171 employees of a manufacturing firm were obtained. Extrinsic rewards' perceptions were obtained through George and Zhou's (2002) measure. Measures of creative style, Kirton's (1976) adaptive versus innovative style, and job complexity were also obtained. The findings indicated that adaptors working on relatively simple jobs found extrinsic rewards motivating for creative work. When, however, innovators were working on complex problems, a weaker relationship between extrinsic rewards and creativity was observed. Thus, the value of extrinsic rewards may depend on both the style by which people approach creative work and the complexity of the work being done, such that rewards are likely to prove greater value in late-cycle as opposed to early-cycle work where intrinsic motivation is more critical.

Of course, rewards are not the only way leaders may motivate creativity. Leaders might encourage followers to invest identity in the mission, or alternatively, they might attempt to increase followers' feeling of self-efficacy with regard to creative work (Jaussi, Randel, & Dionne, 2007). Some support for this proposition has been provided in a study by Tierney and Farmer (2002). They developed a measure assessing employees' beliefs about their capability for creative work and they obtained managerial ratings of employee creativity in a technology and a manufacturing firm. They found that creative self-efficacy could be distinguished from job self-efficacy. More centrally, creative self-efficacy was found to be positively related to supervisory assessments of creativity. Thus, actions taken by leaders to build employee confidence in their capability for creative work may, in fact, motivate creativity.

Interactions

One way leaders might attempt to build feelings of creative self-efficacy is through positive exchange relationships – especially positive exchange relationships where the leader both calls for and evidences creativity. However, studies of leader–member exchange indicate that positive exchange relationships between a leader and followers might promote creativity through a number of other mechanisms. For example, positive exchange relationships might promote the development of requisite expertise – expertise is known to be critical to the performance of creative work (Damanpour, 1991). Alternatively, positive exchange relationships might encourage the information exchange known to contribute to creative work (Ancona & Caldwell, 1992). Along somewhat different lines, positive exchange relationships might result in more perceptions of leader support, more positive affect, and better management

of the emotions associated with the uncertainties of creative work (Zhou & George, 2003).

In fact, a number of studies provide some support for these propositions. For example, Scott and Bruce (1994) administered a measure of leader–member exchange to 110 scientists and examined working in 22 research and development groups. They found a positive relationship between their measure of exchange and managers' ratings of employee creativity. In still another study along these lines, Tierney et al. (1999) obtained multiple measures of creativity (e.g., supervisory ratings, invention disclosures, research reports) for 191 research and developmental personnel who also were asked to complete a measure of leader–member exchange. Again, a positive relationship was obtained between leader–member exchange and creativity. However, these relationships were stronger for followers evidencing an adaptive, as opposed to an innovative, approach to creative work – presumably because innovators evidence a more autonomous work style.

The Tierney et al. (1999) study is of interest, in part, because it suggests that the effects of positive exchange relationships between leaders and followers may be rather complex. A positive exchange relationship induces feelings of follower trust in the leader (Graen & Uhl-Bein, 1998). And, given the ambiguity and conflict that often surrounds creative work, trust in the leader may prove critical (Mumford & Hunter, 2005). Carmeli and Spreitzer (2009) asked 172 employees to appraise their own creative behavior and thriving, or self-initiated learning, along with energy devoted to creative work. Three months earlier, participants were asked to complete measures describing their trust in their supervisor and connectivity to others in their work. It was found that trust in the supervisor led to connectivity at time 1 which, led to thriving at time 2, which, in turn, contributed to creativity at time 2. Not only does this study underscore the importance of trust in the leader to creative work but also it underscores the complex mediational relationships by which trust, and positive exchange relationships, contribute to creativity, with connectivity to others and thriving moderating these effects. Hopefully, future research will serve to articulate other moderators and mediators of the effects of leader–member relationships on creativity.

Teams

The Carmeli and Spreitzer (2009) article is, however, also of interest because it indicates that the effects of leader–member exchange on creativity may be contingent of how these exchanges influence followers' interaction with other members of a team. In fact, the available evidence indicates that most creative work is accomplished in teams (Abra, 1994). However, the influence of teams on creative performance is not assured (Paulus, 2000). Thus, it is commonly found on brainstorming, or idea production tasks, that nominal groups (individuals working alone) typically outperform teams due to the operation of inhibitory social psychological processes such as normative pressure and social loafing.

One study intended to examine how team process influences performance in creative work has been conducted by Taggar (2002). He asked business students to produce solutions to problems calling for creative thought. As students worked in teams, team process variables were assessed: (1) team citizenship, (2) performance management, (3) effective communication, (4) involving others, (5) providing feedback, (6) reaction to conflict, and (7) averting conflict. It was found that each of these seven variables made a unique contribution to predicting creative problem-solving even when relevant individual-level influences were taken into account. What is of note in this regard, however, is that leader behavior may influence all of these team processes. For example, leaders may act to ensure that conflict is approached as a technical rather than as a personal issue. Similarly, leaders may expressly acknowledge contributions to the team as well as technical work. Thus, leaders may prove critical in ensuring effective team performance during work on creative tasks. In fact, attempts by leaders to create team processes that stress citizenship, trust, and effective communication have been consistently found to contribute to team performance (e.g., Cooper & Kleinshmidt, 2000; Keller, 1989; Madjar, Oldham, & Pratt, 2002; Thamhain, 2003).

As important as it is for leaders to manage the process of teams working on creative projects, leaders appear to exert two other noteworthy effects on creative teams. Mumford, Feldman, Hein, and Nago (2001) examined the effects of shared mental models on teams of undergraduates developing creative solutions to business problems. Some groups were provided with task-relevant training, some groups were provided with task-irrelevant training, and some were provided with no training. It was found that training, regardless of task relevance, induced better creative performance than no training, presumably due to the team's adoption of a shared mental model. Leaders, by articulating, and acting on, a clear mission, of course, influence the adoption of shared mental models. A recent study by Pearce and Ensley (2004) is noteworthy in this regard because it suggests that a leader's induction of shared mental models may

have a complex set of effects on team performance. Creative performance was measured through behavioral reports obtained from team members, managers, and customers of 71 teams responsible for production process innovations. Measures of shared mental models were obtained along with measures of team social behavior – team potency, social loafing, teamwork, altruism, and courtesy. It was found that shared mental models were strongly related to measures of team innovation obtained from all three sources. Moreover, the availability of these shared mental models resulted in decreased social loafing, increased team potency, increased altruism, increased courtesy, and increased teamwork. Thus, the availability of shared mental models, models relevant to a leader's articulation of a mission, appears to result in more effective patterns of exchange among team members.

Another way leaders influence the performance of teams working on creative tasks is through the leader's selection of team members. Perhaps the most critical consideration in this regard is assembling a team that has requisite expertise (Damanpour, 1991). The importance of expertise, however, has led to the emergence of another question. How diverse should the expertise be for those assigned to creative teams? In fact, a number of studies have examined the requirements for diversity in creative teams, with many studies stressing the need for cross-functional teams (Brown & Eisenhardt, 1995; Cooper & Kleinschmidt, 2000; Griffin, 1997; Lovelace, Shapiro, & Weingart, 2001). For example, Thamhain (2003) obtained measures of the success of 74 new project teams and found that cross-functional cooperation and support was positively related to innovation ($r = 0.40$).

Although evidence is available indicating that a range of expertise in creative teams is beneficial, not all studies support this conclusion (Gebert, Boerner, & Kearney, 2006). Keller (2001) studied 93 new product development and applied research teams drawn from various industries. The work performed by these teams was assessed with respect to technical quality, schedule performance, and budget performance. Additionally, functional diversity, external communication, cohesiveness, and stress were assessed. It was found that technical, schedule, and budget performance were positively related to functional diversity, but that functional diversity decreased team cohesiveness, in part, as a result of increased stress. These findings are noteworthy because they suggest that leaders must manage diversity relevant to task demands if they are to ensure successful creative projects. What is unclear at this point is exactly what considerations – for example, internal and external communication (Anderson, Glassman, McAfee, & Pinelli, 2001), team commitment (Adams & Day, 1998), and professional versus business identity (Gebert et al., 2006) – moderate or mediate these relationships.

Systems exchange

Of course, the findings obtained with regard to cross-functional teams indicate that creative efforts do not exist in isolation from a broader organizational environment. In fact, the available evidence indicates that most creative work in organizations is costly both in terms of the resources required for this work (Nohari & Gulati, 1996) and in terms of disruption of ongoing organizational activities (Gopalakrishnan, Bierly, & Kessler, 1999). As one might expect based on these costs, and the risks associated with creative work, size, resources, and top management support have all been found to be critical to the success of innovative efforts (Chandy & Tellis, 2000; Damanpour, 1996; Dougherty & Hardy, 1996; Jelinek & Schoonhoven, 1990; Klein, Conn, & Sorra, 2001). In fact, sustained top management support and sustained organizational resources (Klein et al., 2001) have been found to be critical forces shaping the success of creative work in organizations.

The dependence of creative efforts on organizational support, however, broaches a fundamental question: How do organizations react to creative efforts? Dougherty and Heller (1994) conducted in-depth interviews with those involved in developing innovative products within 15 large firms. The material obtained in these 134 interviews was coded to identify sources of illegitimacy in the creative effort. Eight sources were identified that led to perceptions of illegitimacy: (1) no creativity evidenced, (2) inappropriate product evaluation, (3) departmental barriers, (4) departmental classes in view, (5) team maintenance problems, (6) no structural fit, (7) no strategic fit, and (8) no climate fit. Failed and canceled projects were found to score higher on all of these dimensions. These findings are noteworthy because they suggest that a critical role played by leaders is to establish the legitimacy of the creative effort (Shalley & Gilson, 2004). Broadly speaking, two mechanisms exist by which creative efforts are legitimated: (1) championing and (2) strategic planning.

Championing involves selling creative work to others (Howell & Higgins, 1998; Markham & Aiman-Smith, 2001). In one recent study, Howell and Boies (2004) identified 28 noteworthy innovations in 88 firms. In-depth interviews were conducted with project champions and non-champions. Interview data were coded with respect to contextual knowledge, normative knowledge, flexible role orientation, idea generation, idea promotion-selling, and idea promotion-packaging. They found that champions differed from non-champions in that (1) they were involved in, and supportive of, the creative effort and (2) they used both contextual and normative knowledge to package and sell creative work. These findings are noteworthy because they suggest that the leaders of creative efforts must acquire knowledge about both the organization's strategies and its norms, and they must be able to package and sell creative work to other organizational constituencies within this context. These 'sales' efforts, moreover, must begin early on in a cycle of creative work and must be maintained over time to insure stability in requisite resources and support.

Although leaders must sell creative work, sales efforts are unlikely to prove successful unless based on substance. This observation led Mumford et al. (2008) to agree that strategic planning is critical to the leadership of creative efforts. Within this view, the role of the leader is to identify fundamentals, basic phenomena, either technical or process oriented, critical to the strategy being pursued by the organization. Systematic exploration of these fundamentals provides a basis for sustained support while building the absorptive capacity organizations need to both develop and field creative work (Cohen & Levinthal, 1990; Gopalakrishnan & Damanpour, 2000). Although evidence bearing on the plausibility of this model is lacking, it does suggest that the leaders of creative efforts must conceptualize a strategy and initiate ongoing organizational learning if creative efforts are to succeed (Senge, 1990).

CONCLUSIONS

Before turning to the broader implications of our observations, certain limitations of the present effort should be noted. To begin, in the present effort we focused on models of leadership in creative work. As a result, many contingencies that shape leader behavior – for example, firms' evaluation systems (Hitt, Hoskisson, Johnson, & Moesel, 1996), political norms within the firm (Mumford & Hunter, 2005), or alliances among firms (Osborn & Marion, 2009) – have not been discussed. Nonetheless, it should be recognized that these variables do influence the behavior of leaders responsible for creative efforts.

It should also be recognized that we have not considered every theory that might be relevant to understanding the leadership of creative efforts. For example, little has been said about organizational structure, although structure is known to influence innovation (Damanpour, 1991;

Woodman, Sawyer, & Griffin, 1993), and, leaders do, to some extent, create structure. Instead, in the present effort we have focused on those theories that explain the performance of an individual leader who has been designated as a leader of a creative effort (Howell & Boies, 2004).

Along related lines, it should be recognized that we have only examined models of leadership. We have not examined organizational variables that might moderate the impact of each of these models. For example, Friedrich, Mumford, Vessey, Beeler, and Eubanks (2010) have examined the relevance of each of these models to Kimberly and Evanisko's (1981) distinction between technical and process innovations, finding that cognitive, control, and team models are more relevant to understanding technical innovations while motivation, interactions, and systems exchange are more relevant to understanding process innovations. Similarly, Beeler, Shipman, and Mumford (in press) have examined how stage of product development moderates the impact of these models. They argue that some models, such as cognition, are important in all stages. Other models, such as control and climate, prove important in early stages while motivation and leader interactions become more important in the later stages of innovative efforts. Of course, these are not the only potential moderators. For example, model impact might be moderated by whether radical versus incremental innovations are under consideration (Ettlie, Bridges, & O'Keefe, 1984; Tushman & O'Reilly, 1996), the degree of technological development (Hughes, 1989; Wise, 1992), the organization's strategic environment (Dean & Sharfman, 1996; Miles & Snow, 1978), and field of work (Baer, 2003; Csikszentmihalyi, 1999). Hopefully, future work will serve to delineate the impact of these, and other, potential moderators of the relevance of each of these theories' bearing on the leadership of creative efforts.

Even bearing these limitations in mind, we believe that the present effort does point to some important conclusions about the leadership of creative work. Perhaps the first, and most important, conclusion that should be drawn in this regard is that the leadership of creative work is complex – in fact, exceptionally complex. At least seven theoretical models have been proposed to account for the leadership of creative work (e.g., cognitive, control, climate). More centrally, all of these theories have evidenced some validity as models of what leaders must do to ensure creativity and innovation. Thus, it appears that the effective leadership of creative efforts may be unusually demanding (Mumford, Scott, Gaddis, & Strange, 2002). These demands are noteworthy because they suggest that organizational

interventions intended to prepare people to lead these efforts may be particularly important.

These interventions, however, cannot follow a simple 'cookbook' approach. The leadership of creative efforts does evidence some attributes of typical leadership behavior. Cases in point may be found in the importance of leader–member exchange (Tierney et al., 1999) and control (Keller, 1989). By the same token, the research examined in the present effort suggests that three unique aspects of leadership take on special significance when one examines innovation. First, in leading creative work, leader cognition becomes especially important (Mumford, Scott, Gaddis, & Strange, 2002). Secondly, the leader's ability to define a climate that will support innovation becomes of great concern (Elkins & Keller, 2003). Thirdly, how leaders go about integrating creative work with other ongoing organizational activities appears uniquely important (Howell, & Boies, 2004). Hopefully, future work will focus on these uniquely critical aspects of leadership in creative work.

Although a more thorough examination of the uniquely critical aspects of leadership is required, the present effort suggests an additional step must be taken. Traditionally, studies of creative leadership have been based on one model. What is clear, however, is that these models are all interrelated. Leader cognition influences systems integration and team formation. The climate defined by a leader influences how motivation is induced and how leader–follower interactions are perceived. Given these likely relationships among the models of leadership that have been proposed, it should seem clear that there is a need for research expressly intended to explore these cross-model dependencies. Indeed, such research may prove critical to developing a general model of the leadership of creative efforts (Mumford, Eubanks, & Murphy, 2006).

The kind of research called for above is a demanding and time-consuming undertaking. It is essential, however, because it will provide organizations with critical evidence needed to prepare people to lead creative efforts (Mumford, Hunter, Eubanks, Bedell-Avers, & Murphy, 2007). Organizations must appraise critical conditions to identify relevant leader behaviors and applicable theories. Interventions must be built around these conditions. For example, broad organizational exposure may not be critical for early-stage technical development efforts but it may be critical for late-stage systems integration efforts (Cardinal & Hatfield, 2000).

This kind of disciplined approach to leader development called for above has, frankly, been rare. By the same token, the leadership of creative efforts is a complex phenomenon. And, perhaps more centrally, it is an aspect of leadership that is likely to become progressively more important to the success and survival of organizations. Given these observations, it seems clear that the kind of systematic research called for above is warranted. Hopefully, the present effort will provide background for further research along these lines.

ACKNOWLEDGMENTS

We would like to thank Tamara Friedrich, Amanda Shipman, Sam Hunter, and Katrina Bedell-Avers for their contributions to the present effort

REFERENCES

Abra, J. (1994). Collaboration in creative work: an initiative for investigation. *Creativity Research Journal, 7,* 1–20.

Adams, J. E. & Day, G. S. (1998). Enhancing new product development performance: an organizational learning perspective. *Journal of Product Innovation Management, 15,* 403–422.

Amabile, T. M. (1985). Motivation and creativity: effects of motivational orientation on creative writers. *Journal of Personality and Social Psychology, 48,* 393–399.

Amabile, T. M., Conti, R., Coon, H., Lazenby, J., & Herron, M. (1996). Assessing the work environment for creativity. *Academy of Management Journal, 39,* 1154–1184.

Amabile, T. M., Hadley, C. N., & Kramer, S. J. (2002). Creativity under the gun. *Harvard Business Review, 80,* 52–61.

Amabile, T. M., Hennessey, B. A., & Grossman, B. S. (1986). Social influences on creativity: the effects of contracted for reward. *Journal of Personality and Social Psychology, 50,* 14–23.

Amabile, T. M., Schatzel, E. A., Moneta, G. B., & Kramer, S. J. (2004). Leader behaviors and work environment for creativity: perceived leader support. *The Leadership Quarterly, 15,* 5–32.

Ancona, D. & Caldwell, D. (1992). Demography and design: predictors of new product team performance. *Organization Science, 3,* 321–341.

Anderson, C. J., Glassman, M., McAfee, R. B., & Pinelli, T. (2001). An investigation of factors affecting how engineers and scientists seek information. *Journal of Engineering & Technology Management, 18,* 131.

Anderson, N. R. & West, M. A. (1998). Measuring climate for work group innovation: development and validation of the team climate inventory. *Journal of Organizational Behavior, 19,* 235–258.

Andrews, F. M. & Farris, G. F. (1967). Supervisory practices and innovation in scientific teams. *Personnel Psychology, 20,* 497–515.

Arvey, R. D. & Dewhirst, H. D. (1976). Goal-setting attributes, personality variables, and job satisfaction. *Journal of Vocational Behavior, 9,* 179–188.

Arvey, R. D., Dewhirst, H. D., & Boling, J. C. (1976). Relationships between goal clarity, participation in goal setting, and personality characteristics on job satisfaction in a scientific organization. *Journal of Applied Psychology, 61,* 103–105.

Ayers, D., Dahlstrom, R., & Skinner, S. J. (1997). An exploratory investigation of organizational antecedents to new product success. *Journal of Marketing Research, 34,* 107–116.

Baer, J. (2003). Evaluative thinking, creativity, and task specificity: separating wheat from chaff is not the same as finding needle in haystacks. In M. A. Runco (ed.), *Critical creative processes.* Cresskill, NJ: Hampton, pp.129–152.

Baer, M., Oldham, G. R., & Cummings, A. (2003). Rewarding creativity: When does it really matter? *The Leadership Quarterly, 14,* 478–486.

Barnowe, J. T. (1975). Leadership and performance outcomes in research organizations. *Organizational Behavior and Human Performance, 14,* 264–280.

Basadur, M., Runco, M. A., & Vega, L. A. (2000). Understanding how creative thinking skills, attitudes, and behaviors work together: a causal process model. *Journal of Creative Behavior, 34,* 77–100.

Baughman, W. A. & Mumford, M. D. (1995). Process analytic models of creative capacities: operations involved in the combination and reorganization process. *Creativity Research Journal, 8,* 37–62.

Beeler, C. K., Shipman, A., & Mumford, M. D. (in press). Managing the innovative process: the dynamic role of leaders. *Psychology of Aesthetics, Creativity, and the Arts.*

Besemer, S. P. & O'Quin, K. (1999). Confirming the three-factor creative product analysis matrix model in an American sample. *Creativity Research Journal, 12,* 287–296.

Brophy, D. R. (1998). Understanding, measuring, and enhancing individual creative problem-solving efforts. *Creativity Research Journal, 11,* 123–150.

Brown, S. & Eisenhardt, K. (1995). Product development: past research, present findings, and future directions. *Academy of Management Review, 20,* 343–378.

Cardinal, L. B. (2001). Technological innovation in the pharmaceutical industry: the use of organizational control on managing research and development. *Organization Science, 12,* 19–37.

Cardinal, L. B. & Hatfield, D. E. (2000). Internal knowledge generation: the research laboratory and innovative productivity in the pharmaceutical industry. *Journal of Engineering & Technology Management, 17,* 247–272.

Carmeli, A. & Schaubroeck, J. (2007). The influence of leaders' and other referents' normative expectations on individual involvement in creative work. *The Leadership Quarterly, 18*(1), 35–48.

Carmeli, A. & Spreitzer, G. M. (2009). Trust, connectivity, and thriving. Implications for innovative behaviors at work. *Journal of Creative Behavior.*

Castrogiovani, G. J. (1996). Pre-start-up planning and the survival of new small businesses: theoretical linkages. *Journal of Management, 22,* 810–822.

Caughron, J. J. & Mumford, M. D. (2009) Project planning: the effects of using formal planning techniques on forecasting and plan development. *Creativity and Innovation Management, 17,* 1–12.

Chalupsky, A. B. (1953). Incentive practices as viewed by scientists and managers of pharmaceutical laboratories. *Personnel Psychology, 6,* 385–401.

Chandy, R. K. & Tellis, G. J. (2000). The incumbent's curse? Incumbency, size and radical innovation. *Journal of Marketing, 64,* 1–17.

Christiaans, H. H. C. M. (2002). Creativity as a design criterion. *Creativity Research Journal, 14,* 41–54.

Cohen, W. M. & Levinthal, D. A. (1990). Absorptive capacity: a new perspective on learning and innovation. *Administrative Science Quarterly, 35,* 128–152.

Connelly, M. S., Gilbert, J. A., Zaccaro, S. J., Threlfall, K. V., Marks, M. A., & Mumford, M. D. (2000). Predicting organizational leadership: the impact of problem solving skills, social judgment skills, and knowledge. *The Leadership Quarterly, 11,* 65-86.

Cooper, R. G. & Kleinschmidt, E. J. (2000). New product performance: what distinguishes the star products. *Australian Journal of Management, 25,* 17–46.

Csikszentmihalyi, M. (1999). Implications of a systems perspective for the study of creativity. In R. J. Sternberg (ed.), *Handbook of creativity.* Cambridge, England: Cambridge University Press, pp. 313–338.

Dailey, L. & Mumford, M. D. (2006). Evaluative aspects of creative thought: errors in appraising the implications of new ideas. *Creativity Research Journal, 18,* 367–384.

Damanpour, F. (1991). Organizational innovation: a meta-analysis of effects of determinants and moderators. *Academy of Management Journal, 34,* 555–590.

Damanpour, F. (1996). Organizational complexity and innovation: developing and testing multiple contingency models. *Management Science, 42,* 693–722.

Dean, J. W. & Sharfman, M. P. (1996). Does decision process matter: a study of strategic decision making effectiveness. *Academy of Management Journal, 39,* 368–396.

Dewey, J. (1910). *How we think.* Boston, MA: Houghton.

Dougherty, D. & Hardy, B. F. (1996). Sustained innovation production in large mature organizations: overcoming organization problems. *Academy of Management Journal, 39,* 826–851.

Dougherty, D. & Heller, T. (1994). The illegitimacy of successful product innovation in established firms. *Organization Science, 5,* 200–281.

Eisenberger, R. & Cameron, J. (1996). Detrimental effects of reward: Reality or myth? *American Psychologist, 51,* 1153–1166.

Ekvall, G. & Ryhammer, L. (1999). The creative climate: its determinants and effects at a Swedish University. *Creativity Research Journal, 12,* 303–310.

Elkins, T. & Keller, R. T. (2003). Leadership in research and development organizations: a literature review and conceptual framework. *The Leadership Quarterly, 14,* 587–606.

Ericsson, K. A. & Charness, W. (1994). Expert performance: its structure and acquisition. *American Psychologist, 49,* 725–747.

Ettlie, J. E., Bridges, W. P., & O'Keefe, R. D. (1984). Organizational strategy and structural differences for radical versus incremental innovation, *Managing Science, 30,* 65–74.

Farris, G. F. (1972). The effect of individual roles on performance in innovative groups. *R&D Management, 3,* 23–28.

Feist, G. J. (1999). The influence of personality on artistic and scientific creativity. In R. J. Sternberg (ed.), *Handbook of creativity.* Cambridge, England: Cambridge University Press, pp. 273–296.

Feldman, D. H. (1999). The development of creativity. In R. J. Sternberg (ed.), *Handbook of creativity.* Cambridge, England: Cambridge University Press, pp. 169–188.

Finke, R. A., Ward, T. B., & Smith, S. M. (1992). *Creative cognition: theory, research, and applications.* Cambridge, Massachusetts: MIT Press.

Friedrich, T. L., Mumford, M. D., Vessey, W. B., Beeler, C., & Eubanks, D. (2010). Leading for innovation: re-evaluating leader influences with regard to innovation type and complexity. *International Studies of Organization and Management.*

Gebert, D., Boerner, S., & Kearney, E. (2006). Cross-functionality and innovation in new product development teams: a dilemmatic structure and its consequences for the management of diversity. *European Journal of Work and Organizational Psychology, 15,* 431–458.

George, J. M. & Zhou, J. (2002). Understanding when bad moods foster creativity and good ones don't: the role of context and clarity of feelings. *Journal of Applied Psychology, 87,* 687–697.

Gonzalez-Roma, V., Peiro, J. M., & Tordera, N. (2002). An examination of the antecedents and moderator influences of climate strength. *Journal of Applied Psychology, 87,* 465–473.

Gopalakrishnan, S. & Damanpour, F. (2000). The impact of organizational context on innovation adoption in commercial banks. *IEEE Transactions on Engineering Management, 47,* 14–25.

Gopalakrishnan, S., Bierly, P., & Kessler, E. H. (1999). A reexamination of product and process innovations using a knowledge-based view. *The Journal of High Technology Management Research, 10,* 147–166.

Graen, G. B. & Uhl-Bien, M. (1998). Relationship-based approach to leadership: Development of leader–member exchange (LMX) theory of leadership over 25 years: applying a multi-level multi-domain perspective. In F. Dansereau & F. J. Yammarino (eds), *Leadership: the multi-level approaches.* Stamford, CT: JAI Press, pp. 103–134.

Greenberg, E. (1992). Creativity, autonomy, and the evaluation of creative work: artistic workers in organizations. *Journal of Creative Behavior, 26,* 75–80.

Griffin, A. (1997). PDMA research on new product development practices: updating trends and benchmarking best practices. *Journal of Product Innovation Management, 14,* 429–458.

Grosse, D. (2007). Leadership in R&D projects. *Creativity and Innovation Management, 16,* 447–456.

Hitt, M. A., Hoskisson, R. E., Johnson, R. A., & Moesel, D. D. (1996). The market for corporate control and firm innovation. *Academy of Management Journal, 39,* 1084–1196.

Houndshell, E. A. (1992). Invention in the industrial research laboratory: individual or collective process? In R. J. Weber,

& D. N. Perkins (eds), *Inventive minds: creativity in technology*. New York: Oxford University Press, pp. 273–291.

Howell, J. M. & Boies, K. (2004). Champions of technological innovation: the influence of contextual knowledge, role orientation, idea generation, and idea promotion on champion emergence. *The Leadership Quarterly, 15,* 123–143.

Howell, J. M. & Higgins, C. A. (1988). Champions of technological innovation. *Administrative Science Quarterly, 35,* 317–341.

Howell, K. M. & Avolio, B. J. (1993). Transformational leadership, transactional leadership, locus of control, and support for innovation: key predictors of consolidated-business-unit performance. *Journal of Applied Psychology, 78,* 891–902.

Hughes, T. P. (1989). *American genesis: a history of the American genius for invention.* New York: Penguin.

Hunter, S. T., Bedell, K. E., & Mumford, M. D. (2005). Dimensions of creative climate: a general taxonomy. *Korean Journal of Thinking and Problem Solving, 15,* 97–116.

Hunter, S.T., Bedell-Avers, K.E., & Mumford, M.D. (2007). Climate for creativity: a quantitative review. *Creativity Research Journal, 19,* 69–90.

James, L. R., James, L. A., & Ashe, D. K. (1990). The meaning of organizations: the role of cognition and values. In B. Schneider (ed.), *Organizational climate and culture.* San Francisco, CA: Josey-Bass, pp. 40–84.

Jaussi, K. S. & Dionne, S. D. (2003). Leading for creativity: the role of unconventional leader behavior. *The Leadership Quarterly, 14,* 351–368.

Jaussi, K. S., Randel, A. E. & Dionne, S. D. (2007). I am, I think I can, and I do; role of personal identity, self-efficacy, and cross-application of experiences in creativity at work. *Creativity Research Journal, 19,* 247–258.

Jelinek, M. & Schoonhoven, C. B. (1990). *The innovation marathon: lessons learned from high technology firms.* Oxford, England: Blackwell.

Jung, D. I. (2001) Transformational and transactional leadership and their effects on creativity in groups. *Creativity Research Journal, 13*(2), 185–195.

Kahai, S. S., Sosik, J. J., & Avolio, B. J. (2003). Effects of leadership style, anonymity, and rewards on creativity-relevant processes and outcomes in an electronic meeting system context. *The Leadership Quarterly, 14,* 369–376.

Kasof, J. (1995). Explaining creativity: the attribution perspective. *Creativity Research Journal, 8,* 311–366.

Keller, R. T. (1989). A test of the path-goal theory of leadership with need for clarity as a moderator in research and development organizations. *Journal of Applied Psychology, 74,* 208–212.

Keller, R. T. (1992). Transformational leadership and the performance of research and development project groups. *Journal of Management, 18,* 489–501.

Keller, R. T. (1997). Job involvement and organizational commitment as longitudinal predictors of job performance: a study of scientists and engineers. *Journal of Applied Psychology, 82,* 539–545.

Keller, R. T. (2001). Cross-functional project groups in research and new product development: diversity, communications, job stress, and outcomes. *Academy of Management Journal, 44,* 547–559.

Keller, R. T. (2006). Transformational leadership, initiating structure, and substitutes for leadership: a longitudinal study of research and development project team performance. *Journal of Applied Psychology, 91*(1), 202–210.

Kimberly, J. R. & Evanisko, M. J. (1981). Organizational innovation: the influence of individual, organizational and contextual factors on hospital adoption of technological and administrative innovations. *Academy of Management Journal, 24,* 689–713.

Kirton, D. (1976). Adaptors and innovators: a description and measure. *Journal of Applied Psychology, 61,* 622–629.

Klein, K. J., Conn, A. B., & Sorra, J. S. (2001). Implementing computerized technology: an organizational analysis. *Journal of Applied Psychology, 86,* 811–824.

Krause, D. (2004). Influence-based leadership as a detriment of the inclination to innovate and of innovation-related behaviors. *The Leadership Quarterly, 15,* 499–524.

Lapierre, J. & Giroux, V. P. (2003). Creativity and work environment in a high-tech context. *Creativity and Innovation Management, 12,* 11–23.

Laursen, K. & Salter, A. (2006). Open for innovation: the role of openness in explaining innovation performance among U.K. manufacturing firms. *Strategic Management Journal, 27,* 131–150.

Licuanan, B., Dailey, L. R. & Mumford, M. D. (2007) Idea evaluation: error in evaluating highly original ideas. *The Journal of Creative Behavior, 41,* 1–27.

Lonergan, D. C., Scott, G. M., & Mumford, M. D. (2004). Evaluative aspects of creative thought: effects of appraisal and revision standards. *Creativity Research Journal, 16,* 231–246.

Lovelace, K., Shapiro, D. L, & Weingart, L. R. (2001). Maximizing cross-functional new product teams' innovativeness and constraint adherence: a conflict communications perspective. *Academy of Management Journal, 44,* 779–793.

Luria, B. (2008) Climate strength–How leaders form consensus. *The Leadership Quarterly, 19,* 42–53.

McCrae, R. R. (1987). Creativity, divergent thinking, and openness to experience. *Journal of Personality and Social Psychology, 52,* 1258–1265.

McGourty, J., Tarshis, L. A., & Dominick, P. (1996). Managing innovation: Lessons from world class organizations. *International Journal of Technology Management, 11,* 354–368.

MacKinnon, D. W. (1962). The nature and nurture of creative talent. *American Psychology, 17,* 484–495.

Madjar, N., Oldham, G. R., Pratt, M. G. (2002). There's no place like home? The contributions of work and nonwork creativity support to employees' creative performance. *Academy of Management Journal, 45,* 757–787.

Maidique, M. & Zirger, B. J. (1984). A study of success and failure in product innovation: the case of the U.S. electronics industry. *IEEE Transactions in Engineering Management, 31,* 192–203.

Maier, N. R. F. & Hoffman, L. R. (1965). Acceptance and quality of solutions as related to leaders' attitudes toward disagreement in group problem-solving. *Journal of Applied Behavioral Science, 1,* 373–386.

Maier, N. R. F. & Janzen, J. C. (1969). Are good problem solvers also creative? *Psychological Reports, 24,* 139–146.

Maier, N. R. F. & Solem, A. R. (1962). Improving solutions by turning choice situations and problems. *Personnel Psychology, 15,* 151–157.

Marcy, R. T. & Mumford, M. D. (2007). Social innovation: enhancing creative performance through causal analysis. *Creativity Research Journal, 19,* 123–140.

Markham, S. K. & Aiman-Smith, L. (2001). Product champions: truths, myths, and management. *Research Technology Management, 44,* 44–50.

Marta S., Leritz, L. E., & Mumford, M. D. (2005). Leadership skills and group performance: situational demands, behavioral requirements, and planning. *The Leadership Quarterly, 16,* 97–120.

Miles, R. E. & Snow, C. C. (1978) *Organizational strategy, structure, and process.* New York: McGraw-Hill, 1978.

Mossholder, K. W. Dewhirst, H. D. (1980). The appropriateness of management-by-objectives for development and research personnel. *Journal of Management, 6,* 145–156.

Mouly, V. S. & Sankaran, J. K. (1999). The 'permanent' acting leader: insights from a dying Indian R & D organization. *The Leadership Quarterly, 10,* 637–651.

Mumford, M., Baughman, W., Maher, M., Costanza, D., & Supinski, E. (1997). Process-based measures of creative problem-solving skills: IV. category combination. *Creativity Research Journal, 10,* 59–71.

Mumford, M. D. (2000). Managing creative people: strategies and tactics for innovation. *Human Resource Management Review, 10,* 1–29.

Mumford, M. D. (2002). Social innovation: ten cases from Benjamin Franklin. *Creativity Research Journal, 14,* 253–266.

Mumford, M. D. (2003). Where have we been, where are we going? Taking stock in creativity research. *Creativity Research Journal, 14,* 107–120.

Mumford, M. D. & Gustafson, S. B. (1988). Creativity syndrome: integration, application, and innovation. *Psychological Bulletin, 103,* 27–43.

Mumford, M. D. & Gustafson, S. B. (2007). Creative thought: cognition and problem solving in a dynamic system. In M. A. Runco (ed.), *Creativity research handbook: Volume II.*Cresskill, NJ: Hampton, pp. 33–77.

Mumford, M. D. & Hunter, S. T. (2005). Innovation in organizations: a multi-level perspective on creativity. In F. Dansereau & F. J. Yammarino (eds), *Research in multi-level issues: Volume IV.* Oxford, England: Elsevier, pp 11–74.

Mumford, M. D. & Licuanan, B. (2004). Leading for innovation: conclusions, issues, and directions. *The Leadership Quarterly, 15,* 163–172.

Mumford, M. D., Bedell-Avers, K. E., & Hunter, S. T. (2008). Planning for innovation: a multi-level perspective. In M. D. Mumford, S. T. Hunter, & K. E. Bedell (eds), *Innovation in organizations: a multi-level perspective.* Oxford, England: Elsevier, pp. 107–154.

Mumford, M. D., Eubanks, D., & Murphy, S. R. (2006). Creating the conditions for success: best practices in leading for innovation. In J. A. Conger & R. E. Riggio (eds), *The practice of leadership: developing the next generation of leaders.* San Francisco, CA: Jossey-Bass, pp. 129–141.

Mumford, M. D., Feldman, J. M., Hein, M. B., & Nago, D. J. (2001). Tradeoffs between ideas and structure: individual versus group performance in creative-problem solving. *Journal of Creative Behavior, 35,* 1–23.

Mumford, M. D., Hunter, S. T., Eubanks, D. L., Bedell-Avers, K. E., & Murphy, S. T. (2007). Developing leaders for creative efforts: a domain-based approach to leader development. *Human Resource Management Review, 17,* 402–417.

Mumford, M. D., Marks, M. A., Connelly, M. S., Zaccaro, S. T., & Reiter-Palmon, R. (2000). Development of leadership skills: experience and training. *the Leadership Quarterly, 11,* 87–114.

Mumford, M. D., Mobley, M. I., Uhlman, C. E., Reiter-Palmon, R., & Doares, L. (1991). Process analytic models of creative capacities. *Creativity Research Journal, 4,* 91–122.

Mumford, M. D., Schultz, R. A., & Osburn, H. K. (2002). Planning in organizations: performance as a multi-level phenomenon. In F. J. Yammarino & F. Dansereau (eds), *Research in multi-level issues: the many faces of multi-level issues.* Oxford, England: Elsevier, pp. 3–63.

Mumford, M. D., Schultz, R. A., & Van Doorn, J. R. (2001). Performance in planning: processes, requirements, and errors. *Review of General Psychology, 5,* 213–240.

Mumford, M. D., Scott, G. M., Gaddis, B. H., & Strange, J. M. (2002). Leading creative people: orchestrating expertise and relationships. *The Leadership Quarterly, 13,* 705–750.

Murphy, S. E. & Ensher, E. A. (2008). A qualitative analysis of charismatic leadership in creative teams: the case of television directors. *The Leadership Quarterly, 19,* 335–352.

Nohari, K. & Gulati, D. (1996). Is slack good or bad for innovation? *Academy of Management Journal, 39,* 799–825.

Noice, H. (1991). The role of explanations and plan recognition in the learning of theatrical scripts. *Cognitive Science, 15,* 425–460.

O'Connor, G. C. (1998). Market learning and radical innovation: a cross case comparison of eight radical innovation projects. *Journal of Product Innovation Management, 15,* 151–166.

Oldham, G. R. & Cummings, A. (1996). Employee creativity: personal and contextual factors at work. *Academy of Management Journal, 39,* 607–634.

Osborn, R. N. & Marion, R. (2009). Contextual leadership, transformational leadership and the performance of international innovation seeking alliances. *The Leadership Quarterly.*

Osburn, H. & Mumford, M. (2006). Creativity and planning: training interventions to develop creative problem-solving skills. *Creativity Research Journal, 18,* 173–190.

Pant, P. N. & Starbuck, W. H. (1990). Innocents in the forest: forecasting and research methods. *Journal of Management, 16,* 433–460.

Parnes, S. J. & Noller, R. B. (1972). Applied creativity: the creative studies project: part results of the two-year program. *Journal of Creative Behavior, 6,* 164–186.

Paulus, P. B. (2000). Groups, teams, and creativity: the creative potential of idea-generating groups. *Applied Psychology 49*(2), 237–262.

Pearce, C. L. & Ensley, M. D. (2004). A reciprocal and longitudinal investigation of the innovation process: the central role of shared vision in product and process innovation teams (PPITs). *Journal of Organizational Behavior, 25,* 259–278.

Pelz, D. C. (1963). Relationships between measures of scientific performance and other variables. In C. W. Taylor, & F. Barron (eds), *Scientific creativity: its recognition and development.* New York: Wiley, pp. 302–310.

Pelz, D. C. & Andrews, F. M. (1966). Autonomy, coordination, and simulation in relation to scientific achievement. *Behavioral Science, 12,* 89–97.

Pelz, D. C. & Andrews, F. M. (1976). *Scientists in organizations.* Ann Arbor, MI: Institute for Social Research.

Perez-Freije, J. & Enkel E. (2007). Creative tension in the innovation process: how to support the right capabilities. *European Management Journal, 14,* 5–18.

Pirola-Merlo, A., Haertel, C., & Mann, L. (2002). How leaders influence the impact of affective events on team climate and performance in R&D teams. *The Leadership Quarterly, 13,* 561–581.

Redmond, M. R., Mumford, M. D., & Teach, R. J. (1993). Putting creativity to work: leader influences on subordinate creativity. *Organizational Behavior and Human Decision Processes, 55,* 120–151.

Robinson, R. B. & Pearce, J. A. (1988). Planned patterns of strategic behavior and their relationship to business-unit performance. *Strategic Management Journal, 20,* 691–710.

Root-Berstein, R. S., Berstein, M., & Garnier, H. (1995). Correlations between avocations, scientific style, work habits, and professional impact of scientists. *Creativity Research Journal, 8,* 115–137.

Salomo, S., Weise, J., & Gemunden, H. G. (2007). NPD planning activities and innovation performance: the mediating role of process management and the moderating effect of product innovativeness. *Journal of Product Innovation Management, 24,* 285–302.

Scott, G. M., Lonergan, D. C., & Mumford, M. D. (2005). Conceptual combination: alternative knowledge structures, alternative heuristics. *Creativity Research Journal, 17,* 79–98.

Scott, S. G. & Bruce, R. A. (1994). Determinants of innovative behavior: a path model of individual innovation in the workplace. *Academy of Management Journal, 37,* 580–607.

Senge, P. M. (1990). *The fifth discipline.* London: Century Business.

Shalley, C. E. & Gilson, L. L. (2004). What leaders need to know: a review of social and contextual factors that can foster or hinder creativity. *The Leadership Quarterly, 15*(1) 33–53.

Shalley, C. E. & Zhou, J. (2008). Organizational creativity research: a historical overview. In J. Zhou & C. E. Shalley (eds) *Handbook of organizational creativity.* New York: Taylor & Francis, pp. 3–32.

Sharma, A. (1999). Central dilemmas of managing innovation in large firms. *California Management Review, 41,* 65–85.

Shin, S. J. & Zhou, J. (2003) Transformational leadership, conservation, and creativity: evidence from Korea. *Academy of Management Journal, 46,* 703–714.

Shipper, F. & Davy, J. (2002). A model and investigation of managerial skills, employees' attitudes, and managerial performance. *The Leadership Quarterly, 13,* 95–120.

Simonton, D. K. (1990). *Psychology, science, and history: an introduction to historiometry.* New Haven, CT: Yale University Press.

Sternberg, R. J. (1986). Toward a unified theory of human reasoning. *Intelligence, 10,* 281–315.

Sternberg, R. J. (2008). We want creativity! No we don't. In F. Dansereau, & F. J. Yammarino (eds), *Multi-level issues in strategy and methods.* Oxford: Elsevier, pp. 43–104.

Taggar, S. (2002). Individual creativity and group ability to utilize individual creative resources: a multilevel model. *Academy of Management Journal, 45,* 315–330.

Thamhain, H. J. (2003). Managing innovative R&D teams. *R&D Management, 44,* 297–322.

Thamhain H. J. & Gemmill G. R. (1974). Influence styles of project managers: some project performance correlates. *Academy of Management Journal, 17,* 216–224.

Tierney, P. & Farmer, S. M. (2002). Creative self-efficacy: its potential antecedents and relationship to creative performance. *Academy of Management Journal, 45,* 1137–1148.

Tierney, P., Farmer, S. M., & Graen, G. B. (1999). An examination of leadership and employee creativity: the relevance of traits and relationships. *Personnel Psychology, 52,* 591–620.

Trevelyan, R. (2001). The paradox of autonomy: a case of academic research scientists. *Human Relations, 54,* 495–525.

Tushman, M. L. & O'Reilly, C. A. (1996). Ambidextrous organizations: managing evolutionary and revolutionary change. *Management Review, 38,* 8–30.

Vincent, A. H., Decker, B. P., & Mumford, M. D. (2002). Divergent thinking, intelligence, and expertise: a test of alternative models. *Creativity Research Journal, 14,* 163–178.

Waldman, D. A. & Atwater, L. E. (1992) The nature of effective leadership and championing processes at different levels in an R&D hierarchy. *Journal of High Technology Management Research 5,* 233–245.

Ward, T. B., Patterson, M. J., & Sifonis, C. M. (2004). The role of specificity and abstraction in creative idea generation. *Creativity Research Journal, 16,* 1–9.

Weber, R. N. & Perkins, D. J. (1992). *Inventive minds: creativity in technology.* New York: Oxford University Press.

Weisberg, R. W. (2006). Expertise and reason in creative thinking: evidence from case studies and the laboratory. In J. C. Kaufman & J. Baer (eds), *Creativity and reason in cognitive development.* New York: Cambridge University Press, pp. 7–42.

Weisberg, R. W. & Hass, R. (2007). We are all partly right: comment on Simonton. *Creativity Research Journal, 19,* 345–360.

West, M. A., Borrill, C. S., Dawson, J. F., Brodbeck, F., Shapiro, D. A., & Haward, B. (2003). Leadership clarity and team innovation in health care. *The Leadership Quarterly, 14,* 393–410.

West, M. A., Hirst, G., Richter, A., & Shipton, H. (2004). Twelve steps to heaven: successfully managing change through developing innovative teams. *European Journal of Work and Organizational Psychology, 13,* 269–299.

Wise, G. (1992). Inventions and corporations in the maturing electrical industry. In R. J. Weber & D. N. Perkins (eds), *Inventive minds: creativity in technology.* New York: Oxford University Press, pp. 291–310.

Woodman, R. W., Sawyer, J. E., & Griffin, R. W. (1993). Toward a theory of organizational creativity. *Academy of Management Review, 18,* 293–321.

Yukl, G. (2001). *Leadership in organizations.* Englewood Cliffs, NJ: Prentice-Hall.

Zhou, J. & George, J. M. (2003). Awakening employees creativity: the role of leader emotional intelligence. *The Leadership Quarterly, 14,* 461–478.

Zuckerman, H. (1977). *The scientific elite.* New York: Free Press.

PART V

Emerging Perspectives

Followership and Follower-Centred Approaches

Michelle C. Bligh

To treat leading and following as simultaneous is to redistribute knowing and doubting more widely, to expect ignorance and fallibility to be similarly distributed, and to expect that knowledge is what happens between heads rather than inside a single leader's head.

Karl Weick (2007, p. 281)

Let no one say that he is a follower of Gandhi. It is enough that I should be my own follower. I know what an inadequate follower I am of myself, for I cannot live up to the convictions I stand for. You are not followers but fellow students, fellow pilgrims, fellow seekers, fellow workers.

Gandhi (1940/1957)

INTRODUCTION

It is a tribute to the rising interest in followership that there are now pervasive reminders in both academic and business publications that 'the essence of leadership is followership' and that 'without followers there can be no leaders.' In fact, there are some clear indications that interest in followership has been steadily increasing, despite declarations that it is 'outmoded,' 'out of tune' and 'discordant' with the dominant melody of contemporary organizations (Rost, 2008, p. 53). Google searches for the word 'leader' on

September 1, 2009 generated 247 million items about leaders, and for 'follower' only 11.3 million items. This 22:1 ratio of leader-follower items is significantly lower than the 57:1 ratio that Karl Weick reported in 2006 (Weick, 2007). In addition, several edited volumes have recently been devoted entirely to followership (Riggio, Chaleff, & Lipman-Blumen, 2008; Shamir, Pillai, Bligh, & Uhl-Bien, 2007), and the number of articles in leadership-oriented journals (e.g., *Leadership* and the *Leadership Quarterly*) that explicitly focus on followership and follower-centred perspectives has been growing. Bligh and Kohles (2008) conducted a content analysis of the *Leadership Quarterly* articles from 1990, the first year *LQ* was published, through 2008. They found that over this 19-year period, just 14% of the articles published included some version of the word follower in the abstract or title. Despite this still relatively unbalanced equation, there is growing recognition that leaders follow and followers lead, blurring any semblance of clear distinctions in contemporary organizations and research studies.

This chapter is a review of the literature on followership that challenges traditional assumptions of what it means to lead and what it means to follow. It is an attempt to summarize a growing stream of research that relaxes the assumption that leaders are fundamentally important in their own right, and that leaders are always inherently critical to the leadership process (Meindl, 1993, 1998; Meindl, Ehrlich, & Dukerich, 1985). While followers have always been recognized as an important part of the leadership process, the study of followership has emerged as a critical, even 'controversial' (Kelley, 2008) stream of theorizing and research that has provided an alternative to the 'mainstream' leadership tradition. In the process of its development, it has helped to crystallize what leadership research looks like and what it has left out. It is in the development of this critical approach within the leadership field that some of the most interesting advances have been made, and it is in the emergence of this alternate perspective that followership has the greatest contribution yet to make. As Weick (2007) puts it, follower-centred approaches deepen almost any leader-centric analysis: when we shift questions of perception and attention from leaders to followers, then inevitably new issues arise and new questions are raised.

In the sections that follow, I provide a historical overview of some of the primary theories of followership, the research streams that have begun to coalesce within this broad tradition, and conclude with what I see are some of the pressing issues for the field as well as future directions these issues may take. Despite the recent growing interest in followership, the vast majority of research continues to focus on leaders and leadership. Within this broader tradition, those studies that do focus on followers often do so from within a very limited perspective, treating followers as 'an undifferentiated mass or collective' (Collinson, 2006, p. 179). However, it is a favorable reflection of the growing interest in followership and follower-centred approaches that it is no longer possible to devote adequate space and attention in a single chapter to all of the work that has been done under this broad umbrella. Therefore, I attempt to provide a summative survey of some of the prevailing perspectives that have shaped our current understanding of what constitutes 'followership.'

In a recent review, Bligh and Kohles (2008) found that articles on followers fell into three broad categories: (1) *follower attributes* relevant to the leadership process, including follower perceptions, affect, identity, motivation, and values; (2) *leader–follower relations*, such as the active role followers play in dynamic leadership processes; and (3) *follower outcomes* of leadership behaviors, such as performance, creativity, or other dependent variables and unspecified effects that leaders have on followers. The focus of this chapter is on the first two categories, which explicitly tackle the proverbial 'other side' of the leadership coin, and thus represent a critical departure from treating followers as outcomes in the 'typical leadership study' (Hunter, Bedell-Avers, & Mumford, 2007).

THE EVOLUTION OF LEADERSHIP AND FOLLOWERSHIP: A HISTORICAL PERSPECTIVE

Building on Kuhn's (1970) work, Reichers and Schneider (1990) pointed out that scientific concepts exhibit a predictable sequence of development. The first stage in the sequence is introduction and elaboration, when a new concept is either borrowed, invented, or discovered. In general, this stage is characterized by attempts to legitimize the new concept and focus on its definition, importance, and utility for augmenting existing knowledge and understanding. In many ways, much of the current work on followership is still in this first stage of introduction and elaboration. However, evidence is beginning to emerge that followership is entering the second stage of conceptual development, one of evaluation and augmentation (Reichers & Schneider, 1990). During this stage, critical reviews of the concept begin to emerge and clearly distinguished traditions begin to develop. A recent example is Baker's (2007) description of the four basic tenets that define active followership: (a) that followers and leaders are roles, not people with inherent characteristics; (b) that followers are active, not passive; (c) that followers and leaders share a common purpose; and (d) that followers and leaders must be studied in the context of their relationship.

As Hollander (1995, p. 56) pointed out, 'followership is periodically rediscovered as important to leadership, despite a long tradition of usage' that has emerged and re-emerged since at least the sixth century BCE. Meindl (1990) similarly highlights this cycle in his observation that 'leadership comes and goes and comes around again,' suggesting that leadership and followership ebb and flow in a predictable, even faddish, cycle. In a historical review of the field of leadership, Pearce and Conger (2003) pointed to the roots of the leader–follower dichotomy in the Industrial Revolution, its emphasis on control and oversight, and scientific management. Within this context, early management scholars emphasized distinctions between leaders and followers, and 'spent considerable time trying to figure out ways to prevent followers from shirking responsibilities' (p. 6). Mary Parker Follett's (1924) work provided an early exception to this prevailing approach. Her writings on leader–follower relations emphasized leadership as a partnership in reciprocal following, but the social and economic context of the 1920s and 1930s effectively suppressed any paradigmatic shifts in the relationships between leaders and followers until nearly a century later.

Despite a long tradition of sporadic attention to followership, it was not until the late twentieth century that the tradition of followership began to more fully emerge and gain momentum (see also Baker, 2007). James Meindl and his colleagues introduced and developed the romance of leadership in the 1980s as a fundamentally follower-centred approach that did not disregard the importance of leaders, but instead directed attention toward the importance of followers' processes of attribution and sensemaking in organizations. Around the same time, Kelley's (1988) influential article 'In Praise of Followers' sought to redraw the map of leadership research, with followership in the middle rather than at the periphery (Kelley, 2008). Chaleff (1998) also argued persuasively that followers have a moral responsibility to both leaders and organizations to act courageously, and that, rather than serving leaders, both leaders and followers serve a common purpose from complementary roles (see also Chaleff, 2008). Within a short time period, numerous authors were arguing for shifting approaches to leadership and followership. Hosking (1988) pointed out that 'we need to understand leadership, and for this, it is not enough to understand what leaders do' (p. 147). Hollander (1992) echoed this sentiment, arguing that leadership is more accurately viewed as a process rather than as a person. As the twentieth century drew to a close, Warren Bennis (1999) decried 'the end of leadership,' pointing out that the traditional top-down approach to leadership 'was not only wrong, unrealistic and maladaptive but also, given the report of history, dangerous' (p. 71).

Related research traditions helped to further erode traditional leader–follower distinctions, including that of shared leadership (Pearce & Conger, 2003), self-management/self-leadership (Manz, 1986; Manz & Sims, 1980), leader–member exchange (Graen & Uhl-Bien, 1995; Anand et al. Chapter 23, in this volume), and substitutes or neutralizers of leadership (Kerr & Jermier, 1978). All of these theories relaxed the assumption that leadership behaviors must occur within formal hierarchical roles. Lord and Brown's (2003) work went even further, advocating a process-oriented and reverse-engineered approach to leadership centred around followers. That is, rather than describing what leaders do, they examined the relationship between these activities and outcomes, and then attempted to understand why leadership effects occur, 'The most defensible strategy for leadership research and practice is to understand factors central to subordinates' motivation, affect, and development and then work backwards to analyze how leaders might influence these processes' (p. 6). Other approaches, such as Uhl-Bien's (2006) relational leadership theory and Uhl-Bien, Marion, and McKelvey's (2007)

leadership complexity theory, also treat leadership as an interactive dynamic relationship between organizational actors from which adaptive outcomes (e.g., learning, innovation, and adaptability) emerge (Marion & Uhl-Bien, 2001; see also Uhl-Bien and Marion, Chapter 34, in this volume). Other relevant discussions include Gronn's (2002) appeal for distributed leadership, which also critiqued the leader–follower dichotomy and emphasized interdependence, coordination, and the reciprocal influence (see Gronn, Chapter 32, in this volume). Similarly, Prince (2005) drew on the Eastern tradition of Taoism to promote an approach that treats leadership and the use of power as a fluid set of interrelations. Taken together, these perspectives formed a coalescing tradition in the leadership field that sought to relax assumptions that leaders and followers are always distinctly different actors with fundamentally distinct characteristics and behaviors, and focused increased attention on the interactive relationship at the core of the leadership process.

THEORIES OF FOLLOWERSHIP

Kelley's (1988, 1992) work offered one of the first explicit theories of followership. He defined followers in terms of two dimensions: independent/critical thought and passive/active. Based on these two dimensions, he offered five basic styles of followership: the sheep, the yes-people, the alienated, the pragmatics, and the star followers. This initial framework led to a number of related questions, including: What assumptions do leaders (and followers) make about the various followership styles? Do certain mixes of follower styles create more favorable situations for leaders? Can people move easily from one followership style to another? Kelley (2008, p. 5) points out that his initial work was explicitly designed to put a stake in the ground and declare, 'We need to pay attention to followers.' Kelley's influential and initially controversial framework began a discussion around why followership was most frequently associated with negative stereotypes, yet stopped short of problematizing the leader–follower dichotomy or questioning the nature of leadership and followership (see also Kelley, 2004).

The romance of leadership as a follower-centric approach

It was the work of James Meindl and colleagues that began to address these latter issues more directly within mainstream leadership research, marking the beginning of a truly follower-centric approach to leadership. Meindl (1995, p. 330) articulated his follower-centred approach as 'an alternative to theories and perspectives that place great weight on "leaders" and on the substantive significance to their actions and activities.' Meindl did not reject or minimize the importance of leadership, but simply emphasized that 'it is easier to believe in leadership than to prove it' (Meindl, 1990, p. 161). Meindl's legacy has primarily been enacted as a critique of the cultural and societal fascination with leadership, and the prevailing emphasis on heroism, charisma, and the glorification of leadership in the face of any real proof of its efficacy (Bligh, Pillai, & Uhl-Bien, 2007b).

The romance of leadership perspective developed by Meindl et al. (1985) provided convincing evidence that leaders and leadership issues often become the favored explanations for both positive and negative outcomes in and around organizations. In addition, subsequent research has demonstrated that people value performance results more highly when those results are attributed to leadership, and that a halo effect exists for leadership attributes: if an individual is perceived to be an effective leader, his or her personal shortcomings and poor organizational performance may be overlooked (Meindl & Ehrlich, 1987). Meindl pointed out that this one-sided emphasis on the positive forms of leadership can be dangerous, for it suggests that leaders are inherently positive forces for individuals, organizations, and humanity as a whole. Meindl et al. (1985, p. 100) also asserted that this 'continuing infatuation with leadership, for whatever truths it yields about the qualities and behavior of our leaders, can also be used to learn something about the motivations of followers.' This observation proved influential in spawning empirical evidence that approaches ratings and perceptions of leaders' behaviors were not 'objective' measures of leadership, but rather as important insights into how *followers* conceptualize leader behaviors and their potential impacts (real or otherwise) (e.g., Bligh et al., 2007a).

Other researchers built upon the romance of leadership to examine societal constructions of leadership that are produced and consumed in the popular press (Bligh & Meindl, 2004; Jackson & Guthey, 2007). Images of 'great' leadership figures feed our appetite as a society for leadership products and behaviors that promise to enrich or improve followers' lives, fixating attention on the personas and characteristics of leaders while relegating followers to the peripheral shadows or outside of the picture altogether (Meindl, 1990). In their examination of the 'Celebrity CEO Backlash,' or the period of media recrimination and criticism directed against former business heroes, Jackson and Guthey (2007) illustrate how visual images in the popular media can work to *deconstruct* images of business leaders and set in play multiple or even conflicting leadership images at the same time. Work in this tradition has highlighted our collective desire to believe in an 'omnipotent leader' (Schilling, 2007, p. 616), painting leaders as 'heroes' or 'villains' to be elevated or blamed for organizational successes and failures (Collinson, 2005a). It also points out the emphasis on leadership effectively mitigates the responsibility and accountability of followers (Ba Banutu-Gomez, 2004; Uhl-Bien & Pillai, 2007). Other research has pointed out that leaders themselves may utilize self-deception and impression management techniques to effectively 'woo' followers into believing in the inflated potency and efficacy of the leader (Gray & Densten, 2008; Kets de Vries, 2001).

From follower-centric approaches to the study of followership

Building on the romance of leadership approach, Uhl-Bien and Pillai (2007) offered a corollary to the romance of leadership, which they termed the subordination of followership. Historically, they point out that 'follower' often has a pejorative connotation in leadership research, evoking images of passivity, conformance, compliance, inferiority, and a lack of drive and ambition. They assert that prototypical followership behaviors involve some sort of deference to the leader, and that in more hierarchical contexts, followers are more likely to construct their roles based on status differentials, resulting in reduced responsibility-taking and initiative and increased reliance on the leader for motivation. In contrast, Uhl-Bien and Pillai suggest followers can also more actively construct their roles as partners, participants, and co-leaders and co-followers. Collinson (2006) echoes this sentiment, pointing out that followers are not hapless beings that exist at the mercy of their leaders. Instead, followers are often active, powerful players in the leadership process (see also Shamir, 2007).

Carsten et al. (2010) distinguished follower*ship* approaches from follower-*centric* approaches to leadership (i.e., Meindl, 1995), in that the issue of interest is not follower perspectives of leadership but instead *follower perspectives of followership*. Rather than considering how followers view their leaders and their leaders' behaviors, a focus on followership considers how followers view their own behaviors and roles when engaging with leaders (see also Uhl-Bien & Pillai, 2007). Carsten et al.'s research demonstrated that followership holds 'a multiplicity of meaning,' in that individuals develop followership schema along a continuum from more passive and obedient at one end to more proactive at the other. Furthermore, they found that followership constructions were related to leadership styles (more authoritarian vs supportive/empowering) and organizational climate (more bureaucratic/ hierarchical vs empowering). Thus, in alignment with Meindl's (1995) arguments, social constructions of followership appear to be the product of both individual schema and relevant contextual variables within an organization.

Role orientations and leader–follower states

Recently, a number of authors have attempted to develop theoretical frameworks to categorize different approaches to followership. Howell and Mendez (2008) offered three perspectives, or role orientations, on followership: followership as an interactive role, followership as an independent role, and followership as a shifting role. In approaching followership as an interactive role orientation, followers complement and support the leader, and in its most effective form, are as critically important to achieving team and organizational goals as the leadership process. In this approach, effective followers demonstrate knowledge and competence, build collaborative relationships, defend the leader, exert influence on the leader, and support him or her. In the second role orientation, followers are treated as independent actors in organizations. In addition, this orientation emphasizes follower substitutes for leaders in the context of more highly skilled, trained, knowledgeable, and self-deterministic followers who can take on behaviors and tasks that historically have been carried out by hierarchical leaders. Finally, Howell and Mendez (2008) point out a third followership role orientation, which reflects alternating leader and follower roles. In this approach, followers monitor and interpret the environment to respond to dynamic changes, actively participate in decision-making when appropriate, challenge the team, and role-model effective team behaviors. Howell and Mendez (2008) outline three primary antecedents of follower role orientations, including followers' self-concept, the leader's expectations, and organizational factors such as the interdependence of tasks and reward systems.

In presenting what he terms a 'new leadership–followership paradigm,' Stech (2008) similarly delineated three different approaches to the study of leaders and followers: (1) the leader–follower paradigm, which focuses on the individual leader as an exemplar or a 'hero'; (2) the leader–follower

position paradigm, which emphasizes the formal, hierarchical, and bureaucratic organization in which leaders are defined by their positions of authority; and (3) the leader–follower *state* paradigm, in which leadership and followership are states or conditions (or roles, cf. Howell & Mendez, 2008) that can be occupied at various times by different individuals. The first approach follows the tradition of the Great Leader, which Meindl and colleagues challenged in the romance of leadership; the second approach is reflective of the hierarchical differentiation between leaders and followers, in the tradition of the Industrial Revolution; and the third approach is very much in line with Collinson's (2005b, p. 1436) call for 'multiple, shifting, contradictory and ambiguous identities of "leaders" and "followers."' In addition, it echoes the words of Visa founder Dee Hock (1999, p. 72): 'In the deepest sense, distinction between leaders and followers is meaningless. In every moment of life, we are simultaneously leading and following.'

Within the followership tradition, a number of theorists have also vocally problematized the meaning of followership itself, and what using the labels of 'leader' and 'follower' continue to signify. Hosking (2007) proposed moving toward a postmodern discourse of leadership as a process that goes beyond 'overly simple "outsider" assumptions' about who are leaders and who are followers, embracing the possibility of distributed leadership, taking followers' involvement in leadership seriously, and giving space to developing 'followers' into leaders. From this approach, practitioners and researchers must embrace multiple local leadership constructions that involve all participants in research (not just hierarchical leaders and top management). Others argue for a poststructuralist approach to leadership and followership that focuses on relational realities involving constructions of the self in relation to others, and explores how someone is constructed as a leader or follower and how these realities are created and changed (Collinson, 2006; Uhl-Bien & Pillai, 2007). Uhl-Bien and Pillai argued that socially constructed views of followership influence both attributions of leadership and attributions by followers about themselves and their own roles and participation in the leadership process. For instance, prototypical followership interpretations involve deference to the leader, particularly when there are hierarchical constructions of leadership and followership. Collinson (2006) presented an alternative way of conceiving identity and power and examined a wider repertoire of follower selves, exploring in particular conformist, resistant, and dramaturgical identities.

Similarly, drawing on post-structuralist perspectives, Collinson (2005b) considered leader–follower relations as mutually constituting and co-produced, explicitly highlighting the tensions, contradictions and ambiguities that often characterize shifting asymmetrical and interdependent leadership dynamics. He went on to outline how three interrelated 'dialectics' (i.e., control/resistance, dissent/consent and men/women) shape ambiguous and potentially contradictory conditions, processes and consequences. Collinson (2005b, p. 1422) pointed out that since asymmetrical power relations are always bidirectional, leaders are always somewhat dependent on the led, while followers always retain some degree of autonomy and discretion. Reconceptualizing followers in this way as knowledgeable and proactive agents highlights the 'repertoire of possible agencies' they have at their disposal.

ASKING NEW QUESTIONS AND QUESTIONING OLD ANSWERS

New approaches to followers and followers' perceptions have been extrapolated and enacted in a multitude of ways that encourage leadership research to both ask new questions as well as question traditional leader-centric assumptions and answers. These questions include how followers construct leadership (Meindl, 1995), and how followers engage in traditional leader influence processes (e.g., self-leadership and shared leadership, Manz & Sims, 1980; Pearce & Conger, 2003) ranging from *co*-leadership to *collective* leadership/followership (Offermann, 2004; Offermann & Scuderi, 2007). Other researchers have begun to explore how followers' personal characteristics influence perceptions of leadership (Schyns & Felfe, 2006), the critical role of followers' attributional processes in leadership (Meindl, 1995), followers' implicit theories and schemas (De Vries & van Gelder, 2005; Medvedeff & Lord, 2007), followers' social identities (Collinson, 2006; Hogg, 2008), and followers' psychological needs (Lipman-Blumen, 2007, 2008).

In part as a response to these needs, followers socially construct leadership (and followership, Uhl-Bien & Pillai, 2007) through their interactions with one another, which has been examined in groups (van Knippenberg, van Knippenberg, & Giessner, 2007) and in social networks (Mayo & Pastor, 2007; Pastor, Meindl, & Mayo, 2002). Followers construct these views of leadership and followership through cognitive inference processes by which they surmise that leadership has occurred (Lord, 2008; Medvedeff & Lord, 2007) and by looking to reference points that exist in their social groups, which become a critical

source of information about leadership and social reality (Hogg, 2008; van Knippenberg et al., 2007). Follower-centred approaches thus highlight the importance of inter-follower processes from a number of different angles: followers are not just connected to leaders, they are also connected to other followers. Researchers must also consider *inter*-follower processes to get a better understanding of leadership (Mayo & Pastor, 2007; Pastor et al., 2002). An important emphasis here is that sensemaking is integral to the process of leadership, and individuals learn the meaning of leadership behaviors through their interactions both with leaders and with one another.

Thus, the field has begun to empirically examine followers' ratings and perceptions of leaders' behaviors as important insights into how followers conceptualize leader behaviors and their potential impact (Schyns & Bligh, 2007). More radically, follower-centred perspectives move away from traditional conceptualizations of leaders and followers to describe leadership as distributed, contested, and contradictory (Collinson, 2000, 2005a, 2005b, 2006, 2008; Hosking, 2007), involving the explicit recognition that followers have long shared leadership with those who have led (Offermann & Scuderi, 2007). Followers can actively counteract the effect of destructive and toxic leaders by holding leaders accountable, creating term limits and departure options, and even calling upon their own enduring ambivalence about leaders to drive themselves to action (Lipman-Blumen, 2007, 2008). Whereas followers may be more or less susceptible to a charismatic leader to lead them out of crisis, they can and do exercise their rights to vote an ineffective leader out of office (Pillai et al., 2007).

In addition, a seemingly infinite number of traditionally leader-centric constructs can be fruitfully reexamined from a follower-centric approach (Weick, 2007). For example, Jaussi, Stefanovich, and Devlin (2008) pointed out that followers can and do leverage who they are as followers as the driving force for innovation and creativity in organizations. Carsten and Bligh's (2007, 2008) work similarly illustrated that followers are not just passive recipients of a leader's vision: they are actively involved in constructing the meaning of the vision to their own work roles, and they develop emotional investment or skepticism and resistance in response to a leader's vision. Other examples of this type of reframing from a follower-centred perspective include whistleblowing as responsible followership (Alford, 2008), authentic follower development (Avolio & Reichard, 2008), bullying (Lipman-Blumen, 2008), and even the infamous Milgram obedience experiments (Blass, 2008).

A further example of viewing more leader-centric phenomenon from a follower-centric lens is provided in shifting approaches to charismatic leadership. Mayo and Pastor (2007) point out that followers who are more agreeable (one of the Big 5 personality factors; see McCrae & Costa, 1991) and emotionally intense are also more likely to succumb to the charisma 'virus.' In addition, followers who are high in both closeness centrality and in-betweenness centrality within a given social network are most likely to spread charismatic attributions. More anxious followers are more likely to socially construct and project qualities on a leader to help allay their fears (Beyer, 1999a). In circumstances of crisis or ambiguity, exceptional or 'charismatic' qualities in a leader may be actual, attributed, or exaggerated. As Shamir and Howell (1999, p. 260) put it, post-crisis followers 'will readily, even eagerly, accept the influence of a leader who seems to have high self-confidence and a vision that provides both meaning to the current situation and promise of salvation from the currently acute distress.' Pillai and Meindl (1998) found that followers more often used charismatic criteria for emergent leadership in situations of crisis. And after the terrorist attacks of September 11, 2001, Bligh et al. (2004) provided evidence that the ambiguity and uncertainty surrounding the crisis set the stage for more charismatic attributions of President George W. Bush.

Several other examples highlight that a follower-centred approach has begun to be realized more broadly outside the realm of charismatic leadership as well. Meindl (1990, p. 198) argued that follower-centred approaches could complement existing leader-centric approaches through increased 'focus on the social psychological processes that take place among followers, independent of, or controlling for the actions and traits of the leader.' For example, Kark and Van Dijk's (2007) theory explicitly recognizes the potential of bidirectional influence: in their model, followers play an active role, activating a certain regulatory focus among leaders, and thus affecting a leader's style and behavior. Other recent theoretical work has explored how temporal influences affect both leaders and followers, and ultimately the effectiveness of the leadership process and relationship (Bluedorn & Jaussi, 2008).

Perhaps most importantly, follower-centric approaches have recently begun to tackle the 'big issues' happening in the world, such as how followership can help us unravel issues of fundamentalism and extremism, dictatorship, corrupt governments, and corporate abuses of power (Kelley, 2008). Lipman-Blumen (2007, 2008) described the strong needs of followers to have

leaders who can keep them safe in uncertain situations and provide vision and direction, particularly in times of crisis or ambiguity. Along with Kellerman (2004), this work has raised the important issues concerning how followers are co-implicated in bad leadership and destructive outcomes (see also Padilla, Hogan, & Kaiser, 2007). However, important questions remain concerning how followers can actively resist leaders, and what societal and individual-level factors inhibit them from doing so (Uhl-Bien & Carsten, 2007). Padilla et al. (2007) outlined two types of followers that support destructive leadership, conformers and colluders. Conformers passively allow bad leaders to assume power because their unmet needs and immaturity make them vulnerable. Colluders, on the other hand, support destructive leaders because they want to promote themselves in an enterprise consistent with their own worldview. As Ba Banutu-Gomez (2004, p. 147) pointed out, 'followers can evaporate a leader's mask of power merely by dis-believing in it. Authority does not reside in those who issue orders; rather, authority lies with*in* the *responses* of persons to whom those orders are addressed.' Yet we know little about the conditions surrounding how this form of authority operates, and what factors encourage followers to exercise their authority more or less readily.

IMPLICATIONS AND UNANSWERED QUESTIONS

The research reviewed in this chapter brings to mind a wide-ranging agenda for research into follower perceptions of leadership and followership, inter-follower processes, the role of context in understanding leader–follower processes, and the role of follower cognitions, personalities, attitudes, and emotions in understanding dynamic leader–follower relations. In addition, it suggests some important practical implications as well. First and foremost, organizations should consider adopting policies and practices that encourage proactive followership. For example, Microsoft has identified 'comfort around authority' as one of the 10 core competencies for its staff. Other organizations have begun to experiment with radical transparency in order to facilitate the breakdown of hierarchical leader–follower distinctions. In addition, Chaleff (2003, 2008) outlined practical conditions that must be in place in order to promote and exercise courageous followership. First, the follower must value the leader and the talents he or she brings. Chaleff cited Baldassare Castiglione, author of *The Book of the Courtier* and a contemporary of Machiavelli. According to Castiglione, the aim of the courtier is to so win the favor of the prince by good deeds so that, when he sees the mind of the prince inclined to an evil action, he can speak up and bring the prince back to a path of virtue. Similarly, courageous followership requires a foundation of trust so that the leader knows that the follower supports both his interest and the mission.

Paradoxically, a second necessary precondition is having the courage to risk the relationship by speaking truth to power. The follower who is not willing to do so cannot be effective in balancing out the tendency for power to corrupt those in a leadership position. And finally, courage alone may often not be enough. Followers must also develop the skills to speak up credibly and assertively so that leaders will pay attention. In addition, followers must be able to accurately gauge how and when to raise sensitive topics. Through role-playing activities, followers can learn how to overcome inhibitions against being too assertive in the face of authority, as well as how to raise issues forcefully enough to be heard, particularly in times of ambiguity, crisis, or turbulence.

Future directions

Part of the followership legacy is the establishment of an ongoing research tradition that approaches leadership as a complex and socially constructed phenomenon involving not only leaders but also followers and the contexts in which leaders and followers interact. It is in the development of this followership legacy, I have argued, that the most significant contributions have been made and will continue to be made as we tackle the 'big issues' of the twenty-first century.

Below are some specific research questions that remain relatively unexplored:

Defining leadership and followership processes

- How do both leaders and followers play an important and active role in managing dynamic leader–follower processes?
- What are the key affective and cognitive mechanisms that influence constructions of leadership and followership?
- What is the process by which 'followership' is socially constructed, and what factors cause it to be constructed in different ways? What is the role of organizational culture and structures in suppressing or fostering a climate for effective followership?

- What role does social contagion play in the spread of leader and follower constructions? Can followers empower one another to step up and take leadership responsibility?
- How do courageous followers act as leaders themselves, testing their reality through conversation with others and building coalitions with others who can help them get their message heard?

Contextual and cultural influences on leadership and followership

- What is the role of different types of contexts on leader–follower attributions?
- What contexts (e.g., organizational change, restructuring, leadership turnover) are particularly ripe for follower constructions of charismatic, authentic, or effective leadership? What can be learned through exploring the perspectives of organizational members who are experiencing organizational change (as opposed to those of leaders or external audiences)?
- Is truly shared or distributed leadership possible during a crisis? What kinds of situations would be more or less conducive to distributed, collaborative, or shared leadership?
- What cultural factors impact implicit theories of followership? Do cultural barriers (e.g., power distance, collectivism, uncertainty avoidance) inhibit some followers from questioning authority?

Romancing leaders and subordinating followers

- How do both leaders and followers contribute to romanticizing the importance of leaders and downplaying the role of followers in both sustaining the status quo as well as contributing to larger organizational and societal changes?
- What are some of the key underlying mechanisms through which charismatic leadership attributions are made? Who are the first followers to succumb to the charisma or toxic leadership 'virus' in specific contexts (e.g., situations of crisis, organizational change or restructuring)?

Ethical Implications of leader–follower processes

- Is a whistleblower simply a disenfranchised courageous follower? How can we create contexts where constructive dialogue is not seen as treason, but rather as a mechanism for an organization to self-correct internally before a dangerous situation explodes?

- Is proactive followership an antidote to toxic leaders? How do we socialize people early in their education to balance respect for authority with the ability to challenge people in authority?
- How can leaders and followers be trained to see that enabling people to speak freely is not just in the communal interest, but in the leader's own self-interest as well?
- How can followership and follower-centred approaches augment the ethical debate surrounding the use of power and authority?

Finally, one of the major issues and debates that continues to confront the burgeoning field of followership is seemingly semantic, yet also strikes close to the heart of many of the theoretical traditions reviewed above. As Rost (2008, p. 57) succinctly put it, 'The word *followers* is inconsistent with the postindustrial understanding of leadership.' Followers and followership still retains the 'baggage' of the Industrial Revolution, with its connotations of subordination, submission, passivity, and lack of control. Attempts to overthrow these industrial vestiges of followership with connotations of dynamic, active, intelligent, influential, responsible, and involved followers have been met with resistance, or at least limited success. Rost (2008) contended that if we do not change the word *follower*, its use can only continue to promote a view of leadership that is Great Leader, good management in orientation. Within this seemingly basic semantic debate surrounding the word *follower* lie a number of important questions regarding the future of followership: specifically, should we discard the word *follower* altogether, and refer instead to *participants, contributors, members, associates,* or *collaborators*? Alternately, should we continue to invoke adjectives to promote a more postindustrial approach to followership, modified to reference a proactive, participative approach, such as 'courageous followers' or 'powerful followers'?

In many ways, this debate reflects how much work is still left to be done in moving toward the study of leadership and followership as complementary, and equally important, organizational processes. As Burns (2005, p. 12) noted, 'Leadership, in common parlance, is "good."' Unfortunately, followership in common parlance is all too often 'bad.' This false dichotomy does little to advance our understanding of either leadership or followership. And invoking positive adjectives fails to provide a satisfactory solution for followership, any more than invoking a negative adjective (e.g., destructive, toxic, aversive) represents a suitable antidote to our prevailing assumption that leadership, by default, is positive. If the world is truly becoming flatter, as Friedman (2005) has argued, then our approaches to leadership and followership must begin to explicitly incorporate 'the multiple, shifting, contradictory and ambiguous identities of "leaders" and "followers"' (Collinson, 2005b, p. 1436). These shifting identities are impossible to capture with dichotomies of good and bad, leader and follower, or even courageous and destructive. It may be less that the term 'followership' is an 'outmoded concept' as Rost (2008) has argued, and more that our simplistic dichotomies are increasingly out of step in organizations with blurring hierarchies and creative working arrangements. Yet this does not undermine the fact that followers still do matter, in both industrial and the postindustrial uses of the term: they matter for both proactive and negative outcomes, and they can be romanticized and demonized, lauded and blamed, and constructed and deconstructed. Existing industrial terms such as *supervisor* and *subordinate* capture one type of leader–follower relationship, and *collaborators* captures another. Yet all fall under the purview of leadership and followership, fundamentally challenging both our terminology and our methods of inquiry to capture and portray them accurately.

From this perspective, the field of followership is truly still in its infancy (Kelley, 2008). Yet its resurgence represents more than a simple fad that will quietly expire once again. Regardless of what we call them, followers have always played a role in the most important managerial and societal problems of the time. As Rost (2008, p. 61) pointed out, if the world is truly flattening, it is not a result of people being followers. It is because people, whether as leaders, followers, participants, collaborators, or contributors, have 'been involved in dynamic processes that have caused the death knell of hierarchy, authoritarianism, elitism, and power derived from wealth and corruption.' Followership has already claimed a role in the leadership challenges of the twenty-first century, and future research should continue to tackle these challenges from both sides of the equation, emphasizing the dynamic, interpersonal processes that fundamentally define the leader–follower relationship.

ACKNOWLEDGMENTS

The author would like to thank Melissa Carsten, Jeffrey Kohles, and Rebecca Reichard for their comments on earlier versions of this chapter.

REFERENCES

Alford, C. F. (2008). Whistleblowing as responsible follower-ship. In Riggio, R. E., Chaleff, I., & Lipman-Blumen, J. (eds), *The art of followership* . San Francisco, CA: Jossey-Bass. (pp. 237–251).

Avolio, B. J. & Reichard, R. J. (2008). The rise of authentic followership. In R.E. Riggio, I.chaleff, & J.Lipman-blumen (eds), *The art of followership: how great followers create great leaders and organizations*. San Francisco, CA: Jossey-Bass. pp. 325–337.

Ba Banutu-Gomez, M. (2004). Great leaders teach exemplary followership and serve as servant leaders. *Journal of American Academy of Business,*143–151.

Baker, S. D. (2007). Followership: the theoretical foundation of a contemporary construct. *Journal of Leadership & Organizational Studies, 14*(1), 50–60.

Bennis, W. J. (1999). The end of leadership: exemplary leadership is impossible without full inclusion, initiatives, and cooperation of followers. *Organizational Dynamics, 28*(1), 71–79.

Beyer, J. M. (1999). Taming and promoting charisma to change organizations. *The Leadership Quarterly*, 10, 307–330.

Blass, T. (2008). What can Milgram's obedience experiments contribute to our understanding of followership? In R.E. Riggio, I. Chaleff, & J. Lipman-Balmen (eds), *The art of followership: how great followers create great leaders and organizations*, San Francisco, CA: Jossey-Bass. pp. 195–208.

Bligh, M. C. & Kohles, J.C. (2008). Leading or following? contemporary notions of followership in academic research. Presented at the annual meeting of the Society of Industrial and Organizational Psychology, San Francisco, CA, April 2008.

Bligh, M. C., Kohles, J. C., Justin, J. E., Pearce, C. L, & Stovall, J. (2007a). When the romance is over: follower perspectives of aversive leadership. *Applied Psychology: an International Review, 56*(4), 528–557.

Bligh, M. C., Kohles, J. C., & Meindl, J. R. (2004). Charisma under crisis: presidential leadership, rhetoric, and media responses before and after the September 11th terrorist attacks. *The Leadership Quarterly, 15*(2), 211–239.

Bligh, M.C. & Meindl, J. R. (2004). The cultural ecology of leadership: an analysis of popular leadership books. In D. M. Messick & R. M. Kramer (eds) *The psychology of leadership: new perspectives and research,* London: LEA Press, pp. 11–52.

Bligh, M. C., Pillai, R., & Uhl-Bien, M. (2007b). The social construction of a legacy: Summarizing and extending follower-centered perspectives on leadership. In B. Shamir, R. Pillai, M. C. Bligh, & M. Uhl-Bien (eds), *Follower-centered perspectives on leadership: a tribute to the memory of james R. Meindl*. Greenwich, CT: Information Age Publishing, pp. 265–277.

Bluedorn, A. C. & Jaussi, K. (2008). Leaders, followers, and time. *The Leadership Quarterly, 19*(6), 654–668.

Burns, J. M. (2005). Leadership. *Leadership, 1,* 11–12.

Carsten, M. K., Uhl-Bien, M., West, B. J., Patera, J. L., & McGregor, R. (2010). Exploring social constructions of followership: a qualitative study. *The Leadership Quarterly, 21*(3), 543–562.

Carsten, M. K. & Bligh, M. C. (2008). Lead, follow, *and* get out of the way: involving employees in the visioning process. In R.E. Riggio, I. Chaleff, & J. Lipman-Blumen (eds), *The Art of followership: how great followers create great leaders and organizations,* San Francisco, CA: Jossey-Bass, pp. 277–290.

Carsten, M. K. & Bligh, M. C. (2007). Here today, gone tomorrow: follower perceptions of a departing leader and a lingering vision. In B. Shamir, R. Pillai, M. C. Bligh, & M. Uhl-Bien (eds), *Follower-centered perspectives on leadership: a tribute to the memory of James R. Meindl.* Greenwich, CT: Information Age Publishing, pp. 211–241.

Chaleff, I. (2003). *The courageous follower* (2nd edn). San Francisco, CA: Berrett-Koehler.

Chaleff, I. (2008). Creating new ways of following. In R.E. Riggio, I.chaleff, & J. Lipen-Blumen (eds), *The art of followership: how great followers create great leaders and organizations.* San Francisco, CA: Jossey-Bass. pp. 67–88.

Collinson, D. L. (2000). Strategies of resistance: power, knowledge and subjectivity in the workplace. In K. Grint (ed.), *Work and society: a reader* Cambridge: Polity Press, pp. 163–198.

Collinson, D. L. (2005a). Questions of distance. *Leadership, 1*(2), 235–250.

Collinson, D. L. (2005b). Dialectics of leadership. *Human Relations, 58*(11), 1419–1442.

Collinson, D. L. (2006). Rethinking followership: a post-structuralist analysis of follower identities. *The Leadership Quarterly, 17,* 179–189.

Collinson, D. L. (2008). Conformist, resistant, and disguised selves: a post-structuralist approach to identity and workplace followership. In R.E. Riggio, I. chaleff, & J. Lipman-Blumen (eds), *The art of followership: how great followers create great leaders and organization.* San Francisco, CA: Jossey-Bass, pp. 309–324.

De Vries, R. E. & van Gelder, J-L. (2005). Leadership and need for leadership: testing an implicit followership theory. In B. Schyns & J. R. Meindl (eds), *Implicit leadership theories: essays and explorations,* Geenwich, CT: Information Age Publishing, pp. 277–303.

Follett, M. P. (1924). *Creative experience.* New York: Longmans Green.

Follett, M. P. (2003). *Dynamic administration: the collected papers of Mary Parker Follett.* New York: Routledge.

Friedman, T. (2005). *The world is flat: a brief history of the twenty-first Century.* New York: Farrar, Straus and Giroux.

Gandhi, M. K. (1957). *The story of my experiments with truth.* Boston, MA: Beacon Press.

Graen, G. B. & Uhl-Bien, M. (1995). Relationship-based approach to leadership: development of leader–member exchange (LMX) theory of leadership over 25 years: applying a multi-level multi-domain perspective. *The Leadership Quarterly, 6*(2), 219–247.

Gray, J. H., & Densten, I. L. (2007). How leaders woo followers in the romance of leadership. *Applied Psychology: an International Review, 56*(4), 558–581.

Gronn, P. (2002). Distributed leadership as a unit of analysis. *The Leadership Quarterly, 13*(4), 423–452.

Hock, D. (1999). *Birth of the chaordic age.* San Francisco, CA: Berrett-Koehler.

Hogg, M. A. (2008). Social identity processes and the empowerment of followers. In R.E. Riggio, I. Chaleff, & J. Lipman-Blumen (eds), *The art of followership: how great followers create great leaders and organizations.* San Francisco, CA: Jossey-Bass, pp. 267–276.

Hollander, E. P. (1992). The essential interdependence of leadership and followership. *American Psychological Society,* Cambridge Press, pp. 71–75.

Hollander, E. P. (1995). Ethical challenges in the leader–follower relationship. *Business Ethics Quarterly, 5*(1), 55–65.

Hosking, D. M. (1988). Organizing, leadership, and skillful process. *Journal of Management Studies, 25*(2), 147–166.

Hosking, D. M. (2007). Not leaders, not followers: a postmodern discourse of leadership processes. In B. Shamir R. Pillai, M. C. Bligh, & M. Uhl-Bien (eds), *Follower-centered perspectives on leadership: a tribute to the memory of James R. Meindl.* Greenwich, CT: Information Age Publishing, pp. 243–264.

Howell, J. P., & Mendez, M. J. (2008). Three perspectives on followership. In Riggio et al. (eds.), *The art of followership: How great followers create great leaders and organizations.* San Francisco, CA: Jossey-Bass, pp. 25–40.

Hunter, S. T., Bedell-Avers, K. E., & Mumford, M. D. (2007). The typical leadership study: assumptions, implications, and potential remedies. *The Leadership Quarterly, 18*(5), 435–446.

Jackson, B. & Guthey, E. (2007). Putting the visual into the social construction of leadership. In B. Shamir, M. C. Bligh, & M. Uhl-Bien (eds), *Follower-centered perspectives on leadership: a tribute to the memory of James R. Meindl.* Greenwich, CT: Information Age Publishing, pp. 167–186.

Jaussi, K. S., Stefanovich, A., & Devlin, P. G. (2008). Effective followership for creativity and innovation. In R. E. Riggio, I. Chaleff, & J. Lipman-Blumen (eds), *The art of followership: how great followers create great leaders and organizations.* San Francisco, CA: Jossey-Bass, pp. 291–307.

Kark, R. & Van Dijk, D. (2007). Motivation to lead, motivation to follow: the role of the self regulatory focus in leadership processes. *Academy of Management Review, 32*(2), 500–528.

Kellerman, B. (2004). *Bad leadership.* Boston, MA: Harvard Business School Press.

Kelley, R. E. (1988). In praise of followers. *Harvard Business Review, 66*(6), 141–148.

Kelley, R. E. (1992). *The power of followership.* New York: Doubleday.

Kelley, R. E. (2004). Followership. In J. M. Burns, G. R. Goethals, & G. J. Sorenson (eds), *Encyclopedia of leadership.* Oxford: Sage Reference/Berkshire, pp. 504–513.

Kelley, R. E. (2008). Rethinking followership. In R. Riggio, I. Chaleff, & J. Lipman-Blumen (eds), *The art of followership: how great followers create great leaders and organizations.* San Francisco, CA: Jossey-Bass, pp. 5–16.

Kerr, S. & Jermier, J. (1978). Substitutes for leadership: their meaning and measurement. *Organizational Behavior and Human Performance, 22,* 374–403.

Kets de Vries, M. (2001). The leadership mystique. In K. Grint (ed.), *Leadership: classical, contemporary and critical approaches.* Oxford: Oxford University Press, pp. 250–271.

Kuhn, T. S. (1970). *The structure of scientific revolutions,* (2nd edn). Chicago: University of Chicago Press.

Lipman-Blumen, J. (2007). Toxic leaders and the fundamental vulnerability of being alive. In B. Shamir, R. Pillai, M. C. Bligh, & M. Uhl-Bien (eds) *Follower-centered perspectives on leadership: a tribute to the memory of James R. Meindl.* Greenwich, CT: Information Age Publishing, pp. 1–17.

Lipman-Blumen, J. (2008). Following toxic leaders: in search of posthumous praise. In R. E. Riggio, I. Chaleff, & J. Lipman-Blumen (eds), *The art of followership: how great followers create great leaders and organizations.* San Francisco, CA: Jossey-Bass, pp. 181–194.

Lord, R. G. (2008). Followers' cognitive and affective structures and leadership processes. In R. E. Riggio, I. Chaleff, & J. Lipman-Blumen (eds), *The art of followership: how great followers create great leaders and organizations.* San Francisco, CA: Jossey-Bass, pp. 255–266.

Lord, R. & Brown, D. (2003). *Leadership processes and self-identity: a follower-centered approach to leadership.* Mahwah, NJ: Erlbaum.

McCrae, R. R. & Costa, P. T. (1991). Validation of the five-factor model of personality across instruments and observers. *Journal of Personality and Social Psychology, 52,* 81–90.

Marion, R. & Uhl-Bien, M. (2001). Leadership in complex organizations. *The Leadership Quarterly, 12:* 389–418.

Manz, C. C. (1986). Self-leadership: toward an expanded theory of self-influence processes in organizations. *Academy of Management Review, 11,* 585–600.

Manz, C. C., & Sims, H. P., Jr. (1980). Self-management as a substitute for leadership: A social learning theory perspective. *Academy of Management Review, 5*(3), 361–367.

Mayo, M. & Pastor, J. C. (2007). Leadership embedded in social networks: looking at inter-follower processes. In Shamir et al. (Eds.), *Follower-centered perspectives on leadership: a tribute to the memory of James R. Meindl.* Greenwich, CT: Information Age Publishing, pp. 93–114.

Medvedeff, M. E. & Lord, R. G. (2007). Implicit leadership theories as dynamic processing structures. In B. Shamir, R. Pillai, M. C. Bligh, & M. Uhl-Bien (eds). *Follower-centered perspectives on leadership: a tribute to the memory of james R. Meindl,* Greenwich, CT: Information Age Publishing, pp. 19–50.

Meindl, J. (1995). The romance of leadership as a follower-centric theory: a social constructionist approach. *The Leadership Quarterly, 6*(3), 329–341.

Meindl, J. R. (1990). On leadership: an alternative to the conventional wisdom. *Research in Organizational Behavior, 12,* 159–203.

Meindl, J. R. (1993). Reinventing leadership: a radical, social psychological approach. In J. K. Murnighan (ed), *Social* psychology in organizations. Englewood Cliffs, NJ: Prentice Hall, pp. 89–118.

Meindl, J. R. (1998). The romance of leadership as a follower-centric theory: a social construction approach. In F. Dansereau & F. J. Yammarino (eds), *Leadership: the multiple-level approaches—Part B: contemporary and alternative.* Stamford, CT: JAI Press, pp. 285–298.

Meindl, J. R. & Ehrlich, S. B. (1987). The romance of leadership and the evaluation of organizational performance. *Academy of Management Journal, 30,* 91–109.

Meindl, J. R., Ehrlich, S. B., & Dukerich, J. M. (1985). The romance of leadership. *Administrative Science Quarterly, 30,* 78–102.

Offermann, L. (2004). Leader–follower relationships. In J. M. Burns, G. R. Goethals, & G. J. Sorenson (eds), *Encyclopedia of leadership.* Boulder, Sage Reference/Berkshire, pp. 828–833.

Offerman, L. R. & Scuderi, N. F. (2007). Sharing leadership: who, what, when, and why. In B. Shamir, R. Pillai, M. C. Bligh, & M. Uhl-Bien (eds), *Follower-centered perspectives on leadership: a tribute to the memory of James R. Meindl.* Greenwich, CT: Information Age Publishing, pp. 71–92.

Padilla, A., Hogan, R., & Kaiser, R. B. (2007). The toxic triangle: destructive leaders, susceptible followers, and conducive environments. *The Leadership Quarterly, 18*(3), 176–194.

Pastor, J. C., Meindl, J. R., & Mayo, M. (2002). Network effects model of attributions of charismatic leadership. *Academy of Management Journal, 45*(2), 410–420.

Pearce, C. L. & Conger, J. A. (2003). All those years ago: the historical underpinnings of shared leadership. In C. Pearce & J. Conger (eds), *Shared leadership: reframing the hows and whys of leadership.* Thousand Oaks, CA: Sage, pp. 1–18.

Pillai, R., Kohles, J. C., & Bligh, M. C. (2007). Through thick and thin? Follower constructions of presidential leadership amidst crises, 2001–2005. In B. Shamir, R. P. Pillai, M. C. Bligh, & M. Uhl-Bien (eds) *Follower-centered perspectives on leadership: a tribute to the memory of James R. Meindl.* Greenwich, CT: Information Age Publishing, pp. 135–165.

Prince, L. (2005). Eating the menu rather than the dinner: Tao and leadership. *Leadership, 1*(1), 105–126.

Reichers, A. E. & Schneider, B. (1990) Climate and culture: an evolution of constructs. In B. Schneider (ed.), *Organizational climate and culture.* San Francisco, CA: Jossey-Bass. pp. 5–39

Riggio, R. E., Chaleff, I., & Lipman-Blumen, J. (eds). (2008). *The art of followership: how great followers create great leaders and organizations.* San Francisco, CA: Jossey-Bass.

Rost, J. (2008). Followership: an outmoded concept. In R. E. Riggio, I. Chaleff, & J. Lipman-Blumen (eds), *The art of followership: how great followers create great leaders and organizations.* San Francisco, CA: Jossey-Bass, pp. 53–64.

Schilling, J. (2007). Leaders' romantic conceptions of the consequences of leadership. *Applied Psychology: An International Review, 56*(4), 602–623.

Schyns, B. & Bligh, M. C. (2007). Introduction to the special issue on the romance of leadership—in memory of James R. Meindl. *Applied Psychology: an International Review, 56*(4), 501–504.

Schyns, B. & Felfe, J. (2006). The personality of followers and its effect on the perception of leadership: an overview, a study, and a research agenda. *Small Group Research, 37*(5), 522–539.

Shamir, B. (2007). From passive recipients to active co-producers: followers' roles in the leadership process. In B. Shamir, R. Pilli, M. C. Bligh, & M. Uhl-Bien (eds), *Follower-centered perspectives on leadership: a tribute to the memory of James R. Meindl.* Greenwich, CT: Information Age Publishing, pp. ix–xxxix.

Shamir, B. & Howell, J. M. (1999). Organizational and contextual influences on the emergence and effectiveness of charismatic leadership. *The Leadership Quarterly, 10*(2), 257–283.

Shamir, B., Pillai, R., Bligh, M. C., & Uhl-Bien, M. (eds) (2007). *Follower-centered perspectives on leadership: a tribute to the memory of James R. Meindl.* Greenwich, CT: Information Age Publishing.

Stech, E. L. (2008). A new leadership–followership paradigm. In R. E. Riggio, I. Chaleff, & J. Lipman–Blumen (eds), *The art of followership: how great followers create great leaders and organizations.* San Francisco, CA: Jossey-Bass, pp. 41–52.

Uhl-Bien, M. & Pillai, R. (2007). The romance of leadership and the social construction of followership. In B. Shamir, R. Pillai, M.C. Bligh, & M. Uhl-Bien (Eds.), *Follower-centered perspectives on leadership: a tribute to the memory of James R. Meindl.* Greenwich, CT: Information Age Publishing, pp. 187–210.

Uhl-Bien, M. (2006). Relational leadership theory: exploring the social processes of leadership and organizing. *The Leadership Quarterly, 17*(6), 654–676.

Uhl-Bien, M. & Carsten, M. K. (2007). Being ethical when the boss is not. *Organizational Dynamics, 36*(2), 187–201.

Uhl-Bien, M., Marion, R., & McKelvey, B. (2007). Complexity leadership theory: shifting leadership from the industrial age to the knowledge era. *The Leadership Quarterly, 18*(4), 298–318.

van Knippenberg, D., van Knippenberg, B., & Giessner, S. R. (2007). Extending the follower-centered perspective: leadership as an outcome of shared social identity. In Shamir, R. Pillai, M. C. Bligh, & M. Uhl-Bien (eds), *Follower-centered perspectives on leadership: a tribute to the memory of James R. Meindl.* Greenwich, CT: Information Age Publishing, pp. 51–70.

Weick, K. E. (2007). Romancing, following, and sensemaking: Jim Meindl's legacy. In B. Shamir, R. Pillai, M. C. Bligh, & M. Uhl-Bien (eds.), *Follower-centered perspectives on leadership: a tribute to the memory of James R. Meindl.* Greenwich, CT: Information Age Publishing, pp. 279–291.

32

Hybrid Configurations of Leadership

Peter Gronn

An alternative [to the reductionist stance of most theories] would be to treat leadership as a multi-dimensional phenomenon and analyze leaders' relations to their contexts and to the outcomes they achieve as configurational problems. (Meyer et al., 1993, p. 1189)

INTRODUCTION

This chapter argues for a revised unit of analysis in leadership. In doing so, it addresses the challenge thrown down in the lead quotation. There are two ways of understanding what these authors had in mind. On the one hand, the configurational problem to which they referred is concerned with a specific body of literature on configurations of organizational activities (reviewed later in the discussion) that arose mainly in reaction to contingency theory. On the other hand, by enquiring 'how might different configurations of leadership traits, leadership behavior, and influence styles be associated with leadership effectiveness', Meyer et al. (1993, p. 1189) were allowing for the possibility that leadership was itself configured. It is this latter idea that provides the revised analytical focus advanced by the chapter. The argument used to develop it is built around a conception of parts–whole relations, in which configurations of practice constitute units of leadership analysis. This means that, when investigating the practice of leadership for diverse purposes – which might range from simply understanding practices to

intervening to try to alter them with a view to their realignment, improvement or increased effectiveness – a useful first step for scholars may be to eschew the normative typologizing that typifies much scholarship in the field in favour of mapping or contouring leadership configurations. In respect of parts–whole relations, leadership configurations represent social (or organizational) wholes. The elements or parts that integrate to some degree to comprise an overall configured whole consist of numerous role set relations. These role set relations, it will be shown, manifest themselves in diverse ways, rather than narrowing around a norm of convergence, with the consequence that configurations are most appropriately characterized as hybridized.

As more and more leadership scholars try to think themselves out of or beyond the heroic impulse that came to dominate the field for the last quarter century or so, a number of post-heroic alternatives are currently under consideration (for a summary see Drath et al., 2008). Part of the aim of this chapter about unit revision is to query the fitness for purpose of perhaps the most popular of those alternatives, distributed leadership (or, as it is sometimes referred to, shared or dispersed leadership or even leaderfulness). Far from being a new idea, distributed leadership has resurfaced over the previous decade and attracted a large following. There are a number of shortcomings with distributed leadership that are highlighted in the chapter, but the fundamental difficulty with it stems from what might be termed a migration problem. This arises out of parts–whole relations. When it was originally articulated (Gibb, 1954), distributed leadership formed part of a binary relationship with focused leadership. From a levels-of-analysis perspective, the primary focus of scrutiny by social psychologists of leadership in Gibb's day was small groups and their dynamics, in which case micro-level influence could be principally concentrated in just one leader (who could be shown to be disproportionately influential) or it could be distributed, meaning that there were multiple leaders (who may have emerged at different stages in the career of a group). In subsequent discussions in the field, however, an upwards migration or transposition problem appears to have occurred. This was due to a presumption that what may have characterized part relations (i.e., interaction within small groups) applied automatically or by default to the relations of wholes (i.e., entire organizations).

Such a presumption is invalid, as Markham and Markham's (1995, pp. 344, 351–353) poignant levels-of-analysis criticism of self-management and self-leadership demonstrated. They provided a good illustration of the errors entailed in such reasoning by indicating how conceptual scaling-up to the team level on the basis of empirical findings at the individual level was not necessarily argued for explicitly in the accounts they reviewed, but was often left unspecified. This meant that processes applying at one level did not necessarily apply at the next. A parallel act of unjustified migration seems to have occurred in respect of characterizing the leadership of both small groups and organizations. Thus, when, as part of a broad critique of what Bryman (1992, p. 1) dubbed the 'new leadership', a monopoly of leadership by formally positioned upper-echelon individuals was queried for its implicit heroism, there was a tendency corresponding to the one identified by the Markhams for writers (including the present author) to substitute distributed for focused leadership as an alternative unit of analysis encompassing relations across the whole, and not just within a part (i.e., small group leadership) as was originally proposed (Gibb, 1954, p. 884). Once more the movement upwards tended to be made unquestioningly. As is demonstrated in more detail shortly, however, an unforeseen consequence of this presumed elevation or substitution of part relations for that of wholes has been confusion about the significance of individuals and where they fit in accounts of leadership that purport to be distributed. The proposed reworking of parts–whole leadership relations around role sets and configurations is intended as a means of resolving this confusion and providing a more robust basis for post-heroic alternatives when refocusing analyses within the field.

To develop this argument, the chapter commences with a review of leadership's persistent susceptibility to heroism and the continued reassertion of heroic leadership, despite the apparent obsolescence of what became known as the 'great man' view of leadership. I then show how leadership has been inextricably bound up historically with coordination and decision making, and also historically how a variety of leadership formations has been prevalent, not merely the leadership of individuals, let alone heroic individuals. This longitudinal perspective on leadership highlights the importance of the hybrid forms it frequently takes. After discussing the place of hybridity in the social sciences generally, I undertake a critical review of recent research into distributed leadership in education – a field in which the uptake of distributed leadership has been high. Despite the claims of authors that their educational research offers evidence of distribution, I show how each set of findings in fact reveals variations of mixed leadership practice. It is on the basis of this revised reading of other scholars' evidence that I propose configurations and role sets as the core components of units of leadership analysis. Finally, the chapter concludes with a consideration of some issues arising out of the argument and their implications for future leadership research.

HEROICS

For the previous quarter century or so, the field of leadership has been dominated by views of leaders as exceptional individuals. Such views are evident in a number of sources, including general writings and scholarly studies. Exceptionality was characterized by Yukl (1999, p. 292), for example, as a heroic bias and by Copland (2002) as a myth of superiority. The antecedents of exceptionality were many and varied. One prominent strand was disdain for managers and management. The roots of this anti-managerial antagonism were evident in 1950s criticism of the stifling of the rugged individualism of a bygone US entrepreneurial age, and the production of rank upon rank of cloned organization men (Whyte, 1963) – presumably an unanticipated consequence of the twentieth-century managerial revolution documented by Burnham (1962). Subsequently, this negative disposition was etched more sharply into a binary of leaders and managers, and the presumed superiority of the former (Zaleznik, 1977), a view which later attained its apogee in the rather dismissive claim that while leaders do right things managers are preoccupied with doing things right (Bennis & Nanus, 1985). A second key ingredient can be sourced to Weber's (1970) concept of charisma. This was an idea that mostly inhabited the intellectual margins during the 1950s and 1960s – thanks, probably, to three factors: the recency of English translations of Weber's work; bitter collective memories of the brutal messianic leadership of 1930s Asian and European fascist and communist dictators; and instability evident in a succession of post-World War II regimes led by colourful ex-colonial nationalist figures, especially in Africa and Asia. By the mid-1970s, however, charisma had finally been domesticated for its application in business management and psychology (House, 1977). Yet another angle on exceptionality was provided by Meindl et al. (1985), who detected persistent evidence of a romance of leadership. Meindl was not the first scholar to suggest that romanticization of the deeds of individuals was a deeply culturally embedded tendency, because earlier Hook (1992 [1945], p. 4) had claimed that every nation's history 'is represented to its youth in terms of the exploits of great individuals – mythical or real'. Moreover there was a universal cultural propensity for leaders to be exalted as heroes, for which Hook fingered school systems as complicit – although his claim about universality is only partially correct as the leadership of individuals (let alone their canonization) has been far from the norm historically (see below).

These recent tendencies to accord prominence in leadership to individuals and to inflate their agency were reinforced during the period under discussion by the reassertion of trait-based approaches to leadership. Stogdill's review of more than 40 years of trait studies is often seen as sounding the death-knell of supposedly great leaders, because it concluded that 'a person does not become a leader by virtue of the possession of some combination of traits', in which case 'an adequate analysis of leadership involves a study of leaders not only but of situations' (Bass, 1990, p. 76). In his summary of a follow-up review of a further 20 years or so of trait studies by Stogdill, however, Bass (1990, p. 78) provided an early hint of a fight-back, by claiming that his predecessor's conclusions about situational factors had been miscited. The result was that personal factors in leadership were being underemphasized. Although Bass (1990, p. 87) was careful initially in insisting that personality as a factor differentiating leaders 'does not represent a return to the pure trait approach', subsequently he directly identified his concept of transformational leadership with the revival of this trait way of thinking: 'in the 1980s, revised analyses and new evidence turned the tide back towards the person' (Bass, 1998, p. 121). More recently, Zaccaro (2007) has argued for traits not merely as a basis for differentiating leaders from non-leaders (along with leader effectiveness and leader emergence) but also for predicting the membership of both categories. Zaccaro's (2007, p. 7) definition of traits is: 'relatively coherent and integrated patterns of personal characteristics reflecting a range of individual differences' that foster effectiveness. Despite these attempts to resuscitate traits, unanswered questions remain. One concerns precisely how contextual factors interrelate with these new trait clusters. Another is whether tighter specification and a more robust methodological grounding of traits (than may have been attainable by Stogdill) are sufficient to dampen or deflect the continued imputation of heroic status to leaders, particularly given the way heroism reinforces the tendency of leaders to exaggerate their control over their successes (March & Weil, 2005, p. 117).

An important by-product of the heroic legacy in leadership has been to residualize or ignore the possibility of credible alternatives to focused individual perspectives on leadership. Distributed leadership, for example, which had been already foreshadowed by a succession of authors as far back as the late 1940s (see Gronn, 2008, pp. 145–148), had been marginalized almost to the point of invisibility during the leadership's resurgence in the early 1980s. As is often the case in the movement of ideas, however, ruling illusions breed reactions. During the previous decade or so, distributed leadership has reasserted itself in both the general field of leadership and in subfields such as educational leadership. Such has been the rapidity of its phoenix-like ascent that distributed leadership represents a new point of intellectual convergence that is fast approaching hegemonic status. Prior to a discussion of its recent revival, the close connection of leadership with decision making and collectively coordinated action is highlighted, along with historical alternatives to one-person leadership.

LEADERSHIP'S LEGACY[1]

In conventionally understood terms, leadership tends to be associated with the influential and direction-setting behaviour of individuals, particularly with regard to the making of decisions and the coordination of collective endeavour (Drath et al., 2008). While such prototypical understanding may be deeply embedded culturally, it obscures considerable historical and natural world knowledge (see also Grint, Chapter 1, in this volume).

Decision making among many animal species contrasts markedly with that of humans. In this realm the idea of leadership by one creature is nonsensical. Bees and other insects, for example, practice swarming behaviour. This pattern is instanced by the murmuration patterns of starlings and the torus formations of fish (i.e., where a school rotates around an empty core). Swarming is quintessential evidence of group-mindedness (Wilson et al., 2004, p. 2). Here, creatures rely on distributed intelligence to synchronize their collective movement to solve such problems as their need to locate food, to rest and nest, and to find security from predation. A swarm attempts to devise 'a collectively intelligent solution' (Surowiecki, 2004, p. 27). Typically, this requires each swarm member to rely on local decision rules (concerned with alignment, attraction and avoidance) 'to maintain personal space and to avoid collisions' (Couzin et al., 2005, p. 513). A swarm, then, is a complex computational system that facilitates consensus without any need for a division of labour along leader–follower lines. As adaptive evolutionary responses to environmental stimuli, such phenomena as swarming, schooling, flocking and hiving confound human expectations about problem solving and decision making: swarm members mediate and transmit information by such sensory modalities as vision, temperature, pressure, sound and odour (e.g., ants' pheromone trails), yet there 'there is no centralized controller' (Couzin, 2007, p. 715). Instead, informational awareness is determined by prior swarming experiences and information is transferred between more and less experienced members. This reliance on parallel neighbourhood decision making means that leadership – if this idea makes any sense in a swarm context – is dispersed rather than 'control being hierarchical with one (or a few) leader(s) controlling group-members' actions' (Couzin, 2008, p. 36).

In the case of the African primates (chimpanzees, bonobos and gorillas), there are some similarities with humans. Groups of primates, for example, are known to establish dominance hierarchies and alpha male primates are despotic (Boehm, 2001, pp. 16–30). Genetically, humans are predisposed to establish dominance and submission hierarchies (Boehm, 2001, p. 147) and, even when dominance-based hierarchical relations themselves and their effects can be mitigated, increased group membership sizes are still conducive to the creation of hierarchies for productive purposes (Rubin, 2000). This is because continued productive self-organization by small collaborating groups is difficult with more than about six people. Beyond this figure, control by an individual member becomes more likely, with the reason being that the number of one-to-one relations entailed increases rapidly and creates mounting interpersonal complexity (Johnson, 1982, p. 392). The basis of this claim is the following formula: paired relations = $(n^2 - n)/2$ (where n = group size). Thus, when group membership increases from 4 to 6, the corresponding number of one-to-one relations escalates from 6 to 15 and to 21 with an increase of 7 members.

Even though human leadership's legacy may be assumed to be one of hierarchical subordination (e.g., Simmel, 1950, pp. 181–203), hunter-gatherers, chiefdoms and early states provide evidence of diverse leadership patterns. Here there are two points of significance. First, for about 94,000 of the 100,000 years of human history, people lived in acephalous hunter-gathering societies in which a strong sense of collective egalitarianism trumped hierarchy. Nomadic individuals had 'no real authority over each other' and there was 'the closest approximation to equality known in any human societies' (Woodburn, 1982, p. 431). According to Boehm (2001), band members with pretensions to be dominant leaders were controlled by the practice of reverse dominance hierarchy: i.e., vigilant collective rank and file levelling intended to prevent disproportionate sharing of influence, breeding opportunities or large game meat (Boehm, 1996, p. 775). Secondly, it was only with the transition to sedentary settlement patterns as recently as 3,000 to 6,000 years ago that early chiefdoms arose (and solo leadership began consolidating itself). Here, leadership became concentrated in the hands of single warriors or warrior elites, rather than band groups, with the hierarchy of decision makers expanding in size whenever the number of decisions required exceeded 'an individual's personal capacity to make decisions' (Earle, 1987, p. 289). The interesting variation on this incipient monarchy, however, was dyarchy (or dual authority) between a priest and warrior, which was 'a consistent structural feature of proto-Indo-European society' (Kristiansen, 2001, p. 93). In ancient (or seventh century BCE) Sparta, for example, there were two simultaneous *basileis* (village officials rising to kingly status). Dyarchies were common across Europe from Crete to Scandinavia. This particular division of leadership labour was a solution to the problem of reconciling the competing claims to superordinate authority of the secular and the sacred domains.

HYBRIDIZATION

From a historical perspective, then, this indicative body of the evidence suggests that hybrid practices of leadership may have constituted the norm. That is, decision making and co-ordination were facilitated by varied leadership formations, which either succeeded one another sequentially or coexisted as hybrids (Ferguson, 1991, p. 170), mainly in the guise of individuals, dyads, groupings, networks or elite strata – including nascent democratic fora in Greek city-states and even, during the pre-Constantine Roman Empire, a tetrarchy of four co-emperors (Freeman, 2003, p. 158). These historical illustrations raise a question for contemporary leadership: What does it mean to describe social and organizational phenomena (e.g., entities, objects, structures, practices) as hybrid?

To begin with, clarification of hybrid and hybridity is required. From an analytical point of view, the likelihood of hybrid classification status requires that there be deficiencies, shortcomings or problems with existing schemes that categorize phenomena. In the event that a particular instance of something is found to ill-fit a prevailing classification, for example, this triggers a need for new categories and reclassification. If, on the one hand, an altogether new category is devised, then this counts as an example of displacement or super-session, in which case an orthodox classification is rendered redundant by a new one. If, on the other hand, the relationship between two existing categories is reworked, so that attributes of each are combined or connected in differing proportions, then the process of arriving at an outcome is one of hybridization, of which the outcome itself is a hybrid form. Typically, hybridity is antipathetic to categories whose relationship is binary or dualistic. Thus, the utility of simple opposites and polarities (such as black and white colours) is subverted due to their inability to accommodate different shadings or gradations between the two. It is because of this kind of reasoning that some scholars view disruption as an inherent property of hybridity (Young, 1995, p. 26). For discourse analysts, for example, hybridity refers to 'transgressive processes that displace conceptual boundaries between discourses that are generally seen as distinct' (Gilmour, 2006, p. 19). Here, transgression obliterates boundaries. In doing so, hybridizing processes subvert the idea of object purity, for a hybrid combines elements once thought of as separate and discrete. From this perspective, the notion of object purity may be dismissed as little more than an essentialist myth.

But to call into question the purity of two objects which yield a hybrid when they are combined prompts one further inquiry: If it is good enough for two objects to be rendered impure by virtue of their hybridization, then doesn't it follow that all objects are inherently impure? In effect, then, each and every phenomenon may be a hybrid. On this point, Kalra et al. (2005, p. 84) concede that 'there is nothing gained' by such ironical reasoning, for it also means that 'the coherence of other agreed terms begins to fade'. Rather than venturing down an ontological cul-de-sac (i.e., the infinite regress of all objects potentially being hybrids), however, other scholars (e.g., Latour, 1993) have chosen to highlight the proliferation of hybrids as a challenge to habitual categories. Nowhere in the recent past in the social sciences have these developments associated with hybridity been more manifest than in both post-colonial and cultural studies. The broad consensus in these two domains of scholarship is that, historically, hybridity fell from grace after a nineteenth century apotheosis, only to rise subsequently and to continue rising. While attention is often drawn to its botanical and biological associations (Young, 1995, p. 6) – in particular the deliberate mixing and cross-breeding of species of plants and animals – the nineteenth- and twentieth-century entanglements of hybridity elevated it to a central tenet of mutation in theories of race and culture (e.g., eugenics). There it provided a doctrinal bulwark in imperial views about racial identity, purification, contamination, difference and degeneration which legitimated an ideology of white, European superiority and natural ascendancy. In a variant of this theme, some commentators (e.g., Frenkel & Shenhav, 2006, p. 856) have even suggested that the colonial encounter *itself* was an inherently hybrid experience – with the effects of colonization on both colonizer and colonized being mutually felt (although differently and unequally). In more recent reworkings of the idea of hybridity, it tends to be seen as a third or in-between space. Highlighting its creative potential in this regard, for example, Papastergiadis (1997, p. 258) interprets hybridity as 'an energy field of different forces'.

From this more positive perspective there is an impressive number of instances of hybridized spaces, roles, conceptual revisionism and theories that have appeared in a number of literatures. These include not only cultural products and traditions (Smith, 2004, p. 245), as might be anticipated, but also phenomena as diverse as the adoption of hospital-based medical-manager clinical director roles (Kitchener, 2000), the therapeutic reconstitution of hospitals as patient home spaces (Gilmour, 2006), the historically hybrid origins of a reworked canon of management and organization studies (Frenkel & Shenhav, 2006), practices, outcomes and knowledge transfer approaches in multinational corporations (Frenkel, 2008), diversity management of non-governmental organizations; NGOs (Schwabenland & Tomlinson, 2008), and the diffusion of hybridized globally adaptational corporate cultures of management (Shimoni & Bergmann, 2006).

LEADERSHIP: DISTRIBUTED OR HYBRIDIZED?

Despite these developments, and the historical record of varied and even hybrid leadership practice, hybridity has figured rarely, if at all, in contemporary leadership scholarship. In fact leadership continues to be a domain of inquiry in which well-rehearsed binaries, such as leader–follower, leadership–followership, superior–subordinate and leader–manager, retain a tenacious grip. Nonetheless, leadership inquiry is susceptible to reconstitution along the lines of creative hybridity. Gibb's (1954) focused–distributed leadership dualism opened up one such possibility for reconstruction (although still within a leader–follower discourse), in the guise of a pendulum-like movement between these two types of leadership – as was implied in the earlier depiction of a quarter century's developments in the field (and see Bolden et al., 2009, p. 275). The argument of this chapter, however, is slightly different. Rather than the reality of leadership and the way it is represented by scholars being a kind of grossly staged movement in which one description supplants the other – as in the chronological sequence T1: focus > T2: distribution > T3: focus > T4: distribution, etc. – the two descriptive categories might be more accurately thought of as polarities at either end of a continuum of possibilities, rather than as binary opposites. Such an understanding would allow for contextualized degrees of focus *and* distribution to coexist at different hierarchical levels in organizations. Thus, even though 'distributed' may recently have captured scholars' imagination, the unit of analysis in empirical investigations of leadership contexts is less likely to boil down to a hard and fast choice between an individual leader or some version of a leadership plurality, and is more likely to comprise a *hybrid mixture*.

EDUCATIONAL LEADERSHIP

Before expounding on the idea of leadership as a configured organizational whole, research in the area of leadership in education is used to illustrate the above claim. The education sector has been selected for two reasons. First, it has spawned a significant amount of distributed leadership research (indeed, perhaps more than any other sector), particularly in schools, although also in further and higher education institutions. Secondly, education (especially school education) is highly instructive for a broadened understanding of leadership because it operates as part of the service sector in which the kinds of commercial imperatives governing the work of firms and corporations (which provide the contextual focus for much leadership research) cease to apply. Moreover, because education operates simultaneously in a much more tightly regulated policy environment (particularly in England, where the present author is located), leaders are constrained in uniquely challenging ways (see below).

The examples summarized encompass changing expectations of leadership practices, aspects of routine or regular practices, and instances of leaders attempting to change practices. In the seven studies reviewed, some authors acknowledge explicitly the limitations of the descriptor 'distributed', while in the majority of cases distributed remains their preferred interpretive label. This retention occurs despite the fact that in a significant amount of the documented activity, individual leadership still figures prominently. The phrasing of each subheading indicates the particular ways in which, for the present author at least, the data provide evidence of hybrid patterning.

1. Hybrid practice as coexisting dissonant leadership preferences

In the first of three interview studies considered in this section, Collinson and Collinson (2009) show how the leadership of an individual tends to be hierarchically positioned, while at the same time distributed sources of influence are laterally aligned and how the influence of the former does not suddenly become redundant when the latter assumes prominence. There were 140 informants in the authors' study of seven English further education (FE) colleges, and in their views of effective institutional leadership these informants expressed strong expectations of both vertical and lateral leadership. Most people perceived distributed leadership as top-down delegation, rather than bottom-up engagement (Collinson & Collinson, 2009, p. 10). Furthermore, at the same time as they 'preferred a consultative leadership style', they also 'valued leaders who were clear and decisive'. Taken together, the authors characterize these predilections as blended leadership in which 'apparent dichotomies in heroic and post-heroic perspectives' are interpreted by respondents as 'mutually-compatible and equally-necessary for leadership effectiveness' (all quotes from Collinson & Collinson, 2009, p. 9).

2. Hybrid practice as permeable leadership spaces and identities

Whitchurch (2008) interviewed 54 senior and middle managers in the UK, the USA and Australia. On the basis of the participants' self-reports (in two sets of interviews) of their identities and role spaces, she found that while about half of the English subsample considered themselves to be bounded professionals (i.e., they operated within conventionally prescribed role parameters), the remainder engaged with role boundaries in much more fluid and informal ways. About a third, for example, saw themselves as working across boundaries between dichotomous professional and academic domains, another group ignored such boundaries altogether and the roles of a final group spanned both domains. These findings are indicative evidence of emerging mid-level university role portfolios (in which there is strong scope for project-based leadership in institutional partnerships, community links and development, etc.) that were more pronounced in the UK than in the USA and Australia. Typically, those who found themselves less constrained by role boundaries inhabited third spaces which comprised 'mixed teams of staff who work on short-term projects such as bids for external funding and quality initiatives' for which professional staff were 'less concerned with a fixed body of knowledge than on maintaining an up-to-the minute portfolio of experience' (Whitchurch, 2008, pp. 386, 388).

3. Hybrid practice as a mix of orchestrated and emergent leadership

As part of their analysis of distributed leadership in 12 UK universities Bolden et al. (2009) conducted interviews with 152 university leaders, about 20% of whom were vice-chancellors (or their equivalents) and deputies. The authors supplemented this material with documentary evidence and workshop feedback. The research informants espoused a 'great degree of support' for leadership that was shared across an institution (Bolden et al., 2009, p. 261). When the various forms taken by university leadership are examined closely, this study provides strong and unequivocal evidence of preferences for the following mixture of practices (Bolden et al., 2009, pp. 263–266):

- devolved and delegated decision making
- numerous individuals acting alone or collaboratively within and across levels
- tension-free role blending by staff who were content to augment their academic identities when managing research, but also experiences of role-tension and conflicting identities when those same staff tried to blend academic allegiance and commitment with management in areas other than research
- utilization of teams and committees
- co-leading relationships between professional managers and academic heads

Noting the similarity between their findings and those of Collinson and Collinson, Bolden et al.

(2009, p. 270, original emphases) concluded in relation to the totality of this mix that their informants drew 'sharp attention to the need for *both* top-down *and* bottom-up leadership'. While also noting that the commitment to distributed leadership in universities is mostly rhetorical, when compared with what informants report about enacted reality elsewhere when these authors articulated a model of practice (Bolden et al. 2008, p. 364), they suggested that 'hybrid' offered a more plausible mode of representing this mix than 'distribution'.

4. Hybrid practice as simultaneous multiple individual leaders and co-leading pairings

Spillane et al. (2007) investigated leadership practice for a six-day period by using an experience sampling method (ESM) to track the daily activities engaged in by 42 US school principals and their colleagues. As part of ESM, the principals were randomly beeped on 15 occasions each day, at which times, using handheld computers, they were required to complete a 10-item questionnaire. The activities engaged in by principals were coded into four categories: administrative; curriculum and instruction; professional growth; and fostering relationships. The results indicated that for about two-thirds of the time principals self-reported themselves as leading; either solo or paired with individuals from 11 co-leader categories. For about a third of the time that they felt they were not leading; individuals from 12 other categories of leaders substituted for principals, with such individuals defined as those who 'have responsibility for executing the activity' (Spillane et al., 2007, p. 110). Thus, leadership in 'Cloverville' school district combined both hierarchically positioned leadership, and paired informal leadership with both fellow position holders in the organizational spine and others beyond the hierarchy. So prominent were professional pairings that 47% of all activities were co-led.

5. Hybrid practice as project teacher team leaders, their teams and other leaders

Timperley (2005) described the literacy leadership of seven primary schools in Auckland, New Zealand, during a four-year government-sponsored initiative which, following the provision of external professional development for teachers, was intended to improve the literacy skills of disadvantaged children. School literacy team meetings were observed, the dialogue recorded and analysed, and interviews were conducted with principals, team leaders and teachers. The quality of responses of team meetings to students' achievement data from teachers' own and other classes varied, with two schools' teacher teams responding quickly to the data and national benchmark summaries of reading achievement scores and reconsidering the requisite teaching implications, while all five of the remaining schools had not responded until Year 3 (Timperley, 2005, pp. 402–404). In one of these five schools, for example, it was not until the broadly non-directive approach taken originally by the team leader was modified (so that aggregated student cohort achievement data were replaced with individual student achievement scores benchmarked against national norms) that remedial teaching strategies were collaboratively devised. In this case study of distribution, it was individual leaders (teacher literacy leaders) who influenced colleagues' collective practices (teacher teams) and who also persuaded other individual leaders (principals) to offer release time and professional development for literacy teachers (Timperley, 2005, pp. 410, 416).

6. Hybrid practice as expert–teacher leader collaboration to influence teachers

The influence of school districts on classroom teaching in disadvantaged New Jersey schools receiving special funding for a US Mathematics–Science partnership project was analysed by Firestone and Martinez (2007). In 12 state-aided poor schools in three districts participating in university partnerships, district curriculum supervisors intervened to scrutinize classroom teaching closely by monitoring (i.e., observing classes and examining test scores), obtaining and allocating resources (e.g., instructional materials and time schedules) and providing professional development. Although teacher leaders were 'largely the creatures of the districts' and 'occupied formal positions created by the districts to work with other teachers' (Firestone & Martinez, 2007, p. 23), their efforts blended with the work of district experts. One district's approach to influencing teacher leaders was directive, another's was collegial, while the third relied on specialist pedagogical expertise (such as constructivism). Overall, the results highlight the importance of aligning professional practices to ensure that solo and paired actions were as complementary as possible, which meant that leadership was shared between two sets of individuals, with districts operating

'at a distance', and relying on formal authority and substitutes for leadership, while teacher leaders relied more on 'close relationships to lead' (Firestone & Martinez, 2006, p. 9).

7. Hybrid practice as shared teacher leading contingent upon a focused leader

Finally, in eight schools (four elementary and four secondary) in southern Ontario, Canada, Leithwood et al. (2007) reworked Gronn's (2002, pp. 430–431) holistic category of three forms of concertive action into four modes of practice, each of which was tested for its alignment or misalignment of four leadership functions: direction setting; people development; organizational redesign; and instructional management. With a focus on the potential of 'unconstrained forms of distributed leadership' to 'leverage organizational expertise', Leithwood et al. (2007, p. 47) were particularly interested in the engagement of informal or 'nonadministrator leaders'. After surveying teachers who nominated instances of non-administrator leaders, school and district informants were interviewed by Leithwood and colleagues. The occurrence of planful and aligned forms of distribution was found to be 'unlikely in the absence of focused leadership on the part of the school's formal leader' because these forms depended on the establishment of facilitating structures (Leithwood et al., 2007, p. 55). Teacher team leadership was also found to require principals' monitoring and intervention to move forward stalled agendas: in short, teacher leaders needed to be led. Within this broad pattern, there was evidence of differentiated and specialized performance of the four leadership functions; more colleagues working together on complex tasks rather than simple ones; and, prototypical attributions of leaders matching those teachers with formally designated leader status. Personal qualities were the most frequently nominated prototypical characteristics for distinguishing leaders (regardless of whether their status was formal or informal), with the likelihood of their influence increasing when the requisite personal qualities were combined with task-related expertise.

Summary

The above sets of empirical findings by no means exhaust the range of possibilities for leadership practice. On the other hand, they do provide solid indicative evidence that when leadership is mapped it is likely to be hybridized, with that hybridity manifesting variability and divergence. (The full significance of this absence of narrowing convergence around a norm or mode should become evident shortly.) Because most of the analyses offer mainly one-off snapshots, the extent of the fluidity, flexibility and durability of these hybrid forms and the through-time influence of levels of context (e.g., international, national, local) on each hybrid pattern remains unclear. As leadership practices go, there are also few indications from these studies of their effectiveness, efficiency and consequences (both intended and unintended). Equally, knowledge about the circumstances which gave rise to them is uneven. On the other hand, the examples have clear implications for the relationship of parts and wholes.

HYBRIDIZED AND CONFIGURED LEADERSHIP

Taking as a departure point the preceding evidence of practice that warrants the designation of hybrid, in this section I endorse a holistic approach to leadership. As foreshadowed earlier, I suggest that the unit of leadership analysis is a configuration, with configuration taken as equivalent to a social whole, and with the various parts that make up a configurational whole consisting of a series of role sets. There are two senses of configuration. First, there is the overall complex of an organization's activities and their interconnection, along with the pattern of resource usage that arises out of its division of labour. For commercial organizations these might entail functions such as production, sales, marketing and distribution, whereas for schools these would include, for example, the interdependencies among such elements as learning and teaching, curriculum, assessment and personnel appraisal (see Fiss, 2009, p. 429). Secondly, there is the subject of this chapter: the overall configuration of leadership. This maps onto the first activity configuration and manifests a degree of integration or 'system-ness' that derives from the extent of the interdependence of the parts achieved by the former.

Parts–whole relations foreground a number of important ontological questions concerned with the emergence of social phenomena and their hierarchical structuration into levels or layers of complexity. These questions include the following. First, how much of the meaning and significance of parts is attributable to their own integrity, *sui generis*, or to their membership and relationship within a whole? Secondly, if wholes comprise a number of parts, does this mean that they are mere aggregations of those parts or is an emergent whole more than the sum of its parts, and in some sense irreducible to them? If the latter, then to what extent is this holism due to upwards or downwards causation, or is the causation bidirectional?

ROLE SETS AS PARTS

Merton's (1957, p. 110) definition of a role set was 'that complement of role-relationships in which persons are involved by virtue of occupying a particular social status'. Role sets have general social application and are structured relations in which persons and groupings linked to the occupants of various status positions communicate their (often diverse) sets of expectations. In respect of managerial role set relations (and, presumably, those of leaders), Fondas and Stewart (1994, p. 87) highlighted the importance for a focal manager of 'an environment of role senders who hold expectations about appropriate behaviour, send signals to communicate those expectations, and react to the manager's behaviour with rewards and punishments'. To ensure that relations within role sets are genuinely reciprocal, the reactive behaviour of managers that is implied in this remark needed to be complemented, in the authors' view, by the ability of managers to shape and modify the expectations of role senders.

Curiously, attributes such as role set size and numbers of role senders seem not to have figured prominently in these discussions. Moreover, there is scant recognition that managers (and leaders) may accord priority to some role sets ahead of others and why that might be (e.g., due, perhaps, to their longevity as a valued formation, and their control of prized information and resources). A clear implication of Fondas and Stewart's (1994, p. 95) emphasis on such role set characteristics as interpersonal interaction and attraction, however, is that while the universe of potential role sets in an organization may be great in number, the salient ones are likely to be small in membership size. In the cut and thrust of decision making, it is in leaders' tightly interconnected sets of relations that judgements about their intentions and motivations, and the consistency of the match between the expectations held of them as leaders and the quality of their actual leadership performance, are either reinforced or found to be wanting. Needless to say, such judgements are the basis on which trust is accorded or withheld. Examples of leaders' role set memberships in the previous review of hybrid practices include such plural–member units as pairings and partnerships (e.g., principal–teacher, district expert–teacher leader, professional manager–academic head) and groups (e.g., project work groups, teams, committees). Among the other well-documented examples of small-number groupings (Alvarez & Svejenova, 2005, esp. pp. 111–171; see Gronn, 2002, pp. 434–437) there are also executive triads or constellations (e.g., Hodgson et al., 1965) and organizational networks – both intra-organizational (e.g., de Lima, 2008) and extra-organizational (e.g., Hadfield, 2007).

As to the structural sources of parts relations, there are two of them. Mouzelis (2008, pp. 108–115, 228) refers to these as institutional and figurational. The first is rule-governed and role-based, and entails normative expectations, while the second comprises the socially patterned interactions of organization members in modes, and for motives, peculiar to them. A more commonsense way of expressing this distinction is to differentiate formal (or official) and informal (or unofficial) sets of relations. In everyday reality, the two types interweave. Barnard (1982, p. 116), for example, claimed that informally-sourced relations tend to be seed-beds for formal relations, whereas Dalton (1959, p. 222) cautioned against 'exclusive reliance on this couplet' because it ignored 'the whole confused middle ground where there are "mixtures" – or, in other words, what I have referred to as hybrid practices. Both sources shape an organization's overall performance and outcomes which, presumably, is why Sayles (1993, p. 230) suggested that managers 'need to learn to continuously "rejiggle" or reconfigure the interfaces among jobs or functions', because 'no work structure can stay static for long in a dynamic organization'. Dalton's example of executive relations at the Milo Fractionating Centre, where 'the existence of informal power positions create[d] a pressure on the formal framework to accelerate new positions and reassignments beyond the "normal" rate of promotion and retirement' (Dalton, 1959, p. 30; and see also pp. 226–238), is a good illustration of this point. Provided, then, that the notion of a role set is a suitable proxy for part relations in leadership, why might 'configuration' function as a parallel proxy for the idea of leadership taken as a whole?

CONFIGURATIONS AS WHOLES

The choice of appropriate terminology with which to designate emergent holistic structures is by no means arbitrary. Thus, while configuration may commend itself, it is merely one of a number of likely candidate terms for encompassing the totality of leadership practice. Indeed, some leadership scholars already make use of configuration – albeit in passing or in a light touch way (e.g., Denis et al., 1996, p. 676; Drath et al., 2008, p. 637; Leithwood et al., 2007, p. 58), and mostly without defining it, elaborating it or using it in the parts–whole manner that is proposed here. Other alternatives include complex, constellation, conglomeration, gestalt, archetype, assemblage or ensemble. There may be more.

While space precludes rehearsal of the respective merits of these other possibilities, the alternative to configuration with probably the strongest claim to potential adoption is 'constellation'. Having already been used to designate an instance of a role set (in the guise of an executive role constellation), however, this term 'has form', so to speak. It was Hodgson et al. (1965, p. xii) who initially employed constellation to describe an upper-echelon cluster of three managers whose close working relations these authors said formed a 'relatively integrated whole'. The precise number of persons appears not to have been a critical defining attribute in their elucidation of this idea, because a subsequent field study by one of the co-authors (Levinson) also cited a 'relatively close-knit dyad' (Newton & Levinson, 1973, p. 137) as an instance of an executive role constellation. Likewise, Hodgson et al.'s (1965) idea was utilized by Denis et al. (1996, p. 677) to describe and track shifting leadership relations among four main sets of actors during a 15-year reform phase in a Quebec public hospital. Equally, then, if constellation has form, so too does configuration. There are three senses in which it does. First, configuration features prominently in discussions of social research methodology in which it is a key component of a comparative case analysis strategy. This is an approach that is anchored in fuzzy set designs which has been proposed as a kind of third-way alternative to idiographic single case narratives, on the one hand, and variable-based linear analyses, on the other. Here, cases are conceived of as set-theoretic configurations of conditions (both necessary and sufficient) along with the causal relations between these conditions. Ragin (2000, p. 68), for example, insists that the logic of cases is configurational because 'different parts of the whole are understood in relation to one another and in terms of the total picture or package that they form'. Secondly, configuration has been used by social theorists to elucidate sets of institutionally patterned relations, especially those that may have acquired structural dominance and longevity. Thus, in his history of power, Mann (1986) analyses the interplay of four main network-based sources of power (ideological, military, economic and political) and shows how in different historical epochs these have crystallized in both intended and unintended ways to form particular power configurations. Thirdly, as part of a rethink of contingency theory, configurational reasoning has been prominent since the 1980s in business management, where it has been adopted to try to account for both proliferating and differentiated organizational forms.

CONCEPTUALIZING CONFIGURATIONS

It is this third area, in which evolutionary assumptions and reasoning are strongly evident, that is especially pertinent to leadership. For this reason, succeeding subsections of the chapter review a selection of a rather large and unwieldy corpus of literature that has accrued on organizational configurations. Due regard is paid to the pitfalls that have been identified in order to cement the case for utilizing configurations in leadership, in a way that is consistent with the suggestion in the chapter's lead quotation.

Configuration theory is one of a number of theories that arose during the 1980s which sought to account for organizational change (Greenwood & Hinings, 2006, pp. 815–816). Scholarly contributions on configurations proliferated in that decade, peaked in the 1990s and then fell away, although interest has recently been revived (Fiss, 2007, 2009; McPhee & Poole, 2001; Siggelkow, 2001, 2002). Proponents of configurations have tended to be united in their quest for holistic synthesis, with their focus overwhelmingly on firms as the exemplary organizational type. The major bone of contention that has divided proponents and critics has been concerned with the *a priori* typological, as distinct from empirical taxonomic, bases in which configurations are mostly grounded (Donaldson, 1996; Fiss, 2009, p. 428; McPhee & Poole, 2001, pp. 511–512; Meyer et al., 1993, p. 1175; Miller, 1996, pp. 506–507, 1999, pp. 29–33). At the outset of this debate, Miller and Mintzberg (1983, p. 62) focused on the structural elements of organizations and reacted against what they believed was a research bias in organization studies in favour of 'testing for simple, circumscribed relationships instead of searching for or constructing rich, insightful patterns'. To this end, these authors suggested that the range of organizational attributes should be synthesized and reduced to just five organizational types: simple structures; machine bureaucracies; professional bureaucracies; divisionalized forms; or adhocracies. (Subsequently, these five have been added to and allowance made for hybrids; see McPhee & Poole, 2001, pp. 515–518.) But this five-fold structural set left at least two questions begging: Why did reduction to such a small

number occur? And, given the existence of a vast and diverse population of organizations across the planet, why did that small number converge on these five in particular?

In answer to both questions, these authors provided a Darwinian explanation: internal adaptive practices within particular organizations were dictated by environmental selection pressures. Overall varietal retention and survival at the population level were determined by the need to secure a compatible fit, with the preferred pattern of adaptation (at least in those circumstances in which a choice for agents was permitted) being piecemeal – i.e., small changes in the interests of stability, predictability, reduced costs and retention of existing interdependencies, rather than wholesale configurational change (Miller, 1986, p. 236; Miller & Mintzberg, 1983, pp. 69–71; and see Miller 1990, pp. 781–783 for a more detailed elucidation).

CONFIGURATIONS AND THEIR IMPACT

This turned out to be a first-cut mode of reasoning explanation. What was its explanatory virtue? In one way it endorsed the through-time continuity of organizational responses to external pressures, with long periods of stability interspersed by occasional short bursts of structural modification. In another way, it sanctioned a plurality of pathways to the achievement of successful organizational outcomes (irrespective of how these may have been defined) rather than privileging a one-best-way. There is a direct parallel here between this latter reasoning and that of the fuzzy set logic foreshadowed earlier, in which sets of case configurations are assumed to manifest alternate causal recipes for the attainment of similar or shared outcomes (see Ragin, 2008, p. 110). Subsequently, Miller has modified and developed in a series of publications this initial articulation of configurations, with successive refinements of the reasoning in each instance manifesting increased acknowledgement of organizational complexity, along with an awareness of the significance of the interdependencies that make for such complexity.

Miller (1981) began by expanding the explanatory reasoning for convergent structural configurations as singular responses to environmental pressures in order to incorporate the need for an internally consistent set of organizational attributes and to create space for the strategic agency of decision makers. The effect of these modifications was subsequently articulated as a tripartite set of configurations (Miller, 1986, p. 235) – i.e., strategic, structural and environmental – which were 'interlinked' by 'natural congruences' among them. For illustrative purposes, Miller omitted professional bureaucracy and aligned the remaining four structurally configured commercial types with corresponding configurations of strategy. Later, overall organizational variety was claimed to be restricted by four 'imperatives' – environment, strategy, structure and leadership – with imperatives being seen as causes and configurations as effects (Miller, 1987, p. 686). Later still, Miller (1990, p. 772) used executive personality interchangeably with leadership. And, in an early gesture in the direction of hybrid practices, he also suggested that if single imperatives could be dominant in some firms, in others they could operate in combination – although at the time when he wrote he said there was 'little empirical evidence and still less theory to support any cogent discussion of hybrids' (Miller, 1987, p. 697). Finally, not only did Miller make allowance for differences in configurational imperatives *among* firms but also for variations *within* firms over time.

In this lineage of reasoning, then, it is apparent that the links between configured structures and the strategic management and leadership of organizations were being tightened to the point that they were almost conceptually inextricable. From there it was but a short step in reasoning to try to link particular configurations to levels of performance accomplishment and (especially in firms) competitive advantage (Miller, 1996, p. 509).

CRITICISMS OF CONFIGURATIONS

The most trenchant critic of Miller's typological approach to linking performance to configurations has been Donaldson (1996). His criticism is twofold: first, by generating insufficient numbers of configurations, typological convergence has been emphasized at the expense of divergence; secondly, the intricacies of the interdependent relations between the parts comprising such configurations have been oversimplified.

On the first point, the narrowing effect of convergence on a handful of types results in the glossing of a number of problems. One consequence is to divert analysis from how particular types came to be what they are, and how they interrelate. That is, to take two of Miller's examples, if instances of complex machine bureaucracies are deemed to have grown or emerged from simple structures, then a series of historically intermediate and path-dependent configurations would have been required to facilitate this through-time development, with each having its own

requisite (and distinctive) fit with its environment. There are likely, therefore, to be more than four of five configurations. A closely related point concerns the starkly demarcated and contrasting types. It is unclear whether and how such distinctions can accommodate incremental organizational growth over time and also whether they allow for variations in *degrees* of configuredness (e.g., in the strength of the presence of a defining attribute) rather than differences in *kind* (Donaldson, 1996, pp. 113–114). On the second point, one consequence of Miller's articulation of distinct types (especially divisional forms, adhocracies and machine bureaucracies) is to accentuate their homogeneity at the cost of categorical variation and heterogeneity. Another, stemming from assertions about interlinked organizational elements or attributes, is to obscure the nature of the casual relations between them (Donaldson, 1996, pp. 115–119). The net effect of configurational reasoning, therefore, in Donaldson's (1996, p. 127) view, has been to reduce complex organizational reality to a series of 'stark, but simplistic caricatures'.

CONFIGURATIONS RECONFIGURED

Despite these criticisms, configurational reasoning has undergone a revival. The focus has switched latterly to the search for mechanisms that accomplish environmental fit or equifinality. Essentially, the 'fit' hypothesis, as it is known, is expressed as: 'organizations facing specific environmental or other contingencies are likely to resemble a type that is especially called for by those contingencies' (McPhee & Poole, 2001, p. 514). There are two strands of work concerned with fit. In their separate approaches to rectifying the current dearth of empirical studies of configurations each offers a means of avoiding the dangers of functionalism that may be implicit in a phrase like 'called for by' in the extract just quoted.

The first strand is historical and analyses the developmental pathways and processes through which organisations progressively achieve a requisite or desired fit with their environments. In the first of two case studies, Siggelkow (2001, p. 839) analysed 'the developmental journey' of Liz Claiborne, a US women's fashion apparel manufacturer (founded in 1976). Siggelkow distinguishes internal and external fit: internal coherence of activities, on the one hand, and their appropriateness, on the other hand, given the presence of particular external environmental conditions. In relation to each sense of fit, he mapped the shifting interaction pattern among five key elements (or retailing choices) of Claiborne's overall market strategy. For Siggelkow, decisions made by managers (relying on their mental maps of organizational performance) as a result of both internally- and externally-sourced changes were found to be fit-conserving or fit-destroying (potentially in either a benign or detrimental sense). In the second case study of the Vanguard Group (a US mutual funds provider), Siggelkow (2002, p. 126) distinguished different types of elements (or components of activity domains), especially core and elaborated (with the latter supporting the former), along with a series of processes that were 'intimately related to the creation and further elaboration of organizational elements'. The four processes, arrived at by backward mapping through company archival sources (Siggelkow, 2002, p. 134), were patching, thickening, coasting and trimming. Patching meant the adoption of new components, while trimming entailed their elimination. Thickening referred to the reinforcement of core activities (e.g., by augmenting or more tightly integrating components) and coasting to letting them be. By these means, a series of characteristic developmental trajectories or pathways were arrived at, based around varying degrees of incremental changes, growth spurts, punctuated equilibrium or linear progression, in response to environments that could be turbulent, volatile or stable.

The second strand takes the 'equivocal' nature of the evidence of a performance–configuration relationship as its departure point and links this idea to the set-theoretic approach signaled earlier (Fiss, 2007, p. 1180). Here, in the interests of remedying the disconnect between configurational theorizing and empirical research (Fiss, 2007, p. 1183), the focus is on the patterning of organizational attributes (i.e., Siggelkow's elements) and the ways in which these are likely to exhibit different outcomes 'depending on how they are arranged' (Fiss, 2007, p. 1181). A set-theoretic approach entails comparative case analyses in which a selection of cases is utilised to arrive at necessary and sufficient combinations of causal attributes that enable organizations (once again, firms) to achieve high performance. Set fuzziness, rather than crispness, allows for the expression of threshold values for the inclusion of attributes in sets to be numbered partially (as in 1 = fully in, 0.80 = mostly in, etc.) rather than in simple binary terms (i.e., 1 = in, 0 = out). Apart from the promise of empirical observation of organizational configurations afforded by set theory, this approach also commends itself by facilitating improved practice due to the potential identification of 'more than one sufficient combination of design features that leads to high performance' (Fiss, 2007, p. 1189). In short, a set-theoretic perspective makes possible the charting of the relative simplicity or density of the multiple interdependencies between the parts of configurations.

CONFIGURING THE LEADERSHIP OF SCHOOLS

Notwithstanding what has been summarized as the slightly chequered, albeit productive, life course taken by this broad body of configurational theorizing over about three decades, empirical studies of configurations generally are still disappointingly few in number. Nevertheless, to revert back to the educational contexts reviewed earlier, schools offer uniquely interesting and promising laboratories for field observations of two points at the heart of the configurational literature that are crucial for leadership. The first point is Miller's (1986, p. 236) claim that 'each element makes sense in terms of the whole'. The second point is Siggelkow's (2001, p. 838) suggestion that tightness of fit 'raises the incentive for management to optimally configure and adjust all of its choices'.

Regarding the first point, there is a poignant illustration of configured leadership in Coburn's (2006) ethnography of the implementation of the California Reading Initiative (CRI), a policy designed to improve early years reading instruction in the American state of California. Coburn devoted a year's fieldwork to investigating CRI in an urban elementary school during which period she tried to better understand the dynamics of framing and implementing policy. From a large body of observational and interview data, Coburn (2006, p. 365) generated a total of 95 frames (or ways in which teachers and leaders typically defined problems or aspects of problems) associated with reading instruction. These were arranged in six thematic areas and, in the face of strong pre-existing teacher autonomy norms, about 50 frames in total were found to be successful in generating 'resonance', or were especially influential in persuading teachers to change their instructional practices.

Coburn's study is not an analysis of leadership per se, although she does devote considerable article space to a discussion of the key roles played by a range of school leaders in the micro-processes of problem framing. In essence, with regard to just one key area of pedagogy, her naturalistic account provides the kind of through-time discussion of the operation of a leadership configuration (Coburn, 2006, esp. pp. 364–369) that in research terms so far has been conspicuous by its absence. No 'solitary decision maker' (p. 364) stood out in her case study because 'teachers and teacher leaders were active participants *with* the school principal in articulating problem definitions and engaging in counterframing' (p. 364, original emphasis). On the other hand, professional interactions and negotiations were 'shaped by relations of authority' (p. 366), in which case the principal did have greater influence on problem framing, except with the caveat that her influence was 'always contingent upon her ability to construct frames that generated resonance' among sufficient numbers of teachers (p. 366). Provided that the principal endorsed them, then, particular ways of framing problems would resonate, yet they were much less likely to resonate if she opposed them. Here, both the principal's positional authority and her skill in framing gave her a rhetorical edge (p. 367). At the same time, there were numerous occasions when her preferred way of framing was countered successfully by those of teachers (pp. 367–368). Framing and counter-framing also took place in role sets such as grade-level teacher groups (large and small) and informal professional networks (especially in order to mobilize dissent), and teacher colleagues also influenced each other on a face-to-face basis (p. 368). Another prominent role set was the school leadership team (of classroom and resource teachers, along with the principal). Likewise, influential individual teachers 'were often able to create rhetorical bridges that helped their close colleagues connect particular frames with their own beliefs and experiences, thus facilitating resonance' (p. 369). Although Coburn does not explicitly foreground specific instances of leader pairings or threesomes, a number of the role set examples summarized earlier in the historical and contemporary review sections of this chapter were evident to some degree and at varying times in the processes documented in her research.

The second point about tightness of fit inducing optimal configuring is currently amply evident in England, where numerous and extensive policy changes in government schooling have taken place since 1988. Unlike firms, schools generally operate in highly-regulated, non-marketized (or at best partially marketized) environments. In this regard, English schools in particular represent the antithesis of the image of loosely-coupled systems as originally propounded by Weick (1976, p. 1), for whom tightly-coupled rationality in education was a rarity. Indeed, so tight has the fit become recently between English schools and the policy environment in which they operate that the likelihood of sealing off a breakdown in one portion of the overall organizational system, as Weick (1976, p. 7) claimed was universally common when he wrote, is exceedingly difficult if not impossible.

Indeed, these English developments may be characterized (and have been by numerous critics) as archetypically self-disciplining in the Foucaultian sense. The reason is that the entirety of the work of schools is very rigidly defined by, and measured through, external inspection against a range of examination-based student learning improvement performance targets. Inspection encompasses student achievement on national tests taken at three key student progression stages, with all school data recorded and stored on, and retrievable from, a system-wide database. These data are accessible to schools and inspectors, through an IT system known as 'RAISE on-line'. This IT enables inspectors to penetrate to the level of individual data profiles of specific children and to require explanations from schools in instances where students do not perform at anticipated levels as predicted on diagnostic tests of learning potential, which prompts the question of whether and to what extent school personnel 'know they are being watched' (McPhee & Poole, 2001, p. 524)?

With schools required to meet a range of government, local authority and other targeted performance measures, the consequences for failure are very serious and can include loss of grant or project income, diminished status, public humiliation and even the sacking of headteachers. In such circumstances, the day-to-day operational elements of schooling are so delicately balanced that if one gets out of kilter with the remainder the risk of a downwards spiraling vicious circle becomes genuinely real. For this reason, there is a strong incentive for schools to tightly and continuously monitor the performance of both their teachers and students through extensive data collection and tracking systems. To this end, schools devote considerable energy to the alignment and integration of teaching and learning with resource allocation, performance review, staff appraisal and optimum ways of identifying, fostering and the re-configuring of their overall leadership talent pools.

DISCUSSION AND CONCLUSION

This chapter has advanced an argument for configuration as the unit of leadership analysis. The rationale was two-fold. First, the aim was to try to transcend the individual–distributed divide that currently characterizes leadership and, by extension, to provide an alternative to the pendulum-swinging tendency which produces this divide. That is, the heroic resurgence that occurred over roughly two decades from the early 1980s appears to have plateaud and declined, and has been superseded by a renewed recognition of distribution (especially, although not only, in educational leadership). Potentially problematic consequences arise when pendulums swing. One, in a field which as was suggested is already highly susceptible to binary thinking, is to create yet one more binary or dualism, to the effect that leadership is either focused on an individual in a leader-centric manner or it is distributed in a collectivized and leaderful sense. The other consequence is to fall victim to a similar kind of narrowing convergence for which the proponents of configurations reviewed in the chapter have been said to be guilty, except that in this instance a convergence template which prioritizes the leadership of the many has been substituted for a template of the leadership of the one.

The second rationale was to try to better align the ways in which scholars theorize leadership with the hybrid actualities and emergent complexities of reality. To this end, two sources of empirical evidence were utilized. First, notwithstanding the strong sense of hierarchical positioning and superordination implicit in individually focused (not to mention heroic) leadership, along with any claims to its normality, the glimpse of part of the historical record in the early section of the chapter sought to vitiate such an assumption. Even though tendencies towards hierarchical individualism among humans were shown to parallel the behaviour of some primates, such tendencies were also shown to be far from inexorable and quite out of step with the holistic pattern of decision making accomplished by creature swarming. Rather, the human pattern for most of the long-run of the history of mankind has been for acephalous groupings to prevail, and for institutionalized pairings of leadership to coexist alongside city-state democracies and systems of kingship. Secondly, a range of contemporary instances of research purporting to be distributed was also reassessed as a prelude to suggesting how leadership relations might be reworked advantageously in parts–whole terms. This strategy was consistent with the recommendation of Meyer et al. (1993, p. 1178) that 'rather than trying to explain how order is designed into parts of an organization, configurational theorists try to explain how order emerges from the interaction of those parts as a whole'.

Of the considerable amount of unfinished research business that remains, four items are worthy of priority. First, with so much of the organizational configuration literature devoted to themes of convergence and divergence, and to some extent hybridity, questions need to be asked about the range of potential variation in leadership configurations. While the indicative evidence from existing studies summarized in this chapter points towards leadership hybridity, the anticipated outcomes of empirical studies of its patterning are unclear: these might indicate that hybrid mixtures narrow around a small handful of gestalts or that they diverge in unpredictable ways. Much will depend on the impact of external environmental imperatives and how these are experienced by the agents and agencies concerned. Secondly, regardless of whether the answer to this initial question favours divergent or convergent patterning, the next logically sequenced research priority would be to ascertain the consequences (both intended and unintended) of the population of configurations. That is, what contribution do particular ways of configuring leadership make to the overall performance effectiveness of organizations in respect of their missions and why is this?

Thirdly, there is also a powerful argument for tracking leadership hybridity over time, both retrospectively (as in the cases of fit discussed earlier) and prospectively in order to ascertain broad developmental trajectories. Not only would this approach answer the repeatedly raised objections in leadership to its cross-sectional design bias but also it would broaden understanding of at least three other evolutionary factors: (1) how alterations in the configuring of leadership relate to wider organizational-level realignments of core activities; (2) whether and why the coupling of leadership to these core areas varies in the degree of its tightness or looseness; and (3) the extent to which leadership configurations tend to be biased mainly in the direction of design (e.g., deliberate structuring initiatives) or emergence (e.g., evidence of self-organization) in the division of labour, and whether the balance between these two features varies over time and why. Finally, given that the environmental imperatives which impinge on organizations seem to differ by sector (at least when taken at face value) and shape their fit, increased recognition may have to be accorded to the peculiar factors which constrain and enable the work of different categories of leaders. Doesn't the fact that the business of schools is concerned with learning (or caring in the case of hospitals) for example, require researchers to begin thinking in terms of domain-specific, rather than generic, leadership knowledge and practice? If so, then, such determinants may go some way to affording leadership configurations their distinctive texture. Hopefully, all of these issues and questions point to the kind of reinvigorated and productive research agenda that opens up when a configuration becomes the unit of leadership analysis.

NOTE

1   This section draws on parts of Gronn (2009).

REFERENCES

Alvarez, J.L. & Svejenova, S. (2005) *Sharing executive power: roles and relationships at the top.* Cambridge: Cambridge University Press.

Barnard, C. (1982) *The functions of the executive.* Cambridge, MA: Harvard University Press.

Bass, B.M. (1990) *Bass & Stogdill's handbook of leadership: theory, research and managerial applications.* New York: Free Press.

Bass, B.M. (1998) *Transformational leadership: industrial, military, and educational impact.* Mahwah, NJ: Lawrence Erlbaum.

Bennis, W. & Nanus, B. (1985) *Leaders: the strategies for taking charge.* New York: Harper.

Boehm, C. (1996) Emergency decisions: cultural-selection mechanics, and group selection, *Current Anthropology*, 37(5): 763–793.

Boehm, C. (2001) Hierarchy in the forest: the evolution of egalitarian behaviour. Cambridge, MA: Harvard University Press.

Bolden, R., Petrov, G., & Gosling, J. (2008) Tensions in higher education leadership: towards a multi-level model of leadership practice, *Higher Education Quarterly*, 62(4): 358–376.

Bolden, R., Petrov, G., & Gosling, J. (2009) Distributed leadership in higher education: rhetoric and reality, *Educational Management, Administration & Leadership*, 37(2): 257–277.

Bryman, A. (1992) *Charisma and leadership in organizations.* London: Sage.

Burnham, J. (1962) The *managerial revolution*. Harmondsworth: Penguin.

Coburn, C.E. (2006) Framing the problem of reading instruction: using frame analysis to uncover the microprocesses of policy implementation, *American Educational Research Journal*, 43(3): 343–379.

Collinson, D. & Collinson, M. (2009) 'Blended leadership': employee perspectives on effective leadership in the UK further education sector, *Leadership*, 5(3): 365–380.

Copland, M.A. (2002) The myth of the superprincipal, *Phi Delta Kappan*, 82(7): 528–533.

Couzin, I. (2007) Collective minds, *Nature* (2007), 445: 715.

Couzin, I. (2008) Collective cognition in animal groups, *Trends in Cognitive Science*, 13(1): 36–43.

Couzin, I.D., Krause, J., Franks, N.R., & Levin, S.A. (2005) Effective leadership and decision-making in animal groups on the move, *Nature*, 433: 513–516.

Dalton, M. (1959) *Men who manage: fusions of feeling and theory in administration.* New York: John Wiley and Sons.

de Lima, J.A. (2008) Department networks and distributed leadership in schools, *School Leadership & Management*, 28(2): 159–187.

Denis, J-L., Langley, A., & Cazale, L. (1996) Leadership and strategic change under ambiguity, *Organization Studies*, 17(4): 673–699.

Donaldson, L. (1996) *For positivist organization theory: proving the hard core* London: Sage.

Drath, W.H., McCauley, C.D., Palus, C.J., Van Velsor, E., O'Connor, P.M.G., & McGuire, J.B. (2008) Direction, alignment, commitment: toward a more integrative ontology of leadership, *The Leadership Quarterly*, 19(6): 635–653.

Earle, T.K. (1987) Chiefdoms in archaeological and ethnohistorical perspective, *Annual Review of Anthropology*, 16: 279–308.

Ferguson, Y.H. (1991) Chiefdoms to city-states: the Greek experience. In T. Earle (ed.), *Chiefdoms: power, economy, and ideology.* Cambridge: Cambridge University Press, pp. 169–192.

Firestone, W.A. & Martinez, M.C. (2007) Districts, teacher leaders, and distributed leadership: changing instructional practice, *Leadership and Policy in Schools*, 6(1): 3–35.

Fiss, P.C. (2007) A set-theoretic approach to organizational configurations, *Academy of Management Review*, 32(4): 1180–1198.

Fiss, P.C. (2009) Case studies and the configurational analysis of organizational phenomena. In D. Byrne & C.C. Ragin (eds.), *The Sage handbook of case-based methods.* London: Sage, pp. 424–440.

Fondas, N. & Stewart, R. (1994) Enactment in managerial jobs: a role analysis, *Journal of Management Studies*, 31(1): 83–103.

Freeman, C. (2003) *The closing of the Western mind: the rise of faith and the fall of reason.* London: Pimlico.

Frenkel, M. (2008) The multinational corporation as a third space: rethinking international management discourse on knowledge transfer through Homi Bhaba, *Academy of Management Review*, 33(4): 924–942.

Frenkel, M. & Shenhav, Y. (2006) From binarism back to hybridity: a postcolonial reading of management and organization studies, *Organization Studies*, 27(6): 855–876.

Gibb, C.A. (1954) Leadership. In G. Lindzey (ed.), *Handbook of social psychology*, Vol 2. Reading, MA: Addison-Wesley, pp. 877–917.

Gilmour, J.A. (2006) Hybrid space: constituting the hospital as a home for patients, *Nursing Inquiry*, 13(1): 16–22.

Greenwood, R. & Hinings, C.R. (Bob) (2006) Radical organizational change. In S.R. Clegg, C. Hardy, T.B. Lawrence & W.R. Nord (eds), *The Sage handbook of organization studies*, 2nd edn. London: Sage, pp. 814–842.

Gronn, P. (2002) Distributed leadership as a unit of analysis, *The Leadership Quarterly*, 13(4): 423–451.

Gronn, P. (2008) The future of distributed leadership, *Journal of Educational Administration*, 46(2): 141–158.

Gronn, P. (2009) Leadership: its genealogy, configuration and trajectory. Inaugural Lecture, University of Cambridge (17 June).

Hadfield, M. (2007) Co-leaders and middle leaders: the dynamic between leaders and followers in networks of schools, *School Leadership & Management*, 27(3): 259–283.

Hodgson, R.C., Levinson, D.J., & Zaleznik, A. (1965) *The executive role constellation: an analysis of personality and role relations in management*. Boston; MA: Graduate School of Business Administration, Harvard University.

Hook, S. (1992 [1945]) *The hero in history: a study in limitation and possibility*. New Brunswick, NJ: Transaction.

House, R.J. (1977) A 1976 theory of leadership. In J.G. Hunt & L.L. Larson (eds), *Leadership: the cutting edge* carbondale, IL: Southern Illinois University Press, pp. 189–207.

Johnson, G. (1982) Organizational structure and scalar stress. In C. Renfrew, M.J. Rowlands, & B.A. Segraves (eds), *Theory and explanation in archaeology: The Southampton Conference*. New York: Academic Press, pp. 389–421.

Kalra, V.S., Kaur, R., & Hutnyk, J. (2005) *Diaspora and hybridity*. London: Sage.

Kitchener, M. (2000) The 'bureaucratization' of professional roles: the case of clinical directors in UK hospitals, *Organization*, 7(1): 129–154.

Kristiansen, K. (2001) Rulers and warriors: symbolic transmission and social transformation in Bronze Age Europe. In J. Haas (ed.), *From rulers to leaders*. New York: Kluwer, pp. 85–104.

Latour, B. (1993) *We have never been modern* (trans. C. Porter). Hemel Hempstead, Herts: Harvester Wheatsheaf.

Leithwood, K., Mascall, B., Strauss, T., Sacks, R., Memon, N., & Yashkina, A. (2007) Distributing leadership to make schools smarter: taking the ego out of the system, *Leadership and Policy in Schools*, 6(1): 37–67.

McPhee, R.D. & Poole, M.S. (2001) Organizational structures and configurations. In F.M. Jablin & L.L. Putnam (eds), *The new handbook of organizational communication: advances in theory, research, and methods*. London: Sage, pp. 503–543.

Mann, M. (1986) *The sources of social power*, Vol 1: *A history of power from the beginning to A.D. 1760*. Cambridge: Cambridge University Press.

March, J.G. & Weil, T. (2005) *On leadership*. Malden, MA: Blackwell.

Markham, S.E. & Markham, I.S. (1995) Self-management and self-leadership reexamined: a levels-of-analysis perspective, *The Leadership Quarterly*, 6(3): 343–359.

Meindl, J.R., Ehrlich, S.B., & Dukerich, J.M. (1985) The romance of leadership, *Administrative Science Quarterly*, 30(1): 78–102.

Merton, R.K. (1957) The role set: problems in sociological theory, *British Journal of Sociology*, 8(2): 106–120.

Meyer, A.D., Tsui, A.S., & Hinings, C.R. (1993) Configurational approaches to organizational analysis, *Academy of Management Journal*, 36(6): 1175–1195.

Miller, D. (1981) Toward a new contingency approach: the search for organizational gestalts, *Journal of Management Studies*, 18(1): 1–26.

Miller, D. (1986) Configurations of strategy and structure: towards a synthesis, *Strategic Management Journal*, 7: 233–249.

Miller, D. (1987) The genesis of configuration, *Academy of Management Review*, 12(4): 686–701.

Miller, D. (1990) Organizational configurations: cohesion, change, prediction, *Human Relations*, 43(8): 771–789.

Miller, D. (1996) Configurations revisited, *Strategic Management Journal*, 17(7): 505–512.

Miller, D. (1999) Notes on the study of configurations, *Management International Review*, 39(2): 27–39 (Special Issue).

Miller, D. & Mintzberg, H. (1983) The case for configuration. In G. Morgan (ed.), *Beyond method: strategies for social research*. Beverley Hills; CA: Sage, pp. 57–73.

Mouzelis, N.P. (2008) *Modern and postmodern social theorizing: bridging the divide*. Cambridge: Cambridge University Press.

Newton, & Levinson, D. (1973) The work group within the organization: a sociopsychological approach, *Psychiatry*, 36: 115–142.

Papastergiadis, N. (1997) Tracing hybridity in theory. In P. Werbner, & T. Modood, (eds), *Debating cultural hybrity: multi-cultural identities and the politics of anti-Racism*. London: Zed Books, pp. 257–281.

Ragin, C.C. (2000) *Fuzzy-set social science*. Chicago, IL: University of Chicago Press.

Ragin, C.C. (2008) *Redesigning social inquiry: fuzzy sets and beyond*. Chicago, IL: University of Chicago Press.

Rubin, P.H. (2000) Hierarchy, *Human Nature*, 11(3): 260–264.

Sayles, L.R.. (1993) *The working leader: the triumph of high performance over conventional management principles*. New York: Free Press.

Schwabenland, C. & Tomlinson, F. (2008) Managing diversity or diversifying management?, *Critical Perspectives on International Business*, 4(2–3): 320–333.

Shimoni, B. & Bergmann, H. (2006) Managing in a changing world: from multiculturalism to hybridization—the production of hybrid management cultures in Israel, Thailand, and Mexico, *Academy of Management Perspectives*, 20(3): 76–89.

Siggelkow, N. (2001) Change in the presence of fit: the rise, the fall and the renaissance of Liz Claiborne, *Academy of Management Journal*, 44(4): 838–857.

Siggelkow, N. (2002) Evolution toward fit, *Administrative Science Quarterly*, 47(1): 125–159.

Simmel, G. (1950) *The sociology of Georg Simmel*, (Ed. and Trans. K.H. Wolff). New York: Free Press.

Smith, A. (2004) Migrancy, hybridity, and postcolonial literary studies. In N. Lazarus (ed.), *The Cambridge companion to postcolonial literary studies*. Cambridge: Cambridge University Press, pp. 241–261.

Spillane, J., Camburn, E.M., & Pareja, A.S. (2007) Taking a distributed perspective to the school principal's working day, *Leadership and Policy in Schools*, 6(1): 103–126.

Surowiecki, J. (2004) *The wisdom of crowds: why the many are smarter than the few*. London: Abacus.

Timperley, H.S. (2005) Distributed leadership: developing theory from practice, *Journal of Curriculum Studies*, 37(4): 395–420.

Weber, M. (1970) *From Max Weber*. London: Routledge & Kegan Paul.

Weick, K.E. (1976) Educational organizations as loosely coupled systems, *Administrative Science Quarterly*, 21(1): 1–19.

Whitchurch, C. (2008) Shifting identities and blurring boundaries: the emergence of *third space* professionals in UK higher education. *Higher Education Quarterly*, 62(4): 377–396.

Whyte, W.H. (1963) *The organization man*. Harmondsworth: Penguin.

Wilson, D.S., Timmel, J.J., & Miller, R.R. (2004) Cognitive co-operation: when the going gets tough, think as a group, *Human Nature*, 15(3): 1–15.

Woodburn, J. (1982) Egalitarian societies, *Man*, 17(3): 431–451.

Young, R.J.C. (1995) *Colonial desire: hybridity in theory, culture and race*. London: Routledge.

Yukl, G. (1999) An evaluation of conceptual weaknesses in transformational and charismatic leadership theories, *The Leadership Quarterly*, 10(2): 285–305.

Zaccaro, S.J. (2007) Trait-based perspectives of leadership, *American Psychologist*, 62(1): 6–16.

Zaleznik, A. (1977) Managers and leaders: Are they different?, *Harvard Business Review*, 55(3): 67–78.

33

Moving Relationality: Meditations on a Relational Approach to Leadership

Dian Marie Hosking

CONSTRUCTING RELATIONS: INTRODUCING ENTITATIVE AND RELATIONAL-PROCESSUAL DISCOURSES

'It was my first murder' – was how my colleague Maurice Punch began his ethnography of police work. Since I had no dramatic introduction I borrowed his. My first leadership handbook (much more prosaic than a murder) was Stogdill's (Stogdill, 1974). I remember using it when I was a PhD student researching Fiedler's model of leadership effectiveness (Fiedler, 1967). More than 30 years later I was invited to write about relational leadership for what is, I believe, the third handbook. Now that I come to think of it, my reply was perhaps rather bold. I said I would love to write such a chapter but only if I could write about what I meant by the term 'relational' and only if I could use the space to play with some moving possibilities; we had a deal.

But now what? Time to fill space? I recall Ted Hughes' poem 'The Thought-Fox' – a poem about the process of writing the poem – beginning with the blank page – outside in the night-time garden a fox emerges from the shadows… and fills the page with its passing. So perhaps I could begin with some foxy reminiscences… with a tale…of an approach…of wanderings and wonder…a moving tale of relational processes.

Looking back it seems I wandered into leadership. I followed a growing curiosity which was less about leadership and more about person–world relations. I was curious about the ways social theories differentiated person and world and, having done so, 'put them back together' in relation. I had recently come across the contingency approach, a variant of systems thinking, which combined information about, for example, organizations, organizational environments and organizational effectiveness. Fiedler was one of the earliest contingency models which, in his case, combined variables he thought to be implicated in leadership effectiveness. He aimed to predict the latter by combining talk about the leader, talk about the context or 'leadership situation', and performance data – each separately defined and measured.

Fiedler defined the leader as one who 'directs and controls' the task-relevant activities of a work group. He obtained information about the leader by asking leaders to describe their Least Preferred Co-worker (the LPC questionnaire). He then correlated leaders' LPC scores with group performance data (which he viewed as a measure of the leader's effectiveness). These correlations were plotted on a graph in which the vertical axis ranged from −1 through 0 to +1 (the size of the co-relation); the horizontal axis combined high and low levels of three 'situational' measures: group atmosphere, the leader's position power and the level of structure in the group's task to produce eight distinguishable 'leadership situations'.

Fiedler claimed that a data plot involving over 800 work groups showed that high LPC scorers were more effective than low in some defined situations, whereas the opposite was the case in other situations. Many accepted his claims and so directed their attention to the LPC measure – which seemed to predict – but no-one knew why. LPC scores were variously investigated as potential signifiers of a leader's 'leadership behavior', of some leadership trait, and of 'cognitive complexity' – how complexly leaders could know 'self' and 'other' or world, so to speak.

At first I was intrigued by the idea that the way leaders perceived 'the world' might be connected with their leadership effectiveness. However, to cut a long story short, I came to have serious doubts about Fiedler's model and about the entire contingency approach. My doubts included the following:

- selecting and centering one particular person (in this case, 'the leader') and focusing on individual characteristics and behaviors gives too much significance to that individual;
- treating 'the leadership context', 'world' or 'other' as 'out there', independent of the leader, draws too sharp a boundary between self and not-self;
- differentiating self and other in these ways over-emphasizes stable things with stable characteristics and means that processes can only happen within and between things; and
- differentiating self and other in these ways turns relating into an instrumental process potentially valuable for self through (a) producing knowledge about and (b) achieving power over other.

My fellow social psychologist Ian Morley and I used the term '*entitative*' to summarize all theoretical/empirical approaches that embrace the above constructions of self, other and relations (Hosking and Morley, 1991). Later I came across the work of another social psychologist, Edward Sampson, who linked these constructions to what he called 'the western project' in which 'dominant groups construct (…) serviceable others' (Sampson, 1993). He spoke of this 'monological and self celebratory' construction as being oriented around the notion of (i) a singular and rational self (ii) who is able to know other as other really (or probably) is, (iii) who can speak for and about other (followers, women, other ethnic groups…), and (iv) can use other in the rational pursuit of (supposedly) rational goals and interests.

Samson emphasized the moral/ethical aspects of this construction. For example, he mobilized feminist and postcolonial critiques (e.g., Flax, 1987; Harding, 1986, 1998) to make connections with dominance relations in areas such as race and gender, centering the issue of whose claims to know receive warrant, whose claims go unheard and whose are 'heard' but evaluated and reconstructed in dominance relations. In broad summary, various critiques of the 'entitative approach' and Western individualism point to (i) the ways in which relations are connected to persons who are assumed to possess a stable and bounded self together with individual knowledge, who performs individual acts and who relates to other in terms of what other can do for self… (ii) the relative neglect of power and politics, for example, through an emphasis on one universal rationality and abstract, objective knowledge 'from nowhere'; (iii) the ethical/moral issues involved in constructing a 'serviceable other'; and (iv) the implications that these practices might have for the future of humanity and the planet (see Sampson, 1993; Gergen, 1994).

By the time I finished my PhD on Fiedler's contingency model I was actively investigating other possible constructions of persons, processes and relations and how these might be manifested in leadership theories and (research) practices. Over the years, and together with many co-authors, I have explored various possibilities. So, for example, in the book *A Social Psychology of Organising*, Ian Morley and I developed a view of organizing leadership as a *relational process* that is simultaneously social, cognitive and political. We defined social processes as those in which 'participants (in organizing) construct a sense of who they are (identity) in relation to a context which consists importantly of other people and their constructions' (Hosking and Morley, 1991 p. xi). We proposed that these same processes should also be seen as 'cognitive' in that they involve sensemaking. By this, we meant that social processes construct local-cultural realities that reflect particular orderings of fact and value. We further proposed that these same processes are 'political' inasmuch as they support particular local-cultural constructions or valuations – and not others – constructions that are more or less open to otherness.

In this context we theorized leadership as a special kind of organizing process. We used the term 'leadership' to refer to contributions that achieve acceptable influence; we defined leaders as those whom participants see to make consistent contributions of this sort and come to expect to do so. In other words, *we defined leadership relationally* according to how contributions are supplemented, and *centered extended leadership processes* rather than bounded, 'self contained' individuals (e.g., Hosking, 1988; Hosking and Morley, 1988, 1991). In theorizing relational processes, we spoke of the '*mutual creation*' and *'emergence' of self and other*. In other words, we viewed self as fundamentally relational and ongoing rather than characteristic of some pre-existing entity engaging in 'backwards and forwards transactions, to produce rational outcomes. We spoke of processes as more or less helpful and, in this sense, more or less skillful, of the importance of actively open-minded thinking, conversations and dialogues – including those which 'build relationships in which followers turn into leaders' (Hosking and Morley, 1991, p. 256). To my mind, we said a great deal that was useful about a possible relational approach to leadership and I shall return to these themes in a while.

Meanwhile, I was also in conversation with Helen Brown during the time she was a participant observer in women's groups. In a subsequent publication, Helen and I argued that 'entitative' constructions of individuals, leadership and organization were gendered, masculine-cultural constructions (e.g., Brown and Hosking, 1986; see also Brown, 1992). Again we attempted to articulate a relational-processual view. In this case we explored *relational processes as themselves 'the product'*. We argued that 'the process is the product' when it allows participants to enjoy a certain (positively valued) way of being in relation rather than being reduced to a (instrumental) means to link inputs and outcomes. In this case, the local social ordering of value included ways of relating characterized by distributed leadership and heterarchy. It was important to us that this work added 'another voice' (Gilligan, 1993) to contrast with the more usual emphasis on focused leadership, appointed leaders, and (gendered) hierarchy.

The same year that Ian and I had our book published, Peter Dachler and Ken Gergen invited me to a small workshop in St Gallen, Switzerland. A few years later the three of us brought out an edited book based on the workshop, calling it *Management and Organization: Relational Alternatives to Individualism*. As I remember, we puzzled a great deal over what title to give the book and we had lengthy discussions over the many things we wanted to signify by the term 'relational'. In general, we wanted to signify a shift from entitative assumptions to what we called 'active processes of relations' – viewing the latter as 'the matrix from which the conception of both individual selves and social structures spring' (Hosking, Dachler and Gergen, 1995, p. xii). Once again, the issue of how further to develop a relational approach was very much in the foreground.

Peter Dachler and I wrote a chapter which we called 'The primacy of relations in constructing organizational realities'. We proposed that:

the key issue in any relational approach lies not in matters of content, e.g., competitive vs collaborative relationships, and not in justifying the truth value of propositional statements; the central issue is epistemological. (Dachler and Hosking, 1995, p. 1)

Although we used the term 'epistemological', we emphasized that a relational approach blurs the (entitative) distinction between ontology (what exists) and epistemology (what we can know). We asserted: 'What is experienced as real or true depends on (usually implicitly) held assumptions about processes of knowing' (p. 1) and it is these 'knowing' processes that give existence (ontology), for example, to individuals, leadership, and organization.

Illustrating the above, entitative constructions treat for example, persons, leaders, and contexts as 'out there' and available to be observed and known by an independent observer. In contrast, a relational epistemology (we could say ontology) views for example, entities, knowledge, power..., as constructions made in ongoing relational processes – and these are processes in which the 'observer' participates. We argued that these processes construct and reconstruct relational realities in all kinds of actions and focused on *language as action* rather than as a way to represent entities. We proposed that processes be viewed as ongoing in the sense that actions (or 'texts') supplement preceding actions, whereas at the same time, making themselves available for possible supplementation. In sum, we (a) blurred the (post)positivist distinction between ontology and epistemology, (b) shifted emphasis to relational construction processes, and (c) directed attention to relational realities as ontology in the sense of (d) being made in local-cultural, local-historical processes.

Our account of relational processes was illustrated through reference to existing and possible narratives of leadership. We began by emphasizing that, in comparison with the entitative approach, everything changes. First, relational theorizing centers 'empty' relational processes, so to speak. Since relational realities are theorized as local (rather than universal) rationalities, *their 'content' must be allowed to emerge* rather than be prespecified by the theorist/researcher (see Alvesson and Deetz, 2000). It also became clear that a relational perspective invites different questions – about how rather than what. For example, a relational approach might ask how distributed leadership could be constructed and maintained (i.e., constantly re-constructed). Similarly, we might become curious about the ways ongoing act-supplement processes (re)construct Western individualism and 'hard' self-other differentiation (e.g., Berman, 1981, 1990). One particular question continues to intrigue me. It concerns the possibility of 'soft' self–other differentiation: How are such relations be constructed and how might leadership be part of and contribute this? In the context of this relational approach, it no longer makes sense to ask which narrative of leadership is correct or to complain that different narratives of leadership 'do not add up'. Instead, we are invited to direct our attention to the ways in which relational processes open up or close down possibilities and what this means for identities and relations, including the space for others and to be other.

Reflecting on the many live conversations, research and writing projects in which I have participated, Sandra Harding's reconstruction of the 'voyage of discovery' metaphor comes to mind. But the 'post-colonial voyage' is not (in order) to conquer and possess, but rather a process of (re) learning possible worlds and ways of being in relation (Harding, 1998). I would like to use the rest of this chapter to further develop what I have already said about a possible 'relational approach' to leadership. So I will center relational processes and view leaders and leadership, science and scientist – all relational realities – as always emergent in relational processes.

When considered as a 'social science perspective' (Alvesson and Deetz, 2000) this approach could be said to embrace a set of voices that variously emphasize historicism, phenomenology and hermeneutics. A historical voice is reflected in the view that understandings and practices, *including 'scientific' ones*, are 'inside' rather than 'outside history'. The phenomenological voice centers everyday life worlds as local-cultural 'relational' realities, rather than centering the assumption of a single 'real reality' that science can know more or less objectively. Science then is viewed as one local-cultural relational reality or 'form of life' (Wittgenstein, 1953) which 'goes on' in relation to other forms of life. A hermeneutic voice directs attention to language and the ways it reflects and (re)constructs, shall we say, local-historical, local-cultural practices and conventions (Hosking and Morley, 2004, p. 319).

I shall bring these 'voices' together in a way that *gives ontology to ongoing relational processes*. I shall speak of leaders and leadership, science and scientists – indeed all identities and related forms of life – as '*constituted*' in relational processes. This is a 'constitutive' rather than a 'mediative' view of science (Woolgar, 1986). It is vitally important to note that it offers a very distinctive relational view. It contrasts with other 'relational' perspectives of leadership (e.g., Uhl-Bien, 2004) by being constitutive, by including scientists and their community-based traditions in the general line of theorizing of relational processes, and by its dialogical view of personhood (Hosking, 2006, 2007).

PARTICIPATION AND THE DIALOGICAL VIEW OF PERSON

It's been a while since we heard from Sampson. It's time for him to come out of the undergrowth; he has been yapping at the shadows of Western individualism for long enough. As we already know, he is not alone. Like many other social theorists he has articulated a view of person and self–other relations that differs from the egocentric, monological, Western view of personhood. As we have seen, this (we could call it 'eco-logical') view treats self as a relational construction made in relational processes. What has not yet been made explicit is that this implies, not one, but *many selves 'situated' in particular relations with particular others*. In this view, other is intimately connected (related) to (or should I say with) self. When theorizing these relational processes language-based interactions are usually centered and variously conceptualized using concepts such as conversation, dialogue, discursive activity, and narrative or storytelling (e.g., Edwards and Potter, 1992; Gergen, 1994; Hermans, Kempen, and van Loon, 1992; Hosking and Morley, 1991; Sampson, 1993). I need to say a little bit about these language-based processes so that I can then explore their possible connections with leadership.

Hermans and his colleagues can help us with this (Hermans, Kempen, and van Loon, 1992). Their approach was to contrast what they saw as the cultural specificity of Western individualism with the notion that all persons, in all cultures and at all times, listen to and tell stories and, in these ways, socially construct particular ways of relating self and world. They drew from writers such as Vico to argue that mind and body are inseparable and 'in history' while also actively making history – knowing and doing are the same (Hermans, Kempen, and van Loon, 1992, p. 24). History making was theorized as narrating and narrating was theorized as a *dialogical* process. This is where the work of Russian literary theorist Mikhail Bakhtin comes in. Bakhtin had noted that, rather than having one narrator dominate and speak for others, Dostoevsky allowed each character their own voice. Dostoevsky's *narratives were produced by a 'polyphony' of voices in dialogical relation* rather than 'a multitude of characters within a unified objective world' (Hermans, Kempen, and van Loon, 1992, p. 27). What is important here is that the metaphor of the polyphonic novel shows that one person can live in many *I* positions in many coexisting worlds, that several may enter into dialogue with one another and, indeed, may agree or disagree.

Polyphonic narrating is possible because persons can engage in imaginal dialogues (where they can imagine a future and reconstruct a past) in addition to 'actual' dialogues in interactions with 'real' presences. So *the dialogical self is social* '...in the sense that other people occupy positions in the multi-voiced self' (Hermans, Kempen, and van Loon, 1992, p. 29). Unlike the monological view of person, there is no centralized and singular self attempting to control other. Indeed, as they remark, the Western-cultural 'tendency to centralization' may encourage practices that center one self in dominance relation with others 'thereby reducing the possibility of dialogue that, for its full development, requires a high degree of openness for the exchange and modification of perspectives' (Hermans, Kempen and van Loon, 1992, p. 30). Looking ahead, we can begin to imagine the significance of this for a relational view of leadership processes, a view that links the dialogical self and dialogue to openness, listening, and history making.

Sampson (1993) also centered a dialogic view of person. He wrote at length about what he called 'the dialogic turn', which he saw as a turn to 'celebrating the other' (rather than the self). He wrote:

> ...what stands out when we look at what people do together is language as communication in action. Because we have become so intent on searching deeply within the individual's psyche for the answers to all our questions about human nature, we usually fail to see what sits right before us, a dominating conversations feature of our lives with others: conversations. It is time now to take conversations seriously. (p. 97)

He singled out four key features of conversations. First, they go on between people; even when people are alone, 'their thinking occurs in the form of inner conversation or dialogue' (p. 97). Secondly, conversations are public (we could also say, social) because they involve signs that are generally shared by a particular community. Thirdly, conversations implicate addressivity – they are addressed by someone to (an)other(s); they are what we humans do i.e., *conversation* is *action* (rather than *about* action). And fourthly, conversations involve verbal and non-verbal, symbolic and written material. For Sampson, 'These four features link person and other in such an intimate way that disentangling the bonds that join them becomes an exercise in futility' (Sampson, 1993, p. 98). Borrowing from Bakhtin, he continued: 'The argument, in short, is that we gain a self in and through a process of social interaction, dialogue, and conversation with others' (Sampson, 1993, p. 106). And so, *by being constituted in*

conversations, each person is a multiplicity, 'multiplicity is the norm'.

Again, to be very clear, these dialogic, narrative, conversational processes are processes in which *all* aspects of relational realities are in ongoing, emergent (re)construction. These processes (re) create particular 'language games' together with their related 'forms of life' (Wittgenstein, 1953), which we then take to have their own independent existence or, in other words, to be how things 'really are' (e.g., Bohm, 2004). So, for example, as Sampson remarked: 'Our conversations both express and presuppose a reality which, in expressing what is presupposed, we help to create' (Sampson, 1993, p. 108). I should also add that the grounds for these lines of argument are found in many literatures, including those that focus on language (e.g., Wittgenstein, 1953), on social development and social relations generally (e.g., Mead, 1934; Vygotsky, 1978), on 'mind', cognition, and 'discursive' processes (see, e.g., Billig, 1987, Edwards and Potter, 1992; Wertsch, 1991), on feminism and feminist critiques, for example, of science and social relations (e.g., Flax, 1987; Harding, 1986, 1998), on the social construction of relational realities (e.g., Gergen, 1994), and on the nature of consciousness and historical-cultural variations in the same (e.g., Berman, 1981, 1990; Bohm, 2004; Ong, 1967).

This relational perspective re-constructs the entitative narrative of knowledge and power. *Knowledge* is now seen as social-relational, constructed in action, situated and moving, and intimately interconnected with power. *Power* now is linked to how self and other can be – in relation. The apparent presence or relative absence of multiplicity must now be seen in terms of power. So, for example, when dialogues are constrained such that one party acts as if they know and can speak for other – when the voice of other is not heard or distorted – when other is judged in relation to some supposed universal rationality – then we can say these are *ego*-logical processes constructing dominance or 'power over' (Dachler and Hosking, 1995; Gergen, 1995; Sampson, 1993). *Eco*-logical processes embrace the 'power to' be in different but equal relations – as in the case of the women's groups mentioned earlier (Hosking, 2000). They also include the 'power to' voice different selves (e.g., as parent, green activist, health service user, Buddhist etc.) and not just one (e.g., self as a manager). Returning to leadership, we shall need to explore ways in which conversations, narratives or dialogues can open up (or close down) multiplicity in all these aspects.

This dialogical view is closely related to work that talks of a 'participative' worldview. In this context, 'participation' refers to much, much more than, for example a leadership style, a way of handling management–labor relations, a preferred approach to national governance or a liberal ideology. Rather, *participation is viewed as a relational way of being and knowing* (Reason, 1994). So, for example, the anthropologist and cybernetician Gregory Bateson argued something like this in his *Steps to an Ecology of Mind* (Bateson, 1972). For Bateson, a proper understanding of mind would be to see it as extended or 'immanent' – not only in the human body – but throughout the entire living world. Bateson is one of a number of social theorists who argue that humankind's 'fall from grace' involved the construction of many dis-engagements or separations – separating self from other, separating thought from emotion, separating sacred from secular and so on. A 'return to grace' (Bateson, 1972) or to an 'enchanted world' (Berman, 1981) requires that 'individual mind' be re-viewed as part of 'larger mind', which is 'comparable to God and is perhaps what some people mean by 'God'' (Bateson, 1972, p. 461). For Bateson and many others, re-engagement is essential for recovering wisdom, ecological balance and long-term survival of the planet. This requires re-connecting with participative ways of knowing, with ways that re-join the many levels of mind, including 'computations of the heart' (Bateson, 1972, p. 464; see also Reason, 1994; Reason and Bradbury, 2001; Hosking, 2000).

Many have suggested that 'participating consciousness' underwent an 'epochal' shift to non-participation. This shift has been linked with many changing cultural practices, especially with changes in communications – from oral/aural cultural practices dominated by sound, speaking, hearing, and listening to literate cultures in which visual forms (especially written texts) and visual observation dominates (Berman, 1981; Berendt, 1992; Levin, 1989; Ong, 1967). However it is also possible to see participatory thought, not in some dualistic 'either-or' relation, but as the ever-present background of literal thought. For example, the physicist David Bohm, one of the Dalai Lama's 'scientific gurus', wrote 'I suggest that we are constantly doing participatory thought…it has never gone away' but 'literal thought claims we are not doing it at all' (Bohm, 2004, p. 98). For this reason, claims Bohm, literal thought is incoherent. If, as Bohm further suggests, literal, subject–object ways of relating continue to dominate, then *the fundamental interrelatedness of thoughts, bodies, cultures, nature and the cosmos cannot be understood*. We will be unable to understand what it is to be human, unable to be relationally responsive to other – other selves, other people, nature and the cosmos. It seems to me that we have now come to the heart of what *this sort* of relational perspective can offer.

A RELATIONAL APPROACH TO LEADERSHIP

I have suggested that relational processes can be more or less open – open to multiple self–other relations, to the voices of others, to the 'many levels of mind' and to ongoingness. I have further argued that, instead of assuming that hard self–other differentiation is how things really are or should be, hard differentiation should be seen as an ongoing construction made in language-based processes. This invites us to explore how ongoing relational processes could construct *soft self–other differentiation* and to reflect on how leadership might emerge and contribute to such processes.

It seems timely to do just this. We seem to be facing issues of interconnectedness such as climate change, global communications, increasing inequalities in financial wealth and economic infrastructure, loss of biodiversity, destruction of forests, landscapes and communities, pollution… issues which may not be tractable to yet more 'knowing that', more 'power over', more instrumental ways of relating. In other writings I have suggested that all this gives us enough good reasons to (re-)learn and (re)construct practices of soft self–other differentiation, to (re)learn more participative ways of relating. This clearly is how some, for example, feminists, ecologists, Buddhists…, want to be (to 'go on') – in relation (Hosking, 2000; Hosking and Kleisterlee, 2009). This relational constructionist perspective, together with its special interest in eco-logical ways of relating, perhaps should be viewed less in terms of knowledge and truth (as is the case with other[social] science perspectives) and more in terms of *ethics* (e.g., Levinas, 1989) *and local (interconnected and extended) pragmatics*. For me, this is where a relational approach to leadership has greatest promise.

I have theorized relating as a language-based process using concepts such as narrative, conversation and dialogue. In this view of process, the present both re-produces some previous local-cultural, local-historical constructions and acts in relation to possible and probable futures. In other words, both the past and possible futures are implicated in the ever-ongoing present, 'in the now' so to speak. This invites us to explore 'nowness' and how it might be more or less open to other possible selves, to other persons and other possible worlds. One possibility is to reconsider relating in terms, for example, of *extending hospitality* without attempting to know or to achieve 'power over' other. 'Hospitality' for Derrida meant, 'I open up my home… I give place to them… I let them come…' (Derrida, 2000, p. 25).

He adds that hospitality might include careful attention to language (following Emmanuel Levinas, who suggested that language *is* hospitality) but might also 'consist in suspending language... and even the address to the other.... Keeping silent is already a modality of possible speaking' (Derrida, 2000, p. 135). What follows are meditations on some qualities of relating that seem required for there to be room for other, for other to be invited and hosted in different but equal relations.

Dialogue and relationally engaged leadership

Conversation has become increasingly popular in connection with transformative change work. Approaches such as appreciative inquiry (Cooperrider and Shrivastva, 1987) assume a relational, dialogical view of person and processes, whereas others such as participative action research are attached to a participative worldview (Reason and Bradbury, 2001). They are all ways of working that can open up 'power to' rather than close down through 'power over'. Approaches of this sort: (a) work through multiple dialogues, rather than through top-down leadership edicts and the avoidance of dialogue; (b) work with many different self–other relations, rather than a single hierarchy of knowledge and expertise; (c) work with what is already (potentially) available and with what participants believe to be relevant, rather than imposing mono-logical constructions of leaders or outside experts; and (d) invite and support many lines of action, rather than requiring or imposing consensus. Dialogical processes can facilitate multiple community-based voices and can help multiple communities (as 'forms of life') to participate such that other realities can be 'allowed to lie' rather than being questioned, grasped, judged, and re-constructed by a particular, knowing and structuring agent.

There are some social science approaches that explicitly center 'dialogue'. They include the Public Conversations Project (Chasin, Herzig, Roth, Chasin, and Becker, 1996), work using the language of 'transformative dialogues' (Gergen, McNamee, and Barrett, 2001),' dialogue conferences' (Toulmin and Gustavsen, 1996) and the MIT Dialogue Project (e.g., Isaacs, 1993, 1996). The former draw most heavily from research and theory in communication studies, social psychology, family therapy and cybernetic systems theory, and action science, for example, using the work of Bakhtin (e.g., Wertsch, 1991), Gregory and Catherine Bateson (Bateson and Bateson, 1987),

Watzlawick (Watzlawick, 1978; Watzlawick, Weakland and Fisch, 1974); the MIT Dialogue Project draws more heavily on David Bohm's writings. Whatever their particular lineage, these approaches use the term 'dialogue' to refer to *a special kind of conversation.*

In its 'purest' form, dialogue is free from selfish attempts to know and control other (Bateson, 1972; Bateson and Bateson, 1987) and goes on in conversations that have no agenda (Bohm, 2004). Dialogue, as a special kind of conversation goes on in slow, open, and curious ways of relating characterized: (a) by a very special sort of listening, questioning, and being present; (b) by willingness to suspend one's assumptions and certainties; and (c) by reflexive attention to the ongoing process and one's own part in it. Rather than constructing separate, fixed, or closed realities, for example, of self (other) and one's own (others) position, dialogical practices open up to relationality and to possibilities, and open up space for self and other to co-emerge: this is what Bohm called flow.

At least in the circles I move in, dialogical practices seem to be increasingly emphasized. They seem to offer an alternative to dis-engaging, dis-heartening, and dis-enchanting ways of being in relation. Dialoging can provide a way out of stuckness; in relational processes characterized by dialogue it becomes possible to let go of entifying practices that construct relatively solid, stable, singular entities trying to build knowledge about and power over other (knowable and formable) entities. Dialoging can help to bring forth and support appreciation (rather than judgment and critique), discussion of what can be done (rather than what cannot), and a sense of relational responsibility (rather than blaming others). Dialoging makes space for ongoing emergence, for improvisation. Practicing dialogue as a 'discipline of collective inquiry' (Isaacs, 1996), participants can learn how to learn, can learn to open up to possibilities – to other constructions of what is real and good. Relationally engaged leadership can be thought of as ongoing in practices that invite and support this 'discipline' and the practice of hospitality.

Leadership and light structuring

Specifying the design of some research or organizational change program, producing written rule books and job specifications, and single-voiced leadership can all be viewed as examples of one local 'form of life' (Wittgenstein, 1953) or 'elite' (Alvesson and Deetz, 2000), attempting to control other 'forms' – to control what, when and how in relation to (the elite's) specified standards. Much the same could be said of the therapist who relates to his patient on the basis of some content-rich story of health and illness or of the leader who applies some theory of leadership when relating, for example, to his followers or team. These are forms and practices that are 'already knowing'. In contrast, what I am calling light structuring gives more space for emergence and improvisation, for dance and play, for 'being in the now'. Part of what this means is that it becomes possible to be 'relationally responsive' (McNamee, Gergen, and associates, 1999) to whatever comes up in any particular moment and possible to make space for multiple 'local forms of life' to be voiced, heard, and related to.

Light structuring is an important aspect of dialoguing, a practice which, as I have said, has to be practiced. Usually, participants are invited to agree to certain rules of engagement that help them to learn (while practicing) the 'collective discipline' of dialogue. These usually include rules such as, for example, don't interrupt, do not attempt to persuade others, use respectful language, ask questions only for clarification, listen to your listening, and so on (e.g., Chasin et al., 1996). Minimal structures such as these can help to block or interrupt already solidified patterns and, in this way, help to open up new possibilities. The idea is to provide enough but not too much structure: i.e. to provide a container, so to speak, that invites and supports the gradual emergence of slow, open, coherent, in-the-present-moment performances.

Improvisation has been much discussed in this context: for example, using improvisational jazz or theater to illustrate and/or develop skillful practice. While improvising, participants could be said to discover the future that their actions invite, as it unfolds, by being relationally responsive and by being ready to connect with what cannot be seen or heard ahead of time. This is possible, for example, through making space for multiple equal voices – minimizing or doing away with hierarchy – and making space for 'distributed leadership' (Brown and Hosking, 1986). Improvising in the context of light structuring means being open to whatever is presented, relating to whatever it is as 'workable' and open to emerging possibilities. You could also call this an appreciative orientation: there is no good or bad, no mistake, no bum note – everything is related to as workable. Relating in these ways involves being ready to dare, to leap into the unknown, and perhaps, like Picasso, 'refusing to appeal to the familiar' by repeating some already established pattern or form. I love the way my colleague Frank Barrett, himself a very talented jazz pianist, speaks of improvisation as 'cultivating surrender' (Barrett,

2006). It seems to me this relational practice could make a valuable contribution to leadership processes.

Light structuring seems to be a matter of 'as light a structure as possible'. But this doesn't mean always light, which would become heavy by becoming another design principle, by becoming unresponsive to the particular moment. Structuring can be thought of as 'light' to the extent that goes on in multiple, temporary, and variable forms rather than some singular and stable form. For example, temporary groups might emerge in relation to particular projects and, like a sand or flower mandala, be allowed to dissolve as the project is completed. And, last, structuring can be thought of as 'light' when 'empty' of some prespecified content or 'what', just like the present construction of leadership. Perhaps this is why Bohm proposed that dialogue meetings should be held in which there is no preset agenda (Bohm, 2004). Practices such as 'appreciative inquiry' (Cooperrider and Shrivastva, 1987) are also relatively 'empty' methodologies, intended to facilitate and support a certain kind of process. In light structuring, leadership is not provided by one individual and does not fix and separate; rather, it is a relational practice, ongoing in and supportive of dialogues, emergent processes, relational responsiveness, multiplicity, and appreciation (Hosking and Kleisterlee, 2009). We could call this 'relationally engaged' leadership, which is ongoing in practices of soft self–other differentiation.

Sound leadership and heart-felt listening

Cultural-historical variations in communication forms have been linked with differing constructions of person and world and their relations (e.g., Berman, 1981; 1990; Bergquist, 1996; Berendt, 1992; Corradi Fiumara, 1990; Levin, 1989; Ong, 1967; Toulmin, 1992). According to Ong, 'one of the most striking and informative' differences between oral/aural cultures and cultures dominated by the alphabet and print concerns their relationship with time. In oral/aural cultures, and in the absence of 'look up' facilities, the past is present in what people say and do, in the performances of epic singers, storytellers and poets, in the arts of oratory and rhetoric... performances that join play, celebration, and community with learning. In oral/aural cultures, the word is clearly a vocalization, a happening, an event... experienced as 'contact with actuality and with truth' (Ong, 1967, p. 33).

Implicit in our discussion of dialogue and light structuring were two important themes that now need repetition and slower development. One is the theme of being in the present (rather than already known and already knowing); we could call this '*being in the now* rather than the know'; the other, interrelated theme, is *listening*. There are important connections to be made between nowness, listening, and what some call 'compassionate action'. Pema Chödrön's way of talking about compassion seems particularly relevant since it is clearly situated in what I am are here calling 'soft self–other differentiation'. She speaks of compassionate action: as not shutting down on self or others; as being open and nonjudgmental (appreciative); as letting go of fixed views; as being fully present 'on the spot', and as 'deep listening' (e.g., Chödrön, 1995).

Talk of listening, feeling, and compassion can seem 'flaky' and irrational when understood in relation to hard self–other differentiation. The latter usually manifests in an emphasis on talk (*logos*) rather than listening (*legein*) and talk and listening are understood as individual action. Furthermore, in the context of hard self–other differentiation, listening is storied in a self-centered way: as something that the knowing and influencing subject does – for their own instrumental purposes – in order to 'grasp' something (Corradi Fiumara, 1990; Heidegger, 1975). In the context of hard self–other differentiation, listening is *disheartened* by being tied to interests in 'aboutness knowledge'. In Western individualism, the knowing and influencing subject is assumed to be largely closed to other: to other as other possible selves, to 'other' as body and not mind, to 'other' as other people and 'other' sentient and non-sentient 'things'. But listening shifts into a very different context without these familiar 'hard differentiations'.

When part of soft self–other differentiation, listening or *legein* – what Corradi Fiumara called 'the other side of language' – gains prominence relative to talk as *logos*. In this context, listening becomes understood as embodied, heart-felt participation in relational processes characterized by dialoguing and light structures. Perhaps there's a connection here with Bohm's suggestion that, 'If we consider that it's also necessary to reach or contact the unlimited, then there must be silence – a lack of occupation' (Bohm, 2004, p. 107); so listening need not be 'for' some-thing. Indeed, rather than for producing 'aboutness knowledge', listening can now be understood in relation to participatory knowing. Listening then becomes sensing and feeling or 'being with' the phenomenal world; listening is heart-felt, engaged relating. Returning again to Corradi Fiumara, listening – in the sense of *legein* – 'allow(s) sounds, overtones, multiple

voices… to be heard' – allowing rather than grasping. Heidegger linked *legein* to 'hearkening and heeding'; he connected listening with being – understood as a particular local manifestation of a singular, unifying whole. This brings us back to dialogue and opening up to the *logos*. Listening – in the sense of *legein* – allows space for what is; rather than molding or structuring other, listening allows *both* multiplicity *and* wholeness or, as others have said 'not two, not one' (Chogyam Trungpa, 2002).

RELATIONAL CONSTRUCTIONISM AS PRACTICE

The relational constructionist perspective I have outlined deals with 'the how' of constructing and says little about the 'what' or 'content'. This makes sense given that it is intended to speak about multiple, local realities and relations, rather than the one way things probably are (assuming some universal rationality), and about 'developing' or ongoing realities, rather than stable realities as 'content'. Perhaps it can be thought of as a postmodern (and indeed Buddhist) recognition of, and turning towards, emptiness. Indeed, I have sometimes found myself referring to this orientation as 'empty theory'. This relative emptiness is one of the ways relational constructionism differs from other social science perspectives. I should also add that this perspective should *not* be related to as a theory. For example, it is not about causal relationships between variables and it is not stated in a way that invites or is amenable to 'testing'. Relational constructionism makes no predictions, has no interest in control, does not offer explanations, and is not oriented towards producing objective knowledge of independently existing entities.

In contrast to work done out of other social science perspectives, 'theory' is not the point, nor is theory testing, nor is knowing what is or was the case. Rather, I suggest that relational constructionism be thought of as *a way of orienting to practice* – to ongoing relational processes and the ways they (re)construct particular relational realities – such as self as a knowing and power-full agent (scientist, leader, consultant) in relation to some 'serviceable other' (Sampson, 1993). The orientation is intended to have practical effects and to develop practical wisdom (Toulmin and Gustavsen, 1996). So, for example, there is no need (although of course one could) to treat social practices as either theory construction or empirical work. Similarly, there is no need for inquirers to view their inquiry as the instrumental means to say something 'about' some-thing from a detached observer position. When viewed from a relational constructionist standpoint, inquiry does not discover 'what is' in order to provide the basis for some subsequent ('evidence-based') intervention, but rather offers a view of *inquiry as a process of (re)constructing realities and relations* (Pearce, 1992). The objects of inquiry are the very processes themselves, the relational processes: as they coordinate or organize activities; as they make identities and relations; as they constitute and live a certain 'form of life' (Wittgenstein, 1953); and as they construct different but equal, or different and unequal orderings of power and value (Hosking, 2007).

Of course the 'inquirer' may participate in the inquiry process in many different ways. Other social science perspectives could be said to require researchers to do research 'on' and 'about' other. But relational constructionism also makes meaningful the possibility of doing research 'with' others (Pearce, 1992). This means working in ways that minimize a priori assumptions about local rationalities and their (hierarchical or otherwise) relations and in ways that avoid centering scientific rationality above others. This could mean, for example, joining with organizational or community participants to perform some sort of participative or collaborative inquiry (Friere, 1982; Reason and Bradbury, 2008) that might help (perhaps in quite different ways) the various participating forms of life. To quote Darin Weinberg on 'The philosophical foundations of constructionist research'. 'The practical point of doing constructionist studies has very often been to promote a better way of thinking and, more important, living...' (Weinberg, 2008, p. 15). But, I should add, in the relational constructionist orientation, this 'promoting' is viewed as ongoing.

Consistent with my meditations on dialogue in the context of leadership, performing research *with* others seems to call for dialogue. This is definitely not the case in other social science perspectives, which view dialogue (a) in the context of methodology (where it should be minimized since it reduces experimenter control), and (b) as an individual act by other (the research object), which provides potential data. These practices privilege the local rationality of science and so relations of what some have called 'power over'. Conducting inquiries 'with' others means working in and through dialogues and so opening up the possibility of becoming more multi-logical – of multiple local rationalities. Work of this sort that is presented as inquiry includes 'generative metaphor intervention' (Barrett and Cooperrider

1990; Barrett, Thomas, and Hocevar, 1995); appreciative evaluation (McNamee, 2006), 'responsive evaluation' (Greene and Abma, 2001), and participative action research or 'action science' (Reason and Bradbury, 2008). These all 'go on' in ways that aim to open up spaces for new kinds of conversation and for new ways of being in relation, and open up possibilities for multiple local realities (as forms of life, not individual subjectivities) to coexist and be appreciated as different but equal.

This discussion about relational processes implies that we have to learn how to work in these soft, slow, heart-felt ways as we 'go along' (in practice) in dialogues and reflection. Joe Jaworski wrote about this in his book *Synchronicity* (1996). The book could be read as yet another (masculine-cultural) heroic tale. But what he talks about resonates with relational constructionism and the discussion about learning another way of being in the world. You could say it was a story of how things 'fell apart' and how he learned self-reflection, 'self discovery' and 'surrender' – to a new kind of commitment and to a larger purpose in life. Jaworski wrote about his transition from separateness to relatedness. Part of what this involved was a growing desire and commitment to serve something beyond himself. For him, this was to create a leadership institute that was oriented towards 'servant leadership' – serving with compassion and heart. After a number of years and all kinds of experiences, he described himself as making the leap of confidence: he gave up his job and his business and dedicated himself to creating the Institute.

But after 'the leap' came the void – 'a domain without maps'. He wrote about falling into 'traps' which were his 'old ways of being', his old 'habits'. The first was 'the trap of responsibility', which was to see himself as indispensable, responsible for everyone and everything, and so making the focus on him rather than what he called the larger calling. Secondly was 'the trap of dependency', which meant that he became too dependent on his original plan, stopped being flexible, stopped listening, and became more fearful. Thirdly was the 'trap of overactivity'. This came from having people in the organization who were not 'aligned with the dream', 'resulting in deep incoherence in the organization' (Jaworski, 1996, p. 127). He wrote that getting out of this trap required individual and collective reflection: 'unless we have the individual and collective discipline to stay anchored, we will eventually lose the flow' (p. 129); he went on to emphasize 'the discipline of dialogue' – taking the time for regular 'get togethers', continual reflection, and re-nurturing.

CONCLUSIONS

At the beginning of this chapter I borrowed from Ted Hughes's poem 'The Thought-Fox', indicating that, through some 'foxy reminiscences', I would present a very particular and moving tale of relational processes and leadership. Of course this has meant that other 'relational' approaches to leadership (e.g., Koivunen, 2007; Kupers, 2007; Uhl-Bien, 2006) have been left in the shadows. It seems to me good news indeed that interest in relational approaches to leadership is blossoming. Jerry Hunt, who made an enormous contribution to leadership studies, considered 'the relational perspective and [the approaches within it]... to be at the forefront of emerging leadership thrusts' (Hunt and Dodge, 2000, p. 448). Of course, the term 'relational' is given many different meanings in the context of very different social science perspectives. However, what seems to me important is that such differences are recognized and respected (see Uhl-Bien, 2006), rather than glossed or subjected to a universalizing 'better/worse' critique.

My own hope is that we shall see continuing exploration of *eco*-logical constructions and relational processes as they make and re-make self–other and relations. Given the work that has already been done, it seems that this must give more space to the body, to feelings and the senses, to what some would call wisdom, and to ways of opening up to otherness. Increasingly world leaders, managers, and consultants are (re)connecting 'sacred' and secular (e.g., Senge, Scharmer, Jaworski, and Flowers, 2004). Maybe 'relationally engaged leadership' can provide the difference that really makes a difference; maybe, this is the fox emerging from the shadows.

REFERENCES

Alvesson, M. and Deetz, S. (2000) *Doing critical management research*. London: Sage.

Barrett, F. (2006) Living in organizations: lessons from jazz improvisation. In D.M. Hosking and S. McNamee (eds), *The social construction of organization*. Malmo, Sweden: Liber and Copenhagen Business School Press, pp. 269–277.

Barrett, F. Cooperrider, D. (1990) Generative metaphor intervention: a new approach for working with systems divided by conflict and caught in defensive perception. *The Journal of Behavioural Science*, 26(2): 219–239.

Barrett, F. Thomas, G.F. and Hocevar, S. P. (1995) The central role of discourse in large scale change: a social construction perspective. *The Journal of Applied Behavioural Science*, 31(3): 352–372.

Bateson, G. (1972) *Steps to an ecology of mind*. San Francisco, CA: Chandler.

Bateson, G. and Bateson, M.C. (1987) *Angels fear: toward an epistemology of the sacred*. New York: Macmillan.

Berendt, J.E. (1992) *The third ear*. New York: Henry Holt & Co.

Berman, M. (1981) *The re-enchantment of the world*. Ithaca, NY: Cornell University Press.

Berman, M. (1990) *Coming to our senses*. New York: Bantam Books.

Bergquist, W. (1996) Postmodern thought in a nutshell: where art and science come together. In J. Shafritz, and J. Ott. (eds), *Classics of organisation theory*, 4th edn. Orlando,FL: Harcourt.

Billig, M. (1987) *Arguing and thinking: a rhetorical approach to social psychology*. Cambridge: Cambridge University Press.

Bohm, D. (2004) *On dialogue*. London: Routledge.

Brown, H. (1992) *Women organizing*. London: Routledge.

Brown, H. and Hosking, D.M. (1986). Distributed leadership and skilled performance as successful organization in social movements. *Human Relations*, 39(1), 65–79.

Chasin, R., Herzig, M., Roth, S., Chasin, L., and Becker, C. (1996). From diatribe to dialogue on divisive public issues: approaches drawn from family therapy. *Mediation Quarterly*, 13(4), 323–344.

Chödrön, P. (1995) *When things fall apart*. Boston, MA: Shambhala Publications.

Cooperrider, D.L. and Shrivastva, S. (1987) Research into organizational change and development. In R.W. Woodman and W.A Pasmore (eds), *Appreciative inquiry into organizational life*. Amsterdam: Elsevier B.V.

Corradi Fiumara, G. (1990) *The other side of language: a philosophy of listening*. London: Routledge.

Dachler, H.P. and Hosking, D.M. (1995) The primacy of relations in socially constructing organizational realities. In D.M. Hosking, H.P. Dachler, and K.J. Gergen (eds), *Management and organization: relational alternatives to individualism*: Aldershot: Avebury, pp. 1–29.

Derrida, J. (2000) *Of hospitality*. Stanford, CA: Stanford, University Press.

Edwards, D. and Potter, J. (1992) *Discursive psychology*. London: Sage.

Fiedler, F.E. (1967) *A theory of leadership effectiveness*. New York: McGra-Hill.

Flax, J. (1987) Postmodernism and gender relations in feminist theory. *Signs: Journal of Women in Culture and Society*, 12(4), 621–643.

Friere, Paulo (1982) 'Creating alternative research methods: learning to do it by doing it. In *Creating knowledge: a monopoly? Participatory research in development*. B. Hall, A. Gillete, and R. Tandon (eds), New Delhi: Society for Participatory Research in India.

Gergen, K.J. (1994) *Realities and relationships: soundings in social construction*. MA: Cambridge, Harvard University Press.

Gergen, K.J. (1995) Relational theory and the discourses of power. In D.M. Hosking, H.P. Dachler, and K.J. Gergen (eds), *Management and organization: relational alternatives to individualism.* Aldershot: Avebury, pp. 29–51.

Gergen, K., McNamee, S., and Barrett, F. (2001), Toward transformative dialogue. *International Journal of Public Administration*, 24(7/8), 679–707.

Greene, J. and Abma, T.A. (2001) *Responsive evaluation*, San Francisco, CA: Jossey-Bass.

Gilligan, C. (1993) *In a different voice: psychological theory and women's development.* Cambridge, MA: Harvard University Press.

Harding, S. (1986) *The science question in feminism.* Milton Keynes: OUP.

Harding, S. (1998) *Is science multicultural?* Bloomington, IN: Indiana University Press.

Heidegger, M. (1975) Early Greek thinking. Quoted in Corradi, Fiumara (1990) *The other side of language: a philosophy of listening.* London: Routledge.

Hermans, H., Kempen, H., and Van Loon, R. (1992) The dialogical self. Beyond individualism and rationalism. *American Psychologist*, 47(1), 23–33.

Hosking, D.M. (1988) Organizing, leadership and skilful process. *Journal of Management Studies*, 25(2), 147–166.

Hosking, D.M. (2000) Ecology in mind, mindful practices. *European Journal for Work and Organizational Psychology*, 9(2), 147–158.

Hosking, D.M. (2006) Bounded entities, constructivist revisions and radical re-constructions. *Cognitie, Creier, Comportament (Cognition, Brain, Behavior)* 9(4), 609–622.

Hosking, D.M. (2007) Not leaders, not followers: a postmodern discourse of leadership processes. In B. Shamir, R. Pillai, M. Bligh, and M. Uhl-Bien (eds), *Follower-centered perspectives on leadership.* Greenwich, CT: Information Age Publishing, pp. 243–264.

Hosking, D.M. and Morley, I.E. (1988) The skills of leadership. In J.G., Hunt, R. Baliga, P. Dachler, and C. Schriesheim (eds), *Emerging leadership vistas.* Lexington, MA: Lexington Press.

Hosking, D.M. and Kleisterlee, E. Centering the path. Critical Management Studies Conference, University of Warwick, England. July 2009 & http://www.relational-constructionism.org/pages/publications/articles.php

Hosking, D.M. and Morley, I.E. (1991) *A social psychology of organising.* London: Harvester Wheatsheaf.

Hosking, D.M. and Morley, I.E. (2004) Social constructionism in community and applied social psychology. *Journal of Community and Applied Social Psychology*, 14, 318–331.

Hosking, D.M.; Dachler, H.P., and Gergen, K.J. (eds) (1995) *Management and organization: relational alternatives to individualism.* Aldershot: Avebury.

Hunt, J. and Dodge, G.E. (2000) Leadership déjà vu all over again. *The Leadership Quarterly Review of Leadership*, 11(4), 435–458.

Isaacs, W.M. (1993) Taking flight: dialogue, collective thinking and organizational learning. *Organizational Dynamics*, 22(2), 24–39.

Isaacs, W.M. (1996) The process and potential of dialogue in social change. *Educational Technology*, Jan/Feb, 20–30.

Jaworski, J. (1996) *Synchronicity.* San Francisco, CA: Berrett-Koehler.

Koivunen, N. (2007) The processual nature of leadership discourses. *Scandinavian Journal of Management*, 23, 3.

Kupers, W. (2007) Perspectives on integrating leadership and followership. *International Journal of Leadership Studies*, 2(3), 3–30.

Levin, D. (1989) *The listening self: personal growth, social change, and the closure of metaphysics.* London: Routledge.

Levinas, E. (1989) *The Levinas reade.* S. Hand (ed.). Oxford: Blackwell.

McNamee, S. (2006) Appreciative evaluation in an educational context inviting conversations of assessment and development. In D.M. Hosking and S. McNamee (eds), The social construction of organization. Malmo, Sweden: Liber and Copenhagen Business School Press, pp. 211–224.

McNamee, S. Gergen, K. and associates (1999) *Relational responsibility: resources for sustainable dialogue.* Thousands Oaks, CA: Sage.

Mead, G.H. (1934) *Mind, self, and society.* Chicago, IL: University of Chicago Press.

Ong, W.J. (1967) *The presence of the word.* New Haven, CT: Yale University Press.

Pearce, W. Barnett (1992) A camper's' guide to constructionisms. *Human Systems: the Journal of Systemic Consultation & Management*, 3: 139–161.

Reason, P. (1994) *Participation in human inquiry.* London: Sage.

Reason, P. and Bradbury, H. (eds) (2001) *Handbook of action research: participative inquiry and practice*, London: Sage.

Reason, P. and Bradbury, H. (eds) (2008) *Handbook of action research: participative inquiry and practice*, 2nd ed. London: Sage.

Sampson, E.E. (1993) *Celebrating the other.* London: Harvester Wheatsheaf.

Senge, P., Scharmer, C.O., Jaworski, J., and Flowers, B.S. (2004) *Presence. exploring profound change in people, organizations and society.* London: Nicholas Brearley Publishing.

Stogdill, R.M. (1974) *Handbook of leadership: a survey of theory and research.* New York: Free Press.

Toulmin, S.E. (1992) *Cosmopolis: the hidden agenda of modernity.* Chicago, IL: University of Chicago Press.

Toulmin, S. and Gustavsen, B. (1996) *Beyond theory. Changing organizations through participation.* Amsterdam/ Philadelphia: John Benjamins Publishing Company.

Trungpa, Chogyam (2002) *Cutting through spiritual materialism.* Boston, MA: Shambhala Publications.

Uhl-Bien, M. (2004) Relational leadership approaches. In G.R. Goethals, G.J. Sorenson, and J.M. Burns (eds), *Encyclopedia of leadership.* New York: Sage.

Uhl-Bien, M. (2006) Relational leadership theory: exploring the social processes of leadership and organizing, *The Leadership Quarterly*, 17: 654–676.

Vygotsky, L.S. (1978) *Mind in society: the development of higher psychological processes.* M. Cole, V. John-Steiner, S. Scribner, and E. Souberman (eds), Cambridge, MA: Harvard University Press.

Watzlawick, P. (1978) *The language of change.* New York: W.W. Norton.

Watzlawick, P., Weakland, J., and Fisch, R. (1974), *Change: principles of problem formation and problem resolution.* New York: W.W. Norton.

Weinberg, Darin (2008) The philosophical foundations of constructionist research. In J. Holstein, J. Gubrium (eds), *Handbook of constructionist research.* London: Guilford Press, pp. 13–40.

Wertsch, J.V. (1991) *Voices of the mind. A sociocultural approach to mediated action,* London: Harvester Wheatsheaf.

Wittgenstein, L. (1953) *Philosophical investigations* (G.E.M. Anscombe trans). Oxford: Blackwell.

Woolgar, S. (1996) Psychology, qualitative methods and the ideas of science. In J.T.E. Richardson (ed.), *Handbook of qualitative research methods for psychology and the social sciences.* Leicester: BPS Books, pp. 11–25.

34

Complexity Leadership Theory

Mary Uhl-Bien and Russ Marion

INTRODUCTION

The field of leadership is in the midst of a paradigm shift, in which traditional models are giving way to new conceptualizations of leadership and organizing. Predominant theories, such as transformational leadership and leader–member exchange (LMX), are reaching maturity, the stage Hunt and Dodge (2000) refer to as Consolidation/Accommodation in the evolution of concepts – their major contributions have already been made, research is matter-of-fact, and overall research declines (Reichers & Schneider, 1990). More significantly, they are insufficient to explain the complex realities of leadership and management today (Lewin, 1999; Marion & Uhl-Bien, 2001; Pearce & Conger, 2003; Plowman & Duchon, 2008). As described by Hamel (2009), the principles of 'modern' management are over 100 years old. We need to develop new foundations for leadership: 'Scholars and practitioners must rebuild management's underpinnings [which] will require hunting for new principles in fields as diverse as anthropology, biology, design, political science, urban planning, and theology' (Hamel, 2009, p. 93).

Complexity leadership scholars are doing just this – using complexity concepts from the physical sciences to develop new foundations for theorizing about leadership. Similar to biology and physics, where complexity radically transformed views regarding orderliness of the universe (Wheatley, 1992), complexity is helping leadership scholars overcome the limits of bureaucratic logics in thinking about the dynamics of order in organizational life. Complexity is providing a new lexicon for leadership research and practice – one that considers leadership as occurring in both formal and informal processes, and as emerging in and interacting with complex interactive dynamics.

Although the language is new, complexity focuses on concepts of informal organization and leadership emergence that are age old. We have known them since the earliest writings in the study of management and leadership (Barnard, 1938; Follett, 1924; Roethlisberger & Dickson, 1939; Selznick, 1949). Despite this, organizational studies chose to focus on formal structures and systems of organizations, adopting the zeitgeist of the times (Hunt & Dodge, 2000) by assuming predictable states of adaptation to the environment (Burns & Stalker, 1961; Galbraith, 1973; Katz & Kahn, 1978; Lawrence & Lorsch, 1967; Scott, 1987) and static equilibrium models (e.g., contingency theory, punctuated equilibrium, ecology, strategic choice) (Brown & Eisenhardt, 1997; Eisenhardt & Tabrizi, 1995; Stacey, 1995). As management scholars have discovered, these models do not fit today's contexts of dynamic and continual change (Browning, Beyer, & Stetler, 1995; Eisenhardt & Schoonhoven, 1990).

Because of this a new, 'dynamic equilibrium,' paradigm has emerged in organizational studies in the last two decades (Anderson, 1999; Boisot & Child, 1999; Davis, Eisenhardt, & Bingham, 2009; Galunic & Eisenhardt, 2001; Meyer, Gaba, & Colwell, 2005; Osborn & Hunt, 2007; Pettigrew et al., 2003). Complexity leadership theory provides a leadership model to fit with this emerging, dynamic organization paradigm (Uhl-Bien, Marion, & McKelvey, 2007). It describes a model for the 'leadership of emergence' in organizations and social systems (Lichtenstein & Plowman, 2009).

In this chapter we overview the field of complexity leadership and position it in the dynamic organization paradigm in organization studies

(Eisenhardt & Tabrizi, 1995; Lewin, 1999). Because complexity leadership is an emerging area in the field and unfamiliar to many leadership scholars, we begin with a chronological review that describes how complexity theory entered into management and leadership discourse. We then provide an overview of the current state of the field. We conclude by discussing methodological issues associated with studying complexity leadership and identifying the most promising areas for future research.

Due to space limitations we do not provide a detailed review of complexity principles – excellent resources are available discussing complexity science as it relates to organizations (Anderson, 1999; Cilliers, 1998; Marion, 1999; Stacey, Griffin, & Shaw, 2000) and leadership (Hazy, Goldstein, & Lichtenstein, 2007; Uhl-Bien & Marion, 2008; Wheatley, 1998). We refer readers who are interested in learning more about core complexity concepts and principles to those and other sources (e.g., Kauffman, 1995; Mainzer, 1997; Waldrop, 1992).

CHRONOLOGICAL DEVELOPMENT OF COMPLEXITY APPROACHES TO LEADERSHIP

For many leadership scholars and practitioners, the first exposure to the promise of complexity for the study of organizational leadership was Margaret Wheatley's *Leadership and the New Science* (Wheatley, 1992, 1999). In this book, Wheatley described the possibilities of the 'new science' of complexity for advancing scientific management principles, based in Newtonian mechanics, to 'scientific leadership' principles, based in complexity and complex adaptive systems. According to Wheatley, 'scientific leadership' shifts the perspective from managerial leadership, grounded in hierarchical ordering and control, to a complexity view of leadership as emergent order that arises in the combinations of many individual actions. Leadership from this perspective acknowledges the deep relationship between individual activity and the whole (Wheatley, 1992).

Applying the metaphor of 'living systems' found in complexity to leadership in organizations, Wheatley introduced concepts such as emergence and self-organizing processes. From this view, change results not from top-down, preconceived strategic plans or mandates of any single individual or boss, but from local actions that occur simultaneously around the system linking up with one another to produce powerful emergent phenomena.

Wheatley described how, in complexity, management would not be about command-and-control but sharing information and catalyzing 'local' connections to generate emergence and adaptability (Wheatley, 1999). Leadership would not lie in formal structure, but in the interconnected actions of individuals acting out of personal values or vision and engaging with one another through dialogue.

In 1995, Ralph Stacey conveyed a similar theme with his article applying complexity to strategic change (see also Stacey, 1996). Stacey suggested that complex adaptive systems offer a superior alternative to predominant static views. Rather than organizations tending toward *equilibrium* (stability, regularity, and predictability) as described by strategic choice and ecology views, Stacey proposed that strategic change is more accurately described using complexity concepts of *far from equilibrium* states. In equilibrium, change is driven by negative feedback processes toward predictable states of adaptation to the environment. In far from equilibrium (i.e., complexity), creative, innovative and continually changing behavior is driven by negative *and* positive feedback to 'paradoxical states of stability and instability, predictability and unpredictability' (Stacey, 1995, p. 478). As described by Stacey (1995, p. 478):

> The transformational process is one of internal, spontaneous self-organization amongst the agents of a system, provoked by instabilities, and potentially leading to emergent order ....*The dynamics of success then have to do with being kept away from equilibrium adaptation in states of instability, irregularity and unpredictability.* [emphasis added]

In other words, Stacey introduced to leadership the powerful but paradigm-shifting concept that changeable organizations are those in which informal feedback networks are sustained *away from equilibrium* (i.e., edge of chaos). Instead of order and control, these organizations operate on 'disorderly' dynamics of contradiction, conflict, tension, and dialogue (cf. Heifetz & Laurie, 2001). Moreover, these dynamics occur primarily in the informal network system – not the formal stabilizing systems – in the organization.

The role of strategic management, then, is not to reduce the level of uncertainty (i.e., diminishing surprise in the organization) but to accept and even promote uncertainty, surprise, unknowability, and open-endedness. In direct contrast to leadership approaches advocating the critical role of organizational leaders in establishing vision and aligning employees around that vision, Stacey says that in changeable systems it is not possible to specify meaningful pictures of a future state (i.e., a vision): '...consensus around some picture of a future state removes the chaos which change-able systems must experience if they are to inno-vate' (p. 491). Rather than focusing on individual leaders and actions of those at the top, Stacey (1995) suggested strategic management research should focus on leadership in the group dynamics and spontaneously self-organizing political and organizational learning processes through which innovation occurs.

Furthermore, given that managers operate para-doxically – in a formal hierarchy with a focus on efficiency and control while also in informal net-works seeking to undermine these hierarchies and controls to allow for creativity and changeability – Stacey (1995) states that research programs exploring the dual processes of formal and infor-mal leadership are of paramount importance for strategic management. He calls for research inves-tigating how leaders affect and are affected by the informal networks of which they are a part, as well as how leaders encourage these networks to engage in promoting conflict and dialogue within bounda-ries. Consistent with shared leadership perspec-tives, Stacey describes the need for attention to 'leadership which is located not simply in one person but shifts from person to person according to task needs or emotional states of groups of people operating in informal networks' (p. 492).

In a separate series of studies in high-velocity organizations, Kathleen Eisenhardt provided empirical evidence that, in retrospect, is consistent with Stacey's assertions. Eisenhardt was drawn to complexity when traditional equilibrium-based and contingency views were not able to explain findings regarding organizations operating in rap-idly changing industries. Eisenhardt, like Stacey (1995), began to suggest that complexity approaches are better suited for development 'of a more dynamic organizational paradigm' that cap-tures key features of firms that are 'continuously adaptive' (Eisenhardt & Tabrizi, 1995).

For example, Eisenhardt and Schoonhoven (1990) described a 'surprising result' in which effects of the founding team and environment grew – rather than faded – with time, similar to amplifying effects and sensitive dependence on initial conditions in chaos theory (Gleick, 1987). They proposed that chaos dynamics may have been at play and could represent an interesting avenue for future research.

In Eisenhardt and Tabrizi (1995), the authors called into question traditional depictions of organic processes as lacking structure (Burns & Stalker, 1961; Lawrence & Lorsch, 1967). Their findings show that these organizations *do* have structure, just not structures that match descrip-tions in the literature. These structures combine elements of both adaptation and formal control. For example, continuously changing organizations

have fast processes in uncertain situations that are 'improvisational,' in that they combine real-time learning through design iterations and testing (i.e., adaptation), but also have the focus and discipline of milestones (i.e., formal structure). Moreover, they have leaders who, rather than restricting information, suppressing conflict, and centralizing decision-making (i.e., formal structure and con-trol), allow for the essential dynamics of real-time interaction, intuition, and improvisation (i.e., adaptation). These leaders allow for flexibility (i.e., adaptation) while also having high-level reporting relationships that give them final deci-sion-making authority on key issues of budget, team composition, and project timetable (i.e., formal structure). They conclude (p. 108):

> Thus our work joins a small but growing number of studies that challenge the relevance of organic processes to effective organization (Jelinek and Schoonhoven, 1990; Weick, 1993; Brown and Eisenhardt, 1995b) and relate closely to emergent ideas on balancing order and disorder within com-plex, adaptive systems.

Similarly, Browning et al. (1995) 'found' complexity when they were analyzing data from their qualitative research in the semiconductor industry. Investigating how cooperation can arise and persist in a highly competitive industry, their data did not fit systems theories positing internal processes toward homeostasis. They realized, instead, that their findings were better explained by complexity theory. For example, individual con-tributions became self-amplifying in that they 'gave birth to a moral community and created structures that in turn created other structures' (p. 145). Moreover these activities occurred in an environ-ment in which the top leader's non-directive lead-ership style created an egalitarian culture that encouraged innovation and self-organization. In this managerial environment, individuals in the organization could structure situations and activi-ties according to needs. They could 'create struc-tures that fit the moment' (p. 142) – allowing them flexibility and fluidity to modify structures they found useful and keep inventing new ones.

In 1997, Brown and Eisenhardt used complexity theory to explore continuous change in the context of multiple-product innovation. They challenged punctuated equilibrium models assuming radical and intermittent change, suggesting instead that: 'While the punctuated equilibrium model is in the foreground of academic interest, it is in the back-ground of the experiences of many firms' (p. 1). Their findings show that many organizations are more accurately described as continuously changing, and such organizations are 'semistruc-tured' rather than over-structured (mechanistic) or under-structured (organic). Semistructures are sufficiently rigid to allow change to happen, but not so rigid that change cannot occur: while some responsibilities, meetings, and priorities were set, the design process itself was almost completely unfettered.

According to their data, the most adaptive organizations – those that exhibited the most prolific, complex, and continuous change – were poised at the 'edge of chaos that exists between order and disorder' (p. 29). This 'dissipative equilibrium...requires constant managerial vigilance to avoid slipping into pure chaos or pure structure' (p. 29). In these systems, unsuccessful managers were those who engaged in too much structuring. These managers used what could be considered traditional leadership approaches – they began with the future, developed a strategy (i.e., planning and visioning), and then worked to execute (i.e., implementation). In so doing, they kept getting bogged down, however, in implementation – in the day-to-day business. They were continually waylaid by problems with current product development and a focus on maintaining current revenues. Managers in successfully changing organizations neither rigidly planned nor chaotically reacted. They began by getting rid of lock-step and bureaucratic process, increasing communication, and adding project-level responsibilities, and then 'choreographed transitions' between past and future projects that were neither haphazard nor rigid. This involved looking out to the future to identify next opportunities, eventually linking current and future projects in seamless transitions (see also Brown & Eisenhardt, 1998).

The findings from Eisenhardt (Brown & Eisenhardt, 1997; Eisenhardt & Schoonhoven, 1990; Eisenhardt & Tabrizi, 1995) and Browning et al. (1995), combined with the writings of Stacey (1995) and Wheatley (1992), began to suggest a new view of management as more fluid, enabling, and adaptive than predominant theorizing at the time. By the end of the 1990s, evidence was beginning to mount for the potential of complexity to offer a new paradigm for management and leadership. This sentiment was crystallized in a special issue of *Organization Science* focusing on the implications of the science of complexity for the field of organizational studies. As stated by Arie Lewin (1999, p. 215):

This rediscovery of the characteristics of open systems begs a reexamination of the underlying management logic that dominates the view of the role of managers....The idea that organizations can naturally evolve effective strategies, structures, and processes and self-adjust to new strategies and environmental changes *implies that managers should facilitate, guide, and set the boundary conditions in which successful self-organization can take place.* [emphasis added]

This new managerial logic would focus on things such as managing the organizational levers of dissipative energy; designing organizational systems that facilitate emergent processes such as improvisation, product champions, and emergent strategies; and openness to bottom-up processes and acceptance of equifinal outcomes (Lewin, 1999).

In an article introducing complexity to leadership research in 2001, Marion and Uhl-Bien made a similar call for a new leadership logic grounded in complexity. Describing complexity as a science of complexly interacting systems, they argued that complexity changes the dialogue in leadership away from managing and controlling and toward *enabling*. Instead of viewing leadership as interpersonal influence, they described complexity leadership as providing linkages to 'emergent structures' within and among organizations. At the macro leadership level (e.g., leadership *of* the organization; Boal & Hooijberg, 2001), this means that the focus of leadership should be on how to foster and speed up the emergence of distributed intelligence (DI) (McKelvey, 2008). At the micro level (e.g., leadership *in* the organization, Boal & Hooijberg, 2001), this means creating the conditions that enable productive, but largely unspecified, future states:

This recognizes that leaders cannot control the future (e.g., determinism) because in complex systems such as organizations, unpredictable (and sometimes unexplainable) internal dynamics will determine future conditions. Rather, micro-level complex leaders need to influence networks, creating atmospheres for formation of aggregates and meta-aggregates (e.g., the emergent structure concepts of complexity theory to be discussed below) in ways that permit innovation and dissemination of innovations so critical for 'fitness' of the firm. (Marion & Uhl-Bien, 2001, p. 391)

Drawing from Marion's 1999 book *The Edge of Organization*, they explained these dynamics as a combination of microdynamic (e.g., correlation, interaction, and randomness) and macrodynamic forces. Microdynamics represent bottom-up (emergent) behaviors that occur when individuals interact, leading to both coordinated behavior and random behavior (i.e., aggregation). Macrodynamics represent the emergence of the larger systems from the interactions at the micro-level. Macro-level behaviors are driven by the microdynamics and characterized by 'bottom-up' coordination and non-linear behavior to generate emergence and self-organization (rather than leader-designed outcomes).

Applying this to al-Qaeda, Marion and Uhl-Bien (2003) offered an illustration of complexity leadership. Arguing that the nature of Islamic militancy spawned a complexly structured organization led according to complexity leadership principles, they showed how al-Qaeda emerged through a process of aggregation and autocatalysis characteristic of complex adaptive systems. Rather than resulting from strategic plans of a set of leaders, al-Qaeda emerged through a process of bottom-up aggregation (i.e., linking-up of various terrorist cells) enabled by direct and indirect leadership processes (e.g., forging alliances that helped increase the power of the network, capitalizing on opportunities emerging out of network dynamics, serving as tags to catalyze al-Qaeda's structure and activities). Al-Qaeda leaders did not create this movement; they were created by it. Thus, the authors conclude, the case shows that leadership is not necessarily a person or a formal role but a phenomenon created by, and residing in, a complex adaptive system.

As Marion and Uhl-Bien were beginning their complexity work, Ralph Stacey was rapidly advancing the concepts he initiated in the 1990s into a perspective known as complex responsive processes (Stacey, 2000; 2001b; Stacey, Griffin & Shaw, 2000). Beginning with Mead's responsive processing (1934), Stacey described a social process as one in which each gesture from one animal calls forth a response from another, and together, gesture and response form a social act (Stacey, 2000; 2001b). From this perspective, the social is a responsive process of meaningful signaling in continuous cycles of cooperative and competitive interaction (Stacey, 2000; 2001b). Intellect plays a role in this process, but, contrary to traditional perspectives, Stacey proposes that mind is not an autonomous individual first thinking and then choosing an action; rather, it is individuals in relationship *continuously evoking and provoking responses in one another* (with responses influenced by past history). In this process, Stacey argues, both individual mind and social emerge in relationships between people – i.e., Stacey sees mind and social as occurring in 'the space between' (cf. Bradbury & Lichtenstein, 2005).

Whereas this presents a radical departure from traditional positivist and realist views, it is consistent with complexity notions of emergence (Goldstein, 2007; Marion & Uhl-Bien, 2001). Stacey elaborates Mead's (1934) concept of social by using complexity concepts to explain how interactions between large numbers of agents, each responding to others on the basis of local organizing principles, produce coherent patterns with the potential for novelty. In this way, complexity explains the way in which global coherence can arise in the context of large numbers of local interactions. When richly connected enough (i.e., edge of chaos), this process of self-organizing interaction can produce coherent and novel patterns in itself, and this occurs *without any blueprint or program* (cf. Uhl-Bien, 2006). With this, Stacey returns to his position in the 1995 article regarding the importance of recognizing paradoxical states of stability/instability and predictability/unpredictability at the same time (2001a). His point:

> Interaction itself is sufficient to account for coherent pattern in relating. There is no need to posit causal powers in some system above, beneath, behind or in front of that interaction. (Stacey, 2001a, p. 462)

Applied to leadership, Stacey makes a strong case for moving beyond the dominant voice in management theory that speaks in the language of design, regularity, and control. Instead, he calls for researchers to acknowledge the voices from the fringes of organization theory, complexity sciences, psychology, and sociology that define a participative perspective (Stacey et al., 2000; Streatfield, 2001). From this view, managers are not *outside* the organization system, which is thought of as an objective, pre-given reality that can be modeled, designed, and under their control; instead, they are themselves members of the complex networks they form, and through their intersubjective voices they interact to co-evolve a jointly constructed reality (cf. Fairhurst & Grant, 2010; Hosking 2007; Hosking, Dachler, & Gergen, 1995). This suggests, then, that managers/leaders are not 'in control' even though they may be 'in charge' (Stacey et al., 2000; see also Stacey & Griffin, 2008; Streatfield, 2001).

Back in the USA, Marion and Uhl-Bien were hearing strong interest in pursuing the potential of complexity for advancing leadership theory and research. In response they organized two conferences in 2005 – the first at the Center for Creative Leadership (Greensboro, NC) with Ellen Van Velsor and Cindy McCauley, and the second at George Washington University (Executive Leadership Program), with Margaret Gorman and Jim Hazy. These conferences were designed to bring together top leadership scholars with complexity scholars to explore the possibilities for advancing a new theory of complexity leadership. The conferences resulted in two books (Hazy et al., 2007; Uhl-Bien & Marion, 2008) and two special issues (*Emergence: Complexity & Organization*, Vol. 8, Issue 4, 2006; *The Leadership Quarterly*, Vol. 18, Issue 4, 2007). They also resulted in collaborations and publications, as conference participants set out to develop and investigate theoretical frameworks for the study of complexity leadership.

Today, complexity leadership research is burgeoning, with writing increasing exponentially since 2005. To describe the current state of the field, in the section below we present the major theoretical framework for the study of complexity leadership and review related research with respect to this framework.

CURRENT STATE OF THE FIELD

From the review above we can see the core concepts that comprise a complexity approach to leadership. Complexity leadership theory is the study of leadership based in complexity science (Hazy et al., 2007; Uhl-Bien & Marion, 2008); it is grounded in a complexity, rather than a bureaucratic (Weber, 1947), paradigm. It assumes that leadership is not generated in authority and control (i.e., the formal managerial structure) but in the interconnected actions of individuals acting out of personal values or vision, and engaging with one another through dialogue (Wheatley, 1992). From this perspective, order is not designed and directed, but emergent from the combinations of many individual actions: Local actions that occur simultaneously around the system link up with one another to produce powerful emergent phenomena (Lichtenstein & Plowman, 2009; Uhl-Bien & Marion, 2009). In this way, complexity suggests very much a shared, or distributed, view of leadership (Gronn, 2002; Pearce & Conger, 2003).

Complexity leadership theory acknowledges the deep relationship between individual activity and the whole (Wheatley, 1992). It focuses on the rich interplay between local and global. As described by Goldspink and Kay (2004), complexity helps bridge the micro–macro divide in the social sciences by helping explain the relationship between the constitutive elements of the social system (people) and the emergent phenomena resulting from their interactions (e.g., organizations). In this way, levels of analysis are not so much about individual, dyad, group, organization (levels generated from hierarchical, linear, bureaucratic ordering) but about how phenomena emerge from the complex and non-linear interplay between heterogeneous agents and complexity dynamics.

For many leadership scholars this will be hard to get one's head around. This is because our leadership training is heavily positivist, and we typically don't even know it. We are trained in a scientific method that advocates reductionism (studying individual level variables) and determinism (showing linear causality) (Marion & Uhl-Bien, 2001; Stacey, 1995). But there is a new science, one in which change and constant creation

signal new ways of maintaining order and structure (Wheatley, 1992). Complexity leadership advances leadership theory and research into this new science and its new scientific method (Hazy et al., 2007; Uhl-Bien & Marion, 2008). By offering a leadership theory to fit the emerging dynamic organizational paradigm (Eisenhardt & Tabrizi, 1995), it takes leadership out of the Industrial Age and places it into the modern, connectionist Knowledge Era (Uhl-Bien et al., 2007).

Knowledge Era organizations are poised at the 'edge of chaos' that exists between order and disorder, stability and instability – continuously changing, rather than giving in to equilibrium, stability-seeking tendencies (Eisenhardt & Tabrizi, 1995; Pettigrew et al., 2003; Stacey, 1995). In essence, they must attempt to operate as complex adaptive systems (Martin & Eisenhardt, 2010). Yet keeping an organization in an adaptive state (i.e., far from equilibrium, edge of chaos) is counter to everything we have been taught and assumed (Plowman & Duchon, 2008). Moreover, it is no easy task. As shown by Houchin and MacLean (2005), stabilizing forces in organizations are strong – in conditions of anxiety caused by disequilibrium, the pressures on managers to seek equilibrium in the form of comfort and security are often overwhelming. Organizational managers give in to these pressures to reduce anxiety by taking actions that avoid conflict, maintain control and minimize change, thereby creating complex *recursive* rather than complex *adaptive* systems. As Houchin and MacLean (2005) point out, complex recursive systems, because they do not adapt, often experience only short-term survival.

Although complexity approaches describe how organizations maintain an adaptive, rather than recursive, state the findings of Houchin and MacLean (2005) require complexity scholars to acknowledge that organizations are *not* naturally complex adaptive systems. Instead they are bureaucracies (Hales, 2002). As we know, bureaucracy is not designed to be adaptive (Heckscher, 1994). *We argue that this is why complexity leadership is needed: complexity leadership offers managers and leaders a framework for understanding how they can help organizations operate more like complex adaptive systems.* Complexity leadership does this by enabling and interacting with complex adaptive dynamics in organizations (Hazy, 2006; Marion & Uhl-Bien, 2001; Uhl-Bien et al., 2007). The primary role of complexity leadership is to show how, in contexts of larger organizing frameworks (most often bureaucracy), organizational leaders can create conditions suitable to complex adaptive dynamics, and then interact with these dynamics to generate productive outcomes for the firm (Uhl-Bien & Marion, 2009).

To grasp this, we need to understand two key concepts: (1) complexity leadership functions and (2) complexity dynamics and emergence. Therefore, we turn to these next.

Complexity leadership functions

One of the challenges in advancing a paradigm of complexity leadership theory is in addressing terminology. As can be seen from the review above, complexity clearly suggests an alternative view of leadership. But what is this view, and how can it be described?

Some scholars do not give it a specific name, instead referring to it simply as a new view of leadership (Stacey et al., 2000; Wheatley, 1992, 1999). These scholars, not without justification, argue that the distributed and interactive view of leadership is the true reality of leadership and therefore we should acknowledge that reality and move ahead.

Other scholars recognize that complexity suggests additional forms of leadership. For example Hazy (2006), drawing from complexity concepts, identified three new forms of leadership associated with complexity: leadership of convergence, leadership of variety, and leadership of unity. Leadership of convergence catalyzes the activities of a system toward a particular attractor. Leadership of variety catalyzes an exploration and experimentation process to increase the variety of possibilities available to the system and also creates the conditions that enable transformation from one attractor to another. Leadership of unity balances tension and catalyzes coherence and a sense of oneness in the system over time. Surie and Hazy (2006) added another kind of leadership: generative leadership. Generative leadership is defined as leadership that fosters innovation, organizational adaptation, and high performance over time. It does this by seeking out, fostering, and sustaining generative relationships that yield new learning relevant for innovation.

Drawing from organization and management theory, Uhl-Bien et al. (2007) offered a slightly different perspective. They identified three functions of leadership: administrative, adaptive, and enabling. Administrative leadership is managerial leadership associated with the bureaucratic elements of organizations. It occurs in formal, managerial roles and reflects traditional management processes and functions aimed at driving business results: strategic direction and alignment, budgeting, resource allocation, regulatory, scheduling, etc. It aligns organizational members with the business needs of the firm (e.g., through efficiency and control). It comprises the *administrative function* of the organization.

Adaptive leadership, similar to Stacey's complex responsive processing (Johannessen & Aasen, 2007), reflects the 'complexity' view of leadership. It describes leadership as emerging in and from the dynamic interaction of heterogeneous agents as they work interdependently in organizations. It occurs in the complex adaptive systems of organizations. Adaptive leadership varies from Stacey's view, however, in its focus on adaptive work (cf. Heifetz, 1994). As defined by Uhl-Bien and Marion (2009), adaptive leadership is an informal leadership process that occurs in intentional interactions of interdependent human agents (individuals or collectives) as they work to generate and advance novel solutions in the face of adaptive needs of the organization (cf. Heifetz & Laurie, 2001; Johannessen & Aasen, 2007). It is productive of new ideas, innovation, adaptability, and change (Uhl-Bien et al., 2007). It comprises the *adaptive* function of the organization.

Hence, the model presented by Uhl-Bien and Marion (Uhl-Bien & Marion, 2009; Uhl-Bien et al., 2007) identifies two primary functions related to leadership in organizations: administrative and adaptive. The administrative function drives toward business results; the adaptive function drives toward innovation (product innovation) and adaptability (process innovation). The administrative function is motivated toward efficiency and control (e.g., exploitation) while the adaptive function is motivated toward creative interaction and innovation (e.g., exploration).

These two functions operate in dynamic tension with one another (Houchin & MacLean, 2005). This tension is reflected in pressures from administrators to bureaucratize organizational processes (e.g., formalization) and pressures from organizational members to operate and adapt more informally and flexibly. For example, Christiansen and Varnes (2007) described how numerous micro-decisions and negotiations that occur in a networked dynamic tend to preempt the decision making of managers, thus relegating manager meetings to the role of approval or non-approval. Eisenhardt and Tabrizi (1995) describe the suppressing effect of the administrative function on adaptive processes: 'The results also show that planning and rewarding for schedule attainment are ineffective ways of accelerating pace' (p. 84). Koch and Leitner (2008) found evidence for purely emergent bottom-up processes, in which employees intrinsically and without explicit orders took initiative to innovate in ways that deliberately bypassed and even ignored formal processes (e.g., financial incentive systems, suggestion schemes, patent rules), often keeping these activities secret until they were mature enough to be presented to management. Osborn and Marion (2009) found that, in alliances, administrative leadership in the form of transformational leadership was useful for returning profit to the mother institution but dysfunctional for innovation within the alliance itself. Similar findings were reported by Martin and Eisenhardt (2010).

To address the dynamic tension between administrative and adaptive functions, complexity leadership theory introduces a third leadership function: enabling leadership (Uhl-Bien & Marion, 2009; Uhl-Bien et al., 2007). Enabling leadership operates in the interface, the dynamic tension, between the administrative and adaptive functions. It recognizes both needs of the organization as legitimate, so it works to 'loosen up the organization – stimulating innovation, creativity and responsiveness and learn[ing] to manage continuous adaptation to change – without losing strategic focus or spinning out of control' (Dess & Picken, 2000, p. 19).

Enabling leadership does this in two ways. First, it enables adaptive climates and conditions conducive to complexity dynamics (Uhl-Bien & Marion, 2009; Uhl-Bien et al., 2007). Adaptive climates create relational dynamics characterized by rich interaction, interconnectivity, and information flow (cf. Anderson, Issel, & McDaniel, 2003; Lichtenstein & Plowman, 2009; Plowman, Solansky, et al., 2007; Regine & Lewin, 2000). For example, adaptive climates are characterized by such things as empowerment, trust, psychological safety, networking, and rewards for collaboration and creativity that allow for members to openly share, disagree, and conflict over ideas and perspectives (cf. Edmondson, 1999; Heifetz & Laurie, 2001). They see conflict not as destructive, but as the 'fuel that drives system growth and enables learning and adaptive behaviors, which make innovation possible' (Andrade, Plowman, & Duchon, 2008, p. 24). Adaptive climates provide resources (time, budget, expertise, heterogeneity) and space (physical layout, location; Barry & Price, 2004; Thomke & Nimgade, 2007) that encourage complexity dynamics (e.g., adaptive tension, conflicting constraints, aggregation). This type of enabling leadership recognizes the value of highly adaptive leaders and enables them by allowing latitude, resources, protection, and sponsorship. Moreover, it protects adaptive dynamics from the stifling and suppressing elements of administrative leadership and bureaucracy.

Secondly, enabling leadership loosens up the administrative structures and systems to help adaptive leadership advance and champion innovative outcomes into the formal system. When adaptive outcomes emerge they need to be incorporated into the system to generate business results. Enabling leadership helps break down barriers that might shut out adaptive initiatives along the way or inhibit them from getting heard by the right audience. They do this by clearing hurdles,

providing protection, and opening administrative channels. Enabling leaders also provide cover for adaptive initiatives (e.g., high-level sponsorship), help adaptive leaders get to the right audience, and use their authority to help the initiative gain visibility (e.g., become tags; Boal & Schultz, 2007; Hunt, Osborn, & Boal, 2009; Marion & Uhl-Bien, 2001; Plowman, Solansky, et al., 2007). For example, as found by Plowman, Solansky, et al. (2007) in their study of emergence in Mission Church, when the administrative leaders began to see the breakfasts in a new light, the Sunday morning program took on a new meaning:

> [The leader's] exact words were 'that café needs a kick in the pants' and those were his exact words and so I thought okay and once that whole transition was made from getting two pastors out of preaching to ten people at 9 o'clock and go serve the 200 who were sitting right below you, you know, that was huge. I think that was huge....
>
> From that moment on when [the leader] decided to get involved .... that's when it really evolved. (p. 352)

Hence, complexity leadership theory (CLT) identifies three leadership functions (Uhl-Bien & Marion, 2009; Uhl-Bien et al., 2007). CLT proposes that adaptability occurs in the adaptive function; the adaptive function generates and advances adaptive outcomes (e.g., product innovation, process innovation, learning) for the firm. These adaptive outcomes are converted into business results by the administrative function. Because these two functions operate in dynamic tension, enabling leadership works in the interface of adaptive and administrative to maintain appropriate entanglement between these functions (Uhl-Bien & Marion, 2009; Uhl-Bien et al., 2007).

Complexity dynamics and emergence

A key contribution of complexity to leadership research is the study of interactive dynamics and emergence. Contrary to conventional leadership research, which largely examines individuals, absent context or process (Osborn, Hunt, & Jauch, 2002), the essence of CLT is that leadership is generated in the context of richly networked interactions. *Complexity is at its core a theory of interactive dynamics and emergence.* While complexity leadership certainly acknowledges individuals with respect to leadership *functions* (not styles, e.g., individuals can engage in one or more functions), in CLT leadership functions are considered in terms of how they interact with complexity dynamics. Thus, CLT is a pure contextual theory of leadership (Osborn et al., 2002): it sees leadership as embedded in context.

Although CLT is consistent with social construction views of leadership (Fairhurst & Grant, 2010), it adopts a different focus. Instead of examining socio-emotional processes (e.g., meaning-making, trust, power), it seeks to identify social mechanisms (Hedström & Swedberg, 1998) associated with complexity dynamics – CLT examines complexity dynamics as 'social mechanisms' (Hedström & Swedberg, 1998) that arise when humans interact under complexity conditions (Uhl-Bien et al., 2007). In complexity, social mechanisms are not variables; they are not individual-level constructs, but dynamic, non-linear processes. They are predictable in a *non-linear* sense – in their process but not in their outcomes (Uhl-Bien & Marion, 2009).

Complexity dynamics are the force behind emergence in complexity theory. Emergence occurs when 'system-level order spontaneously arises from the action and repeated interaction of lower level system components without intervention by a central component' (Chiles, Meyer, & Hench, 2004, p. 502; see also Lichtenstein, 2000; Plowman, Baker, et al., 2007). Emergence describes a situation in which order does not result from imposition of an overall plan by a central authority, but from the action of interdependent agents purposefully pursuing individual plans based on local knowledge and continuously adapting to feedback about the actions of others (Chiles et al., 2004; Hayek, 1988; Stacey, 1995; Tsoukas & Chia, 2002).

Emergence dynamics include social mechanisms such as conflicting constraints, correlation, and amplification (Lichtenstein & Plowman, 2009; Marion & Uhl-Bien, 2003; Plowman, Solansky, et al., 2007; Uhl-Bien et al., 2007). Conflicting constraints is an initiating mechanism that helps foster generation of new ideas and initial adaptations. It occurs under conditions of interdependence when interacting agents, brought together by common need, must work through adaptive tension generated by heterogeneous perspectives to produce an adaptive response (e.g., an idea for doing something differently, a change in process, a variation from standard procedure; see also Marion & Uhl-Bien, 2001).

Correlation and amplification are aggregation mechanisms. Correlation occurs when interacting agents compromise a measure (but not all) of their individual need preferences to the needs of others and the emerging alliance (Marion & Uhl-Bien, 2001). Marion and Uhl-Bien (2003) found correlation dynamics occurring in training camps in al-Qaeda, where nationalistic differences were set aside in pursuit of common goals. Plowman, Solansky, et al. (2007) found in their case study of Mission Church that correlation was fostered by church leaders who used common language to foster meaning, collective action, and organizational identity among church members and staff.

Amplification occurs when incipient networks that formed to generate a creative or adaptive endeavor expand to include formal and informal supporters. Formal supporters may include organizational structures that will play roles in advancing the idea, such as marketing, legal, branding departments. Informal support may include groups whose own ideas can benefit from alliance or who can piggyback on the original idea. Lichtenstein & Plowman (2009) argue that leaders foster amplification by allowing experiments, encouraging rich interactions, and supporting collective action (see also Lichtenstein, 2000). Chiles et al. (2004) examined the development of Branson, Missouri, into the musical giant it has become. They found that positive feedback processes enhanced an amplification process that helped account for the rapid development of that town. Plowman et al. (2007) studied radical change in a declining, inner-city church, and found that small changes occurred to amplify the actions of an emergent change. Tsoukas and Chia (2002) observed that recursive feedback tended to amplify small ideas into large ones.

Learning is a by-product outcome of these complexity dynamics. Learning occurs when ideas collide, merge, diverge, elaborate in sets, or are extinguished. It emerges from the interaction of ideas, tasks, information, resources, beliefs, worldviews, visions, and adaptive agents. According to Fonseca (2002), knowledge emerges as individuals and social settings interact to create meaning. Schreiber, Marion, Uhl-Bien, and Carley (2006) simulated the capacity of a system to learn, and found that moderate levels of coupling plus moderately demanding vision produced better learning than did low coupling and vision or high coupling and vision. Allen (2001) argued for what he called the fundamental importance of microdiversity in generating learning within a group.

A different perspective of emergence is offered by Goldstein (2007), who argues that bottom-up self-organization cannot occur without significant enabling and constraining factors (e.g., managerial influence). He describes emergence from the standpoint of *self-transcending constructions*, in which pre-existing order is transformed into emergent order. From this perspective, emergent order does not appear 'out of the blue' (i.e., order is not free, Goldstein, 2007; see also Osborn & Hunt, 2007). It comes from a continuous build-up of structures along with an ongoing shifting and merging of structures with one another to generate new structures. It is not self-organizing in a pure sense, but rather emergent organizing in the contexts of already-existing structures (cf. Uhl-Bien & Marion, 2009). As described by Goldstein (2007), the leader's role in such contexts is to 'recognize, identify, foster, sift, provide, shape and constrain resources of order to be used for emergent modifications' (p. 91).

Goldstein's perspective is consistent with Hunt, Osborn, and Boal's (2009) complexity model of strategic leadership, which emphasizes managers' roles in patterning of attention and network development. These processes are proposed to stimulate social construction to create new information and knowledge from the dialogue and discussion of all participants. They may also influence complexity dynamics of N, K, P, and C: 'new individuals within the system may be included (a change of N), new combinations of interaction may be fostered (a change in K), new schema may emerge (a change in P), and new connections with those traditionally outside the system may be made (a change in C)' (Hunt et al., 2009, p. 514 see also Kauffman, 1995; Marion, 1999; Osborn & Hunt, 2007; Schneider & Somers, 2006).

Support for these dynamics is offered by Osborn and Marion (2009), who found that leaders who engaged in attention-patterning behaviors, consolidated the interactive dynamics of the groups (e.g., Goldstein's K and P), thus enhancing creativity. Moreover, consistent with pattern recognition, Plowman et al. (2007) found that leaders interpret adaptations as they began to accumulate and skillfully used language by giving meaning to emergent changes and drawing attention to the pattern that was forming.

In addition to the perspectives above, Cunha and Cunha (2006) offer a complexity view of strategic management. Similar to Uhl-Bien et al.'s (2007) entangled adaptive and administrative functions, they suggest that a complexity theory of strategy involves a combination of freedom with a clear organizational infrastructure of strategy, design, and process that allows strategic improvisation to flourish. From this perspective, complexity leaders manage to achieve a 'paradoxical state' of ample freedom (of employees) and strong control (provided by clear strategic direction):

> Through improvisation and simple rules, organizational members become empowered to make decisions, and strategy takes the form of strategic decision making at many organizational levels, in the context of an enabling organizational design. (p. 844)

Finally, Goldstein, Hazy, and Lichtenstein (2010) suggest that truly adaptable organizations are those in which leaders (i.e., managers) create 'ecologies of innovation' by encouraging and supporting experiments in novelty and building new organizational pathways that allow these experiments to materialize into novel offerings and improvements. They present a framework for leadership to help spawn emergence that comes about through a recognition, amplification, and dissemination of seeds of innovation that come from micro-level diversity or experiments in novelty. As they describe, a primary objective of generative leadership (cf. Surie & Hazy, 2006) in facilitating emergence is fostering and amplifying novelty generation within an ecology of innovation.

In sum, complexity leadership theory is a process theory of leadership that seeks to understand the complexity dynamics comprising the social mechanisms of emergence in organizations. It assumes that adaptive leadership is embedded in context and generated in 'the space between' (Bradbury & Lichtenstein, 2005): it arises when interacting agents operating under conditions of complexity generate adaptive responses in organizations. These responses emerge when adaptive leadership and complexity dynamics work to generate innovation, adaptability, and learning for the firm. Complexity dynamics are social mechanisms associated with generation of new ideas (e.g., conflicting constraints) and flow of these ideas within the organization (e.g., correlation, amplification). Managers (i.e., enabling leaders) can help foster these dynamics by enabling complexity conditions and dynamics and supporting adaptive leadership processes.

Organizations that operate in accordance with complexity leadership are characterized by rich adaptive functions producing adaptive leadership and complexity dynamics, and flexible administrative functions (administrative leadership) that capitalize on these dynamics to produce strong business results for the firm. In such organizations, strategic leadership is not restricted to actions of those at the top, but emerges from the actions and interactions of individuals as they make adaptations in local contexts throughout the organization (Tsoukas & Chia, 2002).

CONCLUSIONS

The field of complexity leadership is still quite young. Borrowing again from Hunt and Dodge (2000), complexity leadership approaches are clearly in the Introduction Elaboration stage of the evolution of concepts (Reichers & Schneider, 1990). In this stage, scholars attempt to legitimize the concept with books and articles to educate people about the topic. They also offer preliminary findings to provide evidence of the concept as a real phenomenon (Hunt & Dodge, 2000).

From the books and articles that have appeared in the last decade we can see evidence of both of these – education about the concept (e.g., Hazy et al., 2007; Stacey et al., 2000; Uhl-Bien & Marion, 2008) and preliminary findings to support its legitimacy (e.g., Lichtenstein & Plowman, 2009; Martin & Eisenhardt, 2010; Plowman, Baker, et al., 2007; Plowman, Solansky, et al., 2007).

Complexity leadership scholars now need to engage in programmatic empirical research. Much of this work is already under way, and we expect to see a variety of empirical studies appearing in the literature in the next five years. Given that the ontology of complexity is closer to critical realism (Goldspink & Kay, 2004; Reed, 2009) than the logical positivism of conventional leadership theories (e.g., transformational leadership, LMX implicit leadership theories), we expect that most of this research will not use traditional survey methodologies but instead more qualitative and agent-based modeling approaches, including grounded theory, rigorous case studies (e.g., Chiles et al., 2004; Plowman, Baker, et al., 2007), dynamic network analysis (Carley, 1992, 1997; Carley & Hill, 2001; Uzzi & Spiro, 2005), simulation and modeling (Davis, Eisenhardt, & Bingham, 2007; Harrison, Lin, Carroll, & Carley, 2007), and network studies (Kilduff, Crossland, & Tsai, 2007).

Moreover, the study of complexity dynamics will adopt more of a process than a variance theory approach (Mohr, 1982) consistent with mechanism-based theorizing (Davis & Marquis, 2005). As described by Chiles et al. (2004, p. 502):

> Unlike traditional variance theory, which uses variation in a small set of well-defined independent variables to explain variance in a dependent variable and to predict specific outcomes of simple phenomena, process theory calls for a high level of abstraction, predicts how general patterns of change will unfold, and develops post hoc explanations of a sequence of events over time by telling a story about how or why a phenomenon evolved from the temporal ordering and interaction of myriad events.

Using process theory and mechanism-based theorizing, complexity leadership scholars can investigate complexity dynamics that comprise mechanisms of emergence – dynamics such as conflicting constraints, correlation, amplification, etc. Complexity leadership scholars should also investigate the conditions under which these dynamics occur. According to complexity theory, these conditions will be generated in dis-equilibrium (e.g., far-from-equilibrium, edge of chaos) (Lichtenstein & Plowman, 2009) and fostered by heterogeneity, interdependence, dynamic interaction, and adaptive tension (Uhl-Bien & Marion, 2009).

Complexity leadership scholars also need to investigate complexity leadership functions. For example, as described by Stacey (1995), research is needed to identify how leaders affect and are affected by the informal networks of which they are a part, as well as how leaders encourage these networks to engage in complexity dynamics. We also need to examine adaptive leadership not as an individual behavior but as a collective leadership process, and enabling leadership as a function distinct from empowerment. Moreover, a complexity theory of strategy suggests that rather than focusing on strategic leadership as the behaviors of those at the top, we must explore strategy as emergent within the organization and identify the enabling organizational designs that foster it (Cunha & Cunha, 2006; Stacey, 1995).

The findings of MacLean and colleagues (Houchin & MacLean, 2005; MacIntosh, MacLean, & Burns, 2007; MacLean & MacIntosh, 2002) suggest important areas for future research. First, the findings reported in MacIntosh et al. (2007) that only two of 25 organizations they studied achieved levels of fluidity, innovation, and performance consistent with edge of chaos states, indicates that maintaining organizations in adaptive states may be one of the greatest challenges faced in organizations today. We believe this indicates all the more reason to generate greater understanding of how organizations can engage in complexity leadership practices that help them overcome pressures to return to equilibrium and instead act in ways that enable adaptive states. However, this recommendation comes with a caution. MacIntosh et al.'s (2007) findings that managers' attempts to generate disequilibrium in organizations used 'unhealthy' organizational practices (e.g., rapid job rotation, high performance demands, circulating organizational fictions such as rumor and counter-rumor) indicate that complexity leadership scholars need to be careful that managerial actions used to generate 'edge of chaos' conditions do not result in deteriorating health outcomes for organizational members.

In conclusion, as demonstrated by this review, complexity leadership theory offers a rich and rigorous theoretical framework that identifies important new directions for leadership research. It is situated in the dynamic organizational paradigm investigating firms that are 'continuously adaptive' (cf. Eisenhardt & Tabrizi, 1995). CLT suggests that adaptive states are those poised at the edge or chaos between order and disorder. Maintaining these states requires constant managerial vigilance to avoid slipping into pure chaos or pure structure.

A critical implication of CLT is this: *complexity leadership theory recognizes that although organizations are bureaucracies, they do not have to be bureaucratic*. According to complexity leadership, a key role of managers is to facilitate, guide, and set the boundary conditions in which successful emergence (e.g., self-organization) can take place and be effectively entangled with organizational systems. A key role of adaptive leadership is to engage with complexity dynamics to generate and advance adaptive outcomes for the firm.

Although complexity approaches represents a sharp break from orthodox perspectives by adopting ontological assumptions rooted in dynamic tension, emergent novelty, perpetual disequilibrium, and increasing heterogeneity, they do not render past paradigms obsolete – instead, they go a step beyond these paradigms while remaining complementary to them (Chiles et al., 2004). The same is true of complexity leadership theory. By focusing on the entangled nature of administrative and adaptive leadership functions, and their interactions with the dynamics of complexity and emergence in organizations, complexity leadership offers an exciting advancement to leadership theory while adding new pieces to help fill in the complex puzzle of leadership in organizations and social systems.

REFERENCES

Allen, P. M. (2001). A complex systems approach to learning in adaptive networks. *International Journal of Innovation Management*, 5(2), 149–180.

Anderson, P. (1999). Complexity theory and organization science. *Organization Science, 10*(3), 216–232.

Anderson, R.A., Issel, L., & McDaniel, R. (2003). Nursing homes as complex adaptive systems: relationship between management practice and resident outcomes. *Nursing Research, 52*(1), 12–21.

Andrade, L., Plowman, D., & Duchon, D. (2008). Getting past conflict resolution: a complexity view of conflict. *Emergence: Complexity and Organization (E:CO), 10*(1), 23–28.

Barnard, C. I. (1938). *The functions of the executive*. Cambridge, MA: Harvard University Press.

Barry, H. & Price, I. (2004). Quantifying the complex adaptive workplace. *Facilities, 22*(1), 8–18.

Boal, K. & Hooijberg, R. (2001). Strategic leadership research: moving on. *The Leadership Quarterly, 11*(4), 515–549.

Boal, K. & Schultz, P. (2007). Storytelling, time, and evolution: the role of strategic leadership in complex adaptive systems. *The Leadership Quarterly, 18*(4), 411–428.

Boisot, M. & Child, J. (1999). Organizations as adaptive systems in complex environments: the case of China. *Organization Science, 10*(3), 237–252.

Bradbury, H. & Lichtenstein, B. M. B. (2005). Relationality in organizational research: exploring the space between. *Organization Science, 11*(5), 551–564.

Brown, S., & Eisenhardt, K. (1995b). Product innovation as core capability: The art of dynamic adaptation. Working paper, Department of Industrial Engineering and Engineering Management, Stanford University.

Brown, S. L. & Eisenhardt, K. M. (1997). The art of continuous change: linking complexity theory and time-paced evolution in relentlessly shifting organizations. *Administration Science Quarterly, 42*(1), 1–34.

Brown, S. L. & Eisenhardt, K. M. (1998). *Competing on the edge: strategy as structured chaos.* Boston, MA: Harvard Business School Press.

Browning, L.D., Beyer, J.M., & Stetler, J.C. (1995). Building cooperation in a competitive industry: Sematech and the semiconductor industry. *Academy of Management Journal, 38*(1), 113–151.

Burns, T. & Stalker, G. M. (1961). *The management of innovation.* New York: Barnes and Noble.

Carley, K. (1992). Organizational learning and personnel turnover. *Organizational Science, 3,* 20–46.

Carley, K. (1997). Organizational adaptation. *Annals of Operations Research, 75,* 25–47.

Carley, K. & Hill, V. (2001). Structural change and learning within organizations. In A. Lomi & E. R. Larsen (eds), *Dynamics of organizational societies.* Cambridge, MA: AAAI/MIT Press, pp. 63–92.

Chiles, T. H., Meyer, A. D., & Hench, T. J. (2004). Organizational emergence: the origin and transformation of Branson, Missouri's musical theaters. *Organization Science, 15*(5), 499–519.

Christiansen, J. K. & Varnes, C. J. (2007). Making decisions on innovation: meetings or networks? *Creativity & Innovation Management 16*(3), 282–298.

Cilliers, P. (1998). *Complexity and postmodernism: understanding complex systems.* London: Routledge.

Cunha, M. P. & Cunha, J. V. (2006). Towards a complexity theory of strategy. *Management Decision, 44*(7), 839–850.

Davis, G. F. & Marquis, C. (2005). Prospects for organization theory in the early twenty-first century: institutional fields and mechanisms. *Organization Science, 16*(4), 332–343.

Davis, J. P., Eisenhardt, K. M., & Bingham, C. (2007). Developing theory through simulation methods. *Academy of Management Review, 32*(2), 480–499.

Davis, J. P., Eisenhardt, K. M., & Bingham, C. (2009). Optimal structure, market dynamism, and the strategy of simple rules. *Administrative Science Quarterly, 54,* 413–452.

Dess, G. & Picken, J. C. (2000). Changing roles: leadership in the 21st century. *Organizational Dynamics, 28*(3), 18–34.

Edmondson, A. (1999). Psychological safety and learning behavior in work teams. *Administrative Science Quarterly, 44*(2), 350–383.

Eisenhardt, K. M. & Schoonhoven, C. B. (1990). Organizational growth: linking founding team, strategy, environment, and growth among U.S. semiconductor ventures, 1978–1988. *Administrative Science Quarterly, 35*(3), 504–529.

Eisenhardt, K. M. & Tabrizi, B. N. (1995). Accelerating adaptive processes: product innovation in the global computer industry. *Administrative Science Quarterly, 40*(1), 84–110.

Fairhurst, G. & Grant, D. (2010). The social construction of leadership: a sailing guide. *management Communication Quarterly, 24*(2), 171–210.

Follett, M. P. (1924). *Creative experience.* New York: Longmans Green.

Fonseca, J. (2002). *Complexity and innovation in organizations.* London: Routledge.

Galbraith, J. R. (1973). *Designing complex organizations.* Reading, MA: Addison Wesley.

Galunic, D. C. & Eisenhardt, K. M. (2001). Architectural innovation and modular corporate forms. *Academy of Management Journal, 44*(6), 1229–1249.

Gleick, J. (1987). *Chaos: making a new science.* New York: Viking.

Goldspink, C. & Kay, R. (2004). Bridging the micro–macro divide: a new basis for social science. *Human Relations, 57*(5), 597–618.

Goldstein, J. (2007). A new model of emergence and its leadership implications. In J. Hazy, J. Goldstein, & B. Lichtenstein (eds), *Complex systems leadership theory.* Mansfield, MA: ISCE Publishing.

Goldstein, J., Hazy, J., & Lichtenstein, B. (2010). *Complexity and the nexus of leadership: leveraging nonlinear science to create ecologies of innovation.* Englewood Cliffs, NJ: Palgrave Macmillan.

Gronn, P. (2002). Distributed leadership as a unit of analysis. *The Leadership Quarterly, 13*(4), 423–451.

Hales, C. (2002). 'Bureaucracy-lite' and continuities in managerial work. *British Journal of Management, 13,* 51–66.

Hamel, G. (2009). Moon shots for management. *Harvard Business Review,* February, 91–98.

Harrison, J.R., Lin, Z., Carroll, G.R., & Carley, K.M. (2007). Simulation modeling in organizational and management research. *Academy of Management Review, 32*(4), 1229–1245.

Hayek, F. A. (1988). *The fatal conceit.* London: Routledge.

Hazy, J. K. (2006). Measuring leadership effectiveness in complex socio-technical systems. *Emergence: Complexity and Organization (E:CO), 8*(3), 58–77.

Hazy, J., Goldstein, J., & Lichtenstein, B. (2007). *Toward a theory of leadership in complex systems.* Mansfield, MA: ISCE Publishing Company.

Heckscher, C. (1994). Defining the post-bureaucratic type. In C. Heckscher & A. Donnellon (eds), *The post-bureaucratic organization: new perspectives on organizational change.* Thousand Oaks, CA: Sage, pp. 14–62.

Hedström, P. & Swedberg, R. (1998). *Social mechanisms: an analytical approach to social theory.* Cambridge: Cambridge University Press.

Heifetz, R. A. (1994). *Leadership without easy answers.* Cambridge, MA: Harvard University Press.

Heifetz, R. A. & Laurie, D. L. (2001). The work of leadership. *Harvard Business Review, 79*(11), 131–141.

Hosking, D. M. (2007.). Not leaders, not followers: a postmodern discourse of leadership processes. In B. Shamir, R. Pillai, M. Bligh, & M. Uhl-Bien (eds), *Follower-centered perspectives on leadership: a tribute to the memory of James R. Meindl.* Greenwich, CT: Information Age Publishing, pp. 243–264.

Hosking, D. M., Dachler, H. P., & Gergen, K. J. (eds). (1995). *Management and organization: relational alternatives to individualism.* Brookfield, USA: Avebury.

Houchin, K. & MacLean, D. (2005). Complexity theory and strategic change: an empirically informed critique. *British Journal of Management, 16*(2), 149–166.

Hunt, J. G. & Dodge, G. (2000). Leadership deja vu all over again. *The Leadership Quarterly, 11,* 435–458.

Hunt, J. G., Osborn, R., & Boal, K. (2009). The architecture of managerial leadership: stimulation and channeling of organizational emergence. *The Leadership Quarterly, 20*(4), 503–516.

Jelinek, M. & Schoonhoven, M. (1990). The Innovation Marathon. London: Basil-Blackwell.

Johannessen, S. & Aasen, T.M.B. (2007). Exploring innovation processes from a complexity perspective. Part I: theoretical and methodological approach. *International Journal of Learning and Change, 2*(4), 420–433.

Katz, D. & Kahn, R. L. (1978). *The social psychology of organizations,* 2nd edn. New York: John Wiley and Sons.

Kauffman, S. (1993). Origins of order: Self-organization and selection in evolution. Oxford: Oxford University Press.

Kauffman, S. A. (1993). *The origins of order.* New York: Oxford University Press.

Kauffman, S. A. (1995). *At home in the universe: the search for the laws of self-organization and complexity.* New York: Oxford University Press.

Kilduff, M., Crossland, C., & Tsai, W. (2007). Pathways of opportunity in dynamic organizational networks. In M. Uhl-Bien & R. Marion (eds), *Complexity leadership, part 1,* Vol. 5. Charlotte, NC: Information Age Publishing, pp. 83–100.

Koch, R. & Leitner, K. (2008). The dynamics and functions of self-organization in the fuzzy front end: empirical evidence from the Austrian semiconductor industry. *Creativity and Innovation Management, 17*(3), 216–226.

Lawrence, P. R. & Lorsch, J. W. (1967). *Organization and environment.* Cambridge, MA: Harvard University Press.

Lewin, A. (1999). *Complexity: life at the edge of chaos,* 2nd edn. Chicago: University of Chicago Press.

Lichtenstein, B. (2000). Emergence as a process of self-organizing: new assumptions and insights from the study of nonlinear dynamic systems. *Journal of Organizational Change Management, 13,* 526–544.

Lichtenstein, B. & Plowman, D. (2009). The leadership of emergence: a complex systems leadership theory of emergence at successive organizational levels. *The Leadership Quarterly, 20*(4), 617–630.

MacIntosh, R., MacLean, D., & Burns, H. (2007). Health in organization: towards a process-based view. *Journal of Management Studies, 44*(2), 206–221.

McKelvey, B. (2008). Emergent strategy via complexity leadership: using complexity science and adaptive tension to build distributed intelligence. In M. Uhl-Bien & R. Marion (eds), *Complexity leadership, part 1: conceptual foundations* Charlotte, NC: Information Age Publishing, pp. 225–268.

MacLean, D. & MacIntosh, R. (2002). One process, two audiences: on the challenges of management research. *European Management Journal*, 20, 383–92.

Mainzer, K. (1997). *Thinking in complexity*, 3rd edn. New York: Springer-Verlag.

Marion, R. (1999). *The edge of organization: chaos and complexity theories of formal social organizations*. Newbury Park, CA: Sage.

Marion, R. & Uhl-Bien, M. (2001). Leadership in complex organizations. *The Leadership Quarterly, 12*, 389–418.

Marion, R. & Uhl-Bien, M. (2003). Complexity theory and al-Qaeda: examining complex leadership. *Emergence: a Journal of Complexity Issues in Organizations and Management, 5*, 56–78.

Martin, J. A. & Eisenhardt, K. (2010). Rewiring: cross-business-unit collaborations in multibusiness organizations. *Academy of Management Journal, 53*(2), 265–301.

Mead, G. H. (1934). *Mind, self, and society*. Chicago: University of Chicago Press.

Meyer, A., Gaba, V., & Colwell, K. (2005). Organizing far from equilibrium. *Organization Science, 16* (5), 456–473.

Mohr, L. B. (1982). *Explaining organizational behavior*. San Francisco, CA: Jossey-Bass.

Osborn, R. & Hunt, J. G. (2007). Leadership and the choice of order: complexity and hierarchical perspectives near the edge of chaos. *The Leadership Quarterly, 18*(4), 319–340.

Osborn, R., Hunt, J. G., & Jauch, L. R. (2002). Toward a contextual theory of leadership. *The Leadership Quarterly, 13*(6), 797.

Osborn, R. & Marion, R. (2009). Contextual leadership, transformational leadership and the performance of international innovation seeking alliances. *The Leadership Quarterly, 20*(2), 191–206.

Pearce, C. L. & Conger, J. A. (2003). *Shared leadership: reframing the hows and whys of leadership*. Thousand Oaks, CA: Sage.

Pettigrew, A. M., Whittington, R., Melin, L., Sanchez-Runda, C., van den Bosch, F., Ruigrok, W., & Numagami, T. (2003). *Innovative forms of organizing*. London: Sage.

Plowman, D. & Duchon, D. (2008). Dispelling the myths about leadership: from cybernetics to emergence. In M. Uhl-Bien & R. Marion (eds), *Complexity leadership, part 1: conceptual foundations*. Charlotte, NC: Information Age Publishing, pp. 129–154.

Plowman, D., Solansky, S., Beck, T., Baker, L., Kulkarni, M., & Travis, D. (2007). The role of leadership in emergent, self-organization. *The Leadership Quarterly, 18*, 341–356.

Plowman, D. A., Baker, L. T., Beck, T. E., Kulkarni, M., Solansky, S. T., & Travis, D. V. (2007). Radical change accidentally: the emergence and amplification of small change. *Academy of Management Journal, 50*(3), 515–543.

Reed, M.I. (2009). Critical realism: philosophy, method or philosophy in search of a method? In A. Bryman and D. Buchanan (eds), *The Sage handbook of organizational research methods*. London: Sage, pp. 430–448.

Regine, B. & Lewin, R. (2000). Leading at the edge: how leaders influence complex systems. *Emergence: a Journal of Complexity Issues in Organizations and Management, 2*(2), 5–23.

Reichers, A. E. & Schneider, B. (1990). Climate and culture: an evolution of constructs. In B. Schneider (ed.), *Organizational climate and culture*. San Francisco, CA: Jossey-Bass, pp. 5–39.

Roethlisberger, F. J. & Dickson, W. J. (1939). *Management and the worker*. Cambridge, MA: Harvard University Press.

Schneider, M. & Somers, M. (2006). Organizations as complex adaptive systems: implications of complexity theory for leadership research. *The Leadership Quarterly 17*(4), 351–365.

Schreiber, C., Marion, R., Uhl-Bien, M., & Carley, K. (2006). Multi-agent based simulation of a model of complexity leadership. Paper presented at the International Conference on Complex Systems, Boston, MA.

Scott, W. R. (1987). *Organizations: rational, natural, and open systems*, 2nd edn. Englewood Cliffs, NJ: Prentice Hall.

Selznick, P. (1949). *TVA and the grass roots*. Berkeley, CA: University of California Press.

Stacey, R. D. (1995). The science of complexity: an alternative perspective for strategic change processes. *Strategic Management Journal, 16*(6), 477–495.

Stacey, R. D. (1996). *Complexity and creativity in organizations*. San Francisco, CA: Berrett-Koehler.

Stacey, R.D. (2000). The emergence of knowledge in organizations. *Emergence, 2*(4), 23–39.

Stacey, R.D. (2001a). What can it mean to say that the individual is social through and through? *Group Analysis, 34*, 457–471.

Stacey, R. D. (2001b). *Complex responsive processes in organizations: learning and knowledge creation*. London: Routledge.

Stacey, R. D. & Griffin, R. W. (2008). What contribution can insights from the complexity sciences make to the theory and practice of development management? *Journal of International Development, 20*(6), 804–820.

Stacey, R. D., Griffin, D., & Shaw, P. (2000). *Complexity and management: fad or radical challenge to systems thinking*. London: Routledge.

Streatfield, P. J. (2001). *The paradox of control in organizations*. London: Routledge.

Surie, G. & Hazy, J. (2006). Generative leadership: nurturing innovation in complex systems. *Emergence: Complexity and Organization, 8*(4), 13–26.

Thomke, S. & Nimgade, A. (2007). *Ideo product development. Harvard Business School case (9-600-143)*. Boston, MA: Harvard Business School Publishing.

Tsoukas, H. & Chia, R. (2002). On organizational becoming: rethinking organizational change. *Organization Science, 13*(5), 567–582.

Uhl-Bien, M. (2006). Relational leadership theory: exploring the social processes of leadership and organizing. *The Leadership Quarterly, 17*, 654–676.

Uhl-Bien, M. & Marion, R. (2008). *Complexity leadership, part 1: conceptual foundations*. Charlotte, NC: Information Age Publishing.

Uhl-Bien, M. & Marion, R. (2009). Complexity leadership in bureaucratic forms of organizing: a meso model. *The Leadership Quarterly, 20*, 631–650.

Uhl-Bien, M. Marion, R., & McKelvey, B. (2007). Complexity leadership theory: shifting leadership from the industrial age to the knowledge era. *The Leadership Quarterly, 18*(4), 298–318.

Uzzi, B. & Spiro, J. (2005). Collaboration and creativity: the small world problem. *American Journal of Sociology, 111*(2), 447–504.

Waldrop, M. M. (1992). *Complexity: the emerging science at the edge of order and chaos.* New York: Simon & Schuster.

Weber, M. (1947). *The theory of social and economic organization* (A. H. Henderson & T. Parsons, trans.). Glencoe, IL: Free Press.

Weick, K. E. (1993). The collapse of sensemaking in organizations: the Mann Gulch disaster. *Administrative Science Quarterly, 38*(4), 628–652.

Wheatley, M. J. (1992). *Leadership and the new science: learning about organization from an orderly universe.* San Francisco, CA: Berrett-Koehler.

Wheatley, M. J. (1999). *Leadership and the new science,* 2nd edn. San Francisco, CA: Berrett-Koehler.

35

Spirituality and Leadership

Mario Fernando

INTRODUCTION

The aim of this chapter is to discuss the link between spirituality and leadership in the workplace. Fairholm (1996) is credited as being one of the first scholars to 'put the terms spiritual and leadership together to explain spirituality in context of workplace leadership' (Dent et al., 2005, p. 628). Generating 344,000 hits on Google Scholar, 'spiritual leadership' is quickly gaining recognition as an attractive leadership form to study and practice across education, healthcare, psychology and management disciplines. The growing interest of spiritual leadership among management scholars is demonstrated by the rising number of journal articles (e.g. Aydin and Ceylan, 2009; Baglione and Zimmerer, 2007; Benefiel, 2005a; Dent et al., 2005; Fernando et al., 2009; Fry and Cohen, 2009; Geroy et al., 2002; Kardag, 2009; Kriger and Seng, 2005; Reave, 2005), special issues (e.g. *The Leadership Quarterly*, 2005) as well as books devoted to the topic (e.g. Benefiel, 2005; Fernando, 2007; Hicks, 2002).

This interest has been further fuelled against a backdrop of the recent highly publicized irresponsible business leadership practices that were linked to the global financial crisis and corporate collapses. One of the key lessons to be learned from these events is 'that it takes responsible leadership and responsible leaders to build and sustain a business that is of benefit to multiple stakeholders (and not just to a few risk-seeking individuals)' (Maak, 2007, p. 329). According to Maak, the popular response shown by many businesses with initiatives such as the UN Global Compact and the Business Leader's Initiative on Human Rights are clear indicators that organizations are actively seeking ways to promote responsible leadership. Thus, in support of this interest, a number of leadership scholars believe that leadership theories should serve leaders to become more responsible and to lead responsibly in a global stakeholder society. Those who work in this domain argue that a spiritually-driven leadership approach can serve to create a much needed balance between the enhancement of profits, people and the planet. It is in this context that this chapter provides an opportunity to review the state of play within the spiritual leadership domain and examine the most significant theories, empirical studies and debates within this young but growing field.

The 'spiritual' element of spiritual leadership in the management literature has been largely shaped by theory, measurement and construct development in the workplace spirituality field. The current workplace spirituality literature has been influenced by developments in fields as diverse as religious studies, psychology, healthcare and management. It originated and developed almost wholly in the West, within mostly a Judaeo-Christian perspective (Fernando, 2007). Conceptualizing the role of religion has been the focus of much debate within the workplace spirituality discourse for nearly three decades (see Dent et al., 2005). A review of workplace spirituality research indicates that there are several views of the proper role of religion in the conceptualization of workplace spirituality. In this chapter, we first examine the role of religion in spiritual leadership. This is followed by a discussion of the influence of spirituality on leadership and a review of the more prominent theories that have endeavored to link spirituality with leadership. After reviewing these theories of spiritual leadership, we review the most significant empirical studies on the topic.

The chapter closes by making some recommendations for the future development of spiritual leadership inquiry.

THE ROLE OF RELIGION IN SPIRITUAL LEADERSHIP

There are a multitude of definitions of spirituality in the religious studies, healthcare, psychology, management and other literatures. Some workplace spirituality researchers identify and define spirituality within a religious context (Dent et al., 2005; Fernando and Jackson, 2006; Kriger and Seng, 2005). Other management scholars have defined spirituality as being devoid of any religious connection; as an inherent characteristic of all humans which encompasses the sacredness of everything; as being non-denominational, broadly inclusive and embracing everyone; and involving the experience or achievement of a godlike self through connection (Dent et al., 2005; Fernando, 2007; Mitroff and Denton, 1999; Smith and Rayment, 2007). For example, Dehler and Welsh (1994) define spirituality as 'a subconscious feeling that energizes individual action in relation to a specific task... an animating life force, an energy that inspires one toward certain ends or purposes that go beyond self' (p. 19).

One key contributing factor to the wide variety of definitions of spirituality is the role of religion in the characterization of spirituality. Not surprisingly, therefore, the definition and theory development of spiritual leadership has also been shaped by this discussion of the role of religion in workplace spirituality. For example, in a recent call for papers by *Organization* on Theology, Work and Organization, the guest editors (Sørensen et al., 2010) note that the concept of work is rooted 'in the Judeo-Christian tradition, which understands work as the burden imposed upon man after he had been expelled from Paradise'[sic] (p. 412). Highlighting the importance of studying the role of religion on leadership, they claim that a similar view applies to leadership in organizations, 'revolving around terms like charisma, spirit, inspiration, sacrifice, and humility' (p. 412). To understand the ways in which religion could influence leadership, we need to examine what religion is.

A comprehensive and useful definition of religion has been provided by Geertz (1973). It offers a helpful explanation for the existence of so many diverse views of the role of religion in formulating spirituality. According to Geertz (1973), a religion is (1) a system of symbols which acts to (2) establish powerful, pervasive and long-lasting moods and motivations in men [sic] by (3) formulating conceptions of a general order of existence and (4) clothing these conceptions with such an aura of factuality that (5) the moods and motivations seem uniquely realistic (p. 90). The internal aspects of religion – elements 2, 3, 4 and 5 – help to connect with a transcendental reality, an experience which engulfs the total person, transporting them, so far as they are concerned, into another mode of existence. In these experiential (internal) aspects of religion, the formal and institutionalized rules, procedures, symbols and rituals (external) seem absent. Similarly, in the workplace spirituality literature, systems of symbols and rituals appear to be absent too – commentators tend to deny any significance to these external aspects of religion. But, as Geertz (1973) describes, this external element of religion helps to clothe the conceptions of a general order of things with such an aura of factuality that it helps to move the believers beyond the realties of everyday life to wider realities. The distinct relationship between the external and internal elements of religion makes an important contribution to the current debate on the role of religion in workplace spirituality.

The same division of views is also reflected in the spiritual leadership discourse. For example, Dent et al. (2005) note that there is still very limited scholarship that links religion with leadership. Several scholars believe that spiritual leadership should be directly linked to religion (e.g. Benefiel, 2005; Fernando, 2007; Hicks, 2002; Kriger and Seng, 2005) whereas others (e.g. Giacalone et al., 2005) consider that spiritual leadership should be viewed from a non-religious perspective. To these scholars, religion is institutional, dogmatic and rigid whereas spirituality is personal, emotional and adaptable to an individual's needs (Hicks, 2002, p. 380). According to Fry (2003), spirituality is one of several basic needs that individuals need to satisfy.

> The purpose of spiritual leadership is to tap into the fundamental needs of both leader and follower for spiritual well-being through calling and membership, to create vision and value congruence across the individual, empowered team, and organization levels...to foster higher levels of employee well-being, organizational commitment, financial performance, and social responsibility. (Fry and Cohen, 2009, pp. 266–267)*

---

*   With kind permission from Springer Science+Business Media: Journal of Business Ethics, Spiritual Leadership as a Paradigm for Organizational Transformation and Recovery from Extended Work Hours Cultures, 84, 2009, 266-267, L. Fry and M. Cohen.

Despite empirical evidence suggesting that leaders who genuinely operate from religious principles are likely to be highly committed to the well-being of their staff members as well as other organizational stakeholders, Dent et al. (2005) lament that little research has been conducted into the spiritual or religious beliefs leaders may hold, and how those beliefs may impact leaders' actions. They voice a concern that 'many authors write as if there is no belief system that accompanies someone's spirituality' (p. 642). Dent et al. call for theory development that recognizes that 'any form of spirituality also includes practices and beliefs (i.e., a religion) and that the accompanying beliefs are an important, if not more important, element of how someone's spirituality is manifest in his or her leadership' (p. 642).

I concur with the observation that spiritual leadership has been largely characterized by management scholars as being non-religion based. One contributing factor for this non-religion-based characterization could be due to the perceived risks and complexities associated with promoting a religion-based leadership in the workplace. Most obviously, it can lead to arrogance that a particular faith is better and morally superior to another (Fernando and Jackson, 2006). However, a closer look at several spiritual leadership definitions suggests that key elements of these definitions actually represent religion-based themes. For example, Fry (2003) defines spiritual leadership as 'the values, attitudes, and behaviors necessary to intrinsically motivate one's self and others so that they have a sense of spiritual survival through calling and membership' (pp. 694–695). He describes the notion of calling as 'the experience of transcendence or how one makes a difference through service to others and, in doing so, derives meaning and purpose in life' (p. 703). As Reave (2005) rightly observes, 'calling is defined as a response to a call – an expressed need coming from within or from a Higher Power. The response may take the form of service to an ideal or service to God, and may only indirectly involve others' (p. 663). Thus, although not explicit, the characterization of spiritual leadership in the management literature includes notions of religion either implicitly or explicitly.

THE INFLUENCE OF SPIRITUALITY ON LEADERSHIP

According to Druskat (1994), leaders of spirituality-based organizations such as parish churches have been shown to generally score higher on measures of leadership effectiveness than leaders in other settings. After administering the Multifactor Leadership Questionnaire (MLQ) to 3,352 sisters, 1,541 brothers and 1,466 priests in the Roman Catholic Church in the USA, Druskat found that these spiritual leaders were rated significantly higher in transformational leadership capability than leaders in the general population. Despite the revelations of clergy abuse, cover up and organizational hypocrisy (see Reave, 2005), the majority of these individuals followed a model for spiritual success, not the recommendations of leadership research. This prompts Reave (2005) to ask 'Why, then, did they score significantly higher on measures of leadership effectiveness?' (p. 664). We will try to answer this question by briefly turning our attention to several prominent leadership approaches, and how the business context has shaped a growing need to recognize the contribution that spirituality can and should make in fostering effective leadership.

Although workplace spirituality scholars for some time have acknowledged the importance of leadership to the development of their field, until recently, leadership scholars have not acknowledged such a relationship between leadership and workplace spirituality. For example, in Fernando (2007), I observed that Zwart's (2000) study of 266 American business leaders failed to find any linkages between the transformational leadership of Bass and Avolio (1989) and the dimensions of spirituality identified by Beazley (1998). But after reviewing over 150 studies, Reave (2005) notes of a 'clear consistency' between what she identify as spiritual values such as integrity, honesty and humility, and spiritual practices connected with leadership effectiveness such as showing respect for others, demonstrating fair treatment, expressing care and concern, and listening responsively (p.655).

Reflecting Reave's views, an increasing number of recent leadership contributions suggest the need to integrate spirituality with the leadership discourse (Fernando et al., 2009; Fry and Cohen, 2009; Smith and Rayment, 2007). Some even suggest an overlap between authentic and servant leadership approaches with spiritual leadership (see for example Avolio and Gardner, 2005). As theorists and researchers attempt to better understand the linkage between spirituality and leadership, a consensus is emerging that the linkage appear to be much more complex than a blanket assertion that there is a strong spiritual component in leadership.

As Fukushige and Spicer (2007) suggest, the Full Range Leadership (FRL) model of Bass (1985) and Bass and Avolio (1997) has perhaps been the most cited source for leadership researchers in the past two decades. The FRL model describes the distribution of leadership behaviours, ranging from completely inactive (laissez-faire) to transactional behaviours to transformational behaviours. Transactional and transformational leadership are seen to be in a continuum rather than being mutually exclusive (Bass and Avolio, 1994; Yammarino, 1993). As the FRL model is more fully described in Chapter 22 of this Handbook, we will not examine this model in detail here. However, at this stage, it is important to note that the spiritual dimension of the FRL model, particularly that of the transactional and transformational styles, has been noted by leadership scholars such as Sanders III et al. (2003). Later in this chapter, we examine the proposition that as leaders' spirituality deepens, leaders have the greater potential to progress from practising transactional to transformational leadership.

Of the different leadership theories, transformational leadership has most often been linked to spirituality. The influence of transformational leaders 'distinguished on the hierarchical scale of moral development measured by Kohlberg's conceptualization' (Popper et al., 2000, p. 269) was classified as being more morally advanced than transactional leaders, and more successful in motivating their followers to move beyond 'Maslow's (1954) need hierarchy from needs for safety and security to needs for achievement and self-actualization' (Bass, 1995, p. 467). But several scholars have pointed to the weaknesses in transformational leadership, including the underlying assumption of a unidirectional influence flowing from the leader to the follower; the over-identification with the leader, creating loyal and obedient followers; and the overdependence on the leader (see Fernando et al., 2009). Reave (2005) notes that, although transformational theories describe the process of how leaders influence follower motivation, they have so far not addressed the source of the leader's own motivation. As a causal factor, she contends that spiritual motivation and faith is often described in the literature as the origin of the transformational leader's motivation. But for decades, leadership research has failed to generate a useful theory that explains this spiritual motivation and the contribution of the faith of the leader.

Transformational leadership has also been criticized for lacking a moral and ethical base (Bass and Steidlmeier, 1999; Kanungo, 2001). For transformational leadership to be 'authentic' (see Parry and Proctor-Thomson, 2002), it must 'incorporate a central core of moral values' (Bass and Steidlmeier, 1999, p. 210). Although transformational leadership is 'moral in that it raises the level of human conduct and ethical aspiration of both leader and led' (Burns, 1978, p. 20), and transactional leadership is not moral in that it is self-absorbing and manipulative, Kanungo (2001) argues that the ethical justification for transformational leadership is not that clear; neither is the assertion that transactional leadership is devoid of a moral base. According to Kanungo (2001, p. 258), unless leaders are able to transform everyone and create absolute unanimity of interests, transformational leadership produces simply a majority will that represents the interests of the strongest faction. Such leadership, then, may not always protect the basic interest of the weak from the self-interest of the strong. Thus, although transformational leadership has been linked to spirituality, and seems to be more morally advanced than transactional leadership, there is a void in the leadership literature of a leadership style that is based on spiritual motivation that is moral and authentic, and represents the interests of both the leader and the led.

To overcome some of the conceptual weaknesses of transformational leadership a few variants have been proposed, such as authentic leadership and servant leadership. As Chapter 26 of this Handbook is devoted to authentic leadership, we limit our discussion here to servant leadership. This leadership style is sometimes treated synonymously with spiritual leadership (Sendjaya and Sarros, 2002). Servant leaders' service orientation is aimed at enabling 'wise organizations' (Barbuto and Wheeler, 2006). Scholarly contributions to defining and conceptualizing servant leadership engage many of the underlying themes and concepts of spiritual leadership. Greenleaf (1977) first conceptualized the concept of servant leadership, describing it as a process beginning with the 'natural feeling that one wants to serve first, then conscious choice', making one to 'aspire to lead' (p. 12). Daft (1999) presented four underlying precepts of servant leadership: service before self; listening as a means of affirmation; creating trust; and nourishing followers to become whole. All of these are based on the notion of connectedness, a key concept in spiritual leadership (see Fernando, 2007). Smith et al. (2004) compared the differences between transformational and servant leadership, and suggested that servant leadership leads to a spiritual generative culture. In one of the rare empirical studies on servant leaders, Sendjaya and Sarros (2002) found that servant leaders possess inner consciousness and a sense of mission, which give meaning and purpose to their own lives and those of others. These researchers describe this attribute as transcendent spirituality – behaviours of the leader which manifest an inner conviction that something or someone beyond self and the material world exists and makes life complete and meaningful.

Thus, servant leadership has been described with a transcendental spiritual element, common with the characterization of 'spiritual' in spiritual leadership (Fernando, 2007; Hicks, 2002). However, for some commentators this overlap between several new positive forms of leadership is a cause for concern. According to Avolio and Gardner (2005), areas of overlap between the authentic and spiritual leadership theories include integrity, trust, courage, hope and perseverance (or resilience). The spiritual leadership theory of Fry (2003), which we shall consider shortly, includes an implicit recognition of the role of leader self-awareness, with a focus on vision and leader values and attitudes that are broadly classified as altruistic love and hope/faith. However, according to Avolio and Gardner (2005), 'these values/attitudes are also described as leader behaviors, producing some confusion regarding these constructs and their role in spiritual leadership' (p. 331). Thus, these new variants of spiritual leadership and the resulting overlap in constructs calls for greater clarity and refinement of spiritual leadership.

KEY SPIRITUAL LEADERSHIP THEORIES

While there is a growing recognition of the importance of an ethical leadership style in the general leadership literature (Barling et al., 2008), early empirical attempts at testing the relationship between spirituality and leadership found that the characteristics of leaders do not commonly encompass notions of spirituality (Dent et al., 2005). These researchers suggest that both spirituality and leadership share the problem of not having a specific and widely accepted meaning. Neither term has generated a consensus with respect to its definition. Mixing two vague concepts like spirituality and leadership was expected to result in an even fuzzier concept (Sendjaya and Sarros, 2002).

Spiritual leadership has been variously described as '… creating a vision wherein organization members experience a sense of calling in that their life has meaning and makes a difference and establishing a social/organizational culture based on altruistic love whereby leaders and followers have genuine care' (Fry, 2003, p. 695); 'the directing of self and others to achieve collective purpose from a sense of shared community' (Kriger and Seng, 2005, p. 798); and 'as demonstrated through behavior and reflective practice, and the ethical, compassionate, and respectful treatment of others' (Reave, 2005, p. 663). There are only a handful of scholars who make regular contributions to the spiritual leadership discourse and Louis (Jody) Fry's theory of spiritual leadership

(2003, 2005) is the most extensively tested and validated in a variety of settings. Fry's spiritual leadership theory is centred on organizational transformation and development designed to create an intrinsically motivated, learning organization (Fry, 2005).

According to Fry, spiritual leadership involves the growth of spiritual well-being of the leader and the follower 'through calling and membership, to create vision and value congruence across the individual, empowered team, and organization levels and, ultimately, to foster higher levels of organizational commitment and productivity' (Fry and Cohen, 2009, p. 269). The source of spiritual leadership is an inner life or spiritual practice that, as a fundamental source of inspiration and insight, positively influences development of (1) hope/faith in a transcendent vision of service to key stakeholders and (2) the values of altruistic love. Over 100 organizations have participated in studies that have applied Fry's theoretical framework, involving schools, military units, cities, police and for-profit organizations. The central feature of Fry's work is that it provides a 'consensus on the values, attitudes, and behaviors necessary for positive human health, psychological well-being, life satisfaction, and ultimately, corporate social responsibility' (Fry & Cohen, 2009, p. 270).

Fry's spiritual leadership theory was recently applied to the transformation of dysfunctional extended work hour cultures. In the study, Fry and Cohen (2009) explain the apparently contradictory condition whereby one can seem to be obsessed with work yet have high levels of psychological well-being, positive human health and organizational commitment and productivity. Fry and Cohen (2009) point out that the 'enthusiastic workaholic' will be energized by a job that is intrinsically motivating. They argue that, to the extent that the spiritual leadership paradigm is implemented, enthusiastic workaholics will be intrinsically motivated, experience competence, autonomy, relatedness and spiritual well-being. Explaining the contrary position where low levels of psychological well-being, positive human health and dysfunctional organizational behaviour of 'non-enthusiastic workaholics' are involved, Fry and Cohen point out that the 'non-enthusiastic workaholic' is primarily motivated by extrinsic rewards that can appear to be quite effective. However, they are neither adequate nor productive motivators and may even be detrimental to organizational performance over the long run. First, extrinsic rewards assume people are driven by lower needs and act to diminish intrinsic rewards since the motivation to seek an extrinsic reward, whether a bonus or approval, leads people to focus on the reward rather on the nature of the work they do to achieve it. This type of reward-seeking behaviour necessarily diminishes the focus and satisfaction people receive from the process of working. In addition, extrinsic rewards are temporary and targeted to short-term success but often at the expense of long-term quality (p. 271). Thus, giving people extrinsic rewards undermines their interest in the work itself to the point that, if there is a lack of intrinsic rewards, performance levels out or stays barely adequate to reach the reward. This situation can also cause dysfunctional organizational behaviours to the extent that people will do what it takes to get the reward even if it ultimately hurts the organization's effectiveness (p. 272). While confirming the spiritual leadership causal model and the reliability and validity of its measures, Fry and Cohen (2009) claim that results 'support a significant positive influence of spiritual leadership on employee life satisfaction, organizational commitment and productivity, and sales growth' (p. 269).

Thus, Fry treats spiritual leadership 'more as an observable phenomenon occurring when a person in a leadership position embodies spiritual values such as integrity, honesty, and humility, creating the self as an example of someone who can be trusted, relied upon, and admired' (Reave, 2005, p. 663). However, I concur with Reave (2005) that spiritual leadership is also demonstrated through behaviour, through reflective practice and the ethical, compassionate and respectful treatment of others. Despite Avolio and Gardner's (2005) concerns noted earlier about Fry's spiritual leadership theory, it is the most cited and tested spiritual leadership theory. As Fry and Cohen (2009) suggest, the theory needs to be refined and, as more empirical validation of the theory takes place using mixed methodologies and across different cultural settings, it is likely that this spiritual leadership theory will become the dominant theory in the field in much the same way as transformational leadership. Nonetheless, there have been other researchers who have proposed theories linking leadership with spirituality.

For example, Sanders III et al. (2003) proposed a model that comprises three dimensions of spirituality: consciousness, moral character and faith. They combined the managerial aspects of transactional leadership theory with the charismatic aspects of transformational leadership theory to enhance leader effectiveness. In this model, transactional, transformational and transcendental leadership styles are connected through three continua (Geroy et al., 2005, p. 23; Sanders III et al., 2003, p. 20). First, the locus of control continuum refers to the extent to which individuals differ in terms of their beliefs about whether they control the outcomes in their lives (i.e. internal locus of control), or the outcomes are controlled by factors such as luck and other people (i.e. external locus

of control) (Blakely et al., 2005). Applying Sanders III et al.'s (2003) model to transcendental leadership, Fernando et al. (2009) note that the locus of control relates to transactional, transformational and transcendental leadership types, and is important in determining the quality of relationships or exchanges that develop between the leader and followers. Some researchers have found a positive relationship between an internal locus of control and high-quality leader–follower exchanges (Kinicki and Vecchio, 1994; Martin et al., 2005). An internal locus of control 'was positively related to ratings of transformational leadership' (Howell and Avolio, 1993, p. 899), meaning that transactional leaders are characterized by an external locus of control, while transformational leaders are characterized by an internal locus of control, and are more likely to use rationality when attempting to influence others (Barbuto and Moss, 2006). Transcendental leaders are even more internally focused than transformational leaders, because they are 'spiritually focused, which compels them to consciously place greater importance on the dynamics of the immaterial (i.e. inner spirit), as opposed to the material (i.e. body)' (Sanders III et al., 2003, p. 25).

The second continuum is the spirituality continuum. According to Sanders III et al. (2003), as leaders' internal moral values and spirituality deepen, they progress from primarily practising transactional to transformational leadership. As leaders move from low spirituality to high spirituality, they also move from transactional leadership through transformational leadership to transcendental leadership (Fernando et al., 2009). The last continuum is labelled the effectiveness continuum. Strong evidence supports the claim that a transformational leadership style is more effective than a transactional leadership style (Burpitt, 2009; Howell and Avolio, 1993). Sanders III et al. (2003, p. 25) argued that because transcendental leaders possess all of the same effectiveness traits as transformational leaders, as well as having a higher internal locus of control and high spirituality, they should be just as, if not more, effective than transformational leaders. Cardona (2000) argued a slightly different point. He believes that the closer economic and social exchange relationship between transformational and transcendental leadership results in the highest possible value-added partnerships being developed. Thus, Sanders III et al.'s (2003) model captures the transactional, transformational and transcendental theories of leadership along a hierarchical continuum (Sanders III et al., 2003, p. 27). As leaders progress from an external to an internal locus of control, and from low to high spirituality, they move from transactional to transformational to transcendental leadership styles. The more internal a leader's locus of control and the higher the leader's spirituality, the more effective they are. Effectiveness is the dependent variable of locus of control and spirituality.

The two theories to link spirituality and leadership that are presented here are distinctly different, but both focus on the leader with little attention to the impacts upon the follower. The spiritual leadership inquiry is in an embryonic stage and as issues regarding frameworks, measurements and empirical methods are addressed and further developed, these theories linking spirituality with leadership are likely to be more refined and comprehensive, addressing the leader, follower and also the situation characteristics of the leadership process.

MAJOR EMPIRICAL FINDINGS AND RESEARCH METHODS

Workplace spirituality is frequently asserted to provide greater meaning at work, superior ethical practices and greater effectiveness and profitability. There is a limited (although increasing) amount of research throwing light on these assertions. While in the early formative years of the field, much of the work in this area was based more on hope than academic rigor, and was criticized for adopting an overly prescriptive approach, the current workplace spirituality research seems to have made significant strides towards focusing more on the attributes of the content rather than the concept (Mitroff and Denton, 1999) and process rather than the outcome variables (Lips-Wiersma, 1999). Despite support from clinical (de Klerk, 2005), neurotheological (Newberg et al., 2001) and psychological (Strong, 1998) studies that link spirituality with improvements in overall mental and physical health, well-being and meaning-making ability of life, workplace spirituality researchers have been criticized for their reluctance to develop definitions of the concept because of its ethereal and abstract nature. But if the claims regarding workplace spirituality are valid, the benefits to derive at individual, organizational and society levels are too vast to gloss over or ignore because of its ethereal and abstract nature. Thus, several scholars, including Wilber (1998), Gibbons (2000), Fornaciari and Lund Dean (2005; 2001), Dent et al. (2005), Benefiel (2005a) and Fry (2003), have called for the academic community to adopt innovative methodologies to comprehend and apply the concept of workplace spirituality in business organizations.

Despite the conceptual and operational difficulties associated with examining spiritual leadership, spiritual leadership scholars have recently undertaken and published several important studies. One of the first empirical studies on spiritual leadership used structural equation modelling on a sample from the US army (Fry et al., 2005). The aim of this study was to test the Spiritual Leadership Theory causal model that hypothesizes positive relationships between the qualities of spiritual leadership, spiritual survival and organizational productivity and commitment. The study used longitudinal data from a newly formed Apache Longbow helicopter attack squadron at Ft. Hood, Texas (p. 835). These researchers developed a methodology for establishing a baseline for future organizational development interventions. The three dimensions of spiritual leadership, two dimensions of spiritual survival, and organizational commitment and productivity were measured using survey questions developed for the spiritual leadership theory. A total of 181 soldiers, representing 91% of the target population, responded to the first survey. A second survey administered approximately five months later was combined with the first survey to test the Spiritual Leadership Theory structural equation causal model. There were 189 respondents in the second survey. The second survey also focused on the qualities of vision/mission, altruistic love, hope/faith, meaning/calling, and membership as key components of spiritual survival to examine their impact on organizational commitment and productivity (p. 841). The researchers found strong initial support for the Spiritual Leadership Theory and its measures.

A more recent quantitative study examined the relationship between spiritual leadership and organizational culture, also using structural equation modelling (Kardag, 2009). Using the spiritual leadership behaviour of managers as the independent variable and the organizational culture as the dependent variable, 2,447 primary school teachers working in 32 primary schools in Turkey took part in the study. The spiritual leadership scale consisted of performance and attendance components with five subscales of commitment, vision, productive, belongingness and belief. The organizational culture scale consisted of four subscales (managerial, social, value and aim).

Spirituality has been frequently linked to ethical cognition, and is an important factor in determining how individuals perceive the ethicality of a situation. A study by Giacalone and Jurkiewicz (2003) demonstrate that an increase in individual spirituality leads to an increased tendency to perceive questionable business practices as being unethical. They conclude that that higher spiritual awareness can lead to greater ethical concern.

Thus, spiritual well-being, viewed as an outcome of experiencing spirituality, should also influence ethical orientations. Fernando and Chowdhury (2010) examined the relationship between spiritual well-being and ethical orientations in decision making of senior executives in Australian organizations. Results showed that spiritual well-being, in particular the communal aspects of spiritual well-being correlated with and were predictive of idealism (Forsyth, 1980). However, the relationship between spiritual well-being and relativism was found to be weak. The authors conclude that predictive power of communal well-being on the idealism of Australian executives' decision making could be due to the stronger presence of social attributes such as volunteerism, mateship and the dominance of Christian values in Australia.

Another major challenge facing spiritual leadership scholars is the challenge of demonstrating a causal link between spiritual leadership and organizational performance. In an exploratory study, Fry and Matherly (2006) tested Fry's (2003) Spiritual Leadership Theory model and its impact on organizational performance using a sample of 347 workers employed in 43 wholesale distributorships of a large electrical products company. The results provided support for the Spiritual Leadership Theory as a significant and important driver of organizational commitment and productivity as well as sales growth. More recently, Aydin and Ceylan (2009) examined the impact of spiritual leadership on organizational learning capacity and organizational development in Turkey. Using 578 employees, the study measured Fry's (2003) spiritual leadership dimensions of vision, hope/faith, altruistic love, meaning/calling and membership. The results indicated that organizational learning capacity has a positive significant correlation with each spiritual leadership dimension. However, the total explained variance of organizational learning capacity reliant on spiritual leadership was insignificant.

In a rare cross-cultural study on spiritual leadership, Baglione and Zimmerer (2007) examined the spirituality, values and leadership beliefs and practices of US and Chinese business leaders. They found, perhaps surprisingly, that Chinese business leaders believed more strongly in the positive impact of spirituality on the conduct of business. The Chinese business leaders responded more positively to all items concerning economic benefit to organizational climate, proactive workforce and to the existence of strong and positive organizational values and beliefs.

In another quantitative study, Field (2004) examined the question regarding the strength of the relationship between spirituality and transformational leadership. Participating in a multi-part survey, business leaders in the US hi-tech industry were asked to complete the Multifactor Leadership Questionnaire Short Form 5X (which measures transformational leadership), the Spiritual Well-Being Scale and the Spiritual Transcendence Scale and the Marlowe–Crowne Social Desirability Scale. The study found support for a positive correlation between transformational leadership and spirituality.

The high number of quantitative studies compared to the number of qualitative studies of spiritual leadership reflects a similar trend in the workplace spirituality field and, as is discussed in Chapter 2, leadership studies in general. Fornaciari and Dean's (2003) study of peer-reviewed empirical articles published during the early stages of workplace spirituality (1996–2000) reveals that 68% of the 26 articles reviewed used quantitative methods. In response to the growing number of quantitative studies on the topic, there is a view among workplace spirituality scholars of the futility of 'trying to factor analyze God' (Fornaciari and Lund Dean, 2001, p. 335). Citing Hunt (1999), and his concern with the preponderance of survey-based studies on leadership, Benefiel (2005a) calls for more qualitative studies to overcome the challenge of measuring spirituality in organizations based on non-positivist ways of knowing, such as ethnomethodological techniques, qualitative techniques and tradition-based stories (p. 726).

One qualitative method that spiritual leadership scholars could use more is the case study method (see Benefiel, 2005a; Fernando et al., 2009 for examples). Defined by Yin 'as an empirical inquiry that investigates a contemporary phenomenon within its real life context, when the boundaries between phenomenon and context are not clearly evident, and in which multiple sources are used' (1989, p. 23), individual case studies of leaders are appropriate for gathering and analysis of data. In spiritual leadership studies, the case study method has potential to be used over other qualitative methods for several reasons. First, these studies examine the contemporary phenomenon of spiritual leadership, investigating the case in a real-life context. Multiple sources of data, such as in-depth personal interviews, public documents and observations of leaders, could be used to ensure the quality of the data. Secondly, the case study approach allows the spiritual leadership researcher to examine the meanings rather than events, answering the 'Whys' and the 'Hows' rather than the 'Whats'. Thirdly, this approach allows comparing and contrasting individual spiritual leader cases to draw conclusions about emerging themes between different leaders. Linked with grounded theory methodology, a multiple case study design of several leaders can be used to generate robust and compelling data. Thus, instead of a large number of data, the qualitative approach suits spiritual leadership research, allowing the researcher to seek meaning at a greater depth than allowed by quantitative methods.

In conclusion, these recent empirical studies conducted in different organizational settings using different research methods provide hope for further refinement of definitions, constructs and variables of spiritual leadership. This trend will no doubt help attract more scholars to the growing field of spiritual leadership.

THE FUTURE OF SPIRITUALITY AND LEADERSHIP

There are several ways that spiritual leadership research might profitably advance. A first step would be to study influential business leaders who actively adopt a spiritual leadership approach to leading organizations. Robert Ouimet is a case in point. He is the Chairman and CEO of Holding OCB Inc., Cordon Bleu International and Ouimet-Tomasso, a producer and marketer of Italian pasta frozen food products in Canada. Ouimet is recognized by workplace spirituality scholars for drawing on spirituality to achieve the balance between an organization's responsibility to each employee and the responsibility to make profits. Ouimet (2003) believes that the two responsibilities are constantly in conflict, but are fundamental to the daily operation of his business. However, the representation of these leaders should ideally cross the North American and European base to other parts of the world (e.g. see Fernando et al., 2009). Such a showcasing and 'storytelling' of influential business leaders (Driscoll and McKee, 2007) in diverse cultural settings would promote the growth and dissemination of the spiritual leadership phenomenon and highlight the pragmatic values of spiritual leadership.

Secondly, more empirical studies on spiritual leadership need to link with established concepts, constructs and variables from other fields linked to spirituality. For example, spiritual leadership should continue to develop on the more established constructs and variables in the fields of psychology, religious studies and philosophy domains to extend the research base and infuse further methodological rigour and academic credibility.

Thirdly, although qualitative methods in spiritual leadership studies are being adopted by few scholars, quantitative methods have been used in the majority of the reported empirical studies. Spiritual leadership scholars could adopt more qualitative methods in empirical work. Observing that empirical studies of spirituality in organizations

have been gaining ground, Benefiel (2005a) notes that workplace spirituality scholars have contributed to the task of defining and measuring spirituality and assessing its impact on organizational performance. Claiming that empirical studies of spiritual leadership are not far behind, she however identifies a critical need to respond to the 'growing epistemological critique of the existing empirical studies of organizational spirituality' (p. 724). In addition, spiritual leadership scholars could also adopt mixed-method approaches in spiritual leadership empirical work. According to Sydenstricker-Neto (1997), mixed-method approaches generate creative alternatives to traditional or more monolithic ways of conceiving and implementing evaluation. For example, adding the qualitative flesh to the quantitative findings is a good strategy to overcome some of the challenges facing spiritual leadership research. According to Caracelli and Greene (1997), these alternative methods project a genuine effort to be reflexive and more critical of the evaluation practice, and more useful and accountable to broader audiences. In terms of the use of scale development in quantitative methods, Fornaciari et al. (2005) note that the field is 'experiencing vigorous empirical investigation using a variety of instruments, both old and new' (p. 45). However, after examining 168 studies using scales to measure spirituality in the management, spirituality and religion literature, they find 'scale development practices within the SRW [Spirituality, Religion and Work] domain are sometimes inconsistent'. They recommend 'well-articulated guides to help construct scales that have integrity' (p. 45).

Finally, much like workplace spirituality research was a decade ago, except for a handful of studies, spiritual leadership studies are also limited mostly to the North American and European research settings. Despite gaining some ground in broadening our discussion on spiritual leadership to include globally relevant research settings, and promoting an interfaith and inclusive dialogue, much more is yet to be achieved. Comparative studies similar to that of Baglione and Zimmerer's (2007) leadership and spiritual beliefs study of US and Chinese business leaders should serve to broaden the relevance of spirituality and leadership. This work would also provide an extraordinary opportunity to examine the interplay of Eastern spiritual traditions on established leadership approaches. Heelas (1992) suggests that the phenomenal growth in the interest in workplace spirituality could have been due to a desire to adopt Eastern views of life by Western society, and the consequent adoption of Eastern religious notions by the West. In Fernando (2007), I propose that as a result of this adoption, the workplace spirituality movement contains a host of

Eastern notions of religion and spirituality. Some of these Eastern notions, such as connectedness, self-expression, self-growth, and the potential goodness of the human (which were also notions of early Christian spirituality), are now central and the most frequently discussed concepts in the current workplace spirituality discourse. Indeed, the pioneering work of Mitroff and Denton on the spirituality of corporate America urges organizations to evolve from the values-based to the spiritually-based organization that 'will incorporate a deeper set of texts and practices from both Eastern and Western traditions' (1999, p. 183). Trevino (2000) observes that she was surprised to find this call for the use of texts and practices from Eastern traditions because, in any case, much of what is sometimes called New Age spirituality draws from these.

However as Wilber (1998) points out:

We intend to explore a sensitive question, but one which needs to be addressed – the superficiality that pervades so much of the current spiritual exploration and discourse in the West, particularly in the United States. All too often, in the translation of the mystical traditions from the East (and elsewhere) into the American idiom, their profound depth is flattened out, their radical demand is diluted, and their potential for revolutionary transformation is squelched. (in Joseph, 2002, p. 213)

Thus, future research in the field could focus more on cross-cultural and comparative studies. For example, studies could examine how spirituality and leadership practices are enacted in Chinese, Japanese, Indian and other business settings.

CONCLUSIONS

The aim of this chapter was to discuss the link between spirituality and leadership in the workplace. Despite support from cross-disciplinary studies linking spirituality with improvements in overall mental and physical health, well-being and meaning-making ability of life, we have observed that leadership theories have focused in varying degrees on one or more aspects of the physical, mental or emotional elements of human interaction in organizations, neglecting the spiritual component. More recently, however, a growing number of empirical studies on spiritual leadership have examined the role and influence of spirituality on leadership in a variety of organizational settings. This trend augurs well for the future of spiritual leadership, which is poised to grow as a field of inquiry supported by methodological rigour and credibility. Of particular interest would be to see how the field evolves to fulfil its potential to become the foundation of leadership theories in which the degree of spirituality experienced by leaders, followers and other stakeholders in the leadership process becomes the focal point to explain the effectiveness of leadership in a wide range of institutional and cultural contexts.

REFERENCES

Avolio, B. J. and Gardner, W. L. (2005). 'Authentic leadership development: getting to the root of positive forms of leadership'. *The Leadership Quarterly*, 16(3), 315–338.

Aydin, B. and Ceylan, A. (2009). 'The effect of spiritual leadership on organizational learning capacity.' *African Journal of Business Management* 3(5), 184–190.

Baglione, S. and Zimmerer, T. (2007). 'Spirituality, values, and leadership beliefs and practices: an empirical study of U.S. and Chinese business leaders.' *International Journal of Business Strategy*, VII(2), 32–40.

Barbuto, J. E. J. and Moss, J. A. (2006). 'Dispositional effects in intra-organizational influence tactics: a meta-analytic review.' *Journal of Leadership & Organizational Studies*, 12(3), 30–53.

Barbuto, J. E. J. and Wheeler, D. (2006). 'Scale development and construct clarification of servant.' *Leadership Group & Organization Management*, 31(3), 300–326.

Barling, J., et al. (2008). 'Pseudo-transformational leadership: towards the development and test of a model.' *Journal of Business Ethics*, 81, 851–861.

Bass, B. and Avolio, B. (1989). 'Potential biases in leadership measures: how prototypes, leniency and general satisfaction related to ratings and rankings of transformational and transactional leadership constructs.' *Educational and Psychological Measurement* 49, 509–527.

Bass, B. and Avolio, B. (1994). *Improving organisational effectiveness through transformational leadership*. London: Sage.

Bass, B. and Avolio, B. (1997). *The Full Range Leadership Development Manual for the Multifactor Leadership Questionnaire*. Redwood City, CA: Mind Garden.

Bass, B. M. (1985). *Leadership and performance beyond expectations*. New York: Free Press.

Bass, B. M. (1995). 'Theory of transformational leadership redux'. *The Leadership Quarterly*, 6(4), 463–478.

Bass, B. M. and Steidlmeier, P. (1999). 'Ethics, character, and the authentic transformational leadership behavior.' *The Leadership Quarterly*, 10(2), 181–217.

Beazley, H. (1998). Meaning and measurement of spirituality in organisational settings: development of a spirituality assessment scale (Honesty, Humility, Service to others). The George Washington University, USA.

Benefiel, M. (2005). *Soul at work: spiritual leadership in organizations*. New York: Church Publishing.

Benefiel, M. (2005a). 'The second half of the journey: spiritual leadership for organizational transformation'. *The Leadership Quarterly*, 16, 723–747.

Blakely, G. L., et al. (2005). 'The effects of nationality, work role centrality, and work locus of control on role definitions of OCB.' *Journal of Leadership and Organizational Studies*, 12(1), 103–118.

Burns, J. M. (1978). *Leadership*. New York: Harper & Row.

Burpitt, W. (2009). 'Exploration versus exploitation: leadership and the paradox of administration.' *Journal of Behavioral and Applied Management*, 10(2), 227–246.

Caracelli, V. J. and Greene, J. C. (1997). 'Crafting mixed-method evaluation design'. In J. C. Greene and V. J. Caracelli (eds), *Advances in mixed-method evaluation: the challenges and benefits of integrating diverse paradigms.* New Directions for Program Evaluation No. 74. San Francisco, CA: Jossey-Bass.

Cardona, P. (2000). 'Transcendental leadership.' *The Leadership and Organizational Development Journal*, 21(4), 201–207.

Daft, R.L. (1999). Leadership Theory and Practice. New York: The Dryden Press.

de Klerk, J. J. (2005) Spirituality, Meaning in Life and Work Wellness: A Research Agenda. *International Journal of Organizational Analysis.* 13 (1), 64–68.

Dehler, G. E. and Welsh, A. M. (1994). 'Spirituality and organizational transformation: Implications for the new management paradigm.' *Journal of Managerial Psychology*, 9(6), 17–26.

Dent, E., et al. (2005). 'Spirituality and leadership: an empirical review of definitions, distinctions, and embedded assumptions'. *The Leadership Quarterly*, 16(5), 625–653.

Driscoll, C. and McKee, M. (2007). 'Restoring a culture of ethical and spiritual values: a role for leader storytelling.' *Journal of Business Ethics*, 73, 205–217.

Druskat, V. U. (1994). 'Gender and leadership style: transformational and transactional leadership in the Roman Catholic Church'. *The Leadership Quarterly*, 5, 99–119.

Fairholm, G. (1996). 'Spiritual leadership: fulfilling whole-self needs at work.' *Leadership and Organisation Development Journal*, 17(5), 11–17.

Fernando, M. (2007). *Spiritual leadership in the entrepreneurial business: a multifaith study.* Cheltenham, UK: Edward Elgar.

Fernando, M. and Chowdhury, R. M. M. I. (2010). 'The relationship between spiritual well-being and ethical orientations in decision making: an empirical study with business executives in Australia.' *Journal of Business Ethics.* 95(2), 211–225.

Fernando, M. and Jackson, B. (2006). 'The influence of religion on business leaders' decision-making: an inter-faith study.' *Journal of Management and Organization*, 12(1), 23–39.

Fernando, M., et al. (2009). 'The spiritual dimension in leadership at Dilmah Tea.' *Leadership & Organization Development Journal*, 30(6), 522–539.

Field, D. (2004). The relationship between transformational leadership and spirituality in business leaders. School of Leadership Studies, Regent University.

Fornaciari, C. and Dean, K. (2003). Research in spirituality, religion, and work: empirical methods during the founding years. Management, Spirituality and Religion Group. Academy of Management Meeting, Seattle, Washington.

Fornaciari, C. and Lund Dean, K. (2001). 'Making the quantum leap: lessons from physics on studying spirituality and religion in organizations.' *Journal of Organizational Change Management*, 14(4), 335–351.

Fornaciari, C. J., et al. (2005). 'Scale development practices in the measurement of spirituality.' *International Journal of Organizational Analysis*, 13(1), 28–49.

Forsyth (1980) A Taxonomy of Ethical Ideologies. *Journal of Personality and Social Psychology.* 39(1), 175–184.

Fry, L. (2003). 'Toward a theory of spiritual leadership'. *The Leadership Quarterly*, 14(6), 693–727.

Fry, L. and Cohen, M. (2009). 'Spiritual leadership as a paradigm for organizational transformation and recovery of extended work hours cultures.' *Journal of Business Ethics*, 84, 265–278.

Fry, L. W. (2005). 'Introduction to the *The Leadership Quarterly* Special Issue: toward a paradigm of spiritual leadership'. *The Leadership Quarterly*, 16(5).

Fry, L. W. and Matherly, L. L. (2006). Spiritual leadership as an integrating paradigm for positive leadership development. Gallup International Leadership Summit, Washington, DC.

Fry, L. W., et al. (2005). 'Spiritual leadership and army transformation: theory, measurement, and establishing a baseline'. *The Leadership Quarterly*, 16, 835–862.

Fukushige, A. and Spicer, D. (2007). 'Leadership preferences in Japan: an exploratory study.' *Leadership & Organization Development Journal*, 28(6), 508–530.

Geertz, C. (1973) *The Interpretation of Cultures: Selected Essays Basic Books.* New York.

Geroy, G. D., et al. (2005). 'The CCM model: a management approach to performance optimization.' *Performance Improvement Quarterly*, 18(2), 19–36.

Giacalone, R. A. & Jurkiewicz. C. L. (2003) *Handbook of Workplace Spirituality and Organisational Performance* M.E. Sharp. New York.

Giacalone, R., et al. (2005). 'From advocacy to science: the next steps in workplace spirituality research'. In R. Paloutzian and C. Park (eds), *Handbook of the psychology of religion and spirituality.* New York: Guilford Press, pp. 515–528.

Gibbons, P. (2000). Spirituality at work: definitions, measures, assumptions, and validity claims. Academy of Management Annual Conference, Toronto, Canada.

Greenleaf, R. K. (1977). *Servant leadership: a journey into the nature of legitimate power and greatness.* New York: Paulist Press.

Heelas, P. (1992). 'The sacralisation of the self and New Age capitalism in social change'. N. Abercrombie and A. Warde (eds), In *Contemporary Britain*. Cambridge: Polity Press.

Hicks, D. A. (2002). 'Spiritual and religious diversity in the workplace: implications for leadership'. *The Leadership Quarterly*, 13(4), 379–396.

Howell, J. M. and Avolio, B. J. (1993). 'Transformational leadership, transactional leadership, locus of control, and support for innovation: key predictors of consolidated-business-unit performance.' *Journal of Applied Psychology*, 78(6), 891–903.

Hunt, J. (1999). 'Transformational/charismatic leadership's transformation of the field: an historical essay'. *The Leadership Quarterly*, 10(2), 129–144.

Joseph, M. (2002). Leaders and spirituality: a case study, University of Surrey, UK.

Kanungo, R. N. (2001). 'Ethical values of transactional and transformational leaders.' *Canadian Journal of Administrative Sciences*, 18(4), 257–265.

Kardag, E. (2009). 'Spiritual leadership and organizational culture: a study of structural equation modeling.' *Educational Sciences: Theory and Practice*, 9(3), 1391–1405.

Kinicki, A. J. and Vecchio, R. P. (1994). 'Influences on the quality of supervisor–subordinate relations: the role of time-pressure, organizational commitment, and locus of control.' *Journal of Organizational Behavior*, 15(1), 75–83.

Kriger, M. and Seng, Y. (2005). 'Leadership with inner meaning: a contingency theory of leadership based on the worldviews of five religions'. *The Leadership Quarterly*, 16(5), 771–806.

Lips-Wiersma. M. (1999). *The Influence of `Spiritual Meaning-Making' on Career Choice, Transition and Experience*. Unpublished Doctoral Dissertation, Auckland University, Auckland, New Zealand.

Maak, T. (2007). 'Responsible leadership, stakeholder engagement, and the emergence of social capital'. *Journal of Business Ethics*, 74(4), 329–343.

Martin, R., et al. (2005). 'The role of leader–member exchanges in mediating the relationship between locus of control and work reactions.' *Journal of Occupational and Organizational Psychology*, 78, 141–148.

Mitroff, I. and Denton, E. (1999). 'A study of spirituality in the workplace.' *Sloan Management Review*, 40(4), 83–92.

Newberg, A., D 'Aquili, E. & Rause, V. (2001) Why God Won 'T Go Away Ballantine. New York.

Ouimet, J. R. (2003). *The Golden Book: reconciliation of human wellbeing with productivity and profits*. Quebec, Canada: Ouimet-Cordon Bleu Inc.

Parry, K. and Proctor-Thomson, S. (2002). 'Perceived integrity of transformational leaders in organisational settings.' *Journal of Business Ethics*, 35(2), 75–97.

Popper, M., et al. (2000). 'Transformational leadership and attachment.' *The Leadership Quarterly*, 11(2), 267–289.

Reave, L. (2005). 'Spiritual values and practices related to leadership effectiveness.' *The Leadership Quarterly*, 16(5), 655–687.

Sendjaya, S. and Sarros, J.C. (2002). Servant Leadership: Charting Its Origin, Development, and Application in the Organization. Journal of Leadership & Organizational Studies, 9(2), 57–64.

Sanders III, J. E., et al. (2003). 'From transactional to transcendental: toward an integrated theory of leadership.' *Journal of Leadership and Organisational Studies*, 9(4), 21–31.

Smith, B. N., et al. (2004). 'Transformational and servant leadership: content and contextual comparisons'. *Journal of Leadership & Organizational Studies*, 10(4), 80–91.

Smith, J. A. and Rayment, J. J. (2007). 'The global SMP fitness framework: a guide for leaders exploring the relevance of spirituality in the workplace.' *Management Decision*, 45(2), 217–234.

Sørensen, B., et al. (2010). 'Call for papers – special issue on theology, work and organization '*Organization*, 17, 412–413.

Strong, S. (1998) Meaningful Work in Supportive Environments:Experiences with the Recovery Processes. *American Journal of Occupational Therapy*. 52(3), 1–38.

Sydenstricker-Neto, J. (1997). 'Research design and mixed-method Approach: a hands-on experience'. http://www.socialresearchmethods.net/tutorial/Sydenstricker/bolsa.html Retrieved 30 April 2010.

Trevino, L. (2000). 'A spiritual audit of corporate America: a hard look at spirituality, religion and values in the workplace [book review].' *Personnel Psychology*, 53(3), 758–761.

Wilber, K. (1998). *The marriage of sense and soul: integrating science and religion*. New York: Broadway Books.

Yammarino, F. J. (1993). 'Transforming leadership studies: Bernard Bass' leadership and performance beyond expectations'. *The Leadership Quarterly*, 4(3–4), 379–382.

Yin, R. K. (1989). *Case study research: design and methods*. Newbury Park, CA: Sage.

Zwart, G. (2000). The relationship between spirituality and transformational leadership in public, private and non-profit sector organizations. Unpublished Dissertation Abstracts International University of La Verne, CA.

36

Discursive Approaches to Leadership

Gail T. Fairhurst

INTRODUCTION

The purpose of this chapter is to demonstrate the ways in which scholars who study organizational discourse within a broadly social constructionist framework have rethought the concept of leadership with a social and cultural lens. Not all social constructionists are interpretive, critical, and/or poststructuralist in orientation, but discursive leadership scholars typically are Fairhurst and Grant (2010). The dominant lens in organizational leadership, individual and cognitive, is the leitmotif of leadership psychology. By contrast, a social and cultural lens emphasizes leadership discourse, communication, and relational stances (Alvesson & Sveningsson, 2003a, 2003b; Barge, 2004; Collinson, 2005; Cooren, 2007; Cunliffe, 2001, 2009; Fairhurst, 2007; Grint, 2000, 2005; Gronn, 2002; Hosking, 1988; Kelly, 2008; Taylor & Robichaud, 2006; Tourish & Vatcha, 2005; Vine et al., 2008).

No doubt the emergence of this new lens is a ripple effect of the linguistic turn within the social and organizational sciences (Alvesson & Kärreman, 2000a; Rorty, 1967). It is also a reaction to leadership psychology's overriding concern for leaders' or followers' inner motors, and a belief that leadership is best studied from the point of view of actors instead of researchers. Discursive approaches to leadership thus seek to understand leadership as an occasioned 'form of life,' to borrow from Wittgenstein (1953). Its socio-historical and local situated-ness is treated very seriously despite its endurance as a powerful idealization for societies and cultures throughout history (Fairhurst, 2009). Many leadership psychologists focus on the latter

and are forever seeking generalizable knowledge and that right and final definition of leadership that will unlock the clues to its mysteries. No such project defines the discursive leadership scholar, whose interests are in understanding the ways in which language and communication are put to use as a series of 'doings' that construct leadership in situ (Kelly, 2008).

Discourse is the central and defining term associated with this more situated view of leadership. As intimated above, the term 'social constructionist' is quite broad given the wide variety of leadership scholars who adopt the term (Fairhurst & Grant, 2010). Discourse also covers areas beyond language and communication to include Foucault's (1972, 1995) socio-historical systems of thought that resource the communication process. To aid clarity, Alvesson and Kärreman (2000b) refer to social interaction as little 'd' discourse and a more Foucauldian view as big 'D' Discourse. As we will see, a d/Discursive view of leadership problematizes the interpretive flexibility of terms like 'leadership' and 'management' and helps to unpack how competing truth claims about these terms both emerge and coexist.

Discursive approaches to leadership also have their own way of talking – their own language of leadership – whose distinctiveness is perhaps best understood via a critique of leadership psychology's more post-positivist orientation. Table 36.1 details six areas of difference between discursive approaches to leadership and leadership psychology: object of study, ontology, power, agency, analytic focus, and praxis. Although a comprehensive discussion of these differences has been published by me elsewhere (Fairhurst, 2007),

Table 36.1   Key differences between discursive and psychological lenses*

	Discursive Lens	Psychological Lens
Object of study	Discourse	Mental theater
Ontology	Decentered subjects/thin actors	Essences
Power	Encompassing views of power and influence	Power and influence as dualisms
Agency	Reflexive agency	Untheorized/exaggerated agency
Analytic Focus	Textual, con-textual	Variable analytic
Praxis	Communication as primary, more meaning-centered, and distinct from discourse	Communication as secondary and transmissional

*Adapted from Fairhurst (2007, 2008).

a brief discussion of them in this chapter is worthwhile because they supply an organizing framework for the research on the discursive leadership approaches to be presented here. Due to page limits, emphasis will be given to representative research; more comprehensive accounts of the literature lie elsewhere (Cunliffe, 2009; Fairhurst, 2009; Fairhurst & Grant, 2010; Putnam & Fairhurst, 2001).

Before moving on, I should also note that newcomers to organizational discourse research may find several of its concepts strikingly mundane (Edwards, 1997). For example, when leadership can impact life-and-death struggles in high-reliability police organizations, conversational turn-taking or category use may seem like minutia (Fairhurst, 2008). But to borrow Staw's distinction (1985) between research that is *problem driven* versus *literature driven*, the study of *d/D*iscourse generally gets its import from the former not the latter. As such, discursive research tends not to concern itself with gaps in the literature, inconsistent findings, or converging evidence, but instead focuses on localized problems, issues, or tensions in which there is meaning (negotiation) work and coordinated action of some kind. In a very visceral sense then, discursive approaches to leadership and leadership psychology undertake different kinds of research, which this chapter aims to show. Its possible complementarity with leadership psychology will be among the subjects of discussion at the chapter's end.

OBJECT OF STUDY: DISCOURSE VS MENTAL THEATER

To understand the concept of 'discourse' fully, one should become familiar with the following schools of thought that place *d/D*iscourse, language, and/or

communication at their core: ethnomethodology (Boden, 1990; Garfinkel, 1967), conversation analysis (Boden, 1994; Drew & Heritage, 1992; Heritage, 1997), interaction analysis and its coding schemes (Bakeman & Gottman, 1986; Fairhurst, 2004), speech act analysis (Cooren, 2001; Cooren & Fairhurst, 2004; Searle, 1979), discursive psychology (Edwards & Potter, 1992; Potter, 2003; Potter & Wetherell, 1987), poststructuralist analysis (Foucault, 1972, 1990, 1995), critical discourse analysis (Fairclough, 2003; Fairclough & Wodak, 1997), narrative approaches (Boje, 2001; Czarniawska, 2004; Gabriel, 2004), semiotics (Greimas & Courtes, 1982; Hodge & Kress, 1988), and the like. As one might expect from such a substantial list, definitions and orientations toward the term 'discourse' vary substantially. As mentioned above, I follow the lead of Alvesson and Kärreman (2000b) who parsimoniously distinguish between *d*iscourse and *D*iscourse and, as necessary, points in between.

Generally speaking, as an object of study leadership psychology appears enamored with 'mental theater,' Cronen's (1995) term for psychologists' need to 'get beneath and behind experience to fret out the connections among cognitions, emotions, and behaviors' (p. 29). A quick perusal of *The Leadership Quarterly* will find that leadership psychologists frequently build and test causal models filled with a host of cognitive and affective variables impacting or impacted by leadership behavior. Applied to the post-positivist study of psychological processes, these models will do just fine. However, the interaction they study is mostly statistical (Hosking & Morley, 1991). Any sense of coordinated action or real experience is lost to their method of choice – surveys and seven-point scales whose strengths lie in retrospective *summaries* of behavior.

By contrast, organizational discourse analysts study *d/D*iscourse in leader–member talk-in-interaction, interview discourse, or discursive formations either as stand-alone systems of thought or in dialogically grounded communicative practices. As demonstrated below, discursive scholars generally prefer to study the actual processes of social interaction versus asking leadership actors to look back and self-report on same.

Little 'd' discourse

For example, focusing on little 'd' discourse, Fairhurst and Cooren (2004) undertook a relational control coded interaction analysis, an episodic speech act analysis, and an ethnomethodology-informed conversation analysis to analyze police supervisors' rescue of a wounded officer. Studying the sequences and temporal forms of control patterns and task completions in the police interaction of the first two analyses, leadership comes off as a much more distributed phenomenon based on a wider distribution of influential acts of organizing. Such an outcome was also evident in Vine et al.'s (2008) study in which co-leaders dynamically shifted task and maintenance-oriented roles to share the performance of leadership. The more traditional focus of leadership psychology has been a designated leader due to role occupancy (Gronn, 2002).

In Fairhurst and Cooren's (2004) conversation analysis, emphasis was placed on the category-based, interactional work of the police supervisors and other actors as they made claims about the world and their actions accountable (Sacks, 1992). Such analyses showed all leadership actors to be continual category users, whether they were coordinating the rescue; creating or invoking social or organizational roles and identities; relationally positioning themselves; engaging in sensemaking and social theorizing; setting and solving problems; or resolving contested problem formations.

In a study surrounding the controversy of the first openly gay US Episcopalian bishop, Sheep (2006) studied the ways in which category elasticity or 'stretch' enabled Episcopalian leaders to embrace or reject multiple, conflicting, or ambivalent identities in talk. Category elasticity was constructed metaphorically in discourse with phrasings such as 'the straw that broke the camel's back' and 'tipping point' by a group of people who had reached their limit on compromise over controversial issues (thus constructing the limit of their elasticity). Sheep also demonstrated how leaders' construction of their factionalized identities, either as held in tension with references to 'communion' or as irreconcilably different with references to 'schism,' counted as 'moral performance.' Shifting contexts of divergent Episcopalian Discourses, emphasized either 'inclusion' or 'biblical authority', legitimated 'morality.'

Bryman (2004) characterizes the mainstream literature's view of leadership as the management of meaning as a 'lofty and slightly nebulous' notion, divorced from mundane, immediate, instrumental, and material concerns and likely restricted to senior leaders charged with organizational change (p. 754). However, a discursive view demonstrates how leadership actors in everyday situations routinely bring the 'management of meaning' to life with detail and specificity as category users. Analysis of almost *any* segment of discourse of the police rescue or Episcopalian leaders reveals not only continuous categorization work but also its entrenchment in the mundane, immediate, instrumental, and material aspects of organizational life.

Big 'D' Discourse

Leadership scholars often disagree on a definition of leadership (Alvesson & Sveningsson, 2003a; Barker, 1997; Rost, 1991), perhaps because they fail to question the naturalness or the take-for-granted way in which the concept is viewed. Consider du Gay and Salaman (1996) who argue that what management 'is' and how it is to be performed (and, by implication, as something either synonymous with or different from leadership) is historically rooted in larger Discourses of the day. For example, to handle the turbulence of late twentieth- and twenty-first-century new market economies marked by global outreach, technological advance, and cost-saving labor practices, organizations sought senior executives who could effectively reshape their organizations to compete in a global environment. In the double hermeneutic of the academy and the business press, 'managers' became the technicians with day-to-day know-how and skill, while 'leaders' were cast as change masters (Bryman, 1992; 1996; Fairhurst & Sarr, 1996; Hickman, 1990; Kanter, 1983; Kotter, 1990; Pondy, 1978; Rost, 1991; Zaleznik, 1977).

With visionary and verbal acuity, leaders could transform organizations and win over employees' minds and hearts frequently beyond the terms of their formal employment contract (Bennis & Nanus, 1985; Kotter, 1990; Kouzes & Posner, 1995). Transformational (Bass, 1985, 1988), charismatic (Conger & Kanungo, 1987; House, 1977; Shamir, House & Arthur, 1993), and visionary (Bennis & Nanus, 1985; Westley & Mintzberg, 1989) leadership theories (discussed at length in Chapters 3 and 16 of this Handbook) thus emerged as part of the neo-charisma Discourses that purported to explain leaders' extraordinary capabilities in terms of charisma, personal appeal, and a powerful vision for change. For many leaders, the transition to business celebrity was not far behind (Guthey, Clark & Jackson, 2009; Jackson, 2001).

By capitalizing on colloquial uses of the term 'leadership' during this era not as 'an individual quality to be obtained by careful selection procedures' but 'the *effectiveness* of an individual in a specific role within a specific group united for a particular purpose' (Miller & Rose, 1990, p. 22, emphasis added), neo-charisma Discourses sought to equate transforming leadership with 'true' leadership (Bryman, 1992). By comparison, an examination of several previous management *D*iscourses, for example, that of the Industrial Revolution (early twentieth century), human relations (1940s–1950s), human resources (1960s), or Total Quality (1970s–1980s), shows that the terms 'leadership' and 'management' are with few exceptions largely interchangeable. It also shows that, following Foucault (1980, 1995), the politics of (leadership) truth vary by historical era.

To recap, leadership psychologists are enamored with leadership actors' cognitive and affective orientations, while *d*iscursive approaches focus on the dynamics of their social interaction and *D*iscursive socio-historical systems of thought focus on what leadership or management 'is' and how it is to be performed.

ONTOLOGY: THIN ACTORS/DECENTERED SUBJECTS VS ESSENCES

A social constructionist stance opposes essentializing theory in which things are what they are because that is the true nature of things (Hacking, 1999). Thus, for leadership phenomena, its underlying form or *essence* merely awaits discovery. Such a stance underlies Grint's (2000) critique of traditional leadership theories for essentializing leaders (for example, trait theories of leadership), the context (such as situational leadership theories) or person–context combinations such as when a strong leader and a crisis coincide (contingency theories of leadership) (see Antonakis, Chapter 20 and Yukl, Chapter 21, in this volume).

Such theorizing is emblematic of the kind of work that has led organizational scholars over the years to bemoan both the lack of agreed-upon definitions of leadership and a body of consistent findings to the point of arguing for its diminishment or abandonment as a concept (Calder, 1977; Davis-Blake & Pfeffer, 1989; Kerr & Jermier, 1978; Martin, 1992; Meindl, Ehrlich & Dukerich, 1985; Pfeffer, 1978; Rost, 1991, 1993; Salancik & Pfeffer, 1977). Grint (2000) proposes to help resolve these issues by rejecting essentializing

theory in lieu of leadership as social construction. The latter supplies analysts with the tools to grapple with communication's unending detail and variety, including sensemaking, vocabularies, and ways of talking (Fairhurst, 2007; Pye, 2005).

Grint's (2000, 2005) work on the paradoxes of leadership is exemplary here. Through in-depth case history analyses of several political and organizational leaders, he focuses on the contested nature of leadership interaction and the inventive, creative aspects of leadership-making that explains why it is more art than science. As such, Grint highlights persuasion rather than reason or rationality and irony rather than truth. He does so by focusing on the collective identities upon which much leadership rests, which are not 'reflected' in empiricist data as much as they are 'forged' amidst challenge and conflict. Outcomes are far less predictable as a result, despite a literature body whose writers, especially in the US business press, often confidently proclaim the opposite.

Kelly and colleagues (Kelly, 2008; Kelly et al., 2006) likewise adopt a non-essentialist leadership approach using ethnomethodology and Wittgenstein's (1953) notions of 'forms of life' and 'language games.' Ethnomethodology eschews essentialism by forcing analysts to understand leadership from the perspective of the actors involved. Analysts must look to *how* members occasion and account for leadership behavior through their stock of taken-for-granted knowledge, knowledge that surfaces the inseparability of language, meaning, and action.

By doing so, leadership is repeatedly constituted as a form of life via a series of 'language games.' The latter expression is unfortunate in this day and age because it suggests a mere focus on language, much as Pondy (1978) cast leadership as a language game, or as the pejorative expression 'game playing' implies (conjuring up images of manipulation and deceit). Kelly's use of the term, à la Wittgenstein (1953), is about patterns and routines among leadership actors whose logics are always organized from within the interactions themselves, not the putatively enduring qualities of the actors involved, the situations they face, or some combination thereof. Leadership thus has no single essence:

> Leadership itself is *not* a language game, but rather a *family resemblance* among language games; games which are themselves built upon a stock of taken-for-granted interpretive resources. As such leadership should be treated as what Wittgenstein (1958: aphorism 71) calls a 'blurred concept' around and through which language games orient themselves and can be played out in the practical accomplishment of other kinds of work. (Kelly, 2008, p. 775)

Unless such a move is made, Kelly argues that leadership study is destined to 'continue to occupy that paradoxical space...in which leadership is both potentially real and knowable, but upon closer inspection just manages to slip out of sight' (p. 776). Too little focus on actors' situated enactments and accounts will perpetuate such a dynamic.

However, in a direct challenge to the social constructionist and ethnomethodological arguments of Grint and Kelly, respectively, is Hammersley (2003), who finds fault in their rejecting of attitudes, motives, personalities, strategic orientations and the like as explanatory devices. He critiques discursive approaches for focusing so heavily on publicly available, cultural resources that they fail to capture anything that is unique or specific about actors in favor of what any member of a linguistic community could or would do. In a rejoinder to this critique, Potter (2003) argues that 'a certain kind of thinness,' best characterized as lacking 'a predefined model of the human actor,' is necessary in order to focus on social practices, the constitutive role of language, and the contributions of the cultural (pp. 78–79). More poststructuralist approaches go much further than thin actors to focus instead on decentered subjects, in which the self is neither fixed nor essentialized but multiplicatively located in d/Discourse and where Discourse articulates various subjectivities with both empowering and disempowering effects. As the discussion at the end of the chapter reveals, Hammersley's critique raises key questions for discursive scholars related to behaviors that are distinctive to leadership actors across time and context.

To summarize, theories within leadership psychology tend to fix leadership in the person, the situation, or person–situation combinations. Discursive approaches to leadership research are less essentializing, preferring instead to focus on the situated and linguistic, cultural construction of leadership.

POWER: ENCOMPASSING VS DUALISTIC VIEWS OF POWER AND INFLUENCE

Collinson (2006) argues that the mainstream leadership literature treats power and influence as distinct processes (see Gordon, Chapter 14, in this volume). Power is associated with forced compliance, and thus is viewed negatively as a repressive property exercised in a top-down manner. Influence is associated with voluntary compliance and is often the very embodiment of the term 'leadership' (Antonakis, Cianciolo & Sternberg, 2004; Rost, 1991; Yukl, 2002), in

Collinson's words, a 'positive process of disproportionate social influence' (pp. 181–182). Conventional wisdom has it that leadership fails when leaders must resort to their authority to gain compliance. Such a view also explains our admiration for charismatic leaders who excel at the influence game: for example, Barack Obama, whose meteoric rise to the top of American politics in just four short years was propelled by a spellbinding speech at the 2004 Democratic National Convention.

A discursive perspective eschews a power–influence dualism, adopting instead a much more encompassing view of power and influence, one that integrates their various forms and conceives of them in both positive and negative terms. Discourse scholars typically draw from critical management studies (CMS) here because its poststructuralist, neo-Marxist, and postcolonial schools of thought are shot through with power (Cunliffe, 2009; Collinson, Chapter 13, in this volume), despite widespread disagreement over use of the terms 'leadership' versus 'management' (Fairhurst & Grant, 2010).

For example, the poststructuralist view draws heavily from Foucault (1990; 1995) for whom power is local, relational, and embedded in specific technologies governed by Discourses with the power to discipline. Such technologies are usually aided by surveillance systems that turn individuals into knowable and calculable objects (Miller & Rose, 1990), thus revealing the individualizing effects of power, especially as individuals come to discipline themselves around that which a Discourse normalizes.

Drawing from investigations of the power dynamics in performance management technologies such as the performance appraisal (Newton, 1994; Newton & Findlay, 1996; Townley, 1989, 1992, 1993), Fairhurst (2007) examined 360-degree feedback and executive coaching as key leadership development technologies. The use of 360-degree feedback is emblematic of Foucault's (1995) examination technology with its panoptic surveillance capabilities. Executive coaching is emblematic of Foucault's (1990) confessional technology because a quasi-therapeutic relationship develops between coach and leader who is usually an alpha male, the targeted object of executive coaching Discourse. Such a Discourse can be found in books like *Alpha Male Syndrome* (Ludeman & Erlandson, 2006), which targets the worst of alpha male leadership behavior for extinction. Targeted behavior might include an overriding need for control, the acting out of such a need, and reliance on masculinity Discourses to maintain an instrumentalism and emotional distance in social relationships. Disciplinary techniques include calibrated levels of hard-hitting emotional feedback from the alpha's coworkers and tools like a 'defensiveness scale' to help him control his reactivity. Tools such as these show how alpha male leaders are positioned to be, in the words of Shapiro (1992), 'passive receptors' of meaning as much as they are its managers and transformative agents.

Ironically, in *Alpha Male Syndrome* alpha females' leader behavior does not rise to the level of 'syndrome' because women's stylistic 'softness' creates the opposite problem of not being alpha-enough to be seen as natural leaders. Female leaders are thus urged to emulate their male colleagues to a certain degree because 'alpha' is tantamount to being a 'leader.' Yet, when executive coaching advances what is often regarded as the feminine cure of empathy, listening, and shared control for extreme alpha-ness, such labeling is largely bereft of any feminine association. Women have no chance to be 'natural leaders' because gender differences are inscribed in such a way that it naturalizes masculinity and males as the leadership norm and 'others' the female leader (Fairhurst, 2007; Fairhurst et al., 2011).

Using a Foucauldian framework to investigate a more full-blown view of power dynamics in executive coaching reveals a subtlety that goes well beyond the simple dualism of forced versus voluntary compliance, a dualism often perpetuated in leadership psychology. Discursive approaches to leadership favor the more encompassing view of power and control that CMS approaches afford, which forthcoming research in this review will also show.

AGENCY: REFLEXIVE VS UNTHEORIZED/ EXAGGERATED AGENCY

Bryman (1996) argues that, 'Leadership theory and research have been remarkably and surprisingly uncoupled from the more general field in which they are located' (p. 289). Gronn (2000) and Robinson (2001) suggest this is because leadership psychology often undertheorizes task performance. Hosking (1988) argues that mainstream leadership researchers conceptualize the organization as an already formed entity instead of in a state of becoming. Consequently, leaders are often untheorized as agents while overriding relational concerns, the object of their measurement, supersede any link between leadership and influential acts of organizing. Interestingly, Gronn (2000) makes the case for exaggerated agency based on a pervasive sense of individualism and leader-centrism in leadership psychology. Leadership is thus romanticized (Bligh & Schyns, 2007; Meindl et al., 1985) or hero-anointing (Yukl, 1999).

Discursive approaches tend to emphasize reflexive agency, which is based on the more general ethnomethodological argument of Garfinkel (1967) wherein action is organized from within. Leadership actors are knowledgeable agents reflexively monitoring the ongoing character of social life as they continuously orient to and position themselves with respect to others in interaction. Moreover, language use offers us a window on human agency (Boden, 1994). However, discursive approaches vary in how much knowledgeability they attribute to actors, the role of multiple and competing Discourses, and how the material intervenes to constrain human action. The last two topics are frequent concerns within CMS and are addressed separately below.

Multiple Discourses

Through Discourse, agency becomes a key issue by specifying subjectivities with both empowering and disempowering effects, effects that can be magnified in the case of multiple and competing Discourses. For example, in their study of the Discourse of strategy, Laine and Vaara (2007) observed senior management's use of a strategy Discourse to gain control of an organization during a tumultuous time, while other leadership actors resisted through competing strategizing Discourses that enabled them to carve out a space of action (Daudi, 1986; Holmer-Nadesan, 1996). In particular, middle managers found room to maneuver by deploying an entrepreneurial Discourse, while engineers distanced themselves from both senior and middle management strategy Discourses to preserve a threatened professional identity.

Laine and Vaara's (2007) work builds on Knights and Morgan's (1991) agenda-setting work on strategy Discourse and the agency and identities of leadership actors, in particular, by highlighting actors other than senior management who engage in strategizing. Moreover, their findings also support Zoller and Fairhurst's (2007) notion of resistance leadership in which the seemingly incongruous literatures of critical theory and leadership psychology can be bridged to understand the emergence of resistance leaders.

Materiality

On the subject of how the material (the physical world) and the institutional (such as social or economic structures) intervenes to constrain human action, the work on discourse and technology is instructive. For example, Leonardi and Jackson (2004) studied a merger of high-technology companies and found that company leaders used a technologically determinate *D*iscourse to situate the merger in technological rather than cultural terms. Leonardi (2008) argues that leaders will often leverage a *D*iscourse of technological determinism to create a *D*iscourse of inevitability that subtly works at the level of perception and that 'plays on perceptions as the primary interface with the world in a way that makes certain (human-technological) relationships appear natural and uncontestable' (p. 979). Such efforts at control may stymie more organic technology adoption processes based on localized individual or task orientations. In bringing a critical discursive orientation to this topic, Leonardi's goal is to encourage more reflexive agency for those subject to the *D*iscourses of technological determinism and inevitability and also demonstrate the ways in which the material can be discursively enrolled in social construction processes. This is yet another application of CMS within the leadership arena.

Materiality gets a different treatment from leadership scholars who focus on non-human agency, such as in Parry and Hansen (2007), where the organizational story becomes the leader. More ambitiously, Fairhurst and Cooren (2009) use actor-network theory (Callon, 1986; Latour, 2005) to study charismatic leadership presence and its corresponding phenomena of leadership 'absence.' They sought to understand the magical or mesmerizing effect that some leaders have by focusing on all that they make present (for example, through texts, the body, technologies, *D*iscourses, and so on) and how such features cohere in a distributed actor network of human and non-human hybrid forms.

Neither leadership presence nor absence is considered an 'empirical given' but involves a complex analytic judgment of authors/narrators gauging the impact of various human and non-human actants in network construction, in conjunction with a set of historical/network conditions, and an articulation of the relevant *D*iscourses that give meaning to such constructions and conditions. By conceiving of the world as a plenum of agencies (Cooren, 2006) – i.e. as filled with beings with variable ontologies that 'make a difference' in situ a key aspect of leadership consists of making these actants present or absent amidst other human and non-human networking. Such an approach explains the attributed leadership 'presence' of US New York Mayor Rudy Giuliani and California Governor Arnold Schwarzenegger and the leadership 'absence' of Louisiana Governor Kathleen Blanco following the crises (9/11, California wildfires, and Hurricane Katrina, respectively) that befell their communities.

A key mission of discursive leadership approaches then is to explicitly acknowledge the reflexive agency of leadership actors and counter claims of exaggerated agency by focusing on the space of action created by multiple *D*iscourses and how the material world works to constrain the agency of all too human leadership actors.

ANALYTIC FOCUS: TEXTUAL, CON-TEXTUAL VS VARIABLE ANALYTIC

Leadership psychology's research is in the main post-positivist and variable analytic, which complements their essentializing theories. Context is not unimportant, but it is usually restricted to a few key variables of interest. Alternatively, little 'd' *d*iscourse analysts are neither concerned with the search for essences nor causal connections among variables. Instead, they want to know *how* a text functions pragmatically, *how* leadership is brought off in some here and now moment of localized interaction. In like fashion, big 'D' *D*iscourse analysts ask, *What* kind of leadership are we talking about? What cultural forces at play define what leadership 'is' and how it is to be performed in a particular social setting at a given historic moment (Biggart & Hamilton, 1987)? Because building generalizable theory is not an overriding concern, discourse scholars embrace a thicker description of the context, including both immediate and the cultural/political conditions favored within CMS (Fairhurst, 2009). Local knowledge is the aim, as text and con-text inevitably merge; that which is text one moment for the discourse analyst is con-text the very next.

The concept of 'text' has great currency in organizational discourse research because it can signify written records, memory traces, spoken discourse, or verbal routines. Texts also possess qualities like inscription and 'restance' (the capacity to be revisited) and may even become a metaphor for the organization itself with its abilities to layer and interweave (Cooren, 2001; Derrida, 1988; Taylor & Van Every, 2000).

For example, Vaara and Tienari (2008) examined micro-level discursive legitimation processes in a media text announcing a plant closing and relocation to another country. The CEO's words authorizing the closure were buttressed by the journalist's use of company share prices, thus introducing the 'market' as the ultimate authority in contemporary global capitalism. The positioning of the firm as a multinational corporation also legitimated future profitability as a motive to close even when the plant was not underperforming. Finally, a 'lifeboat' argument was used to justify the plant closure so that other plants in the country could survive. Vaara and Tienari thus demonstrate how this media text functions to legitimate change with significant social and material consequences in the form of a transfer of production and job loss.

Similarly, Craig and Amernic (2004) discursively analyzed two Enron-related texts, one just before the collapse of the firm (a 'Letter to Shareholders' from Ken Lay and Jeffrey Skilling in Enron's *Year 2000 Annual Report*) and the other after the collapse (Anderson CEO Joseph Berardino's written testimony to the US Congress in December 2001). Anderson Consulting was Enron's auditor and was thus positioned to stop or call attention to Enron's egregious accounting practices. For example, the 'Letter to Shareholders' voices the language of sports and war metaphors, with boasts of success 'by any measure' that reek of hyperbole and self-referential superlatives. The Letter also claims to be 'laser-focused' 'on earnings per share,' a measure whose technical construction is highly susceptible to manipulation according to Craig and Amernic.

By contrast, Berardino's frames his testimony before Congress in ways that marginalize the connection between accounting and auditing practices – and Anderson's culpability – with the collapse of Enron. He frames problems as systemic, issues as elusive, and an investigation not yet complete. He refers to the complex, arcane nature of accounting practices only to underscore the point with blinding explanations of specific accounting issues. With his greatest sympathy seemingly held for shareholders, he voices a *D*iscourse of resilient capitalism, which is not one of a broken economic system, merely one in need of tweaking as the 'market' remains the ultimate arbiter. Through Craig and Amernic's textual analyses of two leadership performances, we see the ways it which texts shape and are shaped by larger *D*iscourses of the day.

To recap, in leadership psychology the research is often positivist and variable analytic with a restricted view of the context. Discursive approaches to leadership tend to embrace the context, the close relationship between text and context, and the power-infused interplay among *D*iscourse(s) and *d*iscourse.

PRAXIS: COMMUNICATION AS PRIMARY VS COMMUNICATION AS SECONDARY

Communication bears an often-confused relationship to discourse (Fairhurst & Putnam, 2004). In articles from communication journals, 'communication' usually refers to a meaning-centered, constitutive use of language, whereas the term suggests an individually-oriented transmission or

general interaction process for those outside the communication discipline (Jian, Schmisseur & Fairhurst, 2008). For the latter, communication is often a simple transmission, an input or output of the cognitive domain of interest where meanings are rarely problematized (Axley, 1984). Organizational discourse analysts also tend not to study communication as a lived experience because they say relatively little, in direct terms, about the moment-to-moment lived dynamics of communicating actors. Unless the communicative experience is made central, communication is easily relegated to a secondary role.

In a challenge to this view, communication scholars Barge and Fairhurst (2008) argue that issues of praxis hinge on the distinction between 'communication' and 'discourse.' This is because communication speaks to key process issues – co-creation, connection, uniqueness, and emergence – all of which are associated with the *experience* of interacting with others much more so than the texts of discourse. (Think of communication as the 'doing' and text as the 'done.') Sensemaking, positioning, and play are three communicative practices necessary to understand leadership in-the-making according to these authors. Similarly, Ashman and Lawler (2008; Lawler, 2005) focus on leadership as a lived experience using existentialist concepts and principles such as 'being-in-the-world,' intersubjectivity, and dialogue. Such terms focus on the tension between the subjective experience of being led and the recognition of mutual engagement.

The communicative experience of leadership is also the subject of Western's (2008) use of critical theory to stimulate critical thinking skills about the dominance and privileging of certain 'leadership ideas, discourses and knowledge forms' and the marginalization of others with the 'explicit ethical aim of emancipation' (p. 9). This work is representative of a growing group of critical management educators who are trying to infuse management education with a sense of ethics, moral responsibility, reflexivity, and relational responsibility (Anthony, 1998; Cunliffe, 2004; 2009; Deetz, 1995; Fournier & Grey, 2000; Perriton & Reynolds, 2004; Sinclair, 2000; Watson, 1994). As Watson's (2001) work on negotiated narratives and Fairhurst's (2011) work on framing suggest, oftentimes this is done using insights achieved through discursive analyses.

Thus, in this emerging praxis literature, communication is not a secondary phenomenon as it is in leadership psychology. Instead, leadership-in-the-making takes center stage as a communicative, lived experience whose logics and vocabularies we are only beginning to discover as the next discussion suggests.

THE PATH FORWARD

The emergence of discursive approaches to leadership is testimony to the continued vitality of the leadership concept. Moreover, discursive leadership approaches are neither shackled by the lack of definitional agreement over the term, nor a body of inconsistent findings over whether and how leadership makes a difference, two issues that have been an albatross around the neck of leadership psychology for decades. However, there will be many who question the utility of a d/Discursively oriented science that does not strive for generalization.

What discursive leadership approaches and leadership psychology uniformly share are concerns over relevance and praxis. Regarding *relevance*, the key question here is: What are we learning about leadership through d/Discourse? We are learning that with an emphasis on little 'd' discourse, leadership is often much more distributed because we are able to track a wider distribution of influential acts of organizing. Leadership as the management of meaning also comes to life when we examine how leadership actors craft their category use in their everyday talk. Thus, leadership as the management of meaning is not the sole province of senior leaders advocating change, but is grounded in the routine, mundane aspects of organizational life for all leaders.

An examination of big 'D' Discourse reveals the socio-historical basis for conceiving of leadership, and thus explains why the concept morphs periodically to reflect the conditions of the world in which it resides. Moreover, recognizing the socio-historical basis of leadership does not necessarily commit the analyst to one specific view of leadership because discursive leadership places much more of a premium on (cultural) members' methods rather than those of analysts. Thus, leadership is indeed a language game – or, more accurately, a collection of games – as members figure out what leadership is in the context of what they do and persuade themselves and others that they are doing it (Kelly, 2008). An abundance of leadership language games does not spell error variance.

Importantly, we are learning of the subtle ways in which power is infused in leadership development technologies where leaders are much less the ultimate agents and managers of meaning and more like passive receptors of meaning. They discipline themselves in response to the presumed gaze of their role set as 360-degree feedback and executive coaching get institutionalized as performance management technologies. We also see how the positive regard for women leaders in books like *Alpha Male Syndrome* (Ludeman & Erlandson, 2006) continues a long tradition of disqualifying women as 'natural leaders,' albeit unintentionally.

We are learning about how to create the conditions for reflexive agency in leadership research, and how agency is enabled through multiple and competing *D*iscourses with various empowering and disempowering subjectivities. We are also seeking to uncover a view of agency that unlocks the secrets of the interface between the material and symbolic worlds. Such efforts are paying dividends in concepts like leadership presence and absence, once thought to be too abstract to study. Finally, we are learning how texts function as leadership positioning and legitimation devices, how they layer and interweave, and function as linguistic resources for future accounting(s) by leadership actors.

There is certainly a lot that we do not yet know, including clarification of that which individuals bring to the leadership relationship and that which culture supplies. Hammersley's (2003) critique of discursive approaches raises key questions for discursive leadership scholars related to behaviors (attitudes, motives, personalities, strategic orientations) that are distinctive to leadership actors across time and context. Potter (2003) correctly stipulates that the discursive bias is cultural in favor of what any member of a linguistic community could or would do.

Ostensibly, this should create the ideal conditions for multi-paradigm work (Deetz, 1996; Gioia & Pitre, 1990; Hassard, 1991; Schultz & Hatch, 1996; Weaver & Gioia, 1994). As the Hammersley–Potter debate suggests, leadership psychology and discursive approaches to leadership focus on different questions. Leadership psychologists typically ask cause–effect 'Why' questions ('Why do leaders or followers act a certain way?'), while *d*iscourse scholars ask 'How' questions ('How is leadership brought off?') and *D*iscourse scholars ask 'What' questions ('What kind of leadership are we talking about?') (Fairhurst, 2007).

Problems surface, however, when researchers of one stripe venture into territory best covered by the other's perspective. For example, little 'd' *d*iscursive leadership scholars are often qualitative and argue by example (Jackson, 1986). However, this does not stop some from making unwarranted quantitative claims in their research based on a presumed pattern rather than an empirical demonstration of same. At the same time, leadership psychologists' overreliance on self-report data often ignores the fact that relationships are codefined. They use such data as a proxy for interaction process as if a single relational reality can be presumed (Fairhurst, 2007). Multi-paradigm work may thus be difficult, but it is necessary to understand the multiplicity of questions surrounding leadership in the twenty-first century.

Moreover, there is still much to know about the power of *Discourse* to discipline leaders through leadership development technologies, relationship expectations, or organizational strictures. This is necessary not just to supply a counterweight to the hero-making tendencies of neo-Charisma *Discourses*, but to understand how the constraints and enablements of leadership-making work in tandem in situ.

In addition to issues related to the relevance of discursive leadership approaches and what we learn from them, the second key issue is *praxis* and how can we best help leaders and followers. In many ways, this area is still in its nascent stages even as social constructionists (Cooperrider, Barrett & Srivastva, 1995; Hacking, 1999), action theorists (Argyris & Schon, 1978, 1996; Schon, 1983), and now critical management educators (Anthony, 1998; Barge & Fairhurst, 2008; Cunliffe, 2004, 2009; Deetz, 1995; Fournier & Grey, 2000; Perriton & Reynolds, 2004; Watson, 1994, 2001) have made important contributions.

However, according to the Boston Change Process Study Group and, specifically, the work of Tronick (2007) and Stern (2004) in mother–infant interactions and therapy contexts, what we need is a language of the present and not a language of third-party observation. The latter can inform the former, much as discursive research informs critical management education. But there is still much to learn because, as the Boston Group suggests, a language of the present lights up with affect, different ways and types of knowing involving mind and body, and meaning on possibly multiple levels. It is certainly a tall order, but one worth pursuing in an increasingly complex world in need of leadership solutions.

REFERENCES

Alvesson, M. & Kärreman, D. (2000a). Taking the linguistic turn in organizational research. *Journal of Applied Behavioral Science, 36*, 1125–1149.

Alvesson, M. & Kärreman, D. (2000b). Varieties of discourse: on the study of organizations through discourse analysis. *Human Relations, 53*, 1125–1149.

Alvesson, M. & Sveningsson, S. (2003a). The great disappearing act: difficulties in doing 'leadership'. *The Leadership Quarterly, 14*, 359–381.

Alvesson, M. & Sveningsson, S. (2003b). Managers doing leadership: the extra-ordinization of the mundane. *Human Relations, 56*, 1435–1459.

Anthony, P. (1998). Management education: ethics versus morality. In M. Parker (eds), *Ethics and organization*. London: Sage, pp. 269–281.

Antonakis, J., Cianciolo, A. T. & Sternberg, R. J. (2004). Leadership: past, present and future. In J. Antonakis, A. T. Cianciolo & R. J. Sternberg (eds), *The nature of leadership*. Thousand Oaks, CA: Sage, pp. 3–15.

Argyris, C. & Schön, D. A. (1978). *Organizational learning: a theory of action perspective*. Reading, MA: Addison-Wesley.

Argyris, C. & Schön, D. A. (1996). *Organizational learning II: theory, method and practice*. Reading, MA: Addison-Wesley.

Ashman, I. & Lawler, J. (2008). Existential communication and leadership. *Leadership, 4*, 253–269.

Axley, S. R. (1984). Managerial and organizational communication in terms of the conduit metaphor. *Academy of Management Review, 9*, 428–437.

Bakeman, R. & Gottman, J. M. (1986). *Observing interaction: an introduction to sequential analysis*. Cambridge, UK: Cambridge University Press.

Barge, J. K. (2004). Reflexivity and managerial practice. *Communication Monographs, 71*, 70–96.

Barge, J. K. & Fairhurst, G. T. (2008). Living leadership: a systemic, constructionist approach. *Leadership, 4*, 227–251.

Barker, R. A. (1997). How can we train leaders if we do not know what leadership is? *Human Relations, 50*, 343–362.

Bass, B. M. (1985). *Leader and performance: beyond expectations*. New York: Free Press.

Bass, B. M. (1988). Evolving perspectives on charismatic leadership. In J. A. Conger & R. N. Kanungo (eds), *Charismatic leadership*. San Francisco, CA: Jossey-Bass, pp. 40–77.

Bennis, W. G. & Nanus, B. (1985). *Leaders: strategies for taking charge*. New York: Harper & Row.

Biggart, N. W. & Hamilton, G. G. (1987). An institutional theory of leadership. *Journal of Applied Behavioral Science, 23*, 429–442.

Bligh, M. C. & Schyns, B. (2007). The romance lives on: contemporary issues surrounding the romance of leadership. *Leadership, 3*, 343–360.

Boden, D. (1990). The world as it happens: ethnomethodology and conversation analysis. In G. Ritzer (eds), *Frontiers of social theory: the new synthesis*. New York: Columbia University Press, pp. 185–213.

Boden, D. (1994). *The business of talk: organizations in action*. Cambridge, UK: Polity Press.

Boje, D. (2001). *Narrative methods for organizational and communication research*. London: Sage.

Bryman, A. (1992). *Charisma and leadership in organizations*. London: Sage.

Bryman, A. (1996). Leadership in organizations. In S. R. Clegg, C. Hardy & W. R. Nord (eds), *Handbook of organization studies*. London: Sage, pp. 276–292.

Bryman, A. (2004). Qualitative research on leadership: a critical but appreciative review. *The Leadership Quarterly, 15*, 729–770.

Calder, B. J. (1977). An attribution theory of leadership. In B. M. Staw & G. R. Salancik (eds), *New directions in organizational behavior*. Chicago, IL: St. Clair Press, 179–202.

Callon, M. (1986). The sociology of an actor-network. In M. Callon, J. Law & A. Rip (eds), *Mapping the dynamics of science and technology*. London: Macmillan.

Collinson, D. L. (2005). Dialectics of leadership. *Human Relations, 58*, 1419–1442.

Collinson, D. L. (2006). Rethinking followership: a post-structuralist analysis of follower identities. *The Leadership Quarterly, 17*, 179–189.

Conger, J. A. & Kanungo, R. M. (1987). Toward a behavioral theory of charismatic leadership in organizational settings. *Academy of Management Review, 12*, 637–647.

Cooperrider, D., Barrett, F. & Srivastva, S. (1995). Social construction and appreciative inquiry: a journey in organizational theory. In D. Hosking, P. Dachler & K. Gergen (eds), *Management and organization: relational alternatives to individualism.* Aldershot: Avebury Press, pp. 157–200.

Cooren, F. (2001). *The organizing property of communication.* Amsterdam/Philadelphia: John Benjamins.

Cooren, F. (2006). The organizational world as a plenum of agencies. In F. Cooren, J. R. Taylor & E. J. V. Every (eds). *Communication as organizing: empirical and theoretical explorations in the dynamic of text and conversation.* Mahwah, NJ: Lawrence Erlbaum, pp. 81–100.

Cooren, F. (ed) (2007). *Interacting and organizing: analyses of a board meeting.* Mahwah, NJ: Lawrence Erlbaum.

Cooren, F. & Fairhurst, G. (2004). Speech timing and spacing: the phenomenon of organizational closure. *Organization, 11*, 797–828.

Craig, R. J. & Amernic, J. H. (2004). Enron discourse: the rhetoric of a resilient capitalism. *Critical Perspective on Accounting, 15*, 813–851.

Cronen, V. E. (1995). Coordinated management of meaning: the consequentiality of communication and the recapturing of experience. In S. J. Sigman (eds), *the consequentiality of communication.* Hillsdale, NJ: Lawrence Erlbaum, pp. 17–65.

Cunliffe, A. L. (2001). Managers as practical authors: reconstructing our understanding of managerial practice. *Journal of Management Studies, 38*, 350–371.

Cunliffe, A. L. (2004). On becoming a critically reflexive practitioner. *Journal of Management Education, 28*, 407–426.

Cunliffe, A. L. (2009). *A very short, fairly interesting and reasonably cheap book about management.* Los Angeles, CA: Sage.

Czarniawska, B. (2004). *Narratives in social science research.* London: Sage.

Daudi, G. (1986). *Power in the organization.* Cornwall: T.J. Press.

Davis-Blake, A. & Pfeffer, J. (1989). Just a mirage: the search for dispositional effects in organizational research. *Academy of Management Review, 14*, 385–400.

Deetz, S. A. (1995). *Transforming communication, transforming business: building responsive and responsible workplaces.* Cresskill, NJ: Hampton Press.

Deetz, S. A. (1996). Describing differences in approaches to organization science: rethinking Burrell and Morgan and their legacy. *Organization Science, 7*, 190–207.

Derrida, J. (1988). *Limited inc.* Evanston, IL: Northwestern University Press.

Drew, P. & Heritage, J. (eds) (1992). *Talk at work: interaction in institutional settings.* Cambridge, UK: Cambridge University Press.

du Gay, P. & Salaman, G. (1996). The conduct of management and the management of conduct: contemporary managerial discourse and the constitution of the 'competent manager'. *Journal of Management Studies, 33*, 263–282.

Edwards, D. (1997). *Discourse and cognition.* London: Sage.

Edwards, D. & Potter, J. (1992). *Discursive psychology.* London: Sage.

Fairclough, N. (2003). *Analysing discourse: textual analysis for social research.* London: Routledge.

Fairclough, N. & Wodak, R. (1997). Critical discourse analysis. In T. A. van Dijk (eds), *Discourse as social interaction.* London: Sage, pp. 258–284.

Fairhurst, G. T. (2004). Textuality and agency in interaction analysis. *Organization, 11*, 335–354.

Fairhurst, G. T. (2007). *Discursive leadership: in conversation with leadership psychology.* Thousand Oaks, CA: Sage.

Fairhurst, G. T. (2008). Discursive leadership: a communication alternative to leadership psychology. *Management Communication Quarterly, 21*, 510–521.

Fairhurst, G. T. (2009). Considering context in discursive leadership research. *Human Relations, 62*(11), 1607–1633.

Fairhurst, G. T. (2011) *The power of framing: creating the language of leadership.* San Francisco, CA: Jossey-Bass.

Fairhurst, G. T., Church, M., Hagen, D. E. & Levi, J. T. (2011) Whither female leaders? Executive coaching and the alpha male syndrome. In D. Mumby (eds), *Discourses of difference.* Thousand Oaks, CA: Sage, pp. 77–100.

Fairhurst, G. T. & Cooren, F. (2004). Organizational language in use: interaction analysis, conversation analysis, and speech act schematics. In D. Grant, C. Hardy, C. Oswick, N. Phillips & L. Putnam (eds), *The Sage handbook of organizational discourse.* London: Sage, pp. 131–152.

Fairhurst, G. T. & Cooren, F. (2009). Leadership as the hybrid production of presence(s). *Leadership, 5*, 1–22.

Fairhurst, G.T. & Grant, D. (2010). The social construction of leadership: A sailing guide. *Management Communication Quarterly, 24*, 171–210.

Fairhurst, G. T. & Putnam, L. L. (2004). Organizations as discursive constructions. *Communication Theory, 14*, 5–26.

Fairhurst, G. T. & Sarr, R. A. (1996). *The art of framing: managing the language of leadership.* San Francisco, CA: Jossey-Bass.

Foucault, M. (1972). *The archeology of knowledge and the discourse on language.* London: Tavistock.

Foucault, M. (1980). *Power/knowledge: selected interviews and other writings 1972–1977.* New York: Pantheon.

Foucault, M. (1990). *The history of sexuality: Volume 1.* New York: Vintage/Random House.

Foucault, M. (1995). *Discipline and punish.* New York: Vintage/Random House.

Fournier, V. & Grey, C. (2000). At the critical moment: conditions and prospects for critical management studies. *Human Relations, 53*, 7–32.

Gabriel, Y. (2004). Narratives, stories, and texts. In C. H. D. Grant, C. Oswick, N. Phillips, & L. Putnam (eds), *Sage handbook of organizational discourse.* London: Sage, pp. 61–77.

Garfinkel, H. (1967). *Studies in ethnomethodology*. Englewood Cliffs, NJ: Prentice Hall.

Gioia, D. A. & Pitre, E. (1990). Multiparadigm perspectives on theory building. *Academy of Management Review, 15*, 584–602.

Greimas, A. J. & Courtes, J. (1982). *Semiotics and language: an analytical dictionary*. Bloomington, IN: Indiana University Press.

Grint, K. (2000). *The arts of leadership*. Oxford, UK: Oxford University Press.

Grint, K. (2005). Problems, problems, problems: the social construction of 'leadership'. *Human Relations, 58*, 1467–1494.

Gronn, P. (2000). Distributed properties: a new architecture for leadership. *Educational Management and Administration, 28*, 317–338.

Gronn, P. (2002). Distributed leadership as a unit of analysis. *The Leadership Quarterly, 13*, 423–451.

Guthey, E., Clark, T. & Jackson, B. (2009). *Demystifying business celebrity*. London: Routledge.

Hacking, I. (1999). *The social construction of what?* Cambridge, MA: Harvard University Press.

Hammersley, M. (2003). Conversation analysis and discourse analysis: methods or paradigms. *Discourse & Society, 14*, 751–781.

Hassard, J. (1991). Multiple paradigms and organizational analysis: a case study. *Organization Studies, 12*, 279–299.

Heritage, J. (1997). Conversation analysis and institutional talk. In D. Silverman (eds), *Qualitative research: theory, method and practice*. London: Sage, pp. 161–182.

Hickman, C. R. (1990). *Mind of a manager, soul of a leader*. New York: John Wiley.

Hodge, R. & Kress, G. (1988). *Social semiotics*. Cambridge, UK: Polity Press.

Holmer-Nadesan, M. (1996). Organizational identity and space of action. *Organization Studies, 17*, 49–81.

Hosking, D. M. (1988). Organizing, leadership and skilful process. *Journal of Management Studies, 25*, 147–166.

Hosking, D. M. & Morley, I. E. (1991). *A social psychology of organizing: people, processes and contexts*. New York: Harvester/Wheatsheaf.

House, R. J. (1977). A 1976 theory of charismatic leadership. In J. G. Hunt & L. L. Larson (eds), *Leadership: the cutting edge*. Carbondale, IL: Southern Illinois University Press, pp. 189–207.

Jackson, B. (2001). *Management gurus and management fashions: a dramatisitic inquiry*. London: Routledge.

Jackson, S. (1986). Building a case for claims about discourse structure. In D. G. Ellis & W. A. Donohue (eds), *Contemporary issues in language and discourse processes*. Hillsdale, NJ: Lawrence Erlbaum, pp. 129–147.

Jian, G., Schmisseur, A. & Fairhurst, G. T. (2008). Organizational discourse and communication: the progeny of Proteus. *Discourse & Communication, 2*, 299–320.

Kanter, R. M. (1983). *The changemasters*. New York: Simon & Schuster.

Kelly, S. (2008). Leadership: a categorical mistake? *Human Relations, 61*, 763–782.

Kelly, S., White, M. I., Martin, D. & Rouncefield, M. (2006). Leadership refrains: patterns of leadership. *Leadership, 2*, 181–201.

Kerr, S. & Jermier, J. M. (1978). Substitutes for leadership: their meaning and measurement. *Organizational Behavior and Human Performance, 12*, 374–403.

Knights, D. & Morgan, G. (1991). Corporate strategy, organizations, and subjectivity: a critique. *Organization Studies, 12*, 251–273.

Kotter, J. P. (1990). *A force for change: how leadership differs from management*. New York: Free Press.

Kouzes, J. M. & Posner, B. Z. (1995). *The leadership challenge: how to keep getting extraordinary things done in organizations*. San Francisco, CA: Jossey-Bass.

Laine, P.M. & Vaara, E. (2007). Struggling over subjectivity: a discursive analysis of strategic development in an engineering group. *Human Relations, 60*, 29–58.

Latour, B. (2005). *Reassembling the social: an introduction to actor-network theory*. New York: Oxford University Press.

Lawler, J. (2005). The essence of leadership? Existentialism and leadership. *Leadership, 1*, 215–231.

Leonardi, P. M. (2008). Indeterminacy and the discourse of inevitability in international technology management. *Academy of Management Review, 33*, 975–984.

Leonardi, P. M. & Jackson, M. H. (2004). Technological determinism and discursive closure in organizational mergers. *Journal of Organizational Change Management, 17*, 615–631.

Ludeman, K. & Erlandson, E. (2006). *Alpha male syndrome*. Boston, MA: Harvard Business School Press.

Martin, J. (1992). *Cultures in organizations: three perspectives*. Oxford: Oxford University Press.

Meindl, J. R., Ehrlich, S. B. & Dukerich, J. M. (1985). The romance of leadership. *Administrative Science Quarterly, 30*, 78–102.

Miller, P. & Rose, N. (1990). Governing economic life. *Economy and Society, 27*, 1–31.

Newton, T. (1994). Discourse and agency: the example of personnel psychology and 'Assessment Centres'. *Organization, 15*, 879–902.

Newton, T. & Findlay, P. (1996). Playing God? The performance appraisal. *Human Resource Management Journal, 6*, 42–58.

Parry, K. W. & Hansen, H. (2007). The organizational story as leadership. *Leadership, 3*, 281–300.

Perriton, L. & Reynolds, M. (2004). Critical management education: from pedagogy of possibility to pedagogy of refusal? *Management Learning, 35*, 61–77.

Pfeffer, J. (1978). The ambiguity of leadership. *Academy of Management Review, 2*, 104–112.

Pondy, L. R. (1978). Leadership is a language game. In J. M. W. McCall & M. M. Lombardo (eds), *Leadership: Where else can we go?* Durham, NC: Duke University Press, pp. 88–99.

Potter, J. (2003). Discursive psychology: between method and paradigm. *Discourse & Society, 14*, 783–794.

Potter, J. & Wetherell, M. (1987). *Discourse and social psychology*. London: Sage.

Putnam, L. L. & Fairhurst, G. T. (2001). Discourse analysis in organizations. In F. M. Jablin & L. L. Putnam (eds), *The new handbook of organizational communication*. Thousand Oaks, CA: Sage, pp. 78–136.

Pye, A. (2005). Leadership and organizing: sensemaking in action. *Leadership, 1*, 31–50.

Robinson, V. M. J. (2001). Embedding leadership in task performance. In K. Wong & C. W. Evers (eds), *Leadership for quality schooling*. London: Routledge/Falmer, pp. 90–102.

Rorty, R. (ed). (1967). *The linguistic turn: recent essays in philosophical method*. Chicago, IL: University of Chicago Press.

Rost, J. C. (1991). *Leadership for the twenty-first century*. New York: Praeger.

Rost, J. C. (1993). Leadership development in the new millenium. *Journal of Leadership Studies, 1*, 92–110.

Sacks, H. (1992). *Lectures on conversation, Vols. 1 and 2*. Oxford: Blackwell.

Salancik, G. R. & Pfeffer, J. (1977). Constraints on administrative discretion: the limited influence of mayors on city budgets. *Urban Affairs Quarterly, 12*, 485–498.

Schön, D. A. (1983). *The reflective practitioner: how professionals think in action*. New York: Basic Books.

Schultz, M. & Hatch, M. J. (1996). Living with multiple paradigms: the case of paradigm interplay in organizational culture studies. *Academy of Management Review, 21*, 529–557.

Searle, J. R. (1979). *Meaning and expression: studies in the theory of speech acts*. Cambridge, UK: Cambridge University Press.

Shamir, B., House, R. J. & Arthur, M. B. (1993). The motivational effects of charismatic leadership: a self-concept based theory. *Organization Science, 4*, 577–594.

Shapiro, M. (1992). *Reading the postmodern polity*. Minneapolis, MN: University of Minnesota Press.

Sheep, M. L. (2006). When categories collide: a discursive psychology approach to the elasticity of multiple identities. © ProQuest Dissertations & Theses. Cincinnati, Ohio, University of Cincinnati, 202 pages.

Sinclair, A. (2000). Teaching managers about masculinities: Are you kidding? *Management Learning, 31*, 83–101.

Staw, B. M. (1985). Repairs on the road to relevance and rigor: some unexplored issues in publishing organizational research. In L. L. Cummings & P. J. Frost (eds), *Publishing in the organizational sciences*. Homewood, IL: Irwin, pp. 96–107.

Stern, D. N. (2004). *The present moment in psychotherapy and everyday life*. New York: W.W. Norton & Co.

Taylor, J. R. & Robichaud, D. (2006). Management as metaconversation: the search for closure. In F. Cooren (eds), *Interacting and organizing: analyses of a board meeting*. Mahwah, NJ: Lawrence Erlbaum.

Taylor, J. R. & Van Every, E. (2000). *The emergent organization: communication at its site and surface*. Mahwah, NJ: Lawrence Erlbaum.

Tourish, D. & Vatcha, N. (2005). Charismatic leadership and corporate cultism at Enron: the elimination of dissent, the promotion of conformity and organizational collapse. *Leadership, 1*, 455–480.

Townley, B. (1989). Selection and appraisal: reconstituting 'social relations'. In J. Storey (eds), *New perspectives in human resource management*. London: Routledge.

Townley, B. (1992). In the eye of the gaze: the constitutive role of performance appraisal. In P. Barrar & C. Cooper (eds), *Managing organizations in 1992*. London: Routledge.

Townley, B. (1993). Performance appraisal and the emergence of management. *Journal of Management Studies, 30*, 27–44.

Tronick, E. (2007). *The neurobehavioral and social-emotional development of infants and children*. New York: W.W. Norton & Company.

Vaara, E. & Tienari, J. (2008). A discursive perspective on legitimation strategies in multinational corporations. *Academy of Management Review, 33*, 985–993.

Vine, B., Holmes, J., Marra, M., Pfeifer, D. & Jackson, B. (2008). Exploring co-leadership talk through interactional sociolinguistics. *Leadership, 4*, 339–360.

Watson, T. (1994). Towards a managerially relevant but non-managerialist organization theory. In J. Hassard & M. Parker (eds), *Towards a new theory of organizations*. London: Routledge, pp. 209–224.

Watson, T. (2001). Beyond managism: negotiated narratives and critical management education in practice. *British Journal of Management, 12*, 385–396.

Weaver, G. R. & Gioia, D. A. (1994). Paradigms lost: incommensurability vs structurationist inquiry. *Organization Studies, 15*, 565–590.

Western, S. (2008). *Leadership: a critical text*. London: Sage.

Westley, F. & Mintzberg, H. (1989). Visionary leadership and strategic management. *Strategic Management Journal, 10*, 17–32.

Wittgenstein, L. (1953). *Philosophical investigations*. Oxford: Blackwell.

Yukl, G. (1999). An evaluation of conceptual weaknesses in transformational and charismatic leadership theories. *The Leadership Quarterly, 10*, 285–305.

Yukl, G. (2002). *Leadership in organizations*, 5th edn. Upper Saddle River, NJ: Prentice Hall.

Zaleznik, A. (1977). Managers and leaders: Are they different? *Harvard Business Review, 55*, 67–78.

Zoller, H. M. & Fairhurst, G. T. (2007). Resistance as leadership: a critical, discursive perspective. *Human Relations, 60*, 1331–1360.

37

Being Leaders: Identities and Identity Work in Leadership

Amanda Sinclair

INTRODUCTION

Identity has been a central concern of social theorising for several decades, making appearances in the work of sociologists (Berger and Luckmann, 1966; Giddens, 1991), social psychologists (Gergen 1991) and cultural theorists, many of whom question psychological accounts of identity as an individual developmental accomplishment.

In this chapter I explore the ways in which ideas about identity have increasingly made their way into the study of leaders and leadership. Two broad and very different sets of understandings and prescriptions emerge from this work. On the one hand are more critical accounts of the production of leadership identities. This research examines the political and discursive processes by which manager and leader identities are manufactured, controlled and occasionally resisted (Alvesson and Sveningsson, 2003; Carroll and Levy, 2008; Collinson, 2003; Linstead 2006; Sveningsson and Larson, 2006; Thomas and Linstead, 2002; Thomas et al., 2004; Ford et al., 2008; Keenoy et al., 2009; Caza and Jackson, Chapter 26, Collinson, Chapter 13 and Fairhurst, Chapter 36, this volume). Often building on the work of Foucault, there is an interest in where subjectivities and prescribed identities do not overlap and what happens in these identity spaces of tension and contradiction.

On the other hand is a substantial and growing popular literature which offers advice on how leaders can be more effective by adapting, presenting and performing themselves (their identities). Here the emphasis is often unapologetically about how to be 'great' – how to build, maintain and project an authentic, effective leadership persona (Goffee

and Jones, 2005; George et al., 2007). In the latter genre, identity is usually assumed to be a unitary coherent construction produced by the individual, who is then exhorted on a treadmill of self-improvement (and, conveniently, leadership development and education) to either make the self watertight attractive or, alternatively, to reinvent to improve prospects for success and recognition. Such advice sits alongside and is fed by burgeoning forces encouraging the commoditization and marketing of the self: the leader as a brand. The vision or ideal is of a perfectible self-as-leader, including an appealing but 'fictional belief in the self as an autonomous entity' (Roberts, 2009).

The chapter examines these ways of thinking about identities and leadership, including some of the risks. Drawing on my experiences working with leaders, I argue the need to explore the construction of leadership identities in both a more critical and more mindful way. I also suggest that those of us who study and write about leadership should be explicit about our own identity work. 'Taking the lead' from a couple of examples (see Brewis, 2004; Hearn, 2004), I suggest that exploring the production of our own selves – as leaders of leadership scholarship – may be a foundational platform or gesture from which to make a reflexive contribution on leadership and identities.

IDENTITIES AND LEADERSHIP

The focus of this chapter is on identities in leadership and leadership identities. Defining leadership identities as experienced and projected selves or personas that aspire to 'look' like leadership, I suggest that new pressures are accruing on leaders to produce and project a coherent, convincing sense of themselves (Sveningsson and Larson 2006). Leaders are both authors of and objects in identity production, their efforts sometimes described as 'identity work' (Alvesson and Willmott, 2002).

Identities and how they are constructed and maintained has been an important focus of study across a range of disciplines for over half a century. Early interest often came from psychological perspectives that treated identity as an individual developmental accomplishment. The focus was on how people develop and maintain an integrated and coherent sense of who they are, sometimes equated with measures of psychological health. The famous psychoanalyst Erikson, building on the work of Freud and Jung, argued that the serious study of identity was the basis of adult ethics: 'And this alone permits the individual to transcend his *(sic)* identity – to become as truly individual as he will ever be, and as truly beyond all individuality' (1974, p. 42).

Yet early sociologists (Berger and Luckmann, 1966; Giddens, 1991), radical psychologists (Goffman, 1959), social psychologists (Gergen, 1991) and cultural theorists have questioned such psychological accounts, showing the role of social forces and institutional power in identity-making. The production of self is never done in isolation and is an ongoing negotiation, not a once and for all achievement.

More recently, theorists of organisation have applied identity concepts to explore questions of how selves are intricately crafted, performed and play out in organizations (Karreman and Alvesson, 2004; Kondo, 1990). Scholars examining the impact of economic ideologies and associated managerial trends document the impacts of such changes on self-identity – or how managers see themselves – for example, among police officers (Davies and Thomas, 2003) and public sector managers (Ford, 2006).

Societies regulate the identities that may be taken up and individual leaders conform to and struggle against societal and organizational scripts of who they should be as leaders. Increasing attention is being paid in leadership research to mapping these processes of identity regulation, including the interactions with other markers of identity such as gender and race (Essers and Benschop, 2009; Thomas et al., 2004); the impact on identity processes of trends such as globalization and the international mobility of markets and labour; and of processes of resistance (Prasad and Prasad, 2002). Here the focus is on both collectively organized and 'micro-political' acts of resistance whereby individuals negotiate and resist

a panoply of identity pressures, including the commandment to 'be yourself!'

While scholars have therefore paid considerable attention to the dynamics of identity production and resistance in organizations, there is a smaller amount of research on how identity pressures accrue in leadership and what leaders should do with them. Some of this work confirms that even senior, ostensibly powerful people in organizations feel deeply powerless in the face of pressures to be a certain self. They resort to 'tactical responses', such as 'dis-identification' or distancing themselves by producing other more authentic selves, but may experience further 'self-alienation' where self becomes foreign or alien (Costas and Fleming, 2009). Drawing together and building on this emergent work is one of the purposes of this chapter.

PRESSURES TO PRODUCE A LEADERSHIP IDENTITY

By the late 1980s, in those Western societies which have predominantly shaped business and management thinking, leadership became an accepted moral good (Sinclair, 2007). People working in schools, in community organisations, not-for-profit sectors, in sports, in medicine and health, as well as incorporations and bureaucracies are all encouraged to 'be' or 'become' leaders (Alvesson, 2002; Ford and Harding, 2007; Gabriel, 2005).

The resulting identity pressures accrue via multiple popular and academic discourses of leadership (Fairhurst, 2007). A substantial body of social psychological research known as 'social identity theory', advises leaders on how to moderate and craft their own identities to match the identities of groups of followers, thereby eliciting higher levels of motivation (Hogg, 2003; Shamir et al., 1993). As described below, this and other research has informed a wave of popular advice on how to craft personas, lives and legacies to be an 'authentic' leader. From a leader's point of view, this may involve authoring a biographical self-narrative or composing and telling a compelling story about oneself. As Ford et al., summarise 'where leadership used to be a series of tasks or characteristics, it is now an *identity* (authors' emphasis)' (2008, p. 28).

At an institutional level, aspiring leaders are also subject to increasing levels of surveillance and discipline around producing the 'right' identity. Leaders are subject to image 'makeovers' and coached in presentation and communication styles. They must cultivate their personas to engender confidence among stakeholders and share markets. They must be judicious about how and in what forums they lend their 'presence', yet avoid overexposure. Photographs of leaders proliferate in business magazines and there are now, in Australia at least, 'beauty' pageants for business leaders in which panels select top leaders in particular categories: for example 'Young Entrepreneur' or 'Best Director'. Such events are choreographed and stage-managed to convey the requisite levels of gravitas with a calculated hint of 'quirkiness' or individuality.

Leaders are thus encouraged to work on creating an individual 'brand' that transcends their organisation and feeds the romantic (Meindl et al., 1985) or saviour (Gabriel, 1997) myths that often underpin contemporary appetites for leadership (Gemmill and Oakley, 1992). Furthermore, it's not just the track records or the mental acumen that is the focus of this image crafting – bodies that are upright and uncontaminated by vulnerabilities are also often employed in the selling of leadership selves (Sinclair 2005, 2009).

The many pressures described above impinge on leaders who feel compelled to manage their identities (Collinson, 2003; Linstead, 2006; Sveningsson and Larson, 2006; Thomas and Davies, 2005; Thomas et al., 2004). The leader is not outside the process but enmeshed in it and new leadership discourses, such as 'just being yourself' and 'being authentic', may heighten anxiety to demonstrably secure one's identity as a leader. Despite such efforts, there often remains an inescapable predictability about these representations of leadership, creating what Guthey and Jackson (2005) describe as an 'authenticity paradox': pressure to manufacture an 'authentic persona', which, by its very process renders that authenticity impossible.

It is important to note that while leaders may have always been engaged in this process two trends in social surveillance may have magnified identity pressures. The first is proliferating media channels which increase scrutiny of and speculation about leaders' lives. Even those who formerly have been able to work inconspicuously, such as bureaucrats or community leaders, now often find themselves feted as role models in magazines and websites. These pressures are part of a wider phenomenon termed 'the commoditization of the self', whereby the self, or physical parts of the self, are treated as market objects that may be bought and sold. Corporate leaders such as Richard Branson become brands: the individual leader is the product. Aspects of individual leader identity become issues of studious strategic deliberation: for example, whether a male CEO is clean shaven or allowed a five o'clock shadow.

The second trend is the measurement and management of leader performance, which is now a pervasive aspect of organisational life. Appraisal processes, feedback instruments and other techniques of selection and promotion mean that most leaders are regularly tested against and expected to have their identities conform to organisationally specified norms of success. Yet, recent evidence from the global financial crisis suggests that many CEOs escape being held to account for their financial performance at the helm of their companies. Perhaps while pressures to produce a convincing leadership identity are endemic, they rarely work in rational, evidence-driven ways.

CRITICAL PERSPECTIVES ON THE PRODUCTION OF LEADERSHIP IDENTITIES

As suggested above and despite some claims, identity work is revealed to be rarely a process of the leader simply crafting and projecting a self. Foucault's work (1972, 1994) has drawn attention to the history and unfolding of 'technologies of the self': the ways in which individuals internalise controls and self-discipline to regulate selves. In their important contribution to identity theorising, Alvesson and Willmott build on the work of Foucault and Giddens to conceptualise at least three contributing influences to the production of identities: the narrative of self-identity; organisationally and societally mediated identity-regulation; and identity work, which includes the individual's efforts to maintain a sense of self that has meaning, coherence and distinctiveness.

As Rose (1989, 1996) has warned, and Baritz (1960) foreshadowed several decades earlier, the methods and interests of the social sciences and psychology introduce to the production of personhood, or leadership in this case, new technologies of measurement (performance appraisal processes, 360-degree feedback instruments, selection tools, etc.), new definitions of normality, new intents and new webs of power.

Followers are important though often neglected participants in processes of leadership identity-making (Collinson, 2006; Gronn, 2002). Theorists coming from both psychoanalytic and social psychological perspectives point to the importance of followers, projections and fantasies in endowing the identity of leader on certain individuals (Denhardt, 1981; Kets de Vries and Miller, 1984). Hogg et al. (2003) maintain that perceived leadership depends on the degree to which an individual leader is seen to embody or be 'prototypical' of the group's identity.

Who is deemed an authentic leader and why is indelibly tied to a society's myths and history which in the Australian case is interwoven with assumptions of masculinity, physical toughness and self-reliance (Sinclair, 1994). An example are the recollections of former Australian Prime Minister Kevin Rudd about his eviction from his childhood home after his father's death. This segment of Rudd's leadership was used in the 2006 election to establish his 'battler' credentials, and to show the roots of his claimed economic conservatism.

Furthermore, available leadership spaces and societal readiness to endow leadership capital are already deeply inscribed by gendered and cultural assumptions (Eagly and Karau, 2002). Women leaders in traditionally male-dominated environments experience particular pressures to produce non-threatening leadership selves, to camouflage aspects of their gender, their children and sexualities (Sinclair, 1995; Thomas and Davies 2005; Thomas et al., 2004). Male leaders also experience pressure to conform to often narrowly prescribed understandings of how they should look and who they should be (Connell 2000). Particular types of leadership selves are thus being demanded and produced in the search for authenticity and they are, in deep and self-disciplining ways, agents for maintaining the cultural status quo. This is despite frequent claims for leaders to be agents of 'transformation' or to 'just be yourself'.

Collinson has noted that 'there is an irreducible ambiguity' at the heart of identity construction, where individuals are held in tension between their own attachment to notions of self and their vulnerability to others' opinions of them (Collinson 2006, p. 182). Attempts to clarify or discover a 'true' leader identity thus 'reinforce, rather than resolve the very ambiguity and insecurity identity strategies are designed to overcome' (ibid.).

Some forms of leadership development often have an interest in exploiting this anxiety and hold out the illusion of leadership perfectible through self-discovery (Carden and Callahan, 2007; Carroll and Levy, 2008). Leadership development can therefore become an opportunity for intense identity socialisation.

A focus on fixing individual identities also mirrors and feeds the individualising and narcissism already enshrined in economic doctrine. The view here is that the market will work best in the 'war for talent' by paying the most to the most talented elite of leaders to perfect themselves.

It may be useful to also pause and identify some of the assumptions often made in the business literature. Perhaps pre-eminent is the assumption that leaders should invest time in improving themselves and rendering their leadership more inspiring or influential because, in that way, they can direct followers' behaviours, values and actions toward those that the leader (and perhaps their organisation) understand to be valuable.

The influential work of Daniel Goleman provides a good example. In a book (Goleman, 2006) and article in *Harvard Business Review* (Goleman and Boyatzis, 2008) the value of 'social intelligence' to leaders is advocated. Examples are given where people at work respond better to leaders with social intelligence and he admiringly cites a study showing that 'top performing' leaders elicited laughter from their subordinates three times as often, on average, as mid-performing leaders. Whereas, on the one hand, it seems like a demonstrably good thing to value social skills in leaders, this example is one of many in the leadership literature where organisational purposes remain obscured or are benignly aligned with the interests of leadership. The process of self-perfecting in order to be a more efficient agent of organisational purposes is not necessarily nor always towards which leadership should be aiming.

Critical theorists have also highlighted the oppression that lurks painfully in our ways of being ourselves. We experience a particular self as the only one, getting attached to and fiercely defending that way of being. As Brewis describes '(w)e commit ourselves to a particular version of self, giving us a platform from which to think and act, and we simultaneously begin to reject anything that does not conform to that self' (2004, p. 29). For Foucault, identity becomes an obsession: people think they have to "uncover" their "own identity" and that their own identity has to become the law, the principle, the code of their existence' (1994, p. 166). Yet Foucault also shows the ways we relate to a dynamic self are open to change. Greater freedom lies not in the business of discovering the self, nor necessarily discovering new truths of the self, but in commitment to a practice of choosing how to relate to the selves we are producing.

Similarly, in her book entitled *Giving an Account of Oneself*, Butler (2005) argues that we can never fully know ourselves. She says 'the forms of rationality by which we make ourselves intelligible, by which we know ourselves and offer ourselves to others, are established historically and at a price (2005, p. 121). According to Butler, we need to pay attention and try to understand 'the truth regimes' – those authored by us and located in societies – which function to tell us who we are. At the same time, we also need to grasp that our efforts to know ourselves and present ourselves as whole are inherently flawed. According to Butler, it is in this understanding of the limits in knowing self that is the basis of a form of morality with others.

DOING IDENTITY WORK WITH LEADERS

I've argued above that identity pressures are endemic in leadership and that leaders are either unwittingly or reflectively engaged in responding, colluding and resisting. In this section I describe some of the work I have been doing with MBA and other students, with executives on programmes and in coaching situations exploring identities. I often label this as 'identity work' and the ideas and processes we draw on are informed by the critical perspectives outlined above. My intent in this work is not to help people discover themselves or re-connect to true selves, or even bring their 'whole' selves to their work, though sometimes there are valuable insights that come from such impulses. My observation is that leaders are often enslaved by identity processes and giving people new ways of understanding identities helps them reflect on, selectively resist and re-direct energies and identifications. This identity work with others has unfolded alongside my own efforts to be different in leadership and work differently with my shifting self-identities. In the following, I describe my work with others and then offer an account of my own identity work.

There are three guiding principles in my leadership teaching and development work on identity: a commitment to reflective learning; to experiential learning from the here and now of the class process; and to applying critical perspectives. Each of these arises from particular ways of thinking about learning and its purposes (see Sinclair 2007). For me it is the explicit interweaving of the three that provides a workable foundation for exploring leadership in the classroom and with leaders.

If and when I have the opportunity to work with people over an extended duration (several months) or intensively over several days, I introduce some critical perspectives on identity. These include the ideas of our identities as multiple and potentially contradictory, as constantly being negotiated as they are being performed. We critique the notion of a single perfectible leadership identity and, tested against her or his experience and with others, most individuals readily grasp that the business of being ourselves rarely proceeds smoothly or according to plan. We read articles on authentic leadership and most see that the ideal of finding a permanent authentic self to apply to leadership is illusory. The goal is not to discover self but to get better at observing the processes and practices in identity-in-action, to perhaps be less reactive and more mindful as various apparitions of identity needs appear (Atkins, 2008). Sometimes my intent includes encouragement to relinquish habits of relentless goal-seeking too: that is, to act as if there is value in being present to and learning from what's happening now rather than waiting for the main game.

Depending on the context and group, we work critically with ideas about power and emotion,

reflecting on and experiencing how structural bases of power exert pressure and encourage self-policing of identities. Individuals often arrive with assumptions about power, emotion, gender and so on and they take up a position in the group from which to enact those assumptions. With encouragement, many begin to understand the places from which those assumptions have originated. Some experiment with different ways of 'doing' power, emotion and gender in the group and they are encouraged to notice how this impacts on them, their leadership and the group's learning.

A key part of identity work, as I teach it, is to go back into backgrounds, histories and childhood. This is intended not to fix people or to act as therapy but to help them begin to unpack and work consciously with their beliefs, practices and assumptions about authority and leadership. My interest in backgrounds comes from several important places: my doctoral study under two psycho-analytically inclined political scientists and, not least, making sense of my own history and its impacts. In my experience, helping people think about their backgrounds and their early experiences of leadership and groups is often a very insight-laden and freeing step. It gives people an understanding of why they've developed particular ways of approaching power and authority (or lack of it). In making patterns more visible and comprehensible, it gives leaders the possibility of choosing whether to continue to be completely contained by that approach or whether to experiment. Along with critical ideas, for example about gender, the process provides new understanding of the structural and organisational obstacles to any such change: the limits to individual agency. There are also sometimes quite profound insights into what may be at stake, personally, in being different.

The three examples from my work that follow provide a sense of the range of contexts and outcomes from working explicitly on identities in leadership. The first is a colleague who does excellent work herself in leadership development with women, academics and in organisations. She attended a week's programme which I co-facilitated. In spite of her successes, it seemed that almost always underpinning her work was waiting for the recognition of her father/managers. Some work environments activated for her a much earlier place. In fact she had become so habituated to waiting but never receiving acknowledgement that she had missed important recognition of her work. The insight she gained through identity work is that she had built her identity around waiting for acknowledgment that may not be forthcoming. She made a decision to experiment with not waiting for recognition: with bringing to consciousness the old place and, sometimes in small ways, not placing herself in it. A recent email from her confirmed that she feels she now creates a different space in her leadership work: giving more freedom and permission to herself and others, which includes to be present to what comes up without making judgements.

Another example of the potential of exploring family and gender identity constructions comes from my work with, and research of, a senior Australian woman leader. In our numerous interviews, discussions and work together, we have traversed many themes of background and identities, including gender identity, and the ways these are constantly being revisited, produced and negotiated in her roles as a leader in male-dominated environments. In her own family, it was her brothers who were expected to go on to university and achieve. Yet, as is not uncommon for many young women, there were also extraordinarily high expectations of her to 'get on with things' and 'get things done' – with a minimum of fuss. When we explored the impact of these dynamics, she has been a little taken aback. However, other comments she has made suggest that these insights have given her a deeper understanding about her leadership, including strengths such as her courage, and commitment to change and areas of challenge, for example a ready propensity to take total responsibility on her shoulders. In the public spaces where her own identity seems up for debate – where stereotypes are circling amid ambiguity about how she should act and be seen as leader – I have seen her pause, sometimes name the tensions she is experiencing, and actively experiment with being different.

In the third example, I was teaching an executive group and we were working through some ideas about identities, such as those described above and exercises which encourage participants to explore the themes and strands of identity that have shaped them and continue to regulate them, and consider what identity questions they are working on now. At the end of the session I walked out with one of the participants, who told me the session had felt like it had nearly knocked him over: it had 'hit him in the chest'. Belatedly, and as we talked, I realised that he is an indigenous man and someone who self-identifies strongly as Aboriginal. He has been initiated into cultural practices and is closely guided by elder men. For him, our work that day raised issues about his Aboriginality and his leadership that defy simple resolution and go to the heart of how he sees himself. For example, should he continue in a role working with Indigenous communities or should he pursue a leadership role beyond the bounds of his strong cultural identity, in the latter case perhaps risking rejection or being seen as positioning himself above members of his community? These identity-related tensions are built into the structure of being for many Indigenous Australians. They are created by the political and ideological context that regulates how and which identities may be taken up. In this example, racial and cultural identities already prefigure and constrain leadership. Negotiating through such contradictions is a fact of life for many undertaking leadership work.

My own Whiteness, in contrast, gives me a pre-existing freedom and relative invisibility in not having to think about, or be identified by, my race. But it also creates an obligation. For me, it re-emphasised the importance of not making assumptions about identity from the relatively blind position of my own privilege (Sinclair, 2007). This man's response powerfully demonstrated that identity work for him is deeply embodied, which he demonstrated in talking about the whack in the chest.

These three examples show three leaders engaging very differently in identity work. Despite the differences, my overwhelming experience is that critical ideas and theories about identities are often valuable to people doing a wide range of leadership. It helps them understand and get perspective on the multiple and often conflicting identity pressures from which their own approaches to leadership spring. The ideologies and structures that constrain them become more visible, yet people also feel supported to undertake experimentation in doing their leadership and in being. Also, the persistently fickle pressures from followers on identity become more visible. A particular peril associated with wanting to be a leader is getting caught up in always performing to follower fantasies. Identity work often helps leaders get some understanding of these temptations and seductions (Sinclair, 2009) and navigate through them in a way that allows for disappointment and disillusion – on both sides of the leader and follower relationship.

I have been deeply touched by the work that leaders do and the changes in understanding that are, in many cases, sustained and sustaining. People often seem happier, more open and feel less trapped. Paradoxically, perhaps they seem freer from themselves and the burden of continually producing a version of themselves. There is less egocentrism and narcissism, not more. Importantly, from a leadership point of view, work on identities seems to free leaders to pay attention to others and to intervene thoughtfully in what's really going on.

BEING IN LEADERSHIP: MY OWN IDENTITY WORK

Alongside the research and teaching described above, has been my own identity work. The first time I started thinking about identity and connecting it to my leadership was about 12 years ago, when my brother and grandfather died within a few months of each other. Both had lived for their work, in very different ways.

I started to think then more deeply about how I wanted to be in my life and for what. I also recognised I was one of the key obstacles to me being different. The following year, when I had my fourth child and wrote *Doing Leadership Differently*, I was looking for a way to both intellectually and practically be different, and by that I mean less driven, more compassionate towards myself and others, continuing to critique and innovate but in less punishing fashion.

Of course, quite quickly, I found myself back enacting the familiar self – working very hard and beating myself up for not doing many things well enough. In 2003 I resolved to resign. When I told my boss, he provided the option of leave without pay and I completed my yoga teacher training the following year. Yoga and the Eastern philosophy, Buddhism and meditation I studied and practiced taught me a whole lot of new things: ways of thinking about self, identity and the mind, ways of stepping back from my self and observing many habits of producing myself. These ideas have substantially influenced my own thinking about identities and informed my practices of identity work.

My evolving understanding of identities and identities in leadership thus derive from what ostensibly seem very disparate sources: Foucault, feminism, Buddhism and neuroscience, among others. Despite their eclecticism and perhaps contradictions, they have deepened my insights into what I might do to reduce oppression and create conditions for freedom and openness for others and myself. Let me say a little about these diverse influences on my own identity work.

Foucault's later work resumes an interest in what he calls 'practices of the self' (1994). Here he was not retreating from the structural – the way discourses and power operate at a meta-narrative level – but was adding in to that analysis new ideas about how we might think and be with ourselves in the face of these conditions. For Foucault, freedom lies in our ongoing commitment to practices that put a persistent value on reflexivity and seeing things as they are, rather than getting caught up in the truths we are told about them.

Buddhism and many Eastern philosophies also encourage scepticism towards self, and particularly the pompous, demanding and self-important self that is ego. For Foucault, self is a big production, a highly engineered but fragile palace. In Buddhism, self is an illusion – though a captivatingly plausible one.

Where reading Foucault has helped me intellectually to understand the topography and the

traps of self-making, meditation and mindfulness practices have helped me cultivate a set of practices for observation and intentional intervention in self-production. They have created a capacity to catch myself in the perpetual and often slightly ridiculous process of defending and securing myself: common self-talk phrases like, 'Why don't they understand me?' 'If only I could be left alone', 'If only they'd appreciate me, life would be easy'. Of course these phrases continue to circulate, particularly in circumstances where I am trying to 'be' different and feel a large discrepancy between the self that I feel others may be expecting and the one I am interested in being and believe is potentially more helpful to others. Yet I can and do simultaneously understand that these are all ways of thinking about the self that assumes the self to be precious and need defending. They are ways of entrenching a self, of lending it solidity which I don't actually need to engage in.

Buddhism teaches that stepping back from that clutter of upholding and securing a needy self gives access to a different set of possibilities of being. Some call it a wider consciousness, a knowledge that the self is not separate – that the idea of the separate individual is a doctrine which also holds us in the desperate effort to discover and prove ourselves.

Here I want to bring in feminism and the work of scholars like Butler (2005) and Benjamin (1998). From a very different direction, they highlight how performance of our identities often requires definition and subordination of the 'other': how we use others in order to be ourselves. Benjamin is interested in charting a different territory of inter-subjective space where we are truly with, and present to others without this instrumentality. For me this is again a very Buddhist idea and one which some other leadership researchers are exploring under the label of 'presencing' (Scharmer, 2007; Senge et al., 2005).

In her book, *Giving an Account of Oneself*, Butler offers an unexpectedly compassionate view of identity and ethics. She reminds us that ' "becoming human" is no simple task and it is not always clear when or if one arrives' (2005, p. 103). While we may wish ourselves to be 'whole perspicacious beings', a morality based on a hastily constructed authenticity of being true to oneself is insufficient. Rather, perhaps morality entails refraining from self-assertion and recognising 'the way social forces take up residence within us, making it impossible to define ourselves in terms of free will' (2005, p. 106). According to Butler this understanding – of the limits in knowing self – is the basis of a new form of morality with others. For her, a moral path lies in confronting our narcissistic wish for complete self-knowledge, understanding that we are all products of our histories and places, and gently, almost tenderly, acknowledging the impossibility of a self that is fully transparent to itself. As Roberts explains, her starting point is not the 'violent' or aggressive pursuit of an ideal but 'to observe all the ways in which I cannot give an account of myself; the ways in which I can never quite know what it is that I am doing'(Roberts 2009, p. 25).

Finally, let me say a few words about neuroscience and the emerging evidence that patient, purposeful attention changes our physiology, which in turn supports changes in emotional and psychological experiences: our being. This work – which comes from many different places – takes as its starting point two things. First, the fact that the mind and brain are not the same thing – consciousness is more than physiology. The mind is not reducible to neural connections and the mind can exercise some control and choice about how the brain reacts. This research demonstrates the second new understanding: enormous neural plasticity.

The work of analyst Norman Doidge (2007) provides many fascinating examples of how patient mindful attention can create new and different functioning for people. Examples cover the spectrum from physical functioning where neural damage had seemed to render such functioning impossible through to substantial changes in mental functioning as an outcome of therapy. In my work I am particularly interested in these latter changes: i.e. the way we can alter ways of thinking about ourselves and others and our ways of being in the world, and the fact that over time, our physiology supports these changes. My own experience of meditative and mindful practices is that this is so. My ways of being and ways of being myself have been amenable to modest change. Others also notice.

At the same time, I have many reservations about this science and the way in which some neuroscientific researchers are claiming to say new things about identity, when all that is really being charted is new understandings of physiology. Among leaders and especially corporate leaders there is a frightening appetite for this happy coming together of 'mind studies', science and leadership. As Foucault might have observed, new regimes of truth are being erected with little consideration of who gets power to do what in the process. Equally, Buddhists have durably cautioned about habits of spiritual materialism: the way insights get harnessed to new ego-enhancing projects.

CONCLUSIONS

When organisational theorists such as Alvesson and Wilmott began exploring identities in organisational life, there was an invitation, I believe, to begin to be reflexive about our own identity-making. Collinson (2005) says there should be more attention to the 'multiple, shifting, contradictory and ambiguous identities of leaders and followers' (2005, p. 1436). Yet in our rush as researchers to chart this rich territory, we risk ignoring the processes by which our research constitutes our own identity work. At a basic level it is likely that we use observations of others as a device to secure a self. Furthermore, we may inadvertently be contributing to the construction of a hierarchy in identity-making (Ainsworth and Hardy, 2004), where the efforts of some are subject to scrutiny while our own are above it. Although it may be inevitable that our own identity work is accomplished via our analyses of leadership, it seems essential that we pause to notice that and consider the consequences.

The possibility that I am interested in and have attempted to explore in this chapter is how might leaders – indeed ourselves – be in these identity spaces reflexively. How might leaders get some distance from and not be so captured by the business of producing themselves? I have drawn on leadership, critical, feminist and other writers who show that identities are not ours to craft. I have also drawn on ideas from and my experience of meditation, mindfulness and the perhaps implausible junction where psychoanalysis meets Buddhism (Epstein, 1995), to describe some of my own efforts to be in leadership lightly: with a less pressing need to be myself and with more freeing impacts on those around me. From a leadership point of view, my observation is that when leaders are less engrossed in being themselves, they are better at providing leadership – they are more present, more able to see what's going on and more able to be open and connected to others.

REFERENCES

Ainsworth, S. and Hardy, C. (2004) 'Discourse and identities'. In D. Grant, C. Oswick and L. Putnam (eds), *The Sage handbook of organizational discourse*. london: Sage, pp. 153–173.

Alvesson, M. (2002) *Understanding organizational culture*. London: Sage.

Alvesson, M. and Willmott, H. (2002) 'Identity regulation as organizational control; Producing the "appropriate" individual', *Journal of Management Studies*, 39: 619–644.

Alvesson, M. and Sveningsson, S. (2003) 'Good visions, bad micromanagement and ugly ambiguity: contradictions of (non-) leadership in a knowledge intensive organisation', *Organization Studies*, 24(6): 961–988.

Atkins, P. (2008) 'Responding not reacting'. In P. t'Hart and J. Uhr (eds), *Public leadership: perspectives and practices*. Canberra: ANU E Press, pp. 73–92.

Baritz, L. (1960) *The servants of power: a history of the use of social science*. Middetown, CT: Wesleyan University Press.

Benjamin, J. (1998) *Shadow of the other: intersubjectivity and gender in Psychoanalysis*. New York: Routledge.

Berger, P. and Luckmann, T. (1966, 1971) *The social construction of reality: a treatise in the sociology of knowledge*. Harmondsworth: Penguin.

Brewis, J. (2004) 'Refusing to be "me"'. In R. Thomas, A. Mills and J. Helms Mills (eds), *Identity politics at work: resisting gender, gendering resistance*. London: Routledge, pp. 23–39.

Butler, J. (2005) *Giving an account of oneself*. New York: Fordham University Press.

Carden, L. and Callahan, J. (2007) 'Creating leaders or loyalists? Conflicting identities in a leadership development program', *Human Resource Development International*, 10(2): 169–86.

Carroll, B. and Levy, L. (2008) 'Identity construction in leadership development'. Paper given at the Studying Leadership Conference, Auckland, December 2008.

Collinson, D. (2003) 'Identities and insecurities: selves at work', *Organization*, 10(3): 527–547.

Collinson, D. (2005) 'Dialectics of Leadership' *Human Relations*, 58(11): 1419–1442.

Collinson, D. (2006) 'Rethinking followership: a post-structuralist analysis of follower identities', *The Leadership Quarterly*, 17(2): 179–189.

Connell, R. (2000) *The men and the boys*. Cambridge: Polity Press.

Costas, J. and Fleming, P. (2009) 'Beyond dis-identification: a discursive approach to self-alienation in contemporary organizations', *Human Relations*, 62(3): 353–378.

Davies, A. and Thomas, R. (2003) 'Talking cop: discourses of change and policing identities', *Public Administration*, 81(4): 681–699.

Denhardt, R. (1981) *In the shadow of organization*. Lawrence, KS: Regents Press of Kansas.

Doidge, N. (2007) *The brain that changes itself: stories of personal triumph from the frontiers of brain science*. New York: Viking.

Eagly, A. and Karau, S. (2002) 'Role congruity theory of prejudice toward female leaders', *Psychological Review*, 109: 573–598.

Epstein, M. (1995) *Thoughts without a thinker: psychotherapy from a Buddhist Perspective*. New York: Basic Books.

Erikson, E. (1974) *Identity: youth and crisis*. London: Faber & Faber.

Essers, C. and Benschop, Y. (2009) 'Muslim businesswomen doing boundary work: The negotiation of Islam, gender and ethnicity within entrepreneurial contexts', *Human Relations*, 62(3): 403–423.

Fairhurst, G. (2007) *Discursive leadership: in conversation with leadership psychology*. Thousand Oaks, CA: Sage.

Ford, J. (2006) 'Discourses of leadership: gender, identity and contradiction in a UK public sector organisation', *Leadership*, 2(1): 77–99.

Ford, J. and Harding, N. (2007) 'Move over management: We are all leaders now?', *Management Learning* 38(5): 475–493.

Ford, J., Harding, N. and Learmonth, M. (2008) *Leadership as identity: constructions and deconstructions*. Basingstoke: Palgrave Macmillan.

Foucault, M. (1972) *The archeology of knowledge*. London: Routledge.

Foucault, M. (ed. P. Rabinow, trans. R. Hurley and others) (1994) *Ethics, subjectivity and truth*. London: The Penguin Press.

Gabriel, Y. (1997) 'Meeting God: when organizational members come face to face with the supreme leader', *Human Relations*, 50(4): 315–342.

Gabriel, Y. (2005) 'MBA and the education of leaders: the new playing fields of Eton' *Leadership*, 1(2): 147–163.

Gemmill, G. and Oakley, J. (1992) 'Leadership: an alienating social myth', *Human Relations*, 45(2): 113–129.

George, B., Sims, P. McLean, A. and Mayer, D. (2007) 'Discovering your authentic leadership' *Harvard Business Review*, February, 129–138.

Gergen, K. (1991) *The saturated self: dilemmas of identity in everyday life*. New York: Basic Books.

Giddens, A. (1991) *Modernity and self-identity: self and society in the late modern age*. Cambridge: Polity Press.

Goffee, R. and Jones, G. (2005) 'Managing authenticity: the paradox of great leadership', *Harvard Business Review*, 83(12): 86–98.

Goffman, E. (1959) *Presentation of self in everyday life*. London: Penguin.

Goleman, D. (2006) *Social intelligence: the new science of human relationships*. London: Hutchinson.

Goleman, D. and Boyatzis, R. (2008) 'Social intelligence and the biology of leadership', *Harvard Business Review*, September.

Gronn, P. (2002) 'Distributed leadership as a unit of analysis', *The Leadership Quarterly*, 13(4): 423–451.

Guthey, E. and Jackson, B. (2005) 'CEO portraits and the authenticity paradox', *Journal of Management Studies*, 42(5): 1057–1082.

Hearn, J. (2004) 'Personal resistance through persistence to organizational resistance through distance'. In R. Thomas, A. Mills and J. Helms Mills (eds), *Identity politics at work: resisting gender, gendering resistance*. London: Routledge, pp. 40–63.

Hogg, M., Martin, R. and Weeden, K. (2003) 'Leader–member relations and social identity'. In D. Van Knippenberg and M. Hogg (eds), *Leadership and power: identity processes in groups and organizations*. London: Sage, pp. 18–33.

Karreman, D. and Alvesson, M. (2004) 'Cages in tandem: management control, social identity and identification in a knowledge-intensive firm', *Organization*, 11(1): 149–175.

Keenoy, T., Ybema, S., Beverungen, A., Ellis, N., Oswick, C. and Sabelis, I. (guest eds) (2009) Special issue on constructing identity in organizations. *Human Relations*, 62(3).

Kets de Vries, M. and Miller, D. (1984) *The neurotic organization*. San Francisco, CA: Jossey-Bass.

Kondo, D. (1990) *Crafting selves: power, gender and discourses of identity in a Japanese workplace*. Chicago, IL: University of Chicago Press.

Linstead, A. (2006) *Managing identity*. Basingstoke: Palgrave Macmillan.

Linstead, A. and Thomas, R. (2002) 'Losing the plot? Middle managers and identity', *Organization*, 9(1): 71–93.

Meindl, J., Erlich, S. and Dukerich, J. (1985) 'The romance of leadership', *Administrative Science Quarterly*, 30: 78–102.

Prasad, A. and Prasad, P. (2002) 'Otherness at large: identity and difference in the new globalized organizational landscape'. In I Aaltio-Marjosola and A. Mills (eds), *Gender, identity and the culture of organizations*. London: Routledge, pp. 57–71.

Roberts, J. (2009) 'No-one is perfect: the limits of transparency and an ethics of 'intelligent' accountability', *Accounting, Organizations and Society*, doi: 10.1016/j.aos.2009.04.005.

Rose, N. (1989) *Governing the soul*. Cambridge: Cambridge University Press.

Rose, N. (1996) *Inventing our selves: psychology, power and personhood*. Cambridge: Cambridge University Press.

Scharmer, O. (2007) *Theory U: leadership from the future as it emerges*. Cambridge, MA: Society for Organizational Learning.

Senge, P., Scharmer, O., Jaworski, J. and Flowers, B. (2005) *Presence: exploring profound changes in people, organizations and society*. London: Nicholas Brealey Publishing.

Shamir, B., House, R. and Arthur, M. (1993) 'The motivational effects of charismatic leadership: a self-concept based theory', *Organization Science*, 4(4): 577–594.

Sinclair, A. (1994) *Trials at the top*. Melbourne: The Australian Centre.

Sinclair, A. (1995) 'Sexuality in leadership', *International Review of Women and Leadership*, 1(2): 25–38.

Sinclair, A. (2005) 'Body possibilities in Leadership', *Leadership*, 1(4): 387–406.

Sinclair, A. (2007) *Leadership for the disillusioned: beyond myths and heroes to leading that liberates*. Sydney: Allen.

Sinclair, A. (2009) 'Seducing leadership: stories of leadership development' *Gender, Work and Organization*, 16(2): 266–284.

Sveningsson, S. and Larson, L. (2006) 'Fantasies of leadership: identity work', *Leadership*, 2(2): 203–224.

Thomas, R. and Davies, A. (2005) 'Theorising the micro-politics of resistance: discourses of change and professional identities in the UK public services', *Organization Studies*, 26(5): 683–706.

Thomas, R. and Linstead, A. (2002) 'Losing the plot? Middle managers and identity', *Organizations*, 9(1): 71–93.

Thomas, R., Mills, A. and Helms Mills, J. (eds) (2004) *Identity politics at work: resisting gender, gendering resistance*. London: Routledge.

38

The Virtual Leader

David M. Boje, Alison Pullen,
Carl Rhodes and Grace Ann Rosile

INTRODUCTION

This chapter provides a critical review and evaluation of the idea and practices of the 'virtual leader'. Although the issue of virtuality has been taken up in leadership studies in relation to 'virtual teams' (see Martins, Gilson and Maynyard, 2004), here we are using the term 'virtual' in quite a different way. By our definition, a virtual leader is a leader who is not actually an embodied person, even though still performing leadership functions for the organization – virtual in the sense of being effectively a leader without being human. The virtual leader is an image of an organization leader, actual or fictional, that has been simulated and virtualized through the mass media – a leader who is purposefully created by an organization but who is variably distanced from association with, or representation of, a real person. Drawing on Baudrillard's (1983) theorization of the process of simulation, we explore how an important and potent dimension of contemporary leadership is its increasing mutation away from the materiality of the leader towards a simulated leadership enabled by changes in mass media technology and popular culture.

The virtual leader tends towards becoming 'hyperreal' – a copy of a leader void of an original. With virtualization, leadership can be enhanced and empowered such that it is no longer about the actions of persons, but rather is performed for and on the organization by the cultural 'imaginary' of what leadership signifies. Leadership is a function of this imaginary in that it exceeds the confines of the human body and, in so doing, can increase the potency and ability of leadership. The virtual leader, we maintain, can enhance the capacity for transformational leadership in organizations, and

for organizational transformation (Boje and Rhodes, 2005b). This 'hyperreal' leadership is a potent fantasy of leadership where leadership is disembodied in practice, yet accelerated in effectiveness. Moreover, the embodied representations of the virtual leader are also manifestations of gendered affects which are enormously powerful in shaping organizational identity and performance.

The chapter unfolds in four stages. First, we offer a brief introduction to the notion of the virtual leader as an example of an absent referent (Adams, 1991). Second, we offer a rehearsal of Boje and Rhodes' (2005a)[1] analysis of virtual leadership. Three orders of virtual leadership are discussed and then illustrated with examples from the fast food industry: (1) the virtual leader as an imitation of a *former flesh-and-blood leader*; (2) the virtual leader as a *creative re-representation of a former leader*; and (3) the virtual leader as a *fabricated leader* with no direct relation to an actual person. Having discussed these three orders, we then go on to consider in the last section the relations between gender and virtual leadership. Here we explore how gendered norms infiltrate virtual leadership, such that while the virtualization of leadership is a radical departure from conventional ideas of leadership, it also serves to reinforce established, repressive gender stereotypes. This leads us to conclude more generally that despite changes in its cultural expression, leadership remains problematically located within a dominant masculine model. In the final stage of the chapter we problematize this gendered reading to consider a more radical form of virtualized leadership – where the virtual is presented paradoxically – representationally embodied and yet disembodied by its virtual presence. In bringing the chapter to a close, we argue that virtual leadership has the capacity to transcend the persistent gender dualisms prevalent in leadership research, even though this potential is largely waiting to be realized.

VIRTUAL LEADERSHIP AND THE ABSENT REFERENT

What is the relationship between 'real' embodied leadership and virtual leadership? The virtual leader enjoys the paradoxical power of the 'absent referent', as well as the durability of the virtual image (Adams, 1991). We borrow this idea of the absent referent from Adams, who uses it to show how the 'meat-eater' is kept separate from not only the animal being eaten but also from the female body, often objectified as a pin-up girl with choice portions (thigh, breast, rump) in ads for meat consumption. As an example, Mickey Mouse evokes the presence of that absent person, sometimes as Walt Disney's alter ego, and other times as the idealized worker who always does what Walt wants. The paradox is that when Walt is present, a photo or animated image of Mickey is then relegated to a mere artifact associated with Walt's other toon-possessions. It is only in Walt's absence that Mickey has the power to evoke the presence of the virtual leader. This is also true of the power of virtual image in the absence of the worker, when Mickey represents Mickey Mouse work, or emotional labor. It is not that the virtual becomes a water-downed version of the real, but, more powerfully, it is that the image can be shaped into whatever the situation demands.

As we explore in more detail below, the same can be said of Ronald McDonald, as the alter ego of the departed Ray Kroc, the former owner and leader of McDonald's. When fat burgers are in, Ronald can be portly. When the public wants nutritious food, Ronald can be slimmed down. The morphing and shaping by design occurs in other McDonald's characters, such as Hamburglar. The absent referent is the animal, and one also forgets that there are real workers doing the McWork. When marketers want a younger image for the corporation, Ronald or Hamburglar get younger. No real person could exercise such flexible leadership.

Similarly, we see that the virtual leader may be portrayed most effectively in the media when the actual leader is absent (or never existed). Thus, when Sam Walton, founder of Wal-Mart, was alive, as a leader his comments were not often quoted in the *WalMart Annual Reports*. After his death, his leader-like statements were selectively chosen and re-presented in the annual reports to exploit Sam's leadership power after his death (the ghost of Sam). The paradox is that Sam's statements were quoted in the annual reports much more frequently after his death than when he was alive (and potentially able to refute them) (Boje and Rosile, 2008). Thus, the virtual leader may be more visible and powerful than an actual embodied leader, and in fact the virtual leader which is based on a 'real' person may be most effective in the absence of that 'real' person. An absent referent cannot refute words being put in her or his mouth.

So, to begin with we can surmise that while any leader's public image may be viewed as a virtual representation of the 'real' leader, it seems that the absence of the referent (the 'real' leader) provides an opportunity for others to build, evoke, and exploit the virtual leader. Recognizing those behind-the-scenes others is a key part of virtual leadership, and a step towards unmasking the operations of power sometimes attributed to leaders.

THREE ORDERS OF VIRTUAL LEADERSHIP

To further explore the way that virtual leadership operates we now turn to the discussion of virtuality in Jean Baudrillard's 1983 book *Simulations*. In this book Baudrillard explores the historical changes that have occurred in terms of how we understand the relationship between representations and reality. His particular focus is on how in contemporary times the idea that such representations are reflective of an underlying reality has been radically brought into question. Starting with the Renaissance period, Baudrillard argues that with the growth of the bourgeoisie as a new class in Europe, the relationship between signs and reality began to radically alter. Emerging at this time was the idea of the *counterfeit*, such that clear demarcation is made between a representation and an original. Paying particular reference to architecture and art work, the counterfeit is seen as an imitation of reality; the idea is that while reality is still seen to exist, the counterfeit is a distorted or inaccurate imitation of it.

With the dawn of the Industrial Age, Baudrillard noted the emergence of yet another symbolic order, that of *production*. At this time the development of mass production technologies enabled representations to go beyond being just imitations or counterfeits: for the first time, objects could be endlessly reproduced as copies of each other without needing to be related to any notion of an original. Unlike an imitation, the mass-produced item reproduced an image of itself, and the idea that there was an original material to be copied began to dissipate. In the contemporary era, Baudrillard noted a third symbolic order ushered in with the move from mechanical to digital technology. In this third order, there is no discernable difference between representations and originals. Representations are now understood as copies without originals that replace an actual reality with a simulated *hyperreality*. Our consideration of virtual leadership uses Baudrillard's three orders – counterfeit, production and simulacra – to explore the different extent to which leaders can be virtualized in the mass media and the effects of this virtualization in terms of leadership. We note, too, that in Adams' (1991) terms as we progress through each stage of simulation the referent becomes progressively more absent. On this basis, we now turn to a review of these three orders using examples of virtual leaders in the fast-food industry.

The virtual leader as an imitation of a former flesh-and-blood leader

Between 1989 and his death in 2002, Dave Thomas, the founder of the Wendy's hamburger restaurant chain, appeared in all of the company's more than 800 television commercials. He was even listed in the *Guinness Book of World Records* for the longest-running advertising campaign featuring the founder of a company. Thomas founded *Wendy's Old Fashioned Hamburgers* on 15 November 1969, leading its franchising in the early 1970s, taking it public in 1976 (with 500 locations), and later transforming it into *Wendy's International Inc.* Following a merger with another fast-food organization in 2008, Wendy's is now part of the Wendy's/Arby's Group, Inc., the third largest fast-food corporation in the world. As part of this group, Wendy's continues to operate as an independent brand, with 6,600 outlets in 22 countries.

Even though Thomas' leadership of Wendy's clearly took the company to commercial success, it was in 1989 that he started an even more dramatic role as Wendy's spokesperson in their comical, sometimes whacky TV commercials that helped the company rebound from a difficult period in the mid-1980s when earnings sank. These commercials presented Thomas not as a suited corporate leader, but as a 'regular guy'. Wearing a short-sleeved white shirt and a red tie, the commercials would find Thomas in very

unlikely situations such as driving a racing car while the actual driver ate a burger. Thomas' role in these television commercials marked a significant shift in his leadership function. Indeed, although corporate leaders are seldom very well known to the public, 'wearing a Wendy's apron, Thomas was one of the nation's most recognized television spokesmen' (CNN Money, 2002).

Thomas' transition from chief executive officer (CEO) to celebrity status television spokesperson illustrates the first order of virtual leadership. Through the commercials, Thomas became an image of his former self and, importantly, this was an image of leadership divorced from his corporate role as a manager and executive. The TV Thomas was an imitation or counterfeit of his alter ego as a corporate leader. Baudrillard (1983) remarks that the counterfeit marks a place where theatre takes over social life. It is in this way that Thomas's commercials became theatrical – he was playing the role of himself as a regular guy, rather than as an extremely successful and wealthy entrepreneur. As a symbol for Wendy's he was still very much 'tied somehow to the world' (Baudrillard, 1983, p. 85), but he was not tied completely to his alter ego corporate self. There is an alteration between the mass media Thomas and the boardroom Thomas, but the difference between them does not disturb the fact that they are one and the same person.

As he was beginning to be virtualized, what Thomas could do as a leader changed. He took on more of a mythical role in establishing Wendy's as an organization guided by old-fashioned values and commonsense business practice. Wendy's exploited this successfully by virtualizing Thomas in the image of a folk hero. In 2005, the organization claimed that:

> The long running Dave Thomas™ campaign made Dave one of the nation's most recognizable spokesmen. North Americans loved him for his down-to-earth, homey style. As interest in Dave grew, he was often asked to talk to students, business or the media about free enterprise, success and community services.[2]

Even after Thomas' death Wendy's continues to draw on his character in its public image, even though he does not appear in the most recent advertising campaigns. He is still featured heavily on Wendy's website as 'the man behind the hot 'n juicy hamburger.'[3] In 2002, Wendy's even commenced an advertising campaign based on the slogan 'prepared Dave's way'.

Wendy's used Thomas' virtualization to establish a particular image for the corporation that achieved the transformational leadership task of promulgating its corporate values (House and Shamir, 1993). With Thomas as virtual leader, Wendy's was able to create a corporate image that supported its ongoing success. This transformation was such that the task of the virtualized transformational leader was that of 'influencing outsiders to have a favorable impression of the organization and its products, [and] gaining cooperation and support from outsiders upon whom the organization is dependent' (Yukl, 1999, p. 39). Even to this day the organization uses Thomas as the bedrock of its way of doing business. As Wendy's former chairman and CEO Jack Schuessler said several years ago: 'quality is a way of doing business that must extend […] throughout the entire enterprise. Dave Thomas declared that years ago when he declared the words "Quality is our Recipe" ' (cited in Finan, 2005, p. 4). Thomas' virtualized leadership focused on setting an example to others through his down-to-earth style (Bass, 1999) and on propagating a set of organizational values (House and Shamir, 1993). These are functions that still live on after his death, and are enabled in part because of how his saturated media persona became so well known. Indeed, Thomas' own values are still publicized by the organization: 'quality is our recipe', 'do the right thing', 'treat people with respect', 'profit is a not a dirty word' and 'give something back'. The first of these values is registered by Wendy's as a trademark and is used as a marketing slogan.

What we find with Wendy's was an attempt to approach the first order of the virtual leader through the mass mediatization of Thomas. By making him a household name as a regular guy, a good father and grandfather, Wendy's was able to create an image of corporate leadership distanced from the goings on in the boardroom and the stock market and, instead, to have a leader who could promote the traditional values of community, care and honesty that it aspired to. The result is that Thomas is virtualized only in a fairly minimal way, because his leadership relied on an embodied presence – even after death.

The virtual leader as a creative re-representation of a former leader

Whereas Dave Thomas illustrates the first order of virtual leadership, it is Colonel Sanders, the iconic image of KFC, who takes this leadership in the direction of the second order – as a creative re-representation. The development of the Colonel's virtualization, however, does pass through the first order, as we shall see. The story of KFC starts in 1952 when the original Harland Sanders (born 9, September 1890), who was at the time living on his social security cheque, decided to devote his life to opening a chicken franchising business that he named Kentucky Fried Chicken. Sanders had for a long time been a cook: indeed, his title of Colonel was not earned through military service but was given to him in 1935 by then Governor of Kentucky Ruby Laffoon for his contribution to Kentucky cuisine. By 1964, when Sanders sold the business to investors for $2 million, Kentucky Fried Chicken had 600 outlets. In 1969 the company went public, with Sanders being the first shareholder. In early 2009, KFC has in excess of 11,000 restaurants in over 80 countries.[4]

Although officially ending his ownership of Kentucky Fried Chicken almost 40 years ago, Colonel Sanders was still very much a part of the corporation. He quickly came out of retirement to be paid an annual salary as a corporate spokesperson and as a pitchman in television commercials. For example, in one commercial the Colonel was kidnapped by a 'housewife' and interrogated in an abandoned warehouse; but he still refused to give up his famous 11 herbs-and-spices secret recipe. Sanders also had a candid, individualistic style, and a theatrical presence. Together, this made him a frequent TV talk show guest. He continued to travel 250,000 miles a year and do TV ads until his death in 1980. Up until this point, Sanders, like Thomas at Wendy's, had only started to become a first-order virtual leader. He represented the corporation's espoused values through his being mass mediatized as a heroic leader with a unique and virtuous character. Whereas Thomas was the regular guy, Sanders was the eccentric Southern gentleman replete with white suit, red shoe lace tie and exaggerated white beard. This masculine father-like character gave the organization an aura of authenticity with his 'secret' herbs and spices and his living out the American dream through his epic rags to riches story. Even today, his photograph appears on the main page of KFC's website looking down paternally at an array of fried chicken products.[5] His stylized image also graces the containers in which the food is served.

For the 10 years immediately after his death the image of Colonel Sanders only played a minor role at Kentucky Fried Chicken. His picture still appeared in the stores, and there was still the secret recipe, but there was no more mass media coverage through advertisements and television appearances. After a fall in consumer interest, the need to reinvigorate Kentucky Fried Chicken led to a revival of the older campaign with Sanders look-alikes in 1990. Still operating in the first order of virtual leadership, the new theatrical image was an imitation of Sanders' imitation of himself. It did not prove successful. Things changed, however, when on 9 September 1993 an animated version of Sanders was released. It was in this period that the company changed its branding from Kentucky Fried Chicken to KFC, thus silencing the word 'fried' to respond to a demand for healthy eating! The new Sanders was even more virtualized to meet the requirements of the new brand strategy. He was a cartoon Colonel and, while replete with his familiar string tie, goatee, white suit and cane, the real Colonel was increasingly absent. Actor Randy Quaid provided the voice.

What KFC did was to restyle the deceased corporate founder's first-order virtual leadership by contemporalizing his virtual essence for a new generation of consumers, systematically orchestrated in an animated Colonel. The new Colonel was more distanced from the actual person that its image was representing. In Baudrillard's (1983) terms, the new image liquidated the real of the first order and absorbed its appearance. In this order, rather than an imitative theatre there is a repetitive production whereby the image becomes further removed from the actual original so as to be a copy of itself – as in the case of mass production. In terms of virtual leadership, however, the animated Colonel failed to take on leadership qualities, rendering him instead a foolish cartoon. He was narrated as both the founder of the organization and as a cartoon character, but the second narration lacked any form of leadership. Furthermore, although the first-order Colonel performed a leadership function in terms of embodying the corporation's values, the animated Colonel moved towards the second order of simulacra, but lost his leadership edge. Gone was the individualized style and the personal embodiment of virtues – the new Colonel continued to fulfil a marketing function, but not a leadership one. The body of the Colonel was an artifact, commodified in a new genre of advertising. This Colonel was virtualized through the mass media to attract younger consumers, but in the process his leadership capacity was significantly diminished.

Despite the corporation's continued use of the Colonel's image to establish a sense of authenticity, his 'leadership' has not been used to address organizational transformation outside of the realm of marketing and advertising. In the case of Colonel Sanders, the increasing levels of virtualization meant that his representation was less and less able to provide a leadership function, thus questioning the success of disembodied forms of leadership. While based on a highly masculine representation of the Colonel, the cartoon de-genders Colonel Sander's hyper-masculine legacy through gimmickry.

The virtual leader as a fabricated leader with no direct relation to an actual person

With Dave Thomas, we saw a movement towards a first order of virtual leadership. In Colonel Sanders, we saw the unrealized potential for a second order. It is in Ronald McDonald, however, that we see the most successful virtual leader and the one who is the most virtualized and whose referent is more absent. Ronald has appeared in many incarnations since his humble beginnings as an entertainer at a Washington, DC franchise of McDonald's in the early 1960s. American children have ranked him as second only to Santa Claus as the most recognizable person (Royle, 2000) thanks to the massive media coverage of his character in television advertisements, live shows, merchandising and videos.

Ronald's leadership capacity is clearly demonstrated in the series of events following the death of CEO Jim Cantalupo on 19 April 2004. Ironically, Cantalupo (a cheeseburger and fries lover), died of heart failure just when he was to celebrate McDonald's most highly successful corporate reorientation: to become a nutritious and fitness-conscious chain. As CEO, Cantalupo was tasked with turning around a corporation that had just had 14 consecutive months of same-store sales decline, a stock price that was at the lowest point in nearly a decade, and a downgrading of its credit rating by Standard and Poor. In less than 16 months as CEO, Cantalupo's campaign introduced salads and other nutritional food sources, slowed franchise proliferation, and refocused McDonald's towards a 'back to basics' approach of customer service. The result was increased same-store sales and reversal of the sagging stock price (stock rose 70.8% during Cantalupo's tenure as CEO, from $16.08 in December 2002 to $27.46 in April 2004).

By 6 a.m. on the same day as Cantalupo's death, the Board convened (in teleconference, but with several members attending in person) to implement its formal succession plan. By 7 a.m. Charlie Bell was the new CEO. Bell's story, as it was publicized by McDonald's, told of a rags-to-riches American dream (even though he was Australian) that saw him start his career as a 15-year-old fry clerk who made the climb to CEO. This was a reversal of the *McJob* (Coupland, 1991) image of dead end, no-skill work in fast food outlets. Immediately following Bell's appointment, Ronald took on yet another leadership task. The Board commissioned full-page advertisements of Ronald commemorating Cantalupo. The advertisements presented a photo of Ronald in human clown form, with a tear running down his right cheek. As the tear made his clown makeup run, there was a caption that read, 'We miss you Jim.'[6] The advertisement, distributed just two days after Cantalupo's death, appeared in eight major news outlets, including *the Wall Street Journal*, the *New York Times* and *USA Today*. Translated versions were placed in major dailies around the world.

What is most interesting about the tear advertisement is that it was Ronald, not Charlie Bell (the new CEO) or a Board member, who gave emotion to corporate grief. A clown, full of excess, dealing with hard emotions; an attempt to make light a leaderless ship. As we will explore, this is an indicative demonstration that Ronald has achieved the status of a third-order virtual leader. In the 'Ronald's tear' example, Ronald had the charismatic influence to appeal to people around the world, and to meet the strategic goal of sustaining corporate image cohesion in a time of crisis. In this capacity Ronald did what actual transformational leaders do: He worked to influence people to ensure the organization achieves its strategic corporate objectives (Kapica, 2004). The clown replacing the corporate man is surely inspired by Bahktin, or the fool in King Lear by Shakespeare. His leadership involved espousing the company's vision (Shamir, House and Arthur, 1993), influencing outsiders to have a favourable impression of the corporation (Yukl, 1999), showing determination and confidence, setting an example (Bass, 1999) and communicating enthusiasm and inspiration (Rafferty and Griffin, 2004).

Even though virtualized former owners of KFC and Wendy's performed in comedic, even clownlike ways, with Ronald, McDonald's has gone the full way towards a third order of virtual leadership and a fully absent referent. Ronald approaches being a hyperreal leader in that he is generated by a model of a 'real without origin' (Baudrillard, 1983, p. 2). What this means is that while the first two orders of virtual leadership retain the epic narrative associated with a single leader, with Ronald 'the system puts an end to the myth of its origin and to all the referential values it has itself secreted along the way' (p. 113) such that 'the contradiction between the real and the imaginary is effaced' (p. 142). He even cries human tears. In Baudrillard's terms, Ronald's leadership approaches an aesthetic hallucination of reality (p. 148). For the corporation, this means that Ronald can perform a much greater variety of leadership functions because he is no longer constrained by the limitations of an actual person – although he in part imitates and extends the function of transformational leadership, he does not need to imitate or have to refer to any actual person, and as a result his capacity for leadership

is advanced. Corporate power never had it so good. Ronald as a male clown operates without the hyper-masculinity associated with male forms of leadership. In this way, the aggressive leadership function of McDonald's is masked by the more androgynous masquerade of Ronald, the clown.

FEMININE VIRTUAL LEADERS

Ronald McDonald, Colonel Sanders and Dave Thomas are not individuals who leadership research traditionally defines as transformational leaders, with the likes of Richard Branson and Steve Jobs typically viewed as acting as ideal role models for aspiring leaders. As we have illustrated, however, once virtualized in the mass media, leaders can still perform leadership functions. In part virtual leaders are substitutes for traditional leadership (Howell, 1997; Howell and Dorfman, 1981; Jermier and Kerr, 1997; Kerr and Jermier, 1978). This substitution can operate at a transactional level, where the virtual leader is, in our examples, a spokes-character or an iconic symbol for selling fast food. It can also operate at a transformational level, where the virtual leader is stylized and orchestrated to mimic leadership virtues as well as to provide the organization with a means to narrate a new identity. Although in part this suggests that such leadership might be collapsing into media and marketing, it also suggests that the creation of successful brand icons themselves is not tantamount to the creation of virtual leaders; the virtual leader is better thought of as one particular variety of such iconography that is used, intentionally or unintentionally, for leadership purposes. Whereas brand icons work to signify certain aspects of an organization's identity for its customers, virtual leaders go further by seeking to develop and transform it. Indeed, as we have explored, the leadership potential of the virtual leader varies qualitatively in relation to the character of the icon itself. Hence while marketing is a necessary condition for the virtualization of leadership, it is not a sufficient one. Leadership narratives and simulation are also necessary.

What is clearly evident in our illustration of virtual leadership so far is that all of the leaders we have discussed – whether they are real or virtualized – are men. Furthermore, Sanders and Thomas clearly exhibit a wealth of masculinity, and this is perhaps unsurprising given the observation that 'the dominant type of behaviour deemed appropriate for managers in contemporary organizations coincides with the image of masculinity' (Ford, 2006, p. 81). To have one's virtualized leaders gendered as men makes sense, because it is the image of the man that is culturally accepted as being associated with leadership – to drive organizations, to penetrate markets, to harness community, and in our case of fast food, to put food on the table for the American family. Indeed, it has been suggested that the leadership behaviours associated with femininity have long been largely a secret (Rosener, 1995), such that to read leadership is to read male (Oseen, 2002) even though its rhetoric and research have traditionally been void of gendered analysis. To become a successful female leader equates, as Wajcman (1998) claims, to 'managing like a man'. Indeed, management has long been thought of as synonymous with masculinity (Due Billing and Alvesson, 2002; Kerfoot and Knights, 1993; Pullen, 2006; Pullen and Simpson, 2009) and studies of leadership largely assume masculinity as the norm (Oseen, 2002; Pullen and Rhodes, 2008) whether its gendered nature is highlighted or not.

Due Billing and Alvesson discuss the differences between masculine and feminine orientations to leadership, suggesting that the former involves 'instrumentality, autonomy, result-orientation, etc. something which is not particularly much in line with what is broadly assumed to be typical for females' (2002, p. 144). They propose that female oriented leadership would be more participatory, non-hierarchical, flexible and group-oriented. But as they caution 'constructing leadership as feminine may be of some value as a contrast to conventional ideas on leadership and management but may also create a misleading impression of women's orientation to leadership as well as reproducing stereotypes and the traditional gender division of labour' (p. 144). In other words, the gender dialectic remains intact as feminine forms of leadership are introduced in a subservient relationship to dominant male models of leadership. Indeed, the problem of gender labelling (Due Billing and Alvesson, 2002) has been problematized in relation to women's leadership values (Gherardi, 1995; Höpfl, 2003; Pullen, 2006; Pullen and Rhodes, 2008), recognizing the commodification of femininity. Despite some research suggesting that masculine leadership is more effective, other research suggests that sex advantage in leadership is overstated (e.g. Vecchio, 2002). Furthermore, there are debates surrounding the gendered nature of leadership that question whether femininity disrupts leadership success and female progression. Korabik (1990), for example, proposed an androgynous model of leadership for women that has the potential to overcome bias towards feminine women. But androgyny is not neutral; the suppression of the feminine is a neutering (after Höpfl, 2003). Our point in relation to women's leadership is

that leadership research has been constrained by a dependence on gender categories; specifically, that to be a female leader you either need to practice masculinity or you need to harness particular feminine skills that women are presumed to naturally possess (Fondas, 1997). But you must not be too feminine and you must not be too different. And if androgyny is a preferred option, then this is a risky strategy which destroys feminine otherness.

To consider the gendered nature of virtual leadership, we start by exploring female virtual leaders. Just as there are far fewer female leaders in organizations, so are too there fewer virtual female leaders. When female virtual leaders do exist, however, they take on quite different forms to their male counterparts. In the cases of Sanders and Thomas, in particular, masculinity is a dominant characteristic and virtue. Commonly, female virtual leaders are fictional, either made-up characters, or developed by using a woman's name and avatar to respond to particular audiences, especially a female, domestic audience. As a case in point, we consider Betty Crocker of the General Mills food company, a woman who never actually existed but who was fabricated in the early 1920s as the company's response to requests for answers to baking questions. In 1921, managers decided that signing the responses personally would be more 'intimate' and so they combined the last name of a retired company executive, William Crocker, with the first name 'Betty,' which was thought of as 'warm and friendly.' With these actions General Mills engaged in a direct commodification of the feminine as a marketing strategy. The famous Betty Crocker signature came from a secretary who won a contest among female employees. The same signature still appears on Betty Crocker products. In 1924, Betty Crocker was given a voice for the first cooking show on American Radio. The success of Betty Crocker stemmed, we argue, from everyday women needing to identify with a public female figure, a domestic goddess to aspire to.

Until 1936, Betty Crocker was an invented cultural icon; then she was given a face.[7] Artist Neysa McMein brought together all the women in the company's Home Service Department and 'blended their features into an official likeness.' So while Crocker was fictional, she represented, and was created from, real women – an ideal type to which they might aspire. The widely circulated portrait reinforced the popular belief that Betty Crocker was a real woman. Over eight decades, Crocker's face changed seven times: she became younger in 1955; she became a 'professional' woman in 1980; and in 1996 she became multicultural, acquiring a slightly darker and more 'ethnic' look. Interestingly, dressed in a red jacket and white blouse (that changed with fashion changes through the decades), Crocker presented formally, professional, strong and very much in control. But was Crocker a feminist icon of her day, given her ability to lead the women of America?

By 1945, the virtual character was voted as being the second most famous woman in America after Eleanor Roosevelt. Through blanket media coverage, Betty Crocker led the General Mills Company through changing cultural demands placed on the organization through the twentieth century by being a feminine representation that American women could both identify with and hope to become. Her leadership success was bounded to her image of professional domesticity and this was about being a good American house-wife, which spoke directly to the desires of the women who bought her products. Her virtual leadership was tied inextricably with her brand. Although this demonstrates a form of leadership, in the case of Betty Crocker the virtualization is the creation of hyper-femininity – she is more feminine than feminine. Akin to Ronald McDonald, this sees her emerge through the third order of simulation, but instead of being disembodied as a fabricated leader, her visual shows that she is 'all woman'. From a leadership perspective this is most effective, but we can add that what is virtual-ized is a highly contained and conservative image of femininity. Crocker is the uber-housewife who, unlike the masculine virtual leaders, provides a form of leadership based on serving male organi-zation. Crocker exudes domesticity (and possibly servitude), so while virtualized, her position in the organizational order is 'other'. She is the 'good woman' that we were once told needed to be behind every man – and indeed she remains behind the woman who is behind every man. A construc-tion of corporate necessity, a service provided for women's service in the home.

In stark contrast to Crocker, we take as our second example of feminine virtual leadership Aunt Jemima of the Quaker Oats Company. Crocker had the image of an idealized middle American housewife; Aunt Jemima, on the other hand, received much criticism. Aunt Jemima is a trademark for pancake flour, syrup and other breakfast foods. The trademark dates to 1893, although the Quaker Oats Company first regis-tered the Aunt Jemima trademark in April 1937. The term 'Aunt Jemima' is sometimes used col-loquially as a female version of the derogatory label 'Uncle Tom'. In this context, the slang term 'Aunt Jemima' refers to a black woman who is perceived as obsequiously servile or acting in, or protective of, the interests of white people.[8]

Aunt Jemima started out as a character in the image of an American black maid or cook – a 'mammy' – and then gradually evolved through the cultural perceptions of black women in (white) American culture (see Hooks, 1999 for an academic discussion of black women in America). Indeed, like Crocker, Aunt Jemima led her organi-zation through the cultural changes of the century, as reflected in dominant and hegemonic images of femininity. Aunt Jemima was depicted as a plump, smiling, bright-eyed, African-American woman, originally wearing a kerchief over her hair. In marketing materials she was originally depicted as a former slave. From 1890 to the 1960s Aunt Jemima was played by a series of actresses who depicted the characteristics of the original fic-tional and cartoon character. The Aunt Jemima image has been modified several times over the years. In her 1989 make-over, as she reached her 100th anniversary, the 1968 image was updated, with her kerchief removed to reveal a natural hair-style and pearl earrings. This image remains on the products to this day. Aunt Jemima depicted an ideal that all American families were supposed to need – a maid that could provide stability of serv-ice at home. There is a paradox in Aunt Jemima's leadership abilities at an organizational level, and her subordination as a black maid for American families. Given the offensiveness that the Aunt Jemima trademark caused to African-Americans, it is bitterly ironic that this is the first time in his-tory that a black woman has provided virtual leadership. Furthermore, although a 'mammy', Quaker Oats commodified otherness, the presence of the other as a trademark, which had the capac-ity to change opinion. This, however, is only within the realm of pancakes and syrup.

With the examples of Aunt Jemima and Betty Crocker, we can see clearly that it is not just men who are virtualized for organizational purposes: indeed, both of these characters, like Ronald McDonald, represent an advanced stage of virtu-alization in that they are imitations that do not have an original in terms of a flesh-and-blood person. But, in stark contrast, both Aunt Jemima and Betty Crocker are based on the flesh of real women – women identify with real women and not clowns. The Ronald masquerade is humorous; Crocker and Jemima have no humour, and for many are sad and repressive. Through their virtu-alization, the female virtual leaders do not signify actual leaders but are brought together through an amalgam of cultural stereotypes of femininity put to the service of the organization that they repre-sent. In these cases, femininity becomes branded for the emotional labour desired by the organiza-tion. Although the gender of male leaders is largely implicit (although neglected) (see Oseen, 2002), the gendered character of female leaders – and their bodies – are commodified by their excessive femininity and their being associated with what are traditional female forms of labour, in this case cooking (and being a good cook at that). Female virtual leaders are also strongly associated with their physical form. They are coupled with the cultural stereotypes of being maternal and feminine – nurturing, caring, servile, unthreatening, soft especially in the case of Aunt Jemima. Indeed, they try to create a sense of cultural community, garnering the support of their nations.

Both Betty Crocker and Aunt Jemima are little more than mascots for their respective companies. Neither has a person portraying them in public appearances, nor do they have virtual or cartoon images making statements or taking action. Instead, they are the virtualization of the symbolic and figurehead functions of leadership. They are not inspirational and transformational, as are our male fast-food virtual leaders. Thus, we see gender stereotyping reflected in the virtualization of leadership. Furthermore, as evidenced by the lack of female virtual leaders in the fast-food industry, there appear to be fewer female exemplars in the realm of virtual leadership, mirroring the under-representation of women leaders in the corporate world in general. One estimate indicates 12.5% of Fortune 500 executives are women, and only 3.8% of Fortune 500 top officers are women (Nelson and Quick, 2002). The glass ceiling appears to extend to the realm of virtual leaders. But as our discussion of female leaders and their relationship to femininity suggests, theorists of gender and leadership get caught within and between the production of gender dualisms. Bowring rightly states that gender dualisms underlying leadership research rest on the understanding that

> the male is the universal, neutral, subject, thus creating the female Other as a crucial partner to the universalist claims that it makes about leadership. Thus, leaders are separate from followers (non-leaders), and males as leaders, separate from females (non-leaders). (Bowring, 2004; p. 383)

In our examples of Aunt Jemima and Betty Crocker we have seen that they do not have the leadership prowess of their male counterparts. In our analysis we have reinforced the production of gender stereotypes on two levels: first, we have equated femininity with female leadership and masculinity with masculine leadership; and, secondly, we have argued that feminine leadership, even when the leader is fictional, relies on women's material bodies, thereby reinforcing the embodiment of women's lives in organizations. If we are to imagine different possibilities for female leaders and the importance of femininity in leadership research, we need to start thinking differently – thinking beyond categorization (Bowring, 2004; Calás and Smircich, 1993; Oseen, 2002), because there are harmful effects to continually placing

such value on the differentials between feminine and masculine leadership (Calás and Smircich, 1993 cited in Bowring, 2004, p. 384). As such, virtual leadership, and leadership more generally, is caught within what Butler (1990) calls the heterosexual matrix. Butler, drawing on Foucault, questions categories of gender and sexuality. Gender is a discursive, performative act, ever changing within power relations. To challenge the gendered dialectic of virtual leadership, we need to think beyond heteronormative leadership theories and images of virtual leadership.

Through an excessive masquerade (see Pullen and Rhodes, 2010), Ronald McDonald the clown transcends the criticisms of hegemonic masculinity which we could mount of Sanders and Thomas. Ronald's masquerade is an androgynous gender performance, but McDonald's recognized the limits to Ronald's gender-neutral masquerade. To contemporalize Ronald in popular culture, we turn to an example which shows the queering, of virtual leadership. By queering we mean the challenge and subversion of heterosexual relations, following gender and sexuality as socially constructed and emergent (Butler, 1990; Sedgwick, 1990). Recognizing that Ronald was not popular in every country, McDonald's responded. His statues have mostly been removed in UK stores and in 2005 he was restylized, and his gender changed in Japan.[9] Taking the Japanese reincarnation as an illustration of queering, Ronald is female, young, wearing a 1960s-inspired red-and-white top with yellow dress, yellow gloves and red high heels. Ronald is very feminine and highly sexualized. In one photograph there is a seductive pose into the lens of the camera, lips pouting and leather gloves poised on the lip. Flowing auburn red shoulder-length hair floats around a feminine face. In another photograph there is a young man, wearing a 1960s-inspired red suit with yellow accessories. He has long red hair. This boy and Ronald as female look very similar, and are very feminine. Is this McDonald's attempt to transcend gender roles? The images capture a certain playfulness, elusiveness and seductiveness. Furthermore, this potential gender blurring, and the co-presence of boy with the female Ronald, may be an attempt to upset heterosexual norms through elusiveness.

In contemporary times we may wish to argue that the future of leadership research requires the advancement of thinking less conservatively about gendered leadership roles, placing more emphasis on the deconstruction of a gender binary that continues to simplify both gender and sexuality in organizations. These masquerades of gender (see Pullen and Rhodes, 2010) enable the real and fantasy and the male and female to be transcended, but perhaps only when we queer leadership theory can we fully take part in the debate (see Parker, 2002 on the queering of organizational theory). Offering a subversive take on gender, Bowring claims:

> If queer is 'an attempt to disrupt, to subvert, to set aside, compulsory heterosexuality, and the gendered binary oppositions that come with it' (Hollinger, 1999: p. 25) then it is a powerful way of moving towards fluidity in the theorizing and practice of both gender and leadership. All that is required is for us to subvert taken-for-grantedness by understanding that cause and effect are not always what we assume them to be. (Bowring, 2004, p. 402)

It leaves us wondering whether the virtual leaders illuminated here will remain the cultural icons and organization trademarks that they currently are.

CONCLUSIONS

In the discussion above, we have explored how leaders can become virtualized at three different levels: a first order, where the virtual leader is an imitation of an actual human leader; a second order, where the virtual leader is a re-representation and mutation of an actual human leader; and a third order, where the virtual leader operates independently of any relation with an actual human leader. As the level of virtualization increases, the distinction between the human leader and the virtual leader becomes more and more blurred. Following Adams (1991), the referent is increasingly blurred. Dave Thomas' cartoon counterfeit is still recognizably a copy of him. Colonel Sanders, as he has been modified throughout the years, continues to slip away from his referentiality to the original founder of the organization. In the cases of Ronald McDonald, Betty Crocker and Aunt Jemima, their leadership requires no person for them to be imitating; although we add that Ronald's clown form makes him appear less 'real' than any of the others. Both Ronald and Betty have experienced 'make-overs.' Ronald got thinner to accommodate the nutrition emphasis of the early 2000s, and Betty's whole look was updated successively to keep her contemporary. Such changes are more easily mandated by corporations when their virtual leaders are of the third-order simulacra, with no real person to offer potentially embarrassing inconsistencies. Moreover, this is not so much a replacement of the actual leaders of organizations – instead, it marks an extension of potency of leadership.

While any of the three orders of virtual leadership can perform leadership functions, it is at the third level – that of the hyperreal – that transformational

leadership is most potent. The first order of the virtual leaders such as Thomas and the Colonel can be used to depict an epic story of masculine leadership: for example, romanticizing an epic past by presenting a 'rags to riches' storyline. If transformational leadership at an organizational level involves rethinking and reorienting significant aspects of an organization's image, values and practices (Pawar and Eastman, 1997; Yukl, 1999), then the virtualization of an entrenched epic leader might well become a hindrance. This is the case because the legendary status of the founder will always be backward-looking and nostalgic. This explains why Thomas as virtual leader was used to maintain an image of traditional American values for the corporation, but was not used to directly respond to the fast-food nutrition crisis and, more recently, was dropped from the advertising campaigns all together. It also explains that when the Colonel made the transition to a second level of virtualization, his leadership capacities were diminished: he could not portray a new KFC because, although distanced from it, he was still associated with the original Colonel and his epic heritage. In the case of Ronald McDonald, however, we find that at in the third order of the virtual leader his full transformational leadership was realized. As a *hyperreal* virtual leader, Ronald is not limited by the actuality of any leader before him, and is therefore able to metamorphose into the type of character that can perform the leadership function the organization deems that it requires.

What our discussion has also shown is that while the virtualization of leadership marks an important shift in its functioning, it also reproduces and amplifies the gender stereotypes and norms present in actual leadership. It is through this virtualized reproduction that gender becomes excessive in the way it is used to exemplify leadership – this is indeed the case for both the male and female virtual leaders. This works such that the male virtual leaders are glorified as entrepreneurs, and typify particular character traits – traits largely coterminous with 'transformational leadership' and its association with stereotypes of heroic and individualistic masculinity (cf. Kark, 2004). In the case of the female virtual leaders, the same tendency is present – they are both hyperreal and hyper-feminized, most especially in terms of representing an exaggerated femininity centred around caring and nurturing roles performed in a domestic labour context.

In conclusion, virtual leadership offers the corporation greater control over its leadership function. In addition, the virtual leader examples we have discussed strongly reflect corporate gender-based biases. The virtual leader's success in terms of transformational potential may depend on the corporation's ability to simulate the spark and charisma of the great leader. Ronald McDonald may be the precursor of an era of super-hero-like leaders rivalling Santa Claus in name recognition, able to shed real tears as easily as pounds of body weight, and able to be in many places at once, tirelessly doing good works around the globe at the corporation's bidding. And while corporations are busy creating the supermen of virtual leadership, the Betty Crockers and Aunt Jemimas are standing by holding the capes, all dutifully loyal Lois Lanes. So, even though virtualization may enhance the power of leadership, it does little to dispel its gendered culture. If it is the case that 'a new symbolic structure must be created if new ways of thinking about the leader and of leadership are to be thought which create a space for women other than as imitation men or excavated women' (Oseen, 2002: 170), then despite all of its symbolic manipulation, virtual leadership does not do this. Indeed, an important conclusion from our discussion of virtual leadership is that the need for feminine leadership to be unbounded from the realms of women and their subordination remains pressing.

NOTES

1 These beginning parts of the chapter are based on an updated summary of Boje and Rhodes (2005a).

2 Quoted from the special section of the Wendy's website devoted to Dave Thomas' legacy (http://www.wendys.com/dave/flash.html, accessed 3 March 2005).

3 http://www.wendys.com/about_us/, accessed 25 February 2008.

4 This data comes from the KFC website, http://www.kfc.com/about/, accessed 26 February 2008.

5 http://www.kfc.com/, accessed 28 February 2009.

6 The tear ad (without caption) as it ran in a colour version in USA Today on 21 April 2004 can be seen at http://www.adage.com/images/random/ronald0421_big.jpg, accessed 9 July 2004.

7 See http://chnm.gmu.edu/features/sidelights/crocker.html, accessed 24 February 2009.

8 See http://en.wikipedia.org/wiki/Aunt_Jemima, accessed 16 February 2009.

9 See http://peaceaware.com/McD, accessed 18 February 2009.

REFERENCES

Adams, C.J. (1991) Ecofeminism and the eating of animals, *Hypatia*, 6(1): 125–145.

Bass, B.M. (1999) Two decades of research and development in transformational leadership, *European Journal of Organizational Psychology*, 8: 9–32.

Baudrillard, J. (1983) *Simulations*. New York: Semiotext(e).

Boje, D. and Rhodes, C. (2005a) The virtual leader construct: the mass mediatization and simulation of transformational leadership, *Leadership*, 1(4): 407–428.

Boje, D. and Rhodes, C. (2005b) The leadership of Ronald McDonald: double narration and stylistic lines of transformation, *The Leadership Quarterly*, 17(1): 94–103.

Boje, D. and Rosile, G. (2008) Specters of Wal-Mart: a critical discourse analysis of stories of Sam Walton's ghost, *Critical Discourse Studies*, 5(2): 153–179.

Bowring, M. (2004) Resistance is not futile: liberating Captain Janeway from the masculine–feminine dualism of leadership, *Gender, Work and Organization*, 11(4): 381–405.

Butler, J. (1990) *Gender trouble*. London: Sage.

Calás, M. and Smircich, L. (1993) Dangerous liaisons: the 'feminine-in-management' meets 'globalization', *Business Horizons*, 36(2): 71–81.

CNN Money (2002) Wendy's founder dead at 69, January 8, 2002; http://money.cnn.com/2002/01/08/companies/wendys_obit/. Site visited on 3 March 2005.

Coupland, D. (1991) *Generation X: tales for an accelerated culture*. New York: St. Martin's Press.

Due Billing, Y. and Alvesson, M. (2002) Questioning the notion of feminine leadership: a critical perspective on the gender labelling of leadership, *Gender, Work & Organization*, 7(3): 144–157.

Finan, K. (2005) Wendy's: the state of the enterprise, *Wendy's Magazine*, January 2005 (available at http://www.wendys-invest.com/main/enterprise1204.pdf, visited 3 March 2005).

Fondas, N. (1997) Feminization Unveiled: Management Qualities in Contemporary Writings, *Academy of Management Review*, 22(1): 257–282.

Ford, J. (2006) Discourses of leadership: gender, identity and contradiction in a UK public sector organization, *Leadership*, 2(1): 77–99.

Gherardi, S. (1995) *Gender, symbolism and organizational Cultures*. London: Sage.

Hollinger, V. (1999) (Re)reading queerly: science fiction, feminism, and the defamiliarization of gender, *Science Fiction Studies*, 26(1): 23–40.

Hooks, B. (1999) *Yearning: race, gender and cultural politics*. Boston, MA: South End Press.

Höpfl, H. (2003) Becoming a (virile) member: women and the military body, *Body & Society*, 9(4): 13–30.

House, R.J. and Shamir, B. (1993) Toward the integration of transformational, charismatic, and visionary theories. In M. Chemers and R. Ayman (eds), *Leadership theory and research: perspectives and directions*. New York: Academic Press, pp. 81–107.

Howell, J.P. (1997) Substitutes for leadership: their meaning and measurement' – an historical assessment, *The Leadership Quarterly*, 8(2): 113–116.

Howell, J.P. and Dorfman, P.W. (1981) Substitutes for leadership: test of a construct, *Academy of Management Journal*, 24: 714–728.

Jermier, J.M. and Kerr, S. (1997) Substitutes for leadership: their meaning and measurement – Contextual recollections and current observations, *The Leadership Quarterly*, 8(2): 95–101.

Kapica, C. (2004) The role of quick serve restaurants in wellness. Slide presentation to 26th American Overseas Dietetic Association Conference, Nicosia, Cyprus, March 27. Slides available online at http://www.cydadiet.org/april2004/cathyKapica.pdf.

Kark, R. (2004) The transformational leader: Who is (s)he? A feminist perspective, *Journal of Organizational Change Management*, 17(2): 160–176.

Kerfoot, D. and Knights, D. (1993) Management, masculinity and manipulation: from paternalism to corporate strategy in financial services in Britain, *Journal of Management Studies*, 30(4): 659–677.

Kerr, S. and Jermier, J.M. (1978) Substitutes for leadership: their meaning and measurement. *Organizational Behavior and Human Performance*, 22: 395–403.

Korabik, K. (1990) Androgyny and leadership style, *Journal of Business Ethics*, 9(4/5): 283–292.

Martins. L.L., Gilson, L.L. and Maynyard, M.T. (2004) Virtual teams: What do we know and where do we go from here, *Journal of Management*, 30(6): 805–835.

Nelson, D. and Quick, J. (2002) *Organizational behavior.* Cincinnati, OH: South Western.

Oseen, C. (2002) Luce Irigaray, sexual difference and theorizing leaders and leadership, *Gender, Work & Organization*, 4(3): 170–184.

Parker, M. (2002) Queering management and organization, *Gender, Work & Organization*, 9(1): 146–166.

Pawar, B.S. and Eastman, K.K. (1997) The nature and implications of contextual influences on transformational leadership, *Academy of Management Review*, 22: 80–110.

Pullen, A. (2006) *Managing identity.* London: Palgrave.

Pullen, A. and Rhodes, C. (2008) 'It's all about me!': gendered narcissism and leaders' identity work, *Leadership*, 4(1): 5–25.

Pullen, A. and Rhodes, C. (2010) Revelation and masquerade: gender, ethics and the face. In R. Simpson and P. Lewis (eds), *Concealing and revealing gender.* Basingstoke: Palgrave.

Pullen, A. and Simpson, R. (2009) Managing difference in feminized work: men, otherness and social practice, *Human Relations*, 62(4): 561–587.

Rosener, J.B. (1995) *America's best kept secret: utilizing women as a management secret.* Oxford: Oxford University Press.

Royle, T. (2000) *Working for McDonald's in Europe.* New York: Routledge,

Sedgwick, E. (1990) Epistemology of the Closet, Berkeley: University of California Press.

Shamir, B., House, R.J. and Arthur, M.B. (1993) The motivational effects of charismatic leadership: a self-concept based theory, *Organizational Science*, 4: 577–594.

Vecchio, R.P. (2002) Leadership and gender advantage, *The Leadership Quarterly*, 13(6): 643–671.

Wajcman, J. (1998) *Managing like a man: men and women in corporate management.* Pittsburgh, PA: Pennsylvania University Press.

Yukl, G. (1999) An evaluative essay on current conceptions of effective leadership, *European Journal of Work and Organizational Psychology*, 8: 33–48.

Author Index

Subject Index